THE OXFORD
COMPANION TO
SPANISH LITERATURE

THE OXFORD COMPANION TO SPANISH LITERATURE

EDITED BY

PHILIP WARD

1978

CLARENDON PRESS · OXFORD

Oxford University Press, Walton Street, Oxford OX2 6DP

OXFORD LONDON GLASGOW
NEW YORK TORONTO MELBOURNE WELLINGTON
IBADAN NAIROBI DAR ES SALAAM LUSAKA CAPE TOWN
KUALA LUMPUR SINGAPORE JAKARTA HONG KONG TOKYO
DELHI BOMBAY CALCUTTA MADRAS KARACHI

ISBN 0 19 866114 2

© PHILIP WARD 1978

Set by Eta Services (Typesetters) Ltd., Beccles, Suffolk
Printed in Great Britain
by Richard Clay & Co. Ltd., Bungay, Suffolk

PREFACE

The Oxford Companion to Spanish Literature follows its precursors in attempting to provide, in a single alphabetical sequence, a one-volume reference manual of information likely to be of value to readers of literature in the Spanish language. Most space is devoted to authors and to specific works. The term 'authors' traditionally, in these Companions, comprises not only creative writers but also the major critics, historians, religious writers, philosophers, scholars, and others contributing significantly to the literary life of the countries concerned.

This general statement requires qualification for the present *Companion*, as it does for other Oxford Companions. In the first place, a great deal of literature in Spanish has been written beyond the geographical confines of Spain, and this necessitates the inclusion of entries on the more important authors and books, not only of Spain, but also of Argentina, Bolivia, Chile, Colombia, Costa Rica, Cuba, Dominican Republic, Ecuador, El Salvador, Guatemala, Honduras, Mexico, Nicaragua, Panama, Paraguay, Peru, Philippines, Puerto Rico, Uruguay, and Venezuela. The literatures of Portugal and Brazil are excluded, but languages of Spain other than Castilian are represented: Basque, Catalan, and Galician.

Exigencies of space have made it impossible to include most of the historical and political references traditional to earlier Companions. Another departure has been the inclusion of bibliographical material on rather a wide scale, on the ground that information of this kind is very much less accessible to readers of Spanish in anglophone countries than it is to readers of English or French literature.

The period covered is from Roman Spain to 1977. In the belief that dead authors are not necessarily more interesting than the living, I have chosen to include many young writers. It is probably true to say that of all Latin American writers, the majority are alive and writing today. Despite this bias, I have tried to treat all periods and genres with equal thoroughness.

The Oxford Companion to Spanish Literature began to take its present shape in 1966: slips slowly written in my spare time in Libya followed me first to Malta (where I worked full-time on the *Companion* for eighteen months after the Libyan Revolution), then to Egypt and Indonesia (where I worked for Unesco), and finally to Cambridge, where the references were checked again, and the work brought to a temporary halt by publication.

The listing of sources in such a massive work written over twelve years is quite impossible. Suffice it to say that I have checked original works wherever feasible, submitted entries to living writers to be checked and amended, and utilized the expertise of scholars in four continents. Thus the work has not had to depend on the fallibility and ignorance of the single compiler whose name appears on the title-page (though it can hardly have escaped his weaknesses completely), but may justly be termed the compendium of several hundred. Especial thanks and acknowledgements are due to the editorial staff of the Oxford University Press for their support, and for the detailed assistance of their anonymous expert advisers. Finally, as in all else, I must add a tribute of love and gratitude to my wife and daughters, who have allowed this enterprise to reach a consummation which we know all too well was devoutly to be wished. Notification of errors and omissions will be gratefully received and carefully considered for incorporation in any future edition.

February 1978 Ph.W.

NOTE

All entries are arranged in the order of the English, not the Spanish, alphabet, in the belief that most of the users will be more familiar with English than with Spanish. Thus *Ll* is filed between *Lk* and *Lm* instead of after *Lz*; *Ch* is filed between *Cg* and *Ci* instead of after *Cz*. Accents, tildes, and hyphens are treated as though they do not exist for purposes of order. Ecclesiastics and religious writers are normally to be found under their first name (Juan de la Cruz, *San*), whereas secular writers normally appear under their mother's name (Cervantes Saavedra, Miguel de) and not under their last name, which is normally their father's. Titles beginning with an article (*el, la, los, las*) are filed under the first word after that article. Writers with one or more pen-names are usually to be found under their real name, with a reference from each pseudonym.

The entries are arranged by the principle of 'something before nothing', giving the following sequence:

RODRÍGUEZ
RODRÍGUEZ ÁLVAREZ
RODRÍGUEZ DE LA CÁMARA
RODRÍGUEZ DE LENA
RODRÍGUEZ DEL PADRÓN
RODRÍGUEZ DE MONTALVO
RODRÍGUEZ MARÍN

Spanish usage ignores *y* and *de* in such cases as NAVARRO Y LEDESMA and MARTÍNEZ DE TOLEDO, but I have preferred to give both their normal value when filing.

A place of publication is only shown if it is *not* the capital city of the author's native country.

ABBREVIATIONS

AIEC	*Anuari de l'Institut d'Estudis Catalans*
b.	born
BAE	Biblioteca de Autores Españoles series
BHS	*Bulletin of Hispanic Studies*
BRAE	*Boletín de la Real Academia Española*
c.	*circa*, about
c.	century
ch.	chapter
comp.	compiled
ed.	edited, editor
edn.	edition
fl.	flourished
Fla.	Florida
FMLS	*Forum for Modern Language Studies*
Fr.	*Fray*
Ill.	Illinois
introd.	introduced, introduction
l.	line
ltd.	limited
Mass.	Massachusetts
Md.	Maryland
MS.	manuscript
NBAE	Nueva Biblioteca de Autores Españoles series
N.C.	North Carolina
n.d.	no date of publication in source
N.J.	New Jersey
n.p.	no place of publication in source
N.Y.	State of New York
P.	*Padre*
PMLA	*Publications of the Modern Languages Society of America*
pt.	part
q.v.	which see
RABM	*Revista de Archivos, Bibliotecas y Museos*
RBAM	*Revista de la Biblioteca, Archivo y Museo del Ayuntamiento de Madrid*
S.	*San*
ser.	series
St.	Saint
trans.	translated
UNAM	Universidad Nacional Autónoma de México
Wis.	Wisconsin

A

ABAD or ABADIANO, Diego José (1729–79), b. Jiquilpán, Mexico. A Jesuit poet, author, as Didacius Josephus Abadius, of Latin works including the poem *De Deo Deoque Homine Heroica* in two parts: the first a Summa Theologica and the second a life of Christ. It was highly considered in its time. A Madrid edition of 1769 was succeeded by others dated 1773 (Venice), 1775 (Ferrara), and 1780 (Cesena). For Menéndez y Pelayo 'this book takes its modest place in the long and brilliant catalogue of Christian poems in Latin'. After the Jesuits were expelled from Mexico in 1767 by order of Charles III, Abad went to Ferrara, then to Bologna, where he died.

ABAD, Per, probably the 14th-c. copyist of the poem of the *Cid* (q.v.) in its sole extant MS. The explicit gives his name thus, and the date of transcription as the 'mes de Mayo de 1345 años', a Julian date corresponding to the Gregorian 1307. His name occurs also in histories of Spanish literature as 'Per Abbat', 'Pedro Abad', and similar forms.

See J. Horrent, 'Notes de critique textuelle sur le CMC' in *Mélanges . . . M. Delbouille* (Gembloux, 1964), vol. 2, pp. 275–82.

ABAD DE AYALA, Jacinto (*fl.* 1641), a minor novelist of the Golden Age whose only recorded work is the *Novela del más desdichado amante, y pago que dan mugeres* (1641), a brief love story popular in its time.

Abad Don Juan de Montemayor, Gesta del, a *gesta* recorded in the first half of the 14th c. Its author may have been a Leonese, possibly from Astorga. The earliest complete edition was that of Valladolid (1562) and the first scholarly one that by R. Menéndez Pidal (Dresden, 1903).

The plot concerns a child, found abandoned by the abbot Don Juan and educated by him. The boy when adult turns Muslim and fights against the Christians besieging Montemayor, a town in Portugal between Coimbra and Figueira. The abbot, unable to withstand the siege by his protégé, decides to kill the women, children, and aged of Montemayor, and lead the men in a last stand. The Christians rout the enemy, and Don Juan beheads Don Zulema (as the infidel leader called himself). On returning victorious to Montemayor, the men find their wives, children, and old people miraculously restored to life. The legend became very popular in Spain, where it appears in several novels of the Golden Age.

ABARBANEL or ABRAVANEL, Isaac (1437–1508), b. Lisbon. Author of a commentary on the Old Testament (1483). Treasurer successively to the kings of Portugal, Spain, and Naples. He offered Ferdinand V the Catholic 30,000 ducats to prevent the expulsion of the Jews in 1492, but in vain. He was the father of Judah Abarbanel (q.v.). His most significant theological work was *Rosh emuna* ('Principles of the faith'), which attempts to give the Kabbala intellectual respectability. Instead of dividing religion into separate dogmas, he recommends the acceptance of the Law *in toto*. His other works include '*Ateret zegenim* ('Crown of the ancients'), on Divine Providence, and *Nif'alob Elohim* ('The wonders of God') on the Creation, miracles, and prophecy.

ABARBANEL, Judah (Spanish: León Hebreo; Latin: Leo Judaeus, *c.* 1460–*c.* 1521), b. Lisbon. Son of Isaac Abarbanel (or Abravanel), whose family fled to Italy when the Spanish Jews were expelled in 1492. His neo-Platonist *Dialoghi d'amore* (written *c.* 1502), were three dialogues between Love and Knowledge on the essence, nature, universality, and origin of love, and were influenced by Giovanni Pico della Mirandola and by Marsilio Ficino's *Dialogo sopra l'amore*. Abarbanel was even more indebted to Hispano-Jewish tradition as exemplified in the work by Avicebron (q.v.) known in its Latin version as the *Fons Vitae* (the original is lost), and the neo-Aristotelian system of Maimonides (q.v.). Abarbanel's ideas influenced many writers: Calvi in his *Tractado de la hermosura* (Milan, 1576), the Conde de Rebolledo in his *Discurso de la hermosura y el amor* (written 1652), Castiglione, Bembo in *Gli Asolani*, Fray Luis in his *Oda a Salinas*, and also Cervantes, in Book IV of the *Galatea* (qq.v.). The best Spanish version was made by the Inca Garcilaso de la Vega (q.v.). Pontus de Thiard's French translation became fashionable among the Pléiade group and Denis Sauvage produced another in the 16th c. Abarbanel lived as a physician in Genoa and Naples, where he died.

ABATI Y DÍAZ, Joaquín (1865–1936), b. Madrid. Writer of over 120 comic plays and libretti for *zarzuelas*, many written in collaboration with Carlos Arniches, Enrique García Álvarez, Antonio Paso, and Gregorio Martínez Sierra. Abati's theatre is notable for lively wit, simplicity of plot, and colourful detail. Among his best-known works are *El orgullo de Albacete*, *El gran tacaño*, *Tortoza y Soler*, and *El premio Nobel*.

ABAUNZA, Pedro (1599–1649), b. Seville. A scholar who wrote commentaries on Martial (unpublished), and on the Decretals, the latter included in Meerman's *Novus thesaurus iuris civilis et canonici* (7 vols., The Hague, 1751–4).

'ABBAD, Abu 'Abdullah Muhammad Ibn (1371–), b. Ronda. Of a noble family, he travelled to Tlemcen, Salé, and Fez, where he became *imam* and *katib* of the Karawiyin Mosque. Notable for his ascetic life and doctrines, he instructed many disciples, and left the valuable *Comentarios a las 'Sentencias' de Ibn 'Ataullah*.

'ABDULMALIK BIN HABIB (796–853), b. Cordova. A grammarian, scholar, and the first historian of Muslim Spain. The MS. of his *History* is in the Bodleian Library, Oxford. A naïve writer, he mixes facts and legends indiscriminately and lacks method.

ABELLA CAPRILE, Margarita (1901–), b. Buenos Aires. Poet who has travelled and lived in Europe. Among her collections are *Nieve* (1919) and *50 poesías* (1938). She was for a time editor of the Buenos Aires daily *La Nación*.

Abel Sánchez, a novel by Miguel de Unamuno (q.v.) published in 1917. Unamuno subtitled this existentialist novel of ideas *Una historia de pasión*, declaring it 'acaso la más trágica de mis novelas'. It deals with the biblical problem in the story of Cain and Abel: why did Cain have to suffer punishment if evil had been implanted in him by God? The narrator, Joaquín Monegro, stands for Cain as opposed to the serene egotist Abel Sánchez. Abel marries Joaquín's fiancée Helena and is then unfaithful to her. Joaquín marries another woman and is faithful to his wife, but does not love her, and when Abel's son marries Joaquín's daughter, their son gives all his affection to Abel and none to Joaquín. Unamuno departs from biblical precedent when Cain is given a chance to let Abel die but as a doctor saves his life. The busy, humanitarian Joaquín is destroyed by jealousy of the confident artist Abel, and jealousy, resentment, and

hatred are more significant than any of Unamuno's human protagonists. As a novel of ideas, *Abel Sánchez* succeeds, even if the individuals seldom come to life.

ABEN. for Arabic names beginning with this word, see under Ibn.

ABENALCUTIA, see Qutia, Abu Bakr ibn al-.

Abencerraje y de la hermosa Jarifa, La historia del, a short novel of unknown authorship which first appeared in Antonio Villegas' *Inventario*, written in or before 1551 and published at Medina del Campo, 1565. Its inclusion in the *Diana* of Montemayor ensured its general popularity. The plot concerns the love of Abindarráez, prisoner of Rodrigo de Narváez (q.v., mayor of Antequera), and Jarifa, daughter of the mayor of Coín. Abindarráez is allowed to seek the hand of Jarifa, having given his word to return to Rodrigo. He does return, with Jarifa. The events described are generally believed to be based on fact. Frontier ballads on the theme preceded the novel. Lope de Vega used the story in his play *El remedio en la desdicha*, and mentioned it in his play *La Dorotea*, where the familiar convention of the Sentimental Moor is allied to the pastoral.

ABEN EZRA, see Ezra, Moses ben.

ABOAB, Isaac (*fl. c.* 1300), Spanish Hebrew compiler of *Menorath ha-Ma'or*, (Constantinople, 1514), a collection of religious and ethical writings.

Abolicionista español, El, the periodical (1865–72) of the Spanish anti-slavery movement. It was replaced in 1872 by *La propaganda*.

ABRAVANEL, see Abarbanel.

ABREU GÓMEZ, Ermilo (1894–1971), b. Mérida, Mexico. Professor of Spanish literature, playwright, novelist, and critic. A prolific writer, whose works include *El corcovado* (1924), on Mexico; a literary interpretation of the *Popol Vuh* (q.v., 1950); studies on Sor Juana Inés de la Cruz (q.v.), a critical bibliography of Ruiz de Alarcón (q.v., 1939), *Quetzalcoatl, sueño y vigilia* (1947), and *Martín Luis Guzmán* (1968).
   See Cecilia Silva de Rodríguez, *Vida y obras de Ermilo Abreu Gómez* (Fort Worth, Texas, 1975).

ABRIL, Manuel (1884–1946), b. Madrid. Poet, dramatist, journalist, art critic, and writer for children. His first verses appeared in *Canciones del corazón y de la vida* (1904), and *Hacia la luz lejana* (1914). His comedies *Un caso raro de veras* and *La* *princesa que se chupaba el dedo* were both successful. He satirized the bourgeoisie in the novel *La Salvación* (*Sociedad de Seguros del Alma*) (1931).

ABRIL, PEDRO SIMÓN (*c.* 1530–*c.* 1595), b. Alcaraz de la Mancha, near Toledo. Spanish Renaissance humanist, who wrote in Castilian (*Apuntamientos de como se deuen reformar las doctrinas y la manera de ensenallas* (1589) as well as in Latin. For over 25 years he taught Greek and Latin in Saragossa University, writing his own grammars and teachers' guides: *Latini idiomatis docendi ac discendi methodus* (1561), and *De lingua latina vel de arte grammatica* (1567); he also wrote a Greek and a Latin grammar in Spanish. His prodigious number of translations from Greek and Latin enriched contemporary Spanish culture and revived classical modes of thought and feeling. He translated Aristotle's *Politics* (1584) and *Logic* (1587); speeches by Aeschines and Demosthenes; Aesop's *Fables*; the *Cratylus* and *Gorgias* of Plato, and some of Cicero's letters. Abril also put into Castilian all the plays of Terence then known, the *Medea* of Euripides, and the *Pluto* of Aristophanes (unpublished). His version of the *Comedias* of Terence appeared first in 1577, though the best edition is that of Valencia (1762).

ABRIL, XAVIER (1905–   ), b. Lima. Peruvian poet. Author of *Hollywood* (stories, 1922), he has moved from surrealism to neosymbolism. His later books include *Difícil trabajo* (1935) and *Descubrimiento del alba* (1937).

ABU 'L-AFIA, TUDRUS BEN YEHUDA (1247–*c.* 1303), b. Toledo. Spanish Hebrew scholar and poet who, nevertheless, neglected the Hebrew traditions. As a young man he enjoyed the patronage of Alfonso X. After his flight from Toledo to Aragón and Barcelona his poems, previously profane and even licentious, became ascetic and religious. The *Divan* of Tudrus, entitled *Gan ha-Meshalim we ha-Hidoth* (2 vols. ed. D. Yellin, 1932–4) is more important for insights into its period than for its literary merit.
See I. F. Baer, 'Tudrus ben Yehuda ha-Levi and his times', *Zion* (Jerusalem, 1937), N.S., vol. 2, pp. 19–55. He is not to be confused with his namesake Abu 'l-Afia Tudrus ha-Levi ben Yusuf ben Tudrus (see next entry).

ABU 'L-AFIA, TUDRUS HA-LEVI BEN YUSUF BEN TUDRUS (d. after 1285). Head of the Jewish community of Castile, he exercised great influence over Alfonso X. He was the author of Biblical and Talmudic commentaries with cabbalist tendencies; his Talmudic commentary *Osar ha-kabod* ('Treasury of glory') contained references to the mystical Zohar

('Splendour'). He exchanged verses with his contemporary Abraham Bedersi. He is not to be confused with his namesake Tudrus ben Yehuda Abu 'l-Afia (see previous entry).

ABU 'L-BIQA AR-RUNDI or ABULBECA DE RONDA (*fl.* 13th c.), Arab Andalusian poet known principally for his elegy on the loss of Valencia and Murcia to Jaime of Aragon, and Cordova and Seville to Fernando III 'el Santo'. Juan Valera (q.v.) translated this elegy into Spanish in the manner of the elegiac *coplas* of Jorge Manrique (q.v.), because he believed they were influenced by it, although this theory is no longer accepted.

Abulia, term in psychology denoting loss of will-power. Unamuno introduced the word in 1890 (*Ensayos*, vol. 1, p. 207) to account for Spain's alleged decadence, and the term was taken up by Ángel Ganivet (q.v.) in his *Idearium español* (q.v., 1897), where it was contrasted with the idea of *voluntad* (will-power).

Academia Cadálsica, a literary circle named after José Cadalso y Vázquez (q.v.), who arrived in Salamanca in 1771, despairing at the loss of his mistress, the actress María Ignacia Ibáñez, but was soon made to forget his misery in the congenial company of Meléndez Valdés and Iglesias (qq.v.). The circle grew to include Forner (q.v.) and in 1774 Fray Diego González and Fray Juan Fernández de Rojas (qq.v.). The group, strongly influenced by the attractive figure of Cadalso, known at Court and abroad, wrote bucolic poetry derived from Fray Luis de León and Garcilaso de la Vega (qq.v.). The key book of the group might be considered to be Cadalso's *Ocios de mi juventud* (Salamanca, 1773). The Academia Cadálsica was succeeded by the Parnaso Salmantina and the Arcadia Agustiniana (qq.v.).

Academia del Buen Gusto, a private academy founded in 1749 by the Condesa de Lemos, at whose house it met. It became a forum for the introduction of French taste in Spain, supporting Luzán's (q.v.) defence of Boileau's principles against the Golden Age drama of Spain. Its secretary was the playwright Agustín Gabriel de Montiano y Luyando. One of its members was Luis José Velázquez, whose *Orígenes de la poesía castellana* (1754), written in the manner and under the influence of Luzán, appeared in a superior German edition translated and annotated by J. A. Dieze (1769). Another advocate of 'good taste' was the critic Blas Antonio Nasarre y Férriz, who tried to prove in his preface to Cervantes' plays (1749) that Cervantes wrote them only to parody the works of Lope de Vega.

Academia de los Nocturnos, a private academy formed on the model of the Jesuit literary academies, and active in Valencia 1591–3. It met weekly in the home of Bernardo Catalán de Valeriola. Among its founder-members was Gaspar de Aguilar (q.v.). Each member took a 'nocturnal' pseudonym, such as 'Secreto' (Guillén de Castro), 'Sombra' (Aguilar), 'Descuido' (Francisco Desplugues), 'Relámpago' (Gaspar Mercader), 'Miedo' (Tárrega), 'Sosiego' (Miguel Beneito), or 'Centinela' (Rey de Artieda). This was the only private academy known to have published its proceedings and the poems read and discussed at its meetings. Martí Grajales edited the *Cancionero de los Nocturnos* (Valencia, 1905–12, 4 vols.). Its successor was Los Montañeses del Parnaso, founded in 1616 by Guillén de Castro (q.v.).

Academia Española, see REAL ACADEMIA ESPAÑOLA.

Academy (Greek: *akademeia*), a grove near Athens named after the hero Akademos or Hekademos. Plato's house and garden were here, and it was here that he opened his school of philosophy. A second Academy, teaching modified Platonism, was founded about 250 B.C. by Archesilaos; a third by Carneades about 213 B.C. Justinian closed the Academy as such, but 'the groves of Academe' is still a popular expression for the world of scholarship.

The most important academy in Spain is the Real Academia Española (q.v.); others include the Academia de Buenas Letras (1729), the Real Academia Sevillana de Buenas Letras (1751), the Real Academia de Ciencias, Bellas Letras y Nobles Artes (1810) of Cordova, and the Institut d'Estudis Catalans (1907).

See J. Sánchez, *Academias literarias en el Siglo de Oro español* (1961), and W. F. King, 'The Academies and seventeenth-century Spanish literature', *PMLA*, vol. 75 (1960), pp. 367–76.

ACAICO, IPANDRO, Arcadian name of Ignacio Montes de Oca (q.v.).

ACEBAL, FRANCISCO (1866–1933), b. Gijón. Novelist. His first success, *Aires de mar* (1900), was achieved in competition with Pérez Galdós and Echegaray. He then produced *Huella de almas* (1901), *De mi rincón* (short stories, 1901), *Dolorosa* (1904), *El calvario* (1905), *Rosa mística* (1909), and *Penumbra* (1924). He also wrote plays influenced by Benavente and Pérez Galdós.

Acento, Grupo, a Guatemalan literary movement forming part of the so-called Generation of 1940. Its organ was the magazine *Acento*. The main influences on it were Joyce, Valéry, Kafka, Alberti, Neruda, and García Lorca, and these tastes were shared by members of the later, more militant, Saker Ti group (q.v.). The members included Raúl Leiva, Carlos Illescas, Enrique Juárez Toledo, and Otto-Raúl González.

ACEVEDO or AZEVEDO, ALONSO DE (1550–c. 1620), b. Vera de Plasencia. Epic poet and prebendary of Plasencia Cathedral. His *Creación del mundo* (Rome, 1615; reprinted in vol. 29 (1854) of the BAE), is an epic poem of seven cantos derived partly from Tasso's *Il mondo creato* (1600–7) and partly from *La Sepmaine*, by the Gascon du Bartas. He avoids the latter's verbal extravagance, but the poem is rather heavy and slow to develop. He appears, speaking Italian, in the *Viaje del Parnaso* of Cervantes (q.v.).

ACEVEDO DÍAZ, EDUARDO (1851–1924), (1) b. La Unión, Uruguay. Journalist, politician, and novelist. He participated in both the Revolución Blanca (1870–2) and the Revolución Tricolor (1875), and sought refuge in Argentina, where he died. His historical trilogy *Himno de sangre* (*Ismael*, 1888; *Nativa*, 1890; *Grito de gloria*, 1893) influenced by Pérez Galdós (q.v.), was the foundation of the Uruguayan novel. His energy and epic imagination suggest the influence of Zola. His best-known novel is *Soledad* (1894), an early, significant example of *gauchismo*; other writings include *Gesta de gloria* (1889), *Brenda* (1890), and *Lanza y sable* (1914). He founded the political daily *El Nacional* in 1896.

(2) (1882–). Son of the above. Argentinian novelist. He has twice won the Premio Nacional de Literatura. His regional novels include *Argentina te llamas* (1934), *Ramón Hazaña* (1932), and *Eternidad* (1937), the first two set in the pampas, and the last in Buenos Aires.

ACEVEDO GUERRA, EVARISTO (1915–), b. Madrid. Humorist. He wrote under the pseudonyms 'Cam', 'Evaristóteles', and 'Fernando Arrieta', for the magazines *La Codorniz*, *Informaciones*, *Pueblo*, and others. Among his books are *Los ancianitos son una lata* (1955), *49 españoles en pijama y 1 en camiseta* (1959), and *Triunfé en sociedad hablando mal de todo* (1963).

ACEVEDO HERNÁNDEZ, ANTONIO (1887–1962), Chilean novelist, essayist, and dramatist, whose novels (often about brigandage) include *Manuel Lucero* (1927), *El Roto Juan García* (1938), and *Pedro Urdemalas* (1947). His best book,

Chañarcillo (1956), is like most of the others set in Creole society.

ACOSTA, José de (1539–1600), b. Medina del Campo. When he was about twelve he entered the Society of Jesus, and was sent as a missionary to Peru from 1571 to 1587, eventually becoming Provincial of his order. In 1588 he became the first Jesuit professor of theology at Salamanca University. His *De natura novi orbis* (1589) was a preliminary version of the *Historia natural y moral de las Indias* (1590), translated into English by E. Grimstone (London, 1604). A storehouse of facts, the work drew high praise from Humboldt. It deals with the history and geography of Mexico and Peru, and the religious and political systems of their inhabitants. Acosta was an apologist of Spanish colonialism. His other works include *De procuranda salute Indorum* and catechisms in the Aimará and Quichua tongues.

ACOSTA, José María (1881–   ), b. Almería. Novelist, by profession a military engineer. His first novel *Amor loco y amor cuerdo* (1920) was his best. He produced six other novels and two volumes of *novelas cortas* in the twenties. His literary taste and style were formed by friendship with Francisco Villaespesa (q.v.).

ACOSTA, Oscar (1933–   ), Honduran poet. *Poesía: selección, 1952–1971* (Madrid, 1976) is distinguished by excellent craftsmanship, simplicity, and clarity.

ACOSTA DE SAMPER, Soledad (1833–1903), b. Bogotá. Colombian historian and historical novelist. Her most frequent pseudonyms were 'Aldebarán' and 'Bertilda'. *Los piratas en Cartagena* (1885) is accounted the best of her books. Others include *Los españoles en América*, *Un hidalgo conquistador*, *El tirano Aguirre*, and *Vasco Núñez de Balboa*. She edited the feminist *La mujer*, 1878–82.

ACOSTA ENRÍQUEZ, José Mariano (*fl.* 1779–1816), Mexican author of *Sueño de sueños* (*c.* 1800), in which Quevedo, Cervantes, and Torres Villarroel (qq.v.) journey with the author to Hell and discourse of many things, in particular the current literary fashions. The concept is derived from Torres Villarroel, and Quevedo's own *Sueños* (q.v.).

ACOSTA Y BELLO, Agustín (1886–   ), Cuban poet. His first book, *Ala* (1915), dealt with patriotism and courtly love. *Hermanita* (1923) was followed by lyrics on the sugar industry in *La zafra* (1926) and the simple poems of *Los camellos distantes* (1936), his best book

Últimos instantes (1941), and *Las islas desoladas* (1943).

'A Cristo crucificado', a moving sonnet of the 16th c. which appears in most anthologies of Spanish verse and has been attributed to, among others, S. Francisco Xavier, S. Ignacio de Loyola, Fray Pedro de los Reyes, and (with the greatest degree of probability) Fray Miguel de Guevara (q.v.). It is similar in style to the sonnets in the *Rimas sacras* of Lope de Vega (q.v.), but an attribution to him is no more convincing than the rest.

ACUÑA, Hernando de (*c.* 1520–*c.* 1580), b. Valladolid. A soldier-poet who served in Germany, Italy, and Tunisia. His widow published his *Varias poesías* (1591) which were greatly influenced by Petrarch. Acuña translated some of Ovid, the first four books of Boiardo's *Orlando innamorato*, and Olivier de la Marche's *Le Chevalier délibéré*, which he supposedly versified from a prose rendering of the French text by Charles V. Acuña's version was published in English in 1594 as *The Resolved Gentleman*.

ACUÑA, Manuel (1849–73), b. Saltillo, Coahuila. Mexican poet whose unhappy love affairs and ill-health led him to commit suicide. A Romantic atheist, Acuña wrote *El pasado* (1872), a passionate play against the crimes he associated with Christian society and religious fanaticism. His poetry is materialist, and his love poetry is not of the lyrical type common in the more superficial Romanticism, but darkly toned with melancholy and bitterness. His chief models were Espronceda, Larra (qq.v.), and Byron. See Marcelino Estrada Zalce, *Manuel Acuña: ausencia y presencia* (1959).

ACUÑA DE FIGUEROA, Francisco (1790–1862), b. Montevideo. Uruguay's first significant writer, he composed the national anthem in 1833. A humorist and satirist. His *Obras completas* (1890, 12 vols.) include *Diario histórico del sitio de Montevideo en los años 1812–34* (2 vols.), 1,450 epigrams in an *Antología epigramática* (2 vols.) and *Poesías diversas* (8 vols.).

ADÁN, Martín, pseudonym of Rafael de la Fuente Benávides (q.v.).

ADOLPH, José B., Peruvian short-story writer and novelist. His narratives are enriched by two influences rather unusual in Spanish American fiction: philosophy and science fiction. His short stories are collected in *El retorno de Aladino* (1968), *Hasta que la muerte* (1971), and *Invisible para las fieras* (1972).

Adolph's novel *La ronda de los generales* (1973) is in the tradition of Guillermo Thorndike's *Las rayas del tigre* and Mario Vargas Llosa's *Conversación en 'La Catedral'*, which take past Peruvian military regimes for their theme. Adolph takes for his theme, however, a possible future government.

ADRET, SOLOMON BEN (1235–c. 1310), b. Barcelona. Chief Rabbi of Spain and an authority on Spanish-Hebrew law and religion. Half of his *Responsa,* or answers to problems, were collected in seven volumes published between 1539 and 1568. He wrote numerous cabbalistic works and several hymns. He was a practitioner of gematria, the arithmetical-geometrical Cabbala.

AFÁN DE RIBERA, FULGENCIO (18th c.), satirist and *costumbrista* whose best work was the anonymously published satire *Virtud al uso y Mística a la moda, destierro de Hipocresía en frase de exortación a ella* (1729). Probably influenced by the *Libro de todas las cosas* of Quevedo, it attacks hypocrisy in both religious and secular life and was reprinted in vol. 33 (1854) of the BAE; and a more recent edition appeared in 1952. Uriarte argued convincingly against the pamphlet's attribution to P. Isla (q.v.) in his *Catálogo de obras anónimas,* vol. 3 (1906).

Afrancesados ('Frenchified Spaniards'), the name for those in Spain who supported the rule of Joseph Bonaparte. The term is generally pejorative in implication. *Afrancesamiento* was born with the installation of the Bourbons on the throne of Spain, and was a natural product of the Encyclopaedist movement of France and the Enlightenment (see ENLIGHTENMENT IN SPAIN). Many intellectuals and writers are counted among the *afrancesados,* including Quintana, Meléndez Valdés, Lista, and Moratín (qq.v.). The *afrancesados* and the 'patriots' opposed each other on the dynastic question when the Napoleonic armies occupied Spain in 1808, though they agreed that the cause of Spain should come first. On the return of Fernando VII to Spain in 1814, the *afrancesados* were punished according to the degree of their complicity with the Bonaparte regime. Those who had already fled to France were forbidden to return until the amnesty of 1820.

The major apologia for the *afrancesados* was written by P. Félix Reinoso (q.v.): *Examen de los delitos de infidelidad a la patria imputados a los españoles bajo la dominación francesa* (Auch, 1816).

See M. Méndez Bejarano, *Historia política de los afrancesados* (1912); M. Artola Gallego, *Los afrancesados* (1953); and H. Juretschke, *Los afrancesados en la Guerra de Independencia* (1962).

Afro-Cubanism, see ORTIZ, Fernando.

AGRAZ, JUAN (15th c.), conventional love poet. He is best known for three elegies: *Dezir de la muerte del conde de Niebla* (1468), *Dezir quando murió el Maestre de Santiago,* and *Coplas a la muerte del conde de Mayorga.* Eduardo Rincón has edited the first and third in his *Coplas satíricas y dramáticas de la Edad Media* (1968).

ÁGREDA, Sor MARÍA CORONEL DE JESÚS DE (1602–65), b. Ágreda, Soria, into a devout family, all of whom entered the religious life in 1619. Her parents founded the Convent of the Immaculate Conception in Ágreda, and she became Abbess there at the age of 25, after a special dispensation because of her youth. She experienced several mystic visions, of which the most famous concerned a council of the powers of evil to overthrow the Roman Catholic faith and the Spanish state. On hearing of this vision, Philip IV went to visit her in 1643. Their correspondence, maintained until 1665, was edited by F. Silvela in *Cartas de la Venerable Madre...* (1885). Valbuena Prat called her the 'S. Teresa of the Baroque'. An early work on the life of the Virgin was destroyed on the orders of her confessor, and her main work, the *Mística ciudad de Dios, milagro de su omnipotencia y abismo de la gracia. Historia divina, y vida de la Virgen Madre de Dios... manifestada en estos últimos siglos por la Misma Señora a su esclava Sor María de Jesús,* was the centre of a prolonged dispute because of its insistence on the fact of the Immaculate Conception, a doctrine not officially recognised until 1854. Bossuet spoke out strongly against it. It was placed on the Index for some time, but eventually removed at the behest of the Franciscans of Spain, to which country its circulation was to be confined. Her unaided authorship of the *Mística ciudad* is open to question, and as her correspondence with the King was interrupted during the absence of her Franciscan confessor, it may be concluded that she acted as a mouthpiece for the Franciscans. Sor María's other books include *Escala espiritual para subir a la perfección,* and *Leyes de la esposa: conceptos y suspiros del corazón para alcanzar el último y verdadero fin del agrado del Esposo y Señor.*

AGUADO, Fray PEDRO DE (c. 1520–90), b. Valdemoro, Madrid. Franciscan missionary who went to South America in 1560, and in 1573 became Provincial of the Franciscans in the Nuevo Reino de Granada. His best work, *Historia de Sta. Marta y del Nuevo Reino de Granada,* was edited by J. Becker for the Real Academia de la Historia, as was his *Historia de Venezuela* (1916–17 and 1918–19 respectively). An eye-witness to many of the events he describes, Fray Pedro is an important primary source for historians.

AGUADO HERNÁNDEZ, EMILIANO (1907–), b. Cebolla, Toledo. Drama critic. His volume of plays *Teatro* has won the Premio Nacional de Literatura, but it is as an essayist that he is best known, for *Del siglo XVIII a nuestros días* (1941) and *El arte como revelación* (1943).

Agua y el vino, Denuestos del, see DENUESTOS DEL AGUA Y EL VINO.

AGUAYO, *Fray* ALBERTO DE (1469–1525), Dominican scholar and poet. The first prior of the Monastery of S. Cruz la Real in Granada after the city was taken by the Catholic Sovereigns in 1492. He translated the *De consolatione philosophiae* of Boethius (1518).

Agudeza y arte de ingenio (Huesca, 1648), a greatly enlarged and revised edition of Baltasar Gracián y Morales' (q.v.) *Arte de ingenio, tratado de la agudeza en que se explican todos los modos, y diferencias de conceptos* (1642).

This second edition, subtitled *Tratado de los estilos,* is the most significant Spanish book on *conceptismo* (q.v.) and among the chief works of Baroque literary criticism. Its aesthetic creed was enduring and profound. It used the *Acutezze* of Pellegrini as a model for showing how the best authors employed 'wit', as *agudeza* may be defined, in the sense that the English Metaphysical poets understood 'wit'. Gracián declared both obscurity and brevity to be essential to good writing: the combination of these two qualities renders his most typical specimens designedly impenetrable to the common reader. These specimens are drawn from Góngora, and from such *conceptistas* as Quevedo and Jáuregui (qq.v.). Gracián defined *concepto* as 'un acto del entendimiento que exprime la correspondencia que se halla entre las cosas': the more recondite the connection, the better the *concepto* was considered to be. *Agudeza* he defined as the *concepto*'s ornament, arguing that they are equally necessary and are most successful when best combined. The edition of *Agudeza* by Evaristo Correa Calderón in Gracián's *Obras completas* (1944) has been superseded by the same editor's 2-volume annotated edition (1969) for Clásicos Castalia.

See T. E. May, *An interpretation of Gracián's 'Agudeza y arte de ingenio' (Hispanic Review,* vol. 16, 1948) and *Gracián's idea of the 'concepto'* (ibid., vol. 18, 1950).

AGUILAR, GASPAR HONORAT DE (1561–1623), b. Valencia. Dramatist. His *comedia El mercader*

amante is praised by the Canon of Toledo in *Don Quijote,* I, 48. His comedies are of three kinds: *de capa y espada* (q.v.), such as *La venganza honrosa*; religious, such as *El gran Patriarca S. Juan de Ribera*; and *de ruido* (q.v.), such as *La gitana melancólica* and *Los amantes de Cartago.*

His poetry is not of high quality, but his epic *La expulsión de los moros de España* (1610) enjoyed a certain vogue. He was one of the founder-members of the Academia de los Nocturnos (q.v.).

AGUILAR CATENA, JUAN (1888–), b. Úbeda. Journalist, short-story writer, and romantic novelist in the traditional style of colourful description. His principal works are *Los enigmas de María Luz* (1919), *Herida en el vuelo* (1921), *Disciplinas de amor* (1923), *Nuestro amigo Juan* (1924), *La ternura infinita* (1926), *Un soltero difícil* (1928) *¡Va todo!* (1929), *Dos noches* (1930), *Úrsula, examíname* (1931), and *Lo que yo haría* (1947).

AGUILERA MALTA, DEMETRIO (1909–), b. Guayaquil. Ecuadorian poet, essayist, novelist, short-story writer, and playwright. He first attracted attention with the notable collection of short stories *Los que se van* (Guayaquil, 1930), a collective work with Joaquín Gallegos Lara and Enrique Gil Gilbert (q.v.), who formed with him, José de la Cuadra, and Alfredo Pareja the Grupo de Guayaquil (q.v.).

While in Spain studying offset printing, Aguilera Malta was surprised by the outbreak of the Civil War. He joined the republican troops as a reporter, writing *¡Madrid! reportaje novelado de una retaguardia heroica* (Barcelona, 1937), in the same style as *C.Z. (Canal Zone) Los Yanquis en Panamá* (1935), vivid accounts of topical events. His plays were well received in a country poorly supplied with dramatists: the best are *Lázaro* (with influences of Marcel Pagnol) in *Revista del Colegio Nacional Vicente Rocafuerte* (Guayaquil, vol. 18, no. 53, pp. 15–42); and *Infierno negro* (1967), on the plight of the Negro in history. His 15 plays are studied in Gerardo Luzuriaga's *Del realismo al expresionismo: el teatro de Aguilera Malta* (1971). The short stories *Siete lunas y siete serpientes* (1970) reiterate the plea for social justice for the poor and deprived which he first adumbrated in *Los que se van.*

His novels have shown a steady advance towards maturity and complexity. The powerful protagonist of *Don Goyo* (1933) symbolises in himself the creative strength of the jungle, while *La isla virgen* (1942; reworked in 1954) shows the jungle peopled by the sons of Don Goyo, who unite with the undergrowth and the wild beasts to overcome the blind force of progress. His subsequent novels form a series of

'Episodios americanos': *Una cruz en la Sierra Maestra* (1960) on the Cuban revolution; *La caballeresa del sol* (1964) on Bolívar's mistress Manuela Sáenz; *El Quijote de El Dorado* (1964), on the explorer Orellana; *Un nuevo mar para el rey*, on Balboa's discovery of the Pacific and his love for an Indian girl; and *El secuestro del general* (1973), an effective satire against dictatorship. His 'magic realism' is an important part of the style which has been increasingly adopted in the later novels of Asturias, Carpentier, and above all García Márquez (qq.v.). See REALISMO.

AGUILÓ Y FÚSTER, MARIANO (1825–97), b. Palma de Mallorca. Poet and bibliographer of the Catalan Renaissance. His *Bibliografía Catalana* was awarded the Biblioteca Nacional prize in 1860. His romantic poetry, for the most part in Mallorquín and Catalan, was collected in *L'enteniment y l'amor, Esperança, Amorosas, Libre de la mort*, and *Fochs follets*. He was proclaimed 'Mestre en Gay Saber' in 1866.

AGUIRRE, DOMINGO (1864–1920), b. Ondárroa. Basque novelist. His *Garoa* (1912), expressing nostalgia for an idyllic past, was translated into Castilian as *El helecho*. His earlier books are less important. They include the historical novel *Auñemendiko lorea* (1898) and the *costumbrista* novel *Kresala* (1906).

AGUIRRE, JOSÉ MARÍA (1896–1933), Basque lyric poet, who writes under the pseudonym of 'Xabier de Lizardi'. Aguirre's lyrics *Biotz-begietan* (San Sebastián, 1956), are considered the most haunting and original in the Basque language. He also wrote the humorous prose tales *Itz-lauz* (1934).

AGUIRRE, MANUEL AGUSTÍN (1904–), b. Loja, Ecuador. Leftwing poet and founder of *La Tierra*, the Ecuadorian socialist party journal, in 1944. After the haiku-like *Poemas automáticos* (Guayaquil, 1931), he veered to more political themes in *Llamada de los proletarios* (Guayaquil, 1935). *Pies desnudos: poemas de la infancia* (Loja, 1943) was published by his friends without his consent. Aguirre's *Lecciones de Marxismo* (2 vols., University of Quito, 1950–1) were answered by Gustavo Miranda Ribadeneira's *La única solución del problema social* (1958).

AGUIRRE, NATANIEL (1843–88), b. Cochabamba. Bolivian statesman and historical novelist. His best novel, *Juan de la Rosa: memorias del último soldado de la independencia* (1885), expresses a liberal's dislike for conventional attachment to the colonial past. His *Obras* appeared in 1911.

AGUIRRE, RAÚL GUSTAVO (1927–), Argentinian surrealist poet. He has edited *Poesía Buenos Aires*, having translated into Spanish Char, Apollinaire, and Emily Dickinson, among others. His own poetry has been collected in several volumes, the most distinctive being *El tiempo de la rosa* (1945), *La danza nupcial* (1951), and *Alguna memoria* (1960).

AGUIRRE MORALES, AUGUSTO (1888–1957), Peruvian historical novelist. His *La Medusa* (1916) was strongly influenced by d'Annunzio and Maeterlinck, and his reconstruction of Inca society *El pueblo del sol* (vol. 1, 1924; complete, 1928), was influenced by Flaubert's *Salammbô*.

Aguja de navegar cultos (1613), a brief prose satire by Francisco de Quevedo y Villegas (q.v.) which attacks Góngora and the other *culterano* poets of the day for their use of alleged gibberish. It begins with a poem offered as a *receta* ('recipe') for learning to write poems like Góngora's in a day. The literary feud sustained between Quevedo and Góngora from 1603 until the latter's death in 1627 produced other lampoons by Quevedo, including a proclamation against worthless poets in *El buscón* (q.v., ch. X); *La culta latiniparla* against female imitators of Góngora who would call eggs 'globes of the cockerel's wife'; and *Cuento de cuentos*, an example of a story so verbose, complex, and circuitous that it becomes impossible to disentangle. These works all are in Quevedo's *Obras completas* (2 vols., 1961) ed. by F. Buendía.

AGUSTÍ, IGNACIO (1913–), b. Llissá del Vall, Barcelona. Novelist and journalist writing in both Catalan and Castilian. He first became famous with his realistic Castilian novel *Mariona Rebull* (1941), about the rise of a working-class family in Barcelona to the ranks of the upper-middle classes. The saga begins in 1865 and is intended to finish in about 1944. Other volumes in the sequence—called *La ceniza fue árbol* (1916) are *El viudo Ríus* (1945), *Desiderio* (1957), *19 de julio* (1966), and *Guerra civil* (1972).

AGUSTINI, DELMIRA (c. 1890–1914), b. Montevideo. Uruguayan poet. A happy childhood in cultivated surroundings was followed by marriage with a man incapable of valuing her sensibilities, who eventually killed her and then committed suicide. *Los cálices vacíos* (1913) contained selections from her first two books (*El libro blanco*, 1907, and *Cantos de la mañana*, 1910) and new work. The best edition of *Poesías completas* is that by Manuel Álvar (Barcelona, 1971). Her letters have been edited by Arturo

Sergio Visca: *Correspondencia íntima* (1969). On her poetry see *La poesía de Delmira Agustini* (1968) by A. S. Visca and others; on her life and work see Roberto Bonada Amigo, *Delmira Agustini en la vida y en la poesía* (1964).

AHRIMAN or ANGRA MAINYU, in Zoroastrian theology, the principle of evil in perpetual conflict with Ormazd, the principle of goodness. In Spanish literature, Ahrimán was the pseudonym of Azorín (q.v., i.e. José Martínez Ruiz).

AIRAS or AYRAS, JOAN (13th c.), b. Santiago de Compostela (?). A merchant and a prolific poet, who formed part of the literary circles of Alfonso X (q.v.) and Don Dinis. He wrote many *cantigas* (q.v.), including 50 *de amigo*, 25 *de amor*, and 10 *de burlas*, also pastorals and *tensones* (qq.v.). Arias was edited by Braga in his *Canzoniere portoghese della Biblioteca Vaticana* (Halle, 1875); his works are full of prosaic interludes and subject to frequent failure of inspiration.

AIRÓ, CLEMENTE (1919–), b. Madrid. Spanish novelist and short-story writer exiled in Colombia since 1941. His collections of short stories include *Viento de romance* (1947), *Cardos como flores* (1955), and *5 y...7: cuentos de una misma historia* (1967). His novels are *Yugo de niebla* (1948), *Sombras al sol* (1951), *La ciudad y el viento* (1961), on decadence and corruption in city life, and *El campo y el fuego* (1971) which, though set in the countryside, shows how inexorably city men control the land. Airó edits the influential Bogotá magazine *Espiral*.

See E. Irizarry, 'Novela colombiana. Dos voces de novelista en Clemente Airó', *Espiral*, no. 134 (March 1975), pp. 13–27.

ALARCÓN, ABEL (1881–), Bolivian novelist, whose historical novels deal with Inca times (*En la corte de Yáhuar-Huákac*, 1915) and the colonial period (*Era una vez...*, 1935). The latter is diffuse and incoherent, but it remains worth reading for scenes of Bolivian life carefully assembled from historical records. Alarcón has translated Tagore's *Gitanjali*.

ALARCÓN Y ARIZA, PEDRO ANTONIO DE (1833–91), b. Guadix. Novelist. He abandoned the study of law, when his family was plunged into financial difficulty, and returned from Granada to his home town to study for the Church. He ran away in 1853 to gain a literary reputation in Madrid but failed to make a mark then, or on his return home, as a politician. Later exploits in Madrid included the editing of the fiercely anti-clerical magazine *El látigo*, and

a resulting duel (1855) against José Heriberto García de Quevedo (q.v.) who fired in the air after Alarcón had missed. From that time all his efforts were devoted to literature. His play *El hijo pródigo* (1857) was a failure, and his *Poesías* are without interest. It is in his novels, and above all in his short stories, that Alarcón achieved lasting repute. He first became famous with a vividly patriotic *Diario de un testigo de la guerra de África* (1859; new edn., 1975), an account of the Moroccan campaign of 1859–60, during which he was wounded. His travels in Italy provoked an excellent travel book: *De Madrid a Nápoles pasando por París, Ginebra, etc.* (1861).

He began to write novels influenced by Balzac and George Sand, producing his first at the age of 18: *El final de Norma* (1855), a fantastic adventure romance. The *cuadros de costumbres* he published in *Cosas que fueron* (1871) reveal the influence of Fernán Caballero (q.v.). His amusing *españolista* short-story *El sombrero de tres picos* (q.v., 1874) is his best-known work; it was turned into a ballet by Manuel de Falla and into an opera by Hugo Wolf. His novel *El escándalo* (q.v., 1875), written after the liberal triumph in the political crisis of 1868, showed that his revolutionary fervour was now transformed into extreme conservatism. The violent Andalusia of *El niño de la bola* (1880) is a very different *ambiente* from the easy-going world of *El sombrero de tres picos*, and Alarcón's progress towards artistic and psychological maturity is very marked. The character Pepito is often supposed to be a self-portrait. *La pródiga* (1882) concluded on a feebler note a trilogy (including *El escándalo* and *El niño de la bola*) dealing with an individual's reactions to society and its *mores*, doomed always to defeat. In the same year Alarcón published his short novel *El capitán Veneno*, a variation, quickly written like his other fiction, on the theme of Moreto's *El desdén con el desdén*. After the failure of *La pródiga*, attributed by the author to a conspiracy, Alarcón wrote no more fiction, and published only one book during the last ten years of his life: the autobiographical *Historia de mis libros* (1884). *Novelas completas* (Buenos Aires, 1942) was edited, with a thematic index, by J. Gil.

See J. F. Montesinos, *Pedro Antonio de Alarcón* (Saragossa, 1955); E. Pardo Canalís, *Pedro Antonio de Alarcón* (1966); and A. Ocaño, *Alarcón* (1970).

ALARCÓN Y MENDOZA, JUAN RUIZ DE, see RUIZ DE ALARCÓN Y MENDOZA, Juan.

ALAS Y UREÑA, LEOPOLDO ENRIQUE GARCÍA (1852–1901), b. Zamora. Novelist, short-story writer, and critic who wrote under the pseudonym 'Clarín'. In 1869 his family moved to

Oviedo, where he studied law, and after a year in Saragossa he was eventually appointed Professor of Law in 1883. He was a close friend of Armando Palacio Valdés (q.v.). Influenced as a young man by *krausismo* (q.v.), he later rejected it and satirized what he believed to be its mystical eccentricities in his story *Zurita* (1886). Since his death he has become well-known as a novelist, in particular for *La regenta* (q.v., 1884) in which the heroine is destroyed by the spite and jealousies of small-town life in Vetusta, which is in fact Oviedo thinly disguised.

During his lifetime Alas was always best-known for his criticism. He was probably the most important Spanish critic in the last quarter of the century, and his mordant comments and reasoned arguments provided an essential antidote to the automatic approval given to most new books on their appearance at that time, though even he suffered lapses of excessive benevolence. His reviews were collected in *Mezclilla* (1889), *Solos* (5 vols., 1890–98), and *Palique* (1893).

'Azorín' (q.v.) criticized his early style as being pompous and verbose, too much influenced by his legal training. His writing gradually became more tender, concise, and even humorous, as in the novel *Su único hijo* (1890) and in some of his later stories, collected in the volumes *Pipá* (1886), *El Señor* (1893), *Cuentos morales* (1896), and *El gallo de Sócrates* (1901). A four-volume edition of his *Obras completas* appeared between 1913 and 1929.

See W. E. Bull and V. E. Chamberlin, *Clarín: the critic in action* (Norman, Okla., 1963); and S. Beser, *Leopoldo Alas, crítico literario* (1968).

Alba, a brief lyric used by Castilian and Galician-Portuguese troubadours to express grief at parting from their lovers at dawn. The word *alba* ('dawn') often occurs in the refrain. Its greatest practitioner was the Provençal poet Giraut de Bornelh, whom Dante praises as one of the great triad (with Arnaut Daniel and Bertrand de Born) in *De vulgari eloquentia*.

S. M. Stern (q.v.) and E. M. Wilson describe the *alba* in Iberian literature in *Eos: an enquiry into the theme of lovers' meetings and partings at dawn in poetry* (The Hague, 1965, ed. A. T. Hatto). Dionisia Empaytaz has compiled an *Antología de albas, alboradas y poemas afines en la Península ibérica hasta 1625* (1974). See also ALBORADA.

ALBA, BARTOLOMÉ DE (*fl.* 1634), he translated plays by Lope de Vega (*El animal profeta, San Julián*, and *La madre de la mejor*) into Nahuatl (1641) for performance in Mexico.

Albeldense, Cronicón, the first of the early *Cronicones* (q.v.).

ALBERDI, JUAN BAUTISTA (1810–84), b. Tucumán, Argentina. Political and legal writer. As a result of persecution by Rosas he fled to Montevideo in 1838, where he wrote polemical journalism and practised law. After moving to practise law in Chile, he wrote his most important book: *Bases para la organización política de la Confederación Argentina* (1852), and lesser works, such as *Elementos de derecho público provincial* (1853). He served the Confederación from 1855 to 1862, returning to Buenos Aires in 1879 to a hero's welcome and reconciliation with his two opponents Mitre and Sarmiento. He became disillusioned with the government formed after the fall of Rosas and left again for Paris, where he died in penury. His well-known satire on Sarmiento's regime, *Peregrinación de luz de día; o, viajes y aventuras de la verdad en el Nuevo Mundo* is among the most memorable works in the *Obras completas* (24 vols., 1886–95).

He was the founder of Argentinian *costumbrismo* in his *Memoria descriptiva de Tucumán* (1834); he signed his articles on *costumbrismo* 'Figarillo', after Larra's pen-name 'Fígaro'.

Paul Groussac (q.v.) declared Alberdi to be 'the Argentinian who, in a slightly gallicised form, has put into circulation during the past forty years the greatest number of ideas in his country's interest'.

ALBERT I PARADÍS, CATARINA (1869–1966), the best-known modern woman writer in Catalan. She wrote realistic novels and short stories of the Costa Brava under the pseudonym 'Víctor Català', the finest of her novels being *Solitud* (1905). Her other works include *Drames rurals* (1902), *Caires Vius* (1907), *Ombrívoles* (1910), *Un film* (1926), *Viola mòlta* (1950), and *Jubileu* (1951).

ALBERTI, RAFAEL (1902–), b. Puerto de S. María, Cádiz. Poet and playwright. He began life as a painter; *A la pintura* (1948), reissued in an illustrated edition in 1968, has been called 'perhaps the finest attempt in any language to convey the essence of pictorial art in poetry'. He began to write poetry in 1923, and his *Marinero en tierra* (q.v.) won the Premio Nacional de Literatura on its publication in 1925. *La amante* (1926) was followed by *Cal y canto* (1927), in which successful *romances* show the influence of the traditional Spanish ballads. Traces of Garcilaso and Vicente are also evident. His admiration for Góngora led him to write an unfinished *Soledad tercera*.

Alberti's best poems are probably those in *Sobre los ángeles* (q.v., 1929): they are abstract, difficult, and often surrealistic. His later books are more laboured, though Gaos was to write even of *Sobre los ángeles*: 'el surrealismo de

Alberti parece más fruto de una deliberada actitud mimética que de una honda convicción interior'.

From 1931, Alberti became involved with politics as a Marxist, and after the Civil War went into exile in Argentina, where he returned to the themes of and attitudes of his youth. His *Poesías completas* (Buenos Aires, 1961), was followed by *Suma taurina* (verse, prose, and drama, Barcelona, 1963); *Poemas de amor* (1967); *Roma, peligro para caminantes, 1964–1967* (Mexico City, 1968); *Libro del mar* (Barcelona, 1968); *Poemas anteriores a 'Marinero en tierra'* (Barcelona, 1969); *Los ocho nombres de Picasso* and *No digo más que lo que no digo, 1966–1970* (Barcelona, 1970). The socially-committed poems of *El poeta en la calle* (amplified edn., Paris, 1970) reflect his politics: he had worked for the monarchy's downfall in 1931 and was awarded the Lenin Peace Prize. His plays, less successful than his poetry, include *Fermín Galán* and *El hombre deshabitado* (both 1931). His autobiography is *La arboleda perdida. Libros I y II de memorias* (Buenos Aires, 1959). Alberti returned to Spain from exile in 1977.

See E. González Lanuza, *Rafael Alberti* (Buenos Aires, 1965); R. Marrast, *Aspects du théâtre de Rafael Alberti* (Paris, 1967); S. Salinas de Marichal, *El mundo poético de Rafael Alberti* (1968); and M. Bayo, *Sobre Alberti* (1974).

ALBÓ, Joseph (c. 1380–1444), a Spanish Hebrew philosopher, he continued the tradition of his teacher Hasdai Crescas (q.v.), in *Sefer ha-'iqqarim* ('Fundamentals of the Faith') which has been edited in 5 vols. with an English translation by I. Husik (1930).

Alborada, a brief lyric, often with a homosexual implication, used by Galician-Portuguese troubadours to express joy in being reunited with their lovers at dawn. The 13th-c. poet Nuno Fernandes Torneol makes the theme ironic by employing the typically merry refrain to describe a girl's distress on being abandoned by her lover. See also ALBA.

ALCALÁ, *Fray* PEDRO DE (*fl.* 1505), philologist. His *Vocabulista en aravigo* (1505) is our main source for the Arabic of Spain, showing both its peculiarities of pronunciation and its debt to the Romance language of the period. The dialect transcribed is that of Granada.

ALCALÁ GALIANO, ANTONIO (1789–1865), b. Cádiz. Orator, statesman, and writer, the uncle of Juan Valera (q.v.). He belonged to various Masonic and revolutionary societies, such as La Fontana de Oro (q.v.). When Fernando VII put down the rebellion of 1823, Alcalá Galiano,

condemned to death for subversion, fled to England (where he was the first person to occupy a chair of Spanish literature). After Fernando's death, he returned in 1834 and applied the ideas of Montesquieu and the English Utilitarians he had learned abroad in his writing for the *Westminster Review* and the *Revue Trimestrielle* as well as for Spanish periodicals. His autobiographical *Recuerdos de un anciano* (1878) and *Memorias* (1886) are useful sources for the period, and are commended by Menéndez y Pelayo for a candour unusual in modern Spanish literature.

Of his other books possibly the most valuable is his translation and continuation of Dunham's history of Spain to which Alcalá Galiano contributed vols. 5–7. At first an opponent of Boehl von Faber (q.v.), who supported Schlegel's advocacy of Romanticism, Alcalá Galiano came to agree with his views, and he expounds Romantic tenets in the prologue to *El moro expósito* by the Duque de Rivas (q.v.), much as Hugo had done in the preface to his own play *Cromwell*.

ALCALÁ YÁÑEZ DE RIBERA, JERÓNIMO DE (1563–1632), b. Segovia. He studied medicine in Valencia and later practised in Segovia. He wrote minor devotional works, such as *Milagros de Nuestra Señora de la Fuencisla* (1615), and *Verdades para la vida cristiana* (1632). But he is best remembered for a picaresque novel *Alonso, mozo de muchos amos* (q.v., 1624–6), known in later editions as *El donado hablador*.

ALCALÁ Y HERRERA, ALONSO (1599–1682), b. Lisbon. Poet and merchant. A short-story writer of considerable ingenuity, whose chief contribution to the Baroque is the *Varios effectos de amor en cinco novelas ejemplares. Y nuevo artificio de escrevir prosas, y versos, sin una de las cinco letras vocales, excluyendo Vocal diferente en cada novela* (1641). In this curiosity, *Los dos soles de Toledo* is written without using the letter *a*; *La carroza con las damas* without *e*; *La perla de Portugal* without *i*; *La peregrina ermitaña* without *o*; and *La serrana de Cintia* without *u*. This 'nuevo artificio' was already known in Spanish from a ballad reproduced in the anonymous picaresque novel *La vida de Estebanillo González* (1646).

Alcalá y Herrera also wrote *Iardim anagramático* (1654), of which the second part contains religious verses in Spanish, and the rest is in Portuguese and Latin; and *Corona, y ramillete de flores salutíferas; antídoto del alma, consuelo de afligidos; y desengaño del mundo* (1682).

Alcalde de Zalamea, El, a play written c. 1643 by Pedro Calderón de la Barca (q.v.).

Soldiers quartered in the village of Zalamea disturb the community. Captain Álvaro de

Ataide, billeted on Pedro Crespo, abducts his daughter Isabel and rapes her in a wood. When Crespo runs to her defence, he is tied to a tree where he can hear her cries. Álvaro is finally hunted down and wounded by Isabel's brother Juan before soldiers can come to his aid. Isabel then finds her father, and tells him what has happened. The crux of the play lies in the different solutions at the outraged man's disposal. He might kill Isabel (who has, innocently, brought dishonour on his family); or kill the Captain; or try to keep the matter secret; or persuade the Captain to marry Isabel.

The village scribe enters to announce to Crespo his election as mayor. He is now forbidden by his official position to duel with Ataide or to hush the matter up, and as a loving father he repudiates the thought of killing Isabel, though the hotheaded Juan with his conventional views on honour does unsuccessfully attempt this. He begs Ataide to marry the girl after his arrest. When he refuses, Crespo hands him over for civil execution instead of delivering him to the military authorities for court-martial. The general, Lope de Figueroa, incensed at the alcalde's having exceeded his authority, orders the destruction of Zalamea. But King Philip II appears and decides in favour of the alcalde, appointing him mayor for life. Calderón's moral is that Crespo has preferred justice (open dealing and refusal to duel) and love (refusing to kill Isabel) to the rough justice of *honor* according to which he should have killed the Captain with his own hands.

Like Don Juan in Tirso's *El burlador de Sevilla* (q.v.), Ataide is a disruptive force in society, while Pedro Crespo upholds the concepts of harmony and order. The play has been wrongly considered revolutionary and realistic; in fact it is conservative in spirit and stylized in structure. Calderón's treatment of the source of the play is discussed in A. E. Sloman's *Dramatic craftsmanship of Calderón* (Oxford, 1958).

See also P. Halkhoree, *Calderón de la Barca: 'El Alcade de Zalamea'* (London, 1972).

ALCÁNTARA, FRANCISCO JOSÉ (1922–), b. Haro, Logroño. Novelist. *La muerte le sienta bien a Villalobos* (Barcelona, 1955) won the Premio Nadal in 1954. In 1961 his *Historia de Esmeralda* (at that time not yet published in Spain) was published at Freiburg as *Sie kommen, Don Antonio.*

ALCÁZAR, BALTASAR DEL (1530–1606), b. Seville. Soldier and *jocoso* poet. A writer of racy, humorous light verse, he never considered his *jeux d'esprit* worthy of publication. His friend Francisco Pacheco preserved what little survives of his work, which combines fluency with grace

and rhythm. Of a gay disposition, he well deserves the praise of Jáuregui; 'no sólo superior a todos, sino entre todos singular'. His numerous epigrams, influenced by Martial, are stylish and not without malice, his sonnets workmanlike and the love poems often exquisite. But his most characteristic verses are those celebrating the creature comforts, such as *La cena jocosa*. In *Tres cosas me tienen preso*, the poet proclaims equal affection for his lady, smoked ham, and aubergines in melted cheese. Collections of his works made by Espinosa (1605), López de Sedano (1776–8), Estala (1797), and de Castro (1854), were superseded by Rodríguez Marín's edition published by the Real Academia Española in 1910.

ALCHARISI, see HARIZI, Judah ben Shlomoh al-.

ALCOCER, PEDRO DE (16th c.), b. Toledo. Historian, whose *Hystoria ... de la imperial ciudad de Toledo* (1554) is of great interest for its accumulation of facts and legends. He also wrote a *Relación de algunas cosas que pasaron en estos reinos desde que murió la reina católica doña Isabel, hasta que acabaron las Comunidades en la ciudad de Toledo* which remained unpublished until 1872.

Alcor, Paraguayan literary review, begun in 1955 by the critic Rubén Bareiro Saguier (b. 1930) and the playwright Julio César Troche, to publish the so-called Generation of '50, mainly poets from the Academia Universitaria and the Faculty of Philosophy in Asunción. Contributors include Ramiro Domínguez and José Luis Appleyard (qq.v.) as well as Carlos Villagra Marsal (b. 1932) and Elsa Wiezel (b. 1927).

The members of this group reveal in their works a sense of melancholy, nostalgia for a lost paradise (their youth was scarred by the civil war of 1947), and occasionally that anger felt by children at adult betrayal. The key book of the movement is Appleyard's *Entonces era siempre* (1946).

ALCOVER I MASPONS, JOAN (1854–1926), b. Palma de Mallorca. His Castilian *Poesías* (1887) were followed by work in Catalan collected by M. Ferra in *Poesies completes*. His best work is not popular in style, but deserves to be better known for its delicacy and gentle melancholy, in particular in the elegies on the death of his four sons, and in *La Cançó de la Balanguera.*

ALDANA, COSME DE (16th c.), b. Valencia. The brother of Francisco de Aldana (q.v.), whose works he edited posthumously. In the year of his brother's death he published in Italian a verse *Discorso contra il volgo, in cui con buone raggioni si riprovano molte sue false opinioni* (Florence, 1578), which he later revised and translated as *Invectiva contra el vulgo y su maledicencia*, reprinted in vol. 36 (1855) of the BAE. Leaving the service of the Medici family in Florence, he joined the retinue of the Grand Constable Velasco in Milan and wrote so many flattering sonnets to his protector that Velasco turned on him and called him an ass. In retaliation, Aldana wrote the mock-heroic *Asneyda: Obra irrisoria de las necedades más comunes de las gentes*, but died before it could be printed, and Velasco's agents traced and destroyed so many of the MSS. that the work is feared lost. The only account of it is given by Suárez de Figueroa in his *Passagero* (qq.v.).

Aldana also wrote *Sonetos y octavas ... en lamentación de la Muerte de su Hermano el Capitán Francisco de Aldana* (Milan, 1587) and *Segunda parte* (Florence, 1587).

ALDANA, FRANCISCO DE (1537–78), b. Naples? Poet who was unjustifiably neglected until recently. He wrote sensual love sonnets, often in a pastoral setting; religious poems such as the *Canción a Cristo crucificado*; and mythological poetry, including a *Fábula de Faetonte*.

Because of his environment and reading, his work possesses Italian characteristics, such as intellectual vigour; the then fashionable neo-Platonism, seen at its finest in the important *Carta para Arias Montano sobre la contemplación de Dios y los requisitos della* written in 1577 and edited by Cossío in 1935; and freedom in the treatment of physical love, as in the sonnet *¿Cuál es la causa, mi Damón?* His imagery and vocabulary were strikingly original, and led Cervantes (himself a soldier, like Aldana) to call him 'el divino'.

Aldana was killed at al-Qasr al-Kabir (Alcazarquivir), Morocco, during the ill-fated expedition of King Sebastián of Portugal. His brother Cosme edited the *Primera parte de las Obras que hasta agora se han podido hallar del capitán Francisco de Aldana* (Milan, 1589) and a *Segunda parta ...* (Madrid, 1591). E. L. Rivers edited his *Poesías* (1957) for the Clásicos Castellanos and also wrote *Francisco de Aldana, el divino capitán* (Badajoz, 1955). A Rodríguez-Moñino edited Aldana's *Epistolario poético completo* (Badajoz, 1946) and M. Moragón Maestre edited the *Obras completas* (2 vols., 1953).

ALDEBARÁN, pseudonym of Soledad Acosta de Samper (q.v.).

ALDECOA, IGNACIO (1925–69), b. Vitoria. Novelist and short-story writer considered by some to be the most important writer of the Generation of 1954, the second post-war generation, as Cela (q.v.) is believed to head the first. He was married to the writer Josefina Rodríguez. After two books of poetry *Todavía la vida* (1947) and *Libro de las algas* (1949), Aldecoa turned to the novel. He said of his school: 'We do not write books about books, we are disciples of nobody, and we do not wish to dominate anybody. We follow one path: the novel of reality and lyricism in present-day Spain'. His first novel, *El fulgor y la sangre* (Barcelona, 1954), explores the state of Spain through the reminiscences of five women married to guardias civiles, who are in turn tied to their lonely castle somewhere in Castile, where 'they were set in the world for the sole purpose of fulfilling their duty'. Aldecoa said 'I am convinced that there is a Spanish reality, at once harsh and tender, that· has hardly been touched on in our novels', a deficiency for which he sought to make up by concentrating on those less colourful and less pleasant aspects of Spanish life which the tourist tends to overlook. The other two books in his trilogy *La España Inmóvil* dealt with gipsies: *Con el viento solano* (Barcelona, 1956), and bull-fighting (a novel written in 1958 called *Los pozos* but not yet published). His other novels are *Gran Sol* (Barcelona, 1957), and *Parte de una historia* (Barcelona, 1967). Aldecoa's shorter novels and stories include *Vísperas de silencio* (1955), *Espera de tercera clase* (1955), *El corazón y otros frutos amargos* (1959), *Caballa de pica* (1961), *Arqueología* (1962), *Neutral córner* (1962), *Pájaros y espantapájaros* (1963), and *Los pájaros de Baden-Baden* (1965). He wrote two travel books: *Cuaderno de Godo* (1961) and *El país vasco* (1962).

ALDRETE or ALDERETE, BERNARDO JOSÉ DE (1565–1641), b. Málaga. Antiquary. He became Canon of Cordova Cathedral in 1614. An elegant prose style distinguishes his linguistic and antiquarian studies: *Del origen, y principio de la lengua castellana ò romance que oi se usa en España* (Rome, 1606) and *Varias antigüedades de España, África, y otras provincias* (Antwerp, 1614).

ALEGRÍA, CIRO (1909–67), b. Huamachuco Province, Peru. Peruvian novelist, educated in Trujillo, one of his teachers being César Vallejo (q.v.). He was prevented from finishing his studies and was several times imprisoned for his political activities on behalf of the Aprista party of Victor Raúl Haya de la Torre (q.v.), and was finally exiled to Chile in 1934. His trilogy on the oppressed Indian continues, at a much higher artistic level, the work of Clorinda Matto de Turner (q.v.). *La serpiente de oro* (1935, awarded the Premio Nacimiento) was translated into

English as *The golden serpent* (New York, 1963). This first novel deals with a primitive Indian settlement beside the river Marañón, and was written while Alegría was working as a journalist in Chile. He entered a tuberculosis sanatorium in 1936, and during convalescence wrote *Los perros hambrientos* (q.v., 1938). His best novel is *El mundo es ancho y ajeno* (q.v., 1939), and others include *Duelo de caballeros* (1963) and *Lázaro* (Buenos Aires, 1973). Alegría worked for the U.S. Office of War Information and the Coordinator of Inter-American Affairs during World War II, and taught for some time at Puerto Rico University.

His importance is twofold: he was a fine artist, and he was a social thinker who explored the extent to which he believed the Peruvian Indian could control his own destiny to the best advantage. In this his books follow the tradition of Enrique López Albújar and presage the achievement of José María Arguedas (qq.v.).

ALEGRÍA, FERNANDO (1918–), b. Santiago. Chilean left-wing novelist, poet, and literary critic. His *avant-garde* poem *Instrucciones para desnudar a la raza humana* has been illustrated by the Chilean painter Matta and translated by Matthew Zion and Lennart Bruce (San Francisco, 1968). He has studied and taught in the U.S.A., especially in California, and won the Farrar and Rinehart Literary Prize in 1943 for his novel *Lautaro: joven libertador de Arauco*. He had already published *Recabarren* (1938), on the life of a socialist (later communist) organiser of the Federación Obrera in Chile who committed suicide in 1925; and another short novel, *Leyenda de la ciudad perdida* (1941). *Camaleón* (1950) was a political novel on corruption in Chile. His volume of political stories *El poeta que se volvió gusano* (1956) was followed by *Caballo de copas* (1957), a picaresque novel set in San Francisco.

In addition to numerous articles on Chilean literature, Alegría has published *Ideas estéticas en la poesía contemporánea* (1939), *Ensayo sobre cinco temas de Thomas Mann, Walt Whitman en Hispanoamérica*, and *La poesía chilena: orígenes y desarrollo del siglo XVI al XIX* (Mexico City, 1954), *Literatura y revolución* (1971) and the novel *Amerika, Amerikka, Amerikkka* (1970).

ALEIXANDRE Y MERLO, VICENTE (1898–), b. Seville. Poet. He studied in Málaga, and qualified as a lawyer in Madrid. Indifferent health prevented a normal career, and from 1925 he devoted himself to poetry. His first verses appeared in Ortega y Gasset's *Revista de Occidente* (qq.v.). He was a prominent member of the Generación del 1927 (q.v.). His first book, *Ámbito* (1928), is permeated by the influence of Guillén and Salinas (qq.v.), who also belonged to that movement. Aleixandre experimented with surrealism in *Espadas como labios* (1932), *Pasión de la tierra* (1935), *La destrucción o el amor* (1935) which won the Premio Nacional de Literatura, and *Poemas paradisíacos* (1942). His best work is generally thought to be *Sombra del paraíso* (1944). In 1949 he was elected a member of the Real Academia Española (q.v.). Later books included *Mundo a solas* (1950), *Nacimiento último* (1953), *Historia del corazón* (1954), and *Los encuentros* (1958), the last a series of impressions of contemporary writers. His *Poesías completas* (1960) ran to 864 pages, but were supplemented later by the impressive *En un vasto dominio* (1962), and *Retratos con hombre* (1965).

Since Aleixandre's *Obras completas* appeared in 1968, he has published *Poemas de la consumación* (1968), *Antología del mar y de la noche* (1971), *Poesía superrealista* (1971), and *Diálogos del conocimiento* (Barcelona, 1975), dialogues on death, knowledge, and experience. The latest complete edition is *Antología total* (Barcelona, 1975). Like all surrealist writers, Aleixandre is difficult to approach at first, but he is concerned with fundamental questions of existence and humanity, and has exercised considerable influence in Spain. He won the Nobel Prize for Literature in 1977.

See L. de Luis, *Vicente Aleixandre* (1970). There is also the English-language study by K. Schwartz, *Vicente Aleixandre* (New York, 1970).

Alejandrino, a Spanish verse form composed of two hemistichs with seven syllables each; not to be confused with the French alexandrine, a line of twelve syllables; nor with the Portuguese alexandrine, a line of thirteen.

The Spanish *alejandrino* derives its name from Alexander the Great, whose epic and legendary deeds were celebrated in this metre in the *Libro de Alejandre* (q.v.). Other examples of the *mester de clerecía* (q.v.) in *alejandrinos* are the *Libro de Apolonio* and the Canciller López de Ayala's *Rimado de Palacio* (qq.v.).

Among the early masters of the metre are Gonzalo Berceo (q.v.). Darío (q.v.) varied the *alejandrino's* form slightly by accenting the 3rd and 6th syllables of each hemistich, as in his *Sonatina* from which these lines are drawn:

La princesa está triste . . . ¿Qué tendrá la
| princesa?
los suspiros se escapan de su boca de fresa,
que ha perdido la risa, que ha perdido el color.

Aleluyas, verses printed below wood-block prints or other illustrations on broadsheets (see PLIEGOS SUELTOS) initially of a religious nature but subsequently secular. Their vogue fluctuated from the end of the 15th c. to well into the 19th, and their part in spreading literacy, when printed books were scarce in Spain, is being studied by scholars such as Julio Caro Baroja (q.v.).

ALEMÁN, MATEO (1547–1615), b. Seville. Novelist. The son of the Jewish prison doctor of Seville, he studied medicine in Salamanca and Alcalá. After being imprisoned for debt in 1580, 1594, and 1601, he went to Mexico in 1608 with his protector and patron, Archbishop García Guerra, whose biography he published in 1613. Alemán's other minor works include the biography *San Antonio de Padua* (1603), and *Ortografía castellana* (1609). His *Guzmán de Alfarache* (q.v.) is the first and most popular picaresque novel.

D. McGrady's *Mateo Alemán* (New York, 1968) is a good general introduction based on Francisco Rodríguez Marín's fundamental *Discursos leídos ante la Real Academia Española* (2nd edn., Seville, 1907) and *Documentos referentes a Mateo Alemán y a sus deudos más cercanos, 1546–1607* (1933).

ALEXANDER THE GREAT, Alexander III of Macedon (356–323 B.C.), son of Philip II. See ALEXANDRE, Libro de, and ALJAMÍA (for the *Recontamiento del rey Alixandre*).

Alexandre, Libro de, a *mester de clerecía* (q.v.) poem of 10,700 lines in the *cuaderna vía* (q.v.) which introduces classical themes (here the exploits of Alexander the Great) into Spanish literature. The authorship is disputed. Juan Lorenzo de Astorga, mentioned in the 14th-c. MS. in the Biblioteca Nacional, Madrid, was probably only the copyist. Gonzalo de Berceo has been suggested as author but the secular classical learning shown in the text does not correspond to his other writings. The Archdeacon Jofré de Loaysa and even Alfonso 'el Sabio' himself have been proposed, but the evidence is not convincing. Its date is usually given as *c.* 1240, roughly contemporary with that of the *Libro de Apolonio* (q.v.).

The author dwells admiringly on Alexander's prowess in battle, his nobility, generosity, and his eagerness for knowledge. Among the anachronisms which, for some modern readers, may detract from the book's impact by their unintentional humour, are the concealment of Achilles in a monastery and the appointment of Aristotle as a doctor of the Church. But the style is generally so exuberant that such errors are quickly forgotten. Among the finest passages are a poem to May, descriptions of the tomb of

Darius, and of Alexander's tent, and the narration by Alexander of the Trojan War, using as sources Benoît de Sainte-More's *Roman de Troie* and Guido delle Colonne's *Historia troiana.* Moral discourses inserted in the work suggest that it may have been intended as a *speculum principis.*

There is a good edition by R. S. Willis: '*El libro de Alexandre' : texts of the Paris and the Madrid manuscripts* (Princeton, 1934). The same author has written *The relationship of the Spanish 'Libro de Alexandre' to the 'Alexandreis' of Gautier de Châtillon* (Princeton, 1934) and *The debt of the Spanish 'Libro de Alexandre' to the French 'Roman d'Alexandre'* (Princeton, 1935).

ALFONSO, PEDRO (*fl.* 1106), b. Huesca. Compiler of an important collection of tales, *Disciplina clericalis.* Alfonso, a convert from Judaism, was baptized in 1106. His 33 stories are taken in the main from Arabic sources and are written in bad Latin. Proverbs and aphorisms originally from Persian, Indian, and other Asian traditions are included, as are licentious tales. There are editions by A. González Palencia (1948); and by Eberhard Hermes (London, 1977) with an English translation by P. D. Quarries.

ALFONSO X, *King of Castile* (1221–84), b. Toledo. Called 'el Sabio'. Son of Fernando III and Beatrice of Swabia. he continued the Reconquest begun by his father, whom he succeeded in 1252. He liked to call himself 'King of the Three Religions' and was at times benevolent towards the Jews, if less so towards his Muslim subjects. He will be considered here only as writer, editor, scholar, and patron of the arts. It is doubtful to what extent he contributed to the writing of the great works of scholarship he initiated, subsidised, and brought (in most cases) to fruition, but there can be no doubt that he and his collaborators wrought the first significant classics of Castilian prose. 'The learned' king's productions are usually classified under four heads: history, law, science, and poetry.

(a) *History.* As a co-ordinator of research, Alfonso had no medieval equal. The first part of the *Grande e General Estoria* was begun *c.* 1272, and the fourth finished in 1280. The fifth and sixth parts were written between 1280 and 1284, the year of his death. A universal 'history', it mixes myth with more factual material. Its chronology stops with the parents of the Virgin Mary. It is the first national history in a vernacular European language. The most important of the enterprises in historical research at the Court of Alfonso X, however, was the *Primera Crónica General, o sea Historia de España que mando componer Alfonso el Sabio y se continuaba bajo Sancho IV en 1289* (the title of R. Menéndez

Pidal's edition, 1906). Begun in 1270, it was still in progress in 1289 and may have been finished much later. The first two parts are based on Lucas de Tuy's Latin chronicle and Ximénez de Rada's preface in the *Historia gothica*. Biblical, classical, and Arab sources as well as *cantares de gesta* were all utilized by the collaboraators in later parts: Bernardo de Briheuga, Garci Fernández de Toledo, Juan Gil de Zamora, Jofré de Loaysa, and Suero Pérez, among many others. Under Alfonso's direction the chronicle reached the period of King Rodrigo and the loss of Spain to the Moors in 711, and it was brought up to his own times in the reign of Sancho IV. Three other chronicles are based on Alfonso's *Crónica general*: (1) the *Crónica abreviada* of Juan Manuel; (2) the *Segunda crónica general* or *Crónica de 1344*; and (3) a lost version known from four adaptations, namely the *Tercera crónica general* of Florián de Ocampo, the *Crónica de veinte reyes*, and the *Crónica de Castilla* on which is based the *Crónica particular del Cid*.

(b) *Law*. *Las siete partidas* (q.v., 1256–63) is a compilation of laws, predominantly from Roman law, intended to systematize known practices ('seven' is esoteric rather than arithmetical in connotation) and forms an encyclopaedia of Spanish medieval life. It was compiled by Jacobo or Jacome Ruiz, 'el maestre de las leys', Samuel Halevy, Juan Alfonso, Archdeacon of Santiago de Compostela, and Fernán Martínez, among others. Alfonso appears to have helped with the editing. It is hardly surprising that this single work did not accomplish its grand aim of unifying the Castilian legal system—an objective achieved only in 1348. But it is surprising that Spanish legislation still derives in great part from Alfonso's work, and that until quite recently Florida and Louisiana drew part of their statutes from the *Siete partidas*.

(c) *Science*. Alfonso's contributions to science were transmissions rather than creations. The *Lapidario* has been edited by J. Fernández Montaña (1881) and *Libros del saber de astronomía* by Rico y Sinobas (5 vols., 1863–7). The *Libro de los juegos de acedrex, dados e tablas* has been edited by A. Steiger (1941). All three works were translated or adapted from Arabic sources by Jewish scholars.

(d) *Poetry*. As a poet, Alfonso preferred the more highly developed, expressive and musical Galician-Portuguese dialect to Castilian. He is considered the writer of at least 400 *Cantigas de Santa María* composed to be sung to music, many of them concerning miracles allegedly worked through the Virgin's intercession. To the narrative element of the *mester de clerecía* (q.v.) Alfonso X added lyricism, fusing the two in a way new to Hispanic literature.

ALFONSO XI (1312–50), supposed author of the first troubadour song recorded in Castilian, which appears in the *Canzoniere portoghese della Biblioteca Vaticana* (ed. E. Monaci, Halle, 1875). Part of the *Libro de montería* has also been attributed to him.

Alfonso XI, Poema de, a verse chronicle written, probably in 1348, by a *juglar* who witnessed some of the events he describes in the reign of Alfonso XI.

It is one of the last works of the *mester de juglaría* (q.v.). The writer named in stanza 1841, *yo Rodrigo Yannes la noté/en lenguaje castellano*, is now believed to have translated the text from a lost Galician original. Carolina de Michaëlis (q.v.) suggested that Yáñez might have been Leonese, familiar with Galician. The author drew on vernacular poetic tradition, and borrowed from the *Libro de Alexandre* and the *Poema de Fernán González*, among other sources.

The poem consists of nearly 10,000 octosyllabic lines rhyming abab, and is most successful in social commentary and descriptions of battles. It has been edited by Yo ten Cate (2 vols., Amsterdam, 1942; Madrid, 1956).

See Diego Catálan Menéndez-Pidal, *Poema de Alfonso XI: fuentes, dialecto, estilo* (1953).

Alghero, Sardinia, an enclave in Sardinia in which Catalan was the official language until 1720, when the House of Savoy took control of the island. Catalan was used unofficially long afterwards.

Catalan writers of Alghero include the poet Sire, whose popular song *¿Qué faré, pobre de mi ...?* is reminiscent of the Hispanic-Arab survivals. Jacint Lluis Soffi (1742–1816) is the author of religious and satirical poems of mediocre worth and a memorable sonnet glossing the *Stabat Mater*. Other sonneteers include Canon Vitelli and Josep d'Arcaine. Alghero poetry tends to be more parochial and circumstantial than that of other Catalan areas, as demonstrated by the brothers Domènec (1758–1829), Mateu Lluís (1761–1818), and Joan Francesc Simon (1761–1819).

See E. Toda, *La poesia catalana a Sardenya* (Barcelona, n.d.) and A. Ballero de Candia, *Alghero* (Cagliari, 1961), pp. 399–405.

Alguacil alguacilado, El, the second of the *Sueños* of Francisco de Quevedo (qq.v.).

Alhambra (Arabic: *al-hamra*, 'the red'), the palace of the Moorish kings at Granada, built mainly in the 13th c. Washington Irving's *Legends of the Alhambra* (1832) includes many of the traditional stories of the palace.

Aljamía (Arabic: *al-'ajamiya*, 'indistinct' and used of foreign speech).

A term originally applied to the particular form of corrupt Latin spoken by mozárabes (q.v.), in which sense the word occurs in the *Poema de Alfonso XI* (q.v.): *Dixieron los escuderos/ Sabedes bien la arauia,/¿Sodes bien uerdaderos/De tornarla en aljamía?*

Later, and more commonly, it was the Moorish name for Castilian. *Poemas aljamiados* are those written in the Spanish language with Hebrew or Arabic characters. Mudéjares (q.v.) and Jews gradually forgot their mother tongues and spoke only Castilian, while retaining their original scripts. The earliest example of *literatura aljamiada* was until recently thought to be the *Poema de Yúsuf* (q.v.) of the 14th c., but most of these clandestine MSS. are of the 16th c. The *mufti* of Segovia, 'Isa Jabr (usually Ice de Gebir in Spanish), wrote an important *Kitab Segobiano* (1462), to spread Islam in Spain, and most of the other surviving MSS. are missionary in character, even the fairy tale *La doncella Carcayona*, whose theme is 'la ilahu ill' Allah' ('There is no other god but Allah').

Only one other *aljamiado* author is known by name: the Mancebo de Arévalo, who wrote *Sumario de la relación y exercicio espiritual, Tafsira*, and *Breve compendio de nuestra Santa Ley*, the last written in collaboration with Baray de Reminjo, *faqih* of Aragón. The so-called *Recontamiento del rey Alixandre*, another example of *aljamiada* literature, was published by Guillén Robles (1886). It deals with prodigious happenings to Alexander the Great, among its sources being Greek and Persian legends.

S. M. Stern (q.v.) has recently traced the history of *aljamiado* writing back to the 10th c. through his research into the *kharjas* (q.v.).

ALMAFUERTE, pseudonym of Pedro Bonifacio Palacios (q.v.).

ALMANZOR, see MANSUR, Al-.

Alma y del cuerpo, Disputa del, see DISPUTA DEL ALMA Y DEL CUERPO.

Almohades (Arabic: *al-Muwahhidūn*, 'the monotheists').

A Muslim sect and ruling dynasty arising in the 12th c. in north-west Africa. The founder, Muhammad ibn Tumart, proclaimed himself Mahdi (Messiah) and accused all other Muslims of heretical polytheism. He and his successor 'Abd al-Mu'min seized Fez and Marrakish in 1128. In 1147 they entered Spain, superseding the Almorávides (q.v.), and bringing with them the philosophy and science of the Middle East.

The Almohades dominated Muslim Spain until the Battle of Las Navas de Tolosa (1212).

Almorávides (Arabic: *al-Murābitūn*, 'the holy ones'). A Muslim sect and ruling dynasty arising in the 9th c. in north-west Africa. They expanded as far south as the Sudan, and in 1080 founded Marrakish. At the request of the Spanish Muslims, they entered Spain in 1086 under Yusuf ibn Tashfin to re-establish the political unity of Islam, winning the important battles of Sagrajas (1086) and Uclés (1108). Their dynasty declined and was overrun in 1148 by the Almohades (q.v.). It was during the Almoravid period that the Cid (q.v.) flourished. Without the Almoravid incursions, Spain would have reverted to Christian control much earlier.

A lo divino ('in religious terms'), a literary treatment, which turned popular secular themes into religious themes by the use of Christian allegory, metaphor, or symbolism. Particularly common during the Golden Age, versions *a lo divino* being made of e.g. *Las Obras de Boscán y Garcilaso* by Sebastián de Córdoba (Granada, 1575; ed. G. R. Gale, Ann Arbor, 1971), and of the *Idea de un Principe Politico Christiano Representado en cien Empresas* (Münster, 1640), of Diego de Saavedra Fajardo (q.v.), which was rendered *a lo divino* by Francisco Núñez de Cepeda as *Idea del buen pastor representada en empresas sacras* (Lyons, 1682).

ALOMAR, GABRIEL (1873–1940), b. Palma de Mallorca. Futurist poet (writing in Catalan), political ideologist, and diplomat. On the proclamation of the Republic he was appointed Spanish ambassador to Rome (1931) and later to Cairo. He wrote several volumes of poetry, including *La columna de foc* (1904), *El Futurisme* (1904), *El frente espiritual* (1918), and essays collected as *Verba* (1919). Then came *La formación de sí mismo* (1920) and *La política idealista* (1922), in which he argues that law does not have to adapt itself to human nature, but that human nature should conform to the law.

ALONE, pseudonym of Hernán Díaz Arrieta (q.v.).

ALONSO, AMADO (1896–1952), b. Lerín, Navarra. A philologist and literary critic, he studied phonetics under Menéndez Pidal and Navarro (qq.v.) in the Centro de Estudios Históricos in Madrid, and continued his studies in Hamburg. He created the Library of Hispano-American Dialectology in the Buenos Aires University and in 1939 helped to found the *Revista de Filología Española*. He taught at Harvard University from 1946. Among his many important works are *El problema de la lengua en América* (1935), *Castellano, español, idioma nacional* (1942), *Estudios lingüísticos* (2 vols., 1951–3), *De la pronunciación medieval a la moderna en español* (vol. 1, 1955), and *Materia y forma en poesía* (1955).

ALONSO, DÁMASO (1898–), b. Madrid. Critic, poet, and philologist. He was a pupil of R. Menéndez Pidal (q.v.), to whose chair of Romance Languages he was appointed in 1939 after lecturing in Germany, the U.S.A., England, and Peru. Alonso has written under the pen-name Alfonso Donado.

His *Poemas puros: poemillas de la ciudad* (1921) are imagist; his later poetry develops into a freer, more complex style: *Oscura noticia* (1944; 3rd edn., with *Hombre y Dios*, 1959), *Hijos de la ira* (1944; 3rd edn., 1958), and *Gozos de la vista*, hitherto unpublished in book form. *Poesías escogidas* appeared in 1969.

He translated James Joyce's *Portrait of the artist as a young man* as *El artista adolescente* (1926) and he has also made Spanish versions from Gerard Manley Hopkins and T. S. Eliot. Editions of the *Enchiridion* and *Paraclesis* of Erasmus (1932) show his interest in foreign literature, but he is best known for his editions and critical studies of Spanish writers, particularly Góngora. The rediscovery of Góngora began in 1927 with Alonso's edition and prose version of the *Soledades*, and *La lengua poética de Góngora*, which won the Premio Nacional de Literatura for that year but was not published until 1935. *Ensayos y estudios gongorinos* (1955) was followed by *Góngora y el 'Polifemo'* (1960), which is not only an edition and study of the *Fábula de Polifemo y Galatea* but an anthology and useful general survey of Góngora.

He has also written *La poesía de San Juan de la Cruz* (1942) and *Vida y obra de Medrano* (vol. 1, 1948; vol. 2, 1958). His critical methods are shown most clearly in *Poesía española* (1950; 5th edn., 1966) and in *Seis calas en la expresión literaria española* written in collaboration with Carlos Bousoño (1951; 3rd edn., 1963): here he distinguishes between the exterior form and the interior form of a work and investigates how far they combine successfully. His method is intended to display the timeless uniqueness of a work, for he believes that only a historian of culture should display the continuity of a tradition.

Poetas españoles contemporáneos (1952) is a personal book and in its impressionism contrasts with Alonso's other works, which include *Menéndez Pelayo, crítico literario* (1956), *De los siglos oscuros al de oro* (1958), *Primavera temprana de la literatura europea* (1961), *Del siglo de oro a este siglo de siglas* (1962), and *Cuatro poetas españoles* (1962), in which he declares a reduced interest in Góngora's formal values.

The best bibliography of Alonso's work is still F. Huarte Morton's in *Papeles de Son Armadans* (vol. 11, 1958). A. P. Debicki has published the first general study of him in English: *Dámaso Alonso* (New York, 1970).

ALONSO DE HERRERA, GABRIEL and HERNANDO, see HERRERA, Gabriel and Hernando Alonso de.

ALONSO DE MADRID, Fray (*fl.* 1521), b. Madrid. One of the major Franciscan ascetic writers (q.v.). His *Arte para servir a Dios* (Seville, 1521) is known to have influenced S. Ignacio de Loyola and S. Teresa de Ávila (qq.v.). It was edited with Alonso's other *Obras* by M. Mir in vol. 16 (1911), of the NBAE, and more recently by Fray Atanasio López (Barcelona, 1942). Fray Alonso also wrote *Espejo de ilustres personas* (Burgos, 1524). What little is known of his life and work has been published by J. Christiaens: *Alonso de Madrid: contribution à sa biographie et à l'histoire de ses ecrits* (*Les Lettres Romanes*, 1955).

Alonso, mozo de muchos amos (1624–6), by Jerónimo de Alcalá Yáñez de Ribera (q.v.). A picaresque novel, known in later editions as *El donado hablador*, owing something in manner and matter to *Lazarillo de Tormes* and *Marcos de Obregón* (qq.v.).

Alonso, a lay brother in a monastery, relates the story of his life and his many masters including a mean parish priest, a brutal soldier, an irreverent and irate sacristan, and a Valencian widow whose house was misery and misfortune itself. After returning the poorer from his adventures in Mexico, Alonso joined a theatrical troupe, became a servant in a convent, lived among gipsies, and married an old widow of Saragossa whose two sons purged him of all his wickedness. Although Alonso remains too shadowy, many of the 'masters' are drawn wittily and mordantly. Unlike Lazarillo, he dares to moralize to his masters on their sins and follies, with the unfortunate results only to be expected. The first part (1624) was so popular that it was reprinted in Barcelona (1625) and a second part published in Valladolid (1626).

ALONSO Y TRELLES, JOSÉ (1860–1924), b. Navia, Oviedo. He settled early in Uruguay, where he wrote *gauchesco* poetry for *El Fogón* and other magazines under the pen-name 'Viejo Pancho'. His collection *Paja brava* (1916) includes some of the most typical *gaucho* writing of its time, despite the fact that Alonso y Trelles was of European origin. His best-known play is *¡Guacha!* (1913).

Alphonsine Tables, a translation of astronomical tables compiled by az-Zarqali (q.v.).

ALSINA, José Arturo (1900–), b. Tucumán, Argentina. Dramatist. Alsina moved to Paraguay when young, and all his plays have been produced there: in 1926 *La marca de fuego* and the comedies *Flor de estero* and *Evangelina,* and in 1927 *El derecho de nacer.* His work was influenced by Ibsen.

ALTAMIRANO, Ignacio Manuel (1834–93). b. Torda (now Ciudad Guerrero), of Nahuatl-speaking and illiterate parents. Mexican journalist, poet, and novelist. He took part in the War of Reform (1858–1861), becoming a member of Congress in 1861. He contributed to many periodicals, and founded *El Renacimiento.* He has been called 'the American Danton'. Like Mármol and Isaacs (qq.v.), Altamirano was an important sentimental novelist, following Hugo, Balzac, and Dickens, though he hoped to begin a national tradition based on the familiar *costumbrismo.* His best-remembered works are *Clemencia* (1869), a novel set during the French intervention in 1863, and *El Zarco* (1900; translated by Mary Alt, London, 1951) on banditry in Mexico. He occupied several posts in the Mexican government, and was appointed Consul General to Spain in 1889.

The most up-to-date bibliography of Ignacio Manuel Altamirano is that by R. E. Warner (1955). His *Obras literarias completas* appeared in 1959.

See C. N. Nacci, *Ignacio Manuel Altamirano* (New York, 1970).

ALTAMIRA Y CREVEA, Rafael (1866–1951), b. Alicante. Historian, jurist, and literary critic. A teacher at the Institución Libre de Enseñanza (q.v.), Altamira was from 1916 professor of American Civil and Political Institutions at Madrid University. He also taught at Oviedo, and was a judge at the International Court of Justice, The Hague.

He wrote more than 60 books, including *Historia de España y de la civilización española* (5 vols., 1900–11); the short stories *Cuentos de Levante* (1895) and *Cuentos de mi tierra* (1925), and the novel *Reposo* (1903).

See V. Martínez Morellá and others (eds.), *Homenaje de la ciudad de Alicante a Rafael Altamira* ... (Alicante, 1973).

ALTOLAGUIRRE, Manuel (1905–59), b. Málaga. Poet and printer. He showed Republican sympathies during the Civil War, and later chose to go into exile. He was a founding director of the magazine *Litoral* (1927–9).

Despite the influence of Jiménez, which dominated *Las islas invitadas* (1926; 2nd enlarged edn., Mexico City, 1936), Altolaguirre soon found an individual voice, taking for his principal themes love, loneliness, and suffering. His poetry includes *Soledades juntas* (1931), *La lenta libertad* (1936), *Nube temporal* (Havana, 1939), and *Fin de un amor* (1949). His *Poesías completes, 1926–1959* (Mexico City, 1960) were followed by *Vida poética* (Málaga, 1962). He compiled a useful *Antología de la poesía romántica española* (1933) and translated Shelley's *Adonais,* and two plays by Pushkin. Altolaguirre's prose includes *Garcilaso de la Vega* (1933) and a chapter of an unpublished novel 'El caballo griego', in *Papeles de Son Armadans,* vol. 10, no. 30 (1958).

See M. L. Álvarez Harvey, *Cielo y tierra en la poesía de Manuel Altolaguirre* (1972).

Alumbradismo, the *alumbrados, iluminados,* or *dexados* formed a specific movement and a general current beyond the figures who traced their roots back to the Gnostics. They first achieved notoriety (for their alleged heterodoxy) in Toledo from 1516 and were increasingly persecuted from the first Inquisitorial edict of 1525, which denounced the following attitudes, among a total of forty-eight: that in a state of *dejamiento* ('abandonment', or in mystic terms, 'trance'), works are unimportant; and that external acts such as religious ritual and even prayer are worthless and even harmful. In the 17th c. the doctrine of *alumbradismo* found a sympathiser in Miguel de Molinos (q.v.). Juan de Valdés (q.v.), a major *alumbrado,* argued for the existence of Divine knowledge without the intervention of priests; thus the movement led inevitably to Protestant sympathies on the one hand, or ecstatic mysticism on the other, and Juan de la Cruz, Teresa de Jesús and other mystics were inevitably classed as heretical *alumbradistas* by the Inquisition.

See M. Menéndez y Pelayo, *Historia de los heterodoxos españoles* in *Obras completas* (1940–).

ALVARADO, Huberto (1925–), Guatemalan poet, whose first collection *Sombras de sal* (1947) was a sensitive act of homage to man as the centre of the universe. Alvarado has also published literary and political essays, and is notable for founding in 1947 the Grupo Saker Ti (q.v.) which continued, in a more radical vein, the movement of artistic renewal begun in Guatemala by the Grupo Acento (q.v.).

ÁLVAREZ, José Sixto (1858–1903), b. Gualeguaychú. Argentinian writer of *costumbrista* short stories and travel books. He wrote under the pseudonym 'Fray Mocho', and his middle name was Ceferino not Sixto, which is commonly given. He studied in Paraná, and settled as a journalist in Buenos Aires in 1879. After working on *El Nacional, La Pampa, La Patria Argentina*, and *La Nación*, he founded the magazine *Caras y caretas*, which later published stories by Güiraldes (q.v.). In 1906 he published in book form *Cuentos de Fray Mocho* taken from its pages. Many of his books were ephemeral, but three are still read: *Memorias de un vigilante* (1897), in which he used the pen-name Fabio Carrizo; *Un viaje al país de los matreros* (1897), a travel book on Entre Ríos; and *En el mar austral* (1898), a 'travel book' hoaxing his critics who gave him credit for observation but accused him of lacking imagination. In fact Fray Mocho never visisted Patagonia, despite the vividness of his account of experiences there. His *Vida de los ladrones célebres y sus maneras de robar* (1887), like the *Memorias* above, was derived from his experiences as a police official.

ÁLVAREZ, MIGUEL DE LOS SANTOS (1817–92), b. Valladolid. Minor Romantic poet in the tradition of his friend Espronceda, whose *El diablo mundo* (qq.v.) Álvarez continued (1852), but without the genius or craft of the model. Involved in the radical politics of the time, Álvarez was forced to flee to France in 1848. He returned in 1852, became Governor of Valladolid in 1854 and joined the diplomatic service two years later. Most of his writing was occasional. *La protección de un sastre* (1840), a caustically humorous novel, is more effective than the stories in *Tentativas literarias* (1864).

ÁLVAREZ DE CIENFUEGOS, NICASIO, see CIENFUEGOS, Nicasio Álvarez de.

ÁLVAREZ DE TOLEDO Y PELLICER, GABRIEL (1622–1714), b. Seville, of a Portuguese family. Poet and historian. He became librarian and secretary to Felipe V and was one of the founder-members of the Real Academia Española (q.v.). His poetry, apart from a burlesque *Burromaquia* written in his youth, is mystical and philosophical in tone. Torres de Villarroel (q.v.) edited his *Obras póstumas poéticas, con la Burromaquia* (1744). The first volume of his *Historia de la Iglesia y del mundo* appeared in 1713.

ÁLVAREZ DE VILLASANDINO, ALFONSO (c. 1345–c. 1425), b. Villasandino, Burgos. Also known as 'de Illescas'. He was a poet at the courts of Henry II and John I of Castile. He wrote on amatory, mercenary, and religious subjects (Fitzmaurice-Kelly calls him 'an importunate beggar'). His satire is clever and his technical skill is often evident in an uneven

body of verse. He was employed as a writer of love songs by Pero Niño, Conde de Buelna (q.v.).

His early work was in Galician, but he later wrote in Castilian. He is represented in the *Cancionero de Baena* (q.v.) by over 100 poems—more than any other contributor.

ÁLVAREZ GATO, JUAN (c. 1433–c. 1509), b. Madrid. Poet and courtier. He was steward to Queen Isabella in 1495. His delicate *villancicos*, satires, and religious lyrics were praised by Gómez Manrique (q.v.) and collected by J. Artiles Rodríguez as *Obras completas* (1928). A *Breve suma de la santa vida del reverendísimo e bienaventurado fray Fernando de Talavera* has been attributed to him.

See F. Márquez Villanueva, *Investigaciones sobre Juan Álvarez Gato* (1974), a supplement to the *BRAE*.

ÁLVAREZ LLERAS, ANTONIO (1892–1956), b. Bogotá. Colombian dramatist and novelist, and a founder of modern Colombian theatre. He writes on contemporary themes in a realistic and severely moral manner. Bayona Posada considers his *El virrey Solís* 'without doubt the best historical play of Spanish America'. His other plays include *Víboras sociales* (1911), *Como los muertos* (1916) and *Los mercenarios* (1924). *Ayer, nada más . . .* (1930) is his finest novel, dealing with the interior and exterior worlds of Bogotá.

ÁLVAREZ MURENA, HÉCTOR ALBERTO (1924–), Argentinian essayist, novelist, and short-story writer, who wrote as Hector A. Murena. Though he has published several books of verse and the play *El juez*, Álvarez is best known as an essayist.

El pecado original de América (1954) is described by the author as an autobiography of the mind. America's 'original sin' is historical—the feeling that America is a punishment for an unknown crime. Unlike other states, and also those of Latin America with a living Indian heritage, Argentina is subject to a peculiar type of nationalism which has to survive without a past. Murena criticizes the Borges of the 50s and his *Martín Fierro* group for creating an artificial, meaningless nostalgia. He views culture as an aid against reality and the sense of guilt.

Ensayos sobre subversión (1963) argues that the man of letters is necessarily subversive in defying time; hitherto Latin America has tolerated its writers because the human has been sacrificed to the political and the demands of 'nature' (J. E. Rivera's *La vorágine* or Hernández's *Martín Fierro*), or to an isolated intellectualism. Writers seek to be dominated either by capitalism or by

Marxism, whereas their value to society should lie in their determination not to be so exploited. *Homo atomicus* (1961) is an equally pessimistic view of the situation of contemporary man, presaging the destruction of mankind whether the modern age is viewed as a new Middle Ages or as a 'post-historic' period.

His novels include a trilogy of the Peronist period (*La fatalidad de los cuerpos*, 1955; *Las leyes de la noche*, 1958, and *Los herederos de la promesa*, 1965), echoing the disillusion of his essays *Historia de un día*, and a Quevedo-like *Epitalámica* (1969), the first volume of a projected seven showing the modern world as a grotesque tragicomedy which is also a series of clever parodies of contemporary authors, usually those whom he considers overvalued. *F.G.: Un bárbaro entre la belleza* (1972) is the biography of a fictitious poet, including his 'work'. His short stories are less original, owing a good deal to Poe, Quiroga (q.v.), and Kafka. The collections are *Primer testamento* (1946) and *El centro del infierno* (1956).

See Noé Jitrik, 'Un novelista oblicuo', *Ficción*, no. 23 (1960), pp. 52–70.

ÁLVAREZ QUINTERO BROTHERS, Serafín (1871–1938), Joaquín (1873–1944), playwrights. Both were born in Utrera and died in Madrid. After studying in Seville, the brothers formed a lasting dramatic association based on Andalusian *costumbrismo*. Their first, precocious, work *Esgrima y amor* (1888) was shown in Seville's Teatro Cervantes and some 200 popular, cheerful *sainetes* and comedies followed, not a few of them repetitive: *La reja* (1897), *El patio* and *Los galeotes* (1900), *Las flores* (1901), the zarzuela *La reina mora* with music by Serrano (1903), *El genio alegre* (1906), and many more. Their first success was *El ojito derecho* (1897). These gay novelettes for the stage are sentimental, easily acted, and offer little matter for reflection, but the wit is abundant and the dialogue both vivid and racy. A typical comedy of the better sort is *Las de Caín* (q.v., 1908). Both brothers were members of the Spanish Academy.

ÁLVARO DE CÓRDOBA, PAULO (c. 800–c. 861), b. Cordova. Christian writer probably of Jewish origin. His Latin is faulty, Arabic being the official language of his period, but he varies in style from the complex and ornate in the anti-Muslim *Indiculus luminosus* (854) to the simply-expressed *Vida de San Eulogio* (860) which defends Christianity among the *mozárabes* through the life of his master and friend. He also wrote *Confessio* in the tradition of St. Augustine, 15 poems in rhetorical Latin, *Lamentum* formerly ascribed in error to Isidore of Seville, and letters (*Epistolario*, ed. J. Madoz, 1947, with a critical study). The *Liber scintillarum* commonly attributed to Paulo Álvaro was known in the previous century.

See C. M. Sage, *Paul Albar of Cordoba: studies on his life and writings* (Washington, 1943).

Amadís de Gaula, the title (and hero) of one of the earliest and undoubtedly the most influential of Peninsular romances of chivalry, surviving in Garci Rodríguez de Montalvo's version (Saragossa, 1508, probably not the first). The unique copy is in the British Library.

The full title of the version known to us, written about 1492, is *Los quatro libros del virtuoso cauallero Amadís de Gaula*. Montalvo claims to have written only the fourth book, and to have reworked the first three from earlier texts. These early versions are mentioned in the *Rimado de Palacio* of Pedro López de Ayala (q.v.), and the story was known before 1325. In the 15th-c. Portuguese chronicle of Gómez d'Azurara, *Amadís* is ascribed to Vasco de Lobeira, who is known to have fought in the Battle of Aljubarrota (1385), and Menéndez y Pelayo suggested that the book's sentiment is Portuguese or Galician. But the Knights of the Round Table seem to be closer to the spirit of Amadís. Certainly the Breton cycle of *libros de caballería* (q.v.) formed the basis for the exploits of Amadís, one of the knights whose characteristics included single-minded devotion to one woman, loyalty to one's overlord, fanatic hatred of the infidel, absorption in the pursuit of what has come to be known as 'quixotic' justice, and defence of the oppressed. Amadís was the apotheosis of these virtues. S. Ignacio Loyola loved the book and S. Teresa wrote an imitation of it.

Amadís is the illegitimate child of King Perion of Gaul and Princess Elisena of England. Shut in a box by his mother and thrown in a river, he was washed up and reared by Gandales of Scotland. His love for Princess Oriana is told at length; then follow the episodes of his knighting, the recognition by his parents, his enchantment in the palace of Arcalaus and his salvation by two wise maidens, the battle between Amadís and his brother Galaor, his penitence on the rock under the name Beltenebros, the battle with the monster Endriago on Devil's Island, and his marriage with Oriana.

In 1955 a MS. fragment of the pre-Montalvo *Amadís* was discovered, and from this it seems that Montalvo reduced the original, tightening up the style considerably; he also inserted a large number of moralising reflections and courtly letters and speeches which later—in France at least—were taken as models to be imitated in real life. The original *Amadís* seems to have ended tragically when Amadís was slain by his son Esplandián, whom he had fought incognito, and Oriana committed suicide by hurling herself from a window. Montalvo, on the other hand, maintains that Amadís never died, but that in time his deeds were eclipsed by those of his son, so that eventually his memory faded from the minds of men. Thus he makes the hero immortal, and shifts the story in the direction of myth and fantasy, qualities even more marked in the works of his successors and imitators.

The narrative of giants, dragons, and magicians is interspersed with episodes concerning minor characters whose feeble stature and exploits contrast with those of Amadís and the beautiful Oriana. Given its consistent tenor of exaggeration, the book's style is pleasant enough (the lack of didacticism in the first three parts was a novelty) and Juan de Valdés (q.v.) went so far in his *Diálogo* as to say that 'deben leerle todos los que quieran aprender el castellano'. Its appeal during several centuries can be seen from the many editions and imitations, as well as from the fascination *Don Quijote* (q.v.) still exerts. For, though *Don Quijote* is a satire against novels like *Amadís* (in fact it pillories only the later extravagances among *libros de caballería*), a good part of its readability stems from the paradox of its predecessors' absurdities placed for once in a realistic setting, with common people both involved in the action and commenting on it.

The original *Amadís* had already idealized to some extent the hero's life and deeds. Amadís is clearly modelled upon Lancelot; both Amadís and Lancelot arrive unknown at the court of great kings and there fall in love with ladies close to the monarch; both have protectors with magical powers (the Dame du Lac, Urganda) and also magical foes (Morgane, Arcalaus); each hero wins an enchanted residence (Joyous Gard, Insula Firme); both have sons whose exploits finally outdo their own (Galahad, Esplandián), and both boys are brought up in secret by hermits (Nascien, Nasciano); both fall out with their monarchs, and there is war; the hero, supported by his powerful kinsmen (Gawain, Galaor) in earlier conflicts, now finds them tragically ranged against him (Gawain serves Arthur; Galaor, Lisuarte). But while Lancelot is an adulterous traitor, Amadís is in the right; he is secretly married (validly by medieval Spanish law which recognised clandestine unions as valid civil contracts) to Oriana, who is the King's daughter, not his wife, and Lisuarte had sought to marry her to the Emperor of Rome. The marriage had been in secret as Amadís' noble birth, as son to Perión and Elisena, was not then known. Thus the lovers are able to remain strictly moral while 'enjoying' all the excitement of an illicit relationship, and their child is born in wedlock

(Galahad, of course, was not in any case the son of Guinevere).

This desire to raise the moral tone is also found in the Castilian versions of the romances of Tristram and Lancelot—the translators tend to play down burlesque or anti-chivalrous sentiments, and to minimize the adultery of heroes and heroines, a reflection perhaps of the more primitive, rather less sophisticated society of late medieval Castile, where the continued presence of the Moors to the South could long help to justify the view that the knightly way of life should be presented in a generally favourable light.

Imitations of *Amadís* generally lacked the facility of narrative and variety of invention of the original. Written in a spirit of total exaggeration, they unintentionally mocked the real virtues of the ascetic knight. It has been suggested that the *conquistadores* were strongly influenced by the *libros de caballería* and by *Amadís* in particular; Díaz del Castillo writes on his first view of Mexico City: 'we were amazed and said how it resembled the enchanted towers and temples that are found in the pages of *Amadís*'. (California was named after an imaginary realm in this book, just as Patagonia was named after a land in *Palmerín*.) Sequels to this secular best-seller were quick in coming. To Montalvo's four books a fifth *Las sergas de Esplandián* (Seville, 1510) was added by Garci Ordóñez de Montalvo and Páez de Ribera either wrote or edited a sixth. A seventh on *Lisuarte de Grecia* (son of Esplandián and grandson of Amadís) was published anonymously. Juan Díaz wrote an eighth novel in which Amadís dies an old man, but he was born again in Feliciano de Silva's *Amadís de Grecia* and subsequent books.

Gil Vicente (q.v.) wrote a *Tragicomedia de Amadís de Gaula*. In Cervantes' famous chapter of literary criticism in *Don Quijote*, Pt. I, ch. 6, *Amadís* is saved from the flames as 'el mejor de todos los libros que deste genero se han compuesto'.

AMADOR DE LOS RÍOS, JOSÉ (1818–78), b. Baena. Historian. His best works were an *Historia social, política y religiosa de los judíos en España y Portugal* (3 vols., 1875–6); an *Historia crítica de la literatura española* (7 vols., 1861–5; a 7 vol. facsimile reprint was completed in 1969), which concludes with the reign of Ferdinand and Isabel and is, in the main, superseded; and an *Historia de la Villa y Corte de Madrid* (1861–4), written in collaboration with Juan de Dios de la Rada y Delgado and Cayetano Rosell y López.

He translated the Psalms from the Hebrew, and edited the *Obras* of the Marquis of Santillana. His son Rodrigo (q.v.) was also an historian.

AMADOR DE LOS RÍOS, RODRIGO (1843–1917), b. and d. Madrid. Historian. He was the son of José Amador de los Ríos (q.v.). In 1911 he was appointed Director of the Museo Arqueológico Nacional. Among his numerous scholarly publications were *Inscripciones árabes de Sevilla* (1875), *Inscripciones árabes de Córdoba* (1879), and volumes on Burgos, Huelva, Albacete, Santander, and Murcia in the series *España: sus Monumentos y sus Artes*.

Amante liberal, El, one of the *Novelas ejemplares* (q.v., 1613) by Miguel de Cervantes Saavedra (q.v.), classified as 'inventive' in the traditional divisions.

Turkish corsairs land at Trapani, on the coast of Sicily. They enter a garden where the beautiful Leonisa is relaxing with her family, her betrothed Cornelio, and her despised admirer Ricardo. All escape but Leonisa and Ricardo, who vainly offers all his fortune to the pirate for the freedom of Leonisa. After many adventures, Ricardo and the renegade Muhammad save Leonisa and bring her back to Trapani, where Ricardo surrenders her to Cornelio. Leonisa, however, moved by the generosity and courage of her saviour, rejects Cornelio and marries Ricardo.

Amantes de Teruel, Los, a Spanish legend based on Boccaccio's *novella* of Girolamo and Silvestra. The Teruel poet Juan Yagüe de Salas, who claimed in his *Los amantes de Teruel: epopeya trágica* (Valencia, 1616) to have copied a local *Historia de los amores de Diego Juan Martínez de Marcilla y Isabel de Segura* (allegedly 1217), was a forger. Juan Pérez de Montalbán, Tirso de Molina (qq.v.), and several others adapted the theme, but the best-known version is the play (1837) by Juan Eugenio Hartzenbusch (q.v.).

The complicated plot concerns the separation of two lovers, Diego and Isabel. Diego has been given six years to acquire enough wealth to marry Isabel. This he achieves, but is captured by the Moors. In Valencia Queen Zulima falls in love with him and tells Isabel he is dead. On his release he is captured by bandits in the pay of Zulima before he can prevent Isabel marrying his rival, and both lovers die of sorrow.

The legend has been studied by E. Cotarelo y Mori: 'Sobre el origen y desarrollo de la Leyenda de los Amantes de Teruel', *RABM* (1903), and more recently in J. Caruana's '"Los Amantes de Teruel", ¿Tradición? ¿Traducción? ¿Historia?' in *Los amantes de Teruel* (Teruel, 1958). There is an opera on the subject by Tomás Bretón (1889).

AMARILIS, see ANÓNIMAS PERUANAS.

AMAT DE CORTADA I DE SENTJUST, RAFAEL D', BARON OF MALDÀ (1746–1819), b. Barcelona. Catalan autobiographer. Though Comas calls the Baron of Maldà the most important prose writer of Catalan in his time, he has also described the Baron's style as 'molt pobre i defectuós' (very poor and defective). The immensely detailed memoirs covering the period 1769 to 1816 fill some sixty volumes and, except for a few fragments which have been published, remain in MS. in the possession of the author's heirs.

The book is entitled *Calaix de sastre en que s'explicarà tot quant va succeint a Barcelona i veïnat des de mig any de 1769, a les que seguiran les dels demís anys esdevenidors per divertiment de l'autor i de sos oients, anexes en el dit Calaix de sastre les més mínimes frioleres*, and gives a remarkable picture of the society of Barcelona.

See A. Comas, *Historia de la literatura catalana*, vol. 4 (Barcelona, 1964), pp. 526–48.

Amauta, Peruvian *avant-garde* magazine founded in 1926 and edited by José Carlos Mariátegui (q.v.). On his death in 1930, it was taken over by Ricardo Martínez de la Torre, but survived for only three numbers. John E. Englekirk in his article on 'La literatura y la revista literaria en Hispanoamérica' (*Revista Iberoamericana*, vol. 28, January–June 1962, pp. 9–73), called *Amauta* the most important Marxist journal in Spanish at that time encouraging social realists such as César Falcón. In the first number Mariátegui declared that *Amauta* was 'not a platform open to all winds of the spirit. We make no concession to the fallacy of tolerating ideas. For us there are good ideas and bad ideas'. But his editorial line was not so doctrinaire as that of the contemporary Argentine review *Claridad* (q.v.), and *Amauta* found room for Xavier Abril, Martín Adán, and Alfredo González Prada as well as for Vallejo, Peralta, and Albert Hidalgo. *Amauta* imported many new ideas from Europe, introducing Grosz, Freud, Shaw, Unamuno, Gorki, and Trotski.

AMBROGI, ARTURO (1875–1936), b. San Salvador. Journalist and *costumbrista*. In 1894, having already published a series of essays called *Bibelots* (1893), he founded with other young writers *La Pluma*, a magazine following the modernism of Darío (q.v.) Ambrogi later became well known for a vigorous, colloquial prose style. His *Cuentos y fantasías* appeared in 1895. His own favourite book was *El libro del trópico* (1907), regional stories displaying his narrative skill at its best. He travelled in Chile and Argentina, but made an international reputation with his travel book *Sensaciones del Japón y de la China* (1915). This work and his other descriptions of landscapes are remarkably detailed and precise, showing the influence of Azorín (q.v.). He was Director of the National Library of El Salvador between 1919 and 1925.

AMÉRICA, JUANA DE, honorific title accorded to Juana de Ibarbourou (q.v.).

Americanismo, literary Americanism is the implicit or explicit intention of Latin American writers to impart to their work a sense of indigenous tradition, whether Indianist or deriving from the richness of Nature, as opposed to the Europeanism of certain authors nostalgic for Spain and the Roman and Christian West of Europe.

Americanist movements descending from the many oral traditions of the American Indian peoples (most of them still active today though ill-documented) include the realist novel (with debts to Zola), such as *Raza de bronce* (1919) by the Bolivian Alcides Arguedas (q.v.), *Huasipungo* (1934) by the Ecuadorian Jorge Icaza (q.v.), or *El mundo es ancho y ajeno* (1941) by the Peruvian Ciro Alegría; Gaucho literature (q.v.), which reached its peak in the sardonic narrative poem *Martín Fierro* (q.v., 1872), by the Argentinian José Hernández (q.v.); and Afro-Cubanism, exemplified by Fernando Ortiz (q.v.).

The rise of Romanticism stressed the plight of the Indian caught up in a world which he could not control; the influence of realism on Americanist writing increased the genuine concern by writers throughout the continent, many of them of Indian or *mestizo* race themselves; modernism, though influenced by French Parnassianism, was born in Latin America and flourished there; while the vision of such leading contemporaries as the Colombian Gabriel García Márquez, the Cuban Alejo Carpentier, and the Guatemalan Miguel Ángel Asturias (qq.v.) is intelligible only in the light of Americanist fantasy and reality.

Linguistic *americanismos* (such as *seseo* and *yeísmo*) are peculiarities of the Spanish spoken in Latin America.

Amigo Manso, El (1882), one of the *Novelas españolas contemporáneas* by Benito Pérez Galdós (q.v.).

Máximo Manso is a young philosophy professor influenced by *krausismo* (q.v.). His high ideals are neither noticed nor respected by the Spain of his time, nor by the poor governess Irene, niece of Doña Cándida, a friend of Máximo's mother.

Peña, Manso's shrewd but complacent and shallow pupil, succeeds with Irene and in life generally, while the noble Manso is too shy and inexperienced to declare his love. He even curbs his jealousy and persuades Peña's ambitious mother, his neighbour the rich widow Doña Javiera Rico, to agree to Peña's marriage with Irene.

El amigo Manso is a quiet novel, with a simple plot subtly constructed. Its technique foreshadows the *nívola* of Unamuno (qq.v.).

AMORIM, ENRIQUE (1900–60), b. Salto, Uruguay. Uruguayan novelist and short-story writer of the Argentine Boedo Street School (q.v.). Almost all his novels are set in the pampas and towns of Argentina. His style was plain, even pedestrian, but his imagination was powerful and his narrative sense flawless. His first novel *Tangarupa* (1929) was influenced by Quiroga (q.v.), and *El paisano Aguilar* (Buenos Aires, 1934) was a variation on the theme of *Don Segundo Sombra* (q.v.). But Amorim began to find his own voice in his later novels: *La edad despareja* (1939), a denunciation of the spiritual impoverishment of the modern world; *El caballo y su sombra* (1941; English version by R. L. O'Connell and J. G. Luján, New York, 1943), on the conflict between serfs and immigrants; *La luna se hizo con agua* (1944); the unsuccessful *roman à thèse La victoria no viene sola* (1952); *Zanga* (1952); *Corral abierto* (1956), on the relationship between poverty and crime; *Todo puede suceder* (1956); *Los montaraces* (1957); *La desembocadura* (Buenos Aires, 1958), which tries to sum up the history of the country through the life of a typical pioneer; and the posthumously published *Eva Burgos* (Buenos Aires, 1960), on the tragedy of a prostitute's rise to affluence and her suicide.

See K. E. A. Mose, *Enrique Amorim: the passion of a Uruguayan* (New York, 1972), with a good bibliography.

AMORÓS, JUAN BAUTISTA (1856–1912), b. Madrid. Novelist and short-story writer who wrote under the pen-name 'Silverio Lanza' and was a pioneer in the writing of psychological fiction. *El año triste* (1883) was his first novel. His best books were: *Ni en la vida, ni en la muerte* (written against *caciquismo* on account of which a lawsuit was brought against him); *Mala cuna y mala fosa*; and *Artuña*. His short stories were collected in *Cuentecillos sin importancia* and *Cuentos para mis amigos*. Always eccentric, he died a recluse. Ramón Gómez de la Serna (q.v.), who wrote the obituary and epilogue to his *Páginas escogidas e inéditas* (1918), was influenced by Amorós.

Anaglifo, nonsense verse form devised by Dalí, Buñuel, García Lorca, and contemporaries. Three nouns are to be used in four lines, the second of which must be 'la gallina'; the first and third must have no relation with each other.

Anales Castellanos, two lists of facts and dates covering world and Spanish history from 618 to 1126. Together they form one of the earliest texts in the Spanish language.

Anales de la Universidad de Chile, founded in 1843, this is one of the earliest of all Latin American scientific and literary journals. It still appears. One of its most important features is the section 'Críticas y Reseñas Bibliográficas', a principal source of Chilean literary bibliography. Among its editors have been Guillermo Feliú Cruz (1954–63) and subsequently Álvaro Bunster.

Anales de los Xahil, an important collection of pre-Columbian legends and historical facts of the Cakchiquel tribe of Guatemala, written in the Cakchiquel tongue; it is also known by the alternative title *Memorial de Tecpán-Atitlán* in support of their claim to the lands they occupy. The compilers were the Indian Hernández Arana Xahilá and Francisco Díaz Geburá Quej. Their manuscript was found in 1844 by Juan Gavarrete and first translated into Spanish (through a French version) by José Antonio Villacorta. The most impressive section is the account of the capture of princesses which led to the bloody conflict between the Quichua and Cakchiquel Indians.

Anales Toledanos, three lists of facts and dates covering the period from 'the beginning of the world' to the reign of Fernando III; their sole interest is philological, as examples of early Castilian. The first two *Anales* were written in the reign of Fernando III *el Santo* between 1219 and 1250, the second probably by a *moro latinado.* The third brought the chronology up to 1391.

ANASTASIO EL POLLO, pseudonym of Estanislao del Campo (q.v.).

ANDERSON IMBERT, ENRIQUE (1910–), b. Córdoba, Argentina. Literary historian, critic, novelist, and short-story writer. His major book is the comprehensive *Historia de la literatura hispanoamericana* (6th edn., 1971), translated by John V. Falconieri as *Spanish-American literature: a history* (1963). With Eugenio Florit he has compiled *Literatura hispano-americana: antología e introducción histórica* (1960).

His novels are *Vigilia* (1934), a study of adolescence, and *Fuga* (1953). His *cuentos* have been collected in *Las pruebas del caos* (1946), *El Grimorio* (1961), *El gato de Cheshire* (1965), *La sandía y otros cuentos* (1969), and *La locura juega al ajedrez* (1971). Most of these stories are filled with paradox, fantasy and spirits, as if seen in visions and dreams. He has published over 20 books of essays and criticism, the latter including *La originalidad de Rubén Darío* (1967) and *Genio y figura de Sarmiento* (1967).

ANDRADE, OLEGARIO VÍCTOR (1839–82), b. Alegrete, Brazil. Argentinian poet and journalist whose Romantic poetry, inspired by Hugo and influenced by Manuel José Quintana (q.v.) was collected in *Obras poéticas* (1887). The sonorous verse often came near to bathos, but in *Atlántida* and *Prometeo* his repetitive style was redeemed by a genuine vision of the greatness of his Continent. The best edition of his work is that of the Academia Argentina de Letras (Clásicos Argentinos, 1943) with a study by E. F. Tiscornia.

Prometeo is, in the poet's words, 'un canto al espíritu humano, soberano del mundo, verdadero emancipador de las sociedades esclavas de tiranías y supersticiones'. His most popular poem was *El nido de cóndores,* inspired by the return to Argentina of the body of San Martín, the Argentine general and politician, liberator of Peru and Chile, who had died in exile in France in 1850. Andrade also wrote some lyrical verse in a more restrained manner, such as *La vuelta al hogar, El consejo maternal,* and *Las flores del guayacán.*

ANDRENIO, pseudonym of Eduardo Gómez de Baquero (q.v.).

ANDRÉS, *Padre* JUAN (1740–1817), b. Planes, Valencia. Jesuit scholar, expelled with his Order in 1767. He was appointed librarian to the King of Naples and there wrote one of the earliest cultural histories of Europe: *Origen, progresos y estado actual de toda la literatura,* (translated into Spanish by his brother Carlos in 10 vols., 1784–1806, from the Italian original in 7 vols., Parma, 1782–99). Andrés noted the influence of Arab culture on European civilization in his *Cartas sobre la música de los árabes* included in Giovanni Battista Toderini's *Letteratura turchesca* (Venice, 1787). *Cartas familiares* (4 vols., 1786–93, reprinted in 5 vols., 1791–4) introduced many foreign ideas into Spain, continuing the tradition of Feijoo (q.v.). His tastes were exclusively neoclassical: he considered Tasso's *Gerusalemme liberata* the most perfect epic ever written, and failed to appreciate not only Lope and Calderón, but also Dante and Shakespeare.

ANDÚJAR, Juan de (15th c.), poet at the Court of Alfonso V in Naples whose works were preserved in the *Cancionero de Stúñiga*. His panegyric on the King, in 15 *coplas de arte mayor*, is entitled 'Loores al Señor Rey don Alfonso' and appears in the *Rimas inéditas del siglo XV* (Paris, 1851), compiled by E. de Ochoa, pp. 381–6. The influence of Dante on Spanish poets generally was less widespread than that of Petrarch, but Andújar is an exception: his 'Visión de amor' is a direct imitation of canti IV and V of Dante's *Inferno*. Another allegorical poem, 'Cómo procede la fortuna', relates in octosyllables the fate of various legendary or historical figures such as Cleopatra, Semiramis, and Dido and Aeneas.

ÁNGELES, *Fray* Juan de Los, see Juan de Los Ángeles, *Fray*.

Ángel Guerra (1890–1), a semi-autobiographical novel by Benito Pérez Galdós (q.v.) important for its treatment of his common themes of mental abnormality, religious conversion, mercy, and humility.

Ángel Guerra is a rich young widower who quarrels with his mother, Doña Sales, an authoritarian woman who somewhat resembles the protagonist of *Doña Perfecta* (q.v.). He leaves her for a life of immorality with the prostitute Dulcenombre; he also participates in a Republican revolt. After the death of Doña Sales, Ángel returns home, where he falls in love with Lorenza (Leré for short), the governess of his young daughter Ción. When Ción dies, Ángel proposes to Leré, but she refuses, and enters a convent in her native Toledo, to which city he follows her. Ángel is converted from his agnosticism, and with the energy earlier devoted to political causes, dedicates his life and fortunes to founding a Brotherhood of Mercy, intending Leré to be the head of its women members. He hopes also that his new way of life will atone for the death of Doña Sales, hastened by her grief at his sins. Ángel begins to prepare for the priesthood, and leads a life of extreme asceticism; he experiences mystic visions and hallucinations, and devotes himself to charity. This leads him to accept into his order two criminals, the Babel brothers, brothers of Dulcenombre, who rob and wound him. Ángel refuses to identify his attackers, and dies joyfully, leaving his fortune to the poor. The author's abiding interest in abnormal psychology is evident in the character of Ángel as well as in the often perverse and criminal secondary characters. His growing belief in the Sermon of the Mount as the only solution to human problems is developed in later 'novelas españolas contemporáneas' (q.v.) such as *Nazarín*, *Misericordia*, and *Halma* (qq.v.).

ANGHIERA, Pietro Martire d', see Mártir de Angleria, Pedro.

ANGLERIA, Pedro Mártir de, see Mártir de Angleria, Pedro.

Anglo-Catalan Society, The, a society bringing together Catalans in Britain and Britons interested in Catalonia. It was formed in 1954 and in 1976 had more than 100 members. The society's presidents have been F. W. Pierce (1955–7), R. B. Tate (1958–62), A. H. Terry (1962–5), D. W. Lomax (1966–9), J. L. Gili (1969–73), and R. D. F. Pring-Mill (1974–). The Society holds an annual conference at a British university. It is strictly apolitical. It played a major part in organizing the Third International Colloquium of Catalan Language and Literature in Cambridge in 1973. During this colloquium the formal constitution of the Associació Internacional de Llengua i Literatura Catalanes was approved. The address of the Society in 1976 was c/o Dr. Alan Yates, Department of Hispanic Studies, The University, Sheffield S10 2TN.

ANICETO EL GALLO, pseudonym of Hilario Ascasubi (q.v.).

ANÓNIMAS PERUANAS, two 17th-c. Peruvian women poets, one wholly anonymous and one using the pseudonym 'Amarilis', who wrote, respectively, 'Discurso en loor de la poesía', published in Diego Mexía's *Primera parte del Parnaso Antártico* (1608), and 'Epístola a Belardo', addressed to Lope de Vega (q.v.), who added it to the end of his *Filomena* (1621).

M. Menéndez y Pelayo claimed to identify 'Amarilis' as Doña María de Alvarado, a descendant of Gómez de Alvarado, who founded the city of León de Huanaco. Asenjo Barbieri and Millé y Jiménez have attributed the 'Epístola' to Lope himself, while other names have been suggested by Mendiburu (Isabel de Figueroa), Miró Quesada (María Rojas y Garay), and Riva Agüero (María Tello de Sotomayor).

ANTONIO, Nicolás (1617–84), b. Seville. Bibliographer and scholar, whose private library is reputed to have contained more than 30,000 volumes. His *Bibliotheca hispana vetus* (Rome, 1672) is the first serious attempt to list all books written in Spain from Roman times up to 1500; his posthumous *Bibliotheca hispana nova* (Rome, 1696) brings the work up to 1670. Antonio's work was later revised by Pérez Bayer (Madrid, 1783–88).

Apolonio, Libro de, an anonymous *mester de clerecía* (q.v.) poem of 2,600 lines in the *cuaderna vía* composed (according to Marden) about 1235–40, and probably based on a lost prose version in Latin. The extant text is full of Aragonesisms. The work is in the so-called Byzantine genre, in which pirates and shipwreck recur, lovers are separated and finally reunited. Many such tales were told on the theme of Apollonius, Prince of Tyre, most of them based on the *Historia Apollonii regis Tyri*. The original is weak in structure and inconsistent in motivation, but the Spanish poet improves on it in both respects. The MS. is in the Escorial. Apolonio is a forerunner of the 'compleat knight' in the later *libros de caballería* (q.v.).

Apolonio discovers the incestuous love of the King of Antioch and his daughter, and is forced to flee to Tarsus. An abundance of fantastic events and coincidences ends equally arbitrarily with the hero's virtue and trust in God rewarded. Characters are either good or evil as in most medieval literature, lacking the complexity in the hero's character shown in the book of *Alexandre* (q.v.). The *Libro de Apolonio* has been edited by C. C. Marden (Baltimore, 1917–22) and by G. B. de Cesare (Venice, 1974), and translated into modern Spanish by P. Cabañas (Valencia, 1955).

APPLEYARD, José Luis (1927–), Paraguayan poet of the Generation of '50; a contributor to *Alcor* (q.v.). His first book was *Entonces era siempre* (1946) and his second *El sauce permanece* (1947). He then collaborated in a joint volume *Poesía* (1953) with Ramiro Domínguez (q.v.) and others. In 1961 he won the Municipal Drama Prize (Asunción) with *Aquel 1911*, on the theme of national independence, and in 1965 published his long poem *Tres motivos de Don Carlos* with a revised impression of *El sauce permanece* (1965). *Imágenes sin tierra* (1964) is a novel.

Aprismo, a movement founded by Víctor Raúl Haya de la Torre (q.v.).

Aquelindo, Cervantes' name for the verse form otherwise known as *perqué* (q.v.).

ARANGUREN, José Luis L. (1909–), b. Ávila. Philosopher, theologian, and essayist. Professor of Ethics and Sociology at Madrid University. He has been influenced by Unamuno and Ortega y Gasset (qq.v.). His many books include *La filosofía de Eugenio d'Ors* (1945), *El catolicismo y el protestantismo como formas de existencia* (1954), *Crítica y meditación* (1957), *Ética* (1958), *La ética de Ortega* (1958), *La cultura española y la cultura establecida* (1975), and *Estudios literarios* (1976).

Araucana, La, an epic poem by Alonso de Ercilla y Zúñiga (q.v.). The finest of the Golden Age epics, *La Araucana* is generally recognised as the first work in Spanish of literary merit produced about the American continent.

It was published in three parts (Madrid, 1569; Saragossa, 1578; and Madrid, 1589), totalling 35 cantos. A revised edition published in Madrid in 1597 contained 37 cantos, and the two extra cantos may not be by Ercilla.

The theme is the conquest of Chile, in which the author had taken part in 1555. The book opens with a description of the land and people. The Araucano Indians, having chosen their leader Lautaro by a trial of strength, force the Spaniards to retreat from La Concepción to Santiago, sacked by the Araucanos in a previous engagement. Lautaro celebrates victory and prepares to attack the forces led by Francisco de Villagrán. Defeated, he dies with those Indians who refuse to surrender. The rest of the Araucanos meet in assembly. Ercilla inserts at this point a vision of the Battle of S. Quentin, just as later he 'foresees' the Battle of Lepanto. The Spaniards advance into Arauco, capturing the *caudillo* Galvarino and cutting off his hands. Galvarino still urges his 'senate' to resist and Ercilla describes their fatal struggle, praising the Indians' courage as they are defeated. Galvarino dies, and the Araucano heroes Tucapel and Rengo, wounded in a duel, are reconciled by their leader Caupolicán, who is taken prisoner and, about to die, accepts Christianity. The Spaniards go on to explore the lands they have conquered, and the poem concludes with a defence of Philip II's right to the throne of Portugal.

Ercilla had been humiliated by his commanding officer, García Hurtado de Mendoza, whose part in the victory he minimizes in *La Araucana* to gain revenge. Hurtado de Mendoza retaliated by employing the Chilean poet Pedro de Oña (q.v.) to write a rival *Arauco domado*, which has been edited by J. T. Medina (Santiago de Chile, 1917). This was only the first of several imitations of Ercilla's great epic. *La Araucana* suffers from only a few of the *longueurs* to which the genre is normally prone. The best modern edition of *La Araucana* is by J. T. Medina (5 vols., Santiago de Chile, 1910–18).

ARAY, Edmundo J. (1936–), Venezuelan poet, short-story writer, university teacher, and economist. He formed part of the Sardo group, and in 1961 helped to found the magazine *El techo de la ballena*. In *La hija de Raghú* (1956), *Nadie quiere descansar* (1961), and *Sube para bajar*

(1963), Aray explores the universalist themes, new to Venezuelan literature, that preoccupy many other writers of his generation, such as Alfredo Silva Estrada (b. 1934) and Ramón Palomares (b. 1935).

ARBÓ, Sebastià Joan (1902–), b. San Carlos de la Rapita, Tarragona. Novelist, short-story writer, and biographer. His early novels of the countryside around Tortosa, written in Catalan and published in Barcelona, were generally more successful than the later books, often of Barcelona life, written in Castilian for a wider public. His first novel was *L'inútil combat* (1931) translated into Castilian as *La luz escondida*. *Terres de l'Ebre* (1934) won the Fastenrath Prize of the Real Academia Española when translated as *Tierras del Ebro* (1956). His first book originally written in Castilian was *Sobre las piedras grises* (1948), which won the Premio Nadal for 1949. Other books of his early period were *Camins de nit* (1936), translated as *Caminos de noche*; and *Tino Costa* (1946), the author's favourite novel. He has subsequently published *María Molinari* (1949), the picaresque *Viejas y nuevas andanzas de Caretas* (pt. 1, 1955; complete edn., 1959), *Nocturno de alarmas* (1957), *Entre la tierra y el mar* (Valencia, 1966), which won the Premio Blasco Ibáñez, and *La Espera* (1968).

His biographies include *Pío Baroja y su tiempo* (1964), *La vida trágica de Mosén Jacinto Verdaguer* (1952 in Catalan, 1970 in Castilian), *Cervantes*, and *Oscar Wilde* (1960). His childhood reminiscences are entitled *Los hombres de la tierra y del mar* (1962). Arbó has written two plays: *La ciutat maleïda* (1935) and *Nausica* (1937).

ARBOLEDA, Julio (1817–62), b. S. Vicente de Timbiquí, Barbacoas. Colombian poet, politician, and soldier, called by his compatriots 'el Gigante de los Andes'. The unfinished MS. containing 24 cantos of his Romantic legendary epic *Gonzalo de Oyón* was burnt in the Revolution of 1851, but fragments were reconstructed and published by Miguel Antonio Caro in *Poesías* (New York, 1883).

The poem is based on incidents in the Spanish conquest of Popayán and, as Arboleda had travelled in Europe, the contemporary influence of Byron was allowed to permeate both vocabulary and style. Arboleda spent most of his life in active politics, was imprisoned for his liberal beliefs, and became president-elect of Nueva Granada. He was murdered by an assassin in the Berruecos Mountains.

Arcadia, a mountainous area in the central Peloponnesus traditionally the home of the god Pan. Because there were no towns, Arcadia

was early associated with the pastoral ideal of rural peace and harmony. The first known appearance of the phrase *Et in Arcadia ego* is as a legend in a picture by Guercino (1590–1666) in which simple shepherds find a skull. The words below it, 'I (meaning Death) am even in Arcadia', have been misunderstood by later generations as 'I also have lived in Arcadia', implying 'In the past I once knew great peace'.

In Spain the theme of Arcadia is linked with the pastoral tradition in the *Égloga de Plácida y Vitoriano* by Juan del Encina (q.v.) and the poetry of Garcilaso de la Vega (q.v.). The Arcadian tradition in prose can be traced from the *Menosprecio de corte y alabanza de aldea* (q.v., 1539) of Guevara to the rural essays of Azorín (qq.v.). Secular peace was a natural choice for treatment *a lo divino*: the Catalan *Espill de la vida religiosa* (1515) was translated as a *Tratado llamado el desseoso y por otro nombre, Espejo de religiosos* (Seville, 1530).

Arcadia. Prosas y Versos (q.v.) is a pastoral romance in prose (with verse inserted) written by Lope de Vega at the suggestion of Antonio, Duque de Alba, and published in 1598. It filled vol. 6 of Lope's *Obras sueltas* and was reprinted ten times up to 1620. It was generally believed to narrate real experiences of the Duke and his circle, and many such books (like that of Gálvez de Montalvo: *El pastor de Fílida*, 1582) are known *romans à clef*. Lope's *Arcadia* borrows its title from Sannazaro's (1504, translated into Spanish in 1549), but it is much nearer in style to *Los siete libros de la Diana* (1559?) of Montemayor, *Los cinco libros de la Diana enamorada* (1564) of Gil Polo, and the *Galatea* (1585) of Cervantes (qq.v.).

Arcadia Agustiniana, a literary circle in Salamanca deriving its name from the Augustinian priest Fray Diego Tadeo González (q.v.), known as 'Delio'. The group was the immediate successor (1775–80) to the Parnaso Salmantino (q.v.).

The members included Iglesias de la Casa ('Arcadio'), Juan Meléndez Valdés ('Batilo'), Fernández de Rojas ('Liseno'), and Forner ('Amintas'). Jovellanos ('Jovino') corresponded with the circle from Seville.

As its name suggests, the Arcadia encouraged the writing and publication of pastoral poetry, including *letrillas* and anacreontic eclogues.

Arcadia. Prosas y Versos (1598), a pastoral novel written by Lope de Vega (q.v.) for his patron Antonio Álvarez de Toledo, Duke of Alba, while residing 1592–4 in Alba de Tormes. Lope described it as an 'historia verdadera'.

Anfriso the hero is the Duke of Alba, Belisarda the Duke's Toledan lover, Bresinda the Duke's mother, Brasildo the well-known musician Juan Blas de Castro, and the minor character Belardo Lope himself. Anfriso is in love with Belisarda, who is betrothed by her parents against her will to the wealthy fool Salicio. Anfriso, believing that Belisarda is in fact in love with Olimpo, courts Anarda and finally consults the enchantress Polinesta. She recommends him to serious pursuits such as study and these in the end lead him to the holy temple of *desengaño*, translatable in part as 'disillusion' but probably more accurately as 'self-knowledge'.

Modelled on the successful *Diana* of Montemayor (qq.v.), Lope's *Arcadia* was followed by the essay *Pastores de Belén* (q.v.) in the *a lo divino* genre. Tedious perhaps to the modern reader, it was reprinted 15 times during Lope's lifetime. The most striking feature, apart from the variety of poetic forms and styles, is the wealth of references to classical mythology, an indication of the range of Lope's reading as well as of the learning expected in an average reader. *Arcadia* can be found in vol. 38 (1856; reprinted 1950) of the BAE, pp. 45–136, but the best edition is that of E. S. Morby (1975) in Clásicos Castalia.

See J. Scudieri Ruggieri's 'Notas a la "Arcadia" de Lope de Vega' (*Cuadernos Hispanoamericanos*, vol. 54 (1963), pp. 577–608) and R. Osuna, *La 'Arcadia' de Lope de Vega* ... (1973), a supplement to the *BRAE*.

ARCADIO, the pastoral name of José Iglesias de la Casa (q.v.) in the literary group known as the Parnaso Salmantino (q.v.).

ARCE DE LOS REYES, AMBROSIO (*c.* 1621–61), b. Madrid. Playwright and poet. His *comedias*, written in the manner of Lope de Vega, were very popular in his time, in particular *Cegar para ver mejor*, on St. Lucy of Sicily; *El hechizo de Sevilla*, on slavery and ransom; *El Hércules de Hungría*, on the Hungarian wars against the Turks; and *La mayor victoria de Constantino*.

ARCE DE VÁZQUEZ, MARGOT (1904–), b. Caguas, Puerto Rico. Literary critic. Her best books are *Garcilaso de la Vega* (Madrid, 1930) and a critical biography, *Gabriela Mistral: persona y poesía* (1958). Among her essays are several on Puerto Rican writers such as Tomás Blanco, Rubén del Rosario, and Luis Palés Matos. Her essays on Puerto Rico itself were collected in *Impresiones* (1950). She is a leading contributor to the island's literary review *Asomante* and has taught at Puerto Rico University.

ARCHPRIEST OF HITA, see RUIZ, Juan.

ARCHPRIEST OF TALAVERA, see MARTÍNEZ DE TOLEDO, Alfonso.

ARCICIO, pseudonym of Juan de Arguijo (q.v.).

ARCINIEGAS, GERMÁN (1900–), b. Bogotá. Colombian diplomat and man of letters. He has taught sociology in Colombia, served twice as Minister of Education, and represented his country as ambassador in Paris. His major contributions consist of far-ranging anthologies and surveys of Hispanic-American culture, which he has taught at several American universities. After *Jiménez de Quesada* (1939), *Los alemanes en la conquista de América* (1941), *Este pueblo de América* (1945), and *Biografía del Caribe* (1945; translated as *Caribbean: sea of the New World*, 1946), he edited *The green continent: a comprehensive view of Latin America by its leading writers* (New York, 1947), *The State of Latin America* (1953), *El continente de siete colores* (1965; translated as *Latin America: a cultural history*, New York, 1967), and *Genio y figura de Jorge Isaacs* (Buenos Aires, 1967).

See Federico Córdova, *Vida y obra de Germán Arciniegas* (Havana, 1950).

ARCINIEGAS, ISMAEL ENRIQUE (1865–1938), b. Curití. Colombian poet, diplomat, and journalist; editor of *El Nuevo Tiempo*. A prolific poet from his youth (his early works include *En Colonia* and the Romantic *Inmortalidad* influenced by Bécquer), he ended his career as a Parnassian, in such poems as *Códice antiguo* and *La balada del regreso*. He selected his own *Antología poética* (Quito, 1932), from *Poesías* (1897) and *Cien poesías* (1911). He translated many French poets, including Hugo, Lamartine, and Heredia.

ARCIPRESTE DE HITA, see RUIZ, Juan.

ARCIPRESTE DE TALAVERA, see MARTINEZ DE TOLEDO, Alfonso.

ARDERÍUS FORTÚN, JOAQUÍN (1890–), b. Lorca, Murcia. Novelist and journalist. Beginning with surrealist techniques in the aphoristic *Mis mendigos* (1915), Arderíus developed the modern Spanish anarchist novel in *Así me fecundó Zaratustra* (1923); *Yo y tres mujeres* (1924), combining female fetishism with male sexual fears; *Ojo de brasa* (1925), in which nihilism reaches a point of 'liberation' in gratuitous infanticide; *La duquesa de Nit* (1926), in which the sexual extravagance of a duchess provokes her family's downfall; *Los príncipes iguales* and *El baño de la muerte* (both 1928); *Los amadores de Manqueses* and *Justo 'el Evangélico'* (both 1929), the latter a parody of Christ's Passion subtitled 'novela de sarcasmo social y cristiano'; and *El comedor de la Pensión Venecia* (1930).

During the Second Republic (1931–6), Arderíus' nihilism gave way to slight, though sarcastic, interest in social problems. In *Lumpenproletariado* (1931), a hungry rebel intellectual and a woman debate a choice between purity of conscience and the need for daily bread. *Campesinos* (1931), filled with vulgarisms, is a deliberately shocking exposure of life in rural Spain in which Arderíus spares neither the afflicted nor the exploiters in his anarchic wrath. *Crimen* (1933?) successfully combines the thriller and the socialist pamphlet. Though an isolated, eccentric figure, Arderíus influenced such writers as José Díaz Fernández and Manuel D. Benavides.

ARENALES, RICARDO, pseudonym of Miguel Ángel Osorio Benítez (q.v.).

ARENAS, BRAULIO (1913–), Chilean surrealist poet of the Generation of '38, whose work contrasts with that of his contemporary Nicanor Parra (q.v.) in its verbal extravagance, violent imagery, and wilful discontinuities. Arenas's poetry and ideas were published first in the magazine *Mandrágora* (q.v., 1938–41) and later in his own review *Leitmotiv* (1942–3), and were a liberating influence on the younger Chilean poets. He has written *La casa fantasma* (1962), *Ancud, Castro y Achao* (1963), and *En el confín del alma* (1963).

ARÉVALO MARTÍNEZ, RAFAEL (1884–), b. Guatemala City. Poet, playwright, essayist, novelist, and short-story writer. He made his name with the short novel *El hombre que parecía un caballo* (1915), the most original story of the period in Latin America, allegedly a caricature of the Colombian poet Miguel Ángel Osorio (q.v.), better known under his pseudonym Porfirio Barba Jacob. The success of this work and its sequel *El trovador colombiano* led to similar psychological fantasies (they lack any action of note): *El señor Monitot* (1922), Monitot being an elephant; *La oficina de paz de Orolandia* (1925); *Las noches en el palacio de la Nunciatura* (1927); *La signatura de la esfinge* (1933); and *El mundo de los Maharachías* (1938). His other prose writings range from the *Influencia de España en la formación de la nacionalidad centroamericana* and *Nietzsche el conquistador* (both 1943) to *Ecce Pericles* (1946), the last on the dictator Manuel Estrada Cabrera, the *Señor Presidente* of the novel by Asturias (q.v.).

Arévalo Martínez is the most important Guatemalan poet of his generation: *Juglerías* (1911); *Maya* (1911); *Los atormentados* (1914); *Las rosas de Engaddi* (1918); *Llama* (1934); 35 *poemas* (1944); *Por un caminito así* (1947); and *Poemas* (1958). An edition of his *Obras escogidas: prosa y poesía* appeared in 1959.

ARGENSOLA, BARTOLOMÉ LEONARDO DE (1562–1631), b. Barbastro. Poet and historian. A leader of the so-called Aragonese School (with his brother Lupercio and Esteban Manuel de Villegas, qq.v.). His poetry is restrained and classical, and he took Fray Luis de León (q.v.) as his model when composing religious odes and sonnets. Appointed royal chronicler of Aragón on the death of his brother, Bartolomé wrote the *Primera parte de los anales de Aragón* (Saragossa, 1630), a comprehensive continuation (1516–20) of Zurita (q.v.). He also wrote light verse, for example a warning against palmistry, and *Conquista de las islas Malucas* (1609; ed. M. Mir, Saragossa, 1891). His *Rimas* were collected with those of Lupercio in 1634, and there is a recent edition by J. M. Blecua (2 vols., 1974) in Clásicos Castellanos.

See M. Mir, *Bartolomé Leonardo de Argensola* (Saragossa, 1891) and J. Aznar Molina, *Los Argensola* (Saragossa, 1939).

ARGENSOLA, LUPERCIO LEONARDO DE (1559–1613), b. Barbastro. Poet, historian, and playwright. A leader of the so-called Aragonese School (with his brother Bartolomé and Esteban Manuel de Villegas qq.v.) whose simpler, less ornate poems were written in reaction to the *culto* style of Góngora then in vogue. Lupercio's poetry was eclectic in inspiration, often drawing on Horace, Virgil, and Garcilaso. His version of the Horatian ode *Beatus ille* is among the finest in Spanish. His best known original poems are *Al sueño* and the charming tercets of his *Descripción de Aranjuez*. Not content with attacking the *gongoristas*, he sent a memorandum to Philip II warning him against the licentiousness of the popular theatre. He was royal chronicler of Aragón until his death (when he was succeeded by his brother) and wrote *Información de los sucesos de Aragón en los años de 1590 y 1591* (1808). He was also employed in Naples, where he founded the Academia de los Ociosos while Secretary of State to the Viceroy, the Conde de Lemos. He burnt all his poems while there, but his son Gabriel had taken copies of most of them and was able to publish a posthumous edition of the two brothers' *Rimas* in 1634. Lupercio's *Rimas* are edited by A. Blecua in Clásicos Castellanos.

Lupercio wrote three tragedies in the manner of Seneca: *Filis* is now lost, *Alejandra* and *Isabela* are grim and violent.

See Otis Green, *The life and works of Lupercio Leonardo de Argensola* (Philadelphia, 1927; trans. F. Ynduraín, Saragossa, 1945).

ARGOTE DE MOLINA, Gonzalo (1548–98), b. Seville. Humanist and private librarian whose books and museum were visited incognito by Philip II. Among his writings were a *Discurso sobre la poesía castellana* appended to his edition of the *Conde Lucanor* (q.v.). Argote also edited *Historia del Gran Tamorlán* (Seville, 1582) by Ruy González de Clavijo (q.v.). His *Nobleza de Andalusía* (1588) is an important genealogical work.

ARGUEDAS, Alcides (1879–1946), b. La Paz. Bolivian historian and novelist, a diplomat in Paris, London, and Bogotá. His *Historia general de Bolivia* (1922), a vast compendium of facts and figures, is still a major work of reference, though it lacks historical method and sober analysis.

The first five volumes of his unfinished *Historia de Bolivia* appeared 1921–29. His attitude is that of a pessimistic patriot, for whom the past is a dreadful warning. His sympathies for the Indian peasants of Bolivia emerge strongly in *Pueblo enfermo* (1909), an indictment of the organized oppression against them. His major novel, *Raza de bronce* (q.v., 1919), a re-working of *Wata Wara*, a tale he had published in 1904, attacks those who exploit the Aimará for their own ends, whether priests, Creole landowners, or *mestizo* servants. Less impressive are his other novels, *Pisagua* (1903) and *Vida criolla* (1905) which describes life in La Paz around 1900. The *Obras completas* were published in 1959 (Mexico City, 2 vols.)).

See A. Arguedas, 'La historia de mis libros, o el fracaso de un escritor', in *Cuba Contemporánea*, no. 30 (1922), pp. 376–419; Fausto Reinaga, *Alcides Arguedas* (1960); and Moisés Alcazar, *Alcides Arguedas: etapas de la vida de un escritor* (1963).

ARGUEDAS, José María (1911–69), b. Andahuaylas, Apurímac. Peruvian novelist and folklorist, who wrote in Quechua and Spanish. He wrote *Canto kechwa* (1938) and *Canciones y cuentos del pueblo quechua* (1949, English translation *The singing mountaineers*, Austin, Texas, 1971). *Yawar Fiesta* (1940; revised edn. 1948), related Quechua ritual to present-day customs. *Diamantes y pedernales* (1954) was followed by his last novel of the Andean countryside: *Los ríos profundos* (q.v., Buenos Aires, 1958), dealing with man's potential gentleness in harsh natural surroundings—like his other books it is largely autobiographical. *El Sexto* (1961) again showed how men can rise above their environment, even, as here, in the prisons of Lima during the Benavídez dictatorship. For J. M. Oviedo, the work of Arguedas 'is no longer a mere document, but becomes the revelation of the human condition itself, superior to death or to [human]

justice'. The title of his novel *Todas las sangres* (Buenos Aires, 1964) refers to the complexity of Peru's racial mixture; he urges society to respect all these elements equally without discrimination. His last novel *El zorro de arriba y el zorro de abajo* (Buenos Aires, 1970) was written on psychiatric advice to deter him from committing suicide, and remained unfinished because it failed to do so. There is a bibliography by William Rowe in *Revista Peruana de Cultura*, nos. 13–14 (1970), pp. 179–97.

See César Levano, *Arguedas: un sentimiento trágico de la vida* (1970); Gladys C. Marín, *La experiencia americana de José María Arguedas* (Buenos Aires, 1973); and Sara Castro Klarén, *El mundo mágico de José María Arguedas* (1973).

ARGÜELLO, Agenor (20th-c.), Nicaraguan ultraist writer, author of *Ánforas de silencio* and an important literary study: *Los precursores de la poesía nueva en Nicaragua* (1963).

ARGÜELLO, Santiago (1872–1940), b. León, Nicaragua. The most significant Nicaraguan poet to emerge after Rubén Darío (q.v.), who praised him in both the *Viaje a Nicaragua* and *Historia de mis libros*. While remaining under the shadow of Darío, Argüello moved steadily away from idealism towards a Christian pantheism. Love of the Nicaraguan landscape was present, from his first book: *Primeras ráfagas* (León, 1897). His best collection is *Ojo y alma* (Paris, 1908). After various travels and teaching posts, Argüello was appointed Minister of Education in 1939. The most useful anthology of his work is *Poesías escogidas y poesías nuevas* (1935). This contains (pp. 5–52) the longest critical assessment of the author yet to have appeared.

ARGÜELLO, Solón (1880–1920), Nicaraguan modernist poet (not to be confused with Santiago Argüello, q.v.), who fought with Zapata in Mexico and was murdered there.

ARGÜELLO MORA, Manuel (1845–1902), b. San José. Costa Rican writer of both historical and contemporary novels, such as *La trinchera* and *Elisa Delmar*. His most notable work was *Costa Rica pintoresca: sus leyendas y tradiciones: colección de novelas, cuentos, historias y paisajes* (1899). The nephew of President Juan Rafael Mora, he fled the country when his uncle was overthrown in 1859, and they travelled together to Nicaragua, New York, and thence to Europe.

ARGUIJO, Juan de (1567–1623), b. Seville. Poet in the tradition of Fernando de Herrera (q.v.). He was a patron of the arts, and prominent in the literary life of Seville. He died in poverty. His *silva* (q.v.) *A la vihuela* is excellent, and his 60-odd sonnets on classical themes are well turned. His epigrammatic terseness can often be traced to Latin originals.

He lived for several years in Madrid, where he made the acquaintance of Lope de Vega, Góngora, and the Argensola brothers (qq.v.). Rodrigo Caro (q.v.) in *Varones insignes de Sevilla* described Arguijo as 'no solo elegantísimo poeta, sino el Apolo de todos los poetas de España'. Many of his poems were signed 'Arcicio'. His *Poesías* have been edited by A. de Castro for vol. 32 (1854) of the BAE; by Benítez Claros (1968); and by Stanko B. Vranich for Clásicos Castalia (1971).

ARIAS MONTANO, BENITO (1527–98), b. Fregenal de la Sierra. Theologian and poet. For long a Professor of Oriental Languages at the Escorial, he was persuaded to abandon the life of a recluse to supervise the printing of the Antwerp Polyglot Bible of 1569–72 (the *Biblia Regia de Ámberes*, a scholarly work of splendid appearance). While in Flanders he enriched the library of Philip II at the Escorial by judicious book-collecting on a grand scale. He was particularly interested in Jewish antiquities and wrote a number of philosophical and theological works and some distinguished poetry in Latin. His poetry in Spanish imitated that of his friend Fray Luis de León (q.v.) and, like his mentor, Arias Montano made his own version of the Song of Songs, calling it *Paráfrasis sobre el Cantar de los Cantares*. This was edited by Boehl von Faber (q.v.) in *Floresta de rimas antiguas castellanas* (Hamburg, 1825). He was recalled from Italy to answer charges brought by the Inquisition at the instigation of León de Castro, and although acquitted he retired from public life. *A la hermosura exterior de Nuestra Señor*, usually attributed to Fray Luis de León, has also been ascribed to Arias Montano.

See B. Rekers, *Benito Arias Montano* (London, 1972).

ARIBAU Y FARRIOLS, BONAVENTURA CARLES (1798–1862), b. Barcelona. Catalan poet, literary editor, and economist. Aribau's distinguished career included a period as Director of the Spanish Mint and Treasury. His romantic *Oda a la Pàtria* is usually considered the first work of the Catalan Revival. He joined Rivadeneyra (q.v.) in planning and administering the Biblioteca de Autores Españoles (q.v.), a fundamental, if uneven, series of Spanish classics, and wrote the prologues to editions of Cervantes, Moratín, and 16th and 17th-c. Spanish novels. As an economist, he propagated his protectionist theories in his own magazine *La verdad económica* (1861).

ARIDJIS, HOMERO (1940–   ), b. Contepec, Michoacán. Mexican poet. He studied journalism and edited the magazine *Correspondencias*. He was given a Guggenheim Fellowship in the U.S.A. in 1966–7 and was visiting professor at New York University in 1969–71.

He was somewhat influenced by Octavio Paz (q.v.) in his early verse collections, such as *La musa roja* (1958) or *Los ojos desdoblados* (1960), but later books are assured and personal: *La difícil ceremonia* (1963), *Antes del reino* (1963), *Mirándola dormir* (1964), and *Quemas las naves* (1975). Kenneth Rexroth has edited a bilingual edition of Aridjis's verse, *Los espacios azules/Blue spaces* (New York, 1974). *La tumba de Filidor* (1961) is a collection of short stories.

Ariel, by the Uruguayan José Enrique Rodó (q.v.), is an essay of some 100 pages conceived at the end of the Spanish-American War of 1898, and published in 1900. It achieved sudden and lasting fame for its memorable expression of popular ideas. Shakespeare's Ariel symbolises the power of spiritual nobility over materialism, of reason over unreason, altruism over selfishness, and intelligence over the brutishness of Caliban. Youth must have confidence in its ability to mould a new future, for joy, hope, and enthusiasm are necessary to renew society, although they must be used in conjunction with reason: the Greek ideal of thought balancing action must be maintained, and the study and love of beauty is one way of achieving this harmony. Rodó goes on, unjustifiably perhaps, to identify Caliban with utilitarianism and the materialistic culture of the U.S.A. and Ariel with altruism, aestheticism, and the civilization of Latin America. (The Cuban Jesús Castellanos (q.v.) opposed this simplistic view and maintained that Cuba was more materialistic than the U.S.A.). Rodó's excellent style conceals the contradictions in much of his argument, and the book quickly gave rise to a cult of *arielismo* in reaction against the incipient Nordomania (the indiscriminate following of Germanic ideas) prevalent during 1898–9. As a consequence it improved the extent and quality of education in Latin America and raised the self-confidence of younger Latin American intellectuals.

Rodó was among the first to praise modernism in literature, with an acute preface to the 2nd edition of the *Prosas profanas* (1889) of Darío (q.v.). *Arielismo* was also decisive in halting the spread of nationalism in Latin America for some years in the interests of a wider regional understanding. Rodó took his symbols from Ernest Renan's *drame philosophique, Caliban* (1878), in which Caliban, representing the cynical masses, uses his strength to exploit Prospero's intelligence. Rodó did not however agree that the rise of the masses meant the death of spiritual life, and argued that, with wider and better educational opportunities, a great society could emerge if it combined the Hellenic virtues of grace and moderation with the Christian virtue of charity. *Arielismo* was preached as an educational doctrine throughout most Latin-American countries in the early years of the 20th c., and achieved its greatest literary resonance in Rubén Darío's *Cantos de vida y esperanza* (1905), of which the opening poem was dedicated to Rodó.

ARIZA, JUAN (1816–76), b. Motril. Romantic writer of plays with mainly national and patriotic themes, among them *Alonso de Ercilla* (1848), *Hernando del Pulgar* (1849), and *El primer Girón* (1850). His novels are influenced by Dumas *père*, and are also mainly concerned with Spanish history: perhaps the best is *El dos de mayo* (1846). Another novel, *Viaje al infierno* (1848), is a political satire. Ariza died in Cuba.

ARJONA, JUAN DE (*c.* 1560–1603), b. Granada. A priest from Puente de Pinos who translated the *Thebaid* of Statius so magnificently, in *octavas* (q.v.), that Lope de Vega called him 'nuevo Apolo granadino, pluma heroica y soberana.' He died after translating the first nine books; the other three were completed in 1618 by Gregorio Morillo, chaplain to the Archbishop of Granada. The complete version appeared in vol. 36 (1855) of the BAE.

ARJONA Y DE CUBAS, MANUEL MARÍA DE (1771–1820), b. Osuna. Minor poet. Canon of Cordova Cathedral. He founded the Academia Horaciana and revitalised the Academia de Buenas Letras in Seville in 1793. His best-known poem is the neoclassical *Las ruinas de Roma* (1808), inspired by a visit to Rome. He also wrote some pleasing odes, including *A la memoria* and *La ninfa del bosque*. *Poesías* appeared in vol. 63 (1871) of the BAE.

ARLT, ROBERTO (1900–42), b. Buenos Aires. Novelist, short-story writer, and playwright. His four novels are *El juguete rabioso* (1926); *Los siete locos* (1929) and its sequel *Los lanzallamas* (1931), which deal with the adventures of a gang of madmen who plot to overthrow the capitalist world; and *El amor brujo* (1932). *El jorobadito* (1933) is a collection of *cuentos*. *Aguafuertes porteñas* are sketches of life in Buenos Aires. There is something of Quevedo's *Sueños* about the grotesque, pessimistic world of Arlt, for whom 'human beings are monsters waddling in the shadows', automata in the horrors of the city. Unlike the patrician Larreta (q.v.), Arlt had to write quickly, for he was also a busy journalist. His fiction suffers from this haste, from inconsequential episodes, extravagance, and lack of planning, but his imaginative power still attracts a great number of readers. His plays are *África*, *Trescientos millones* (1932), *La isla desierta*, and *El fabricante de fantasmas* (1936). His *Novelas completas y cuentos* (3 vols.) appeared in 1963.

Armada, La Invencible ('The Invincible Armada'), a fleet of 130 ships, as well as smaller vessels, dispatched in 1588 by King Philip II to sail to Flanders for the purpose of transporting the Spanish forces of the Duke of Parma to England. Under the Duke of Medina Sidonia, the fleet was put to flight by the English Navy led by Lord Howard of Effingham, with the assistance of Drake, Hawkins, Frobisher, and others. The psychological effect of the defeat of the hitherto 'invincible' Spanish fleet was considerable in Spain, although some two-thirds of the ships did in fact return safely. The fleet was quickly re-equipped and became stronger than ever before. Some of the Spanish ships had English pilots and the Duke of Parma's army included companies of English exiles led by English noblemen.

See Garrett Mattingly, *The Armada* (Boston, 1959).

ARMAS Y CÁRDENAS, JOSÉ DE (1866–1919), Cuban critic writing under the pseudonym 'Justo de Lara'. His best book was *Cervantes y el 'Quijote'* (Havana, 1905), superseded in its biographical section by the work of Luis Astrana Marín (q.v.) but otherwise still important for its insights into Cervantes' methods of satirizing Philip III and the Duque de Lerma, who were impoverishing Spain still more by wars against the infidel. *El 'Quijote' y su época* (1915) continued these researches.

Armas published his essays in two volumes: *Ensayos críticos de literatura inglesa y española* (1910) and *Estudios y retratos* (1911).

ARNAO, ANTONIO (1828–89), b. Murcia. Poet and *zarzuela* librettist. With his fellow-Murcian José Selgas (q.v.), Arnao represents the anti-Romantic tradition in his period. His historical plays on national figures such as King Rodrigo and Garcilaso caused no interest, and his verse has not stood the test of time, despite Menéndez y Pelayo's characteristically kindly verdict that it is carefully constructed and lexically pure. These verses were collected in *Himnos y quejas* (1851), *Melancolías* (1857), *La campaña de África* (1860), *El caudillo de los ciento* (1866), *Poesías religiosas* (1872), the posthumous *Soñar despierto* (1891), and many more.

ARNICHES Y BARRERA, CARLOS (1866–1943), b. Alicante. Prolific author of *sainetes* (q.v.), the acknowledged master with the Álvarez Quintero brothers (q.v.) of the *género chico* (q.v.). Of over 200 one-act *sainetes* (then set to music as *zarzuelas*, q.v.) that he wrote on Madrid life and customs, many were written in collaboration with Abati, García Álvarez, López Silva, Fernández Shaw, and others. Those he wrote alone have been collected by E. M. del Portillo in *Obras completas* (1948). His most popular *sainetes* include *Alma de Dios, El señor Badanas, Don Quintín el amargao*, and *La señorita de Trevélez*. A special issue of *Cuadernos de literatura contemporánea* (1943) is devoted to his work, and has a bibliography by Arregui. His plays suffer from sentimentality and they are often slipshod in grammar and vocabulary, but his theatrical abilities are undeniable and his neologisms gave more to the popular speech of Madrid than he borrowed. He wrote to Julio Cejador (q.v.). 'Aspiro sólo con mis sainetes y farsas a estimular las condiciones generosas del pueblo y hacerle odiosos los malos instintos. Nada más'.

AROLAS, *Padre* JUAN (1805–49), b. Barcelona. Poet and journalist. He became a priest at 16, and joined the teaching order of the *Escuelas Pías*, working in Valencia 1835–42. His highly emotional nature (he died insane) made him temperamentally unsuited to his vocation; his love poems, influenced by Hugo, are more erotic than was usual in the Romantic period. His religious nature is indebted to Lamartine's, while both Rivas and Zorrilla influenced his *Leyendas* and *Romances históricos*. Selections from his *Poesías caballerescas y orientales* (1840) and *Poesías religiosas, orientales, caballerescas y amatorias* (1842) were edited by L. L. Rosselló and J. Olea in *Poesías escogidas* (1921). The Clásicos Castellanos edition of his *Poesías* was by José R. Lomba y Pedraja.

ARRABAL, FERNANDO (1932–), b. Melilla, Spanish-speaking Morocco. Spanish dramatist. He studied law in Madrid, but has lived in France and written in French since 1954. His plays are concerned with cruelty and innocence, violence and evil, and attempt to show the absurdity of reconciling the various moralities that coexist in society. He acknowledges a debt to Beckett, but Esslin (in his *Theatre of the absurd*, 1962) has shrewdly indicated how far he is influenced by Dalí. Three volumes of his *Théâtre* have so far been published by Julliard in Paris. Vol. 1 (1958) includes *Oraison, Les deux bourreaux, Fando et Lis*, and *Le cimetière des voitures*; vol. 2 (1961): *Guernica, Le labyrinthe, Le tricycle, Pique-nique en campagne*, and *La bicyclette du*

condamné; vol. 3 (1965); *Le couronnement, Le grand cérémonial, Concert dans un oeuf*, and *Cérémonie pour un noir assassiné*.

In *Orchestration théâtrale* (first acted 1959) Arrabal attempted a play without dialogue, using the movement of abstract shapes from the world of Miró or Calder. His enthusiasm for chess and games has led to a series of formal ritual dramas such as *L'architecte et l'Empereur d'Assyrie* (1967) for two characters, brilliantly staged by Jorge Lavelli in 1967. He has also written *Baal Babylone* (Paris, 1959) and *L'enterrement de la sardine* (Paris, 1961).

ARRÁIZ, ANTONIO (1903–), b. Barquisimeto. Venezuelan novelist and poet. After the precocious *avant-garde* poems of *Áspero* (1924), Arráiz turned to the novel, and produced a powerful (often autobiographical) narrative of the life of political prisoners under the Gómez dictatorship (1908–35) in *Puros hombres* (Lima, 1938). *Dámaso Velázquez* (1943), later named *El mar es como un potro*, is a brutal, vivid novel set in a Caribbean community of smugglers, pearl-fishers and treasure-hunters. *Todos iban desorientados* (1951) is a clever social satire which analyses the downfall of a number of families. Arráiz also wrote an animal fable, *Tío tigre y tío conejo* (1945), illustrating typical Venezuelan attitudes. His *Suma poética* (1966) contains a good essay on Arráiz by Juan Liscano.

ARREOLA, JUAN JOSÉ (1918–), b. Ciudad Guzmán, Mexico. Short-story writer and actor. His first stories appeared in little magazines in Guadalajara during the early forties. He edited *Pan*, with his friend and contemporary Juan Rulfo (q.v.), and *Eos*. His ingenious *Varia invención* appeared in 1949. This was followed by *Confabulario* in 1952, and a collected edition of his *Cuentos* in 1955.

Punta de plata (1958) was a bestiary of satirical fables that he later included with his previous two books and newer stories in *Confabulario total, 1941–1961* (1962) translated by George D. Schade (Austin, Texas, 1964). His play *La hora de todos* (1954) won the first prize in the INBA Drama Festival. *La feria* (1963) is a fantastic compilation of fragments from Isaiah and Ezekiel, the Apocrypha, colonial archives, and the author's childhood memories of his home town. His latest book is *Palindronia* (1971). Arreola's memorable style has been influenced by that of Borges (q.v.) but it is more barbed and witty, less erudite and compassionate.

ARRIAZA Y SUPERVIELA, JUAN BAUTISTA (1770–1837), b. Madrid. Poet. He spent some years in the Navy but was discharged in 1798 because of defective vision. He joined the diplomatic service and served some time in London. His facile verses were published in *Primicias* (Paris, 1797), *Ensayos poéticos* (1799), and *Poesías líricas* (1822). The poems in his *Poesías patrióticas* (London, 1810) were so predictable in celebrating every birth, wedding, coronation, or death that he was nicknamed 'the official poet'. Arriaza is best known for poems on the War of Independence, especially for a composition on the Dos de Mayo. He translated Boileau's *Art poétique* into Spanish (1807). His *Poesías* were collected in vol. 67 (1875) of the BAE by L. A. de Cueto.

ARRIETA, FERNANDO, pseudonym of Evaristo Acevedo Guerra (q.v.).

ARRIETA, RAFAEL ALBERTO (1889–), b. ranch, south of Buenos Aires. Literary historian and poet. Professor of European Literature at La Plata University, where he himself had graduated. He edited (1917–18) the magazine *Atenea* and also edited and contributed to a six-volume *Historia de la literatura argentina* (1960), and won the Premio Nacional de Filosofía for his *Don Gregorio Beeche y los bibliógrafos americanos de Chile y del Plata* (1942). His collections of poetry include *Alma y momento* (1910), *El espejo de la fuente* (1912), *Las noches de oro* (1917), *Fugacidad* (1921), *Estío serrano* (1926), and *Tiempo cautivo* (1947).

ARRUFAT, ANTÓN (1935–), Cuban playwright. A playwright of the absurd, Arrufat is obsessed by time and its effect on human beings. *El caso se investiga* (1957) ridicules police methods in a manner reminiscent of Mack Sennett's silent films. *El vivo al pollo* (1961), inspired by *El velorio de Pachencho* by the Rebreno brothers, deals with a woman's decision to have her husband embalmed in order to have him forever by her side. She eventually marries the embalmer, and her late husband becomes the best advertisement for their business. The way in which routine can corrupt and pervert the human spirit is explored in *El último tren* and *La repetición* (both 1963). *Todos los domingos* (1965) concerns a rich woman, now confined to a wheelchair, who had been abandoned by her fiancé twenty years earlier and now pays young men, dressed exactly like her fiancé, to visit her every Sunday. The last of these impersonators is killed by her nurse-companion with a pair of scissors as the crone cackles insanely. *Los siete contra Tebas* (1968), based on *The seven against Thebes* of Aeschylus, provoked a bitter reaction from the Castro regime for its allegedly anti-revolutionary stance.

See L. F. Lyday and G. W. Woodyard (eds.),

Dramatists in revolt: the new Latin American theater (Austin, Texas, 1976).

ARTEAGA, ESTEBAN DE (1747–99), b. Moraleja de Coca, Segovia. Writer on aesthetics. Expelled from Spain with his fellow-Jesuits in 1767, he left the Order in 1769 and lived in Italy, writing in both Italian and Spanish. Arteaga was the most distinguished Spanish writer on aesthetics of the period. As well as the *Investigaciones filosóficas sobre la belleza ideal* (1789), edited by Miguel Batllori (1943), he wrote *La rivoluzione del teatro musicale italiano dalla sua origine fino al presente* (3 vols., Bologna, 1783–8), *Memorias para servir a la historia de la música española* (1789), and *Della influenza degli arabi sull' origine della poesia moderna in Europa* (1791).

See Eva Marja Rudat, *Las ideas estéticas de Esteban de Arteaga* (1971).

Arte mayor, in Spanish verse, *coplas* or *versos, de arte mayor* are lines of nine to fourteen (infrequently even more) syllables, usually with four rhythmic stresses, two to each hemistich, and a caesura. The term is most often used of a twelve-syllable line with a strong caesura after the sixth syllable, a line especially popular in the 15th c. Various groupings of stressed and unstressed syllables are possible, but the rhythm is anapaestic rather than iambic.

Arte menor, in Spanish verse, *versos de arte menor* are lines of two to eight syllables usually requiring no more than one rhythmic stress, though they may have two.

Arte nuevo de hacer comedias (1609), a verse treatise by Lope de Vega (q.v.) on the 'new art of writing plays' read in self-justification before a Madrid literary society. Lope suggests the following ideas for the aspiring dramatist: choose any subject, even royalty (though Philip II was known to take offence at commoners acting the parts of kings and queens); mix comic and tragic in the same play; disregard the unities of time and place; divide your play into three *jornadas* (or acts) for exposition, complication, and denouement; and maintain suspense to the last line, or the audience will leave. Use domestic language in domestic scenes, and plenty of wit and epigrams. Make the dialogue fit the character, and do not forget in Act III what you had written in Act I. Make the verse-form fit the situation, so that for example those speaking of tragic themes employ tercets. Use mystery, satire, and puns. Above all, do not write about how to write plays, but go and see them: that is the best way to learn.

The 'new' elements of Lopean theory and practice were conceived in opposition to the classical drama, adhering closely to Aristotelean unities, and were rejected by opponents of Lope such as Francisco Cascales (q.v.). Lope's witty *Arte nuevo* has been translated by W. T. Brewster for *Papers on playmaking*, edited by Brander Matthews (New York, 1927).

Arthurian Literature in Spain, the Arthurian romances of Europe were a significant part of the oral and written traditions from the late 12th c. None remained unchanged by time or the crossing of national or linguistic borders, and most acquired passages from sources beyond the original legends surrounding King Arthur and his Knights of the Round Table.

References to the *matière de Bretagne* first appear in the Peninsula in Catalonia towards the close of the 12th c., and the Provençal verse romance *Jaufré* (by a disciple of Chrétien de Troyes), composed *c.* 1200, was dedicated to a king of Catalonia. Many French Arthurian works in prose and verse were known in Catalonia from the 13th c. onwards, and several were translated. Arthurian literature seems to have reached Castile later, Castilian translations appearing to date from the early 14th c. Though much enjoyed, Castilian Arthurianism was limited to a small number of works: (a) a version of the French Post-Vulgate cycle (1230–40) now known as the *Roman du Graal*; of the three parts, the first was entitled *Libro de Josep Abarimatia*, and concerned the early history of the Grail; the second told the story of Merlin and the setting-up of the Round Table and was published as *Baladro del Sabio Merlín* from the end of the 15th c.; the third dealt with the Grail Quest, and was published in the early 16th c. as *La Demanda del Sancto Grial*. This cycle of romances was far more popular in Castile than was the so-called Vulgate cycle, although this was known, and is represented by (b) a long manuscript fragment of the 16th c. entitled *Lanzarote de Lago*; (c) the story of Tristan and Yseut, of which two versions survive, a long 14th-c. fragment and the printed *Tristán de Leonís*, published first in 1501; the 1534 edition had a sequel relating the adventures of the hero's son and was entitled *Corónica de don Tristán de Leonís y del rey don Tristán el Joven*. Both the manuscript and the printed versions derive from a common source, probably in Italian rather than French; (d) *Tablante de Ricamonte*, a prose rendering of *Jaufré*, of which at least seven editions were published between 1513 and 1629. This appears to have been the only Arthurian work of which Cervantes had direct knowledge (he mentions it in *Don Quijote*, I, 16), and retained a certain appeal after the romances of Tristan, Merlin and the Grail Quest ceased to be published in the 1530s.

Editions of some Spanish Arthurian romances can be found in: A. Bonilla y San Martín, *Libros de caballerías* (NBAE VI, Madrid, 1907); G. T. Northup, *El cuento de Tristán de Leonís* (Chicago, 1928); and P. Bohigas Balaguer, *El baladro del sabio Merlín* (3 vols., Barcelona, 1957–62).

See also W. J. Entwistle, *The Arthurian legend in the literatures of the Spanish peninsula* (London, 1925); M. R. Lida de Malkiel, 'Arthurian literature in Spain and Portugal' in *Arthurian literature in the Middle Ages*, ed. R. S. Loomis (Oxford, 1959), pp. 406–18; A. Deyermond, 'The lost genre of medieval Spanish literature', *Hispanic Review*, vol. 43, 1975, 231–59; J. B. Hall, '*Tablante de Ricamonte* and other Castilian versions of Arthurian romances', *Revue de Littérature Comparée*, vol. 48, 1974, 177–89. See also Caballería, Libros de.

ARTIGAS FERRANDO, Miguel (1887–1947), b. Blesa, Teruel. Scholar and librarian, from 1915 to 1930 Director of the Biblioteca Menéndez y Pelayo in Santander and from 1930 Director of the Biblioteca Nacional in Madrid. He helped to direct the national edition of the *Obras completas* of Menéndez y Pelayo (Santander, 1940–59), in 65 volumes and wrote studies entitled *Menéndez y Pelayo* (1927) and *La vida y la obra de Menéndez Pelayo* (1939). He has written three critical and biographical books on Góngora: *Don Luis de Góngora y Argote* (1925), *Semblanza de Góngora* (1928), and *La vida y la obra de Góngora* (Saragossa, 1939).

ASBAJE, Juana de, see Juana Inés de la Cruz, Sor.

ASCASUBI, Hilario (1807–75), b. Posta de Fraile Muerto (now Bell-Ville), Argentina. *Gauchesco* poet and journalist, who opposed the dictator Rosas and after two years in prison escaped and fled to Montevideo (1832). He developed the *gaucho* tradition of Juan Gualberto Godoy and Bartolomé Hidalgo (qq.v.) in one-man magazines such as *El arriero argentino* (2 September 1830, 1 issue only), for which he wrote under the pen-name 'Gaucho Cordobés'; *El gaucho en campaña* (4 issues in 1839); and *El gaucho Jacinto Cielo* (12 issues in 1843). Much of his writing was ephemeral and has disappeared: but two editions were collected in his lifetime: *Trovos de Paulino Lucero* (2 vols., 1853) and *Paulino Lucero; o, Los gauchos del Río de la Plata cantando y combatiendo contra los tiranos de las Repúblicas Argentina y Oriental del Uruguay, 1839–1851* (Paris, 1872). He edited the satirical magazine *Aniceto el Gallo* using the title as his pen-name; 14 numbers and a special bulletin appeared between 19 May 1853 and 1 October 1859. It was reprinted in Paris in 1872.

Ascasubi's most significant contribution to Gaucho Literature (q.v.) is *Santos Vega* (q.v.), a long narrative poem. Its first two parts, consisting of 1,080 lines, appeared in 1850–1 under the title of *Los mellizos de La Flor*. Its theme is that of the twins, one virtuous and one criminal, whose lives are described by the *payador* Santos Vega.

Ascasubi finished his poem in Paris in 1871–2 in a total of 12,604 lines, publishing it as vol. 1 of his *Obras completas* (Paris, 1872).

See Manuel Mújica Láinez, *Vida de Aniceto el Gallo (Hilario Ascasubi)* (1943); and E. F. Tiscornia, *Poetas gauchescos: Hidalgo, Ascasubi, del Campo* (1940).

Ascetic Writers, *ascética* (Greek: *asketes*, a monk or hermit, from *askein*, to exercise) traditionally consists of the first two or three spiritual degrees: the purgative (mortification of the body, and prayer); the illuminative; and the contemplative, 'estado beatífico' or 'matrimonio espiritual' of S. Juan de la Cruz (q.v.). *Mística* is attained only by those who have mastered all three degrees. St. Thomas Aquinas differentiates between acquired virtues (*ascética*) and gifts of grace (*mística*).

The Stoic tradition of Seneca, which taught that virtue could be attained through self-discipline, merged in Spain with the teachings of the Church to produce a wave of ascetic literature beginning *c.* 1496 with *Breve e muy provechosa doctrina de lo que deue saber todo christiano* of Fray Hernando de Talavera (q.v.), written in clear prose and intended for a popular audience. Ascetic literature, stimulated by the *Ejercicios espirituales* (Rome, 1548) by Ignacio de Loyola (q.v.), reached its apogee in the reign of Philip II (1556–98), when many of the best writers wrote on religious topics and several thousand books and pamphlets were published on the subject. *Ascética* is not easily separable from *mística* in the works of such authors as Fray Luis de Granada (q.v.), and Menéndez y Pelayo's list of ascetic writers includes S. Juan de la Cruz and S. Teresa (qq.v.), usually considered mystics, and thus omitted here.

Augustinians: Fray Luis de León, Beato Alonso de Orozco, Fray Hernando de Zárate, Fray Pedro de Vega, Santo Tomás de Villanueva and Fray Pedro Malón de Chaide;

Dominicans: P. Melchor Cano, P. Alonso de Cabrera, Fray Luis de Granada;

Franciscans: Fray Alonso de Madrid, Francisco de Osuna, Fray Bernardino de Laredo, S. Pedro de Alcántara, Diego de Estella, Fray Juan de los Ángeles, and Sor María de Jesús de Ágreda;

Jesuits: P. Alonso Rodríguez, P. Luis de la Puente, P. Juan Eusebio Nieremberg, P. Luis de

la Palma, P. Pedro de Rivadeneyra, and S. Francisco de Borja;

Others: Beato Juan de Ávila, Fray Hernando de Talavera, and Alejo Venegas del Busto.

A representative collection of the ascetic writers was edited by M. Mir in vol. 16 (1911) of the NBAE. Fray Alonso de Madrid (q.v.) wrote the *Arte para servir a Dios* (Burgos, 1521). Fray Bernardino de Laredo is the author of a *Subida del Monte Sión por la vía contemplativa* (1535). Alejo Venegas del Busto (q.v.) wrote the *Agonía del tránsito de la muerte con los auisos y consuelos que cerca della son prouechosos* (Toledo, 1537), and Beato Juan de Ávila compiled a confidential sermon directed to a pupil based on Psalm 44 and called *Audi, filia, et vide* (written 1530, publ. 1556). The greatest ascetic writer was Fray Luis de Granada (q.v.), especially in his magnanimous *Guía de pecadores* (2 vols., Lisbon, 1556–7) and his *Introducción al símbolo de la fe* (Salamanca, 1583).

ASÍN Y PALACIOS, MIGUEL (1871–1944), b. Saragossa. Arabist. After obtaining a theological degree, he studied Arabic under Julián Ribera (q.v.). His first book was *Algazel: dogmática, moral y ascética* (1901). In 1903 he was appointed to the chair of Arabic in Madrid University in succession to Gayangos and Codera, and founded (1933) the important journal *al-Andalus*, which has been largely responsible for the high level of Spanish Islamic studies in recent decades. His life's work was to reveal the great extent of cross-cultural influences between Islam and Christianity, in books such as *Averroísmo teológico de Santo Tomaso d'Aquino* (1904); *La escatología musulmana en 'La Divina Comedia'* (1919), in which he was the first to prove that Dante's vision (including a Hell of ice) was derived in part from Muslim accounts of the ascension of Muhammad; *El Islam cristianizado* (1931); *La espiritualidad de Algazel y su sentido cristiano* (4 vols., 1934–41); and *Huellas del Islam. S. Tomás de Aquino. Turmeda. Pascal. S. Juan de la Cruz* (1941). As a teacher, Asín trained Arabists of great distinction, among them Emilio García Gómez (q.v.).

Asno erudito, El (1782), a malicious attack on Tomás de Iriarte y Oropesa and his neoclassical literary theories by Juan Pablo Forner (qq.v.) in the form of a fable.

Association of Hispanists of Great Britain and Ireland, The, a society founded in 1955 to bring together academics interested in Spain, Portugal, and Latin America. The Association's presidents have been Ignacio Llubera (1955), A. A. Parker (1957), J. W. Rees (1959), E. M. Wilson (1961), R. F. Brown (1963), L. J.

Woodward (1965), C. A. Jones (1967), J. Manson (1969), F. W. Pierce (1971), D. J. Gifford (1973), and M. Wilson (1975). The Society had a membership of over 300 in 1976, and holds an annual conference at a British university.

Astracanada, a broad farce, often dependent on ambiguous situations and puns, created in about 1900 from the witty comedy of the previous generation by Pedro Muñoz Seca (q.v.) and his collaborators, among them Enrique García Álvarez (q.v.). The genre has remained paramount on the Madrid stage as undemanding and easy entertainment.

ASTRANA MARÍN, Luis (1889–1960), b. Villaescusa de Haro, Cuenca. Scholar. He wrote a biography *William Shakespeare* (1930) and translated Shakespeare into Spanish. His major contribution, however, is a massive *Vida ejemplar y heroica de Miguel de Cervantes de Saavedra* (1948–58) in seven volumes. He edited the *Obras completas* of Quevedo (2 vols., 1932), Calderón (1932) and Juan Martínez de Cuéllar's *Desengaño del hombre* (1928) in the series Los Clásicos Olvidados. He also wrote *Cristóbal Colón* (1929) and a useful *Vida azarosa de Lope de Vega* (Barcelona, 1935).

ASTURIAS, Miguel Ángel (1899–), b. Guatemala City. Major novelist. He studied law in the National University of Guatemala, and ancient American cultures under Georges Raynaud at the Sorbonne. Raynaud had already translated the *Popol Vuh* into French, and Asturias undertook the Spanish translation with the Mexican scholar M. González de Mendoza. The *Leyendas de Guatemala* (1930) were produced during these years, but it was with his novel *El señor Presidente* (q.v., 1946) that Asturias achieved fame. Until the publication in 1969 of *Conversación en 'La Catedral'* by Mario Vargas Llosa (q.v.), this novel, inspired by the Estrada Cabrera regime of Guatemala which fell in 1921, was the best Latin American novel of dictatorship.

His later novels are less successful, partly because of their inaccessible vocabulary and verbal extravagance. Although understandable, his hostility to the U.S.A. becomes tedious and perhaps unconvincing when seen against the over-simplified picture of native virtue conjured up by Asturias, himself almost fully European by education. These later novels are *Hombres de maíz* (q.v., Buenos Aires, 1949), *Viento fuerte* (1950), *Papa verde* (1954) *Los ojos de los enterrados* (1960), the last three comprising a trilogy attacking U.S. imperialism in Central America; and *Mulata de tal* (Buenos Aires, 1963).

His verse written between 1918 and 1948 was published in *Poesía: sien de alondra* (1949). Eight political stories were published in *Weekend in Guatemala* (1956), inspired by the overthrow (with the aid of the C.I.A.) of the government of Arbenz Guzmán in 1954, after which Asturias was deprived of his citizenship and exiled for eight years in Argentina.

He was given the Lenin Peace Prize in 1966, the year he was appointed Guatemalan ambassador in Paris, and he received the Nobel Prize for Literature in 1967.

Subsequent books include *El espejo de Lida* (Mexico City, 1967), *Maladrón* (Buenos Aires, 1969), *Viernes de Dolores* (Buenos Aires, 1972), and *América, fábula de fábulas* (Caracas, 1972).

See the foreword by Pablo Palomino to the *Obras completas* (3 vols., Madrid, 1968); P. F. De Andrea, *Miguel Ángel Asturias: anticipo bibliográfico* (Mexico City, 1969); Giuseppe Bellini, *La narrativa di Miguel Ángel Asturias* (Milan, 1966; Spanish translation, Buenos Aires, 1970); Marta Pilon, *Miguel Ángel Asturias: semblanza para el estudio de su vida y obra* (1968); and H. F. Giacoman (ed.), *Homenaje a Miguel Ángel Asturias* (New York, 1971).

Atalaya de la vida umana, the sub-title of the second part of *Guzmán de Alfarache*, a novel by Mateo Alemán (qq.v.).

Atenea, the important Chilean literary review founded in 1924 by Enrique Molina as the magazine of the University of Concepción, established in 1919. The magazine is still in existence. Its editors have included Eduardo Barrios, Domingo Melfi, Luis Durand, Raúl Silva Castro, and Milton Rossel.

Most of Chile's leading writers have appeared in its pages and a number of its critical essays have dealt with international literature.

Another periodical called *Atenea* was edited by Rafael Alberto Arrieta (q.v.) in La Plata, Argentina, during 1918–19.

AUB, Max (1903–72), b. Paris. Novelist, short-story writer, dramatist and essayist. He had a French mother and German father. His family left for Spain in 1914, and later took Spanish citizenship. Aub was educated in Valencia, but travelled over the eastern half of Spain for his father's business. With García Lorca, Alberti, Cernuda (qq.v.) and others he is considered one of the 'Generation of 1927'. In 1938 he collaborated with André Malraux on a film that is now called *Sierra de Teruel*.

Aub lived in Mexico City from 1942, and all his novels about the Spanish Civil War were published there: *Campo cerrado* (1943), *Campo de sangre* (1945), *Campo abierto* (1951). The *avant-*

garde Jusep Torres Campalans (1958) includes an interview between author and the imaginary hero, a list of contemporary world events, and a catalogue of the hero's paintings, some of which are reproduced in colour. The novels which the author considered his most important are *Yo vivo* (1953), *Las buenas intenciones* (1954), *La calle de Valverde* (1961), *Campo del moro* (1963), *Juego de cartas* (1964), *Historia de mala muerte* (1965), *Campo de los almendros* (1968), and the stories collected in *Últimos cuentos de la guerra de España* (Caracas, 1969). One of his earliest stories, the fantastic *Fábula verde* (Valencia, privately printed, 1933), tells of a woman attracted not by meat or fish, but by the more sensuous 'flesh' of fruit and vegetables. She magically brings forth a 'daughter'—an apple. She eats the apple.

Aub's epistolary novel *Luis Álvarez Petreña* (1934) concerns the despair of a suicide. His plays are also important; they include *Narciso* (1928), *Teatro incompleto* (1931), *San Juan* (1943), *Morir por cerrar los ojos* (1944), *Deseada* (1950), *No* (1952), and *Retrato de un general* (1969).

In *La obra narrativa de Max Aub, 1929–1969* (1973), Ignacio Soldevila Durante suggests that Aub's favoured themes are life as a myriad of intersecting labyrinths, and solitude versus sociability.

AULNOY, MARIE-CATHERINE JUMELLE DE BERNEVILLE, *Comtesse d'* (c. 1650–1705), a French writer of fairy-tales, who wrote a number of 'travel books' now believed to have been compiled from other sources, or at any rate embroidered (see *Fantasías y realidades del viaje a Madrid de la condesa d'Aulnoy*, 1943, by G. Maura Gomazo and A. González de Amezúa).

Her *Relation du voyage d'Espagne, 1679–80* (3 vols., The Hague, 1693) has been edited by R. Foulché-Delbosc in *Revue Hispanique* (vol. 67, 1926).

Auto de los Reyes Magos, an anonymous liturgical verse play of 147 lines in four scenes on the Three Kings (the designation *auto* is recent), found in Toledo Cathedral Library *c.* 1785. Its possible sources have been studied by Winifred Sturdevant in *The 'Misterio de los reyes magos': its position in the mediaeval legend of the Three Kings* (Baltimore and Paris, 1927). She suggests a derivation from a liturgical Epiphany play imported from France by a Gascon priest who had settled in Toledo. Each of the Magi appears in turn and decides to follow the Star to Bethlehem; they then appear before Herod, who orders them to find the Messiah so that he too may worship Him. When they leave he reveals his anger, and his rabbis quarrel over

the mystery of Christ's birth which they cannot understand. It has been suggested that although the MS. ends abruptly here, the *auto* may not be a mere fragment, but could be a prologue to the offering of gifts by members of the congregation in the churches where it would be performed. This suggestion is now generally rejected.

The play was edited by R. Menéndez Pidal (who dated it at about 1200) in the *Revista de Archivos, Bibliotecas y Museos* (1900) and reprinted in Ford's *Old Spanish readings* (Boston, 1911). Shortly after the play was composed, Alfonso X (q.v.) in his *Siete Partidas* proscribed all church drama except plays on the angel's announcement to the shepherds, the adoration of the Magi, and the Resurrection.

Autos sacramentales, one-act plays (*autos*) performed at the feast of Corpus Christi, originally confined in theme to the Eucharist; later dealing allegorically with a variety of subjects but still ending with the 'discovery' of a large host and chalice; and finally degenerating into farces. The allegory of the Eucharist had a historical, legendary, or religious setting. The adjective *sacramental* was first used of them in the second half of the 16th c., but the first allegorical *auto* is probably the *Auto de la Pasión* (*c.* 1500) of Lucas Fernández (q.v.) who is known to have been present at the Corpus Christi festivals of 1501 and 1503. The first *auto* known to have taken the Eucharist as its specific theme is the *Farsa sacramental* of Hernán López de Yanguas; later writers in the genre include Diego Sánchez de Badajoz (active from 1525–47), Gil Vicente (in whose *Auto de la fe* Faith explains the origins and mysteries of Christianity to shepherds), Rojas Zorrilla in *El rico avariento*, Lope de Vega in *Las aventuras del hombre*, Mira de Amescua in *Las pruebas de Cristo*, Tirso de Molina in *El colmenero divino*, and Calderón (qq.v.), who brought the *auto sacramental* to the apogee of its allegorical intensity with Old Testament subjects like *La cena de Baltasar*, *Sueños hay que verdad son*, *A tu prójimo como a tí* (from the New Testament), and such philosophical and theological *autos* as *El gran teatro del mundo*, *El veneno y la triaca*, and above all *La vida es sueño* (q.v.).

The *autos* were performed in cities and villages on moveable carts (*carros*), which were easily converted into stages or dismantled, and pulled by oxen. These *carros* bore scenic towers, from which actors could come on to the stage and to which they could retire; the towers might be topped with a globe which might open to reveal God on His throne, or the symbols of the Eucharist at the end of the *auto*. The carts would be aligned before a temporary stage, and beyond this some temporary seating might be erected, e.g. along part of one side of the

Madrid Plaza Mayor for performances there. Being put on in the open air, *autos sacramentales* gave far greater scope for visual spectacles (including scene changes and elaborate machinery) than was possible with plays staged in the *corral* theatres with their limited facilities and lack of space.

As a result of the influence of French taste, *autos sacramentales* were forbidden by law in June 1765, but performances in isolated villages continued, and Lamarca records (*Teatro de Valencia*, 1840) a performance in Valencia as late as 1840.

Calderón had the monopoly of writing *autos* for Madrid from 1649. He stated in a letter to the Duke of Veraguas dated 1680, the year before his death, that he had written seventy *autos sacramentales* (Vicente García de la Huerta's *Teatro Hespañol*, 1785, vol. III, part II).

Autos viejos, the common designation of a MS. in the National Library of Madrid entitled *Colección de autos, farsas y coloquios del siglo XVI* which preserves 96 plays belonging mainly to the first half of the 16th c. All are anonymous except one attributed to Jaime Ferruz of Valencia and another to Lope de Rueda (q.v.). The *autos* are one-act plays, not to be confused with the later *autos sacramentales* (q.v.), here described as *farsas*.

The themes are the Nativity, the Passion, the Resurrection, episodes from lives of the Saints, the Virgin Mary, and scenes from both Old and New Testaments. Technically, the plays are still primitive, marking little advance over their medieval forebears. The foolish shepherd, in some of the *autos*, however, foreshadows the use of the *gracioso* or comic character in the theatre of the Golden Age.

The only complete edition (replacing the partial edition by E. González Pedroso in vol. 68 of the BAE) is that of Leo Rouanet (4 vols., 1901).

AVELLANEDA, Alonso Fernández de, see Fernández de Avellaneda, Alonso.

AVELLANEDA, Gertrudis de, see Gómez de Avellaneda, Gertrudis.

AVELLANEDA Y LA CUEVA, Francisco de (1622–c. 1675), Dramatist—after the manner of Calderón (q.v.)—and censor of plays at the Court in Madrid. His best-known plays are *El divino calabrés San Francisco de Paula* written with Matos Fragoso (q.v.), and *Cuantas veo, tantas quiero*, written with Sebastián Rodríguez de Villaviciosa published in vol. 47 of the BAE. Among his *sainetes* are *El sargento Conchillos*, *El hidalgo de la Membrilla*, *La hija del doctor* and *Noches de invierno y perdone el enfermo*.

Avellano, Cofradía del, literary circle formed in Granada by a group of writers, including Ángel Ganivet (q.v.), Gabriel Ruiz de Almodóvar, Nicolás María López, Matías Méndez Vellido (these four collaborated in *El libro de Granada*, Granada, 1899), Melchor de Almagro San Martín, and Antonio J. Afán de Rivera. The name derives from the Fuente del Avellano, on the outskirts of Granada, where the group used to meet.

AVEMPACE (d. 1138), Abu Bakr Muhammad ibn Yahya, surnamed Ibn as-Sayah and popularly known as Ibn Bajja, a name corrupted by the European schoolmen into Avempace or Avenpace. b. Saragossa. Philosopher, physician, mathematician, astronomer, and musician. He was in Seville during 1118, after which we find him in Africa, enjoying high esteem among the Almorávides (q.v.). An opponent of neo-Platonism, he was one of those learned Muslims who kept the Aristotelean tradition alive in tolerant Almoravid Spain, when in Asia it was regarded as heretical. His chief contributions to learning were the commentaries on Aristotle's *Physics*, *De generatione et corruptione*, and *Meteora*, from which he became known as 'the Commentator'. But he is also important as an original writer on mathematics, and the concept of the soul, and as the author of a *Hermit's guide* or *Guide to the solitary*, later used by Averroes and Moses of Narbonne in the 14th c. His work was known to Thomas Aquinas and influenced the *Visión delectable* of Alfonso de la Torre (q.v.). His reply to the Persian al-Ghazzali's *Destruction of the philosophers* was called the *Destruction of the destruction*, in which Avempace defended Avicenna.

AVENDAÑO, Francisco de (*fl.* 1551), playwright. His sole known work, *Comedia Florisea* (1551; reprinted 1553) shows the influence of Encina and Torres Naharro. After a comic prologue, Muerto (a victim of misfortune) and Floriseo (a victim of unrequited love) vow to commit suicide together, but are mocked by a passing shepherd before they carry out their plans. Eventually Blancaflor is reunited with her missing Floriseo in a comic wedding scene, while Fortuna crowns the proceedings with a gift of 1,000 ducats to the young couple and the promise of plenty for Muerto. Avendaño probably wrote this amusing and well-constructed play to celebrate the marriage of Juan Pacheco, a relative of Avendaño's patron, a Marqués de Villena (Diego López Pacheco?).

J. P. Wickersham Crawford (*Spanish drama before Lope de Vega*, 1922, p. 79) was wrong in attributing to Avendaño the innovation of transforming five acts into three, for the *Auto de*

Clarindo (Toledo, 1535?) of Antonio Díez is one of some three-act plays written earlier. The *Florisea*, which is in verse, has been edited by A. Bonilla y San Martín in 'Cinco obras dramáticas anteriores a Lope', *Revue Hispanique* vol. 27 (1912).

See also Ludwig Pfandl, 'Die "Comedia Florisea" von 1551' in *Zeitschrift für Romanische Philologie*, vol. 39 (1917).

Aventuras, inventos y mixtificaciones de Silvestre Paradox (1901), the first novel in the trilogy *La vida fantástica* by Pío Baroja y Nessi (qq.v.).

AVICEBRON, see GABIROL, Solomon ben Judah ibn.

ÁVILA, *Beato* JUAN DE, see JUAN DE ÁVILA, *Beato*.

ÁVILA, JULIO ENRIQUE (1892–), b. San Salvador. A graduate in chemistry and pharmacy, who has become known for his poetry, at first influenced by Darío but later, according to Juan Ramón Uriarte, 'unclassifiable . . ., belonging to no literary *ism*'. Ávila's first collection was *Fuentes de alma* (1917), followed by *El poeta egoísta* (1922), the novel *El vigía sin luz* (1927), concerning a blind boy who discovers an interior world, the prose poem *El mundo de mi jardín* (1927), and *Galerías* (1942).

ÁVILA Y ZÚÑIGA, LUIS DE, see ZÚÑIGA Y ÁVILA, Luis de.

AXULAR, PIARRES DE (1556–c. 1640), b. Urdax, Navarra. Possibly the best Basque prose stylist. He studied in Salamanca, and was appointed sub-dean in Pamplona in 1595 and dean in Lérida the following year. In 1609 he was appointed parish priest of Sare (Labourd, French Basque provinces) despite the protests of the French. His book *Guero* (1643) is one of the few devotional works written in Basque, not merely translated from Castilian. Though J. de Urquijo has indicated the influence of Fray Luis de Granada (q.v.), Axular's work is often intensely personal, with well-chosen arguments *ad hominem* and fine Basque translations from the Latin. An ascetic work bearing entirely on the conduct of the average man, it possesses virtually no mystical or speculative features. Another part was promised but apparently never written. The 1864 edition entitled *Gueroco Guero*, is a revision by Inchauspe with many changes. There is a facsimile (1958?) by J. de Urquijo and a new edition, *Gero* (Zarauz, 1954).

See J. de Urquijo, 'Axular y su libro', in *Revista Internacional de Estudios Vascos*, vols. 5 and 6 (1911–12).

AYALA, *El Canciller* PERO LÓPEZ DE, see LÓPEZ DE AYALA, Pedro.

AYALA, FRANCISCO (1906–), b. Granada. Novelist, short-story writer, and essayist. He studied in Germany in 1929–30, and translated Rilke and Thomas Mann. He taught sociology and political science in Madrid University from 1933–36, but went into exile during the Civil War, teaching sociology in Buenos Aires (1939–50), where he founded the magazine *Realidad*, and later in Puerto Rico (where he founded *La Torre*), Princeton, New York, and Chicago.

Ayala wrote his first novel, *Tragicomedia de un hombre sin espíritu* (1925), in 1923, in which year he gained his first degree at Madrid University. His other apprentice works were *Historia de un amanecer* (1926), *Medusa artificial* (1928), and *El boxeador y un ángel* (1929). His first important book was *Cazador en el alba*, first published in the *Revista de Occidente* (1929) and the following year in book form. This relates the thoughts of a simple cavalryman one morning while convalescing after a fall. The style is limpid and, as an exercise in creating a character from amorphous memories and vague dreams, the book is a remarkable *tour de force*. *Los usurpadores* (Buenos Aires, 1949) consists of six stories, some of them written just after the Civil War, connected by Ayala's conviction that the power exercised by one person over another is a usurpation and leads to catastrophe. *La cabeza del cordero* (Buenos Aires, 1949; 2nd edn. with a new story 'La vida por la opinión', 1962) shows a continuing, though attenuated, obsession with the Civil War. His more recent books are satirical to the point of caricature: *Historia de macacos* was first published in *Sur* (Buenos Aires, 1952) then as a book (Madrid, 1955); *Muertes de perro* (Buenos Aires, 1958) and *El fondo del vaso* (Buenos Aires, 1962) are black stories of social despair in the tradition of Torrente Ballester (q.v.), offering no hope in the present collapse of moral values.

Seven later stories were collected in *El as de bastos* (Buenos Aires, 1963). Ayala's selection *Mis páginas mejores* appeared in 1965 and his collection *Obras narrativas completas* in 1969. As well as the lengthy *Tratado de sociología* (Buenos Aires, 1947), Ayala has written numerous essays on politics and sociology such as *El escritor en la sociedad de masas* (1955), *Tecnología y libertad* (1959), *De este mundo y el otro* (1963), and *De raptos, violaciones y otras inconveniencias* (1966).

AYGUALS DE IZCO, Wenceslao (1801–73), b. Vinaroz, Castellón. Popular novelist whose success was due mainly to the sensationalism of his pictures of low Spanish life influenced by the Parisian novels of Eugène Sue. His novels were published in parts (like those of Manuel Fernández y González, q.v.), and their tenor was furiously anticlerical, like his journal *El dómine Lucas*. *María; o la hija de un jornalero* (1845–6) is a characteristic novel, dedicated to Sue, with an abundance of vague social protest which hints at the naturalism of the future while failing to offer the historical accuracy or the serious understanding of complex events, of the novel's main source: *El señor de Bembibre* (1844) by Enrique Gil y Carrasco (q.v.), a book which genuinely applied to Spain the vision and skill learnt from Sir Walter Scott.

Ayguals' serial stories were read avidly by the lower classes in Madrid. He also wrote a number of plays and a philosophical poem, *El derecho y la fuerza* (1866). Ayguals founded the important Madrid printing house Sociedad Literaria.

See Blas María Araque, *Biografía de don Wenceslao Ayguals de Izco* (1881).

AYLLÓN, Perálvarez de, nothing is known of Ayllón beyond his authorship of a dramatic eclogue entitled *Comedia de Preteo y Tibaldo, llamada disputa y remedio de amor*, published in Toledo in 1553 after having been completed by Luis Hurtado de Toledo (q.v.), who added 256 lines. This rather static drama concerns the sufferings caused by love and the remedies available, for which Ayllón draws on Ovid's *Remedia amoris*, together with the qualities of women whom Ayllón admires and defends, turning for his arguments to *El triunfo de las donas* of Juan Rodríguez de la Cámara. The text was edited by Bonilla y San Martín in 1903, and the work was studied by Homero Serís in a contribution to a book of studies in honour of Bonilla (1926).

¡Ay, Panadera!, see ¡Di, Panadera!

AZA, Vital (1851–1912), b. Pola de Lena, Asturias. Playwright. After studying and practising medicine, he began to write *sainetes* (q.v.), some with Miguel Ramos Carrión (q.v.). His first premiere, *¡Basta de matemáticas!* at the Variedades (1874), was highly successful, and thereafter he wrote more than seventy plays. The centenary of his birth was celebrated by Aguilar's publication of an anthology of his best plays in the Colección Crisol (1951).

AZAÑA Y DÍAZ, Manuel (1880–1940), b. Alcalá de Henares. Statesman and literary critic. Director of *La Pluma* (1920–3) and *España* (1923–4). Minister of War and President of the Council from 1931–3. President of the Republic 1936–9. After writing several books on Juan Valera (q.v.) including *Vida de don Juan Valera* (1926), *La novela de 'Pepita Jiménez'* (1928), and *Valera en Italia* (1929), Azaña compiled two books of essays: *Plumas y palabras* (1930) and *La invencion del 'Quijote' y otros ensayos* (1931).

His *El jardín de los frailes* (1926) is a partly autobiographical novel inspired by his adolescent experiences in the Colegio de Agustinos at El Escorial. Azaña translated *The Bible in Spain* of Borrow. He died in exile at Montauban, France.

AZCÁRATE, Gumersindo de (1840–1917), b. León. The son of Patricio de Azcárate (1800–86), he wrote a number of philosophical works including *Del materialismo y positivismo contemporáneos* (1870). Gumersindo also became a social and political philosopher, an advocate of *krausismo* (q.v.), and adhered to the utilitarian theories of Herbert Spencer. He studied law at Oviedo University, and for many years represented León as a Republican in the Spanish Cortes.

His best-known works are *Estudios económicos y sociales* (1876), *Estudios filosóficos y políticos* (1877), *La constitución inglesa y la política del continente* (1878), *Ensayo sobre la historia del derecho de propiedad* (3 vols., 1879–83), *Tratados de política* (1883), *El régimen parlamentario en la práctica* (1885), and an interesting *Minuta de un testamento publicada y anotada por W . . .* (1876) which summarises his beliefs. His liberal attitudes were strongly condemned by the ultra-religious, ultra-patriotic Menéndez y Pelayo (q.v.).

AZCOAGA IBAS, Enrique (1912–), b. Madrid. Poet and art critic. His collection of essays on literature, 'Línea y acento' was highly commended by the Premio Nacional de Literatura committee in 1933, but remains unpublished at the author's wish. He edited the magazine *Atlántida* and later *La Hoja Literaria* in 1933 with A. Serrano Plaja and A. Sánchez Barbudo in Buenos Aires, where he lived 1951–63. Of his many collections of poetry, the latest include *El canto cotidiano* (Buenos Aires, 1943), *Cancionero de Samborombón* (Buenos Aires, 1960), *España es un sabor* (1964), *Del otro lado* (1968), *Olmeda* (Salamanca, 1970), and *Primera antología de poemas truncados* (Málaga, 1971). He has written the useful *Panorama de la poesía moderna española* (Buenos Aires, 1953) and many monographs on art, such as *Los dibujos de Gregorio Prieto* (1948) and *La mejor pintura asturiana* (Buenos Aires, 1957). His novel *El empleado* (1949) is a meticulous picture of tedium in office life.

See J. G. Manrique de Lara, 'Enrique Azcoaga' in *El Libro Español* (January 1977), pp. 13–15.

AZEVEDO, see ACEVEDO.

AZORÍN (1873–1967), pseudonym of José Martínez Ruiz, who first used the pen-name 'Cándido' in *La crítica literaria en España* (1893), then 'Ahrimán' in his book of satire and criticism *Buscapiés* (1894), and finally settled on 'Azorín', a common surname in the Spanish Levant, which he used in his semi-autobiographical trilogy.

b. Monóvar, Alicante (where a museum including his library has been opened in his memory). Essayist and novelist who studied law in Valencia, Granada and Salamanca. He began as a sentimental anarchist like Unamuno, Baroja, and Maeztu, but ended as a conservative. He went to Madrid to make a career as a journalist, but was dismissed from *El Imparcial* for his outcry against famine and injustice in Andalusia. Gradually, however, he lost faith in political action as shown in the seminal trilogy *La voluntad* (Barcelona, 1902) which deals with a crisis of lack of will, *Antonio Azorín* (1903), and *Las confesiones de un pequeño filósofo* (1904), which utilized his experiences at a religious boarding school. His sensitive book on the Castilian soul, *El alma castellana* (1899), had been praised by Menéndez y Pelayo and Clarín, but it was only with the trilogy that the term 'Generación del '98' began to assume coherence and an ideology.

Antonio Azorín is the typical nihilist of the Generation, imbued with Schopenhauer's melancholy. Only faith can restore optimism, but Antonio and his friend Yuste even lack faith. The three novels have no traditional framework of plot, but consist of philosophical speculation interspersed with sketches of Martínez Ruiz's childhood and youth. He rejected all earlier fiction as too contrived and moved from his own fiction to the essay form, occasionally erudite but more frequently impressionistic and carefully wrought, dealing in moods, the atmosphere of places (usually in Castile), and his favourite writers in a style of which Ramón Pérez de Ayala described as: 'Plasticity, incomparable fineness. Pictorial values and spiritual content. Stylistic wealth and sobriety, and at the same time classical influences. His early nihilism has now developed towards an elegant Horatian scepticism.' Such essays are collected in *Los pueblos* (1905), *La ruta de Don Quijote* (1905), *España: hombres y paisajes* (1909), *Lecturas españolas* (1912), *Castilla* (1912), *Clásicos y modernos* (1913), *Los valores literarios* (1913), *Al margen de los clásicos* (1915), *Rivas y*

Larra (1916), *Un pueblecito* (1916), *El paisaje de España* (1917), *Los dos Luises* [León and Granada] *y otros ensayos* (1921), *Una hora de España* (1924), *Racine y Molière* (1924), *Escritores* (1956), and *De Valera a Miró* (1959). He tried his hand at drama about 1930 but failed. His short stories, the best of which appeared in *Blanco en azul* (1929), were collected in *Cuentos* (1956). He wrote two other novels: *Félix Vargas* (1928), later retitled *El caballero inactual*; and *Superrealismo* (1929), later retitled *El libro de Levante*.

The first major book on Azorín was by Werner Mulertt (in German, Halle, 1926; Spanish version, 1930), followed by E. Díez-Canedo's *Azorín* (1930). Later studies include *Las novelas de Azorín* (1960) by J. M. Martínez Cachero; *Azorín as a literary critic* (New York, 1962) by E. I. Fox; *Ante Azorín* (1964) by Ramón Pérez de Ayala; and M. M. Pérez López, *Azorín y la literatura española* (1974). *Clausura de un centenario* (1974), by F. Sáinz de Bujanda, is a bibliographical guide.

AZUELA, MARIANO (1873–1952), b. Lagos de Moreno, Jalisco. Mexican novelist who studied medicine, and served as an army doctor during the Mexican Revolution. Disillusioned, he wrote a fine novel on the subject in *Los de abajo* (q.v., El Paso, Texas, 1916), Enrique Munguía has translated this as *The underdogs* (New York, 1929), and Azuela himself adapted the story for the stage. *Los caciques* (1917) and *Las moscas* (1918) also dealt with the Revolution of 1910, while the satire *La luciérnaga* (Madrid, 1932) narrates with pity the life of the poor whites and Indians of Mexico City. His earlier novels were *María Luisa* (1907), *Los fracasados* (1908), *Mala Yerba* (1909), *Andrés Pérez, maderista* (1911) and *Sin amor* (1912). Azuela's later books were the novelized biography *Pedro Morena, el insurgente* (Santiago, Chile, 1935), *El camarada Pantoja* (1937), *San Gabriel de Valdivias* (1936), *Regina Landa* (1939), *Avanzada* (1940), *La nueva burguesía* (Buenos Aires, 1941), *La marchanta* (1944), *La mujer domada* (1946), the working-class novel *Sendas perdidas* (1949), and two posthumously-published novels: the angry *Esa sangre* and the satirical *La maldición* (1955). Azuela wrote literary criticism in *Cien años de novela mejicana* (1947). His *Obras completas* appeared in 3 vols. (1958–60).

Throughout his work, Azuela is a confirmed pessimist: his characters are often mere vehicles for his own preoccupations and his psychological insights are rarely profound or consistent, but each plot is convincing and elaborate, the writing is clear and concise, and techniques from French naturalism are adroitly used to illuminate the vast national upheaval of the Revolution through an accumulation of separate incidents.

See Luis Leal, *Mariano Azuela, vida y obra* (1961) and the same author's *Mariano Azuela* (New York, 1971), the latter in English; and Azuela's *Epistolario y archivo* (1971).

Azul (Valparaíso, 1888), a volume of poems and stories in Romantic vein by the Nicaraguan Modernist poet Rubén Darío (q.v.). The book was almost immediately recognized as a new step in Spanish literature, with strong echoes from the contemporary French writers whom Darío admired. The prose was openly sensual and concerned the artist in opposition to traditional values, while the poetry offered new technical opportunities of metre and line-length for younger poets writing in Spanish, and charm and delicacy in dealing with erotic love in an ideal world. Juan Valera (q.v.) made the young poet's reputation and a second edition appeared in 1890 in Guatemala with additions and Valera's foreword. Few books can have had a more lasting impact on Spanish poetry.

B

BACARISSE, Mauricio (1895–1931), b. Madrid. A minor poet and essayist, author of *Los terribles amores de Agliberto y Celedonia* (1931), a novel that won the Premio Nacional de Literatura for that year. His French ancestry was evident in his poetry which to some extent echoes Verlaine and Mallarmé. His first collection was *El esfuerzo* (1917), in which social themes are treated ironically. *El paraíso desdeñado* (1928) was followed by *Mitos* (1929). He translated Verlaine and the *Oedipus Rex* of Sophocles. Bacarisse frequented the *tertulia* of the Café de Pombo in Madrid founded by R. Gómez de la Serna (q.v.).

See M. Fernández Almagro, 'Mauricio Bacarisse' in *Revista de Occidente*, vol. 31 (1931).

BADIA I MARGARIT, Antoni Maria (1920–), b. Barcelona. Philologist. Among his numerous works are a *Gramática histórica catalana* (1950), a *Gramática catalana* (1962), and *Llengua i cultura als països catalans* (Barcelona, 1964). *La llengua catalana ahir i avui* (Barcelona, 1973) is a collection of 15 articles on Catalan and its disadvantages as a minority language.

BAENA, Juan Alfonso de, minor Jewish poet whose main contribution to Spanish literature was the compilation of the *Cancionero* (1445) still known by his name. It was offered to Juan II, for whom Baena wrote a *Decir* which does not appear in the collection. The unique copy is in the Bibliothèque Nationale, Paris.

The *Cancionero de Baena* is an important source for our knowledge of trends in poetry from the late 14th c. to the early 15th. Some of the poems are in Galician, but the majority are in Castilian, then climbing to the ascendancy which it was to maintain thereafter. Menéndez Pelayo commented ruefully that the *Cancionero* offers 'muchos versos y muy poca poesía', but this can be said of many anthologies, and the *Cancionero* is historically interesting in showing the transition from the *mester de clerecía* (q.v.) style of López de Ayala (q.v.), the oldest poet represented, towards a new courtly poetry and the introduction of Italian metres.

Thus one finds poems full of *galleguismos* (for example by Gonzalo Rodríguez, Archdeacon of Toro), and those of Macías and Rodríguez del Padrón (qq.v.), the moral and reflexive verse of Ferrán Sánchez de Calavera (q.v.), the Seville poets Ruy Páez de Ribera, the *converso* Ferrán Manuel de Lando, the two Martínez de Medina, and the innovatory Dantesque allegory of Francisco Imperial (q.v.).

In all 54 named poets and 576 compositions are included. Baena's introduction should be read for his views of the nature of poetry and the problems of versification.

El Cancionero de Juan Alfonso de Baena (*siglo XV*) edited by P. J. Pidal (1851), the facsimile edition by H. R. Lang (New York, 1926), and the critical edition by J. M. Azáceta (3 vols., 1966) are of interest.

See also W. Schmid, *Der Wortschatz des 'Cancionero de Baena'* (Berne, 1951) and J. Piccus, 'El Dezir que fizo Juan Alfonso de Baena' in *Nueva Revista de Filología Hispánica*, vol. 12 (1958), pp. 335–56.

BÁEZ, Cecilio (1862–1941), Paraguayan historian and polymath, the author of 50 books and numerous essays. A liberal and positivist, he was President of the Republic from 1905–6. Báez's profession was university teaching: he held chairs in sociology, Roman law, and other disciplines. His books include *Ensayo sobre la libertad civil* (1893); *Ensayo sobre el doctor Francia y la dictadura en Sud América* (1910), where he takes the unorthodox view that Francia's dictatorship was essential to the growth of resilient independence in Paraguay; *Historia del Paraguay* (1910); *Los elementos de la civilización cristiana* (1913); *Historia colonial del Paraguay y Río de la Plata* (1926); and the 2-volume *Historia diplomática del Paraguay* (1931–2).

Bailes ('dances'). The term is used in Golden Age literature to denote compositions for music, song, and dance, performed (usually) between the second and third acts in three-act *comedias*. An example of a *baile* is *Las flores* by Alonso de Olmedo, performed as an interlude in Calderón's *Hado y divisa* (1680), preceded by a *loa*, and with an *entremés El labrador gentilhombre* between Acts 2 and 3.

Some *bailes* use song throughout; those partly spoken are known as *bailes entremesados*. Cervantes used *bailes* in four of his *entremeses*. *Bailes* were written by many authors, including Quiñones de Benavente, Quevedo, Navarrete y Ribera, Monteser, Villaviciosa, Diamante, and Marchante. The most comprehensive collection is that of E. Cotarelo y Mori in his *Colección de entremeses, loas, bailes, jácaras y mojigangas* (2 vols.) in vols. 17–18 (1911) of the NBAE, pp. CLXIV–CCLXXIII.

BALAGUER, Victor (1924–1901), b. Barcelona. Catalan poet, dramatist, and historian. Major contributor to the restoration of the Jocs Florals and Catalan Revival, a 'mestre en gay saber'. His plays were scarcely more than sequences of dramatic monologues with scanty plots, but the *Tragedias* (1876) in Catalan made possible the important plays of Àngel Guimerà (q.v.). Of his poems, the most characteristic are the religious *La Verge de Montserrat*, the Catalan patriotic poem *Lo llibre de la patria*, and the Petrarchesque *Lo llibre del amor*. His many historical works, mostly in Castilian, include *Los frailes y sus conventos* (1851), *Historia de Cataluña* (1860–3), and *Historia de los trovadores* (1879). There is an edition of the *Obras completas* (39 vols., 1882–99), and an essay on Balaguer by F. Gras y Elías in his *Siluetes de escriptors catalans del sigle XIX* (Barcelona, 1909).

BALART, Federico (1831–1905), b. Pliego, Murcia. Art critic, minor poet, and liberal journalist writing under the pseudonyms 'Nadie' and 'Cualquiera'. It was only late in life, after the death of his wife, that Balart turned to poetry, showing in *Dolores* (1894) moods ranging from wild grief to quiet melancholy. Less impressive are *Horizontes* (1897), whose tone is often querulous, and the posthumously-published *Sombras y destellos* (1905) and *Fruslerías* (1906). The *Poesías completas* (2 vols., Barcelona,

1929) omit the third and fourth titles, the best edition being *Obras poéticas* (Buenos Aires, 1946). *Impresiones: literatura y arte* (1894) and *El prosaísmo en el arte* (n.d.) are books of criticism.

BALBUENA, Bernardo de (1562?–1627), b. Valdepeñas, Spain. Poet, generally considered Mexican since he was taken to Nueva Galicia (Mexico) when an infant of two or three. He studied at Mexico University c. 1585–90, then joined the Church. Balbuena rapidly became dissatisfied with provincial life and returned to Mexico City in search of literary fame, publishing there his *Grandeza mexicana* (1604). This was in a style not very different from that of his contemporary Luis de Góngora (q.v.), an abstract poetry that at times seems to depart from the subject altogether and enjoy its own patterns. This descriptive poem in hendecasyllabic tercets with quatrains at the end of each part, is influenced by Italian models, and Balbuena's *Siglo de Oro en las selvas de Erífile* (1608, 2nd edn., 1821), written in Mexico in 1585–90, derives from Sannazaro's *Arcadia*, the descriptive elements being far more significant than the narrative.

Balbuena travelled to Spain in 1606, obtaining a doctorate in theology at Sigüenza University, and after seeking preferment at the court, was named Abbot of Jamaica in 1608 and served there from 1610 to 1622. He wrote there *El Bernardo, o Victoria de Roncesvalles* (Madrid, 1624), the best epic on this popular subject in Spanish and often reprinted, the most convenient modern edition is that of the Universidad Nacional Autónoma de México (1941; 2nd edn., 1954). Based on the *Orlando* epics of Boiardo and Ariosto, this poem of 40,000 lines is in *octavas reales*, with accentuated Baroque mannerisms and more narrative and descriptive elements than true epic quality. It is in vol. 18 (1851) of the BAE and in a critical edition by A. Salo (San Feliu de Guixols, 1914).

Balbuena was appointed Bishop of Puerto Rico, where his library was burnt during a raid by Dutch pirates in 1625. A useful selection of his work can be found in '*Grandeza mexicana*' *y fragmentos del 'Siglo de oro' y 'El Bernardo'* (ed. F. Monterde, 1941; 2nd edn., 1954).

See John van Horne, *Bernardo de Balbuena. Biografía y crítica* (1940) and José Rojas Garcidueñas, *Bernardo de Balbuena: la vida y la obra* (1958), the latter with a good bibliography.

BALBUS, Lucius Cornelius (*fl.* 40 B.C.), b. Gades (now Cádiz). Known as 'Balbus Maior'. His family was granted citizenship of Rome by Pompey the Great in 72 B.C. and Balbus Maior went to Rome, where he quickly attained high office and was adopted by Theophanes of

Mitylene in 59 B.C. Caesar entrusted him with the administration of Rome during his absence in Gaul, and it is against the charge of illegal usurpation of the *civitas* brought against Balbus Maior that Cicero delivered the oration *Pro Balbo*, securing his acquittal.

The first provincial to be elevated to the status of consul (in 40 B.C.), Balbus Maior sided with Caesar and later Octavian against Pompey in the Civil Wars. To him are ascribed the *Ephemerides* on the life of Caesar; *Lustrationes*, a book on the rites; and more certainly a correspondence on literary and other matters with his eminent friend Cicero.

His nephew (of the same name) is known as Balbus Minor. He built a new town and harbour area at Gades.

Baldomera: novela (la tragedia del cholo americano), a novel by the Ecuadorian writer Alfredo Pareja Diezcanseco (q.v.), published in Santiago de Chile in 1938, reappearing in Quito (1957) in the series Novelas Ecuatorianos. The history of Guayaquil from 1896, when fire gutted half the town, to 1922, when demonstrators were slaughtered for agitating against the devaluation of sugar and the consequent famine, is told through the biography of a lower-class *zamba* who earns a living hawking cheap food through the streets. The novel is a vivid chronicle of the events leading up to the massacre of 1922, a theme also used by Pedro Jorge Vera in *Los animales puros* (1946), and by Joaquín Gallegos Lara in *Las cruces sobre el agua* (1946).

Ballads, see ROMANCES.

BALLAGAS, EMILIO (1910–54), b. Camagüey. Important Cuban poet who collaborated with both strands of the *avant-garde* ('pure' poetry and later social protest poetry) and drew attention to the sonorous and verbal beauty of Afro-Cuban rhythms both by his own examples and in two seminal books: *Antología de la poesía negra hispanoamericana* (Madrid, 1935; 2nd edn. 1944); and *Mapa de la poesía negra americana* (Buenos Aires, 1946).

In *Júbilo y fuga* (1931) his rejection of the real world is due partly to his own temperament at that time, but mainly to his models, Juan Ramón Jiménez, García Lorca, and Alberti (qq.v.). The *Cuaderno de poesía negra* (1934) showed how a poet who was not a Negro could assimilate the musicality and rhythm of Negro folk singers, a lesson quickly learnt by his contemporaries. Then followed *Elegía sin nombre* (1936), *Nocturno y elegía* (1938), and the neo-Romantic *Sabor eterno* with its themes of frustrated and lost love. *Nuestra Señora del mar* (1943)

was an unsuccessful attempt at religious poetry, and the neo-classical *Cielo en rehenes*, first published in the *Obra poética* (1955) is yet another view of an experimental writer looking for fresh styles.

See the *Órbita de Emilio Ballagas* (1965, ed. R. Antuña); and A. P. Rice, *Emilio Ballagas: poeta o poesía* (Mexico City, 1967).

BALMES URPIÁ, JAIME LUCIANO (1810–48), b. Vich. Philosopher and, in the words of Menéndez y Pelayo, 'el mejor periodista político de la España del XIX'. He studied at Vich seminary and Cervera University, was ordained a priest in Vich, and there taught mathematics until 1840, when he devoted all his time to politics and writing. He founded and wrote in *La Sociedad* (2 vols., Barcelona, 1943–4) and *El Pensamiento de la Nación* (3 vols., Barcelona, 1844–6).

He achieved instant fame and popularity in Spain by his first work: an attack on the Protestant Guizot's *Histoire générale de la civilisation en Europe* (1828) entitled *El protestantismo comparado con el catolicismo en sus relaciones con la civilización europea* (4 vols., 1842–4; 15th edn., 2 vols., Barcelona, 1951).

El criterio (Barcelona, 1845), which became widely popular, was followed by *Cartas a un escéptico en materia de religión* (Barcelona, 1846; centenary edn., Barcelona, 1946); his most extensive work in original philosophy, the metaphysical *Filosofía fundamental* (1846); *Escritos políticos*; and *Filosofía elemental* (both 1847; the latter ed. R. Cardiel Reyes (Mexico City, 1973) in Colección Sepan Cuantos). Basing his thought on scholastic theology, Balmes is often persuaded to reject Thomism by using common sense, for which characteristic he is most often praised in Spain. Descartes and Leibniz also influenced him. The fervour of his crusading Roman Catholic spirit and the directness of his style (though it has little other merit) were factors in his early election to the Real Academia Española.

The *Obras completas* (Barcelona, 1925, 33 vols.) have now been superseded by the 8-vol. edition by the Fundación Balmesiana (Barcelona, 1948–50).

See J. M. Castro y Calvo, *Balmes* (Vich, 1951) and Juan de Dios Mendoza, *Bibliografía balmesiana* (Barcelona, 1961).

BALSEIRO, JOSÉ AGUSTÍN (1900–), b. Barceloneta. Puerto Rican essayist and poet. His two novels *La ruta eterna* (Madrid, 1923) and *En vela mientras el mundo duerme* (Madrid, 1953) have little merit, like his earlier poetry, *La copa de Anacreonte* (Madrid, 1924) which is closely imitative of Darío's modernism, and *Música* *cordial* (1926). But his later verse is interesting, especially *Pureza cautiva* (1946), and the subsequent *Saudades de Puerto Rico* and *Vísperas de sombra*. For some years Professor of Hispanic Literature at Miami University, Balseiro early made a name as a critic of music and literature in *El Vigía* (3 ser., Madrid 1928–42), *Novelistas españoles modernos* (1933), *El Quijote de la España contemporánea* (1935) on Unamuno, *Expresión de Hispanoamérica* (3 ser., 1960–64), and *Seis estudios sobre Rubén Darío* (Madrid, 1967).

BANCES CANDAMO, FRANCISCO ANTONIO DE (1662–1704), b. Avilés, Asturias. Playwright, drama critic, and historian. After studying philosophy, law, and canon law at Seville University, Bances Candamo set out for Madrid to make his fortune as a playwright. His first recorded play at court was *Por su Rey y por su dama* (1685; modern edn. by D. W. Moir being prepared, with *La piedra filosofal*), performed in celebration of the birthday of the Holy Roman Emperor. It is the first of Bances Candamo's didactic plays, seeming to favour Charles II's abandonment of the Low Countries at whatever price. The plot deals with the shrewdness of Hernán Tello Portocarrero against the French defenders of Amiens in 1597.

Bances Candamo was appointed official playwright to the king in 1687, but his outspoken plays, which showed how seriously he took his dramatic duties, led to his resignation in 1693–4 after the performance of his major trilogy, of which the first *comedia* was *El esclavo en grillos de oro* (1692). It is legendary that after the performance of this play he received a chest wound which was caused as a result of an opponent objecting to the satirical content of this *comedia*, which deals with a conspiracy by the senator Ovinius Camillus to overthrow the Emperor Trajan and reign in his stead. Trajan learns of the plot and condemns the senator to govern and thus to discover that kingship is merely 'slavery in fetters of gold'. When Ovinius is due to be inducted as emperor, he pleads instead to be killed; Trajan spares his life and nominates his own son Hadrian to succeed him. The play was understood by the court to attack the fallen Count Oropesa (1685–91) and Charles's own maladministration since then, and to stress the need for a known heir. Bances Candamo returned to the south as a treasury official until the anger of the court had abated, returning to Madrid in 1696–7 when his last play *¿Cuál es afecto mayor: lealtad, sangre, o amor?* again failed to influence Charles's policy. Dismissed once more from his treasury post, he died on a routine inspection in the village of Lezuza.

Bances Candamo is a more significant writer, within the Calderonian circle, than has been commonly acknowledged. Luzán praised him for 'su ingenio, su elegante estilo, sus noticias no vulgares y por cuidado grande que manifestó en la verisimilitud, decoro, y propiedad de los lances y de las personas'.

His *Obras dramáticas* (2 vols., 1722) also contain *La piedra filosofal* (ed. M. Cattaneo, 1974), a sequel to the ideas in Calderón's *La vida es sueño* (q.v.); the *costumbrista El duelo contra su dama;* two plays on themes from Lope, *El español mas amante y desgraciado Macías* and *El sastre del Campillo;* and a historical play on Queen Christina of Sweden, *Quién es quien premia el amor.* A number of his plays were reprinted with less than meticulous care in vols. 49 (1859) and 58 (1865) of the BAE. His poems were published in *Obras lyricas* (1720), edited by J. del Río Marín, the latest edition by F. Gutiérrez, (Barcelona, 1949).

Yet Bances Candamo's main contribution to Spanish literature may well be the *Theatro de los theatros de los passados y presentes siglos* composed in three different versions and edited by D. W. Moir (London, 1970). The first is a defence of decorum in the theatre and of poetic truth against mere historical truth, written (1689–90) specifically against attacks by the Jesuit Ignacio de Camargo. The second and third (1692–4) make up parts of an incomplete universal history of the drama from ancient Greece. The second states his view of writing plays for kings as *decir sin decir*, or conveying ideas without openly preaching: 'historias vivas que, sin hablar con ellos, les han de instruir con tal respeto que sea su misma razón quien de lo que ve tome las advertencias, y no el ingenio quien se las diga. Para este decir sin decir, ¿quién dudará sea menester gran arte?' In Moir's view, Bances Candamo's *Theatro* stands, with P. Guerra's *Aprobación* to the *comedias* of Calderón, as the best Spanish dramatic criticism of the century.

See also F. Cuervo-Arango y González Carvajal, *Don Francisco Antonio de Bances Candamo: estudio bibliográfico y crítico* (1916).

BANCHS, ENRIQUE J. (1888–1968), b. Buenos Aires. Argentinian neoclassical poet and journalist. He wrote little for publication after four collections of poetry written between the ages of 19 and 23: *Las barcas* (1907), the jubilant *El libro de los elogios* (1908), *El cascabel del halcón* (1909), and the 100 sonnets gathered in *La urna* (1911), which are esteemed among the best in the literature of Argentina. His *Oda a los padres de la patria* (1910) appeared in the magazine *Nosotros.* His name has come to symbolize to many of his compatriots the illusory search for perfection in art. His collected *Obra poética* (1907–1955) appeared in 1973.

BÁÑEZ, *Fray* Domingo (1528–1604), b. Medina del Campo. Dominican theologian who became involved in an important controversy with the Jesuit Miguel de Molinos (q.v.). The controversy, known as *De auxiliis*, centred on the question of how divine grace can assist a believer to salvation and the extent to which his free will may co-operate with God to that end. Báñez and the Dominicans taught that Grace is an act of predestination, and accused the Molinists of attributing too much power to human free will, and of tending towards the Pelagian heresy which held that believers might attain salvation without divine grace. The Molinists argued that Báñez and the Dominicans tended towards the Calvinistic heresy that God Himself predestines some souls to Heaven and some to Hell. The controversy started in 1588 and reached such a pitch that Pope Paul V banned further discussion in 1607, but *De auxiliis* continued to stir up bitter feelings well into the middle of the 17th c.

Báñez was the spiritual director of S. Teresa de Ávila (q.v.), and some of his letters to her are reprinted in vol. 55 (1861) of the BAE.

The question of free will versus determinism is reflected in a number of Golden Age plays, of which perhaps the best-known are *La vida es sueño* by Calderón (qq.v.) and *El condenado por desconfiado* (q.v.), attributed to Fray Gabriel Téllez (q.v.).

BARAHONA DE SOTO, Luis (1548–95), b. Lucena. Poet and prose writer. He studied in Granada and was a doctor in Osuna. He became a member of the literary *tertulia* of Venegas, and took part in the 4-month war against the *moriscos* in the Alpujarras rising. A graceful and melodious lyric poet in *Fábulas de Vertumno* and *Acteón*, the latter paraphrasing Ovid's *Metamorphoses*, Barahona turned to the Italianate mode in his elegies and satires, especially the *Égloga de las hamadríades*, which anticipates Góngora. He is best known for *Primera parte de la Angélica* (1586; ed. in facsimile, Archer Huntington, New York, 1904), usually called *Las lágrimas de Angélica*, which is one of the best continuations in Spanish of Ariosto's *Orlando furioso*, yet lacks his model's wit and fantasy. However the priest in *Don Quijote* (I.vi.) confesses that 'I should have wept if I had ordered such a book consigned to the flames, for its author was one of the most famous poets not only in Spain but in the world . . .'.

Barahona himself announced a sequel but it was never carried out and it was left to Lope de Vega (q.v.) to write it: *La hermosura de Angélica*. Many lines have charm and vitality, but the impact of the whole is dissipated by the excessive number of episodes. Fragments of Barahona's intended sequel to his own book survive in the best Castilian treatise on hunting: his *Diálogos sobre la montería*.

His *Poesías* are to be found in vols. 35 (1855) and 42 (1857) of the BAE.

See *Homenaje a Barahona de Soto* (Málaga, 1898) and F. Rodríguez Marín, *Luis Barahona de Soto: estudio biográfico, bibliográfico y crítico* (1903).

BARALT, Rafael María (1810–60), b. Maracaibo. Venezuelan historian and neoclassical poet. He went to Spain in 1843, where he eventually succeeded in his aim of becoming a member 'de número' of the Academy, despite the ignorance of comparative grammar displayed in his *Diccionario matriz de la lengua española* and *Diccionario de galicismos*, about whose author Menéndez Pelayo declared, 'parece . . . preocupado sólo con levantar un muro entre el Castellano y el Francés, suele dar en decisiones caprichosas que parecen hijas del mal humor más que de un sistema racional y consecuente'.

Baralt unsuccessfully imitated Fray Luis de León and the ode 'Cristóbal Colón' by Góngora. His prose is urbane, conventional, and nowadays little read, though a statue to Baralt as an apostle of good taste was erected in Maracaibo. He edited a compilation of Ramón Díaz's historical writings: *Resumen de la historia antigua y moderna de Venezuela* (2 vols., Paris, 1841). An *Antología* (1961) only reached vol. 1. An edition of the *Obras* appeared in 1963.

BARBA JACOB, Porfirio, pseudonym of Miguel Ángel Osorio Benítez (q.v.).

BARBERENA, Santiago Ignacio (1850–1916), b. Guatemala. Scholar and historian who lived most of his life in El Salvador. His major work was the unfinished *Historia de El Salvador* (2 vols., 1914–17), but he also produced an invaluable *Descripción geográfica y estadística de El Salvador* (1892) and detailed *Monografías departamentales* (1909).

BARCO DE CENTENERA, Martín (1544–c. 1605), b. Logrosán, Extremadura. Epic poet of mediocre talent, whose work is didactic rather than heroic. After studying at Salamanca he accompanied Juan Ortiz de Zárate's expedition to Paraguay, becoming archdeacon of the Cathedral of Asunción and Villa Rica (1575–80). His *Argentina y conquista del Río de la Plata, con otros acaescimientos de los Reynos del Perú, Tucumán, y estado del Brasil* (Lisbon, 1602) may possibly have aimed to rival the success of the *Araucana* of Ercilla (qq.v.). This poem was long read as an important historical document, and Fr. Lozano borrows extensively from it for his *Historia de la* conquista del Paraguay, Río de la Plata y Tucumán (c. 1750), but although reliable for the author's experiences in Zárate's expedition, it is untrustworthy for earlier events, for which Centenera uses accounts written by opponents of Martínez de Irala.

BAREA, ARTURO (1897–1957), b. Madrid. Novelist and short-story writer whose political affiliations made it necessary for him to leave Spain in 1939. He settled in England and, with the exception of the war stories in Valor y miedo: relatos (Barcelona, 1938), his books appeared in English before they found Spanish publishers. Barea first showed his ability to create a complete character in The broken root (London, 1952; La raíz rota, Buenos Aires, 1953), but his one acknowledged masterpiece is the confessedly autobiographical trilogy The forging of a rebel (3 vols., London, 1941–4; La forja de un rebelde, Buenos Aires, 1951). His superb control of a host of characters in this panorama of his intellectual and active youth and early maturity made him a respected figure in England, where he was invited to write Lorca: the poet and his people (1944) and Unamuno (1952). He died in Berkshire. His widow Ilsa issued his stories El centro de la pista (1960) posthumously.

Barlaam and Josaphat, a Christian adaptation of a legend of Buddha, which reached Europe through Greek from an Arabic paraphrase of the Sanskrit Lalita-Vistara. A young prince, Josaphat, is shielded from a knowledge of old age, illness and death until he encounters a blind man, a leper and an aged hermit (Barlaam), after talking to whom he is converted to Christianity and is reconciled with the world as it is and as it will be.

The Greek version by St. John Damascene (printed with a facing English translation by G. Woodward and H. Mattingley, London, 1914) was first translated into Spanish by Juan de Arce Solórzano (1608), but a Latin version was available in Spain as early as the 12th c. It was introduced into Spain through the Libro de los Estados (q.v.) by the Infante Juan Manuel (q.v.) written about 1330, and later gave Lope de Vega (q.v.) the theme for his comedia Barlaán y Josafat (1618) and for La vida es sueño (written in 1635; 1636) by Pedro Calderón de la Barca (qq.v.). There is a study by G. Moldenhauer, Die Legende von Barlaam und Josaphat auf der iberischen Halbinsel: Untersuchungen und Texte (Halle, 1929).

BARLETTA, LEÓNIDAS (1902–), b. Buenos Aires. Argentinian short-story writer and novelist. With Max Dickmann (q.v.) and Lorenzo Stanchina, Barletta initiated the prole-

tarian novel of the 1920s, using techniques drawn from Russian realists to show the plight of the deprived in Cuentos realistas (1923), Vientos trágicos (1924), Los pobres (1925), Vidas perdidas (1926), his best book Royal Circo (1927), Los destinos humildes (1938), Cómo naufragó el capitán Olssen (1942), and La señora Enriqueta y su ramito (1943).

Barletta's strength lies partly in the rapid sequence of events in his work, and partly in his expert construction.

He inaugurated a Teatro del Pueblo in 1931; this became a significant influence in Argentinian dramatic history. He wrote Viejo y nuevo teatro (1960) from his immense experience in the theatre. A member of the Boedo Street group (q.v.), he wrote Boedo y Florida: una versión distinta (1967).

BAROJA Y NESSI, PÍO (1872–1956), b. San Sebastián. Major novelist and perhaps the most widely-read of his generation in Spain today. C. J. Cela (q.v.) has called him Spain's 'only European novelist' in the sense that Baroja, 'seven-eighths Basque and one-eighth Italian' in his own words, bore no liking for Castilian Spain and used mainly French models in his early writing. According to his racial theories, the Germans and the English are superior, the Jews and the Mediterranean races inferior; he classed himself with the former. An egomaniac, an eclectic in philosophy who professed at one time or another to be a disciple of Kant, Nietzsche, and Schopenhauer, Baroja was an original in most senses. He studied medicine and practised in Cestona (a small Basque town) for a year, but returned dissatisfied shortly after and in 1896 joined his brother Ricardo (q.v.) in the family bakery in Madrid. There he wrote in his spare time, visited Paris, and was befriended by Azorín.

A morose, shy man who was never to marry, Baroja had been told by teachers from the age of four that 'he would never amount to anything', and when he turned to writing full-time in 1902 his aim was to prove his detractors wrong. Altogether he composed an 8-volume autobiography, the Memorias (1955); three biographies; two plays, of which one was a novel in dialogue; a book of verse with which he was unhappy; nine books of essays; four collections of short stories; five books of longer stories, and 66 novels, most of which were conceived in cycles, usually of three books each.

Tierra vasca consists of La casa de Aizgorri (q.v., 1900), El Mayorazgo de Labraz (q.v., 1903), Zalacaín el aventurero (q.v., 1909) and La leyenda de Juan de Alzate (1922). La vida fantástica (q.v.): Aventuras, inventos y mixtificaciones de Silvestre Paradox (1901) which is the first true Barojian book, *Camino de perfección* (1902) and *Paradox, rey* (1906). *La lucha por la vida: La busca, Mala hierba, Aurora roja* (all 1904), a trilogy on Madrid's lower depths of which Gregorio Marañón said that it opened the eyes of his generation to the condition of the poor and underprivileged. *El pasado: La feria de los discretos* (1905), *Los últimos románticos* (1906), and *Las tragedias grotescas* (1907). *La raza: La dama errante* (1908), *La ciudad de la niebla* (1909), and *El árbol de la ciencia* (1911), the last being in Azorín's view the novel which 'resume, mejor que ningún otro libro, el espíritu de Baroja' and which illustrates the autobiographical transformations operated by Baroja, through the figure of the materialistic, sceptical and republican Andrés Hurtado. *Las ciudades: César o nada* (1910), *El mundo es ansí* (1912), and *La sensualidad pervertida* (1920). *El mar: Las inquietudes de Shanti Andía* (1911), *El laberinto de las sirenas* (1923), *Los pilotos de altura* (1929), and *La estrella del capitán Chimista* (1930). *Agonías de nuestro tiempo: El gran torbellino del mundo* (1926), *Las veleidades de la fortuna*, and *Los amores tardíos* (both 1927). *La selva oscura: La familia de Errotacho* (1931), *El cabo de las Tormentas*, and *Los visionarios* (1932). *La juventud perdida: Las noches del Buen Retiro* (1934), *El cura de Monleón* (1936), and *Locuras de carnaval* (1937). *Las novelas de París: Susana* (1938), *Laura, o la soledad sin remedio* (1939) and *El hotel del Cisne* (1946).

The 22 volumes of *Memorias de un hombre de acción* (1913–1935) consist of 14 novels and eight vols. of shorter episodes connected with the life and times of Baroja's distant relative, Eugenio de Aviraneta e Ibargoyen (1792–1872). The titles are *El aprendiz de conspirador* and *El escuadrón del Brigante* (both 1913), *Los caminos del mundo* (1914), *Con la pluma y con el sable* and *Los recursos de la astucia* (1915), *La ruta del aventurero* (1916), *La veleta de Gastizar* and *Los caudillos de 1880* (1918), *La Isabelina* (1919), *Los contrastes de la vida* (1920), *El sabor de la venganza* (1921), *Las furias* (1922), *El amor, el dandyismo y la intriga* (1923), *Las figuras de cera* (1924), *La nave de los locos* (1925), *Las mascaradas sangrientas* (1927), *Humano enigma* (1928), *La senda dolorosa* (1929), *Los confidentes audaces* and *La venta de Mirambel* (1931), *Crónica escandalosa* and *Desde el principio hasta el fin* (1935).

The greatest of Baroja's novels are those of the first period, up to 1912, when his autobiographical heroes develop, when his nihilism and energy are at their peak, and when his creative power and style make their greatest impact. Novels from 1913 onwards are often repetitive in ideology, language, and personalities but the technique is often no less brilliant. The final period from 1937 is one of waning powers and mechanical writing in which little of interest is produced apart from the often disconnected but frequently absorbing *Memorias*.

Baroja's themes are poverty, social and moral injustice, hypocrisy, and the need for compassion in a world where officialdom has none to give. Though not himself poor, he was not ashamed to be seen mixing with vagrants and tramps, and indeed once complained that his only companions were social outcasts, cats and dogs. González Ruano described him in his Madrid period as 'resembling a beggar dressed in a suit snatched from a corpse'. His art is equally simple, since he fills his books (like a tramp his pockets) with whatever comes to hand. His haste in writing was due not to economic necessity but to the nature of his own personality, which could not bear to revise and polish. Baroja's thought is that of a revolutionary, but his style is as traditional as that of an imitator of Dickens or Scott. He acknowledged the influence of Dickens, but earlier reading (Montepin and Sue in his father's library) proved more pervasive in his later, more pedestrian novels.

Even now most of Baroja's iconoclastic books are available only in expurgated editions, apart from the expensive *Obras completas* (8 vols., 1946–51). The standard life is Miguel Pérez Ferrero's *Vida de Pío Baroja* (Barcelona, 1960). Sebastià J. Arbó's *Pío Baroja y su tiempo* (Barcelona, 1964) by contrast is unsystematic, though useful for anecdotes. Two important works are *Baroja en el banquillo* (2 vols., Saragossa, n.d. [1947–8]), a critical anthology edited by José García Mercadal: and *Baroja y su mundo* (2 vols., 1961) edited by Fernando Baeza, with a supplement listing characters and a thematic index to the works.

See also Carlos Longhurst, *Las novelas históricas de Pío Baroja* (1974). In English there is the translation by Anthony Kerrigan *The restlessness of Shanti Andía and other writings* (Ann Arbor, 1959) and a useful introduction *Pío Baroja* (New York, 1971) by Beatrice P. Patt in Twayne's World Authors series.

BAROJA Y NESSI, RICARDO (1871–1953), b. Rio Tinto mines, Huelva. Painter and writer, whose main claim to fame was that he was a brother of Pío Baroja (q.v.). His adventure stories and recollections of life in the Basque country are less well known than those of his brother but some are effective, especially the complicated *La nao 'Capitana': cuento español del mar antiguo* (1935), the Basque tale of the 17th c. *Carnashu*, and an interesting threefold tale, *Clavijo*, which tells of the seduction of a girl by José de Clavijo y Fajardo (1730–1806) in the words of them both and also through those of the girl's brother Beaumarchais, the author of *Le barbier de Séville* and *Le mariage de Figaro*.

Baroja's *Gente del 98* (Barcelona, 1952) was reprinted as *Gente de la generación del 98* (Barcelona, 1969).

BARQUERO, EFRAÍN (1931–), Chilean neo-surrealist poet. He studied in the Faculty of Philosophy and Education in the University of Chile and was chief editor of *La Gaceta de Chile* when it was directed by Pablo Neruda (q.v.). His youthful *La piedra del pueblo* (1954) was rhetorical in style and social in theme. Since *La compañera* (1956) his themes have become domestic, his mood serene and his style brief to the point of epigram in *Enjambre* (1959), *El pan del hombre* (1960), *El regreso* (1961), and *Maula* (1962). A characteristic poem of charm and quirky surrealism is *Mi amada está tejiendo*, already a popular anthology piece in collections such as Miller Williams, *Chile: an anthology of new writing* (Kent State U.P., 1968).

'Barraca, La', a university theatre group established by the Spanish Government in 1932 and directed by the young playwrights Federico García Lorca (q.v.) and Eduardo Ugarte. The purpose of 'La Barraca' was to employ university students to take serious drama to the provinces. They rehearsed in Madrid, then travelled across the country in a lorry with their stage properties.

The repertory (1932–6) included Calderón's *La vida es sueño*, Lope de Vega's *Fuenteovejuna*, 'Tirso de Molina's' *El burlador de Sevilla* and the *entremeses* of Cervantes (qq.v.). Lorca was impressed by the demand for classic plays outside Madrid. He not only directed them, but abridged them with care and sensitivity, learning ⹂stagecraft and becoming inspired to write important work for the Spanish repertory. Manuel Altolaguirre (q.v.) took over as director of the group in 1936, its last season.

See F. Masini, *Federico García Lorca e 'La Barraca'* (Bologna, 1966) and Luis Sáenz de la Calzada, *'La Barraca': teatro universitario* (1976).

BARRANTES Y MORENO, VICENTE (1829–98), b. Badajoz. Poet and satirist, whose review *Las Píldoras* was banned by the Government. He wrote two minor historical novels: *Juan de Padilla* (2 vols., 1855–6) and *La viuda de Padilla* (1857), and a number of stories: *Narraciones extremeñas* (2 vols., 1873) and *Cuentos y leyendas* (1875). His philosophical poetry in the style of Campoamor (such as *Días sin sol*) is relatively unattractive; Barrantes' most enduring work consists of the *Baladas españolas* (1853), in particular *Esposa sin desposar* and *Santa Isabel y Murillo*. He also wrote several works under the pseudonyms 'Publicio' and 'Abate Cascarrabias'.

See Antonio Cortijo Valdés, *Biografía del excelente señor don Vicente Barrantes* (1874).

BARRENECHEA, JULIO (1910–), b. Santiago. Chilean poet. Opposed to the government of President Ibáñez in 1931, he worked for the cause of socialism, and was elected a socialist deputy for Santiago. He served in the diplomatic corps in Colombia and India. Barrenechea is a serious and melancholy writer, characterized by good taste and moderation. The *Poesía completa* (Quito, 1958) contains most of his writing, from the youthful *El mitín de las mariposas* (1930) and *El espejo del ensueño* (1935) to *Rumor del mundo* (1942), *El libro del amor* (1946), *Vida del poeta* (1948), and *Diario morir* (1954). There is an *Antología* (1961) of his best work.

BARRENECHEA Y ALBIS, JUAN DE SÁNCHEZ (d. 1707?), friar working in Chile who wrote in 1693 a fantastic 'history' entitled *Restauración de la Imperial y conversión de almas infieles*, which many scholars hold to be the first novel written in Chile. Behind the pretensions of the historian of the Spanish conquest of the Araucanian Indians is a love story of Rocamila and Cantabo.

BARRERA Y LEIRADO, CAYETANO ALBERTO DE LA (1815–72), b. Madrid. Bibliographer and biographer whose masterpeice was the *Catálogo bibliográfico y biográfico del teatro antiguo español desde su origen hasta mediados del siglo XVIII* (1860; facsimile edn., London, 1968). His *Nuevo biografía de Lope de Vega* appeared in vol. 1 of the Academy's edition of Lope's works (1890), and is significant for its new data using the important correspondence between Lope and the Duque de Sessa. Berrera was also well known in his day for work on the apocryphal *Quijote* of 'Avellaneda', for a biography and edition of Rioja (q.v.), and *Adiciones a las poesías de don Francisco de Rioja* (Seville, 1872).

BARRETT, RAFAEL (1876–1910), b. Gibraltar? Short-story writer and essayist claimed by Gibraltar, Spain, Argentina, and Paraguay. He left Europe for Latin America in 1903 and remained there. His contemporary stories of misery, despair, and suffering offer a picture of Paraguay free of the illusions of past glories celebrated by the Argentinian Martín de Goycoechea Menéndez (q.v.). In chronological order, his works are: *Lo que son los yerbales* and *Moralidades actuales* (both Montevideo, 1910), the fictional *Cuentos breves* (Montevideo, 1911), the pamphlet *El terror argentino* (1912), *Mirando vivir* and *Al margen: críticas literarias y científicas* (both Montevideo, 1912), *Ideas y críticas*

(Montevideo, 1915?), and *Diálogos, conversaciones y otros escritos* (Montevideo, 1918).

Barrett's *Obras completas* (Buenos Aires, 1943) reached a 2nd edition (2 vols.) in 1954. His *Cartas íntimas* (Montevideo, 1967) have been edited by Francisca López Maiz de Barrett.

See Ramiro de Maeztu and Emilio Frugoni, *Lo que son los yerbales paraguayos: semblanzas de Barrett* (Montevideo, 1926); J. R. Forteza, *Rafael Barrett: su obra, su prédica, su moral* (Buenos Aires, 1927), and Víctor Massuh, *En torno a Rafael Barrett* (Tucumán, 1943).

BARRIENTOS, Fray Lope (1382–1469), Bishop of Segovia and confessor to King Juan II. He was ordered by the king to burn the library of the alleged magician Enrique de Villena (q.v.) and reportedly did so, but it is believed that at least some books were saved and used by him in an unpublished treatise on divination commissioned by the king but apparently never published. J. de M. Carriazo attributed to Fray Lope the *Refundición de la Crónica del Halconero* (1946).

See L. G. A. Getino, *Vida y obras de fray Lope de Barrientos* (Salamanca, 1927).

BARRIONUEVO, Jerónimo de (1587–1671), b. Granada. Letter-writer and poet. He studied at Alcalá and Salamanca, spent some time with the Marqués de Santa Cruz in Italy, and then retired to a comfortable position at the Cathedral of Sigüenza. This gave him time in Madrid (1653–8), where he wrote the Dean of Saragossa a long series of letters on contemporary life and customs in Madrid, now of great importance for an understanding of the period. These *Avisos* are dated from 1 August 1654 to 24 July 1658, and have been edited with a biography and critical notes by A. Paz y Meliá (1892–3) in 4 vols. of the Colección de Escritores Castellanos. Virtually a journalistic gossip column of its day, the collection of *Avisos* discusses not only political and foreign news, but also details of crimes, new plays, fiestas, and fashion.

Barrionuevo is recorded to have written 900 poems, an *entremés* called *El berraco de Río Salido*, and five plays: *La venganza del hermano y valiente Barrionuevo*, *El laberinto de amor y panadera de Madrid*, *El retrato que es mejor: Santa Librada*, *El Judas de Fuentes*, and *La honra que está mas bien*.

BARRIOS, Miguel de (1635–1701), b. Montilla. Hispano-Jewish poet of Portuguese ancestry who served in the Spanish army as a Christian convert, but reverted to Judaism and to his original name, Daniel Levi, when he settled in the Low Countries.

An open supporter of Góngora in his intention: 'alcanzar y aun sobrepasar a Góngora',

Barrios wrote too much too hastily, and generally with little taste. His published works are *Flor de Apolo* (Brussels, 1665; 2nd edn., as *Las poesías famosas y comedias*, Antwerp, 1674), *Coro de las musas* (Brussels, 1672), *El sol de la vida* (Antwerp, 1679), *Bello Monte de Helicona* (Brussels, 1686) and *Estrellas de Jacob sobre Flores de Lis* (Amsterdam, 1686). His plays were spectacular; one contained eight duels and another twelve. *Pedir favor al contrario* and *El canto junto al encanto* are the least uninteresting of his dramatic works.

A few of his poems are in vol. 42 (1857) of the BAE but perhaps only the affecting *sonetos dobles fúnebres* on the death of his wife can be read with any enjoyment today.

See K. R. Scholberg, *La poesía religiosa de Miguel de Barrios* (Columbus, Ohio, 1962).

BARRIOS HUDTWALCKER, Eduardo (1884–1963), b. Valparaíso. Chilean novelist and dramatist. After the death of his father in 1889 he went to Lima, returning to Chile in 1899. He spent two years in the Santiago military academy, but was discharged in 1902. He then went back to Lima and made an abortive rubber expedition to the Eastern Andes. After a brief period in the Panama Canal Zone, he worked from 1904–8 in a nitrate company's office in northern Chile, where he published *Del natural* (Iquique, 1907), his first novel. Barrios subsequently worked as secretary to the pro-Rector of Santiago University, and as shorthand reporter in the Chilean Congress; in 1925 he was Copyright Registrar in the National Library and in 1927 General Superintendent of Libraries, Museums, and Archives. He was Minister of Education briefly in 1927–8 until the fall of the dictator Ibáñez, whom he supported, and again later. In 1937–43 he was manager of a *finca* in the central valley of Chile where he met the prototype of the main character in his most important novel, *Gran señor y rajadiablos* (1948), set in the 19th c. The book's style is not outstanding, but it is ambitious in its virtual repudiation of an earlier, naturalistic style. J. Walker argues in *Bulletin of Hispanic Studies*, vol. 49, no. 3 (July 1972) that its most lasting value is that of a philosophical statement.

His other works of significance are the stories in *El niño que enloqueció de amor* (1915), the city novel *Un perdido* (1918), and the curious novel *El hermano asno* (1922) contrasting the personalities of two Franciscans, one aware of his carnal desires and anxious to subdue them, and the other—acclaimed as a saint for his penances— quite unaware of his hidden urges and overtaken by them at the close of the novel. This novel was translated for Ángel Flores' collection of Latin American fiction *Fiesta in November* (Boston, 1942). The lesser fiction of Barrios includes the stories *Páginas de un pobre diablo* (1923), *Y la vida sigue . . .* (1925), *Tamarugal* (1944), and the novel *Los hombres del hombre* (1950), an uneven work using the first person narrative which worked so well in *El niño . . .* and *El hermano asno*.

Barrios also wrote plays, including *Mercaderes en el templo* (1910) first performed in 1911, but not collected in either *Obras completas* (2 vols., 1962) or in *Teatro escogido* (1947); *Lo que niega la vida* (1913), first performed in 1914; and *Vivir*, first performed in 1916.

Early books by Barrios concentrated on the primacy of emotion over reason, but his later works stressed the need for self-discipline in order to avoid emotional excesses. The best work on Barrios is J. Orlandi Araya's and A. Ramírez Cid's *Eduardo Barrios: obras, estilo, técnica* (1960) with a good bibliography. N. J. Davison's *Eduardo Barrios* (New York, 1970) in Twayne's World Authors series is the only account in English.

BARROS ARANA, Diego (1830–1907), b. Santiago. Chilean historian. He was for long a political exile in Uruguay and Brazil. In Spain he devoted much of his time to archival records (largely in Seville and Simancas) towards his *Historia general de Chile* (1884–6) which provided the factual background for Blest Gana's novel *Durante la reconquista* (1897). His lesser works include *Estudios históricos sobre Vicente Benavides y las campañas del Sur* (1850), *El general Freire* (1851), *Historia general de la independencia de Chile* (1854), *Vida y viaje de don Fernando de Magallanes* (1864), *Riquezas de los antiguos jesuitas en Chile* (1872), *Bibliografía de obras anónimas y pseudónimas sobre la historia, la geografía y la literatura de América* (2 vols., 1882, 1913).

Barros Arana's *Obras completas* (Santiago, 1908–14) are in 15 vols. The *Bibliografía de don Diego Barros Arana* (Temuco, 1907) is by Víctor M. Chiappa.

BARTRINA Y DE AIXEMÚS, Joaquin Maria (1850–80), b. Reus. Catalan poet and journalist. A sceptic and materialist, he was influenced by Leopardi, though less in *Páginas de amor* than in poems such as *Epístola* and *De omni re scibile*. *Algo* (Barcelona, 1876) made his reputation, which was enhanced by J. Sardá's edition of Bartrina's *Obras en prosa y en verso* (Barcelona, 1881), and *Obras poéticas* (Barcelona, 1939).

See J. Roca y Roca, *Memoria biográfica de Joaquín María Bartrina* (Barcelona, 1916).

BASTERRA, Ramón de (1888–1928), b. Bilbao. Poet and diplomat. His obsession with the greatness of Spain and the Hispanic idea led him to construct fanciful historical and cultural theories in which he saw the saviour of civilization in the Roman Catholic, imperial and Latin way of life against the Protestant, liberal, and Anglo-Saxon life.

He served as a diplomat in Italy, where he found ample 'proof' of his theories; in Rumania, where his prose study *La obra de Trajano* (1921) connected an emperor of Iberian origin with the limits of the Roman empire; and in Venezuela, where his idiosyncratic *Los navíos de la Ilustración: una empresa del siglo XVIII* (1925) stressed the impact of the Real Compañia Guipuzcoana de Caracas on the future of Latin America to the diminution of other factors. Basterra was a notable eccentric. He died insane.

Basterra's poetry is interesting for what D'Ors has shrewdly called his 'cerebral feelings'. Dominated almost entirely by his emotions, he consciously deified his concept of reason: the result is mythical personification of his ideal of the Roman element in Spanish life, Vírulo, whose name combines manliness, strength and virility. He used traditional metres in the often baroque poems collected as *Las ubres luminosas* (Bilbao, 1923) and *Vírulo. I: Las mocedades* (1924), but the new metres of *modernismo* (q.v.) began to emerge in *Los labios del monte* (1925) and more especially in his most enduring creation, *Vírulo. II: Mediodía* (1927). The *Obra poética* was recently collected (Bilbao, 1958) and G. Díaz Plaja, author of *La poesía y el pensamiento de Ramón de Basterra* (Barcelona, 1941), published Basterra's *Papeles inéditos y dispersos* (1970).

BATAILLON, Marcel (1896–1977), French Hispanist whose most important work is *Erasme et l'Espagne* (Paris, 1937), corrected by the author for the Spanish translation of Antonio Alatorre (Mexico City, 1950; 3rd rev. edn., 1967). Bataillon has contributed numerous monographs to scholarly reviews, some of which have been collected as *Varia lección de clásicos españoles* (Madrid, 1964). His other books include *Le roman picaresque* (Paris, 1931), '*La Célestine*' *selon Fernando de Rojas* (Paris, 1961), *Études sur Bartolomé de las Casas* (Paris, 1966), *Novedad y fecundidad del 'Lazarillo de Tormes'* (1968), and *Pícaros y picaresca* (1969). He has translated Sarmiento and Unamuno into French. He established Alfonso Valdes's authorship of the *Diálogo de Mercurio y Carón* and has deprived Cristóbal de Villalón (q.v.) of two works previously thought to be his: the *Viaje de Turquía*, which Bataillon attributes to Andrés Laguna (q.v.) and *El crotalón* (q.v.) to an Italian naturalized as a Spaniard.

BATILO, poetic name of Juan Meléndez Valdés (q.v.).

BATRES MONTÚFAR, José (1809–44), b. San Salvador. Guatemalan poet, with a classical background, who fought for Guatemala against El Salvador and was taken prisoner in 1828. On his release the next year, he found his house sacked and his family fled to Antigua. Reduced to poverty, he studied engineering and was travelling in Nicaragua as an engineer with his brother Juan in 1837, when Juan contracted a fever and died. José returned to Guatemala in 1838 sick in mind and body and, after a few years of parliamentary and literary activity, he too met an early death.

His best-known works are the *Tradiciones de Guatemala,* three narratives in *octavos reales,* and a madrigal often anthologised called *Yo pienso en tí,* a declaration of love to Adela García Granados, or possibly Luisa Meany. His *Poesías* were first collected, with a prologue by José Milla (q.v.), in 1845. There have been subsequent editions, of which the centenary volume of *Poesías* (1944) is especially notable.

BAUZÁ, Francisco (1849–99), b. Montevideo. Uruguayan historian and critic. A diplomat and politician initially supporting the dictator Santos, Bauzá abandoned his position when Santos began his religious persecution. After finding no success with his immature *Poesías* (1869), Bauzá shrewdly turned to history, writing a fine *Historia de la dominación española en el Uruguay* (1882). His lesser works include *Estudios literarios* (1885) and *Estudios constitucionales* (1887).

BAYO Y SEGUROLA, Ciro (1859–1939), b. Madrid. Travel writer and novelist. At 16, Bayo was already a Carlist political prisoner in Minorca, and his life followed the same pattern of adventure almost to the end. From Minorca he went to Cuba, returning to Spain to study law but failing to qualify due mainly to his restlessness, which led him across Europe and Latin America. He worked as a primary school teacher in Argentina, Bolivia, and elsewhere. In Sucre he founded *El Fígaro.* His most familiar works are *El peregrino entretenido: viaje romancesco* (1910), which has been edited with a bibliography and the best study of Bayo to date by Joaquín de Entrambasaguas (Barcelona, 1959); and *Lazarillo español: guía de vagos en tierras de España por un peregrino industrioso* (1911), issued in the same year as his *Vocabulario criollo: español suramericano.* Of his many other books, the most significant are *El peregrino en Indias: en el corazón de la América del Sur* (1912), *Bolívar y sus tenientes* and *La Colombiada* (1912), *Romancerillo*

del Plata and *Orfeo en el infierno* (1913), and *Por la América desconocida* (4 vols., 1920).

Baza de espadas (1958), the third, incomplete, novel in the cycle *El ruedo ibérico* by Ramón del Valle-Inclán (qq.v.).

BÉCQUER, Gustavo Adolfo (1836–70), b. Seville. Major Romantic poet, and almost alone in his quiet rejection of conventionality and bombast. His real name was Gustavo Adolfo Domínguez Bastida. Orphaned when a boy, he studied in the naval college of San Telmo until it was closed in 1850, and then became apprenticed to the painter Antonio Cabral. On an impulse he left for Madrid in 1854 with dreams of making a literary sensation, but to make enough money was forced to produce hack libretti for *zarzuelas* now forgotten. He lived on the brink of penury, aggravated in 1857 by an attack of haemoptysis, and relieved only by his appointment as censor of novels, a post which he held from 1864 to 1865 and from 1866 to 1868. He was a frequent contributor (often anonymously) to *El Contemporáneo,* the newspaper founded by José Luis Albareda, from 1860 to 1865. In 1858 he had fallen in love with Julia Espín, daughter of a teacher at the Conservatoire in Seville, but had avoided approaching her because of his awareness of the social gulf between them. She inspired several of the *Rimas.* In 1861 he married Casta Esteban Navarro. His brother Valeriano, a painter with whom he collaborated closely, especially after Gasset y Artime founded *La Ilustración de Madrid* in 1870 and opened his pages to them, joined Gustavo Adolfo in Madrid, and animosity soon marred the marriage, since he resented Casta. Bécquer spent some time in Novierca (Soria), leaving for Seville in 1863, but when his condition deteriorated in 1864 he went to the monastery of Veruela (N. Spain). There he wrote the charming, *costumbrista Cartas desde mi celda* for *El Contemporáneo.*

It was during 1867–8 that he composed most of the *Rimas* but he lost the MS. during the 1868 Revolution, and modern editions print only what he could recall from his lost drafts.

In September 1870, after only a few months' work for *La Ilustración,* Valeriano died. Gustavo Adolfo, who had separated from his wife as a result of his brother's jealousy, continued to write to her during the separation, and lived with her again after his brother's death until he himself died in December 1870.

The only book he published in his lifetime was the *Historia de los templos de España* (vol. 1, 1857), with Juan de la Puerta. After his death a group of friends financed the publication of Bécquer's *Obras* (2 vols., 1871), the profits to be paid to the widow and children. The second edition contained the same number (79) of *Rimas*, but the third (1881) contained more prose writings, including *Cartas de una mujer*. The 1949 *Obras completas* (ed. M. Sánchez de Palacios), if not complete, is at least comprehensive in its coverage of all genres practised by Bécquer, including 24 *tradiciones y costumbres españolas*, 20 *leyendas*, 10 *cartas desde mi celda*, 4 *cartas a una mujer*, 15 *ensayos literarios*, 94 *rimas*, and 18 *motivos del arte*.

There has been no diminution in the appreciation of Bécquer's *Rimas* since they were first collected, despite the fact that they are confessional in tone and are not aimed at a wide audience. His themes are love and hope, misery and solitude, with their consequent despair, and the mysteries of human life and art, in particular poetry. He was influenced by various writers beginning with the forgotten F. Rodríguez Zapata (1813–89). Later he read Heine and Byron, and probably Alfred de Musset. His rhymes are often mechanical, and it has been argued with some plausibility that he was most authentically poetic in his prose *leyendas*, some of which (like *Los ojos verdes* on Fernando's dying for love of a mermaid) derive from Hoffmann; others (e.g. *Es raro*) from Madrid *costumbrismo*; others (e.g. *El caudillo de las manos rojas*) from exotic sources. Perhaps the impression given by Bécquer's poetry of reverie and suggestion can best be summed up by Lamartine's maxim: the best poetry is that which remains unwritten. Bécquer's language is never rhetorical and is in fact often colloquial, verging on the openly trivial, but the effect is magically impressionistic.

See the convenient edition of the *Rimas* (1963) by J. P. Díaz in Clásicos Castellanos. Iglesias Figueroa produced *Páginas desconocidas* (3 vols., 1923), and Ganallo Fierros *Páginas abandonadas* (1948). J. de Entrambasaguas, *La obra poética de Bécquer en su discriminación creadora y erótica* (1974), includes the collected poems.

There is a portrait of Bécquer with his family by his brother Valeriano in the Provincial Museum in Cádiz. The best biography is Rica Brown's *Gustavo Adolfo Bécquer* (Barcelona, 1963) but others may still be read with profit, especially José Pedro Díaz's *Gustavo Adolfo Bécquer: vida y poesía* (Montevideo, 1953) and E. L. King's *Gustavo Adolfo Bécquer: from painter to poet* (Mexico City, 1953). On the *Rimas* see R. de Balbín Lucas, *Poética becqueriana* (1969) and on the legends, M. García-Viñó, *Mundo y trasmundo de las 'Leyendas' de Bécquer* (1970). R. Benítez produced an *Ensayo de bibliografía razonada de Gustavo Adolfo Bécquer* (Buenos Aires, 1961). A special issue of *Quaderni ibero-americani* (nos. 39–40) was devoted to Bécquer in 1971.

BEDREGAL, JUAN FRANCISCO (1883–1944), b. La Paz. Bolivian satirist, poet, critic, and short-story writer. A Franciscan who became Rector of San Andrés University in La Paz, Bedregal was the mildest of satirical writers, aiming to correct without giving offence. He published only two books: *La máscara de estuco* (1926) and *Figuras animadas*, the latter containing his most celebrated piece, *Don Quijote en la ciudad de La Paz*. His prose style is exceptionally pure, and his voice strangely quiet in Bolivia, whose literature had been marked by bitterness and acrimony. His works are not stories, but 'pseudostories' in the sense used by Miguel Serrano in his *Antología del verdadero cuento en Chile* (1938), weaving fictional elements around a core of recorded fact, but neglecting the element of fantasy.

BEJARANO, LÁZARO DE (c. 1501–c. 1575), b. Seville. Poet in the circle of Gutierre de Cetina (q.v., c. 1531–4). Bejarano left for the Americas in 1535 and is recorded in Santo Domingo, Hispaniola (now the Dominican Republic) in 1541. He is credited by Giuseppe Bellini (whose *La letteratura ispano-americana* (Florence, 1970) reprints a satire of 1552 by Bejarano against Alonso de Maldonado, President of the High Court of Santo Domingo) with having introduced the Italian metres into Mexico and Central America. His daring satires against clergy and politicians earned his indictment by the Inquisition in 1558. His lost *Diálogo apologético* defended the rights of Indians to administrative and social justice.

Belarmino y Apolonio (1921), a novel by Ramón Pérez de Ayala (q.v.) which attracted little attention on publication but has since been described by Jean Cassou as 'after *Don Quijote*, one of the greatest Spanish books.' César Barja suggests that 'love is the formula of harmonious solution of the dialectic opposition between Belarmino y Apolonio'. The novel's only weakness lies in the uneasy juxtaposition of heterogeneous elements. It is based on a theory of 'visión diafenomenal': the exploration of dual perspective, rather as if both Sancho and Quijote were to narrate the same events in the same book. Characters are known by different names to different people. The plot revolves around the elopement of Pedrito and Angustias, but the real dispute is between the two shoemakers of the title, the philosopher Belarmino and the dramatist Apolonio. Pérez de Ayala handles the language with assurance and masters a wide range of styles. The novel's influence can be seen in many contemporary writers, among them Julio Cortázar and Ernesto Sábato (qq.v.).

BELDA, Joaquín (1880–1937?), b. Madrid. Erotic novelist and broad humorist. While critics have been generally sceptical of the value of Belda's many novels, Cansinos Assens (in his *La nueva literatura*, vol. 2 (1925), p. 213) described the author of *La suegra de Tarquino* (1909) and *La Coquito* (1915) as 'el *Don Quijote* exterminador de esos otros libros de caballerías eróticos . . . con dedos ungidos de óleo báquico ha escrito su epitafio burlesco'.

In addition to his many short stories and a biography, *Máiquez, actor, guerrillero y hombre de amor* (n.d.), Belda wrote the following novels which attracted wide popularity and huge sales in the second and third decades of the century: *¿Quién disparó?* (1909), *Memorias de un suicida* and *Saldo de almas* (1910), *La piara* and *La Farándula* (1911), *Alcibíades-Club* (1912), *El pícaro oficio* (1914), *Una mancha de sangre* (1915), *De aquellos polvos . . .* (1916), *Más chulo que un ocho*, *Las noches del Botánico* and *Las chicas de Terpsícore* (all 1917), *La Diosa Razón* (1918), *El compadrito* (1920), *Carmina y su novio* (1921), *El faro de Biarritz* (1924), *Se ha perdido una cabeza* (1929), and *Me acuesto a las ocho* (1930).

BELEÑO, Joaquín (1921–), b. Panama City. Novelist. His bitter, partly autobiographical *Luna verde* (1950) achieved fame outside Panama for its denunciation of racial discrimination, neglect, and poverty in the American Zone. His next novel, *Gamboa road gang* (1960), was based on the experiences of the Panamanian Lester León Greaves.

BELISA, the name used by Lope de Vega (q.v.) in his poetry for his first wife, Isabel de Urbina, to whom he was married from 1588 to 1594.

BELL, Aubrey FitzGerald (1881–1950), British Hispanist who lived in Portugal and Canada for many years. His study of the Spanish Renaissance led him to controversial views, one of which was that the Spanish Renaissance began as early as 1400 and lasted for fully three centuries. His travel book *The magic of Spain* (1912) was the result of years spent walking to remote villages, especially in Castile. Later books on Portuguese and Spanish literature included *Gil Vicente* (Oxford, 1921); *Portuguese bibliography* (Oxford, 1922) and its sequel 'Selective Bibliography of Portuguese Literature, 1922–1937' compiled with Melissa A. Cilley in *Hispania* (Stanford but since 1949 at Wallingford, Conn.), vol. 22 (1939), pp. 381–9; *Benito Arias Montano* (1922); *Spanish Galicia* (1922); *Studies in Portuguese literature* (Oxford, 1922), translated by A. de Campos and J. G. de Barros e Cunha (Coimbra, 1931); *The*

Oxford book of Portuguese verse (Oxford, 1925); *Luis de León: a study of the Spanish Renaissance* (Oxford, 1925); *Contemporary Spanish literature* (New York, 1925; 2nd edn., New York, 1933); and *Castilian literature* (Oxford, 1938), which emphasized Bell's view of the dominance of the Castilian spirit in Spanish writing.

BELLI, Carlos Germán (1927–), Peruvian poet and journalist who worked as a government clerk from 1946 and taught at the San Marcos University in Lima and in the U.S.A. *Poemas* (1958), *¡Oh hada cibernética!*, *El pie sobre el cuello* (1964), and *Por el monte abajo* (1966) were collected in *El pie sobre el cuello* (Montevideo, 1967). A later work is *Sextinas y otros poemas* (Santiago de Chile, 1970), using the conceits of 17th-c. poetry wittily in bureaucratic and technological contexts. A tone of ironical resignation to the age of 'progress' has given way to a greater variety of theme, often uniting traditional forms, such as the sextina in the *Sextina de Kid y Lulú*, with contemporary images and surrealistic diction. Belli's latest collection is *¡Oh hada cibernética!* (Caracas, 1971), and a new book incorporating all his published work is due from Seix Barral (Barcelona).

See Javier Sologuren, *Tres poetas, tres obras: Belli. Delgado. Salazar Bondy* (1969, pp. 7–40) and James Higgins, 'The poetry of Carlos Germán Belli' in *BHS*, vol. 47, no. 4 (October 1970), pp. 327–39.

BELLIDO CORMENZANA, José María (1922–), b. San Sebastián. Playwright. He has a law degree from Valladolid but has never practised. To spend more time on writing he sold his interest in a San Sebastián hotel and has become one of the most interesting of 'unofficial' playwrights in Spain.

Whatever he writes is allegorical, mixing humour and tragedy in an absurd or potentially absurd situation. The one-act *El pan y el arroz, o geometría en amarillo* has a certain resemblance to Ionesco's *Les chaises* in its accumulation, this time of beautiful yellow children, whose multiplication frustrates the dream of power entertained by a group representing power: the army, business, intellectuals, and the financial and land-owning class. Symbolism, mostly referring implicitly to Spain, recurs in *Escorpión* (1962), *Fútbol* (1963) with its images of partisanship and hysteria hardly distinguishing supporters of Real Madrid or Barcelona from Spanish patriots, *El día sencillo* (1964), and *Tren a F* (1964). In the last, a train full of passengers is crossing a plain towards F, which is never described. The train is decrepit and constantly breaking down, in contrast to the other trains and buses speeding across the plain. The passengers, who are also shareholders, do not change vehicles for fear that no other will have the secret of access to the only tunnel leading to F. This religious satire makes the most of the passengers' smugness and prophecy of disaster to the passengers in the other vehicles.

Los relojes de cera (1967) is set in a totalitarian state where time has stood still but, to fool the tourists, soldiers are kept constantly on the move to put forward the hands on the wax clocks. *Solfeo para mariposas* (1969), like *La nau* (1969) by Josep Benet (q.v.) centres on a room concealing a secret. Here, orders are given to generals from a room in an unknown military headquarters. Sex is used to infuse decaying army leaders with the energy to carry out these orders of destruction.

Bellido's latest plays foresake symbolism for realism, and he seems to be attracted by the commercial theatre in such plays as *Rubio cordero* (1970), which deals sensitively with the ethical and political issues involved in the kidnapping of foreign diplomats.

See George E. Wellwarth, *Spanish underground drama* (Philadelphia, 1972), pp. 51–63 and translations of *El pan y el arroz* (Robert Lima) and *Tren a F* (Ronald Flores) in *The new wave Spanish drama* (New York, 1970, ed. George E. Wellwarth).

BELLO, ANDRÉS (1781–1865), b. Caracas. Venezuelan philosopher, grammarian, and poet. He travelled to England as an aide to Bolívar and López Meléndez, and his humanism stems from his two periods in Europe, the second lasting until 1829. His *Alocución a la poesía* (1823) is a fragment of a poem that was to have been called *América*. In form it is a neo-classical `silva`; its invocation to Independence refers indirectly to the wars for political independence in Latin America. At the request of the Chilean government, he reformed their educational system, living in Chile 1829–65 and founding the Colegio de Santiago, which was to become the University. His important *Filosofía del entendimiento* (1881) introduced Latin America to the ideas of Locke, J. S. Mill, and Berkeley. His greatest contribution to philology was the *Gramática de la lengua castellana* (1847) which, with the addition of notes by Rufino José Cuervo, is still used today. In a polemic against Sarmiento (q.v.), Bello defended neo-classicism against Romanticism, but he translated Byron and Hugo. He wrote *Silvas a la agricultura de la zona tórrida* (1826), the second of his *Silvas americanas*, which combine a Virgilian manner with Bello's love for his native flora. His *Obras completas* began to appear in 1952, with vol. 1: *Poesías*. E. Rodríguez

Monegal has written a study on Bello entitled *Este otro Andrés Bello* (Caracas, 1969).

BELMONTE Y BERMÚDEZ, LUIS DE (1587?–1650?), b. Seville. Playwright, poet, and biographer. He composed *Vida del Padre Maestro Ignacio de Loyola* (Mexico City, 1609) and poems, of which only two are known to survive: *La aurora de Cristo* (1616) and *La Hispálica*, edited by S. Montoto (Seville, 1921). Despite acute difficulties, it seems that some 25 plays can be attributed to Belmonte, some in co-authorship, as with *La renegada de Valladolid* (considered to be by Belmonte, Moreto, and Martínez de Meneses), which first appeared in *Primera parte de Comedias escogidas . . .* (1652). He is a close follower of Lope, and *El diablo predicador y mayor contrario amigo* (q.v.) first published in the *Parte sexta de comedias de los mejores ingenios de España* (Saragossa, 1653) is ascribed to him, following a play entitled *Fray Diablo* attributed to Lope. These two plays assigned to Belmonte appear in vol. 45 (1858) of the BAE.

Among his other plays are *Darles con la entretenida* in *Parte 31 de las mejores comedias* (Barcelona, 1638), *El príncipe perseguido* in *El mejor de los mejores libros que han salido de Comedias nuevas* (Alcalá, 1651), *Amor y honor* in *Segunda parte de Comedias escogidas* (1652), *El mejor tutor es Dios* in *Parte 28 de Comedias nuevas* (1667), and *Los trabajos de Ulises* in *Parte 45 de Comedias nuevas* (1679).

See W. A. Kincaid, 'Life and works of Luis Belmonte Bermúdez' in *Revue Hispanique*, vol. 74 (1928), pp. 1–260.

BEÑA, CRISTÓBAL DE (1777?–1833), b. Extremadura. Fabulist. Studied at Alcalá University. Imitating La Fontaine and Iriarte (q.v.), Beña attacked tyranny and bad government in fables such as 'La piedra de anular y el cuchillo' and 'La escalera de mano y el farolero'. He published these and other poems in *Lira de la libertad* (London, 1831) after being exiled for his involvement in a conspiracy against the French. He contributed to the *Memorial literario* (1784–1808) in its third phase, 1800–08.

BEN ADRET, SOLOMON, see ADRET, Solomon ben.

BENAVENTE, *Fray* TORIBIO DE (d. 1569), b. Benavente, Zamora, Spanish Franciscan also known as 'Motilinía', who features in Mexican literary histories because all his published work was written in, and about, Mexico. He was one of a group of Franciscans who left for Mexico under Fray Martín de Valencia in 1524 and who, on their arrival in

Mexico, caused a good impression by their humble garb and demeanour. The people called them *motilinía* (the poor ones), and Fray Toribio thenceforth assumed this name. He was the first evangelist in Guatemala and Nicaragua, and in 1530 founded in Mexico the city of Puebla (de los Ángeles). He was appointed Deputy Provincial in 1546 and Provincial in 1548, serving until 1551. He composed many occasional writings on behalf of the Indians, such as an appeal for tax reductions, but is best known for the *Memoriales* (1541; ed. Luis García Pimentel, 1903) and the major *Historia de los indios de Nueva España*, probably completed in about 1541, and certainly used in MS. by later historians, but not published in any form until an abridgment appeared in London in 1848. The first full edition appeared in Mexico City ten years later. There is a good life and bibliography in the edition of Fray Daniel Sánchez (1941). The *Historia* consists of three parts: the rites and ceremonies of the Aztecs recorded so soon after the conquest that Motilinía's account can be regarded as the most trustworthy ever set down by a Spaniard; a firsthand account of their conversion; chronology and astronomy among the Aztecs, and other unusual features of their thought and culture.

BENAVENTE Y MARTÍNEZ, JACINTO (1866–1954), b. Madrid. Playwright to whom is generally attributed the revitalization of the Spanish drama at the turn of the century, which followed the melodrama of intrigue made popular by Echegaray (q.v., whom incidentally Benavente did not attack when an opportunity occurred in the controversy of 1905).

The son of a famous and well-loved doctor, Jacinto enrolled in Madrid University in 1882 to study law, but abandoned his studies in 1885 on the death of his father and devoted himself to travelling, reading, and writing. He was for some time impresario of a circus which visited Russia, and his firsthand knowledge of most societies, particularly the upper classes, gave him abundant material for the social satire which marked his early plays in particular. His most serious play, *El nido ajeno* (first performed in 1894), was too extreme in its criticism to be popular, unlike the more innocuously satirical *Gente conocida* (1896) in which the aristocracy of Madrid condemns itself for cynicism, corruption, and immortality, without the need for moralizing on the part of the author. This play made a great success, and launched Benavente's historic career, during which the artifice and intrigue of the contemporary theatre was gradually replaced by an awakening social conscience. Good taste and sweet reason overcame the vociferous cardboard characters

then fashionable. In *La noche del sábado* (1903), Benavente began to include the whole of decadent European society within his sights, from high society down to circus folk. A prolific writer of uneven powers, Benavente reached his 53rd play with *Los intereses creados* (q.v., 1907), probably his best play for its Machiavellian hero Crispín, nominally a lackey but in reality a puppetmaster, and for its impressive use of masks to exploit and parody simultaneously *commedia dell'arte* elements.

Benavente founded the Teatro de los Niños in 1909 and some of his most interesting works are for children's theatre, particularly *El príncipe que todo lo aprendió en los libros* (1909), which is in fact too sophisticated for most children.

He spent much time in journalism 1908–12, contributing a weekly column to *El Imparcial*, and in 1912 was elected a member of the Real Academia Española. During the First World War Benavente took the German side, as did most of the army, clergy, and aristocracy of Spain. His plays became tendentiously conservative in tone, and were attacked both from the artistic and the personal point of view by most intellectuals and critics, especially Ramón Pérez de Ayala (q.v.) in his reviews and essays collected in *Las máscaras* (2 vols., 1917–19). Upset by these attacks, which he considered to be motivated by political animosity, Benavente abandoned playwriting 1920–4, but, after being awarded the Nobel Prize for Literature in 1922, was honoured twice by the Madrid city authorities in 1924, when *Lecciones de buen amor* received its première. During the Civil War 1936–9 he lived withdrawn in Valencia, still writing, and in 1945 he produced his 150th play, *Nieve en mayo*. Altogether he wrote 172 plays, three in the year of his death; feminist *Cartas a una mujer* (3 vols., 1893–1902); six volumes of table-talk, *De sobremesa* (1910–16); poems influenced by Bécquer and Campoamor, *Versos* (1893); and the fascinating *Recuerdos y olvidos: memorias* (1962). Collected editions began early with *Teatro* (38 vols., 1903–31) and the 4th edition of the *Obras completas* (begun 1947) reached vol. 10 in 1969.

See Ángel Lázaro, *Vida y obra de Benavente* (1925; reprinted 1964); Walter Starkie, *Jacinto Benavente* (London, 1924) a work in English of great critical merit; and a recent summary by Marcelino C. Peñuelas, *Jacinto Benavente*, translated for Twayne's World Authors series by Kay Engler (New York, 1968).

The 'school' of Benavente remained far behind their master in artistic and dramatic appeal. They were, principally, Manuel Linares Rivas (1878–1938), Gregorio Martínez Sierra (1881–1947) and the Argentina-born Enrique Suárez de Deza (1906– , qq.v.).

BENEDETTI, MARIO (1920–), b. Paso de los Toros, Uruguay. Uruguayan novelist, short-story writer, critic, and poet. In 1948 he resuscitated the magazine *Marginalia*, which ceased publication with its sixth issue in December 1949.

His short stories of urban life in offices, homes, and streets are laconic sketches of trivial moments in wasted lives. He described in a lecture, for instance, how civil servants in Montevideo are obliged to arrive twenty minutes before work because there are not enough chairs for all of them. His collections of stories are *Esta mañana* (1949), *El último viaje y otros cuentos* (1951), and the economically-written *Montevideanos* (1959).

Benedetti's novels include *Quién de nosotros* (1955), *La tregua* (1960), and *Gracias por el fuego* (1965). His poetry lies uneasily between the private fantasy and the conventional view of public figures in intellectual circles (against the United States; in favour of Fidel Castro) in *Contra los puentes levadizos* (1967), which expands the subject-matter of *Poemas de la oficina* (1956) and *Noción de patria* (1963). His literary criticism reflects a lively, essentially unscholarly mind: *Literatura uruguaya siglo XX: ensayo* (1963; 2nd enlarged ed., 1969) and *Letras del continente mestizo* (1967). His latest books are *Inventario* (1967); *La muerte y otras sorpresas* (1968); *Los poetas comunicantes* (1972), interviews with ten Spanish-American poets; *Letras de emergencia* (1973), poetry and prose with a political bias written 1968–73; and *El país de la cola de paja* (1973), collected essays on contemporary Uruguay.

See J. Ruffinelli (ed.), *Mario Benedetti* (1973).

BENEGASI Y LUJÁN, JOSÉ JOAQUÍN (1707–70), b. Madrid. Comic (and occasionally serious) poet of means who entered the religious life in 1763. He was the son of Francisco Benegasi (1656?–1742?), whose humorous verse is included in the 1744 and subsequent reprints of José Joaquín's *Poesías líricas, y joco-serias* (1743). He wrote verse lives of the saints: *Vida de San Benito de Palermo* (1750) in *seguidillas;* and *Vida de San Dámaso* (1752) in *redondillas*. The following plays are recorded: *La campana de descansar,* an *entremés*; two *bailes*: *El amor casamentero* and *El ingeniero apurado*; and a *Comedia (que no lo es) burlesca: Llámenla como quisieren* (1753).

BENET GOITA, JUAN (1927–), b. Madrid. Spanish novelist, short-story writer, and essayist. He qualified as an engineer in 1954, and spent many years in his profession in rural areas of León, Asturias, and the Basque provinces, as well as travelling to Finland and other European countries. His first novel was *Volverás a Región* (Barcelona, 1967), an original and often tantalizing work followed by *Meditación* (Barcelona, 1969), which won the Biblioteca Breve prize.

His first short stories were in *Nunca llegarás a nada* (1961), quite different from those in *Sub rosa* (Barcelona, 1973), which are experimental, with shifting narrators and unresolved mysteries. Events and intentions are seen as if through a fog. The use of passive-reflexive verbs assists Benet's depersonalizing process, and photographs accompanying the text heighten a sense of illusion, false perspective, and strange viewpoints.

BENET I JORNET, JOSEP (1940–), Catalan playwright. His plays 'Cançons perdudas' (first performed 1966), *Marc i Jofre o els alquimistes de la fortuna* (first performed 1968; Barcelona, 1970), and *La nau* (1969) are all set in the imaginary state of Drudania, which might possibly stand for Catalonia, for Spain, or for Earth. *La nau* takes place in a spaceship carrying a million passengers from Drudania to colonize the distant stars. In this parable of the Fall of Man, the Technicians arrange the 'suicide' of a curious passenger who has dared to penetrate to the Engine Room and must not be allowed to divulge its secret (which is that there is nothing there) to his fellow-passengers. 'Cançons perdudas' has so far only appeared in a volume entitled *Fantasia per a un auxiliar administratiu* (Palma, 1970). Like Manuel de Pedrolo (q.v.), Benet is a Catalan whose enforced symbolism has paradoxically removed parochialism from his writings, and added a note of universality lacking in contemporary Castilian writing for the commercial theatre.

BENÍTEZ, JUSTO PASTOR (1895–1962), Paraguayan historian, diplomat, and journalist who lived in exile for 25 years. A believer in the cult of the hero, Benítez saw the hero not only in military and political figures but also in writers and artists. Of his formidable output possibly the most enduring books are *Bajo el signo de Marte* (Montevideo, 1934), on the War of the Chaco; *Algunos aspectos de la literatura paraguaya* (Rio de Janeiro, 1935); *La vida solitaria del Dr José Gaspar de Francia* (Buenos Aires, 1937), on the reclusive Paraguayan dictator; *Estigarribia, el soldado del Chaco* (Buenos Aires, 1943); *El solar guaraní* (Buenos Aires, 1947); and, probably his most important essay, *Formación social del pueblo paraguayo* (1955).

See Alejandro Marín Iglesias, 'Notas para la historia de un hombre libre: Justo Pastor Benítez' in *Alcor*, no. 43 (March–April 1967).

BEN LABRAT, Dunash ha-Levi, see Labrat, Dunash ha-Levi ben.

BERAGÜE, Pedro de, see Veragüe, Pedro de.

BERCEO, Gonzalo de (c.1190–after 1264), b. Berceo, Logroño. Religious poet, who served the monastery of San Millán as a legal administrator, possibly for some time also as a notary, and was responsible during part of his career for the financial administration. His importance is partly historical, since he is the first Castilian poet known to us by name, writing in copla 489 of the Vida de San Millán: 'Gonzalvo fue so nomne qui fizo est tractado, /en Sant Millan de suso fue de niñez criado, /natural de Berceo, ond Sant Millan fue nado'.

His writings can be divided into three groups: the four hagiographies, three on local saints, and an unfinished work on the martyrdom of St. Lawrence; the three works on the Virgin Mary, whose cult was established in the West (later than the East) by the 10th c.; and two doctrinal works in rhymed prose of lesser value: the Sacrificio de la misa (in vol. 57, 1864, of the BAE and ed. A. G. Solalinde, 1913); and De los signos que aparescerán antes del Juicio (ed. Clemente Canales Toro, Santiago de Chile, 1955).

Berceo's literary significance lies in his ability to weld together the classical-rhetorical tradition, the ecclesiastical tradition of the sermon and the exhortation, and the popular tradition of the minstrels (juglares). For example, the Vida de Santo Domingo de Silos is based on the Latin Vita Sancti Dominici of the Abbot Grimaldus, yet in that work Bereo refers to himself as a juglar no fewer than four times.

The critical edition by J. D. Fitzgerald (Paris, 1904) should be supplemented by the critical palaeographical edition by Alfonso Andrés (1958) and the latter's article in BRAE, vol. 4 (1917) and the more recent edition by T. Labarta de Chaves (1972) in Clásicos Castalia.

Berceo's first hagiography was the Vida de San Millán, patron saint of his own monastery, a disingenuous choice because his monastery needed a constant supply of funds, and Berceo conceived the idea of using a forged document prepared by his contemporary, the monk Fernandus, to exhort Castilians to pay tribute to the monastery. The poem consists of the story of the saint's life, of his alleged miracles, including his appearance with St. James (Santiago) in the sky during a battle against the Moors. After the Christian victory, the King of León decrees that all his subjects pay tribute to St. James at Compostela, and Fernán González that all Castilians offer tribute to S. Millán de la Cogolla. The source of the poem is the prose life in Latin by S. Braulio. Like his other

important poems, Berceo's life of S. Emilianus is written in cuaderna vía (q.v.), a metre probably introduced either by Berceo or by the poet of the Libro de Alexandre (q.v.). There are modern editions of the Estoria de San Millán by Gerhard Koberstein (Münster, 1964) and by Brian Dutton (London, 1968).

His third hagiography was the Vida de Santa Oria, written on another local saint towards the end of his life. Its Latin source is no longer extant. The poem relies on allegory more than the others do, describing visions of heaven more than the saint's good works in life.

The devout Milagros de Nuestra Señora belong to a genre that spread from the 12th to the 14th cs. and passed from Latin (as in Berceo's prose source stories) to the vernacular. The date of composition seems to be late in Berceo's career; the structural skill varies from the inspired (such as the second and ninth) to the awkward (such as the first and the tenth); and the intention seems always to recommend whole-hearted devotion to the Virgin rather than to offer information on her life and supposed miracles. Contemporary Marian collections were the Latin prose book by Gil de Zamora and Alfonso X's Cantigas de Santa Maria in Galician-Portuguese. Los Milagros de Nuestra Señora (q.v.) has been edited for Clásicos Castellanos by A. G. Solalinde (1922), and for Támesis Books by B. Dutton (London, 1971) as vol. 2 of Berceo's Obras completas, a projected 5-volume set, of which vol. 3 (London, 1975) contains El duelo de la Virgen, Los himnos, Los loores de Nuestra Señora, and Los signos del Juicio Final.

See J. Artiles, Los recursos literarios de Berceo (1964); C. Gariano, Análisis estilístico de 'Los Milagros de Nuestra Señora' (1965); and T. A. Perry, Art and meaning in Berceo's 'Vida de Santa Oria' (New Haven, 1968).

BERENGUER CARISOMO, Arturo (1905–), b. Buenos Aires. Argentinian literary critic and playwright. His two interests joined in Las ideas estéticas en el teatro argentino (1947) and Teatro argentino contemporáneo (Madrid, 1959). He has also compiled the brief Literatura argentina (Barcelona, 1970) and a specialized study Los valores eternos en la obra de Enrique Larreta (1946). His best-known plays are Por el prestigio de la primavera, which won the Premio Argentores of 1946 and La piel de la manzana, winner of the Premio Nacional de Teatro 1949–51.

See Berenguer's Curriculum vitae, 1921–1947 (1947).

BERGAMÍN, José (1897–), b. Madrid. Essayist and literary critic. His major significance in the Spanish intellectual environment of the mid-1930s was the editing of the 'Catholic and Republican' journal *Cruz y Raya* (1933–6), selections from which have been published as *Antología de 'Cruz y Raya'* (1974). At the same time he was making collections of essays and aphorisms: *El cohete y la estrella* (1922), reminiscent of Pascal and Gómez de la Serna; *Tres escenas en ángulo recto* (1923), *Carácteres* (Málaga, 1926), the aphorisms *El arte de birlibirloque* (1930; reprinted with additional material, 1961), *Mangas y capirotes* (1933), *La cabeza a pájaros* (1934), *Disparadero español* (3 vols., 1936–40), *Detrás de la cruz* and *El pozo de la angustia* (both Mexico City, 1941), *La voz apagada* and *El pasajero* (both Mexico City, 1943), *La muerte burlada* (Mexico City, 1945), *Melusina y el espejo* (Montevideo, 1952), *Medea la encantadora* and *Fronteras infernales de la poesía* (both Montevideo, 1954), *La corteza de la letra* (Buenos Aires, 1958), *Lázaro, Don Juan y Segismundo* (1959), *Al volver* (Barcelona, 1962), *De una España peregrina* (1972), *Beltenebros y otros ensayos sobre literatura española* (Barcelona, 1973), two religious essays *El clavo ardiendo* (Barcelona, 1974) previously published in France as *Le clou brûlant* (Paris, 1972), and *La importancia del demonio y otras cosas sin importancia* (1974).

Bergamín's neo-Catholic position is near that of Jacques Maritain. He attacks reason as the worst enemy of truth, and opposes current trends towards literalism in literature and reason as a guiding factor in human life. He has a preoccupation with Spain and its position in the world which recalls that of the Generation of 1898. His style is difficult, highly personal, metaphorical, and lyrical. He went into exile in Mexico following the Spanish Civil War. Recently his works have been permitted publication in Spain, but he is still better known in France than in Spain.

BERGANTIÑOS, EL BARDO DE, the name by which Eduardo Pondal Abente (q.v.), the Galician poet, was usually known.

BERGUEDÀ, GUILLEM DE (*c.* 1140–*c.* 1194), Catalan troubadour writing in Provençal. He was a friend of Bertran de Born and Richard Coeur de Lion and inherited from his father five important castles. It appears that he treacherously murdered the wealthy Ramon Folc de Cardona in 1175. He composed excellent *sirventes* attacking his enemies, praising his friends, and declaring that every lady was in love with him. His finest poem is a *planh* or elegy for Ponç de Mataplana, a valiant knight whom Guillem had earlier vilified just as vehemently as he laments his loss here. Editions of Guillem have been made by M. de Riquer in 'El trovador Guilhem de Berguedan y las luchas

feudales de su tiempo' in *Boletín de la Sociedad Castellonense de Cultura*, vol. 29 (1958) and elsewhere. The best general account of Guillem is also by M. de Riquer, in his *Història de la literatura catalana*, vol. 1 (1964), pp. 74–94.

BERMÚDEZ, *Frai* JERÓNIMO (1530?–1599?), Galician playwright and poet who studied theology in Salamanca and, using the pen-name 'Antonio de Silva', introduced classical Greek tragedy into Castilian with 'Nise lastimosa' and 'Nise laureada (published together as *Primeras tragedias españolas* . . . (1577) on the Portuguese theme of Inés (anagram) de Castro (q.v.). The first was a mere adaptation of the Portuguese tragedy *Inés de Castro* (written between 1553 and 1567) by Antonio Ferreira, but the second is an original work by Bermúdez who has less inspiration than Ferreira, and inserts rhetorical passages more reminiscent of Seneca than Euripides. Editions followed by J. J. López de Sedano in *Parnaso español* (1772) and by E. de Ochoa in *Tesoro del teatro español* (Paris, 1838).

His poem *El Narciso* has been edited by P. Gutiérrez in the Bibliófilas series (1953).

See M. L. Freund, 'Algunas observaciones sobre "Nise lastimosa" y "Nise laureada" de Jerónimo Bermúdez' in *Revista de Literatura*, vol. 19 (1961), pp. 103–12; and F. J. Sánchez Cantón, 'Aventuras del mejor poeta gallego del Siglo de Oro, Fray Jerónimo Bermúdez' in *Cuadernos de Estudios Gallegos*, vol. 20 (1965), pp. 225–42.

BERMÚDEZ, RICARDO J. (1914–), b. Panama City. Panamanian poet, who studied architecture at Southern California University, and from 1945 has taught the subject in the Panama University. He has been Minister of Education. His poetry appeals to a cultivated minority, *Poemas del ausencia* (1937), *Elegía a Adolfo Hitler* (California, 1941), *Adán liberado* (Buenos Aires, 1944), *Laurel de ceniza* (1952) and *Cuando la isla era doncella* (1961). Once a theosophist, he turned towards positivism.

BERMÚDEZ DE CASTRO Y DÍEZ, SALVADOR (1814–83), b. Jérez de la Frontera. Romantic poet. Among his titles were Príncipe de Santa Lucía, Duque de Ripalda and Marqués de Lema y de Nápoles. Bermúdez was a diplomat, who served as ambassador in Mexico (1844–7) and in Paris (1865).

His *Ensayos poéticos* (1840) have an important introduction in which the poet blames the spirit of the age for any frigidity or discontent that the reader can observe: 'tal vez en estos ensayos hay algunos que son triste muestra de un escepticismo desconsolador y frío. Lo sé, pero no es mía la culpa: culpa es de la atmósfera emponzoñada que hemos respirado todos los hombres de la generación presente...'. (His novel arrangement of stresses in the octave was known as *bermudinas*.)

Bermúdez also wrote *Antonio Pérez* (1841), the biography of a Secretary of State during the reign of Philip II.

See J. García Aráez, 'Don Salvador Bermúdez de Castro' in *Revista de Literatura*, vol. 4 (1953), pp. 73–120.

BERNÁLDEZ, ANDRÉS (*c.* 1450–1513), historian. Chaplain to Diego Deza (1443–1523), Archbishop of Seville, and author of *Historia de los reyes católicos don Fernando y doña Isabel* (2 vols., Granada, ed. F. de G. Ruiz de Apodaca; 2 vols., Seville, 1869–70), and C. Rosell in vol. 70 (1878) of the BAE and again in the Colección Crisol (1946). A selected *Antología* by O. de Medeiros appeared in 1945.

As a historian, Bernáldez is longwinded, credulous, bigoted, anti-Jewish, and almost idolatrous in his homage to Columbus, whom he knew personally and whose MSS. he was permitted to use. No fewer than fourteen chapters of the history, which covers the period 1488–1513, are devoted to Columbus.

BERNÁRDEZ, FRANCISCO LUIS (1900–), Argentinian poet. His youth was spent in Spain, where modernist poets influenced his early books: *Orto* (1922), *Bazar* (1922), *Kindergarten* (1924), and *Alcándara* (1925). He contributed to the magazine *Martín Fierro* (q.v., 1924–7), but his later, religious, work is more characteristic: *El buque* (1935), *Cielo de tierra* (1937), *La ciudad sin Laura* (1938), *Poemas elementales* (1942), *Poemas de carne y hueso* (1943), *El ruiseñor* (1945), *Las estrellas* (1947), *El ángel de la guarda* (1949), *La flor* (1951), and *El arca* (1954). In his recent books he uses the 22-syllable line in a prose poetry akin to that of Claudel. He is a master of the sonnet, as in 'Homenaje a Garcilaso' and 'Soneto lejano'.

BERNARDO DEL CARPIO, a possibly legendary figure, conceivably of French origin, who in Spanish epic becomes a Leonese noble defecting from allegiance to a sovereign who allies himself to an invader, in this case Charlemagne. The original epic, of about A.D. 1200, now lost, is retold in several prose chronicles, including the *Chronicon mundi* (1236) of Lucas, bishop of Túy (q.v.), while other chronicles omit all mention of Bernardo. The epic's original motive was to make a nationalistic reply to the extravagant claims made in the opening lines of the *Chanson de Roland* to the effect that it was Charlemagne with his Franks who had liberated much of Spain from Moorish occupation. Rodrigo de Toledo's version of the story follows a probably later Spanish epic; the *Crónica general's* fusion of both is unsatisfactory.

According to the surviving ballads on Bernardo, the childless Alfonso II (El Casto) disinherited his heir and nephew Bernardo, alleging he was a bastard. Bernardo denies this, implying that his parents were married in secret perhaps. To prevent Bernardo's inheriting the realm, Alfonso plans to bestow it on Charlemagne. This leads to the conflict between Bernardo and Roland, Charlemagne's nephew, at Roncevaux (Spanish: Roncesvalles).

Plays on the life of Bernardo include *La libertad de España por Bernardo del Carpio* by Juan de la Cueva, *Las mocedades de Bernardo* by Lope de Vega, and Hartzenbusch's *Alfonso el Casto* (1841).

Epic poems on the theme include Agustín Alonso's *El verdadero suceso de la famosa batalla de Roncesvalles* (1583), Francisco de Villena's *Hazañas del Bernardo del Carpio* (1585), *España defendida* (1612) by Suárez de Figueroa, and the best of them all, Bernardo de Balbuena's *El Bernardo, o Victoria de Roncesvalles* (1624), deriving to some extent (as regards structure and content) from the *Orlando* epics of Boiardo and Ariosto, but in 40,000 lines of *octavas reales* certainly benefiting from the zest and descriptive detail taught by the Italian masters. Balbuena's text is available in vol. 18 (1851) of the BAE, but is better presented in A. Salo's critical edition (San Feliu de Guixols, 1914).

See T. Heinermann, *Untersuchungen zur Entstehung der Sage von Bernardo del Carpio* (Halle, 1927); W. J. Entwistle, 'The "Cantar de Gesta" of Bernardo del Carpio' in *Modern Language Review*, vol. 23 (1928), pp. 307–22 and 432–52; J. B. Horrent, *La Chanson de Roland* (Paris, 1951), pp. 462–83; and R. Lapesa and others, *Romanceros del rey Rodrigo y de Bernardo del Carpio* (1957).

BERNAT Y BALDOVÍ, JOSEP (1810–64), b. Sueca, Valencia. Playwright. After studying law at Valencia University, he became a judge, and a member of the Cortes for Sueca in 1844. He was well known for a long series of *artículos de costumbres* in *El Sueco*, *El Tabalet*, and *La Donsanga*. His plays, notable for a wry sense of humour and somewhat vulgar realism, include *El Gafau o El pretendiente labriego*, *La viuda i l'escolá*, and *Pataques y caragols o La tertulia de Calau*.

His most original contribution to the 19th-c. Catalan Revival was a series of *milacres* (miracle-plays), reviving a medieval tradition of open-air religious performances, celebrating the life and work of S. Vicente Ferrer. *El rei moro de Granada* (published and first performed Valencia, 1860) is one of these, in which the saint converts Aldora, daughter of the Moorish King of Valencia, who curses God and is then carried by two devils into Hell.

See Salvador Carreres, *Homenaje al centenario de José Bernat Baldoví* (Valencia, 1910).

BERRO, ADOLFO (1819–41), b. Montevideo. Uruguay's first romantic poet. In 1839 he was appointed assessor of the defender of slaves by the Higher Tribunal of Justice, and wrote *La emancipación y mejora intelectual de las gentes de color* in the same year. His *Poesías* (1840) contained a wide variety of work, including the social (*El esclavo* and *La cárcel*), the religious (*Ecos de la voz del Señor*), the ballad (*Población de Montevideo*, in the manner of the Duque de Rivas, q.v.), historical ballads, and *Yandabayú y Liropeya*, drawn from an incident in *La Argentina* by Barco de Centenera (q.v.). Berro's prologue to his poetry declares his goal is simplicity, elegance, and morality in both ends and means. Though his work nowhere attains full maturity, the colour, descriptive vigour, and movement of his ballads are undeniable.

BERTILDA, a pseudonym of Soledad Acosta de Samper (q.v.).

BERTINI, GIOVANNI MARIA (1900–), b. Barcelona. Italian Hispanist and editor of *Quaderni Ibero-Americani* (Turin), first published in 1946 and currently published from the Associazione per i Rapporti Culturali con la Spagna, il Portogallo e l'America Latina, Via Po 19, 10124 Turin.

Among his more outstanding contributions are *Fiore di romanze spagnole* (Modena, 1939), *Studi e ricerche ispaniche* (Milan, 1942), *Profilo estetico di S. Giovanni della Croce* (Venice, 1944), *Poesie spagnole del 600* (Turin, 1946), *Testi spagnoli del secolo XV* (Turin, 1950), *Romanze novellesche spagnole in America* (Turin, 1957), and with C. Acutis and P. L. Avila, *La romanza spagnola in Italia* (Turin, 1970).

Bertini translated A. Valbuena Prat's *Historia de la literatura española* into Italian (Turin, 1961) and edited Gracián's *Oráculo manual* (Milan, 1954), *Il 'Refranero' attribuito al Marqués de Santillana*, and *Testi rinascimentali spirituali spagnoli e italiani* (Turin, 1970).

BERTIS, JUAN FELIPE (1837–99), b. San Salvador. Humanist and *literato* who established a chair of Literature in El Salvador University. Thirty-five of his essays on various subjects were collected in *Ciencia y literatura* (1941). A fervent Roman Catholic, Padre Bertis has also written distinguished essays on

classical orators such as Demosthenes and Cicero.

Bertsulariak (Basque: 'improvisers', singular, *bertsulari*). In the Basque country, they were the professional poets and storytellers who went from village to village, like medieval troubadours, retailing gossip and enlivening the evenings with their ballads, epics, and stories. Also known as *koblariak*, they were more frequently women, but most in recent years have been men, often engaging in verbal combat at fairs, and being advertized on posters much like wrestlers. The conventional themes used in contests (such as emigrant v. stay-at-home) are only revealed to the *bertsulariak* a few minutes before the match.

BETANCOURT, JOSÉ VICTORIANO (1813–75). Cuban essayist. An advocate by profession, Betancourt contributed 50 essays on manners to newspapers and magazines. While retaining a sense of humour in his writings, he was seriously involved in reformist politics, and was forced to flee to Mexico for his implication in the revolutionary movement of 1868. 'Los curros de Manglai' is a typical essay, describing the plight of Negroes forced to live as outlaws and robbers, on the fringes of society; others include 'Me quiero casar', 'El día de los ingleses', and 'El médico pedante y las viejas curanderas'.

BIANCHI, EDMUNDO (1880–), Uruguayan naturalistic playwright. Bianchi's early works in the study of moral and physical degradation caused some mild interest, but the public he had won was lost when he failed to discover new veins of content or style and he suffered almost total neglect during the latter part of his life. His earlier plays included *Futuro* (1902), *La quiebra* (1910), *Orgullo de pobre* (1912), and *Perdidos en la luz* (1913). Later works are *La senda oscura* and *El hombre absurdo* (both 1932), his best-known play *Los sobrevivientes* (Buenos Aires, 1942) first performed in 1939, *La sinfonía de los héroes* (1940), and *El oro de los mártires* (1941).

Biblia Políglota Complutense, see COMPLUTENSIAN BIBLE.

Biblioteca Americana, La, a journal founded in 1823 by Andrés Bello (q.v.) in London. It ceased publication in 1824, and was succeeded in 1826 by *El Repertorio Americano* (q.v.).

Biblioteca de Autores Españoles, an important series of Spanish classics, begun in 1846 by Bonaventura Carles Aribau (q.v.) and the publisher Manuel Rivadeneyra, which passed from the ownership of the latter's heirs to the Real Academia Española (q.v.). It came to an end in 1880, having comprised 71 volumes. They were of unequal merit, but many can still be used with profit today, and their main importance (it can be argued) was to familiarise the public at no great expense with one view of the corpus of Spanish literature understood in its broadest sense to include historical, geographical, and religious works. Menéndez Pelayo (q.v.) intended to produce a comprehensive continuation of the BAE with his Nueva Biblioteca de Autores Españoles (q.v.), but only 28 volumes of that series appeared, beginning in 1905, and none were commissioned after he died in 1912.

A second series of the BAE (vols. 72–225) appeared between 1954 and 1970. Two volumes of indices are available: one to vols. 1–70 (vol. 71, 1953) and the other to vols. 72–225 (vol. 226, 1970).

Biblioteca Nacional, Madrid, the Spanish National Library was created from a nucleus known as the Queen Mother's Library as early as 1637, but it was founded officially as the Royal Library in Madrid by Philip V in the year 1712, with a collection of some 8,000 MSS. and printed books, of which roughly a quarter had come from the original nucleus.

The library moved in 1809 and then again in 1826 before Isabel II authorized work to begin on the present building in 1866. It was not opened to readers until 1894. It has been a legal deposit library from its foundation, and now contains over 2½ million volumes, including over 26,000 MSS., more than 3,000 incunabula, and at least 50,000 rare books. Its address is Avenida de Calvo Sotelo 20, Madrid.

Bibliotecas Nacionales, The National Libraries of Central and South American countries were established as follows:

Year	Country	Address
1777	Colombia	Apartado 2525, Bogotá.
1792	Ecuador	Aptdo. 163, Quito.
1810	Argentina	Mexico 566, Buenos Aires.
1810	Brazil	Avda. Rio Branco 219–39, Rio de Janeiro.
1813	Chile	Av. B. O'Higgins, Santiago.
1816	Uruguay	Guayabo 1793, Montevideo.
1821	Peru	Avda. Abancay, Apdo. 2335, Lima.
1833	Venezuela	San Francisco a Bolsa, Caracas.
1836	Bolivia	Calle Bolívar, Sucre.
1857	Mexico	Av. Uruguay 67, Mexico City.
1867	El Salvador	San Salvador.
1869	Paraguay	Mariscal Estigarriba 93, Asunción.
1879	Guatemala	10a Calle 9–31, Entre 9a y 10a Avenidas, Guatemala City.
1880	Honduras	6a Av. Salvador Mendieta, Tegucigalpa.
1882	Nicaragua	Calle del Triunfo 302, Apdo. 101, Managua.
1888	Costa Rica	Calle 5, Avdas 1/3, San José.
1892	Panamá	Apdo. 3435, Panama City.
1901	Cuba	Apdo. Oficial 3, Plaza de la República, Havana.

Bidpai, Fables of, see CALILA E DIGNA.

BILBAO, JOSÉ ANTONIO (1919–), b. Asunción. Paraguayan poet. He qualified as a lawyer in 1946, but rather than practise he lived on his ranch and engaged in commerce.

El claro arrobo (1946), *Verde de umbral* (1953), *La estrella y la espiga,* and *Cuaderno de bitácora* (1961), all published in Buenos Aires, reflect his joy in life and acceptance of traditional religious ideas, especially in the eclogues for which he is best known. Though he has kept apart from the other members of the Generation of 1940 (such as Plá and Roa Bastos, qq.v.), he has been influenced by Herib Campos Cervera (q.v.).

BILBAO, MANUEL (1827–95), Chilean historical novelist. His novels were serialized and suffered thereby, rarely attaining the quality of those by his model, Dumas *père.* He achieved enormous fame, however, with *El inquisidor mayor, o historia de unos amores* (1852), on the trial of the Frenchman François Moyen in colonial Lima by the Inquisition. Its anti-clerical tone is echoed in Bilbao's other books, including *El pirata de Guayas* (1865) and *Vida de Francisco Bilbao* (1866).

BIOY CASARES, ADOLFO (1914–), b. Buenos Aires. Argentinian short-story writer and novelist. His first books of short stories were *Caos* (1934) and *Luis Greve muerto* (1937), but he achieved fame with the novella *La invención de Morel* (1940; English translation by Ruth Simms, Austin, Texas, 1964), in which a machine first copies and then reproduces the appearances of reality in space and time by means of a projector. Similar fantastic stories followed: *Plan de evasión* (1945) and *La trama celeste* (1948), using the devices of double identity, tricks of memory, simultaneous worlds (in the title story of the latter), telepathy and supernatural machines. Later books included *El sueño de los héroes* (1954), *Historia prodigiosa* (1956), and *Guirnalda con amores* (1959).

Bioy Casares is married to Silvina Ocampo (q.v.), with whom he has written the detective novel *Los que aman, odian* (1946). With his friend Borges (q.v.), he has edited the authoritative compilation *Poesía gauchesca* (2 vols., Mexico City, 1955) and written, under the pseudonym 'Honorio Bustos Domecq', the detective stories in *Seis problemas para Don Isidro Parodi* (1942) and *Dos fantasías memorables, Un modelo para la muerte* (1946). Together with his wife and Borges, Bioy Casares has compiled *Antología de la literatura fantástica* (1940) and an equally valuable *Antología poética argentina* (1941). His latest works are *El gran serafín* (1967), *Diario de la guerra del cerdo* (1969) and *Dormir al sol* (1973).

See his autobiography, *Años de mocedad: recuerdos* (1963); and D. P. Gallagher, 'The novels and short stories of Adolfo Bioy Casares' in *BHS*, vol. 52, no. 3 (July 1975), pp. 247–66.

BIZCARRONDO, INDALECIO (1831–76), b. Donostiarra. Basque Romantic poet writing under the pseudonym 'Vilinch'. His face was disfigured in a childhood accident, and he died after being wounded by a shell. Lack of formal education did not hinder his power and fluency of expression. A writer of charm and gentleness, he is occasionally overcome by moods of satire and bitter humour. His vocabulary is limited and provincial, but all the more appreciated for its obvious sincerity. His books were published posthumously: *Neurtitzak eta neurri gabeko itzak* (San Sebastián, 1911) and *Bilintx'en bertsuak* (Rentería, n.d.)

See D. Azcue's lecture 'Vilinch', in *El Día* (San Sebastián, May 1931).

BLANCO, ANDRÉS ELOY (1897–1955), b. Cumaná. Venezuelan poet. His first book was *Canto a la espiga y al arado* (1916), but he achieved instant fame in 1923 when the Spanish Real Academia de la Lengua awarded him first prize for his *Canto a España*. In 1928 he was jailed for opposition to the dictator Juan Vicente Gómez. He returned to Venezuela after the death of Gómez in 1935, and in 1946 was appointed President of the National Assembly. When the first free elections were held in 1947 and Rómulo Gallegos (q.v.) was elected President, he appointed Blanco his Foreign Minister, and after the coup of 1948 Blanco went into exile with Gallegos, spending most of his time in Cuba and Mexico. His political essays were collected in *Navegación de altura* (1948); he tried the biographical essay in *Vargas, albacea de la angustia* (1947), poetic prose in *Malvina recobrada* (1957), and the drama in *Abigail* (1931). His poetry grew steadily in stature from *Tierras que me oyeron* (1921) to the less conventional *La aeroplana clueca* (1935), and

the important *Barco de piedra* (1937) and *Baedeker 2000* (1938). His best book is his last, *Giraluna* (Mexico City, 1955) published in the year when he died in a car crash.

BLANCO, TOMÁS (1900–), Puerto Rican historian and essayist. He attempted the short novel in *Los vates* (1949) and poetry in *Los cinco sentidos* (1955), but excelled in the historical and literary criticism genres, the outstanding books being *Prontuario histórico de Puerto Rico* (Madrid, 1935), *El prejuicio racial en Puerto Rico* (1942), and *Sobre Palés Matos* (1950), on a leading poet of Puerto Rico.

BLANCO-FOMBONA, RUFINO (1874–1944), b. Caracas. Venezuelan writer and politician who was jailed during the early years of Juan Vicente Gómez's dictatorship (1908–1935) but fled to Europe and founded the important Editorial América in Madrid in 1914. He returned to Venezuela on Gómez's death.

He began writing as a modernist poet influenced by Rubén Darío (q.v.) in *Pequeña ópera lírica* (1904) and the more mature *Cancionero del amor infeliz* (1917). A mediocre short-story writer, Blanco-Fombona published *Cuentos americanos* (Paris, 1903) first in French and the following year in the original Spanish in Madrid. *El hombre de hierro* (Madrid, 1907) was written in jail; his other novels, *Cantos de la prisión y del destierro* (Madrid, 1911) and *El hombre de oro* (Madrid, 1915) written in exile. All three are mediocre.

His greatest contribution was in the field of the essay and literary criticism, beginning with *Letras y letrados de Hispano-América* (Paris, 1908) and *La evolución política y social de Hispano-América* (Madrid, 1911) and continuing with a stream of valuable studies: *Grandes escritores de América, siglo XIX* (Madrid, 1917), *El conquistador español del siglo XVI* (Madrid, 1922), the seminal *El modernismo y los poetas modernistas* (Madrid, 1929), and *El espejo de tres faces* (Santiago de Chile, 1937).

A useful anthology of Blanco-Fombona, *Obras selectas*, has been edited by G. Márquez (Madrid, 1958). His autobiographical *Camino de imperfección: diario de mi vida, 1906–13* (1929) should be read in conjunction with F. Carmona Nenclares, *Rufino Blanco-Fombona* (1944).

BLANCO WHITE, JOSÉ MARÍA (1775–1841), b. Seville. Poet, journalist, and religious polemicist. On arriving in Andalusia from Ireland, his family changed its name to Blanco y Crespo, a name used interchangeably with Blanco White by the author. Brought up as a Roman Catholic, he was ordained in 1800, but became sceptical after reading Feijoo and

Fénelon, and became a liberal. In 1810 he left for England, where he founded *El Español* (1810–13) to crusade against Spanish colonialism. His first book, *Letters from Spain, by Don Leucadio Doblado* (London, 1822) established his reputation in England, where he was befriended by Southey, Lord Holland, J. S. Mill and Mrs. Hemans. After conversion to Anglicanism in the 1820s, when he lived in Oxford and Dublin, he settled in Liverpool in the 1830s and there became a Unitarian, writing his *Practical and internal evidence against Catholicism* (2nd edn., 1826) and *Second travels of an Irish gentleman in search of a religion* (2 vols., Dublin, 1833), occasioned by T. Moore's *Travels of an Irish gentleman in search of a religion*.

In 1824–5 he edited *Variedades, o Mensagero de Londres*. Coleridge considered 'Mysterious night' the finest sonnet in English. Blanco White's poetry, influenced by Quintana and Arjona (qq.v.), is found in vol. 67 (1875) of the BAE. Menéndez Pelayo wrote of him from the Spanish viewpoint in his history of Spanish heretics, but the best lives are his own autobiography, *Life of the Reverend Joseph Blanco White written by himself* (ed. J. Hamilton Thom, 3 vols., London, 1845; and trans. by A. Garnica, (1975) and the corrective *Vida y obras de don José María Blanco y Crespo* (1921) by Mario Méndez Bejarano.

BLANCO Y CRESPO, JOSÉ MARÍA, see BLANCO WHITE, José María.

Blanquerna, a Utopian novel by Ramon Llull (q.v.) written in Montpellier *c.* 1283–95 and edited by Monsenor Salvador Galmés in Els Nostres Clàssics (Barcelona, 1914). *Blanquerna* is not only the first major novel in Catalan (and still one of the most absorbing), it is also reputed to be the first novel in any Romance language after the French prose Arthurian romances. A detailed picture of life and conditions in the late 13th c., the novel takes its theme from the notions of Christian reformation that Llull propounded elsewhere in theological and philosophical terms.

Blanquerna is the son of Evast and Aloma, who arrange for his marriage to Tana. But Blanquerna decides to enter a monastery, and Tana enters a convent. Blanquerna reforms his monastery according to his ideals and when elected bishop reforms his diocese. Elevated to cardinal and finally to Pope, Blanquerna realises that high office is incompatible with spiritual progress and retires to solitary life as a hermit. He is sought out by the Emperor and when they meet they converse about the contemplative life in the *Libre d'Amic e Amat*, the section based according to Llull's preface on

Sufi writings but delightfully coloured by troubadour motifs traceable to Llull's early writings, which he destroyed in contempt.

The language of *Blanquerna* is poetic and brilliantly varied, displaying Llull's scholarship and gift for metaphor. A deep thinker incapable of following the traditional Christian *apologia* of the time, Llull mastered the subtlety of Muslim theology and the sonority of the Arabic phrase.

Blanquerna was translated into Castilian in the 18th c. and into English by E. Allison Peers (1926). R. Pring-Mill contributed 'Entorn de la unitat del Libre d'Amic e Amat' to *Estudis Romànics*, vol. 10 (1962).

BLASCO IBÁÑEZ, VICENTE (1867–1928), b. Valencia. Novelist and travel writer who left home early to work as amanuensis to the popular novelist Fernández y González (q.v.). He learned from him the techniques of rapid composition, forceful description of people and their customs, and ways of achieving suspense and keeping the reader's interest on every page. He has little sense of humour and no sense of irony, but the vigour of his writing is undeniable and in his few Valencian stories and novels, such as the masterpiece *Cañas y barro* (1902), all the drama and tension of Zola have been brought into Spanish without effort or miscalculation.

His unpopular political opinions caused him great trouble, including prison sentences and exile from 1890 to early 1891, when he returned to Spain to found the daily *El Pueblo*. He was active in political life, founding the Blasquista party in opposition to the Sorianistas of Rodrigo Soriano, but in 1909 gave this up and travelled to South America, where he lectured. He took the part of the Allies in World War I, earning the French Légion d'Honneur. In 1920 he was given a degree by the George Washington University. Finally exiled when Primo de Rivera came to power in 1923, he died in Menton a rich man due to the ever-growing popularity of his vigorously-written novels.

A writer conscious of the manliness of his heroes, he took his principal figures not only from political life and agitators for social justice, but also from the fishermen of Valencia, bullfighters, and ordinary labourers. His later works suffer from his easy popularity, and are more loosely written, lacking the hard edge of bitterness and personal suffering which characterized the Valencian novels of his youth.

His first period is also his best: that of the regional novels *Arroz y tartana* (1894), on the Valencian middle class; *Flor de Mayo* (1895), on Valencian fisherfolk; *La barraca* (1898), on the evil of usury; *Entre naranjos* (1900), on the relations between an artist and a politician;

Sónnica la cortesana (1901), a historical novel about Hannibal's sack of Sagunto, based on the history of Silius Italicus (*Punica*, A.D. 1st c.) and inspired by Flaubert's *Salammbô* (1862); and the magnificent *Cañas y barro* (1902), turning on the love of Tonet and Neleta in the Albufera.

Thesis novels written 1903-5 include the most interesting *La catedral* (1903), in which the revolutionary protagonist Gabriel Luna dies while trying to prevent the jewels of the Madonna from being stolen: *El intruso* (1904), set in Bilbao, is the story of the piety of Sánchez Morueta and is an overt attack on the Jesuits; *La bodega* (1905) tells of the death of the anarchist Fernando Salvatierra in the country near Jérez, at the hands of the brother of the woman he had violated; in the Madrid novel *La horda* (1905), Maltrana believes in social equality but fights to secure privileges for his son.

Blasco Ibáñez wrote (1906-9) a series of psychological novels: *La maja desnuda* (1906), on the painter Mariano Renovales; *Sangre y arena* (1908), centring on the *torero* Juan Gallardo, with much vivid *costumbrismo* of the bullring and the *aficionados* of all social classes; *Los muertos mandan* (1908), two different novels about the hero Jaime Febrer; and *Luna Benamor* (1909), on love frustrated by anti-Jewish prejudice.

The European or cosmopolitan novels of Blasco Ibáñez were written between 1916 and 1919. The first is *Los cuatro jinetes del Apocalipsis* (1916), an undistinguished but highly popular story of World War I and its ramifications in contemporary society; the second *Mare Nostrum* (1918), on the submarine war and decidedly hostile to Germany; and the third *Los enemigos de la mujer* (1919), which sees the war from the viewpoint of rich aristocrats in Monte Carlo. His historical novels 1925-9 include: *El Papa del mar* (1925), a defence of Pedro Luna; *A los pies de Venus* (1926), on the Borgias; *En busca del Gran Kan* (1928), a novel on Columbus; and *El caballero de la Virgen* (1929), on the *conquistador* Alonso de Ojeda.

Blasco intended to write an American cycle of Balzacian proportions, of which *Los Argonautas* (1914) was only the prologue. Of this great cycle, only *La tierra de todos* (1922) was completed, taking as its heroine a Helen of the New World who provokes a civil war. Three adventure novels appeared 1922-30: *El paraíso de las mujeres* (1922), *La reina Calafia* (1923), and *El fantasma de las alas de oro* (1930). His four travel books are *En el país del arte* (1896), on Italy; *Oriente* (1907), on cities between Geneva and (as it then was) Constantinople; *La Argentina y sus grandezas* (1910); and the often brilliant *La vuelta al mundo de un novelista* (3 vols., 1924-5).

Blasco's short stories, like his novels, are finest when most deeply engaged in regional social problems and psychology. These are *Cuentos valencianos* (1893), *La condenada y otros cuentos* (1896). His long stories appear in: *El préstamo de la difunta* (1921), *Las novelas de la Costa Azul* (1924), *Las novelas del amor y de la muerte* (1927), and *El adiós a Schubert* (1927). The *Obras completas* (40 vols., Valencia, 1923-34) have been superseded by the edition in 3 vols. (Madrid, 1964-5).

See E. Gascó Contell, *Genio y figura de Vicente Blasco Ibáñez* (1957; 2nd edn. 1967) with a good bibliography; A. Grove Day and E. Knowtton, *V. Blasco Ibáñez* (New York, 1962); Enric Sebastià, *Valencia en les novelles de Blasco Ibáñez* (Valencia, 1966); and J. N. Loubès and J. L. León Roca, *Blasco Ibáñez, diputado y novelista* (Toulouse, 1972).

BLECUA, José Manuel (1913–), b. Alcolea de Cinca. Literary critic and professor of Spanish Literature at a number of universities, most recently at Barcelona. He has written a brief *Historia de la literatura española* (2 vols., Saragossa, 1942) and a detailed study of the *Cántico* of Jorge Guillén (q.v.), as well as several anthologies, *Los pájaros* . . ., *Las flores* . . ., and *El mar en la poesía española* (1943-5), the most important being *Floresta de lírica española* (1957; 2nd end., 2 vols., 1968). Blecua has published editions of the *Libro infinido* of Don Juan Manuel (q.v., Saragossa, 1934) the 2nd edition (Granada, 1952) also includes Manuel's *Tractado de la Asunción*); the *Laberinto de fortuna* of Juan de Mena (q.v., Clásicos Castellanos, 1943); the Saragossa University Library's three-volume *Cancionero de 1628* (1945); J. Alfay's *Poesías varias de grandes ingenios españoles* published in Saragossa, 1654 (Saragossa, 1946); the *Rimas inéditas* of Herrera (q.v., 1948); the *Rimas de Lupercio y Bartolomé Leonardo de Argensola* (2 vols., Saragossa, 1950-1); Quevedo's *Lágrimas de Hieremías castellanas* with E. M. Wilson (1953); Lope de Vega's *La Dorotea* (q.v., 1955); a privately-printed edition of 200 copies of Augusto Ferrán's *La soledad* (Santander, 1955); and the *Poesías* of Quevedo (Barcelona, 1963).

BLEST GANA, Alberto (1830-1920), b. Santiago. Chilean novelist. Son of an Irish doctor and a Chilean woman, Blest Gana studied at Santiago military academy and 1847-52 continued his education in France, then returning to teach at the academy until 1855, when he retired to devote all his time to writing.

His early novels were written before he came under the decisive influence of Balzac: *Una escena social* (1853), *Los desposados* (1855), *Engaños y desengaños* (1855), *El primer amor* (1858), and others. Their plots are romantic, and the language full of the clichés and threadbare style that bedevil Blest Gana's work throughout his long career. His major theme is that of innocence defiled, or in economic terms the exploitation of the mind and spirit of man for material ends. He is the father of the Chilean social novel, elevating the anecdotal *costumbrismo* to full documentary stature. The poverty and careless-ness of his style prevented him from attaining the position of a great novelist.

His first successful novel was *La aritmética en el amor* (1860), striking in its ambitiousness as the first Chilean novel to portray recognizable Chilean contemporary characters, but whereas Balzac (his model) dealt with extremely complex stratification in society, Blest Gana was forced to work with Chile's social rigidity, which offered him much less scope. It was followed by *El pago de las deudas* (1861), *Martín Rivas* and *El ideal de una calavera* (both 1862), and *La flor de la higuera* (1864), the last published in the year when he drafted *Durante la reconquista*, an historical novel set on the eve of Independence. Blest Gana destroyed this draft and during a long diplomatic career wrote little, publishing a new draft of his Independence novel in 1897, *El loco Estero* (1909) on the Santiago of his youth, and the interesting *Los transplantados* (1904), on a rich Latin American innocent (Mercedes Canalejas) who is deceived into a marriage of convenience by a poor European aristocrat and commits suicide.

Sus mejores páginas (1961), selected with a biographical-critical study by Manuel Rojas, should be supplemented by the collection *Costumbres y viajes: páginas olvidadas* (1947).

See 'Alone', *Don Alberto Blest Gana* (1940), and the important studies by Raúl Silva Castro, *Blest Gana y su novela 'Durante la reconquista'* (1934), *Alberto Blest Gana* (1941), and his newer, shorter study, *Alberto Blest Gana* (1955).

BLOMBERG, HÉCTOR PEDRO (1890–1955), b. Buenos Aires. Argentinian poet, short-story writer, and novelist. His childhood was spent in Paraguay, and he travelled in Brazil and Europe before settling in Buenos Aires as a journalist on *La Nación* and *La Razón*. His poetry is popular in tone, its atmosphere often senti-mental or tragic: *A la deriva* (1912), *La canción lejana* (Barcelona, 1912), *Las islas de la inquietud* (1914), *Gaviotas perdidas* (1921), and *Bajo la Cruz del Sur* (1922), are all of variable quality.

His best book was the collection of short stories *Las puertas de Babel* (1920); other collec-tions were *Los soñadores de bajo fondo* and *Los peregrinos de la espuma* (both 1924). His most important play, set in the Rosas period, was *La sangre de las guitarras* (first performed 1930). Among his dramatic poems were *Pancho*

Garmendía and *Los pastores de estrellas* (both 1922). His novels included *La otra pasión* (1925), and *Naves* (1927), in which he reverted to his favoured themes of history and the sea. Among his essays were *Martí, el último liberador* (1945) and *Poetas que cantaron al indio de América* (1950).

Blood, Purity of, see LIMPIEZA DE SANGRE.

BOBADILLA, EMILIO (1862–1921), b. Cárdenas. Cuban poet, novelist, and satirist better known by his pen-name, 'Fray Candil'. He lived for many years in France and Spain.

His novels are sensational and poorly con-structed, imitated from Felipe Trigo (q.v.) and Octave Mirbeau: *Novelas en germen* (Madrid, 1900), *A fuego lento* (Barcelona, 1903), *En la noche dormida* (Madrid, 1903), and *En pos de la paz* (Madrid, 1917). It is for his aggressively sarcastic essays that 'Fray Candil' is now remembered: *Escaramuzas: sátiras y críticas* (1888), *Capirotazos: sátiras y críticas* (1890), *Triquitraques: críticas* (1892), *Solfeo, crítica y sátiras* (1894), and *La vida intelectual: folletos críticos* (1895) all published in Madrid. *Artículos periodísticos* (1952) is a useful anthology selected by Domingo Mesa and Surama Ferrer.

Bobadilla wrote much poetry in the Romantic manner, perhaps influenced by Núñez de Arce even more than by Herrera y Reissig or J. Asunción Silva: *Relámpagos* (1884), *Fiebres* (Madrid, 1889), and *Vórtice* (1903). Bobadilla is best viewed as a poet through the *Selección de poemas* (1962) produced in Havana. Little of his travel sketches can be read with profit today, for he reported art exhibitions of the time unaware of the true currents, and lacked both depth and sympathy in his portrait of London, and in the rather better *Viajando por España* (1910).

See G. Barinaga Ponce de León, *Estudio crítico-biográfico de Emilio Bobadilla (Fray Candil)* (1926).

Bocadas de oro (or the *Bonium*), one of the most important collections of medieval wisdom-literature, translated into Castilian at the command of Alfonso 'el Sabio' (q.v.) from the *Book of sayings* of Abu 'l-Wafa Mubashir ben Fati' (12th c.) and edited by Hermann Knust in *Mitteilungen aus dem Eskurial* (Tübingen, 1879), pp. 66–394.

Bonium, King of Persia, departs for India to question wise men about knowledge, truth, and wisdom. Their replies form the bulk of the book, which was well loved and often reprinted in the 15th- and 16th-cs. The *sententiae* attributed to Indian philosophers are in fact derived from Greek philosophy and a Greek philosopher introduces each chapter. Caxton's *Dictes and sayings of the philosophers* (1477) was the English adaptation by the Earl of Rivers of the *Bocadas de oro*.

BOCÁNGEL Y UNZUETA, Gabriel (1603–58), b. Madrid. Poet. Librarian to the Cardinal-Infante Don Fernando. The *Rimas y prosas, junto con la Fábula de Leandro y Ero* (1627) are influenced by Góngora and Jáuregui within the tradition of *culteranismo* (q.v.). He also wrote a number of occasional poems (such as that on the feast of St. John the Baptist in Madrid, 1648); and panegyrics (such as that on the Infante Carlos, 1633). Generally, Bocángel's love poetry is pedestrian, but at its best it achieves a sensuous quality, with sharply visual images. He wrote a play, 'El emperador fingido', which appeared in *Parte 43 de Comedias nuevas* (1678) pp. 207–42. R. Benítez Claros edited the *Obras* (2 vols., 1946) of Bocángel for the Biblioteca de Antiguos Libros Hispánicos, and also wrote the standard *Vida y poesía de Bocángel* (1950).

Bodas de sangre, a play by Federico García Lorca (q.v.) first performed in 1933. It is the first of his three folk tragedies, the second being *Yerma*, and the last *La casa de Bernarda Alba* (qq.v.). Leonardo Félix, the only named character, abducts the bride, his former sweetheart, on her wedding day. The lovers run through the forest, encountering the Moon, who asks for blood, and Death as a beggar-woman. The bridegroom, whose father and brother had been killed by the Félix family, pursues Leonardo and in the struggle both men are killed. The bride goes to the bridegroom's mother to console her, and offers her throat for sacrifice, but the mother ignores her completely and the play ends as it began with the woman's dread of a small knife that can slaughter a 'bull' of a man. The play's imagery is elemental, the vocabulary tautly precise yet vivid with poetry. The use of a chorus adds depth to a rural tragedy about honour and the helplessness of women and tenderness in a brutish male world.

Though the play was inspired by newspaper accounts of an actual event in the province of Almería which Lorca had read many years before, his sources also include folk tales and the technique of fusing music and drama from the Golden Age *comedia*, death symbolism reminiscent of Maeterlinck, and the verbal charm and archaic atmosphere of Valle-Inclán (q.v.). The play was first published in 1935.

Boedo Street group, a literary group of the 1920s named after a run-down lower-class area of Buenos Aires inhabited mostly by Creole immigrants, in contrast to the Florida Street group (q.v.). Members included Roberto Arlt, Álvaro Yunque (Arístides Gandolfi Herrero), César Tiempo (Israel Zeitlin), Enrique Amorim, Olivari, González Tuñón, Guijarro, Riccio, Barletta, Elías Castelnuovo, and Mariani. However, membership of the two groups became steadily more fluid with the passing years, and Mariani, for example, wrote in the elegant, pure style of Florida Street. Their stated aim was to 'llevar al verso, al cuento, a la novela, al ensayo, al teatro, a la crítica, esa visión definitiva que en las masas comenzaba a encenderse como una posibilidad inmediata'. These anarchists, marxists, and often well-meaning liberals without extremist ideology were joined by some Jewish writers in *Los Pensadores*, later called *Claridad*. The preferred medium of the Boedo Street group was the novel.

BOEHL VON FABER, Cecilia (1796–1877), b. Morges, Vaud, Switzerland. Novelist and *costumbrista*, writing as 'Fernán Caballero'. She was the daughter of the Hamburg Hispanophile Johann Niklaus Boehl von Faber (q.v.).

Brought up as a Roman Catholic by her father, a convert, Cecilia married a young infantry captain, Antonio Planells, at the age of 19, but he died in Puerto Rico within a year. In 1822 she married again, this time the Marqués de Arco Hermoso, living in his homes in Seville and in the country, where she gathered most of the material for use in her books of rural life and manners. After the Marqués died in 1835, she remarried for the last time in 1837: her third husband was Antonio de Ayala, and it was because of her newly reduced circumstances that she was forced to consider publishing her writings. *El Heraldo* first published *La Gaviota* (2 vols., 1856; ed. J. Rodríguez-Luis, Barcelona, 1972) as a *folletín* in 1849, and this 'novela original de costumbres españolas' written originally in French was promptly hailed as the work of a new Walter Scott. It was composed in reaction to the vapid, sensational *folletines* then popular in daily newspapers, and quite apart from the plot gave a real insight into the way that Spaniards were then behaving and speaking. The story is that of the failed marriage of Stein, a German doctor, and the daughter of a fisherman, la Gaviota, who falls in love with a bullfighter and leaves her husband to become a professional singer. Dr. Stein leaves for the U.S.A., and la Gaviota finally returns home, her voice ruined, to marry a barber. The scenes of Andalusian life, the real *raison d'être* of the novel, are utterly convincing as far as they go, but even here 'Fernán Caballero' has made a conscious selection of these elements she believes to be 'picturesque'. *La Gaviota* has been edited by G. W. Umphrey and F. Sánchez y Escribano (1931).

Then followed *Clemencia* (2 vols., 1852), in which an unhappily married woman accepts her lot with fortitude; *Cuadros de costumbres populares andaluces* (Seville, 1852); *La farisea* (1853), based on the Puerto Rican experiences of her first marriage; *Lágrimas: novela de costumbres contemporáneas* (Cádiz, 1853); *La familia de Alvareda: novela original de costumbres populares* (1856), first drafted in German thirty years earlier and most recently edited by L. Hernández Alfonso (1963); *Una en otra, Callar en vida y perdonar en muerte* and *Con mal o con bien a los tuyos te ten* (all 1856); *Un servilón y un liberalito, o tres almas de Dios* (1857) edited by N. L. Weisinger (Philadelphia, 1924); *Relaciones* (1857); and the short *cuadro de costumbres Deudas pagadas* (1860).

'Fernán Caballero' aimed to provide truth, *naturalidad* and patriotism, for which some case can be made; but her faults of literary judgement make heavy demands on the modern reader.

Her first *Obras completas* were in 19 vols. (1855–8); the 2nd in 17 (1905–14) in Colección de Escritores Castellanos; the 3rd beginning in BAE (5 vols., 1961), vols. 136–40, edited with a good bibliography by J. M. Castro y Calvo. Fernán Caballero was an inveterate letter-writer, and three collections of her letters have appeared: *Cartas* (1919, ed. Diego de Valencina); *Epistolario* (Barcelona, 1922, ed. A. López Argüello); and *Cartas inéditas* (1961, ed. S. Montoto). Though unfashionable, she still commands affection as a Hispanophile, as can be seen in the *Recuerdos de Fernán Caballero* (Bilbao, 1910) by L. Coloma and the modern studies by J. F. Montesinos, *Fernán Caballero: ensayo de justificación* (Mexico City, 1961); J. Herrero, *Fernán Caballero: un nuevo planteamiento* (1963); S. Montoto, *Fernán Caballero: algo más que una biografía* (Seville, 1969).

BOEHL VON FABER, JOHANN NIKLAUS (1770–1863), b. Hamburg. German Hispanist, businessman, and literary critic. He was German consul in Cádiz and a convert to Roman Catholicism. The father of Cecilia Boehl von Faber (q.v.), Johann Niklaus first took the limelight with articles in the Cádiz press (1814) expounding Schlegel's favourable views on the traditional Spanish ballad and the 'irregular' drama of the Spanish Golden Age which was then out of fashion. These articles led to a dispute with Alcalá Galiano (q.v.), who attacked him from the neoclassical standpoint, being supported by the liberal José Joaquín de Mora who in June 1818 managed to prevent

further articles by Boehl von Faber from appearing. The question became political, the liberals supporting French neoclassical theories, and the conservatives such as Boehl, López Soler, and Agustín Durán (qq.v.) considering themselves as the upholders of the Christian tradition and wrongly identifying it with the contemporary world view of romanticism.

Barred from local periodicals, Boehl published a trio of pamphlets entitled *Pasatiempos* (1818–19) under the pseudonym 'El Alcalde de Daganzos', published together in book form as *Vindicaciones de Calderón, y del teatro antiguo español contra los afrancesados en literatura* (1820). The polemic, studied by C. Pitollet in *La querelle calderonienne* (Paris, 1909), was of course won by the Hispanophiles led by Boehl, who was elected honorary member of the Real Academia Española. Anticipating A. A. Parker and Valbuena Prat, among others, Boehl was also among the first to claim that Calderón's religious *autos* were as valuable as the secular comedies, asserting that 'la verdadera poesía es el prototipo de un mundo del todo espiritual.'

As a scholar, Boehl made two important contributions: the *Floresta de rimas antiguas castellanas* (Hamburg, 1825) and *Teatro anterior a Lope de Vega* (1832). For details of his important library, see the provisional catalogue in *RABM*, vol. 9 (1883), pp. 180–7, 204–33 and 312–9.

BOFARULL Y DE BROCÁ, ANTONIO DE (1821–92), b. Reus. Historian and playwright. Founder of the satirical review *El Hongo* and drama critic under the pen-name 'Lo Coblejador de Moncada'. He contributed to the liveliness of the Catalan literary Revival, and the renewal of the Jocs Florals. His plays included *Pedro 'el Católico', rey de Aragón* (1842), and *Roger de Flor* (1845), while his only historical novel was the mediocre *Blanca o la huérfana de Menargues* (1876). He is best known for his historical works, for which he drew on the Archives of the Kingdom of Aragon as its Director for many years: *Crónica de Pedro IV 'el Ceremonioso'* (1845), *Hazañas y recuerdos de los catalanes . . . hasta el enlace de Fernando con Isabel* (1846), *Historia de don Jaime I* (1848), and *La confederación catalana-aragonesa: historia crítica civil y eclesiástica de Cataluña* (1878).

BOFILL I MATES, JAUME (1878–1933), Catalan poet epitomizing the style of *Noucentisme* (q.v.). Bofill is more serious and ironic than his friend Josep Carner (q.v.) in *La muntanya d'ametistes* (1908), the medievalistic *Somnis* (1913), *La ciutat d'ivori* (1918) on his ideal city, and *Sàtires* (1928). Bofill used the pen-name 'Guerau de Liost'. His collected works are in *Obra poètica completa.Proses literàries* (Barcelona, 1948).

BOIL, CARLOS, see BOYL VIVES DE CANESMAS, Carlos.

BOIX Y RICARTE, VICENTE (1813–80), b. Játiva. Playwright, historian, and poet. A melodramatic novelist in the tradition of Dumas, Boix wrote *El encubierto de Valencia* (1852) and the voluminous but unreliable *Historia de la ciudad y reino de Valencia* (3 vols., 1845). His *Obras poéticas* appeared in two volumes: *Poesías históricas y caballerescas* (Valencia, 1850) and *Poesías líricas y dramáticas* (Valencia, 1851). There is a broader selection of his work in *Obras literarias selectas* (Valencia, 1880).

See L. Querol Roso, 'Vicente Boix, el historiador romántico de Valencia', in *Anales del Centro de Cultura Valenciana*, vols. 12–14 (1951–3).

BOJ, SILVERIO, pseudonym used in the early works of Walter Guido Wéyland (q.v.).

Bolívar, see REVISTA DE LAS INDIAS.

BOLLO, SARAH (1904–), b. Montevideo. Uruguayan poet and critic. Her poetry, in reaction against the feminine erotic poetry conventional in Latin America, concentrates on spiritual sensibility. Her play *Pola Salvarrieta* (perf. 1944; publ. 1945), is a verse tragedy set in the Bolívar period, with a Colombian heroine.

The publication of her poetry began with the immature *Diálogos de las luces perdidas* (1927) and *Nocturnos del fuego* (1931). *Las voces ancladas* (1933) consisted of prose poems. Her personal voice became audible in *Regreso* (1934), *Baladas del corazón cercano* (1935), *Ciprés de púrpura* (1944), and *Ariel prisionero, Ariel libertado* (1948), which were the basis for a selection published in 1948 as *Antología lírica.* Subsequent books have included *Espirituales* (1963), *Tierra y cielo* (1964), and *Diana transfigurada* (1964).

She has written the standard *Literatura uruguaya, 1807–1965* (2 vols., 1965) and the following lesser studies: *La poesía de Juana de Ibarbourou* (1935), the essays *Sobre José Enrique Rodó* (1951) and *El modernismo en el Uruguay: ensayo estilístico* (1951), and *Delmira Agustini: espíritu de su obra* (1963).

BOMBAL, MARÍA LUISA (1910–), b. Viña del Mar. Chilean novelist, who studied philosophy and literature at the Sorbonne. She is the author of two novels, avoiding both Chilean fictional stereotypes of *criollismo* and neorealism: *La última niebla* (1935), rewritten with her husband in a longer English version in New York as *House of mist* (1947); and *La amortajada*

(1938), a book translated as *The shrouded woman* (New York, 1948) and described by Jorge Luis Borges as a 'libro de triste magia . . . de oculta organización eficaz'.

La última niebla tells the story, with a haunting and persistent use of fog and mist as symbol and simile, of a married woman lacking true love. It has been compared to Hoffmann's fiction, to the technique of Virginia Woolf, and at points resembles the work of Barrios and d'Halmar (qq.v.) in its subjectivism. The second edition of 1941 added two novelettes, also centred on unhappy love. *La amortajada* is the story of a corpse, told in the first person through the use of flashbacks.

BONILLA, ABELARDO (1899–), b. Cartago, Costa Rica. Literary historian, essayist, and in *El valle nublado* (1944) a novelist of ideas, quietly attacking political hypocrisy and corruption. His *Historia de la literatura costarricense* (2 vols., 1959) was commissioned by the University of Costa Rica.

Bonium, another title given to the *Bocadas de oro* (q.v.).

BOOZ, MATEO, pseudonym of the Argentinian novelist Miguel Ángel Correa (q.v.).

BORGES, JORGE LUIS (1899–), b. Buenos Aires. One of the greatest short-story writers in world literature, and an incomparable essayist whose writings have exercised an immense influence far beyond the boundaries of his native Argentina. Borges is also a poet, but his narrative excellence frequently tends to override his lyrical inspiration. His prose style combines brevity, elegance, and ambiguity in tales of striking originality. His early years were spent in Buenos Aires, but his grandmother was English and he stresses that he learnt to read English (devouring Robert Louis Stevenson with appreciation) before Spanish.

He studied in Geneva from 1914–18, then travelled in France, Germany, and Majorca until he settled in Spain in 1919, joining the Grupo Ultra in Madrid. He left for Buenos Aires in 1921 and there spread the renovatory message of *ultraísmo* (q.v.) in magazines such as *Prisma, Proa, Nosotros,* and *Martín Fierro* and in his first book *Fervor de Buenos Aires* (1923).

The first series of *Proa* ran from 1922 to 1923, but the co-founder Macedonio Fernández (q.v.) resigned, and Borges founded a second series (1924–5) with Ricardo Güiraldes (q.v.), Pablo Rojas Paz, and Brandán Caraffa. From 1925 Borges was invited to contribute to the Sunday supplement of the daily *La Prensa* and thenceforth contributed to most magazines of any value in Argentina, and especially to *Sur* (q.v.). His biography is largely the story of the evolution of his reading and intellectual development. The only external incidents of note were his dismissal by Perón from his post as Director of the National Library for daring to sign a manifesto against Perón, and Borges's increasing blindness, both of which difficultuties Borges faced with the stoicism marking his literature. A profound student of occidental and oriental systems of thought, he has nevertheless remained a sceptic. A man of universal culture, he subtly introduces paradox and metaphor from the most diverse sources, and it can be said that his essays and stories constitute a series of literary problems which he states in brief, and attempts to resolve with economy and grace. His essays are *Inquisiciones* (1925), *El tamaño de mi esperanza* (1926), *El idioma de los argentinos* (1928), *Evaristo Carriego* (1930), *Discusión* (1932), *Las kenningar* (1933), *Historia de la eternidad* (1936) which also includes 'Las kenningar', *Nueva refutación del tiempo* (1947), *Aspectos de la literatura gauchesca* (Montevideo, 1950), *Antiguas literaturas germánicas* (with Delia Ingenieros, Mexico City, 1951), *Otras inquisiciones* (1952), *El 'Martín Fierro'* (with Margarita Guerrero, 1953), *Leopoldo Lugones* (with Betina Edelberg, 1955), and the miscellany *Elogio de la sombra* (1969), which includes stories and poems.

Borges's first book was a collection of poetry, and he has continued to compose poetry throughout his life on his central preoccupations of time and timelessness, ambiguity of identity, paradox, and the cyclical nature of knowledge and history. After *Fervor de Buenos Aires*, he published *Luna de enfrente* (1925) and *Cuaderno de San Martín* (1929), later repudiated as being too doctrinally 'ultraistic' in tone. His subjects in the early poems are often Creole and regional, showing the provincial side to his literary character which seldom appears in his stories. The *Antología personal* (1961), *Obra poética, 1923–1967* (1967), *Nueva antología personal* (1968), and the poems in the miscellany *Elogio de la sombra* (1969) reflect a metaphysical tendency. There is an excellent bilingual *Selected poems 1923–1967* (London, 1968) with translations by thirteen poets.

But Borges is celebrated above all for his magnificent stories; *Historia universal de la infamia* (1935; revised and augmented in *Obras completas*, 1954), the first great if laconic work in the tradition of Latin American 'magic realism' which was to culminate in the masterpieces of Gabriel García Márquez (q.v.); *El jardín de senderos que se bifurcan* (1941); *Artificios* (1944); *Ficciones, 1935–44* (q.v., 1944; new edn. in *Obras completas* as *Ficciones*, 1956, collecting the two previous anthologies); *El Aleph* (1949; new edn.

in *Obras completas*, 1957); *La muerte y la brújula* (anthology with some new stories, 1951); *El hacedor* (q.v., 1st edn. in *Obras completas*, 1960); *Cuentos* (1968); *Elogio de la sombra* (1969); *El informe de Brodie* (1970); and *El Congreso* (1971); and *El libro de arena* (1975).

Most of Borges's writings have been translated into English, though selections of stories have overlapped with confusing titles, since several translators have been occupied with his work. He has admitted the influence of Chesterton and other profoundly 'English' writers, including Lewis Carroll. His stories have been described by D. P. Gallagher as 'not only coolly lucid cerebral games but often highly affective, poetic expressions of the fragility of the world and of man'. The element of play so frequently involved led Borges to collaborate with Adolfo Bioy Casares (q.v.) in detective stories under the joint pseudonym of 'H. Bustos Domecq': *Seis problemas para don Isidro Parodi* (1942), *Dos fantasías memorables* (1946), and *Crónicas de Bustos Domecq* (1967). As 'B. Suárez Lynch', they published *Un modelo para la muerte* (1946).

Borges has produced several anthologies: *Antología clásica de la literatura argentina* (n.d., but 1937) with P. Henríquez Ureña; *El compadrito: su destino, sus barrios, su música* (1947) with S. Bullrich Palenque; *Cuentos breves y extraordinarios* (1953) with A. Bioy Casares; *Manual de zoología fantástica* (1957) with Margarita Guerrero, enlarged as *El libro de los seres imaginarios*; and *El matrero* (1970).

The literature on Borges is daunting: see H. J. Becco, *Jorge Luis Borges: bibliografía total, 1923–1973* (1973). Among the indispensable items are the special issue of *L'Herne* (Paris, 1964), with a good bibliography and iconography; A. M. Barrenechea, *La expresión de la irrealidad en la obra de Borges* (Mexico City, 1957); Georges Charbonnier, *Entretiens avec Jorge Luis Borges* (Paris, 1967); J. Alazraki, *La prosa narrativa de Jorge Luis Borges* (1968; 2nd edn., 1974); M. Ferrer, *Borges y la Nada* (London, 1971); 'Autobiographical essay' in *The Aleph and other stories, 1933–1969* (London, 1971, pp. 201–60) edited and translated by N. T. di Giovanni; and the special issue of *Iberoromania*, May 1975.

BORJA, ARTURO (1892–1912), b. Quito, Ecuador. Poet, who was the son of Luis Felipe Borja, the commentator on the Civil Code. Borja introduced post-Modernism to Ecuador from France, which he visited as a boy. His posthumous collection *La flauta de ónix* (1920) consists of twenty-seven of his poems and three in homage from his friends.

BORJA, CÉSAR (1852–1910), b. Quito, Ecuador. Poet, politician and doctor. Exiled for his political views, Borja returned as Minister of Public Education when the liberals came to power. His major work is *Flores tardías y joyas ajenas* (1909) in the first section of which his poetical themes are childhood, love of nature, and his various hatreds. The *Joyas ajenas* are versions of the major French poets of his period, especially Baudelaire and Hérédia.

BORJA Y ARAGÓN, FRANCISCO DE (1581–1658), Spanish poet descended from the ruling house of Aragón and from the Italian Borgia family. He was Prince of Squillace, Italy (Spanish: Esquilache) and Viceroy of Peru (1615–21). He founded in Lima the Universidad de San Marcos.

Through his friendship and literary affinity with the brothers Leonardo de Argensola (qq.v.), Borja resisted *culteranismo* except in such works as *El canto de Antonio y Cleopatra*. His courtly poems are elegant but relatively simple. The best of his 300 ballads or 'romances artísticos' are excellent. His *La Passión de Nuestro Señor Iesu-Christo* (1638), written in *tercetos*, is collected in the *Obras en verso* (1639, several times reprinted). He wrote a dull epic poem to celebrate deeds of his ancestor Alfonso V of Aragon: *Nápoles recuperada por el rei don Alonso* (Saragossa, 1651). In his old age, Borja translated *Meditaciones y oraciones* (Brussels, 1661) the Latin treatises attributed to Thomas à Kempis. Borja's works appear in vols. 16, 29, 42 and 61 of the BAE.

See Juan de Dios Barros, *Don Francisco de Borja: su vida y sus obras* (Valencia, 1954); A. González Palencia, 'Noticias biográficas del virrey poeta Príncipe de Esquilache (1577?–1658) in *Anuario de Estudios Americanos* (Seville), vol. 6 (1949), pp. 73–160; and R. del Arco, 'Don Francisco de Borja, poeta anticulterano' in *Archivo de Filología Aragonesa* (Saragossa), vol. 3 (1950), pp. 83–126.

BORRÁS, TOMÁS (1891–), b. Madrid. Prolific but almost forgotten novelist. He studied with Navarro Ledesma at the Instituto de San Isidro. His best work has been achieved in the short story: *Noveletas* (1924), *Cuentos con cielo* (1943), *La cajita de los asombros* (1947), *Algo de la espina y algo la flor* (1954), and *Pase usted, fantasía* (1956), among others.

Believed to have written more than 5,000 articles from the age of 12, Borrás also explored other genres, such as the dramatic, in *La esclava del Sacramento* (1943), a *biografía dramática* set in Madrid between 1840 and 1865. But most of his working life was spent on the novel, his more interesting works including *La pared de tela de araña* (1924; 2nd edn., 1960), set in Morocco and offering *costumbrista* scenes of Moroccan

life, especially as regards the relations between the sexes; *Checas de Madrid* (Cádiz, 1940), with hallucinatory visions of a terrorized city; *La sangre de las almas* (n.d., but 1947; 2nd edn., 1955), a moving illustration of the contrast between revolutionary theory and practice, in places too exaggerated to be plausible; *La mujer de sal* (1925), set in a provincial Spanish city, and revolving around the ménage of a talented but irresolute painter, whose girl-friend commits suicide when he takes an interest in a wealthy woman.

The critics have ignored his work, but it is possible to find interest in his use of shrewd dictatorial figures as heroes and their variation from one book to another, and his treatment of dialect. He lacks profundity, and the relationships among characters are never adequately filled out.

See J. de Entrambasaguas, 'Tomás Borrás' in *Las mejores novelas contemporáneas*, vol. 6 (1960), pp. 1261–1315.

BORROW, GEORGE (1803–81), British author of *Lavengro* (1851) and *The Romany Rye* (1857). Borrow was the Spanish agent for the British and Foreign Bible Society 1835–40, a period covering much of the First Carlist War of 1833–9, and was also *The Times* correspondent in Spain. His works on Spain are a compound of fact and picaresque fancy. *The Zincali, or an Account of the Gypsies in Spain* (1841) was followed by *The Bible in Spain* (1843). The latter has been translated into Spanish by Manuel Azaña (q.v.).

BOSCÀ ALMUGAVER, JOAN (Castilian: JUAN BOSCÁN DE ALMOGÁVER, 1487?–1542), b. Barcelona. Poet and translator. Tutor to the young Don Fernando, future Duke of Alba. Though he lived most of his life in court circles, his most significant themes are the domestic virtues, love of his wife and children, the pleasures of home and the simple, honest life. At the court of Carlos V he befriended Garcilaso de la Vega (q.v.), and this friendship proved to be the vital element in the introduction of Italian metres and the Italianate temperament into Spain. In 1526 the Venetian ambassador, Andrea Navagero, invited Boscà to attempt the Italian style. Boscà, already familar with the Provençal hendecasyllabic line normal in Catalan lyric poetry, quickly learnt the new accentuation and showed his compatriots the new metres, not only *octavas reales* (which became the dominant metre in Spanish Renaissance epic verse) but also sonnets and tercets. There are many pleasing moments in Boscà's work, but it suffers from diffuseness, a certain lack of suppleness so evident in Garcilaso, frequent woodenness and a tendency to triviality. He began to collect his work, but died before it was published, and his widow Ana Girón de Rebolledo, to whom Boscà's most charming love poetry was addressed, collected and published it as *Las Obras de Boscan y algunas de Garcilasso de la Vega repartidas en Quatro libros* (Barcelona, 1543). The first book contains Boscà's earlier, pre-Italian poetry; the second his Italianate works; the third 'Epístola a Mendoza' in tercets, an allegory 'Octava rima' which begins well but becomes diffuse with the interpolation of 85 new octaves into the original 50 of Bembo's *Stanze* on which it is modelled, and 'Leandro' in 2,793 lines of free verse based on the *Hero and Leander* of Musaeus; and the fourth book contains Garcilaso's greatly superior work. The work was an instant success, and until 1570 Boscà's poetry continued to be issued with that of his poetically superior friend. The first edition is bibliographically significant too, marking the transition from Gothic to roman type in Spanish 16th-c. printing. The first edition is distinguished from two pirated editions by its repetition of ff. 19, 20, 21, 22, and 118.

Garcilaso sent Boscà Castiglione's *Cortegiano*, and he translated it as *Los quatro libros del Cortesano*, edited by M. Menéndez y Pelayo as *Anejo 25* (1942) to the *Revista de Filología Española*. Critical editions of Boscà's complete works have been prepared by W. I. Knapp (1875) and by M. de Riquer and others (Barcelona, 1957). Riquer has published and annotated newly-discovered poems in MS. 359 of the Central Library of Barcelona, in *Juan Boscán y su cancionero barcelonés* (Barcelona, 1945).

See Antonio Gallego Morell, *Bibliografía de Boscán* in *Revista Bibliográfica y Documental*, fasc. I–IV (1949).

BOSCÁN DE ALMOGÁVER, JUAN, see BOSCÀ ALMUGAVER, Joan.

BOTELHO DE CARVALHO, MIGUEL (*fl.* 1622), Portuguese poet who wrote almost exclusively in Castilian, the exception being *La Filis* (1641), a poem in octave stanzas which begins in conventional pastoral style but quickly achieves interest with an account of Botelho's own life and adventures. His major works are *La Fábula de Píramo y Tisbe* (Madrid, 1621), *Prosas y versos del Pastor de Clenarda* (Madrid, 1622) another pastoral romance, and *Rimas varias y tragi-comedia del Mártir de Ethiopia* (Rouen, 1646).

See Sousa Viterbo, 'Miguel Botelho de Carvalho' in *Dois poetas seiscentistas* (Lisbon, 1906) and D. P. Testa, 'An analysis of the "heroic" style of M. Botelho de Carvalho's "Fábula de Píramo y Tisbe"' in *Revista de Estudios Hispánicos*, vol. 2 (1968), pp. 183–92.

BOTELHO GOSÁLVEZ, RÁUL (1917–), b. La Paz. Bolivian novelist and short-story writer. The long stories of *Borrachera verde* (1938) are comparable, even in their brevity, to the indigenist violence of Rivera's *La vorágine* (q.v.) and caused great interest. *Coca: motivos del Yunga paceño* (1941) is a novel mixing modernism with social realism. *Altiplano* (Buenos Aires, 1945) is perhaps his best novel, confronting two families, the Huancas and the Condoris, who live near Lake Titicaca. It is a book very similar to *El mundo es ancho y ajeno* by Ciro Alegría (q.v.) *Vale un Potosí* (1949), a book of short stories imitating Valle-Inclán, was followed by the novels *Tierra chúcara* (1957) and *El Tata Limachi* (1967), enlarged from a short story on the corruption of a young priest's idealism in an isolated Indian parish.

Los toros salvajes y otros relatos (1965) combines humour, fantasy, and that streak of magic realism then becoming common in Latin American narrative. Botelho Gosálvez has also published a book of essays, *Vendimia del viento* (1967), whose dominant theme is the need for social justice.

BOUSOÑO, CARLOS (1923–), b. Boal, Asturias. Poet and critic who has taught literature at Wellesley College (U.S.A.) and Madrid University.

Subida al amor (1945) is a volume of poems concerned with repressed love, religion and Spain; *Primavera de la muerte* (1946) contrasts themes of death and love, and was followed by books progressively discovering a world of the senses: *Hacia otra luz* (1951), which adds *En vez de sueño* to the first two books) and *Noche del sentido* (1957). Subsequent works were *Poesías completas* (1960), *Invasión de la realidad* (1962); *Oda a la ceniza* (1967), and *Las monedas contra la losa* (1973). The last two won the Premio Crítica for 1968 and 1974 respectively.

Elegant, and in his ambiguity an opponent of the laconic, epigrammatic school, Bousoño is also a notable critic: *La poesía de Vicente Aleixandre* (1950; 3rd edn., 1968); *Seis calas en la expresión literaria española* (1951; 3rd edn., 1966) with Dámaso Alonso; and the challenging *Teoría de la expresión poética* (1952; 4th edn., 1966), which seeks to identify a possible scientific basis for the study of poetry.

See José Olivio Jiménez, *Diez años de poesía española, 1960–1970* (1972), pp. 33–60 and 243–79.

BOYL VIVES DE CANESMAS, CARLOS (1577–1617), b. Valencia. Playwright of the Lope de Vega circle, who met Lope in Valencia. Boyl is one of the less interesting of the Valencian school, which also included Guillén de Castro,

Gaspar de Aguilar, Tárrega, and Ricardo del Turia, but *El marido asegurado* has real merit. First published in the *Segunda parte de laureados poetas valencianos* (1616), it was reprinted with a *loa* in vol. 43 (1857) of the BAE, and edited by E. Juliá in vol. 2 (1929) of *Poetas dramáticos valencianos*. Deriving from Italian sources and Cervantes' *El curioso impertinente*, the plot concerns the trial made by King Segismundo of Naples of the love and loyalty of his betrothed Menandra of Sicily, who had previously been pledged to Duke Norandino. The series of tests is engineered by his exchanging rôles with his court favourite Manfredo, and Menandra passes all tests, her sister Fulgencia marrying Manfredo.

Boyl was a member, using the name 'Recelo', of the Academia de los Nocturnos. His poetry was collected in *Silva de los versos y loas de Lisandro* (Valencia, 1600). He was murdered by an unknown assailant near the cathedral in Valencia.

See H. Mérimée, *L'art dramatique à Valencia* ... (Toulouse, 1913), and Martí Grajales, *Poetas valencianos* (1927).

BRAÑAS, César (1900–), b. Antigua, Guatemala. Poet, novelist, and literary critic. His first book, *Sor Candelaria: leyenda lírica*, was published when he was 16, and in the years from 1918 to 1939 he published seven others. In 1922 he founded, with Alejandro Córdoba and Carlos Gándara Durán, the daily *El Imparcial*, in whose pages most Guatemalan writers have appeared.

Brañas' first book of verse, *Antigua* (1921), celebrated his native city, but he broke new ground with an elegy on the death of his father in ten cantos, *Viento negro* (1938), one of the most beautiful of its generation. *El lecho de Procrusto* (1943) is a collection of sonnets. His *costumbrista* novels are *Tú no sirves* and *La vida enferma*.

BRANNON, Carmen (1899–), b. Armenia, Sonsonate, El Salvador. A poet of mixed parentage (Irish on her father's side), who is generally considered to be the outstanding woman contemporary lyric writer in Central America. *Estrellas en el pozo* (1934) echoes the work of González Martínez (q.v.), and the influence of García Lorca pervades *Romances de norte y sur* (1946), but in *Sonetos* (1947) and especially in *Donde llegan los pasos* (1953) she found an authentic voice, intelligent and aptly metaphorical. She wrote two autobiographical works: the prose *Tierra de infancia* (1958) and the poetic *Fábula de una verdad* (1959).

BRAU, Salvador (1842–1912), b. Cabo Rojo. Puerto Rican playwright and essayist. A prolific journalist, Brau collected his ephemera in *Ecos de la batalla* (1886) and his longer and more substantial essays in *La campesina* (1866), *Las clases jornaleras* (1882), *La herencia devota* (1886), and *La danza* (1887). *Hojas caídas* (1909) is an unremarkable collection of poems. His novels caused little interest, the best being *La pecadora* (1881), but his historical writings were important: *Puerto Rico y su historia* (1894), *Historia de Puerto Rico* (1904), and *La colonización de Puerto Rico* (1930).

Brau achieved instant and lasting success as a playwright. His works, all in three acts and in verse, are *Héroe y mártir* (1870), based on the Castilian *comunero* revolt of 1520; *De la superficie al fondo* (1874), a comedy on a matchmaker and her daughter; *La vuelta al hogar* (1877), a tale of romance and piracy in 19th-c. Puerto Rico; and *Los horrores del triunfo* (1887), a patriotic play on the Sicilian Vespers.

See Cristóbal Real, *Salvador Brau: estudio biográfico-crítico* (1910).

BRENAN, Gerald (1894–), b. Malta. British travel writer and literary historian who, except for a few years, has lived in Spain since 1920. *The face of Spain* (London, 1950) was followed by his best book, the evocative *South from Granada* (London, 1957). His enthusiastic survey *The literature of the Spanish people* (Cambridge, 1951) was described by B. W. Wardropper in *Modern Language Notes* (1952, pp. 345–6) as 'a work of persuasion, a vigorous personal account of Spanish literature, [but] a dangerous tool for students, and an inappropriate one for scholars'. *The Spanish labyrinth* (1943) was a political commentary of great value to contemporary analysts. His latest study is *St. John of the Cross: his life and poetry* (Cambridge, 1972). Brenan's autobiographical works include *A life of one's own* (London, 1973) and *Personal record, 1920–1972* (London, 1974).

BRENES MESÉN, Roberto (1874–1947), b. San José, Costa Rica. Poet and philologist. One of the most significant modernists in Costa Rica, he opened the way for a new simplicity, purity of form, and freedom of rhythm in his lyrics *En el silencio* (1907), *Voces del ángelus* (1916), *Pastorales y jacintos* (1917), *Los dioses vuelven* (1928), *En busca del Grial* (Madrid, 1935), *Poemas de amor y de muerte* (1943), and *Rasur; o, semana de esplendor* (1946). His prose works include *Gramática histórica y lógica de la lengua castellana* (1905), and two books dating from the period after he joined the Theosophical Society in 1908: *Metafísica de la materia* (1917), and *El misticismo como instrumento de investigación de la verdad* (1921).

BRETÓN DE LOS HERREROS, Manuel (1796–1873), b. Quel, Logroño. Playwright and poet, he became secretary to the Real Academia

Española (to which he was elected as a member in 1837) and from 1847 Director of the National Library. Left an orphan when a boy, Bretón enlisted as a volunteer in the army 1812–22 during which period he lost an eye, possibly in a quarrel over a girl. He wrote over 200 dramatic works in all, of which some 50 were original and the rest translations and adaptations.

His first period extends to 1831, and is marked by *costumbrismo* deriving largely from Fernández de Moratín the younger (q.v.). His lack of originality in these plays, accentuated by the repetition of types, was heavily criticised by Larra and others. Incensed at this criticism which he felt to be unjust (see the prologue to his *Obras*, 1850), Bretón pilloried Larra in his play *Me voy de Madrid*. Yet there is much truth in the accusation of monotony, even in his second period, beginning in 1831 with the popular success of *Marcela, o ¿cuál de los tres?* (q.v.), in which a vivacious young woman is confronted by three equally disagreeable, caricatured suitors and chooses none of them. He followed this with *Un tercero en discordia*, in which the heroine Luciana is again faced with a choice among three suitors, one jealous, one complacent, and the third simple and sincere who emerges as the victor. The plot is simplicity itself; the whole interest of these plays revolves around Bretón's malicious but never embittered views of the middle classes and their foibles, just as Ramón de la Cruz (q.v.) shows the lower classes in his *sainetes*. Bretón moralizes, but far less openly than his early master Moratín, and he develops a personal style that Eugenio de Ochoa calls 'bretoniano' in plays such as *¡Muérete y verás!* (1837), an attack on Romanticism; and *A Madrid me vuelvo*, which ridicules the Romantic view of village life as a kind of Paradise.

Of his many translations, it is necessary to list only a handful: Racine's *Mithridate* and *Andromaque*, several works of Scribe, Guimond de la Touche's *Iphigénie en Tauride*, and Casimir Delavigne's *Les enfants d'Edouard* (1833), on the Princes in the Tower, a play which Bretón unobtrusively improved.

He recreated various Golden Age plays for the contemporary stage, among them *Con quien vengo, vengo* by Calderón, *Las paredes oyen* by Ruiz de Alarcón, and *Los Tellos de Meneses* by Lope de Vega.

Elena (1834) is the most interesting of Bretón's essays in the Romantic theatre for which he was unsuited by literary ancestry and personal inclination. Others include *Don Fernando el Emplazado*, on the Carvajales; and *Vellido Dolfos*, centring on the siege of Zamora. The first edition of Bretón's *Obras* (1850) was superseded by that in 5 vols. (1883–4). A volume of his

Teatro in Clásicos Castellanos (1929) contains *¡Muérete y verás!* and the very popular *El pelo de la dehesa* (q.v.). The latter, like its sequel, *Don Frutos en Belchite*, combines neoclassical and Romantic elements.

Bretón's poetry looks back to the anacreontics and *letrillas* of Meléndez Valdés (q.v.), and the *Poesías* (1831) also include comic and satirical poems. He also wrote the long *La desvergüenza* (1856). His popularity was always high during his lifetime, Valera describing him in 1860 as 'el príncipe de nuestros poetas cómicos'.

See Miguel de Molíns, *Bretón de los Herreros: recuerdos de su vida y de sus obras* (1883) and G. Le Gentil, *Le poète Manuel Bretón de los Herreros et la société espagnole de 1830 à 1860* (Paris, 1901).

BRIEBA, Liborio E. (1841–97), Chilean historical novelist, whose serialized adventure novels of the War of Independence are in the line of Dumas *père* and not that of Pérez Galdós (q.v.), despite the collective title of *Episodios nacionales* which he gave them. A primary school teacher, Brieba instilled moral and patriotic fervour into his widely-read books, the best of which were *Los Talaveras* (1871) and *El capitán San Bruno, o el escarmiento de los Talaveras* (1875). Brieba's style was hectic, and his treatment superficial and partisan.

Bringas, La de, see LA DE BRINGAS.

Broadsheets, Broadsides, see PLIEGOS SUELTOS.

BROCENSE, El, the common designation of the Renaissance humanist Francisco Sánchez de las Brozas (q.v.).

BROSSA CUERVO, Joan (1919–), b. Barcelona. Catalan poet who edited the magazine *Algol* and was one of the leaders of the Dau al Set group. His major book is *Poesia rasa* (Barcelona, 1970), consisting of several hundred poems written 1943–59, many of them previously published (all in Barcelona) in *Em va fer Joan Brossa* (1951), *Poemes civils* (1961), and *El saltamartí* (1969). Now demonstrably one of the leading Catalan writers of his generation, Brossa has shown certain affinities to Foix and the French surrealists. His later poems include those of *Cappare* (1973) and *La barba del cranc* (1974).

His plays have, perhaps unjustly, not obtained equal recognition with the poems, but they are important contributions to the theatre of the absurd: *La jugada, La xarxa, Or i sal, El bell lloc, Gran Guinyol* and *Aquí al bosc. Teatre complet* (vol. 1, Barcelona, 1973) collects Brossa's plays written 1945–54.

BRULL, MARIANO (1891–1956), Cuban poet.
By profession a diplomat, Brull was fluent in
French, translating the *Cimetière marin* of Valéry
into Spanish. He considered modernism
decadent, and first published lyrics of traditional
type in *La casa del silencio* (1916). The influence
of Enrique González Martínez and Juan Ramón
Jiménez appeared in the pure poetry of *Poemas
en menguante* (Paris, 1928). A poet who relied
greatly on the use of metaphor, Brull also used
the free invention of sounds made familiar by the
Dadaists. His later collections were *Canto
redondo* (1934), *Solo en rosa* (1941), *Tiempo en
pena* (1950), and *Nada más que* . . . (1954).

BRUNET, MARTA (1901–67), b. Chillán.
Chilean novelist and short-story writer. Her
first novels were steeped in Zolaism, but during
a period with the diplomatic service in Buenos
Aires she met writers of the *Sur* circle and was
inspired, particularly by Eduardo Mallea
(q.v.), to take a more subtle, psychological
approach. In both periods her subjects are
women; men are mere ciphers in the background, never developed into real characters.
   Works of her first period are the novel
Montaña adentro (1923), the short stories *Don
Florisondo* (1925), the novels *Bestia dañina* (1926)
and *María Rosa, flor del Quillén* (1929), and the
short stories *Reloj del sol* (1930). Her second
period is completely different, beginning with
the short stories *Aguas abajo* (1930) and partially
abandoning *criollismo* for a more international
style, with more technical elaboration, and
themes such as the conflict between illusion and
reality and the eternal problem of the frustrated
woman.
   Humo hacia el sur (1946) is a novel in which the
conservative forces confront ideas of progress
and lose. A short novel, *La mampara* (1946) deals
with a resentful woman incapable of attaining
her desires, as do the stories in *Raíz del sueño*
(1949). *María Nadie* (1957) attempts to juxta-
pose Brunet's two manners: the Creole attitude
in the first part of the book, and modern sexual
and urban problems in the second; the heroine
is deliberately nebulous and recalls several
female characters in Virginia Woolf's novels.
Amasijo (1962) is Brunet's first attempt to study
a male, and here the hero is a homosexual due to
oppressive maternal love who finally commits
suicide. Her *Obras completas* were published in
1963. There is a useful *Antología de cuentos* (1962)
selected, with a bibliography, by Nicomedes
Guzmán.

BRYCE ECHENIQUE, ALFREDO (1939–   ),
Peruvian novelist and short-story writer who
has lived in Europe since 1964. His novel *Un
mundo para Julius* (1971) is a brilliant description

of the downfall of a powerful Lima family in a
style owing something to the stream-of-consciousness technique of James Joyce's *Ulysses*.
His stories in *La felicidad ja, ja* (1974) are narrated
from within the characters, rejecting the
traditional technique of the omniscient narrator/
creator. The above books are studied in *Ínsula*
nos. 332–3 (July 1974) by Wolfgang A. Luchting
and Jorge Campos respectively. The same issue
contains Bryce's story 'Los indios'.
   See also W. A. Luchting, *Alfredo Bryce:
humores y malhumores* (1975).

Buen amor, El libro de, by Juan Ruiz (q.v.),
see LIBRO DE BUEN AMOR, EL.

BUENO, MANUEL (1874–1936), b. Pau, France.
Journalist and man of letters. Bueno's father was
Argentinian and his mother from Bilbao. Except
for a short time in Latin America, Bueno spent
all his life in Spain and considered himself a
Spaniard. Among his plays are *La mentira del
amor* (1907) and *El talón de Aquiles* (1908). He
wrote a great deal of drama criticism, collecting
some of it in *El teatro en España* (1910).
   His greatest efforts were put into short
stories and novels, though even these are now
forgotten. The collections of short stories are
Viviendo (1897), *A ras de tierra* and *Almas
y paisajes* (both 1900), and *En el umbral de la
vida* (1919); his many novels include *Corazón
adentro* (1906), *Jaime el Conquistador* (1912), *El
dolor de vivir* (1924), and *Poniente solar* (1931).
They are fluently written but lack the imaginative power and ability in construction of his
master Baroja (q.v.). His favourite themes are
God and immortality, death and suicide. The
best biobibliographical summary available is
that in J. de Entrambasaguas' *Las mejores
novelas contemporáneas* (1961), pp. 237–79.

BUENO MENÉNDEZ, SALVADOR (1917–   ),
b. Havana. Literary critic and historian, he has
written for the Cuban National Commission of
Unesco *Contorno del modernismo en Cuba* (1950) and
Medio siglo de literatura cubana, 1902–1952 (1953).
He has edited an *Antología del cuento en Cuba,
1902–1952* (1953), written an *Historia de la
literatura cubana* (1954), and contributed a brief
essay on 20th-c. Cuban literature to Montezuma
de Carvalho's *Panorama das literaturas das
Américas* (vol. II, 1958, pp. 435–64).

BUERO VALLEJO, ANTONIO (1916–   ), b.
Guadalajara. Most important Spanish playwright of his generation. On the outbreak of the
Civil War he interrupted his education to serve
as a medical orderly on the Republican side and
was jailed for political reasons until 1945. He

began to write plays after regaining his liberty and in 1949 his first two plays both won important prizes: the Lope de Vega for *Historia de una escalera*, a full-length social drama on the lines of Elmer Rice's *Street scene*; and the one-act *Palabras en la arena*, on adultery and the need for mercy. His second full-length play was the existentialist *En la ardiente oscuridad* (written in 1946; first performed 1950), in which a home for the blind represents Spain, the human situation, or merely itself. *La tejedora de sueños* (1952) is on the theme of Penelope's expectation of Ulysses' return, and her disillusion. Then follow works of lesser impact: *La señal que se espera* (1952), *Casi un cuento de hadas* (1953), *Madrugada* (1953), *Irene o el tesoro* (1954), and *Hoy es fiesta* (1956). *Las cartas boca abajo* (1957) is a more successful play on failure and frustration.

Buero began a series of historical dramas with *Un soñador para un pueblo* (1958), which deals with Esquilache's failure to modernize Spain in the reign of Carlos III. *Las meninas* (1960) is a masterly 'fantasía velazqueña' using the author's own experience of painting. *El concierto de San Ovidio* (1962) takes place in pre-revolutionary Paris. Then followed *Aventura en lo gris* (1963), *El Tragaluz* (1967), *La doble historia del Dr. Valmy* (world première by the Gateway Theatre in Chester, 1968), *El sueño de la razón* (1970), and *Llegada de los dioses* (1971). He has won numerous prizes, and has translated Shakespeare (*Hamlet*) and Brecht (*Mutter Courage*).

Buero has been considered a polemical writer in ultra-conservative Spain; though such a view is hardly justified, he has in G. G. Brown's view 'restored some seriousness and dignity to the Spanish theatre'.

See R. Mueller, *Antonio Buero Vallejo: Studien zum spanischen Nachkriegstheater* (Cologne, 1970); R. L. Nicholas, *The tragic stages of Antonio Buero Vallejo* (Chapel Hill, N.C., 1972); and R. Domenech, *El teatro de Buero Vallejo* (1973). A bibliography by Kronik appeared in *Hispania*, vol. 54 (1971), pp. 856–68, and interest is growing.

BUFANO, ALFREDO R. (1895–1950), Argentinian poet, whose fluent verse became steadily less rhetorical with each of his thirty-odd books. Though most, including his *Mendoza, la de mi canto* (1943), were occasioned by sentimental love and the domestic peace he found in San Rafael, Mendoza, his last two collections were occasioned by travels in Spain: *Junto a las verdes rías* (1950), and Morocco: *Marruecos* (1951). His best book, owing something to the *Melpómene* of Arturo Capdevila (q.v.), is the *Misa de Requiem* (1920), in which suffering displaces the sentiment of his earlier work.

Bulletin Hispanique, a scholarly quarterly founded in 1898–9 by G. Cirot, E. Mérimée, A. Morel-Fatio, P. Paris, and G. Radet and published for the University of Bordeaux, by Éditions Bière, 18–22 rue du Peugue, Bordeaux.

Bulletin of Hispanic Studies, a scholarly quarterly founded in 1923 by E. Allison Peers. The original title, *Bulletin of Spanish Studies*, was changed in 1950. It is still edited at the Institute of Hispanic Studies, Liverpool University, and is published by Liverpool University Press, 123 Grove Street, Liverpool L7 7AF.

BUÑUEL, LUIS (1900–   ), b. Calanda. Filmmaker. He made his reputation with the surrealist films *Un chien andalou* (1928) and *L'âge d'or* (1930), collaborating with Salvador Dalì (q.v.). Though Buñuel came from a comfortable middle-class family, was a good pupil at his Jesuit school, and studied literature and philosophy at Madrid University, these two films of powerful originality shocked contemporary audiences by their juxtaposition of images which can be understood symbolically (fighting scorpions and the Catholic church in *L'âge d'or*; or sexual repression and death and decay in the equally anti-clerical *Chien andalou*). *Land without bread* (1932) showed a starving Spanish community of cripples and mental defectives.

External pressures prevented Buñuel from directing more films until he emigrated to Mexico in 1946. There he made fifteen other films, now with conventional plots which enabled them to be shown in commercial cinemas but maintaining his aesthetic and philosophic standards. These films, which include the excellent *Los olvidados* (1950) and *Arcibaldo de la Cruz* (1955), never lose his poetic vision, patient observation of human malice and cruelty, and anarchic cynicism towards church and state.

His third period is that of international recognition as a major artist. It began with *Nazarín* (1958) based on the novel by Pérez Galdós (q.v.), and continued with *Viridiana* (1961) and *La voie lactée* (1969) a comic parody of the pilgrimage to Santiago de Compostela. *The discreet charm of the bourgeoisie* (1972) and *Le fantôme de la liberté* (1974) indicate that age has not mellowed the critic of hypocrisy.

See José Francisco Aranda, *Buñuel* (Barcelona, 1970) and the same editor's *Os poemas de Luis Buñuel* (Lisbon, 1975), with a Portuguese translation preceding the text.

BURGOS, FAUSTO (1885–1951), b. Tucumán, Argentina. Regional novelist and short-story writer, whose prolific output was marred to some extent by the haste of a busy journalist.

His best novels were partly autobiographical:
Los regionales (1939), influenced by Pereda (q.v.),
and *Aire de mar* (1943).

BURGOS, FRANCISCO JAVIER DE (1778–1849),
b. Motril, Granada. Neoclassical poet, playwright, and translator of Horace, Virgil's
Georgics, and the *De rerum natura* of Lucretius. He
studied for the priesthood, but was never
ordained and became a lawyer instead. Under
the French occupation he was appointed sub-
prefect of Almería and in 1812 emigrated to
Paris. From 1822 he directed *El Imparcial* and
was elected to the Real Academia Española in
1827. His neoclassical poetry has been published
in vol. 67 (1875) of the BAE. His poems *La
primavera, El porvenir,* and *A la constancia* are
particularly praised. Of his plays, only *El
baile de máscaras* (1832) is remembered.

BURGUILLOS, TOMÉ DE, Lope de Vega's
pseudonym used when publishing *Rimas
humanas y divinas . . .* (1634) which included *La
gatomaquia* and other works.

***Burlador de Sevilla y convidado de piedra,
El,*** a *comedia* by Fray Gabriel Téllez (q.v.)
written under the pseudonym of 'Tirso de
Molina'. The first major dramatization of the
legend of Don Juan Tenorio (see DON JUAN).
The surviving text of 1630 is believed to be an
imperfect version of an earlier play by Tirso or
another writer.

A Sevillian nobleman, Don Juan Tenorio,
has seduced Duchess Isabela in Naples by
coming to her at night pretending to be her
lover; escaping to Spain he is shipwrecked and
comes ashore at Tarragona. There he is given
shelter by Tisbea, a fisherwoman whom he
seduces with the promise of marriage, and then
deserts.

Back in Seville he intercepts a note of assignation from Ana de Ulloa to her fiancé the
Marqués de la Mota and enters her room, disguised as Mota. He attempts to assault her, and
when she cries out in terror, her father the
Comendador Don Gonzalo rushes to her but is
killed by Don Juan, who gets away unrecog-
nised. Mota is suspected of the outrages and
taken prisoner.

Meanwhile Don Juan is attending a peasant
wedding, and dazzles the bride-to-be Aminta
with his display of wealth, after which he
seduces and abandons her too.

In a Seville church he finds the effigy of the
Comendador above his tomb, insults it, and
invites it to dine with him. The statue accepts
the mocking invitation and in return offers to
show Tenorio the Ulloa family sepulchre. The
arrogant libertine accepts, but on shaking hands

he feels the fire of Hell in the stone statue's grip,
and cries out for mercy. It is too late: he is
dragged down into the inferno.

Tirso the Mercedarian friar attacks the immorality of the contemporary nobility (Spanish
scholars wryly suggest that Farinelli, in his
Italia e Spagna, need not have looked so hard for
Italian ancestors) accusing them of undermining the security of the social order. He combines this invective with a message against
human arrogance before divine retribution. For
Don Juan is not merely a libertine condemned
for his moral laxity: his four seductions are
accompanied by treachery, *lèse-majesté,* violation
of the laws of hospitality, murder, and the
defilement of the sacrament of marriage. Don
Juan's opposite is the King of Castile, who
attempts, through arranging marriages for
Juan's victims, to repair the damage caused by
the libertine to the social fabric; this contrast
between disorder and harmony is common to
many Golden Age Spanish dramas.

Some commentators see Juan as the type of
the mocking atheist (capable not only of wilful
murder, but mockery of his victim, an old man),
but Juan is in fact a believer whose fault is too
overweening a confidence in a long life with
ample time to repent of his sins. 'Tan largo me
lo fiáis,' he cries.

The sources of Tirso's creation (for this is one
of the few cases of a literary type without
classical antecedents) have been traced to a
controversial play *Tan largo me lo fiáis* (by
Tirso?), which may however be later, to *El
infamador* by Juan de la Cueva (q.v.), to *La
fianza satisfecha* (adapted by John Osborne as
A bond honoured) of Lope de Vega, and to *El
rufián dichoso* by Cervantes, as well as to four of
Tirso's own plays: *La ninfa del cielo, La dama del
olivar,* and the second and third plays in the
Santa Juana trilogy. Sloman (*BHS,* vol. 42,
1965, pp. 18–33) views *Tan largo* as the earlier
play and *Burlador* as a superior successor, both
descended from a source no longer extant.

But Tirso's innovation lies precisely in the
pairing of two unconnected dramatic ideas:
the heartless libertine and the stone guest. The
style is highly *culterano,* especially in the speeches
of Tisbea, who is only a fisher girl, and altogether Tirso's commoners speak less · convincingly than those of Lope, for example.

See J. Casalduero, 'El desenlace de "El
burlador de Sevilla"' in *Estudios sobre el teatro
español* (1962); and D. Rogers, 'Fearful sym-
metry: the ending of "El burlador de Sevilla"'
in *BHS,* vol. 41 (1964), pp. 141–59.

Buscapié, El, a key to obscure passages or to
unidentified characters in Spanish literature,
and the title of two different works purporting

to elucidate the real nature of the *Quijote* (for which see George Ticknor, *History of Spanish literature*, 6th American edn., 3 vols., New York, 1891, vol. 3, appendix D). A substantial literature surrounds one of the works, a forgery alleged to be by Cervantes according to its editor, Adolfo de Castro (Cádiz, 1849).

Daniel Defoe declared *El Quijote* to be 'an emblematic history of, and a just satire upon, the Duke of Medina Sidonia, a person very remarkable at the time in Spain' (see Wilson's *Life of De Foe*, 1830, vol. 2, p. 437).

Buscón, llamado Don Pablos, exemplo de Vagamundos, y espejo de Tacaños, Historia de la vida del, a picaresque novel by Francisco de Quevedo (q.v.), written between 1603 and 1608 and first published, probably without the author's consent, in Saragossa (1626). It is remarkable more for its violence and brilliant caricatures than for its narrative, which reproduces many incidents familiar from *Lazarillo de Tormes* and *Guzmán de Alfarache* (qq.v.). Already, at the age of 23, Quevedo demonstrates the depth of his malice and the brilliance of his verbal powers.

According to F. Lázaro Carreter, in his critical edition (Salamanca, 1965), none of the three extant MSS. is autograph. Quevedo probably rewrote the *Buscón* since a hundred or so crucial changes (mainly early in the book) can be traced in the MS. used for Américo Castro's 2nd edition (Clásicos Castellanos, 1927), which superseded his 1st edition (1911).

Pablos, the *buscón* ('petty thief' or 'rogue') of the title, is the son of a thief and a witch, and nephew of the Segovia town hangman. He runs away from home to be the servant of a wealthy young man, attending first his school and later Alcalá University (here Quevedo uses his own reminiscences, wildly distorted). When his father dies, he leaves Pablos enough money to become independent, and the young confidence trickster goes to court in the hope of a rich marriage. He fails and is reduced to card-sharping. Pablos is forced to leave Madrid and then Seville in quick succession, eventually emigrating to America.

A promised sequel was apparently never written. There is a good recent translation (with *Lazarillo de Tormes*) entitled 'The swindler', by Michael Alpert in *Two Spanish picaresque novels* (Harmondsworth, 1969).

Parker and others have argued that *El buscón* is not only a humorous and satirical work, marking the zenith of the picaresque tradition, but also contains a complex symbolic structure, involving a parallel with the life of Christ (whose example Pablos explicitly rejects on his first morning as a freshman with the words 'I am not *Ecce homo*'). The life of a petty thief and swindler comes to stand for the life of the sinner, moving as a human figure through a stylized world of caricature. His failure is due to his misuse of the divine gift of free-will, for Pablos takes a cold and calculated decision to lead a life of vice rather than virtue, and can blame only himself for the disasters that consequently befall him.

See A. A. Parker, 'The psychology of the "pícaro" in "El Buscón"' *Modern Language Review*, vol. 42 (1947), pp. 58–69; P. N. Dunn, 'El individuo y la sociedad en "La vida del buscón"' *Bulletin Hispanique*, vol. 52 (1960), pp. 375–96; and C. B. Morris, *The unity and structure of Quevedo's 'Buscón'* (Hull, 1965).

BUSTAMANTE, José Rafael (1881–1961), b. Quito. Ecuadorian *costumbrista* novelist and essayist. His only novel was first published serially in *Letras* (1915) and only in 1935 in book form (reprinted in 1960) as *Para matar el gusano*. It is a delicate portrayal of social conflict between the poor yet honest Robert and the arrogant, wealthy George who takes to drink after an unhappy love affair. Written in a plain, moving style, the novel gives a fine picture of the Ecuador mountains. Bustamante also wrote *Consideraciones sobre la libertad* (1938).

BUSTAMANTE CARLOS INCA, Calixto, see Carrió de la Vandera, Alonso.

BUSTILLO ORO, Juan (1904–   ), b. Mexico City. Mexican playwright. By profession an advocate, Bustillo Oro was convinced of the necessity for revolution in Mexico, but his plays reflect an almost wholly pessimistic outlook. He collaborated with Mauricio Magdaleno (q.v.) in the Teatro de Ahora group.

His best plays deal with agrarian problems, judicial corruption, and the difficulty of the humble, honest man in the face of society. *Masas: reportaje dramático en tres tiempos y un final* describes the assassination of a man of integrity whose brother-in-law agrees to be made a puppet by the general who rules behind the scenes. *Los que vuelven* is a disillusioned story of emigrants. *Justicia, S.A.* shows the venality of a judge, Santos Gálvez, who 'works' for the local *cacique* Hilario Salgado, to the point of knowingly signing the death warrant of an innocent man. These three plays were collected in *Tres dramas mexicanos*: *Los que vuelven, Masas, Justicia* (Madrid, 1933).

Bustillo Oro wrote many plays, including *Tiburón* and *Una lección para maridos*, but his most durable tragedy is *San Miguel de las Espinas* (included in *Teatro mexicano del siglo XX*), set in San Miguel, in the north of Mexico, where successive generations squabble about a dam without any attempt at mutual assistance or understanding. A. Magana Esquivel called this trilogy "de muy profundo y doloroso realismo".

BUSTOS DOMECQ, HONORIO, the pseudonym of Jorge Luis Borges and Adolfo Bioy Casares (qq.v.) for their joint fictions such as *Seis problemas para Don Isidro Parodi* (1942), parodies —as their title suggests—of detective-story solutions provided by a jailed man from his cell.

C

Caballería, Libros de, a Spanish fictional genre deriving from the so-called post-Vulgate cycle (1230–40) of the French Arthurian romances of chivalry (see ARTHURIAN LITERATURE IN SPAIN).

The first indigenous Spanish romance (*c.* 1300) was the *Caballero Cifar* (q.v.), probably written by the Toledo priest Ferrán Martínez and first published in Seville in 1512. Then followed a fictional chronicle of the Crusades, the *Gran conquista de ultramar* (q.v.), incorporating the legend of the Swan Knight. *Amadís de Gaula* (q.v.), the greatest of the almost certainly indigenous Spanish *libros de caballería*, is known as early as the mid-14th c. The work is neo-Arthurian in character (whereas the *Caballero Cifar* had relied on the *Thousand and one nights* or related oriental sources) and the book's immediate and lasting success from its first publication in 1508 (in a reworking by Garcí Rodríguez de Montalvo, q.v., of about 1492) led to both a renewed interest in Arthurian romance as well as to the writing and publication of a host of imitations, of which the most interesting are those comprising the *Palmerín* cycle (q.v.).

The fall of Troy was known in Spain mainly through the *Roman de Troie* of Benoît de Sainte-Maure (mid-12th c.) and this work was the source of the *Historia troyana polimétrica* (q.v.), though not of the 14th-c. *Sumas de historia troyana* of Leomarte, which is derived from the *General estoria* and from Guido delle Colonne's 13th-c. *Historia destructionis Troiae*. The 13th-c. *Alexandre* and *Apolonio* (q.v.) are further examples of the romance of chivalry of the 14th and 15th cs. in Spain. Hapless lovers divided by fate, the jealousy of others, and misunderstandings after a series of bizarre adventures, are the central themes in such stories as *Flores y Blancaflor*, the *Historia del muy valiente Clamades y de la linda Claramonda*, and the *Libro del esforçado cavallero Partinuplés*.

Some *libros de caballería* were written *a lo divino* (q.v.), in some cases to circumvent the rising moral and ecclesiastical opposition, though the only Spanish example to achieve more than ephemeral fame was *Joyas de la rosa fragante*, in which Christ, as the Knight of the Lion, overcomes the Knight of the Serpent with the assistance of twelve paladins.

Of the independent Catalan romances of chivalry, the most significant was the 15th-c. *Tirant lo Blanch* (q.v.).

The chivalresque genre lost its popularity with the rise of the picaresque and pastoral; it is not true that *Quijote* killed the vogue for books of chivalry by satire and ridicule (see the critical assessment of many *libros de caballería* in the bookburning episode, *Quijote* I, 6), for apart from a few reprints none had appeared since the *Historia de Policisne de Beocia* (1602) by J. de Silva y Toledo. The genre was already dying at the end of the 16th c.

A useful compilation by J. Amezcua, *Libros de caballerías hispánicos* (1973), includes extracts from *El Caballero del Cisne*, *El Caballero Cifar*, *Amadís de Gaula*, *Tirante el Blanco* (translated from Catalan), *Palmerín de Oliva*, and *Crónica del emperador Clarimundo*.

See Pedro Bohigas Balaguer, 'Orígenes de los libros de caballería', in G. Díaz-Plaja, (ed.), *Historia general de las literaturas hispánicas* vol. 1 (Barcelona, 1949), pp. 521–41.

CABALLERO, FERNÁN, the pseudonym of Cecilia Boehl von Faber (q.v.).

CABALLERO CALDERÓN, EDUARDO (1910–), Colombian novelist, essayist, and travel-writer. He founded the Guadarrama publishing house in Madrid and has worked in the diplomatic service in Spain and Latin America and as the Buenos Aires correspondent of *El Tiempo*, Bogotá.

His novel *El Cristo de espaldas* (Buenos Aires, 1952) is based on the Colombian civil war of 1948–58 during which 200,000 peasants died. A young liberal priest sent from his seminary to an Andean village opposes the conservative government, the local *cacique* and the Church.

The Bishop, at the end of the five days of the novel, orders the young, idealistic priest to return to the seminary: Christ has been forced to turn his back on Colombia.

Manuel Pacho (Barcelona, 1966) is the story of a boy who sees his whole village massacred while he hides in a tree. He carries his father to be buried in the nearest consecrated ground, a long way off, through swamps. While suffering thirst, hunger, and exhaustion he is forced to mutilate his father's body to make it lighter, and he eventually reaches the village, the people are more concerned to learn which way the troops went than to give burial to the stinking and mutilated corpse. Caballero Calderón's dry narrative avoids all the pitfalls of sentimentality or brutality, concentrating on a plain evocation of a simple peasant's suffering.

His subsequent novel *El buen salvaje* (1966) was awarded the Premio Nadal. *Siervo sin tierra* (1954) is devoted to a peasant's obsession with owning one small piece of land.

Caballero Calderón has written many essays on Latin America's relationship with the world, such as *Suramérica, tierra del hombre* (1942), and *Latinoamérica, un mundo por hacer* (1957).

Caballero Cifar, El, the first original full-length novel recorded in Spanish in the chivalresque genre, surviving in two MSS., one in the National Library of Spain and the other in the National Library of France. The author, who certainly knew the *lais* of Marie de France and the works of Chrétien de Troyes, wrote the novel in the first half of the 14th-c., and may have been Ferrán Martínez, Archdeacon of Madrid.

The plot is concerned with the involved adventures of the knight Cifar, his wife Grima, and his sons Garfín and Roboán. The life of St. Eustace is secularized, and there is much didactic matter drawn from oriental sources. The storytelling style is that of the Byzantine tales of Heliodorus. A feature of the book is the squire Ribaldo, a predecessor of the *pícaro* of Golden Age fiction, the *gracioso* of Golden Age drama, and of the later Sancho Panza himself.

The best edition is that by M. de Riquer (2 vols., Barcelona, 1951) with a study. See also R. M. Walker, *Tradition and technique in 'El libro del Cavallero Zifar'* (London, 1974).

Caballero de Olmedo, El, the titles of three famous Spanish plays.

(1) *Comedia de El Caballero de Olmedo*, written in 1606 and attributed by E. Juliá Martínez to the actor Cristóbal de Morales. It was edited by Schaeffer (Leipzig, 1871) and again by Juliá (1944).

(2) *El caballero de Olmedo*, a tragedy by Lope de Vega Carpio (q.v.), first published in Parte

XXIV of his *Comedias* (Saragossa, 1641 and since re-edited many times, notably by Jean Sarrailh (Paris, 1935), Inez Macdonald (Cambridge, 1935) and J. M. Blecua (Saragossa, 1959). This version was probably written about 1620–5. M. A. Buchanan (*Modern Language Notes*, vol. 22, 1907, pp. 215–8) proposed Tirso de Molina (q.v.) as one of the alleged co-authors of this play, one of the few genuine tragedies in Golden Age drama.

(3) *El caballero de Olmedo*, a parody probably of the play by Lope, written by Francisco Antonio de Monteser (q.v.), and first published in the *Mejor libro de las mejores comedias* (1653).

The tragedy by Lope de Vega is one of the masterpieces of world theatre but, as N. D. Shergold has indicated in 'Lope de Vega and the other "Caballero de Olmedo"' in *Studies in Spanish literature of the Golden Age presented to Edward M. Wilson* (ed. R. O. Jones, London, 1973), Lope almost certainly used his recollection of the earlier play or a copy of it when writing his own version. Deriving ultimately from the *Celestina* (q.v.) and its tradition, even explicitly in Act II where the *gracioso* calls the hero Calisto and the heroine Melibea, the play has an equally tragic ending and can be considered the culmination of the *Celestina* story in dramatic terms.

Don Alonso, a knight of Olmedo, comes to the fair of Medina and falls in love with Doña Inés, who is dressed as a peasant. He persuades the go-between Fabia to take Inés a love sonnet. Inés is equally infatuated with Alonso, although her father Don Pedro has agreed to her betrothal with Don Rodrigo and to her sister Leonora's betrothal with Don Fernando. Inés leaves a ribbon to show her feelings for Alonso, but Rodrigo discovers it and meets her next day, wearing it. Forced by her father to marry this man whom she loathes, Inés feigns a religious vocation and is given two teachers of Latin to prepare her for convent life. These 'teachers' turn out to be Fabia and Tello, Alonso's servant, who thus maintain communication between the lovers.

King Juan II arrives in Medina, and a great *fiesta* is organized, at which the prowess of Alonso becomes evident and much praised, especially when he saves the life of Rodrigo, acutely ashamed at this humiliation by his rival. Alonso returns home along the solitary road to Olmedo, disturbed by his thoughts and by the appearance of a shadowy figure (una sombra). He hears a peasant singing a traditional *cantarcillo* 'Que de noche le mataron / al caballero, / la gala de Medina, / la flor de Olmedo'. The peasant urges Alonso to return to Medina, but Alonso continues and is ambushed by Rodrigo and his friends. Tello, who is following his master, finds him dying, takes him home to Olmedo, and obtains justice against the murderous knights from King Juan II.

Duncan Moir has justly observed that 'as a skilfully constructed tragedy, *El caballero de Olmedo* is excellent; as a carefully unified and disturbing dramatic poem, it is superb'.

See William C. McCrary, *The goldfinch and the hawk: a study of Lope de Vega's tragedy 'El Caballero de Olmedo'* (Chapel Hill, N.C., 1966) and J. W. Sage, *Lope de Vega: 'El Caballero de Olmedo'* (London, 1974).

Caballo verde para la poesía. A poetry magazine printed in Madrid by Manuel Altolaguirre and edited by Pablo Neruda (qq.v.). The first issue appeared in October 1935, and Neruda tells in his autobiography *Confieso que he vivido* (Barcelona, 1974), pp. 168–9, how the sixth number, dedicated to Julio Herrera y Reissig, remained unpublished in July 1936 due to the outbreak of civil war. Humberto Díaz Casanueva and Rosamel del Valle were the main collaborators, but Neruda also included contributions from Cernuda, Miguel Hernández, García Lorca, Aleixandre, and Guillén (qq.v.). A reprint of 1974 (nos. 1–4) has a prefatory letter by Neruda and an introductory note by J. Lechner.

CABANILLAS ENRÍQUEZ, RAMÓN (1873–1959), b. Cambados, Pontevedra. Poet writing in the Galician language. A contributor to the important review *Nos* and collaborator with the Seminario de Estudos Galegos, Cabanillas was a writer of great versatility and accomplishment capable of sea poetry in *Vento mareiro* (Havana, 1915), narrative verse from three Celtic poems in *A noite estrelecida* (1926), and love poetry of great expressive power and formal economy in *A rosa de cen follas* (1927). His work in the field of oral poetry is gathered in *Antífona da cantiga* (Vigo, 1951) and in his other poems he celebrated his native Cambados and international themes with equal success. He wrote the plays *A man de Santiña* and, with Antón Villar Ponte, the historical-legendary *O mariscal* (1926).

CABANYES, MANUEL DE (1808–33), b. Villanueva y Geltrú, Barcelona. Pre-Romantic poet whose virtues included a genuine inspiration, and use of direct and simple language. He was influenced, through Luis de León, by Horatian epithets, turns of phrase and sentiments, but not metres. He read widely in English, with an especial affection for Thomas Moore and Byron, though he rejected the Byronic tendency to disillusion. He translated Alfieri's *Mirra* early in 1831 and in the following year, with his close friend 'Cintio' (Joaquín Roca

y Cornet) published a version of *Las Noches de Torquato Tasso* (Barcelona, 1932). He was struck down with phthisis, dying a few weeks after the publication of his only book, *Preludios de mi lira* (Barcelona, 1833) and after hearing on his deathbed that his beloved, separated from him by her mother, was finally permitted to marry him. The fullest edition of his poems was *Producciones escogidas* (Barcelona, 1858) but the *Poems* (Manchester, 1923), ed. by E. Allison Peers also contain some letters to 'Cintio'. His poetry, of which perhaps the best example is the hendecasyllabic *A Cintio*, was praised by Menéndez y Pelayo in *Horacio en España* (vol. 2, 2nd end., 1885, p. 161): 'Cabanyes tenía lo que faltó a Moratín: ideas, sentimientos, y vida poética propia'.

The most substantial work on Cabanyes is M. Romano Colangeli, *Classicismo e romanticismo in Manuel de Cabanyes* (Lecce, 1967).

CABELLO DE CARBONERA, MERCEDES (1845–1907), b. Moquegua. Peruvian novelist. A member of Juana María Gorriti's Lima *tertulia*, and a writer of 'escandalosa reputación y gran talento', to quote V. García Calderón. Her first three novels were *Los amores de Hortensia* (1888), *Sacrificio y recompensa* (1886), and *Eleodora* (1887), equally insipid and sentimental. But *Blanca Sol* (1889) broke new ground as the first Zolaesque novel to be written in Peru, analysing the vices and hypocrisy of Peruvian high society. *Las consecuencias* (1890) attacks gambling again, this time in a rural setting. Her last novel *El conspirador: autobiografía de un hombre público* (1892), the memoirs of a fictional party leader who is deserted by his few friends and jailed, was her best. Cabello claimed scientific objectivity for her work, but her denunciations of Bello and his like are all too subjective to substantiate the claim. Her essay *La novela moderna* (1892) was reprinted in 1948.

See A. Tamayo Vargas, *Perú en trance de novela* (1940).

CABRAL, MANUEL DEL (1907–   ), b. Santiago de los Caballeros. The most important contemporary poet of the Dominican Republic. The fact that all his early books appeared during the repressive dictatorship of Trujillo (1930–61) hardly affected his outspoken social-protest poetry on behalf of the Negro and mulatto in the Antilles, such as the bitterly ironic poem on a Haitian witch-doctor, capable of any kind of magic except the transformation of his own poverty to wealth: 'Haitiano brujo / hace tu vela prieta maravillas / tú dices. / Tengo el destino entre mis manos, / Sí- / Haitiano brujo, el Futuro / prisionero en la llama de tu vela. / Pero, / ¿y tu sonrisa de pobre?'

His later work benefits by a broader choice of themes and a gentler attitude to society and to love, which he divides into four categories: romantic, sexual, literary, and metaphysical. His range of expression is as wide as his subject-matter.

Cabral's *Antología tierra* (Madrid, 1949) contains the best work from *Pilón* (1931), *Color de agua* (1932), *Doce poemas negros* (1935), *Biografía de un silencio* (1940), *Trópico negro* (1942), *Compadre Mon* (1943), *Sangre mayor* (1945), and *De este lado del mar* (1949).

The *Antología clave, 1930–1956* (1957) is a different selection, with poems from *Los huéspedes secretos* (1951), *Sexo y alma* (1956), and *Dos cantos continentales y unos temas eternos* (1956). Since then, Cabral has published a literary autobiography *Historia de mi voz* (Santiago, Chile, 1964), a revealing account of the inner workings of a major poet's mind, and the following collections of new poetry: *Pedrada planetaria* (1958), *Carta para un fósforo no usado y otras cartas* (1958), *Catorce mudos de amor* (1962), *La isla ofendida* (1965), and *Los anti-tiempo* (1967). Cabral has also written two volumes of prose-poems: *Chinchina busca el tiempo* (1945) and *30 parábolas* (1956), and *El presidente negro* (1973), a novel.

CABRERA, CLAUDIO ANTONIO DE, the pseudonym adopted by Diego de Saavedra Fajardo (q.v.) for his *Juicio de Artes y Sciencias* (1655), better known as the *República literaria*.

CABRERA DE CÓRDOBA, LUIS (1559–1623), b. Madrid. Historian. A courtier, who took part in the Armada. His best work is the biographical *Felipe Segundo, rey de España* (pt. 1, 1619; pt. 2, 4 vols., 1876–7). This was the source of Pérez de Montalbán's important play *El segundo Séneca de España*.

Cabrera's virtues are accuracy and brevity, but these are to a great extent offset by his unfortunate style; he takes little trouble to plan a chapter or to explain the complex and often difficult chains of events which he narrates, rendering many pages virtually unreadable. He thus cannot be said to practise the tenets laid down in his manual *De historia, para entenderla y escrivirla* (1611). A relatively minor work, though with some important details, is the *Relaciones de las cosas sucedidas en la Corte de España, desde 1599 hasta 1614* (1857).

CABRERA INFANTE, GUILLERMO (1929–), Cuban novelist, short-story writer, and film critic for *Carteles*, a magazine which ceased publication in 1960. His film reviews were collected in *Un oficio del siglo XX* (1963). In 1959 he founded *Lunes*, a weekly literary supplement

to *Revolución*, and edited it until it was banned in 1961. He then entered the diplomatic service, but was deprived of his position in 1965. His short stories of the Batista period, *Así en la paz como en la guerra*, have been translated into French, Italian, Polish, Czech, Russian, and Chinese. An unpublished version of his novel *Tres tristes tigres* won the Premio Biblioteca Breve in 1964 under the title *Vista del amanecer en el trópico*; it was not published in its uncensored form until 1967. The book, set in the Havana of Batista's last months, is superficially a guide to the city's night life, decked out with scintillating verbal extravagance such as vigorous neologisms and clever puns. But below the surface Cabrera Infante savages the cultural decadence of pre-revolutionary Cuba, rarely missing his mark. He now lives in exile.

See J. Ríos (ed.), *Guillermo Cabrera Infante* (1974) which includes a fragment of *Cuerpos divinos*, then in preparation.

CADALSO Y VÁZQUEZ, JOSÉ (1741–82), b. Cádiz. Poet and satirist. One of the most influential figures (with Jovellanos and Forner, qq.v.) of the late 18th c., and heir to the Stoic-*desengaño* tradition of Quevedo and Gracián (qq.v.). He was educated at the Jesuit school in Cádiz, and studied English, French, German, and Italian, travelling widely in Europe and then returning to the capital in 1758. He enlisted for the Portuguese campaign in 1762 and was made knight of Santiago in 1766, the year he met Jovellanos. In 1768 he was exiled from Madrid for allegedly writing the 'Calendario manual', a MS. which caused offence to a number of society ladies; he spent two years in Aragón composing the poems *Ocios de mi juventud* (Salamanca, 1773), the best of which are addressed to 'Filis', the actress María Ignacia Ibáñez, who played Doña Ava in his tragedy *Don Sancho García* in January 1771 and died in the following April.

In 1772 he was regular in his attendance at the famous *tertulias* (literary gatherings) at the San Sebastián inn, Madrid, and published *Los eruditos a la violeta* and the *Suplemento*, a satire on the pretentious 'scholarship' of those who pontificate a great deal but read and study not at all. The success of this amusing parody, in the form of 'lessons' in poetry, philosophy, law, mathematics and much else, led Cadalso to compose *Un buen militar a la violeta* (1790), a similar parody on military knowledge. He spent part of 1773–4 in Salamanca, where he met Juan Meléndez Valdés (q.v.) and other poets of the School of Salamanca, and in those two years composed the works for which he is best remembered: *Cartas marruecas* (q.v., 1793) and *Noches lúgubres* (q.v., 1798) both first serialized in the *Correo de Madrid* (1789–90). He was promoted to colonel in 1782 a fortnight before being killed at the siege of Gibraltar.

Cadalso's love story, his energetic patriotism, his fearless attack on institutions based on hypocrisy, and the melancholy side of his nature all made him a figure of abiding interest to the Spanish Romantics.

See N. Glendinning, *Vida y obra de Cadalso* (1962) and F. Ximénez de Sandoval, *Cadalso: vida y muerte de un poeta soldado* (1967).

CÁDIZ, Beato Diego José (1743–1801), b. Cádiz. Capuchin religious writer whose secular name was José Caamaño García Texeiro. His style was very popular in its time for simplicity, being free of the *conceptismo* and *culteranismo* (qq.v.) then considered *de rigueur* even in sermons. Among his most celebrated works was *Afectos de un pecador arrepentido* (Barcelona, 1776). His contribution to literary history was the attack on theatrical licence entitled *Dictamen sobre asunto de comedias y bailes* (Pamplona, 1790). Editions of his *Obras completas* were begun in 1796 and 1856 but not completed.

CAIRASCO DE FIGUEROA, Bartolomé (b. 1540), b. Gran Canaria, Canary Islands. Poet, playwright, and Canon of the Cathedral of Las Palmas. *Templo de la Iglesia militante, o Flos sanctorum* (3 vols., Lisbon, 1612) is a long poem of 5,000 *octavas*. A selection from his *Definiciones poéticas morales y cristianas* was reproduced by A. de Castro in vol. 42 (1857) of the BAE. This defines in verses of varying metre and quality terms such as Gratitude, Alms, Music, Faith, Hope and Charity. Some of his hitherto unpublished plays have appeared as *Obras inéditas: I: Teatro* (Santa Cruz de Tenerife, 1957).

CALAVERA, Ferrant de, see Sánchez de Talavera, Ferrant (the form preferred by Marcelino Menéndez y Pelayo).

CALDERÓN, Fernando (1809–45), b. Guadalajara, Nueva Galicia (now Jalisco). Mexican playwright and poet of liberal ideas, who suffered harassment early in his political career, but later rose to administrative power in Zacatecas. His poetry is often derivative, as for example when he complains of imaginary sorrows in the early Romantic vein. However, his *Obras poéticas* (1844) were reprinted several times.

It was in the theatre that he excelled, and perhaps above all in the splendid comedy *A ninguna de las tres* (1854), a riposte to the *Marcela o ¿cuál de las tres?* of Bretón de los Herreros (q.v.). In this he criticizes the prevalent mania for things French, political hypocrisy, and the defective education of girls and women in Spain and Mexico. There is an edition by Francisco Monterde (1944) in the Biblioteca del Estudiante Universitario.

Calderón's other plays included the five-act verse historical drama *Ana Bolena* (1854); *Hernán, o la vuelta del cruzado* (1854; ed. C. González Peña, 1945), set in the time of the Crusades; the chivalresque four-act verse play *El torneo* (1865); the neoclassical verse tragedy *Muerte de Virginia por la libertad de Roma* (Zacatecas, 1882) in three acts; and the prose comedy *Los políticos del día* (Zacatecas, 1883), complete only as far as scene IX. Considered by some critics the finest playwright that Mexico has so far produced, Calderón achieved greater success on the stage than on the printed page; he was a master of stagecraft, dramatic construction and spirited dialogue, emotion and plot. *Dramas y poesías* (1959) is an edition of his works by Francisco Monterde in the Colección de Escritores Mexicanos.

CALDERÓN DE LA BARCA, Pedro (1600–81), b. Madrid. Major dramatist of the Golden Age. He and his school, or cycle, are commonly distinguished from Lope de Vega (q.v.) and his school by stylistic differences; where the latter rely on rapid and lyrical composition, the former seek special effects deriving from *culteranismo* and *conceptismo*, and greater care with the use of language and in the construction of the play's form and shape. Further, Calderonian drama is often more doctrinal and didactic than Lope's work. Thematically they rely on much the same source material, though Calderón, by his unique understanding and mastery of the *auto sacramental* genre, must be considered superior.

Calderón studied under the Jesuits from nine to fourteen, matriculated from Alcalá in 1614, and studied Canon Law at Salamanca until 1620, when he abandoned his promising ecclesiastical career and returned to Madrid. There he led a somewhat violent life with his eldest brother Diego and a younger brother José; their conflict with Diego de Velasco ended in the murder of Velasco. Pedro's first known *comedia* (*Amor, honor y poder*) dates to 1623, following which year the playwright travelled in Flanders and northern Italy and on his return in 1625 entered the service of the Duke of Frías. Most of his plays were first performed in the theatre of the Royal Palace and it is to Calderón's appointment as official court playwright that we owe many of the masterpieces that in other hands might have been merely 'occasional'.

A second violent incident concerning one of Calderón's brothers occurred when the latter was wounded by Pedro de Villegas, son of the actor Antonio de Villegas, who fled into a Trinitarian convent. Calderón and some constables violated the convent, where Lope de Vega's daughter Marcela was staying. Lope de Vega protested, as did Fray Hortensio Paravicino (q.v.) in a famous sermon mocked by Calderón's *gracioso* (clown) in his play *El príncipe constante*. Despite his brushes with the law and the Church, Calderón never lost the royal favour and in 1637 was made Knight of Santiago and began his military service with the Duque del Infantado, being wounded in a hand during the Catalan Revolt. For supporting Philip IV in the siege of Lérida and other signal services, Calderón was awarded a monthly pension of 30 escudos in 1642. A few years later an illegitimate son was born to his mistress, who probably died early for there is no contemporary information on these events. In 1651 he was ordained a priest and appointed Chaplain of the New Sovereigns in Toledo, though he made frequent visits to Madrid and continued to write secular plays as well as the celebrated series of sacramental *autos* and plays of greater length. When the Patriarch of the Indies censured him for writing plays, though an ecclesiastic, and then commissioned him to create new *autos* for Corpus Christi, Calderón retorted with wholly justifiable indignation 'o es malo o es bueno: si es bueno, no me obste, y si es malo no se me mande'. It was apparently 'bueno' for there is no noticeable diminution in the number of plays he wrote. In 1663 he was named Chaplain of Honour to His Majesty and spent even more of his time composing large-scale works and *autos*; indeed, Calderón's prestige stood if anything even higher after the death of his protector Philip IV and during the reign of his successor.

As to his contemporary fame, Menéndez y Pelayo observes that 'rara vez se ha visto ejemplo de una popularidad igual no parecida siquiera a la de Calderón entre sus contemporáneos; realmente la de Lope fue más ruidosa, pero no tan honda ni tan duradera'.

Though four *Partes* of Calderón's plays were published in his lifetime, not one was edited by him and not a single text can be described as approved. *Primera parte de las Comedias* (1636; 2nd edn., 1640) and *Segunda parte* (1637; 2nd edn., 1641) were collections of twelve plays each (as was customary at the time) made by Calderón's brother José. They undoubtedly did much to supersede the more garbled versions, though there is no certainty that Calderón himself provided his brother with original autograph versions. *Tercera parte* ... (1664) was prepared by Calderón's friend Sebastián Ventura de Vergara. A *Quarta parte* (1672) carries a prologue by Calderón specifically rejecting the

authorship of a long list of plays attributed to him. A spurious *Quinta parte* (1677) contained four plays not by Calderón and six others nominally his but disfigured by numerous errors and amendments. Twelve *Autos sacramentales* ... *Primera parte* (1677) are authentic. The best modern edition of these last is that by A. Valbuena Prat (1926–7) in Clásicos Castellanos.

There is no entirely satisfactory classification of Calderón's plays, but the secular drama has been divided by Díez-Echarri and Roca Franquesa as follows:

Tragedies. *El pintor de su deshonra; El mayor monstruo, los celos* (q.v.); *El médico de su honra* (q.v.); *A secreto agravio, secreta venganza.*

Histories. (a) National: *Amar después de la muerte; El príncipe constante* [q.v., on Portugal]; *La niña de Gómez Arias; El alcalde de Zalamea* (q.v.) [not in fact historical]; *El sitio de Breda;* and (b) Foreign: *El cisma de Inglaterra; La hija del aire* (q.v.); and *La gran Cenobia.*

Comedies of manners. *La dama duende* (q.v.); *Casa con dos puertas mala es de guardar; Guárdate del agua mansa.*

Palace Plays: *La banda y la flor* and *No siempre lo peor es cierto.*

Mythological Plays. *Eco y Narciso; Ni amor se libra de amor; La fiera, el rayo y la piedra;* and *El mayor encanto, amor.*

Philosophical Plays. *La vida es sueño* (q.v.) and *En esta vida todo es verdad y todo es mentira.*

Plays of Chivalry. *El castillo de Lindabridis* and *La puente de Mantible.*

Zarzuelas. El laurel de Apolo and *La púrpura de la rosa.*

Entremeses. El dragoncillo; El pésame de la viuda; Carnestolendas; and *La casa de los linajes.*

The care that Calderón expends on a much smaller number of works than Lope's is clear to modern readers, who find, however, that a certain imaginative quality and fantasy is lacking in Calderón which is found in a play such as *El caballero de Olmedo* (q.v.) of Lope de Vega. Lope is more varied in his source material while Calderón can be accused of monotony in the numerous love intrigues of the plays of manners, while even such expert dramas as *El pintor de su deshonra* and *A secreto agravio, secreta venganza* suffer from lack of differentiation, occasionally even in detail. Much has been written too against characterization in Calderón, in which identical types recur and the tendency towards symbolism militates against depth and interest of character, though a valuable corrective is to be found in A. A. Parker, *The approach to the Spanish drama of the Golden Age* (London, 1957). His use of language is typical of the later Golden Age in its complexity. Like the tragic heroes and villains in Lope and Tirso, those of Calderón seem violent in speech and action alike. As Valbuena Prat has observed, 'instead of natural humanity, Calderón depicts characters with exaggerated, disproportionate virtues and failings'.

His religious drama is classifiable into the full-length plays and the *autos sacramentales*. The religious plays are:

Biblical. *Los cabellos de Absalón*; *La sibila de oriente*; and *Judas Macabeo*.

Occasional. *El gran príncipe de Fez, don Baltasar de Loyola* (a Jesuit apologia).

Saints. *El mágico prodigioso* (q.v.); *Las cadenas del demonio*; *Los dos amantes de cielo*; and *El José de las mujeres*.

Pious Legends. *La devoción de la Cruz* (q.v.); *El purgatorio de San Patricio*; *Orígen, pérdida y restauración de la Virgen del Sagrario*. *La devoción de la Cruz* (q.v.) is an astonishing play of crime, violence, and incest in which Eusebio's lifelong devotion to the Cross is seen as the mode of his redemption.

Calderón's *autos sacramentales* are not the mere pious interludes dignified by that title in the works of some of his contemporaries but usually of a stature comparable with his secular drama or *La devoción de la Cruz*. They vary in length from about 1,000 to 2,000 lines, and deal in sweeping images: the world as market in *El gran mercado del mundo*, or as theatre in *El gran teatro del mundo*. He reworked some of his *comedias* as *autos*: these include *El pintor de su deshonra* and *La vida es sueño*.

The *autos sacramentales* can be analysed into the following categories:

Philosophical and Theological. *La vida es sueño*; *El pintor de su deshonra*; *El gran teatro del mundo*; *El gran mercado del mundo*; *Pleito matrimonial del alma y el cuerpo*; *Lo que va del hombre a Dios*; and *El veneno y la triaca*.

Mythological. *Los encantos de la culpa* (an allegorical form of the *comedia El mayor encanto, amor*); *El divino Orfeo*; *El laberinto del mundo*; *El divino Jasón*; and *Andrómeda y Perseo*.

Old Testament. *La torre de Babilonia*; *El árbol del mejor fruto*; *Sueños hay que verdad son*; *Primero y segundo Isaac*; *La cena del rey Baltasar*; *Las espigas de Ruth*; and *Mística y real Babilonia*.

New Testament. *El tesoro escondido*; *La siembra del Señor*; *Llamados y escogidos*; *El día mayor de los días*; and *A tu prójimo como a ti*.

Historical-legendary. *El cubo de la Almudena*; *La protestación de la fe*; *Al santo rey don Fernando* (Parts I & II); *La devoción de la Misa*; and *A María el corazón*.

Occasional. *Las órdenes militares*; *Los misterios de la Misa*; and *No hay instante sin milagro*.

Marian. *La hidalga del valle*.

The above selection of the major plays and *autos* can be considered among the representative masterpieces of a writer ranked by Spanish scholars with Shakespeare for variety and language. The playwrights who collaborated with Calderón include Rojas Zorrilla, Moreto, Cubillo de Aragón, Coello, Enríquez Gómez, Diamante, Hoz y Mota, Juan Vélez de Guevara, Matos Fragoso, and Ramírez de Arellano (qq.v.).

The non-dramatic works of Calderón are universally passed over, except by the percipient Curtius, who notes the importance of the *Deposición a favor de los profesores de la pintura* in the history of 17th-c. art theory; but there is a powerful *romance* on the penance of St. Ignatius at Manresa, and the similarly Ignatian poem *Psalle et sile* on the inscription on the choir-screen of Toledo, edited by Leopoldo Trenor (Valencia, 1930–9).

No satisfactory editions have been made of the complete works of Calderón, many copying the mutilated texts produced by J. de Vera Tassis y Villarroel (9 vols., 1685–91); this stricture applies to the BAE editions by J. E. Hartzenbusch (4 vols., 1848–50), but less to the *Dramas* edited by L. Astrana Marín (1932; 3rd edn., 1945) with forty plays and to the *Comedias* edited by A. Valbuena Briones (1956) with 52 plays. There are critical editions of many individual plays (q.v. under title).

There is a useful collection of essays, *Critical essays on the theatre of Calderón* (ed. Bruce W. Wardropper, New York, 1965) and many other studies, including A. E. Sloman, *The dramatic craftsmanship of Calderón* (Oxford, 1958); E. Cotarelo y Mori, *Ensayo sobre la vida y obras de Calderón* (1924); A. L. Constandse, *Le Baroque espagnol et Calderón de la Barca* (Amsterdam, 1951); and Harry W. Hilborn, *A chronology of the plays of D. Pedro Calderón de la Barca* (Toronto, 1938). Brief studies include those of A. Valbuena Prat, *Calderón* (Barcelona, 1941) and Everett W. Hesse, *Calderón de la Barca* (New York, 1967).

Among English versions of Calderón none attains verbal fidelity and literary felicity in equal measure, but there are some successes in Edward FitzGerald's *Eight dramas of Calderón* (London, 1906); better are *Four plays* translated by Edwin Honig (New York, 1961) with *Secret vengeance for secret insult*, *Devotion to the Cross*, *The mayor of Zalamea*, and *The phantom lady*); best of all is Roy Campbell's *The surgeon of his honour* (Madison, Wis., 1960).

Calila e Digna, El libro de, a rendering, made at the instance of Alfonso X, 'el Sabio' (q.v.), of the *Pançatantra*, a Sanskrit collection of moral fables written for an Indian monarch. The *Pançatantra* was transmitted to Europe through a lost Old Persian translation by Barzuya and an Arabic version by 'Abdullah ibn al-Muqaffa', from which all modern versions have been made. The version known to Alfonso was put into Castilian in 1251, and then into Latin (by Raymond de Béziers) in 1313. The version which became widely popular in medieval Europe was the Latin rendering of John of Capua (1263–78) from the Hebrew. The book is also known as *Kalila wa Dimna*, in Arabic, and the *Fables of Bidpai*, the last word being a corruption of 'bidbah', the title of the chief scholar at the court of an Indian prince.

See I. Montiel, *Historia y bibliografía del Libro de Calila e Dimma* (1975).

Calisto y Melibea, La [tragi]comedia de, see CELESTINA, La.

CALLE, MANUEL J. (1866–1918), b. Cuenca, Ecuador. Journalist. Prolific writer of polemics in his newspaper column *Charlas* and elsewhere. His literary essays were collected under the title *Biografías y semblanzas* (1920), but he is best known for a book aimed at the younger generation: *Leyendas del tiempo heroico: episodios de la Guerra de la Independencia* (Guayaquil, 1905).

CALVETE DE ESTRELLA, JUAN CRISTÓBAL (1526?–1593), b. Sariñena, Huesca. Humanist who studied at Alcalá and attended Prince Philip (later Philip II) as a courtier. His eye-witness account, *Felicísimo viaje del príncipe don Felipe, hijo de Carlos V, a Alemania y a Flandes* (Antwerp, 1552, ed. M. Artigas, 1930), contains an absorbing, detailed description of a tournament offered to Carlos V by the Queen of Hungary in 1549. This illustrates how deeply ingrained into the contemporary European imagination the feats of errantry of the *libros de caballería* (q.v.) had become. Calvete also wrote a poem on the life of Carlos V (1590); an encomium of the Duke of Alba in Latin (trans. López de Toro, 1945), *Túmulo imperial, adornado de historias* ... (Valladolid, 1559); and an account of the capture of a North African city, *De Aphrodisio expugnato, quod vulgo Aphrica vocant* (Antwerp, 1551).

CALVO SOTELO, JOAQUÍN (1905–), b. Corunna. Playwright whose attitude is that of the Catholic middle classes, though not un-critical of them. Of his 50 or so plays, many are melodramatic, uneven, and full of clichés. He has written in three genres: the farce, the straight *comedia*, and the thesis play. The first is exemplified by *El contable de estrellas* (1937) and *Tánger* (1945), and the third by *La muralla* (q.v., 1954), *La ciudad sin Dios* (1960), and *El poder* (1965). The second is the genre he has cultivated most, from the early *Una comedia en tres actos* (1930) and *A la tierra, kilómetros 500,000*

(1932) to the diplomatic trilogy consisting of *Una muchachita de Valladolid* (1957), *Cartas credenciales* (1961), and *Operación embajada* (1962), *Micaela* (1964), based on a story by J. A. Zunzunegui, *El proceso al Arzobispo Carranza* (1964), *La condesa Laurel* (1965), *El inocente* (1969), and *Una noche de lluvia* (1969).

Cal y canto (1929), a collection of poems by Rafael Alberti (q.v.) written under the influ-ence of both *ultraísmo* and Góngora (qq.v.). The poems in the latter category, including *Soledad tercera*, show his technical virtuosity at its most brilliant, the intricate concepts and images deserving careful study. There are also a number of *romances* in the manner of Góngora often with a bitter, deflating irony reminiscent of Quevedo. The *ultraísta* poems take con-temporary themes and attempt to reflect them in breathless cacophony.

See S. Salinas de Marichal, *El mundo poético de Rafael Alberti* (1968).

CAM, pseudonym of Evaristo Acevedo Guerra (q.v.).

CAMBA, JULIO (1882–1962), b. Villanueva de Arosa, Pontevedra. Spanish humorist whose caricatures are invariably good natured, even in his satire on the U.S.A., *La ciudad automática* (1932). Camba was employed as a journalist in Argentina (as was his brother Francisco Camba, 1884–1947), France, the U.S.A., and Turkey. He wrote a number of witty and sympathetic sketches including *Las alas de Ícaro* (1913), *Alemania* (1916), *Londres* (1916), *Playas, ciudades y montañas* (1916), *Un año en el otro mundo* (1917), *La rana viajera* (1920), *Sobre casi nada* (1928), the satire on Spain *Haciendo la República* (1934) and *Millones al horno* (1958). Camba's *Obras com-pletas* (1948) are in two volumes.

CAMBACERES, EUGENIO (1843–88), b. Buenos Aires. Argentinian satirical novelist and liberal politician who, being an agnostic, proposed the separation of Church from State in Argentina in 1871. He abandoned Parliament with 'una ilusión menos y un desengaño mas' ('one illusion less and one disillusion more').

His first books *Potpourri* (1881) and *Música sentimental* (1884), published in Paris with the common sub-title '*silbidos de un vago*', showed a misanthropy far beyond anything in Groussac, Eduardo Wilde, or Lucio Vicente López (qq.v.). Their chief defect is a discordantly happy ending. His best novel *Sin rumbo* (1885), heavily influenced by Zola, is spoilt by a melo-dramatic ending out of key with the *costumbrismo* of earlier episodes. Otherwise the book is memorable, especially in the psychological study of the hero Andrés. Cambaceres' last novel was the determinist *En la sangre*, serialized in *Sud América* during 1887; dealing with hereditary defects, it also was influenced by Zola.

CAMERINO, GIUSEPPE (*fl.* 1624), Italian novelist whose *Novelas amorosas* (1624) were written in Spanish at the height of the vogue for sentimental love tales in the Golden Age. Though the work was praised by Lope de Vega, Ruiz de Alarcón, Vélez de Guevara, and Guillén de Castro (qq.v.), the twelve *novelas* have been described by Díez-Echarri and Roca Franquesa as 'de lo más insípido que puede darse en su género'. They were reprinted in 1736 and in a modern edition by F. Gutiérrez (Barcelona, 1955).

Camerino's other Spanish works were *Discurso político sobre estas palabras: A fee de hombre de bien* (1631) and *La Dama Beata* (1654 [but 1655]).

See E. Levi, 'Un episodio sconosciuto nella storia della novella spagnuola', *BRAE*, vol. 21 (1934), pp. 687–736.

Camino, El (Barcelona, 1950), a novel by Miguel Delibes (q.v.).

A quietly-told and effective story of country life in Spain which achieved immediate success. Daniel, 'El Mochuelo', is eleven, and the novel deals with his sleepless night spent looking back at his childhood in his native village which he is to leave in the morning for the provincial capital where he will begin his secondary education—the path from boyhood to manhood. In the prologue to vol. 2 of his *Obras completas* (1966), Delibes suggests that his interest in the countryside and the instinctive tenderness with which he regards such areas and their inhabitants . . . may signify, rather than recognition of the virtues of the country, a feeling of pity because of its abandonment.

The noval has been translated as *The path* by J. & B. Haycraft (New York, 1961).

CAMINO CALDERÓN, CARLOS (1884–1956), b. Lima. Peruvian novelist and writer of *tradiciones* partly based on folktales. His most celebrated work is the novel of Independence *La Cruz de Santiago: memorias de un limeño* (Trujillo, 1925), his first work after *Ildefonso* (1924). His other books included *El Caballero de Santiago* (1935); *Anecdotario de los libertadores* (1941), *El daño* (1942), a regional novel of rural Peru; *La ilusión de Oriente* (1943), *Tradiciones de Trujillo* (1944), *Tradiciones de Piura* (1944), *Diccionario folklórico de Perú* (1945), *Mi molino* (1947), and *Cuentos de la costa* (Trujillo, 1954).

Camino de perfección (1902), the second novel in the trilogy *La vida fantástica* by Pío Baroja y Nessi (qq.v.).

Camino de perfección, El (Évora, 1583), an ascetic work by S. Teresa de Jesús (q.v.), first published under the title *Tratado que escriuió la Madre Teresa de Jesús a las hermanas religiosas de la Orden de Nuestra Señora del Carmen del monesterio del Señor sant Josef de Áuila*, teachings of the first convent of the Discalced Carmelites that she founded in 1562.

It was begun in 1565 at the request of her spiritual director Fray Domingo Báñez (q.v.) and teaches the way of perfection through humility, poverty, obedience, mortification, and prayer. The *Camino* has been reprinted in Clásicos Castellanos (2 vols., 1929–30).

CAMPEADOR, EL CID, see CID, Cantar de mio.

CAMPILLO, NARCISO DEL (1835–1900), b. Seville. Poet and short-story writer. A member of Valera's *tertulia*, and friend of Bécquer (qq.v.), Campillo was influenced by the classical tradition from Virgil through Luis de León, and equally by the Romanticism of Zorrilla and Espronceda (qq.v.). He taught literature in Cádiz (1865–9) and then in Madrid, where he edited the influential review *El Museo Universal*. *Memoria y teoría del estilo* (Cádiz, 1865) and *Retórica y poética* (1871) date from this period.

Campillo's verses were spontaneous, eclectic, and essentially mediocre: *Poesías* (Seville, 1858), and *Nuevas poesías* (Cádiz, 1867). These have been supplemented by *Cartas y poesías inéditas* (1923). Campillo also wrote a number of short stories, including ten in the collection *Cuentos y chascarrillos andaluces* (1896; reprinted 1898), which has 39 others by Valera, 15 by the Conde de las Navas and 11 by Thebussem; *Una docena de cuentos* (1879); *Nuevos cuentos* (1881); and *Cuentos y sucedidos* (1891).

CAMPO, ÁNGEL DEL (1868–1908), b. Mexico City. Mexican short-story writer, novelist, and humorist. Writing as 'Micrós', he published three collections of quirky, often gentle short stories: *Ocios y apuntes* (1890), *Cosas vistas* (1894), *Cartones* (1897). His *cuadros de costumbres* have been claimed as the best in the great tradition of 'El Pensador Mexicano' (Fernández de Lizardi), 'Fidel' (Prieto), and 'Facundo' (Cuéllar) (qq.v.). They were written under the pseudonym 'Tick-Tack' for newspapers and a selection can be found in the *Obras* (Mexico City, 1958).

Campo also wrote two novels: *La sombra de Medrano*, which has never been published complete; and *La Rumba* (first serialized in *El*

Nacional, 1890–1), named after a fictional shop in a poor district. A wretched seamstress, Remedios, is seduced by a brutal salesman, whom she eventually murders. Campo showed a good understanding of the middle as well as of the lower classes. Urbina wrote of him, 'No ve en grande, pero ve en detalle y límpidamente. Su dibujo es asombroso; su color brillante y enérgico'.

See A. Fernández del Castillo, *Micrós (Ángel del Campo). El drama de su vida . . .* (Mexico City, 1946), a biography and a good anthology.

CAMPO, ESTANISLAO DEL (1834–80), b. Buenos Aires. Argentine soldier, journalist, and *gaucho* poet (see GAUCHO LITERATURE). He used the pen-names 'Anastasio el Pollo' and (less frequently) 'El Pardo' and was a declared disciple of Hilario Ascasubi (q.v.).

Campo's most influential work, *Fausto* (1866), a poetic dialogue for *gauchos* in six episodes, was occasioned by a performance of Gounod's *Faust* in Buenos Aires. A superstitious *gaucho*'s naïve account of the opera is amusing because he believes that he has witnessed a genuine manifestation of black magic in the Teatro Colón. This tendency to see the *gaucho* as a figure of fun did not survive the *Martín Fierro* of Hernández (qq.v.). The Peuser edition (Buenos Aires, 1951) is the best, with a study and facsimile of the original MS. by Amado Alonso, and an introduction by Emilio Ravignani. Campo's earliest *gaucho* poetry appeared in *Los Debates*, a Buenos Aires daily. His collected *Poesías* (1870) were revised twice, the best edition being the 3rd of 1875.

See M. Mujica Láinez, *Vida de Anastasio el Pollo* (1948).

CAMPOAMOR, RAMÓN DE (1817–1901), b. Navia, Asturias. Post-Romantic poet. After a period in which he felt a religious vocation, and another in which he briefly took up medical studies, Campoamor turned to politics and literature. His first verses, *Ternezas y flores* (1840), he later described as being without merit, and neither *Ayes del alma* nor *Fábulas* (both 1842) brought him fame, but *Doloras* (1845; enlarged edn., 1886) was greeted as major lyric poetry. Serene and optimistic like his friend Valera (q.v.), Campoamor rejected a suggested laurel-wreath for his poetry. 'Quizá', Félix Ros has wittily indicated, 'por temor a una emoción fuerte' ('Perhaps for fear of a deep emotion'), thus revealing the weakness of this follower of Espronceda, whose significance was precisely in the expression of strong feelings. Throughout his poetic career Campoamor attempted without success the epic and philosophic poem: *Colón* (Valencia, 1853), *El drama universal* (1862), and *El licenciado Torralba* (1881). Critics and public alike, however, appreciated his shorter poems, especially *Doloras, Los pequeños poemas* (1871), and *Humoradas* (1886).

A man of great wealth, influence, and prestige, Campoamor was a distinguished member of the Moderate party and obtained, as well as a number of sinecures, the governorships of Castellón, Alicante, and finally Valencia. The themes of his poetry were a personal philosophy and love; and he attempted the reconciliation of traditional Catholic beliefs with the prevailing 19th-c. European drift towards scepticism and positivism. *El personalismo* (1835) and *Lo absoluto* (1865) were the result and, though almost unreadable today because of their *naïveté*, make interesting reading for the student of philosophical fashions. Campoamor wrote the valuable theoretical *Poética* (1883) which has been studied by Vicente Gaos in *La poética de Campoamor* (1955; 2nd edn., 1969). Campoamor's poetic achievement in no way matched his precepts, which can be summarized as follows: first, clarity and significance of ideas and diction; second, the transmutation of these ideas into vivid imagery; and finally, the expression of this imagery in rhythmic language avoiding the empty 'poetic' phrase. Campoamor was reacting against the bombast of the Romantics, and was to influence Bécquer and Bartrina in Spain; Darío, Nájera, and Asunción Silva in Spanish America.

The best editions of his works are *Poesías* edited by C. Rivas Cherif (1956) in Clásicos Castellanos; and the Aguilar *Obras poéticas completas* (1929; 5th edn., 1949).

See A. González Blanco, *Campoamor: biografía y estudio crítico* (1912) and R. Hilton, *Campoamor, Spain and the world* (Toronto, 1940).

CAMPOS, JOSÉ ANTONIO (1868–1939), b. Guayaquil, Ecuador. Journalist, writing mainly on political and literary topics. His humorous columns appeared over the pseudonym 'Jack the Ripper'. Several such collections were published in Guayaquil, notably *Cintas alegres* (Guayaquil, 1919) and *Cosas de mi tierra* (Guayaquil, 1929).

CAMPOS CERVERA, HÉRIB (1908–53), b. Asunción. Paraguayan poet and critic, he was one of the founders of the Modernist literary review *Juventud* (q.v.) but turned to surrealism in 1926. For several years he lived in the Chaco of western Paraguay, and later worked as a journalist in Buenos Aires. Commonly known as the leader of the Paraguayan Generation of '40, Campos Cervera wrote his first important poems in 1940–2 ('Hachero' and 'Sembrador'). He left only one book of poetry, *Ceniza redimida*

(1950), but his influence was profound, especially on Augusto Roa Bastos and Elvio Romero (qq.v.). His themes encompass death, private nostalgia (in 'Un puño de tierra') and, often less successfully, problems of work, war, and politics.

Campos de Castilla (1912), a collection of poems by Antonio Machado y Ruiz (q.v.) marking an abrupt change in both style and content from the modernist introspection of the *Soledades* of 1903. He rejected the *modernista* aesthetic, writing 'no amo los afeites de la actual cosmética / ni soy un ave de esas del nuevo gay-trinar'.

In *Campos de Castilla* Machado ponders national issues, including the decadence and backwardness of the people and land of Spain, and laments the passing of old glories. However, his pessimism is mitigated by the realization that nothing is permanent, not even decadence, and that Spaniards can regain the energy and initiative they once displayed. Images of temporality and flux (such as birds in flight or herds on the move) show the influence of Bergson, and Machado's philosophy of action that of Unamuno.

Machado had given up the Bohemian life of Madrid in 1907 for the quieter life of a schoolmaster in Soria (Old Castile) and had married Leonor, a girl of sixteen, eighteen years younger than him. Recollections of the happy interlude with his wife, who died of tuberculosis in 1912, are included in the greatly-expanded second edition of 1917. These poems on Leonor, and the hope that she may have survived death, were composed in Baeza, an Andalusian city to which he had moved after the years in Soria; other poems written in Baeza return to the national themes, and show Machado's belief that the faults he found in Old Castile are no less evident in the south. His interest in the land and people, and the hope for a revival, led him to write 'La tierra de Alvargonzález' and to typify the attitude of the Generación de 1898 (q.v.). The book is by no means limited to national concerns: the prevalent laziness, greed, and violence he castigates are to be found in all societies, and a number of biblical references make this point quite clearly.

See A. Terry, *Antonio Machado: 'Campos de Castilla'* (London, 1973).

Canaima (1935), a novel by the Venezuelan Rómulo Gallegos (q.v.). A key document in the development of literary *criollismo* (q.v.), the book stands between *La vorágine* of Rivera and *Los pasos perdidos* of Carpentier (qq.v.) in the tradition of the conflict between city dwellers and the jungle which fascinates them. Canaima

is an Indian name for the forest god who represents evil in the Guayana region of Venezuela. Gallegos never lived in the area, but visited this and most other regions of Venezuela briefly during electoral campaigns and read widely of local conditions. The central figure is Marcos Vargas, a man from Ciudad Bolívar who is tempted by the jungle, but the jungle itself dominates all else and Vargas merely survives, as neither victor nor vanquished. Gallegos hints that Vargas's son may end the exploitation of Negro and Indian, the *cacique* system and the cult of *machismo* (masculinity) which lend themselves to violence for its own sake. Vargas failed because he tried to become greater than Nature herself for the satisfaction that such a victory would give him. Gallegos argues that Venezuela needs both an American sense of nature and harmony, and a European social conscience and feeling for the rights of man, together with technological training.

Gallegos appears to conclude with an ideal synthesis of *civilización* and *barbarie* reminiscent of *Doña Bárbara* (q.v.).

CANCELA, ARTURO (1892–1956), Argentinian short-story writer and, in the words of Carmelo M. Bonet, 'accidental novelist' of the *Historia funambulesca del profesor Landormy*, a book influenced by Anatole France.

The important work *Tres relatos porteños* (1922) contains 'El cocobacilo de Herrlin,' 'Una semana en holgorio', on the 'Tragic Week' of January 1919, and 'El culto de los héroes'. The first two are quietly satirical, the third a subtle parable of a poor Asturian emigrant, who becomes rich by hard work in Buenos Aires, and his daughter, raised as a rich girl, who is ashamed of her father. Juan Martín and his daughter Juana María are recognised as universal types in Argentinian society.

Cancela's profound anglophilia led to his being influenced by G. K. Chesterton and to his invention of an Englishman whose life he relates. Cancela has parodied the Eastern tale in *Babel* (1919) and in *El suicida y el león de Persia*.

CÁNCER Y VELASCO, JERÓNIMO DE (c. 1594–1654), b. Barbastro. Playwright and poet, impoverished but of noble birth, who found protection with the Counts of Luna and de Niebla. He was a friend of some notable playwrights of the time, among them Moreto, Pedro Rosete Niño, and Antonio de Huerta. A witty, clever improviser, he excelled at wordplay in the *conceptista* manner and at Quevedesque satire. Fray Andrés Ferro de Valdecebo, in *El templo de la fama*, described Cáncer as 'unique in the art of the pun, and the first to give puns a soul . . .'.

The only plays Cáncer is known to have written without collaborators are *La muerte de Baldovinos*, banned by the Inquisition in 1790, and *Las mocedades del Cid*, both burlesques. The rest, written usually with two other authors, each of the three composing one act for the insatiable audiences of the time, include the following written with Matos and Moreto: *Caer para levantar, El bruto de Babilonia, Hacer remedio el dolor*, and *La adúltera penitente*. With Rosete and Martínez he wrote *El arca de Noé* and *El mejor representante San Ginés*. The standard of these collective works ranges from the shoddy to the inspired, but most are pedestrian works written with the sole aim of making money quickly. Cáncer's selected plays can be found in vol. 14 (1850) of the BAE, and his talented, original *entremeses* in vols. 17–18 (1911) of the NBAE.

Obras varias, including some of his poetry, appeared in two widely divergent editions, both dated 1651. A selection of his verse, including sonnets, *décimas* and *tercetos*, appears with *Vejamen que dió siendo secretario de la Academia* (poking fun at his friends and fellow-dramatists) in vol. 42 (1857), of the BAE. Other such *Vejamenes literarios* were edited by El Bachiller Mantuano [A. Bonilla y San Martín] (1909).

Cancionero General de Hernando del Castillo, see CASTILLO, Hernando del.

CÁNDIDO, the first pseudonym of José Martínez Ruiz, best known as Azorín (q.v.).

CANDIL, *Fray*, the pseudonym of the Cuban satirist Emilio Bobadilla (q.v.).

CANÉ, MIGUEL (1851–1905), b. Montevideo, where his father, of the same name, had gone into exile. Argentinian journalist and man of letters, whose deft touch enlivened even the early works, *Ensayos* (1877). *Charlas literarias* followed in 1879, then *Notas y impresiones* (1901), and *Prosa ligera* (1903).

Cané is recognised as the leader of the Generation of 1880 and is remembered mainly for an evocative autobiography of his years at boarding-school: *Juvenilia* (1884) published in the same year as his memorable travel book *En viaje*. He was the first Argentinian to translate a play by Shakespeare: *Enrique IV* (1900).

See R. Sáenz Hayes, *Miguel Cané y su tiempo* (1955).

CAÑETE, MANUEL (1822–91), b. Seville. Critic and minor poet. An arch-conservative in politics, he was an 'idealist' in literature like Valera, and an opponent of the liberalism represented by Leopoldo Alas ('Clarín'). He

was a drama critic in Madrid for many years, latterly with *La Ilustración Española y Americana*.

Poesías (Granada, 1843) was mediocre, and his plays are forgotten, with the possible exception of *El duque de Alba* (1845). Cañete was admitted to the Real Academia Española in 1857. He edited a number of early dramatists: Lucas Fernández, Jaime Ferruz, Agustín de Rojas, Francisco de las Cuevas, and Alonso de Torres, and among his critical and historical studies of the theatre are *Sobre el drama religioso español antes y después de Lope de Vega* (1862), and *Teatro español del siglo XVI* (1885).

CAÑIZARES, JOSÉ DE (1676–1750), b. Madrid. Playwright of the Calderonian school, like Antonio de Zamora (q.v.). Appointed to the household of the Duque de Osuna, at the age of 14 he composed his first *comedia, Las cuentas del Gran Capitán*, already showing a reaction to the contemporary neoclassical taste that was finally to dominate Spanish drama throughout the 18th c. and to overshadow his own work.

His plays were performed, and remained widely popular, in Madrid from 1704 to 1742, particularly the *comedias de figurón* (q.v.) such as the outstanding satire on Salamanca university life *El dómine Lucas*, which improves on the Lopean original. This is one of his texts in vol. 49 (1859 and reprints) of the BAE, the others being the historically-based *El picarillo en España, Señor de la Gran Canaria*, with excellent characterization; *Abogar por su ofensor, y Barón del Pinel*; *El honor da entendimiento, y el más bobo sabe más*; *La más ilustre fregona*, from the Cervantine exemplary novel; *Por acrisolar su honor, competidor hijo y padre*, from a lost original by Lope de Vega; and *Yo me entiendo y Dios me entiende*. Cañizares wrote *También por la voz hay dicha*, an imitation of Calderón's *El alcaide de sí mismo*. He also wrote *zarzuelas*, among the best being *Angélica y Medoro*. Cañizares' *Comedias escogidas* (2 vols., 1828–33) was the most extensive selection ever made, consisting of 24 plays.

See A. V. Ebersole, *José de Cañizares, dramaturgo olvidado del siglo XVIII* (1974).

CANO, JOSÉ LUIS (1912–), b. Algeciras. Poet, anthologist, and critic. He belonged to the group associated with the Málaga review *Litoral*, founded the poetry series Adonais in 1943 (editing it until 1963), and since the date of its first appearance in January 1946 has been secretary to the monthly book review *Ínsula* (q.v.).

His poetry collections, mostly inspired by Málaga, are: *Sonetos de la bahía* (1942), *Voz de la muerte* (1944), *Las alas perseguidas* (1946), *Otoño en Málaga y otros poemas* (Málaga, 1955), *Luz del tiempo* (Málaga, 1962), and *Poesía* (Barcelona, 1964).

Cano has written biography: *García Lorca* (Barcelona, 1962); critical studies: *De Machado a Bousoño* (1955), and *Poesía española del siglo XX* (1960). His anthologies have greatly assisted in making known the best current Spanish poetry: *Antología de poetas andaluces contemporáneos* (1952), *Antología de la nueva poesía española* (1958), *El tema de España en la poesía española contemporánea* (1964), and *Antología de la lírica española actual* (1964). Later works include *Poesía española contemporánea* (1974), articles first published in *Ínsula; and La poesía de la Generación del 27* (2nd edn., 1973).

CÁNOVAS DEL CASTILLO, Antonio (1828–97), b. Málaga. Spanish conservative politician largely responsible for the restoration of the Bourbon dynasty. He was the nephew of Serafín Estébanez Calderón (q.v.) whose life and times he narrated in '*El Solitario*' *y su tiempo* (1883).

He graduated in law in 1853, was appointed minister in 1864 and Prime Minister in 1874. He edited the monumental *Historia general de España* (18 vols., 1890–4), wrote three volumes of essays and lectures including *Problemas contemporáneas* (1884), a volume of poetry, *Obras poéticas* (1887), *Arte y letras* (1887), and *Estudios del reinado de Felipe IV* (2 vols., 1888) in the Colección de Escritores Castellanos. *La campana de Huesca* (1852) is a historical novel of the 12th c. Cánovas also wrote the interesting *Historia de la decadencia de España desde Felipe II hasta Carlos II* (1910). He was assassinated by the Italian anarchist Angiolillo.

See A. M. Fabie, *Cánovas del Castillo . . . estudio biográfico* (Barcelona, 1928); M. Fernández Almagro, *Cánovas* (1951); and the historical novel *Cánovas* (1912) by Benito Pérez Galdós (q.v.).

CANO Y MASAS, Leopoldo (1844–1936), b. Valladolid. Soldier and popular playwright. He won his reputation in the shadow of his master Echegaray (q.v.). Beginning with historical plays such as *El más sagrado deber* (1877) which dealt with the Second of May, he moved into the theatre of ideology and morality with plays such as *El código de honor* (1881), making a national reputation with *La Pasionaria* (1883), a forceful melodrama in which a woman avenges herself on her seducer. He attempted the Greek tragic manner with *La opinión pública* (1878) and the symbolist manner with *La mariposa* (1879), on the theme that human beings may not know happiness in this life. *Los laureles de un poeta* (1878) seems to have been a parody of Echegaray by way of reaction against his master.

Cantar de Fernán González, a lost epic. See Fernan González, Poema de.

Cantar de mio Cid, see Cid, Cantar de mio.

Cantar de Roncesvalles, see Roncesvalles, Cantar de.

Cantares, poems originally intended to be sung or set to music and deriving from the oral tradition. *Cantares de gesta* such as *Bernardo del Carpio* or the *Cantar de mio Cid* (qq.v.), are poems on epic themes. 19th-c. Romanticism produced a revival of the *cantar* genre, inspiring such important 20th-c. poets as Antonio Machado and García Lorca (qq.v.).

Cantares, Libro de los, the familiar title of the book known until 1898 as the *Libro de buen amor* (q.v.).

Cántico espiritual, the popular title of the mystical poem, *Canciones entre el alma y el Esposo*, and its prose commentary written 1576–8 by S. Juan de la Cruz (q.v.) and first published in Brussels. The longest work of S. Juan, it consists of forty stanzas in the *lira* metre (q.v.). The theme is the progressive stages to be reached towards union with God: the purgative (stanzas 1–12); the illuminative (stanzas 13–21); and the unitive (stanzas 22–40).

The *Cántico* consists of dialogues in which the 'universal essences' postulated by S. Juan (the Soul, the Creator, and the Created) act out the drama of the mystic experience. It enacts in the present tense the search for the Creator which is eventually rewarded. The Bride seeks out the cause of her despair, asking all living creatures where she can find God, and passes through the dangers of natural reasoning. S. Juan considers the Soul to be feminine—the Bride, and the Creator as masculine—the Bridegroom; this assigning of gender to religious concepts is indefensible theologically, but makes a powerful poetic point in its sexual imagery. At last the Bride sees her Lover's eyes reflected in the pool into which she gazes. The two join in love in an atmosphere of intensifying ecstasy.

The *Cántico* was probably influenced directly by the poems of Garcilaso (q.v.), and by the *a lo divino* version of Garcilaso by Córdoba Sacedo (q.v.). The symbolism is drawn from The Song of Songs, while the vocabulary is often evocative of the *libros de caballería* (q.v.) then popular.

A convenient edition of both poem and commentary is that of M. Martínez Burgos (1924) in Clásicos Castellanos, based on the MS. of the Carmelites of Jaén.

See D. Chevallier, *Le Cantique Spirituel de Saint Jean de la Croix* (Brussels, 1930) and J.

Krynen, *Le Cantique spirituel de Saint Jean de la Croix commenté et refondu au XVIIe siècle* (Salamanca, 1948).

Cantigas, brief, usually narrative, poems characteristic of the Galician-Portuguese literature of the Middle Ages, and intended to be sung. The name derived from the Luso-Galician *cantegas*, and the form reached its height in the 420 *Cantigas de Santa María* of Alfonso 'el Sabio' (q.v.).

There are three principal forms: the *cantigas de amigo* (in which a girl addresses a young man), the earliest examples being the *kharjas* (q.v.) of the Mozarabic period; the *cantigas de amor* (sung by a man to the woman he loves to lament her disdain and express his devotion); and the *cantigas de burlas* or *de escarnio*, satirical in intent and mocking other *trovadores* or vices of the time.

The Archpriest of Hita, Juan Ruiz (q.v.), describes a type of *cantiga* less important in its surviving examples: the *cantiga de danza*, sung as he says by 'escolares y de ciegos, para pedir limosna por puertas'. The Archpriest also describes and offers examples of the *serranilla*, in essence another type of *cantiga*. See COSSANTE.

The *cantiga de estribillo* stanza, modifying the *kharja*, normally consists of three parts: the *estribillo* itself, usually of four lines; an often unrhymed four-line *mudanza*; and a *vuelta* also of four lines. A typical rhyme-scheme in the *Cantigas* of Alfonso 'el Sabio' might be abab: cdcd: cdcb. The usual number of syllables is eight, though the *cantiga* is extremely varied in line-length.

Canto general (Mexico City, 1950), a major poem by the Chilean poet Pablo Neruda (q.v.), begun in 1938, adapted in the late 1940s during composition to reflect the history of the country from the Marxist point of view as a commission by the Communist Party, and continued after its first publication. Later editions appeared in 1952, 1955, and 1963 (2 vols.), the latter both in Buenos Aires.

Neruda's purpose is to write a new Marxist social history of the Continent, with the miners, farmers, and private soldiers in the foreground, and the generals and presidents in the background.

The work consists of fifteen very disparate *cantos* on: the earliest America, as yet unnamed; the Inca city of Machu Picchu; the Conquest; the Liberation; the betrayal of the Liberation (the first five being thus in rough chronological order, though with some temporal dislocation); the general invocation of America; the 'Canto general de Chile' which was earlier the intended complete poem; a poem to (and ostensibly by) ordinary people; an appeal to the common people of the U.S.A.; Neruda's flight originally from González Videla to the Urals; a miners' strike in Punitaqui; letters to other writers; the 1949 'New Year's Carol for the People in Darkness'; and the comprehensive and often contradictory conclusions 'The Great Ocean' and 'I am', in which he challenges a comparable North American 'epic' poet, Walt Whitman.

A dominant theme is the wealth, beauty, and natural order of the poet's continent, contrasted with the poverty, ugliness, and chaos resulting from man's ruthless exploitation of nature and his fellows. Critics have tended to judge the propaganda passages harshly, yet they are vital to a vivid treatment of the socio-political issues at stake.

The *Canto general*, while no more than a small part of Neruda's immense work, can be called a successful culmination of that epic tradition first adumbrated by José Santos Chocano, Andrés Bello, and José Joaquín Olmedo (qq.v.). There is a good selection from the text (with an English translation) in Neruda's *Selected poems* (London, 1970, pp. 164–279, ed. Nathaniel Tarn).

See E. Siefer, *Epische Stilelemente im 'Canto General' von Pablo Neruda* (Munich, 1970); and F. Riess, *The word and the stone: language and imagery in Neruda's 'Canto general'* (Oxford, 1972).

CANTÓN, ALFREDO (1910–), b. Emperador, Panama. Novelist. He received his secondary education in Nicaragua, then studied at Panama University and at Washington University, St. Louis, Missouri. His novels include *A sangre y fuego* (Costa Rica, 1935), *Rojas y pálidas* (Barcelona, 1935), *El ciego del Bulabá* (1946), and *Juventudes exhaustas* (1959) which won the first prize of the Brazilian *Cruzeiro Internacional*, where the novel was subsequently serialized. Cantón's experiences as labourer and farmhand are used in his books, whose deficiencies are a certain prolixity and political *naïveté*.

Capa y espada, Comedias de ('Cloak and sword plays'), in Spanish Golden Age drama (also known as *comedias de ingenio*), so called because the protagonists are usually gentlemen or even noblemen who wear a cloak and carry a sword; the lower classes, where they appear, wear their everyday dress. The settings are normally realistic, and usually in Spain.

The first recognised play in this genre is the *Comedia Himenea* by Bartolomé de Torres Naharro (q.v.), though Bances Candamo (q.v.) asserts that Diego de Jiménez Enciso was the first to write in the genre and most of the Golden Age dramatists wrote them, the most accomplished being those by Pedro Calderón de la Barca (q.v.). In his *Geschichte der dramatischen*

Literatur und Kunst in Spanien (Frankfurt/Main, 1854), Adolf Schack states that *comedias de capa y espada* are based entirely on external circumstances and there are no inner motives, typical examples being *La dama boba*, *La discreta enamorada*, and *El acero de Madrid* by Lope de Vega (q.v.). They are also called plays of 'character' such as *El vergonzoso en palacio* (q.v.) and plays of 'intrigue' such as *Don Gil de las calzas verdes*, both by 'Tirso de Molina', the pseudonym of Fray Gabriel Téllez (q.v.).

CAPDEVILA, ARTURO (1889–1967), b. Córdoba, Argentina. University professor, Romantic poet, and essayist. His best books are the quiet, melancholy *Melpómene* (1973), and *La fiesta del mundo* (1922) which contains the jubilant 'Canción de la recién nacida'. His autobiographical trilogy consists of *El tiempo que se fue* (1926), *Córdoba del recuerdo* (1937), and *Córdoba azul* (1940).

CAPELLÁN DE LA VIRGEN, EL, a familiar epithet for S. Ildefonso de Toledo (q.v.).

CAPMANY SURIS Y DE MONTPALAU, ANTONIO DE (1742–1813), b. Barcelona. Historian and literary critic. Giving up his early military ambitions, Capmany spent some time in the Sierra Morena as a colonist in Olavide's project for agricultural renewal, but returned to Madrid to become permanent secretary of the Real Academia de la Historia. On the French invasion he sought refuge in Cádiz, where he became a respected deputy to the Cortes.

The influential *Filosofía de la elocuencia* (1777) was revised for the much better London edition of 1812. The *Teatro histórico-crítico de la elocuencia española* (5 vols., 1780–94) was a largely justifiable defence of Spanish literature against its critics, such as Masson de Morvilliers. Capmany's major work is the closely-researched *Memorias históricas sobre la Marina, Comercio, y Artes de la antigua ciudad de Barcelona* (4 vols., 1779–92). He also edited *Antiguos tratados de paces y alianzas entre algunos reyes de Aragón y diferentes príncipes infieles de Asia y Africa* (1786; reprinted 1974 with new indices).

See J. Forteza, *Juicio crítico de las obras de don Antonio de Capmany y de Montpalau* (Barcelona, 1857) and E. Giralt i Raventós, *Ideari d'Antoni de Capmany* (Barcelona, 1965).

CARAMILLO, CRISPÍN, pseudonym of Cándido María Trigueros (q.v.).

CARBALLIDO, EMILIO (1925–), b. Córdoba, Veracruz. Mexican playwright and short-story writer. As a neo-realist he has brought daily life

to the theatre, exemplified by his first play to be produced (1950) *Rosalba y los Llaveros*. As a poetic and fantastic dramatist he created the modern *auto sacramental La zona intermedia* in 1950. His other neo-realist works are 'La danza que sueña la tortuga', first performed in 1955 as *Las palabras cruzadas*, and published in *Teatro mexicano del siglo XX*, vol. 3 (1956); *Felicidad*, first performed in 1955 and published the same year in *Concurso nacional de teatro*; and *D.F.* (1957), containing 9 one-act plays in the first edition and 14 in the second of 1962. His other fantastic plays are *La hebra de oro* (1956) and the important *El día que se soltaron los leones*, *El relojero de Córdoba* and *Medusa* (published with *Rosalba y los Llaveros* in *Teatro*, 1960), which combine his two modes in a new style. His short novels *La veleta oxidada* (1956), *El norte* (1958; trans. Margaret S. Peden, *The north*, Austin, Texas, 1969), and *Las visitaciones del diablo* (1965) show a master realist with a sure psychological touch. *La caja vacía* (1962) is a collection of ten realist short stories set in the province of Veracruz.

CARBALLO CALERO, RICARDO (1910–), b. El Ferrol. Galician poet. Professor of Galician literature in Santiago University. His academic studies include *Sete poetas galegos* (1955), *Aportaciones a la literatura gallega contemporánea* (1955), *Contribución ao estudio das fontes literarias de Rosalia* [de Castro] (1959), *Historia da literatura galega contemporánea* (1963; 2nd greatly enlarged edn., 1975), and *Gramática elemental del gallego común* (2nd end., 1968).

His regional novel *A xente da barreira* (1963) has a 19th-c. setting; his plays are *Farsa das zocas* (1963) and *A arbre* (1965); his collections of poetry include *Vieiros* (1931), *O silenzo axionllado* (1934), *Anxo de terra* (1950), *Poemas pendurados d'un cabelo* (1952), and *Salterio de Fongoy* (1961).

Cárcel de amor, La (Seville, 1492), the most important 15th-c. Spanish novel of courtly love, by Diego de San Pedro (q.v.).

The lover Leriano is taken by the allegorical figure of Desire to a 'prison of love' with gilded marble pillars, high towers, twisting stairs, a dark entrance, and symbolic decorations. The narrator then acts as the go-between, taking letters from Leriano to the princess Laureola. These letters are in many places rhetorical in the style of the time, but elsewhere a new note of eloquent passion and delicacy can be found. Just as the lovers' difficulties seem to be resolved, Leriano dies of hunger.

The *Cárcel de amor* shows each of the three characteristic elements of courtly love as defined by Gaston Paris in his seminal *Lancelot du lac* (*Romania*, vol. 12, 1883, pp. 459–534): the recognition of a moral principle behind human love; the altruistic gift of lover to beloved; and the lover's recognition of the beloved's absolute superiority. *La cárcel de amor* was influenced by an early version of the *Amadís de Gaula*, the legend of the Grail, Boccaccio, Dante, and the Castilian translation of *De duobus amantibus historia* of Aeneas Sylvius Piccoloini, as well as the Bible. Diego de San Pedro eliminates the verse sections which had to some extent marred his own earlier *Arnalte e Lucenda* (Burgos, 1491, but written much earlier), and modernizes the style by eradicating many Latinate elements. Some 16th-c. editions include a sequel or *cumplimiento* by Nicolás Núñez in which the character-narrator is visited by the ghost of Leriano.

The novel's extraordinary vogue, as the most popular *novela sentimental* of the Renaissance, can be judged from the fact that it was re-printed at least 24 times in the 16th c., and was translated no fewer than 20 times. The English version by Lord Berners (*c.* 1540) encouraged the literary movement known as Euphuism, so called from John Lyly's *Euphues* (2 vols., London, 1578–80).

There are editions of the *Cárcel* by Gili y Gaya in Clásicos Castellanos (1950), by M. Menéndez y Pelayo in NBAE (1907), by Cieza (1967), and by Keith Whinnom and Dorothy S. Severin (in *Obras*, 3 vols., 1971–, in Clásicos Castalia).

See B. W. Wardropper, 'El mundo sentimental de la "Cárcel de amor"' in *Revista de Filología Española*, vol. 37 (1953), pp. 168–93 and F. Márquez, '"Cárcel de amor", novela política' in *Revista de Occidente*, vol. 4 (1966), pp. 185–200.

CARDENAL, ERNESTO (1925–), b. Granada, Nicaragua. Important Nicaraguan poet and critic. After studying at Columbia University, and spending some time in Nicaragua, Cardenal returned to the U.S.A. in 1957 to the Trappist monastery in Gethsemane, Kentucky, where the Trappist poet Thomas Merton lived. His retreat there is recorded in *Gethsemani, Ky.* (1961), and about this time he also published *Hora O* (Mexico City, 1960) and *Epigramas* (Mexico City, 1961) which are by contrast bitter satires upon and denunciations of Latin American corruption and injustice. Cardenal's strength is the remarkable balance between the contemplative and the active elements in his poetry, which is strongly influenced by Pound, Eliot, William Carlos Williams, and Chinese and Japanese poets. His critics have suggested that much of his work reads like translations from English, but it would be equally just to point to the parallel of his social poetry with that of Neruda (q.v.). According to J. M. Oviedo, Cardenal's poetic feat lies in the ability to make us see that the history of America is a prediction, that this Utopia did once happen, and that recent signs announce it in the midst of the hecatomb.

Cardenal lives on an island in the Gran Lago of Nicaragua in a Christian community which he founded there, and discusses passages from Guevara or Marx, as well as from the Bible, with his congregation.

Cardenal's *Antología* (Buenos Aires, 1971) contains new work as well as poems preserved from the earliest volumes and from *Salmos* (Medellín, 1964; definitive edn., Buenos Aires, 1969); *Oración por Marilyn Monroe y otros poemas* (Medellín, 1965); *El estrecho dudoso* (Madrid, 1966); and *Vida en el amor* (Buenos Aires, 1970). He has subsequently published the visionary poem *Homenaje a los indios americanos* (León, Nicaragua, 1969); the inspirational *En Cuba* (Buenos Aires, 1972), in which Cardenal acknowledges the faults of Castro's Cuba but claims to find there that 'the Vallejo-era of America had begun (the new man, and man brother of man)'; the Nerudian *Canto nacional* (Mexico City, 1973); and *Oráculo sobre Managua* (1973).

See M. Benedetti, *Los poetas comunicantes* (Montevideo, 1972) for a long interview with Cardenal, among others.

CARDONA, JENARO (1863–1930), b. San José. Costa Rican novelist and poet. Cardona's *El primo* (1905) was the first Costa Rican novel of manners, depicting high society at the turn of the century. His other novel was *La esfinge del sendero* (Buenos Aires, 1916; reprinted San José, 1970), which tackles the problem of celibacy and the Roman Catholic priest with psychological insight and refreshing irony. His short stories were collected in *Del calor hogareño* (1929).

CARDONA PEÑA, ALFREDO (1917–), b. San José. Costa Rican poet and critic. In 1938 he moved to Mexico City. Cardona is thought to be the best Costa Rican poet of his generation; he wrote *El mundo que tú eres* (Mexico City, 1944), *Poemas numerales 1944–1948* (Guatemala City, 1950), and *Zapata* (Mexico City, 1954). His later style is free in rhythm and metre; in content he respects the historical and legendary past, while showing little of the chauvinism typical of many Latin American writers. He has won the Premio Centroamericano de Poesía (Guatemala City, 1948) and the Premio Interamericano de Poesía (Washington, 1951). His literary criticism has been collected in *Pablo Neruda y otros ensayos* and *Semblanzas mexicanas* (both Mexico City, 1955).

CARDOSO, ONELIO JORGE (1914–   ), b. Calabazar de Sagua, Las Villas province. Cuban short-story writer. His themes and character are drawn from the Cuban peasantry, but he shows an equal understanding of urban and rural life. His works include *Taita, diga Usted cómo* (Mexico City, 1945), *El cuentero* (Las Villas, 1958), *Cuentos completos* (1960; 2nd enlarged edn., 1965), *Gente de pueblo* (Las Villas, 1962), *La otra muerte del gato* (1964), *El perro* (1965), and *Iba caminando* (1966).

CARDOZA Y ARAGÓN, LUIS (1904–   ), b. Antigua, Guatemala. Poet, essayist, and art critic. He studied literature, philosophy, and art in Europe, spending several years during his youth in France, where he studied French poetry and the works of García Lorca. His complex poetry is influenced by surrealism: *Luna Park* (Paris, 1923), *Maelstrom* (Paris, 1926), *La torre de Babel* (Havana, 1930), *El sonámbulo* (Mexico City, 1937), and *Pequeña sinfonía del Nuevo Mundo* (Guatemala City, 1949). His best essays appear in *Guatemala: las líneas de su mano* (Mexico City, 1955), in which Cardoza y Aragón advocates a revolution at once political, social, economic, and cultural, after which all Guatemalans would have equal opportunities. He has written acutely on Mexican art, especially in *Pintura mexicana contemporánea* (Mexico City, 1953), and *México: pintura activa* (Mexico City, 1961).

CARDOZO, EFRAÍM (1906–   ), Paraguayan historian, whose publications *El Chaco en el régimen de las intendencias* (1930) and *El Chaco y los virreyes* (1934) led to his active participation in peace-negotiations with Bolivia in 1938, after the Chaco war. In Cardozo's view, the crucial factors in the evolution of Paraguayan national character were not economic, geographic, or racial, but the ideas of God and Freedom. He propounded this idea in his lecture *El sentido de nuestra historia* (1953) and subsequently in his book *El Paraguay colonial* (1959). In 1959 he published an important two-volume *Historiografía del Paraguay*.

Cards, Playing, see NAIPES, LOS.

CARNER I PUIG-ORIOL, JOSEP (1884–1970), b. Barcelona. Catalan expatriate poet, who revived Catalan as a literary language with Guerau de Liost (q.v.) and became the leading figure in the *noucentisme* movement with Eugeni d'Ors (q.v.). His first book was *Llibre dels poetas* (Barcelona, 1904). He was an assiduous contributor, with subtle irony, to *La Veu de Catalunya*, which he helped to edit over a period of many years. His early poetry was often playful, lacking the gravity and dedication of his later work: *Primer llibre de sonets* (1905), *Els fruits saborosos* (1906), *Segon llibre de sonets* (1907), *Verger de les galanies* (1911), *Les monjoies* (1912), *La paraula en el vent* (n.d. [1914]), *Auques i ventalls* (1914), *Bella terra, bella gent* (1918), *L'oreig entre els canyes* (1920), the last published in the year in which he founded Amics de la Poesia. He began a diplomatic career in 1921, living for a period in Costa Rica, France, Chile, and Mexico. After the Civil War he lived in Mexico and Belgium, teaching at universities. He continued to write in Catalan and, with Carles Riba (q.v.), was the major influence on the younger Catalan poets. His later books especially offer an insight into the potential wealth of Catalan imagery and metaphysical depth: an example is the long poem *Nabí* (1941), in which the familiar biblical story of Jonah becomes the kernel of a disquisition on faith and despair. Books of his expatriate period include *La inútil ofrena* (1924), *El cor quiet* (1925), *Sons de lira i flabiol* (1927), *El veire encantat* (1933), *La primavera al poblet* (1935), *Lluna i llanterna* (1935), *Paliers* (1950, with facing French translations), *Llunyania* (1952), *Arbres* (1954), *Obra completa. I: Poesia* (1957), *Bestiari* (1964), and *El tomb de l'any* (1966). His collections of short stories include *La creació d'Eva i altres contes* (1922) and *Les bonhomies* (1925). His translations are wellknown for their fidelity: among the best are those from Shakespeare, Hans Christian Andersen, and Villiers de l'Isle Adam. The first volume of a new collection of Carner's *Escrits inèdits i dispersos, 1898–1903* appeared in 1974.

See A. Manent, *Tres escritores catalanes: Carner, Riba, Pla* (1973).

CARO, JOSÉ EUSEBIO (1817–53), b. Ocaña, Colombia. Colombian Romantic poet. At first attracted to rationalism, he later became a Christian. In 1836 he founded the literary magazine *La Estrella Nacional* and the following year edited the liberal paper *El Granadino*. His civic and philosophic poetry boldly claimed freedom of conscience for all men, modelled on Byron. *En alta mar* is an impressive philosophic poem, perhaps his best together with *La libertad y el socialismo*. On the election of José Hilario López in 1849, Caro went into exile in the U.S.A., and after his return four years later soon died of yellow fever. He was the father of Miguel Antonio Caro (q.v.). Anthologies of his work appeared after his death: *Obras escogidas en prosa y verso* . . . (1873), *Poesías* . . . (Madrid, 1885), and *Antología: verso y prosa* (1951). Caro's *Epistolario* appeared in 1953.

See J. L. Martín, *La poesía de J. E. Caro* (1953).

CARO, Miguel Antonio (1843–1909), b. Bogotá. Colombian essayist and critic, President of Colombia, 1892–8, and son of José Eusebio Caro (q.v.). His early poetry was of little merit: *Poesías* (1866), *Horas de amor* (1871), and *Bolívar y los Incas* (1888), but his versions of Virgil's *Eclogues* and *Georgics* are probably the best in Castilian. The Instituto Caro y Cuervo in Bogotá re-edited Caro's works, among them *Poesías latinas* and *Versiones latinas* (both ed. J. M. Rivas Sacconi, 1951), *Estudios de crítica literaria y gramatical* (2 vols., 1955), a new edition of the Caro and Cuervo *Gramática de la lengua latina* (1895; 1972), and a new edition of Caro's *Obras completas* (vols. 1–2, 1962–72) first published in 5 vols. (1918–28).

See I. Hernández Normán, *Miguel Antonio Caro: vida y obra* (1961).

CARO, Rodrigo (1573–1647), b. Utrera. Archaeologist, antiquary, and minor poet. Caro was among the first Spaniards to investigate historic monuments and ruined cities in a manner anticipating modern methods. After the brief *Santuario de Nuestra Señor de Consolación, y antigüedad de la Villa de Vtrera* (Osuna, 1622), he published the important *Antigüedades, y Principado de la ilustríssima ciudad de Sevilla y Chorographia de su convento iurídico, o antigua chancillería* (Seville, 1634), supplemented by *Adiciones* . . . in *Memorial Histórico Español*, vol. 1, (1851), pp. 345–458. He also wrote *Varones insignes en letras naturales de la ilustrísima ciudad de Sevilla* (Seville, 1915), a volume of correspondence (ed. S. Montoto).

His poetry was conceived in the rhetorical mould of Herrera but free of gongorism. It includes 'A la villa de Carmona' (in the Seville *Revista de Ciencias, Literatura y Artes*, vol. 2 (1856), pp. 445–450, a *silva*; and *Silva a Sevilla antigua y moderna* first published in 1634 and edited by M. Romero Martínez in the Seville *Archivo Hispalense*, vol. 8 (1947), pp. 25–36. Caro is primarily remembered for the often reworked *Canción a las ruinas de Itálica*, formerly attributed to Francisco de Rioja, which is concerned with the ruins of the great Roman city of Itálica, near Seville. In verses of careful workmanship but lacking lyrical power, Caro helped to establish a tradition of antiquarian nostalgia in Spain. J. M. Rivas Sacconi's edition of Caro's *Canción* also contains an introduction, Latin translation, and notes by M. A. Caro (Bogotá, 1947). Caro's *Obras* (2 vols., 1883–4) has an essay on Caro by M. Menéndez y Pelayo reprinted in the latter's *Estudios y discursos de crítica histórica y literaria*, vol. 2 (1941), pp. 161–96.

See A. Sánchez y Sánchez Castañer, *Rodrigo Caro* (Seville, 1914), M. Morales' more ample *Rodrigo Caro* (Seville, 1947), and A. del Campo, 'Problemas de la "Canción a Itálica"' *Revista de Filología Española*, vol. 41 (1957), pp. 47–139.

CARO BAROJA, Julio (1914–), b. Madrid. Ethnologist and historian; son of the publisher Rafael Caro Raggio and nephew of the novelist Pío Baroja (q.v.).

He was Director of the Museo del Pueblo Español in Madrid (1944–55), and ran a course (1957–60) in general ethnology at Coimbra University (Portugal). Among his many distinguished works are *Los pueblos del norte de la Península Ibérica* (1943); *Los pueblos de España* (1946); *Los vascos* (1949; 3rd edn., 1971); *Las brujas y su mundo*; *El señor inquisidor y otras vidas por oficio* (1968); *Teatro popular y magia* (1974); and *De la superstición al ateísmo* (1974). His most enduring contribution to literary history is likely to be the important *Ensayo sobre la literatura de cordel* (1969), but Caro Baroja himself believes his best work to be the 3-vol. study *Los judíos en la España moderna y contemporánea*.

His *Obras completas* published to 1974 are vol. 1, *Estudios vascos*; vol. 2, *Vecindad, familia y técnica*; vol. 3, *Vasconiana*; vol. 4, *De la vida rural vasca*; vol. 5, *Brujería vasca*; and vol. 6, *Introducción a la historia social y económica del pueblo vasco*.

CARPENTIER, Alejo (1904–), b. Havana. Cuban novelist, of Franco-Russian parentage. In 1924 he became editor of *Carteles*, at that time the most important magazine in Cuba, and helped to found the Grupo Minorista. He was imprisoned in 1927 for signing the Minority Group's manifesto against the dictator Machado. Carpentier escaped from Cuba with a false passport, and worked as a journalist in Paris until his return to Cuba in 1939. He went into voluntary exile in Venezuela in 1945, first running a radio station in Caracas, then teaching at the Central University in Caracas, where he lived until 1959.

His best novel so far is *Los pasos perdidos* (q.v., Mexico City, 1953; trans. H. de Onís, *The lost steps*, London, 1956), thought by J. B. Priestley to be 'one of the major works of our time'. He has also written *¡Ecué-Yamba-O!* (Madrid, 1933), on the African element in Cuban art and life; the story *Viaje a la semilla* (1944, in an edition limited to 100 copies; reprinted in *Guerra del tiempo* and *Tres relatos*, below); *El reino de este mundo* (Mexico City, 1949; trans. H. de Onís, *The kingdom of this world*, New York, 1957); *El acoso* (1956); *Guerra del tiempo* (Mexico City, 1958), a novel and three stories about time; *El siglo de las luces* (Mexico City, 1962) set in the West Indies during the French Revolution (trans. J. Sturrock, *Explosion in a* *cathedral*, London, 1963); *Tientos y diferencias* (Mexico City, 1964); *Tres relatos* (Montevideo, 1967); *Literatura y conciencia política en América Latina* (Madrid, 1969); *La ciudad de las columnas* (Barcelona, 1970); the story *El derecho de asilo* (Barcelona, 1972); and the novel *El recurso del metodo* (Mexico City, 1974). The last, an ironic and bitter denunciation of the dictator Gerardo Machado, similar to Asturias' *El señor presidente* and García Márquez's *El otoño del patriarca*, traces the traffic in ideas and stereotypes between Europe and Latin America in the later 1920s and early 1930s.

Concierto barroco (Mexico City, 1974) is another ambitious short novel, in which a prosperous Creole leaves Mexico with his Negro servant for Spain and Italy. The style gradually becomes more ornate and baroque as the principal characters regress in time. Disguised as Montezuma, the *indiano* meets Handel, Vivaldi, and Scarlatti and, partly through a Vivaldi opera of 1709 based on the defeat of Montezuma, the novel turns into a search for a composite Latin American identity in which the Negro too finds a place. Musical analogies are expertly introduced and finely handled by Carpentier, the author of *La música en Cuba* (Mexico City, 1946).

See G. Pogolotti, *Alejo Carpentier: 45 años de trabajo intelectual* (1966); K. Müller-Bergh, *Alejo Carpentier: estudio biográfico-crítico* (New York, 1972), with a 19-page bibliography; and *Asedios a Carpentier: once ensayos críticos sobre el novelista cubano* (New Haven, 1973, ed. K. Müller-Bergh).

CARPIO, BERNARDO DEL, see BERNARDO DEL CARPIO.

CARRANZA, EDUARDO (1913–), Colombian poet, and leader of the Piedra y Cielo group, so-called from the magazine in which they came to the fore about 1935. The group rejected the national poet Guillermo Valencia (q.v.), and named their magazine after a book by Juan Ramón Jiménez. A poetry of bold metaphor, love of the homeland, and addresses to Christ, Carranza's work has appeared in the following collections: *Azul de ti: sonetos sentimentales* (Salamanca, 1952), written between 1937 and 1943; *Canciones para iniciar una fiesta* (Madrid, n.d. [1953]), written between 1935 and 1950; *Los pasos contados* (Madrid, 1970), written between 1935 and 1968. He has also translated Rabindranath Tagore and Rémy de Gourmont.

CARRASQUILLA, TOMÁS (1858–1940), b. Santodomingo, Antioquia. Colombian novelist. His law studies at Antioquia University were interrupted by the long-drawn-out Civil War and never resumed. By far the most interesting and popular regional novelist of Antioquia, Carrasquilla possesses a true flair for reproducing colloquial language. *Frutos de mi tierra* (1896; ed. Seymour Menton, 1972) is spontaneous, humorous, and packed with anecdote. Its subject in general is the exploitation of provincial people by those of the city—a common theme in Carrasquilla—and its central figures are an avaricious brother and sister. Carrasquilla's satirical treatment of human beings as animals makes the novel at one level a fable. His later books included *Salve, Regina* (1903), *Grandeza* (1910), *El Padre Casafús* (Madrid, 1914), *Entrañas de niño* (Madrid, 1914), *Ligia Cruz, Superhombre* (1926), *El Zarco* (1925), and *La Marquesa de Yolombó* (Medellín, 1928), an 18th-c. historical novel about a woman made rich by the mines. In 1928 Carrasquilla suffered a fall which confined him to a wheelchair, and he was completely blind by 1934, having to dictate one of his best works, *Hace tiempos* (3 vols., 1935–6). Carrasquilla also wrote a number of regional folktales: *En la diestra de Dios Padre* (1897), in which a peasant outwits the Devil in a style reminiscent of the Palma *Tradiciones peruanas*. *Dominicales* (Medellín, 1934) contains *cuadros de costumbres* commenting on some aspect of Saturday or Sunday life, such as the boy who sets out to impress the whole neighbourhood by his original attire and becomes a laughing-stock. There is an edition of Carrasquilla's *Cuentos* (Medellín, 1956) by B. A. Gutiérrez. The latest edition of the *Obras completas* is that of Medellín (1964).

See N. Mango, 'Tomás Carrasquilla: una bibliografía' in *Revista Interamericana de Bibliografía*, vol. 9 (1959), pp. 249–54; K. L. Levy, *Life and works of Tomás Carrasquilla* (thesis, Toronto, 1956; Spanish trans. Medellín, 1958); N. Sylvester, *The homilies and dominicales of Tomás Carrasquilla* (Liverpool, 1970).

CARRERA ANDRADE, JORGE (1903–), b. Quito. Ecuadorian poet, anthropologist, literary historian, and diplomat. He was Gabriel Mistral's secretary in Marseilles, and his earliest influences were French: Baudelaire, Jammes, and Renard. He has translated Valéry, Reverdy, and other French writers. Carrera Andrade founded the Editorial Asia-America in Japan and published the *haiku*-like poems of *Microgramas* (Tokyo) in 1940. Poems from numerous earlier books were selected for *Registro del mundo: antología poética, 1922–1949* (Quito, 1940), a book superseded first by *Lugar de origen* (Caracas, 1945), then by *Edades poéticas, 1922–1956* (Quito, 1958), and by *Obra poética completa* (1976).

William Carlos Williams has written of Carrera Andrade: 'The images are so extraordinarily clear, so related to the primitive, that I think I am seeing as an aborigine saw and sharing that lost view of the world. It is a sad pleasure, but a great one'. H. R. Hays is the translator of *Selected poems* by Carrera Andrade (Albany, N.Y., 1972).

See E. Ojeda, *Jorge Carrera Andrade: introducción al estudio de su vida y de su obra* (New York, 1972), with a good bibliography.

CARRERE MORENO, EMILIO (1881–1947), b. Madrid. Prolific poet, journalist, short-story writer, and novelist, although his dozen novels are nowadays neglected. He carried the bohemianism of his life into his fiction, with naturalism borrowed from Zola and Madrid *costumbrismo* mingled with mild eroticism. Few pages in his novels are attractive, and the language is irritatingly pseudo-archaic for its unintentional anachronisms; they include *El reloj del amor y de la muerte* (1915), *Aventuras de Amber el luchador* (1920), *La torre de los siete jorobados* (1924), and *La calavera de Atahualpa* (n.d. [1925]).

Carrere, a lifelong devotee of his native city, was made official historian of Madrid. His best play was *La canción de la farándula* (1912). As a poet he was influenced by Verlaine (whom he translated) and Darío (q.v.) in *El caballero de la muerte* (1909), *Del amor, del dolor, y del misterio* (1915), and *Dietario sentimental* (1916).

An edition of *Obras completas* (15 vols.) appeared between 1919 and 1922.

CARRIEGO, EVARISTO (1883–1912), b. Paraná. Argentinian Creole poet and journalist, whose devotion to the suburbs of Buenos Aires (to which his family moved in 1887) was recorded in his apprentice *Misas herejes* (1908) and the posthumous *La canción del barrio* (1913), tinged with the socialism later taken up with drums and trumpets by the Boedo Street group (q.v.). A month after his death the National Theatre presented his one-act play 'Los que pasan'. José Gabriel wrote *Evaristo Carriego* (1921) on his life and work, while the fourth volume of the *Obras completas* of Jorge Luis Borges (q.v.) is *Evaristo Carriego* (1955), stressing the relation between Carriego and the suburbs which he tended both to exalt and to exemplify.

CARRILLO E., FRANCISCOI (1925–), Peruvian poet and anthologist. Among his books of verse are *Rimas de juventud* (1945), *Provincia* (1961), *Cuzco* (1962), and the collected poems, *En busca del tema poético* (1965). His poems often seem to be rueful statements of the misery and poverty of others seen helplessly from outside. A good selection has been translated in *Peru: the new poetry*, by M. Ahern and D. Tipton (London, 1970), pp. 20–26.

Carrillo's important anthologies include *Las 100 mejores poesías peruanas contemporáneas* (1961); *Antología de la poesía peruana joven* (1965); and *El cuento peruano, 1904–1966* (1966).

CARRILLO Y SOTOMAYOR, LUIS DE (1581/2?–1610), b. Cordova. Nobleman, galley-captain, poet, and literary critic, who was educated at Salamanca. He later moved in literary circles in Naples, where he met Giambattista Marino, whose *Adone* (1623) was to set a new fashion in ornament, imagery, and conceits.

In his *Libro de la erudición poética*, edited by M. Cardenal Iracheta for the Biblioteca de Antiguos Libros Hispánicos (1946), Carrillo argues that Spanish poetry should revert to the sonorous diction and seriousness of Latin literature. Poetry should be written purely for the intellectual élite, and should be full of classical allusions, unusual metaphors, and recherché vocabulary, including the archaic. His book constitutes the main apologia for the *culteranismo* (q.v.) movement. An edition of his *Obras* published in 1611 was replaced by a corrected version in 1613. There is a more recent edition by Dámaso Alonso (1936), in which Alonso incidentally repudiates the theory that Góngora's *Polifemo* was influenced by Carrillo's *Fábula de Acis y Galatea*. Carrillo translated Ovid and Seneca. There is a new edition by F. Randelli Romano of Carrillo's *Poesie: introduzione, testo, traduzione e commento*, vol. 1: *Sonetti* (Florence, 1971).

CARRIÓ DE LA VANDERA, ALONSO (c. 1715–after 1778), b. Gijón. Spanish colonial administrator and travel-writer. He arrived in Mexico in 1735, but preferred Lima and lived there for much of the rest of his life, first from 1746 as *corregidor* and from 1771 as inspector of posts. As 'Concolorcorvo' he wrote the piquant, often amusing *El lazarillo de ciegos caminantes . . . sacado de las memorias que hizo don Alonso Carrió de la Vandera, por Don Calixto Bustamante Carlos Inca, alias Concolorcorvo* (Gijón, 1773 [sic]—in fact published in Lima late in 1775 or early in 1776). This useful guidebook about the road from Buenos Aires to Lima has been described by Jean Franco as 'como una bocanada de aire fresco en un mundo colonial mal ventilado' and its picaresque elements have led some literary historians to label the book as a novel. Carrió's sympathies are with the upper-class Creoles and, more ambivalently, with Spain. At the same time he castigates the slavish imitation of

European models and in a few places castigates the Spanish regime strongly enough to have induced him to disguise his authorship. This was proved by Marcel Bataillon in his *Introducción a Concolorcorvo y a su itinerario de Buenos Aires a Lima* (*Cuadernos Americanos*, Mexico City, July–August 1960).

El lazarillo was reprinted in Buenos Aires in 1946. There has been an English translation by W. C. Kline (Bloomington, Indiana, 1966). E. Carilla, in his annotated edition of *El lazarillo* (Barcelona, 1973) insists that the book is not a precursor of the Spanish-American novel but a travel book intended to portray towns and people as the author actually saw them.

CARRIÓN, ALEJANDRO (1915–), b. Loja, Ecuador. Poet, novelist, and short-story writer. He founded the influential review *Letras del Ecuador* and edited for a time *El Tiempo* of Bogotá. He has for many years contributed a political column to the Ecuadorian daily *El Universo* under his pen-name 'Juan Sin Cielo', and in 1956 founded the Quito review *La Calle*. His first writings appeared in the reviews of the Elan group (q.v.). *La manzana dañada* (1948) consists of autobiographical stories about his childhood. *La espina* (Buenos Aires, 1959) is a novel of solitude.

Carrión's poetry, collected in *Poesía* (1961), is dominated by disillusionment, at times metaphysical, at others Romantic, moving from an observation of nature or people to a conclusion reflecting the author's innate pessimism, as in 'Buen Año ¡Nunca hace buen año para los labradores!' (There is never a Happy New Year for the workers!).

CARRIÓN, BENJAMÍN (1897–), b. Loja, Ecuador. Son of the Romantic poet Manuel Alejandro Carrión. Widely-travelled essayist and critic, he wrote a novel on intellectual despair: *El desencanto de Miguel García* (Madrid, 1929). He was Ecuador's ambassador to Mexico and he transformed the Instituto Cultural Ecuatoriano into the Casa de la Cultura Ecuatoriana. Politically of the extreme left, he supported Castro's regime in Cuba. His first book was his brilliant, sympathetic *Los creadores de la nueva América* (Madrid, 1928), on José Vasconcelos, Manuel Ugarte, F. García Calderón, and Alcides Arguedas. *Mapa de América* (Madrid, 1930) deals with the following writers: Teresa de la Parra, Jaime Torres Bodet, Vizconde de Lascano Tegui, Pablo Palacio, and Carlos Sabat Ercasty. *Atahuallpa* (Mexico City, 1934) is on the conquest of the Inca Empire. Later books are not so important, but *El nuevo relato ecuatoriano* (2 vols., 1950–1) is a useful summary and anthology.

CARRIÓN, DIEGO and FERNANDO GONZÁLEZ, INFANTES DE. The poet of the *Cantar de mio Cid* (q.v.) makes them enemies of the Cid. It was long held that they probably were not historical figures, but Ramón Menéndez Pidal has indicated that they were the sons of a Conde don Gonzalo Ansúrez as is stated in the poem at lines 2,268 and 2,441. They were probably born *c.* 1075. Their father was not Conde de Carrión at the time of the events narrated in the poem, but their uncle (the famous Pedro Ansúrez) was. Their marriage to the Cid's daughters, and the consequences of their ill treatment of the girls are certainly pure fiction. The enmity indicated in the poem, however, may have a factual origin in the rivalry between the Cid and their uncle Pedro in and after the wars of 1072.

Their literary significance (they appear in some famous ballads) has been assessed by T. R. Hart in 'The Infantes de Carrión', *BHS*, vol. 33 (1956), pp. 17–24.

CARRIÓN, MIGUEL DE (1875–1929), Cuban novelist, doctor, and journalist. Influenced by V. Blasco Ibáñez (q.v.), Carrión wrote novels of psychological realism and social analysis concerned with hypocrisy and false values. A scientific positivist, he attacked false religious vocations in *El milagro* (1903), written in 1896–7, and in the connected novels *Las honradas* (1918) and *Las impuras* (1919) made the familiar point that honour and 'honour' are often misunderstood for base motives. *La esfinge* was left unfinished and not published until 1961. *La última voluntad* (1903) is a volume of short stories.

See A. Montori, 'La obra literaria de Miguel de Carrión' in *Cuba contemporánea*, vol. 21 (1919), pp. 337–52.

CARRIZO, FABIO, pseudonym of José S. Álvarez (q.v.).

CARRIZO, JUAN ALFONSO, modern Argentinian scholar and research-worker in the field of folk-song, who has collected more than 22,000 songs at first-hand, with the help of his wife. His books include *Antecedentes hispano-medioevales de la poesía tradicional argentina* (1945) and four collections: *Antiguos cantos populares argentinos*, known as the *Cancionero de Catamarca* (1926), *Cancionero popular de Salta* (1933), *Cancionero popular de Jujuy* (1935), the *Cancionero popular de Tucumán* (Tucumán, 1937), and the *Cancionero popular de La Rioja* (Tucumán, 1942).

CARTAGENA, ALFONSO DE SANTA MARÍA DE (1384–1456), b. Burgos. Humanist. Son of the Great Rabbi of Burgos, Solomon Ha-Levi, who chose to be baptized in July 1390 as Pablo

García de Santa María, and was created Bishop of Cartagena in 1401. Alfonso de Santa María was named Bishop of Burgos in 1435, but took up his appointment as late as 1439, because he was representing Castile at the Council of Basle. There he made a celebrated Latin speech *Sobre la precedencia del Rey Católico sobre él de Inglaterra en el Concilio de Basilea* reprinted in vol. 116 (1959) of the BAE. He also published a claim that the Canary Islands belonged to Castile and not to Portugal. Alfonso's Episcopal Palace in Burgos was a school of learning for many, including his followers Rodrigo Sánchez Arévalo and Diego de Rodríguez Almela.

Alfonso's poetry is lost: that which appears under his name in the *cancioneros* was probably by his younger brother Pedro. He compiled materials for *El Valerio de las historias*, modelled on the didactic history of Valerius Maximus, and edited with *Compilación de las batallas campales* (a compendium of major battles since biblical times) by Diego de Rodríguez Almela (Murcia, 1487). In the same year appeared Cartagena's *Doctrinal de los cavalleros* (Burgos), borrowing a good deal from the *Siete partidas* of Alfonso 'el Sabio'. His Christian works include *Tractado que se llama el oracional de Fernand Pérez porque contiene respuesta a algunas questiones que fizo* ... (Murcia, 1487) and *Defensorium unitatis christianae*, edited by P. Manuel Alonso (1943) for the Consejo Superior de Investigaciones Científicas. Alfonso was a notable translator and commentator: *Cinco libros de Séneca* (Seville, 1491) and *Tullio de Oficiis* [*sic*] *y de senectute en romance* (Seville, 1501), but he was not (*pace* P. de Gayangos), the author of *Amadís de Gaula* (q.v.).

See Hernando Pulgar's *Claros varones de Castilla* for a portrait of Alfonso, and R. P. Luciano Serrano, *Los conversos Don Pablo de Santa María y Don Alfonso de Cartagena* (1942).

CARTAGENA, Teresa de (*fl.* 1450), b. Cartagena. Religious writer who may, as J. Amador de los Ríos claimed, have been the granddaughter of the Jewish convert Pablo de Santa María and the niece of Alfonso de Cartagena (q.v.). This is unlikely, according to M. Serrano y Sanz, who published excerpts from her work in *Apuntes para una biblioteca de escritoras españolas desde el año 1401 al 1833*, vol. 1 (1903), which is vol. 268 of the BAE.

A MS. in the Escorial library contains, among other works, Teresa's *Arboleda de los enfermos* and *Admiratio operum Dey*, which were edited by L. J. Hutton in anejo XVI (1967) of the *Boletín de la Real Academia Española*. The former work stresses the need to bear infirmity with fortitude, while the latter discusses the spiritual favours granted to souls by God and, incidentally and with some asperity, defends her authorship of the *Arboleda*, which had been doubted in print by some male writers.

Cartas eruditas y curiosas, en que, por la mayor parte, se continúa el designio del Theatro crítico universal (5 vols., 1742–60), essays in the form of letters by Fray Benito Jerónimo Feijoo y Montenegro (q.v.). A series of 163 letters, dealing with very diverse subjects, which served to awaken the spirit of curiosity and intellectual debate then unfashionable in Spain. Feijoo is fearless in his attacks on false miracles ('Sobre la multitud de milagros') and on false pedantry ('El estudio no da entendimiento'), and, while he is often credulous and less rigorous than a modern reader would require, in his 18th-c. context he marks a new emphasis on the experimental as opposed to the dogmatic.

There is no unabridged modern edition of the *Cartas*. The fullest is in the 4-vol. *Obras* in the BAE and a 1-vol. selection by A. Millares Carlo is available in Clásicos Castellanos (1928).

Cartas marruecas, a book in epistolary form by José Cadalso y Vázquez (q.v.), composed in 1774, serialized in the *Correo de Madrid* (posthumously) in 1789, and first published in 1793.

Three imaginary correspondents exchange letters: Gazel, an Arab who had come to Spain in his country's diplomatic service, Nuño Núñez, a Christian friend of the Arab, and Ben Beley, a wise old Moor and friend of Gazel. The book, which does not survive in an autograph MS., deals with the character of Spain, but Cadalso is so careful to avoid offending the censors that he claims to omit questions of religion and politics, thus removing the two most interesting potential subjects. However, he discusses the corruption of politicians, nepotism, praises patriotism and the paternalistic Bourbon kings, attacks the Habsburgs for furthering their personal political ambitions at the expense of the nation's wellbeing, defends marriage and the family, praises poetry and fulminates against bad translators and those who corrupt the language, and attacks the bullfight and the institution of hereditary nobility based on paper deeds instead of actual deeds.

Though the form of Cadalso's book is borrowed from that of Montesquieu's *Lettres persanes* (1721) and Goldsmith's *Chinese letters* (1760–1), themselves modelled on Giovanni Paolo Marana's *L'espion du Grand Seigneur* (Paris, 1684–6), the matter is so far removed from his predecessors' that the traditional charge of plagiarism against Cadalso is unfair. The Clásicos Castellanos edition by J. A. Tamayo (1935) has been superseded by that of L. Dupuis and N. Glendinning (London, 1966).

CARTUJANO, El, alternative name for Juan de Padilla (q.v.).

CARVAJAL, María Isabel (1888–1949), b. San José. Costa Rican journalist and poet writing as 'Carmen Lyra'. She wrote a number of good children's books, such as the novel *En una silla de ruedas* (1918), *Las fantasías de Juan Silvestre* (1918), and the traditional stories of *Los cuentos de mi tía Panchita* (1920) retold in popular language. As a convinced Communist she was forced to leave the country after the uprising of 1948. She settled in Mexico City, where she died.

CARVAJAL, Micael de (*c.* 1501–*c.* 1576), b. Plasencia. Playwright. His important *Tragedia Josefina* was written in 1535 and, according to a note in Fernando Colón's *Abecedarium*, was probably published in the same year in Salamanca. The recently-discovered Seville edition of 1545 may approximate more closely to the lost *editio princeps*, and was thus edited by J. E. Gillet (Princeton, 1932) in preference to the shorter versions of Palencia (1540), used by Manuel Cañete for his edition published by the Sociedad de Bibliófilos Españoles (1870) and of Toledo (1546).

Carvajal's play, in 4,256 lines of *redondillas dobles*, dramatises those parts of Genesis that tell the story of the sale of Joseph by his brothers, his life at the Pharaoh's court, and the death of Jacob. The characterization of Zenobia is particularly notable.

Carvajal also wrote most of an *auto sacramental* called *Las Cortes de la muerte*, which Luis Hurtado de Toledo (q.v.) completed and published as his own work in 1557. This, together with Juan de Pedraza's *Farsa llamada danza de la Muerte* (1551; reprinted in vol. 58 (1865) of the BAE), is one of the most outstanding *danses macabres* in the Spanish 16th-c. theatre. The theory that *Las Cortes de la muerte* was finished by Hurtado de Toledo has been disputed by A. Rodríguez Moñino.

CASACCIA, Gabriel (1907–), Paraguayan novelist considered the best of his generation. His first novel was *Hombres, mujeres y fantoches* (1930), foreshadowing the exploration of naturalism and *costumbrismo* in the play *El bandolero* (1932), the stories collected in *El guahú* and *El pozo* (both 1938), and the novel *Mario Pareda* (1940).

His best book is *La babosa* (1952), a Joycean novel set near Asunción in the village of Areguá, which is in fact the main protagonist, each character appearing as a voice of the village: Ramón Fleitas, the failed writer brought down by drink and gambling, his concubine-servant Paulina, and the sisters Ángela and Clara. Casaccia subsequently published *La llaga* (1963), which won the Argentinian Kraft Prize, and *Los exiliados* (1966), which won the prize of the Argentinian weekly *Primera Plana*. The latter is set in a border town of Argentina, where refugees from Paraguay are fretting away their lives.

Casa de Aizgorri, La (Bilbao, 1900), the first novel in the *Tierra vasca* trilogy by Pío Baroja (q.v.).

First planned as a play, it is in effect a novel in dialogue. Baroja conceived the work after visiting a distillery in Pasajes, near San Sebastián, which he transformed into a symbol of the ruin and degradation of the inhabitants of Arbea. The surviving members of the once-illustrious Aizgorri are degenerate (Don Lucio and his son Luis), madmen or idiots. Baroja sounds a note of hope when Lucio's daughter Agueda overcomes her mad visions and looks toward a future based on hard work and honesty with her fiancé Mariano in the iron foundry. The Basque element is unimportant in this novel, being confined largely to the superstitious rantings of the servant Melchora. Baroja had not yet found his true voice.

Casa de Bernarda Alba, La (1946), a play by Federico García Lorca (q.v.) written in 1934, and first performed in 1945 (Buenos Aires). Bernarda Alba (alba, 'white') is a fanatical, recently-widowed mother of five unmarried daughters kept in seclusion to avoid a breath of scandal in a small country town. Angustias (whose name is symbolic) is thirty-nine: the youngest, Adela, is twenty. Adela, repressed like her sisters, falls in love with Angustias' *novio* and hangs herself when she is told (falsely) that he is dead. No male character appears at all, thus increasing the sense of sexual frustration.

The backcloth of *La casa de Bernarda Alba* is white for chastity. Lorca's belief in following one's natural instincts and in the freedom of women is here at its most articulate and poetic. The power of gossip to stifle the expression of physical love and stimulate hypocrisy is powerfully conveyed in what Torrente Ballester has called 'el drama formalmente más perfecto de todo el teatro español contemporáneo'.

Casa de las Américas, a significant bi-monthly Cuban cultural magazine edited by the poet Roberto Fernández Retamar (q.v.) and published since 1960 by the Casa de las Américas in Havana. Its contributors are drawn from Cuba and other countries in Central and South

America, and their quality is usually very high. Politically, it reflects the socialist ideas of the Cuban leadership.

CASAL, JULIÁN DEL (1863–93), b. Havana. Cuban modernist poet influenced by Gautier, Baudelaire, Zorrilla, and Bécquer. He abandoned his university studies when his family lost their small sugar estate, taking a job as a minor civil servant. Always delicate, Casal died of tuberculosis, having lost his post because of his articles in the press (signed 'El Conde de Camors') which attacked the Spanish governor-general. He preferred the beauty of art to that of nature, praising in *La canción de la morfina* that 'dicha artificial / que es la vida verdadera'.

Hojas al viento (1890) is a collection of neo-Romantic poetry characterized by an attitude of hopeless love and bitterness, the theme of perfection in art denied to our lives, and a style of refinement and exoticism. *Nieve* (1892; enlarged edn., Mexico City, 1893) achieves greater plasticity and realism, combining elements such as symbolism and Parnassianism, at that time considered mutually exclusive, and hence marking some originality. *Bustos y rimas* (1893), published posthumously, is comparable with the work of Darío (q.v.) for its confident modernism, renewing poetic forms in an atmosphere totally hostile to his achievement. The *Poesías completas* (1945) edited by M. Cabrera Saqui have now been superseded by the centenary edition: *Poesías* (1963).

His prose includes *Bustos*, the satirical sketches in *La sociedad habanera* (1888), short stories and impressionistic criticism. *Crónicas habaneras* (Las Villas, 1963) and *Selected prose* (Alabama, 1949) are useful, and his collected prose works have appeared in 3 vols. (Havana, 1963–4).

See R. M. Cabrera, *Julián del Casal: vida y obra poética* (New York, 1970), with a good bibliography; and *Julián del Casal: estudios críticos sobre su obra* (1974), by E. Figueroa and others.

CASAL, JULIO J. (1889–1954), b. Montevideo. Uruguayan poet. He spent many years as a diplomat in Spain, beginning there his magazine *Alfar* (continued in Montevideo from 1910) and publishing there his early books *Regrets* and *Allá lejos* (both 1913), *Cielos y llanuras* (1914), *Nuevos horizontes* (1921), *Huerto maternal* (1921), *Humildad* (1922), *Cincuenta y seis poemas* (1923), *Árbol* (1925) and *Poemas* (1926).

His later books left modernism behind, being serious and meditative, even somewhat heavy: *Colina de la música* (1933), *Cuaderno de otoño* (Buenos Aires, 1947), *Recuerdo de cielo* (1949), and the posthumous *Distante álamo* (1956). In the

766-page *Exposición de la poesía uruguaya desde sus orígenes hasta 1940* (1941), Casal erred on the side of generosity, the anthology containing more compositions of the 'stuffed owl' variety than is normally permissible. There is a good selection of his work entitled *Poesía* (1964).

CASALDUERO, JOAQUÍN (1903–), b. Barcelona. Literary critic and historian. He has taught in Spanish universities, also at Strasbourg, Marburg, Cambridge, Oxford, and in the U.S.A. The sensitive *Contribución al estudio del tema de Don Juan en el teatro español* (Northampton, Mass., 1938; reprinted with a new introd., 1975) established Casalduero as an original critic but it is as a Cervantist that Casalduero has achieved the highest recognition: *Sentido y forma de los 'Novelas ejemplares'* (Buenos Aires, 1943), . . . *de 'Los trabajos de Persiles y Sigismunda'* (Buenos Aires, 1947), . . . *del 'Quijote'* (1949), and . . . *del teatro de Cervantes* (1951).

He did not inherit the medievalist interests of his mentor Ramón Menéndez Pidal (q.v.), though he covered a wide range of themes: *Vida y obra de Galdós* (Buenos Aires, 1943), *Jorge Guillén*, '*Cántico*' (Santiago de Chile, 1946), *Espronceda* (1961), *Estudios sobre el teatro español* (1962), and *Estudios sobre literatura española* (1962).

See *Homenaje a Casalduero* (1972), edited by Rizel Pincus Sigele and Gonzalo Sobejano, with a good bibliography.

Casamiento engañoso, El, one of the *Novelas ejemplares* (q.v., 1613) by Miguel de Cervantes Saavedra (q.v.). It has been convincingly described by Pamela J. Waley in *BHS*, vol. 34 (October 1957) as a tale interlocking and unified with *El coloquio de los perros* (q.v.). They are edited together in a critical edition by A. Gonzalez de Amezúa (1912) and an annotated edition by F. Rodríguez Marín (1918).

Ensign Campuzano tells his friend Peralta how he was cheated into marriage by a certain Estefanía who claimed to own a grand house and its furnishings. These were later discovered to belong to Doña Clementa Bueso, who had left her supposed friend in charge of her property while on pilgrimage. Campuzano amazes Peralta, at the conclusion of his tale, by bringing out notes of a dialogue he claims to have overheard between two hospital dogs, Cipión and Berganza.

See also L. J. Woodward, 'El casamiento engañoso y El coloquio de los perros' in *BHS*, vol. 36 (1959).

CASAS, *Fray* BARTOLOMÉ DE LAS, see LAS CASAS, *Fray* Bartolomé de.

Casa verde, La (Barcelona, 1966), a novel by the Peruvian Mario Vargas Llosa (q.v.). The author described this novel as a story of man's alienation, of his discovery of sex, and of his choice of violence as the basis for human relations. Using five different autobiographical experiences, the book was rewritten three times before he was satisfied with it.

Technically, the novel is complex, especially in dialogue, on which Vargas Llosa relies to create atmosphere and character. Coherent interior monologue, dream monologue, fragmented dialogue, and the fusion of dialogues from different times and places are among the devices used to present the multiplicity of life in contemporary Peru, which for the author is a hell dominated by the church and the military. The settings are the city of Piura (the first to be colonized by the Spaniards in Peru) and the jungle trading-post of Santa María de Nieva, on the Marañón river.

The 'casa verde' is a brothel, symbolically the jungle, and by extension the green Earth where life goes on despite human error and evil. The parallel lives which are described here include those of a Japanese contrabandist who falls sick and ends in a leper colony; a jungle girl educated in a convent who is expelled and finds herself in a brothel; a slum boy who becomes a sergeant but is punished for a misdemeanour and on leaving the army finds that his *macho* code of honour leads him to jail, which he leaves only to find his wife (the jungle girl) in a brothel; the smuggler's wife Lalita; and others, all trapped in a web of contradictions and hypocrisies seemingly natural to the world we live in. *La casa verde* has been translated as *The green house* by Gregory Rabassa (New York, 1968; London, 1969).

CASCALES, FRANCISCO DE (1564–1642), b. Fortuna, Murcia. Historian and literary critic. Cascales fought in Flanders and travelled in France and southern Italy before settling as official historian of Murcia, in which capacity he compiled *Discurso de la ciudad de Cartagena* (Valencia, 1598) and *Discursos históricos de la . . . ciudad de Murcia* (Murcia, 1621; 3rd edn., 1874). As a humanist and critic he won the respect and friendship of Saavedra Fajardo and Carrillo y Sotomayor (qq.v.), though his unfinished *Epopeya del Cid* displays a lame imagination. His dialogue *Tablas poéticas* (q.v., Murcia, 1617; 2nd edn., 1779) and anthology *Florilegium artis versificatoriae* (Valencia, 1639) were overshadowed by the erudite and often sympathetic *Cartas philológicas* (Murcia, 1638; 2nd edn., 1779) which attacks Góngora. These have been reprinted in Clásicos Castellanos (3 vols., 1930–41).

See J. García Soriano, *El humanista Francisco Cascales: su vida y sus obras . . .* (1924) and A. García Berrio, *Introducción a la poética clasicista: Cascales* (1975).

CASCARRABIAS, *Abate*, a pseudonym used by Vicente Barrantes y Moreno (q.v.).

CASO, ANTONIO (1883–1946), b. Mexico City. Mexican philosopher. A leading intellectual, who became founding secretary of the Ateneo de la Juventud (1909) and Rector of the University of Mexico (1920–3), Caso founded the Universidad Popular in 1913 with the important mission of spreading education to the underprivileged majority. A Bergsonian intuitionist, he wrote a number of works on philosophy, the chief example being *La existencia como economía, como desinterés y como caridad* (1919).

See *Homenaje a Caso* (1947), published by the Centro de Estudios Filosóficos.

CASONA, ALEJANDRO, pseudonym of Alejandro Rodríguez Álvarez (q.v.).

CASTELAR, EMILIO (1832–99), b. Cádiz. Essayist and novelist. A Republican politician who mocked the much-vaunted charity of Isabel II in a satirical article published in *La Democracia*, which he had founded in 1864. Condemned to death in 1865, Castelar escaped to Paris and stayed there until the Revolution of 1868. He became President in 1874. He was a prolific novelist of minor importance: *Ernesto* (1855), *Alfonso 'el Sabio'* (1856), *La hermana de la Caridad* (1857), *Lucano* (1857), *Fra Filippo Lippi* (1877), and *Nerón* (1891).

Castelar was a famous speaker and his *Discursos* created a lasting impression on the Republican side, being influenced by Krause, Hegel, Michelet, Renan, Victor Hugo, and 'Clarín'. His major works in the field of history are *La civilización en los cinco primeros siglos del cristianismo* (1859), *La fórmula del progreso* (1867), *Tragedias de la historia* (1881), and *La revolución religiosa* (1880–83). 'Azorín' had a high regard for his work, asserting that 'la prosa castellana es otra desde Castelar'. Castelar's autobiography, which stops in 1870, was not published until 1922.

See A. Sánchez del Real, *Emilio Castelar: su vida y su carácter* (Barcelona, 1873) and Benjamín Jarnés, *Castelar, hombre del Sinaí* (1935).

CASTELLANOS, JESÚS (1879–1912), b. Havana. Cuban short-story writer and novelist, and an admirer of Rodó (q.v.).

La conjura (Madrid, 1909) is a short novel in which the idealistic doctor Augusto Román (a somewhat Quijotesque figure) is destroyed by business interests and social hypocrisy. *La manigua sentimental* (1910) tells the exploits of a soldier with General Maceo's forces during the struggle for independence. His novel 'Los Argonautas' was left unfinished at his death, but a series of essays on great men *Los optimistas* (Madrid, 1918) appeared posthumously.

CASTELLANOS, JUAN DE (1522–1607), b. Alanís, Seville. Poet. In his youth he decided to explore the New World and he wandered over much of the West Indies and northern parts of South America, finding employment as a soldier, miner, and pearl-fisher. He witnessed a number of important events in the Spanish colonization of America. In Cartagena he composed his first known poems: 'Discurso del capitán Francisco Drake' and 'S. Diego de Alcalá', in *octavas rimas*. He then became prebendary of Tunja, settling for 40 years among the Chibcha Indians to compose his mighty epic in verse *Elegías de varones ilustres de Indias*, in imitation of Ercilla's *La Araucana* (qq.v.).

The poem consists of 119,000 lines in *octavas reales*. It is divided into four parts, each of which is subdivided into so-called 'elegies' since the protagonist invariably dies during its progress; each 'elegy' is subdivided into cantos.

In the first part, Castellanos describes the voyages of Columbus, the conquest of the Antilles and the journey up the Orinoco. The second part is devoted to events in Venezuela and the third to events in Cartagena, Popayán, and Antioquia. The fourth, the *Historia del Nuevo Reino de Granada*, concerns Tunja, Santa Fe, and neighbouring cities and towns. Much of the poem is merely a verse rendering of a prose narrative and little more, but occasionally, as N. Bayona Posada has indicated, the author 'adquiere el tono inconfundible de los poemas primitivos, porque se asoma con ojos de niño a un mundo inédito'.

The *Obras* of Castellanos have been introduced by M. A. Caro (4 vols., Bogotá, 1955). See M. G. Romero, *Joan de Castellanos: un examen de su vida y de su obra* (Bogotá, 1964) and his essay 'Aspectos literarios de la obra de don Joan de Castellanos' in *Boletín Cultural y Bibliográfico* (Bogotá), vol. 4 (1961) and later vols.

CASTELLANOS, ROSARIO (1925–), b. Mexico City. Mexican poet and novelist. She spent her childhood in Comitán, Chiapas, but returned to Mexico City for her university education, later studying also at Madrid University.

She achieved recognition as a poet in 1948 with *Trayectoria del polvo* and *Apuntes para una declaración de fe*, following these books with *De la vigilia estéril* (1950), *Dos poemas* (1950), *El rescate*

del mundo (Tuxtla Gutiérrez, 1952), *Poemas 1953–1955* (1957), *Al pie de la letra* (Xalapa, 1959), and *Lívida luz* (1960). She is perhaps best known not for her intimate, feminine poetry praising her homeland and urging social justice, but for her fiction: *Ciudad Real* (Xalapa, 1960) and *Los convidados de agosto* (1964), both volumes of short stories; and the novels *Balún Canán* (1957; translated by Irene Nicholson as *The nine guardians*, London, 1958), a story, poorly constructed but in all other respects compelling, of a young girl's reactions to class prejudice, revolution and its aftermath, and the exploitation of the Indian in her adopted Comitán.

Even more impressive is *Oficio de tinieblas* (1962), again part-anthropological, part-autobiographical and also set in Chiapas province; this is better constructed than her first novel, and occasionally borrows *avant-garde* techniques of story-telling to good effect. Castellanos has published the essays *Sobre cultura femenina* (1950) and *Juicios sumarios* (1966).

CASTELNUOVO, ELÍAS (1893–), b. Montevideo. Argentinian short-story writer much esteemed for the Gorkiesque stories which appeared in magazines early in the 1920s and for his contribution to *Los Nuevos* (the title of an anthology), with Mariani, Yunque, Barletta, Amorím, Cendoya, and Pinetta.

His own *Notas de un literato naturalista* (1923) admitted a debt to Zola. Though a materialist, and inclined to show the darker side of life, Castelnuovo reveals a positive side in his pity for lepers, beggars, and madmen, and his scorn for the rest of the world which is too complacent in its good fortune to feel compassion for the unlucky. His works are *Tinieblas* (1924), *Entre los muertos* (1925), *Carne de cañón* (1926), *Calvario* (1929), *Malditos*, and *Larvas* (both 1931), the last a chronicle of juvenile delinquency and police brutality. Castelnuovo also wrote a play, *La noria*, c. 1940.

Castigo sin venganza, El, a four-act tragedy by Lope de Vega Carpio (q.v.) written in 1631 and first published (Barcelona) in 1634. Its plot is taken from the eleventh tale in *Novelle* by Matteo Bandello, which is based on a historical event. The central character is the vicious Duke of Ferrara, who is married to a young noblewoman, Casandra. He abandons her for other women, while Casandra, who had fallen in love with the Duke's bastard son Federico without knowing his identity, commits incest with him in the Duke's long absence during the Holy Wars. Aurora, whom the Duke had wished to marry to Federico, informs him of what has occurred and he is convinced of his wife's guilt on overhearing an angry scene between

Casandra and Federico. Later, the Duke ties up Casandra, conceals her identity, and says she is a traitor. He then orders Federico to kill the 'traitor' and when his son, despite presentiments of disaster, does kill Casandra, the Duke summons his guards and orders them to kill his son, who has murdered the Duchess of Ferrara.

Lope's ability to make the Duke a living, and not altogether detestable, character (on his return to Ferrara he declared himself to be reformed) turns a domestic melodrama into high tragedy full of irony. The best edition of the play is that by C. A. Jones (Oxford, 1966).

See E. M. Wilson, 'Cuando Lope quiere, quiere' in *Cuadernos Hispanoamericanos*, nos. 161–2 (1963), pp. 265–98; and V. Dixon and A. A. Parker, '"El castigo sin venganza": two lines, two interpretations' in *Modern Language Notes*, vol. 85 (1970), pp. 157–66.

CASTILLEJO, Cristóbal de (*c.* 1491–1450), b. Ciudad Rodrigo. Poet. At fifteen he became a page to Charles V's brother, the Archduke Ferdinand, returning to his service after becoming a Cistercian priest. In 1539 he travelled to Venice, joining the household of the Spanish ambassador Diego Hurtado de Mendoza. When his former patron became King Ferdinand of Austria, Castillejo joined him in Vienna but apparently derived no benefits from the patronage.

Castillejo defended the traditional Spanish verse forms (such as the ballad and the *villancico*), at a time when the newer Italian metres were becoming more popular, in *Contra los que dejan los metros castellanos y siguen los italianos* (*c.* 1540), in which a few Italianate sonnets were included as mockery.

His preferred metre was the octosyllabic, both uniform and in *pie quebrado* form. Thematically, Castillejo's work can be divided into three groups: the moral and devotional, such as the *Diálogo entre la verdad y la lisonja* (Alcalá, 1614); love poetry of the courtly mode, such as the poem to Ana de Aragón; and the conversational, informal group, including the *Diálogo que habla de las condiciones de las mugeres* (Venice, 1544; ed. L. Pfandl in the *Revue Hispanique*, vol. 52, 1921) on the medieval topos of the faults and virtues of women.

The best example of the first group is the satirical *Diálogo y discurso de la vida de corte* in the tradition of the *Menosprecio de corte* by Guevara (q.v.). The best example of the second group is *Sermón de amores del maestro buen talante llamado fray Nidel de la orden del Fristel* (1540; ed. R. Foulché-Delbosc in *Revue Hispanique*, vol. 36, 1916). The *Diálogo entre el autor y su pluma* has been edited by E. Werner in *Revue Hispanique*, vol. 71, 1927. Adolfo de Castro edited a selection

of Castillejo's verses in vol. 32 (1854), pp. 105–252, of the BAE. All Castillejo's plays are lost, with the exception of some fragments of *Farsa de la Constanza* (in vol. 32 of the BAE), for which see J. P. Wickersham Crawford, 'The relationship of Castillejo's "Farsa de la Constanza" and the "Sermon de Amores"' in *Hispanic Review*, vol. 4 (1936), pp. 373–5.

Las Obras of Castillejo were first edited by J. López de Velasco in a censored version dated 1573, and have been newly edited by J. Domínguez Bordona (4 vols., 1926–8) for Clásicos Castellanos.

See C. L. Nicolay, *The life and works of Castillejo* (Philadelphia, 1910).

CASTILLO, Eduardo (1889–1938), Colombian modernist poet influenced by French Parnassians and known as one of the Centenarios. His poems are tender, melancholy, and pessimistic.

His best-known work is *El árbol que canta* (n.d. [1938]). There is a good government-sponsored anthology, *Obra poética* (1965). His *Duelo lírico* (1918) centred on the figure of Guillermo Valencia (q.v.), whom Ángel María Céspedes attacked and Castillo chose to defend.

CASTILLO, Hernando del (*fl.* 1510), compiler of the so-called *Cancionero General de Hernando del Castillo*. This has the literary and documentary importance for the reigns of Enrique IV and the Catholic Monarchs which the *cancioneros* of Baena (q.v.) and Stúñiga (q.v.) possess for the reigns of Juan II and Alfonso V of Aragón respectively.

The *Cancionero General de muchas y diversas obras de todos i los mas principales trovadores de España en lengua castellana . . .* (Valencia, 1511) contains 1033 poems by 128 named poets and many more unnamed. The poems have been divided into the following main groups: satirical, moral and didactic, devout, gallant, and those for jousts and tournaments. Most of the well-known writers of the age are included, among them the Manriques, Cota, Sánchez de Badajoz, Álvarez Gato, Santillana, Mena, Montoro, and Diego de San Pedro. The Toledo edition of 1520 prints 167 new poems, omits many more, and alters others previously printed. The first edition appeared in a facsimile reprint by Rodríguez Moñino in 1958, and the Toledo edition was published in a New York facsimile in 1904. The book was popular, and influenced several generations of poets through frequent reprints, notably those of Valencia (1540), Saragossa (1554), and Antwerp (1557).

CASTILLO ANDRACA Y TAMAYO, Fray Francisco del (1716–70), b. Piura. Peruvian playwright and poet. A blind lay brother, known as 'El ciego de la Merced' after the order which he joined at the age of fourteen, he spent his life in meditation and study. A prolific balladeer and clever improviser of lyrics on the manners of 18th-c. Lima, Castillo Andraca wrote *sainetes* and plays imitating French neo-classical drama. His *Obras* have been edited by Padre Rubén Vargas Ugarte (1948).

Castillo Interior, o tratado de las Moradas, El (Salamanca, 1588), a mystical work by Santa Teresa de Jesús (q.v.) and one of the capital documents of Western mysticism.

It was written in 1577, in the Carmelite convent of Toledo, at a period when Santa Teresa's enemies were trying to deport her to Spanish America, fearing her potential to reform the Church. She had experienced mystical visions for more than ten years, including the famous episode of the cherubim transfixing her heart with a golden arrow. She saw a vision of a glittering castle with many halls, 'just as there are many mansions in heaven', and set out to describe the seven abodes or *moradas* leading to union with God. The first three constitute the *vía purgativa* in which the soul remains burdened with sin: the ascetic doctrine is that of the *camino de perfección* (q.v.). The next three abodes are those of the *vía iluminativa*, the purely mystical experiences of those purified by ascetic practices. In the sixth *morada*, the suffering of the soul, wounded by the love of the Bridegroom, at last turns into pleasure, and in the seventh the Bride achieves mystical union with God.

The sources of Teresa's writing, long considered original, include the Bible and martyrology, Thomas à Kempis, the *Confessions* of St. Augustine, Fray Luis de Granada (q.v.), Fray Alonso de Madrid (q.v.), and Fray Pedro de Alcántara (q.v.).

T. Navarro Tomás edited *Las moradas* for the Clásicos Castellanos in 1916, and a second edition appeared in 1922.

CASTILLO PUCHE, José Luis (1919–), b. Yecla, Murcia. Novelist and travel-writer who first attracted attention in 1952 with *Memorias íntimas de Aviraneta* (1952) on Baroja. His novels are *Sin camino* (Buenos Aires, 1956), written in 1947; *Con la muerte al hombro* (1954); *El vengador* (Barcelona, 1956); *Hicieron partes* (1957); *Paralelo 40* (Barcelona, 1963); and *Oro blanco* (1963). He has been called a Catholic moralist, and his skill in realistic observation was evident from *Sin camino*. It is an ironic account of a seminarist torn between a late vocation and his anarchic self-questioning, set in the early days of war. *América de cabo a rabo* (1959) was his first

travel book, followed by *El Congo estrena libertad* (1961).

CASTILLO SOLÓRZANO, Alonso de (1584–1648?), b. Tordesillas, Valladolid. Picaresque novelist and dramatist. His father was in the service of the Duque de Alba and he himself found patrons in the Marqués del Villar and two successive Marqueses de los Vélez.

His best play is *El mayorazgo figura*, first published in *Los alivios de Casandra* (Barcelona, 1640), which deals with the adventures of a pretentious idiot, and appears with *El marqués del Cigarral* in vol. 45 (1858) of the BAE. Castillo Solórzano's *entremeses* appear, selected, in vol. 17 (1911) of the NBAE.

He is remembered above all as a picaresque storyteller in a *Decamerone*-style framework, with a courtly or at least urban milieu. These escapist stories are virtually devoid of moral teaching; they often seem mechanical, as though the author cannot tell his characters apart, and he does not dwell on any deeper motives behind the surface of his intricate plots. They include *Tardes entretenidas* (1625), *Jornadas alegres* (1626), *Tiempo de Regozijo, y Carnestolendas de Madrid* (1627), *Lisardo enamorado* (Valencia, 1629; ed. E. Juliá Martínez, 1947), *Las Harpías en Madrid, y coche de las estafas* (Barcelona, 1631; ed. E. Cotarelo y Mori with *Tiempo de regocijo*, 1907), *Noches de plazer, en que contiene doze Nouelas* (Barcelona, 1631; ed. E. Cotarelo y Mori, 1906 and reprinted in Barcelona, 1914 and 1922), *La niña de los embustes, Teresa de Mançanares, natural de Madrid* (Barcelona, 1632; ed. E. Cotarelo y Mori, 1906 and reprinted in 1929), *Los amantes andaluzes: historia entretenida* (Barcelona, 1633), *Fiestas del Iardín* (Valencia, 1634, containing four stories and three plays: 'Los encantos de Bretaña', 'El fantasma de Valencia', and 'El marqués del Cigarral'), the celebrated *Aventuras del bachiller Trapaza, quinta essencia de Embusteros, y Maestro de Embelecadores* (Saragossa, 1637; later editions in 1944 and 1949) and its even better sequel *La garduña de Sevilla, y anzuelo de las bolsas* (1642; ed. F. Ruiz Morcuende, 1922 and revised 1942 for Clásicos castellanos), *La quinta de Laura* (Saragossa, 1649), and *Sala de recreación* (Saragossa, 1649). R. O. Jones's somewhat scathing view of *La garduña de Sevilla* is that it is 'representative of the whole group in its monotonous parade of would-be ingenious trickery and in its general shallowness', but this view is too severe in the light of the author's clear intention to provide amusing reading such as was then available to Italians. Castillo also wrote hagiography for the popular market, and satirical and light verse collected in *Donayres del Parnaso* (2 vols., 1624–5).

See P. N. Dunn, *Castillo Solórzano and the decline of the Spanish novel* (Oxford, 1952).

CASTILLO Y GUEVARA, *Venerable Madre* MARÍA FRANCISCA JOSEFA DEL (1671–1742), b. Tunja, Boyacá. Colombian autobiographer and religious writer. Her father was from Illescas (Toledo) and her mother was a Colombian Creole. Of the family of eight, four others also entered religious orders. María Francisca herself joined the Order of Poor Clares at the age of 20, after a very strict and conventional upbringing. She wrote her autobiography (*Vida*, Philadelphia, 1817; Bogotá, 1942) at the instruction of her confessor P. Francisco Herrera, and a pathetic, charming work entitled in the MS. 'Afectos espirituales' and published as *Sentimientos espirituales* (pt. 1, 1843; pt. 2 as pp. 305–80 of A. Gómez Restrepo's *Historia de la literatura colombiana*, 1945–6). The latter work was judged, over-generously, to be on a par with the writings of S. Teresa de Ávila by Menéndez y Pelayo. María Francisca also wrote poetry but this is not known to have been published.

CASTRO, AMÉRICO (1885–1972), b. Rio de Janeiro. Spanish critic and historian, a disciple of Ramón Menéndez Pidal and of F. Giner de los Ríos (qq.v.). He taught first in Spain, later in Latin America, and finally in the U.S.A., at Princeton and Harvard. A. M. de Lera characterized Castro as 'quizá el más esforzado y profundo investigador de la realidad histórica de España.' His views in such books as *España en su historia: cristianos, moros y judíos* (Buenos Aires, 1948) and *La realidad histórica de España* (Mexico City, 1954, new edn., 1966) are that the co-existence of Christian, Moor, and Jew was the decisive factor in the development of Spanish culture, and that any historical work which does not take into account this fundamental diversity of tradition must eventually misunderstand the nature of the Spanish people. Castro's position was elaborated in *Origen, ser y existir de los españoles* (1959), revised as *Los españoles* (Madrid, 1965), *De la edad conflictiva* (Madrid, 1961), *Sobre el nombre y el quien de los españoles*, and *Españoles al margen* (both Madrid, 1973). This position has been attacked comprehensively by Claudio Sánchez-Albornoz and others.

Much of Castro's work has been less controversial, however: *Lengua, enseñanza y literatura* (1924), *Don Juan en la literatura española* (1924), *El pensamiento de Cervantes* (1925), *Santa Teresa y otros ensayos* (1932), *Lo hispánico y el erasmismo* (Buenos Aires, 1942), *Castilla la gentil* (Mexico City, 1944), *Antonio de Guevara* (Princeton, N.J., 1945), and *Cervantes y los casticismos españoles* (1966).

Castro has written studies of and edited Mal Lara, Quevedo, Lope de Vega, Rojas Zorrilla, Tirso de Molina, and many other classical writers. There is a bibliography by A. Brent and E. Kirsner in *Semblanzas y estudios españoles* (1956).

CASTRO, INÉS DE, the subject of a Spanish literary tradition preceding Pero López de Ayala, who mentions the legend in his *Crónica del rey Don Pedro*. The ballads about Doña Isabel de Liar describe a love affair identical with that between Inés and Pedro. The legend may have originated in Portugal, where the early *Trovas a morte de D. Inês de Castro* appeared in the *Cancioneiro Geral* compiled by Garcia de Resende (1516). Camões alluded to Inés in Canto III of *Os Lusíadas*:

> *misera e mesquinha*
> *que, depois de ser morta, foi Rainha*

and Antonio Ferreira wrote the Greek-inspired *Tragédia . . . de D. Inês de Castro*, which in turn inspired the *Nise lastimosa* and *Nise laureada* of Fray Jerónimo Bermúdez (q.v.), who lived for some time in Portugal.

Suárez de Alarcón is the author of a poem entitled *La Infanta coronada*. Mexía de la Cerda's involved *Tragedia famosa de doña Inés de Castro* was printed in 1612.

A lost *comedia* by Lope de Vega called *Doña Inés de Castro* is mentioned in his *El peregrino en su patria* (q.v., 1618). The most successful treatment of the subject is the *Reinar después de morir* of Vélez de Guevara. Matos Fragoso added a second part with the title of *Ver y creer*. The latest notable version of the fertile theme is *La reine morte* of Henry de Montherlant. Ramón de la Cruz parodied the legend in his *sainete Inesilla la de Pinto*, and there is a brief work entitled *Doña Inés de Castro*, by Comella, which is worthy of note.

The facts according to Fernão Lopes appear to be these: in 1340 the lovely Galician Inés de Castro went to the court of Portugal as lady-in-waiting to Don Pedro's wife, the Infanta Constanza. Inés and Pedro fell in love, and two sons were born to them without the general knowledge of the court. After Constanza died, however, the affair was discovered and Inés was killed by unnamed assassins on the banks of the Mondego, near Coimbra, not far from what has come to be called *a quinta das lágrimas*. The date usually accepted for the political assassination is 1355.

CASTRO, ÓSCAR (1910–47), b. Rancagua. Chilean poet, short-story writer, and novelist. His poetry is characterized by delicacy of feeling and expression, and first attracted attention in 1936 with *Responso a García Lorca*. He abandoned his early masters Huidobro and

Lorca for the gongorism of *Camino en el alba* (1940) and *Viaje del alba a la noche* (1941). His short stories sprang from the same provincial source as his verse. They were collected in *Huellas en la tierra* (1940), *La sombra de las cumbres* (1944), and *Comarca del jardín* (1953). Castro also cultivated the novel with good results: *Llampo de sangre* (1950) set in the copper mines, is in the 'magic realist' vein; *La vida simplemente* (1951) shows an innocent boy in a brutal world; *Lina y su sombra* (1958) portrays the life and times of a woman ill-treated by her gambling lover. Hernán Poblete Varas compiled a useful if brief *Antología* (1952).

See T. Lago, *Tres poetas chilenos* (1942), the other poets studied being Nicanor Parra and Victoriano Vicario (qq.v.).

CASTRO, ROSALÍA DE (1837–85), b. Santiago de Compostela. Poet and novelist who wrote in Galician and Castilian. At 15 she discovered that she was the illegitimate daughter, possibly by a priest, of Doña Teresa de Castro. She left Galicia at 19, publishing in Madrid her first book, *La flor* (1857), where the eneasyllabic verse form of 'La rosa del camposanto' (written in 1851) predates the so-called 'innovations' of Darío (q.v.). In 1820 Rosalía married the Galician art critic and historian Manuel Martínez Murguía, but although she had six children and a secure family life, she was often bored and recalled in her poems and fiction a lost love from her adolescence who may have been Aurelio Aguirre, the hero in her novel *Flavio* (1861). In 1863 she published *A mi madre* in Castilian and *Cantares gallegos*, the latter reprinted in its centenary year in Salamanca (ed. R. Carballo Calero). This latter book was influenced by the *baladas* of Trueba and Ruiz Aguilera; its delightful songs found their way into popular memory so quickly and deeply that many are nowadays cited as authentic folksongs, though they were created specifically for this book by Rosalía. Esperanza, the heroine of her novel *La hija del mar* (Vigo, 1859), a persecuted outcast of unknown parents who finally drowns herself, seems partly based on Rosalía, while critics have identified as her husband the Señor de la Albuérniga of *El caballero de las botas azules* (Lugo, 1867).

The collection of Galician poems *Follas novas* (1880) was followed by her masterpeice, in Castilian: *En las orillas del Sar* (1884; trans. S. Griswold Morley, Berkeley, 1937). Rhyme here largely gives way to assonance and, as D. L. Shaw points out, 'the starting point for many of the poems is a deeply rooted spiritual malaise'. A depressive, Rosalía died of cancer, mourned by the whole Galician people.

Her *Obras completas* (1909–11) were reduced from 4 volumes to one in the Aguilar edition of 1944 (4th edn., 1958). *Poesías* (ed. R. Carballo Calero, 1973) contains *Cantares gallegos*, *Follas novas*, and *En las orillas del Sar*.

See M. Murguía, 'Rosalia de Castro' in his *Los precursores* (1885), pp. 169–200; M. P. Tirrell, *La mística de la saudade*, a study of her poetry (1951); J. Costa Clavell, *Rosalía de Castro* (Barcelona, 1967); K. K. Kulp, *Manner and mood in Rosalía de Castro* (1968), J. Filgueira Valverde, *Rosalía de Castro no seu fogar* (1974); and M. Mayoral, *La poesía de Rosalía de Castro* (1974).

CASTRO Y BELLVÍS, GUILLÉN DE (1569–1631), b. Valencia. Dramatist of the school of Lope de Vega (q.v.). He spent some time as a captain of coastguards, and was a founder-member (as 'Secreto') of the Academia de los Nocturnos. In 1623 he was appointed a Knight of Santiago. Castro was married twice: to the Marquesa Girón de Rebolledo, apparently unhappily, in 1595; and to Ángela Salgado in 1626.

Castro's most outstanding achievement was the accomplished adaptation of the *Romancero* to Golden Age drama, a contribution which reached its highest point in his *Las mocedades del Cid* (q.v.), a play in two parts first published in 1618. *El conde de Irlos* and *El conde Alarcos* are similar adaptations from epic and chivalresque material.

Los mal casados de Valencia, one of his *comedias de capa y espada*, is believed to rely partly on autobiographical matter.

Another such *comedia* is *El Narciso en su opinión* (q.v.), which possibly influenced Moreto's *El lindo don Diego* (qq.v.). Among his historical plays are *Pagar en propia moneda*, *La humildad soberbia*, and *La justicia en la piedad*. *El amor constante*, first published with *El caballero bobo* in *Doze comedias famosas, de quatro poetas naturales de . . . Valencia* (Barcelona, 1609), is a fast-moving family tragedy ending with a controversial justification for tyrannicide.

Of his three adaptations from Cervantes for the theatre, possibly the most interesting is *Don Quijote de la Mancha*, which concentrates on the episode of Cardenio and Lucinda; the others are of *El curioso impertinente* and *La fuerza de la sangre*. Castro also wrote the mythological plays *Progne y Filomena* and *Los amores de Dido y Eneas*. The most complete edition of Castro's works this century is the *Obras* edited by E. Juliá in 3 vols. (1925–7). Castro's works are believed to have first appeared in a clandestine edition of 1613 or 1614, and the first licit edition, *Primera parte de las comedias*, came out in Valencia in 1618; the *Segunda parte* appeared in the same city in 1625. Seven of his plays were edited by R. de Mesonero Romanos in vol. 43 (1857) of the

BAE, and C. Bruerton wrote 'The chronology of the "Comedias" of Guillén de Castro' in *Hispanic Review*, vol. 12 (1944).

See also R. Monner Sans, *Don Guillén de Castro: ensayo de crítica biobibliográfica* (Buenos Aires, 1913); F. Martí Grajales, 'Biobibliografía de Guillén de Castro' in *Anales del Centro de Cultura Valenciana*, vol. 4 (1931), pp. 171–220; and William E. Wilson, *Guillén de Castro* (New York, 1973), in Twayne's World Authors series.

CASTRO Y ROSSI, ADOLFO DE (1923–98), b. Cádiz. Scholar and historian who wrote accounts of the reigns of Philip II and Ferdinand VII. For some time his Cervantic hoax *Buscapie* (q.v.) deluded certain writers. He wrote a satirical novel in the picaresque genre: *Aventuras literarias del iracundo extremeño don Bartolomé Gallardete* (1831), histories of Cádiz and Jérez (both 1845), and a useful *Historia de los judíos en España* (1847). For the BAE he compiled a collection of literary curiosities mistitled *Curiosidades bibliográficas*, vol. 36 (1855) and two volumes of *Poetas líricos de los siglos XVI y XVII*, vols. 32 and 42 (1854–7, reprinted 1861–5).

CATALÀ, VÍCTOR, see ALBERT I PARADIS, Catarina.

CAVIEDES, JUAN DEL VALLE Y, see VALLE Y CAVIEDES, Juan del.

Cecial, Tomé, a neighbour of Sancho Panza, in Cervantes' *Quijote* (q.v.). In Part II of the novel he sets out, disguised with a false nose, as the squire of Sansón Carrasco who, himself disguised as a knight, plans to challenge Quijote, defeat him, and send him home.

The satirist Juan Pablo Forner (q.v.) adopted 'Tomé Cecial' as a pseudonym.

CEJADOR Y FRAUCA, JULIO (1864–1927), b. Saragossa. Literary critic, historian, and Professor at Madrid University. His major works were the *Tesoro de la lengua castellana* (1908–14) and *Historia de la lengua y literatura castellana* (14 vols., 1915–20), but he also produced many conscientious editions of the classics, such as Gracián, Alemán, Quevedo, and the Archpriest of Hita. His novels and miscellaneous essays are neglected. Other works include *Fraseología y estilística castellana* (4 vols., 1921–5), *La verdadera poesía popular castellana* (1921–4), and two posthumous works: the autobiographical *Recuerdos de mi vida* (1927) and *Vocabulario medieval castellano* (1929).

CELA TRULOCK, CAMILO JOSÉ (1916–), b. El Padrón, Corunna. His mother was English, and his brother is the novelist Jorge C. Trulock

(q.v.). Novelist, travel writer, short-story writer, poet, and leader of the *tremendistas* (see TREMENDISMO).

Among his best works is *La familia de Pascual Duarte* (q.v., 1942). This marked a new direction in Spanish literature with sober, concise, and dramatic writing almost cinematographic in quality. His later novels are very different: *Pabellón de reposo* (1944); *Nuevas andanzas y desventuras de Lazarillo de Tormes* (1944); the excellent neo-realist *La colmena* (q.v., Buenos Aires, 1951) describing a few days in and around a sordid Madrid cafe during 1943; *Mrs. Caldwell habla con su hijo* (Barcelona, 1953) in which a senile woman mourns her dead child; *La Catira* (Barcelona, 1955) subtitled '*historias de Venezuela*' and using Venezuelan words (explained in a glossary) to tell a Venezuelan story; *Tobogán de hambrientos* (Barcelona, 1962); and *Vísperas, festividad y octava de San Camilo del año 1936 en Madrid* (1969), on the lower classes in Madrid during the early days of the Civil War.

Cela's short stories include *Esas nubes que pasan* (1945); *El bonito crimen del carabinero y otras invenciones* (1947); *El gallego y su cuadrilla* (1951); *El molino de viento y otras novelas cortas* (Barcelona, 1956), which has been described as a provincial *Colmena*; *La familia del héroe* (1965); *El ciudadano Iscariote Reclús* (1965); *Viaje a USA* (1967); and *Nuevas escenas matritenses* (7 vols., 1965–6), which are *esperpentos* (q.v.), in the tradition of Spanish black humour. His collections of poems are *Pisando la dudosa luz del día*, written in 1936 but not published until 1945, and *Cancionero de la Alcarria* (1948).

Viaje a la Alcarria (1948) is a brilliant series of travel sketches; his other essays in the same genre include *Del Miño al Bidasoa* (1952), *Primer viaje andaluz* (1959), *Viaje al Pirineo de Lérida* (1965), *Madrid* (1966), and *Barcelona* (1970).

There is a useful collection of *Mis páginas preferidas* (1956); and 8 vols. of his *Obras completas* have already appeared (1972).

In 1956 he founded one of the best literary magazines in Spanish: *Papeles de Son Armadans*, which he edits.

See Paul Ilie, *La novelística de Camilo José Cela* (1963); R. Kirsner, *The novels and travels of Camilo José Cela* (Chapel Hill, N.C., 1966), and also in English, D. W. McPheeters, *Camilo José Cela* (New York, 1969).

CELAYA, GABRIEL, pseudonym of Rafael Múgica (q.v.).

Celestina, La, the name commonly given to the famous dialogue novel by the *converso* Fernando de Rojas (q.v.). The earliest surviving edition (Burgos, 1499), containing sixteen 'auctos' or acts, was published anonymously, and entitled *Comedia de Calisto y Melibea*. Later editions reveal the author's identity in an acrostic, and a prefatory letter claims that Rojas completed (allegedly in a fortnight) the work of a predecessor who is not named, and who wrote only the first act and part of the second. Editions from 1502 include five more acts (generally accepted as the work of Rojas) after act fourteen, with additions to most of the others, and the title is changed from *Comedia* to *Tragicomedia*.

Calisto, a nobly-born youth, enters the orchard of the Jew Pleberio in pursuit of a hawk, and there sees the lovely Melibea, Pleberio's daughter, with whom he falls in love. She rejects him, so Sempronio, his dishonest servant, advises Calisto to use the guile of the old go-between and procuress Celestina, who will win over the girl by some means or another, even by witchcraft if need be.

Celestina obtains an audience with Melibea, and in a dialogue of great psychological penetration, is at first defeated by Melibea's modesty, which will not allow her to confess love for Calisto, but at last triumphs by urging compassion: 'Yo dexo un enfermo a la muerte que con sola una palabra de tu noble boca salida que le lleve metida en mi seno, tiene por fe que sanará'.

Calisto's servants Sempronio and Pármeno are seen in Celestina's hut by the river in the company of their mistresses, the whores Elicia and Areusa. They learn that Calisto has given Celestina money and a gold necklace for her trouble, and when she enters they demand their share, which she refuses. The ruffians stab her, but are caught by the authorities, and executed in public the following day.

The 16-act version comes to a quick and effective climax with the seduction of Melibea by Calisto, his death on falling from the high wall around the garden, the touching lamentations of Melibea, who commits suicide by jumping from a tower, and the chorus-like moralizing of her parents.

The 21-act version is not only longer, but also introduces at a late stage a new character, Centurio, a *miles gloriosus*. The last two acts are the same in both versions save for the dénouement: in the earlier version Calisto falls to his death after seducing Melibea, but in the expanded version he returns home safely, and continues to meet her for a month; then Elicia and Areusa (friends of Celestina) enlist Centurio to make Calisto pay for the deaths of their lovers and Celestina. While Calisto is in Melibea's house one night, Centurio's toughs attack Calisto's followers who are awaiting him outside; he goes to their aid and falls from his ladder to his death.

Probably intended more for reading aloud to a group than for dramatic performance, *La Celestina* is included by Marcelino Menéndez y Pelayo (q.v.) in his *Orígenes de la novela* (vol. 3, pp. 219–458).

That Rojas's unhappy background of forced conversion and discrimination led him to complain of this treatment in *La Celestina* is argued by Garrido Pallardó (*Los problemas de Calisto y Melibea y el conflicto de su autor*, 1957) and Serrano Poncela (*El secreto de Melibea*, 1959) who believe that Melibea's parents are *conversos*, and so Calisto the nobly-born Castilian *cristiano viejo* is prohibited from marrying her or courting her openly. This theory is plausible but unnecessary, given the many precedents (as in the *Libro de buen amor*) in medieval Spain for employing a go-between.

The book's sexual licence and verbal obscenity apparently caused the Inquisition no concern, for though later they excised some anti-clerical passages, the book was reprinted at least sixty times in the 16th c. As a morality, *La Celestina* demonstrably serves the cause of good against evil, as shown by the well-deserved bad ends that so many of the characters meet, and by the dreadful consequences of *loco amor*.

La Celestina is the most remarkable work produced in 15th-c. Spain, and its influence has been enduring and profound. Its unity is exceptional for a work of its length. Its universality lies not merely in the deepening love of Calisto and Melibea, but also in the 'picaresque' scenes between the servants and their women, which follow Terence in the parallel of masters and servants in love, in the despair of Pleberio and Alisa at their daughter's death and dishonour, and above all in the thorough and often humorous delineation of the *alcahueta* Celestina, the culmination of the Trotaconventos (q.v.) tradition, and the most important character in the book. She is a sorceress though totally human in her hypocritical 'wise' sayings, utterly worldly, and shrewd in her dealings with each successive foil.

Rojas's choice of language has often been criticized for incongruous Latinisms, and it is true that he is never slow to reveal his Salamancan education, but for the most part his vocabulary is perfectly chosen to match each character.

His sources include the Bible, and many classical authors including Homer, Virgil, Terence, Plautus, and the *Pamphilus* (also used by Juan Ruiz in the *Libro de buen amor*, q.v.), Petrarch, and Diego de San Pedro (q.v.).

There are six principal sequels to *La Celestina*: the *Segunda comedia de Celestina* (Medina del Campo, 1534, by Feliciano de Silva, q.v.); the *Tercera Celestina* of Gaspar Gómez de Toledo

(1536; ed. by M. E. Barrick, Philadelphia, 1973); the *Tragicomedia de Lisandro y Roselia* (1542) of Sancho Sánchez de Muñón; *Tragedia Policiana* (1547) by Sebastián Fernández; *Comedia Florinea* (1554) by Rodríguez Florián; and *Comedia Selvagia* (1554) by Alonso de Villegas; all studied by Pierre Heugas in *La Célestine et sa descendance directe* (Bordeaux, 1973). But the figure of Celestina recurs throughout Peninsular literature in numerous imitations, direct and indirect: from the 'alcoviteira' of Gil Vicente to Lope de Vega's Gerarda in *La Dorotea* and Fabia in *El caballero de Olmedo*.

M. Criado de Val and G. D. Trotter have published a new critical edition of *La Celestina* (1958; 3rd corrected edn., 1970) which follows the Seville version of 1502, with variants from those of Burgos (1499) and Seville (1501).

There is an early translation by James Mabbe (1631) and more recent versions by P. Hartnoll (1959) and J. M. Cohen (Harmondsworth, 1964).

The book has been studied by numerous scholars, including Marcel Bataillon, *La 'Célestine' selon Fernando de Rojas* (Paris, 1961), and María Rosa Lida de Malkiel (*Two Spanish masterpieces: the Book of Good Love and the Celestina* (Urbana, Illinois, 1961) and *La originalidad artística de 'La Celestina'* (Buenos Aires, 1962).

Celoso extremeño, El, one of the *Novelas ejemplares* (q.v., 1613) by Miguel de Cervantes Saavedra (q.v.).

A rich Extremaduran, Felipe de Carrizales, returns at the age of 68 from Peru with a handsome fortune but on learning that he has neither family nor friends surviving in Extremadura, resolves to stay in Seville. There he manages to find a pretty fourteen-year-old girl to marry, but due to the discrepancy in their ages he is seized by mad jealousy, turns his house into a fortress, acquires a Negro eunuch as guard, and even forbids any male cat or dog to enter.

In spite of all these precautions a youth called Loaysa manages to win the confidence of the eunuch and all the other servants and, Carrizales being drugged, tries to win the love of the honest Leonora. They eventually fall alseep, innocently, and are found by Carrizales who assumes that they are lovers but suddenly realizes the madness of his earlier behaviour and offers his wife a rich legacy in contrition without living to hear her explanation. Sad at the loss of her husband and unwilling to marry Loaysa, Leonora enters a convent.

The major studies of this cautionary tale against marital jealousy include F. Rodríguez Marín, *El Loaysa de 'El celoso extremeño': estudio histórico-literario* (Seville, 1901;); and Joaquín

Casalduero, *Sentido y forma de los 'Novelas ejemplares'* (Buenos Aires, 1943).

Cena del rey Baltasar, La, an *auto sacramental* by Pedro Calderón de la Barca (q.v.) first performed at Madrid in 1634 and published in *Navidad y Corpus Christi, festejados por los mejores ingenios de España* (1664).

This religious play, taken from Daniel, 5, is set in Babylon, where King Belshazzar, already married to Vanity, is about to marry for a second time, Idolatry, Empress of the East. The king boasts of his ancestors, his military glories, and his temporal power. Vanity promises him new glory and Idolatry urges him to erect statues to make him adored like all the gods: who on earth can divide the King from his two wives? Perhaps nobody; perhaps, suggests the captive Jew Daniel, the vengeful hand of God. Belshazzar, enraged, is about to execute the Jew when a mysterious fear stays his hand. Death comes to Daniel and promises him retribution, but Daniel begs Death to remind Belshazzar of his mortality before making the fatal move. Brought quickly to the king by Thought, Death offers him a memoir reminding him that he is no more than dust; the memoir is torn up by Vanity, so that the king believes the visitation was an illusion and is lulled to sleep by the songs of Vanity. After bad dreams, the king is presented by his queen Idolatry with a banquet so sumptuous that the goblets used are the sacred drinking vessels from the temple at Jerusalem. Death mixes with the servants and passes a poisoned drink to the king whose hour is nearly come. Suddenly, amid a terrible uproar, a hand moves across the palace banqueting hall and writes *Mane tecel fares*. Idolatry now sees that God rejects her. Daniel offers her the vision of the Sacrament, and Idolatry bends down in humility before the chalice and host.

See the translation by R. G. Barnes in *Three Spanish sacramental plays* (San Francisco, 1969), and A. A. Parker, *The allegorical drama of Calderón* (Oxford, 1943 and reprints), pp. 156–196.

Ceniza fue árbol, La, a sequence of novels published in Barcelona by Ignacio Agustí (q.v.) in which five have so far appeared: *Mariona Rebull* (1944); *El viudo Ríus* (1945); *Desiderio* (1957); *19 de julio* (1966); and *Guerra civil* (1972). Written in Castilian, the work is a realistic saga of Barcelona life as reflected in the lives of the Rebull and Ríus families, starting in the year 1865 and intended to finish in about 1944. Agustí's conservative technique shows the influence of Galdós (q.v.) but his awareness of contemporary events and manners is less acute.

CEPEDA SAMUDIO, ÁLVARO (1926–), Colombian short-story writer and novelist, considered in his own country to rank with García Márquez, Rojas Cerazo, and Alberto Sierra, as one of the four major contemporary Colombian writers of fiction.

Todos estábamos a la espera (1954) is a picture of contemporary, technological man lost in the urban jungle he has created; wry, tense, and acid by turns, the stories comment on allegedly universal dehumanization. *La casa grande* (1962) is a novel reconstructing a family's past through letters.

Cerco de Numancia, El, a tragedy by Miguel Cervantes de Saavedra (q.v.), see NUMANCIA.

CERDÁ Y RICO, FRANCISCO (1739–1800), b. Castalla, Alicante. Scholar and editor of medieval and Golden Age texts, such as the *Crónica de Moncada* and the writings of Luis de León, Sepúlveda, González de Salas, and Cervantes de Salazar.

See Ángel González Palencia, *Don Francisco Cerdá y Rico: su vida y su obra* (1928), reprinted in his *Eruditos y libreros del siglo XVIII* (1948).

CERNA, ISMAEL (1856–1901), b. El Paxte hacienda, Chiquimula, Guatemala. Romantic poet and playwright who admired Hugo, Lamartine, and Byron. He abandoned in turn philosophy, medicine, law, theology, and the army. His family was persecuted under the regime of General Justo Rufino Barrios, and Cerna fled for a while to El Salvador. In prison for rebellion in 1878 he wrote his poem 'En la cárcel' against Barrios, collected with his other verses in *Poesías* (Santa Ana, El Salvador, 1901?). He was gaoled in 1884 but released the following year on the death of Barrios. His most important play is *La penitenciaria de Guatemala* (Guatemala City, 1891), a three-act national drama in verse. Its success encouraged him to write 'Vender la pluma' and 'La muerte moral' of which the MSS. are now lost.

CERNUDA, LUIS (1902–63), b. Seville. Major poet of the Generation of 1927 (or 1925, according to his own terminology). He studied under Pedro Salinas in Seville, then taught in Toulouse (1928–9) and at the end of the Civil War left Spain for Britain. He taught at the universities of Glasgow 1939–43, Cambridge 1943–5, and London 1945–7. During 1947–51 he taught at Mount Holyoke College (U.S.A.) but spent his last twelve years mainly in Mexico.

His favourite themes are solitude, melancholy, homosexual love, and the desire for an impossible ideal. The manner is introverted and often bitter, and form varies from the classical,

with *décimas* and *cuartetas*, to modern free verse. His first book *Perfil del aire* (Málaga, 1927), later retitled *Primeras poesías*, has been reissued in a critical edition by Derek Harris (London, 1971). This was followed by *Égloga, elegía, oda* (1927–8); *Un río, un amor* (1929), affected like the next two works by surrealism; *Los placeres prohibidos* (1931); *Donde habite el olvido* (1932–3), with its title taken from Bécquer; *Invocaciones* (1934–5); *Las nubes* (1937–8), on the tragic destiny of the Spaniard; *Como quien espera el alba* (1941–4), on the grief of exile; *Vivir sin estar viviendo* (written 1944–9); and *Con las horas contadas* (completing the 1958 edn. of *La realidad y el deseo*) and *Desolación de la quimera* (completing the 4th (1964) edn. of *La realidad y el deseo*). In some ways his best book, *Desolación de la quimera* is also regrettably bitter, attacking poets such as Guillén, whose influence on *Perfil del aire* he once admitted and now repudiates. Cernuda asserts that the poet's rewards are 'la aridez, la ruina y la muerte'. He wrote two works of poetic prose: *Ocnos* (London, 1942; 3rd edn., Xalapa, 1963) and *Variaciones sobre tema mexicano* (Mexico City, 1952) and translated Hölderlin as well as Shakespeare's *Troilus and Cressida*. He wrote *Estudios sobre poesía española contemporánea* (1957), and the two-volume *Poesía y literatura* (1960 and Barcelona, 1964), the first of which contains the important essay on his own work, 'Historial de un libro'. *Tres narraciones* (1974) contains the stories 'El viento en la colina', 'El indolente', and 'El sarao'.

Derek Harris and Luis Maristany have produced a new edition of *Poesías completas* (Barcelona, 1974) and are preparing *Prosas completas*. *The poetry of Luis Cernuda* (New York, 1971) is an anthology of translations edited by D. Harris and A. Edkins.

See Philip Silver, *'Et in Arcadia ego': a study of the poetry of Luis Cernuda* (London, 1965); A. Coleman, *Other voices: a study of the late poetry of Luis Cernuda* (Chapel Hill, N.C., 1969); and Agustín Delgado, *La poética de Luis Cernuda* (1975).

CERRUTO, ÓSCAR (1907–), Bolivian novelist and short-story writer. *Aluvión de fuego* (1935) failed as a novel because its artistry was too conscious and 'poetic', weakening the impact of the author's denunciation of the Bolivian feudal system and his plea for justice for the Indians. Politically, Cerruto is a revolutionary and a socialist. His poetry, such as *Cifra de las rosas*, is abstract to the point of hermeticism. His best writings to date have been the short stories in *Cerco de penumbras* (1958).

CERVANTES DE SALAZAR, FRANCISCO (1514?–75). b. Toledo. Spanish historian of Mexico. After studying at Salamanca University and teaching at Osuna (1550), he left for Mexico in 1551, at first teaching Latin in a school and later Rhetoric on the foundation of Mexico University in 1553. The following year he took holy orders. As the official chronicler, he compiled the *Crónica de la Nueva España* which remained unpublished until 1914 (vol. 1, Madrid) and 1936 (vols. 2 and 3, Mexico City). Now available in an edition by Manuel Magallón (2 vols., 1971) as vols. 244–5 of the BAE, this is the most valuable of all the historical accounts of the Mexican conquest. Cervantes de Salazar not only knew Cortés personally, and made extensive use of his *Relaciones*, but also used the work of López de Gómara (q.v.). The *Obras . . . que ha hecho, glosado, y traduzido* (3 vols., Alcalá, 1546) consist of texts by Mexía, Juan Luis Vives (qq.v.), and Oliva together with important dialogues on the early years of the university and on contemporary life and manners in the Mexican capital. Cervantes' works have been edited, with a Castilian translation, as 'México en 1554' by Joaquín García Icazbalceta in the latter's *Obras*, vol. 6 (1898), pp. 153–346. *Túmulo imperial de la gran ciudad de México* (Mexico City; new edn. by A. Millares Carlo, 1954) contains some often mediocre poems in Latin and Spanish.

See A. Millares Carlo, *Apuntes para un estudio bio-bibliográfico del humanista Francisco Cervantes de Salazar* (Mexico City, 1958) and the same scholar's edition of *Cartas recibidas de España por Francisco Cervantes de Salazar, 1569–1575* (Mexico City, 1946).

CERVANTES SAAVEDRA, MIGUEL DE (1547–1616), b. Alcalá de Hénares. The most famous novelist produced by Spain so far, and one of the acknowledged masters of world literature. The son of a poor surgeon Rodrigo de Cervantes and his wife Leonor de Cortinas. As a boy he studied in Valladolid, then possibly with the Jesuits in Seville, and certainly with Juan López de Hoyos in Madrid.

In 1569 he went to Italy in the service of Cardinal Acquaviva, and in 1570 became a soldier, fighting in the Battle of Lepanto (1571), where he was wounded, losing the use of his left hand. He never lost his vivid admiration for Juan de Austria gained at this time. After six months in Messina hospital he took part in the campaigns of Corfu, Navarino, and Tunis. On his return voyage to Spain in 1575, carrying laudatory letters of recommendation from Juan de Austria, Cervantes was taken prisoner by a renegade pirate and taken to Algiers. Juan's letters lent Cervantes an authority he did not possess, but made his ransom impossibly high, and he made several escape attempts before being eventually ransomed in October 1580.

Once back in Spain he was given minor government positions, such as purchasing and requisitioning for the Armada, and made a little money by writing, but remained poor throughout much of his later life. In 1584 he married Catalina de Salazar y Palacios, but apparently never attained happiness with her. He was imprisoned twice for alleged bookkeeping irregularities or debt. He lived for some time from 1603–4 in Valladolid, and was gaoled there after the death of Gaspar de Ezpaleta at the door of his house. He later separated for some time from his wife. Cervantes' most productive literary period was from 1606, when he moved with the court to Madrid, where he died (on 22 April 1616) and was buried in the Convent of Trinitarian Nuns in Calle de Cantarranas, now known as Calle de Lope de Vega. It was the Trinitarian order which had pleaded with the sovereign for the money with which Cervantes had been ransomed in 1580.

Poetry. Cervantes is not normally considered a poet, but he produced a number of works of some interest in this genre. *Viage del Parnaso* (1614; critical edns. by J. T. Medina (2 vols., Santiago de Chile, 1925), and F. Rodríguez Marín, 1935) consists of 3,000 lines in eight cantos, and is based on the poem of the same title by Cesare Caporali. Cervantes handles the tercet cleverly, but the work is interesting mainly for its view of earlier and contemporary writers, often ironic like the prose *Adjunta. Canto de Calíope*, which is book VI of *La Galatea* (q.v.) contains earlier opinions of writers, this time exclusively contemporary. It consists of 111 lines of *octavas reales* and represents, if somewhat sycophantically at times, an interesting review of poets writing in Cervantes' epoch.

On the other hand the *Epístola a Mateo Vázquez*, written from Algiers to the secretary of Philip II, sheds light on Cervantes' own life, pleading in tercets his case for a rapid ransom.

Lesser verses in the Spanish tradition (*quintillas dobles*) and in the Italian (*liras, tercetos,* and *octavas reales*) are scattered throughout the *obras*, particularly in *La Galatea*; while *romances* can be found in both the *Quijote* and *La gitanilla*. His poetry was never regarded highly until early in the 20th c.; the fact remains that Cervantes is a prose stylist of the first order who never achieves equivalent eminence in even his finest verse.

Plays. Cervantes is probably the most talented and varied playwright before Lope de Vega, with a lifelong addiction to the watching and writing of drama. His early plays are: *El trato de Argel*, imitated by Lope de Vega in *Los cautivos de Argel* and confessedly autobiographical (Cervantes introducing himself with one of his own names, Saavedra), written in sprightly verse, and describing the intrigues of life in Barbary as a captive; and *El cerco de Numancia*, the best tragedy in Spanish before Lope. A precursor of Lope's *Fuenteovejuna* in representing a whole community as patriotic hero, the play is monumentally simple and appealing.

Cervantes' later drama, published in *Ocho Comedias, y ocho Entremeses nuevos, nunca representados* (1615), is again all in verse. The plays are less successful than the marvellous *entremeses*, in which Cervantes showed himself a true master of the playlet in situation, character, and humorous dialogue. The eight plays of his second period are: *El gallardo español, Los baños de Argel,* and *La gran sultana doña Catalina de Oviedo,* all based on captivity and the tension between Moor and Christian; the chivalry plays *La casa de los celos* and *El laberinto de amor* which are so complex in plot as to be totally mystifying and the least original or interesting of the master's work; *La entretenida,* the *comedia de capa y espada* outstanding for its wit and realism; *El rufián dichoso,* the *comedia de santos* on the conversion of Cristóbal de Lugo; and the cleverly-woven *Pedro de Urdemalas* (q.v.), a fine comedy on the *pícaro* who joins the gipsies for love of a girl.

The prose *entremeses* are astonishingly original, showing glimpses of real life enhanced by wit and pointed dialogue; the two verse *entremeses* are believed by reason of their form to antedate the rest: they are *La elección de los alcaldes de Daganzo* and *El rufián viudo. El juez de los divorcios* is a snapshot of married life; *El retablo de las maravillas* is a typical scene of village fun; *La cueva de Salamanca* is a Boccaccio-like satire on complacent husbands; *El vizcaíno fingido* shows a presumptuous and smug woman deceived; *La guarda cuidadosa* is a satire on rivalry in love between Church and Army. Where Calderón will treat such themes with solemnity, Cervantes shows his true universality by laughing in sympathy with human frailty.

Novels. Cervantes' novels, in chronological order, are *Primera parte de La Galatea* (Alcala, 1585), *El ingenioso hidalgo Don Quixote de la Mancha* (Part 1, 1605), *Novelas ejemplares* (1613), *Segunda parte del ingenioso cavallero Don Quixote de la Mancha* (1615), and *Los trabajos de Persiles y Sigismunda, historia setentrional* (1617), published posthumously.

La Galatea (q.v.) is his first attempt at fiction, published at the age of 38 but from internal evidence composed much earlier. It derives from the pastoral tradition imported from the Italian novel popularized by Sannazaro. A splendid example of a genre virtually unread today, *La Galatea* is essential reading for the Cervantist intent on locating sources for material later reworked in exemplary novels and in the *Quixote* itself. The style is homogeneous, perhaps startlingly so for this period of his career, and

there is much to savour in the neo-Platonic ideas drawn from Padre Fonseca and the dialogues of Leo Hebraeus. The promised second part never appeared.

Don Quixote (after the first edition usually spelt *Don Quijote*, q.v.) is the capital work of Spanish fiction with which all subsequent novels of stature are inevitably compared. On the publication of the novel's first part, in 1605, it was immediately acclaimed and reprinted five times. In Cervantes' lifetime it was available in English and French and within the next century it had spread throughout the known world, including Spanish America.

The popularity of *Don Quixote de la Mancha* created a ready public for a collection of twelve *Novelas ejemplares* (1613, q.v.), at least one of which (*Rinconete y Cortadillo*, q.v.) is mentioned as early as *Quijote* I, and most belong to the period 1600–10. They are models of narrative skill in various genres: from the Italianate novel (*Las dos doncellas, El amante liberal, La española inglesa, La señora Cornelia*) to the picaresque (*Rinconete y Cortadillo*); and from the satirical (*El coloquio de los perros* and *El licenciado Vidriera*) to the realistic (*El celoso extremeño, La ilustre fregona,* and *El casamiento engañoso*). *La gitanilla* and *La fuerza de la sangre* are novels of feigned or unmasked identity. Another *novela, La tía fingida,* is found in a MS. also containing the first draft of *El celoso extremeño,* and has been ascribed to Cervantes by Bartolomé José Gallardo and Cejador y Frauca, among others; but denied by Bello, Adolfo de Castro, Icaza, and others, who are almost certainly correct to judge by the analysis carried out by Criado de Val.

In 1614 a certain Alonso Fernández de Avellaneda (q.v.) published in Tarragona *Segundo tomo del Ingenioso Hidalgo don Quijote de la Mancha,* while Cervantes was still working on his own sequel, his *Segunda parte del ingenioso cavallero Don Quixote de la Mancha* appearing the following year in Madrid.

The rest of his life Cervantes devoted mainly to *Los trabajos de Persiles y Sigismunda* (1617) which he managed to complete just before his death, although he had begun it as early as 1609; its ending was apparently hastened by his own sufferings from dropsy, for its last and fourth book contains only 14 chapters, whereas the first three had 23, 22, and 21 respectively. Generations of readers have wondered why, given the superb creation of Quixote, Cervantes should apparently 'retreat' into the traditional Byzantine novel with its complicated plot intrigues and threadbare characterization. Most scholars nowadays lean towards the view of Américo Castro, according to which the unhappy, almost destitute Cervantes preferred a fantasy world 'en la última parte de Noruega, casi debajo del Polo

Ártico' and characters with extraordinary adventures, to the realistic world of some *novelas ejemplares* or the earthy wisdom of Sancho Panza.

Cervantes' overall purpose in the novel is to illustrate man's spiritual adventure by virtuous and vicious examples and so 'enseñar y deleitar juntamente'. Posterity has judged the novel harshly by comparison with *Don Quijote*, but it cannot be ignored by anyone interested in Cervantes' narrative skill.

The following works commonly at one time or another attributed to Cervantes have been rejected as spurious by Luis Astrana Marín: the *entremeses Los mirones, Los habladores, El hospital de los podridos, La cárcel de Sevilla*, and *Doña Justina y Calahorra*; *Refranes*; *Romances*; *Diálogo entre Sillania y Selanio*; the *novela ejemplar La tía fingida*; the *comedia La soberana Virgen de Guadalupe*, the *canción A la elección del arzobispo de Toledo*, and the *carta A don Diego de Astudillo Carrillo*.

The bibliography of Cervantes is immense: see L. Rius, *Bibliografía crítica de las obras de Miguel de Cervantes* (3 vols., 1895–1904); G.-M. del Río y Rico, *Catálogo bibliográfico de la Sección de Cervantes de la Biblioteca Nacional* (1930), consisting of 915 pp.; J. D. M. Ford and R. Lansing, *Cervantes: a tentative bibliography* (Cambridge, Mass., 1931); R. L. Grismer, *Cervantes: a bibliography* . . . (New York, 1946) supplemented by V. R. B. Oelschlager, 'More Cervantine bibliography' in *Hispania*, vol. 33 (1950), pp. 144–50; Alberto Sánchez, *Cervantes: bibliografía fundamental, 1900–1959* (1961) and the same author's contributions to *Anales Cervantinos* (Madrid), *passim*; J. Simón Díaz in vol. 8 (1970), pp. 1–442, of his *Bibliografía de la literatura hispánica*.

There are many editions of the complete works. There is a facsimile edition from early impressions in 7 vols. (1917–23) by the Real Academia Española, but the usual edition recommended is that in 16 vols. (1914–41) by R. Schevill and A. Bonilla y San Martín. For editions of individual works, see under the appropriate title entry.

No single biography is entirely satisfactory, from the *Vida* by G. Mayáns y Síscar (1737) up to date. A purely chronological treatment is recorded by E. Cotarelo y Mori in *Efemérides cervantinas* (1905). Other lives include: S. J. Arbó, *Cervantes* (Barcelona, 1946); M. Herrero-García, *Vida de Cervantes* (1948); L. Astrana Marín, *Vida ejemplar y heroica de Miguel de Cervantes* (7 vols., 1948–58); and J. A. Cabezas, *Cervantes, del mito al hombre* (1967).

Among the thousands of general critical works are: R. Schevill, *Cervantes* (1919); R. Rojas, *Cervantes* (Buenos Aires, 1935, 2nd edn., 1948); J. Cassou, *Cervantes* (Paris, 1936); M. Menéndez y Pelayo, 'Estudios cervantinos' in his *Estudios*

y discursos de crítica histórica y literaria, vol. 1 (1941), pp. 255–356; F. Rodríguez Marín, *Estudios cervantinos* (1947); three books by Azorín: *Con Cervantes* (Buenos Aires, 1947), *Con permiso de los cervantistas* (1948), and his itinerary *La ruta de Don Quijote* (1905) first published as articles in that year's *El Imparcial*; A. Ruegg, *Miguel de Cervantes und sein Don Quijote* (Berne, 1949); Américo Castro, *Hacia Cervantes* (1957; 2nd edn., 1960), and *El pensamiento de Cervantes* (1925); the series of *Sentido y forma* monographs by Joaquín Casalduero devoted to each of Cervantes' works in turn, and all greatly illuminating; E. C. Riley, *Cervantes' theory of the novel* (Oxford, 1962); W. J. Entwistle, *Cervantes* (Oxford, 1940); and W. Krauss, *Miguel de Cervantes: Leben und Werk* (Neuwied, 1966).

Cesante, a Spanish civil servant who has lost his post through a change in government, and expects reinstatement in the next. The classic treatment of the theme is *Miau* (1888) by Benito Pérez Galdós (q.v.), in which the *cesante*, Don Ramón de Villaamil, is reduced to misery and despair by his inability to obtain a new appointment.

CÉSPEDES, AUGUSTO (1904–), b. Cochabamba. Bolivian short-story writer and novelist. Like Díaz Machicao (q.v.), Céspedes both fought in the Chaco War and wrote about it, first in the vigorous stories *Sangre de mestizos* (Santiago de Chile, 1936) which have been described as a 'novela vertebrada en crónicas de intenso realismo'. *Metal del diablo* (1946) is a fierce political tirade in the form of a fictional life of the tin tycoon Simón Iturri Patiño called here 'Zenón Omonte', and would be more of a novel and less of a pamphlet if Patiño had been allowed any human traits. Céspedes' most notorious work is a very biased history of the period 1900–40, *El dictador suicida: cuarenta años de historia de Bolivia* (Santiago de Chile, 1956), on the career of Germán Busch. His later books were *El presidente colgado* (1966) and *Trópico enamorado* (1968).

See Armando Soriano Badani, *El cuento boliviano* (Buenos Aires, 1964), pp. 118–44.

CÉSPEDES Y MENESES, GONZALO DE (1585?–1638), b. Madrid. Novelist and short-story writer. His achievement was to blend courtly and picaresque elements into a genre which reacted against the more sordid situations then popular in fiction. His best works are the semi-autobiographical ('en parte verdaderos y en parte fingidos desengaños'): *Poema trágico del español Gerardo y Desengaño del amor lascivo* (1615) and *Varia fortuna del soldado Píndaro* (Lisbon, 1626), both reprinted in vol. 18 (1851) of the BAE. The former is a source of Fletcher's *Spanish curate* and *The maid in the mill*. He also wrote six short stories: *Historias peregrinas y exemplares* (Saragossa, 1623, ed. E. Cotarelo y Mori, 1906), the best being 'La constante cordobesa', a forerunner of *El burlador de Sevilla* (q.v.).

Céspedes' least interesting writings are the sycophantic, *conceptista* histories: *Historia apologética* (1622) on Aragón during the reign of Felipe II, and *Primera parte de la historia de D. Felipe el IIII* (Lisbon, 1631).

CETINA, GUTIERRE DE (before 1520–1557?), b. Seville. Poet. Italianate in form and feeling, Cetina can be placed midway between Garcilaso de la Vega and Fernando de Herrera (qq.v.) in the Castilian poetic tradition. He translated Petrarch and Ariosto, as well as poets otherwise long forgotten, and mastered the madrigal, especially in *A unos ojos*.

J. Hazañas y la Rúa edited the *Obras* (2 vols., Seville, 1895) of Cetina, and added a romanticized biography emphasising the allegedly autobiographical content of the unhappy love-affair between 'Vandalio' (Cetina?) and 'Amarillida'. Lucas de Torre, however, in 'Algunas notas para la biografía de Gutierre de Cetina', *BRAE*, vol. 11 (1924), pp. 388–407 and 601–26, claimed that the poet had been confused by Hazañas and all other biographers with a different man of the same name.

Cetina's works are available in the edition by A. de Castro in vol. 32 (1854) of the BAE; there are also various anthologies of *Poesías inéditas* in the Seville *Revista de Ciencias, Literatura y Artes*, vol. 4 (1857), pp. 701–61; vol. 5 (1859), pp. 243 and 566–8; and vol. 6 (1860), pp. 166 and 561–2.

See A. M. Withers, *The sources of the poetry of Gutierre de Cetina* (Philadelphia, 1923).

CEVALLOS, PEDRO FERMÍN (1812–93), b. Ambato, Ecuador. Historian and philologist. His *Resumen de la historia del Ecuador desde su origen hasta 1845* (2nd edn. in 6 vols., 1886–9) was intended to supersede the pioneer work of Juan de Velasco (q.v.). *Breve catálogo de errores en orden a la lengua y al lenguaje castellanos* (3rd edn., 1862) was his most significant contribution to philology.

Ch, entries beginning 'Ch' will be found in the order of the English alphabet, between 'Ce' and 'Ci'.

CHABÁS MARTÍ, JUAN (1898–1954), b. Denia, Alicante. Novelist and poet. He taught Spanish literature, first in Genoa, and then, after the Civil War, in Cuba. *Espejos* (1920) is a precocious book of poems influenced by Juan Ramón Jiménez. His novels, influenced by his friend Gabriel Miró (q.v.), are described by Nora as full of 'psychological lyricism'. They are *Sin velas, desvelada* (Barcelona, 1927), *Puerto de sombra* (1928), and *Agor sin fin* (1930). *Fábula y vida* (Santiago, 1955) is a collection of stories and *Vuelo y estilo* (1934) a book of essays.

CHACEL, ROSA (1898–   ), b. Valladolid. Novelist. She spent several years in Italy studying art with her husband Timoteo Pérez Rubio. Before the Civil War she had made a modest literary reputation with a novel *Estación, ida y vuelta* (1930), a remarkable antecedent of the French *nouveau roman*, and with the sonnets *A la orilla de un pozo* (1936).

After 1939 she emigrated to Buenos Aires, then lived for a year or two in New York and Spain, and finally settled in Rio de Janeiro. Her fiction, almost unknown in Spain until 1970 when the Barcelona reprint of *La Sinrazón* (first published in Buenos Aires in 1960) formed vol. 1 of her *Obras completas*, showed a steady advance from the perhaps excessively-coloured *Teresa* (Buenos Aires, 1941), about Teresa Mancha, mistress of Espronceda. The heroine of the *Memorias de Leticia Valle* (Buenos Aires, 1945) is a 11-year-old girl who mischievously seduces a married man. *Sobre el piélago* (Buenos Aires, 1952) is a collection of short stories.

CHAMICO, pseudonym of Conrado Nalé Roxlo (q.v.).

CHAMPOURCIN, ERNESTINA DE (1905–   ), b. Vitoria. Poet. She married the poet Juan José Domenchina (q.v.) and lived in Mexico with him from 1939. Her Basque origins are evident throughout her work, but the early influence of Juan Ramón Jiménez (q.v.) gradually diminished. Thematically, her work is dominated by love. Her books are *En silencio* (1926), *Ahora* (1928), *La voz en el viento* (1931), and *Presencia a oscuras* (1952). Champourcin's only novel, *La casa de enfrente* (1936), is remarkable for the splendidly successful female character Elena.

CHANGMARÍN, CARLOS FRANCISCO (1922–   ), b. Caserío de Leones, Veraguas, Panamá. Poet and short-story writer who has painted, composed well-known folksongs, and become a professional photographer. His stories in *Faragual* (1961) deal with the pathos and tragedy of simple country people in Veraguas. His poetry includes *Punto'e llanto* (1948) and *Poemas corporales* (1956).

Chapbooks, see PLIEGOS SUELTOS.

CHAVES, Fernando (1902–), b. Otavalo. Ecuadorian novelist, who became Director of Quito Public Library. He wrote his novels *La embrujada* (in *Revista de la Sociedad Jurídico-Literaria*, Quito, nos. 106—11, 1923) and *Plata y bronce* (1927) while teaching in a country school. Their significance is that they are the first important *indigenista* novels of Ecuador, and led to the major work in the genre, *Huasipungo* by Jorge Icaza (q.v.). Chaves treated the Indian peasants not as a folklore motif, but as part of the whole national problem. In *Plata y bronce*, Raúl, a white man, loves and seduces a highland Indian girl; the subsequent revenge by the Indians is not based solely on that single incident but, after centuries of exploitation by rapacious landowners, cynical political bosses, and fanatical priests, it becomes the spark that inflames the violence.

Escombros (1958) is in complete contrast to Chaves's earlier fiction in theme, style, and attitude. The angry young *indigenista* has given ground to the melancholy man of the world. Perpetua, a charming but inscrutable woman, is travelling with a man who adores her but remains as isolated as she; much of the novel is taken up by Socratic dialogues in an autumnal atmosphere of loneliness and sterility.

Chivalry, Books of, see Caballería, Libros de.

CHUMACERO, Alí (1918–), b. Acaponeta, Nayarit. Mexican poet and critic. Influenced to some extent by the poetry of Paz and Villaurrutia (qq.v.), Chumacero is the most significant writer to emerge from the Tierra Nueva group which gathered around the magazine *Tierra Nueva* (1940–2) and also included J. Cárdenas Peña, J. González Durán, and Manuel Calvillo. Like the Contemporáneos group, they considered poetry to be an end in itself, serving no social need. Chumacero's books show a gradual refinement of discipline and severity, their themes being desire, love, solitude, and death: *Páramo de sueños* (1944), *Imágenes desterradas* (1948), and *Palabras en reposo* (1956). Perhaps his most enduring achievement is *El viaje de la tribú*, a panoramic examination of human progress seen from much the same vantage point as the *Anabase* of Saint-John Perse.

Cid, Cantar or **Poema de mío,** the greatest, and earliest surviving, literary epic of Castile, celebrating the exploits both real and legendary of the Castilian knight Rodrigo Díaz de Vivar (q.v.). Composed *c.* 1140, or perhaps in the early 13th c., it survived almost intact in a unique MS. of 74 folios copied in the 14th c. by a scribe called Per Abbat or Abad from a

MS. of 1207. A palaeographic edition of this MS., now in the National Library in Madrid, was published by R. Menéndez Pidal as vol. 3 of his *Cantar de mio Cid* (1911; 2nd edn., 1946; 3rd edn., 1956). A photographic facsimile appeared in 1961 (with a reprint of Pidal's palaeographic edn.) and there is a good popular edition in Clásicos Castellanos (1913; 12th edn., 1968) which reproduces Menéndez Pidal's critical edition of 1911. New editions of the text have recently been published by Colin Smith, *Poema de mio Cid* (Oxford, 1972), and by Ian Michael, *Poema de mio Cid* (1976) in Clásicos Castalia.

The *Cantar* (or *Poema*) consists of 3,730 lines divided into three parts: the *Cantar del destierro* (up to line 1,085); the *Cantar de las bodas* (lines 1,086–2,277); and the *Cantar de la afrenta de Corpes* (from line 2,278 to the end).

The first leaf, possibly a second, and two other leaves of the MS. are missing. The lost opening has been conjecturally restored by Menéndez Pidal using such historical sources as the *Crónica de veinte reyes*; he suggests that the poem would have begun by telling how the Cid set out to collect the tribute due to Alfonso VI, King of Castile from King Mu'tamid of Seville. While there, the Cid (with Mu'tamid) defeated the Moors of Granada allied with Count García Ordóñez, and the Cid pulled Ordóñez's beard as an insult. To avenge this, Ordóñez spread the rumour that the Cid had embezzled part of Mu'tamid's tribute and the King believed the charge, exiling the Cid in punishment. The first section now opens as the Cid and his followers leave Vivar for Burgos, where a nine-year-old pleads with him on behalf of the citizens not to demand shelter from them, since if they help the exile they have been threatened by the king with reprisals even to losing 'los ojos de las caras' (l. 46). In order to pay his servants the Cid borrows money from the Jews Raquel and Vidas on the strength of two great chests which they believe to be full of jewels, but are actually filled with sand. In Cardeña the Cid takes leave of his wife Jimena (Díaz, q.v.) and his daughters Sol and Elvira. '¡Ya doña Ximena, la mi mugier tan complida, / commo a la mi alma yo tantos vos quería!' (ll. 278–9). His conquests of Castejón and Alcócer extend his fame and fortune, so that he is able to send Álvar Fáñez to Alfonso with a rich gift and to obtain more troops. The Cid then attacks the region around Alcañiz, and defeats the Moors of Lérida and Count Ramon Berenguer of Barcelona.

Cantar II deals with the Cid's triumphant march on Valencia. He takes Jérica, Onda, Almenara, Murviedro (the ancient Saguntum), and finally Valencia itself, after which he sends another present to the king, beseeching him to permit Jimena, Sol, and Elvira to rejoin him in the conquered city. Alfonso VI agrees, and Álvar Fáñez brings the Cid's wife and daughters to Valencia, where a moving reunion takes place. After an abortive attack on Valencia by the armies of Yusuf, King of Morocco, the Cid sends a third and even more generous tribute to Alfonso. The Infantes de Carrión (q.v.), envious of the Cid's wealth and prestige, seek the hands of Sol and Elvira in marriage; Alfonso solemnly pardons the Cid and allows the double wedding to take place.

In *Cantar* III the Infantes are shown up as cowards and mocked by the Cid's men when a lion escapes in the palace. On their way home, the Infantes, after a night of lovemaking, attack their new brides in the oakwood of Corpes (q.v.), strike them senseless, and leave them to the roaming wild animals. A nephew of the Cid finds the brides and takes them back to him, and the Cid demands justice from the king. Alfonso convenes a court in Toledo, summoning the Infantes to face the Cid, who requests the restitution of the dowries and the swords Colada and Tizón, which had been given to the Infantes, and a judicial combat to satisfy his honour and demonstrate who is in the right.

The champions of the Cid defeat those of the Infantes, and the poem ends with the marriage of the girls to the princes of Navarra and Aragón and the death of the Cid.

Menéndez Pidal suggested that the author of the poem was a *juglar* of Medinaceli whose Castilian patriotism found the subject for his epic in the person of Rodrigo Díaz de Vivar, a just and brave man without rancour, whose regard for the institution of monarchy and respect for the law was matched by his mercy toward his foes. Though a monarchist, the Cid was apparently not a fervent Christian (a pious deathbed scene is an addition by monastic chroniclers), since he is recorded as having fought in league with certain Muslim princes against Christians. C. C. Smith maintains, however, that the author was not a *juglar* but a man of education, and that the epic was originally a written one, adding that the evidence of composition in or near Burgos is very strong.

The complicated question of the poem's form and metre was studied by Menéndez Pidal in *Cantar de mio Cid*, vol. 1, pp. 76–124 and in the *adiciones* to the 2nd and 3rd editions, pp. 1,173–85. It is written in sections or *laisses* of irregular length, with a well-marked caesura in each line and assonantal line-endings instead of rhymes.

The structure of the poem reflects the gradual ascendancy of the Cid, exemplified by the increasingly splendid gifts he sends Alfonso.

Irony marks the three turning points of the action: the exile which the Cid suffers gives him the opportunity of becoming ruler of Valencia; Alfonso's attempt at retribution only succeeds in serving the Infantes' ends; the Infantes' revenge on the Cid by humiliating his daughters only ends in their nobler marriages to the princes of Navarra and Aragón.

The narrative form of the poem is interspersed with lyrical passages and lively dialogue. The characterisation is remarkably vivid: the Cid is a prudent, loving husband, and a loyal subject; Jimena Díaz is a charming, faithful wife; the king is arrogant yet easily swayed by political expediency (a perfect foil for the more idealistic hero); the Infantes are cowardly and vile. The tense drama of the poem is a perfect vehicle for oral performance. In the words of C. C. Smith, 'no verse literature could have had a worthier beginning than this'. Its originality is a feature of the poem which is being stressed by recent scholarship.

There are versions of the *Cantar de mio Cid* in modern Spanish by Pedro Salinas (q.v., 1926), J. Pérez de Urbel, F. López Estrada, and M. Martínez Burgos (all 1955), and Camilo José Cela (q.v., 1957). Recent English translations have been made by J. G. Markley (1961) and by L. B. Simpson (1962) in prose, and by W. S. Merwin (1959) in verse.

See Luis Rubio García, *Realidad y fantasía en el 'Poema de mio Cid'* (Murcia, 1972), and Jules Horrent, *Historia y poesía en torno al 'Cantar del Cid'* (Barcelona, 1973).

Cielito ('little heaven'), in *gaucho* literature, an octosyllabic four-line stanza in colloquial language rhyming in lines two and four. The first line is usually a refrain, as in

> *Cielito, cielo que sí,*
> *lo que te digo Fernando.*
> *Confiesa que somos libres,*
> *y no andés remoloneando.*

The best-known practitioner is Bartolomé Hidalgo (q.v.), author of the above lines.

Cien años de soledad (Buenos Aires, 1967), the masterpiece of the Colombian novelist Gabriel García Márquez (q.v.).

Begun in 1945 as a draft entitled *La casa* and then abandoned, the novel is a history of the mythical town of Macondo seen through a period of seven generations of the Buendía family. Macondo, two years' march from the northern coast of Colombia, was founded by José Arcadio Buendía. His friend Melquíades possesses a Sanskrit MS. about the future of his family; this MS., translated into Castilian, is the novel and Melquíades is discovered to be the narrator. The family propagates itself partly through a strain of incest, names are repeated from generation to generation, and Macondo is subjected to a succession of catastrophes, including civil wars, drought, fruit company imperialism, and a slow and lingering decay.

Rains lasting nearly five years reduce Macondo to its original desolation, poverty, and purity. Biblical analogies are seldom pushed too far but always present—with the Flood, Adam and Eve, and plagues. The humour of the contrast between *civilización* and *barbarie* has never been better done, and for the reader versed in Latin-American literature the parodies of Carpentier, Cortázar, Borges, and others add an extra dimension to the enjoyment of this remarkable novel. It has perhaps become best-known as the leading example of 'magic realism', in which ordinary life is suddenly illuminated by inexplicable occurrences, such as a trail of blood leading evenly and carefully in and out of houses and across streets to the assailant, or the ship marooned in the forest. The characters accept the magic and wonder of human life as perhaps the reader should.

It has been translated by Gregory Rabassa as *One hundred years of solitude* (New York and London, 1970).

CIENFUEGOS, NICASIO ÁLVAREZ DE (1764–1809), b. Madrid. A pre-Romantic Salamancan poet, influenced by Juan Meléndez Valdés (q.v.). His work can be divided into the bucolic and the philosophical, its prevailing atmosphere being that of brooding melancholy, loneliness, and even despair.

His *Obras poéticas* (2 vols., 1816) were collected and published by royal command. The best are considered to be 'La escuela del sepulcro', his early ballad 'El túmulo', and 'Paseo solitario en primavera'.

Cienfuegos also wrote tragedies such as *La condesa de Castilla* (1815) and *Pítaco* (1822). A courageously patriotic editor of *La Gaceta*, he publicly opposed Napoleon's invasion of Spain in 1808, was denounced to Murat, reprieved, but taken to France as a hostage, where he died.

CIEZA DE LEÓN, PEDRO DE (1518–54), b. Seville. Soldier and historian. He left Spain for the New World in 1531, serving under Jorge Robledo, taking part in the foundation of Santa Ana de los Caballeros, and joining Sebastián de Belalcázar in what is now Colombia. In 1547 he arrived in Peru, and witnessed the civil war between the Spanish *conquistadores*. He spent the next three years making detailed geographical and ethnographical notes on the Indians of Peru, and on his return to Spain published *Parte primera de la Chrónica del Perú* (Seville, 1553; reprinted in Antwerp, 1554 and 1555; translated into Italian, Rome, 1555), which appeared in vol. 26 (1853) of the BAE.

Cieza de León's other works all appeared posthumously. *Segunda parte de la Crónica del Perú que trata del Señorío de los Incas Yupanquis y de sus grandes hechos y gobernación* (ed. Manuel González de la Rosa, Edinburgh, 1871, and Manuel Jiménez de la Estrada, 1880) was newly edited by A. M. Salas as *Del Señorío de los Incas* (Buenos Aires, 1943). It has been translated by C. R. Markham as *The second part of the Chronicle of Peru* (London, 1883), the first part having appeared as *The travels of Pedro de Cieza de León A.D. 1532–1550* (London, 1864). *Tercer libro de las guerras civiles del Perú, el cual se llama la Guerra de Quito* (1909) in the NBAE was translated into English in the Hakluyt Library (1913). Cieza de León's *tercera parte* was apparently lost but it was rediscovered by Rafael Loredo, who published some chapters in *Mercurio Peruano* (1956). *Guerras civiles del Perú* (2 vols., 1877) is the fourth part of Cieza's history. The first two parts reprinted together (Buenos Aires, 1922) reached a 3rd edition in 1941.

Cieza de León is an admirable contemporary chronicler. In the view of Raúl Porras, 'trazó el cuadro completo del escenario peruano, describiendo detenidamente, con profundo amor, al Perú; el territorio, sus llanos y sierras, ríos, valles y montañas, las ciudades, el hombre de cada región y sus costumbres, creencias, habitaciones y vestidos . . . Es el primer cronista que emprende la historia de los Incas y que abarca todo el cuadro de la historia peruana, indígena y española'.

See M. Maticorena Estrada, 'Cieza de León en Sevilla y su muerte en 1554: documentos' in *Anuario de Estudios Americanos* (Seville), vol. 12 (1955), pp. 615–74); R. Porras, *Cronistas del Perú* (Lima, 1962); and Pedro R. León, *Algunas observaciones sobre Pedro de Cieza de León y la Crónica del Perú* (1973).

Cifar, El Caballero, see CABALLERO CIFAR, El.

Cigarrales de Toledo (1621), a miscellany by Fray Gabriel Téllez (q.v.), generally known as 'Tirso de Molina'. There are editions by V. Said Armesto (1913) and in Colección Crisol (1954).

The framework of the text, of the type familiar from the *Decamerone* of Boccaccio, is a series of meetings among friends at their country houses ('cigarrales') on the banks of the Tagus during the hot summer months. The host on each occasion entertains his guests with tales, plays, and poems. Among the plays are *El vergonzoso en palacio* (q.v.) and *El celoso prudente*; among the stories, *Los tres maridos burlados*, with clear echoes of Boccaccio. Tirso specifically defends the drama of Lope de Vega in the *Cigarrales*, and also imitates Lope.

See A. Nougué, *L'œuvre en prose de Tirso de Molina* (Toulouse, 1962) and *Tirso de Molina: Les trois maris mystifiés* (Paris, 1966).

CIGES APARICIO, MANUEL (1873–1936), b. Enguera, Valencia. Novelist and essayist. He lived in voluntary or forced exile in Paris before his short-lived appointment as Civil Governor of Ávila during the regime of the Popular Front.

Neglected since his death, he had been something of a celebrity with the publication of the autobiographical tetralogy comprising *Del cautiverio* (1903), *Del cuartel y de la guerra* (1906), *Del hospital* (1906), and *Del periodismo y de la política* (1907). His fiction included *El Vicario* (1905); the two-volume *Luchas de nuestros días* consisting of *Los vencedores* (1908) and *Los vencidos* (1910); *Villavieja* (1914), which pointed to the inevitability of the failure of all sociopolitical reforms in Spain; *El juez que perdió su conciencia* (1925), a political novel showing how the illiterates in rural Spain (estimated then at 70% of the total population), were deprived of civil rights; and his last and finest novel *Los caimanes* (1931), in which the story of the illiterate Román Castalla is movingly told. *Marruecos* (1912) is war journalism; *Joaquín Costa, el gran fracasado* (1930) a biography; and *España bajo los Borbones* (1932) a popular history.

CILLÓNIZ, ANTONIO (1944–), b. Lima. Peruvian poet. His university studies took him to Madrid, and he worked there as archaeologist, travelling salesman, and teacher of languages and literature, before returning to Peru.

His verse is nervous and imaginative, qualities he shares with most of his fellow-poets in *Estos 13* (q.v., Lima, 1973), compiled by José Miguel Oviedo. Cillóniz's books so far are *Verso vulgar* (Madrid, 1967); *Después de caminar cierto tiempo hacia el Este* (1971), which won the 'Poeta Joven del Perú' prize for 1970; *Donde va el tiempo cuando no sopla*, and *En busca de la hierba que crece bajo la sombra del árbol del paraíso*.

Cipreses creen en Dios, Los (Barcelona, 1953), the first novel of a Civil War pentalogy by the Spanish writer José María Gironella (q.v.). It won the National Prize for Literature of 1953, and was followed by *Un millón de muertos* (Barcelona, 1961), *Ha estallado la paz* (Barcelona, 1966), and *Los hombres lloran solos* (Barcelona, 1971). A great deal of research on the period April 1931 to July 1936 in Gerona gave the author a confident basis for his chronicle, which

is in the tradition of Pérez Galdos's (q.v.) generation novels. The action takes place on three levels: that of the central Alvear family; the Spain of the early 1930s of which the Alveares are representative members; and the universal problems of war and death seen by Ignacio Alvear, who is also narrator. Many minor characters add richness to the novel's essentially 19th-c. texture.

Gironella shows how the internal conflicts of Spain made civil war inevitable not only as regards the great issues, but also—for example—in the daily problems of political agitation, the failure of gas and water supplies, and even trivial matters. Julián Marías has suggested that 'Gironella's novel is superior in form to all the others of its kind because it does not neglect any essential dimension of the circumstances, because everything functions dynamically within the narrative' (*La Nación*, Buenos Aires, 13 September 1959).

The novel has been translated by H. de Onís as *The cypresses believe in God* (New York, 1955), and its sequels by Joan MacLean as *One million dead* (New York, 1963) and *Peace after war* (New York, 1969).

CIRLOT, JUAN-EDUARDO (1916–), b. Barcelona). Surrealist poet and critic, whose most creative period (1944–7) coincided with the rise of surrealism between the neo-Romantic stage of 1940–4 and its revival after 1947. The leading practitioners were Julio Garcés, Manuel Segalá, and Cirlot himself, who published *Seis sonetos y un poema de amor celeste* (1943), *La muerte de Gerión* (1943), the influential *En la llama* (1945), *Canto de la vida muerta* (1945), and *Cordero del abismo* (1946). Apart from *Diccionario de los ismos*, Cirlot has written *El mundo del objeto [bajo la luz del surrealismo]* (Barcelona, 1953).

CISNEROS, ANTONIO (1942–), b. Lima. Peruvian poet. His first collections *Destierro* (1961) and *David* (1962) were well received, but Cisneros' international reputation was made by the perceptiveness, irony, and clarity of *Comentarios reales* (1964) and *Canto ceremonial contra un oso hormiguero* (Havana, 1968). The latter won the Casa de las Américas prize for 1968 and both appeared in part as *The spider hangs too far from the ground* (London, 1970).

Cisneros reacts against poeticism by the use of 'hard' images and a satirical approach to the founding fathers of Peru and to the conventions of everyday life. His latest books are *Agua que no has de beber* (Barcelona, 1971) and *Como higuera en un campo de golf* (1972), the latter concentrating for the first time on personal emotions rather than on irony.

CISNEROS, *Cardinal* Francisco Ximénez de, see Ximénez de Cisneros, *Cardinal* Francisco.

CISNEROS, Luis Benjamín (1837–1904), b. Lima. Peruvian novelist and poet, who in Riva Agüero's view was the best Peruvian poet of his generation. Cisneros began as a romantic poet but later made use of the neoclassical *silva* in the manner of Quintana, Bello, and Olmedo (qq.v.).

Known misleadingly as 'the father of the Peruvian novel', Cisneros produced two sentimental novels of little worth: *Julia, o escenas de la vida en Lima* (1860) and *Edgardo, o un joven de mi generación* (1864), and two novelettes: *Amor de nido* (1844) and *Cecilia* (1865). Cisneros' other works included *El pabellón peruano* (1855); *Alfredo el sevillano* (1856), a play; *Ensayo sobre varias cuestiones económicas del Perú* (1866); *Memoria sobre ferrocarriles* (1868); *El negociado Dreyfus* (1870); *Que no hay remedio* (1874); *Memoria y guía estadística de instrucción primaria* (1876); *Aurora amor* (1885); and *De libres alas* (1912). His *Obras completas* appeared in 1939.

See Alfredo Moreno Mendiguren, *Luis B. Cisneros* (1960).

Ciudad y los perros, La (Barcelona, 1963), a novel by the Peruvian Mario Vargas Llosa (q.v.).

Described (by Andrés Sorel in *Cuadernos Hispanoamericanos*, no. 201 (1966), p. 724) as 'la mejor novela de lengua española desde *Don Segundo Sombra*' (q.v.), the book is set in the Leoncio Prado military academy, which Vargas Llosa himself briefly attended, in Lima (the 'ciudad' of the title).

A bully, Jaguar, organizes a small secret society and sets out to cheat by stealing chemistry examination papers, choosing by lot Porfirio Cava to obtain the papers. Ricardo Arana (nicknamed 'El Esclavo') has been tormented by the Jaguar and denounces Cava, who is expelled. Some time later Arona is deliberately or accidentally killed, probably by Jaguar, on a rifle range. Alberto Fernández, one of Arana's few friends, tries to prosecute Jaguar for the death and is assisted by an honest junior officer, Gamboa, but the colonel hushes up the affair to protect the 'good name' of the academy. Jaguar marries Teresa, a girl who had also been loved by Arana and Fernández, and chooses to work in a bank. Fernández agrees to follow the career chosen for him by his parents.

Outwardly an attack on militarism as exemplified by a particular institution, the novel achieves much more than the description of brutality, deceit, and Darwinian oppression by extending the analogy of the academy to the city at all levels (the families of Jaguar and Alberto, as well as political circles), to Peru in general, and consequently to all human society. Vargas Llosa's determinism makes a brutal environment corrupt innocent boys, and Alberto into a hypocritical and adulterous 'Don Juan' figure like his father; only the Jaguar seems to be able to break loose from the shackles of his upbringing and environment, but ironically Jaguar's new idealism and loyalty are exploited by the opportunistic Higueras. Vargas Llosa recognizes that the novel, if it is to reflect life in any way, must be open-ended and confusing. Thus, for example, the central enigma of Arana's death is never finally resolved, characters change often without explanation, and do not believe what they claim to believe.

Stylistically, the novel offers a range of devices, among them flashback, counterpoint, multiple and simultaneous perspectives, changing foci for the narrative action, and interior monologues. Chapters are fragmented, but the attentive reader will gradually discover a connection between two events or statements occurring at different places and at different times. Vargas Llosa takes the view that one needs to observe the mental process before describing the act to realize the depth of human hypocrisy and falsehood. Bestiality, homosexual violence, and sadism are seen by him as merely the outward manifestations of lives twisted by deceit. The novel has been translated by Lysander Kemp as *The time of the hero* (New York, 1966).

See Luis Harss, *Los nuestros* (Buenos Aires, 1966), pp. 420–62); Helmy F. Giacoman, *Homenaje a Mario Vargas Llosa* (New York, 1971); and Luis A. Díez, *Asedios a Vargas Llosa* (Santiago, 1972).

Civilización y barbarie: vida de Juan Facundo Quiroga, y aspecto físico, costumbres, y hábitos de la República Argentina (1845), usually known simply as *Facundo*, an important polemical essay by the Argentine Domingo Faustino Sarmiento (q.v.), who was President of the country 1868–74.

The book was written in exile in Chile, where Sarmiento had fled at the age of 18 for his Unionist principles (as opposed to the Federalists led by the dictator Rosas). *Facundo* attacks Rosas through the work's nominal subject, Facundo Quiroga, a *gaucho* soldier and Federalist *caudillo* in the wars against the Unionists; a man who for Sarmiento represented the 'barbaric', violent, ignorant, rural way of life, as opposed to the 'civilized', urban ideals of the Unionists. Direct and biting in its polemical power, *Facundo* is poor history due to its partisan origin, and is now read as a good example of the Argentine Romanticism. R. Rojas, in *La literatura argentina* (vol. 3), has indicated the several contradictions in Sarmiento's ideology and thus in *Facundo*: he condemned the *gauchos* as wild, violent men yet was himself a '*gaucho* of ideas'; he deplored the Indian qualities, yet possessed many himself; he attacked Spain yet was Spanish in many of his words and actions; he called himself a freethinker, yet published works of piety; he recommended Europe as a model for Latin America but nobody was more Argentinian or Latin American than he; he condemned the *caciquismo* so prevalent in his sub-continent yet possessed clear traits of the *cacique* or 'boss' himself.

Rosas, for Sarmiento, was a barbarian who had violated all that was civilized in Argentina. However, in condemning his scapegoat, Sarmiento was guilty of flagrant bias and used language as 'barbaric' as that of his enemies. His secret admiration for the *gauchos* is obvious in his excellent account of their life on the pampas in the first part of the book. They may be backward in terms of European culture, but they are tough and colourful. Sarmiento narrates the life of Facundo, presents an essentially unreliable picture of the Civil Wars, and hints that Rosas may have been behind Facundo's mysterious death. Sarmiento's final recommendations are for the rapid industrialization of the country and mass immigration from Europe. The book was very well received, and was translated into English by Mrs H. Mann as *Life in the Argentine Republic in the days of the tyrants* (New York, 1868). The struggle between the opposing forces of town and country (*civilización* and *barbarie*) has been portrayed in different ways by many Latin American writers since Sarmiento, among them J. Hernández, Azuela, Rivera, Güiraldes, Gallegos, and Icaza (qq.v.).

See A. Palcos, *El Facundo: rasgos de Facundo* (Buenos Aires, 1934) and C. A. Jones, *Sarmiento: 'Facundo'*, an essay for the Támesis Critical Guides to Texts series (London, 1974).

Claridad, an Argentinian literary review which first appeared in July 1926 as successor to *Los Pensadores* (1922), *Dínamo* (1924), *La Campana de Palo* (1925), and *La Revista del Pueblo* (1926).

It was founded by J. P. Barreiro and Gaspar Mortillaro as a voice of the socialist left, of realism and utilitarianism, and of the masses as opposed to the élitist, aesthetic school of *Martín Fierro* (q.v.), successor to *Prisma* and *Proa*. The two groups of writers were named after Boedo Street and Florida Street respectively, where they held their meetings. The promise of *Claridad* was always greater than its performance, and it lasted no longer than its predecessors. Its contributors included Enrique Amorim, Raúl

González Tuñón, José Ingenieros, César Tiempo, Leonidas Barletta, and Carlos Mastronardi.

CLARÍN, see ALAS Y UREÑA, Leopoldo.

CLAVERÍA, CARLOS (1909–74), b. Barcelona. Literary critic. Director of the Spanish Institutes of Munich and (from 1963) of London. Among his essays in literary history were *Cinco estudios de literatura española moderna* (Salamanca, 1945), *Temas de Unamuno* (1952), and *Ensayos hispanosuecos* (Granada, 1954). He became a member *de número* of the Spanish Academy.

CLAVIJERO, FRANCISCO JAVIER (1731–87), b. Veracruz, Mexico. Creole historian. He mastered not only Greek, Latin, French, and Portuguese, but also more than twenty indigenous tongues. A Jesuit priest, he was expelled with his fellows in 1767, establishing himself first in Ferrara and then in Bologna. One of the least biased of all Mexican historians, he is very conscious of the relativity of historical 'truth'. He translated his *Historia antigua de Mégico* into Italian and published it in that language first, as *Storia antica del Messico . . .* (Cesena, 1780). The Spanish MS. was lost for nearly two centuries, reappearing in 1945 as *Historia antigua de México* in an edition by Mariano Cuevas.

Clavijero's *Historia de la Antigua o Baja California* (1852), translated from the first Italian edition, *Storia della California* (Venice, 1789), is a much inferior work, less concerned with its subject than with an apology for Jesuit conduct in California.

See J. Romero Flores, 'Documentos para la biografía del historiador Clavijero' in *Anales del Instituto Nacional de Antropología e Historia*, vol. 1, 1945.

CLAVIJO Y FAJARDO, JOSÉ DE (1730–1806), b. Lanzarote, Canary Islands. Satirist and translator. He was employed in a number of official posts, including that of state archivist to the Secretary of State, after a period in Paris during which he met both Voltaire and Buffon. He translated Buffon's work on natural history and plays by Racine.

He was founder and editor of, and virtually sole contributor 1762–7 to, the satirical weekly *El Pensador* (q.v.). This, with the outspoken attacks by Nicolás Fernández de Moratín (q.v.), was instrumental in securing the prohibition of *autos sacramentales* by royal degree dated 11 June 1765. His seduction of Louise Caron, sister of Beaumarchias, led not to the expected duel, but to a humiliating letter of apology from Clavijo and its acceptance by Beaumarchais. The incident, which took place in 1764, forms the subject of Goethe's romantic tragedy *Clavijo* and is referred to in Beaumarchais' own memoirs.

See A. Carlo Millares, *Biobibliografía de escritores de Canarias* (1932), pp. 177–86.

CLEMENCÍN, Diego (1765–1834), b. Murcia. Priest, scholar, and critic; he was employed as tutor to the children of the Duchess of Benavente, and was also a deputy to the Cortes of 1813, later being appointed Minister of Foreign Affairs and Minister of State. He was also a founder of the National Archaeological Museum, and in 1833 was Librarian to the Regent María Cristina. Among his many contributions to scholarship were an edition of the works of Leandro Fernández de Moratín (4 vols. in 6, 1830–1) for the Real Academia de la Historia, *Elogio de la Reina Católica Doña Isabel* (1820; 2nd edn., 1821), and the best commentary up to that time on Cervantes' *Quijote* (1833–9).

See J. Puyol y Alonso, *Don Diego Clemencín, ministro de Fernando VII. Recuerdos del Ministerio de 7 de julio de 1822* (1929).

Clerecía, Mester de, see MESTER DE CLERECÍA.

Clérigo y el caballero, Disputa del, see DISPUTA DE ELENA Y MARÍA.

COBO, Bernabé (1580–1657), b. Lopera, Jaén. Historian. He set out for the New World in 1596 to find 'El Dorado' in Venezuela's hinterland, but explored a wide area, finding truth stranger than legend. In 1599 he sailed from Panama to Peru, where he entered the Society of Jesus, making his first vows in 1603, and renewing them in 1630. After much travel he was appointed Rector of the Jesuit order in Arequipa in 1618, and spent the period 1630–50 in Mexico. In 1650 he returned to Lima, where he spent the rest of his life.

His major work is the *Historia del Nuevo Mundo* (4 vols., Seville, 1890–5), edited in his collected *Obras* by Francisco Mateos (2 vols., 1959). His minor work is *Historia de la fundación de Lima*, written in Mexico in 1639, published by Manuel González de la Rosa, and reprinted in the 1959 *Obras*.

See Raúl Porras, *Cronistas del Perú* (Lima, 1962).

CODAX or MOXA or DE VIGO, Martin (*fl.* 1220), b. Vigo? Galician poet of love and the sea. Pre-eminently a 'chantre do mar', in the words of Otero Pedrayo, Codax celebrated the beauty of the sea off the Galician coast, using nature as the means of expressing his personal feelings. The seven love poems of Codax surviving in a unique MS. are significant first

because the MS. is the only extant MS. of an individual poet, as opposed to an anthology, of the 13th c. in Galicia; and secondly because the music—with certain lacunae, like the text—is included. The MS. was first published in 1914 in a limited edition (of which only 10 copies were put on sale) by the antiquarian bookseller Pedro Vindel. This edition was superseded by the facsimile edition of C. Ferreira da Cunha, *O Cancioneiro de Martin Codax* (Rio de Janeiro, 1956).

See S. Oviedo y Arce, 'El genuino "Martin Codax", trovador gallego del siglo XIII' in *Boletín de la Real Academia Gallega*, vol. 10 (1916–7), pp. 60–2.

COELLO Y OCHOA, Antonio (1611–82), b. Madrid. Dramatist of the school of Pedro Calderón de la Barca (q.v.) yet influenced too by his friend Lope de Vega Carpio (q.v.). He distinguished himself in the service of the Duke of Albuquerque, and was awarded the knighthood of Santiago. The considerable work he produced for the stage was for the most part written in collaboration: five plays with Calderón, four with Rojas, three with Pérez de Montalbán, and others with his brother Juan Coello, L. Vélez de Guevara, and Solís. For instance, he wrote the second act of an adaptation of Guarini's *Il pastor fido*, the first being by Solís and the third by Calderón. With Vélez and Rojas he collaborated on *La Baltasara*, *El catalán Serrallonga*, and *También la afrenta es veneno*.

The only play he is believed to have written on his own is *Yerros de naturaleza y aciertos de fortuna* (ed. Juliá, 1930), though a tradition states that part was written by Calderón. Others are *El celoso extremeño*, based on the *novela ejemplar* of Cervantes; and an *auto* entitled *La cárcel del mundo*. *El conde de Sex, o dar la vida por su dama*, formerly attributed to King Philip IV by Jovellanos and reprinted in vol. 45 (1858) of the BAE, is now confidently attributed to Coello; however, since Philip IV is known to have written plays, he may well have collaborated in certain scenes. *El conde de Sex* (Robert Devereux, Earl of Essex) concerns the sacrifice of his life by the Earl for his betrothed Blanca, who had conspired against Queen Elizabeth I. Despite the fact that Elizabeth was hated in Spain more than any other monarch of her time, Coello's Queen is a model of regal decorum and, all things considered, a rounded character. This is Coello's finest play, and first appeared in 1638 in part XXXI of the collection of plays known as 'la antigua o de afuera'.

COLL, Pedro Emilio (1872–1947), b. Caracas. Venezuelan modernist short-story writer and essayist. With Pedro César Dominici and Urbaneja Achelpohl (qq.v.), he was a co-founder of the review *Cosmópolis* (1894–5), an ambitious magazine intended, as the title suggests, to reflect a wide variety of literary tendencies in many countries. A man tolerant of most ideas and philosophical systems, Coll was perhaps nearest Renan, Taine, and the sceptics in the essays collected as *Palabras* (1896). *El castillo de Elsinor* (1901) established Coll's reputation as a short-story writer, particularly for 'Opoponax' (influenced by the sensuality of Baudelaire) and 'El diente roto'. More stories can be found in *La escondida senda* (1927) and the useful anthology introduced by Rafael A. Insausti, *Obras* (1966).

COLLANTES DE TERÁN, ALEJANDRO (1901–33), b. Seville. Minor poet who founded, with Rafael Laffón, the Seville magazine *Mediodía* (1926–33). His verse, collected in *Versos* (1926) and *Poemas* (1949), is neo-popularist in style, like some early work by García Lorca and Alberti (qq.v.). His main subject is the city of Seville, its surroundings, people and customs. Among contemporaries connected with the *Generación del 1927* (q.v.), his closest friend was Luis Cernuda (q.v.).

See M. del Pilar Márquez, *Alejandro Collantes de Terán, poeta de Sevilla* (Seville, 1973), with a good bibliography.

Colmena, La (Buenos Aires, 1951), a novel by Camilo José Cela (q.v.).

A long time in the composition (1945–50) and rejected by many publishers, *La colmena* can be read as a view of general philosophical despair (taking its atmosphere of gloom as a pervasive belief) or as an evocation of the spirit of Franco's Spain.

The central character, Martín Marco, drifts from Doña Rosa's café (ejected for his inability to pay), to look at the city 'with the eyes of a sick and harassed child' and visits his married sister, whose husband he detests. He spends some time in Celestino's bar, meets his friend Paco on the street, and spends the night as usual in a store-room in the home of his friend Pablo Alonso. He spends whole mornings scribbling poems on forms at the Banco de España and the Central Post Office. Martín and his friend Ventura Aguado are next found in a café; Aguado is having an affair with Julita, a daughter of Don Roque and Doña Visi, the latter being a sister of Doña Rosa at whose café the opening pages were set. Scattered details which seem trivial in themselves later assume a greater significance, and it could be said that *La colmena* is the novel of trivia, and thus related to an important aspect of the French *nouveau roman*. Martín wanders aimlessly through Madrid, cadging fifty pesetas from Nati Robles, a girl he knew as a student, and experiencing 'a fear that is past under-standing' when he is unable to produce any papers for a policeman. Then, delirious with illness and fear, he seeks refuge in the brothel of Doña Jesusa and finds peace in the arms of the ironically named Pura.

While Martín visits the cemetery on the anniversary of his mother's death, friends learn from the newspapers that he is wanted by the police because his papers are not in order, and his friend Pablo Alonso goes to seek him in his usual morning haunts. Martín obtains a paper from the cemetery attendant but fails to see the notice concerning himself and returns to the city.

The episodic nature of the novel and its repudiation of the chronological treatment of events make it a demanding work. Cela was still under the influence of Nietzsche at this period, and the German's name crops up repeatedly as does the notion of determinism. The influence of the picaresque on Cela is notable.

Cela's imitators have found his technique easy, and produce disconnected anecdotes in banal language without Cela's gift for quick and accurate characterization. He himself declared that *La colmena* is a novel like a watch, 'made up of little parts which are all necessary, each for the other, so that the whole thing can run'. There is an English version, *The hive*, by J. M. Cohen (New York, 1953).

See Paul Ilie, *La novelística de Camilo José Cela* (1963) and D. Henn, *Cela: 'La colmena'* (London, 1974).

COLMENARES, DIEGO DE (1586–1651), b. Segovia. Historian. Chaplain to the Contreras family, and author of the monumental *Historia de la Insigne Ciudad de Segovia y Compendio de las Historias de Castilla* (1637; reprinted 1837), which was annotated in a new edition by Tomás Baeza y González (3 vols., Segovia, 1921–2) and last reissued in 1969.

See Juan de Vera, 'Biografía de Diego de Colmenares' in *Estudios Segovianos*, vol. 3 (1951), pp. 5–115.

COLOMA, CARLOS, *Marqués de la Espina* (1573–1637), b. Alicante. Historian. He continued the *Comentarios* (1592) of Bernardino de Mendoza in *Las guerras de los Estados Baxos desde el año MDLXXXVIII hasta el de MDXCIX* (Antwerp, 1625), reprinted (with Mendoza's book) in vol. 28 (1853) of the BAE. Coloma fought under the Duke of Alba in Portugal in his youth, later serving in Messina and Flanders, so his well-written account is based on personal knowledge. He was made a Knight of Santiago and Governor of Perpignan and the Balearics.

Tacitus was Coloma's model in the historical genre, and he translated his work as *Obras de Caio Cornelio Tacito* (Douai, 1629; 2nd edn., 1794).

COLOMA, *Padre* Luis (1851–1915), b. Jérez de la Frontera. Novelist and short-story writer. He studied law in Seville. While earning a living as a writer in Madrid, he was involved in a scandal, was shot and gravely wounded. In 1873 he decided to enter the Society of Jesus.

His name is connected primarily with only one novel, *Pequeñeces* (2 vols., Bilbao, 1890), which created a furore for its satirical attack on the Madrid aristocracy just before, and in the first year of, the Restoration (1874). It was considered a *roman à clef* for its scenes of naturalism depicted by a Jesuit, despite the fact that its heroine, Currita Albornoz, is converted by a Jesuit in the closing pages. Its title refers to the 'trivialities' shrugged off as venial sins by the aristocracy but considered mortal sins by the Church. This attack on high society in Madrid followed that of Pereda (q.v.) in his weak *La Montálvez* (1888) and preceded that of Palacio Valdés (q.v.) in his more effective *La espuma* (1891). Juan Valera wrote an anonymous 79-page 'letter' from the heroine to Coloma, *Pequeñeces . . . Currita Albornoz al Padre Luis Coloma*, apparently in a light vein but in fact attacking Coloma's literary style and pretensions as well as his ideology.

'Fray Candil' (E. Bobadilla, q.v.) also wrote on the book in his *Críticas instantáneas* (1891). Coloma was influenced by Fernán Caballero (q.v.), and wrote *Recuerdos de Fernán Caballero* (1910). Coloma also attempted the historical novel with *Retratos de antaño* (1895); *La reina mártir* (1902) on Mary Stuart; *El marqués de Mora* (1903); *Jeromín* (1905–7), on the life of Juan de Austria; and *Fray Francisco* (1914) on Contreras (q.v.). His *Obras completas* (19 vols., 1940–2) reached their 4th edition (with a biographical and critical study by R. M. de Hornedo now included) in 1960.

See A. & A. García Carraffa, *Españoles ilustres: El Padre Coloma* (1918).

COLOMBO, Cristoforo, see Colón, Cristóbal.

COLÓN, Cristóbal (1451?–1506), b. Genoa, Italy. Known in English as Christopher Columbus and in his native Italy as Cristoforo Colombo. Explorer credited with the 'discovery' by Europeans of the New World and its first European historian in his *Carta anunciando el descubrimiento de América* (Barcelona, 1493; facsimile edn. by C. Sanz, 1956), soon translated into Latin and distributed throughout Europe.

See J. M. Asensio, 'La carta de Colón con la relación del descubrimiento del Nuevo Mundo' in *La España Moderna*, vol. 34 (1891), pp. 5–21.

The four voyages of Christopher Columbus (ed. and trans. J. M. Cohen, Harmondsworth, 1969) consists of Columbus's log-book, letters, and dispatches with a connecting narrative drawn from the biography by his son Fernando Colón and other contemporary historians. There is an inferior edition of *Relaciones y cartas* (1892) in the Biblioteca Clásica.

The language of Columbus has given rise to much speculation. It has been suggested that he wrote Spanish as a first language; however, R. Menéndez Pidal asserted that his native tongue was the Genoese dialect, but as it was not a written language he learnt to write in Spanish in the Portuguese colony at Genoa, so that his Spanish is full of Portuguese turns of phrase and other features (see *La lengua de Cristóbal Colón* (1942) in Colección Austral). There is a more exhaustive treatment of the question by V. I. Milani, *The written language of Christopher Columbus* (1973).

The finest portrait of Columbus is that by Sebastiano del Piombo (1519) in the Metropolitan Museum of Art.

See R. Llanas de Niubó, *El enigma de Cristóbal Colón* (Barcelona, 1964) and for a broader perspective *The quest for America* (London, 1971) by Geoffrey Ashe and others.

Coloquio de los perros, El, the common title of *El Coloquio que pasó entre Cipión y Berganza*, one of the *Novelas ejemplares* (q.v., 1613) by Miguel de Cervantes Saavedra (q.v.). Probably an integral part of *El casamiento engañoso* (q.v.), the *Coloquio* is as its title suggests a dialogue between two dogs, in which Berganza tells of his picaresque life serving many masters: a butcher's boy who entrusted the dog with gifts of stolen meat for his lady-love, a shepherd who managed to find mutton whenever he fancied it, and a witch who took him for an enchanted man. He finally gave up his picaresque existence and decided to join Cipión in his quiet occupation, helping beggars.

A feature of the story is the bizarre series of philosophical reflections offered by Cipión.

There are critical editions of the *Coloquio* and its frame tale by A. González de Amezúa (1912) and F. Rodríguez Marín (1918), and a fine translation of both by J. M. Cohen in *Blind man's boy* (and) *Two cautionary tales* (London, 1962) in Four Square Classics.

See P. Laín Entralgo, 'Coloquio de los perros' in *Vestigios . . .* (1948, pp. 47–66); O. Belic, 'La estructura de "El coloquio de los perros"' in *Análisis estructural de textos hispanos* (1970, pp. 63–90), and general studies on the *Novelas ejemplares*.

COLUMBUS, Christopher, see Colón, Cristóbal.

Comedia nueva, La (1792), a satirical play (subtitled *El café*) by the neoclassical dramatist Leandro Fernández de Moratín (q.v.) against the bombastic, irregular writers of the age whom he had also attacked in *La derrota de los pedantes* (1789).

Described by Menéndez y Pelayo as the most astonishing satire that he knew in any language, the play concerns the imaginary *El gran cerco de Viena* by Don Eleuterio Crispín de Andorra, composed with the encouragement of his wife and his friend, the comic pedant Don Hermógenes. Though the play is not actually performed, quotations and descriptions give a clear idea of Moratín's targets. These include pseudo-erudition (Don Hermógenes clarifies his Latin tags in *Greek*), convoluted plots, extravagant sets, scenery, and numbers of extras. It was suspected that Moratín's principal victim was the playwright Luciano Francisco Comella (q.v.), who appealed to the public's taste for music and spectacle but lacked subtlety in plot, thought, or characterization. The play has been edited by J. C. Dowling (1970) for Clásicos Castalia.

See René Andioc, *Sur la querelle du théâtre au temps de Leandro Fernández de Moratín* (Tarbes, 1970).

COMELLA Y VILLAMITJANA, Luciano Francisco (1751–1812), b. Vich. Dramatist of the 'irregular' school who opposed the neoclassical or 'regular' school of such playwrights as Leandro Fernández de Moratín (q.v.). He thought his play *El sitio de Calés* (1790) the butt of Moratín's play *El café* (usually known as *La comedia nueva*, q.v.) and was probably correct. He tried to stop the production of *El café* (1792), but in vain. Moratín's valid point was that cheap spectacular effects in quick succession without a reasonable plot or characterization were taking precedence on the Madrid stage over works of wit and depth.

Always intent on being in the fashion, Comella experimented with several genres: the *sainete* in the manner of R. de la Cruz (q.v.); the realistic play in *La familia indigente*; the *comédie larmoyante* in *Cecilia* (1786) and *Cecilia viuda* (1787); a bad play on the popular theme of *Doña Inés de Castro*; the theme of the enlightened despot in the trilogy comprising *Federico II, rey de Prusia*, *Federico II en el campo de Torgau* (criticizing the use of torture), and *Federico II en Glatz*; and the theme of arranged marriages in *El matrimonio por razón de estado*.

See C. Cambronero, *Comella: su vida y sus obras* in *Revista Contemporánea* (1896), vols. 102–4,

passim; and I. L. MacClelland, '"Comellan" drama and the censor' in *Bulletin of Hispanic Studies*, vol. 30 (1953), pp. 20–31.

COMENDADOR GRIEGO, El, the title given by his contemporaries to the classical scholar Hernán Núñez de Toledo y Guzmán (q.v.), also known from his birthplace as 'el Pinciano'. Not to be confused with Alonso López Pinciano (q.v.).

Complutensian Bible, the *Biblia Políglota Complutense* (after Complutum, the Latin name for Alcalá de Henares) planned and patronized by Cardinal Francisco Ximénez de Cisneros (q.v.), was the first complete polyglot Bible. It was begun in 1502 by a team of scholars, including the great grammarian Antonio de Nebrija (q.v.), Demetrios Loukas of Crete, Diego López de Estúñiga, and Hernan Núñez 'el Pinciano' (editing the Greek and Latin sections) and the Hebrew scholars Alfonso de Zamora, Alfonso de Alcalá, and Pablo Coronel.

Printing was started at Alcalá de Henares in 1514 and was completed in 600 copies of six volumes each in 1517, the year of the Cardinal's death. The date of publication was delayed by Pope Leo X until 1520, but the work was not on sale until 1522.

The first four volumes print the Old Testament in Hebrew, Greek, and Latin (volume 1 includes Chaldean in addition); the fifth prints the New Testament in Greek and Latin; the sixth has a Hebrew–Chaldean vocabulary, a Hebrew grammar, and an index of names. The Greek type used in setting the Complutensian Bible has been called the finest of its kind ever designed.

This Bible was intended to incorporate the latest advances in scholarship and textual criticism, but eventually proved to be conservative, and was superseded finally by the Antwerp Polyglot Bible (1569–72) prepared under Benito Arias Montano (q.v.).

Conceptismo, the use of literary conceits or wit (*agudeza*), paradox, and ambiguity, as well as difficult images and metaphors, and hence literary *matter* rather than the *manner* of *culteranismo* (q.v.).

Conceptismo can be traced back to Renaissance writers such as Garcilaso and Fray Luis de León (qq.v.), but as a recognizable style or movement it is generally considered to have gained momentum with the publication of *Conceptos espirituales* (1600–12), poetry *a lo divino* by Alonso de Ledesma (q.v.). Quevedo and Gracián (qq.v.) are the acknowledged masters of the style, but *agudeza* was cultivated by most late 16th- and 17th-c. Spanish writers.

Gracián was unable to arrive at a very precise definition of *agudeza* that would exclude symbols and similes; in his *Agudeza y arte de ingenio* (q.v., Huesca, 1648) he suggested that the writer should combine obscurity with brevity, unusual ideas with striking metaphors, and serenity with violence. The aim was to establish a conceptual similarity despite a contrast of two terms in an image. A purpose behind *conceptismo* was to read signs which would lead to an understanding of the occult relationships between all things in the universe, a medieval idea. For the philosophical significance of *conceptismo*, see *Oculta filosofía* (1643) by Juan Eusebio Nieremberg (q.v.).

Until recently it was widely believed that *conceptismo* and *culteranismo* (q.v.) were antithetical, but it is now recognized that examples of *agudeza* abound not only in Quevedo, an acknowledged *conceptista*, but also in the *culterano* Góngora. Both movements seek difficulty of expression and understanding; both are aimed at making the reader think carefully. The *conceptos* are related in this aspect to the *emblemas* (q.v.).

See Andrée Collard, *Nueva poesía: conceptismo, culteranismo en la crítica española* (Waltham, Mass., 1967).

CONCHALÍ, INOCENCIO, a pseudonym used by the Chilean *costumbrista* storyteller and war reporter Daniel Riquelme (q.v.).

CONCOLORCORVO, the pseudonym under which Alonso Carrió de la Vandera (q.v.) wrote *El lazarillo de ciegos caminantes desde Buenos Aires hasta Lima* (Gijón, 1773 [but Lima, 1776]).

CONDE, CARMEN (1907–), b. Cartagena. Poet. Widely considered the leading Spanish poetess of her time. She married the poet Antonio Oliver Belmás (q.v.) and has edited his *Obras completas* (vol. 1, 1971–). A selection of her verses appeared in *Obra poética* (1967), a work notable for its passionate verse celebrating love and life. Mensajes de Poesía (Vigo) published *Homenaje a Carmen Conde* in 1951.

She has also written a number of psychological novels: *Vidas contra su espejo* (1944), *En manos del silencio* (Barcelona, 1950), *Las oscuras raíces* (Barcelona, 1954), and an evocative volume of childhood reminiscences *Empezando la vida* (Tetuán, 1955).

She wrote a number of children's books with her husband, and has written a great deal under the pseudonym 'Florentina del Mar'. In recent years she has published the anthology *Once grandes poetisas américo-hispanas* (1967), and the biographies *Menéndez Pidal* (1969) and *Gabriela Mistral* (1971).

CONDE, JOSÉ ANTONIO (1765–1820), b. Peraleja, Cuenca. Historian, and the foremost student of Muslim Spain until the Dutchman R. Dozy (1820–83). Conde studied at Cuenca and Alcalá, and was librarian at El Escorial and subsequently in the Royal (now National) Library in Madrid. He was a pedestrian writer, but his work was important in helping to counter the prevalent Hispanocentric view of Mediterranean history. The *Historia de la dominación de los árabes en España, sacada de varios manuscritos y memorias arábigas* (3 vols., 1820–1) was carefully (and often adversely) criticized by Dozy (q.v.).

See P. Roca, 'Vida y escritos de don José Antonio Conde' in *Revista de Archivos, Bibliotecas y Museos*, vols. 8–12 (1903–5), and Manuela Manzanares de Cirre, *Arabistas españoles del siglo XIX* (1972?).

Conde Lucanor et de Patronio, El libro de los Enxiemplos del, a collection of fables after oriental models, chiefly Arabic, completed in 1335 by the Infante Don Juan Manuel (q.v.). The work thus antedates Boccaccio's rather similar *Decamerone* by more than a decade.

There are 51 moral tales in the first part (and three other brief sections), each starting with a question asked by the young Count Lucanor of his old and trusted adviser, this being the form used in the Buddhist *Milinda-Pañha* ('Questions of [King] Menander').

The subject-matter is varied, but love is rarely mentioned. The Infante is a perfectionist in his style, which is dignified and concise; he keeps an adroit balance between the serious moral and the amusing anecdote. Where the fables of Aesop and the *Calila e Digna* (q.v.) are confined to animal figures, Juan Manuel prefers human beings. His post-medieval self-assurance is evident equally in the expunging of miraculous or fantastic elements, in his individuality of style, and in his oft-expressed need for protection from mutilation of works by illiterate reciters or bad copyists.

One story is of the *homne que iba cargado de piedras preciosas et se afogó en el río*, against the excessive love of worldly goods; another served as Shakespeare's inspiration for *The taming of the shrew*; in another, the weak unite to defeat the strong in a tale of two horses against a lion; others concern the progressive enlightenment of kings and princes, as in Juan Manuel's own *Libro infinido* and other works in the genre of *De regimine principum* (q.v.). The most elegant *enxiemplo* (modern Spanish: *ejemplo*) is that in which a woman married to one of Saladin's soldiers asks Saladin, who is pursuing her himself, to name the finest quality a man may possess, before he may possess her. Her own answer is 'a sense of shame', 'que era madre et cabeza de todas las bondades'.

The *editio princeps* is that of G. Argote de Molina (Seville, 1575). The version edited by P. de Gayangos in vol. 51 (1857) of the BAE has been superseded by those of H. Knust (Leipzig, 1900), E. Juliá Martínez (1933), and J. M. Blecua (in Clásicos Castalia, 1969), while versions in modern Spanish have been made by J. Loveluck (Santiago de Chile, 1950) and E. Moreno Báez (Valencia, 1953). There is an English version by James York, *Count Lucanor; or, the fifty pleasant tales of Patronio* (London, 1924).

See E. Lunardi, *'El Conde Lucanor' di don Juan Manuel* (Lugano, 1953, with text, Italian translation, and good study); and E. Caldera, 'Retorica, narrativa e didattica nel "Conde Lucanor" ' in *Miscellanea di Studi Ispanici*, vol. 14 (Pisa, 1966–7), pp. 5–120.

Condenado por desconfiado, El, a Golden Age theological *comedia* ascribed by most scholars to 'Tirso de Molina', the pseudonym of Fray Gabriel Téllez (q.v.). It was written *c.* 1624, though not published (in the *Segunda parte de las Comedias del Maestro Tirso de Molina*) until 1635.

As a play on the theme of human arrogance in the face of divine retribution, it is often considered a companion-piece to Tirso's *Burlador de Sevilla* (q.v.). It should be seen in the context of the views of the Jesuit Luis de Molina (q.v.), who had stressed the importance of free-will in a famous controversy with the determinist Domingo Báñez (q.v.), a Dominican.

Paulo, a hermit obsessed with the fear of damnation, rather than with the love of God or altruistic thoughts of service, is told by the devil that he will meet the same fate as Enrico, son of Anareto. When Paulo leaves his lonely hermitage for Naples to discover what manner of holy man Enrico can be, he discovers that he is a seducer, thief, and assassin. Paulo's shock reveals his true arrogance, and he vows revenge on God for this cruel trick. Enrico, however, so loves his father that he will sacrifice anything for him: this is his saving grace.

The next meeting is full of suspense. Paulo ties Enrico to a tree, blindfolds him and convinces him that his last hour has come in order to provoke repentance and consequent salvation and thus ensuring his own. Enrico refuses to repent, preferring to trust in God's mysterious mercy, and urging the same view on Paulo. Paulo, while hating him, cannot condemn Enrico to death because that would condemn him too.

In the third act, Enrico is in gaol and condemned to die, but repents when urged to do so by Anareto, and is saved. Paulo, rejecting for a second time the angel offering salvation through the grace of God, dies in despair and goes to Hell. Tirso's conclusion is that Divine mercy is granted to those who deserve it by their thoughts and works, providing they retain their trust in God, rather than to those enmeshed in arid theology. The unexpected ending agrees with Lope's dictum that the audience should not be able to anticipate the denouement of a play.

Tirso's lively treatment of a fundamental theological problem is excellent; language and versification are brilliant and varied.

Among those who deny Tirso's authorship of *El condenado por desconfiado* are José López Tascón, in *Boletín de la Biblioteca Menéndez y Pelayo*, vols. 16–18 (1934–6), who attributes it to Fray Alonso Remón (q.v.); A. Valbuena Prat in his *Historia de la literatura española* (7th edn., vol. 1, 1964, pp. 416–20); and J. Cejador y Frauca, in *Revue Hispanique*, vol. 57 (1923), pp. 127–59. The theme of *santos y bandoleros*, so popular in the Golden Age, was perhaps even better dealt with in Calderón's *La devoción de la Cruz* (q.v.).

See N. Prado, *'El condenado por desconfiado': estudio crítico-teológico* (1907); R. Menéndez Pidal, *'El condenado por desconfiado'* in his *Estudios literarios* (1920), pp. 13–85 [collecting papers of 1902 and 1904]; and T. E. May, *'El condenado por desconfiado': 1. The enigmas; 2. Anareto*, in *BHS*, vol. 35 (1958), pp. 138–56.

CONGRAINS MARTÍN, ENRIQUE (1932–), b. Lima. Peruvian short-story writer and successful businessman. The short stories *Lima, hora cero* (1954) and *Kikuyo* (1955), dealing with slums and poverty in urban Peru, are often tinged with magic and surrealism. His best work is the novel *No una sino varias muertes* (Buenos Aires, 1957), which narrates the events of two days in the life of a bottle-washer, the 17-year-old Maruja, who dreams of owning her own bottle factory.

Contemporáneos, the foremost Mexican literary magazine of the period 1928–31. It published the work of its founder, Bernardo Ortiz de Montellano, and of Xavier Villaurrutia, José Gorostiza, Jaime Torres Bodet (qq.v.), Enrique González Rojo, Bernardo J. Gastelúm, Salvador Novo, Jorge. Cuesta, Elías Nandino, Gilberto Owen, and also Octavio G. Barreda, who was to continue its tradition with his own *Hijo pródigo* (1943–6).

Contemporáneos fostered the cosmopolitan outlook that had been advocated by *La Revista Azul* and *La Revista Moderna* (qq.v.), in particular renewing the cultural ties with France that had been developed between Independence and the Revolution of 1910. It also strengthened the *avant-garde* tendencies that had emerged in important earlier reviews such as *Pegaso* (founded in 1917 by López Velarde, q.v.), *Falange* (founded in 1922), and *Ulises* (founded by Novo and Villaurrutia in 1927), which had taken its title from James Joyce's novel. The most popular themes with *Contemporáneos* writers were chance, solitude, and death.

Manuel Durán has compiled *Antología de la revista 'Contemporáneos'* (1973).

Contrarreforma, the Counter-Reformation, or movement to counteract the process of Protestant Reformation of the Church, was especially strong in Spain, and was led by Philip II. The *Contrarreforma* was also aimed at abolishing the internal abuses of the Roman Catholic Church, and is thus often described as a true *Reforma*. Internal reform was attempted through the sessions of the Council of Trent (q.v.), which took place intermittently 1545–63. New religious orders were established in an effort to renew the Roman Catholic Church: these included the Jesuits, the Aesculapians, and the Capuchins; and other orders were transformed, notably the Carmelites (see S. JUAN DE LA CRUZ and S. TERESA). The ascetic and mystic writers of the 16th c. (among them Luis de Granada, Alonso de Orozco, and Pedro de Alcántara) can properly be understood only in the light of the Counter-Reformation. This movement provoked long-standing and often bitter controversy such as that in *De auxiliis* (q.v.) on the problem of free-will, and a new theology based partly on the anti-Protestant reaction, such as that in the *Tratado de la victoria de sí mismo* by Melchor Cano.

In the drama, Calderón, Tirso de Molina, and many other writers take up themes of the Counter-Reformation, as for example in the *Devoción de la Cruz* of Calderón (qq.v.). The moral content of books became much more emphatic after the Council of Trent, in which Spanish delegates played a prominent part.

CONTRERAS, ALONSO DE (1582–c. 1641), b. Madrid. Autobiographer. Apparently uneducated, Contreras wrote (largely at the encouragement of Lope de Vega, q.v.), his autobiography *Vida del capitán Alonso de Contreras*, first published in the *Boletín de la Real Academia de la Historia*, vol. 37 (1900), pp. 129–270. The first news of Contreras' adventures, enough of which have been authenticated to prove their general veracity, appeared in Lope de Vega's dedication to Contreras of his play *El rey sin reino* (*Parte XX*, 1625). Contreras began to write his story in 1630, and added more at a later date. Of scant literary value, the *Vida* is absorbing for its matter.

After fighting in Italy and Flanders he became

a pirate in the Mediterranean, taking part in the siege of Hammamet in 1601 and seizing Turkish and Barbary ships. He squandered the fortune he made from piracy, had strange adventures in Greece, and fought as a mercenary with the Knights of Malta. Back in Spain he was accused of being chief conspirator with the *moriscos* of Hornachuelos (Badajoz) but was eventually set free. He travelled again, to Flanders, Puerto Rico, Santo Domingo, and Cuba. The Knights of Malta appointed him governor of the island of Pantelleria.

Contreras also wrote the unpublished 'Derrotero del Mediterráneo' (MS. in National Library) copied in the first third of the 17th c. and consisting of 107 leaves in quarto. His major work was reprinted, with a prologue by J. Ortega y Gasset, in 1943.

See A. Morel-Fatio, 'Soldats espagnols du XVIIe siècle: Alonso de Contreras' in *Bulletin Hispanique*, vol. 3 (1901), pp. 135–58, and R. Benítez Claros, 'La personalidad de Contreras' in *Visión de la literatura española* (1963), pp. 117–29.

CONTRERAS, FRANCISCO (1877–1933), Chilean poet, critic, and disciple of Darío (q.v.). Contreras worked in Paris from 1905 until his death, mainly on the staff of *Le Mercure de France*. Influenced there by the poetry of Gautier, Baudelaire, Moréas, and in particular by that of Darío, he produced several books of somewhat derivative verse: *Esmaltines* (1890), *Toison* (1906), *Romances de hoy* (1907), *Almas y panoramas* (1910), *La piedad sentimental* (1911), *Luna de la patria* (1913), and *La varillita de virtud* (1919).

A penetrating critic and reader of new Latin-American literature, he coined the term *mundonovismo* to indicate the changing emphasis from old world themes and attitudes to indigenous themes and attitudes. Among his critical works were *Les écrivains contemporains de l'Amérique espagnole* (Paris, 1920), *L'esprit de l'Amérique espagnole* (Paris, 1931), and *Rubén Darío: su vida y su obra* (Barcelona, 1930; 2nd edn., Santiago, 1937).

CONTRERAS, JERÓNIMO DE (c. 1520–c. 1585), b. Aragón? Novelist. He declared himself in prefaces 'coronista de su Majestad'. He is now remembered not for *Dechado de varios subjectos* (Saragossa, 1572) which eulogizes a large number of celebrated Spaniards, but for *Selva de aventuras* (q.v., Barcelona, 1565), a tale of frustrated love in the Byzantine tradition.

CONTRERAS, RAÚL (1896–), b. Cojutepeque, El Salvador. Poet, playwright, and diplomat who, from 1922, spent many years in

Spain. A major figure of post-modernism in El Salvador. His books include *Armonías íntimas* (1919), *Poesías escogidas* (Barcelona, 1922), *La princesa está triste: glosa escénica en tres actos de la sonatina de Rubén Darío* (Madrid, 1925), and *Presencia de humo* (1959).

The work of 'Lydia Nogales', a poet who appeared on the Central American literary scene in 1946, has been attributed to Contreras.

Conversos ('converts'), a term used of Muslims and more especially of Jews who were obliged to be baptized in order to remain in Spain and retain their possessions. The term usually has a pejorative sense, for it was evident to the authorities that such enforced 'conversion' would often be nominal. The Roman Catholic faith became officially established in Spain during the reign of the Visigothic King Recared I (586–601) but enforced conversion seems to have begun under Sisebut (612–621). The *conversos* played no great part in peninsular life until in the 13th c. Pablo Cristiano took part in open debate with Moishe ben Nahman in Barcelona. During the reign of Juan II of Castile (1407–54) the *conversos*, or *marranos* as they were also known, possessed great power and were apparently instrumental in causing the fall of Álvaro de Luna. One of the great humanists of the period, Alfonso de Santa María de Cartagena (q.v.), was the son of the Great Rabbi of Burgos, but rose to be Bishop of Burgos in 1435. Accusations of practising Jewish religious rites in secret were easily made against *conversos*, and there were massacres of *cristianos nuevos* in 1449 and 1467 (Toledo), 1473 (Cordova), and 1481 (Seville). Ferdinand and Isabella were persuaded to establish the Inquisition against the alleged danger from *conversos*, and in 1481 the wealthy *converso* Diego Susán and others were publicly burnt in Tablada. The flight of many *conversos* to Granada and Portugal was halted by the publication of a general pardon on 6 February 1481 and as many as 2,000 *conversos* took advantage of this, and became reconciled with the Church. Torquemada's period as Inquisitor General (1483–98) is generally considered the apogee of anti-*converso* feeling. Alfonso de Zamora, Professor of Hebrew at the University of Alcalá, wrote *Sefer hokmah Elohim* ('Book of the wisdom of God') as a Christian apologia to Jews, and worked with another *converso*, Pablo Coronel, on the Complutensian Bible (q.v.). The process of assimilation continued with the 16th and 17th cs., since when the issue has steadily decreased in significance.

In literature, *conversos* made a significant contribution to most genres. They included Fray Luis de León, S. Teresa de Ávila, Mateo Alemán, the Santa María and Cartagena families, Fernando de la Torre, Juan de Baena, and Francisco López de Villalobos (qq.v.).

See C. Roth, *A History of the Marranos* (Philadelphia, 1932).

Coplas del Provincial, see PROVINCIAL, Coplas del.

Coplas de pie quebrado, see PIE QUEBRADO.

CORCUERA, ARTURO (1935–), b. Salaverry. Peruvian poet. He teaches at the Universidad Nacional Mayor de San Marcos and is a contributor to *Cuadernos Trimestrales* edited by Marco Antonio Corcuera. His voice is colloquial and his style simple, influenced by Alejandro Romualdo (q.v.). His first book was *Cantoral* (1956) and he has published a dozen others, of which the better-known include *Primavera triunfante*, *Noë delirante* and *Recuerdo y presencia de Javier Heraud* (all 1963), and *Territorio libre* (1969). Apart from his moving poetic memoir of the prematurely deceased Heraud, Corcuera's best work is in the fable genre, such as *Fábula del lobo feroz. La gran jugada o crónica deportiva que trata de Teófilo Cubillas y el Alianza* (1974) takes association football as its theme.

CORDERO, AURELIA (1874–1922), b. Cuenca, Ecuador. Poet. Daughter of Luis Cordero (q.v.), she was a solitary, anguished writer, whose works appeared in a selection by Rigoberto Cordero y León entitled *Aurelia Cordero de Romero León* (1954).

CORDERO, LUIS (1833–1912), b. Déleg, Ecuador. Poet, philologist, lexicographer, and jurist. He was President of the Republic of Ecuador in 1892. He published the epigrammatic *Poesías jocosas*, and was influenced by Victor Hugo, especially in his *Poesías serias* (both 1895). He also wrote in Quichua and composed a Spanish-Quichua dictionary.

CÓRDOBA, GONZALO FERNÁNDEZ DE (d. 1515). He was called 'el Gran Capitán' because of his exploits in recapturing Granada from the Moors (thus completing the eight centuries of Reconquest) in 1492 and subsequently seizing Naples from the French for the Crown of Aragón.

Gonzalo de Córdoba was the last epic hero of Spain. A prose *Vida del Gran Capitán* (Seville, 1527) prepared by Hernando Pérez del Pulgar (q.v.) at the request of the Emperor Charles V was reprinted by Martínez de la Rosa as *Hernán Pérez del Pulgar: bosquejo histórico* (Madrid, 1834). The tedious prose *Chrónica llamada de las dos Conquistas de Nápoles* (Saragossa, 1559) is

attributed in the introduction to Pérez del
Pulgar but is spurious. José de Cañizares (q.v.)
wrote prose sketches of the story of Gonzalo, and
Jean-Pierre Claris de Florian is the author of a
romantic novel *Gonsalve de Cordoue* (1791), but
Gonzalo was celebrated more frequently in
verse.

The first verse epic on Gonzalo, Alonso
Hernández's (q.v.) *Historia parthenopea* (Rome,
1516), benefits from the author's first-hand
knowledge of events, and his determination to
follow their course; Hernández is, however, a
poor poet. The other major heroic poems on
Gonzalo appeared in 1651: the *Neapolisea*
(Granada), by Francisco Trillo y Figueroa (q.v.)
and *Nápoles Recuperada por el Rey Don Alonso*
(Saragossa) by Francisco de Borja (q.v.). The
vogue of the epic was drawing to a close at this
period: Trillo and Borja exemplify the decadence
of the genre.

CÓRDOBA, Fray MARTÍN ALFONSO DE (*c.*
1398–*c.* 1468), b. Cordova. Didactic writer and
Augustinian preacher, close to Juan II and
Enrique IV, who taught in the universities of
Toulouse and Salamanca. Much of his writing
in Latin and Spanish has been lost, but some
works are available in vol. 171 (1964) of the
BAE, with an introduction by P. Fernando
Rubio.

His most important works were *De próspera
y adversa fortuna* dedicated to Álvaro de Luna and
written 1440–53, and edited as *Compendio de la
fortuna* by P. F. Rubio Álvarez (El Escorial,
1958); *Jardín de las nobles donzellas* (Valladolid,
1500, critical edn. by H. Goldberg, N.C., 1974),
written before 1467 for the Infanta Isabel and
defending her right to the throne of Castile; and
Tratado de la predestinación, edited by Aníbal
Sánchez Fraile (Salamanca, 1956). The fourth
book by Fray Martín in the BAE is *Libro del
regimiento de los señores*, also in didactic vein.

CÓRDOBA SACEDO, SEBASTIÁN DE (1545?–
1604?), b. Úbeda. Versifier, who rendered the
influential Italianate poetry of Boscà and
Garcilaso (qq.v.) *a lo divino*, making it more
acceptable to Counter-Reformation Spain. *Las
obras de Boscán y Garcilaso trasladadas en materias
christianas* (Granada, 1575) was fairly popular,
and was reprinted once. The importance of this
bowdlerized classic lies in the fact that S. Juan
de la Cruz (q.v.) was undoubtedly thoroughly
acquainted with it, though he knew the original
texts as well, and studied both metre and content
for adaptation in his own poetry. Other verses
by Córdoba can be read in vol. 35 (1855) of the
BAE.

Glen R. Gale has edited Córdoba's work as
Garcilaso a lo divino (1971) for Clásicos Castalia.

CÓRDOVA, Fray MATÍAS DE (1768–1828), b.
Tapachula, Guatemala. Poet, teacher, and
humanist. Even his utilitarian prose was marked
by a conscientious attention to style. His first
publication was *Utilidad de que todos los indios
y ladinos se vistan y calcen a la española, y medios de
conseguirlo sin violencia, coacción ni mandato* (1798),
followed by *Método de leer con utilidad los autores
antiguous de elocuencia* (1801), *Prelecciones a los
libros de elocuencia* (1801), and *Método fácil de
enseñar a leer y a escribir* (1824–5). But his principal
claim to fame is an epic poem of 417 hendecasyllabic lines: *La tentativa del león y el éxito de su
empresa* (1801), a moral fable imitated by
Antonio Machado y Núñez (*El león y el hombre*),
by José Echegaray (*Consejos de un padre*), by
Louis François Jauffret (*Le lion et l'homme*), and
even by Tolstoy (*Intelligence*). The fable teaches
the supremacy of human beings over the other
animals, and the power of intelligence to subdue
brute strength.

Corno Emplumado, El, a bilingual Mexican
literary magazine (English-Spanish) edited by
Sergio Mondragón and Margaret Randall. It
was founded in 1962 and quickly became
established as one of the most adventurous
journals of new writing from Latin America,
publishing important writers such as Ernesto
Cardenal (q.v.).

COROMINAS, JOAN (1905–), b. Barcelona.
Philologist and lexicographer. Professor of
Romance Philology in Chicago University
from 1946, Corominas was naturalized a U.S.
citizen in 1953. The work for which he will
always be remembered is the essential *Diccionario crítico-etimológico de la lengua castellana*
(4 vols., 1954–7). He produced a number of other
important books: *Mots catalans d' origens aràbic*
(Barcelona, 1936), a complete translation of
Terence into Catalan (4 vols., 1936–59),
Estudios de etimología hispánica (Mendoza, Argentina, 1942), *L'estil i manera de M. J. de Galba i el
de Joanot Martorell* (1953), *Introducció a l'estudi de
la toponímia catalana i altres assaigs toponomàstics*
(1962), a fine critical edition of the *Libro de Buen
Amor* (1967), and *Entre dos llenguatjes* (2 vols.,
Barcelona, 1976).

CORONADO, CAROLINA (1823–1911), b.
Almendralejo, Badajoz. Poet and novelist.
Married to a U.S. diplomat, J. H. Perry, she
took advantage of this immunity to give sanctuary to several liberals on the failure of the
1866 revolution.

Her poetry, raising human love to the semi-
mystical level, was well received all over Spain
from its first publication in 1843. The second
edition of her *Poesías* (1852) was prefaced by

J. E. Hartzenbusch; other editions have appeared in Barcelona (1943) and Badajoz (1953). Her novels were less successful: *Paquita. Adoración* (San Fernando, 1850), *Jarilla* (1851), *La Sigea* (2 vols., 1854), and *La rueda de la desgracia. Manuscrito de un conde* (1873). Among her neglected historical plays were *Alfonso IV de León, Petrarca,* and *El divino Figueroa.*

See R. Gómez de la Serna, *Mi tía Carolina Coronado* (1942) and A. de Sandoval, *Carolina Coronado y su época* (Saragossa, 1944).

Coronel no tiene quien le escriba, El, a short novel by the Colombian Gabriel García Márquez (q.v.), first published in Mexico City in 1961.

The main character is a retired colonel who is still waiting for news of his pension fifty years after the Civil War. His only possession is a fighting cock left to him by his son Agustín, a murdered revolutionary, and although he is starving he will not sell it. The old colonel is to enter the bird for fights as soon as the season begins. All the local people are betting on the bird, for they hope that it will win in the place where Agustín was killed, the local cockpit.

The colonel represents the indomitable courage and irrepressibility of the human spirit in the face of old age, ill health, loneliness, tyranny, and even bad weather. García Márquez's portrait of the old man is enhanced by his terse, objective style.

A translation by J. S. Bernstein, *No-one writes to the colonel* (with *Big Mama's funeral*), was published in New York in 1968.

CORONEL URTECHO, JOSÉ (1906–), b. Granada, Nicaragua. Critic and poet. He studied at universities in the U.S.A., and has published a useful *Panorama y antología de la nueva poesía norteamericana,* for which he is best known outside Nicaragua. He returned home in 1925 to lead an *avant-garde* movement, editing the magazine *Semana* (1926–), in which the new surrealism and ultraism were favoured. A poet of experiment, he wrote traditional poetry for a few years (1939–41), but then returned to his preferred hermeticism. His poems have appeared mainly in magazines, often cerebral, ironic, and esoteric. They largely influenced the subsequent generations of Nicaraguan poets, such as Ernesto Cardenal, Ernesto Mejía Sánchez (qq.v.), and others.

Corpes, the name of the oakwood ('robredo de Corpes') in *Cantar de mio Cid,* l. 2,697 (see CID), where the Infantes de Carrión (q.v.) dishonoured and abandoned their wives Elvira and Sol, the Cid's daughters, in the *Cantar de la afrenta de Corpes,* the third and final section of the epic. The wood was southwest of San Esteban de Gormaz, the 'Sant Estevan' of the text (l. 2,696) but has now disappeared.

CORRAL, PEDRO DEL (*fl.* 1440), Spanish novelist. Author of *Crónica Sarracina,* properly entitled *Crónica del Rey don Rodrigo con la destrucción de España* (Seville, 1499), written *c.* 1443. Corral clearly began from the semi-historical chronicles of Ghazi, the *Crónica general,* and the *Crónica troyana,* but gave up all pretence of factual detail when inventing three 'authorities': Eleastras, Alanzuri, and Carestas. Pérez de Guzmán (q.v.), in his *Generaciones y semblanzas,* loftily dismissed the 'mentira y trufa paladín' of the lewd and presumptuous author. Thus the book is not a chronicle at all, though referred to as such by Ausìas March and others, but one of the influential *libros de caballería* (q.v.). Of scarcely any intrinsic worth, the book is important as the source of the oldest ballads of Rodrigo, and of plays by Hartzenbusch (*La jura en Santa Gadea*) and Zorrilla (*La leyenda del Cid*).

See R. Menéndez Pidal, *Leyendas del último rey godo,* vol. 1 (1906).

CORREA, JULIO (1900–53), Paraguayan poet and dramatist, associated with the review *Juventud* (q.v.), who founded the Guaraní theatre with plays inspired by the Chaco War, and created characters from the people, such as soldiers and peasant women. His first poems appeared in *Cuerpo y alma* (Buenos Aires, 1943). He rejects the concept of art for art's sake, and preaches a literary rebellion, and has influenced the Spanish-language drama in Paraguay by his insistence on the significance of the common people and their plight in times of war. His plays include *Sandía Ýbyguy, Guerra Ayá, Terejó yeby frente, Peicha guarante,* and *Pleito riré.*

CORREA, MIGUEL ÁNGEL (1881–1942), b. Rosario. Argentinian novelist, poet, and dramatist, who frequently used the pen-name 'Mateo Booz'. A journalist and civil servant, he first made a literary reputation with the short novels *El agua de tu cisterna* (1919) and *La reparación* (1920). He subsequently wrote a number of varied full-length novels concerned with social and political problems, including *La tierra del aire y del sol* (1926) on the difficulties encountered by the indigenous people; *La vuelta de Zamba* (1927); *El tropel* (1932), a historical novel on the Rosas period; *La mariposa quemada* (1932); *Aleluyas del Brigadier* (1936), a fictional life of Estanislao López of Santa Fe; *La ciudad cambió de voz* (1938), showing the growth of Rosario from 1870 through the life of an imaginary Spanish immigrant family and their integration into the Argentine middle class.

Santa Fe, mi país (1934) is a celebrated collection of short stories involving legends and superstitions treated with tenderness and sarcasm.

See Laura Milano's brief *Mateo Booz* (Santa Fe, 1964).

Corregidor, until the early 19th c. the title given to the *alcalde* ('mayor' or 'governor') appointed by the king to preside over meetings of local town councils in Spain (*ayuntamientos*) and administer the region in the king's name.

The most celebrated *corregidor* in Spanish fiction is Don Eugenio de Zúñiga y Ponce de León, in *El sombrero de tres picos* by Pedro Antonio de Alarcón (qq.v.).

See the useful study, *El corregidor castellano: 1348–1808, estudios de historia de la administración* (1971) by B. González Alonso.

CORTÁZAR, JULIO (1916–), b. Brussels, of Argentinian parents. Major Argentinian short-story writer, novelist, and critic. His early years were spent first in Belgium and then in Argentina. In 1951 he moved to Paris. He has travelled extensively in the United States, and has worked as a schoolmaster for five years in Buenos Aires. He has said that Jean Cocteau's *Opium* awakened his interest in writing; other influences include Verne, Alfred Jarry, and the Argentinians Arlt and Borges (qq.v.). His first book, *Presencia* (1938), appeared under the pen-name 'Julio Denis'. *Los reyes* (1949) is a dramatic prose poem retelling the Theseus legend. The early short stories in *Bestiario* (1951) already showed Cortázar's agreement with Jarry that 'the true nature of reality lies not in its laws but in the exceptions to those laws'; his phantasmagoric world is a compound of human terror, phobias, and animal fantasies. *Final del juego* (Mexico City, 1956, enlarged edn., Buenos Aires, 1964) shows the same preoccupation with the bizarre and fantastic. *Las armas secretas* (1959) is another collection showing his concern for the anguish of contemporary man and his depersonalized existence. *Historias de cronopios y famas* (1962) takes *Alice in Wonderland* into an Argentina of science fiction, the *famas* being the conventional characters, the *cronopios* green and bristly elements of sudden joy in life, and *esperanzas* brilliant microbes. Cortázar's fantasy assumes the desirability of the poetic and unexpected in a world being deliberately or accidentally made inhuman. *Todos los fuegos el fuego* (1966) continues Cortázar's rebellion against middle-class values of safety and comfort.

His novels have caused an even greater stir than have his short stories (which he has frequently dismissed as 'escapist literature'). *Los premios* (q.v., 1960) is a parable of modern life in the form of a ship's voyage begun as the result of a lottery. The densely-written *Rayuela* (q.v., 1963), influenced to some extent by Marechal (q.v.), can be read in several orders, some of which are proposed by Cortázar himself. Its 62nd chapter gave rise to an independent work: *62. Modelo para armar* (1968).

Cortázar has also produced two miscellanies, or word collages, which reflect in their fragmentation the absurdity of man's existence and the world in which he lives. These are *La vuelta al día en ochenta mundos* (Mexico City, 1967), the title parodying Verne's hectic adventure novel, and *Último round* (Mexico City, 1969).

His recent books include *El perseguidor y otros cuentos* (1967), *Viaje alrededor de una mesa* (1970), *Pameos y meopas* (Barcelona, 1971), *Prosa del observatorio* (Barcelona, 1972), *Libro de Manuel* (1973), the short stories *Octaedro* (1973), and *La casilla de los Morelli y otros textos* (Barcelona, 1973). With Mario Vargas Llosa (q.v.) and Oscar Collazos he has produced the critical *Literatura en la revolución y revolución en la literatura* (Mexico City, 1970).

Cortázar's influence on the later generation of Argentinian novelists has been especially evident in the case of Néstor Sánchez (q.v.).

See Néstor García Canclini, *Cortázar: una antropología poética* (1968); G. de Sola, *Julio Cortázar y el hombre nuevo* (1968); Luis Harss, *Los nuestros* (1968), an interview; R. Escamilla Molina, *Julio Cortázar: visión del conjunto* (Mexico City, 1970); M. E. Filer, *Los mundos de Julio Cortázar* (New York, 1970); H. F. Giacoman (ed.), *Homenaje a Julio Cortázar* (New York, 1972); Joaquín Roy, *Julio Cortázar ante su sociedad* (Barcelona, 1974); and E. Picón Garfield, *¿Es Julio Cortázar un surrealista?* (1975).

Corte de los milagros, La (1927), the first novel in the cycle *El ruedo ibérico* by Ramón del Valle-Inclán (qq.v.).

CORTÉS, ALFONSO (1883–), b. León. Nicaraguan poet, who lived for more than 25 years in the house where Rubén Darío (q.v.) had spent his youth. In 1927 he was pronounced insane. His father and sisters collected his poems written indiscriminately during his youth and maturity, in his periods of madness and lucidity, in *Poesías* (1931; reprinted, León, 1937), *Tardes de oro* (León, 1934), and *Poemas eleusinos* (1935). A symbolist in such poems as *El barco pensativo* and a mystic in *La canción del espacio*, Cortés has been compared with S. Juan de la Cruz (q.v.) by Ernesto Cardenal in the latter's introduction to the work of Cortés in *Nueva poesía nicaragüense* (Madrid, 1949).

CORTÉS, HERNÁN (1485–1547), b. Medellín, Extremadura. *Conquistador* of Mexico who studied humanities at Salamanca University and is believed to have modelled his prose style on that of Julius Caesar. He arrived in Hispaniola (West Indies) in 1504, moving to Cuba in 1511, and to Mexico in 1519. He arrived at the site of the future Vera Cruz, and passed Tlaxcala and Cholula on his way to detain Montezuma in Mexico City. In 1520 he marched against Narváez, defeating him at Cempolán, and re-entering Mexico City only to be expelled within a week. Taking refuge in Tlaxcala, he marched again on Mexico City, beginning the siege on 20 May 1521. On 15 October 1522 he received a letter from the Emperor Charles V recognizing his conquest of Mexico. After an expedition to Guatemala and Honduras in 1524, he returned to Spain in 1528. He spent the decade from 1530 back in Mexico, but died in Spain. His official reports to the Emperor Charles V have been praised for their lucidity and for the sympathy he frequently displays for the besieged Mexican Indians. There are five such reports in the form of letters: the first is lost, and has been replaced in editions of the *Cartas de relación* by a report sent on 10 July 1519 to the Emperor by the Regent of Villa Rica de la Vera Cruz, which tells of the arrival in Mexico and the dispatch of all the gold, silver, and jewels that they could find.

The second letter, dated 30 October 1520 and first published in Seville (1522), tells how Cortés and his men entered the Mexican hinterland, and of their adventures; this is the letter of the *noche triste* (30 June 1520), when more than 500 of the adventurers were killed and forty captured, to be sacrificed later to the Mexican gods. *Carta III* (15 May 1522) is subtitled *de las cosas sucedidas e muy dignas de admiración en la conquista y recuperación de . . . Temixtitán* and was first published in Seville (1523). *La quarta relación* (first published in Toledo in 1525) was sent by Cortés on 15 October 1524. In it he complains of the treachery of Diego Velázquez, Governor of Cuba, his rival for the generalship of the Spaniards in Mexico, and urges the Emperor to send Spaniards to populate the newly-won lands. The fifth letter (3 September 1526), which was not published at the time, tells of the treachery of Cristóbal de Olid, sent by Cortés to conquer Honduras. Cortés had made many enemies at court, who claimed that Cortés had not only murdered his wife and Juan de Garay, but that he had withheld from Charles V the great proportion of his booty. Called to Spain to defend himself against these charges, Cortés was exonerated and given the title of Marqués del Valle de Oaxaca, but significantly not that of Viceroy of New Spain, which he humbly requested.

His literary style is clear and concise, telling of the most extraordinary events almost laconically. *Letters from Mexico* (London, 1972) is a translation by A. R. Pagden with an essay on Cortés, Diego Velázquez, and Charles V by J. H. Elliott. His *Cartas* are in vol. 22 (1852) of the BAE, but the best edition is that published at Graz (1960).

The official history of Cortés's exploits was written by López de Gómara (q.v.), and answered in the name of those who had fought with Cortés by Bernal Díaz del Castillo (q.v.).

The literature on Cortés is immense: see R. H. Valle, *Bibliografía de Hernán Cortés* (Mexico City, 1953) and *Estudios cortesianos* (1948), and *Homenaje a Hernán Cortés* (Badajoz, 1948) issued to mark the quatercentenary of his death. In English there is the translation of Salvador de Madariaga, *Hernán Cortés, Conqueror of Mexico* (1942 and reprints), and Maurice Collis, *Cortés and Montezuma* (London, 1954 and reprints).

CORTÉS DE TOLOSA, JUAN (1590–*c.* 1643), b. Madrid. Novelist. He studied in a Jesuit seminary and became a secretary at the court of Philip III. His *Discursos morales de cartas y novelas* (Saragossa, 1617) have been overshadowed by *Lazarillo de Manzanares, con otras cinco novelas* (1620), edited subsequently by E. Cotarelo y Mori (1901) and by M. I. Chamorro Fernández (1970).

The title story is, as would be expected, an imitation of *Lazarillo de Tormes* (q.v.); but whereas Cortés de Tolosa flattered himself on improving the original, by complexity of plot and multiplicity of characters, he fell short of it.

Cosante, see COSSANTE.

Cosaute, see COSSANTE.

COSCA BAYO, ESTANISLAO DE, see KOTSKA Y BAYO, Estanislao de.

Cossante (properly 'cosaute', French: 'coursault'), a courtly sung dance originating in France which gave its name to a poetic form in which many of the *cantigas de amigo* (q.v.) were composed. The couplets with an invariable single-line refrain are characterized by repetition, parallelism, and interlaced phraseology. The subject-matter is often slight and the treatment is simple and vivid, as in the well-known *Cossante* of Diego Hurtado de Mendoza (q.v.).

The evolution of the *cossante* has been traced by Eugenio Asensio in his *Poética y realidad en el Cancionero peninsular de la Edad Media* (1957).

COSSÍO, JOSÉ MARÍA DE (1893–), b. Santander. Literary critic, who studied at the universities of Valladolid and Madrid. His works, in which a passion for bullfighting predominates, include *Los toros en la poesía española: estudio y antología* (2 vols., 1931), *Romancero popular de la Montaña* (1933), *La obra literaria de Pereda: su historia y crítica* (1934), *Poesía española: notas de asedio* (1936), *Siglo XVII: Espinosa, Góngora, Gracián, Calderón, Polo de Medina, Solís* (1939), *El romanticismo a la vista: tres estudios* (1942), *Los toros* (4 vols., 1943–61) subtitled 'tratado técnico e histórico', *Fábulas mitológicas de España* (1952), and *Cincuenta años de poesía española, 1850–1900* (2 vols., 1960).

COSSÍO, MANUEL BARTOLOMÉ (1858–1935), b. Haro, Logroño. Educator and art critic. A disciple of Giner de los Ríos (q.v.), Cossío devoted his life to the reform of Spanish education, teaching for almost 50 years at the Institución Libre de Enseñanza, Madrid University, and the Museo Pedagógico Nacional, which he directed 1883–1929. In addition to forming a new kind of teacher, involved with the development of sensibility rather than learning by rote, Cossío helped to establish the Misiones Pedagógicas which, in view of the failure to establish a nationwide system of public libraries, made a vital contribution to the dissemination of culture in rural Spain. The Misiones sent teachers with paintings, books, and recordings to all parts of Spain: see his selected writings *De su jornada* (1929). Cossío also produced the major study *El Greco* (1908).

See *Revista de Pedagogía* (Sept. 1935) and J. B. Trend, *The origins of modern Spain* (1934).

COSTA I LLOBERA, MIQUEL (1854–1922), b. Pollença, Majorca. Catalan poet who was made a priest in 1888 and become a Doctor of Theology the following year. One of the neo-classicists (with Alcover, q.v.), Costa i Llobera linked formal richness to linguistic clarity, becoming a 'Mestre en Gay Saber' for his poetic gifts. He combined the Christian and pagan traditions in his best book *Horacianes* (1906) and relied on classical metres. Travels in Italy and elsewhere in Europe enriched his thematic material. His most memorable poem is 'El pi de Formentor' ('The pine of Formentor').

Among his books are *Poesies* (Palma, 1885), *Del ayre i de la terra* (1897), *Líricas* (1899), *Tradicions i fantasies* (Barcelona, 1903), *Poesies* (Palma, 1907), and *Visiones de Palestina* (1908).

COSTA Y MARTÍNEZ, JOAQUÍN (1846–1911), b. Graus, Huesca. Historian, scholar, and reformist politician. He was the son of a poor Aragonese farmer, but was recognized for his outstanding potential by an uncle, who paid for his education. After a brilliant university career, he was elected to the Cortes, but never took his seat. A precursor of the Generation of 1898, Costa was a proponent of *regeneracionismo* and the Europeanization of Spain, rejecting the traditional past as irrelevant to the needs of modern man. The range of work represented in his *Obras completas* (21 vols., Huesca, 1911–24) includes *Teoría del hecho jurídico, individual y social* (1880), *La poesía popular: mitología y literatura celtohispana* (1881), *Estudios ibéricos* (1891), and *El colectivismo agrario en España* (1898). There is a useful selection by J. García Mercadal in *Historia, política social, patria* (1961).

See M. Ciges Aparicio, *Joaquín Costa, el gran fracasado* (1930); R. Pérez de la Dehesa, *El pensamiento de Costa y su influencia en la Generación del 98* (1960); C. Martín-Retortillo, *Joaquín Costa, propulsor de la Reconstrucción Nacional* (Barcelona, 1961); E. Tierno Galván, *Costa y el regeneracionismo* (1961); and two important books by George J. G. Cheyne: *Joaquín Costa, el gran desconocido* (Barcelona, 1972) and *A bibliographical study of the writings of Joaquín Costa* . . . (London, 1972).

Costumbrismo, in literature, the special attention given to the portrayal of manners and customs characteristic of a region or country. The trend towards *costumbrismo* has always been present in some degree from the Golden Age and even earlier, as in the early *entremés* and the realistic *Novelas ejemplares* (q.v.) of Cervantes. But its relative importance grew in the 18th and 19th cs. through the prose *cuadros de costumbres* and verse sketches, when social atmosphere began to be treated with the care previously given only to the plot. Broadly, they can be divided into the neutral or philosophical genre, and the satirical genre exemplified by Sebastián de Miñano's *Cartas del pobrecito holgazán* (1820), with a broader political target. Early *costumbrista* articles appeared in journals such as Clavijo y Fajardo's *El Pensador* (q.v.) and the height of the vogue was the mid-19th c., when *Los españoles pintados por sí mismos* (1850) appeared.

Among the major writers in this genre were 'Fernán Caballero' (the pen-name of Cecilia Francisca Boehl von Faber, q.v.), whose *Cuadros de costumbres* (1857) were set in Andalusia; Pedro Antonio de Alarcón (q.v.), whose *Cosas que fueron* (1871), also set in Andalusia, typify his ability to find both the characteristic and the individual in rural Spain; and José María de Pereda (q.v.), whose *Escenas montañesas* (1864), set in the mountains behind Santander, were the first of a series of sketches he continued to produce sporadically until 1890. Other leading writers of *costumbrista* sketches included Mariano José de Larra, Serafín Estébanez Calderón, and

Ramón de Mesonero Romanos (qq.v.). The movement had an important influence on the regional novel in Spain and Spanish America.

See E. Correa Calderón, *Costumbristas españoles* (1950–2), and J. L. Varela, *El costumbrismo romántico* (1970).

COTA, RODRIGO DE (d. after 1504), b. Toledo? Poet. A Jewish *converso* thought wrongly to be the author of the first act of *La Celestina* (q.v.) and of the *Coplas del Provincial* and *Coplas de Mingo Revulgo* (q.v.). Cota composed *Epithalamium*, a burlesque against the King's Treasurer, who had not invited him to his wedding. He is best known for the *Diálogo entre el Amor y un viejo* in which an old man, who has given up the delights of love, is approached by Love, who stirs up his passions with fair words and brings a young girl to his retreat, itself in ruins like his emotional life. When the old man eventually succumbs, the figure of Love mocks him for his presumptuous folly. The argument is ably developed, with admirable imagery, but it differs from the *debates* (q.v.) in general, since it ends with the clear victory of one of the parties. The style of the last part foreshadows the drama and was twice imitated by Juan del Encina (q.v.). First published in the *Cancionero general* of 1511, the *Diálogo* has been edited most recently by Elisa Aragone (Florence, 1961), with an anonymous and untitled 15th-c. poem usually known as *Diálogo entre el Amor, el viejo y la hermosa*, which seems to be a reworking of Cota's theme in different words and obviously by a different hand.

See Francisco Cantera Burgos, *El poeta Ruy Sánchez Cota (Rodrigo Cota) y su familia de judíos conversos* (1970).

COTARELO Y MORI, EMILIO (1857–1936), b. Vega de Ribadeo, Asturias. Literary scholar and editor. A pupil of Marcelino Menéndez y Pelayo (q.v.), he continued his master's editions and commentaries of the plays of Lope de Vega (q.v.). Many of his contributions were articles to the *Boletín* of the Real Academia Española, to which Cotarelo was elected in 1898, largely on the strength of his excellent study *Iriarte y su época* (1897); he served as secretary from 1913.

Among his major works were *El conde de Villamediana* (1886), *Tirso de Molina* (1893), *Vida y obras de don Enrique de Villena* (1896), *Don Ramón de la Cruz* (1899), *Juan del Enzina y los orígenes del teatro español* (1901), *Lope de Rueda y el teatro español* (1901), *Bibliografía de las controversias sobre la licitud del teatro en España* (1904), *Francisco de Rojas Zorrilla* (1911), the essential *Colección de entremeses, loas, bailes . . .* (vols. 17–18 of the NBAE, 1911), *Luis Vélez de Guevara* (1916–17), and *Pedro Calderón de la Barca* (1924).

Council of Trent, see TRENT, Council of.

Counter-Reformation, see CONTRARREFORMA.

COVARRUBIAS [H]OROZCO, SEBASTIÁN DE (1539–1613), b. Toledo. Canon of Cuenca Cathedral and lexicographer. He was the son of Sebastián de Horozco the proverb-collector; his brother was Juan de Horozco y Covarrubias (q.v.) the religious writer.

His *Tesoro de la lengua castellana o española* (1611) was, with that of Nebrija (q.v.), the most important Spanish dictionary until the *Diccionario de autoridades* was published in 6 vols. by the Real Academia Española (q.v.) between 1726 and 1739. Fray Benito Remigio Noydens reissued the work of Covarrubias with his own revisions and improvements in 1674. A 'Suplemento al Tesoro' compiled by Covarrubias was never printed. As a lexicographer his virtue is his skill in gathering material, but his work lacks the sobriety of Nebrija's and the fullness and accuracy of the *Autoridades*. Martín Riquer published a new edition of the *Tesoro* (Barcelona, 1944). Covarrubias also wrote a collection of *Emblemas morales* (1610; reprinted 1973) different in many respects from that of his brother Juan de Horozco y Covarrubias (1589).

Creacionismo, an *avant-garde* movement which appeared about 1916 almost simultaneously in France (Pierre Reverdy) and in the Spanish-speaking world (Vicente Huidobro, q.v.). Its manifesto can be summed up in Huidobro's words:

> *¿Por qué cantáis la rosa, oh poetas?*
> *¡Hacedla florecer en el poema!*
> *El poeta es un pequeño dios.*

After him, the main practitioners of *creacionismo* in Spanish have been Gerardo Diego and Juan Larrea (qq.v.). Their intention has been 'to write a poem as a new cosmic reality which the artist adds to the sum of nature, and which must possess, like the planets, more than simply centrifugal and centripetal forces' (Huidobro). The main consequences of the movement's spread were a renewal of poetic vocabulary, and its enrichment by more daring juxtapositions of images and metaphors, arising out of the refusal on the part of the poet to reflect the divinely ordered 'real' world, replacing it by the complex magical visions of his own creation.

CRÉMER, VICTORIANO (1908–   ), b. Burgos. Poet and founder of the magazine *Espadaña*, the review of the Espadaña group (q.v.), which emphasized the the social rôle of poetry in distinction to *modernismo*. *Tendiendo el vuelo* (1928) was followed by *Tacto sonoro* (1944), *Caminos de* *mi sangre* (1946), *Las horas perdidas* (1949), *La espada y la pared* (1949), *Nuevos cantos de vida y esperanza, Libro de Santiago* (1954), and *Furia y la paloma* (1956).

CRESCAS, HASDAI (1340–1410), b. Barcelona. Chief Rabbi of Aragon. A philosopher who contributed to the growth of the Renaissance and to the overthrow of the Aristotelian system of Ibn Rushd (or Averroes). His major work is *Or Adonai* (Ferrara, 1555), in the tradition of the school of Nissim Girondí of Barcelona. He also wrote a history of the Aragonese pogrom of 1391, and taught Joseph Albó (q.v.).

CRESPO, RAFAEL JOSÉ (1800–58), b. Alfajarín, Saragossa. Fabulist and epigrammatist. He defended himself, in the prologue to *Fábulas morales y literarias* (Saragossa, 1820), against the charge of unoriginality which he knew would be made by critics. His later works were *Poesías epigramáticas* (Saragossa, 1827), *Don Papis de Bobadilla, o sea, Defensa del Cristianismo y crítica de la seudofilosofía* (Saragossa, 1829), and *Vida de Nuestro Señor Jesucristo* (Valencia, 1840).

CRESPO TORAL, REMIGIO (1860–1939), b. Cuenca, Ecuador. Poet and essayist; Crespo was a prolific writer. His first publication was *Mi poema* (4th edn., 1908) influenced by Núñez de Arce (q.v.) and imbued with juvenile fervour. His other works included *Leyenda de Hernán* (1917) and *Selección de ensayos* (1936).

Criollismo, a movement defined by the Venezuelan Rufino Blanco-Fombona (q.v.) as 'la pintura, *à outrance*, de las costumbres populares, con los tipos y en el lenguaje del bajo pueblo'. The tendency encouraged the development of regional literature. *Criollismo* dominated the literature of Venezuela and Colombia *c.* 1900, its weakness being a tendency to moralize, which was avoided only by exceptional writers such as the Colombian Tomás Carrasquilla. *Criollismo* is at its purest in Ricardo Güiraldes's Argentine novel *Don Segundo Sombra* (qq.v.) and in the early *gaucho* stories of Jorge Luis Borges (q.v.), *gauchismo* being the Río de la Plata equivalent of *criollismo*. Among the movement's chief journals were the Venezuelan *El cojo ilustrado* (1892–1915) and the Cuban *Orígenes* (1944–57).

See the novels of Alejo Carpentier, the Havana poems of Eliseo Diego, and the novel *Peonía* (1890) by the Venezuelan Vicente Romero García.

See also COSTUMBRISMO.

Cristianos nuevos, see LIMPIEZA DE SANGRE.

Cristianos viejos, see LIMPIEZA DE SANGRE.

Criticón, El, a major philosophical novel by Baltasar Gracián y Morales (q.v.) first published in 3 parts, the first (Saragossa, 1651) under the anagrammatic pen-name 'García de Marlones'; the second and third (Huesca, 1653 and Madrid, 1657) under the pen-name 'Lorenzo Gracián'.

The book concerns two types of men: Critilo the man of the world, and Andrenio a man of nature and innocence. In part one Critilo is shipwrecked and finds ashore the young 'noble savage' Andrenio; together they begin a journey across the world, commenting on their adventures and what they see. They visit the Source of Illusion; Queen Artemia, who converts beasts into men; the Inn of the World, with a room for· every vice; and Madrid, where Andrenio falls in love with Falsirena, provoking the famous tirade of Critilo against women.

The second part, corresponding to maturity as the first corresponded to youth, contains the adventures of Salastano (an anagram of Lastanosa, the Maecenas of Gracián, q.v.), an account of his library and museum, and of the Palace of Understanding; in France they discover art and the useful life: there follows an account of the desert of Hipocrinda, or dissimulation, and of the House of Madmen, where all humanity is found.

Part three corresponds to old age and senility. They enter Italy, but before they come to Rome Andrenio becomes invisible (like all others) in the Castle of Adventurers, until the light of disillusion allows him to regain his true shape. The book consequently portrays disillusion as a great benefit to men who wish to understand reality. The allegorical journey ends with the vision of the Wheel of Time (seen from one of the seven hills of Rome) a metaphor for the fragility of human life, and the Cave of Death. The Isle of Immortality is reached only by those who have trodden the pathway of virtue and prudence.

The similarity of *El criticón* to the work of ibn Tufail is now seen to be due to their common source in an oriental tale, but Gracián used many other well-known sources, including the Byzantine tales of Heliodorus, *El Conde Lucanor*, many books by Quevedo but principally *Los sueños*, and Juan de Mena.

Apart from the intrinsic interest of the characters and their doings, the book is remarkable for its careful unity as a composition, its pessimism ('ir muriendo cada día'), balanced by the author's belief in a life beyond this, free from earthly imperfections, and the *conceptista* style of striking originality which he described in his own *Agudeza, o arte de ingenio* (q.v.): 'son los conceptos vida del estilo, espíritu del decir, y tanto tienen de perfección cuanto de sutileza'. An artist difficult to appreciate to the full without many years of devotion, he is among the most rewarding of writers, causing Schopenhauer to declare 'his *Criticón* is for me one of the greatest books in the world'. Its influence can be traced in the *Candide* of Voltaire.

M. Romera-Navarro's critical edition appeared in Philadelphia (3 vols.) in 1938. The latest good edition is that by A. Prieto (2 vols., 1970), and there have been a number of translations.

See G. Schröder, *B. Graciáns 'Criticon': eine Untersuchung zur Beziehung zwischen Manierismus und Moralistik* (Munich, 1966).

Crónica, Paraguayan literary review published from 1913 to 1915. It was the first collective manifestation of modernism in Paraguay, publishing the work of the poets Guillermo Molinas Rolón, Pablo Max Ynsfrán (qq.v.), and Leopoldo Ramos Jiménez, and the short-story writers Leopoldo Centurión (1893–1922) and Roque Capece Faraone (1894–1928), who both died prematurely from drug addiction and alcoholism, imitating the decadence of their literary models.

Crónicas, those histories, normally written by eyewitnesses or drawn from contemporary accounts, which usually lack critical or analytical value, but consist of a partial and often panegyric view of events, not always devoid of legendary or fictitious elements intended to aggrandize the hero(es). The earliest extant work of prose in Spanish is one of a group of brief chronicle-writings in Navarro-Aragonese found at the end of a MS. legal code, the *Fuero general de Navarra*, dated 1186 by its editor.

Used critically, these chronicles (as distinct from the more laconic *cronicones*, q.v.) have often been of great value to historians. One of the most important is the *Estoria de España* (usually known as the *Primera crónica general*) commissioned by Alfonso X, 'el Sabio' (q.v.) in the late 13th c., but there are many others of the 14th c., and particularly of the 15th, such as the *Crónica del rey don Pedro* of López de Ayala, the *Crónica de don Álvaro de Luna* (by Gonzalo Chacón?), and the *Crónica sarracina* of Pedro del Corral.

Cronicones, medieval verse or prose chronicles, called *cronicones* to distinguish them as bare annals or statements of events from the connected historical narratives of the *crónicas* (q.v.). They are normally uncritical as to detail and of variable accuracy.

Those in Latin include the *Epitome imperatorum vel arabum ephemerides*, an anti-Muslim work generally known as the *Cronicón del Pacense* and

covering the years 611–754; the *Cronicón de San Isidoro de León*, in the main accurate records of the years 618–939 in Castile, and thus known also as the *Anales castellanos primeros*, completed up to 1126 by the *Anales castellanos segundos*; the *Cronicón de Alfonso III* (672–866), attributed to Sebastián, Bishop of Salamanca (or Oviedo) in its second, revised format; the *Cronicón Albeldense*, named after the Riojan monastery where it was found, and which is of anonymous authorship up to 883 and from 883 to 978 by the monk Vigila, who gives the *cronicón* its alternative title of *Vigilano*; the *Cronicón del Silense* (718–1054), the *Cronicón Complutense* (281–1065); the *Cronicón de Pelayo*, by a Bishop of Oviedo (982–1109); *Cronicón Compostelano* (362–1126); *Cronicón Lusitano* (311–1222), *Cronicón Burgense* (up to 1250); and the *Cronicón Barcinonense* (958–1308).

The *cronicones* in Castilian are less numerous, including two of Cardeña (797–842 and 856–1327); three *Anales Toledanos*; that of Lucas de Túy, or 'el Tudense'; and the *Historia gothica* or *De rebus Hispaniae* of Rodrigo Ximénez de Rada (q.v.).

For forged annals or chronicles see J. Godoy Alcántara, *Historia crítica de los falsos cronicones* (1868).

Crotalón, El, a satire on contemporary Spain written about 1552 by 'Christophoro Gnosopho', believed by some authorities to have been Cristobal de Villalón (q.v.), and by Marcel Bataillon to have been an Italian naturalized as a Spanish subject. The title is derived from the *crótalo*, an ancient musical instrument of the tambourine family, which can summon a dormant spirit (in this case a cockerel) to life and make it speak.

This Erasmian dialogue between a shoemaker and a cockerel leads into the '*cantos del gallo*' (punning on 'songs of the cockerel') which relate, in the manner of Lucian, his previous incarnations with the intention of ridiculing contemporary customs and hypocrisies. The anecdotes, witty, to the point, and expressed in a fluent style, are among the best of the period.

The *Crotalón* has been edited by the Marqués de la Fuensanta del Valle (1871) and more recently by A. Cortina (Buenos Aires, 1942).

CRUCHAGA SANTA MARÍA, ÁNGEL (1893–1964), b. Santiago. Chilean poet who was awarded the National Prize for Literature in 1948. Cruchaga worked for some time in the Banco Español and also in the National Library, and he became President of the Alianza de Intelectuales. To some extent incapable of establishing an individual style, he moved from an early Romanticism to realism and in later work celebrated the landscapes and nature of Chile, and explored the use of symbolism. His most characteristic trait is obtrusive pietism in *Las manos juntas* (1915), *Job* (1922), and *Afán del corazón* (1933), but this tendency is restrained in *Paso de sombra* (1939), and *Anillo de jade* (1959). *Antología* (Buenos Aires, 1946) contains poems selected by Pablo Neruda, and the less comprehensive *Pequeña antología* (1953) has those chosen by Cruchaga himself.

CRUZ, Sor JUANA INÉS DE LA, see JUANA INÉS DE LA CRUZ, *Sor*.

CRUZ, San JUAN DE LA, *see* JUAN DE LA CRUZ, *San*.

CRUZ CANO Y OLMEDILLA, RAMÓN DE LA (1731–94), b. Madrid. Dramatist whose name is always connected with the best and most characteristic period of the Madrid *sainetes* (q.v.). He began by writing tragedies and comedies, usually adaptations or translations from French or Italian originals, including *Bayaceto* (from Racine's *Bajazet*), *Hamlet* (from Ducis's translation of Shakespeare's play), and *Aecio* (from Metastasio). His first collection, *Teatro* (10 vols., 1786–91), contained 19 serious works and only 47 *sainetes* in an attempt to persuade the reading public at least that he should be taken seriously.

But few were deceived, and it is for his *sainetes* that he has become best known. He insisted that he drew his scenes from real life, but a crisis of some kind is normally involved and it is not his habit to portray humdrum events. His *sainetes* often moralize, unlike the 17th c. *entremeses*, their predecessors, and there is often a major scene-change. He keeps to his models in retaining a predominance of low-life characters, and such *dramatis personae* as the *vizcaíno* speaking comic Spanish. His picture of society is traditionalist, as in the lesson given to a former serving-maid by her aristocratic husband in *La presumida burlada*, and he mocks the novel and the foreign in such *sainetes* as *El petimetre*. The types he portrays (inevitably in the *sainete*) never become characters, and the sequence of scenes never adds up to a careful plot, so the end is either bathetic or inconsequential. Typical of his work is *El alcalde limosnero*, in which a country mayor, responsible for distributing alms, finds girls, a poor nobleman, and a soldier to support. Cruz's *Manolo* is a parodic 'tragedia para reír o sainete para llorar' as he described it, mocking in assonanted hendecasyllables the 'serious' tragedies of the time with their complicated plots and multiple deaths.

Posthumous editions of Cruz's works include *Colección de los sainetes* (2 vols., 1843) in which Agustín Durán edited 120 of his *sainetes*; and two volumes (1915–28) of the NBAE, in which Emilio Cotarelo y Mori assembled 88 *sainetes* (he had prepared another two volumes but died before they could appear). Bertaux has indicated a figure of 450 known *sainetes*, less than half of which have been published. A list of his works was prepared by Cruz himself for Sempere y Guarinos, *Ensayo de una biblioteca española de los mejores escritores del reinado de Carlos III* (6 vols., 1785–9). He also wrote *zarzuelas*, among them *Las segadoras de Vallecas* (1762) and *Las foncarraleras* (1772).

In the Academia de los Árcades, Cruz was known as 'Larissio Dianeo'. His followers included Luceno (q.v.) and the insignificant Ignacio González del Castillo (1763–1800).

See E. Cotarelo y Mori, *Don Ramón de la Cruz y sus obras* (1899), and A. Hamilton, *A study of Spanish manners, 1750–1800 from the plays of Ramón de la Cruz* (Illinois, 1926).

CRUZ VARELA, JUAN DE LA, see VARELA, Juan de la Cruz.

Cuaderna vía ('fourfold way'), the name given to a verse form written by clerics in the monasteries of Old Castile practising the *mester de clerecía* (q.v.) which was superseded early in the 15th c. by the *arte mayor*.

The term was used in the 13th and 14th cs. to denote a stanzaic structure of four fourteen-syllable lines divided by caesura into equal hemistichs of 7 syllables each. One fully consonantal rhyme normally recurs throughout each stanza.

Si estos votos fuessen   lealment enviados,
estos sanctos preciosos   serien nuestros pagados,
avriemos pan e vino,   temporales temprados,
non seriemos com somos   de tristicia menguados.
             —Berceo

The *cuaderna vía* or 'alexandrine' is so-called in stanza 2 of the *Libro de Alexandre*. It is not native to Spain, deriving from either Latin verse of the Middle Ages or French poetry of the 12th c. The rhyme is aaaa, bbbb, etc.

See J. D. Fitzgerald, *Versification of the 'cuaderna vía'* (New York, 1905).

Cuadernos Americanos, a leading Mexican cultural review founded in 1942 by the Mexicans J. Silva Herzog and B. Ortiz de Montellano and the Spaniards León Felipe and Juan Larrea. The emphasis was on literature, politics, economics, and sociology, all from a virtually exclusive Spanish-American viewpoint. Its main contributors included L. Cardoza y Aragón, Chumacero, and Leiva (qq.v.).

Octavio G. Barreda founded in opposition *El Hijo Pródigo* (1943–6), which repudiated Cardoza y Aragón's 'especie de política continental, en que se llegaba al absurdo de dar por acabada a Europa'.

CUADRA, José de la (1903–41), b. Guayaquil. Ecuadorian short-story writer, novelist, and essayist. One of the members of the Grupo de Guayaquil (q.v.). His best novel is *Los Sangurimas* (1934) a neo-realistic story of violence set among the *montuvios* of Ecuador, whom he also studied in the essay *El montuvio ecuatoriano* (1937).

CUADRA, Pablo Antonio (1912–), b. Managua. Nicaraguan poet, essayist, and playwright. The most distinguished man of letters in Nicaragua, he has edited several important literary journals, such as *Vanguardia* (1929–), *Trinchera* (1936–9), the weekly literary supplement to *La Prensa* of Managua (1941–), and *El pez y la serpiente* (1961–).

His own poetry is infused with a deep love for Nicaragua, and a profound attachment to the Spanish Roman Catholic tradition. Oreste Macrí has called him the originator in Central America of a 'nuevo clasicismo rural' in books such as *Poemas nicaragüenses* (Santiago de Chile, 1934), *Canto temporal* (Granada de Nicaragua, 1943), and the collection of poems 1929–49 entitled *Corona de jilgueros* (Madrid, 1949). In *El jaguar la luna* (1959) Cuadra has enlarged his perspective to the whole American continent. Later collections are *Cantos de Cífar* (1971), *Tierra que habla* (1974), and *Esos rostros que asoman en la multitud* (1975).

His essays include *Hacia la cruz del sur* (Buenos Aires, 1938), *Breviario imperial* (Madrid, 1939), *Promisión de México* (Mexico City, 1945), *Entre la cruz y la espada* (Madrid, 1949), and *América o el purgatorio* (Madrid, 1955). His first play was political: *Por los caminos van los campesinos* (1936); his later plays included *La cegua* (1945), *Máscaras exige la vida* (1952), and *Tres obras de teatro nuevo* (1958).

See G. Guardia de Alfaro, *Estudio sobre el pensamiento poético de Pablo Antonio Cuadra* (1971), in which Cuadra's achievement is compared with those of Claudel and Whitman.

CUBILLO DE ARAGÓN, Álvaro (1596?–1661), b. Granada. Playwright of the school of Calderón (q.v.). He studied humanities in Granada University, and spent part of his life as Governor of the Royal Gaol, Calatrava. Always poor, he took every opportunity of writing verse for all likely patrons. His best poem is *Curia leónica* (Granada, 1625), an allegory. The only plays he published in his lifetime appeared in *El enano de las musas. Comedias, y obras diversas, con un poema de las Cortes del León, y del Águila, acerca del Búo gallego* (1654).

Witty and often subtle in dialogue, he was a master of theatrical effect in several styles such as the heroic (*El genízaro de España, y rayo de Andalucía*) and the religious (*Los triunfos de San Miguel*).

The seven plays by Cubillo included by R. de Mesonero Romanos in vol. 47 (1858) of the BAE were *El conde de Saldaña* and its sequel *Hechos de Bernardo del Carpio*; *La perfecta casada*; *Las muñecas de Marcela* and *El Señor de Noches Buenas* (his best plays, ed. also by A. Valbuena Prat (1928) in Clásicos Olvidados); *El amor cómo ha de ser*; and the *comedia de figurón* (q.v.), *El invisible príncipe del baúl*.

See E. Cotarelo y Mori, 'Dramáticos españoles del siglo XVII: Álvaro Cubillo de Aragón' in *Boletín de la Real Academia Española*, vol. 5 (1918), pp. 3–23, 241–80.

CUÉLLAR, Jerónimo de (1622–c. 1666), b. Madrid. Dramatist of the school of Calderón (q.v.). He obtained a minor position at court and in 1650 was made a Knight of the Order of Santiago. The play *El pastelero de Madrigal* (which Manuel Fernández y González (q.v.) made into a novel (1862) of the same title) has been attributed to him, but the only surviving accessible play known to be his is *Cada cual a su negocio y hacer cada uno lo que debe* in vol. 47 (1858) of the BAE, a clever piece of theatre within the norms of theme and treatment familiar from Calderón.

CUÉLLAR, José Tomás de (1830–94), Mexican dramatist and novelist. His first performed play was *Deberes y sacrificios* (1855), followed by *El arte de amar*, *El viejecito Chacón*, *¡Qué lástima de muchachos!*, and *Natural y figura*, the last a satire on French influence and 'false patriots'.

Under the pen-name 'Facundo' he wrote a series of novels known collectively as *La linterna mágica* (6 novels, 1871–2 in the first series and 24 vols., Barcelona, 1889–92 in the second) which in the author's own words 'no trae costumbres de ultramar, ni brevete de invención; todo es mexicano, todo es nuestro, que es lo que nos importa . . .'. These sketches, part fiction and part observation of Mexican life and manners, were influenced by Dumas and Sue, as well as by Mexican writers and Mesonero Romanos. Cuéllar is an urban writer, and more convincing on middle-class life than on aristocratic or proletarian themes. A. Castro Leal has edited some of Facundo's short stories in *Historia de Chucho el Ninfo y La Noche Buena* (1947) and *Ensalada de pollos y Baile y cochino* (1946).

CUERVO, Rufino J. (1844–1911), b. Bogotá. Colombian philologist. He lived in Paris for many years, and died there. The Instituto Caro y Cuervo in Bogotá has set out to provide new editions of all Cuervo's works, and the following have so far appeared: *Obras inéditas* (1944, ed. R. P. Félix Restrepo); *Diccionario de construcción y régimen de la lengua castellana* (vols. 1–2, 1953–4; vol. 3, pts. 1–2, 1959–61); *Obras* (vols. 1–2, 1954); *Disquisiciones sobre filología castellana* (1950, ed. R. Torres Quintero); and the *Epistolario* (vols. 1–5, 1965–72).

CUESTA Y CUESTA, ALFONSO (1912–), b. Cuenca. Ecuadorian novelist and short-story writer, whose fame continues to spread despite his reluctance to be published. He was one of the most original personalities in the Elan group (q.v.) of the Generation of 1933, and is considered one of the most sensitive analysts of child thought and behaviour in Latin America in his short stories *Llegada de todos los trenes del mundo* (Cuenca, 1932) and in a novel, still unpublished, called 'Los hijos', which won second prize for the Novel in the Casa de las Américas contest in Havana (1960).

Cuestión palpitante, La (1883), a series of essays by Emilia Pardo Bazán (q.v.).
'The burning question' of the title is the defensibility of Naturalism, particularly in the novels of Zola. The essays, originally published over twenty weeks from November 1882 to April 1883, in the Madrid newspaper *La Época*, were based on Zola's critical works *Le roman expérimental* (1880) and *Les romanciers naturalistes* (1881). Pardo Bazán's thesis is that Naturalism is mistaken in its determinism, and that Realism offers a wider, more complete and perfect theory of art. 'In Realism, everything is contained except the exaggerations and ravings of the two extreme, and, as a necessary consequence, exclusive schools' [i.e. of Naturalism and Romanticism]. She accuses English novelists (especially the women) of being boring. The polemics caused by Pardo Bazán's articles continued up to 1887, and Juan Valera (q.v.) belatedly entered the controversy in 1886 with his *Apuntes sobre el arte nuevo de escribir novelas*, but by then the issue was moribund. Pardo Bazán's position, which was not long in becoming widely fashionable, was attacked by such traditionalists as Pedro de Alarcón, the Venezuelan Calcaño, and Cánovas del Castillo.
See D. F. Brown, *The Catholic Naturalism of Emilia Pardo Bazán* (Chapel Hill, N.C., 1957) and W. Pattison, *El naturalismo español* (1965).

CUEVA, JUAN DE LA (1543–1610), b. Seville. Playwright and poet. He spent some time in Mexico from 1574 with his brother Claudio, who became an archdeacon and inquisitor. On his return to Spain, Cueva began to write his plays, producing his first in 1579. *Primera parte de las Comedias y Tragedias* (1583; 2nd edn., Seville, 1588) is important primarily, as Marcel Bataillon has said (*Varia lección de clásicos españoles* (1964) pp. 206–13), for the fact of its publication, since few of Cueva's contemporaries took similar trouble to publish their works, which are consequently known imperfectly. Of Cueva's 4 *tragedias* and 10 *comedias*, three are on classical themes: *Tragedia de Ayax Telamón*, *Tragedia de la muerte de Virginia*, and *Comedia de la libertad de Roma por Mucio Scévola*; three are on fictional subjects: *El infamador*, *El viejo enamorado*, and *La constancia de Arcelina*; and of the others the best are on national themes: *Los siete infantes de Lara*, *El saco de Roma*, *La muerte del rey don Sancho*, and *La libertad de España por Bernardo del Carpio* (Exeter, 1974, ed. A. Watson).
His treatment of the story of Virginia (taken from Livy) is the best up to that time, but Cueva's main claim to fame is his technique of adapting stories from ballads and medieval chronicles. This technique formed the backbone of Golden Age dramatic subjects though the absence of Cueva's name from the writings of Lope de Vega and his school implies that they were not conscious of their debt to him.
Cueva's composition was hasty and his plays are of scant literary value; his poems are even weaker. The *Obras* (Seville, 1582) contain much Petrarchist poetry, mainly erotic in theme: *Caro Febeo de romances historiales* (Seville, 1587 [i.e. 1588]) which has been described by Gallardo as 'los peores que se leen en castellano'; the tedious epic *Conquista de la Bética, poema heroico* (Seville, 1603); a selection of poems; and *Egemplar poético, o Arte poética española* edited by J. J. López de Sedano in *Parnaso español*, vol. 4 (1770), pp. 349–70 and vol. 8 (1774), pp. 1–81. *Ejemplar poético* has also been edited by E. Walberg (Lund, 1904) and by F. A. de Icaza (1924) in the Clásicos Castellanos volume that also includes *El infamador* and *Los siete infantes de Lara*.
See E. Walberg, *Juan de la Cueva et son 'Exemplar poético'* (Lund, 1904); G. Guerrieri Crocetti, *Juan de la Cueva e le origini del teatro nazionale spagnuolo* (Turin, 1936); A. Watson, *Juan de la Cueva and the Portuguese succession* (London, 1971); and R. F. Glenn, *Juan de la Cueva* (New York, 1973) in Twayne's World Authors series.

CUEVAS, PLOTINO, pseudonym used by Ramón Pérez de Ayala (q.v.) in his early tetralogy of novels.

Culteranismo, a pejorative term (for its similarity to *luteranismo*) coined in the early 17th c. to describe a learned or 'culto' literary style of extreme artificiality, and in particular a

Latinate syntax and vocabulary, erudite reference to classical and foreign literature, and a poetic diction so replete with neologisms and archaisms as to be virtually unintelligible to the common reader.

The manifesto of what was to become a powerful style or movement (generally, though misleadingly, considered antithetical to *conceptismo*, q.v.) is the *Libro de erudición poética* by Luis Carrillo y Sotomayor (q.v.), first published in Carrillo's *Obras* (1611) and edited separately by M. Cardenal Iracheta (1946).

Carrillo proposes that the poet should immerse himself in classical and mythological sources, and plant hidden meanings that can be divined only by the equally scholarly and patient reader. Obscurity for its own sake is to be avoided, but will often result from elaborate ornament and internal complexity. Carrillo's own *Fábula de Acis* illustrates these precepts, but the leading *culteranista* is Luis de Góngora y Argote (q.v.). He was opposed by Quevedo, on behalf of the *conceptistas*; by Lope de Vega and the folk poets; by Jáuregui, on behalf of the Seville school, and by Pedro de Valencia y Cascales, on behalf of the humanists. Góngora's poetic style was defended by Trillo y Figueroa, Espinosa Medrano, Díaz de Rivas, and García Salcedo y Coronel.

In addition to Góngora's *Polifemo, Soledades*, and *Panegírico*, the main works of *culterano* poetry include those of Tassis y Peralta (Conde de Villamediana), Soto de Rojas, Bocángel, and Polo de Medina.

At its best the school could produce magnificent, sumptuous, and sensual effects, as in the *Polifemo* of Góngora (q.v.). Especially important are the great use of metaphor and the imagery of sights, sounds, scents, and precious stones. The school was attacked for its allegedly confusing hyperbaton and irrelevant classical allusions, and because no suitably elevated matter existed behind its complex style.

See the bibliography under Góngora and related entries; also Andrée Collard, *Nueva poesía: conceptismo, culteranismo en la crítica española* (Waltham, Mass., 1967).

CUNQUEIRO MORA, ÁLVARO (1911–   ), b. Mondoñedo, Lugo. Poet and novelist in Galician, and by profession a journalist. His first book of poems was influenced by surrealism: *Mar ao norde* (Santiago, 1932), but his major poetic source was the treasure of Galician balladry. Already in *Cantiga nova que se chama riveira* (Santiago, 1933) he was expressing *avant-garde* themes in ballad metres and achieving considerable success. He pursued this tendency in *Elegías y canciones* (Barcelona, 1940) but abandoned it after *Dona do corpo delgado*

(Pontevedra, 1950). Most of his later poems remain unpublished.

Among his other books are novels in Castilian such as *Un hombre que se parecía a Orestes* (1969) which won the Nadal Prize of 1968, and *El año del cometa* (1974); essays on Galicia: *Paisajes y retratos* (1936) and *La otra gente* (1975); and travel books: *Merlín y familia* (1957), and an account of the pilgrim route to Santiago de Compostela, where he studied at the university.

Curial e Guelfa, the title usually given to an anonymous 15th-c. Catalan novel surviving in an untitled MS. (in the National Library, Madrid) written between 1435 and 1462 by a novelist familiar with Italian topography probably resulting from residence at the court of Naples.

In the broad tradition of *libros de caballería* (q.v.), *Curial e Guelfa* nevertheless lacks magical and prodigious elements. Curial is merely an excellent military commander challenged by his lady and patroness Guelfa to become a perfect knight, lover, and gentleman. A shy man from a poor home, Curial is tempted by Laquesis, daughter of the Duke of Bavaria (Lachesis in Greek mythology is the decider of lots or destiny among the Three Fates), but after countless adventures finally marries Guelfa. The characterization is usually subtler than in similar fiction of the period, and the outstanding personage is Pere II (1276–89). The immediate source of the book is novel 61 of the Italian 13th-c. *Cento novelle antiche. Curial e Guelfa* was first published by Rubió i Lluch (Barcelona, 1901) but the best edition is that by R. Aramon i Serri (3 vols., Barcelona, 1930–3) in Els Nostres Clàssics.

Pamela Waley, 'In search of an author for "Curial e Guelfa"' in *BHS*, vol. 53 (1976), pp. 117–26, tentatively proposes Ramon de Perellós as the author.

Curioso impertinente, Novela del, a tale intercalated as chapters 33, 34 and part of 35 in the first part of *Quijote* by Cervantes (qq.v.). It is in effect one of the *novelas ejemplares* (q.v.), with a plot and characters similar to those of *El celoso extremeño*.

El curioso impertinente is set in Florence, and is influenced by Boccaccio and earlier developments of the Italian *novella*. The rich Anselmo decides to marry Camila, but is subsequently grieved that his best friend, Lotario, spends less time with him after the marriage than before. Anselmo believes his wife to be loyal and pure, but wishes to test her by putting her in the way of temptation. He finally persuades the reluctant Lotario to test Camila's virtue but when Lotario reports that her respect for Anselmo is perfect, Anselmo decides to test her further by offering money (from Lothario, ostensibly) to overcome her scruples. Lothario, enchanted by Camila's perfect honesty, falls in love with her despite his best intentions, and eventually elopes with her and her servant Leonela. Anselmo is so overcome by the realization of his own folly that he dies of remorse.

See A. S. W. Rosenbach, 'The curious impertinent in English dramatic literature before Shelton's translation' in *Modern Language Notes* (Baltimore), vol. 17 (1907), cols. 357–67; R. Schevill, 'A note on "El curioso impertinente"' in *Revue Hispanique*, vol. 22 (1910), pp. 447–53.

Curioso Parlante, El, the pseudonym used by Ramón de Mesonero Romanos (q.v.) for his *cuadros de costumbres,* or essays on manners.

CURROS ENRÍQUEZ, MANUEL (1851–1908), b. Celanova, Orense. Major Galician poet, considered one of the best of the 19th c. with Rosalía de Castro and Eduardo Pondal (qq.v.). He worked as a journalist throughout his life, his most formative period being that with *El Imparcial* of Madrid (1870–6). He returned to Galicia, since he believed himself the political conscience and the true voice of the people. A secular poet of pronounced liberal ideas, he is the Galician poet nearest to the Portuguese Antero de Quental. His first collection was *Aires*

da miña terra (Orense, 1880), containing the exquisite provincial legend 'A Virxen do Cristal', translated into Castilian by Constantino Llombart (1892). *O divino sainete* (Corunna, 1888) is a long poem in 18 cantos on a journey to Rome with his friend Francisco Añón. *El Padre Feijoo* (first performed in 1879) is a pleasant one-act verse *loa* on an imaginary incident in the life of Feijoo (q.v.).

He settled in Cuba in 1904, and died in Havana. His journalism can be found in *Artículos escogidos* (1911) and a selection of his major writings in *Obras escogidas* (1956).

See D. Gamallo Fierros, *Curros Enríquez* (Havana, 1951).

CUZZANI, AGUSTÍN (1924–), Argentinian dramatist. An anti-realist and expressionist, Cuzzani's work falls frequently into the modern genre of tragic farce typified in Europe by Beckett and Pinter, and often makes a protest against conformity and injustice. *Una libra de carne* (1954) is a reworking of the Shylock story. *El centro-forward murió al amanecer* (1955) is a comprehensive onslaught on the capitalist system. His next two plays were inferior: *Sempronio* (1957) and *Los indios estaban cabreros* (1958), but *Para que se cumplan las escrituras* (1965) surpassed all his earlier plays in its parable of God, man, and computers.

The collection *Teatro* (1960) brought together Cuzzani's writings to date.

D

DABOVE, SANTIAGO (1889–1949), Argentinian storyteller whose work first appeared in book form in the *Antología de la literatura fantástica* (1940) edited by Jorge Luis Borges, Silvina Ocampo, and Adolfo Bioy Casares. His collection 'La muerte y su traje' was withheld from publication by this most solitary of writers, but friends managed to persuade him to allow some stories to appear in magazines.

An original and daring talent, Dabove created fictions of madness, terror, time travel (*El experimento de Varinsky*), and metamorphosis (*Ser polvo*). He enjoyed the friendship of Macedonio Fernández and Borges. Dabove's portrait of the psychotic is too convincing to make pleasant reading, but his style is not without humour and he describes nightmares with clinical care.

DACARRETE, ÁNGEL MARÍA (1827–1904), poet. A disciple of Lista (q.v.), Dacarrete met

Bécquer (q.v.) and became his most important precursor in merging Spanish elements with German, the *soleá* with the *Lied,* and in composing the 'Becquerian' stanza of three hendecasyllables followed usually by a heptasyllable or occasionally by a pentasyllable. Dacarrete contributed to *La América,* founded in 1857, which also published Campoamor, Eulogio F. Sanz, and Castelar. The Anglo-German flavour of the magazine suited Dacarrete, who provided excellent imitations of Heine as well as his own original work. His *Poesías* appeared posthumously (1906).

DALÍ, SALVADOR (1904–), b. Gerona. Catalan painter and writer, who joined the surrealists in 1929 and invented the 'paranoiac-critical method' which, in the words of R. Melville, 'involved the calculated use of delusion and hallucination in order to turn the objects of the real world into an iconography of sexual fears and desires'. This purposive method was contrary to the original emphasis of surrealism on automatic procedures. His reputation was founded in the early 1930s on such paintings as *The persistence of memory* (1931), now in the Museum of Modern Art, New York, incorporating soft watches lolling in a mysterious landscape. His first important book was autobiographical, *The secret life of Salvador Dali* (1942; 3rd English edn., London, 1968), the sequels being *Journal d'un génie* (Paris, 1964), translated as *Diary of a genius* (New York, 1965), and the repetitive *Unspeakable confessions* (London, 1976).

A controversialist and *enfant terrible* by nature, given to outrageous pronouncements, Dalí stated in November 1951: 'Reniego de todo lo anteriormente hecho por mí' (I utterly renounce all I have done hitherto). His judgments on his contemporaries appeared in a bilingual edition (French and English), *Dali on modern art: the cuckolds of antiquated modern art* (London, 1958).

He has made several remarkable films with Luis Buñuel (q.v.), including *Un chien andalou* and *L'âge d'or*, important for their liberating effect on the tradition-bound Spain of their day. Dalí's most significant contribution to literature is *Rostros ocultos* (Barcelona, 1952). The novel's heroine, Mme Solange de Clèda, is the mystical and physical mistress of Count Hervé de Grandsailles, a figure based on the Marquis de Sade. Events are narrated in a misty world of dream and irrationality, in which obsessive eroticism, witchcraft, nightmares, and gratuitous violence play a major part.

Dama boba, La, a play in three acts by Lope de Vega (q.v.), written in 1613 and first published (from a defective copy) in the *Novena parte* (1617) of Lope's plays. The first edition of the autograph MS., which belongs to the National Library in Madrid, was that of the Real Academia Española (1929), reprinted in the Aguilar *Obras escogidas* (vol. 1, 1958) edited by F. C. Saínz de Robles.

La dama boba was written for the famous actress Jerónima de Burgos (who played Nise), wife of Pedro de Valdés, whose company first performed it. Jerónima was living with Lope when he became a priest in 1614.

The parents have arranged a marriage between Liseo and the heiress Finea, a stupid and ignorant girl with a witty, intelligent sister, Nise. The adventurer Laurencio is a member of the poetic circle meeting regularly in Nise's home, and there he learns of Finea's expectations. Nise favours Laurencio of all her admirers, but now Laurencio secretly seeks Finea's affections too. Finea is flattered by his declaration and suddenly improves her appearance and sharpens her wits, much to Nise's jealous concern. Finea and Laurencio privately marry. Unaware of this, Liseo takes a sudden interest in the unexpected access of good sense in Finea, whose father Octavio is pleased, and now forbids Laurencio the house. Finea conceals her new husband in the house, where he is discovered by Octavio. However, Finea and Laurencio reveal that they are married, Nise is now betrothed to Liseo, and three sets of servants are also paired off.

A light and fast-moving comedy, *La dama boba* intrigues by the author's technique; one is never sure whether (and when) Finea is feigning stupidity.

Dama duende, La (1636), a *capa y espada* play in three acts by Pedro Calderón de la Barca (q.v.), possibly first performed in 1629.

On entering Madrid, Don Manuel and his servant Cosmé are accosted by two veiled women who beg them to stop a nobleman from following them. Manuel promises to do so and, shortly after the women have fled, challenges the nobleman (Don Luis), with whom he has a sharp altercation. Swords are drawn but Don Juan, brother of Luis and host of Manuel, arrives in time to prevent bloodshed.

The veiled women arrive home: they are revealed as Doña Angela, widowed sister of Luis and Juan, and her maid Isabel. Angela resents being kept a virtual prisoner in her own house. Her room adjoins that of Manuel, with a connecting door hidden by a large cupboard, and through this door she enters Manuel's room and, with Isabel, searches their new guests' belongings. She leaves a note of thanks for Manuel and Isabel robs Cosmé of his money, filling his purse with charcoal. Cosmé is frightened at the discovery, which strengthens his belief in the 'phantom lady' of the play's title. Eventually the mystery is cleared up and Manuel marries Angela. Calderón obtains dramatic effect by comic means, intrigue, misunderstanding, and the honour motif. *Costumbrismo* is a dominant feature of *La dama duende*.

It has been translated by Edwin Honig and published in *Four plays* (New York, 1961), the others being *A secreto agravio, secreta venganza*, *La devoción de la Cruz*, and *El alcalde de Zalamea*.

DAMIRÓN, RAFAEL (1882–1956), poet, playwright, and novelist from the Dominican Republic. *Del cesarismo* (1911) deals with contemporary political history, but Damirón made his name as a Creole novelist and essayist of manners in *El monólogo de la locura* (1914), *La sonrisa de Concho* (1921), *¡Ay de los vencidos!* (1925),

Estampas (1938), the psychological study of a tough, wicked woman *La cacica* (1944), *¡Hello Jimmy!* (1945), and *Canciones de antaño* (1946). His realist plays were not so successful: *Alma criolla* (1916), and *Cómo cae la balanza, Mientras los otros ríen*, and *La trova del recuerdo* (1917). *Pimentones* (1944) is a selection of articles.

DAMÓN, the Arcadian name adopted by Pedro Estala (q.v.).

DARÍO, RUBÉN (1867–1916), b. San Pedro de Metapa, Chocoyo, Nicaragua. Pseudonym of Félix Rubén García Sarmiento. Major poet who acquired 'Darío' as a nickname from his family. His childhood in León was certainly unhappy, and remained a constant theme in his poetry. Darío was the most influential poet in Spanish of his time, experimenting successfully in many modes and forms, from Parnassianism to Symbolism, and from the Latin hexameter to the sonnet. He coined the term 'modernismo' (q.v.) and became the movement's leading exponent.

He went to Managua and San Salvador as a child prodigy and published a great deal of ephemeral civic verse, his first important book being the Romantic *Azul* (Valparaíso, 1888), containing poems and stories. Juan Valera (q.v.) reviewed this book admiringly, and with additions and his foreword a second edition appeared two years later in Guatemala. Darío's first wife, Rafaela, died in 1892 after only two years of marriage, and he married his second wife, Rosario, in 1893. Darío travelled a great deal then as a diplomat, interesting French writers in Spanish-American culture but above all absorbing and consequently transmitting the new currents of French literature. His Bohemian life and meetings with Valera and Pardo Bazán, Verlaine, Moréas and Gourmont, made Darío a literary lion on his return to Buenos Aires in 1893, where he worked for five years on *La Nación*, the paper for which he had written from abroad since 1889. It was in Buenos Aires that he published *Los raros* (portraits of writers, among them Poe, Bloy, Leconte de Lisle) and *Prosas profanas* (q.v.), both in 1896. The latter was received with ecstasy by the younger generation, and imitated by scores of them in all parts of Latin America both for its daringly exotic language and for its metrical innovations and revivals, which included dissonance, asymmetry, internal rhymes, and a masterly selection of borrowed mannerisms which he made his own. Exotic, nostalgic, and cosmopolitan, *Prosas profanas* was attacked in Buenos Aires by Paul Groussac, but Darío was not discouraged and an augmented edition appeared in Paris in 1901.

He continued his travels in France, England, Austria, and Germany and in 1905 published in Madrid the important *Cantos de vida y esperanza*, in which he turns inward to reflection and outward to more political and social awareness. His personal vision is crystallized, his style less eclectic. His sense of the fleeting life is almost oriental; his deification of the artist as creator is absolute. He separated from his second wife and found in Spain his third companion, Francisca Sánchez. He returned to Nicaragua for the first time in eighteen years in 1906. *El canto errante* (Madrid, 1907) further enhanced his enormous prestige. New books appeared regularly: *Poema del otoño y otros poemas* (Madrid, 1910) and *Canto a la Argentina y otros poemas* (Madrid, 1914) being the best, the fruit of his personal experience and endowed with a rare sense of style. Dissolute, religious, solitary, at times cynical and at other times childlike, Darío, as Azarías H. Pallais stated in his eulogy *Ante el cadáver de Rubén Darío* (León, 1916), is too complex to be susceptible of analysis.

There is a useful edition of the *Obras completas* (2 vols., Madrid, 1971) by A. Méndez Plancarte. On his life, see *La dramática vida de Rubén Darío* (Guatemala, 1952) and *Rubén Darío: su vida y su obra* (Paris, 1930; 2nd edn., Santiago, 1937). On his work, see A. Marasso's *Rubén Darío y su creación poética* (La Plata, 1934), *La poesía de Rubén Darío* (Buenos Aires, 1948; 2nd edn., 1957) by Pedro Salinas; and K. Ellis, *Critical approaches to Rubén Darío* (1974). H. G. Doyle's *A bibliography of Rubén Darío (1867–1916)* was published in Cambridge (Mass.) in 1935.

DARÍO MALDONADO, SAMUEL (1870–1925), Venezuelan essayist, explorer, and poet. His autobiography *Tierra nuestra* has been called an 'emotional inventory' of his country. It is in the form of an exploration through the virgin forest, during which several characters talk. The most interesting discussions are those involving extreme types, such as the decadent littérateur from Caracas, and the dangerously unpredictable village headman.

Darío Maldonado left a long poem in fragments, *Luis Cardozo*, in which the hero, again an explorer and man of the tropics, is seen as a Childe Harold figure in whose mind the refined and primitive elements are battling for supremacy. It is influenced by the Latin American theme of *civilización y barbarie* (q.v.).

DÁVALOS, BALBINO (1866–1951), b. Colima. Mexican poet, diplomat, and translator of Gautier, Verlaine, the *Aphrodite* of Pierre Louÿs, and the *Monna Vanna* of Maeterlinck. His original poetry appeared as *Las ofrendas* (Madrid, 1909), and his critical essays included

Sobre la poesía horaciana en México (1901) and *Discursos leídos ante la Academia Mexicana* (1930).

Dávalos taught Romance languages at Minnesota University and at Columbia University, New York.

DÁVALOS, JUAN CARLOS (1887–1959), b. Salta. Argentinian short-story writer and poet. His verses *De mi vida y de mi tierra* (1914) set the mood of regional autobiography that reappears in *Cantos agrestes* (n.d.) and *Cantos de la montaña* (1921), and in the short stories of *Salta* (1921), *El viento blanco* (1922), and *Airampo* (1925). His best work was collected in *Cuentos y relatos del norte argentino* (1946).

DÁVALOS, MARCELINO (1871–1923), b. Guadalajara, Jalisco. Mexican playwright, short-story writer, and poet. His first play, the melodrama *El último cuadro* (1900) set in Spain, showed the influence of Echegaray, but he turned to a national setting with *Guadalupe* (1903), a morality against alcohol, and in *Así pasan . . .* (1908), showing the pathetic life of a middle-aged actress. Dávalos possessed a keen sense of the theatre, but lacked sensitivity and a feeling for language. His later plays included *El crimen de Marciano* (1909), *Jardines trágicos* (1916), and *¡Indisoluble!* (1916). He also wrote *Monografía del teatro* (2 vols., 1917) and *¡Carne de cañón!* (1915), ten stories about victims of Porfirio Díaz. His collections of poetry are *Iras de bronce* (1916), *Del bajío y arribeñas* (1917), and *Mis dramas íntimos* (1917).

DÁVILA, JOSÉ ANTONIO (1899–1941), b. Bayamón, Puerto Rican Creole poet, son of Virgilio Dávila (q.v.). *Vendimia* (1940) contains many of his poems, enriched by the English-language poetic tradition which he studied in the U.S.A. His simple poems in traditional forms were collected in *Almacén de baratijas* (1942).

DÁVILA, VIRGILIO (1869–1943), Puerto Rican Creole poet whose style, still Romantic in *Patria* (1903), became fully committed to Modernism in *Viviendo y amando* (1912), *Aromas del terruño* (1916), and *Pueblito de antes* (1917). His themes were taken from Puerto Rican life, sometimes too indulgently autobiographical, as in *Un libro para mis nietos* (1928).

De auxiliis, the controversy on predestination and freewill which erupted in 1588 between Fray Domingo Báñez (q.v.) and the Dominicans on the one hand and Fray Miguel de Molinos (q.v.) and the Jesuits on the other. The conflict was officially brought to a halt by Pope Paul V in 1607, but reverberations continued to be felt long afterwards.

Debates, medieval verse dialogues between opposed people or abstractions, such as the *Denuestos del agua y el vino, Disputa del alma y el cuerpo,* and the incomplete *Elena y María* (qq.v.), respectively between water and wine, the soul and the body, and secular and religious love. In many cases an arbitrator gives his verdict, to conclude the *debate.*

The most important use of this type of encounter in Spanish literature is the battle between Carnival and Lent in the *Libro de buen amor* of Juan Ruiz (q.v.).

Décadas (or 'Decads'), a series of ten books into which early copyists divided Livy's *Ab urbe condita* (27–25 B.C.).

Several *décadas* were written by Spanish writers, one of the earliest being the *Décadas* of Alfonso Fernández de Palencia also known as the *Crónicas de Enrique IV*, originally written in Latin and entitled *Gesta hispaniensia ex annalibus suorum dierum colligentis* describing polemically, in the manner of Tacitus, events in Spain 1440–77. It was translated into Castilian by A. Paz y Melia (1904–12).

Fanciful lives of Roman emperors were compiled by Fray Antonio de Guevara (q.v.), *Década de los Césares* (Valladolid, 1539). Juan de Coloma wrote *Década de la Pasión* (Cagliari, 1576). The *Décadas* of Antonio de Herrera y Tordesillas (1549–1625) are subtitled *Historia general de los hechos de los castellanos en las islas y tierra del mar océano* (4 vols., 1601). The *Década Epistolar sobre el Estado de las letras en Francia* (1781; 2nd edn., 1792) by the Duque de Almodóvar was significant for the Duke's defence of French drama against the Spanish; he was ambassador in Paris at the time.

Decasílabos, lines of ten syllables each. A *decasílabo simple* or *dactílico* has a stress on the 3rd, 6th, and 9th syllables.

> *Del salón en el ángulo oscuro*
> *de su dueño tal vez olvidada,*
> *silenciosa y cubierta de polvo*
> *veíase el arpa.*
>
> —Bécquer

A *decasílabo compuesto* combines two pentasyllabic hemistichs, as in 'Oye mis penas, mira mis males' by Sor Juana Inés de la Cruz (q.v.).

DÉCIMA MUSA DE MÉXICO, a title given to Sor Juana Inés de la Cruz (q.v.).

Décimas, stanzas of ten octosyllables with the rhyme scheme abba:ac:cddc. They are also found described as *espinelas,* since Vicente

Espinel (q.v.) was considered to be an outstanding practitioner in his *Rimas* (1591), though he was not the inventor of the form. Among the many poems in *décimas* are *Las moscas y la miel* by Samaniego and *El vértigo* by Núñez de Arce. The form is common in Lope, Tirso, and Moreto, but perhaps reached its height in two speeches by Segismundo in Calderón's *La vida es sueño*: Act I, 103–272, the monologue in prison beginning 'Apurar, cielos, pretendo, / ya que me tratáis así, / qué delito cometí, / contra vosotros naciendo'; and Act II, 2018–2187, beginning 'Es verdad; pues reprimamos / esta fiera condición, / esta furia, esta ambición / por si alguna vez soñamos'.

Decires, short poems first seen in the 15th c., their themes being mainly didactic, political, or courtly, as opposed to the amorous theme predominating in *cantigas* and *canciones*. Their ancestors in Spain were the *Historia troyana*, *Libro de buen amor*, and *Rimado de palacio* (qq.v.). Technically, the *decir* differs from the *canción* in lacking both initial *tema* and *estribillo*; its form is the octosyllabic *copla* of *arte menor*, *real*, *castellana*, or *mixta*.

Decires in *arte mayor* are found in the *Cancionero de Baena* (1445), no. 250 in that collection being the important *Dezir de las syete virtudes* of Francisco Imperial (q.v.), the first known Castilian imitation of Dante. Others writing *decires* include Juan Agraz, Fernán Pérez de Guzmán, the Marqués de Santillana, and Ferrán Sánchez de Calavera. More recently the *decir* was practised by Rubén Darío (q.v.) in his *Dezires, layes y canciones*, using the irregular metre of medieval poetry. This revival (in Darío's *Obras completas*, 21 vols., Madrid, 1923–9) has not been influential.

DÉLANO, Luis Enrique (1907–), b. Santiago. Chilean novelist, short-story-writer, and journalist. Délano joined the staff of *El Mercurio* in 1928 and his first book (apart from juvenilia) is *Viaje de sueño* (1935), short stories. *Cuatro meses de guerra civil* (1937) dealt with the Spanish Civil War to which he returned in his novel *El rumor de la batalla* (1964), a sequel to *El viento del rencor* (1961), on the Chilean Civil War of 1891.

Puerto de fuego (1956) is perhaps his most successful novel, mingling social concern with a conflict of emotions. Délano's other books include *Balmaceda, político romántico* (1937), the novel *En la ciudad de las Césares* (1940), *Viejos relatos* (1941), *Lastarria* (1944), and *Pequeña historia de Chile* (1944).

DEL CID, Juan de Dios (1606–83), b. San Salvador. Poet and scientist who operated the first known printing press in the American continent. At the age of about forty he became a Franciscan, while pursuing other interests such as poetry and the cultivation of the indigo plant. Frustrated by the lack of a press, he built his own, and printed a treatise on the indigo plant *El puntero apuntado con apuntes breves* (1647), thirteen years before the importation of the first press into Guatemala from Spain.

DELGADO, José María (1884–1956), b. Salto. Uruguayan regional novelist and poet. His early *El relicario* (1919) was an unremarkable collection of poems, but *Metal* (1920) revealed a good epic quality. He wrote one play, *La princesa Perla Clara* (1921), and travel books, including *Por las tres Américas* (1929) and *Las viñas de San Juan* (1951), but he is best remembered for his novels of the Salto region, *Juan María* (1941), *Doce años* (1946), and *Las viñas de San Antonio* (1951).

DELGADO, Rafael (1853–1914), b. Córdoba, Veracruz. Mexican novelist of the realist school. His first novel, *La Calandria*, serialized in the *Revista Nacional de Letras y Ciencias*, vol. 3 (1890) and published in Orizaba in 1891, deals with a girl choosing between an honest man of her own class and a depraved dandy. Descriptions make up for defects in the plot, and the style is fluent, modelled on Cervantes and Pereda. *Angelina* (1893) is similar in theme and treatment to the *María* of Jorge Isaacs (q.v.). *Los parientes ricos* (1901–2) and the *costumbrista Cuentos y notas* (1902) were followed by a short novel, *Historia vulgar* (1904).

See Delgado's *Obras completas* (5 vols., Xalapa, 1953).

DELGADO TRESIERRA, Washington (1927–), b. Cuzco. Peruvian poet. He has lived in Lima since 1930, and has taught literature there in several universities and schools, publishing studies of Lope de Vega, Rubén Darío, and Jorge Guillén (qq.v.).

He is co-editor of the magazine *Visión del Perú.* His books of poetry are *Formas de la ausencia* (1955), *Días del corazón* (1957), *Para vivir mañana* (1959), *Parque* (1965), and *Tierra extranjera* (1968).

His mastery of various styles, often in semi-parody, is characteristic of his generation in Peru, which has in general turned against rhetoric and patriotic subjects towards the intimist poetry of Delgado's *La condición humana*, or the bitter but muted condemnation of Church and State oppressions in his poem *Las buenas maneras.* His *Elegía* on Pedro Salinas is one of the finest of its genre in Latin America, and he has written a moving prose elegy on the death of his friend Javier Heraud (q.v.).

See Javier Sologuren, *Tres poetas, tres obras: Belli. Delgado. Salazar Bondy* (1969).

DELIBES, MIGUEL (1920–   ), b. Valladolid. Novelist and journalist. His first novel *La sombra del ciprés es alargada* (Barcelona, 1948) won the Premio Nadal. It is the bitter story of an orphan brought up on pessimism but changed by his love for a young woman, who dies a few days after their marriage. It was only partly successful, like *Aún es de día* (Barcelona, 1949), but his third book, *El camino* (q.v., Barcelona, 1950) won immediate acclaim. His works include a number of travel books: *Un novelista descubre América* (1956), *Por esos mundos* (1961), *Europa, parada y fonda* (1963), *USA y yo* (1966), and *La primavera de Praga* (1968). *Vivir al día* (1968) consists of miscellaneous articles.

Delibes will be remembered for his novels, however, which include *Mi idolatrado hijo, Sisí* (1953), an anti-Malthusian thesis novel set in Valladolid over a period of thirty years; *La hoja roja* (1959), a successful novel on the loneliness of an old man forgotten by the firm for which he worked for 53 years; *Las ratas* (1962), essentially a series of plain anecdotes evoking a forgotten village in Castile and its memorable characters, such as the cave-dwelling Nini and his father Tío Ratero; *Cinco horas con Mario* (1966), almost entirely one long interior monologue; and *Parábola del náufrago* (1969), on the crushing of the individual by bureaucracy and totalitarianism.

Delibes is a passionate small-game hunter (like Alfonso X, Juan Manuel, and Ortega y Gasset, qq.v., all of whom wrote on the sport) and has produced not only three nonfictional works on hunting: *La caza de la perdiz roja* (1963), *El libro de la caza menor* (1964), and *Con la escopeta al hombro* (1970), but important novels in the neorealist manner: *Diario de un cazador* (1955) and *Diario de un emigrante* (1957), in which latter the hunting interest is confined to the earlier pages.

More recent novels include *Un año de mi vida* (1971); *El príncipe destronado* (1973), attempting to depict the mind of a four-year-old child who tries to draw attention from his newly-born sister; and *Las guerras de nuestros antepasados* (1973). After the short stories of *La partida* (1950), Delibes published single stories in a variety of journals and pamphlets and they are best consulted in the continuing *Obra completa*. Two subsequent collections were *Siestas con viento sur* (1959) and *La mortaja* (1970), in which Delibes is clearly preparing sketches for longer works.

See Janet Díaz, *Miguel Delibes* (New York, 1971), in English; and E. Pauk, *Miguel Delibes: desarrollo de un escritor* (1974).

DELICADO, FRANCISCO (c. 1480–after 1533), b. near Cordova? Novelist, editor, and physician. He studied in Spain with Nebrija (q.v.) but, as a Jewish *converso*, was forced to leave the country with the expulsion of the Jews in 1492. He travelled to Rome, and lived there until 1528, writing his anonymous novel *Retrato de la loçana andaluza en lengua española muy claríssima* (Venice, 1528). This is a tongue-in-cheek attack in dialogue on the vices of Renaissance Rome, using the same environment as Aretino uses in his bawdy dialogue *Ragionamenti* (1534–6). The book's language is notable for words of Italian origin and from the Jaén dialect.

On the death of her father, the Cordova-born Aldonza, the 'exuberant Andalusian woman' of the title, travels across Spain with her mother. But then her mother dies too, and Aldonza returns to live with her aunt in Seville. There she meets a young Genoese merchant and elopes with him to Cádiz. The merchant's father thinks she is fortune-hunting and orders her to be murdered but she manages to escape to Rome where most of the novel is set. Her gradual rise to wealth and esteem is told with abundant ironic and scurrilous detail. Like other picaresque heroines, 'she learns from experience', to quote Damiani, 'that deceit and trickery are indispensable weapons for success'. She eventually retires to the isle of Lipari with her manservant Rampín well content with her riches. The influence of *La Celestina* (q.v.), which Delicado edited (Venice, 1531), is unmistakeable.

There is a facsimile edition of the first printing (Valencia, 1950). Three good recent editions are those of Joaquín del Val (1967), Bruno Mario Damiani (1969), and the critical edition by Damiani and G. Allegra (1975).

Delicado also wrote two medical treatises: *De consolatione infirmorum* (Rome, 1525), now lost; and *El modo de adoperare el legno de India occidentale* (Rome, 1525; known only in the Venice edn., 1529), on venereal disease. His *Spechio vulgare per li sacerdoti che administraranno li sacramenti in ciaschedune parrochia* (Rome, 1526?) is also lost. He edited *Amadís de Gaula* (q.v., Venice, 1533) and *Los tres libros del cavallero Primaleón y Polendos su hermano* . . . (Venice, 1534), the latter belonging to the so-called *Palmerín* cycle.

See J. A. Hernández Ortiz, *La génesis artística de 'La lozana andaluza': el realismo literario de Francisco Delicado* (1974); and, in English, Bruno M. Damiani, *Francisco Delicado* (New York, 1974).

DELIGNE, GASTÓN FERNANDO (1861–1913), b. Santo Domingo, the brother of Rafael Alfredo Deligne (q.v.). The most significant poet produced by the Dominican Republic before World War I. Deligne was self-taught, had a fine private library, and for twenty years was an accountant in a business firm in San Pedro de Macorís.

Ars nova scribendi (1897) satirized the *modernistas*, but Deligne finally adopted some of the school's metrical innovations. Henríquez Ureña has described Deligne's best work as 'psychological short stories in verse', such as the spiritual evocations of women: *Angustias* (1885), *Soledad* (1887), and *Confidencias de Cristina* (1892). His fine political poetry, such as *Ololoi* (1899), marked him as a new breed of national poet, neither heroic nor cynical, but a meditator on real problems. His style was concise, and he excelled in descriptive poetry such as *En el botado* (1897) and the ballads of *Romances de la Hispaniola* (1931). Continuing interest in his work is shown by the publication of selected prose and verse in *Páginas olvidadas* (1944) and Fernando A. Amiama Tío's *Contribución a la bibliografía de Gastón Fernando Deligne* (1944).

DELIGNE, RAFAEL ALFREDO (1863–1902), b. Santo Domingo. Essayist and playwright of the Dominican Republic, and brother of G. F. Deligne (q.v.). By profession a lawyer, he was an assiduous contributor to *El Cable* in the Lamb/ Hazlitt mould, writing as 'Pepe Cándido', and he edited with Luis Arturo Bermúdez the review *Prosa y verso* (1894–5). His miscellaneous essays were collected in *Cosas que son y cosas que fueron* and his short stories in *Cuentos del lunes*. A realistic tendency marked his predominantly Romantic verse play *La justicia y el azar* (1894) and his best play, *Vidas tristes* (1901). An anthology, *En prosa y verso*, appeared in 1902.

Delincuente honrado, El, a play in prose by Gaspar Melchor de Jovellanos (q.v.), published under a pseudonym. It states the case against the 1757 edict against duelling on the grounds that it does not distinguish between provoked and provoker. The play was written in 1773 as Jovellanos's contribution to a private competition set in the circle of Pablo de Olavide in Seville, and won great success when first performed in that city the following year. Conventional and rhetorical in its language, it yet marked a new stage in the nascent Spanish social drama.

Don Torcuato, after refusing a challenge, is forced to agree to duel in secret, when he kills the scoundrelly husband of Laura, the lady he afterwards marries. His friend Anselmo is arrested for the crime, so Torcuato honourably confesses and is condemned to death by the judge, Don Justo de Lara, Torcuato's father. After he has been led out to execution, Torcuato is reprieved from death, but sentenced to banishment.

Jovellanos based his play on an actual event which occurred in Segovia in 1758.

DELMONTE, DOMINGO (1804–53), Cuban man of letters who published *Romance*, a collection of Creole ballads, and gathered around him in the 1830s a circle of Romantic novelists. Their common aim was to protest at the continuance of slavery after its legal abolition in 1815 and 1817. Among these writers were Anselmo Suárez y Romero, José Antonio Echeverría, Félix Manuel Tanco y Bosmeniel, and Ramón de Palma.

DELOFFRE, J., a pseudonym used by R. Foulché-Delbosc (q.v.).

De los Nombres de Cristo, see NOMBRES DE CRISTO, De los.

Del rey abajo, ninguno: el labrador más honrado, García del Castañar (1650), the most celebrated *comedia* by Francisco de Rojas Zorrilla (q.v.). It uses the theme of *La estrella de Sevilla* (possibly by Lope de Vega, q.v.), with elements from Lope's *El villano en su rincón* and *Peribáñez* (Calderón's most significant play on the same theme of peasant's honour is *El alcalde de Zalamea*, q.v.). García del Castañar is not a peasant (as in Lope) but a nobleman concealing his ancestry for political reasons and living as a simple landowner. Alfonso XI has received his offer of help against the Moors and comes to make his acquaintance in disguise. Don Mendo is in the royal company, and García mistakes him for the king. Mendo falls in love with García's wife, Blanca, and attempts to seduce her while García is thought absent; and when García returns unexpectedly, Mendo escapes unharmed as García still takes him to be the inviolable king as in Calderón's *El médico de su honra* (qq.v.). García therefore decides to save his honour by killing Blanca, who manages to escape to the court. There García discovers his mistake and kills Mendo instead, ... 'en tanto que mi cuello esté en mis hombros robusto, / no he de permitir me agravie, / del rey abajo, ninguno'.

Succeeding in its aim of reproducing on stage the Castilian ideals of masculine honour and monarchical inviolability, *Del rey abajo, ninguno* has always held an important place on the Spanish stage. Its sources have been studied by J. G. Fucilla in the *Nueva Revista de Filología Hispánica*, vol. 5 (Mexico City, 1951), pp. 381–93. R. R. MacCurdy has recently questioned Rojas Zorrilla's authorship, in *Bulletin of the Comediantes*, vol. 9 (Chapel Hill, N.C., 1957), pp. 7–9. The play was published by Mesonero Romanos in vol. 54 of the BAE (new edn.,

1952) and its popularity may be gauged from the fact that of the fourteen editions of various plays by Rojas Zorrilla that have appeared since 1900, six have contained *Del rey abajo, ninguno.*

Del sentimiento trágico de la vida en los hombres y en los pueblos, see SENTIMIENTO TRÁGICO DE LA VIDA EN LOS HOMBRES Y EN LOS PUEBLOS, Del, a long essay by Miguel de Unamuno (q.v.).

DEMÓFILO, the pseudonym of Antonio Machado y Álvarez (q.v.).

DENEVI, MARCO (1922–), Argentinian novelist, short-story writer, and playwright. The son of an Italian immigrant. Denevi's first significant book was the intellectual thriller *Rosaura a las diez* (1955), concerning the death of a girl in a cheap Buenos Aires hotel and the reactions of four people who knew her, including the suspect, Camilo. The surprise ending is superior to most detective fiction, and Denevi claims to have been influenced by Wilkie Collins's *The woman in white* (1860) and *The moonstone* (1868). Denevi has been termed by Fernando Alegría 'one of the most astonishing of contemporary Argentine writers'. His *Ceremonia secreta* (New York, 1955) won the *Life en Español* prize for the best short novel from Spanish America, describing a 'grand, complex, prolonged, terrifying and fatalistic ritual' in the words of Donald Yates. The collection of short stories and fables *Falsificaciones* (1966) and *Hierba del cielo* (1973) show the influence of Jorge Luis Borges (q.v.).

Antología precoz (1973) includes extracts from two novels, several stories, and short plays. Denevi's plays are ironically expressionist: *Los expedientes* (1957), *El Emperador de la China* (1959), and *El cuarto de la noche* (1962).

The 'magic realism' of García Márquez (q.v.) is never far from Denevi's narrative; man is depersonalized in an increasingly bureaucratic world that offers its own lunacy to replace the chaos it hopes to eradicate. Denevi's vocabulary is rich and allusive, yet not oppressively 'poetic'.

DENIS, JULIO, an early pseudonym, soon abandoned, of Julio Cortázar (q.v.).

Denuestos del agua y el vino, a 13th-c. example of the numerous medieval literary *debates* (q.v.), found at the end of the *Razón feita de amor* (q.v.).

The accidental spilling of a glass of water into a glass of wine provokes this dispute between the two liquids, the water accusing the wine of destroying the reason of those who drink it, while the wine complains that it is weakened and spoiled by the water, and boasts that in the Eucharist it is changed into the blood of Christ. To this the water retorts that it is no less holy, since it is necessary for the rite of baptism.

De regimine principum, a literary genre concerned with the offering of advice to princes or kings also known as 'the mirror of princes', of which the most famous example is Machiavelli's *Il principe* (1513). The *De regimine principum* of St. Thomas Aquinas as transmitted is partly spurious. Of oriental (ultimately Buddhist) origin, the genre was popular in Spain from the time of the Muslim occupation and remained significant until the end of the 17th c. María Ángeles Galino Carrillo listed 81 such works in Spanish and Portuguese in *Los tratados sobre educación de príncipes, siglos XVI y XVII* (1948), to which Ch. V. Aubrun added a further 4 in *Bulletin Hispanique*, vol. 51 (1949), pp. 447–8.

Egidio di Colonna (known in Spain as Gil de Roma) wrote *De regimine principum* in 1284 for Philip the Fair of France. This was turned into Spanish about 1435 by Juan García de Castrogeriz (Barcelona, 1480), but the genre was already common in Spain by then, represented by *Castigos e documentos* once attributed to King Sancho IV and definitely written during his reign, and by the *Libro infinido* of Don Juan Manuel (q.v.), both of which were published by Gayangos in vol. 51 (1857) of the BAE.

Gómez Manrique (q.v.) wrote *Regimiento de príncipes* before 1478; Diego Ortúñez de Calahorra wrote the first part of *L'espejo de príncipes y cavalleros*, which was continued by Pedro de la Sierra and Marcos Martínez; Antonio de Guevara (q.v.) is the author of the *Reloj de príncipes* (Valladolid, 1529), and the genre culminated in the *Idea de un príncipe político cristiano* (1640) of Diego de Saavedra Fajardo (q.v.).

DESCLOT, BERNAT (13th c.), Catalan chronicler writing between 1283 and 1288, and thus contemporary with Ramon Llull and the earliest of the four great Catalan chroniclers. The best MS. is the *Libre del rei En Pere d'Aragó e dels seus antecessors passats*, and the best critical edition is that of M. Coll i Alentorn entitled *Crònica* in Els Nostres Clàssics (5 vols., Barcelona, 1949–51).

The history begins in the reign of Ramon Berenguer IV (1131–62), but passes briefly over the intervening years, concentrating on the reign of Desclot's hero, Pere II (1276–85), and especially on the Catalan-Aragonese intervention in south Italy and France's unsuccessful invasion of Catalonia. Desclot stops short of hagiography, indicating Pere's failings and blaming him for atrocities committed against the French. Facts interest him more than their interpretation, and his Aragonese successor Zurita (q.v.) praises his discriminating use of documents.

J. Rubió's thesis *Consideraciones generales acerca de la historiografía catalana medieval y en particular de la crónica de Desclot* (Barcelona, 1911) has been partly superseded by the relevant section of Marti de Riquer's *Història de la literatura catalana* (vol. 1, Barcelona, 1964).

Desdén con el desdén, El, a Golden Age *comedia de fábrica*, the masterpiece of Agustín Moreto y Cabaña (q.v., 1618–69).

Diana, daughter of the Count of Barcelona, has been studious since her youth and rejects the frivolous flirtations of her circle, claiming that she will not surrender her liberty in marriage. Her suitors, Carlos, Count of Urgel, and Gastón, Count of Foix, are in despair, until Polilla, Carlos's servant, suggests that his master overcome the lady's disdain by disdaining her and feigning love for her friend Cintia; the ruse succeeds. The play is distinguished by its courtly atmosphere, with music, masks, and comedy.

M. M. Harlan concludes in *The relationship of Moreto's 'El desdén con el desdén'* (Indiana University Studies, June 1924) that of the twenty commonly-cited predecessors of the play, only four are close enough to merit the description of model: Tirso de Molina's *Celos con celos se curan*, and three *comedias* by Lope: *Los milagros del desprecio*, *La hermosa fea*, and (especially) *La vengadora de las mujeres*. Moreto's *El poder de la amistad* is an earlier play on the same theme.

Narciso Alonso Cortés has edited the play (with *El lindo don Diego*, q.v.) in Clásicos Castellanos (1916); and there is a later edition by J. H. Parker (Salamanca, 1970).

See Ruth Lee Kennedy, *The dramatic art of Moreto* (Northampton, Mass., 1931–2) and Frank P. Casa, *The dramatic craftsmanship of Moreto* (Cambridge, Mass., 1966).

Desheredada, La (1881), one of the *Novelas españolas contemporáneas* (q.v.) by Benito Pérez Galdós (q.v.).

It marks the beginning of the central period of Galdós's work, combining the presentation of the ugly and corrupt facets of reality with the conversion of 'la vulgaridad de la vida' into 'materia estética', as he himself was to write at the end of *Fortunata y Jacinta* (q.v.). It also exemplifies his interest in abnormal psychology.

Tomás Rufete, having died a lunatic in the Leganés asylum, has left his daughter Isidora papers claiming the marquisate of Aransis. Her uncle Santiago Quijano (the name echoing Quijote's) tells her that she is the natural daughter of the deceased Virginia de Aransis. Isidora comes to Madrid to live in the home of her eccentric but kindly godfather José Relimpio and, having been rejected by the Marquesa de Aransis, Virginia's mother, begins a lawsuit which gradually assumes a central position in her life and thoughts. Blinded by a passion for luxury, Isidora becomes the mistress of the penniless widower, the Marquis of Saldeoro (Joaquinito Pez, son of the Manuel José Ramón Pez who recurs in *La de Bringas*, q.v.), and later of Sánchez Botín and, involved in prostitution, Frasquito Surupa and other lovers. Finally she is persuaded that the documents relative to her claim had been forged by her insane father.

Delusions of grandeur and fantasy, in Galdós's view besetting Spanish vices, are a major theme of the book. The novel never descends into the sentimentality which occasionally betrayed Dickens; Isidora's young brother Mariano (known as 'Pecado' for obvious reasons) is involved in underworld scenes not unlike those of *Oliver Twist*, for example, but the naturalism of Galdós bears more resemblance to known criminal records and less to caricature. Other important characters are the Catalan José Relimpio; and the medical student Augusto Miquis.

See E. Rodgers, 'Galdós, "La desheredada", and Naturalism' in *BHS*, vol. 45 (1968), pp. 285–98.

Deshumanización del arte, La (1925), an essay by José Ortega y Gasset (q.v.) which diagnosed the state of life and literature in the early 1920s as a break from past humanism. Ortega claimed that Debussy had dehumanized music, Mallarmé poetry, Pirandello drama, and the Dadaists art. Techniques of dehumanization vary from surrealism (Tzara, Magritte, Dalí) to subjectivism (Joyce, Proust, Gómez de la Serna q.v.). Essentially an attempt to understand the new as a mere digression from, and reaction to, the old, Ortega's essay was an important stepping-stone towards helping his countrymen come to terms with new art for, if his attitude was less than sympathetic, it was also more than merely vituperative.

DESNOES, Edmundo (1930–), b. Havana. Cuban novelist and short-story writer. His early stories and poems appeared in *Todo está en juego* (1952). *No hay problema* (1961) is a bitterly satirical novel of the Batista years in Cuba. *El cataclismo* (1965) describes the effects of the Revolution on Cubans of all classes. Julio E. Miranda described Desnoes as an 'implacable and tenderly ironic self-critic' (*Nueva literatura cubana*, Madrid, 1971), and it is this autobiographical element that adds greater interest to *Memorias del subdesarrollo* (1965; trans. by the author as *Inconsolable memories*), an existential story of a failure, abandoned by friends and family, told in the first person. *Puntos de vista* (1967) is a volume of essays.

DEÚSTUA, ALEJANDRO (1849–1945), Peruvian positivist philosopher who also wrote on education and aesthetics. His outstanding work was *La cultura nacional* (1937), but it is as a teacher that he is remembered. Among his pupils were Humberto Borja García (1890–1925) and Pedro S. Zulen (1889–1925).

Devoción de la Cruz, La, a religious play on the theme of divine grace by Pedro Calderón de la Barca (q.v.), first published in *Primera parte de comedias . . .* (1640).

The action is set in 13th-c. Italy, although the manners are those of Golden Age Spain. A youth Eusebio, brought up by a man who found him abandoned as a new-born baby, is in love with Julia; Curcio her father and Lisardo her brother do not wish them to marry, having destined Julia to be a nun, thereby frustrating her free will. Eusebio and Lisardo quarrel and fight; the former warns his opponent that his is a charmed life; found under a wayside cross he has a cross-shaped birthmark, and on several occasions the virtue of the Cross has saved his life. Having fatally wounded Lisardo, he takes him to a confessor when begged to do so in the name of the Cross. Curcio tells Julia of how, suspicious that her mother had deceived him and was pregnant by another man, he took her to a lonely spot soon before she was due to give birth; his story is interrupted by news of Lisardo's death, at which he sends Julia at once to a convent, never to see Eusebio again. Persecuted by Curcio, Eusebio is forced to join a gang of bandits, but remains devout, sparing the life of Alberto, an old priest who is writing a book on the Holy Cross and its powers. In a long monologue Curcio reveals more of how Julia was born: as he was about to kill his wife to avenge his suspected dishonour, she clung to a wayside cross and protested her innocence. Having left her for dead, he returned home only to find her there, safe and well, with a baby daughter bearing a cross-shaped birthmark—an obvious miracle. However, another baby had been left in the woods . . .. Meanwhile Eusebio finds his way to the convent, and is reunited with Julia; as she offers to give herself to him he draws back in horror on seeing her birthmark and realizes she is really his sister. He flees and she pursues him, becoming an outlaw herself until she can find him again. They meet once more and are attacked by Curcio and his men who are hunting down Eusebio and his companions; in the fight Eusebio has Curcio at his mercy, but cannot bring himself to kill his enemy

who is his father also. Finally Eusebio is fatally wounded and dies at the foot of a wayside cross, begging God's mercy and forgiveness for his crimes. He is restored briefly to life in order to receive absolution from Alberto—'que tanto con Dios alcanza / de la Cruz la devoción'. Julia returns to her convent, escaping from her frenzied father who tries in vain to slay her for dishonouring his name.

As A. A. Parker suggests (*The approach to the Spanish drama of the Golden Age*, London, 1957, pp. 17–22), the true protagonist of the play is not Eusebio but Curcio, whose cruel and fanatical regard for his honour (cf. Gutierre in *El médico de su honra*) led him to seek to kill not only his innocent wife but also her unborn twins, and whose exemplary punishment is brought about in the course of the play. The sin of the crimes they commit belongs to Eusebio and Julia, but the guilt ultimately belongs to their father, who is shown childless and dishonoured at the end. By contrast Eusebio, who had always been devout, is saved despite his deeds as a bandit; the Cross is a symbol of salvation for him and of the punishment of his perverse father brought about through Eusebio who kills Lisardo, causes Julia to leave the convent and turn to crime, and is finally slain as a bandit before his father's eyes. This theme of the father–son conflict is important also in *La vida es sueño* (q.v.).

La devoción de la Cruz was one of Calderón's early plays, first published in a poor, unauthorized (?) edition in 1634, under the title *La Cruz en la sepultura* and attributed to Lope de Vega. The *santos y bandoleros* theme was a popular one with Golden Age dramatists, who obtained striking moral and aesthetic contrasts by setting virtue against vice, as in *El condenado por desconfiado* by Tirso de Molina (q.v.) and *El esclavo del demonio* by Mira de Amescua (q.v.); the latter play and *La fundación de la Orden de Nuestra Señora de la Merced* by F. A. Tárrega (q.v.) appear to have inspired directly parts of Calderón's play.

S. F. Wexler has edited this play (Salamanca, 1966). See also A. A. Parker, 'Santos y bandoleros en el teatro español del Siglo de Oro', *Arbor*, nos. 43–4 (1949) and Edwin Honig, 'Calderón's strange mercy play' in B. W. Wardropper, *Critical essays on the theatre of Calderón* (New York, 1965).

D'HALMAR, AUGUSTO, see THOMSON, Augusto Goeminne.

Diablo cojuelo, El (1641), a satirical novel by Luis Vélez de Guevara (q.v., 1579–1644). Subtitled in its first edition 'Novela de la otra vida', the book appeared in its first modern critical edition by A. Bonilla y San Martín in

1902, but this was attacked in great detail and was revised in 1910. There is a good edition by F. Rodríguez Marín (1960) in Clásicos Castellanos.

While escaping from justice over the rooftops, the student Don Cleofás Leandro Pérez Zambullo seeks refuge in an astrologer's laboratory, and there unwittingly releases the lame devil of the novel's title. Cleofás is rewarded by the devil in a series of ten *trancos*, or leaps, into which the book is divided. Each shows a feature of the evils and hypocrisies of 17th-c. Spain, since as they fly over the rooftops of Madrid and other cities the lame devil shows Cleofás the realities below them, much as R. Fernández de Ribera had done in *Los anteojos de mejor vista* (Seville, *c.* 1630). The tone of Vélez's satire is mild and affectionate compared with that of his greatest precursor, the Quevedo of *Los sueños* (q.v.). It is also more discriminating in its targets. The novel's style is *conceptista*, its vocabulary erudite and recherché, and its metaphors often outlandish. One *tranco* derides the pretentiously rich who so love their carriage that they live in it, never emerging from one year's end to the next. The fourth *tranco* satirizes contemporary playwrights for whom spectacle outweighs imagination; one wakes other lodgers in the night by shouting 'fire, fire!' and they are pacified only when the innkeeper explains that the poet is merely finishing his play *Troya abrasada*.

El diablo cojuelo, a late example of the Golden Age picaresque novel, is among the most vigorous and comic works of the time, and enjoyed a new vogue when Lesage adapted it for his *Le diable boiteux*. It has been reprinted frequently.

Diablo mundo, El (1840), an unfinished allegorical poem by José de Espronceda (q.v.).

Humanity, in the form of Adam, is permitted the choice between death and understanding on the one hand, or life and perplexity on the other. Entering the world innocent and naked, he cannot make the choice that he knows is right, and takes life. At the realization of love, his initial bondage suddenly ends. Espronceda identifies himself with Adam, and all indications are that he would have ended the poem pessimistically with tragedy and perhaps bitterness. The histrionic power of the poem is undoubted, but Espronceda shows limited literary ability, possibly due to haste in composition. The most impressive section of the poem is the *Canto a Teresa*, which some critics see as a meaningless interpolation. These 44 octaves crystallize his grief after the death of Teresa Mancha, whom he carried off from Paris to Spain. A convenient edition of the poem is that

by J. J. Domenchina in Espronceda's *Obras poéticas completas* (1936).

See J. Casalduero, *Forma y visión de 'El diablo mundo'* (1951).

Diablo predicador y mayor contrario amigo, El, a play attributed to Luis Belmonte y Bermúdez (q.v.), first published in *Sexta parte de Comedias escogidas* (Saragossa, 1653) and reprinted by R. de Mesonero Romanos in vol. 45 (1858) of the BAE.

The devil appears, to exult over the scandal he has caused to the Franciscan cause in Lucca which he plans will lead the populace to drive them out of the city. St. Michael and the infant Jesus descend and Michael sternly bids Lucifer to reconvert the Lucchesi and restore the Franciscans' respectability in the city. The play concerns his grumbling efforts to do this over a period of five months and there is a sub-plot with an attractive heroine. The Guardian Father of the monks and his opposite, the greedy, deceitful *gracioso*, are also sharply delineated. Lucifer completes his task, but is forced to confess his identity and to show that, despite his monk's garb, the flames of hell await him.

Though the author is perhaps not entirely sympathetic to the Franciscan cause, the play was long seen as a devout work, and it was only at the end of the 18th c., for a relatively short period, that its performance was banned. It reappeared on the stage until 1804, when the Inquisition banned it again. The revolution of 1820 gave absolute liberty to theatrical performances and it has been occasionally played since then. Its source was the *Fray Diablo* attributed to Lope de Vega (q.v.).

Diálogo de la lengua, a philological discussion between two Spaniards and two Italians, one of the former being 'Valdés', probably Juan de Valdés (q.v.). Written in Naples in 1535–6, it was first published anonymously as *Diálogo de las lenguas* by G. Mayáns y Síscar in his *Orígenes de la lengua española* vol. 2 (1737), pp. 1–178.

'Valdés' agrees to help his friends who are seeking to improve their knowledge of Spanish, offering the Castilian proverb as a concise model, being both common and pithy. As an Erasmian, 'Valdés' advocates a plain style and verisimilitude, ridiculing the novels of chivalry for their inflated language and fantasy but, like Cervantes later, distinguishing the best from the average. Philology being in its infancy, 'Valdés' understandably makes the mistake of assuming that Greek was once widely spoken in Castile. The book was influenced by Pietro Bembo's *Prose della vulgar lingua* (1525). The delay in its publication was due to the tradition that its author was a heretic; when it finally appeared in 1737, 'as a specimen of pure and easy style', in Ticknor's words, '[it] was lost on the age that produced it'. The attribution of the *Diálogo* to Valdés was questioned by P. Miguélez in *Sobre el verdadero autor del 'Diálogo de la lengua' según el códice escurialense* (1918), but defended in replies by E. Cotarelo in *Boletín de la Real Academia Española*, vol. 5 (1918), vol. 6 (1919), and vol. 7 (1920). Miguélez's attribution (repeated in *La Ciudad de Dios*, 1919) was to Juan López de Velasco. The useful edition by José F. Montesinos in *Clásicos Castellanos* (1928) supports Cotarelo.

DIAMANTE, JUAN BAUTISTA (1625–87), b. Madrid. A prolific minor playwright of the school of Calderón. His mother was a *madrileña* and his father a Sicilian of Greek parentage. During his turbulent youth he killed a man, but was freed when his father gave the man's widow 400 ducats. His wildness did not come to an end on his admission to the Order of St. John of Jerusalem. Diamante wrote numerous *zarzuelas* and other light pieces for the courts of Philip IV and Charles II, but these are no longer acted. Some fifty *comedias* are attributed to him, and a dozen *autos*, *loas*, *entremeses*, and *bailes*.

El honrador de su padre, first performed in 1657, is an often literal translation of Corneille's *Le Cid*, except for Diamante's original third act. *La judía de Toledo*, in vol. 49 of the BAE, pp. 1–18, is attributed to him there, and in James A. Castañeda's edition of Lope's *Las paces de los Reyes, y judía de Toledo* (Chapel Hill, 1962), but H. A. Rennert considers it to be a reworking by Antonio Mira de Amescua (q.v.) of one of his own plays (*Revista Hispánica*, vol. 7, pp. 119–140). *El valor no tiene edad, y Sansón de Extremadura*, reprinted in vol. 49 (1951) of the BAE, pp. 19–41, was followed by *El honrador de su padre*, and the cleverly-constructed *Cuánto mienten los indicios, y el ganapán de desdichas*.

Of his religious plays, *La devoción del Rosario* is an imitation of Calderón's *La devoción de la Cruz* (q.v.) and is inferior to *La Magdalena de Roma*; it concerns the conversion of a young courtesan, her temptation by the devil in the guise of a dead lover, and her resistance with the aid of divine intervention. Not gifted as a writer of popular speech, Diamante was more successful in historical plays such as *La reina María Estuarda*, which describes the life of Mary Queen of Scots from her arrival in England to her death. His plays were published in 1670 and 1674 as the *Primera parte de las comedias* and *Segunda parte . . .*.

See E. Cotarelo y Mori, 'Don Juan Bautista Diamante y sus comedias', in *BRAE*, vol. 3 (1916), pp. 272–97, 454–97.

DIAMONTE, JOAN, an anagram of Joan Timoneda (q.v.).

Diana, Los siete libros de la (Valencia, 1559?), a pastoral novel in Castilian by the Portuguese Jorge de Montemayor (q.v.). It became the most popular of its genre, being reprinted 15 times before 1581, and imitated by other writers in their works, including A. Alonso Pérez (q.v.), Gaspar Gil Polo (q.v.), Cervantes in *La Galatea* (q.v., Alcalá, 1585), Lope de Vega in *Arcadia* (q.v., 1598), and Sir Philip Sidney in *Arcadia* (London, 1590).

Sireno, distraught on learning of the marriage of his beloved Diana to Delio, visits the enchantress Felicia with other unhappy lovers. Her magic potion achieves its purpose of turning Sireno's love for Diana to indifference. Diana, unhappily married, remains unhappy at the end of the novel, but Montemayor promises a sequel, apparently never written (the unfulfilled promise of a sequel was to become common in the pastoral and other genres). Such stories, as in the case of Boccaccio's *Ninfale d'Ameto*, were often *à clef* but if this was the case in Montemayor, the characters have not yet been identified with their prototypes. The book is really an examination of the varieties and intricacies of love. The view taken by Montemayor is that love is a force beyond reason, over which a man and woman have no possible control. As in courtly love familiar from Provençal poets, Montemayor's lovers are all chaste.

Montemayor derived his ethic of love in broad terms from the *Dialoghi d'amore* of Leo Hebraeus, except that Leo stated one 'extraordinary reason' to which love is in fact subject, and this too is denied by the author of *Diana*.

The style of *Diana* is elegant and appropriate to the brief novel's pastoral atmosphere. The harmony of prose passages with the poems is notable. Of the seven books, the fourth (*Abindarráez y Jarifa*) has a Moorish story intercalated after Montemayor's death and appearing for the first time in the Valladolid edition of 1561. The episode of Félix and Felismena is taken from a novella by Bandello and reappears in Shakespeare's *Two gentlemen of Verona*.

Good editions of the *Diana* are those by Francisco López Estrada (1946; 4th edn., 1967) in *Clásicos Castellanos* and E. Moreno Báez (1955) in *Biblioteca Selecta de Clásicos Españoles*. *Diana* was transformed *a lo divino* (q.v.) by the Cistercian Bartolomé Ponce de León, as *Primera parte de la Clara Diana a lo divino* (Saragossa, 1599?).

See Gerhart Hoffmeister, *Die Spanische Diana in Deutschland* (Berlin, 1972).

Diana enamorada, Los cinco libros ` de la (Valencia, 1564), a pastoral novel by Gaspar Gil Polo (q.v.), written to continue and controvert the *Diana* (q.v., Valencia, 1559?) of Jorge de Montemayor (q.v.), following the latter's enormous success. Polo's ethic of love is derived broadly from Pietro Bembo's *Gli Asolani* (1505), which teaches that love is not madness, but reason, and is characterized not by lack of self-control, but by goodness and temperance. This retort was caused by the influence of Leo Hebraeus on the original *Diana*, but Polo's moralizing was considered too tedious in a pastoral novel and Felicia's denunciation of irrational love was dropped after the first edition. Polo condemns Montemayor's ending (as does Cervantes in *Don Quijote*) and shows that magic is not necessary to resolve the plot. His 'improvement' has usually been appreciated as such in both its literary accomplishment and its philosophical position.

Diana, in love with Sireno, meets the shepherdess Alcida, who offers to cure her grief. Diana, repeating Montemayor's sentiment, prefers the pain of love to being cured of it and, in any case, believes the affliction incurable. Alcida however denies this, taking love to be a product of sense and harmony. Diana's husband Delio now appears and falls in love with the virtuous Alcida. She hears another shepherd approaching and escapes. This is Marcelio, Alcida's betrothed.

As in Montemayor, the lovers all make their way to Felicia's palace. But the enchantress offers no magic potions. Gil Polo's solutions are credible; Delio dies of his rash *loco amor* for Alcida, which permits Diana to marry Sireno.

The versification is fluent throughout; especially notable are the alexandrines of the *Epitalamio de Diana y Sireno* and the *versos provenzales* in *coplas* of 12 lines. A good edition with a study by Rafael Ferreres is available in Clásicos Castellanos (1962).

DIANEO, LARISSIO, the name given to Ramón de Cruz Cano y Olmedilla (q.v.) in the Academia de los Árcades.

Diario de los Literatos de España, a quarterly review founded in 1737 by Francisco Manuel de Huerta y Vega, Juan Martínez Salafranca, and Leopoldo Jerónimo Puig. The *Diario* was modelled on *Le Journal des Savants* (1665–1792 and 1816 to date).

It was discontinued in 1742, mainly because it was not sufficiently friendly to the prevailing theories of Luzán (q.v.). The tone of the journal was moderate and eclectic, and there was marked attention to scientific topics. Many authors whose works were reviewed in its columns were incensed by the attitudes of its contributors, who were unafraid to comment adversely, though more frequently the contents of books were summarized without judgement.

Among its contributors were José Gerardo de Hervás (q.v.), who published in it the well-known *Sátira contra los malos escritores* under the pseudonym 'Jorge Pitillas'; Juan de Iriarte; and Gregorio Mayáns y Síscar, author of a critique of Luzán's *Poética*, who was angered by an unfavourable notice of his *Orígenes de la lengua española* and replied with *Conversación sobre el 'Diario de los literatos de España'* (1737).

DÍAZ, JIMENA or XIMENA, wife of the Cid, Rodrigo Díaz de Vivar (q.v.). Modern scholarship has established that she was the daughter of Diego Rodríguez, Count of Oviedo, and granddaughter of Alfonso V of Leon, and thus a cousin of Alfonso VI, but this was unknown to the poet of the *Cantar de mio Cid* (q.v.).

She married the Cid in 1074, and after Valencia was abandoned in 1102 returned to her home in Cardeña, and was there buried with her husband in or shortly after 1113.

Some of the most moving passages in the *Cantar* are devoted to Jimena, such as her prayer for her husband's safety when he goes into exile (ll. 327–65) and her arrival with her daughters María and Cristina (called Elvira and Sol in the poem) in Valencia (ll. 1560–1618) where they are reunited with the Cid.

DÍAZ, JORGE (1930–   ), b. Rosario, Argentina. Chilean playwright, whose plays were first performed in Santiago de Chile as follows: *Un hombre llamado Isla* (1961), *El cepillo de dientes* (1961), *Requiem por un girasol* (1961), *El velero en la botella* (1962), *El lugar donde mueren los mamíferos* (1963), *Variaciones para muertos de percusión* (1964), and *El nudo ciego* (1965). *Requiem por un girasol* was published by the U.S. Ministry of Education in 1963, 'El velero en la botella' and 'El lugar donde mueren los mamíferos' appeared in *Mapocho*, the magazine of the Biblioteca Nacional de Chile, 'Variaciones para muertos de percusión' appeared in *Conjunto* (Havana, 1964), while *Teatro* (Madrid, 1967) contained the one-act 'La víspera del degüello', a black comedy on the end of the world, 'El cepillo de dientes', and 'Requiem por un girasol', mocking the bourgeoisie in the tradition of Jarry and Genet. Díaz has lived in Spain since 1965.

DÍAZ, LEOPOLDO (1862–1947), b. Chivilcoy, province of Buenos Aires. Argentinian poet. Consul in Geneva at the age of 35, Díaz was subsequently appointed ambassador in Norway, Venezuela, and Paraguay. His first collection was *Fuegos fatuos* (Mendoza, 1885), influenced by Bécquer (q.v.). He had already arrived at perfection of form in the somewhat arid *Sonetos* (1888), but he changed completely when Darío (q.v.) arrived in Buenos Aires, as the *Bajo-*

relieves of 1895 demonstrate. A volume of *Traducciones* (1897) made the poetry of D'Annunzio, Leconte de Lisle, and Poe accessible to Argentina. The rhetorical Hellenism of Hérédia's *Les trophées* (1893) marked Díaz's sonnets collected in *Las sombras de Hellas* (Geneva, 1902), *Atlántida conquistada* (Geneva, 1906), and *Las ánforas y las urnas* (Christiania, 1923). A comprehensive *Antología* (1945) included some 20 poems previously unpublished.

See the essay on Díaz in José Enrique Rodó's *La tradición intelectual argentina* (1939).

DÍAZ ARRIETA, HERNÁN (1891–), b. Santiago. Chilean literary critic, historian, and regular reviewer for *La Nación* and *El Mercurio*, under the pen-name 'Alone'. The quasi-autobiographical *La sombra inquieta* (1915) is the diary of a man in the Santiago of 1910. His contributions to Chilean literary history began with the useful *Panorama de la literatura chilena durante el siglo XX* (1931) and the sensitive anthology *Las cien mejores poesías chilenas* (1935; 3rd edn., 1957), continuing with *Don Alberto Blest: biografía y crítica* (1941), shorter than the contemporary book on Blest Gana by Raúl Silva Castro; *Reseña de historia cultural y literaria de Chile* (Buenos Aires, 1945); *Historia personal de la literatura chilena* (1954; 2nd edn., 1962); *Memorialistas chilenos: crónicas literarias* (1960); *Bello en Caracas* (Caracas, 1963); and *Los cuatro grandes de la literature chilena del siglo XX: Augusto d'Halmar, Pedro Prado, Gabriel Mistral, Pablo Neruda* (1963). A useful selection of Alone's writings is *Leer y escribir* (1962).

DÍAZ CALLECERRADA, MARCELO (17th c.), b. Madrid. Poet. Rector of Salamanca University and protégé of Rodríguez de Ledesma. He wrote *Endimión* (1627), a *culterano* narrative poem in *octavas reales*. The poem (ed. C. Rosell in vol. 29 (1854) of the BAE) is divided into three cantos. In the first, Venus is insulted by the moon and incites Love to bewitch her. In the second, the icy goddess is burned by Endymion. In the third she is put to sleep while her love is satisfied. Thematically, Díaz Callecerrada owes a clear debt to Ovid's *Metamorphoses*. Stylistically, the poem is attractive and elegant, meriting Lope's praise in *silva* 7 of his *Laurel de Apolo*.

DÍAZ CANEJA, GUILLERMO (1876–1933), b. Madrid. Novelist. His later books did not fulfil the early promise of *Escuela de humorismo* (1913), *La pecadora* (1914), *La deseada* (1915), *El sobre en blanco* (1918), and *Pilar Guerra* (1920). His style is plain, lacking personality or innovation. His judgment of characters tends to the pious and conventional, especially in the later works: *El vuelo de la dicha* (1921), *La virgen paleta* (1922),

La mujer que soñamos (1924), *Garras blancas* (1925), *La novela sin título* and *El carpintero y los frailes* (1927), and *El misterio del hotel* (1928).

DÍAZ CASANUEVA, HUMBERTO (1905–), b. Santiago. Chilean poet. He studied philosophy and science in Germany, then served as a diplomat in Spain, U.S.A., Algeria, and elsewhere. He returned home to take part in the educational reforms which started in 1928. For political reasons he later went into exile in Uruguay, then taught at Caracas University.

Díaz Casanueva is a hermetic poet, an innovator in rhythm and metaphor. His works include *El aventurero de Sabá* (1926), *Vigilia por dentro* (1930), *El blasfemo coronado* (1941), *Requiem* (1945) for his mother, and *La estatua de sal* (1947).

See Rosamel del Valle, *La violencia creadora* (1959).

DÍAZ CASTRO, EUGENIO (1804–65), b. Soacha, Cundinamarca. Colombian novelist and writer of social sketches, or *cuadros de costumbres*. His best-known work is the novel *La Manuela*, which first appeared in instalments in the important Colombian literary magazine *El Mosaico*. Set in the late 1850s, *La Manuela* (1889) was described by Cejador as 'the most faithful artistic copy of reality and the most finished of the novels so far written in America'.

A conservative, Díaz set out in this book to satirize the well-meaning young city liberal Demóstenes who tries to free Manuela from the *hacendado* Don Tadeo Candillo, and her village from his dictatorship. Though the melodramatic plot is weak, Díaz's novel is still readable for the description of village *fiestas* and working life, contrasting the wealth of the rapacious land-owners and politicians with the misery of the common people. Tadeo is defeated in the political struggle by Demóstenes, but takes revenge by burning down the church in which Manuela is being married to a village youth.

La Manuela has been studied in Salvador Camacho Roldán's *Estudios* (Bogotá, 1935).

El rejo de enlazar (1873) and other novels are forgotten, but the lively sketches in *Una ronda de Don Ventura Ahumada y otros cuadros*, several times reprinted, retain their regional appeal.

DÍAZ COVARRUBIAS, JUAN (1837–59), b. Xalapa, Veracruz. Mexican novelist. Distressed by the early death of his mother and by an unlucky love affair, Díaz Covarrubias joined the liberal troops as a medical assistant in the Mexican Civil War. He was taken prisoner at Tacubaya and shot with his comrades when he was only 21.

His sentimental novels have the common

theme of young love ending in misery; their lack of invention is to some extent offset by his vivid descriptive abilities and the autobiographical episodes of the civil war. The strongest is *Gil Gómez el insurgente, o la hija del médico* (1859) and the weakest a mere sketch for a novel *La sensitiva* (1859), in which the heroine Luisa dies of love for Fernando. *La clase media* (1859) deals with the rehabilitation of a prostitute, who considers herself too humble to marry Román and enters a convent. *El diablo en México* (1860) shows how the pure love of Enrique and Elena is contaminated by material considerations, each marrying another for gain.

DÍAZ DE GUZMÁN, Ruy (c. 1554–1629), b. Asunción. Historian. The son of Alonso Riquelme de Guzmán who, in the company of his uncle the *Adelantado* Álvar Núñez Cabeza de Vaca, came to Río de la Plata and later married Úrsula, the *mestiza* daughter of Martínez de Irala, a central figure in the conquest of Paraguay. Díaz de Guzmán was the first *mestizo* historian of the Río de la Plata. His book was finished in 1612, and was popularly known as *La Argentina manuscrita* to distinguish it from the epic poem (1602) published by Barco de Centenera (q.v.). It was not published until 1835. The full title is *Anales del descubrimiento, población y conquista de las provincias del Río de la Plata*, and there are several incomplete MSS., though the original is lost. His style is clear and the account is modest, but the accuracy of the history is disputed, suffering from the author's excessive credulity, especially concerning legends and miracles recounted throughout as fact, and by his partiality, since it was written partly to exalt the deeds of his father and grandfather. His sources appear to have been primarily oral and traditional. He never questions the religious and political attitudes of the *conquistadores*.

DÍAZ DEL CASTILLO, Bernal (1492–1581), b. Medina del Campo. *Conquistador* and historian of the Mexican conquest. Though an ordinary Castilian soldier, Díaz was educated, and fortunate to have experienced 'one hundred and nineteen battles', sufficient for a lengthy chronicle.

He accompanied Dávila to the New World in 1514, Velázquez to Cuba, Grijalva to Yucatán, and Hernán Cortés in the conquest of Mexico. He was rewarded with an *encomienda* (estate and workforce) in Guatemala, where he lived out the rest of his days. There he read the official history of Cortés's exploits written by López de Gómara (q.v.) and in his indignation at the scanty mention of those who had fought with Cortés, began, when over 70, the *Historia verdadera de la Conquista de la Nueva-España*. He made a fair copy

at the age of 76, but it was not until 1632 that it was first published. It was made available in vol. 26 (1853) of the BAE. Díaz lacks the literary polish of López de Gómara, and is more to the taste of the modern reader. He describes not only events, but also feelings, including his fear before a battle. The book covers the two preliminary expeditions along the Mexican coast, the march on Montezuma's city, the flight of the Spaniards, and the final defeat of Guatemoc in his island-capital. Then follow the intrigues in Spain, Cuba, and Hispaniola, the march through Honduran jungles and the final triumph of Cortés. Against the 'black legend' of Las Casas, Díaz suggests that the *conquistadores* were motivated not only by greed for money, land, and riches, but also by Christianizing zeal, loyalty to Spain, and the abstract notion of glory derived from the exceedingly popular novels of chivalry.

As a writer, Díaz is probably less biased than López; his sense of drama, especially in scenes involving the common soldiers among whom he moved as an eye witness, is not often marred by fantasy. He also acknowledges the Aztec's nobility and generosity where appropriate, though he never wavers from his certainty of Spain's divine inspiration. Díaz's account was used a primary source by W. H. Prescott (q.v.) in his classic history. The most reliable current edition is that of Joaquín Ramírez Cabañas (2 vols., Mexico City, 1955). A complete but pedestrian English version by A. P. Maudslay was issued by the Hakluyt Society (1908–16); an excellent abridged translation by J. M. Cohen was issued in the Penguin Classics series as *The conquest of New Spain* (Harmondsworth, 1963).

DÍAZ DE TOLEDO, Pedro (15th c.), translator of the *Proverbios de Seneca* (Zamora, 1482); editor of the glosses on the *Proverbios* (new edn. introduced by M. Menéndez y Pelayo, 1944) of the Marqués de Santillana (q.v.).

He is the reputed author of 'Diálogo e razonamiento en la muerte del Marqués de Santillana', edited by Paz y Melia in *Opúsculos literarios de los siglos XIV a XVI* (1892), pp. 247–360.

DÍAZ DE VIVAR, Rodrigo (Ruy, Roy) (c. 1040–99), b. Vivar, Burgos. A historical figure whose exploits, some true and some legendary, were recounted in a number of medieval and Renaissance epics and ballads, notably the earliest extant *chanson de geste*, the *Cantar de mio Cid* (q.v., c. 1140). Nothing is known of his birth, but much of his later life is described in the chronicles, such as the conferring of his knighthood by Fernando I in the mosque of Coimbra after he had captured the city in 1064, and his marriage in 1074 (see Díaz, Jimena). He was probably first colloquially called *Cid* (Arabic: *sayyid*, 'lord' or 'master') by the Moorish mercenaries in his *mesnada*, or legion, but the term is not recorded in writing until the *Poema de Almería* of 1147–9. Early sources for his life are the Spanish chronicles of the time, and histories in Arabic, such as the history of Valencia written by Ibn Alcama *c.* 1110 and now lost, and the works of Ibn Bassam (1109). The *Cantar de mio Cid* is merely the most important single work in a great literature on the life of the *Cid*. In the later 14th c. a *Crónica particular del Cid* was incorporated into an early 14th-c. *Crónica de Castilla*. An unknown poet wrote *c.* 1300 a *cantar de gesta* on the youthful exploits of Rodrigo, and this came to be called *Las mocedades de Rodrigo* (q.v.). Numerous ballads derive from these and other sources, since the common people identified the astute, wilful Rodrigo with the spirit of Castile. 'Por Guadalquivir arriba' and 'Tres cortes armara el rey' spring from the *Cantar* narrative, and 'Cabalga Diego Laínez' and 'En Burgos está el buen rey' from the *Mocedades*. Hundreds such were assembled in a *Romancero del Cid* (Lisbon, 1605) that was reprinted 26 times in 152 years.

Guillén de Castro (q.v.) wrote a spectacular drama, *Las mocedades del Cid* (1618), and Corneille's *Le Cid* was a sensational success in Paris in 1636. The *Cantar* itself had been lost to view until the publication of the MS. as the first item in Tomás Antonio Sánchez's (q.v.) *Colección de poesías castellanas anteriores al siglo XV* (1779). *The Cid*, an American film, brought the epic tale to a public of millions with Charlton Heston in the title role and Sophia Loren as Jimena.

Much has been written on the Cid as a person, notably in *La España del Cid* (2 vols., 1929; 5th edn., 1956), by R. Menéndez Pidal (q.v.), abridged in the translation by H. Sutherland, *The Cid and his Spain* (London, 1934; reprinted, 1972). *Las huellas del Cid* (Burgos, 1955) by J. M. Garate Córdoba and Stephen Clissold's *In search of the Cid* (London, 1965) are useful for travellers wishing to retrace the steps of the Cid.

DÍAZ FERNÁNDEZ, JOSÉ (1898–1940), b. Aldea del Obispo, Salamanca. Novelist and journalist, working successively on *El Sol*, *Crisol*, and *Nueva España*. He fought in Morocco in 1921, deriving from his experiences there the raw material for his novel *El blocao* (1928; 2nd edn., also 1928, with prologue). Díaz Fernández is a pacifist, but without polemical partisan opinions. His book is realist in intention, but not ideological. 'I maintain', he wrote in his prologue, 'that there is a single eternal formula for art: emotion'.

He creates no real characters, and is weak in novelistic construction; his strength lies in the effectiveness of his cinematographic narration and his control of language. *La Venus mecánica* (1929) is a curious amalgam of nihilism, *avant-garde* techniques (the narrative is interrupted by interpolated prose poems), and the erotic novel (the heroine Obdulia is a well-born girl with social advantages who nevertheless becomes a prostitute).

DÍAZ LOYOLA, CARLOS (1895–1968), b. Curicó. Chilean poet who wrote under the pen-name of 'Pablo de Rokha'. A turbulent figure, Rokha systematically employed adjectives like 'enorme' and lists of nouns in his 'gigantism' which he borrowed from the rhetoric of Whitman without the latter's breadth of vision. *Los gemidos* (1917) was the last collection in this manner, however; his preoccupation with Marxism and the plight of the Chilean masses made him a self-styled 'intellectual guerrilla' from *Satanas* (1927) and the long poem *Jesucristo* (1930), to political bombast such as *Canto de trinchera* (1933) and *Oda a la memoria de Gorki* (1936). His later collections were equally committed to the Left: *Gran temperatura* (1937), *Cinco cantos rojos* (1938), *Morfología del espanto* (1942), and *Canto al Ejército Rojo* (1944).

Rokha's *Arenga sobre el arte* appeared in 1950, by which time the poetic leadership of Chile was irrevocably Neruda's. *Neruda y yo* was published in 1955.

DÍAZ MACHICAO, PORFIRIO (1909–), Bolivian novelist and essayist. Librarian of S. Andrés University in La Paz. He wrote one collection of short stories: *Los invencibles* (1932) set at the time of the Chaco War and expressing his angry pacifism in the saying 'Spartan mothers do not exist: they never have!'

His main reputation is that of novelist, with *El estudiante enfermo* (Cochabamba, 1938) which deals with sexual problems of university students and a veteran of the Chaco War; *Vocero* (1942) on the press; and *La bestia emocional* (1955) which is both historical and autobiographical. His detailed *Historia de Bolivia* (1954– , in progress) so far covers the years 1920–43 in 5 volumes. Of his volumes of essays, the best-known are 20 *lecciones sobre Bolívar* (1949), *El Ateneo de los muertos* (1956), and *Crónica de crónicas* (1963). Díaz Machicao has compiled two anthologies: *Antología de la literatura boliviana* (4 vols., Cochabamba, 1965) and *Prosa y verso de Bolivia: antología* (3 vols., 1966–7).

DÍAZ MEZA, AURELIO (1879–1933), b. Talca. Chilean playwright who worked on the Talca newspaper *La Libertad* until he left for Santiago in 1899. Apart from his plays, he wrote a fictional biography, *La Quintrala* (the book's subject was also treated by Magdalena Petit, *La Quintrala* and Armando Arriaza, *La tragedia de los Lisperguer*, 1936).

Díaz Meza's first well-known play was *Bajo la selva* (1914), a comedy like the one-act *Amorcillos* (1916). Other plays included *Ricacahuín, En la Araucania*, and *Con su destino*.

He published *Leyendas y episodios chilenos* (11 vols.) between 1925 and 1927.

DÍAZ MIRÓN, Salvador (1853–1928), b. Veracruz City. Mexican poet whose influence on Darío and José Santos Chocano (qq.v.) was considerable. His poem *Sursum* (1884) and his political speeches of 1884–5 indicated that he accepted the view of Hugo and Byron that the poet is a leader of men. He later rejected his Byronic *Poesías* (Xalapa, 1886; 2nd edn., 1901) and all other poetry written before *Lascas* (Xalapa, 1901), an important document in the early Modernist movement. He abandoned social themes and a new fastidiousness in composition became evident; he turned to Quevedo as regards his treatment of Castilian and to Góngora for complexity of metaphor.

His *Poesías completas* (1941) appeared in their 3rd edition in 1952. *Prosas* (1954) was an anthology compiled by L. Pasquel.

Díaz Mirón's writings do not show the violence of his life. He lost his left arm in a fight before an election, went into voluntary exile following his political journalism of 1874–6, but returned to become a deputy in 1878. In 1892, for the second time he killed a man during an electoral campaign and was sentenced to four years in prison. From prophesying glory, his voice turned to contemplation. Once freed, he ran yet again for office and in 1910 was again gaoled for attempted murder, obtaining his release only in 1911 when Madero's revolution broke out. His last drafts for books, 'Astillas' and 'Triunfos', were not published.

See A. Méndez Plancarte, *Díaz Mirón, poeta y artífice* (1954).

DÍAZ-PLAJA, Guillermo (1909–), b. Manresa. Literary historian, critic, and essayist who edited the standard *Historia general de las literaturas hispánicas* (7 vols., 1949–67) and the *Antología mayor de la literatura española*. He has written more than 150 books, writes literary criticism for *ABC* and is Director of the Instituto Nacional del Libro Español.

Some of his original writings are *El arte de quedarse solo y otros ensayos* (1936), *Introducción al estudio del Romanticismo español* (1936, revised 1942) which won the Premio Nacional de Literatura on its first appearance, *El espíritu del Barroco* (1940), *Modernismo frente a Noventa*

y Ocho (1951), *Las estéticas de Valle-Inclán* (1965), and *El oficio de escribir* (1969). Díaz-Plaja's *Poesía junta* appeared in 1967.

DÍAZ RENGIFO, Juan. Jesuit; author of an *Arte poética española con una fertilísima sylva de consonantes comunes, propios, esdrújulos y reflexos y un divino estímulo del Amor de Dios* (Salamanca, 1592). It was expanded, without any notable improvement, by Joseph Vicens from the edition of 1703. In Rengifo's poetics, the *doctrina* (or *utile* of Horace) is given much more importance than the *deleite* (or *dulce* of Horace). Rengifo borrowed the doctrines of Italian theorists such as Antonio da Tempo, adapting them to traditional Spanish metres. His *Sylva de consonantes* or rhyming dictionary was so well-known that Moratín (q.v.), in his *La derrota de los pedantes* (1789), could write: 'Qué es la poesía? El arte de hacer coplas. ¿Y cómo se hacen las coplas? Comprando Rengifo por tres pesetas.'

DÍAZ RODRÍGUEZ, Jesús (1942–), b. Havana. Cuban essayist and short-story writer, who has lectured in Dialectical Materialism at Havana University. His short stories collected in *Los años duros* won the 1966 prize of the Casa de las Américas.

DÍAZ RODRÍGUEZ, Manuel (1868–1927), Venezuelan novelist influenced by Bécquer and Rodó (qq.v.). His socio-satirical novels included clever character-sketches and travel descriptions, but suffered from stilted dialogue. Among his works were *Sensaciones de viaje* (Paris, 1896), *De mis romerías* (Caracas, 1898), and *Sangre patricia* (Caracas, 1902). *Ídolos rotos* (Paris, 1901) was an autobiographical novel.

DÍAZ SÁNCHEZ, Ramón (1903–68), b. Puerto Cabello. Venezuelan novelist and short-story writer. He was a journalist, working on *Ahora* (1936–7), for two years head of publications of the Ministry of Agriculture, and 1942–44 director of the National Printing Office. His first novel *Mene* (1936) uses a documentary technique to tell of life in a village rapidly turned into a big and prosperous town by the arrival of an oil company. *Cumboto* (1950) illustrates the problems of *mestizaje* and black and white relationships on a coconut hacienda near Puerto Cabello, Díaz Sánchez's birthplace. The narrator is a Negro, Natividad, who tells his own history and that of Federico Zeus, a white, as well as that of the attractive adolescent Negress Pascua and others. Fantasy mingles with fact, terror with pity, and past with present. *Cumboto* has been translated by John Upton (Austin, Texas, 1969).

Díaz Sánchez's later novels are less impressive:

Casandra (1958), on a pitiable madwoman with prophetic ability, essentially attacks materialism but fails to bring its hero José Ubert to life; in *Borburata* (1961), a family, once great, abandons the city for a cacao plantation.

Díaz Sánchez has published two collections of short stories: *Caminos del amanecer* (1942) and *La Virgen no tiene cara* (1946), and two distinguished biographies: *Guzmán, elipse de una ambición de poder* (1951), a great panorama of 19th-c. history painted around the figures of Antonio Leocadio Guzmán and his son Antonio Guzmán Blanco, which won the National Literature Prize; and *El caraqueño* (1967), on Simón Bolívar. His major contributions to literary history were *Teresa de la Parra: clave para una interpretación* (1954) and *Paisaje histórico de la literatura venezolana* (Mexico City, 1965).

DÍAZ TANCO, VASCO (149-?–1573?), b. Fregenal de la Sierra, Extremadura. Playwright and poet. He travelled widely, in Portugal, Italy, France, Greece, and Turkey, and was probably a captive among Muslims before 1547, the year of publication of *Libro intitulado Palinodia de la nephanda y fiera nacion de los Turcos, y de su engañoso arte y cruel modo de guerrear . . .* (Orense, 1547). He based this on the *Commentari delle cose dei Turchi* (Venice, 1541) by Paolo Giovio (1483–1552). A facsimile of Díaz Tanco's first edition commemorated its quatercentenary (Badajoz, 1947).

He was a prolific writer, listing in the prologue to his *Jardín del alma cristiana* (Valladolid, 1552) no fewer than 48 titles, some of which were compilations and translations. All 30 of his dramatic works are lost, but *Los viente triumphos* (*c.* 1530, ed. A. Rodríguez Moñino, 1945), a verse history of 20 notable Spanish ships, survives. His Latinate style is reminiscent of Juan de Mena (q.v.).

DICENTA, JOAQUÍN (1893–   ), b. Madrid. Son of the major playwright Joaquín Dicenta Benedicto (q.v.). Himself a dramatist, he achieved success with the verse plays 'Leonor de Aquitania' and 'Son mis amores reales' published with 'Pluma en el viento' in *Obras dramáticas* (1933). With Antonio Paso he wrote *Un pasatiempo bufo-lírico-bailable en un acto* and *Los cuerno del diablo* (1927). His collections of poetry include *El libro de mis químeras* (1912) and *Lisonjas y lamentaciones* (1913), with a prologue by Pérez Galdós. He has written a dramatic trilogy, *Hernán Cortés*.

DICENTA BENEDICTO, JOAQUÍN (1863–1917), b. Calatayud. Liberal playwright and novelist. He began by writing post-Romantic verse melodramas of the Echegaray type such as

El suicidio de Werther (1887), *La honra y la vida* (1888), and *La mejor ley* (1889). His prose drama *Luciano* (1894) was followed by *Juan José* (1906), first performed in 1895. This is a tense drama of the hero's love for Rosa, who does not really love him, but desires a life of comfort. Juan José, a working man, steals for Rosa's sake, but is caught and jailed. Rosa goes to live with his rival Paco. Juan José escapes from jail, kills Paco, and to prevent Rosa from calling out, strangles her. Urged by a friend to run away, Juan José decides to stay and accept punishment: life without Rosa would be unbearable.

An atheist, Dicenta nevertheless respected religious sensibilities. His plays were filled with socialistic liberalism of the kind attacked by Donoso Cortés (q.v.). Generally considered the founder of Spanish social drama, Dicenta is perhaps more interested in ethical drama, but though moral and ethical questions concern him more directly than the lot of the poor, he is nevertheless attributed with the introduction of the common people on the Spanish stage as human characters, and not merely as ideas.

El señor feudal, first performed in 1896, is more significant than *Juan José*. A country girl is dishonoured by the middle class Tío Roque and avenged by her brother. Roque, farm manager to an Andalusian landowner, dotes on his son Carlos, whom he hopes to marry to the granddaughter of the Marquis of Atienza. Tío Juan is the sympathetic hero, his son Jaime being a 'new man', convinced of the need for technological progress, a man of the city. But Jaime retains some of the characteristics of Peribáñez and Pedro Crespo. The Marquis forbids the marriage of his daughter to Carlos, son of Roque, not on class gounds but on moral grounds. Dicenta's third social drama *Daniel* (1906), set in a mining community, is less convincing than the others.

Among his *sainetes* and *zarzuelas* were *El duque de Gandía* (1894), *Curro Vargas* (1898), and *La cortijera* (1899). *El crimen de ayer* (1904) showed an artist in decline, as in the melodramatic *El lobo* (1913), on a convict redeemed by love. Dicenta's autobiographical *Sobrevivirse* shows an artist who loses favour with the public, compromises, but finally realizes that he will not again be appreciated, and commits suicide.

Dicenta's novels, little read today, include *Galerna* (1911), *Los bárbaros* (1912), *Encarnación* (1913), *De la vida que pasa* (1914), *Mi Venus* (1915), and *Paraíso perdido* (1917). *Novelas* (Paris, 1913) comprises 'El idilio de Pedrín', 'Idos y muertos', 'Infanticida', and 'Sol de invierno'.

See A. González-Blanco, *Los dramaturgos españoles contemporáneos* (1st series), 1917).

DICKMANN, MAX (1902–   ), b. Buenos Aires. Argentinian journalist, novelist, and translator.

A member of the Boedo group in Buenos Aires, committed to social reform. His themes include the problems of immigration, Jewish integration, poverty, and injustice. He is a master, with Leónidas Barletta and Lorenzo Stanchina, of the proletarian novel. The short stories collected in *Europa* (1930) were followed by his best-known novel, *Madre América* (1935), an epic in the style of John Dos Passos, whom he translated into Spanish. It takes as a microcosm of Latin America the little town of San Itatí in the Paraná delta, and the characters Gabriel, a fatalist, Perfecto, an idealist, and Faustina, an old witch. The language is brisk and vivid, but Dickmann occasionally slips from the epic to the trivial. *Gente* (1936) contrasts the rise of *nouveaux riches* such as Oscar Lunel with the decadence of the old aristocracy exemplified by Julia Roca-mara. *Los frutos amargos* (1941) is set in Rosario, where Ana Allison, daughter of English parents, marries Walter Phelps. Rosario is a city with many immigrants of whom the English are regarded as the least adaptable, so that the scene is set for a conflict between Walter, an anti-Argentinian and Ana, who tries to become integrated into her new home.

Esta generación perdida (1945) reflects Dickmann's concern with post-war Argentina, the unlikable hero, Francisco San Millán, sacrificing his ex-lover Flora for his own ends. *El motín de los ilusos* (1949) deals with a revolution, but the 'revolutionary' is a shadowy figure and the novel lacks conviction. Dickmann's later works include *Los habitantes de la noche* (1952), *El dinero no cree en Dios* (1958), and *Los atrapados* (1962). Dickmann has attracted little critical attention.

See Ethel Kurkat's 'Max Dickmann: el novelista y el hombre' in *Revista Iberoamericana*, vol. 8, no. 15 (May–November 1944), pp. 49–56.

Dictadura, Generación de la, a name frequently given to the *Generación del 1927* (q.v.).

DIEGO, ELISEO (1920–), b. Havana. Cuban poet and short-story writer whose early work was published in the influential magazine *Orígenes*, founded in 1944 by José Lezama Lima (q.v.) and José Rodríguez Feo.

Diego travelled widely in Europe and the U.S.A., acquiring a profound sympathy with English literature. He is identified with pre-revolutionary circles including Eugenio Florit and Mariano Brull, being concerned with pure poetry rather than with patriotic themes. *En la calzada de Jesús del Monte* (1949) is one of his best collections of poetry, but his short stories are equally successful, especially the volume *Divertimentos* (1946).

DIEGO, JOSÉ DE (1868–1918), b. Aguadilla. Puerto Rican poet and politician. While studying in Spain he was gaoled for agitating in favour of liberal republicanism. While in Barcelona in 1887 he wrote his first book, the essays *Jovillos* (Barcelona, 1904), which are in the patriotic tradition of R. E. Betances and E. M. de Hostos.

Los grandes infames (1885) is a set of 26 sonnets. *Sor Ana* (1887) is an irreverent long poem. His later poetry was published in *Pomarrosas* (Barcelona, 1904), the bombastic patriotic songbook *Cantos de rebeldía* (1916), and the posthumously-published *Cantos de pitirre* (Palma de Mallorca, 1950).

DIEGO CENDOYA, GERARDO (1896–), b. Santander. Poet, anthologist, and musicologist. He studied under the Jesuits at Deusto, at Salamanca, and in Madrid, then taught literature in Soria, Gijón, Santander, and Madrid. He has lectured on music, and has produced good anthologies, among them *Antología poética en honor de Góngora desde Lope de Vega a Rubén Darío*, and *Poesía española contemporánea* (1932; new edn. [1901–34] 1949). He took part in both the *ultraísta* and *creacionista* movements. A poet in many styles, he founded two magazines to reflect his catholic tastes: *Carmen* for the cultivated poem and *Lola* for the simple.

Iniciales (1918) consists of regional and intimate poetry. *El romancero de la novia* (1920; rewritten, 1944) is a youthful collection perhaps too self-indulgent in its sentimentality. *Imagen* (1922) is a *creacionista* work in the mode of Huidobro (q.v.). *Soria* (ltd. edn., Valladolid, 1923; 2nd edn., Santander, 1948) contains sonnets on Spanish subjects. *Manual de espumas* (1924; 2nd edn., 1941) reverts to *avant-garde* techniques, whereas *Versos humanos* (1925), traditional in form, was joint-winner of the National Prize for Literature with Rafael Alberti's *Marinero en tierra* that year.

Later collections follow fashion rather than dictate it: *La sorpresa* (1944), *La luna en el desierto* (Santander, 1949), *Limbo* (Las Palmas, 1951), *Biografía incompleta* (1953). Then followed *Viacrucis* (Santander, 1931), the gongoristic *Fábula de Equis y Zeda* (Mexico City, 1932), *Poemas adrede* (Mexico City, 1932; new edn., 1943), the religious *Ángeles de Compostela* (1940; new edn., 1961), *Alondra de verdad* (1941), *Amazona* (1955; 2nd edn., 1956), *Égloga de Antonio Bienvenida* (Santander, 1956), *Paisaje con figuras* (Palma, 1956), *Canciones a Violante* (1959), *La suerte o la muerte* (1963) on bullfighting, *El Jándalo* (1964), *Poesía amorosa* (1965), *El cordobés dilucidado* (1966), *Vuelta del peregrino* (1967), and *La fundación del querer* (1970).

See A. Gallego Morell, *Vida y poesía de Gerardo Diego* (Barcelona, 1955).

DIEGO DE ESTELLA, Fray (1524–78), b. Estella, Navarra. Franciscan mystical writer. He studied at Toulouse and Salamanca, and was known in the world as Diego Ballesteros y Cruzas. He lived for many years in Portugal, became confessor to Cardinal Granvelle (1517–86) and counsellor to Ruy Gómez de Silva, after whose death Fray Diego returned to his native town to write the mystical prose works which have given him a renown equal to that of Fray Juan de los Ángeles or S. Pedro de Alcántara.

These works were primarily doctrinal, and have little literary appeal apart from their representative quality in the popular devotional writing of the time. They are *Tratado de la vida, loores y excelencias del glorioso apóstol y bienaventurado euangelista san Iuan* (Lisbon, 1554; 2nd edn., Valencia, 1595); *Libro de la Vanidad del mundo* (Toledo, 1562), rewritten in three parts (3 vols., Salamanca, 1574); *In sacrosanctum Iesu Christi Domini nostri Evangelium secundum Lucam enarrationum* (Salamanca, 1575); *Meditaciones devotíssimas del amor de Dios* (Salamanca, 1576; new edn. by Ricardo León in 1920), Diego's most interesting work, in which he examines the meaning of 'the love of God' and shows a truly Franciscan feeling for the beauty of nature; and *Modus concionandi: et explanatio in Psalm. CXXXVI super flumina Babylonis* (Salamanca, 1576; ed. by P. Sagués Azcona, 2 vols., 1951).

See P. Sagués Azcona, *Fray Diego de Estella (1524–1578): apuntes para una biografía crítica* (Pamplona, 1950).

DIEGO DE VALENCIA DE LEÓN, Fray, see VALENCIA DE LEÓN, Fray Diego de.

DIEGO JOSÉ DE CÁDIZ, Beato, see CÁDIZ, Beato Diego José.

DIEGO PADRÓ, JOSÉ I. DE (1896–), b. Vega. Puerto Rican writer who travelled in Spain, France, and the U.S.A. in his youth, and in 1917 enlisted in the U.S. forces in Europe. *La última lámpara de los dioses* (1920; 2nd edn., 1950) is modernist poetry on pagan themes. His novel *En Babia: el manuscrito de un braquicéfalo* (1940) is set in Harlem, the Bowery, and other sleazy parts of New York, the hero being an intellectual, and the heroine a masochistic pervert; it falls into the broad naturalistic tradition of the Puerto Rican novel exemplified by Alejandro Tapia and Manuel Zeno-Gandía.

In 1921 Diego and Luis Palés Matos founded the shortlived movement *diepalismo* (the name being derived from the first three letters of Diego and Palés), which stressed onomatopoeia in poetic language. Early French symbolist influence gave way to traces of Whitman in his later work. Interestingly, Diego denounced the young Afro-Antillian movement (in *El Mundo*, San Juan, 1932) as characterized by 'a lack of mental balance' and 'a morbid attempt to be original'.

DIÉGUEZ OLAVERRI, JUAN (1813–82), b. Guatemala City. Guatemalan poet. A liberal lawyer, he was persecuted until the liberal ascendency after the 27-year rule of Rafael Carrera (1838–65), when he was appointed Professor of Law in Guatemala University. His *Poesías líricas* (1893) were reissued as *Poesías* (1957), the best poem being an elegy for André Chénier called 'El cisne'.

See 'Juan Diéguez' by Salvador Falla in the *Biografías* of the Academia Guatemalteca, pp. 261–343.

DIESTE, RAFAEL (1899–), b. Rianjo, Corunna. Short-story writer, playwright, and essayist whose prose is careful, and often beautiful. A professional journalist, he spent many years with *El Pueblo Gallego*. A radical, he directed the theatre of the Misiones Pedagógicas during the Republican years and left Spain at the end of the Civil War, since when he has lived in Paris, Buenos Aires, Cambridge, and Nuevo León, Mexico. His best stories are collected in *Historias e invenciones de Félix Muriel* (Buenos Aires, 1943; reprinted 1974) and his essays in *La vieja piel del mundo* (1936), *Luchas con el desconfiado* (Buenos Aires, 1948), *Nuevo tratado del paralelismo* (Buenos Aires, 1955), and *Pequeña clave ortográfica* (Buenos Aires, 1959). In the early 1960s, Dieste returned to his home in Galicia.

His best play is *A fiestra valdeira* ('The empty window'), written in Galician in 1926 and first published in 1927. An interesting symbolist work, it deals with the return of the hero Miguel to Galicia after making his fortune in Brazil. A new portrait by a young painter shows him against the background of his former life, among seamen and wharves. His wife and daughter are more conscious of their new wealth, however, and ask for the background to be altered. The villagers subscribe to buy the painting as it is, but Don Miguel refuses to sell the painting he commissioned; he cuts out the background of the sea, and carries this tiny square of canvas away, having paid for the whole painting. Eventually, Miguel's wife and daughter rescue the missing fragment.

DÍEZ-BARROSO, VÍCTOR MANUEL (1890–1936), b. Mexico City. Mexican playwright and drama critic. His first play, *Las pasiones mandan* (1925) is conventional in theme and treatment, but in *Véncete a ti mismo* (1926) first performed in 1925, Díez-Barroso shows the influence of

Freud's ideas on the subconscious and of Pirandello's dramatic technique. Plays first produced in 1926 include *Una lágrima* and *Una farsa*. These were followed by *La muñeca rota* (1927) and *En 'El Riego'* (1929). His best work was *Él y su cuerpo* (first performed and published 1934) on the hero's burial granted to an aeroplane pilot and its aftermath, when the hero confesses to his mother and his friend that he had feigned death out of cowardice. At his own 'funeral' he had been so impressed by the respect shown to his memory by the townsfolk that he can no longer risk the shame of discovery and commits suicide. The play is based on a historical event recorded in Mexico. *Siete obras en un acto* (1935) is the only collection of his one-act plays.

DÍEZ-CANEDO, Enrique (1879–1944), b. Badajoz. Post-modernist poet. Literary critic on *Diario Universal* and drama critic on *El Sol* of Madrid. From 1939 Díez-Canedo lived in Mexico and taught at the Universidad Nacional Autónoma de México.

His poetry, influenced by Darío, Verlaine, and Jiménez, was collected in *Versos de las horas* (1906) and *La visita del sol* (1907); a more original note sounded in *La sombra del ensueño* (1910), *Algunos versos* (1924), and *Epigramas americanos* (1928). *El desterrado* (Mexico City, 1940) contains his poetry of exile. His literary journalism, which first appeared in 1921 (*Conversaciones literarias*, first series), is collected in the *Obras completas* (vol. 1, 1915–20, 1964; vol. 2, 1920–24, 1964; vol. 3, 1924–30, 1965; vol. 4, *Estudios de poesía española contemporánea*, 1965). Díez-Canedo's literary criticism includes *El teatro y sus enemigos* (Mexico City, 1939), *La nueva poesía* (1941), *Juan Ramón Jiménez en su obra* (1944), and *La poesía francesa del romanticismo al superrealismo* (Buenos Aires, 1945).

See R. Blanco-Fombona, 'Un poeta preterido: Enrique Díez-Canedo' in *Motivos y letras de España* (1930).

DÍEZ-CANSECO, José (1904–49), b. Lima. Peruvian social novelist influenced by the *Tradiciones peruanas* of Ricardo Palma (q.v.). *Suzy* (1929), Díez-Canseco's autobiographical novelette of his adolescent love, gave no indication of his future direction in *Estampas mulatas* (1930), a wide-ranging and sympathetic series of realistic sketches of life on the coast and in inland Peru. 'El gaviota' and 'Kilómetro 83' are the best of these ten stories of life in the Chinese community, among Negroes, priests, and criminals. Several first appeared in *Amauta*, and showed the author's mastery of speech rhythms and manners among the dispossessed. César Miró called Díez-Canseco the most Creole of all authors, his sketches and stories being full of animation, wit, and malice. The most deeply-felt observations of Lima are to be found in these works and in those of José Fernando (1903–47). *Duque* (Santiago, 1934) is a blistering satire on Lima's high society, of which Díez-Canseco was a member. His *Obras completas* appeared in 1949.

DÍEZ DE GÁMEZ, Gutierre (1378?–after 1448), Spanish chronicler of *El Victorial: crónica de don Pero Niño, conde de Buelna*, which he finished in 1448. Apart from his somewhat extravagant eulogies of Pero Niño (q.v.), Díez de Gámez writes engagingly, interspersing in his chronicle quotations from the *Libro de Alexandre* (q.v.), maxims and morals, ballads and roundelays, and a fine discourse in ch. 22 similar to that of Cervantes on arms and learning in *Quijote* I.38.

DÍEZ DE MEDINA, Fernando (1908–   ), b. La Paz. Bolivian literary historian, essayist, and controversialist. Profoundly incensed by what he considered the negativism of Alcides Arguedas (q.v.), Díez de Medina attacked him with the positive patriotic call of *Los valores negativos* (1929). In 1941 he published a reply to the U.S. Vice-President Henry Wallace's *The American choice* (1940): *¡Siéntate, hombre del Norte, y atiende al Sur!* and brusquely responded to Tamayo's *Para siempre* with *Para nunca*, pamphlets occasioned by his 'biografía fantástica', *Franz Tamayo, hechicero del Ande* (1942, 3rd edn., 1968). In 1951 he attacked Madariaga's biography *Simón Bolívar* (1949), and Toynbee's section on the Andes in *A study of history* in which Quechua history is discussed.

Díez de Medina founded the reformist political movement *Pachakutismo* in 1948, the first salvo of his attack being his pamphlet *Pachakuti* (1948), meaning 'The Reformer', which was against the powerful mining interests in Bolivia and in favour of the masses, the second *Siripaka* (1949), and the third *Ainoka* (1950). His essays *Thunupa* (1947) and his prose poem *Nayjama* (1950) created a sense of nationalism among the youth of the post-war generation. His *Libro de los misterios* (1951) is symbolic theatre in the style of Claudel; *La enmascarada y otros cuentos* is a collection of fantastic stories lacking much originality, their language inflated rather than poetic; his idiosyncratic history *Literatura boliviana* (1953) was reprinted in Madrid (1959).

DIFÍCIL, EL, pseudonym used in the Academia del Buen Gusto by Alfonso de Verdugo Castilla (q.v.).

¡Di, panadera! Spanish satirical *coplas* written after the Battle of Olmedo (1445), in which Juan II and Don Álvaro de Luna defeated the rebellious barons, only twenty-two men dying altogether. Rincón has suggested that the barons were 'more cruelly dealt with in the *coplas* than on the field of battle'.

The *coplas* are found in two versions: one with the refrain *¡Ay, panadera!*, in the 15th-c. *Cancionero* owned by B. J. Gallardo, and the other in a MS. in the library of M. Menéndez y Pelayo, where they are attributed, almost certainly without foundation, to Juan de Mena. It is the former version which Rincón publishes in his *Coplas satíricas y dramáticas de la Edad Media* (1968).

DISCÉPOLO, ARMANDO (1887–), Argentinian dramatist, who wrote most of his *sainetes* with Rafael de Rosa, among them *El chueco Pintos* on a villager who aims to become the local police chief but ends up in gaol; and *El movimiento continuo. El Conservatorio de La Armonía* satirizes professional musicians, while *Stéfano* (1928) ridicules a failed orchestral musician. Using the popular *sainete* genre as both model and vehicle, Discépolo also created a more ambitious work: *Relojero* (1934), with Pirandellian overtones.

His theme is the continual frustration of human ambition, and his manner is grotesque, in one way anticipating the theatre of the absurd. Three such neo-*sainetes* were collected in *Tres grotescos* (1958).

Discreto, El (Huesca, 1646), a didactic work by Baltasar Gracián y Morales (q.v.). Two editions appeared in 1646.

Like Gracián's *Héroe* and *Oráculo manual*, the book is a handbook for a virtuous and a happy life, which Gracián believes can be achieved only through the exercise of prudence. Among the many maxims are the following: to spend the first third of one's life with the dead (that is, with books written by the ancients and more recent authors), the second third with the living (that is, in conversation with the wise, in travel, and in exploring the wonders of art and nature), and the last third with oneself (in meditation); to bide one's time in patience; to be all things to all men; never to lose one's temper; to be both diligent and intelligent.

Gracián (writing as 'Lorenzo Gracián') takes as his model of the 'prudent man' the *impavidus vir* of Horace, and the 'wise man' of Machiavelli. There is a critical edition by M. Romera-Navarro and J. M. Furt (Buenos Aires, 1960).

Discurso poético contra el hablar culto y oscuro (1624), by Juan Martínez de Jáuregui y Hurtado de la Sal (see JÁUREGUI). An attack on *culteranismo* (q.v.) or *gongorismo* which amplifies the objections already made to the poetry of

Góngora and his school by Jáuregui in the prologue to his *Rimas* (Seville, 1618). Jáuregui also wrote in 1624 *Antídoto contra la pestilente poesía de las Soledades* (specifically against Góngora, q.v.), but this was not published until 1899.

See E. J. Gates, *Documentos gongorinos* (Mexico City, 1960).

Disputa de Elena y María, a 13th-c. *debate* by a Leonese author written in imitation of a Picardy original, *Le jugement d'amour*. Also known as the *Disputa del clérigo y del caballero*, the incomplete text consists of 402 lines of irregular metre and deals with the argument between Elena and María as to the merits of their respective sweethearts, a knight and an abbot. María praises the cleric's comfortable life, with money, servants, and good food. Elena rejoins 'Somos hermanas y fijas de algo, / mais yo amo el mais alto, / ca es caballero armado, / de sus armas esforzado; / el mio es defensor, / el tuyo es orador: / que el mio defende tierras / e sufre batallas y guerras, / ca el tuyo yante e yaz / y siempre está en paz'. They go before a king for his decision, but the MS. ends before the result is awarded.

R. Menéndez Pidal, who found the MS. and published it in facsimile in the *Revista de Filología Española*, vol. 1 (1914), pp. 52–96, refers to its satirical intent and traces its continuity in the *Libro de buen amor* (q.v.). Menéndez Pidal's edition and study in *Tres poetas primitivos* (revised edn., 1958) is in Colección Austral.

See Giuseppe Tavani, 'Il dibattito sul chierico e il cavaliere nella tradizione mediolatina e volgare' in *Romanistisches Jahrbuch*, vol. 15 (1964), pp. 73–79.

Disputa del alma y del cuerpo, a fragment of 37 lines of a late 12th-c. *debate* in *mester de juglaría*. It was found on a parchment dated 1201 in the Monastery of Oña.

It is translated from the French *Débat du corps et de l'âme* which itself derives from the Latin *Rixa animi et corporis*. The theme is the debate between a man's soul and body, each blaming the other for the man's faults during life. In the Oña fragment, only the soul's argument survives.

It was first published by P. J. Pidal as 'Fragmento inédito de un poema castellano antiguo' in *Diario Español* (22 June 1856) and edited with facsimile by R. Menéndez Pidal in *RABM*, vol. 4 (1900), pp. 449–453.

See P. Groult, 'La disputa del alma y el cuerpo: sources et originalité' in *Homenaje a Helmut Hatzfeld* (Washington, 1964). The topos occurs in Golden Age drama, at its best in Calderón's *auto sacramental* 'El pleito matrimonial del alma y del cuerpo' (ed. A. Solalinde) in *Hispanic Review* (1933).

DOBLADO, Leucadio, a pseudonym used by José María Blanco White (q.v.).

DOBLES, Fabián (1918–   ), b. San Antonio de Belén, Costa Rica. Novelist, short-story writer, and poet, of Marxist leanings. He identifies himself with the poor in *Ese que llaman pueblo* (1942). Vivid naturalism pervades this story of a peasant forced to borrow money at exorbitant interest rates in order to marry, his situation deteriorating every day. *El sitio de las obras* (Guatemala City, 1950) explores the problem of the inequitable distribution of land. His other novels include the quasi-surrealist *Una burbuja en el limbo* (1946), in which he created the Costa Rican peasant Tata Mundo, the narrator of the short stories in *Historias de Tata Mundo* (1955) and *El Maijú* (1957). A collection of *Cuentos* appeared in 1971.

DOBLES SEGREDA, Luis (1890–1956), b. Heredia, Costa Rica. Historian, bibliographer, and *costumbrista*. Having taught in Costa Rica, where he became Secretary of Public Education, he went to the U.S.A. and taught geography in Marquette University and Spanish in Louisiana State Normal College. He represented Costa Rica as a diplomat in Argentina, Chile, and several European countries.

Dobles Segreda compiled the notable *Índice bibliográfico de Costa Rica* (9 vols., 1927–36) and devoted much of his time to a detailed record of Heredia: *Por el amor de Dios* (1918) on five beggars; *Caña brava* (1926) on childhood reminiscences; and *Fadrique Gutiérrez* (1954), evoking colonial times.

Doctor Centeno, El (1883), one of the *Novelas españolas contemporáneas* of Benito Pérez Galdós (qq.v.).

The boy Felipe Centeno, who appeared in *Marianela* (q.v., 1878) is a *pícaro* in the sense of serving many masters, as in Jerónimo de Alcalá Yáñez de Ribera's *Alonso, mozo de muchos amos* (qq.v.), as opposed to the low-life sense of *Rinconete y Cortadillo* (q.v.).

El doctor Centeno is a novel of observation, not action. Felipe Centeno, on his way to Madrid 'para estudiar mucho a fin de llegar a ser médico' is given lessons, in return for domestic service, by the schoolmaster-priest Pedro Polo. The scenes at Don Pedro's school, doubtless inspired by Cabra's establishment in Quevedo's *El buscón* (qq.v.), also resemble those at Dickens's Dotheboys Hall in *Nicholas Nickleby*. One evening, while running an errand, Felipe sees Don Pedro on an assignation and is dismissed. The would-be doctor is then taken under the wing of the generous Romantic poet Alejandro

Miquis, who is studying law, and the vivid pictures of Doña Virginia's hostelry where they lodge are reminiscent of Todgers's boarding-house in *Martin Chuzzlewit*. The lovable Alejandro finally dies of consumption, leaving 'Doctor' Centeno on his own again.

This book presents the usurer Torquemada (q.v.) for the first time. Pérez Galdós created a series of four novels about this obsessed anti-hero, who makes his final appearance in *Amadeo I* (1910). The sequel to *El doctor Centeno*, continuing the adventures of Felipe Centeno, is *Tormento* (q.v.).

Dodecasílabos, lines of twelve syllables. The simple, or dactylic type of dodecasyllable is stressed on the 2nd, 5th, 8th, and 11th syllables.

> *Bendice mil veces, bendice, alma mía,*
> *en himno sonoro al Dios de Israel,*
> *que mano y clemente visita su pueblo*
> *y fuerte quebranta el yugo cruel.*
>
> —Lista

A *compuesto* type may consist of either two six-syllable hemistichs or two unequal hemistichs in the combinations 7,5; 5,7; or 8,4, the last noted by Nebrija (q.v.) in his grammar, but rare. The 5,7 *compuesto* was used by Santos Chocano (q.v.) in his *Momia incaica*. Sor Juana de la Cruz (q.v.) often used the 7,5 *compuesto*, as in these lines from the *Nocturnos* (1679):

> —*Plaza, plaza, que sibe vibrando rayos.*
> —*¿Cómo, qué? — Aparten, digo,*
> *y háganle campo.*
> *Abate allá, que viene, y a puntillazos*
> *les sabrá al sol y luna romper los cascos.*

Dolophatos, see Sendebar.

DOMENCHINA, Juan José (1898–1959), b. Madrid. Novelist, poet, and critic. He wrote reviews for *El Sol* as 'Gerardo Rivera' collected as *Crónicas . . .* and *Nuevas crónicas de Gerardo Rivera*. His poetry, *culterano* in diction and baroque in form, is modelled on Quevedo, Valéry, and Juan Ramón Jiménez. The collections are *Del poema eterno* (1917; 2nd edn., 1922), *Las interrogaciones del silencio* (1918; 3rd edn., 1922), *La corporeidad de lo abstracto* (1929), *El tacto fervoroso* (1930), *Dédalo* (1932), *Margen* (1933), *Elegías barrocas* (1934), and *Poesías completas* (1936).

His novels are original and equally cerebral: *El hábito* (1926) and *La túnica de Neso* (1929), the latter showing the neuroses of the intellectual Arturo during the last week of his life.

After his marriage to the poet Ernestina de Champourcin (q.v.) and his exile to Mexico, he published *Destierro* (1942), *Pasión de sombra*

(1944), *Exul umbra* (Mexico City, 1948), *La sombra desterrada* (Mexico City, 1950), *El extrañado: 25 sonetos, 1948–57* (Mexico City, 1958), and the collected *Poesía, 1942–1958* (1975).

See 'Juan José Domenchina, poeta de la sombra' by Concha Zardoya in her *Poesía española contemporánea* (1961), pp. 397–410.

DOMÍNGUEZ, José de Jesús (1843–98), b. Añasca. Puerto Rican poet and historian who studied medicine in Paris and served in the French army during the Franco-Prussian War. He wrote *Los jíbaros de Puerto Rico* and *Prehistoria de Bunken*, as well as the incomplete *Historia del lenguaje y la civilización*.

His early poetry was influenced by Espronceda and Bécquer: *Poesías de Gerardo Alcides* (1879) and *Odas elegíacas* (1883); but *Las huríes blancas* (1886) is a long poem startlingly anticipating the Modernism of Darío (q.v.). Domínguez wrote *El sueño de una cacica* (1892), a one-act play to celebrate the quatercentenary of the discovery of America.

See Ana María Losada, 'Un precursor del Modernismo en Puerto Rico' in *Asomante*, III, 1 (Jan.–March 1947).

DOMÍNGUEZ, Luis L. (1819–98), b. Buenos Aires. Argentinian historian. From 1878 he was in the diplomatic service in Peru, Brazil, U.S.A., Spain, and England. His family left for Uruguay in 1834.

Domínguez is represented in many anthologies by his patriotic poem 'El ombú', but his main achievement is the *Historia argentina, 1492–1820* (1861) described by Sarmiento as excellent.

DOMÍNGUEZ, Ramiro (1929–), Paraguayan poet of the Generation of '50. A contributor to *Alcor* (q.v.); his books include *Zumos* (1962), and *Salmos a deshora* (1963). In 1953 he published *Poesía* with José Luis Appleyard (q.v.) and others.

DOMÍNGUEZ ALBA, Bernardo (1904–), Panamanian poet, novelist, and short-story writer more familiar under his pseudonym 'Rogelio Sinán'. His collection *Onda* (Rome, 1929), proposed a complete break with traditional verse, and influenced among others Gaspar Octavio Hernández (1893–1918) and Roque Xavier Laurenza (b. 1910). Sinán's later poetry included *Incendio* (1944) and *Semana santa en la niebla* (1949). His fiction, erotic and psychological, with a Pirandellian flavour, includes the novel *Plenilunio* (1947), and the short stories in *La boina roja y cinco cuentos* (1954) and *Los pájaros del sueno* (1958). His most recent writing is for the stage but is so far unpublished.

DOMÍNGUEZ BASTIDA, Gustavo Adolfo, see Bécquer, Gustavo Adolfo.

DOMÍNGUEZ CAMARGO, Hernando (1601 ?–1656), b. Bogotá. Colombian epic poet. For some years Domínguez Camargo lived in Lima and was a member of the Jesuit order, but he is believed to have abandoned the Society towards the end of his life, and died as the parish priest of Guatavita.

He is best known as the author of an unfinished, gongoristic poem in 1,117 *octavas reales*, *S. Ignacio de Loyola, fundador de la Compañía de Iesús: poema heroyco* (Madrid, 1666). All the traditional techniques of Góngora and his school were utilized, combining unfamiliar American plant-names with exotic metaphors, classical constructions, and mythology, alliteration, and hyperbaton. An edition by F. Arbeláez (Bogotá, 1956) adds some shorter poems, but the most convenient edition is the *Obras* (ed. R. Torres Quintero, Bogotá, 1966).

Short poems by Domínguez Camargo were included by Jacinto de Evia in his *Ramillete de varias flores poéticas recogidas y cultivadas en los primeros abriles de sus años* (Madrid, 1676), the best being 'A un salto por donde se despeña el arroyo de Chile', inspired by a description of a brook in the second of Góngora's *Soledades*.

The authenticity of most, if not all, of the works attributed to Domínguez Camargo was questioned by Aurelio Espinosa Pólit in *Revista Javeriana* (Bogotá), no. 253 (April 1959).

See Emilio Carilla, *Hernando Domínguez Camargo: estudio y selección* (Buenos Aires, 1948); G. Diego, 'La poesía de Hernando Domínguez Camargo en nuevas vísperas' in *Thesaurus* (Bogotá), vol. 16 (1961), pp. 281–310; and G. Meo Zilio, *Estudio sobre Hernando Domínguez Camargo y su 'S. Ignacio de Loyola, poema heroyco'* (1967).

DOMINICI, Pedro César (1872–1954), Venezuelan novelist. As a journalist and subsequently a diplomat, he resided for many years outside Caracas. He launched the shortlived but significant magazine *Cosmopolis* (1894–5), with Coll and Urbaneja Achelpohl (qq.v.), to embrace all the literary styles of all nations.

Dominici himself was influenced by French poets, especially the Parnassians, and even *Dionysos* (1904), his novel of Alexandria in the 1st c. B.C., owes more to the *Aphrodite* (1896) of Pierre Louÿs than to the historical Greeks, especially as regards the sensualism and exoticism of Dominici's style and vocabulary. But *Dionysos* was a great advance on *La tristeza voluptuosa* (1899), set in Dominici's familiar Latin Quarter of Paris, and he was tempted to more historical reconstructions such as *El triunfo del ideal* (Paris, 1901; 2nd edn., Buenos Aires, 1928) set in the Italian Renaissance period and written in the manner of D'Annunzio. Only in *El cóndor* (1925) did Dominici turn to an indigenous theme, centring on the Inca Atahuallpa's quarrel with Huáscar and the Spanish conquest of Peru.

Dominici called his autobiography *Bajo el sol de otoño: del bosque de mis recuerdos* (Buenos Aires, 1947).

See also Julio Garet Mas, *Semblanzas de Pedro César Dominici* (Montevideo, 1961).

Doña Bárbara (Barcelona, 1929), a famous *novela de la tierra* by the Venezuelan Rómulo Gallegos (q.v.).

Though this is a work in the dominant Latin-American literary movement of *criollismo* (q.v.), in an important sense it is also a transposition of Pérez Galdós's *Doña Perfecta* (qq.v.) to a Venezuelan setting. The lovely Bárbara, a *mestiza*, was raped when young, and has taken vengeance on the male sex by fraud and the unscrupulous use of her body to become the owner of a large *hacienda* north of the Orinoco. She plans to obtain the neighbouring Luzardo estate, but fails to seduce the young Santos Luzardo, who loves Barbara's daughter Marisela. Confronted with what she believes to be the alternatives of surrendering her estate or killing Marisela, she decides on the former, and disappears mysteriously.

The characters take on symbolic roles: Santos Luzardo representing virtue (the missionary aspect of *civilización* opposing the *barbarie* of the *llanos*, or plains) and Doña Bárbara representing savagery and blind instinct. Like the protagonist of Alejo Carpentier's *Los pasos perdidos* (qq.v.), Santos returns to his primal nature to find himself but also to kill that part of the centaur which he knows to be half beast. Gallegos may deplore the wildness of Bárbara, but in the novel he manages to express her significance with vigour and acute sympathy.

See Mariano Picón Salas, *A veinte años de 'Doña Bárbara'* (Mexico City, 1959) and D. L. Shaw, *Gallegos: 'Doña Bárbara'* (London, 1972).

DONADO, ALFONSO, pseudonym of Dámaso Alonso (q.v.).

Doña Luz (1879), a novel by Juan Valera (q.v.).

In *Pepita Jiménez* (q.v.), Valera had explored the theme of a seminarist's vocation being shaken by his unplatonic love of a woman. The hero of that book, Luis, did not choose to take his final vows, but married Pepita instead. In *Doña Luz*, however, Fr. Enrique has been a priest for many years, and has returned from his mission to the Philippines at the age of 40 to recuperate

in the Andalusian town of 'Villafría'. Luz, at twenty-seven, is a more complex character than Valera's other heroines. A victim of pride, she is poor and illegitimate, but being of noble blood she considers the local gentry beneath her, and is still unmarried.

Enrique and Luz are mutually attracted, but when the newly-elected deputy to the district, Don Jaime de Pimentel, arrives and proposes to Luz, she is swept off her feet and marries him. While Pimentel is in Madrid to set up their home, Luz discovers that her mother, whom she had never known, has just died and left her an immense fortune. Luz also learns that Pimentel had known about the inheritance before he proposed to her and she breaks with him. Enrique, deprived both by his vocation and· Luz's marriage of any chance of enjoying her love, suffers an apoplectic stroke and dies. Only on reading a confession he wrote just before his death does Luz recognize that her feelings for Enrique were as deep as his for her.

The novel's moral ambiguity lies in the fact that Valera, in the dedicatory note, proposes platonic love as a solution to Enrique's problem, though we discover that Enrique attempts such a solution and fails. As recently as *Pepita Jiménez* (1874), Valera had categorically rejected platonic love: it is the enforced celibacy of the Church which prevents 'natural love' from taking its course, and critics are now agreed that the dedicatory note was inserted to placate the kind of opposition aroused by *Pepita*.

Valera does not use mystical language ironically in *Doña Luz*, for Enrique's vocation may be genuine though his mysticism is false.

Luz is shown as a victim of reading romantic fiction: she believes in 'true', disinterested love, and is bitterly disappointed that Jaime loves her not despite her poverty (as she had thought) but because of her wealth. Yet she never changes, and she believes that by an effort of will she will be able to make her baby resemble Enrique, who really loved her, when the reader knows, with Valera, that he will probably cause her sorrow, as his father had done. In its examination of impossible ideals (Luz's false view of perfect human love) and of the effects of pernicious fiction, *Doña Luz* owes something to Cervantes' *Quijote*. There is a good edition of *Doña Luz* by Benito Varela Jácome (1970).

See J. F. Montesinos, *Valera o la ficción libre* (1957).

Doña Perfecta (1876), one of the *Novelas españolas de la primera época* by Benito Pérez Galdós (qq.v.).

A young engineer, Pepe Rey, goes to the provincial town of Orbajosa at his father's suggestion to seek the hand of his cousin Rosario, who lives there with her wealthy mother Doña Perfecta and Perfecta's brother-in-law, an engaging bibliophile called Cayetano Polentinos. But Doña Perfecta is quickly induced by her confessor Padre Inocencio (another ironical name) to favour the claims of Jacintillo (son of his niece María Remedios) as a suitor for Rosario.

A fanatical Roman Catholic and Carlist, Doña Perfecta is easily persuaded by Padre Inocencio that the liberal Pepe is both immoral and an atheist, though in fact he is simply frank, tolerant, and loving. War is waged on Pepe, at first hypocritically and, when that fails, openly. Rumours fill the squares of Orbajosa, he is expelled from cathedral worship for alleged irreverence, and finally he is forbidden to see Rosario, who is shut up in her room. But Pepe defiantly declares that he will marry Rosario even without her mother's consent, and arranges to meet her at midnight in the garden of her house. María Remedios informs Perfecta of the plan. Perfecta arranges with the guerrilla leader Caballuco to shoot the young man, and when he is found dead not only states that he committed suicide, but also that he must therefore be denied Christian burial. Pepe's death sends Rosario out of her wits and she is sent to a lunatic asylum. But Perfecta is also going mad at the end of the novel; Inocencio is remorseful and leaves on a pilgrimage to Rome.

The Carlist troubles of the period are clearly if not subtly, reflected in Galdós's *roman à thèse* which offended many Spanish critics, among them Menéndez y Pelayo, by the forcefulness of its attack on the clergy's domination of provincial society in general, and provincial women in particular. The tragic figure of Pepe Rey is comparable to that of Ana Ozores, victim and protagonist of Clarín's *La Regenta* (q.v.). The related novels of Pérez Galdós on religious bigotry are *Gloria* and *La familia de León Roch* (qq.v.). Pepe, like several other later heroes of Galdós, is a Christ-like figure, aged 33 and bearded, sent by his father to a backward community whose members see themselves as a chosen race, who is accused of trying to overthrow religion, and of wanting to destroy the temple (his enemies accused him of hoping to demolish Orbajosa Cathedral). The local people prefer to him the Barabbas-figure of Caballuco and as true 'defenders of the faith' are destroying, like the Jews they so condemn, the man who might well have been the 'saviour' (at least in a material sense) of poor, backward Orbajosa. There is a glimmer of hope in the possibility that, though Pepe will not rise from the dead, the progress and liberalism that he represents will inevitably conquer, just as Christianity flourished after the death of Christ. Various scriptural references help to reinforce the symbolism, such as the 'Yo me lavo las manos' of Inocencio.

Galdós intended the novel as a document in the long debate on religious liberty in Spain, made topical at that moment by discussions in the Cortes. He viewed the accession of the Bourbon monarchy in 1874 as a threat to the libertarian gains made by the Revolution of 1868.

See R. Cardona's introduction to *Doña Perfecta* (New York, 1965); C. A. Jones, 'Galdós' second thoughts on "Doña Perfecta"' in *Modern Language Review*, vol. 54 (1959), pp. 570–3; and J. E. Varey, *Pérez Galdós: 'Doña Perfecta'* (London, 1971).

Doña Rosita la soltera, o El lenguaje de las flores, a play by Federico García Lorca (q.v.) first staged in Barcelona in 1935, but written at least ten years earlier. Though the performance was a triumph, with Margarita Xirgu in the main rôle, the play was condemned as 'political' because of certain comments against the rich, and it never reached Madrid.

The three acts of the play show three periods in Rosita's life: at the age of 20, in 1885; at 35, in 1900; and at 46, in 1911. In Act 1, Rosita, an orphan, is in love with her cousin, who decides to go for a while to help his father in South America. Rosita's uncle, with whom she is living, is preoccupied with the development of new rose types, especially the *rosa mutabile* which is red in the morning, white in the afternoon, and loses its leaves at nightfall. Rosita's aunt gossips endlessly with her housekeeper and with three young ladies who come to visit.

In Act 2, change has come upon Granada with the arrival of industry. Rosita is still waiting for the promised return of her cousin. The three spinsters of the first act return, and the housekeeper remains worried about Rosita's future.

Act 3 takes place in a poorer house to which the women have been forced to move after the death of Rosita's uncle. The cousin writes to say that he has been married for the last eight years, and the last of Rosita's cherished illusions vanishes. Lorca contrasts the fragrant and gentle Rosita (the 'rose' representing both beauty and transience) with the dour and petty struggles for existence which go on around her; his art is to evade the charge of boredom while necessarily inflicting on the audience a realistic portrayal of routine in a dull house inhabited by mainly dull people. Doña Rosita herself is not an individual, but a type, as conceived by Lorca in the *Libro de poemas* (1921). She promises life and beauty like a rose as its petals open and ends like a rose as its petals fall. Lorca considered Rosita a symbol of his lost youth in Granada; some critics have pointed to the similarity between her last scene and the close of Chekhov's play *The cherry orchard*, both nostalgic for a decayed past. The theme of frustrated womanhood recurs in the more important plays *Bodas de sangre* (1933), *Yerma* (1934), and *La casa de Bernarda Alba* (1936, qq.v.).

Don Juan. The origin of the Don Juan theme as that of a heartless libertine punished by divine retribution personified by a stone guest has been attributed by Víctor Said Armesto (*La leyenda de Don Juan*, 1908) to Spanish sources. The modern prototype (though not in fact the earliest chronologically) of plays about Don Juan is the tragedy of *El burlador de Sevilla y convidado de piedra*, by Tirso de Molina (qq.v.), the source of adaptations by Molière, Goldoni, Byron, Pushkin, and Montherlant. Mozart's opera *Don Giovanni* is true to the traditional tragic ending, but Antonio de Zamora (q.v.) leaves the seducer's fate to the imagination of the audience in *No hay plazo que no se cumpla ni deuda que no se pague, y convidado de piedra* which, with Prosper Mérimée's *Les âmes du Purgatoire* (1825) and *Don Juan de Marana; ou, La chute d'un ange* (1836), were the sources of the most popular Spanish play on the subject: José Zorrilla's *Don Juan Tenorio* (1844), in which the hero is redeemed by the love of a chaste woman.

   La Regenta (q.v.) is the major treatment of the theme by Leopoldo Alas (q.v.), who taught Pérez de Ayala (q.v.) at Oviedo University; the latter's *Tigre Juan* follows the theory of Marañón (q.v.) that the Don Juan type is possibly effeminate and probably sexually insecure. Azorín and Jacinto Grau (qq.v.) are among other 20th-c. authors who have employed the Don Juan theme.

DONOSO, José (1924–), b. Santiago. Chilean novelist and short-story writer, who now lives in Spain. His family belonged to the professional classes. After three years at the Instituto Pedagógico of Chile University, he went to Princeton University for two years, obtaining the B.A. in 1951. He taught English at the Instituto Pedagógico of the Catholic University of Santiago and at the School of Journalism in the Chile University. His short stories in *Veraneo* won the Municipal Prize in 1956, and he has also written *El Charleston*.

   His novels *Coronación* (Santiago, 1957) and *Este domingo* (1967) attacked the idle rich in Santiago. *El lugar sin límites* (1967) is set in the countryside, its anti-hero Don Alejo being a wealthy landowner who is also a consummate rogue and lecher.

   El obsceno pájaro de la noche (1970) was revised by the author for the English translation by H. St. Martin and Leonard Mades (New York,

1973; London, 1974) called *The obscene bird of night*. The novel is told largely by a deaf and dumb man who was once secretary to Don Jerónimo, a rich landowner one of whose properties is a squalid Catholic retreat populated by orphans, cripples, and beggarwomen. Iris, an orphan, manages to escape one night and becomes pregnant. The novel, in vivid and often surrealistic language, concentrates on the atmosphere of decay, despair, and delirium which Donoso clearly identifies with the world he lives in. It is one of the most powerful novels to emerge from Spanish America.

   See H. Vidal, *José Donoso: surrealismo y rebelión de los instintos* (1972).

DONOSO CORTÉS, Marqués de Valdegamas, Juan (1809–1853), b. Valle de la Serena, Badajoz. Political and religious essayist. A monarchist and fervent Roman Catholic whose last and most important work collected in his *Obras* (5 vols., 1854–5, ed. G. Tejado) is the *Ensayo sobre el catolicismo, el liberalismo, y el socialismo* (1851). Donoso, then Spanish ambassador to France, describes how he was converted from his youthful allegiance to liberalism, which he now identifies with socialism, and defends Roman Catholicism against both. Translated at once into French and Italian, the book produced much controversy due to its intemperate tone. Fitzmaurice-Kelly observed that 'he writes with eloquence and fire and with a belief in his own infallibility that has no parallel in literature'.

   Carlos Valverde has edited Donoso Cortés's *Obras completas* (2 vols., 1970) for the Biblioteca de Autores Cristianos.

DONOSO NOVOA, Armando (1887–1946), b. Talca. Chilean essayist and critic, who occasionally wrote humorous sketches under the pen-name 'Gilko Orellana'.

   Los nuevos: la joven literatura chilena (Valencia, 1913) was the first of his several texts and anthologies devoted to Chilean letters, the largest being *Nuestros poetas: antología chilena moderna* (1924) and the best *Algunos cuentos chilenos* (Buenos Aires, 1943; 2nd edn., 1945).

   Among his other literary essays were *Bilbao y su tiempo*, *Menéndez y Pelayo y su obra* (both 1913), and *La sombra de Goethe* (Madrid, 1916). Donoso's autobiography is *Recuerdos de cincuenta años* (1947).

Don Quijote de la Mancha, El ingenioso hidalgo, see Quijote de la Mancha, El ingenioso hidalgo Don.

Don Segundo Sombra, (San Antonio de Areco, 1926), an idealized novel of the Argentinian pampas by Ricardo Güiraldes (q.v.), in which the main character, the old *gaucho* seen through the eyes of an admiring boy who grows to manhood in his care, is an epitome of the *gaucho* virtues as the author saw them, and is based upon Don Segundo Ramírez, an old cowboy employed on the Güiraldes ranch and whom the young Ricardo had greatly respected. Apart from nostalgia for his lost childhood, various other factors combined to make his picture of *gaucho* life an attractive and sentimental one: Güiraldes began it when he was in Paris and homesick for the pampas; he was also disillusioned by the bad reception some of his earlier works had had from the Buenos Aires critics and contrasted the superficiality and hypocrisy of such men with the decent, open character of the countrymen he had known as a youth; he finished the novel when he was dying at La Porteña, the family ranch, and this contributes to the elegiac mood of the later part of the work.

In Part I Fabio Cáceres, the narrator, is a young lad adrift in a little country town, rapidly becoming corrupt and dissolute; he remembers with affection the brief period he had spent on his natural father's ranch some years ago, a golden age that seems to have gone for ever. One evening he sees the famous *gaucho* Don Segundo Sombra, a mysterious figure ('más una idea que un ser') who typifies all the qualities of the *gaucho* way of life; in a bar an arrogant town bully picks a quarrel with Sombra, who emerges triumphant by remaining calm and self-controlled and dominating the other by sheer force of character. Fabio witnesses this encounter (which symbolizes the two conflicting attitudes, town and country, within himself) and elects to follow Segundo, to whom he becomes a kind of son. They find work on a ranch and the remainder of the first part shows Fabio acquiring the *gaucho*'s skills and physical toughness under his *padrino*'s guidance. In Part II five years have gone by, Fabio is a young man, and this section appropriately shows him displaying the moral qualities of the *gaucho*: prudence in matters of love, loyalty to friends, temperance, stoicism in the face of accidents and misfortune. At the end of this section he learns that he has inherited an estate on the death of his father (one suspects that Segundo knew all along that the boy was one day going to become wealthy and was aware of his true identity) and that his roving way of life must now give way to a more settled existence: he can no longer be a *gaucho*. Segundo reassures him: being a *gaucho* is a matter of character, a spiritual thing almost, and this is something that Fabio cannot lose despite his wealth. In the course of his life with Segundo he has acquired qualities that he will find essential

in his new life as a man of responsibility and substance, and he is also man enough to bear the change in his life and the parting from Segundo who in the closing lines rides away to merge with the great plains whence he came and which he symbolizes.

The novel is carefully constructed; despite its important documentary side, its folklore and its realistic dialogue, it is nonetheless a very artistic novel, rich in imagery, sometimes rustic, often of a more esoteric and intellectual nature. Some critics have seen the two styles as co-existing rather oddly together, but if we remember the two layers to Fabio's makeup, the young *gaucho* and the later, educated and travelled land-owner, they seem acceptable enough.

See Aristóbulo Echegaray, '*Don Segundo Sombra*': *reminiscencia infantil de Ricardo Güiraldes* (Buenos Aires, 1955); Luis C. Pinto, '*Don Segundo Sombra*' *y sus críticos* (Avellaneda, 1956); Giovanni Previtali, *Ricardo Güiraldes and '*Don Segundo Sombra*'* (New York, 1963); Eduardo Romano, *Análisis de '*Don Segundo Sombra*'* (Buenos Aires, 1967); E. Castelli and R. Barufaldi, *Estructura mítica e interioridad en '*Don Segundo Sombra*'* (Santa Fe, 1968); and José R. Liberal, '*Don Segundo Sombra*' *de Ricardo Güiraldes* (Buenos Aires, 1969).

Dorado, El ('the golden or gilded man'), an epithet for the mythical King of Manoa, a great city of unimaginable wealth situated according to the early explorers on the banks of the Amazon or in the jungles surrounding it. The king was believed to have been covered with oil and then powdered with gold dust, which literally gilded him. Many expeditions, principally from Spain and England (two of them led by Sir Walter Ralegh), set out to find the land of El Dorado. By extension, the epithet refers to any region of fabulous treasures, normally of gold or precious stones.

Voltaire, in *Candide*, shows his hero visiting El Dorado; Milton described it in *Paradise Lost* vi. 411; and Edgar Allan Poe wrote a poem called *Eldorado* (1849).

DORMER, DIEGO JOSÉ (d. 1705), chronicler of Aragón from 1677, continuing the *Anales* (Saragossa, 1663) of Uztarroz. Of his *Progressos de la Historia en el Reyno de Aragón* (Saragossa, 1680), only the first part was published; this is substantially the life of Jerónimo de Zurita (q.v.).

Dormer's later work included *Discursos varios de Historia, con muchas escrituras reales antiguas . . .* (Saragossa, 1683) and *Anales de Aragón desde el año M.D. XXV . . . hasta él de M.D.XL* (Saragossa, 1697). His writings are detailed, mainly accurate, and without affectation. He also wrote *San Laurencio defendido* (1673).

Dorotea: acción en prosa, La, a novel in dialogue by Lope de Vega (q.v.) first published in 1632, reproduced in facsimile by the Real Academia Española (1951) and edited by J. M. Blecua (1955) and by E. S. Morby (Berkeley/ Los Angeles, 1958). The sources of this five-act 'novel' are *La Celestina* (q.v.) and its progeny, and Lope's own youthful love for Elena Osorio (Dorotea). Lope himself states that the play was written when he was young, but internal evidence proves that at least for the most part it is a work of his maturity. It was Lope's own favourite, and Morby has said it is the 'richest, best-planned, most complex work, the one which best summarizes his capacities as a lyric poet, dramatist, and prose writer'.

Dorotea is a rich, well-educated and beautiful woman whose husband had left for the New World five years previously and is presumed dead. Her young suitor, Don Fernando, is poor and her tastes are expensive, so she reluctantly agrees to the marriage proposal of Don Bela, a wealthy 'indiano' (a merchant returned from the Indies), at the insistence of her mother Teodora and a procuress, Gerarda.

Fernando learns of Dorotea's infidelity to him, obtains money from his new mistress Marfisa, and goes to Seville to forget Dorotea. Dorotea, distraught at Fernando's leaving her, swallows a diamond in a vain attempt to commit suicide. Some months later, Fernando returns without having been able to start a new life, and duels with Don Bela, seriously wounding him. But Dorotea now learns of Fernando's liaison with Marfisa and, when the weakened Bela is attacked and killed by ruffians, she feels no longer able to endure worldly love and enters a convent. Fernando enlists in the navy and Gerarda dies of a fall while bringing Dorotea a glass of water, possibly her only uncalculating act. With Calderón's *comedia La vida es sueño* and Quevedo's *Sueños* (qq.v.), *La Dorotea* is one of the key documents in the Spanish literature of disillusion or *desengano*.

The style is artificial as the age required, but the perhaps needless erudition is not only characteristically flowery, but also parodies artifice and includes irony. Gerarda (the Celestina figure), Celia, Don Bela, and Teodora all mock fashionable diction in their own way, most effectively in the maid Celia's 'epitaph' for Gerarda.

See Alan S. Trueblood, *Experience and artistic expression in Lope de Vega: the making of 'La Dorotea'* (Cambridge, Mass., 1974).

D'ORS Y ROVIRA, Eugenio, see Ors y Rovira, Eugenio d'.

Dos doncellas, Las, one of the stories in *Novelas ejemplares* (q.v., 1613) by Miguel de Cervantes Saavedra (q.v.). One of the 'realistic' stories in the volume, the plot concerns Teodosia and Leocadia, both courted by the seducer Marco Antonio Adorno with the promise of marriage; Teodosia had been seduced but Leocadia had resisted. Teodosia, disguised as a man, pursues Adorno to persuade him to marry her. At an inn she chances to meet her brother Rafael and, after explaining her predicament to him, they set off together. They come across some travellers who have been attacked by bandits: one of them is Leocadia, also disguised as a man to pursue Adorno. Rafael guesses she is a woman and obtains her confidence too. All three continue towards Barcelona, where they know Adorno is to embark for Italy. Adorno, wounded in a fight, agrees to marry Teodosia while Rafael proposes successfully to Leocadia. After the recovery of Adorno, all four make a pilgrimage to Montserrat and Santiago.

The 'exemplary' nature of the tale ('indiscretion retrieved by discretion' has been suggested by R. O. Jones) is dubious, indicating that perhaps the collective title *novelas ejemplares* may not have been wholly serious.

See Joaquín Casalduero, *Sentido y forma de las 'Novelas ejemplares'* (Buenos Aires, 1943).

DOZY, Reinhart Pieter Anne (1820–83), b. Leiden. Dutch Arabist specializing in Muslim Spain, whose preparatory works included an edition of al-Marrakishi's *History of the Almohades* (Leiden, 2nd edn., 1881), *Scriptorum Arabum loci de Abbaditis* (Leiden, 3 vols., 1846–63), ibn-Adhari's *History of Africa and Spain* (Leiden, 3 vols., 1848–52), ibn-Badrun's *Historical commentary on the poem of ibn-Abdun* (Leiden, 1848), and his *Dictionnaire détaillé des noms de vêtements chez les Arabes* (1845).

His great work is the *Histoire des Mussulmans d'Espagne, jusqu'à la conquête de l'Andalousie par les Almoravides, 711–1110* (Leiden, 1861), supplemented by *Recherches sur l'histoire et la littérature de l'Espagne pendant le moyen âge* (Leiden, 2 vols., 1849, 3rd edn. completely revised, 1881). This latter is a masterly analysis of the inconsistency in the chronicles concerning the Cid, demolishing most of the legends and showing the Cid in a light less favourable than the Spanish accounts. R. Menéndez Pidal countered some of Dozy's more controversial points in *La España del Cid* (2 vols., 1929), the most authoritative Spanish refutation of the work of Dozy. Dozy's work in Arabic philology was also extensive, culminating in the *Supplément aux dictionnaires arabes* (Leiden, 2 vols., 1877–81) and, with W. H. Engelmann, the *Glossaire des mots espagnols et portugais, dérivés de l'Arabe* (Leiden, 1866). Dozy also edited al-Makkari's *Analectes sur l'histoire et la littérature des Arabes d'Espagne* (Leiden, 2 vols.,

1855–61), and with de Goeje, al-Idrisi's *Description de l'Afrique et de l'Espagne* (1866), and the *Calendrier de Cordoue de l'année 961* (Leiden, 1874), with both Arabic text and a Latin translation. Dozy was less successful as a popularizer in *Het Islamisme* (Haarlem, 1863) and *De Israeliten te Mekka* (Haarlem, 1864), both controversial in character.

DRAGÚN, OSVALDO (1929–), Argentinian playwright who has experimented successfully with classical themes: *La peste viene de Melos* (1956), and indigenous themes: *Tupac Amaru* (1957). The crude realism of *El jardín del infierno* (1959) develops into the more subtle social dramas *Y nos dijeron que éramos inmortales* (1962) and *Milagro en el mercado viejo* (1963). *Heroica de Buenos Aires* (1966) won a prize from the Casa de las Américas, Havana, and Dragún's *Teatro* appeared in 1965.

DROGUETT, CARLOS (1914–), Chilean novelist and short-story writer. Obsessed with violence and death, Droguett is a prolific author whose sympathies lie with the working classes and left-wing students. *Sesenta muertos en la escalera* (1953) won the Nascimento Prize. Its theme is the assassination of students by the police in 1938. *Eloy* (Barcelona, 1960) is a carefully-constructed monologue, inspired by Proust, on the last night before the execution of the Chilean bandit Ñato Eloy. *100 gotas de sangre y 200 de sudor* (1961) is a fictional recreation of the conquest of Chile by the Spaniards with all its horror, 'a terrible conjunction of Apocalypse and Last Judgment'. *Patas de perro* (1965) has for its hero the cripple Bobi; without undue insistence, the reader is led to see each of us in Bobi. *El compadre* (1967) concerns an alcoholic building-labourer, Ramón, whose companion and patron is the figure of a saint in a church. Yet even that sobering aid fails and he gives in to his weakness. Among subsequent novels the best is probably *El hombre que había olvidado* (Buenos Aires, 1968), the protagonists being Mauricio, his girlfriend La Rubia, and a psychopathic murderer of young babies. Man's fear and hopelessness in the world is the Quevedesque theme informing the whole of Droguett's work. *Los mejores cuentos de Carlos Droguett* (1967) contains his best short stories.

DRYANDER, see ENZINAS, Francisco de.

D'SOLA, OTTO (1912–), b. Valencia, Venezuela. Venezuelan poet and a contributor to the review *Viernes*. His lyrics, *Acento* (1935), *Presencia* (1938), *De la soledad y las visiones* (1941), and *El viajero mortal* (1943), are imaginative and

sensual. He uses Surrealism but it does not dominate the formal perfection of his work. He has edited the important *Antología de la moderna poesía venezolana* (2 vols., 1940).

DUBLÉ URRUTIA, DIEGO (1877–1967), b. Angol. Chilean regional poet of Arauco. Dublé Urrutia was a diplomat and lived abroad from 1904 until his retirement. His verse achieved equilibrium between Romanticism, Classicism, and Modernism. *Fontana cándida* (1953) contains works written from 1895 to 1952, including the selections in *Del mar a la montaña* (1903) and *El caracol* (1903). *Veinte años* (1898) is a study of Chilean Creole writing.

DU CHESNE, FRANÇOIS, see ENZINAS, Francisco de.

DUEÑAS, JUAN DE (c. 1405–60?), courtier poet. He lost favour at the court of Juan II and took refuge with the sons of Don Fernando de Antequera in Aragón and Navarra. In the company of Don Alfonso de Aragón, he was taken prisoner at the Battle of Ponza in 1435 (the battle which inspired the Marqués de Santillana's *Comedieta de Ponza*) and while captive in Naples wrote the allegorical octosyllabic *La nao de amor*, edited with his other poems by R. Foulché-Delbosc in *Cancionero castellano del siglo XV*, vol. 22 (1915) of the NBAE, and in vol. 51 (1864) of the Baudry Colección de los Mejores Autores Españoles. Dueñas was challenged in the Marqués de Santillana's brief *Dezir contra los aragoneses* to a literary joust in 1429, and his *Respuesta* appears in vol. 22 (1915), no. 442, pp. 201–2 of the NBAE. Dueñas is still popular for *El pleyto que ovo J. de D. con su amiga*, witty verses in dialogue. On his eventual return to Spain, he lived at the court of Doña Blanca, Queen of Navarra.

Dulcinea del Toboso, the village girl chosen by Don Quijote de la Mancha as his fair lady in the novel by Cervantes (q.v.). Her real name is Aldonza Lorenzo. Sancho Panza describes her as 'a stout-built sturdy wench, who could put the shot as well as any young lad in the parish', but according to Don Quijote 'her flowing hair is of gold, her forehead the Elysian fields, her eyebrows two celestial arches, her eyes a pair of glorious suns, her cheeks two beds of roses, her lips two coral portals that guard her teeth of Oriental pearl, her neck is alabaster, her hands are polished ivory, and her bosom whiter than new-fallen snow'.

DUMONT, CARLOTA, a pseudonym occasionally used by Clorinda Matto de Turner (q.v.).

DUQUE, Aquilino (1931–   ), b. Seville. Poet, novelist, and translator, who lives in Rome. He studied law in the universities of Seville, Cambridge, and Dallas, and travelled widely. He has translated into Spanish works by Roy Campbell, Dylan Thomas, Heinrich Böll, Thomas Mann, Bertolt Brecht, and Anna Akhmatova. His verse collections include *La calle de la luna* (Seville, 1958) and *El campo de la verdad* (1958). In the notable novel *Los consulados del más allá* (Barcelona, 1966), Duque satirized the Cádiz of 1868–9. His earlier work was influenced by Valle-Inclán (q.v.), an influence greatly reduced in subsequent novels such as *El invisible anillo* (1971), *La rueda de fuego* (1971), *La linterna mágica* (1971), and *El mono azul* (Barcelona, 1974).

DUQUE DE ESTRADA, Diego (1589–1647), b. Toledo. Poet, autobiographer, and possibly a playwright, since he lists 17 *comedias* in his romanticized 'autobiography'; however, none of his plays is extant, and Pascual de Gayangos casts doubt on the veracity of Duque de Estrada's narrative in the *Memorial histórico español*, v. 12 (1860) and reprinted *Autobiografías de soldados (siglo XVII)* (1956). This narrative attributes to the author a life packed with escapades, love affairs, and military exploits, together with an aristocratic origin which may be equally imaginary. The life is entitled *Comentarios del desengañado de sí mesmo, prueba de todos estados y elección del mejor de ellos* (1956). Of his poetry, all that survives is *Octavas rimas a la insigne victoria que la Serenísima Alteza del Príncipe Filiberto ha tenido . . .* (Messina). His last years were spent under the name of Justo de Santa María in a monastery in Sardinia.

See Benedetto Croce, *Realtà e fantasia nelle memorie di Duque de Estrada* (Naples, 1928).

DUQUE JOB, EL, pseudonym of Manuel Gutiérrez Nájera (q.v.).

DURÁN, Agustín (1789–1862), b. Madrid. Literary critic and ballad editor. Director of the National Library in Madrid, he collected a fine private library which was acquired by the nation in 1863. His significant *Discurso sobre el influjo que ha tenido la crítica moderna en la decadencia del teatro antiguo español, y sobre el modo con que debe ser considerado para juzgar convenientemente de su mérito particular* (1828) made four points in response to neoclassical attacks on Spanish Golden Age drama: that earlier Spanish drama did not derive from classical Greek drama; that its principles and laws differ and must differ from classical models because its nature differs; that the norms of Spanish drama must be free enough to offer the imagination no inhibition; and that

the oral poetry of the Peninsula which infiltrated so much Golden Age drama should be recognized as a major reason for its success.

His *Discurso* was paralleled by the work in Cádiz of the German consul Nicolás Böhl de Faber (q.v.) and resisted by the neoclassical apologists José Joaquín de Mora, Alcalá Galiano, and others.

Durán's defence of passion above form explicitly rejected the neoclassicism of Leandro Fernández de Moratín (q.v.) and proposed the rehabilitation of Lope, Tirso, and Calderón.

Durán's name is also closely associated with the large collection of ballads known as the *Romancero general* or *Romancero de Durán*. He collected some 1,200 in five volumes published from 1828–32 and reprinted twice: in Paris (1838) and Barcelona (1840); but, dissatisfied with this edition, he prepared a new one of 1,887 ballads for the BAE, vols. 10 (1849) and 16 (1851). His views on the origins of the ballads are now superseded, but the texts and most of the notes are still very useful, as is his *Colección de sainetes* (1843).

Durán wrote two curious 'original' legends matching the originals' form and language: *La infantina de Francia y sus amores con la hija del rey de Hungría* and *Leyenda de las tres toronjas del vergel de amor* (1856), by 'el Trovador'

See D. T. Gies, *Agustín Durán* (London, 1975).

DURÁN, Armando (1938–   ), b. Havana. Venezuelan narrative writer who attended high school in the U.S.A. and received his doctorate from Barcelona University, subsequently teaching Romance languages at Michigan University. His novels are the impressive, short *Contracorrientes* (1969) and *Triángulos* (1971). The influence of Jorge Luis Borges (q.v.) is apparent in stories such as 'José Barcalayo, killer of pests', translated in *Mundus Artium* (Athens, Ohio), Summer 1970.

DURÁN, Manuel (1925–   ), b. Barcelona. Poet and critic. His collections of verse include *Puente* (Mexico City, 1946), *Ciudad asediada* (Mexico City, 1956), *La paloma azul* (Mexico City, 1959), and *El lugar del hombre* (Mexico City, 1965). Among his critical writings are *El superrealismo en la poesía española contemporánea* (Mexico City, 1952) and *La ambigüedad en el 'Quijote'* (Xalapa, 1960). He edited *Lorca: a collection of critical essays* (Englewood Cliffs, N.J., 1962).

DURAND, Luis (1895–1954), b. Traiguén. Chilean novelist and short-story writer. After completing his secondary education, Durand worked in the National Library and was for many years director of *Atenea*. His best fiction deals with peasant life in the far south, near Temuco, on the borderland between whites and Mapuches: above all, *Frontera* (1949), which may lack the style of Rivera and the lyricism of Gallegos but compensates in the fineness of its epic treatment and sense of mystery. A Creole writer of Mariana Latorre's school (q.v.), Durand described the lower classes in realistic terms. His characters have a limited mental horizon and poor powers of expression in the stories collected in *Tierra de pellines* (1929), *Campesinos* (1932), and *Cielos del sur* (1933). Other novels include *Mercedes Urízar* (1935), *Piedra que rueda* (1935), and *El primer hijo* (1939). Durand's essays appeared in *Presencia de Chile* (1942), *Alma y cuerpo de Chile* (1947), and *Gente de mi tiempo* (1953).

E

ECHAGÜE, JUAN PABLO (1877–1950), b. San Juan. Argentinian man of letters who first attracted attention with drama reviews in *El País* (1904–8) as 'Jean Paul' and in *La Nación* (1912–18). His first reviews were collected as *Puntos de vista* (Barcelona, 1905) and *Prosa de combate* (1908). After his second phase as a reviewer he compiled *Un época del teatro argentino, 1904–1918* (Paris, 1918; Buenos Aires, 1926). On his return from European tours he taught theatre history at the National Conservatory, was a founder member of the Academia Nacional de la Historia from 1931, and was President of the National Council for Public Libraries. In 1938, Echagüe was awarded the National Literary Prize in the 'imaginative prose work' section for *Por donde corre el Zonda: fantasmagorías* (1938).

There are useful essays on his work and a detailed bibliography in *Boletín de la Real Academia Argentina de Letras*, vol. 19, no. 73 (July–September 1950).

ECHAGÜE, PEDRO (1800–75), b. Cuyo. Argentinian playwright and novelist. After earning a living at a variety of callings, from commercial traveller to soldier and school inspector, Echagüe edited *El Zonda*, the magazine founded by Sarmiento (q.v.). He wrote a number of novels now forgotten, and two good plays: *Rosas* (1851; second version, 1860), and *Amor y virtud* (1868) which suffer from the melodramatic romanticism of their time. J. A. Leguizamón has written of him 'Dentro de su tiempo y de su medio se nos aparece como un honrado artista, trabajador paciente en la cantera apenas explorada'.

ECHEGARAY, JOSÉ (1832–1916), b. Madrid. Melodramatic playwright who dominated the Spanish stage from 1875 for three decades. By training a mathematician and engineer, Echegaray rose in later life to become Minister of Finance, and was founder of the Bank of Spain.

He began to write plays while in exile in his early forties, and achieved success with his first, *El libro talonario* (1874, produced under the anagram Jorge Hayaseca). This is a drawing-room comedy in which a young wife ingeniously turns the tables on her unfaithful husband. Then followed over 60 plays, some being huge successes, and others complete failures. Echegaray inherited the popular appeal of Tamayo (q.v.) and his influence on his contemporaries and successors was equally detrimental. His versification lacks charm, his characters are mere cardboard, and his grotesque situations are resolved by unlikely and violent events. His sole major virtue is the power to create and maintain suspense, which is why his historical Romantic verse melodramas have lasted better than his other plays, and why his name has been erroneously connected with the Romantic movement. His most famous plays are *En el puño de la espada* (1875); *O locura o santidad* (1877); *El gran galeote* (1881), on the tragic results of malicious gossip; *Dos fanatismos* (1887); *El hijo de Don Juan* (1892), influenced by Ibsen's *Ghosts; Mariana* (1892); *Mancha que limpia* (1895); *La duda* (1898); *El loco dios* (1900); and *A fuerza de arrastrarse* (1905). He was awarded the Nobel Prize for Literature in 1904. The two major editions of his plays are *Obras dramáticas escogidas* (12 vols., 1884–1905) and *Teatro escogido* (1955; 3rd edn., 1959).

He also wrote *Algunas reflexiones generales sobre la crítica y el arte literario* (1894), *Cuentos* (1912), and a posthumously-published autobiography, *Recuerdos* (3 vols., 1917).

See C. Eguía Ruiz, 'Don José Echegaray, ídolo caído de nuestro teatro' in his *Crítica patriótica* (1921), pp. 67–175; and J. Mathías, *Echegaray* (1970).

ECHEGARAY, MIGUEL (1848–1927), b. Quintanar de la Orden, Toledo. Playwright and brother of the playwright José Echegaray (q.v.).

The first of his works to be performed was *Cara y cruz* (1864), and from then until *c.* 1910 he formed, with Vital Aza and Miguel Ramos Carrión, the trio of popular librettists for the *género chico* (q.v.). Among his most celebrated libretti are *El dúo de la Africana* (1893), *Gigantes y cabezudos* (1898), and *La viejecita* (1898). He was elected to the Real Academia Española in 1913.

ECHEVERRÍA, AQUILEO J. (1866–1909), b. San José. Costa Rican poet, called by his friend Darío 'el poeta nacional, el poeta representativo, el poeta familiar'. In retrospect his verses seem sentimental and even commonplace.

His *Concherías* (1905) includes poems written in the language of Costa Rican country people or '*conchos*', and is still very popular among them. In 1908 he went to Europe for his health, and died in Barcelona without seeing the second edition of this book (Barcelona, 1909).

ECHEVERRÍA, ESTEBAN (1805–51), b. Buenos Aires. Argentinian novelist, poet, and essayist. Left an orphan on the death of his mother when he was 17, Echeverría went to Paris in 1825 and, having absorbed the ethos of the *vie de bohème*, returned in 1830 to Argentina. He wrote *Elvira, o la novia del Plata* (1832), *Los consuelos* (1834), and *Rimas* (1837), which included the famous 'La cautiva' set in the pampas and already revealing all the traits of Romanticism. An opponent of the dictator Rosas, he emigrated to Uruguay in 1840, and the following year wrote *El matadero* (published 1871) against Rosas. This is a short novel full of realistic descriptions showing the brutality in the *matadero* or abattoir which symbolizes Argentina under Rosas. Echeverría discussed the literary theories of the Romantic movement in his essay *Fondo y forma de las obras de imaginación*, which rejects Aristotelian theory. Defending the concept of poetry as the supreme form of artistic creation, 'el padre del romanticismo argentino' argues that the artist should be free to select his subject and style; a race will develop canons of literary taste unique to it. Echeverría influenced many writers, including Juan María Gutiérrez (q.v.).

ECHEVERRÍA, JOSÉ ANTONIO (1815–85), b. Venezuela. A Cuban by adoption, Echeverría wrote several books on Cuban historical subjects, but is remembered for a historical novel in the manner of Sir Walter Scott, *Antonelli* (1838), on an imaginary episode in the life of the Italian architect Giambattista Antonelli summoned to construct El Morro castle in Havana by Philip II in 1560.

Echeverría was the copyist, almost certainly the modernizer (and possibly even the author) of what is claimed to be the first Cuban poem, *Espejo de paciencia*, attributed to a certain Silvestre de Balboa, and dated 1608. In exile in New York, he founded with José de Armas y Céspedes a political journal called *La Revolución* (1869).

Edad de Oro, see SIGLO DE ORO.

EDWARDS, JORGE (1931–), b. Santiago. Chilean short-story writer and novelist. Edwards studied law in the University of Chile and has practised law and worked in the Ministry of Foreign Affairs. His most persistent theme is the weakness of middle-class society, and his stories like those of Mario Benedetti (q.v.) in Uruguay, show the pathos, humour, grief, and tragedy inherent in his capital city. These stories have appeared in the collections *El patio* (1952), *Gente de la ciudad* (1961), and *Las máscaras* (1967), the last being clearly superior to the earlier work. *El peso de la noche* (1964) takes its title from the statement by Portales: 'El orden social en Chile se mantiene por el peso de la noche' and attempts to portray the lack of genuine values in contemporary Santiago through the eyes of Cristina, her alcoholic son Joaquín, and her sickly grandson Francisco.

EDWARDS BELLO, JOAQUÍN (1886–1968), b. Valparaíso. Chilean novelist and essayist. He was a direct descendant of Andrés Bello (q.v.) and was educated at the English School in Valparaíso and subsequently in Europe.

His fiction can be divided roughly into two periods: before 1928, when he produced work comparable to that of Blasco Ibáñez (q.v.) and deriving from the naturalism of Zola; and from 1928, when he liberated himself from Zolaism, first of all in the novel *El chileno en Madrid* (1928).

Edwards Bello's early period began with *El inútil* (1910), a novel showing the degradation of a Chilean in Paris which so shocked his contemporaries that he was forced to leave the country. He lived for some time in Brazil, as he described in *Tres meses en Río de Janeiro* (1911). *El monstruo* (1912) takes up the same theme of a Chilean in Paris, but this time the hero is redeemed by his quick return to Chile and the love of a good woman after the social satire has been permitted to take its effect. It is of this novel in particular that A. Torres Ríoseco was thinking when describing the author as 'an American Larra, whipping the naked bodies of his compatriots'. Edwards Bello also wrote *La tragedia del 'Titanic'* (1912), revised as *La muerte de Vanderbilt* (1922); the notorious *El roto* (1920), which for the first time dared to set the Zolaesque situations of the earlier books in Santiago instead of Paris and made an instant *succès de scandale; Cap Polonio* (1929); *Valparaíso, la ciudad del viento* (1931), in which Edwards first appreciated the virtues of his native city, reworking it as *En el viejo Almendral* (1943); *Criollos en Paris* (1933); and *La chica del Crillón* (1935), another satire on Santiago, centred on a society girl fallen low.

Despite the obvious appeal of his narrative ability, Edwards Bello creates characters without real depth and his excessively explicit moral judgements retard the novel's flow.

Églogas (Greek: *eklogé*, 'selected'), in their classical significance, bucolic or pastoral poems. Virgil uses all three classes of eclogue: the narrative, dramatic, and the mixed. Theocritus is generally considered to be the leading Greek practitioner of the genre. In Spanish literature they also take lyrical form, as in the *églogas* of Garcilaso de la Vega (q.v.), and dramatic form, as in those of Juan del Encina and Lucas Fernández (qq.v.). The word idyll is often equated with eclogue in classical writers, but Martínez de la Rosa suggests that the idyll is 'more delicate, and offers more tender sentiments'. Among other leading writers of the *égloga* in Spanish are Herrera, Lope de Vega, Rioja, Pedro de Espinosa, Fernández de Moratín, and Meléndez Valdés (qq.v.).

EGUIARA Y EGUREN, Juan José de (1695–1763), b. Mexico City. Mexican polymath who taught at the university and rejected a high ecclesiastical position to begin the ambitious Bibliotheca Mexicana (vol. 1, 1755, A–C) for which he was unsuited by reason of his gongoristic style, his preference for Latin as opposed to Spanish, and his excessively polemic approach to scholarship. He died before he was able to publish the rest of his work, but prepared D–J which is to be found in MS. in the University of Texas Library at Austin and of which only a few fragments have been published. His work was continued, with greater skill and impartiality, by José Mariano Beristáin de Souza (1756–1817) in the Biblioteca Hispanoamericana Septentrional (1816). Eguiara's attempt at an encyclopaedia of Latin-American authors consists of a polemical sketch of Mexican culture aimed at controverting European ideas of the intrinsic worthlessness of the American intellect and imagination. The 'proof' is given by a sequence of entries by authors' names, but the work is in Latin, and even the titles of the books are given in Latin in a mistaken belief that the work would thus gain in intellectual authority.

Eguiara's lesser works included *Vida del Venerable Padre don Pedro de Arellano, y Sosa, Sacerdote . . .* (1735); and *Selectae dissertationes mexicanae ad scholasticam spectantes theologiam tribus tomis distinctae* (1746), of which only the first volume appeared.

Joaquín García Icazbalceta studied the encyclopaedic works of both Eguiara and Beristáin in his *Obras* (1896), pp. 119–46, and there is a more recent study by A. Millares Carlo, *Don Juan José de Eguiara y Eguren, 1695–1763 y su 'Bibliotheca Mexicana'* (1957).

EGUÍLAZ, Luis de (1830–74), b. Sanlúcar de Barrameda. Novelist and playwright. When only 14, he wrote and had performed in Jérez his one-act play *Por dinero baila el perro*. He studied law in Madrid and embarked on a literary career as a protégé of Eugenio de Ochoa (q.v.).

His weakness as a dramatist was his creation of caricature rather than character, so that in his first serious play, *Verdades amargas* (1853), Carlos is the archetypal hypocrite and Luis the egoist. So it is with *Mentiras dulces* (1859) and *La cruz del matrimonio* (1861), which is his best play in spite of the stereotype figures of Mercedes and Enriqueta. Eguílaz's *Obras dramáticas*, collected in 1864, were published in Paris.

The realistic *costumbrismo* of his historical novel *La espada de San Fernando* (1852) enhances the telling of the conquest of Seville, but Eguílaz's treatment of an important subject is diminished by a slapdash use of language and excessive piety.

EGUREN, José María (1874–1942), b. Lima. Peruvian poet and painter. A man of means, both of whose parents were Basques, Eguren was brought up in the countryside yet had ample experience of life in the city and wrote with equal confidence of both in language of astonishing originality. He is the most outstanding Peruvian poet before César Vallejo, (q.v.).

His first book, *Simbólicas* (1911) gives the misleading impression that he was influenced by the French symbolists; in fact he uses words in some poems for their musical value rather than for their intellectual meaning. He influenced much of the experimentation connected with the *Colónida* group of 1916 which also included E. Bustamante y Ballivián, A. Valdelomar, A. Hidalgo, and J. Parra del Riego. His second book was the important *La canción de las figuras* (1916), and *Poesías* (1929) contained his earlier work and his even more striking new work. Romantic in feeling, classical in language, and occasionally symbolist in expression, *Poesías completas* (Barranco, 1952) was reprinted first in 1961 and then in 1970 with selected prose.

His prose is collected in *Motivos estéticos* (1959). R. Silva Santiesteban edited Eguren's *Obras completas* (1974). A constant theme is Lima and its surroundings. The neologisms (listed by L. A. Sánchez, *Escritores representativos* (3rd edn., 1971), vol. 3, pp. 110–11) show his inventiveness but do not hinder the smooth reading of his dream poems which offer strange thoughts and sudden metamorphoses which were to become widely acceptable with the later Peruvian surrealists led by César Moro (q.v.).

See E. Núñez, *José María Eguren: vida y obra* (New York, 1962) and *La poesía de Eguren* (1932); and Emilio Armaza, *Eguren: análisis poético de la obra* ... (1963).

EICHELBAUM, SAMUEL (1894–1967), b. Domínguez, Entre Ríos. Argentinian dramatist. Working initially within the naturalistic convention, Eichelbaum gradually extended his technical range to encompass emotional realism in contrast to his earlier, purely mechanistic plays showing the degradation of character through external circumstances. With Conrado Nalé Roxlo (q.v.), Eichelbaum is considered the most important playwright of Argentina. He also wrote short stories and novels.

His best-known works are *La mala sed* (1920), *Un hogar* (1922), *La hermana terca* (1924), *Señorita* (1930), *Soledad es tu nombre* (1932), *El viajero inmóvil* (1933), *Pájaro de barro* (1940), *Un guapo del 900* (1940, his best play and an excellent portrayal of Buenos Aires at the turn of the century, dealing with a professional killer), *Un tal Servando Gómez* (1942), *Nadie le conoció nunca* (1956), and *Los aguas del mundo* (1959).

See Jorge Cruz, *Samuel Eichelbaum* (1962).

EIELSON, JORGE EDUARDO (1921–). b. Lima. Peruvian poet and novelist. His early poetry was influenced by Rilke and the French post-symbolists: *Reinos*, a separatum of the magazine *Historia*, no. 9 (1945) and *Dédalo dormido* (1946). *Canción y muerte de Rolando* (1959) first appeared in *El Mercurio Peruano*, no. 207 (June 1944).

In the mid-1950s, Eielson turned to the plastic arts, but has also since written a play (*Maquillaje*), another collection of poetry, *Mutatis mutandis* 1967), and a novel, *El cuerpo de Gulia-no* (Mexico City, 1971).

He has produced with S. Salazar Bondy and J. Sologuren an important anthology *La poesía contemporánea del Perú* (1946) and is represented in the collection *Surrealistas y otros peruanos insulares* Barcelona, 1973), compiled by M. Lauer and A. Oquendo.

EIXIMENIS, FRANCESC (before 1327–1409), b. Gerona. Franciscan who studied in Toulouse, was ordained in Barcelona in 1352, and attained high ecclesiastical office. He acted as ambassador to successive kings, and compiled part of a great projected encyclopaedia on Christian principles and practice, known as *Lo Chrestià*, as well as a number of minor works.

Primer del Chrestià (Valencia, 1483) written 379–81, was the first of the thirteen books

planned. The four completed comprise a total of 2,587 chapters. The second book, *Segon del Chrestià* was written in 1382–3 but never published. The *Terç del Chrestià* was written in 1384, and the first 352 chapters of Eiximenis' 1,060 appeared in Els Nostres Clàssics (3 vols., Valencia, 1929–32). The twelfth book, or *Dotzè del Chrestià*, was written mainly from 1385–6, with interpolations of 1391, and has been inaccurately published by A. Bulbena as *Tractat de regiment de princeps e comunitats* (Barcelona, 1904) giving only the first 68 chapters of the author's original 907. The work is a remarkable source-book for medieval thought and religious belief unchallenged by the sophistication of Metge (q.v.) or the intellectual genius of Llull (q.v.). Eiximenis provides a vivid chronicle of the emergence of the middle class, writing specifically for 'persones simples e legues e sans grans lletres', as he says. He travelled extensively, and it is known that he was in Oxford, Avignon, and various Italian cities. Dialogues learnt in various situations enliven his long work, which is seldom tedious. His insight in stressing *pactisme* (rule by mutual agreement) as the contribution of the Catalan people to the European political tradition is shrewd.

See J. Massó Torrents, 'Les obres de fra Francesch Eximeniç', *AIEC*, vol. 3 (1909–10), pp. 588–692; A. Ivars, 'El escritor fr. Francisco Eximénez en Valencia' in *Archivo Ibero-Americano*, vols. 14–25 (1920–6); and M. de Riquer, *Història de la literatura catalana*, vol. 2 (Barcelona, 1964), pp. 133–96.

El, see under the word following the article, e.g. LICENCIADO VIDRIERA, El.

Elan, Grupo, Ecuadorian literary movement of the 1930s, whose members included Alfonso Cuesta y Cuesta, Alejandro Carrión, Jorge Fernández (qq.v.), José Alfredo Llerena, Augusto Sacotto Arias, Ignacio Lasso, and Humberto Vacas.

Elche, Mystery Play of, a play of indeterminate antiquity, its present form known as the *Misteri d'Elx* dating from the early 17th c. This text is based on the 14th-c. *Representació de la Asumpció de madona Santa Maria*, itself possibly derived from an earlier version. It was published in the *Boletín de la Sociedad Española de Excursiones* as *Auto lírico-religioso en dos actos representados todos los años en la iglesia parroquial de S. M. de Elche los dias 14 y 15 agosto* (1896).

See R. Mitjana, 'El Misterio de Elche' in his *Discantes y contrapuntos* (Valencia, n.d. but 1905) and F. Pedrell, *La fête d'Elche ou le drame lyrique liturgique espagnol* (Paris, 1906).

Elena y María, see DISPUTA DE ELENA Y MARÍA.

ELIPANDUS OF TOLEDO (717–794?), b. Toledo. Goth who became prelate of Spain in 783, succeeding Cixila. He attacked the heresy of Migetius, who taught that the first member of the Trinity was David, the second his descendant Jesus, and the third St. Paul.

Elipandus himself taught that Christ was not the natural son of God, but only his adoptive son through regeneration. This heresy of adoptionism originated in Spain and was supported by Felix of Urgel, who was condemned with Elipandus at the Assembly of Frankfurt of 794.

Seven letters of Elipandus survive; all are reprinted from various sources in M. Menéndez y Pelayo's *Historia de los heterodoxos españoles* (vol. 1, 1880).

See F. C. Saínz de Robles, *Elipando y San Beato de Liébana* (1934) and J. F. Rivera, *Elipando de Toledo* (Toledo, 1940).

ELIZONDO, MARTÍN (1923?–), important Spanish playwright who has lived in exile since the Civil War, like Fernando Arrabal and José Guevara (qq.v.). He is founder and director of Los Amigos del Teatro Español, a group producing Spanish plays for exiles living in France. Elizondo teaches at Toulouse University.

His plays are concerned broadly with the effect of tyranny on the individual, and he has begun to write also in French to present his theme to a wider audience. His plays are *De verdugo a verdugo* (1964); *La garra y la dura escuela de los Perejones* (1966), in which a socially-deprived family, the Perejones, are evicted by a centenarian woman, 'la garra'; *Otra vez el mal toro* (1967), a sardonic view of the futility of all revolutions; *La faim* (1968), on the unequal sharing of the world's food supply; and *Pour la Grèce* (1969), in which the characters rehearse and discuss an unspecified play on the Greek military coup of 1967. The Toulouse première of 1970 was disrupted by a Fascist youth organization, but the audience thought that this was part of the play and the interruption petered out.

See G. E. Wellwarth, *Spanish underground drama* (Philadelphia, 1972).

ELIZONDO, SALVADOR (1932–), b. Mexico City. Mexican novelist, poet, and painter. His *Poemas* (1960) show violent interior passions with traces of surrealism. He achieved fame with his novel *Farabeuf o la crónica de un instante* (1965) which, in the words of George McMurray, is 'a combined climactic moment of orgasm and death, with the resultant atmosphere of eroticism and sadism . . .'. *El hipogeo secreto* (1968) is a less impressive novel on account of its intellectual

aridity, the protagonist seeming to be the words of the novel themselves and the whole process markedly derivative from Joyce or Faulkner. Elizondo has written his autobiography, *Salvador Elizondo* (1966), and has emerged as a significant short-story writer in *Narda o el verano* (1966) and *El retrato de Zoë y otras mentiras* (1969).

Elx, Misteri d', see ELCHE, Mystery Play of.

Emblemas ('emblems'), symbols, and later illustrations, with verse captions. Originating in the medieval period, emblems reached the height of their popularity in the Renaissance, with allegorical allusions to theology, philosophy, history, politics, and morals. They derived their fascination from the common medieval and Renaissance view of the universe as a system of signs which must be deciphered, and served in their turn to popularize this concept. The first important collection was the *Emblemata* (Augsburg, 1531) of the Italian Andrea Alciati (1492–1550), with captions in Latin distichs, imitated widely in Spanish literature, beginning with and continuing with the *Emblemas morales* (Segovia, 1589) of Juan de Horozco y Covarrubias, the *Emblemas moralizados* (1599) of Hernando de Soto, and the *Emblemas morales* (1610) of Sebastián de Covarrubias Orozco.

Ludwig Pfandl, in his *Introducción al estudio del Siglo de Oro* (1929), associated the emblems primarily with the literary baroque, declaring that the *Oráculo manual* of Gracián (q.v.) is in fact no more than a miscellaneous collection of moral emblems, to which the illustrations have not been assigned. Pfandl sees as 'original' the emblems of Saavedra Fajardo, whose *Empresas políticas* (1640) were in fact a close imitation of the *Emblemata politica* (1618) of Jakob Bruck Angermunt. The use of emblems in literary *conceptismo* (q.v.) was commonplace in Golden Age poetry and prose; one of the leading figures in this connection was Alonso de Ledesma Buitrago (q.v.). Preachers of the same period (usually Jesuits) employed emblems in moral instruction.

The standard work is A. Henkel and A. Schöne, *Emblemata: Handbuch zur Sinnbildkunst des XVI und XVII Jahrhunderts* (Stuttgart, 1967).

Enciclopedismo, see ENLIGHTENMENT IN SPAIN.

ENCINA, JUAN DEL (1469–1529?), b. Salamanca. Playwright, musician, and poet, who is known as the father of Spanish Renaissance drama. He studied at Salamanca University, graduating as Bachelor of Law, and took minor orders. He entered the household of the Duke of Alba in 1492 (or as late as 1495 according to another view) and spent several years with him as courtier, playwright, musician, actor, and producer of entertainments. In 1498 he competed for the post of cantor at Salamanca Cathedral and, on losing to Lucas Fernández (q.v.), he left for Rome, where he became a favourite of Alexander VI, a Spanish Pope. Pope Julius II appointed him Archdeacon of Málaga Cathedral in 1509, but Encina was restless and finally obtained the post of Prior to León Cathedral from Pope Leo X and died at León late in 1529 or early in 1530.

His *Cancionero* (Salamanca, 1496; facsimile edn. by E. Cotarelo y Mori, 1928) contained all his poetry and his first eight dramatic eclogues. These short pastoral plays, produced for the Duke of Alba's pleasure at Alba de Tormes, lacked all Italian influence beyond the pastoral convention itself. The *Cancionero* was reprinted several times, with additions, and remained an important source of style and matter for all Spanish playwrights until Lope. Only three of his eclogues followed medieval European Christian dramatic tradition: the second, a Christmas play; and the third and fourth, on the passion and resurrection of Christ. His other plays were secular, truly dramatic in the sense of contrast and tension, and often witty or comic. The *Égloga de Cristino y Febea* may possibly have Italian antecedents; his best plays definitely have. These are the *Égloga de Fileno, Zambardo y Cardonio*, a close adaptation from the Italian poet Antonio Tebaldeo; and the *Égloga de Plácida y Vitoriano* (see PLACIDA Y VITORIANO).

Encina's language is vigorous to the point of innovation, for he created a comic peasant speech known as *sayagués* (q.v.) much imitated by later playwrights. He is a skilled versifier, careful to attribute appropriate language to each character, and though his plots are simple, their structure is careful.

The attribution of the *Auto del repelón* to Encina earlier, and now again by H. López Morales, has been challenged by O. T. Myers in *Hispanic Review*, vol. 32 (1944), pp. 189–210. Urban Cronan's attribution to Encina of the *Égloga interlocutoria* (*Revue Hispanique*, vol. 36, 916) has been dismissed by later writers.

The *Teatro completo* edited by M. Cañete and F. A. Barbieri (1893; reprinted New York, 969) has been largely superseded by H. López Morales' edition of the *Églogas completas* (1968). The *Poesías completas* have been edited by R. O. Jones and H. López Morales (1976) and an anthology of Encina's songs by R. O. Jones and Carolyn Lee (1976).

See J. Richard Andrews, *Juan del Encina: Prometheus in search of prestige* (Berkeley, 1959) and H. López Morales, *Tradición y creación en los orígenes del etatro castellano* (1968).

ENCINAS, *Fray* PEDRO DE (*c.* 1530–95), b. Burgos. Dominican monk who studied at Salamanca and spent most of his life in Huete. His *Versos espirituales, que tratan de la conversión del pecador, menosprecio del mundo y vida de nuestro Señor* (Cuenca, 1596) contains six religious eclogues in *terza* and *ottava rima* (among the earliest in that genre) and other lyrical poems. His works also appeared in the *Séptima y octava parte de Flor de varios romances nuevos* . . . (Alcalá, 1597) and the *Novena parte* . . . (Madrid, 1597). He was cited and praised (in error as 'Ezinas') in the *Buscapié* (q.v.). P. Aguado has produced a modern edition of the *Églogas espirituales* (1924) with a biography of the author.

Endecasílabos, lines of eleven syllables each. The commonest type, as used by Garcilaso de la Vega (q.v.) after the model of Petrarch, is the heroic hendecasyllable, with stresses on the 2nd, 6th, and 10th syllables: '¡Oh más dura que mármol a mis quejas . . .'—Garcilaso, *Egloga primera*.

Other types are emphatic (a mixture of the dactylic and trochaic) stressed on syllables 1, 6, and 10; the anapaestic, stressed on syllables 4, 7, and 10; and the sapphic, stressed on syllables 4, 6, and 10 or 4, 8, and 10.

Eneasílabos, lines of nine syllables each, infrequent in Spanish literature. Used early by Villasandino in the *Cancionero de Baena* (qq.v.), nos. 19, 43, and 45 and subsequently by Valverde, as in the line 'No quieren beber en el río', Darío (author of perhaps the best example, 'El clavicordio de la abuela', Rosalía de Castro, and Salvador Rueda, among others. The trochiac eneasyllable is stressed chiefly on the 4th and 8th, the dactylic on the 2nd and 8th, and the mixed dactylic/trochaic on the 3rd and 8th.

Engaños, Libro de los, see SENDEBAR.

Enlightenment in Spain (Spanish: '*Ilustración*') is a term used to describe an 18th-c. philosophical and religious movement developed by the Englishman Locke and his French successors Montesquieu (*Lettres persanes*, 1723), the prolific Voltaire, Diderot, Rousseau and the epoch-making *Encyclopédie* (1751–80) which gave its name to the alternative Spanish name for its dominant sceptical tendency, *enciclopedismo*. The *Encyclopédie*, embodying the philosophic spirit of the 18th c., attempted to give a consistently rational view of the universe and to expose credulity and superstition. It was attacked by the clergy in France, and in Spain works by the writers cited above were proscribed by the Inquisition except for their verse which was, however, equally imbued with the spirit of enquiry, satire, reason, philosophic optimism, and the search for earthly happiness. New urban policies of detailed planning, methodical philanthropic institutions, and the expulsion of the Jesuits in 1767, all contributed to the spread of the Enlightenment in Spain, which was associated, partly through mere historical accident, with the Bourbon dynasty. The academies and *sociedades económicas* or *de amigos del país* which sprang up throughout Spain also owed much to French models.

Spanish writers connected with the *Ilustración* included Jovellanos, Quintana, Feijóo, and Cadalso (qq.v.). From the second half of the 18th c., science and independent enquiry became increasingly strong, leading to emphasis on satire in the essay form, realism and naturalism in the novel, and to a resurgence of the periodical press (*El Censor* and *Correo de Madrid*) and a new reading public more ready for controversy.

See J. Sarrailh, *L'Espagne éclairée de la seconde moitié du XVIIIᵉ siècle* (Paris, 1954); Richard Herr, *The Eighteenth-Century Revolution in Spain* (Princeton, 1958; Spanish translation, 1964); V. Palacio Atard, *Los españoles de la Ilustración* (1964); G. Anés, *Economía e Ilustración en la España del Siglo XVIII* (Barcelona, 1969); and A. Elorza, *La ideología liberal en la Ilustración española* (1970).

ENRÍQUEZ, CARLOS (1907–57), Cuban novelist. *Tilín García* (1939) dealt with agrarian reform in missionary terms, but *La feria de Guaicanama* (1960) emerged from the strait-jacket of the *roman à thèse* to advocate a wild anarchism based on the exuberant sexuality of D. H. Lawrence's novels and the political extremism deriving from the theories of Bakunin and Kropotkin, undermined to some extent by the dense style of metaphor and hyperbole. *La vuelta de Chencho* (1960) is a very different, straightforward picaresque tale of life in the Cuban countryside.

ENRÍQUEZ, LUIS, see FERNÁNDEZ DE VELASCO, Juan.

ENRÍQUEZ DEL CASTILLO, DIEGO (1433–1504?), b. Segovia. Biographer, chaplain, and counsellor to King Henry IV. His *Crónica del rey don Enrique el Quarto de este nombre* was first published in an undated edition and later by J. M. de Flores in 1787, and by C. Rosell in vol. 70 (1878) of the BAE.

The first version of his chronicle, covering the thirteen years up to 1467, was captured by his enemies after the Battle of Olmedo, and he relied on his memory for rewriting that section, which is consequently the weakest as regards accuracy.

Colourful in detail and vivid in portraiture, Enríquez lacks the serenity and objectivity of the true historian; he favours his king as much as Alfonso Fernández de Palencia (q.v.) attacks him.

See Julio Puyol, 'Los cronistas de Enrique IV: I: Diego Enríquez del Castillo' in *Boletín de la Academia de la Historia*, vol. 78 (1921), pp. 399–415.

ENRÍQUEZ GÓMEZ, ANTONIO (1600–63), b. Segovia. Novelist, poet, and playwright of the school of Calderón, now known to be the 'Fernando de Zárate' who returned from exile in France in 1649 and wrote the plays *Quien habla más obra menos* and *El valiente Campuzano* (in vol. 47, 1858, of the BAE), among others.

His father was a Portuguese Jew, Diego Enríquez Villanueva, and Enríquez Gómez was forced to escape from Spain's religious persecution, taking up residence in France. He published his works there and eventually became secretary to King Louis XIII. His books attacked the excesses of the Inquisition, and he was burnt in effigy in Spain in 1660, arrested by the Inquisition in the following year, and died in gaol.

His poetry first appeared in *Academias morales de las Musas* (Bordeaux, 1642), with four insubstantial Calderonian plays: *La prudente Abigail, Contra el amor no hay engaños, Amor con vista y cordura*, and *A lo que obliga el honor*. The last-named appears with *Celos no ofenden al sol* in vol. 47 of the BAE. Altogether, Enríquez Gómez composed 22 plays under his own name; none of them fully engages the attention, lacking originality in both theme and treatment. Some of his poetry is charming, excellent in the metaphor learned from Góngora. *Sansón Nazareno* (Rouen, 1656) is an heroic poem in 14 cantos following the fashionable mode, and there are few arresting passages in *La culpa del primer peregrino* (Rouen, 1644; 2nd edn., enlarged with more sonnets and *El pasagero*, Madrid, 1735).

Enríquez Gómez's most celebrated book is the satirical novel *El siglo pitagórico, y Vida de don Gregorio Guadaña* (Rouen, 1644), the latter part being a picaresque insertion reprinted without its framework in vol. 33 (1854) of the BAE.

See N. Díaz de Escobar, 'Antonio Enríquez Gómez', in *Boletín de la Academia de la Historia*, vol. 88 (1926).

En torno al casticismo (1902), five essays by Miguel de Unamuno (q.v.).

Originally published as five articles by the magazine *La España Moderna* in 1895, these essays set out to study, like the *Idearium español* (1897) of Ángel Ganivet (qq.v.), the current state of Spain and the methods by which the allegedly defective nation might be regenerated.

Unamuno, a major member of the *Generación del 1898* (q.v.), identifies the malaise of Spain as inertia, the aftermath of an 'historical trance'. 'Accursed history', the tale of kings and noblemen, should be forgotten, and the vital energies of the peasantry should be utilized when studying the discipline of 'intrahistory' (*intrahistoria*). The aim of intrahistory is to examine the eternal and unshakeable tradition of the masses which is equally strong in peace and war. Like Ganivet, Unamuno deplores the weakening of the nation by impossible dreams of eternal imperial and military power. Unamuno attacks the narrow religiosity of Castile which forces all types and complexities into a single, 'simple' unity. Castile stands for either the profligate Don Juan or the vengeance-seeking husband: rarely for the constant lover and husband. The military strive for conquest in Africa; the aristocracy dream of the Golden Age; the peasantry are sunk in apathy; and the middle classes are superstitious. Even the ascetic craves only his own salvation.

Unamuno's solution is to utilize the energies of the Spanish collective human spirit; beneath national forms, he believes, lie universal forms; beneath the crust of caste lies the potential for unity between all classes and people of all political and spiritual persuasions. Thus, whereas Nietzsche proposed a 'suprahistory' which 'would give existence to an eternal and stable character in art and religion', Unamuno proposes through 'intrahistory' to develop the real but obscured potential of the common man so that he is no longer passively obedient to authority, but examines his situation and tries to improve it by his own efforts.

Unamuno's essays were seminal in the development not only of his own thought but also that of his own and succeeding generations. They influenced Ortega y Gasset's philosophy and Antonio Machado's poetry, for instance. See his correspondence with Ganivet, *El porvenir de España* (1912).

See also M. García Blanco, *En torno a Unamuno* (1965); P. Ilie, *Unamuno: an existential view of self and society* (Madison, Wis., 1967); and J. Marías, *Unamuno* (Barcelona, 1968).

ENTRAMBASAGUAS, JOAQUÍN DE (1904–), b. Madrid. Literary critic, essayist, and editor of high reputation, who has specialized on Lope de Vega (q.v.), publishing more than a hundred studies of his work and more than twenty editions. His annotated editions of *Las mejores novelas españolas contemporáneas* (12 vols., Barcelona, 1956) are most useful.

Among his more important studies are *Miguel de Molinos* (1935), *Obras de Pedro Laynez* (1951), *Vicente Espinel, poeta de la reina Ana de Austria*

(1956), *El Madrid de Moratín* (1960), *Lope de Vega y su tiempo* (Barcelona, 1961), *Góngora y Lope en la coyuntura del Renacimiento y el Barroco* (1962), *La obra poética de Bécquer en su discriminación creadora y erótica* (1974), and *Estudios y ensayos sobre Góngora y el Barroco* (1975).

Entre bobos anda el juego (first published in the *Segunda parte de las Comedias*, 1645), a *comedia de figurón* (q.v.), by Francisco de Rojas Zorrilla (q.v.).

The pompous fool, Don Lucas de Cigarral (whose name is the play's sub-title), is a protagonist familiar from Roman comedy, the *commedie dell'arte* and the Spanish *entremeses*, but is here given fuller treatment. Thin as a rake, fussy, rich but avaricious, Lucas has arranged a marriage with Isabela, the daughter of a poor nobleman who thinks this a good way of improving the family fortunes. Lucas sends his cousin Pedro to escort his fiancée from Madrid but, after a series of complications, 'takes his vengeance' on Pedro for falling in love with Isabela, and forces him to marry her.

The play has some entertaining minor characters, among them another of Isabela's suitors, Don Luis, who speaks in an affected gongoristic style; and Don Lucas' sister Alfonsa, who can swoon at will to achieve her own ends. Most of the play is written in verse, but Rojas uses prose for the 'love' letter which Lucas sends to his fiancée, in extreme contrast to the high-flown language used by Pedro to describe the bathing Isabela.

Entre bobos anda el juego has been ed. for *Clásicos Castellanos* (3rd edn., 1944) by F. Ruiz Morcuende.

Entremeses (French: *entremets*, 'side-dish'), short plays, often accompanied by singing, believed to be of religious or semi-religious origin but later purely secular. Works of this kind were recorded at Valencia as early as 1412, but the *entremés* reached the height of popularity with Luis Quiñones de Benavente (q.v.). Few plays were performed between 1620 and 1650 without one or more *entremeses* between the acts (usually the first and second) to provide comic relief, often incongruous with the play but of great importance for the depiction of contemporary customs, drawn mainly from low life.

Joan Timoneda (q.v.) first used the term in his collection of *entremeses*, *Turiana* (Valencia, 1565), and Lope de Rueda (q.v.) wrote a large number, from which Lope de Vega (q.v.) drew subjects and characters for the numerous *entremeses* dubiously ascribed to him in his *Comedias*. Eight of Cervantes' *entremeses* survive, the best being *El retablo de las maravillas* and *La cueva de Salamanca*. Probably the finest writer of *entremeses* was Quiñones de Benavente, who created the immortal character Juan Rana (q.v.). The *entremés* became so popular that, in the early decades of the 17th c., collections of *comedias* often included the *entremeses* that had been performed with them. The first anthology of *entremeses* by various authors appeared in Saragossa in 1640. *Entremeses* have been written by more recent dramatists such as the brothers Álvarez Quintero (qq.v.).

See the study by Eugenio Asensio, *Itinerario del entremés desde Lope de Rueda a Quiñones de Benavente* (1965).

ENZINAS, FRANCISCO DE (1520–52), b. Burgos. Humanist who studied at Louvain, taught Greek at Cambridge, went to Geneva to see Calvin, and died of the plague on his return to Strasbourg.

A disciple of Luther and admirer of Melanchthon, Enzinas hellenized his name to Dryander. He wrote *Breve y compendiosa institución cristiana* (1540) before translating and publishing *Nuevo Testamento de Nuestro Redemptor* (Antwerp, 1543), an offence for which he was jailed in Brussels. He managed to escape from prison and continued writing for the Reformation movement. He translated Livy, Lucian, and Plutarch's *Lives* and composed the important *Historia del estado de los Paises Bajos y de la religión de España* (1558) under the French form of his name, François du Chesne. His absorbing *Memorias* (1543–5) are autobiographical.

See M. Bataillon, *Erasme et l'Espagne* (1937; enlarged Spanish translation, Mexico City, 1950).

Episodios nacionales, the cycle of 46 historical novels by Benito Pérez Galdós (q.v.) spanning the history of Spain from the Battle of Trafalgar, in 1805, to the Bourbon Restoration in 1874. The cycle consists of four sequences of ten novels each, and a fifth of six novels. The immediate model was the cycle of *Romans nationaux et populaires* written by Émile Erckmann and Alexandre Chatrian, collaborating as Erckmann-Chatrian.

The first sequence is on the War of Independence: *Trafalgar* (1873), *La corte de Carlos IV* (1873), *El 19 de marzo y el 2 de mayo* (1873), *Bailén* (1873), *Napoleón en Chamartín* (1874), *Zaragoza* (1874), *Gerona* (1874), *Cádiz* (1874), *Juan Martín, el Empecinado* (1874), and *La batalla de los Arapiles* (1875).

The second sequence concerns the struggle between the liberals and the absolutists up to the death of Fernando VII in 1833: *El equipaje del rey José* (1875), *Memorias de un cortesano de 1815* (1875), *La segunda casaca* (1876), *El Grande Oriente* (1876), *El 7 de julio* (1876), *Los cien mil*

hijos de San Luis (1877), *El terror de 1824* (1877), *Un voluntario realista* (1878), *Los apostólicos* (1879), and *Un faccioso más y algunos frailes menos* (1879).

The third sequence, technically the most accomplished, deals with the Carlist wars: *Zumalacárregui* (1898), *Mendizábal* (1898), *De Oñate a La Granja* (1898), *Luchana* (1899), *La campaña del Maestrazgo* (1899), *La estafeta romántica* (1899), *Vergara* (1899), *Montes de Oca* (1900), *Los Ayacuchos* (1900), and *Bodas reales* (1900).

The fourth sequence covers the period from the marriage of Isabel II in 1846 to the September Revolution of 1868: *Las tormentas del 48* (1902), *Narváez* (1902), *Los duendes de la camarilla* (1903), *La revolución de julio* (1904), *O'Donnell* (1904), *Aita Tettauen* (1905), *Carlos VI en La Rápita* (1905), *La vuelta al mundo de la 'Numancia'* (1906), *Prim* (1906), and *La de los tristes destinos* (1907).

The fifth sequence is the least convincing, since in it Galdós resorts to an excessive use of symbolism and allegory: *España sin rey* (1908), *España trágica* (1909), *Amadeo I* (1910), *La Primera República* (1911), *De Cartago a Sagunto* (1911), and *Cánovas* (1912).

Galdós began by making each sequence integral by means of a single hero (Gabriel Araceli in the first, Salvador Monsalud in the second), but he abandoned this method as his panorama of contemporary history spread. The *Episodios nacionales* are better known in Spain than the *Novelas españolas contemporáneas* (q.v.) because they are more orthodox from the religious viewpoint. They are painstakingly factual where the narrative calls for delineation of historical people and events, but no less realistic on the psychological plane, allowing for the author's liberal and anti-clerical bias (cf. H. C. Berkowitz, *Benito Pérez Galdós, Spanish liberal crusader*, Madison, Wis., 1948).

Two novels which Pérez Galdós grouped with his *Novelas españolas de la primera época* (q.v.) have been judged by many critics to fall more aptly within the framework of the *Episodios nacionales*. These are *La Fontana de Oro* (1867–8), on the revolutionary *tertulia* of 1820–2; and *El audaz: historia de un radical de antaño* (1871), on a Spanish revolutionary's involvement with the events of 1804.

See H. Hinterhäuser, *Die 'Episodios Nacionales' von Benito Pérez Galdós* (Hamburg, 1961, Spanish translation, Madrid, 1963).

Epístola moral a Fabio, an anonymous moral poem in tercets formerly attributed to Bartolomé Leonardo de Argensola (q.v.), when first published in López de Sedano's *Parnaso español* (1768), though one of the MSS. bears a marginalium declaring the poems to be not his but by Francisco de Medrano (q.v.). The work was later attributed to Francisco de Rioja (q.v.) when published in Pedro Estala's *Poesías inéditas de Francisco de Rioja* (1797); to Rodrigo Caro (q.v.) in A. Baig Baños's *Rodrigo Caro: autor de la* 'Epístola moral a Fabio' (1932); and to Andrés Fernández de Andrada (q.v.) by Adolfo de Castro in his *La 'Epístola moral a Fabio'* (Cádiz, 1875), and (more convincingly) by Dámaso Alonso (q.v.) in *Dos españoles del Siglo de Oro* (Madrid, 1960).

Often acclaimed as the major Spanish poem of the 17th c., the *Epístola moral* expounds a Stoic view of life in its acceptance of adversity, its *desengaño* (or disillusion) with the fleeting world of appearances and the transitory nature of life and worldly values, and a meditative tone which makes it the nearest secular counterpart to the poems of Luis de León (q.v.). It has been suggested that the poem influenced Gray's *Elegy*.

The variants in the MSS., numerous and often difficult to resolve, have been studied by R. Foulché-Delbosc in the *Revue Hispanique*, vol. 7 (1900).

ERAUSO, Catalina de (1592?–1635?), b. San Sebastián. Subject of a spurious autobiography. She was of an aristocratic family, and entered a Dominican convent when a girl. After a conflict with the nuns, she escaped in 1607 and wandered all over Spain dressed as a man, playing cards, drinking, and flirting with women. Obtaining a passage on a boat to America, she was appointed estate manager and fought in the Spanish army against the natives. During an illness in 1623, she was examined and her sex discovered. After some time in Spain and Rome, she set out once more for America, but her boat sank, and 'Antonio de Erauso' was declared officially missing.

There is a factual *Memorial de los méritos y servicios del Alférez Erauso* in MS. (in Seville) and it is possibly on the basis of this MS. that the apocryphal *Historia de la monja alférez* (Paris, 1829; reprinted 1919) was written in the first person. It was edited by J. M. Ferrer, with a postscript by Cándido María Trigueros, either of whom may have been the true author. Pérez de Montalbán (q.v.) used the same *Memorial* as the source for his play *La monja alférez*.

ERAUSO Y ZABALETA, Tomás (18th c.), the pseudonym of the author of *Discurso crítico sobre el origen, calidad y estado de las comedias de España, contra el dictamen que las supone corrompidas* (1750) by 'un Ingenio de esta Corte'. This was one of the scathing attacks on Blas Antonio Nasarre (q.v.), who had mocked Lope de Vega and Calderón (qq.v.) in a vituperative prologue to

his reissue of the *Comedias y entremeses de Miguel de Cervantes* (1749).

ERCILLA Y ZÚÑIGA, Alonso de (1533–94), b. Madrid. Epic poet of noble parentage. His *La Araucana* (q.v., first complete edn. of 3 parts, 1589) is the greatest of Spanish epics, though it deals with the relatively insignificant capture by the Spaniards of a small valley in Chile. The work's greatness lies in the brilliance of its description of the Indian chiefs, battles, and landscapes.

Ercilla travelled throughout Europe before coming of age, but felt impelled to take part in the South American adventures, joining Alderete in the invasion of the Arauco valley. After Alderete's death, Ercilla went to Lima, where he fought with García Hurtado de Mendoza. He fell gravely ill in 1560, but recovered and returned to Spain, where he made an advantageous marriage and lived, respected and honoured, at court.

Alonso de Ercilla y Zúñiga by A. J. Aquila (London, 1975) is a bibliography. The best edition of *La Araucana* is that of J. Toribio Medina (1916).

ESCALANTE Y PRIETO, Amós de (1831–1902). b. Santander. Novelist and poet, writing as 'Juan García'. He wrote an impressive historical novel, *Ave Maris Stella* (1877; reprinted 1920), subtitled *historia montañesa del siglo XVII*, whose only weakness is the relative paucity of action. Escalante creates expertly period atmosphere and wholly convincing characters. His more conventional verses in *Poesías* (1907) are best when concentrating on the sea and mountains near Santander. Among his travel books are *Del Manzanares al Darro* (1863), *Del Ebro al Tíber* (1864), *Costas y montañas* (1871), and *En la playa* (1873). His *Obras escogidas* (2 vols., 1956) appeared as vols. 93–4 of the BAE edited by M. Menéndez y Pelayo with a bibliographical introduction by Helen S. Nicholson.

See J. M. de Cossío, *Amós de Escalante: biografía y carácter* (1933), a brief essay.

Escándalo, El (1875), a novel by Pedro Antonio de Alarcón (q.v.).

Regarded by Alarcón as his best work, *El escándalo* is written mostly in dialogue form. The protagonists are Fabián Conde (semi-autobiographical in his attitudes) and Padre Manrique, a Jesuit who guides Conde through a crisis in which he chooses to renounce his social position and fortune in a matter of conscience.

Alarcón was greatly affected (as were most of the writers of his generation) by the Revolution of 1868. Though not a Carlist, he was ultra-Catholic and conservative (a supporter of

Cánovas), and against the progressives. His novel becomes a *roman à thèse*, yet his polemical stance rarely detracts from the beauty of the character-drawing or the verisimilitude of the dialogue and dramatic situations.

See J. F. Montesinos, 'Sobre "El escándalo" de Alarcón' in his *Ensayos y estudios de literatura española* (1959), pp. 170–201; and M. Z. Hafter, 'Alarcón in "El escándalo" ' in *Modern Language Notes*, vol. 83 (1968), pp. 212–25.

ESCARDÓ, ROLANDO (1925–60), b. Camagüey. Cuban poet of the first revolutionary generation who was killed in a car accident. He spent the last year of Batista's dictatorship in Mexico, subsequently returning to work for the Instituto Nacional de Reforma Agraria in Las Villas. Most of his poems are hastily-written but are impressive fragments of a life lived to the full despite the poet's frequent poverty and hunger. Influenced by Vallejo (q.v.), Escardó had however moved towards more individual style in the tense, lyrical poems of *Las ráfagas* (1961) and *El libro de Rolando* (1962).

ESCARRAMÁN, a notorious Sevillian criminal who served ten years in the galleys for his misdeeds. Lope's *auto sacramental La puente del mundo* is preceded by a *Loa del Escarramán* stated by Menéndez y Pelayo to be a paraphrase *a lo divino* of the famous *jácara* (q.v.) of Quevedo, *Carta de Escarramán a la Méndez*. An *escarramán* is also a kind of lewd ballad performed in Spain about 1613 and denounced by the Jesuit P. Juan Ferrer.

ESCAVIAS, PEDRO DE (*fl.* 1470), historian and poet. He was castellan at Andújar (a small Andalusian town), helping Miguel Lucas to hold the Kingdom of Jaén and providing Enrique IV with a reliable southern redoubt. Escavias is known to have written 22 surviving poems (in the *Cancioneros de Gallardo-San Román* and *Oñate y Castañeda*), and a history of Spain entitled *Repertorio de príncipes*, edited together by Michel García (Jaén, 1972). On stylistic evidence Escavias may also be the author of *Hechos del condestable Miguel Lucas de Iranzo*.

See J. B. Avalle-Arce, *El cronista Pedro de Escavias: una vida del siglo XV* (Chapel Hill, N.C., 1972), which publishes recently discovered documents.

Escenas matritenses (4 vols., 1842), a collection of *cuadros de costumbres* by Ramón de Mesonero Romanos (q.v.).

Most late 18th-c. and early 19th-c. Spanish writers produced at least a few sketches of manners, or *cuadros de costumbres*, but the specialists and acknowledged masters were Mesonero Romanos and Serafín Estébanez Calderón (q.v.), 'El Solitario'.

Mesonero Romanos, writing as 'El Curioso Parlante', produced three series beginning with *Panorama matritense* (3 vols., 1835–8), expanded as *Escenas matritenses* (4 vols., 1842), and concluding with *Tipos, grupos y bocetos de cuadros de costumbres* (1862).

Most of the sketches were first published in the reviews *Cartas españolas* and *Semanario pintoresco*, and concentrate on the city and people of Madrid, where many of their readers lived and worked. The sketches are affectionate, lacking the sharp satire of Larra's articles or the objectivity of Estébanez. Mesonero is not to be trusted as an accurate observer, and he strikes the modern reader as excessively didactic. His morality is explicit, and conservative. Some of the best essays are on literary themes (*El Liceo*, *El Parnasillo*) or examples of literary satire (*Las traducciones*, *Costumbres literarias*). He connected immorality with Romanticism in the satire *El romanticismo y los románticos*; idealized the traditional values of Castilian society while realizing that they were fast disappearing; and sought to offset the caricatures of Spanish life propagated by French Romantic writers.

The style is simple and direct and the language that of the middle classes who read the Madrid papers. He aimed to entertain, and to provoke benevolent laughter. Some of his best sketches are 'Las ferias', 'El cesante', 'La almoneda', 'El día de toros', and 'De tejas arriba'.

E. Correa Calderón has produced a recent edition (Salamanca, 1964). Camilo José Cela (q.v.) has written seven volumes of *Nuevas escenas matritenses* (1965–6).

See E. Caldera, 'Il problema del vero nelle "Escenas matritenses" ' in *Miscellanea di Studi Ispanici* (Pisa, 1964), pp. 101–21.

Escenas montañesas (1864), a series of stories and *cuadros de costumbres* by José María de Pereda (q.v.).

Subtitled 'Colección de bosquejos de costumbres tomados del natural', the book contained stories, essays, and sketches all previously published. It attracted little attention, but deserved wider recognition for its new-found frankness about the province of Santander, which Pereda had previously described only in the most flattering way. In a later note, Pereda explained that his mountain scenes 'were not written with a set plan nor at one time, nor are they the work of the mature reflection of a philosopher but the fruit of an impressionable boy's leisure'.

The *cuadros de costumbres* proper include *Los*

bailes campestres, and *Arroz y gallo muerto* on a saint's day feast. *Suum cuique* ('Each to his own') is a short novel in which a *santanderino* goes to Madrid to expedite the settling of a law-suit and returns in disgust with a *madrileño* who at first expresses delight with the Montaña region behind Santander but with the passing weeks understands more of the peasants' roughness and deceit. The two friends finally agree that each person belongs in his original environment, and part amicably.

The shorter stories each present a picture of some aspect of regional life: *La leva* and *El fin de una raza* on Santander's port and seamen; *El requero* on a beachcomber; and *La costurera* on a seamstress.

A second series of Pereda's Santander sketches appeared in 1871, entitled *Tipos y paisajes*; and a third, *Esbozos y rasguñas*, in 1881.

See J. F. Montesinos, *Pereda o la novela idilio* (1969).

Esclavo del demonio, El (Barcelona, 1612), a major theological play by Antonio Mira de Amescua (q.v.) on the well-known medieval theme of Faust and his pact with the devil.

The direct source of the play is Hernando del Castillo's *Historia general de Santo Domingo y de la Orden de Predicadores*, but Mira exchanges the devil's gift of knowledge in the source for his gift of a woman's love in the play.

The play has two male protagonists (Gil and Diego) and two female (Leonor and Lisarda). The figure of the impulsive Lisarda (like Julia in Calderón's later *Devoción de la Cruz*, qq.v.) is especially well conceived and executed.

Diego Meneses is in love with Lisarda and intends to elope with her against her father's wish. On his way, however, he meets the pious Gil, an ascetic canon of Coimbra, who dissuades Diego. But Gil is himself enchanted by Lisarda and seduces her. Lisarda's father Marcelo believes that she has been kidnapped by Diego, and Diego believes that she has gone away with her father. Gil and Lisarda turn outlaws, and happen to capture Marcelo and Lisarda's sister Leonor. Gil now falls in love with Leonor and signs a pact with the devil to obtain her willing love. Diego is then captured by the bandits and he attempts to dissuade Gil in his turn. Lisarda finally pardons Gil, who rejects all the treasures he is offered by the devil and claims Leonor. The devil brings her, but in the form of a skeleton. Gil repents and manages to retrieve the written pact with the devil, and confesses that he was the cause of all the suffering. The souls of both Lisarda and Gil are saved.

The play attempts to justify the doctrine of free will, and is thus a key document in the controversy *De auxiliis* (q.v.).

El esclavo del demonio has been edited by A. Valbuena Prat (1928) in Clásicos Castellanos.

ESCOBAR, ALBERTO (1929–), Peruvian critic, neo-Romantic poet, and anthologist. His poems in *Diario de viaje* (1958) are carefully constructed but by no means academic in style. His best work has been in the field of criticism and the essay: *Asedio en torno del cuento y la novela* (1952), *La narración en el Perú* (with an anthology, 1956), and *Patio de letras* (1965), the last containing studies on the Inca Garcilaso, González Prada, Ricardo Palma, Alegría, and later writers, concentrating on close textual analysis, which has been relatively weak in Latin-American writing. Escobar's anthologies include *El cuento peruano, 1825–1925* (Buenos Aires, 1964) and *Antología de la poesía peruana* (1965).

ESCOBAR, JULIO (1901–), b. Arévalo, Ávila. Novelist and journalist. Beginning in provincial journalism, he joined the staff of *El Imparcial* (Madrid) in 1929. His occasional essays were collected as *Azulejos españoles* (1947) and *Andar y ver* (1949).

Among his novels, which have been praised highly by Madrid critics, are *El hidalgo de Madrigal* (1952), *Teresa y el cuervo* (1954), *Cinco mecanógrafas y un millonario* (1955), *La viuda y el alfarero* (1957), *Una cruz en la tierra* (1960), *El viento no envejece* (1964), *Se vende el campo* (1966), *La sombra de Caín* (1968), *Vargadores de ceniza* (1971), and *El novillo del Alba* (1971), the last awarded the Álvarez Quintero Prize of the Real Academia Española for the best novel over three years.

ESCOBAR Y MENDOZA, ANTONIO DE (1589–1669), b. Valladolid. Jesuit baroque poet. His two long poems are *San Ignacio* (Valladolid, 1613) and *Historia de la Virgen Madre de Dios* (Valladolid, 1618), the latter reworked as *Nueva Jerusalén María* (1625). Both poems use fantastic, ornate word pictures. *San Ignacio* is one of the several epics wrought around the life and legends of the founder of the Society of Jesus. It consists of 18 cantos, and is impregnated with the kind of classical myth that Camões and Góngora had made *de rigueur* in Peninsular verse.

His second poem makes up in decoration what it lacks in original inspiration, audaciously identifying Mary the Mother of God with a New Jerusalem whose foundations were of jacinth, chrysoprase, and many other precious stones.

For the unwitting damage done to the Jesuit cause by Escobar's poetic effusions as ridiculed in Pascal's *Lettres provinciales* (1656–7), see T. Wyzewa, 'Le Père Escobar et les Lettres

Provinciales' in *Revue des Deux Mondes* (March 1872).

ESCOBEDO, Padre FEDERICO (1874–1949*v*, b. Salvatierra, Guanajuato. Mexican poet and translator, who also wrote in Latin. He was forced to discontinue higher theological studies in Granada due to ill health, and returned to Mexico where he published a long series of neoclassical poems with Romantic and modernist tinges, the majority lacking interest because of his limited imagination. His first collection was *Carmina latina* (Puebla, 1902), followed by *Poesías* . . . (Puebla, 1903), and many more, of which the more interesting are *Rapsodías bíblicas, horacianas y soledades canoras* (Tezuitlán, 1923), *La sombre de Virgilio* (Tezuitlán, 1930), and the *Elegía* (1940) to Archbishop Montes de Oca. Escobedo's most enduring writing is a translation of Rafael Landívar's *Rusticatio mexicana: geórgicas mexicanas* (Tezuitlán, 1925).

ESCOIQUIZ, JUAN DE (*fl.* 1798–1814), epic poet, translator, and autobiographer. A man of integrity, Escoiquiz suffered imprisonment and exile in France for refusing to change allegiance as tutor to Ferdinand, Prince of Asturias, on the invasion of the French in 1808. He translated Young's celebrated *Night Thoughts* (1742–5) in 1797 and in the following year published his epic poem in 26 books, *México conquistado* (3 vols., 1798), a failure which derives its meagre interest from the source material taken from *Historia de la conquista de México* of Antonio de Solís (q.v.). The stanzas are awkwardly-constructed, the dullness is rarely relieved by an imaginative insight, and allegorical figures take up too much of what little action there is. Escoiquiz was a political prisoner in France 1808–14, and there translated Milton's *Paradise Lost*. His *Memorias 1807–1808* (1915) have been edited by A. Paz y Melia for the Colección de Escritores Castellanos.

ESCOSURA, PATRICIO DE LA (1807–78), b. Oviedo. Minor Romantic novelist, playwright, and poet. A pupil of Lista, Escosura was a friend of Espronceda and a member of his secret society *Los Numantinos* (see also NUMANCIA) and as such was forced to escape from Spain when the society was threatened.

On his return to Spain he eventually became ambassador, in the Philippines and elsewhere.

He made a name as a historical novelist in the manner of Sir Walter Scott with *El Conde de Candespina* (2 vols., 1832), *Ni Rey ni Roque* (4 vols., 1835) set in 1595, *El Patriarca del Valle* (2 vols., 1846–7), *La conjuración de México, o los hijos de Hernán Cortés* (3 vols., Mexico City, 1850), and the semi-autobiographical *Memorias de un coronel*

retirado (1868). He imitated Espronceda in his legend *El bulto vestido de negro capuz* (1835).

His verse plays enjoyed a measure of popularity, particularly those dealing with familiar historical events and personages: *La Corte del Buen Retiro* (1837) and its sequel *También los muertos se vengan* (1838), *La aurora de Colón* and *Don Jaime el Conquistador* (both 1838), and *Las mocedades de Hernán Cortés* (1845). Among his contributions to scholarship were a study on Calderón's plays prefixed to the Real Academia Española edition (2 vols., 1868), *Manual de mitología* (1845), and *Estudios históricos sobre las costumbres españolas* (1851).

See A. Iniesta, *Don Patricio de la Escosura* (1958), with a bibliography.

ESCRIVÁ, JOAN (*c.* 1450–*c.* 1520), poet writing in Valencian and Castilian. The only biographical datum known is that he was ambassador of Fernando and Isabel at the Vatican in 1497. His verse is inventive, melodious, and often witty, though the *canción Soledad triste que siento* (1511) is serious, and he has written the wistful *villancico* '¿Qué sentís, coraçón mío?' The dialogue 'Una quexa que da a su amiga ante el Dios de amor' is one of the 29 compositions by Escrivá in the *Cancionero General* of Hernando del Castillo (2nd edn., 1514).

The exquisite *canción* 'Ven, muerte tan escondida' addresses death in an apparently lighthearted manner.

See *Cancionero General* (1882, ed. J. A. de Balenchana) in the series of the Sociedad de Bibliófilos Españoles.

ESCUDERO, GONZALO (1903–), b. Quito. Ecuadorian poet and diplomat, the son of the liberal Minister of Education Manuel Eduardo Escudero. He contributed to *El Día* and *La Tierra*. His books include *Los poemas del arte* (1919), *Parábolas olímpicas* (1922), *Hélices de huracán y de sol* (Madrid, 1933), *Altanoche* (1947), *Estatua de aire* (Madrid, 1951), *Materia del ángel* (1953), *Autorretrato* (1957), and *Introducción a la muerte* (1960). Escudero's earlier poetry was influenced by Walt Whitman, but he has narrowed his range from the cosmic to the human since *Altanoche*. He has also written a comedy: *Paralelogramas* (1935).

ESLAVA, ANTONIO DE (b. 1570?), b. Sangüesa, Navarra. Novelist. His eleven long stories in dialogue form appeared in *Primera parte del libro intitulado Noches de Inuierno* (Pamplona, 1609) and several printings in different cities in a few months. It has been edited by González Palencia (1942). No second part appeared.

There is a strong possibility that Shakespeare read Eslava's story 'Do se cuenta la soberbia del rey Nicíforo y incendio de sus naves, y la arte mágica del rey Dardano' and took the kernel of *The Tempest* (1611–12) from it.

This story, with 'Do se cuenta como fue descubierta la fuente del desengaño' and 'Se cuenta el nacimiento de Carlo Magno, rey de Francia y emperador romano' are reprinted in *Cuentos viejos de la vieja España* (comp. by F. C. Saínz de Robles, 1949).

See J. de José y Prades, ' "Las noches de invierno" de Antonio de Eslava', in *Revista Bibliográfica y Documental*, vol. 3 (1949), pp. 163–96.

Espadaña, Grupo, a literary circle formed in León by Victoriano Crémer, Eugenio G. de Nora (qq.v.), and the critic Antonio G. de Lama.

The movement began in May 1944 with the first issue of *Espadaña*, subsequently spreading its belief in the social function of poetry throughout Spain. Adherents include Rafael Múgica, Blas de Otero, Leopoldo de Luis (qq.v.), and Salvador Pérez Valiente.

España invertebrada: bosquejo de algunos pensamientos históricos (1921), a socio-historical meditation on the nature of Spain and the Spanish by José Ortega y Gasset (q.v.).

A nation signifies a dynamic common way of life. When the dynamism fails, this common way of life disintegrates into sections through the process of *particularismo*. Castile created the Spain that we know today, but by retaining centralized power she also destroyed the potential of Spain as a nation. *Particularismo* involves not only the different races that make up Spain, but also its warring classes, each defending its own interest against the others. The reason for Spain's spinelessness is to be found in the absence of an intellectual élite capable of guiding the masses. As a Germanophile, Ortega detects a Germanic element in any true European aristocracy, arguing however that the Visigoths who ruled Spain after the fall of the Roman Empire were decadent, as opposed to the vigorous Franks who guided the rise of France as a nation. There was no difference in potential between the aboriginal Iberians and Gauls: the difference lay in the social structure imposed by the German invaders. The main characteristic of German society was feudalism. The Germanic people were men powerful in mind and body who were more interested in warfare than in farming. The Romance peoples were farmers among whom the term 'people' meant the collectivity of the masses who, in Roman times, were administered by elected officials. The militaristic Germans were most successful (as in England, or Northern Italy)

where the personality of their race was strongest. The Visigoths, lacking a strong personality and an educated élite, able to rule and impose feudalism, never passed through the phase during which (as in France) counties and dukedoms gradually passed under central control, with the result that in Spain the 'Reconquest' took eight centuries, a sign of debility rather than strength. For Ortega, the whole history of Spain, except for a few moments of glory, has been a history of decadence. Without an élite, Spain has been and is likely always to be, a rural country; the only difference between the rich and the poor is the difference between a rich peasant and a poor peasant.

Ortega returned to the theme of an educated élite and the masses in his *Rebelión de las masas* (q.v.).

Española inglesa, La, one of the *Novelas ejemplares* (q.v., 1613) by Miguel de Cervantes Saavedra (q.v.).

After the sack of Cádiz by the English, an English ship's captain captures a Spanish girl aged seven and takes her to England, where she grows up as the daughter of a respected Roman Catholic family. Ricaredo, enamoured of Isabela's beauty and charm, is loved by her in return but before celebrating the marriage the queen demands that the man to be given such a jewel should earn her by his prowess and commands him to fight against the Turkish corsairs in the Mediterranean. He takes a Portuguese galleon which has been captured by the Turks, freeing the Christian slaves, among whom he finds the parents of Isabela, who wish to find their daughter in England. The queen now grants the couple's wish but a jealous lady-in-waiting, who had hoped to marry her son to Isabela, gives her poison which fails to kill her, but causes the disfigurement of her face. The steadfast Ricaredo keeps his vow to marry her but postpones the marriage for two years in order to make a promised pilgrimage to Rome. Ricaredo is delayed on the return journey, and Isabela (gradually recovering her beauty) is on the point of entering a convent when he finally arrives and they are married.

Cervantes' neo-Platonic moral is that love is drawn to something higher than mere physical beauty.

See N. González Aurioles, *Recuerdos auto-biográficos de Cervantes en 'La española inglesa'* (1913).

Espéculo de los legos, El, a didactic work in 91 chapters translated in the 14th c. from the *Speculum laicorum* attributed to the English divine John Howden or Hoveden (13th c.). A large number of *exempla* are mixed with miscellaneous information on many subjects, parables, lives of the saints, and fables. A number of elements are drawn from the *Conde Lucanor* (q.v.).

There is an edition and study by J. M. Mohedano Hernández (1951) which should be used with caution. See the review by P. E. Russell in *Modern Language Review*, vol. 49 (1954).

ESPEJO, EUGENIO FRANCISCO JAVIER (1747–95), b. Quito, Ecuador. Journalist and essayist. Son of an Indian father and a *mestiza*. Qualified in medicine and law, Espejo became through his writings the social conscience of Ecuador and was exiled to Bogotá for two years. On his return he published the first periodical in Quito: *Primicias de la Cultura en Quito* (no. 1, 5 January 1972). He was gaoled for sedition and died in prison. His best-known works are *El nuevo Luciano* (1779; new edn., 1943), intended to alter the Jesuits' plans for education in Ecuador; and the important medical work *Reflexiones . . . acerca de un método seguro para preservar a los pueblos de viruelas* based on instructions sent from Madrid and reprinted in his *Escritos médicos, comentarios e iconografía* (1952).

Esperpentos ('horrible, nauseating persons, or things'), a term employed by Ramón María del Valle-Inclán (q.v.) to describe the technique of systematic distortion in some plays and novels. He first used the word in this aesthetic context in the play *Luces de Bohemia* (1923), whose hero Max Estrella says 'Los héroes clásicos reflejados en los espejos cóncavos dan el esperpento'. Valle-Inclán suggests both that Spanish reality is a grotesque deformation of European tradition, and that to capture the tragic sense of Spanish life one must apply a systematically-deformed aesthetic. The most typical example of Valle-Inclán's esperpentic plays is *Los cuernos de don Friolera* (1921), foreshadowing the later European theatre of the absurd (Adamov, Ionesco, Beckett, and the exiled Spaniard Arrabal). Characters are seen not as heroic or gallant but as grotesque dolls, puppets, or even animals. Valle-Inclán's first esperpentic novel was *Tirano Banderas* (q.v., 1926).

See María Eugenia March, *Forma e idea de los esperpentos de Valle-Inclán* (1969), and A. N. Zahareas, *Visión del esperpento: teoría y práctica en los esperpentos de Valle-Inclán* (1970).

ESPINA, CONCHA (1877–1955), b. Santander. Novelist. She married at 18, and went to Valparaíso with her husband for a few years but they soon returned home, and she was widowed about 1898. Her first book was a collection of poems, *Mis flores* (Valladolid, 1904), and she produced several volumes of short stories, including *Cuentos* (1922), but her fame today

rests on the 17 long novels, beginning with one of her best, *La niña de Luzmela* (1909). She was always conscious of Pereda (q.v.), the great novelist of the Montaña behind Santander, and tried to break away from the regional novel in which he had excelled. Yet these experiments all failed, and despite excessive sentimentality, strained effects, and flabby rhetoric, her Montaña novels are clearly her best.

Her works include *Despertar para morir* (1910), *Agua de nieve* (1911), *La esfinge maragata* (1914), *La rosa de los vientos* (1916) which is possibly the best of her mountain novels, *El metal de los muertos* (1920) a popular novel of mining and miners, *Dulce nombre* (1921), *El cáliz rojo* (1923), *Altar Mayor* (1926), *Copa de horizontes* (1930), and *Retaguardia*, published in 1937, the year of her blindness. She continued to produce novels: *El más fuerte* (1947), *Un valle en el mar* (1950), *Una novela de amor* (1953), and *Aurora de España* (1955). The *Obras completas* (1944) were replaced by a new edition in 2 vols. (1960).

See M. Rosenberg, *Concha Espina* (Los Angeles, 1927), F. Lagoni, *Concha Espina y sus críticos* (Toulouse, 1929), and E. G. de Nora, *La novela española contemporánea* vol. 1 (2nd edn., 1963, pp. 328–41).

ESPINA GARCÍA, ANTONIO (1894–), b. Madrid. Journalist, biographer, and novelist. He edited *La Nueva España* with J. Díaz Fernández. His early poems were influenced by *ultraísmo*: *Umbrales* (1918) and *Signario* (1923) but he is perhaps best known for his intellectual 'dehumanized' novels *Pájaro pinto* (1927) and *Luna de copas* (1929), the latter serialized in *Revista de Occidente*. He was influenced by the writings of Benjamín Jarnés (q.v.), though he lacked Jarnés's powers. His essays include *Lo cómico contemporáneo y otros ensayos* (1928) and *Audaces y extravagantes* (1959). Espina spent much of his writing life on biography, beginning with *Luis Candelas, el bandido de Madrid* (1929) and *Romea, o el comediante* (1935), and concluding with lives of Cánovas del Castillo, Quevedo, and Cervantes.

See E. G. de Nora, *La novela española contemporánea*, vol. 2 (2nd edn., 1968, pp. 197–200).

ESPINÀS, JOSEP MARIA (1927–), b. Barcelona. Catalan novelist, travel writer, and short-story writer. He is also known as an author of Catalan songs. His novels are *Com ganivets o flames* (1954), *Dotze bumerangs* (1954), *El gandul* (1955), *Tots som iguals* (1956; translated as *By nature equal* (New York, 1961), *La trampa* (1956), *L'home de la guitarra* (1957), *Combat de nit* (1959), *L'ultim replà* (1962), and *La collita del diable* (1968). His short stories include *Vestirse per morir* (1958), *Varietés* (1959), and *Els joves* *i els altres* (1960). Among his many travel books, usually records of wanderings on foot, are *Ciutats de Catalunya* (2 vols., 1956-8), *Tarragona* (1963), *Això també és Barcelona* (1965), and *Viatge a la Segovia* (1972).

ESPINEL, VICENTE MARTÍNEZ DE (1550-1624), b. Ronda. Poet, novelist, and musician. He studied at Salamanca University, and then travelled a good deal in Spain and Italy, serving with the troops of Alessandro Farnese at the siege of Maastricht (1579). He may have been taken captive by Barbary corsairs and enslaved in Algiers, but if this episode in his great novel *Marcos de Obregón* (q.v., 1618) is indeed autobiographical, which is dubious, he was quickly ransomed and soon at liberty.

He was known to his contemporaries mainly by his alleged invention of the *décima* (known after him as the '*espinela*') and for adding the fifth string to the guitar. However, the *décima* was known to earlier poets, and Espinel's major contribution was to provide the genre's most elegant and vigorous examples.

Diversas Rimas . . . con el Arte Poética, y algunas Odas de Oracio, traduzidas en verso Castellano (1591) has been edited by D. C. Clarke (New York, 1956).

See Diego Vázquez Otero, *Vida de Vicente Martínez de Espinel* (Málaga, 1948).

ESPINO, ALFREDO (1900-28), b. Ahuachapán, El Salvador, the brother of Miguel Ángel Espino (q.v.). Alfredo Espino was the poet of Cuscatlán, a department of central Salvador, and his only work *Jícaras tristes* (1936) remains popular in his native country.

ESPINO, MIGUEL ÁNGEL (1902-), b. Santa Ana, El Salvador. In his *Mitología de Cuscatlán* (expanded for publication in 1919), Espino displayed the wealth of the aboriginal literature of his native land. His best novel, *Hombres contra la muerte* (Guatemala City, 1942), won the Premio de Literatura Nacional when reprinted in Mexico City (1947). It deals with the lives of men in the forests of British Honduras, and the proximity of death by snakebite or fever. As well as its value as a major social document, the novel contains lyrical passages on the savage beauty of the forest.

ESPÍNOLA, FRANCISCO (1901-), b. Montevideo. Short-story writer and novelist who has written little but ranks as one of Uruguay's leading exponents of the short story for the nine in *Raza ciega* (1926) and the four in *El rapto y otros cuentos* (1950), none written after 1936. *Cuentos* (1961) contains a further three, the thirteen reprinted, and the children's tale

Saltoncito (1930), but he also revised the orthography of his *gaucho* tales, thus depriving them of their regional flavour. Alberto Zum Felde has pointed out that Espínola deals not in characters but in souls: 'de lo esencial y lo abismal del hombre', and this trait serves him less well in his only novel, *Sombras sobre la tierra* (1933), a shapeless but often interesting work centred on the sado-masochistic Juan Carlos, in love with the prostitute La Nena but attracted also to the more conventional Olga. Espínola also wrote *La fuga en el espejo* (1937), a play with surrealistic overtones.

ESPINOSA, JANUARIO (1882-1946), b. Linares. Chilean novelist and short-story writer. He worked as a telegraphist, using this experience in his novel *La señorita Cortes Monroy, telegrafista* (1928). Espinosa, a Creole realist occasionally guilty of careless writing, was a member of the *Generación del Centenario*, with Latorre, d'Halmar, Barrios, and Edwards Bello (qq.v.).

His first book, *Cecilia* (1907), dealt with rural life, but later works concentrated on the urban middle classes: *La vida humilde* (1914), *Las inquietudes de Ana María* (1916), *El juguete roto* (1927), and *Pillán* (1934). *La ciudad encantada* (1942) is a collection of short stories on middle class themes.

ESPINOSA, PEDRO DE (1578-1650), b. Antequera, Málaga. Poet, anthologist, and prose writer, who lived in Granada, Seville, and Valladolid, with an interval as a hermit with the name of Pedro de Jesús. His poems are notable for giving new life to well-worn Italian themes, such as the love of nature and classical mythology: 'La fábula del Génil' is such a work. His religious verse appears in *Salmo de penitencia, importantíssimo para alcançar perdón de los pecados* (Sanlúcar, 1625). He wrote Quevedesque satirical prose in *El perro y la calentura* and *Espejo de cristal* (both Sanlúcar, 1625), and a cynical essay against astrologers, *Pronóstico judiciario de los sucesos deste año 1627 hasta el fin del mundo* (Málaga, 1627) which is included in F. Rodríguez Marín's edition of Espinosa's works (1909). F. López Estrada has edited the *Poesías completas* (1975) in Clásicos Castellanos.

Espinosa, is best remembered, however, for *Primera parte de las Flores de poetas ilustres* (Valladolid, 1605), which was finally completed by the *Segunda parte* prepared by Juan Antonio Calderón in 1896. Espinosa's anthology (ed. J. Quirós de los Ríos and F. Rodríguez Marín, 2 vols., 1896) was remarkably perceptive in its choice, including Luis de León, Barahona de Soto, Góngora, Quevedo, Alcázar, and Lope de Vega, and excluding many poets highly regarded in their day but now forgotten.

See F. Rodríguez Marín, *Pedro de Espinosa: estudio biográfico, bibliográfico y crítico* (1907) and the useful *Homenaje a Pedro Espinosa* (Seville, 1953).

ESPINOSA MEDRANO, JUAN DE (1640?–1688), b. Calcauso. Peruvian *mestizo* playwright, essayist, churchman, and philosopher, Espinosa was known as 'El Lunarejo' from the mole on his face. Legend has it that he was taken from his home village by the Bishop of Cuzco, who heard the lad reciting a poem. A prodigy of learning, Espinosa was teaching at 16 and eventually became Archdeacon of Cuzco. He was the leading baroque writer of Latin America and a late proponent of Góngora's theory and practice in *Apologético en favor de don Luis de Góngora, príncipe de los poetas líricos de España, contra Manuel Faria y Sousa* . . . (1662). He praised Góngora's innovatory treatment of traditional themes, his lyrical brilliance, verbal dexterity, and enrichment of Castilian through Latin words and metres. He is known to have written a play when only 17 (*El rapto de Proserpina*, 1657?) and was especially highly regarded for his *autos sacramentales* and biblical plays. Many works were attributed to him falsely. His best-known play is the *Auto sacramental del hijo pródigo* written in Quechua and set in Peru, the characters being Indian. It is available in Jorge Basadre's anthology *Literatura inca* (Paris, 1938). His other books include *Philosophia Thomistica* (2 vols., Rome, 1688) and a collection of thirty sermons entitled *La nouena marauilla* (1695).

See L. A. Sánchez, *La literatura peruana* (6 vols., 1950–1).

ESPRIU, SALVADOR (1913–), b. Santa Coloma de Farners, Gerona. Major Catalan poet, whose family moved when he was two to Arenys de Mar, on which he based the mythical country of 'Sinera', celebrated in many poems and in his prose fiction. Much of his best work has constituted a meditation on death and is marked by his sense of loss at the passing of the old way of life in such small communities as 'Sinera'. His books of poetry include *Cementiri de Sinera* (1946), *Les cançons d'Ariadna* (1949), *Obra lírica* (1952, including 'Les hores' and 'Mrs. Death', published in Castilian, 1956), *El caminant i el mur* (1955), *Final del laberint* (1955), and *La pell de brau* (1960, published in Castilian as *La piel de toro*, 1968), widely regarded as the most important book to appear in Spain during the 1960s, and much concerned with modern national problems. His *Obra poética* (1963) contained all his previous work, with the new *Llibre de Sinera*, separately published in Castilian in 1966. *Obres completes* began in 1968 with vol. 1: *Poesia*. Subsequent collections include

Setmana santa (Barcelona, 1971; translated into Castilian by B. Losada Castro, 1972).

A precocious prose-writer, Espriu has also written novels: *El doctor Rip* (1932), *Laia* (1932), and *Miratge a Citerea* (1935); and short stories: *Aspectes* (1934), *Ariadna al laberint grotesc* (1935), and *Letizia i altres proses* (1937). His short story 'Tres sorores' has been very highly praised. The fifth edition of his *Narracións* appeared in 1974. Among his essays are those in a volume entitled *Evocació de Rosselló-Pòrcel* (1963).

His plays include *Antígona* and *Fedra* (1950); an 'improvisation for puppets' entitled *Primera història d'Esther* (1948; 3rd edn., 1967); and *Ronda de mort a Sinera* (1966), a theatrical montage by Ricardo Salvat using texts from Espriu.

See J. M. Castellet, *Iniciació a la poesia de Salvador Espriu* (Barcelona, 1971).

ESPRONCEDA, JOSÉ DE (1808–42), b. Almendralejo, Extremadura. Major Romantic poet. After studying with Alberto Lista (q.v.) at his private school in Calle Valverde, Madrid, Espronceda was convicted of revolutionary activity (founding *Los Numantinos*, to which Escosura (q.v.) also belonged) and was banished to the monastery of S. Francisco in Guadalajara. There he started an unsuccessful epic entitled *Pelayo*, in *octavas reales*, on the Moorish conquest of Spain; there is evidence that Lista wrote some parts of this unfinished poem. He emigrated in 1826, first to Gibraltar, then to Lisbon, where he fell in love with Teresa Mancha, daughter of another *émigré*, and finally he followed the Mancha family to London in 1827. Teresa was married to a businessman in Paris but, after Espronceda had fought for libertarian causes in the Netherlands (1828) and on the Paris barricades (1830), he eloped with her to Spain, where she eventually left him. He joined the left wing of the Liberal Party on his return to Spain in 1833, and was a founder-member of the Republican Party in 1840 shortly after his reputation had been made by the Romantic *leyenda*, *El estudiante de Salamanca* (q.v., 1836–7). His lyrical poetry was much admired. The first group is the patriotic cycle beginning with *A la patria* (1829), which attacks the despotism then prevailing in Spain, and the virulent sonnet on the death of Torrijos. Espronceda was a member of the second Romantic generation, as is shown by his call to arms against the Carlists (1835) and *Dos de mayo* (1840), when the first Romantic generation (including Rivas and Martínez de la Rosa, qq.v.) were retreating from their earlier position.

Individualistic poems of rebellion and liberty form another distinct group, including 'Canción del pirata', 'El verdugo', and 'El canto del

Cosaco'. The final group of Espronceda's lyrics is the occasional, and includes 'A una estrella', and the philosophic 'Himno al sol' which contrasts the mutability of human life with the sun's permanence. Espronceda's debt to Byron was overstated in his lifetime by the Conde Toreno who, asked if he had read Espronceda, replied merely, 'I have read Byron'. Espronceda was less influenced by Byron in *El diablo mundo* (q.v.), unfinished at his death. His plays exaggerate the rhetorical faults of his poetry, and his prose is disappointing. *Sancho Saldaña, o el castellano de Cuéllar* (6 vols., 1834) is a curious attempt at the historical novel made popular by Sir Walter Scott; the hero is a victim of existential misery (as it would now be known), desiring a belief in some external principle but constantly encountering disillusion.

Espronceda's *Obras completas* are in vol. 72 (1954) of the BAE, but the lyrical poetry is best read in *Poesías líricas y fragmentos épicos* (1970), edited by R. Marrast and translated from his French edition of 1969. The tragedy *Blanca de Borbón* (1870) has been edited by P. H. Churchman (*Revue Hispanique*, vol. 17 (1907), pp. 549–775).

See J. Cascales Muñoz, *Don José de Espronceda* (1924); Joaquín Casalduero, *Forma y visión de 'El diablo mundo'* (1951) and *Espronceda* (1961); and in particular Robert Marrast, *José Espronceda et son temps: littérature, société, politique au temps du Romantisme* (Paris, 1974).

ESQUILACHE, *Príncipe de,* see BORJA Y ARAGON, Francisco de.

Estados, Libro de los, a didactic work by the Infante Don Juan Manuel (q.v.) written in and shortly after the year 1330. The first 100 chapters deal with worldly education, while the last 50 deal with religious education.

Juan Manuel uses the dialogue, his characters being the heathen king Moraván, his son Johás, a holy man Julio, and a knight Turin. A doctrinal dispute between Islam, Judaism, and Christianity ends with the traditional victory of Christianity.

The *Libro de los Estados* includes the first surviving adaptation in Spanish of the legend of Barlaam and Josaphat (q.v.), but in Juan Manuel's version the young prince's three encounters are condensed into one, with a corpse; while the essentially religious message of asceticism becomes an ethical message of prudence and wisdom. The book, much of it derived from the *Blanquerna* of Ramon Llull (q.v.), has been edited by J. M. Castro y Calvo (1968) and by R. B. Tate and I. R. Macpherson (Oxford, 1974).

ESTALA, PEDRO (*c.* 1740–*c.* 1820), b. Madrid. Essayist and anthologist. An Aesculapian monk who returned to the world, Estala became Rector of Salamanca Seminary. He was protected by Godoy, and when he fell Estala was persecuted and gaoled, so that when the French invaded he passed to their side and published on their behalf *El Imparcial* (1809). He compiled under the name of his barber, Ramón Fernández, the first six vols. of the Colección de Poetas Españoles (1789–98), a series which ultimately ran to 20 vols. Among the poets included were Herrera, Jáuregui, the Argensolas, and Luis de León.

Important essays on Greek tragedy and comedy respectively were prefixed to his translations of *Oedipus rex* (1793) by Sophocles and *Pluto* (1794) by Aristophanes. He defined the chief ideas of Greek drama as the dogma of fatality and the principle of democratic freedom. Among his other works are *Veintiuna cartas ineditas dirigidas a don J. P. Forner, bajo el nombre arcadico 'Damón' para la historia literaria del ultimo tercio del siglo XVIII*, edited by J. Pérez de Guzmán in *Boletín de la Real Academia de la Historia*, vol. 63 (1911), pp. 5–36.

He wrote *Bello gusto satírico crítico de inscripciones para la inteligencia de la ortografía castellana* (1785) under the pen-name Claudio Bachiller Rosillo, and the anonymous *Quatro cartas de un español a un anglómano en que se manifiesta la perfidia del gobierno de la Inglaterra* (1805), which Estala deduces the perfidy of Albion from her alliance with Spain to drive out the invading French, a circumstance which led to Estala's own disgrace and exile to France, where he died.

ESTÉBANEZ CALDERÓN, SERAFÍN (1799–1867), b. Málaga. Scholar, *costumbrista,* bibliophile, and Arabist. He studied law in Granada, and eventually occupied influential positions in the nation, including those of state councillor and senator. Originally of liberal leanings, Estébanez (he used the form Estévanes for himself and his family) became gradually more conservative in his opinions. His early writings were signed 'Safinio', but later he adopted the pen-name 'El Solitario' by which he is generally remembered. His first book was *Poesías del Solitario* (1831), consisting mainly of satirical verses, though his best poem is an elegy on the death of the Duchess of Frías. He contributed to *Cartas españolas* (1831–2) the *Escenas andaluzas* (1847) which made his reputation as an enthusiastic regional writer midway between the plain, sentimental writing of Mesonero Romanos (q.v.) and the more bitter social satire of Larra (q.v.). Estébanez confessed to a 'ciega pasión por todo cuanto huele a España', and his ability to write in a regional and archaic style without moralizing made a great impact on his generation and influenced other Andalusian regional writers such as Fernán Caballero and Juan Valera (qq.v.).

He composed an unfinished history entitled *De la conquista y pérdida de Portugal* (2 vols., 1885), and an unsatisfactory historical novel, *Cristianos y moriscos: leyenda lastimosa* (1838). His complete works have appeared in Colección de Escritores Castellanos (6 vols., 1883–96) and in vols. 78–9 (1955) of the BAE.

See '*El Solitario*' *y su tiempo: biografía de don Serafín Estébanez Calderón y crítica de sus obras* (2 vols., 1883) by his nephew, Antonio Cánovas del Castillo; and ' "El Solitario" en el tiempo', by J. A. Muñoz Rojas, in *Revista de Occidente* (1968), pp. 76–95.

ESTEBANILLO GONZÁLEZ, see González, Estéban.

ESTELLA, Fray Diego de, see Diego de Estella, *Fray*.

ESTORINO, Abelardo (1925–), Cuban playwright, producer, and actor. He has written a number of one-act plays, such as *El peine y el espejo* and *Los mangos de Caín* translated by J. M. Cohen in his anthology *Writers in the new Cuba* (London, 1967). His full-length plays are both complex and important views of the impact of the revolution on Cuban society and individuals: *El robo del cochino* (1961) and *La casa vieja* (1964).

Estos 13, the title of an important anthology of Peruvian poetry (Lima, 1973, ed. José Miguel Oviedo) which revealed the preoccupations of the generation after that of *Los Nuevos* (q.v.).

'These 13' of the title are Manuel Morales, Antonio Cilloniz, Jorge Nájar, José Watanabe, Oscar Málaga, Elqui Burgos, Juan Ramírez Ruiz, Abelardo Sánchez León, Feliciano Mejía, Tulio Mora, José Rosas Ribeyro, José Cerna, and Enrique Verástegui. These poets have been associated with the movement and magazine *Hora Cero*. The poets in general demand that poetry should assist the evolution of society towards freedom and justice, but repudiate 'committed' poetry as such. The most outstanding poet of the group is Verástegui (q.v.) who, with Sánchez León, has been insistent on the intelligent understanding of city life, its potential and its dangers. He is linguistically the most daring and the most culturally varied in tone and subject matter.

ESTRADA, Genaro (1887–1937), b. Mazatlán, Sinaloa. Mexican bibliographer, essayist, poet, and ambassador in Spain. He compiled a memorable anthology, *Poetas nuevos de México* (1916), and is generally considered one of the

Contemporáneos group, though in fact he was on the fringe. He edited the important series Monografías Bibliográficas Mexicanas beginning in 1925, contributing the first himself, on Amado Nervo. He stimulated national bibliography by starting the *Anuario Bibliográfico Mexicano*, though only the 3 vols. covering 1931–3 appeared.

His novel *Pero Galín* (1926) is successful both as a colonialist novel and as a subtle parody of the genre. His poetry is inclined to be *avant-garde*, especially in the collections *Crucero* (1928), *Escalera* (1929), *Paso a nivel* (Madrid, 1933), and *Senderillos a ras* (Madrid, 1934).

Estravagario (Buenos Aires, 1958), a significant collection of poems by the Chilean poet Pablo Neruda (q.v.), which has been translated in a bilingual edition by Alastair Reid as *Extravagaria* (London, 1972). The portentousness and wide implications of the *Canto general* (q.v.) here give way to a relaxed, often playful, mood in which Neruda's easy mastery of technique is turned to delightfully humorous effect in 'Partenogénesis', 'Furiosa lucha de marinos con pulpo de colosales dimensiones', 'Bestiario', and many more. The half-mocking, half-testy 'El miedo' begins characteristically: 'Todos me piden que dé saltos,/que tonifique y que futbole,/que corra, que nade y que vuele./ Muy bien./Todos me aconsejan reposo,/todos me destinan doctores,/mirándome de cierta manera./¿Qué pasa? . . .'.

Estrella de Sevilla, La, a play claimed to be by Lope de Vega (q.v.) by E. Cotarelo y Mori in 'La estrella de Sevilla es de Lope de Vega' (*RBAM*, vol. 7, 1930). This attribution was rejected by R. Foulché-Delbosc in his study and edition in *Revue Hispanique*, vol. 48 (1920), pp. 497–678. The play has been edited by H. Thomas, (Oxford, 1923) and translated into English by P. M. Hayden in Brander Matthews's *The chief European dramatists* (Boston, 1916), pp. 167–92. The play was reworked as *Sancho Ortiz de Roelas* (1800) by C. M. Trigueros (q.v.).

The 'star of Seville', Estrella, is a noblewoman who catches the eye of King Sancho on his arrival in Seville. He learns that she is the sister of Busto Tavera, whom he summons, promising to appoint him General of the Archidona borderland. Busto, astonished at this unaccountable preferment, is further surprised to hear that the king wishes to bestow a dowry on Estrella and find her a good husband. Busto returns home to find Estrella with her fiancé Sancho Ortiz, who is embarrassed to hear that the king wishes to dispose of Estrella to another man. However, Busto assures Ortiz that he will tell the king that Estrella is already promised.

Estrella's maid, in exchange for her freedom,

agrees to let the king into Estrella's boudoir that night, since Busto is not expected home until dawn. Busto, who returns early and catches the king, does not wish to attack his sovereign, and so does not avenge his honour but takes the wretched slave-accomplice to the palace in his rage. Furious, the king looks for one of his courtiers to avenge his honour, and selects Ortiz, who is given a slip of paper bearing the name of the man whom he is to kill for slighting the king. Busto tells Estrella to prepare for the wedding with Ortiz quickly, to avoid greater misfortunes, and goes to look for Ortiz who has now read the name of his future brother-in-law on the paper. He resolves his terrible dilemma by picking a quarrel with Busto and kills him. Estrella is preparing for her wedding, and expecting her fiancé, when her brother's body is brought to her and she learns the identity of his murderer. Ortiz is imprisoned, for the king refuses to reveal who ordered him to kill Busto. Estrella begs that she should be allowed to judge the killer of her brother, and the king agrees, believing that she will order his death. She comes masked to the gaol, releases Ortiz, but is compelled to reveal her identity before Ortiz will agree to escape. When he recognizes her, he refuses to escape. The king will not admit his guilt, until he sees there is no other recourse to save Ortiz's life. Ortiz requests the hand of Estrella in marriage, but when she points out that even though she may love him with all her heart, the shadow of a murdered brother would always come between them, she renounces his hand, and Estrella retires to a convent.

The play is intensely moving, the dialogue swift, and there is no distracting sub-plot.

See J. L. Brooks, ' "Estrella de Sevilla", admirable y famosa tragedia' in the *BHS*, vol. 32 (1955), pp. 8–20.

Estribillo, verse refrain, usually of one to three lines, occasionally preceding the first stanza but more often following each stanza of a *letrilla*, *romance*, *romancillo*, or *villancico*. The refrain may be merely phonic in purpose, or may establish the theme of the song. Many Spanish poets have used the *estribillo*, among them Encina, Quevedo, Góngora, and Lope de Vega.

Estridentismo, a Mexican movement begun in 1922 by Manuel Maples Arce (q.v.) with his poetry *Andamios interiores* (1922) and *Urbe* (1924, translated as *Metropolis* by John Dos Passos, New York, 1929); Salvador Gallardo; Luis Quintanilla; Germán List Arzubide (author of *El movimiento estridentista*, 1926); and Arqueles Vela (author of *El café de nadie*, 1926).

Like the Italian futurist movement, *estridentismo* chose to glorify the industrial future at the expense of the classical or Romantic past, and took as its symbols engines, factories, and energy in all its forms. The movement quickly died when it was overtaken by developments in technology even more staggering than it had anticipated in its manifestos.

Estudiante de Salamanca, El, (2 parts, 1836–7), a verse *leyenda* by José de Espronceda (q.v.). It is the most impressive treatment of the Don Juan theme (q.v.) in Spanish Romantic literature, with the exception of that by Zorrilla (q.v.), and is distinguished by vivid, imaginative scenes of sustained suspense, and an impressive diversity of metre. As usual in Espronceda's work, the influence of Byron is significant.

A cynical student of Salamanca, Félix de Montemar, seduces Elvira de Pastrana with a promise of marriage, but abandons her; after she has written Félix a tender farewell message she dies of grief. Her brother Diego hears of the matter, and returns from Flanders to avenge Elvira, finally encountering Montemar at the gaming table, where he is about to wager Elvira's portrait. The duel is won by Félix, who kills Diego and is about to return to the gaming table when he sees a woman in white praying to a crucifix in the street. He follows her, and on the way meets a funeral cortège which he discovers to be that of Diego and himself.

Apprehensive, he continues to follow the woman, and they enter a door leading to a room full of spectres and ghastly visions. The woman offers her hand, which Montemar feels to be cold as death. The ghost of Diego approaches, telling Félix 'Por fin habéis cumplido vuestra palabra' and when Félix boldly tears aside the veil covering the woman's face he finds only a skull. Before he can draw his sword, the skeleton embraces him and its fatal kiss causes him to fall lifeless to the ground. Next day the word is spread around that the devil has taken the body and soul of Montemar.

The poem has been highly popular since its publication: among modern editions are those of E. Allison Peers (Cambridge, 1922), J. Fradejas Lebrero (Ceuta, 1961), and B. Varela Jácome (Salamanca, 1966).

ESTUPIÑÁN BASS, NELSON (1915–), b. Esmeraldas. Ecuadorian Negro poet and novelist. He has reproduced the local poetry of the Esmeraldas area in *Timuarán y Cuabú*. He is however best known as a novelist, for *Cuando los guayacanes florecían* (1954) set in Esmeraldas during the second decade of the 20th c. when peasants fought as guerrilleros under Col. Carlos Concha against the government of President Leonidas Plaza Gutiérrez; and for *El paraíso* (1958), again set in Esmeraldas and showing how a corrupt cabinet minister's son was lynched for his dictatorial attitude to the local people.

ETCHAHOUNIA, PIERRE TOPET D' (1786–1862), b. Etchahounia, Barcus, Soule, French Basque provinces. Important Basque poet. Forbidden to marry the daughter of poor parents, he cursed his father in the now proverbial 'May God curse Gaztelondo Topet/ and all those who give their hearts to penniless maidens'. Obediently, however, he agreed to a marriage with a woman he disliked and who was reputedly undependable. After beating her, he was gaoled. On his release, hearing that she had again been unfaithful, he killed a man, later found to be innocent, and was gaoled again. His brother and son refused to allow him home, as did his father and wife, and he spent his middle and old age in poverty and exile, wandering as a bard and engaging in competition for poetry prizes. The agnostic verses which have survived bearing his stylistic mark consist predominantly of elegies and satires. He was allowed to return after an alleged reconciliation with the Church, but his family vindictively burnt all his surviving MSS. in a public bonfire shortly after his death. Luckily, his poetry was primarily a folk art and was easily remembered by those with whom he had come into contact. It was collected first by J. D. J. Salaberry in *Chants populaires du Pays Basque: paroles et musique originales* (Bayonne, 1870) and more systematically by P. Lhande and J. Larrasquet in *Le poète Pierre Topet, dit Etchahun, et ses oeuvres* (Bayonne, 1946).

ETCHEBARNE, MIGUEL D. (1915–), b. Tigre, province of Buenos Aires. Argentinian poet who composed poems on the life of the city gangsters or *compadres*. His outstanding work in this difficult genre was *Juan Nadie: vida y muerte de un compadre* (1954) of which Borges has declared 'It is a poem I should have liked to write but couldn't'. At once abstract, universal, and allegorical, the poem is a vivid and credible picture. Etchebarne's other works include *Poema de arroyo y alma* (1937), *El arroyo perdido* (1941), *Religión de soledad* (1943), *Lejanía* (1945), *Soliloquio* (1947), *Campo de Buenos Aires* (1948), and *En este valle de lágrimas* (1949). He has also compiled the anthology *La Pampa* (1946).

ETCHEBERRI, JOANES (*c.* 1590–*c.* 1670), b. Ciboure. Basque poet. He graduated in theology, and wrote two devotional works: *Manual devotionezcoa* (Bordeaux, 1627; 2nd edn., 1669), the first part containing that knowledge considered necessary for a Christian; and the second prayers for different needs; and *Eliçara erabiltceco liburua* (1636), also in verse. *Noelac* (1630?) is a collection of poems on the life and Passion of Christ, the hours, canticles, and hymns in honour of saints, among them the Basque saints Ignatius Loyola and Francis Xavier. Etcheberri is a fluent versifier, inventive in his imagery and charming in his *villancicos*.

ETCHEBERRI DE SARA, JOANES (1668–1749), b. Sare, Labourd, French Basque Provinces. Basque grammarian and essayist. After graduating in medicine, he practised in many villages of the Basque provinces, but his life-work was the propagation of Basque as the principal language of instruction in its areas of colloquial use. His *Lau-urdiri gomendiozco carta, edo guthuna* (Bayonne, 1728) is a letter requesting financial and administrative assistance from the *Biltzar* (provincial assembly) of Labourd to publish a dictionary of Latin, French, Castilian, and Basque.

This assistance was refused, but Etcheberri was able to prepare a Latin grammar in Basque *Eskuarazko hatsapenak latin ikhasteko*, known as *Rudimentos*. His best-known work, a defence of Basque as a literary language which should be encouraged equally with other tongues, was unpopular when originally propounded, but its common-sense view was upheld later by many Basque scholars. The essay, *Eskuararen hatsapenak*, proposes Piarres de Axular (q.v.) as a model and is itself modelled on Axular's style.

J. de Urquijo edited the *Obras vascongadas del doctor labortano Joannes d'Etcheberri* (Paris, 1907). See also Fray L. Villasante, 'Joannes Etxeberri (1668–1744)' in *Boletín de la Real Sociedad Vascongada de los Amigos del País*, vol. 9 (1943), pp. 231–43, and Antonio María Labayen, 'Joannes d'Etcheberri (1668–1749)' in *Eusko-Jakintza*, vol. 3 (1949), pp. 99–103.

EUGENIUS OF TOLEDO, Saint (*c.* 600–57), Visigoth who became Bishop of Toledo (646–57), and the foremost Spanish Latin poet of his age. At the direction of Chindasvinth (642–53), he edited the works of Dracontius. The critical edition of his works is that by F. Vollmer in *Monumenta Germaniae Historica: Auctores antiquissimi*, vol. 14 (Berlin, 1905), pp. 229–91. The poems are simple to the point of ingenuousness, but signs of his wide reading are shown by frequent, unmistakeable echoes of Virgil, Ovid, Horace, and Petronius, as well as early Christian writers. Eugenius' favoured themes include the penalties of old age and the brevity of life, peace, love, and birds. His style can be observed from the following wry passage, parodying classical authors on the delights of summer, in *Carmen* 101: *De incommodis aestivi temporis*: '... Musca nunc saevit piceaque blatta / et culex mordax olidusque cimex, / suetus et nocte vigilare pulex /

corpora pungit'. ('Now the fly and the cockroach black as pitch turn merciless, the mosquitoes and the evil-smelling bedbugs bite, the flea pricks the skin while passing the time of night awake').

Europeo, El, an influential weekly magazine published in Barcelona from late 1823 to mid-1824. Its editorial group, including Bonaventura Carles Aribau and Ramón López Soler (qq.v.), admired Meléndez Valdés and Quintana (q.v.), and translated the European Romantics such as Chateaubriand, Schiller, Klopstock, and 'Ossian'.

In one article, Monteggia definitively justified the use of the term 'romántico' over such competitors as 'romancesco'; in another, *Análisis de la cuestión agitada entre románticos y clasicistas,* López Soler supported Boehl von Faber's interpretation of Christian traditional Romanticism. Menéndez y Pelayo was later to distinguish two prevailing streams of Romanticism: the historical, and the liberal or revolutionary.

EVARISTÓTELES, pseudonym of Evaristo Acevedo Guerra (q.v.).

EVIA, Jacinto de (1620–?), b. Guayaquil. Ecuadorian baroque poet whose gongoristic *Ramillete de varias flores poéticas recogidas y cultivadas en los primeros abriles de sus años* (Madrid, 1675) included work by the Ecuadorian Fr. Antonio Bastidas and the Colombian Hernando Domínguez Camargo (q.v.).

EXIMENO, *Padre* Antonio (1729–1808), Jesuit musicologist who taught in Valencia University. Jovellanos (q.v.), who valued the philosophical teachings of Eximeno highly, stated that the Spaniard restored logic to the sensualistic epistemology of Locke and Condillac, but purged their doctrines of ideas considered by the Church to be theologically inadmissible.

Eximeno is best known for *Dell' origine e delle regole della musica, colla storia del suo progresso, decadenza, e rinnovazione* (Rome, 1774), translated into Spanish by F. A. Gutiérrez (3 vols., 1796). He also wrote a novel, *Don Lazarillo Viscardi, sus investigaciones músicas con ocasión del concurso a un Magisterio de Capilla vacante,* first published by the Sociedad de Bibliófilos Españoles (ed. F. Asenjo Barbieri, 2 vols., 1872–3).

See F. Pedrell, *Padre Antonio Eximeno* (Valencia, 1920) and N. Otaño, *El P. Antonio Eximeno: estudio de su personalidad* (1943).

Expostulatio Spongiae (1618), a defence of Lope de Vega by Alfonso Sánchez de la Ballesta, Francisco López de Aguilar Coutiño, and possibly Lope himself. It was written against the *Spongia* of Pedro de Torres Rámila (q.v.).

EZRA, Abraham ben Meir ben (1092–1167), b. Tudela. Spanish-Hebrew poet, grammarian, and biblical commentator. Abraham was forced to leave Spain in 1140, and is recorded as having taught in Jewish communities in Rome, Salerno, Lucca, Pisa, Mantua, Verona, Béziers, Narbonne, Bordeaux, Angers, and Rouen, usually suffering poverty with wry fortitude. In Dreux he wrote *Fundamenta tabularum astronomicarum* (1154) and in London a treatise on the astrolabe (1160), though his astronomical knowledge is vitiated (inevitably at that period) by an obsession with astrology. Abraham's knowledge of mathematics and astronomy was exceptional, exemplifying the authority enjoyed by Spanish Jews in contemporary scholarship. He wrote principally in Hebrew for the benefit of other Jews and while his prose is uneven in quality, his biblical commentaries were widely used and respected.

D. Rosin edited *Reime und Gedichte der Abraham ibn Ezra* (Breslau, 1885–95) and there is a major study and anthology, *Rabbi Avraham ibn Ezra* (2 vols., Warsaw, 1894), by D. Kahana.

EZRA, Moses ben Jacob ben (c. 1055–c. 1138), b. Granada. Spanish-Hebrew poet, of a wealthy and powerful family. His youthful poems, consisting of 245 light secular pieces on wine, love, spring, and friendship, *Shirei ha-Khol* (ed. H. Brody, Berlin, 1935), reflect a life of ease. There is a bilingual *Selected poems* by S. de Solis-Cohen (Philadelphia, 1934) and a study by A. Diez-Macho, *Mose ibn Ezra como poeta y preceptista* (Madrid, 1953), which also examines Moses's Arabic source on early Judaeo-Spanish poets and poetics, *Kitāb al-muḥāḍara wa 'l-muḏākara,* translated into Hebrew by B. Halper as *Shirat Israel* ('Hebrew poetry', 1924).

It is not recorded whether Moses suffered under the persecution of the Andalusian Jews in 1066, but it may have been then that he studied under Isḥaq ben Yehuda ben Gayyāt (q.v.) at Lucena. He is known to have been in Granada during the Almoravid invasion of 1090, however, for he stayed there for a short time when his family was dispersed. Eventually he too was forced to escape to Christian Spain, where he wrote emotional poetry about his lost Granada. Yehuda ha-Levi wrote a moving poem 'to Moses ben Ezra in Christian Spain' which is translated by David Goldstein in *The Jewish poets of Spain* (Harmondsworth, 1971), p. 147.

F

FABBIANI RUIZ, José (1911–), b. Pana-quire, Miranda. Venezuelan novelist, short-story writer, and literary critic. He has taught literature, and was founding director of the Schools of Library Science and Literature, and of the Centre of Literary Studies at the Universidad Central in Caracas. He was Dean of the Faculty of Humanities and Education 1959–62.

His essays have been collected in *Clásicos Castellanos: Novelas y novelistas* (1944), *Cuentos y cuentistas* (1951), *El cuento en Venezuela* (1953), and *Tres temas de poesía venezolana* (1966).

Fabbiani Ruiz's fiction falls into the category of 'magic realism', beginning with the novel *Valle hondo* (1934) and the stories in *Agua salada* (1939), the novel *Mar de leva* (1941) on events following the fall of the dictator Juan Vicente Gómez in 1935, *Guira es un río de Barlovento* (1946), and *La dolida infancia de Perucho González* (1946), a series of twenty-five sketches from the protagonist's childhood and early service in a number of households, slightly reminiscent of *Lazarillo de Tormes* (q.v.). *A orillas del sueño* (1959), a novel that won the National Literary Prize, deals with the love of the imaginative Magnolia for the boy Crisanto, and their magic world where they meet a bird-hunter, Epifanio, who offers to take Magnolia to the city of dreams. The real world cruelly intervenes when her father is arrested on political grounds and Crisanto's parents die.

Fabliella (Latin: *fabula*, 'story'), a term used by Juan Manuel (q.v.), in his *Libro del Caballero et del escudero* (1326) and elsewhere, to indicate a short story enlivening or illustrating a moral or didactic point. In the *Conde Lucanor* (q.v.), Juan Manuel reduces the moral element. In Juan Ruiz's *Libro de bien amor* (q.v.), *fabliella* means 'proverb'.

FABRA, Pompeu (1868–1948), Catalan grammarian responsible for *Normes ortogràfiques* (1913). He collaborated with Ruyra on the standard dictionary of modern Catalan, the *Diccionari general de la llengua catalana* (1932).

FABREGAT CÚNEO, Roberto (1906–), b. Montevideo. Uruguayan essayist, novelist, and playwright. His essays have been concerned mainly with society and propaganda: *Investigaciones de lógica social* (1943), *La dialéctica del conocimiento* (1944), *Filosofía de la propaganda* (1946), *Caracteres sudamericanos* (1950), and *Propaganda y sociedad* (1961). His plays are *La dama del retrato* (first performed in Buenos Aires, 1950), *Como por arte de magia* (1950), *Luces de cine* and *La verdad llega de noche* (1952), and *El pinar de las tierras altas* (1953). His first fiction was *Los encuentros de Andrés* (1947) and the hallucinatory *Metro* (1962), but Fabregat Cúneo is principally known by *La casa de los cincuenta mil hermanos* (1963), a novel that in its humour and sense of the absurd has been claimed by Benedetti as a true descendant of the Anglo-Saxon sense of fantasy, mingling comedy with the dream state.

Fábula de Polifemo y Galatea (1613), a poem by Luis de Góngora y Argote (q.v.) which retells the story of Acis and Galatea from Ovid's *Metamorphoses*, Book XIII. Acis wins the love of Galatea, who has rejected the Cyclops Polyphemus. Enraged with jealousy, Polyphemus kills Acis with a rock. Acis is turned into a stream by the sympathetic gods. Góngora's treatment of this familiar theme was probably inspired by rivalry on reading Carrillo de Sotomayor's *Fábula de Acis y Galatea* (1611), but, unlike Carrillo, he chose not to follow Ovid closely.

Galatea is at the centre of his poem: she becomes virtually a goddess of love, who seems to preside over the fertility of all Sicily and the love of all Sicilian men. Polyphemus and all Sicilians except Acis are denied the bounty of Galatea's love. Acis, the only fortunate man, dies before he can enjoy it. The poem is thus seen as a warning on the transience of human happiness, like the *romance* on Angélica and Medoro: in both poems the ending is optimistic, in the former the metamorphosis into a stream and the reception of Acis into the sea being conceived as a victory of life over death.

The metre of the 540-line poem is the *octava real* and the line-length is hendecasyllabic.

There is an edition by R. O. Jones in his *Poems of Góngora* (Cambridge, 1966). *Polyphemus and Galatea: the interpretation of a baroque poem*, by A. A. Parker (Edinburgh, 1977), includes a verse translation by G. C. Cunningham.

See Antonio Vilanova, *Las fuentes y los temas del 'Polifemo' de Góngora* (2 vols., 1957) and Dámaso Alonso, *Góngora y el 'Polifemo'* (2 vols., 1961).

Facundo, see Civilización y Barbarie ... .

FALCO, Ángel (1885–), b. Montevideo. Minor Uruguayan poet who achieved notoriety with *Cantos rojos* (1907) in favour of revolution and socialism. His later books were *Vida que canta* (1908), consisting of sonnets; and *Breviario galante* (1910), decadent love poetry. Though guilty of 'los peores resabios de la poesía socializante y modernista' in the words of E. Díez-Echarri and J. M. Roca Franquesa, Falco also wrote patriotic verse, *El alma de la raza* (1910) and *La leyenda del patriarca* (1911) on Artigas's struggle against Spain, and other conventional work.

FALCO, Líber (1906–55), b. Montevideo. Uruguayan poet of innocence and sensibility. Unlike many of his contemporaries, Falco coined no new words and used no contrived metaphors. *Cometas sobre los muros* (1940), *Equis Andacalles* (1942), and *Días y noches* (1946) are collections on time, solitude, and death in tones of quiet sadness and pessimism. These books and a long poem, 'Artigas', published in the weekly *Marcha* in 1954, appeared with other poems previously unpublished in *Tiempo y tiempo* (1956; rev. and augmented in 1963).

See Mario Arregui, *Líber Falco* (1964) and Mario Benedetti's essay in *Literatura uruguaya siglo XX* (2nd edn., 1969), pp. 115–19.

FALCÓN, César (1892–), b. Lima. Peruvian novelist, short-story writer, and essayist. He went to Europe with J. C. Mariátegui (q.v.) in 1920, and remained overseas. His first regional stories of the Central Andes were collected in *Plantel de inválidos* (Madrid, 1921). His three novels are: *El pueblo sin Dios* (Madrid, 1928), which attacked the *caciquismo* and the exploitation of the Indian in the Peruvian Andes and introduced the cinematographic technique into the Peruvian novel; *El buen vecino Sanabria U* (Mexico City, 1947), an ironic attack on the period of Manuel Prado (President of Peru, 1940–45) and on the 'good-neighbour policy' of the U.S.A.; and *Por la ruta sin horizonte* (Mexico City, 1961), on Spain during the Second Republic. His articles and essays appeared in *Crítica de la revolución española* (Madrid, 1931) and *El mundo que agoniza* (Mexico City, 1945).

FALLAS, Carlos Luis (1909–), b. Alajuela, Costa Rica. A self-taught communist novelist, he worked on a banana plantation and was Secretary General of the committee organizing the great banana strike of 1934. From 1944 to 1948 he was a deputy in the National Congress. His best-known novel, *Mamita Yunai* (1941), is like the others an attack on the avarice of the rich, the complacency of the government, and the exploitation by foreign companies such as United Fruit (the 'Yunaited'). His later books include the novels *Gentes y gentecillas* (1947) and

Marcos Ramírez (1952), and three stories collected in *Mi madrina* (1954).

FALLON, Diego (1834–1905), b. Santa Ana (now Falán), Tolima. Colombian poet. He studied in Bogotá (with the Jesuits) and in England. On his return to Colombia, Fallon taught languages, mathematics, and music. He was a member of the group, whose work was published by the magazine *El Mosaico* (1858–72).

A severe critic of his own work, Fallon allowed only one volume, *Poesías* (n.d. [1875]), to appear in his own lifetime. A classicist in *La luna*, *cuartetos* on the theme of silence, and in the *sextillas* of *La palma del desierto*, Fallon often resorted to familiar Colombian landscapes to express his moods.

His verse and various opinions on it by M. A. Bonilla, J. J. Casas, and M. A. Caro were published officially in homage: *Diego Fallon: su obra, juicios sobre ella y estudios sobre su vida* (Ibague? 1934) and there is a useful study by José Joaquín Casas, *Semblanzas: Diego Fallon y José Manuel Marroquín* (1936).

FÁLQUEZ AMPUERO, Francisco (1877– 1947), Ecuadorian poet whose importance as a Parnassian and symbolist in *Gobelinos*, a volume composed mainly of sonnets, was equalled by his translations from his French models, and in particular *Les trophées* by Hérédia (q.v.).

See José Antonio Falconi Villagómez, *Los precursores del modernismo en el Ecuador: César Borja y Fálquez Ampuero* (1959).

Familia de León Roch, La (2 vols., 1878), one of the *Novelas españolas de la primera época* by Benito Pérez Galdós (qq.v.).

Its theme is religious fanaticism (as in *Doña Perfecta* and *Gloria*, qq.v.) and the catastrophe is partly caused (as in *Doña Perfecta*) by a woman's confessor, in this case Padre Paoletti, confessor to María Egipcíaca. León Roch is a young geologist married to the lovely María Egipcíaca, daughter of the impoverished Marqués de Tellería.

Pepa Fúcar, daughter of the wealthy Marqués de Fúcar, has been in love with León since childhood but when he married, she had agreed to marry the opportunist Federico Cimarra. León's happy married life is gradually undermined by his wife's efforts to convert him and, after enduring countless verbal assaults on his scientific humanism, he leaves home after ensuring her financial welfare. He meets Pepa again (living alone after her husband has been presumed drowned at sea) but, while declaring his love for her, León remains faithful to his wife. The worst interpretation is placed on their renewed friendship, and when María Egipcíaca is told of their 'affair', she confronts León, suffers a cerebral haemorrhage, and dies. León and Pepa dream of a happy future together, but in a rather contrived ending, Cimarra reappears and prevents their marriage.

Familia de Pascual Duarte, La, a novel by Camilo José Cela (q.v.) published in 1942. The first important novel produced in Spain after the Civil War, it helped to create the vogue for *tremendismo* (q.v.).

Duarte, an Extremaduran peasant, is the son of an alcoholic father and an unloving mother. Awaiting execution in the death-cell, he tells the story of his life. He was driven to kill in turn his dog, his horse, the seducer of his sister and of his first wife, and then his own mother, spending long periods in prison for these two murders. But Cela helps us to understand that Duarte is at heart a kind and loving person, fond of children and of animals, and horrified by the suffering of others; his unfavourable heredity, primitive environment, and sheer ill-luck combine with his unstable temperament to make him violent in spite of himself.

His most ironic misfortune is being accused of the murder of the local squire Don Jesús at the start of the Civil War, when it is clear from clues in the text that Duarte found Jesús dying after being attacked by a mob and killed him quickly to end his sufferings. It is this act of intended charity that causes the Nationalists to execute him as a supposed left-wing assassin, though Duarte respected both priest and squire and saw no reason to question society at large. Cela's determinism is voiced by Duarte, who unconsciously denies the Church's teaching on free will (and is thus really a heretic) despite being converted shortly before his death. This is one of the many examples of irony pervading the novel.

The book concludes with two conflicting and equally unsatisfactory views of Duarte by men who saw him die: a cynical and contemptuous account by a Civil Guard and a sympathetic one by the prison chaplain. This antithesis reflects the author's implication that clear-cut judgments are impossible; life is too complex for individuals and their actions to be judged simply 'good' or 'bad'. The squalor of backward Spanish villages is merely the background of the novel; its main theme is philosophical rather than social, treating Duarte's condition as a human being rather than as a particular Spaniard in a particular place at a given time. The book's pessimism, its daring rejection of orthodox concepts of retributive justice (in the aftermath of the Civil War), and its negative portrait of traditional Spanish society, all led to its being adversely criticized in some quarters when it first appeared.

FARADI, Abu 'l-Walid 'Abdullah al (962–1013), b. Cordova. Historian, *qāḍi* of Valencia, and owner of a renowned private library. On his return from the pilgrimage to Mecca, al-Faradi was murdered by the Berbers who had taken possession of the city. He wrote on Spanish-Arab poetry, and on the learned writers of Arab Andalusia.

FARIÑA NÚÑEZ, Eloy (1885–1929), a Paraguayan poet who joined the Modernist movement that formed around the magazine *Nosotros* in Buenos Aires. There he became friendly with Leopoldo Lugones (q.v.) and published an epic in blank verse, *Canto secular* (1911), a year after the *Odas seculares* of Lugones appeared. Fariña was a devotee of Latin literature, and his *Canto* owes its scale to Virgil and its style to Horace. His poetry was collected in *Cármenes* (1922). He also wrote critical essays, short stories (*Las vértebras de Pan,* 1914), a neoclassical novel (*Rhodopis,* 1926), several plays, and a valuable collection, *Mitos guaraníes* (1926).

FARINELLI, Arturo (1867–1948), the doyen of Italian Hispanists and an important scholar in the field of comparative literature. Farinelli's doctoral thesis was entitled *Deutschlands und Spaniens literaturische Beziehungen.* Among his most notable contributions were *Grillparzer und Lope de Vega* (Berlin, 1894), translated as *Lope de Vega en Alemania* (Barcelona, 1936); a study of Calderón's *La vida es sueño* entitled *La vita è un sogno* (2 vols., Turin, 1916); *Viajes por España y Portugal desde la Edad Media hasta el siglo: divagaciones bibliográficas* (Madrid, 1920) and *Suplemento* (Madrid, 1930); *Dante in Spagna, Francia, Inghilterra, Germania* (Turin, 1922); *Guillaume de Humboldt et l'Espagne* (Turin, 1924); *Divagazioni erudite* (Turin, 1925); *Ensayos y discursos de crítica literaria hispano-europea* (2 vols., Rome, 1925); *Romanticismo nel mondo latino* (3 vols., Turin, 1927); the magisterial *Italia e Spagna* (2 vols., Turin, 1929); *Divagaciones hispánicas* (Barcelona, 1936); and *Poesía del Montserrat y otros ensayos* (Barcelona, 1940).

Farsas, religious plays of the Middle Ages, often with a comic interlude, as in the *Farsas y églogas al modo pastoril y castellano* of Lucas Fernández (q.v.) and the modern *Farsa de los Reyes Magos* of Rafael Alberti (q.v.). The conventional modern Spanish *farsa* has the sole purpose of making audiences laugh. Another meaning given by the Real Academia Española's dictionary is 'obra dramática desarreglada, chabacana y grotesca'.

FEBRER, Andreu (*c.* 1375–*c.* 1444), b. Vich. Catalan soldier, lyric poet, and translator. His love poetry, arguably the finest of his age after that of Jordi de Sant Jordi, was influenced by Arnaut Daniel, Cerverí, and Dante. Febrer's *Poesías* (ed. M. de Riquer, Barcelona, 1951) also include the 'Sirventesch per lo passatge de Berberia', on a storm that threatened the king's fleet on the way to the Barbary Coast. Later in his life, Febrer turned to translation, and his *La Comedia de Dant Allighier* (ed. C. Vidal y Valenciano, Barcelona, 1878) was both popular and influential in its day.

FEBRES CORDERO, TULIO (1860–1938), b. Mérida, Venezuela. Venezuelan historian, novelist, and short-story writer. A patriarch of the Mérida region, Febres Cordero has been described by M. Picón Salas as adopting an anti-modern and emotionally archaic position. The official archivist of Mérida, he produced *Décadas de la historia de Mérida* (Caracas, 1935) and contributed stories (*Tradiciones y leyendas*) of the area to local magazines. In *Don Quijote en América* he wrote of the old ways 'like a small Walter Scott of the Andes' (Picón Salas).

See José Domingo Tejera, *Tulio Febres Cordero* (Mérida, 1915) and the panegyric by Roberto Picón Lares (1938) delivered before the Athenaeum of Caracas.

FEIJÓO, SAMUEL (1914–), Cuban poet and literary critic. Feijóo is a writer of the region of Las Villas, from which Alcides Iznaga and Allo Menéndez also come. A neo-Romantic, Feijóo united a deep love for Cuban landscapes and folklore with an awareness of the Hispanic tradition both in his original work, such as *Camarada celeste* (1944) and *La hoja del poeta* (1956), and his scholarly editions and anthologies, such as *Colección de poetas de la ciudad de Camagüey* (1958), *Sonetos en Cuba, Cantos a la naturaleza cubana del siglo XIX: selección, El movimiento de los romances cubanos del siglo XIX*, and *Sobre los movimientos por una poesía cubana hasta 1856* (1964). Feijóo also published a travel diary, *Diarios de viaje* (1958).

FEIJÓO Y MONTENEGRO, *Fray* BENITO JERÓNIMO (1676–1764), b. Casdemiro, Orense. Important essayist whose controversial discourses and letters were among the most vigorous and enlightened contributions to Spanish life and literature in the first half of the 18th c. Feijóo became a Benedictine in 1690 and from 1709 taught theology at the monastery of S. Vicente in Oviedo. He wrote there, and carried on a voluminous correspondence both before and after his retirement in 1739. Influenced by the French Enlightenment and by the Spanish tradition of Erasmianism beginning with Juan Luis Vives (q.v., 1492–1540), Feijóo attacked the superstitious ignorance into which the Spanish people and clergy had fallen. He called for a spirit of impartial investigation, a lucid prose style against the excesses caricatured in P. Isla's *Fray Gerundio* (1758), and for experiment rather than acceptance of tradition and dogma. Often known as the Spanish Voltaire, he was in fact conservative in many ways, favouring aristocratic privilege and the continuance of ecclesiastical intervention in state affairs.

His outward life is notable for its lack of incident. He called himself a 'ciudadano libre de la república de las letras' and spent his life composing the treatises for which he is now known, and answering the pamphlets and letters of his critics, among them the Dominican Jacinto Segura, Torres Villarroel, Mañer, and Armesto y Osorio. In 1750, Fernando VI declared that his writings should no longer be attacked, a victory for his allies such as Padre Isla, Sarmiento, and Juan de Iriarte.

His writings are *Carta apologética de la 'Medicina scéptica' del doctor Martín Martínez*; the 118 discourses of the *Theatro crítico universal* (q.v., 9 vols., 1726–40); the 163 letters of the *Cartas eruditas y curiosas* (q.v., 5 vols., 1742–60); the *Justa repulsa de iniquas acusaciones* (1749); and posthumously-published *Adiciones* (1783), *Las poesías* (Lugo, 1899, ed. A. López Peláez), and *Colección de poesías inéditas* (Vigo, 1901, ed. J. E. Areal).

While Feijóo is not a specialist, and is never rigorously concerned with any single problem, his encyclopaedic interests and spirit of enquiry mark him as exceptional in 18th-c. Spain. His essays touched on superstitions and folklore (showing how the ignorant will generalize from a single event without trying to repeat that event to verify their hypothesis), on politics, history and society, language, literature and aesthetics, and most of the sciences. Gregorio Marañón has examined his scientific views in *Las ideas biológicas del P. Feijóo* (1934). Polemics ranged around many of Feijóo's ideas, so liberally expressed. Among these were *Los orígenes de las lenguas gallega y portuguesa, Música de los templos, Milagros supuestos* (he believed that the few true miracles were sufficient; it should not be necessary to invent more), *Defensa de las mujeres*, and *El estudio no da entendimiento*.

There has been no complete reprint of his original collected works. Though neither critical nor unabridged, the fullest edition is that in the BAE, vols. 56 (1952), 141, 142, and 143 (1961), while there are convenient extracts in Clásicos Castellanos: 3 vols. of the *Theatro* (usually modernized as *Teatro*) selected by A. Millares Carlo (1923–5), and 1 vol. of the *Cartas eruditas* (1928).

See J. A. Pérez Rioja, *Proyección y actualidad de*

Feijóo (1965); and I. L. McClelland, *Benito Jerónimo Feijóo* (New York, 1969) the latter in English.

FELIPE CAMINO, León (1884–1968), b. Tábara, Zamora. Poet. He spent his youth in Salamanca and trained as a pharmacist, practising in Almonacid de Zorita in the Alcarria. An inveterate wanderer, he spent some time in Africa before settling in Mexico, at the end of the Spanish Civil War, in 1939. His tone of prophetic idealism has been compared to that of Walt Whitman, whose work he translated into Spanish. He was later influenced by surrealism, and then by social commitment to the poor and helpless. To obtain his striking effects he resorted to a brusquely colloquial style in free verse. *Versos y oraciones del caminante* (pt. 1, 1920; pt. 2, New York, 1930) marked him out as original, but it was not until *El español del éxodo y del llanto* (Mexico City, 1939) that he emerged as a moving poet of exile, unhappy but convinced of being right. *El hacha* (Mexico City, 1939) railed against the annihilation brought by war, and *El gran responsable* (Mexico City, 1940) and *El poeta prometéico* (Mexico City, 1942) involved him further in the lonely struggle to help the under-privileged. He collected his best work in *Antología rota, 1920–1947* (Buenos Aires, 1947; 2nd edn., 1957), following this with *El ciervo* (Mexico City, 1958). Felipe's *Obras completas* appeared in Buenos Aires in 1964.

His work has been studied by L. F. Vivanco in his *Introducción a la poesía española contemporánea* (Madrid, 1957, pp. 143–73).

FELIÚ Y CODINA, José (1847–97), b. Barcelona. Playwright and novelist. A minor dramatist of the neo-Romantic school of Echegaray, Feliú wrote numerous plays, and raised the rural, and *costumbrista*, *sainete* to the level of tragedy. His protagonist is usually a woman of the middle or lower classes in a Spanish country town who has flawless morals and is very attractive. Feliú's treatment is sentimental, conventional, and lacks any modern viewpoint. *María del Carmen* (1895) and *La real moza* (1896) show Feliú's typical heroine in Murcia and Andalusia respectively, but *La Dolores* (1892) first established his name. It was turned into a *zarzuela* by Bretón de los Herreros and into a novel *La Dolores: historia de una copla* by Feliú himself. Luis Fernández Ardavín (q.v.) wrote a sequel, *La hija de la Dolores*.

Dolores, seduced by the barber Melchor and then despised by him, seeks vengeance through her admirers, the *miles gloriosus* Rojas, and the wealthy young man-about-town Patricio. But these are interested more in her favours than in her good name, and it is left to the shy seminarist Lázaro, who has always adored her from afar, to stab Melchor and redeem the heroine's honour. The *copla* on which the work was based is ascribed to the scoundrel Melchor: *Si vas a Calatayud | pregunta por la Dolores, | que es una moza muy guapa | y amiga de hacer favores.*

Feliú translated a section of the short novels of Bandello.

FÉNIX, EL ('the Phoenix'), a term of awe and admiration coined by critics and public alike to describe the fecund and brilliant Golden Age dramatist Lope de Vega Carpio (q.v.).

FERNÁN CABALLERO, the pseudonym of Cecilia Boehl von Faber (q.v.).

FERNÁNDEZ, see also HERNÁNDEZ.

FERNÁNDEZ, FRANCISCO (1842–1922), b. Entre Ríos. Argentinian dramatist whose *Solané* (1872) was the first attempt at a *gaucho* play. A tragedy in four acts subtitled *drama psicosociológico*, it did not capture the authentic *gaucho* experience and is interesting more for its intention than for its achievement. Fernández wrote the patriotic *Sol de mayo* (1877) and *El genio de América*, the morality *El borracho*, the historical drama *Monteagudo*, and *Clorinda*, a play on Venetian aristocracy.

See Ricardo Rojas, *Un dramaturgo olvidado: Don Francisco Fernández y sus 'Obras dramáticas'* (1923).

FERNÁNDEZ, HERIBERTO (1903–27), Paraguayan poet and founder-member of the magazine *Juventud* (q.v.). His first collection was *Visiones de églogas* (Paris, 1925), which treated the countryside as a refuge from reality and was influenced by Juan Ramón Jiménez (q.v.). This was followed by *Voces del ensueño* (Paris, 1926), a profounder book, exploring the human spirit, published after his meeting in Paris with César Vallejo (q.v.). The posthumous *Sonetos a la hermana* (1957) was edited by Miguel Ángel Fernández.

FERNÁNDEZ, JORGE (1912–), b. Quito. Ecuadorian journalist, and novelist of peasant life in *Agua* (1937), and of the middle classes in *Los que viven por sus manos* (Santiago, 1951). He began as a journalist on *El Día*, and moved to *El Comercio*, whose history he wrote in *Tránsito a la libertad* (1956). He also took part in the Elan group (q.v.), but gave up literature for journalism.

FERNÁNDEZ, LUCAS (1474?–1542), b. Salamanca. Playwright, who took the post of *cantor* from Encina (q.v.) at Salamanca in 1498, visited Portugal about 1502, and taught music at Salamanca University from 1522 until his death. The only MS. surviving of the only known copy of his important *Farsas y églogas al modo y estilo pastoril y castellano* (Salamanca, 1514) is in the National Library, Madrid. It consists of three secular plays, three religious plays, and a sung dialogue on love between two shepherds.

The three secular plays are the *Farsa o cuasi comedia del soldado*, deriving directly from Centurio of *La Celestina* (q.v.) and ultimately from the Plautine *miles gloriosus*; the *Comedia de Bras-Gil y Berenguella*, a comic betrothal play introducing into Golden Age drama the *viejo*, here Berenguella's grandfather, rough but kindly; and the *Farsa o cuasi comedia de una doncella, un pastor y un caballero*, introducing the novel idea of a shepherd's unrequited love for a lady. Linguistically, Fernández introduces burlesque rural speech into his secular comedies.

Of the three religious plays, or *autos sacramentales* (q.v.), the most remarkable is the *Auto de la Pasión* for Holy Week, longer than the two plays of Encina on the same subject and dramatically finer. This is the first known conversion play in the Golden Age, taking the pagan intellectual Dionysius the Areopagite from his first meeting with St. Peter, still lamenting the betrayal of Christ the night before by Judas, and his own thrice-spoken disavowal of Jesus. St. Matthew interrupts them, telling them whatever of the Passion they have not yet heard. The three Marys enter in tears and finish the story of Matthew. The prophet Jeremiah, drawn to the scene by the lamentation, foretells the destruction of Jerusalem, and Dionysius joins Peter, Matthew, Jeremiah, and the three Marys in singing the praises of the Saviour.

There is a modern edition of the Madrid MS. by John Lihani (New York, 1969), and a facsimile edition by E. Cotarelo y Mori (1929). The best edition of the *Farsas y églogas* is that by María Josefa Canellada (1976), in which she rejects the *Coplas del Salvaje* as spurious.

See R. Espinosa Maeso, *Ensayo biográfico del Maestro Lucas Fernández* in BRAE, vol. 10 (1923), pp. 567–603; John Lihani, *El lenguaje de Lucas Fernández* (Bogotá, 1973); and A. Hermenegildo, *Renacimiento, teatro y sociedad: vida y obra de Lucas Fernández* (1975).

FERNÁNDEZ, MACEDONIO (1874–1952), b. Buenos Aires. Argentinian philosopher, poet, and short-story writer. He qualified as a lawyer in Buenos Aires at the age of 21, then practised in Asunción for 25 years until his wife, Elena de Obieta, died in 1920, when Fernández returned to Buenos Aires and lived there in virtual retirement until his death.

His writings are unique in Argentinian literature for their technique (a blend of poetry and philosophy) and their content (his subjective idealism being greatly at variance with the positivist trend prevailing in Latin American circles at the time of Fernández's formative years). Always reluctant to publish, Fernández was persuaded by literary friends to release a number of MSS. at intervals, the first being *No todo es vigilia la de los ojos abiertos. Arreglo de papeles que dejó un personaje de novela creado por su arte. Deunamor-El-No-Existente Caballero, el estudioso de su esperanza* (1928), in which a bewildered Buenos Aires public, lamenting the loss that same year of the popular Güiraldes (q.v.), found a compound of truth and paradox revolving around the time-honoured topoi of waking, dreaming, reality and illusion. Fernández teaches pure and transcendental subjectivism, mysticism being the supreme discipline (though not the science propounded by religious writers of the Golden Age). Being, he declared, is 'lo sentido, y únicamente lo sentido por mí y actualmente. El mundo [material] es un sueño de la afección'. The impact of Fernández's blurring of the frontiers between reality and the fictive can be seen clearly in the work of many later Argentinian writers and indeed among his own contemporaries, notably Jorge Luis Borges and Adolfo Bioy Casares (qq.v.). *Papeles de recienvenido* (1930; 2nd edn., 1944) continues the earlier book's philosophic vein, but more humour intrudes, often disconcertingly. Allegory and paradox mark the semi-fictional *Una novela que comienza* (Santiago, 1941), and in 1944 he published *Continuación de la nada*. Later books include the posthumously-published *Poemas* (Mexico City, 1953), *Museo de la novela de la eterna* (1967), and *Selección* (1968).

Two other books were reportedly in manuscript at the time of Fernández's death: *Adriana Buenos Aires, última novela mala* written as 'Isolima Buenos Aires' in 1922 and first published in *Obras completas*, (vol. 5, 1974); and *¿Algo más en metafísica después de William James?* the latter reflecting an intensive correspondence with James during the years 1906–11.

See J. L. Borges, *Macedonio Fernández* (1961); the shorter *Introducción a Macedonio Fernández* (1960) by C. Fernández Moreno, with an excellent bibliography by H. J. Becco; and N. Jitrik, *La novela futura de Macedonio Fernández* (1973).

FERNÁNDEZ, MIGUEL ÁNGEL (1938–), Paraguayan poet. In 1957 he founded the influential Ediciones Diálogo to publish both Paraguayan and foreign poets, virtually ending the country's cultural isolation, and in 1960 he started the magazine *Diálogo*.

In his own work, influenced by Josefina Plá, he is precise in the use of words, avoiding 'la seducción de las palabras hermosas, de las palabras vacías'. *Oscuros días* (1964) and *A destiempo* (1966) show Fernández's essential pessimism.

FERNÁNDEZ, Pablo Armando (1930–   ), b. Delicias, Eastern Province. Cuban poet of the revolutionary period. He was cultural attaché in London until 1965. His early poetry *Toda la poesía* (1961) is derivative, but in *Himnos* (1962) and the impressive *Libro de los héroes* (1964), he 'gives modern Cuban poetry a new beginning' (J. M. Cohen). The latter volume celebrates tersely and graphically the death of his friends during the Revolution as part of the unequal struggle between aspirations to freedom and human mortality. It was influenced by African mythology. His novel *Los niños se despiden* won the Casa de las Américas prize for 1968.

FERNÁNDEZ, Ramón, the barber of Pedro Estala (q.v.), who used this name as a pseudonym when editing the Colección de Poetas Españoles (6 vols., 1789–98).

FERNÁNDEZ, Sebastián (16th c.), author of the anonymous *Tragedia Policiana* (Toledo, 1547), an imitation in 29 acts of *La Celestina* (q.v.). A second edition, corrected by Luis Hurtado de Toledo, exists in a single copy in the National Library, Vienna. M. Menéndez y Pelayo reproduced the first edition in his *Orígenes de la novela*, vol. 3 (1910), pp. 2–59.

FERNÁNDEZ ARDAVÍN, Luis (1891–1962), b. Madrid. Poet and playwright. His early poems appeared in *Meditaciones* (1913) and his later poems in *A mitad del camino* (1944). His more familiar works are his verse plays, such as the historical *Rosa de Francia*, *La vidriera milagrosa* (1925), and *La florista de la reina* (1939); *El doncel romántico*, set in the time of Larra; and *La dama del armiño* (1922), set in El Greco's family ambience in 16th-c. Toledo. Fernández Ardavín's strength is in his versification; his weakness is in his dramatic composition and anachronism. He seized on Feliú's success in *La Dolores* to compose *La hija de la Dolores* (1927). *El hijo* (1921) contains his short stories. He translated Sophocles, Goethe, Balzac, and others.

Tres comedias (*La dama del armiño*, *La florista de la reina*, and *La dogaresa rubia*) are available in Colección Crisol (1944).

FERNÁNDEZ DE ANDRADA, Andrés (17th c.), b. Seville. A captain whose literary significance rests on the attribution by Adolfo de Castro (in *La 'Epístola moral a Fabio'*, Cádiz, 1875) and by Dámaso Alonso (in *Dos españoles del siglo de oro*, 1960) of the anonymous moral poem *Epístola moral a Fabio* (q.v.), considered one of the finest poems of the 17th c.

Apart from the existence of a fragmentary poem on his capture of Larache (1610), very little is known of Fernández de Andrada. Dámaso Alonso identified a contemporary of that name in Mexico, but insufficient evidence has been adduced to confirm that the two were identical.

FERNÁNDEZ DE AVELLANEDA, Alonso, the name, probably a pseudonym, of the author of a spurious *Segundo tomo del ingenioso hidalgo Don Quixote de la Mancha, que contiene su tercera salida: y es la quinta parte de sus aventuras* (Tarragona, 1614). The identity of the author is still in doubt: suggestions include Fray Luis de Aliaga, confessor of Philip III (Rosell and others); an obscure Aragonese poet Alfonso Lamberto (Menéndez y Pelayo); Guillén de Castro (Cotarelo y Mori); Tirso de Molina (Blanca de los Ríos); Joan Martí (Groussac); Andrés de Pérez (Díaz de Benjumea, who afterwards preferred Juan Blanco de Paz); Lope de Vega (León Maínez); Quevedo (Juan Millé y Giménez); Alonso de Ledesma (F. Vindel); and many others, including Cervantes himself.

In this spurious continuation, Cervantes (q.v.) is insulted in the prologue, and in the story Quijote is presented as a madman with neither wisdom nor learning, whose adventures are merely farcical, and who ends up in the madhouse of Toledo. The author claims in the prologue that Cervantes had insulted Lope de Vega, whom he is defending. Cervantes defended himself and his work in his own Part II.

Quijote, no longer in love with Dulcinea, arrives at the jousts of Saragossa (after they are over); suffers mockery at the hands of Don Álvaro de Tarfe; conducts the prostitute Bárbara to Court as 'Queen Zenobia'; and is finally cured of his madness in Toledo at the expense of Don Álvaro, who also provides for Sancho and Teresa Panza, and arranges for Bárbara to enter the House of Penitents. Two important stories intercalated in the book (just as *El curioso impertinente* (q.v.) is intercalated into *Quijote*, Part 1) are *El rico desesperado* and *Los felices amantes*.

Editions include those of Cayetano Rosell, in vol. 18 (1851) of the BAE, M. Menéndez y Pelayo (Barcelona, 1905), Colección Austral (1946), Colección Crisol (1944; 3rd edn.; 1960), and M. M. Villalta (Barcelona, 1961).

See Stephen Gilman, *Cervantes y Avellaneda: estudio de una imitación* (Mexico City, 1951).

FERNÁNDEZ DE CONSTANTINA, Juan (early 16th c.), the compiler of the *Guirnalda esmaltada de galanes y eloquentes dezires de diuersos autores* (1520?) closely related to, but probably earlier than, the *Cancionero de Hernando del Castillo*. Also known as the *Cancionero de Constantina*, this anthology included poets of the reigns of Enrique IV and the Catholic Monarchs. It has been edited by R. Foulché-Delbosc (1914).

FERNÁNDEZ DE CÓRDOBA, Fernando (1809–83), b. Buenos Aires. Autobiographer and historian, who was created Marqués de Mendigorria for his military exploits. He fought in the first Carlist wars (1833–4), serving under his brother Luis, general of the army of the North. Fernández de Córdoba went to Rome leading the Spanish troops to the aid of Pius IX. He was appointed President of the Council of Ministers in 1854 and became Minister of War in 1864, but from 1873 turned to writing. He wrote *Mis memorias íntimas* (3 vols., 1886–9), a remarkable autobiography covering the period from the accession of Fernando VII to the dethronement of Isabel I. His earlier work was the *Memoria sobre los sucesos políticos ocurridos en Madrid los días 17, 18 y 19 de julio de 1854* (1855).

FERNÁNDEZ DE CÓRDOBA, Gonzalo, see Córdoba, Gonzalo Fernández de.

FERNÁNDEZ DE GERENA, Garci, see Ferrandes de Jerena, Garci.

FERNÁNDEZ DE HEREDIA, Juan (1310?–96), b. Munébrega. Historian, soldier, and diplomat. He served Pedro IV of Aragón, to be Grand Master of the Order of St. John of Jerusalem, and fought in the Hundred Years' War and was wounded at Crécy (1346). In an expedition against Turkish pirates, Fernández de Heredia was taken prisoner at Patras (1381), where he was held for three years.

He spent the last years of his life on the histories and translations for which he is now known. His major histories are the *Gran Crónica de España* (MS. 10.133–4 in the National Library, Madrid) and the *Gran Crónica de los Conquiridores* (also in the National Library).

From the first work, A. Morel-Fatio edited *Libro de los fechos et conquistas del Principado de Morea* (Geneva, 1885) and R. Foulché-Delbosc edited *Gestas del rey Don Jaime de Aragón* (1909). The second included biographies of great men of the past, such as Tiberius, Octavius, Mark Antony, Attila, Charlemagne, and Genghis Khan.

The splendid private library assembled by Fernández de Heredia is believed to have passed, in part, to the Marqués de Santillana (q.v.).

Obras (Valencia, 1913) was edited by F. Marti Grajales.

See J. Vives, *Juan Fernández de Heredia, gran Maestre de Rodas* (Barcelona, 1927).

FERNÁNDEZ DE LA REGUERA, Ricardo (1916–), b. Barcenillas, Santander. Novelist. He lived in Chile 1929–39. Most of his working life has been spent writing and teaching at Barcelona University. He is a shrewd observer and his strength is his traditional approach to narrative style. His weaknesses are a lack of conviction in female characterization and, especially in the earlier books, a lack of individuality in the writing. His novels (all published in Barcelona) include *Entre otoño y primavera* (1945), *Un hombre a la deriva* (1947), *El corazón en el río* (1949), the Civil War novel *Cuando voy a morir* (1950) considered by D. Pérez Minik as the best in its genre, *Cuerpo a tierra* (1954), *Perdimos el paraíso* (1955), *Bienaventurados los que aman* (1957), *Vagabundos provisionales* (1959), and *Espionaje* (short stories).

With his wife Susana March (q.v.), Fernández de la Reguera has written several novels in the series Episodios Nacionales Contemporáneos.

FERNÁNDEZ DE LIZARDI, José Joaquín (1776–1827), b. Mexico City. Mexican anti-clerical journalist, poet, fabulist, and playwright. He often used the pseudonym 'El Pensador Mexicano'. He wrote the first Latin-American novel, *El Periquillo Sarniento* (q.v., 3 vols., 1816; complete edn., 5 vols., 1930–31). Self-taught and a fervent disciple of the Encyclopaedists, Fernández de Lizardi was an independent thinker, fearless despite several periods of imprisonment for anti-government propaganda, including one of seven months when he edited *El Pensador Mexicano* (1812–14). His even shorter-lived periodicals included *Alacena de Frioleras* (1815–16), *Las Sombras de Heráclito y Demócrito* (1815), *Caxoncito de la Alacena* (1815), *El Conductor Eléctrico* (1820), *El Amigo de la Paz y de la Patria* (1822, the year in which he declared for the Freemasons and against the Emperor, and was excommunicated for so doing), *El Hermano del Perico* (1823), *El Payaso de los Periódicos* (1823), *Las Conversaciones del Payo y del Sacristán* (1824), and *El Correo Semanario de México* (1826–27).

His career began with the poetry in which he satirized church and government, and unfashionably defended Indians and Negroes against exploitation. He also wrote forty *Fábulas* (1817), imitating Iriarte and Samaniego (qq.v.). Two volumes of his collected *Obras* have so far appeared, vol. 1 (1963) containing the *Poesías y fábulas*, and vol. 2 (1965) the *Teatro*, though his plays have not stood the test of time. It is for his journalism, and more especially for his novels, that Fernández de Lizardi is remembered today.

El Periquillo Sarniento (q.v.) is in the picaresque tradition of *Lazarillo de Tormes* and *El diablo cojuelo* (qq.v.), but it has been attacked by critics such as Sánchez for its excessively moral tone, out of keeping in such a racy novel. *Noches tristes y día alegre* (1818) is an imitation in both style and theme of Cadalso's *Noches lúgubres* (q.v.). The virtuous Teófilo is tested over four nights by Divine Providence; he is imprisoned, finds himself on the brink of a cliff, sees his servant and a friend die, and finds his wife's body in a graveyard. The *día alegre* is caused by his discovery that his wife is still alive. Heavily allegorical, the novel can be seen as a religious statement that it is darkest before the dawn and politically as an act of faith in the future. His moralizing is less obtrusive in this book. *La Quijotita y su prima* (1818) is a slighter work, based on Fénélon and Rousseau, and attacking conventional ideas on education for women. *Vida y hechos del famoso caballero don Catrín de la Fachenda* (1832) is his most assured and successful novel because the hero is more interesting and the author's digressions and solemn moralizing less frequent than in *El Periquillo Sarniento*. A fop, pimp, uneducated actor, boastful soldier, and antisocial in a dozen other ways, Don Catrín is involved endearingly in grotesque situations which he manages to survive, if ruefully, to the end, an unrepentant sinner in an unrepentant society.

Modern editions of *El Periquillo Sarniento* (3 vols., 1949) and *Don Catrín de la Fachenda y Noches tristes y día alegre* (1959) have been prepared by J. R. Spell, author of *The life and works of José Joaquín Fernández de Lizardi* (Philadelphia, 1931).

FERNÁNDEZ DE MINAYA, Fray LOPE (*c.* 1375–after 1438), few details are known about this writer of religious works. The only date known with certainty is 1438 when he was honoured by the Superior of the Augustinians, to whose Toledo house he belonged. He wrote *Espejo del alma*, found in Escorial MS. h-II-14 with *Libro de las tribulaciones* and *Tratado breve de penitencia*, with whose authorship he is consequently also credited. These three works appear in vol. 171 (1964) of the BAE and, with *Opúsculos inéditos*, in the Biblioteca Clásica Augustiniana (El Escorial, 1928).

The *Espejo del alma* describes the three sins which tie men to the world (pleasures of the flesh, avarice, and pride); three motives for rejecting the world (illusions, the certainty of death, and lasting suffering in Hell); and three reasons for uniting with God (the fact that God does not deceive, the excellence of His rewards,

and their eternal duration). The *Libro de confesión* attributed to Fernández de Minaya is now lost but it may have been a translation of St. Antony of Florence's *Summa confessionis* (Sargossa, 1492).

FERNÁNDEZ DE MORATÍN, see MORATÍN, Leandro Fernández de, and Nicolas Fernández de.

FERNÁNDEZ DE NAVARRETE, MARTÍN (1765–1844), b. Abalos, Logroño. Historian and biographer. A member of the Real Academia Española from 1792 and of the Real Academia de la Historia from 1800. He held prominent posts in the Spanish Navy, and much to his indignation was appointed Head of the Navy by Napoleon, whereupon he retired into private life. His *Vida de Miguel de Cervantes Saavedra* (1819) was the first to take into account the papers, which describe his life 1571–82, submitted by Cervantes to King Philip II in 1590, in order to justify a request for a colonial appointment. Fernández de Navarrete also compiled the useful *Colección de viajes y descubrimientos . . . por los españoles desde fines del siglo XV* (1825).

See *Primer centenario de don Martín Fernández de Navarrete: discursos de F. J. Sánchez Cantón, J. F. Guillén Cato y A. Cotarelo Valledor* (1945).

FERNÁNDEZ DE OVIEDO Y VALDÉS, GONZALO (1479–1557), b. Madrid. Soldier and chronicler. He took part in the Reconquest of Granada and fought in Italy under Gonzalo de Córdoba. He travelled to the New World in 1514, 1520, 1526, 1532, 1536, and 1549 and the diffuse account of his impressions is of some importance for his ethnological and topographical observations. His Eurocentric, militaristic attitudes were opposed by the humanitarian historian Fray Bartolomé de Las Casas (q.v.) who, in his own work, was at pains to indicate the numerous errors of fact and interpretation perpetrated by Fernández de Oviedo.

His *Sumario de la natural y general istoria de las Indias* (Toledo, 1526) was reprinted in vol. 22 of the BAE and more recently by J. Miranda (Mexico City, 1950). Fernández y Oviedo's most comprehensive work was the *Historia natural y general de las Indias, Islas y Tierra Firme del mar océano* (vol. 1, Seville, 1535; vol. 2, Valladolid, 1537), edited by J. Amador de los Ríos (4 vols., 1851–4), and by Pérez de Tudela Bueso (5 vols., 1959) as vols. 117–21 of the BAE.

He left unfinished the unpublished 'Batallas y quinquagenas', a sequence of dialogues on the families and the events in Spain under the Reyes Católicos and Charles V, and *Las Quinquagenas de la nobleza de España*, a random compilation of facts and recollections of life and personalities at the court of Spain (ed. V. de la Fuente, vol. 1, 1880).

Twc other works are generally attributed to him: *Reglas de la vida espiritual y secreta theológia* (1549), a pseudo-mystical work ill-according with what we known of his character, and which is in any case a translation from the Italian; and *Libro del muy esforçado e inuencible Cauallero de la Fortuna propiamente llamado don Claribalte* (Valencia, 1519), a chivalresque novel (facsimile edn., 1956) which has also been ascribed to a certain Fernández de Oviedo de Sobrepeñas.

FERNÁNDEZ DE PALENCIA, ALFONSO, see PALENCIA, Alfonso [Fernández] de.

FERNÁNDEZ DE RIBERA, RODRIGO (1579–1631), b. Seville. A satirical novelist and poet, whose best work is *Los anteojos de mejor vista* (*c.* 1628). In this, thanks to a special pair of spectacles, Dr. Disillusion sees the naked reality of life in Seville—and, by analogy, the world—from the top of the Giralda. Fernández satirizes doctors, writers, and other fashionable targets. The work undoubtedly influenced *El diablo cojuelo* of Luis Vélez de Guevara (q.v.), and it may have been influenced by the *Sueños* of Quevedo y Villegas (q.v.), written from 1606 onwards, but not published until 1627. Fernández de Ribera's allegorical satirical and picaresque sketches *El mesón del mundo* is a vehicle for his literary theories. He is a minor representative of that mood of baroque disillusion whose principal exponent is Gracián (q.v.). In his own day the devotional *décimas* of his *Escuadrón humilde levantado a devoción de la Inmaculada Concepción* (1618) were highly regarded. He occasionally used the pseudonym 'Toribio Martín'.

FERNÁNDEZ DE ROJAS, *Fray* JUAN (1750–1819), b. Colmenar de Oreja, Madrid. Poet and satirist. He became an Augustinian monk in 1768, and in 1772 went to Salamanca, where he became a disciple of Fray Diego Tadeo González and, like his mentor, a member of the Parnaso Salmantino, taking the poetic name of 'Liseno'. In his anacreontic and bucolic poetry he was influenced by Cadalso (q.v.). Very little has been published (Menéndez Pidal called his poems 'frías e infelices'), but a few have been edited by P. Conrado Muiños for *La Ciudad de Dios*: the MSS. are in the Augustinian College in Valladolid.

Fernández de Rojas is best known for his prose satire on the encyclopaedists, *Crotalogía, o arte de tocar las castañuelas* (1792), published under the pseudonym 'Francisco Agustín Florencio'. He answered attacks in *Impugnación literaria de la Crotalogía*, using the pen-name 'Juanito López

Polinario'. His other work was an edition of the *Poesías* of Fray Diego Tadeo González (1796).

FERNÁNDEZ DE VELASCO, BERNARDINO, *Duque de Frías* (1701–69?), author of the amusing collection of anecdotes *Deleyte de la discreción y fácil escuela de agudeza* (2nd edn., 1749). This was praised by the Augustinian friar, Martín Salgado: 'books are like stew, one type appealing to some people and a different type appealing to others; but I think that this book is like bread, which tickles all palates'.

A convenient edition is that in Colección Austral (Buenos Aires, n.d. [1947]). Most of the stories display the wit or the wisdom of kings and prelates.

FERNÁNDEZ DE VELASCO, BERNARDINO, *Duque de Frías* (1783–1851), b. Madrid. Poet and playwright. A soldier and diplomat, he represented Spain in England 1820–23. His *Obras poéticas* (1857) show the influence of Quintana and Gallego, particularly in the odes *A Pestalozzi* and *A las bellas artes*. He also wrote a play, *Don Juan de Lanuza* (1837).

FERNÁNDEZ DE VELASCO, JUAN, *Conde de Haro* (d. 1613), the pseudonymous author, in the view of Nicolás Antonio (q.v.) and most other authorities, of *Observaciones del Prete Jacopin, en defensa de Garcilaso de la Vega, contra las Anotaciones que hizo a sus obras Hernando de Herrera* first published by J. M. Asensio in *Controversia sobre sus Anotaciones a las obras de Garcilaso de la Vega* (Seville, 1870). This attack on Herrera is a defence of Francisco Sánchez's edition of Garcilaso.

FERNÁNDEZ DE VILLEGAS, PEDRO (1453–1536), b. Burgos. Translator from the Italian. After living in Rome 1485–90, he made a complete translation into Castilian verse of the *Divina Commedia*, as well as translating Latin authors. In 1496 he is recorded as being archdeacon of Burgos Cathedral and from 1500 in the royal monastery of San Salvador, Oña, as *juez conservador*, a position involving protecting the rights of the monastic community. His books are *La traducción de Dante de lengua toscana en verso castellano . . . con otros dos tratados, uno que se dize querella de la fe, y otro aversión del mundo y conversión a Dios* (Burgos, 1515) and *Sátira dezena del Iuvenal en que reprende los vanos deseos* (Burgos, 1519). As well as Juvenal's tenth satire, selections from Plutarch's *Lives* were translated by Fernández de Villegas.

FERNÁNDEZ FLORES, ISIDORO (1840–1902), b. Madrid. Satirist, critic, and journalist who founded the respected literary supplement known as *Los lunes de 'El Imparcial'*. Writing usually as 'Fernanflor' or 'Un Lunático', he wrote *El teatro de Tamayo* (1882), collected some short stories, *Cuentos rápidos* (1886), and made his entrance speech to the Academy, *La literatura de la frensa* (1898). Two posthumously-compiled volumes of journalism appeared as *Cartas a mi tío* (1903–4).

FERNÁNDEZ FLÓREZ, DARÍO (1909–), b. Valladolid. Novelist, historian, and playwright. His early novels were *Inquietud* (1931); *Maelstrom* (1932), which is part detective-story and part psychological novel on a triple death; and *Zarabanda* (1944), about a group of amoral characters without roots or loyalties.

Fernández Flórez achieved fame and fortune with the much-translated expressionist novel *Lola, espejo oscuro* (1950). Reminiscent of *La pícara Justina* (q.v.), the book relates the career of the prostitute Dolores Vélez, for whom men are 'gargantas cobardes, corrompidas por el miedo, por la vileza de su vida'. It has been suggested that *Lola* imitates Moravia's *La romana*, a greatly superior work.

His later novels were less well received: *Boda y jaleo de Titín Aracena* (1952), *La hora azul* and *Frontera* (both 1953), *Alta costura* (1954), the Don Juanesque *Yo estoy dentro* (1961), and *Señor Juez* (Barcelona, 1958). Fernández Flórez has also written the historical novel *Mío Cid y Roldán* (1939), and the plays *La vida ganada* (1942), and *La dueña de las nubes* (1944).

FERNÁNDEZ FLÓREZ, WENCESLAO (1884–1964), b. La Coruña. Novelist and journalist. Forced to earn his living from the age of 15, when his father died, Fernández Flórez turned out thousands of articles on all aspects of Spanish life, the most durable being the political journalism collected as *Acotaciones de un oyente* (2 vols., 1918–31). Throughout his life a supporter of Franco, he wrote much satire against *avant-garde* writers. His later novels and stories developed into broader attacks on other targets and his earlier realism changed to a more comprehensive social and political critique. In his best novel, *Las siete columnas* (1926), he attempts to demonstrate that Western culture is based on the general practice of the seven deadly sins.

His *Obras completas* (7 vols., 1945–61) omit his first novel *La tristeza de la paz* (1910), *El poder de la mentira* (1916?), *Los mosqueteros* (1918), and the short story 'La calma turbada' which concluded the book *Unos pasos de mujer* (1934).

Fernández Flórez's major fiction included *La procesión de los días* (1914), *Volvoreta* (1917), *Silencio* (1918), the satirical *Ha entrado un ladrón* (1920), the Utopian *El secreto de Barba Azul* (1923), *El ladrón de glándulas* (1929), six ghost

stories in *Fantasmas* (1930), *El malvado Carabel* (1931), *El hombre que compró un automóvil* (1932), *Los trabajos del detective Ring* (1934), the political satires *Una isla en el Mar Rojo* (1938) and *La novela número 13* (1941), and the melancholy fantasy *El bosque animado* (Saragossa, 1943).

A prolific and often popular writer because of his fluent style and humour, Fernández Flórez has not received the critical attention he merits, except that of Eugenio G. de Nora, in *La novela española contemporánea* (vol. 2, 2nd edn., 1968), pp. 7–39, and of M. Gómez-Santos, in *Wenceslao Fernández Flórez* (Barcelona, 1958).

FERNÁNDEZ GUARDIA, RICARDO (1867–1950), Costa Rican historian, dramatist, and writer of short stories. As a child he was sent to Paris, returning to San José in 1883, when he entered the diplomatic service, following his father, the historian León Fernández. He wrote the first play on a Costa Rican theme: *Magdalena* (1902), produced by the Teatro Nacional in San José the same year, but is best known for his historical writings: *Historia de Costa Rica: el descubrimiento y la conquista* (1905), translated into English by H. W. van Dyke (New York, 1913), and *Historia de Costa Rica: la independencia* (2nd edn., 1941).

FERNÁNDEZ MORENO, BALDOMERO (1886–1950), b. Buenos Aires. Argentinian *modernista* poet, who lived in Spain between the ages of six and thirteen, qualified as a doctor in 1912, and practised in the towns of Buenos Aires province from 1917 to 1924, but then gave up medicine to teach literature and write. His first book *Las iniciales del misal* (1915) prefigured in its simplicity and sensibility the line that he was to follow in *Intermedio provinciano* (1916) and the increasingly masterly *Ciudad* (1917), *Campo argentino* (1919), and *El hijo* (1928). His style becomes more elaborate in *Aldea española* (1926), *Poesía* (1929), *Dos poemas* (1936), *Romances* (1938), and *Penumbra* (1951). All passions are restrained until his last book, full of bitter disillusion. A common theme in his poetry is the rootlessness and insecurity which, after his early years in Spain, he experienced in Latin America. The best of his prose, witty and aphoristic, was gathered in *La mariposa y la viga* (1947).

See *Introducción a Fernández Moreno* (1956) by his son César; and E. Carilla, *Genio y figura de Baldomero Fernández Moreno* (1973).

FERNÁNDEZ RETAMAR, ROBERTO (1930–), b. Havana. Cuban poet, editor, and essayist, he abandoned early studies in art and architecture and turned to literature in Havana, Paris, and London. After a time teaching at Yale University, and a short period as Cultural

Attaché in Paris, Fernández Retamar was appointed co-ordinating secretary of the Union of Writers in Cuba. At present he edits the Casa de las Américas magazine in Havana, and teaches literature at Havana University.

His original poetry includes the adolescent rhetoric of *Elegía como un himno* (1950), the vaguely patriotic *Patrias* (1952), and *Alabanzas, conversaciones* (Mexico City, 1955), and the pro-revolutionary work published since, such as *Aquellas poesías* (1958), the collection *Con las mismas manos, 1949–62* (1962), *Historia antigua* (1964), and *Poesía reunida* (1966). More recently he has published *Buena suerte viviendo* and *Que veremos arder* (1970), the latter republished in Spain as *Algo parecido a los monstruos antediluvianos* (1970).

If his revolutionary poetry often seems naive or sentimental, his essays show a stirring belief in the revolutionary ideals of Fidel Castro and in the possibilities for literature during a time of upheaval: the early essays in *La poesía contemporánea en Cuba: 1927–53* (1954) being followed by the pamphlet *En su lugar, la poesía* (1957), *Vuelta de la antigua esperanza* (1959), *Sí a la revolución* (1961), *Papelería* (1962), and *Ensayo de otro mundo* (1967).

FERNÁNDEZ SANTOS, Jesús (1926–), b. Madrid. Novelist, film director, and scriptwriter. *Los bravos* (Valencia, 1954) was greeted by critics as one of the first manifestations of the generation of novelists that included Sánchez Ferlosio, A. M. Matute, Aldecoa, and J. Goytisolo (qq.v.). Gil Novales has characterized Fernández Santos as a novelist of *sobriedad*. His objective realism developed in *En la hoguera* (1957), the stories of *Cabeza rapada* (Barcelona, 1958), *Laberintos* (Barcelona, 1964), and *El hombre de los santos* (Barcelona, 1969). A graduate of the Instituto de Investigaciones y Experiencias Cinematográficas, Fernández Santos has spent the recent years in film-making.

FERNÁNDEZ Y GONZÁLEZ, Manuel (1821–88), b. Seville. Historical novelist, in the manner of Sir Walter Scott, whose novels issued in parts (either serially in magazines or in booklet form) were immensely successful and made him one of the wealthiest writers of his day, though he died in penury as a result of his extravagant living.

The European vogue for the serialized novel, which reached its zenith with Alexandre Dumas *père* in France and Charles Dickens in Britain, also affected Spain, and many writers contributed to the genre: Ramón Ortega y Frías, Enrique Pérez Escrich (qq.v.), Antonio Flores, Wenceslao Ayguals de Izco (1801–73), and Torcuato Tarrago Mateos (1822–89). But

Manuel Fernández y González, whose first novel *El doncel de don Pedro de Castilla* achieved commercial success when the author was only 17, is the characteristic master of the genre, with a gift for creating tension and period atmosphere at the expense of psychological and historical veracity. His three hundred or so novels, issued in some 500 volumes, deal with the semi-legendary, semi-factual twilight world of popular history where an inexhaustible invention, as regards plot and dialogue, creates a spurious, if glittering past where men are divided sharply into heroes and villains. Typical works include *Men Rodríguez de Sanabria: memorias del tiempo de don Pedro el Cruel* (1851); *Los siete Infantes de Lara: leyenda histórica tradicional* (1853); *El cocinero de su Magestad: memorias del tiempo de Felipe III* (1857); *El pastelero de Madrigal: memorias del tiempo de Felipe II* (2 vols., 1862); and *El Conde-Duque de Olivares* (1870).

Many anecdotes are told of Fernández's insufferable conceit and his incredible fecundity. Sometimes he would dictate two novels simultaneously to two secretaries (he employed both Tomás Luceño and Vicente Blasco Ibáñez, qq.v.). He was a member of the literary circle La Cuerda Granadina, which also included Alarcón and Manuel del Palacio (qq.v.).

See F. Hernández-Girbal, *Una vida pintoresca: Manuel Fernández, biografía novelesca* (1931).

FERNANFLOR, a pen-name used frequently by Isidoro Fernández Flores (q.v.).

Fernán González, Poema de (c. 1260), an anonymous narrative poem in the learned *cuaderna vía* metre recalling the exploits of Count Fernán González (c. 915–970) and based on a lost epic, the *Cantar de Fernán González*.

The fragment that survives is in a 15th-c. MS. with important lacunae and ends at stanza 701. It was composed at the Castilian monastery of S. Pedro de Arlanza, allegedly founded by Fernán González, and much of the poem is taken up with the connections between Arlanza, González, and Castile, whose independence from León formed an important part of the hero's struggle, which also involved the Moors and Navarra. The monk who wrote the epic used elements from Berceo, the *Libro de Alexandre*, and a vernacular chronicle the *Liber Regum*, and enlivened his propaganda for the monastery and its real or imagined association with the Castilian hero by inserting vivid battle scenes, González's imprisonment in Castroviejo, and the burial of the Count of Tolosa. The poem is thus a national epic as well as an ecclesiastical work.

Editions have been made by C. Carroll Marden (Baltimore, 1904); R. Menéndez Pidal, in *Reliquias de la poesía épica española* (1951); A.

Zamora Vicente, in Clásicos Castellanos (2nd edn., 1954); and there is a modern Spanish version by E. Alarcos Llorach (Valencia, 1955).

FERRÁN, Augusto (1830–80), Spanish minor poet whose friendship with G. A. Bécquer (q.v.) was mutually fruitful. Both were influenced by Heine, but it seems from the chronology that at least some of Ferrán's *La soledad: colección de cantares* (1861) anticipated poems by Bécquer, who summarized his poetic theories in a prologue. After Bécquer's death, Ferrán went to Chile (1872–77) and died insane. The other work which appeared in his lifetime was *La pereza: colección de cantares originales* (1871).

As well as these two collections, Ferrán's *Obras completas* contained prose legends and translations of Heine.

FERRANDES DE JERENA, Garci (*fl.* late 14th c.), Galician poet who married a Moorish poetess and retired with her to a hermitage. He intended to make the pilgrimage to Jerusalem, but apparently travelled no farther than Málaga. In Granada he renounced Christianity for Islam, but will always be admired for a charming prayer to the Virgin with the *estribillo*:

> *Virgen, flor de espina,*
> *syempre te serví;*
> *sancta cosa e dina*
> *ruega a Dios por mi.*

He allegedly reverted to Christianity in old age and died in Castile, though legend is difficult to separate from fact. His texts are found not only in the *Cancionero de Baena* (*c.* 1443) but in the *Cancionero gallego-castellano* assembled by H. R. Lang (New York, 1902). His *Cantiga Despedida del amor* was long attributed to Alfonso Álvarez de Villasandino (q.v.).

See L. Dolfus, *Études sur le Moyen Âge espagnol* (Paris, 1894).

FERRARI, Emilio (1850–1907), b. Valladolid. Poet and playwright whose full name was Emilio Pérez Ferrari. He was Secretary of the Association of Writers and Artists. He attracted attention with the philosophical poem *Pedro Abelardo* (1884). Such poems as *Un día glorioso* (on the battle of Lepanto), *En el arroyo* (1885), and *Consummatum est* (1889) show the overpowering influence of Núñez de Arce and Zorrilla (qq.v.). His *Obras completas* were published in two volumes in 1908–10.

See J. M. Martínez Cachero's studies in *Archivum* (Oviedo, 1959–60, vols. 9–10).

FERRATER, Gabriel (1922–72), b. Reus. Catalan poet. His first three collections, *Da nuces pueris* (1960), *Menja't una cama* (1962), and *Teoria*

dels cossos (1966), were assembled in the fluent, intelligent *Les dones i els dies* (Barcelona, 1968), in which the dominant themes of love, frustration, and nostalgia are given serious attention by a moral man obeying his private convictions. An admirer of medieval literature and Thomas Hardy, Ferrater uses prosaic language to good effect. He has said, 'I understand poetry to be the description of moments in the moral life of an ordinary man, like myself'.

FERRATER MORA, José (1912–), b. Barcelona. Philosopher, who obtained his doctorate from the University of Barcelona. He has lived in exile since 1939, first in Cuba, and from 1941 in Chile. His major philosophical and cultural works include *Cóctel de verdad* (Madrid, 1935), *España y Europa* (Santiago, 1942), *Diccionario de filosofía* (1942), *Las formas de la vida catalana* (1944), *Unamuno, bosquejo de una filosofía* (Buenos Aires, 1944), *Cuestiones disputadas* (1955), *Cuatro visiones de la historia universal* (Buenos Aires, 1955), *Ortega y Gasset, etapas de una filosofía* (Barcelona, 1958), *La filosofía en el mundo de hoy* (1959), *El ser y la muerte* (1962), *Tres mundos: Cataluña, Europa, España* (Barcelona, 1963).

FERRER, Francesc (*fl.* 1430–80), b. Valencia. A Catalan poet whose *Romanç del setge de Rodas* was probably written from personal experience at the siege of Rhodes. A friend of Pedro Torroella (q.v.), or Torrellas Ferrer was an able versifier, and displays a good knowledge of contemporary poets. Nicolau d'Olwer's critical edition of Ferrer's *Romanç* appeared in *Estudis Universitaris Catalans*, vol. 12 (1927), pp. 376–87.

FERRER, José Miguel (1904–), b. Caracas. Venezuelan minor poet attached to the diplomatic service. His books are *Cuarta dimensión* (1940), *Huésped en la eternidad* (1940), and *Poemas* (1956).

FERRER, Juan (*fl.* 1618), Jesuit and pseudonymous author of *Tratado de las comedias* (Barcelona, 1618) in which, writing as 'Bisbe y Vidal', he attacked the contemporary licentiousness of the Spanish theatre and proposed two changes in the practice of the law: that all plays should be carefully examined and if necessary expurgated before licensing; and that permission for performances should be granted not to professional actors but only to people of the place where the play was to be performed, these to be men and youths known to be respectable.

FERRER DEL RÍO, Antonio (1814–72), b. Madrid. Historian and literary critic. As a young man he went to Cuba, writing for its press as 'El Madrileño'. On his return to Spain he was appointed librarian of the Ministry of Education and eventually became Minister. He wrote literary criticism for *El Laberinto* and *Revista Española de Ambos Mundos*.

His *Galería de la literatura española* (1846) was produced hurriedly to a publisher's deadline, so that its portraits of contemporary writers have more value for their anecdotal quality than for their thoroughness. His best historical work is the inevitably biased *Historia del reinado de Carlos III* (4 vols., 1956), commissioned by Isabel II, who paid the printing bill and gave Ferrer a pension. His best-known poem is the *Oda a la muerte de don Alberto Lista*, Lista being Ferrer's mentor in Madrid.

FERRES, ANTONIO (1925–   ), b. Madrid. A novelist and documentary writer, who teaches in the U.S.A. Skilled in the graphic description of the underprivileged and their environment, he alternates between narrative fiction and the factual documentary. In the first category are *La piqueta* (1959), its theme the demolition of a house on the outskirts of Madrid; *I vinti* (Milan, 1962) published in Spanish as *Los vencidos* (Paris, 1965) with a political bias towards the poor; and *Con las manos vacías* (Barcelona, 1964). In the second category are *Caminando por las Hurdes*, with Armando López Salinas (Barcelona, 1960) and *Tierra de olivos* (Barcelona, 1964), which have been widely translated.

FERRETIS, JORGE (1902–62), b. Río Verde, San Luis Potosí. Mexican novelist and socialist politician who represented his state from 1952 to 1957. He stated that fiction should be dedicated to social objectives, and added moralizing prefaces to each of his novels to emphasize their didactic purpose. His best novel is also his first: *Tierra caliente* (1935), published in Spain as *Los que sólo saben pensar*. This was followed by three long stories in *El Sur quema* (1937), in which the title story deals with a possible labour policy for the Indians; *Lo que llaman fracaso*, on the futile honesty of the lower civil servants confronted with massive corruption higher up; and *Cuando bajan los cuervos*, appealing for medical services to the Indians.

Cuando engorda el Quijote (1937) is a novel of disillusionment against those former revolutionaries who, on attaining power, forget their early idealism. *San Automóvil* (1938) consists of three long stories: 'En la tierra de los pájaros que hablan', 'Carne sin luz', and the title story, which shows the astonishment of a boy when one of his friends is admired simply because he owns a car. The tragic irony is that Ferretis himself was killed in a car accident.

Two collections of short stories followed:

Hombres en tempestad (1941) and *El coronel que asesinó a un palomo y otros cuentos* (1952). Ferretis seems to have been influenced above all by Azuela and Romero (qq.v.).

FERRÚS, PERO (*fl.* 1379), poet. Known as 'el Viejo'. With Macías (q.v.) and his friend López de Ayala (q.v.), the most interesting of the writers represented in the *Cancionero de Juan Alfonso de Baena* (*c.* 1443). He lived in Alcalá near the Jewish ghetto, and he is author of an amusing *debate* between himself and some Jews whose singing woke him in the morning. His best-known work is a dispute with López de Ayala, in which he defends winter against summer in the style of classical *debates*. Bellaguisa is the name which he gives the addressee of a memorable love poem influenced by the Provençal courtly lyric. He mentions Arthur, Lancelot, Tristram, Guinevere, and others of the Arthurian cycle, and shows a knowledge of *Amadís de Gaula* (q.v.).

FIALLO, FABIO (1866–1942), b. Santo Domingo. Possibly the best-known poet native to the Dominican Republic, and its first distinguished short-story writer. Fiallo spent some time in jail for his participation in anti-U.S. demonstrations. There are reminiscences of Heine and Bécquer in his poetry. His first book was *Primavera sentimental* (Caracas, 1902), followed by *Cantaba el ruiseñor* (Berlin, 1910), *Canciones de la tarde* (1920), the comprehensive *La canción de una vida* (Madrid, 1926), and *El balcón de Psiquis* (Havana, 1935). *Sus mejores versos* (Santiago, 1938), is a useful collection of Fiallo's genial, elegant work. His short stories are to be found in *Cuentos frágiles* (New York, 1908) and *Las manzanas de Mefisto* (Havana, 1934).

Ficciones, **1935-1944** (1944), a volume of short stories by Jorge Luis Borges (q.v.). These 'fictions' often start with some factual reference and thus are part-essay and part-fantasy; but many of the fourteen stories of the original collection are wholly fictional. The version of *Ficciones* comprising vol. 5 of the *Obras completas* of Borges (1956) contains three new stories: 'El fin', 'La secta del Fénix', and 'El Sur'. The book is divided into two parts: 'El jardín de senderos que se bifurcan' and 'Artificios'. These works are of powerful intellectual imagination and of a prose style unsurpassed in modern Spanish literature. Allegory, symbolism, fantasy, and metaphysics are combined with the author's wide reading in such masterpieces as 'Tlön, Uqbar, Orbis Tertius'. In a mental universe, distinct from the space we inhabit, exist scholars with their own languages, architecture, and philosophies. 'In Tlön there is no science, no reason: the metaphysicians seek not each truth or the semblance of truth, but astonishment'.

Ficciones also contains the story of Pierre Menard, who 'writes', the *Quijote* afresh, but in the same words; 'La biblioteca de Babel'; 'Las ruinas circulares'; 'Funes el memorioso', whose protagonist remembers every detail of whatever he has ever glimpsed, thought, or read; and 'Tres versiones de Judas', which ironically proposes that the divinity of Jesus could not have been observed without Judas Iscariot's self-sacrifice so that, like Christ, he also was a sacrificial redeemer of mankind.

See J. Alazraki, *La prosa narrativa de Jorge Luis Borges* (Madrid, 1968) and D. L. Shaw, *Borges: 'Ficciones'* (London, 1976).

Fierro, Martín, see MARTÍN FIERRO.

FIGARILLO, pseudonym of Juan Bautista Alberdi (q.v.).

FÍGARO, pseudonym of Mariano José de Larra y Sánchez de Castro (q.v.).

FIGUEROA, FRANCISCO DE (1536–1617), b. Alcalá. Poet, called 'el Divino' in his lifetime. A friend of Cervantes, who praised him in the *Galatea*, he studied in Italy, where he lived as a soldier for some years.

On his deathbed he ordered all his poems to be destroyed; some were burnt, but others were edited by Luis Tribaldos de Toledo (Lisbon, 1625; new edn., 1626, with 6 extra poems), and more have since been published by R. Foulché-Delbosc (in *Revue Hispanique*, vol. 25 (1911), pp. 317–44); by R. Menéndez Pidal (in *BRAE*, vol. 2 (1915), pp. 302–40 and 458–96); and by A. Lacalle Fernández (in *Revista Crítica Hispanoamericana*, vol. 1 (1915), pp. 169–71), the last preceded by a biobibliographical study.

The first poet to acclimatize *versos sueltos* from Italy, Figueroa is a worthy imitator of Horace in *Cuitada navecilla*; of Petrarch in fine sonnets, *canciones*, and *elegías*; and of Garcilaso in the pastoral eclogue *Thirsi, pastor del más famoso rio*. The pastoral *liras Los amores de Damón y Galatea* show him at his best: fluent and imaginative, in his favourite themes of love, nature, and solitude. He wrote equally well in Italian. Figueroa is represented in vol. 42 (1857) of the BAE. His celebrated letter to Ambrosio de Morales (q.v.) from Chartres in 1560 *Sobre el hablar y pronunciar la lengua española* was reprinted in *Memorias de la Real Academia Española*, vol. 8 (1902), pp. 285–98.

Ángel González Palencia produced a new edition of Figueroa's *Poesías* (1943) for the Sociedad de Bibliófilos Españoles.

See E. Mele and A. González Palencia, 'Notas sobre Francisco de Figueroa' in *Revista de Filología Española*, vol. 25 (1941), pp. 333–82.

Figurón, Comedias de, plays which caricature the archetype of the pretentious fool, starting in the Golden Age with Don Lucas de Cigarral in *Entre bobos anda el juego* by Francisco de Rojas Zorrilla (qq.v.), which began a long series of Spanish comedies on the *commedia dell'arte* theme of the old man who tries to marry a young girl who is in love with a young man. The first play to be published with this epithet was Agustín Moreto's *De fuera vendrá quien de casa nos echará* (1654), borrowing a great deal from Lope de Vega's *¿De cuándo acá nos vino?*

In Moreto's play, an absurd aunt is hoaxed into thinking that a youth in love with her niece is in fact paying court to her. Other *comedias de figurón* include Moreto's *El lindo don Diego* (q.v.), perhaps the best-known example of the genre and based on *El Narciso en su opinión* by Guillén de Castro; Antonio de Zamora's *Don Bruno de Calahorra, El hechizado por fuerza*, and *Don Domingo de don Blas*; José de Cañizares *El dómine Lucas* (unrelated to Lope's play of the same title); and *La más ilustre fregona*, adapted from Cervantes' *novela ejemplar La ilustre fregona*.

Finida ('finish'), one or more lines forming the ending (but not an *envío* or invocation) of a *cantiga* or *decir*. It is the equivalent of the Provençal *tornada*. In later Spanish poetry it is known as the *fin* or *fin y cabo*.

FINOT, ENRIQUE (1891–1952), b. Santa Cruz de la Sierra. Bolivian historian and diplomat. His name is primarily associated with the massive *Historia de la literatura boliviana* (Mexico City, 1943; 4th edn., La Paz, 1975), of which the author himself confessed 'es menos historia crítica que nomenclatura o catálogo' and indeed 'annotated bibliography' would be a more accurate description. Satisfactory for the Colonial period and the 19th c., it completely ignored the Indian period and failed to cover the 20th c. The 2nd edition (1955) and the 3rd (1964) were greatly improved by appendices: *El período colonial* by J. de Mesa and T. Gisbert, and *Los contemporáneos* by L. F. Vilela.

Finot's most accomplished book is the *Nueva historia de Bolivia* (3rd edn., 1964), in F. Díez de Medina's view 'el mejor esquema crítico de nuestro pasado', and more valuable than the biased work of Arguedas (q.v.). He has also written *La cultura colonial española en el Alto Perú* (New York, 1935) and *Historia de la conquista del oriente boliviano*.

FITZMAURICE-KELLY, JAMES (1857–1923), British Hispanist. He lacked the formal education of many subsequent Hispanists, but created important cadres of specialists at the universities of Cambridge, of Liverpool (from 1909), and King's College, London (from 1916). He edited the influential *Oxford book of Spanish verse* (1913; 2nd edn., J. B. Trend, 1940) and improved upon his uneven *A history of Spanish literature* (1898) in his French-language revision (Paris, 1913) and more notably in *A new history of Spanish literature* (London, 1926), for long the most handy compendium of the subject in English.

Fitzmaurice-Kelly wrote numerous works, among them *Lope de Vega and the Spanish drama* (Glasgow, 1902), *Chapters of Spanish literature* (1908), *The relations between Spanish and English literature* (Liverpool, 1910), the biography *Cervantes* (1913), an annotated *Quijote*, *Cervantes and Shakespeare*, and *Luis de León* (Oxford, 1921).

FLORANES VÉLEZ DE ROBLES, RAFAEL DE (1743–1801), b. Liébana, Santander. Historian and scholar much respected by his collaborators Juan Antonio Llorente and Llaguno y Amírola. His *tertulia* in Valladolid was celebrated. Unfortunately most of his works have been lost, including the supplement to the *Bibliotheca* of Nicolás Antonio (q.v.), and 'El fuero de Sepúlveda' remains unpublished.

Menéndez y Pelayo published an essay by Floranes with another by Tomás Antonio Sánchez as 'Dos opúsculos inéditos sobre los orígenes de la poesía castellana' in *Revue Hispanique*, vol. 18 (1908), pp. 295–431. *Floranes* (ed. L. Redonet, Santander, 1956), has a useful anthology.

See C. Pitollet, 'Datos biográficos sobre Rafael Floranes' in *Revista de Filología Española*, vol. 10 (1923), pp. 288–300.

FLORENCIO, FRANCISCO AGUSTÍN, the pseudonym under which Fray Juan Fernández de Rojas (q.v.) wrote his *Crotalogía, o arte de tocar las castañuelas*.

FLORENTINO SANZ, EULOGIO, see SANZ Y SÁNCHEZ, Eulogio Florentino.

FLORES, JUAN DE (c. 1470–c. 1525), b. Lérida. Novelist. His two novels, both published in Lérida in 1495, were influenced by Boccaccio, and achieved immediate success. A collaborator, Alonso de Córdoba, added verses to Flores's prose texts.

The *Historia de Grisel y Mirabella, con la disputa de Torrellas y Braçayda* fuses the misogynous strand of Boccaccio's writing with the sentimental. The King of Scotland, on learning that his daughter Mirabella has been caught *in flagrante delicto* with her lover Grisel, arranges a *debate* between Brasaida (the Cressida of the Troy romances) and Pere Torroella (q.v., the author of anti-feminist *Coplas de las calidades de las donas*) to judge the dispute. The latter obtains judgment by a trick, but Grisel throws himself on the flames to save his beloved, wherepuon Mirabella casts herself into the royal lion-pit.

The women of the court put Torroella to death for his malicious *coplas* and his judgment in the case.

The novel was early translated into Italian (as *Historia de Aurelio e Isabella*), into French (1520), and into English (1526).

Flores's other novel also tests the medieval ideal of courtly love in a new situation and vindicates it. The *Breve tractado de Grimalte y Gradissa* is a continuation of *La Fiammetta* by Boccaccio. Fiammetta dies of love for Pánfilo, whom Grimalte challenges to a duel as the cause of her death. Pánfilo rejects the challenge, turning to saintly penitence. Gradissa demands that Grimalte renew his challenge and, after a journey lasting 27 years, Grimalte finds Pánfilo again, still scourging himself. Grimalte now joins him. Fiammetta appears in a vision, condemned by her own impertinence. As with Diego de San Pedro's lovers in *El cárcel de amor*, the outcome of consummated love is tragic in both works by Flores.

B. Matulka's *The novels of Juan de Flores and their European diffusion* (New York, 1931) includes both texts in critical editions. *Grimalte y Gradissa* has been edited by Pamela Waley (London, 1971).

FLORES, MANUEL MARÍA (1840–85), b. San Andrés Chalchicomula, Puebla. Mexican poet. A Bohemian whose amorous verses lacked depth or spirituality, Flores read and translated Victor Hugo, Byron, and Heine. His best-known book, *Pasionarias* (Puebla de Zaragoza, 1874; 2nd edn., 1882), derived much of its imagery and style from Alfred de Musset and caused a scandal by its doctrine that physical love is the supreme justification for life on earth. His most consistent muse was Rosario de la Peña, a well-known beauty, though he boasted of numerous other conquests. The only other book which appeared during his lifetime was *Páginas locas* (Puebla, (1878). Posthumous books include *Poesías inéditas* (1910) and his diary *Rosas caídas* (1953).

See Margarita Quijano Terán, *Manuel M. Flores, su vida y su obra* (1946).

FLÓREZ, JULIO (1867–1923), b. Chiquinquirá. Colombian poet of the *Gruta* group, whose Byronic personality and sentimental poetry assured him of popular appeal. His poetic affinities are largely with Espronceda (q.v.). Flórez died of cancer in the coastal village of

Usiacurí shortly after he had been crowned there as a major poet.

There is a selection of *Sus mejores poesías* (Mexico City, 1951) and his collected *Obra poética* (1970) brings together work from *Horas* (1893), *La araña* (Caracas, 1905), *Cardos y lirios* (Caracas, 1905), *Manojo de zarzas* (San Salvador, 1906), *Cesta de lotos* (San Salvador, 1906), *Fronda lírica* (Madrid, 1908), *Gotas de ajenjo* (Barcelona, 1911?), and the posthumous *Oro y ébano* (n.d.) and *¡De pie los muertos!* (Barranquilla, n.d.).

FLÓREZ DE SETIÉN Y HUIDOBRO, *Fray* ENRIQUE (1702–73), b. Villadiego, Burgos. An historian and Augustinian preacher and professor at Alcalá, Flórez knew Iriarte and Mayáns. He resigned his university post in 1742 to investigate the ecclesiastical archives, and produced 29 volumes in the invaluable series entitled *La España sagrada o Theatro geográfico-histórico de la Iglesia de España* (from 1747), continued to 51 volumes successively under Manuel Risco, Antolín Merino, José de La Canal, and Pedro Sáinz de Baranda. His other works include *Teología escolástica* (6 vols., 1732–8), the popular historical work *Clave historial con que se abre la puerta a la historia eclesiástica y política* (1743); *Medallas de las colonias, municipios y pueblos antiguos de España* (3 vols., 1757–73); and *Memorias de las reinas católicas: historia genealógica de la Casa Real de Castilla y León* (2 vols., 1761; 2 vols., 1945 in Colección Crisol). Flórez cannot be recommended for his style, but in diligence he ranks second to none.

Florida Street group, a literary group of the 1920s named after an elegant, cosmopolitan street in Buenos Aires (unlike the Boedo Street group, q.v.). Members of the group included Jorge Luis Borges, González Lanuza, Bernárdez, Mastronardi, Norah Lange, Marechal, and Molinari. Their *avant-garde* practice was willing to learn from European models, whereas the Boedo Street writers generally worked in the genre of proletarian realism.

The Florida Street writers were published primarily in *Prisma, Proa, Inicial,* and *Martín Fierro.* Verse was their preferred medium, though Borges later turned to the short story.

See Leónidas Barletta, *Boedo y Florida: una versión distinta* (1967).

FLORIT, EUGENIO (1903–   ), b. Madrid. Poet. Of Cuban nationality on the maternal side, and Spanish on the paternal side, Florit is considered a Cuban poet largely because his family left for Cuba when he was 15. Widely travelled since then, he has written much verse, frequently showing the influence of Juan Ramón Jiménez (q.v.).

An official of the Interior Ministry in Cuba from 1927 to 1940, he spent the period 1940–45 as a consular official in the U.S.A. and later turned to teaching Spanish there. He has carefully avoided rhetoric, from his first *32 poemas breves* (1927) to the later collections: *Trópico* (1930), *Doble acento* (1937), *Reino* (1938), *Cuatro poemas* (1940), *Poema mío: poesía completa* (Mexico City, 1947), *Asonante final y otros poemas* (1955), *Antología poética* (Mexico City, 1956), *Siete poemas* (Montevideo, 1960), and *Hábito de esperanza* (Madrid, 1965).

He has compiled several anthologies, among them *Cien de las mejores poesías españolas* (New York, 1965) and (with José Olivio Jiménez) *La poesía hispanoamericana desde el modernismo* (New York, 1968).

See *Eugenio Florit, vida y obra, bibliografía, antología, obras inéditas* (Hispanic Institute, New York, 1943); and O. E. Saa, *La serenidad en las obras de Eugenio Florit* (1973).

FOGASSOT, JOAN (c. 1420–c. 1480), b. Barcelona. One of the poets of the Consistory of the Gaya Ciencia when reconstituted under Ferdinand the Just. Entrusted with a mission of the king to the Duke of Burgundy, Fogassot was in Brussels when he learnt of Prince Carlos's imprisonment and he wrote *Romanç sobre la detenció del príncep de Viana* to appeal against the sentence, which had caused riots in Catalonia.

His allegedly eye-witness account of the arrival at Naples of the envoys of Constantinople to implore aid against the Turks is a pedestrian affair, and hardly seems to be what is claimed.

Fragments of the *Romanç* are provided, with a Castilian translation, in *Ocho siglos de poesía catalana* compiled by J. M. Castellet and Joaquim Molas (1969), pp. 165–71.

FOIX, J. V. (1894–   ), b. Sarriá, Barcelona. Catalan poet, who with Folguera and Salvat-Papasseit (q.v.), is considered to be one of the most significant *avant-garde* writers in Catalan. He has used the surrealist modes of Buñuel, Dalí, and Miró, as well as championing their cause. Gabriel Ferrater (q.v.) has divided Foix's life and work into two parts: before 'the public catastrophe of 1936' and after. A businessman and Catalan nationalist, Foix wrote *Revolució catalanista* (1934), a political statement contrasting with his poems, which often approach the condition of waking dreams, as in some Daliesque paintings. With Josep Carbonell, he edited the magazine *L'Amic de les Arts* (1926–9). His first important collection of poetry was *Sol, i de dol* (1947; dated 1936), followed by *Les irreals omegues* (1949) and *On he deixat les claus* (1953). *Onze Nadals i un Cap d'Any* (1960) contains poems written for Christmas and New Years' greetings.

The *Obres poètiques* (Barcelona, 1964) contains work previously published and the new *Desa aquests llibres al calaix de baix*.

Castilian versions of Foix's poetry have been made by Enrique Badosa in *Antología lírica* (1963). *Diari 1918* (1956) is a collection of four prose poems. Other works in prose include *Gertrudis* (1927), *KRTU* (1932), and *L'estrella d'En Perris* (1963). *Obres completes* (vol. I, *Poesia*, 1974) has been supplemented by *Sol i dol* (1975).

See P. Gimferrer, *La poesia de J. V. Foix* (Barcelona, 1974).

FOLCH I TORRES, JOSEP MARIA (1880–1950), Catalan novelist who wrote of the urban working class in *Aigua avall* (1907) and *Joan Endal* (1909), realistic fiction in the tradition of Oller and Pérez Galdós (qq.v.).

FOLGUERA, JOAQUIM (1883–1919), b. Santa Coloma de Cervelló, Bajo Llobregat. Catalan poet. Considered to be one of the most important figures of the Catalan *avant-garde*, Folguera suffered progressive paralysis from early childhood. He wrote *Poemas de neguit* (1915), *El poema espars* (1917), and *Les noves valors de la poesia catalana* (1919).

FOMBONA PACHANO, JACINTO (1901–51), b. Caracas. Venezuelan poet and member of the Generation of 1918 and the *Viernes* group. The fresh, lyrical Creole poems of *Virajes* (1932) were impressive, but less so than *Las torres desprevenidas* (1940), written during his years at the Venezuelan Embassy in Washington. *Sonetos* (1944) was also incorporated in *Obras completas* (2 vols., 1953). A further edition of *Poesías* appeared in 1964.

FONSECA, Fray CRISTÓBAL DE (1550–1621), b. Santa Olalla, Toledo. Augustinian preacher and ascetic writer. Praised by both Lope de Vega and Espinel for his prose style, Fonseca is best remembered for the two parts of *Tratado del amor de Dios* (Salamanca, 1592 and Valencia, 1608) and the three parts of *Vida de Christo Señor Nuestro* (Toledo, 1596 and 1601 and Madrid, 1605), but he also wrote *Discursos para todos los evangelios de la Quaresma* (1614).

It was Narciso Alonso Cortés who, in *El falso 'Quijote' y Fray Cristóbal de Fonseca* (Valladolid, 1920), first mooted the attribution of the 'Avellaneda' *Quijote* to Fonseca, a view generally rejected.

Fontana de Oro, La, a café in Madrid which served as the informal headquarters 1820–2 of a liberal, revolutionary society opposing the dictatorial monarchy. One of its members was Antonio Alcalá Galiano (q.v.). The café was made famous in fiction by *La Fontana de Oro* (1867–8) by Benito Pérez Galdós (qq.v.).

Fontana de Oro, La (1867–8), the first of the *Novelas españolas de la primera época* (q.v.) of Benito Peréz Galdós (q.v.).

It has been declared by Donald L. Shaw to be 'both the beginning of the serious modern novel in Spain and the opening of Galdós' "historical" period'.

The book is set in the period 1820–3 in Madrid, and shows the struggle of the Liberal minority against the oppressive monarchy of Ferdinand VII. Little of the technical skill of Galdós's later years is apparent in this book, and the happy conclusion, in which Lázaro the liberal returns to the Aragonese countryside, abandoning the unequal struggle, was altered in the second edition to one less happy, and then— definitively—back to the original ending.

The message of Galdós is that violent means are inappropriate to abolish absolutism. His characters are not yet rounded: Lázaro is an insubstantial Romantic politician and his uncle little more than the opposing abstraction. The strength of the novel lies in its observation of Madrid life, particularly that of the lower classes.

FORD, RICHARD (1796–1858), English travel-writer. Educated at Winchester, and Trinity College, Oxford, Ford wrote a *Handbook for travellers in Spain* (London, 1845) long considered the best English introduction to Spain for its charming style, wit, idiosyncratic scholarship, and sympathy for the country and people.

His *Gatherings from Spain* (London, 1846) consisted of selections from the earlier work, with new matter, and was intended especially for ladies. Ford wrote that 'in order to lighten the narrative, the Author has removed much lumber of learning, and has not scrupled to throw Strabo, and even Saint Isidore himself, overboard'.

The very rare first edition of the *Handbook* (London, 1844) was severely truncated by Addington & Murray, his publishers, and it is the full version that Centaur Press reprinted (3 vols., 1966). Ford's *Letters* (London, 1905) were edited by Lord Ernle.

Forja de un rebelde, La (Buenos Aires, 1951), a trilogy of autobiographical novels by Arturo Barea (q.v., English translation, *The forging of a rebel*, 3 vols., 1941–4). A libertarian and a pacifist like his contemporary Sender (q.v.), Barea is influenced by Pío Baroja (q.v.) in *La forja*, set in the wretched Madrid of his youth during the early decades of the century. *La ruta* deals with Barea's military service in Morocco. *La llama*, the third volume, on the siege of Madrid in the Civil War, is the weakest. Barea's strength lies in his seemingly effortless control over a large number of characters.

FÓRMICA, MERCEDES (1918–   ), b. Cádiz. Novelist. By profession an advocate, she has used her skills in the courts, in the popular press, and in the novel to press for social justice, especially for women and above all for married women.

She wrote two novels using the pen-name 'Elena Puerto': *Vuelve a mí* (1944) and *Mi mujer eres tú* (1946), then began her career as a serious novelist with *Monte de Sancha* (Barcelona, 1950), devoted to the crime and vice incidental to war. *La ciudad perdida* (Barcelona, 1951) is set in the post-war period and seems to be influenced by Graham Greene. Her best book so far is *A instancia de parte* (1955), a fictional case for improving the legal rights of women whose husbands can, after twelve years of married life, arrange for a juridical 'adultery' with a mercenary 'lover'. 'The law is a trap into which only women fall' is Fórmica's bitter comment.

FORNARIS, JOSÉ (1827–90), b. Bayamo. Cuban minor poet who, in *Cantos del siboney* (1855), defended the indigenous Siboney Indians against the alleged exploitation by the Carib Indians. With his friend Joaquín Lorenzo Luaces, Fornaris founded the magazine *La Piragua* (1855–6) and edited *Cuba poética* (1855), an anthology reprinted in 1961.

He lived in Europe for several years, returning to Cuba in 1879 after publishing *Cantos tropicales* and *El harpa del hogar* (both Paris, 1878). His songs became popular in the countryside for their strong rhythms and sentimentality. The worst of his poems are heavily didactic and so artistically inferior that, in Raimundo Lazo's view, he belongs 'más a la historia política y social que a la historia literaria de Cuba'. His last collection was *Poesías* (1888).

FORNER Y SAGARRA, JUAN PABLO (1756–97), b. Mérida. Satirist and literary critic who studied in Salamanca. Though he was a man of great erudition, his satire became so intemperate that in 1785 he was banned from publishing more works in that genre. The *Sátira contra los vicios introducidos en la poesía castellana* (1782) won the Real Academia Española prize, however, and he had become notorious for *El asno erudito* (1782; critical edn. M. Muñoz Cortés, Valladolid, 1948), which attacked Iriarte's insensitive ear and pedestrian imagination; for *El ídolo del vulgo*, against V. García de la Huerta's *Raquel*; for accusing Vargas Ponce of being 'a wretched

plagiarist'; and for the satirical novel *Exequias de la lengua castellana* (1782; ed. for Clásicos Castellanos (1925) by Pedro Sáinz y Rodríguez), a work in the mould of Saavedra Fajardo's brilliant *República literaria*. Forner concludes that the Spanish language in his time is not actually dead, but merely swooning from a loss of blood. Fully aware of his capacity to wound, Forner described himself as 'un joven adusto, flaco, alto, cejijunto, de condición insufrible, y de carácter . . . mordaz'. Most of his attacks were written under pen-names, such as 'El Bachiller Regañadientes', 'Tomé Cecial', 'Pablo Segarra', 'Antonio Varas', and 'Silvio Liberio'.

His own poetry, available in vol. 113 (1871), pp. 263–425 of the BAE, is unremarkable, but he felt inspired to defend Spanish writers in the patriotic *Oración apologética por la España y su mérito literario* (1786). He also composed *Reflexiones sobre el modo de escribir la Historia de España* and *Discursos filosóficos sobre el hombre* (1787). There is a critical edition of *Los gramáticos. Historia chinesca* (1970) by J. H. R. Polt, greatly superior to the Clásicos Castellanos edition of the same year.

See M. F. Laughrin, *Juan Pablo Forner as a critic* (Washington, 1943); and M. Jiménez Salas, *Vida y obra de don Juan Pablo Forner y Sagarra* (1944).

Fortunata y Jacinta (4 vols., 1886–7), the greatest novel of Benito Pérez Galdós (q.v.). It forms part of his sequence of *Novelas españolas contemporáneas* (q.v.).

Very long and discursive, this work seems constantly to be eluding the author's control, even though he was at the height of his powers.

The central characters are the self-indulgent Juanito Santa Cruz, his middle-class wife Jacinta Arnáiz, and his lower-class mistress Fortunata, who is married to Maxi Rubín. Beyond the story of this quartet lies 'una selva de novelas entrecruzadas', as well as complex assumptions about the conflict of love and marriage (a theme often baldly ignored in the rest of Galdós's work), the relationship of the classes, and the need to keep up appearances. The illicit relationship produces children, while the marriages are sterile. The crisis comes when Santa Cruz deserts Fortunata for a new mistress, Aurora. Fortunata rises in anger from childbed, assaults Aurora but suffers a haemorrhage from which she realizes she will die, and sends the child to her former rival Jacinta. The gallery of minor figures rivals that in *Bleak House* or in *Anna Karenina*: Guillermina Pacheco, Don Plácido Estupiñá, Doña Lupe, and Feijóo, among many others.

Galdós has here achieved a sweep of imagination based solidly in the Madrid middle classes from the '68 revolution to the Bourbon restoration. The novel has been translated as a Penguin Classic by Lester Clark (Harmonsworth, 1973).

See R. Gullón, 'Estructura y diseño in "Fortunata y Jacinta" ' in *Papeles de Son Armadans*, vol. 48 (1968), pp. 223–316; and G. Ribbans, 'Contemporary history in the structure and characterization of "Fortunata y Jacinta"' in *Galdós studies*, ed. J. E. Varey (London, 1970).

Forum Judicum, see FUEROS.

FOULCHÉ-DELBOSC, RAYMOND (1864–1929), French Hispanist, professor of Spanish in Paris, and founder and director of the important *Revue Hispanique* (1894–1933), which was sponsored from 1905 by the Hispanic Society of America. *Revue Hispanique* published not only Foulché-Delbosc's own major contributions to scholarship, but also those of many leading Hispanists of the time.

Foulché-Delbosc edited the *Cancionero castellano del siglo XV* (2 vols., 1912, 1915) which formed vols. 19 and 22 of the NBAE. He also directed the Bibliotheca Hispánica from 1900 to 1920.

The *Manuel de l'hispanisant* (New York, 1920) which he compiled with L. Barrau-Dihigo is essential for the Hispanist and deserves revision, though so far it has been merely reprinted (most recently in 1970).

FOXÁ, AGUSTÍN DE, *Conde de Foxá* (1903–59), b. Madrid. Novelist, playwright, and poet. He began by publishing poetry: *El toro, la muerte y el agua: poemas* (1930), *La niña del caracol* (1933), *El almendro y la espada: poemas de paz y de guerra* (San Sebastián, 1940), and *Antología poética* (1948).

Foxá planned a series of 'episodios nacionales,' but wrote only one: *Madrid, de corte a checa* (1938), dealing with the end of the monarchy, the Republic and the Revolution in a style so personal as to remind one of the innovations of Valle-Inclán or Gómez de la Serna. A diplomat, Foxá travelled widely and published a travel book, *Por la otra orilla. Crónicas e impresiones de viajes por América* (1961). His verse plays enjoyed success on the Madrid stage: *Cui-Pin-Sing* (1940), first performed in 1938, is set in China and deals with the mission of an Emperor's minister to find the most beautiful girl in the kingdom. The minister finds her but manages to marry her himself, eventually incurring the maximum punishment for this infidelity. *Baile en Capitanía* (1944) is set in Spain during the Second Carlist War (1872–6) and describes the frustrated love of Eugenia de Urbino and the army captain Luis.

See J. I. Luca de Tena, *Agustín de Foxá, Conde de Foxá* in the *BRAE*, vol. 39 (1959), pp. 365–77.

FOXÁ Y LECANDA, NARCISO DE (1822–83), b. San Juan. Puerto Rican poet and prose writer. Foxá was educated in Cuba, and lived there so long that he is included in many anthologies of Cuban writing. His first success was the Moorish ballad 'Alíatar y Zaida', which appeared in the magazine *La Siempreviva* (1839) and in 1846 his *Canto épico sobre el descubrimiento de América por Cristóbal Colón* won the prize of the Havana Lyceum. His uneven *Ensayos poéticos* (Madrid, 1849) include conventional images and poor imitations of Bello's *silvas*.

FOX MORCILLO, SEBASTIÁN (1528?–1560?), b. Seville. Philosopher who studied at Alcalá and Louvain. His major work is *De naturae philosophia seu de Platonis et Aristotelis consensione libri V* (Louvain, 1554), an attempt to reconcile the Platonic ideal with Aristotelian form. He wrote lucid and pertinent commentaries on Aristotle's *Topics* (1548), Plato's *Timaeus* (1552), Aristotle's *Politics*, Plato's *Phaedo* and *Republic* (1556); his original works include *De usu et exercitatione dialecticae* (Louvain, 1554) and *De demonstratione eiusque necessitate* (Basle, 1556), both on logic; *De historiae institutione dialogus* (Paris, 1557); and a most interesting work on style: *De imitatione, seu de informandi styli ratione* (Antwerp, 1554), in which, anticipating Buffon's famous remark, Fox stated that 'it is as easy to recognize the nature and habits of a man by his style, as by his behaviour and by his countenance.'

King Philip II appointed him tutor to Prince Carlos, but Fox's ship was wrecked on its way to Spain and Fox perished with all on board.

See U. González de la Calle, *Sebastián Fox Morcillo: estudio histórico-crítico de sus doctrinas* (1902) and R. Lueben, *Morzillo und seine erkenntnis-theoretische Stellung zur Naturphilosophie* (Bonn, 1911).

FOZ, BRAULIO (1791–1865), b. Fórnoles, Teruel. Novelist, historian, and classicist. In 1823 he took part in the struggle against the French invaders, was captured, and taken to France. Later he taught Latin and Rhetoric in Huesca, and Greek in Saragossa, and wrote *Literatura griega* (1849). He founded *El Eco de Aragón* in Saragossa in 1837, and edited the paper until 1842. Apart from his useful edition of the *Historia de Aragón* by A.S., (4 vols., Saragossa, 1848–9), Foz wrote a play, *El testamento de Don Alfonso 'el Batallador'*, but he is best remembered for his *Vida de Pedro Saputo*, written anonymously and edited by Ynduraín (Saragossa, 1959). Menéndez y Pelayo suggested that if Don Quixote is the symbol of the chivalresque ideal, Pedro Saputo is the symbol of natural reason.

FRANCÉS, José (1883–1965), b. Madrid. Novelist and short-story writer. A follower of Vicente Blasco Ibáñez (q.v.), Francés translated Louÿs, Poe, and Baudelaire. His first novel, *El alma viajera*, is the disillusioned story of a provincial girl who ignores the example and warning of her aunt, a former cocotte; she finally salvages some sort of life with a failed actor. He passed to eroticism with *La guarida* (1911) and to the crime novel with *El crimen del Kursaal* (1911; reprinted as *El misterio del Kursaal*, 1916). *La danza del corazón* (1914) is a superficial treatment of the dilemma between art and life. *La muerte danza* (1915) deals with the war in 1914. His subsequent novels were *La mujer de nadie* (1915), *Como los pájaros de bronce* (1918) praised by E. G. de Nora as a 'verdadera sinfonía de la vida provinciana', *La raíz flotante* (1922) described by the author, who was of Asturian ancestry, as 'la novela de Asturias', *El hijo de la noche* (1923), and *Ella y los demás* (1924).

Francés is not a subtle writer, depending heavily on melodrama for his effects, and he has been grouped with Pedro Mata and López de Haro (q.v.).

FRANCO, Luis Leopoldo (1898–), b. Belén, Catamarca. Argentinian poet of the countryside: a peasant by origin, pagan in his writing, he celebrated life with Whitmanesque ebullience in *El libro del gay vivir* (1923). *Nuevo mundo* (1927) bears the influence of a number of contemporary poets. *Suma* (1938) contained the verse written between 1927 and 1937 and *Pan* the work of the following decade, in which social themes begin to predominate; yet the effect is contrived. Of his stories, the part-legend, part-fable *Los hijos del Llastay* (1926) shows Franco's expressive prose at its best. He was a member of the group of writers whose work was published in the magazine *Martín Fierro* (q.v.).

FRANCO OPPENHEIMER, Félix (1912–), b. Ponce. Puerto Rican poet, who studied at Puerto Rico University where his master's thesis was *La poesía de Jorge Carrera Andrade*. He developed the poetic movement known as transcendentalism with Eugenio Rentas Lucas (1910–) and Francisco Lluch Mora (1925–), rejecting a materialist viewpoint in order to 'lift man up to a plane of high spirituality, without letting him forget his human reality'. The collections exemplifying this view are *El hombre y su angustia* (1950) and *Del tiempo y su figura* (1956).

FRANCOVICH, Guillermo (1901–), historian of Bolivian thought and learning. His best-received book was *La filosofía en Bolivia* (Buenos Aires, 1945), but the massive *El pensamiento boliviano de 1900 al presente* (Mexico City, 1956) has been severely criticized for demonstrating, in the words of one scholar, 'un lamentable desconocimiento del proceso histórico, político y social de Bolivia'. Francovich also wrote *El pensamiento universitario de Charcas* (Sucre, 1948).

Fray Gerundio de Campazas, alías Zotes, Historia del famoso Predicador (2 vols., 1757–68), a satirical novel by the Jesuit P. José Francisco de Isla de la Torre y Rojo (q.v.) written under the name of a priest of Villagarcía de Campos, one Francisco Lobón de Salazar. A third volume, *Colección de varias piezas relativas a la obra de fray Gerundio de Campazas*, appeared in 1787.

The bombastic sermons of Fray Félix Hortensio Paravicino (q.v.) and his followers caused Gregorio Mayáns y Síscar (q.v.) to complain as early as 1725 that their 'only concern is for the meaningless sound of high-flown diction, saying much yet signifying nothing'. Fray Gerundio is a fictional hero of this type, able to preach before he could read or write, and his foolish mentor Fray Blas is another. The Countess d'Aulnoy (q.v.) records (possibly through other informants) in her *Relation du voyage d'Espagne, 1679–80* (1693), how such preachers would act the fool in the streets to win a big congregation. As in the case of Don Quixote, Gerundio's mind is turned by reading: not *libros de caballería*, but rhetorical sermons.

There is virtually no action in the novel, which reads more like a Shavian preface than a work of fiction with its good sense and indictment of hypocrisy: Isla openly corrects Gerundio's notions of education, religion, and morality. Overblown diction is a symptom of immaturity, artificial values, extravagance in dress, and lax morals. Exterior manners are to be valued far less than spiritual grace. Despite his firm denial at the end of the book, Isla definitely caricatured some of his contemporaries.

The first part caused a great stir, and those mocked in it managed to effect an Inquisitorial ban in 1760. The second part then circulated in MS. long before its publication in 1768, but it is superfluous, diluting the book's impact by prolixity without extending the scope of its targets. The style is modelled on Cervantes and Quevedo though suffering from excessive length and lack of variety.

Fray Gerundio was scathingly attacked by P. Matías de Marquina in *El penitente*. There is a thorough study by B. Gandeau, *Les prêcheurs burlesques en Espagne au XVIIIe siécle: étude sur le P. Isla* (Paris, 1891), and a good edition by Russell Perry Sebold (4 vols., 1960–4), in the Clásicos Castellanos.

FRÍAS, Heriberto (1870–1925), b. Querétaro. Mexican novelist and journalist. His novel *Tomóchic* (1892; 2nd edn., Rio Grande City, Texas, 1894), first serialized in *El Demócrata* (1892), was the first prominent protest against the regime of Porfirio Díaz and a notable precursor of the Mexican revolutionary novel. It showed through the narrator Manuel Mercado the popular disgust at government methods to exterminate the rebellious Yaqui Indians. Frías wrote from first-hand experience, and was to use the figure of Manuel Mercado as a fictional identity in other books; *Naufragio* (1895) described student life in Mexico City and *El último duelo* (1896) denounced the practice of duelling. Frías also wrote *¡No llores, hombre!* (Orizaba, 1899), *Leyendas históricas mexicanas* (Barcelona, 1899), *Episodios militares mexicanos* (1901), *El triunfo de Sancho Panza* (1911) in which Mercado is a journalist attacking political corruption, the autobiographical *Miserias de Mexico* (1916), *La vida de Juan Soldado* (1918), and *¿Águila o sol?* (1923) written while Frías was Mexican consul in Cádiz and nearly blind. This is almost a testament, touching in its consistent honesty, for Mercado is still doing battle, this time leading a miners' strike.

See R. Ayala Echavarri, *Heriberto Frías, un novelista revolucionario de antes de la Revolución* (1967).

FRUGONI, Emilio (1880–1969), b. Montevideo. Uruguayan poet, and drama critic (as 'Urgonif') for *El Diario Nuevo*, *La Prensa*, and *El Día* successively. A member of the group which founded the Uruguayan Socialist Party, Frugoni was a deputy from 1917 to 1934. For some years he taught literature in Montevideo University, becoming Dean of the Faculty of Law in 1933–4. His first three books consisted of sentimental love verse: *Bajo tu ventana* (1900), *De lo más hondo* (1902), and *El eterno cantar* (1907). *Los himnos* (1916) marked the beginning of his epic period and was influenced by Verhaeren. His later verse appeared in *Poemas montevideanos* (1923), *Bichitos de luz* (1925), *Epopeya de la ciudad* (1927), *Nuevos poemas montevideanos* (1927), *La canción humana* (1933), *El libro de María Rosa* (1942), *La elegía unánime* (1942), *Poemas civiles* (1944), *Sonetos míos* (1957), and *Los caballos* (1960).

Among Frugoni's prose works are *La sensibilidad americana* (1929), studies of Rodó, Florencio Sánchez, Oribe, Mendilaharsu, and others; *La esfinge roja* (1948), a survey of Communism's impact written while serving as ambassador in Moscow; and *El libro de elogios* (1953).

The Hugoesque style is characteristic of his patriotic poems, while Zum Felde has described his descriptive writing in his poetry as resembling 'el resultado de un hombre paseando con una Kodak'. He consistently opposes the exoticism and Europeanism of the modernists.

See M. L. Díez de Peluffo, *Emilio Frugoni: poesía lírica y social* (1964).

FUENSANTA DEL VALLE, Marqués de la, see Ramírez de Arellano, Feliciano.

FUENTE BENAVIDES, Rafael de la (1908–), b. Lima. Peruvian poet writing under the pseudonym 'Martín Adán'. Mariátegui has called his sonnets 'anti-sonnets'; 'Martín Adán' has also experimented with other traditional verse-forms, such as the ballad and the *décima*.

His books include the poetic novel *La casa de cartón* (1928; 4th edn., 1971); *La rosa de la espinela* (1939); *Travesía de extramares* (1950); *Escrito a ciegas* (1961), and *La mano desasida* (1964), subtitled 'a song to Machu Picchu'. The *Obra poética* of 'Martín Adán' was published in 1971.

See Luis Monguió, *La poesía post-modernista peruana* (1955) and Edmundo Bendezú, *La poética y Martín Adán* (1969).

Fuenteovejuna, a three-act play by Lope de Vega Carpio (q.v.) first published in the *Dozena Parte de las Comedias* (1619). The main themes are resistance to tyranny, and the need for justice, loyalty, and order within a state and within its microcosms—the city, village, and family. The setting is 15th-c. Spain before its anarchic situation was brought under control by the Catholic Sovereigns, Ferdinand and Isabella. The play was written probably between 1612 and 1614, and is one of the acknowledged masterpieces of Spanish Golden Age drama.

Lope's drama was conceived around the already popular saying 'Fuenteovejuna lo hizo'; its source was an incident described in the *Crónica de las tres Ordenes militares* [of Santiago, Calatrava, and Alcántara] (1574) by Rades y Andrada.

Fuenteovejuna is a village suddenly disordered by the cruel conduct of Fernán Gómez, the Comendador of the Order of Calatrava, an avowed rebel against Ferdinand and Isabella. The villagers unite to oppose and kill him, vowing never to reveal the identity of the actual assassins but to assert instead that 'Fuenteovejuna did it'. King Ferdinand eventually pardons the villagers, and harmony is restored. The play also deals with the theme of love and trust as exemplified by the peasants, especially Laurencia and Frondoso. Other themes include the common Golden Age ideas of true and false honour (honour being a moral quality, not a mere accident of noble birth), and the Horatian contrast between *aldea* and *corte*.

Monroy y Silva's *Fuenteovejuna* (ed. with Lope's by F. López Estrada (1969) in Clásicos Castalia) is an unhappy reworking of the Lope model, but there is an important alternative treatment of the material in Tirso de Molina's *La dama del olivar*.

Separate editions of the play include those by A. Castro (1919) in Colección Universal, E. Kohler (Strasbourg, 1952), and T. García de la Santa (Saragossa, 1951).

See essays by G. W. Ribbans and L. Spitzer in J. F. Gatti, *El teatro de Lope de Vega* (Buenos Aires, 1962); H. Hoock, *Lope de Vegas Fuenteovejuna als Kunstwerk* (Würzburg, 1963); Noël Salomon, *Récherches sur le thème paysan dans la 'comedia' au temps de Lope de Vega* (Bordeaux, 1965); and J. B. Hall, 'Theme and structure in Lope's "Fuenteovejuna"' in *FMLS*, vol. 10 (1974), pp. 57–66.

FUENTES, CARLOS (1928–), b. Mexico City. Major Mexican novelist and short-story writer. Fuentes grew up in many countries, since his father was in the diplomatic service. His first book was a collection of six short stories, *Los días enmascarados* (1954; 2nd edn., 1966). Then came his sequence of important novels, beginning with *La región más transparente* (1958; English translation, *Where the air is clear* (New York, 1969)), an ironic title by which Fuentes indicated that the clarity in the air above Mexico City is hardly characteristic of the muddied, confused lives of its inhabitants. Techniques of Galdós and John Dos Passos help to present a panorama of Mexico City from 1910 through the revolutionary period to the mid-fifties; the novel's seriousness made a great impact on younger writers. *Las buenas conciencias* (1959; English translation, New York, 1916) relates the adolescence of a young provincial rebelling against his middle-class family but finally being absorbed into the comforts of his class. *Aura* (1962) is a slight, uncharacteristic exercise in the manner of Henry James.

Fuentes's world fame came with *La muerte de Artemio Cruz* (q.v., 1962; English translation, *The death of Artemio Cruz*, New York, 1964). The collection of stories *Cantar de ciegos* (1964) was followed by the thin *Zona sagrada* (1967), a novel of a film star (Claudia Nervo) who dominates the life and imagination of her son Guillermo, the narrator, but the weight of myth is too much for the characters to carry; *Cambio de piel* (1967; English translation, *A change of skin*, 1968) was an equally ambitious but more successful exploration of myth and man in a world of shadows and absurdity where identities are thrust upon one, and symbols seem to be more meaningful than characters. Four characters of diverse backgrounds (a Mexican professor

and his Jewish American wife, his mistress Isabel and his wife's European Nazi lover) living in a motel recall their early lives and in so doing illustrate European and American history. Fuentes offers an alternative ending to his 'open novel', thus depending on the reader's involvement with history and this tale. The narrator is a cab-driver called Freddie Lambert, after Friedrich Nietzsche and Balzac's *Louis Lambert*.

Cumpleaños (1969) is another novel of myth which takes the whole of space and time for its arena. It is possible that Fuentes believed his themes exhausted in these demanding novels, since he later turned to the essay in *La nueva novela hispanoamericana* (1969) and *Casa con dos puertas* (1970), the latter ranging over drama and contemporary visual art in Mexico as well as literature. Fuentes has been involved in film-making and has also written plays: 'Todos los gatos son pardos' and 'El tuerto es rey', published as *Los reinos originarios* (Barcelona, 1971). The latter was first produced in French in 1970, and shows Donata and her servant awaiting her husband's return. Both are blind but each believes the other can see. Both plays succumb to a lame *deus ex machina* climax, the first ending in rock-and-roll and anti-American slogans; the second in the gratuitous violence with which Donata's husband is murdered by five *guerrilleros*. The *efectismo* of both endings is inconsistent with the tone and structure of the main body of each play.

See H. F. Giacoman (ed.), *Homenaje a Carlos Fuentes* (New York, 1971); and L. Befumo Boschi and E. Calabrese, *Nostalgia del futuro en la obra de Carlos Fuentes* (1974).

FUENTES DEL ARCO, ANTONIO (*fl.* 1717), *Regidor* and *alcalde* of Santa Fe, and the first recorded playwright of Argentina, for his 'Loa representada en Santa Fe en 1717'. In the style of Calderón, the *loa* preceded a performance of Moreto's *comedia No puede ser el guardar una mujer*. Its theme is praise of Philip V of Spain for relieving the city's burden of excise taxes. Discovered by P. Guillermo Furlong, the *loa* was published by J. L. Trenti Rocamora in *Boletín de Estudios Etnográficos de Santa Fe* (1947).

FUENTES Y GUZMÁN, FRANCISCO ANTONIO DE (1643–1700), b. Santiago de los Caballeros, Guatemala. Historian and poet, the great-great-grandson of Bernal Díaz del Castillo (q.v.), who died in Guatemala. He was an alderman of the city of Santiago from the age of 18 until his death. Much of his fluent, shallow, gongoristic poetry is lost, but we possess a verse *Descripción de las fiestas hechas en Guatemala al cumplir Carlos II la edad de trece años* (1675). His best-known work is the *Historia de Guatemala; o, Recordación florida,* edited by Justo Zaragoza (2 vols., Madrid, 1882–3), who published all of the first part of the MS. except book 17. A later edition (3 vols., Guatemala, 1932–3) includes both parts of the MS. in their entirety. In 1957 Heinrich Berlin found a further MS. of Fuentes y Guzmán in the Biblioteca Palafoxiana in Puebla, Mexico, and this book on Hispanic historiography, *Preceptos historiales*, was edited by Ernesto Chinchilla Aguilar and published by the Guatemalan Ministry of Education in 1957.

Fueros, Spanish local charters that culminated in the Hispano-Roman and Visigothic legal code known first as the *Liber Judiciorum*, and afterwards as the *Liber* or *Forum Judicum* (Spanish: *Fuero juzgo*). In the modern edition by Zeumer it is known as the *Lex Reccesvindiana* after King Receswinth (reigned 653–672) though his father Chindaswinth (reigned 642–653) had begun the work of reconciling Visigothic legislation with the multifarious local charters dating back to Roman times.

The *Fuero juzgo* was translated into Castilian in the 13th c. on the orders of Fernando and edited by the Real Academia Española as *Fuero juzgo en latín y castellano* (1815). On its language, see M. Rodríguez Rodríguez, *Origen filológico del romance castellano. Fuero juzgo: su gramática, lenguaje y vocabulario* (Santiago, 1905).

When Fernando's son Alfonso 'el Sabio' (q.v.) succeeded to the throne in 1252, his joint kingdom had two different codes: León retained the *Fuero juzgo* which had been dropped by Castile in favour of common law. Alfonso thus commissioned and promulgated a new *Fuero real*, which was completed in 1255 but did not take immediate effect in all parts of his kingdom. A fifth of it, according to Galo Sánchez, was taken from the *Fuero de Soria*, and more from the *Fuero juzgo*; the *Fuero real* exercised a great influence on the *Siete partidas* of Alfonso 'el Sabio' (q.v.).

The original *fueros* were supplemented by many local *fueros* particular to a province, isolated valley, or in some cases even a village in Catalonia and the Basque country. The central government made determined efforts to wipe out these *fueros*, which often consisted of codified folklore rather than embryonic legislation. In Basque Spain, the *fueros* were abolished only at the end of the First Carlist War (1839) in Navarra, and of the Second Carlist War (1876) in the other three provinces, thus eradicating the last legal traces of Basque autonomy.

Fuerza de la sangre, La, one of the *Novelas ejemplares* (q.v., 1613) by Miguel de Cervantes Saavedra (q.v.).

One night, as the 16-year-old Leocadia returns from her walk along the Tagus in Toledo with her parents, she is seized by the dissolute Rodolfo and seduced while unconscious. On regaining consciousness she fails to recognize her masked seducer but takes pains to remember the room and snatches up as evidence a small crucifix found on a desk. Then she is blindfolded, dragged out to the cathedral, and abandoned there.

She tells her parents what had happened but they are forced to keep silent in order to avoid advertizing her dishonour. Rodolfo meanwhile has gone to Italy. Leocadia eventually gives birth to a handsome baby boy who is reared secretly in a nearby village with the name of Luis or Luisillo. He is brought back to Toledo as a 'nephew' of Leocadia's parents when he is four; at the age of seven the boy is accidentally knocked down and an old gentleman (Rodolfo's father) takes him home to look after him. His 'uncle and aunt' are traced and asked to visit the boy, who is too ill to be moved. When she comes to visit him herself, Leocadia recognizes the boy's sickroom as the one in which she had been violated, and tells her mother. Finally Leocadia's parents resolve to inform Rodolfo's mother, also of course Luisillo's grandmother, of what had happened; and she, already sharply aware of the similarity between Luis and her son (absent seven years in Italy) prevails on Rodolfo to return home and honourably marry Leocadia.

Cervantes' moral concerns a perverted love (lust) transformed into pure love. The crucifix symbolizes the divine love which can help in victory over man's baser instincts.

There is an annotated edition of the tale by J. Givanel Mas (1943) and an essay by Azorín in *Al margen de los clásicos* (1915), pp. 87–105.

See also Joaquín Casalduero, *Sentido y forma de las 'Novelas ejemplares'* (1962).

FUNES, GREGORIO (1749–1829), b. Córdoba, Argentina. Historian and supporter of the May Revolution (25 May 1810), he became a member and later director of the Junta. Deputy for Tucumán in the Congress of 1818, he contributed to *La Abeja Argentina* and *El Centinela* (1822–3), and wrote the manifesto for the Constitution of 1819.

His *Bosquejo histórico de la revolución argentina* is a partisan work whose interest lies in the fact that the author was involved in the deeds he described; it was contributed as an appendix to Rodney and Graham's *Reports on the present state of the United Provinces of South America*, and translated into Spanish by Antonio Zinny as *Historia de la Provincias Unidas del Río de la Plata, 1816 a 1818* (1868; 3rd edn., 1883). Another important work was his *Ensayo de la historia civil* (3 vols., 1816–17).

FURIÓ CERIOL, FADRIQUE (c. 1532–92), b. Valencia. He studied in Paris with Pedro Ramos and others. Of his works, there is an extant copy of *Institutionum rhetoricum* (Louvain, 1554) in the Bodleian Library, Oxford, and a copy of *El Concejo i Consejeros del príncipe* (Antwerp, 1559) in the British Library, London. The latter, of which only the first part was published, was reprinted by A. de Castro in *Curiosidades bibliográficas*, in vol. 36 (1855) of the BAE and is one of the most interesting of the genre *de regimine principum* (q.v.). It was translated into Italian by Alfonso de Ulloa (Venice, 1560), and Latin versions appeared in Cologne in 1568, and in Danzig in 1646.

A man of liberal views, Furió Ceriol proposed that the Bible should be translated into the Romance languages of Europe. This suggestion was denounced as heretical by the Sicilian Bononia, Furió's rejoinder being published as *Bononiam sive de libris sacris convertendis in vernaculam linguam libri II*. The Council of Trent banned this book as well as the *Institutionum rhetoricum*.

FUSTER, JOAN (1922–   ), b. Sueca, Valencia. Essayist, poet, and critic in the Valencian form of Catalan. His early poetry appeared in Valencian: *Sobre Narcís* (Valencia, 1948), *3 poèmes* (Alicante, 1949), *Ales o mans* (Valencia, 1949), followed by *Va morir tan bella* (Valencia, 1951).

Fuster has produced excellent anthologies: *Antología del surrealismo español* (with José Albi, Alicante, 1952), *La poesía catalana fins a la Renaixença* (Mexico City, 1954), *Antología de la poesia valenciana* (Barcelona, 1956), *La poesía catalana* (2 vols., Palma, 1956), and he has translated Falkberget, Camus, and Silone.

His *Obres completes* (4 vols., Barcelona, 1968–75) have started to appear, vol. 1 being *Llengua, literatura, historia*. His collection of essays include *Les originalitats* (Barcelona, 1956), *Figures de temps* (Barcelona, 1957), *Indagacions possibles* (Palma, 1958), *El descrèdit de la realitat* (Palma, 1959), *Nosaltres els valencians* (Barcelona, 1962), *Poetes, moriscos i capellans* (Valencia, 1962), *Diccionari per ociosos* (Barcelona, 1964), *Combustible per a falles* (Valencia, 1967), *Examen de consciència* (Barcelona, 1968), *Heretgies, revoltes i sermons* (Barcelona, 1968), *Babels i babilonies* (Palma, 1972), *Rebeldes y heterodoxos* (Barcelona, 1972), *Literatura catalana contemporània* (Barcelona, 1972), *Exploració de l'ombra* (Barcelona, 1974), and *Contra Unamuno y los demás* (Barcelona, 1975).

G

GABIROL, SOLOMON BEN JUDAH IBN (c. 1021–c. 1057), b. Málaga. Poet and philosopher, called 'Avicebron'. He lived for much of his life in Saragossa, crippled by disease. A friend of Shemuel ha-Nagid (see NAGRELLA), he wrote a Hebrew grammar in verse when only 19, and became equally fluent in Arabic.

He wrote poetry in Hebrew, the best being *Keter malkhut* ('Royal crown'), a philosophical poem with largely biblical sources. *Selected religious poems* was edited by I. Davidson and translated by Israel Zangwill (1923); a smaller selection is available in David Goldstein's *The Jewish poets of Spain, 900–1250* (1965; augmented edn., Harmondsworth, 1971).

Ibn Gabirol is best known, however, as a philosopher, writing in Arabic. *Mukhtar al-jawahir* ('Choice of pearls') is a collection of aphorisms which has been rendered into Hebrew as *Mibhar ha-peninim* by Yehuda ibn Tibbon. *Kitab islah al-akhlaq* ('The book on the improvement of character') is a moral and didactic treatise later translated into Hebrew as *Sefer tiqqun ha-middot*. But his most famous book is *Yanbu' al-hayya* ('Source of life'), familiar in the West under its Latin title *Fons vitae* and important for passing on the neo-Platonic and particularly Plotinian tradition. Translated into Hebrew as *Meqar hayyim*, the book is lost in Arabic, surviving only in its Latin version and edited most recently by C. Bäumler (2 vols., 1945).

See J. M. Millás Vallicrosa, *Selomo ibn Gabirol como poeta y filósofo* (Madrid, 1945). The edition of *Shirei Shlomo ben Yehuda ibn Gabirol* (3 vols., Berlin, 1924–32) is not entirely reliable. There is a good translation of *Keter malkhut* (*The kingly crown*) by B. Lewis (London, 1961).

GABRIEL Y GALÁN, JOSÉ MARÍA (1870–1905), b. Frades de la Sierra, Salamanca. Regional poet who achieved instant fame at the Juegos Florales of Salamanca (1901) with the poem 'El ama'. He wrote dialect poetry in eastern Leonese, erroneously called 'Extremaduran' from the title of his second collection, in which occur 'El Cristo benditu', 'El embargo', and 'Varón', possibly his most successful regional poems. His books include *Castellanas* and *Extremeñas* (both 1902), *Campesinas* (1904), *Nuevas castellanas* (1905), the ineffective *Religiosas*

(1906), and volumes of letters: *Epistolario* (1918) and *Cartas y poesías inéditas* (1919). The *Obras completas* (4 vols., Salamanca, 1905–60) are unsatisfactory, and have been superseded by the Aguado edition (3 vols., 1949).

Gabriel y Galán's verse is prolific, spontaneous, but often careless and unwittingly prosaic to the point of bathos, for he lacked true sensitivity and any great technical ability. But there is no denying his fluency, which won him a wide readership and made his pleasant *cuadros de costumbres* instantly popular.

See A. Revilla Marcos, *José María Gabriel y Galán: su vida y sus obras* (1923); V. Gutiérrez Macías, *Biografía de Gabriel y Galán* (1956); and M. Romano Colangeli, *José María Gabriel y Galán, poeta dell'amore* (Lecce, 1960) and *La poesía di Gabriel y Galán* (Bologna, 1965).

Gaceta Literaria, La, an *avant-garde* literary and political magazine founded in Madrid in 1927 by Ernesto Giménez Caballero (q.v.) and associated with the Generation of 1927. Apolitical in its first two years, it changed course for Fascism in 1929 with the first Spanish Fascist manifesto *En torno al casticismo en Italia*, the abandonment of the magazine by earlier contributors, the appointment of Sáinz Rodríguez as co-editor, and the admission of contributors such as Alberto Insúa, Salaverría, and García Sanchiz. In its first issues, the *Gaceta* published not only the younger writers, but also Baroja, Unamuno, Maeztu, Azorín, and A. Machado.

See Miguel Ángel Hernando, *La 'Gaceta Literaria'* (Valladolid, 1974) and Hildegard H. J. Collins, *Un índice analítico de 'La Gaceta Literaria'* (Austin, 1975).

GAGINI, CARLOS (1865–1925), b. San José. Self-taught Costa Rican philologist and novelist whose father was an architect of Swiss origin, Gagini became director of the national library and archives of Costa Rica. A prolific author and Comtean positivist (in *La ciencia y la metafísica*, 1918), Gagini did his most notable work in philology, culminating in his valuable *Diccionario de costarriqueñismos* (1919). His studies led him to a profound knowledge of Costa Rican customs, which he used in six novels and two collections of short stories. His best novel was *El árbol enfermo* (1918), his worst the curious anti-imperialist *La caída del águila* (1920), inspired by the science-fiction of Jules Verne.

Gaiferos, the kinsman of Roland and husband of Charlemagne's daughter Melisenda, in Spanish romance. When Melisenda is kidnapped by the Moors she is rescued by Gaiferos. This is the subject of an amusing puppet play in *Don Quijote de la Mancha* (q.v.), II, 26.

Gaita gallega, a metre used by early Galician poets, and adopted from them by early Castilian poets. It is not always hendecasyllabic, varying from 9 to 12 syllables in length. Anapaestic cadence is predominant, with stress on the 4th, 7th (and 10th) syllables. An example from the *Cancionero Herberay* is:

    Soy garridilla e pierdo sazón . . .

Among later writers it was used frequently, as by Rubén Darío (q.v.) in such lines as:

    Libre la frente que el casco rehúsa,
    casi desnuda en la gloria del día. . . .

Galatea, Fábula de Polifemo y, see FÁBULA DE POLIFEMO Y GALATEA.

Galatea, La, an 'eclogue' by Miguel de Cervantes Saavedra (q.v.) entitled in the first edition *Primera parte de la Galatea, dividida en seys libros* (Alcalá, 1585; ed. in Clásicos Castellanos by J. B. Avalle-Arce, 2 vols., 1961).

Cervantes' first book, *La Galatea*, appears to have remained in MS. for some long time before its publication. It has few novelistic elements, being a series of loosely-connected episodes in the pastoral mode then in vogue, in which nobles disguised as shepherds and shepherdesses sing of their loves, joys, sorrows, and jealousies in ornate language.

The love of Erastro and Elicio for Galatea is the framework in which 80 poems and many tales are interpolated: the tale of the hermit Silerio, that of Teolinda and Artidoro, and that of Lisandro, Carino, and Leonida. Elicio is rejected by Galatea until her father Aurelio commands her to marry Elicio's rival; only then does she agree to marry Elicio. The dialogue on love between the shepherds Tirsi and Lenio is drawn from the *Dialoghi d'amore* by Leo Hebraeus (q.v.) but elsewhere the sources are unmistakably Sannazaro and such Spanish pastoral novelists as Montemayor and Gil Polo. While Cervantes must have recognized with the subsequent success of *Don Quijote* that his true forte was not the pastoral novel, he continued to promise a sequel to *La Galatea*, even four days before his death, when completing *Los trabajos de Persiles y Sigismunda*.

Some scholars have taken literally Cervantes' remark: 'muchos de los disfrazados pastores . . . lo eran eran sólo en el hábito' and have sought to identify the characters with real people; thus 'Lauso' is believed to be the author; 'Tirsi', Francisco de Figueroa; 'Meliso', Diego Hurtado de Mendoza; 'Siralvo', Gálvez de Montalvo; and Astraliano, Don Juan de Austria. Galatea herself has been conjectured to be Doña Catalina de Palacios, the author's wife.

See F. López Estrada, *La Galatea de Cervantes* (La Laguna, 1948); G. Stagg, 'Plagiarism in

"La Galatea"' in *Filologia Romanza* (Naples), vol. 6, 1959, pp. 255–76; John Brande Trend, *Cervantes in Arcadia* (Cambridge, 1954); and a study by J. Casalduero in *Suma Cervantina* (ed. J. B. Avalle-Arce and E. C. Riley, London, 1973), pp. 27–46.

GALBA, MARTÍ JOAN DE, the writer, according to some authorities, of the last part of the finest of the medieval *libros de caballería* (q.v.) in Catalan, *Tirant lo Blanch* (q.v.). Arthur Terry, however, suggests (in *Catalan literature*, London, 1972, p. 50) that Galba's contribution was fairly slight.

GALDÓS, BENITO PÉREZ, see PÉREZ GALDÓS, Benito.

GALINDO, BEATRIZ (1474?–1534), b. Salamanca. Humanist, widely known for her scholarship as 'la Latina'· She married Francisco Ramírez, called 'el Artillero' for his valour and skill as a soldier, and secretary to Fernando V. Galindo taught Queen Isabel Latin, and is believed also to have advised her on matters of state. She wrote good Latin verse, notes on classical authors, and a commentary on Aristotle.
See F. de Llanos y Torriglia, *Doña Beatriz Galindo, la Latina* (1920).

GALLARDO Y BLANCO, BARTOLOMÉ JOSÉ (1776–1852), b. Campanario, Badajoz. Bibliographer and scholar, whose political and literary satires made him many enemies. The satires included *Diccionario crítico-burlesco del que se titula 'Diccionario razonado manual para inteligencia de ciertos escritores que por equivocación han nacido en España'* (Cádiz, 1811); its sequel the *Cartazo al Censor General . . .* (Cádiz, 1812) reproduced in the essential bibliographical study by A. Rodríguez-Moñino, *Don Bartolomé José Gallardo* (1955); and *Las letras de cambio, o los mercachifles literarios: estrenas y aguinaldos del Br. Tomé Lobar* (Toledo, 1834, reprinted in Madrid the same year).
Though most of Gallardo's writings and collections were lost in Seville on 13 July 1836, five numbers of his magazine *El Criticón* (1835–6) survive. His poems can be found in vol. 67 (1875) of the BAE, and there is a useful *Obras escogidas* (2 vols., 1928).
Gallardo's title to fame rests on the materials he collected for *Ensayo de una biblioteca española de libros raros y curiosos* (1863–89) carefully assembled by Sancho Rayón y Zarco del Valle and recently reprinted by Gredos in Madrid. For his correspondence see *Cartas inéditas . . . a don Manuel Torrigli, 1824–1833* (1955) and *Correspondencia* (1960).

See also M. A. Buchanan, 'Notes on the life and works of Bartolomé José Gallardo' in *Revue Hispanique*, vol. 57 (1923), pp. 160–201.

GALLEGO, JUAN NICASIO (1777–1853), b. Zamora. Poet of the Salamancan school held in high esteem by his contemporaries and author of seven poems of which any one, in the view of Ventura de la Vega, would have assured him fame. Imprisoned as a liberal, he eventually became permanent secretary to the Real Academia Española in 1839, and Canon of Seville Cathedral. Of his seven odes, the best are the stirring *A la defensa de Buenos Aires* (1807) and the patriotic *Al dos de mayo* (1808). He is remembered for the heartfelt elegy *A la muerte de la duquesa de Frías* (1830), but his most characteristic work is the collection of 36 sonnets which have the merit of being impeccable and the demerit of being calculated in every nuance.
There is no satisfactory edition of Gallego's work. The *Obras poéticas* of 1854 were supplemented by other poems in vol. 67 (1875) of the BAE, both being an improvement on the pirated Philadelphia edition of 1829 prepared by the Cuban Domingo del Monte.
See E. González Negro, *Estudio biográfico de Don Juan Nicasio Gallego* (Zamora, 1901).

GALLEGOS, RÓMULO (1884–1968), b. Caracas. Major Venezuelan novelist who took an active interest in the politics of his country, and was exiled during the presidency of Juan Vicente Gómez (d. 1935). Gallegos was elected President of the Republic in 1947 for the period 1948–53, but nine months after assuming office, in November 1948, he was deposed by a military *coup* and remained in exile until 1958.
He first achieved fame with *El último Solar* (1920), known in reprints since 1930 as *Reinaldo Solar*. The theme is the plight of the poor, and the realistic descriptions (see CRIOLLISMO) inevitably criticize the existing state of Venezuelan society. Gallegos' Negroes, *gringos*, plainsmen, and mountain dwellers are all treated with sympathy. His other novels, often dealing with the everyday preoccupations of ordinary people, include *La trepadora* (1925); *Doña Bárbara* (q.v., Barcelona, 1929); *Cantaclaro* (Barcelona, 1934); *Canaima* (q.v., Barcelona, 1935); *Pobre negro* (1937), set on the coast; *El forastero* (1942); *Sobre la misma tierra* (Barcelona, 1943), on life in the oilfields; *La brizna de paja en el viento* (Havana, 1952); and the posthumously-published *Tierra bajo los pies* (1971).
Gallegos' *Obras completas* (2 vols., Madrid, 1958) have been edited by Jesús López Pacheco.
See L. Dunham, *Rómulo Gallegos: vida y obra* (Mexico City, 1957); G. Bellini, *Il romanzo di Rómulo Gallegos* (Milan, 1962); Efraín Subero,

Contribución a la bibliografía de Rómulo Gallegos (1969); and J. Liscano, *Rómulo Gallegos y su tiempo* (1969).

GALLEGOS VALDÉS, LUIS (1917–), b. San Salvador. Critic and essayist. His first collection of critical essays, *Tiro al blanco* (1952), ranged from Cervantes and Quevedo to Azorín, Balzac, and Proust. He contributed 'Panorama de la literatura salvadoreña' to the *Panorama das literaturas das Américas*, vol. II (1958), pp. 495–588.

GALT Y ESCOBAR, ALBERTO (1885–1963), b. Havana. Spanish novelist writing under the pseudonym 'Alberto Insúa' (his father had written novels under the pseudonym 'Waldo Álvarez Insúa'). After spending his childhood in Cuba, he studied law in Madrid, and wrote for the newspapers including *Blanco y Negro*, *Nuevo Mundo*, and *El Liberal*.

He wrote more than seventy novels, some in the erotic manner of Felipe Trigo (q.v.), and others influenced by the psychological realism of Pérez Galdós (q.v.). His style suffers from haste, and his characters seldom develop in the course of a novel, an exception being perhaps Conchita Blanco in *El peligro* (1915). Insúa frequently exploits vice and degradation for their own sake, and even his more carefully-constructed books (such as *Las flechas del amor*, 1912) suffer from melodrama. His first book is a collection of travel notes and essays: *Don Quijote en los Alpes* (1907). He then turned to the novel, completing a trilogy showing society in evolution, *Historia de un escéptico*, comprising *En tierra de santos* (1907), *La hora trágica* (1908), and *El triunfo* (1909), but it was only with the scandal of *La mujer fácil* (1910) that he became widely known, and further erotic stories followed quickly, among them *Las neuróticas* (1910), *La mujer desconocida* (1911), *El demonio de la voluptuosidad* (1911), *Las flechas del amor* (1912), *Los hombres: Mary los descubre* (1913) and *Los hombres: Mary los perdona* (1914), a kind of *éducation sentimentale* of his heroine Mary Pacheco.

Insúa was then sent by the Madrid daily *ABC* to Paris as a war correspondent. When he returned, he published more best-sellers, such as *La batalla sentimental* (1921, which advocated divorce), the famous *El negro que tenía el alma blanca* (1922, later filmed and dramatized), *Dos francesas y un español* (1925), *La mujer, el torero y el toro* (1926), *Mi tía Manolita* (1926), *Humo, dolor, placer* (1928), *El barco embrujado* (1929), *El amante invisible* (1930), *El complejo de Edipo* (1933), and *Nieves en Buenos Aires* (1955).

Insúa's plays (*Amor tardío, Cabecita loca, Una mano suava*) were unsuccessful, but he made a

deep impression with his *Memorias* (2 vols., 1951–2).

See F. Carmona Nenclares, *El amor y la muerte en las novelas de Alberto Insúa* (1928); and J. de Entrambasaguas in *Las mejores novelas contemporáneas* (Barcelona, 1960, pp. 305–38).

GALVÁN, MANUEL DE JESÚS (1834–1910). Dominican novelist whose most celebrated work is *Enriquillo* (Pt. 1, 1879; complete edn., 1882), a work which makes use of material from the historical writings of Las Casas, Juan de Castellanos, and Fernández de Oviedo among others, to document events in Santo Domingo from 1503 to 1533. He falsified history by ending the novel on an optimistic note to show colonization in a good light, though as Galván knew very well the Indians had disappeared from Santo Domingo as a result of Spanish policy. Galván's attitudes changed: at times he believed in white supremacy; at other times he stated that progress was impossible without the active participation of the Indians in society, though he rejected the label of 'Indianophile'. His compromise derives from a firm belief in the Roman Catholic social order and sympathy with the plight of the downtrodden Indians.

See Concha Meléndez, 'El "Enriquillo" de Manuel de Jesús Galván: la tradición indianista en Santo Domingo' in *Hispania* (1934), pp. 97–112. There is a fine translation of the novel by Robert Graves, *The cross and the sword* (London, 1956).

GÁLVEZ, JOSÉ (1885–1957), b. Tarma. Peruvian poet of the second Modernist phase (see MODERNISMO), historian, university teacher of literature, Minister of Justice and Education (1931), and ambassador successively to Colombia and Panama.

His poems, influenced by the early Juan Ramón Jiménez (q.v.), react against the work of José Santos Chocano (q.v.). His books of poetry include *Bajo la luna* (1910), *Jardín cerrado* (1912), and *Canto jubilar a Lima* (1936). Gálvez also wrote *Posibilidad de una genuina literatura nacional* (1915), *La boda* (novel, 1923), *Nuestra pequeña historia* (3 vols., 1928–31), *Estampas limeñas* (1935), and *Calles de Lima y meses del año* (1943).

See A. Oliver Belmás, *José Gálvez y el modernismo* (Madrid, 1974).

GÁLVEZ, MANUEL (1882–1962), b. Paraná. Argentinian realist novelist. After a Jesuit education in Santa Fe, he moved to Buenos Aires and became one of the most perceptive chroniclers of life in the capital, his work being often concerned with social problems. Partial deafness made his intellectual life even more intense. His first books were the poems *El enigma* *interior* (1907), a conventional work of literary suffering; and *Sendero de humildad* (1909), which sounded his first note of originality. Gálvez's lifelong devotion to Spain is revealed in *El solar de la raza* (1913), while travels in Europe produced two books of essays: *El diario de Gabriel Quiroga* and *La vida múltiple*.

La maestra normal (1914) is a well-written realist novel in the style of Galdós and Flaubert. It is the trivial story of a poor girl abandoned by her lover, but whereas Hugo Wast (q.v.) would have treated the theme as an excuse for religious sentiments, Gálvez uses it as a vehicle for a detailed account of life's minutiae in La Rioja early in the century. Provincial bigotry and narrowmindedness bring about the ruin of the young schoolmistress Roselda, after her seduction by an outsider. In 1916 Gálvez founded the Cooperativa Buenos Aires to publish fiction by its members in the Biblioteca de Novelistas Americanos, in which the eight short stories of his *Luna de miel* (1920) appeared. His other important novels are *El mal metafísico* (1916), *Nacha Regules* (1918) the story of a woman forced into prostitution; a book on horse racing and gambling called *La pampa y su pasión*, and *Historia de arrabal*, another *Éducation sentimentale* set in Buenos Aires. He has written a number of novels with a religious setting, notably *La sombra del convento* (1917), and *Miércoles santo*, tales told in the confessional. The War of the Triple Alliance against Paraguay (1865–70) inspired three novels: *Los caminos de la muerte* (1928), *Humaitá* (1929), and *Jornadas de agonía* (1930). He has written a cycle of seven historical novels called *Escenas de la época de Rosas*, and biographies of Rosas, Gabriel García Moreno, Hipólito Irigoyen, and Aparicio Saravia, while his *El general Quiroga* won the National Prize for Literature in 1932. Gálvez was an admirer of Mussolini, and a detractor of Sarmiento (q.v.) in *Vida de Sarmiento* (1945). His main weaknesses are hasty construction, excessive padding, religious bigotry, and lack of depth. His virtues include a Zolaesque candour, a fecundity worthy of his master Galdós, and a wealth of personal zest and experience which enables him to describe Buenos Aires in all its complexity, from high society to the poorest classes.

See Ignacio B. Anzoátegui, *Manuel Gálvez* (1961); Jorge Lafforgue, *Manuel Gálvez* (1967); and J. E. Puente, *Estudio crítico-histórico de las novelas de Manuel Gálvez* (1975).

GÁLVEZ DE MONTALVO, LUIS (1546–91?), b. Guadalajara. Pastoral novelist. A friend of Cervantes, Gálvez claimed to have passed his life idly in the court of the Infantado family. While in Italy he translated *Le lagrime di San Pietro* (1585) by Luigi Tansillo as *El llanto de San Pedro*, a version which F. de Villalobos included in his *Thesoro de divina poesía* (Toledo, 1587); and left unfinished a version of Tasso's *Gerusalemme liberata*.

Gálvez's place in Spanish literature is assured by the warm reception given by the public to *El pastor de Phílida* (1582), a pastoral *roman-à-clef* in which the author is 'Siralvo' and 'Fílida' probably a sister of the Duke of Osuna. The sixth of the seven parts is of the greatest interest to the modern reader for its criticism of the rival schools of Spanish poetry at that time. The best edition is the sixth (Valencia, 1792), with a useful prologue by Mayáns y Síscar.

See J. Catalina García, *Escritores de Guadalajara* (1899), pp. 144–8; and F. Rodríguez Marín, *La 'Fílida' de Gálvez de Montalvo* (1927).

GAMBOA, FEDERICO (1864–1939), b. Mexico City. Mexican novelist, playwright, journalist, and diplomat. He began by translating French plays, his first original play being *La última campaña* (1894), and his others a prose monologue *Divertirse* (1894), *La venganza de la gleba* (Washington, D.C., 1904) considered daring for its social message, *A buena cuenta* (San Salvador, 1907), and *Entre hermanos* (1928).

Gamboa is best known for his novels. He began insecurely with pot-boilers but matured in his naturalistic mode with *Santa* (1903), the story of an ironically-named prostitute. It was the first true Mexican 'best-seller' and was filmed twice in the author's lifetime. Weaker in the construction of his fiction than his French masters, Gamboa nevertheless tells his story well. The *Novelas* (1965) in Letras Mexicanas also include *Apariencias* (Buenos Aires, 1892), *Suprema ley* (Paris, 1896), *Metamórfosis* (1896), *Reconquista* (Barcelona, 1907), *La llaga* (1910), and *Del natural* (1888). His memoirs appeared as *Mi diario* (5 vols., 1907–1938), a sixth volume remaining unpublished.

See Ernest R. Moore, 'Bibliografía de obras y crítica de Federico Gamboa' in *Revista Iberoamericana*, vol. 2, no. 3 (April 1940), pp. 271–9; and A. C. Hooker, *La novela de Federico Gamboa* (Madrid, 1971).

GAMBOA, JOSÉ JOAQUÍN (1878–1931), b. Mexico City, Mexican playwright, and nephew of the playwright Federico Gamboa (q.v.). His work represents the transition from realism (which had been exaggerated to naturalism in some of the plays by his uncle) to symbolism, thus turning back full circle to the early Mexican stage dominated by allegorical writers such as Hernán González de Eslava (q.v.). He also experimented with the *zarzuela* in *Soledad* (1899, written with Miguel E. Pereyra) and one-act plays in *Cuento viejo* (1925) and *Espíritus* (1927).

Though it is usual to divide Gamboa's work into two phases, it is probably more accurate to follow the tripartite classification of Carlos González Peña's edition of Gamboa's *Teatro* (1938), of which vol. 1 contains works of the first phase: *La carne,* later known as *Teresa* (1903); *La muerte* (1904); *El hogar* (1905); and *El día del Juicio,* later called *Un día vendrá* (1908); vol. 2 contains the transitional *El diablo tiene frío* (1923); *Los Revillagigedos* (1925), and *Vía crucis* (1925); and vol. 3 contains works of the allegorical final phase: *Si la juventud supiera* (1927); *El mismo caso* (1929); *Ella,* afterwards entitled *Alucinaciones* (1930); and *El caballero, la muerte y el diablo* (1931).

GÁNDARA, CARMEN (1900–), b. Buenos Aires. Argentinian novelist and short-story writer associated with the magazine *Sur* (q.v.). L. E. Soto has suggested that Gándara's characters are 'indefesos ante el impulso ciego que los precipita a la crisis'. Her story 'La habitada' in the collection *El lugar del diablo* (1948) showed that she could develop into a major artist, a hope fulfilled in *La figura y el mundo* (1958), short stories of great style. *Los espejos* (1951), one of the best Latin-American novels, wryly demonstrates how in superficial present-day society each of us tends to mirror the preoccupations and selfishness of others and of society in general.

GANDOLFI HERRERO, ARÍSTIDES (1889–). Argentinian short-story writer and novelist of the Boedo Street group (q.v.). His fiction, written under the pseudonym 'Álvaro Yunque', deals with the plight of poor children from the viewpoint of social realism, and only occasionally lapses into sentimentality.

His best short stories are in *Zancadillas* (1926), *Barcos de papel* (1926), *Ta-te-tí* (1928), *Jauja* (1929), and *Espantajos* (1930).

His novel *Tutearse con el peligro* is less successful. He has also written poetry influenced by Baldomero Fernández Moreno (q.v.), a play entitled *La muerte es hermosa y blanca,* and an important survey, *La literatura social en la Argentina: historia de los movimientos literarios desde la emancipación nacional hasta nuestros días* (1941).

GANIVET, ÁNGEL (1865–98), b. Granada. Novelist and essayist. Educated in Granada, he later obtained a doctorate in philosophy at Madrid University. His works show a sympathetic understanding of classical thought (especially the Stoicism of Marcus Aurelius, Seneca, and Epictetus), and modern European philosophy, especially that of Nietzsche and Schopenhauer.

He was influenced too by Unamuno (q.v.) whom he met in Madrid and with whom he exchanged an important correspondence published as *El porvenir de España* (1912). Ganivet spent his adult life in the consular service at Antwerp, Helsinki, and Riga, ending it as the result of an unhappy love affair and progressive mental disturbances by drowning himself in the river Dvina, near Riga.

Granada la bella (Helsinki, 1896) is a prose poem to his native city which was followed by two satirical novels: *La conquista del reino de Maya por el último conquistador español Pío Cid* (1897), in which Ganivet's views on the folly of Spain's colonial adventures are aired at length; and the semi-autobiographical *Los trabajos del infatigable creador Pío Cid* (2 vols., 1898). Unfinished at the author's death, the latter work displays the same socio-moral stance, but the hero is ironically described as 'un hombre inteligente, pero desilusionado e incapaz de hacer nada' who nevertheless, in the words of Ángel del Río, 'quiere redimir a España y a un grupo diverso de personajes, inspirándoles la fe y la voluntad que él no tiene'. Thus the social reformer shows the *maestro rural* that he should stay where he is and the servant-girl that learning to read can make a nursing nun of her, while he himself has 'en su alma un vacío inmenso que asusta'. Pío Cid is the prototype of Pío Baroja's heroes (q.v.) and foreshadows Antonio Azorín in *La voluntad* (1902) by José Martínez Ruiz (who took the pseudonym 'Azorín', q.v.). Whereas Pío Cid has the ability to persuade others to an honourable course of action, Antonio Azorín 'no cree en nada'.

Ganivet's *Idearium español* (q.v., Granada, 1897) attempted to define the Spanishness of Spain, her rôle in the world since the Reconquest, and her future prospects. He contrasted Spain with Finland in *Cartas finlandesas* (1905), and in *Hombres del norte* (published with *El porvenir de España,* 1905) revealed himself as one of the few Spaniards to grasp the significance of Ibsen, Nietzsche, Schopenhauer, and other Scandinavian and German writers. He also wrote a *drama místico* entitled *El escultor de su alma* (1906).

Other compilations of Ganivet's writings include *Ángel Ganivet, poeta y periodista* (1918) and *Ángel Ganivet, universitario y cónsul* (1920), both edited by Modesto Pérez; *España filosófica y contemporánea* (1930); and *Cartas íntimas* (Granada, 1936).

An edition of Ganivet's *Obras completas* (10 vols., 1923–30) was superseded by that of M. Fernández Almagro (2 vols., 1943), who has written the standard *Vida y obra de Ángel Ganivet* (Valencia, 1922; 2nd edition Madrid, 1953).

See A. Gallego Morell, *Ángel Ganivet: el*

excéntrico del '98 (Granada, 1965) and *Estudios y textos ganivetianos* (1971).

GAOS, Vicente (1919–   ), b. Valencia. Poet and critic. He taught literature in the U.S.A. 1948–56, and returned there in 1965. He is a brother of the philosopher José Gaos (1902–69) and of the poet Alejandro Gaos (1908–58). He has annotated the *Quijote* (1967) and produced several works of criticism, including *La poética de Campoamor* and *Poesía y técnica poéticas* (both 1955), and *Temas y problemas de literatura española* (1959), but he is best known for his original poetry, beginning with the rather derivative *Arcángel de mi noche, 1939–1943* (1944). Echoes from Garcilaso to Unamuno become slighter in *Sobre la tierra* (1945) and *Luz desde el sueño* (Valladolid, 1947), until in his best book, *Profecía del recuerdo* (Torrelavega, 1956), the poet's authentic voice is finally heard. His subsequent books include *Mitos para un tiempo de incrédulos* (1963) and *Concierto en mí y en vosotros* (Río Piedras, 1965).

GARCÉS, Enrique (*fl.* 1591), b. Oporto. Poet and translator notable for an excellent version of Camões's *Os Lusiadas* (1591) and the *canzoniere* of Petrarch (1591). He lived in Peru from 1555 to 1564.

See G. Lohmann Villena, 'Enrique Garcés: descubridor del mercurio en el Perú, poeta y arbitrista' in *Anuario de Estudios Americanos*, vol. 5 (1948), pp. 439–82; and L. Monguió, *Sobre un escritor elogiado por Cervantes. 'Los versos del perulero Enrique Garcés y sus amigos', 1591* (Berkeley, 1960).

GARCÉS, Enrique (1906–   ), b. Otavalo. Ecuadorian biographer, playwright, and journalist who has occupied high government positions. *Eugenio Espejo, médico y duende* (1944, reprinted 1959) is the most illuminating of several biographies of the Ecuadorian fighter for Independence, while *Rumiñahui* (1953) is an absorbing study of an Inca general who defended the area now known as Ecuador from the Spanish invaders. *Marietta de Veintemilla* (1949) traces the life of a passionate woman who virtually ruled Ecuador during the presidency of her father Ignacio. *Daquilema Rex* (1960?) tells the story of the Indian rebellion in Chimborazo province against President Gabriel García Moreno and the coronation of the Indian Fernando Daquilema as King of Quito: like *Rumiñahui* it asserts the right of Indians to their own lands.

His best plays deal with the middle classes of Quito: *Boca trágica* (1943), *Alondra* (1950), and *Lo que no pudo ser* (1955), the three plays being collected in a new edition by the Casa de la Cultura Ecuatoriana (1957).

GARCÍA, Carlos (*c.* 1575–*c.* 1630). Spanish picaresque novelist known to have lived as a refugee in Paris during the second decade of the 17th c., despite Nicolás Antonio's doubts of his very existence and Sbarbi's identification of him with Cervantes.

La desordenada codicia de los bienes agenos, a work subtitled *antigüedad y nobleza de los ladrones* and published in Paris in 1619, is a picaresque novel important for its grotesque violence and harsh satire. It begins with the confession of Andrés, the protagonist and thief, that he was responsible for the execution of his own parents, and there is much in the book that foreshadows the 'black comedy' of the 20th c. The novel was edited by J. M. Eguren with *La oposición y conjunción de los dos grandes luminares de la tierra. Obra apazible y curiosa en la qual se trata de la dichosa Aliança de Francia y España* in 1877. The latter's first edition was bilingual (Paris, 1617).

See A. Valbuena Prat, *La novela picaresca española* (1943); A. Carballo Picazo, 'Datos para la historia de un cuento' in *Revista Bibliográfica y Documental*, vol. 1 (1947), pp. 425–66, and 'El doctor Carlos García, novelista español del siglo XVII' in the same journal, vol. 5 (1951), pp. 5–46; and J.-M. Pelorson, 'Le docteur Carlos García et la colonie hispano-portugaise de Paris, 1613–1619' in *Bulletin Hispanique*, vol. 71 (1969), pp. 518–76.

GARCIA, Francesc Vicenç (*c.* 1580–1623), b. Tortosa. Catalan poet often known simply as the Rector of Vallfogona. One of the most skilful sonneteers of his day, Vallfogona was stylistically a very careful imitator of the conceits of Góngora and Quevedo (qq.v.), but frequently lacked their taste or finish. The unnatural syntax is unhappily accompanied by often inappropriate Castilianisms. The *Obras de Garceni* (Vallfogona's bucolic name) was published in Barcelona not in 1700 as stated but almost certainly in 1703. The burlesque obscenities caused some difficulties with the Inquisition, the new edition of 1770 being banned in 1782. The 1703 edition was reprinted in 1805 and 1820, and that of 1830 incorporates four new pieces.

GARCÍA ÁLVAREZ, Enrique (1873–1931), b. Madrid. Playwright, chiefly of *zarzuelas* and *sainetes*. With Pedro Muñoz Seca (q.v.), he created the genre known as the *astracanada* (q.v.), or broad farce, in which all the dramatic elements are subjugated to the comic, often using the *double entendre*. Most of his works were written in collaboration, including *El verdugo de Sevilla* and *Los cuatro Robinsones* (with Muñoz Seca); *Alma de Dios* and *El pobre Valbuena* (with Carlos Arniches); and *La alegría de la huerta* (with Antonio Paso). This last, first performed and published in 1900, is set in Murcia. An entertaining musical, this *zarzuela* concerns above all the atmosphere of the Murcian countryside, with its typical characters such as gipsies, and the traditional pilgrimage to the Virgin of Fuensanta. The slight plot concerns the sly Carola, in love with Alegrías, who accepts Juan Francisco (who does not love her) in order to induce her bashful sweetheart to declare his real feelings. This of course he eventually does.

See José Casado, *Las pirámides de sal* (1918).

GARCÍA BACCA, JUAN DAVID (1901–), b. Pamplona. Philosopher considered, in the words of F. Saínz de Robles, to be one of the major philosophers of contemporary Spain, with Ortega y Gasset (q.v.) and Zubiri.

He has taught philosophy in Barcelona University and elsewhere, and has translated the pre-Socratics, Plato, Aristotle, Xenophon, and others. His original works include *Algunas consideraciones sobre el problema epistemológico* (1932), *Introducción a la lógica moderna* (1936), *Interpretación histórica de la lógica clásica y moderna* (1939), *Filosofía en metáforas y parábolas* (Mexico City, 1945), and *Síete modelos de filosofar* (Caracas, 1950).

GARCÍA BALBOA, PEDRO JOSÉ, the secular name of Fray Martín Sarmiento (q.v.).

GARCÍA CALDERÓN, FRANCISCO (1883–1953), b. Lima. Peruvian essayist, critic, and diplomat. Son of a former President of Peru and brother of the important critic and literary scholar Ventura García Calderón (q.v.). A graduate of the University of San Marcos, he undertook minor diplomatic posts in London (1908) and Paris (1910–18) before appointment as Ambassador to Belgium (1918), France (1930–42), and Portugal (1943–9). A more level-headed and objective writer than González-Prada (q.v.) for instance, García Calderón diagnoses the ills of contemporary Peruvian society within the prevailing positivist atmosphere. His works are not historical in the true sense, but essays in sociological observation. His books include *De litteris* (1904), *Hombres e ideas de nuestro tiempo* (Valencia, 1907), *Le Pérou contemporain* (1906; translated into Spanish, 1908), *Les conditions sociologiques de l'Amérique Latine* (1908), *Profesores de idealismo* (Paris, 1909), *Les démocraties latines de l'Amérique* (Paris, 1912), *La creación de un continente* (Paris, n.d. but 1913), *El panamericanismo* (1917), *Ideas e impresiones* (Madrid, 1919), and *Testimonios y comentarios* (1934). Jorge Basadre compiled a useful anthology *En torno al Perú y América* (1954) and

there is a good bibliography by Rafael Heliodoro Valle in the *Mercurio Peruano* (July 1953).

GARCÍA CALDERÓN, VENTURA (1885–1959), b. Paris. Peruvian critic, short-story writer, poet, and diplomat. Brother of Francisco García Calderón (q.v.). He graduated from San Marcos University in Lima. Among his important posts were those of ambassador to Belgium, Switzerland, and Unesco. He was commissioned by his government to edit the important Biblioteca de Cultura Peruana (Paris, 1938). Estuardo Núñez has said of García Calderón: 'a stylish prose-writer, he introduced incidents and personalities from all regions of Peru', in stories such as *Dolorosa y desnuda realidad* (1914), *La venganza del Cóndor* (1924), and *Le sang plus vite* (Paris, 1938), in which the urbane diplomat told in prose of marvellous vitality tales of violent death and urgent passion. His critical essays included *Del romanticismo al modernismo* (Paris, 1910), and *Leopoldo Lugones* (1947). He made important anthologies of verse (*Parnaso peruano*, 2nd edn., Barcelona, 1915) and short stories (*Los mejores cuentos americanos*, 1914). An anthology of his own *Cuentos peruanos* (Madrid, 1952) is perhaps the best introduction to a Peruvian writer better known in France than in his native land.

See R. Gómez de la Serna, *Ventura García Calderón* (Geneva, 1946); Yves Gandos (ed.), *Hommage à Ventura García Calderón* (Paris, 1947); and two books by Luis Humberto Delgado, *Ventura García Calderón* (1947), and *Diálogos con Ventura García Calderón* (1949).

GARCIA DE GUILHADE, JOHAM, see GUILLADE, Xohán de.

GARCÍA DE LA HUERTA, VICENTE (1734–87), b. Zafra. Spanish playwright and poet. He worked in the Royal Library (now the National Library) for a living, but spent ten years as a political prisoner in the North African colony of Oran, where his great play *Raquel* was first performed in 1778. This play, based on Diamante's classic treatment of the tragic love of the Jewess of Toledo for Alfonso VIII and her murder by his vassals, has been described by Duncan Moir as 'the best political play of that age'. *Raquel* (q.v.) has been edited by J. C. Fucilla (Salamanca, 1965) and in *Clásicos Castellanos* by R. Andioc (1971). It observes the unities closely; reduces Diamante's five acts to three, thus heightening the tension; and simplifies the verse forms. *Raquel* was translated into Italian free verse by García de la Huerta's brother Pedro (Bologna, 1782), an exiled Jesuit. His *Agamemnón vengado* (Buenos Aires, 1930) is an interesting version of Sophocles' *Electra* in which García uses metres much more complex and varied than those in *Raquel*.

García's defence of the Spanish dramatic tradition against the Francophiles Iriarte, Samaniego, and their fraternity was somewhat vitiated by his omission from his anthology *Theatro hespañol* (16 vols., 1785–6) of all works by Lope de Vega, Tirso de Molina, and Ruiz de Alarcón. Constantly at war with these powerful literary enemies by pamphlet and verse satire, García was the subject of a cruel epitaph by Iriarte, whose clever final rhyme recalls the lunatic asylum in Saragossa made famous in the spurious *Don Quijote* of Fernández de Avellaneda:

> *De juicio sí; mas no de ingenio escaso,*
> *Aquí Huerta el audaz descanso goza;*
> *Deja un puesto vacante en el Parnaso,*
> *Y una jaula vacía en Zaragoza.*

His *Tragedias* (1786) appeared in the same year as the 2nd edition of his *Obras poéticas* (2 vols., 1778), a selection of which is also available in vol. 61 (1869) of the BAE.

See G. Mancini, 'Per una revisione critica di García de la Huerta in *Studi di Letteratura Spagnola* (Rome, 1964), pp. 267–74; and Russell Sebold, 'Neoclasicismo y creación en la "Raquel" de García de la Huerta' in *El rapto de la mente* (1970), pp. 235–54.

García del Castañar, the hero and sub-title of the play by Francisco de Rojas Zorrilla *Del rey abajo, ninguno* (qq.v.).

GARCÍA DE QUEVEDO, José Heriberto (1816–71), b. Coro, Venezuela. Minor poet and playwright, at court in the period of María Cristina. The gossip of the time alleged that he fell in love with Princess Isabel (the future 'Chaste Queen'), whom he is believed to have addressed when he sang of an earlier Isabel, in his long poem 'A Colón'. In any case he served Isabel II as diplomat in three continents, returning to Venezuela as Spain's chargé d'affaires in time for the April Revolution of 1858, when he wrote a song 'A Caracas' in Romantic vein. He collaborated with Zorrilla, and with the Duque de Rivas in *Contrastes*. His religious poem *María* (1850) is a close imitation of Zorrilla. He wrote ballads; romantic plays of little worth, such as those on Coriolanus, Don Bernardo de Cabrera, and Isabel de Medicis; and the philosophical poems *Delirium* (1850) and *El proscrito* (1853). His *Obras poéticas y literarias* (Paris, 1863) preceded by eight years his accidental death by shooting in Paris during the Commune.

GARCÍA DE RESENDE, see Resende, García de.

GARCÍA DE SALAZAR, Lope (*fl.* 1450), b. Bilbao. Historian. His *Libro de las bienandanças e fortunas* . . . is an important miscellany of local traditions and history. The edition by M. Camarón (1884) had a good biography of the author by A. de Trueba, but has been superseded by that of Ángel Rodríguez Herrero (4 vols., Bilbao, 1967).

J. C. de Guerra has edited García de Salazar's 'Crónica de siete casas de Vizcaya y Castilla, escrita . . . 1454' in *Revista de Historia y Genealogía Española*, vol. 3 (1914).

GARCÍA DE SANTA MARÍA, Álvar (*fl.* 1455), b. Burgos. Historian. A member of a leading Jewish *converso* family, he was attributed by Amador de los Ríos with the *Crónica de don Álvaro de Luna* (Milan, 1546), written between 1455 and 1460 and attributed by Nicolás Antonio to Antonio Castellanos, and by A. D. Deyermond to Gonzalo Chacón (d. 1517). Álvar García is probably responsible for the compilation of the collective *Crónica de Juan II* (q.v.).

See Francisco Cantera, *Álvar García de Santa María: historia de la judería de Burgos y de sus conversos más egregios* (1952).

GARCÍA DE SANTA MARÍA, Pablo (1350–1435), b. Burgos. A member of a leading Jewish *converso* family and tutor to Juan II. Father of Alfonso de Santa María de Cartagena (q.v.) and brother of Álvar García de Santa María (q.v.).

Born Salomon ha-Levi, he chose to be baptized in July 1390 as Pablo García de Santa María, and studied to become a priest. He met the Pope in Avignon, was appointed an archdeacon to the See of Burgos in 1395, and created Bishop of Cartagena in 1401. He became Bishop of Burgos in 1415.

His long historico-allegorical poem *Las siete edades del mundo, o Edades trovadas* was completed before 1404, though dedicated in 1430. The poem, in *octavas reales*, attempts to deal summarily with the whole history of the world to the birth of Juan II. His *Suma de crónicas*, beginning with Hercules, son of Jupiter, purports to narrate the history of Spain up to 1412. Serrano (in *Los conversos Pablo y Alonso de Cartagena*, 1949) demonstrates that Pablo is not the author of part of the *Crónica de Juan II* formerly attributed to him.

See F. Cantera, *Álvar García de Santa María: historia de la judería de Burgos y de sus conversos más egregios* (1952).

GARCÍA DE VILLALTA, José (1798?–before 1846), b. Seville. Minor novelist and playwright, whose political principles led him to leave Spain in 1831 for Paris and Switzerland.

He returned to Spain in 1834 but was seized with his friend Espronceda (q.v.), whose *Poesías* (1840) García was to introduce.

He produced a verse translation of Shakespeare's *Macbeth* and two interesting original plays in the historical genre: *Los amores de 1790* (1838) and *El astrólogo de Valladolid* (1839), but is now remembered for a single historical novel *El golpe en vago: cuento de la decimoctava centuria* (6 vols., 1835).

See E. Torre Pintueles, *La vida y la obra de José García de Villalta* (1959).

GARCÍA GODOY, FEDERICO (1857–1924). b. Dominican Republic. Novelist and critic, best known for his historical trilogy of the struggle against Spain and Haiti: *Rufinito* (1908), *Alma dominicana* (1911), and *Guanuma* (1914), in the fictional tradition of Galván (q.v.). His novel *El derrumbe* (1917) is rare because most copies of it were destroyed by the U.S. forces of occupation for its alleged seditiousness.

Páginas efímeras (1912) is a collection of reviews, somewhat too kind to the now largely forgotten books noted. García Godoy's other critical collections are *La literatura americana de nuestros días* and *Americanismo literario* (both Madrid, 1915), and *La literatura dominicana* and *De aquí y de allá* (both 1916). There is a useful *Antología* (1951) including fiction and non-fiction.

See Rufino Martínez, *Estudio de la labor literaria de Federico García Godoy* (Puerto Plata, 1925).

GARCÍA GÓMEZ, EMILIO (1905–), b. Madrid. An Arabist, he studied under Miguel Asín y Palacios (q.v.) and has been the most influential Spanish scholar in his field since the latter's death. He has been ambassador of Spain in Iraq, Lebanon, and Turkey. His exemplary translations of Hispano-Arabic poetry have reached a wide audience, especially *Poemas arábigoandaluces* (1930), *Cinco poetas musulmanes* (1944) and his version from Ibn Hazm, *El collar de la paloma* (1953), which is masterly. He has studied a source common to Ibn Tufail and Gracián (qq.v.) in *Un cuento árabe*. On the kharjas (q.v.) he has written *Las jarchas mozárabes y los judíos de al-Andalus* (1957) and *Las jarchas romances de la serie árabe* (1966).

GARCÍA GOYENA, RAFAEL (1766–1823), b. Ecuador. Poet, who lived much of his life in Guatemala. He was celebrated as a writer of tercets and of fables. His *Fábulas y poesías varias* (Guatemala City, 1825) were reprinted several times, the most recent edition being that of Carlos Samayoa Chinchilla (1950) with a good introduction in Los Clásicos del Istmo.

See Flavio Guillén, *Un fraile prócer y una fábula poema* (Guatemala City, 1932).

GARCÍA GUTIÉRREZ, ANTONIO (1813–84), b. Chiclana, Cádiz. Playwright. A friend of Larra, Espronceda, Ventura de la Vega, and others of the Romantic generation, he spent a number of years in the military and diplomatic service, especially in England, France, Switzerland, Cuba, and Mexico, before eventually becoming director of the National Archaeological Museum in Madrid in 1872.

Though he wrote more than fifty plays and *zarzuelas* in all, none surpassed in fame the first of them all: *El trovador* (q.v., 1836; ed. J. Ibesse, 1964), which inspired the libretto for Verdi's equally successful opera *Il trovatore* (1853). Yet García Gutiérrez patently failed to live up to the expectations of public and critics alike, for *El paje* and *El rey monge* (both 1837) were quickly forgotten. E. Allison Peers (in *The Romantic Movement in Spain*, 1949) wrote of the former: 'All the faults of third-rate Romantic drama can be found here: unrestrained horror, misdirected emotion, glaring improbabilities of plot and character, false psychology, and the usual exaggerated language'.

It was at the very end of his dramatic career, in *Venganza catalana* (1864) and *Juan Lorenzo* (1865), edited together by J. Lomba y Pedraja (1925) in Clásicos Castellanos, that García Gutiérrez not only regained the attention of the dramatic critics, but probably also realized his greatest potential. The first is a stirring epic tragedy in verse on Roger de Lauria, while the second shows a rebel as the first sacrificial victim of the revolution he helped to create: a drama of morals and action which is undoubtedly its author's finest work. By this time, he had become a member of the Academy (1862) and an accepted senior figure, writing on like Zorrilla into the age which was to be dominated by Manuel Tamayo y Baus (q.v.). His *zarzuelas* were set to music by Arrieta, the best being *El grumete* (1864) and its sequel *La vuelta del corsario* (1865). García Gutiérrez's *Poesías* (1840) have been freshly edited by J. de Entrambasaguas (1947).

See F. Funes, *García Gutiérrez: estudio crítico de su obra dramática* (Cádiz, 1900); and Nicholson B. Adams, *The Romantic drama of García Gutiérrez* (New York, 1922).

GARCÍA ICAZBALCETA, JOAQUIN (1825–94), b. Mexico City. Mexican historian described by Menéndez y Pelayo as 'gran maestro de toda erudición mexicana'. His family was exiled from 1829 to 1836. On their return García Icazbalceta began the education which was to lead him to become the foremost Mexican scholar of his age as collector, editor, and printer. His private library and private press acquired and distributed the fruits of learning on Mexico in general, and on the Mexican 16th c. in particular. He produced a translation of Prescott's *History of the conquest of Mexico* in 1849–50, and then wrote for the *Diccionario universal de historia y geografía* (1852). As an imaginative and resourceful editor he gained the respect of all Americanists with two abundant and careful series: *Colección de documentos para la historia de México* (2 vols., 1858–66), of which a facsimile edition appeared in 1971; and *Nueva colección . . .* (4 vols., 1886–92).

Outstanding among his original works are *Apuntes para un catálogo de escritores en lenguas indígenas de América* (1866), *Don Fray Juan de Zumárraga, Primer Obispo y Arzobispo de México* (1881), and the *Bibliografía mexicana del siglo XVI* (1886), the last having been brought up to date by Agustín Millares Carlo (1954). His important *Vocabulario de mexicanismos*, incomplete at his death, was published in its unfinished state in 1905.

GARCÍA LORCA, FEDERICO (1898–1936), b. Fuente Vaqueros, Granada. Major poet and playwright of universal popularity. He studied in the universities of Granada and later Madrid, where he lived at the Residencia de Estudiantes, an offshoot of the Institución Libre de Enseñanza (q.v.). There he met some of the capital's leading literary figures, including Marquina, Martínez Sierra, and Juan Ramón Jiménez (qq.v.). He became interested in folklore, especially that of inland Andalusia, and in the 1930s travelled around Spain with the Madrid university group 'La Barraca' (q.v.). A pianist and painter of some achievement, he was to use his range of talents within his poetry to provide Spanish literature with a poetry at once musical and painterly in its effects. He then began to travel widely outside Spain, lecturing and writing, and charmed all those he met with his ingenuous enthusiasm and poetic inspiration.

Apart from varied prose sketches and stories, Lorca's work consists of poetry and drama. The collections of poetry are *Libro de poemas* (q.v., 1921), with its echoes of Salvador Rueda, Machado, and Juan Ramón; the *Primeras canciones* (1936) of 1922, which begin to show the signs of originality later associated with the mature Lorca, including the striking metaphors and the folk motifs; the *Canciones, 1921–1924* (Málaga, 1927; 2nd edn., Madrid, 1929); the impressive *Poema del cante jondo, 1921–1922* (1931; 2nd edn., 1937) which gave him world fame for recapturing in text and rhythm the authentic gipsy soul; *Primer romancero gitano, 1924–1927* (q.v., 1928; later edns. *Romancero gitano*), in which

he reaches full maturity. In 1934 he wrote the sombre, stirring masterpiece *Llanto por la muerte de Ignacio Sánchez Mejías* (q.v.), unique for its exploitation of the richness of Spanish sound, rhythm, and assonance, and equalling Lope de Vega for his mastery of the ballad form; and *Poeta en Nueva York, 1929–30* (q.v., Mexico City, 1940), an ambitious cycle written while he was in residence at Columbia University, but arguably marred by a derivative surrealism that seems at odds with his essential nature.

Lorca's drama in each of his styles is distinguished by his great lyrical vision and power. The first style, of Romantic origin, casts the spectator back to the atmosphere of the 19th c. Examples are *Mariana Pineda* (1928) written in 1925, and *Doña Rosita la soltera, o El lenguaje de las flores* (q.v.) first performed in 1935. These plays, like his brief *El paseo de Buster Keaton* or *La doncella, el marinero y el estudiante* offer little more than a glimpse of the playwright that Lorca was to become. This is also true of *La zapatera prodigiosa* and *Amor de Don Perlimplín con Belisa en su jardín* (written in 1930 and 1931 respectively), gentle farces with barely a realistic touch between them, but filled with poetic grace.

It is with the tragic popular drama that Lorca rose to his full stature, however, realizing the powerful connotations of such simple words as 'blood', 'moon', and 'rose', and hinting always at more than he describes in so many words.

Bodas de sangre (first performed in 1933), *Yerma* (1934), and *La casa de Bernarda Alba* (1945, qq.v.) deal with elemental themes of love, passion, sterility, and murder in direct terms, borrowing their movement towards a fatal climax with classical authority. If the first contains too much lyricism and the second too little, then the third achieves a fine balance between dramatic movement and lyrical strength.

Murdered by the Nationalists in Granada at the outset of the Civil War, with an estimated four thousand intellectuals, Lorca was a great loss to Spanish literature and to the world in general. Unlike many of his contemporaries, he continues to be read and loved for his personality and his writings alike. The Aguilar *Obras completas* (ed. Arturo del Hoyo, 1954), which reached 2 volumes in its 1973 edition, also includes his drawings and music, with an excellent bibliography, but *Impresiones y paisajes* (Granada, 1918) is reprinted only incompletely.

See E. Honig, *García Lorca* (Norfolk, Conn., 1944); A. Barea, *Lorca: the poet and his people* (London, 1945; Spanish translation, Buenos Aires, 1956); G. Díaz-Plaja, *Federico García Lorca* (1954); J. Flys, *El lenguaje poético de Federico García Lorca* (1955); *Lorca: a collection of critical essays* (ed. Manuel Durán, Englewood Cliffs,

N.J., 1962); C. Ramos Gil, *Claves líricas de García Lorca* (1967); the biographical *Enfance et mort de García Lorca* by M. Auclair (Paris, 1968); and R. Martínez Nadal, '*El público*': *amor, teatro y caballos en la obra de Federico García Lorca* (Oxford, 1970). On Lorca's death see Ian Gibson, *La represión nacionalista de Granada en 1936 y la muerte de Federico García Lorca* (Paris, 1971).

GARCÍA MÁRQUEZ, Gabriel (1928–), b. Aracataca. Major Colombian novelist and short-story writer; the first to achieve international recognition since Rivera (q.v.) published *La vorágine* in 1928. At the age of 12 García Márquez was sent to a Jesuit college in Bogotá, and at 18 entered journalism, on *El Heraldo* of Barranquilla. In 1954 he went to Europe as correspondent for the liberal *El Espectador*, and there began writing novels. He was stranded without a penny for a year in Paris when his paper was suppressed in 1955, partly because it had printed his interviews with Luis Alejandro Velasco which later appeared in book form as *Relato de un náufrago* (Barcelona, 1970). Velasco had survived falling overboard from a Colombian warship which had been carrying smuggled goods from the U.S.A., and the story led to a political scandal.

García Márquez's selected journalism over the period 1957–9 has been published as *Cuando era feliz e indocumentado* (Barcelona, 1974). In 1959 he became director of the Bogotá office of the Prensa Latina press agency. Since 1961 he has worked in Barcelona and Mexico, directing films and writing fiction. The eleven stories in *Ojos de perro azul* (Barcelona, 1974) were written between 1947 and 1955. The short novel *La hojarasca* (Buenos Aires, 1955; translated by G. Rabassa as *Leaf storm*, London, 1972) is set in Macondo, an imaginary Colombian town based on his native Aracataca. The novel, recounted mainly with the aid of flashbacks, takes place between 2 and 3 p.m. on 12 September 1928 and is told through interior monologue by three characters. They are attending the wake of a doctor who committed suicide but is to be buried in hallowed ground at the insistence of a retired army colonel whose life the doctor had once saved. His next book was *El coronel no tiene quien le escriba* (q.v., Mexico City, 1961), a parable drawn from the lonely, desolate world of rural South America that García Márquez illuminates so memorably. *La mala hora* (Buenos Aires, 1962) rejected by the author, who claims the 1966 edn. to be the first) tells of a poster campaign of vilification in Macondo, the setting also of the stories in *Los funerales de Mamá Grande* (Xalapa, 1962), with vignettes of the town's barber, ineffectual priest, dentist, and the mayor.

Márquez's masterpiece so far is *Cien años de soledad* (q.v., Buenos Aires, 1967) set again in Macondo. At great length the novel shows the isolated, backward, decaying town and its apathetic inhabitants. The faceless authorities are brutal and repressive, and in collusion with the banana company during the boom of 1915–18, when foreigners and adventurers drifted in for a quick profit and then left again. The tone of the book is that of 'magic realism', in which the coming of ice to Macondo is recorded as a prodigy, incest and circular time are commonplace, and a ship is stranded in a forest. Events are seen as by a child, but recorded with subtlety and nostalgia.

García Márquez has since published *Isabel viendo llover en Macondo* (1969); the seven stories comprising *La increíble y triste historia de la cándida Eréndira y su abuela desalmada* (Barcelona, 1972), based on an episode from *Cien años de soledad*; and *El otoño del patriarca* (Barcelona, 1975), in which the life of an imaginary but archetypal Latin American dictator is seen through the lens of 'magic realism'.

Few novelists now writing in Spanish are more highly regarded than García Márquez.

See Miguel Fernández Braso, *Gabriel García Márquez* (Madrid, 1969); *Nueve asedios a García Márquez* (Santiago de Chile, 1969); P. S. Martínez (ed.), *Sobre García Márquez* (Montevideo, 1971); Mario Vargas Llosa, *Gabriel García Márquez: historia de un deicidio* (Barcelona, 1971); Graciela Maturo, *Claves simbólicas de García Márquez* (Buenos Aires, 1972); H. F. Giacoman (ed.), *Homenaje a Gabriel García Márquez* (New York, 1972); Vincenzo Bollettino, *Breve estudio de la novelística de García Márquez* (Madrid, 1973); and an interview in Luis Harss, *Los nuestros* (Buenos Aires, 1966), pp. 381–419.

GARCÍA MONGE, Joaquín (1881–1958), b. Desamparados, Costa Rica. A novelist and short-story writer, García Monge created the Costa Rican *costumbrista* novel of the early 20th c., modelling his realist style on José María de Pereda (q.v.) in *El moto* (1900), written under the pseudonym of 'El Lugareño', and on Émile Zola in *Las hijas del campo* (1900). Another novel, *Abnegación*, appeared in 1902, but his best work, mature in its directness and simplicity, consists of the short stories in *La mala sombra y otros sucesos* (1917 and later edns.), which show the influence of Maupassant. With Magón, Brenes Mesén, and Echeverría (qq.v.), García Monge was instrumental in forging the literary tradition of Costa Rica.

GARCÍA MORENTE, Manuel (1888–1942), b. Arjonilla, Jaén. Philosopher and teacher of philosophy. Beginning as a radical under F. Giner de los Ríos, and in France and Germany,

García Morente, who was appointed professor of philosophy at Madrid University in 1912, was influenced by his close friend Ortega y Gasset (q.v.) towards phenomenology and the philosophy of values. His early studies include *La filosofía de Kant* and *La filosofía de Bergson* (both 1917). *Lecciones preliminares de filosofía* (Tucumán, 1937; 2nd edn., Buenos Aires, 1943), *Orígenes del nacionalismo español* (Buenos Aires, 1938), and *Ser y vida del caballero cristiano* (1945) belong to the period when he had rejected his earlier beliefs, accepted Roman Catholicism, and become a priest.

See Juan Zaragüeta, *Manuel García Morente* (1948); the relevant section in Julián Marías, *Filosofía española actual* (1949); and M. de Iriarte, *El Profesor García Morente sacerdote: escritos íntimos y comentario biográfico* (1951; 3rd edn., 1956).

GARCÍA NIETO, JOSÉ (1914–), b. Oviedo. Poet and founder in 1943 of the magazine *Garcilaso* which was connected with the Juventud Creadora group, concerned with maintaining the national poetic tradition free of foreign models and influences. García Nieto's naturally conservative verse was officially approved, and prolific: *Víspera hacia ti* (1940), *Poesía, 1940–1943* (1944), *Retablo del ángel, el hombre y la pastora* (1945), *Del campo y soledad* (1946), *Tregua* (1951), *Juego de los doce espejos* (Santander, 1951), *Primer libro de poemas. Segundo libro de poemas* (2 vols., 1951 in the Más Allá series), *La red* (1955, winner of the Fastenrath Prize), *Leyendas de la dulce Francia* (1959), *El parque pequeño* (1959), *Geografía es amor* (1961), *Circunstancias de la muerte* (1963), *La hora undécima* (1963), and *Memorias y compromisos* (1966).

See F. Umbral, 'José García Nieto: semblanza directa y esquema biográfico' in *Punta Europa*, no. 83 (Madrid, 1963), pp. 10–19.

GARCÍA PAVÓN, FRANCISCO (1919–), b. Tomelloso, Ciudad Real. Novelist, drama critic, and journalist who has taught History of Drama in the Real Escuela Superior de Arte Dramático in Madrid.

Cerca de Oviedo (1946) is an impressive first novel which was a Nadal finalist in 1945; its strength is in its easy but quirky humour, and its fresh perception of the provinces around Oviedo and Gijón. Subsequent novels have steadily improved on the first: *Los liberales* (Barcelona, 1965), *La guerra de los dos mil años* (Barcelona, 1967), *El reinado de Witiza* (Barcelona, 1968, another Nadal finalist), *El rapto de las Sabinas* (1969), and *Las hermanas coloradas* (1970), winner of the Premio Nadal of 1969.

His short novels have also immense appeal: *Memorias de un caza-dotes* (1953), *Los carros vacíos*

(1965), and *Historias de Plinio* (Barcelona, 1968); perhaps more than his collections of short stories such as *Cuentos de Mamá* (1952), *Las campanas de Tirteafuera* (1955), *Cuentos republicanos* (1961), and *El último sábado* (1974).

GARCÍA SERRANO, RAFAEL (1917–), b. Pamplona. Novelist and *franquista* journalist on such papers as *Arriba*, and the weeklies *Haz* and *7 fechas*. From his first novel *Eugenio, o proclamación de la primavera* (Bilbao, 1938) he declared his interest: 'somos jóvenes, elementales, orgullosos, católicos y revolucionarios' on behalf of the Falange. His later work is somewhat more subtle, but never wavers from the orthodox Nationalist line, and in common with the exiled novels of the left offers little human and permanent to offset the somewhat hysterical politics.

As fictional pamphlets, the novels of García Serrano have a definite importance in the literature of their time, even if artistically they hardly compete with the contemporary fiction of Barea, Max Aub, Gironella, and Mercedes Fórmica (qq.v.). García Serrano's novels include *La fiel infantería* (1943, withdrawn by the censorship for ideological radicalism and reissued in 1958; 4th edn., 1973), *Plaza del Castillo* (1951), *Los ojos perdidos* (1958), *Los sanfermines* (1963), and *Historia de una esquina* (1964).

GARCÍA TASSARA, GABRIEL (1817–75), b. Seville. Poet and diplomat whose verse was written under the influence of Espronceda (q.v.). According to Donald Shaw, Tassara 'thundered out in verse his [own and Donoso Cortés'] version of a Europe madly bent on its own destruction and his prophecy of its ruin'. There is no doubt of the sincerity of Tassara's rhetoric, but its monotonous tenor detracts from its overall impact. The *Poesías* (1872) are mainly concerned with the larger themes of nature, man, and God. *Un himno al Mesías* breathes an atmosphere of religious optimism, but the heated political and satirical message of *A Napoleón*, *Un diablo más*, and *A la guerra de oriente* is that his generation deserves the dire destiny which seems unavoidable.

See M. Méndez Bejarano, *Tassara: nueva biografía crítica* (1928).

GARCÍA TERRÉS, JAIME (1924–), b. Mexico City. Mexican poet and critic who has travelled widely and is considered the most European of Mexican poets. *Panorama de la crítica literaria en México* (1941) is a precocious work, and *Sobre la responsabilidad del escritor* (1949) is a carefully considered essay. *La feria de los días* (1961) is his most important prose book to date, containing left-wing political and literary essays from the column of that title in the magazine *Universidad de México*.

Las provincias del aire (1956) was a collection of poems notable for the tightness and clarity of its language, far exceeded in quality by *Los reinos combatientes* (1961), which gains in suppleness and depth of thought, as well as in extreme care in construction. *La fuente oscura* (Bogotá, 1961) consists of five poems.

GARCÍA TEXEIRO, JOSÉ CAAMAÑO, see under his religious name, CÁDIZ, *Beato* Diego José de.

GARCÍA VELA, FERNANDO, see VELA, Fernando García.

GARCILASO DE LA VEGA (1501?–1536), b. Toledo. Major poet. Born into a noble family, Garcilaso entered the court of Carlos V in 1502 and spent most of his life in that king's service. He took part in an unsuccessful expedition to relieve Rhodes in 1522 and the Tunis campaign of 1535. In 1525 he married Elena de Zúñiga, but in the following year fell in love with a Portuguese lady, Isabel Freyre, to whom he addressed his greatest love poems.

As a result of his unauthorized attendance at the forbidden marriage of one of Carlos V's nephews, Garcilaso was banished in 1532, first briefly to Schut, an island in the Danube, and later to Naples, where he met Tasso, Luigi Tansillo, and the Spanish humanist Juan de Valdés (q.v.).

In 1536 he was fatally injured leading an attack on the fort of Le Muy (near Fréjus) while serving Carlos V in the invasion of France.

His work is important for introducing the so-called 'Italian' style into Spain, using in particular the courtly love conventions enhanced by Petrarch. Extant compositions by Garcilaso comprise two *elegías* in tercets, one addressed to his friend Joan Boscà (q.v., in Castilian 'Boscán'); an epistle to Boscà in free verse; five *canciones*; some verse in traditional metres; some in Latin; and in particular the thirty-eight sonnets and three eclogues, one in *octavas reales* and the others in varied metres.

It is the eclogues which constitute his most significant contribution to the literature of the Spanish Renaissance. Eclogue II (1533) is of 1,885 lines, mainly in dialogue, and concerns the shepherd Albanio (possibly the Duke of Alba, Garcilaso's friend and patron), who has long loved the shepherdess Camila, but is rejected when he tries to violate her. Salicio and Nemoroso, other shepherds, frustrate his attempted suicide. The last third of the poem is Nemoroso's description of his own wild love, and its cure by Severo, a wise man whose vision of

the love and exploits of Fernando de Toledo is also related by Nemoroso. Garcilaso's aim seems to be to show the need for human love to be restrained by reason, and one of his main sources here is the *Orlando furioso* of Ariosto.

Eclogue I (1534–5) was written on the poet's learning of the death in childbirth of Isabel Freyre. The shepherd Salicio laments the cruelty of Galatea, and Nemoroso laments the death of Elisa. The tone of both parts of the poem (the first written possibly as early as 1531) is that of resignation. Both shepherds reflect experiences of the poet. Doña Isabel rejected Garcilaso to marry another man; she died when still young.

Eclogue III (1536) largely comprises a description by some Tagus river-nymphs of the death of Elisa and the sorrows of Nemoroso, and has been described by R. O. Jones (in *The Golden Age: prose and poetry*, London, 1971) as 'an extended metaphor for the recollection of past sorrows which at last return again beneath the waters of oblivion'. Though Sánchez de las Brozas identified Salicio with Garcilaso and Nemoroso with Boscà, both Salicio and Nemoroso represent Garcilaso.

For his own and succeeding generations Garcilaso has represented the Renaissance ideal of the courtly poet-soldier: a man of arms and learning, quick to love yet wise enough to resign himself to love's loss. He and Boscà familiarized Spain with the Italian metres, providing admirable examples of the sonnet, the *canzone* (*canción*), *versi sciolti* (*versos sueltos*), and *ottava rima* (*octavas reales*). Their influence on many writers, including Gutierre de Cetina, Hernando de Acuña, and Francisco de Figueroa (qq.v.) was rapid and widespread. The immediate reaction of traditionalists such as Castillejo (q.v.) was hostile but ultimately unsuccessful. The popularity of Garcilaso's secular verse was a matter of concern to some clerics and others, and Sebastián de Córdoba (q.v.) bowdlerized the original, rendering it *a lo divino* (Granada, 1575). Córdoba's version of Garcilaso and its original are known to have influenced the poetry of S. Juan de la Cruz (q.v.).

Garcilaso quickly acquired the status of a classic author, and his works were edited by Francisco Sánchez de las Brozas, 'el Brocense' (q.v., 1574) and Fernando de Herrera (q.v., Seville, 1580). Herrera offered criticism as well as praise, and was attacked by Juan Fernández de Velasco (q.v.). Among the best of more recent editions are those by E. L. Rivers (*Obras completas*, 1964; and *Poesías castellanas completas* in Clásicos Castellanos, 1969).

See M. Arce Blanco, *Garcilaso de la Vega . . .* (1930; 2nd edn., 1961); R. Lapesa, *La trayectoria poética de Garcilaso* (1948; 2nd edn., 1968); A. Blecua, *En el texto de Garcilaso* (1970); and

E. L. Rivers (ed.), *La poesía de Garcilaso* (Barcelona, 1974).

On Eclogue I, see A. A. Parker, 'Theme and imagery in Garcilaso's first eclogue' in *BHS*, vol. 25 (1948), pp. 222–7. On Eclogue II, see R. O. Jones, 'The idea of love in Garcilaso's second eclogue' in *Modern Language Review*, vol. 46 (1951), pp. 388–95.

GARCILASO DE LA VEGA, 'El Inca' (1539–1616), b. Cuzco. Peruvian historian. The son of the *conquistador* Sebastián Garcilaso de la Vega and the Inca princess Isabel Chimpu Ocllo and also known, from a grandfather, as Gómez Suárez de Figueroa. In 1560 his father died, and he went to Spain to claim his inheritance but was unsuccessful and joined the army, later entering the Church.

His knowledge of the Inca civilization from early life, and his continuing contacts with the Incas by correspondence and visits, ideally fitted him to become the chronicler of his people. In anecdotal freshness and style, his *Comentarios reales* (1609) can be considered the predecessor of the *Tradiciones peruanas* (q.v.) of Ricardo Palma. The *Primera parte de los Comentarios Reales, que tratan del origen de los Incas, Reyes que fueron del Perú* . . . (Lisbon, 1609 [but 1608]) was followed by *Historia general del Perú que trata del descubrimiento de él; cómo lo ganaron los españoles* . . . (Cordova, 1617).

The latest edition of the *Comentarios reales* is that of J. Durand (3 vols., Lima, 1959; 2nd edn., 1968), and of the *Historia general* that of A. Rosenblat (3 vols., Buenos Aires, 1944).

The Inca Garcilaso translated into Castilian the *Dialoghi d'amore* of Leo Hebraeus (Madrid, 1590) and wrote a history of the State of Florida, *La Florida del Ynca* (Lisbon, 1605), more recently edited by J. Durand (Mexico City, 1956).

His *Obras completas* were edited by P. C. Sáenz de Santa María for the BAE (4 vols., Madrid, 1960).

See J. Fitzmaurice-Kelly, *El Inca Garcilaso de la Vega* (Oxford, 1921); R. Porras Barrenechea, *El Inca Garcilaso en Montilla, 1561–1614* (Lima, 1955); and J. G. Varner, *El Inca: the life and times of Garcilaso de la Vega* (Austin, Texas, 1968).

GARIBAY, ÁNGEL MARÍA (1892–1967), b. Toluca. Mexican literary historian of the Nahua people. He became a priest in 1917, studying Nahuatl during his twenty years' missionary activity among indigenous communities all over Mexico. In 1952 he was appointed professor at the Universidad Nacional Autónoma de México, writing the magisterial *Historia de la literatura náhuatl* (2 vols., 1953–4). From 1956

he directed the Seminario de Cultura Náhuatl, the deputy director being Dr Miguel León-Portilla (q.v.). Padre Garibay translated parts of the Old Testament, the tragedies of Aeschylus (1939 and 1962), Sophocles (1962), and Euripides (1964), and was responsible for the best edition of Sahagún's monumental *Historia general* (4 vols., 1956).

Garibay's other works include *La poesía lírica azteca* (1937), *Llave del náhuatl* (1940; 2nd edn., 1961), *Poesía indígena de la Altiplanicie* (1940; 3rd edn., 1962), *Épica náhuatl* (1945, 3rd edn., 1964), *Xochimapictli* (1959, 2nd edn., 1964), an anthology of Nahuatl poetry; the text and translation of *Vida económica de Tenochtitlán*, vol. 1 (1961), *Panorama literario de los pueblos nahuas* (1963, 2nd edn., 1971), *Historiadores de la época colonial* (1964), an anthology called *La literatura de los aztecas* (1964), a study of *Poesía náhuatl* (3 vols., 1964–6), an edition of three 16th-c. documents entitled *Teogonía e historia de los mexicanos* (1965); and Diego Durán's *Historia de las Indias de Nueva España* (2 vols., 1967).

GARIBAY Y ZAMALLOA, ESTEBAN DE (1533–99), b. Mondragón, Guipúzcoa. Basque historian. After studying Greek and Latin at Salamanca and Alcalá universities, Garibay was appointed librarian to Philip II in 1576 and historian in 1592 partly because of the great impression made on the king by his *Los XL libros d'el Compendio historial de las Chrónicas y universal Historia de todos los reynos de España* . . . (2 vols. in 4, Antwerp, 1571; 2nd edn., 4 vols., Barcelona, 1628). A warm friend of the Aragonese annalist Jerónimo de Zurita (q.v.), Garibay was an opponent of the historian Juan de Mariana (q.v.). His other works include *Ilustraciones genealógicas de los Cathólicos Reyes de las Españas, y los Christianíssimos de Francia, y de los Emperadores de Constantinopla* (1596) and a collection of Basque proverbs in *Memorial Histórico Español*, vol. 7 (1854), pp. 1–646. It is possible that Esteban is the Garibay who wrote stories preserved in manuscript in the Real Academia de la Historia and in the National Library and used by A. Paz y Melia in his *Sales españolas* (1890) in the Colección de Escritores Castellanos.

See J. de Urquijo e Ibarra, *El Refranero vasco* (San Sebastián, 1919); F. Arocena, *Garibay* (Saragossa, 1960); and L. María de Lojendio, 'Referencias a la Historia vasca que se contienen en "Los quarenta libros del compendio historial" de Esteban de Garibay' in *Príncipe de Viana* (Pamplona), vol. 30 (1969), pp. 121–46.

GARMENDIA, SALVADOR (1924–), b. Barquisimeto, Lara. Venezuelan novelist and short-story writer. He is Director of Culture at the Universidad de los Andes and editor-in-chief of the university review *Actual*. He quickly attained success with *Los pequeños seres* (1959), which described with ironical realism the drifters and the maladjusted in Venezuelan society. *Los habitantes* (1961) showed the pathetic failures of communication in a family during the course of one day. His third novel *Día de cenizas* (1964) was less successful, but he then published some short stories of impressive penetration and sympathy in *Doble fondo* (1966). *La mala vida* (Montevideo, 1968) is a novel of the seamier side of the Venezuelan oil industry. His latest novel is *Memorias de Altagracia* (1974).

GARRIDO DE VILLENA, FRANCISCO (*fl.* 1583), b. Alcalá. Poet and translator. His books are rare, but were noticed by Nicolás Antonio (q.v.) in his *Bibliotheca hispana nova* (Rome, 1696). Apart from an influential translation of the *Orlando innamorato* (1495) of Boiardo published in Valencia (1555) and known to have been reprinted in Alcalá (1577), Garrido's principal work was an original poem on the Roland cycle, *El verdadero suceso de la famosa batalla de Roncesvalles, con la muerte de los doze pares de Francia* (Valencia, 1555; 2nd edn., Toledo, 1583).

GASPAR, ENRIQUE (1842–1902), b. Valencia. Playwright. Gaspar worked in the consular service in many countries, notably in France, Greece, and Hong Kong. His earliest plays are sentimental, probably unconsciously absorbing the influence of the popular Bretón de los Herreros (q.v.), and are now forgotten. His later plays, in the realist genre, suffer from simplistic theses: *Las circunstancias* (1867) for instance merely attacks hypocrisy; *La levita* (1868) sees society through the snobbery of the frock-coat; and *El estómago* (1874) harps on the need for one's daily bread at the cost of all moral obligations and duties. Gaspar achieved greatness in his last plays: *Las personas decentes* (1890), *La huelga de hijos* (1893), and *La eterna cuestión* (1895), which tackle seriously and without simplification the moral decadence of the middle class, which Gaspar sardonically agrees is the backbone of the nation. The most original and socially objective dramatist of his generation in Spain, he was closest to the manner of Tamayo (q.v.) and foreshadows the theatre of Benavente (q.v.).

See Daniel Poyán, *Enrique Gaspar* (2 vols., 1957).

GASPAR GIL POLO, see POLO, Gaspar Gil.

GASTELUZAR, *Padre* BERNARDO (*fl.* 1686). Basque Jesuit poet whose *Eguia catholicae* (*Catholic truths*, Pau, 1686) was an interesting experiment in producing popular didactic verse for a Basque-reading public. Gasteluzar was influenced by the classical tradition in his variety of metre and his mythological interpolations.

Gaucho Florido, El (1932), a novel by the Uruguayan Carlos Claudio Reyles Gutiérrez (q.v.). A semi-autobiographical work based on *Mansilla*, a short story he wrote in 1893, the novel is set on a ranch, Tala Grande, which recalls Reyles's own Bellavista. Though some critics attack the book for its false nostalgia, others consider that Reyles offers a generally authentic picture of life on an *hacienda*, with its unruly *gauchos* unable to cope with mechanization.

Florido, believing that she is unfaithful, cuts off the hair of his girl Mangacha, having been misled by a malicious rumour spread by Ramón. Learning the truth, Florido cuts out Ramón's tongue and fixes it to Mangacha's door. The lovers flee from the authorities and Mangacha is killed by a bullet intended for Florido, who becomes an outlaw.

See E. Suárez Calimaño, ' "El gaucho Florido" ' in *Nosotros*, vol. 78 (1933), pp. 209–24.

Gaucho Literature, a literary genre deriving from the interest shown by sophisticated writers in the *gaucho*, or nomadic herdsman of the River Plate plains, and especially in the latter's popular songs accompanied by guitar such as the *triste*, *vidalita*, and *cielito*. The first example of true *gaucho* literature was probably the lost *Corro*, by Juan G. Godoy, which is known to have influenced the mock naïveté of poems by Hilario Ascasubi, Bartolomé Hidalgo, and Estanislao del Campo. The masterpiece of *gaucho* fiction is *Don Segundo Sombra* by Ricardo Güiraldes (qq.v.) and the poetic masterpiece is *Martín Fierro* by José Hernández (qq.v.). The poets were neither *gauchos*, nor peasants whose traditional poetry has been published in such anthologies as Carrizo's *Antiguos cantos populares argentinos* (1926) and *Cantares tradicionales del norte*. *Gaucho* poetry is also as different from the Europeanized poetry of Buenos Aires as Wild West films are from the poetry of Robert Lowell; it is characterized by the male virtues of strength, courage, and endurance, by knowledge of the ways of horses and cattle, and by constant travel over huge distances making family life impossible.

See J. L. Borges and A. Bioy Casares, *Poesía gauchesca* (2 vols., Mexico City, 1955), and also CIVILIZACIÓN Y BARBARIE.

GAVEL, HENRI (*fl.* 1922). Basque grammarian who began to publish his *Grammaire pratique de la langue basque* in *Gure Herria* in monthly instalments in 1922 and never completed the monumental task.

GAVIDIA, Francisco (1863–1955), b. San Miguel. Salvadorian poet, short-story writer, and playwright. He abandoned his legal studies for literature, and learnt Latin, Greek, and French in his spare time. On receiving from France a copy of Victor Hugo's *Les châtiments* late in 1880, he studied the French alexandrine and attempted to naturalize the metre into Spanish but failed until Rubén Darío (q.v.) arrived in 1882, when they worked on the new form together. *Versos y pensamientos* (1884) contained the equally rare *Versos* (San Miguel, 1878) and *Pensamientos* (San Miguel, 1880), of which no copies are believed to survive. His excessive studies led to his being sent for a cure to Paris in 1885, but there he threw himself into the Seine without, however, drowning. On returning to El Salvador he learnt German, Italian, English, Sanskrit, and Arabic, and introduced the Greek hexameter into Spanish. In 1895–6 he was appointed to a high position in the Ministry of Education, and he imported modern methods of teaching and created the Free University, doomed to early extinction through lack of funds. The state authorized an edition of his *Obras* to honour his contribution to the nation, publishing the poems *Libro de los azahares* (1913) and *Historia moderna de El Salvador* (2 vols., 1917–18; 2nd edn., 1958). For some time Director of the National Library, Gavidia was a ceaseless enquirer after knowledge in the European Renaissance tradition, and of his polymathic work only a small part has ever been published, including the four-act *Júpiter* (1895), the essays *Salvadoreños ilustres* (1901), *Cuentos y narraciones* (1931), and the long poem *Soteer, o Tierra de Preseas* (1949). Among his many unpublished works are three volumes of Arabic studies, books on education, and an 'Historia de la razón humana'. A man of high principle and devotion to duty, he died poor, but with a state pension and great honour.

See C. M. Ibarra, *Francisco Gavidia y Rubén Darío: semilla y floración del Modernismo* (1958); José Salvador Guandique, *Gavidia: el amigo de Darío* (vol. 1, 1965); and Roberto Armijo and José N. Rodríguez Ruiz, *Francisco Gavidia: la odisea de su genio* (1965).

Gaya ciencia ('the gay science', or 'the art of poetry', 'knowledge'), the poetry of the troubadours, deriving from the Provençal term *gai saber* given currency by the poets of the Toulouse school in the 14th c., also *gay trovar* or *arte de trovar* (Enrique de Villena). *Gaya ciencia* denotes the body of rules and precepts used to compose verse. The Provençal models passed to Catalonia, and it was a Catalan, Ramon Vidal de Besalu, who founded there (in 1323) the Consistory of Gay Science. Ramon Vidal composed a prose

treatise on the poetic art, *Los rasos de trobar*, while the later and more celebrated *Arte de trobar* of Villena (1433; ed. by F. Sánchez Cantón in *Revista de Filología Española*, 1919) was equally firmly based on Provençal precepts.

The careful, often meticulous rules of the troubadour's art are contrasted with the popular verse of the *mester de juglaría* (q.v.).

GAYANGOS Y ARCE, Pascual de (1809–97), b. Seville. Arabist and historian. Educated in France, Gayangos studied Arabic under Silvestre de Sacy and entered the Spanish government service as an interpreter in 1831. He lived in Britain for several years, contributing to many journals, among them *Westminster Review* and *Edinburgh Review*. He abridged the history of Muslim Spain by al-Makhari and the history of Spanish literature by Ticknor (q.v.). On behalf of the British Museum Library he collected and catalogued Spanish manuscripts and early printed books. He taught Arabic in the University of Madrid for some time from 1843 and was elected to the Real Academia de la Historia in 1844. Among his literary works were prologues to the BAE volumes of *Libros de caballerías* (1857), *La Gran Conquista de Ultramar* (1858), and *Escritores en prosa anteriores al siglo XV* (1860). He also edited vols. 13–19 of the *Memorial Histórico Español* of the Real Academia de la Historia.

GAYYAT, Ishaq ben Yehuda ben (d. 1089), b. Lucena. Spanish-Hebrew poet, biblical scholar and Rabbi of Lucena, under whose doctrinal leadership Lucena became the 11th-c. centre of Jewish scholarship in Western Europe. His prolific commentaries on the Talmud (in Arabic) and the Bible were as widely used as his philological studies, and he taught Arabic and Aramaic as well as Hebrew. Among his pupils was Moses ben Jacob ben Ezra (q.v.).

His hospitality was celebrated. When Abu Nasr, grandson of the disgraced Shemuel ha-Levi ben Yosef Nagrella (q.v.), became homeless, ben Gayyat gave him refuge.

His poetry lacks the lyrical flight of the best work by Solomon ibn Gabirol (q.v.), but in poems like 'The greatness of God', ben Gayyat is capable of great sonority, couched in language of humble devotion.

GECÉ, the pen-name used by Ernesto Giménez Caballero (q.v.).

Generación del 1898, a generation of Spanish writers connected, in the words of Donald Shaw, 'by their collective recognition of the inability of the mind to make sense of human existence ...' One of the major legacies of the liberals who supported the Revolution of 1868 (Galdós and 'Clarín' especially) to the Generation was the notion that in the spiritual and ideological regeneration of the individual lay the key to the regeneration of the nation. Though 'Arorín' (q.v.) was by no means the first to use the term, he popularized it in his influential articles later collected in *Clásicos y modernos* (1913).

The year 1898 saw a disastrous war with the U.S.A. and the end, with the loss of Cuba, Puerto Rico, and the Philippines, of the centuries-old Spanish overseas empire. Many Spaniards now saw that a radical adjustment to new political conditions would be necessary. Leaders of the Generation rediscovered the landscape of Old Castile, identifying it with the old Spanish virtues which they claimed had been lost in the apathy and insularity which followed the loss of the last colonies but had, they claimed, gradually been increasing since the end of the Golden Age. They sought to inculcate the old Spanish virtues of stoicism, energy, and bold action. The movement is both radical and traditionalist, finding its voice characteristically in the travel books of Unamuno, the essays of Azorín, and the poems (such as *Campos de Castilla*) of Antonio de Machado (qq.v.).

Whereas the Nietos del '98 (the Generation of 1927) were to contribute essentially to the development of poetry, the chief genres of their ancestors were the novel and philosophical essay. Though the very existence of the group was denied by Baroja, he himself is usually classed as one of its leading novelists, together with Azorín, Unamuno, Pérez de Ayala, and Valle-Inclán (qq.v.). Benavente was their chief playwright, Antonio Machado their most considerable poet, and their essayists and philosophers included such important figures as Ortega y Gasset, Maeztu, Ganivet, Costa, and Unamuno (qq.v.).

Their views were important, searching, and often correct. They sought universality as opposed to parochialism, and intellectually they were respected far beyond the borders of Spain. Time has shown their contribution to the debate of Spain in the world to be of great significance.

See studies on the individual members of the group and H. Jeschke, *Die Generation von 1898* (Halle, 1934; revised Spanish translation, 1954); P. Laín Entralgo, *La generación del noventa y ocho* (1945); L. S. Granjel, *La generación literaria del 98* (1966); D. L. Shaw, *The Generation of 1898 in Spain* (London, 1975). See also GENERACIÓN DEL 1927.

Generación del 1925, Luis Cernuda's description of the group of poets usually known as the Generación del 1927 (q.v.).

Generación del 1927, a group of writers (principally poets, whereas the Generation of 1898 consisted mainly of prose writers) known also as the Nietos del '98, Generación de la Dictadura, and Generación de la *Revista de Occidente*, from the journal in which many of them first came to prominence. Luis Cernuda (a member of the group) referred to it as the Generación del 1925.

The year 1927 was the tercentenary of Góngora's death, and Gerardo Diego wrote a record of the celebrations entitled 'Crónica del centenario de Góngora (1627–1927)' in *Lola*, nos. 1–2 (December 1927–January 1928). Dámaso Alonso published his important edition of Góngora's *Soledades*; José María de Cossío edited Góngora's *romances*; and Diego produced his *Antología poética en honor de Góngora*.

The major influences on the writers of 1927 were Jiménez (b. 1881), Ortega y Gasset (b. 1883), and Gómez de la Serna (b. 1888). Salinas (b. 1892) is the oldest of the group and Altolaguirre (b. 1906) the youngest. Others generally included are Jorge Guillén, Gerardo Diego, F. García Lorca, Alberti, Juan José Domenchina, Dámaso Alonso, Vicente Aleixandre, and Emilio Prados (qq.v.). The school introduced new subjects ('no deben parecerse a nada de lo ya dicho' declared Gómez de la Serna), new words, and had scant respect for traditional rhyme and metre. It is international in its relations and influences (Whitman, Baudelaire, Rimbaud, and Marinetti as well as Góngora) yet hermetic in its chosen public. It is both anti-realist and anti-Romantic, serving pure aestheticism in the tradition of Jiménez and pure statement as in Guillén's: 'Ser. Nada más. Y basta / Es la absoluta dicha'. The metaphor is used as powerfully and constantly as in the work of Góngora.

The most useful anthology of the group is Vicente Gaos, *Antología del Grupo Poético de 1927* (Salamanca, 1965) and the best overall view is that of C. B. Morris, *A generation of Spanish Poets, 1920–1936* (Cambridge, 1969), though there are better and more comprehensive works on each individual poet.

Generaciones y semblanzas, a series of biographical sketches forming the third part of the *Mar de ystorias* (Valladolid, 1512) by Fernán Pérez de Guzmán (q.v.). They were written c. 1450 to describe notable figures of the reigns of Enrique III and Juan II. He acknowledges a responsibility to these persons, writes of his contemporaries only after their death, and sees that fame calls for morality. After a prologue defining his aims and methods, he provides thirty-four examples of his craft, ranging from two or three paragraphs (for Gómez Manrique,

Don Pedro, Conde de Trastamara, and Juan Hurtado de Mendoza) to more substantial essays for Enrique III, Fernando I, and Juan II. His style is laconic: of Catherine of Lancaster, queen of Enrique III, for instance, he says: 'reina alta de cuerpo e muy gruesa, blanca, colorada e rubia. En el talle e meneo del cuerpo tanto pareçía onbre como muger'.

Pérez de Guzmán was aware of his debt to Tacitus; in turn he was to influence Hernando del Pulgar (q.v.) in the latter's *Claros varones de Castilla*.

Editions of *Generaciones y semblanzas* include those of the BAE, vol. 68 (1877), Clásicos Castellanos (1924), and Colección Austral (1947), the last also containing some letters from Pérez de Guzmán and hitherto unpublished chapters from the *Mar de ystorias*. But the best edition is that by R. B. Tate (London, 1964) for Támesis books.

Género chico ('lesser genre'), a term covering the one-act *zarzuela menor* (see ZARZUELA) and the one-act *sainete* (q.v.), as opposed to the *género grande* comprising tragedy, comedy, and opera.

G. G. Brown has defined the essence of the *género chico* as 'its combination of lighthearted representation of popular *tipos* (in the venerable tradition of *pasos* and *entremeses*) and the *costumbrista* vision of a region or city as a picturesque spectacle of which Spaniards might feel justly proud'. There is thus no realistic or cynical attitude to life in Spain shown in these essentially sunny, optimistic works. Music is usually associated with the *género chico*. Many such *sainetes* were written in collaboration, the major writers being Carlos Arniches, Vital Aza, and Ricardo de la Vega (qq.v.). The height of the popularity of the *sainete* (which is even now to be seen on the stage in Madrid and provincial cities) was from 1890 to 1910.

GERCHUNOFF, ALBERTO (1884–1950), b. Proskurov, Kamenets Podolskiy (according to his father's passport, which is probably inaccurate, on 1 January 1883). His family fled from the Ukraine to Argentina, and reached Moisés Ville, Santa Fe, in 1890. There, after his father was killed, his mother took him to the farming commune of Rágil, Entre Ríos, but after encountering hard times they left for Buenos Aires, where Gerchunoff was forced to earn a living by manual labour and could study only at night. After five years of this life, he became a journalist and in 1903 was appointed editor of *El Censor*, an anti-government paper in Rosario. When that closed, he joined the staff of *El País*, and subsequently that of *La Nación*, in the capital. He edited *La Nación* until his death.

His best book is *Los gauchos judíos* (1910), a penetrating sequence of stories from his life in Rágil, where intimations of anxiety and the uncertainty of human fortunes are always muted by the innocence of the pampa, so much less terrible than the anti-semitic hatreds and massacres Gerchunoff had left behind in Russia. The *Cuentos de ayer* (1919) were not quite so vivid. Gerchunoff's satirical novels include *El hombre importante*, on the life of the politician Hipólito Irigoyen; *La clínica del doctor Mefisto*, on psychiatry; and *El hombre que habló en la Sorbona*, against pseudo-intellectuals.

Gestas ('deeds'), in Spanish literature, a body of material, not necessarily accurate or even true, used in a verse *cantar de gesta* or in a prose chronicle, such as *Primer crónica*, for which in 1270 a decree of Alfonso el Sabio (q.v.) sought the assistance of *juglares de gesta*.

See the anthology *Cantares de gesta* (Saragossa, 1971, ed. by C. Guardiola Alcover).

Gesticulador, El, (1944) a play by the Mexican dramatist Rodolfo Usigli (q.v.) written in 1937 and first performed ten years later. The theme is the betrayal of revolutionary ideals.

The 'hero' is a failed professor, César Rubio, who assumes the identity of a murdered rebel. The play ends with the assassination of Rubio, Usigli's most rounded theatrical character, ironically just at the moment when he begins to dream of carrying out the idealistic reforms of his predecessor.

The 2nd edition of the play (1947) carries an epilogue 'La hipocresía del mexicano' and 'Doce notas y un ensayo sobre la actualidad de la poesía dramática'.

Gigante de los Andes, El, see ARBOLEDA, Julio.

GIL, ILDEFONSO-MANUEL (1912–), b. Paniza, Saragossa. Poet and novelist. Gil has taught in U.S. universities since 1962. His early writings were in verse: *Borradores: primeros versos* (1931), *La voz cálida* (1934), *Poemas de dolor antiguo* (1945), *El corazón en los labios* (Valladolid, 1947), *Huella del linaje* (Oporto, 1950), and *El tiempo recobrado* (1950).

Gil emerged as a novelist with *La moneda en el suelo* (Barcelona, 1951), in which a violinist loses his hands in an accident and fails to recover from the blow to his career and his life. In *Juan Pedro, el dallador* (Saragossa, 1953), again the hero is shocked by fate, in his case by the murder of his lover Carmela by his rival, but he recovers from the blow with relative equanimity. Gil's subsequent poetry has included the anthology *Poesía* (Saragossa, 1953) and *Los días del hombre* (Santander, 1968).

GIL, RICARDO (1855–1908), b. Madrid. Poet, educated in Murcia, who qualified as a lawyer but never practised. His work is in the manner of Campoamor (q.v.), influenced by Catulle Mendès and other French poets, as well as by Zorrilla and Bécquer (qq.v.).

His collections are *De los quince a los treinta* (1885); *La caja de música* (1898), which contains the fine lyric 'Abierto está el piano'; and *El último libro* (1909).

Gil Blas de Santillane (4 vols., 1715–35), a picaresque novel by Alain-René Lesage or Le Sage (q.v.). This important work in French relates adventures 'robadas a España y adaptadas en Francia por Lesage' and subsequently 'restituidas a su patria y a su lengua nativa por un español celoso que no sufre se burlen de su nación', as Padre Isla angrily protested in his introduction to his translation.

Within the broad picaresque tradition (and a direct ancestor of Fielding and Smollett's novels), the book nevertheless offers many attractions and originalities. The hero is taken from a decent middle-class environment (unlike the low life milieu of most forerunners) and he is not personally a rogue: he merely attracts rogues during his occasional periods of good fortune. The servant of an ordinary priest early on, Gil Blas rises to become servant to the Duke of Lerma, Chief Minister of the Crown. Intriguing comparisons can be made between the petty thefts and trickery of earlier picaroons, and the chicanery in high places sardonically recalled by Lesage's hero. Like Moll Flanders, Gil Blas repents on facing the near prospect of death. However, he meets a former master now exalted who gives him an estate producing five hundred ducats a year. In some ways the most absorbing volume is the last (books X–XII), in which Gil Blas returns to seek favour at court, and becomes secretary to Lerma's successor, the Count-Duke Olivares, whom he accompanies into exile. He eventually returns to his ideal life as an 18th-c. gentleman of leisure, cultivating his sensibilities and reading the classical philosophers and moralists.

Smollett confessed that his model for *Roderick Random* (1748) was *Gil Blas de Santillane*, which enjoyed a vogue in Spain no less than in France.

GIL GILBERT, ENRIQUE (1912–), b. Guayaquil. Ecuadorian novelist and short-story writer who gradually turned from writing political novels of a crusading tone to overt political action, visiting the U.S.S.R. and other communist countries to express his solidarity with the international working-class movement. He emerged as a short-story writer with eight contributions (one being 'El malo') to the anthology *Los que se van* (Guayaquil, 1930) published with work by Demetrio Aguilera Malta (q.v.) and J. Gallegos, a turning point in Ecuadorian fiction. *Yunga* (Guayaquil, 1933) is another book of short stories, including the celebrated 'El negro Santander'. His first novel is the impressive *Relatos de Emanuel* (Guayaquil, 1939), possibly even more successful than the more popular *Nuestro pan* (Guayaquil, 1942), dealing with the exploitation of rice workers and translated by Dudley Poore as *Our daily bread* (New York, 1943).

GIL POLO, GASPAR, see POLO, Gaspar Gil.

GIL VICENTE, see VICENTE, Gil.

GIL Y CARRASCO, ENRIQUE (1815–46), b. Villafranca del Bierzo, León. Novelist and minor poet. After graduating as a lawyer, Gil worked in the National Library, and later in the diplomatic service in Berlin. With Pastor Díaz, he represents the northern regional group of Spanish Romantic poets for delicate verses such as *La violeta* (1839) and the moving *Elegía a la muerte de Espronceda*, read at the grave of his close friend. The verse collection made by Laverde (1873) has been superseded by the *Obras completas* (1954) in the BAE.

Gil was an interesting prose-writer of travel sketches and notes on manners collected in *Costumbres y viajes* (1961), but it is for *El Señor de Bembibre* (1844) that he is best known, in the words of Díez-Echarri and Roca Franquesa, 'la mejor novela histórica de nuestra literatura'. Using a variety of sources, among them Mariana, Campomanes, and Michelet, Gil worked in the full tradition of Walter Scott then in vogue throughout Europe, creating a plausible conflict between religious duty and human feelings, with excellent descriptions of Leonese scenery and country life. J. del Sino and F. de la Vera e Isla produced a collection *Obras en prosa* (2 vols., 1883).

See D. G. Samuels, *Enrique Gil y Carrasco: a study in Spanish romanticism* (New York, 1939); and Ricardo Gullón, *Cisne sin lago: vida y obras de Enrique Gil y Carrasco* (1951).

GIL Y ZÁRATE, ANTONIO (1793–1861), b. El Escorial. Playwright. After teaching French for some time he went into politics. A member of the *tertulia* El Parnasillo, he was elected to the Real Academia Española. His early plays are inconsequential comedies, such as *Un año después de la boda* and *Cuidado con los novios* (both 1826), but he achieved respect and recognition with a fine neoclassical tragedy on the consort of Pedro el Cruel, *Blanca de Borbón* (1835). The historical play *Carlos II el Hechizado* (1837) is the most impressive of a series including plays on William Tell, Don Álvaro de Luna, and El Gran Capitán. His most important play is undoubtedly *Guzmán el Bueno* (q.v., 1842). E. de Ochoa edited Gil y Zárate's *Obras dramáticas* (Paris, 1850). Gil also wrote a thoughtful discussion, *De la instrucción pública en España* (3 vols., 1855).

See Marqués de Valmar, 'Don Antonio Gil y Zárate' in *Autores dramáticos contemporáneos* (2 vols., 1881–2).

GIMÉNEZ CABALLERO, ERNESTO (1899–   ), b. Madrid. Essayist and journalist who taught at the Instituto Cardenal Cisneros in Madrid. For some time he used the pen-name 'Gecé'. Among his prolific writings in the genial essay form is the autobiographical memoir that first brought him attention: *Notas marruecas de un soldado* (1923). A contributor to *El Sol*, in 1927 he founded *La Gaceta Literaria* (q.v.). A staunch Falangist throughout his life, he was for some time ambassador to Paraguay. *Revelación del Paraguay* (1958) is one of several books celebrating Latin American nations, like *Maravillosa Bolivia* (1957).

His most famous book is *Genio de España* (1932; 4th edn., 1937), which makes up in enthusiasm what it lacks in depth; others include *Roma española* (1941), *España nuestra* (1943), and *El dinero y España* (1964).

See D. W. Foard, *Ernesto Giménez Caballero* (1975) and M. A. Hernando, *Prosa vanguardista en la Generación del '27: Gecé y 'La Gaceta Literaria'* (1975).

GINER DE LOS RÍOS, FRANCISCO (1839–1915), b. Ronda. Educational reformer. After studying at Barcelona and Granada he lived in Madrid from 1863 and followed the *krausismo* of Julián Sanz del Río (qq.v.). He was appointed professor of the Philosophy of Law at the University of Madrid in 1868 but resigned in support of Sanz del Río. Restored to his position when the First Republic was declared, he subsequently fell foul of the Prime Minister Cánovas del Castillo in 1875 and was again removed.

In 1876 he founded with a group of collaborators the Institución Libre de Enseñanza (q.v.) to create a new educational environment equally free of control by Church or State and of pedagogic conservatism. His immense intellectual prestige was used to alleviate problems of juvenile delinquency and penal reform.

His pupils claimed that his conversation was more scintillating than his books, which included *Estudios jurídicos y políticos* (1875), *Estudios de*

literatura y arte (1876), *Estudios filosóficos y religiosos* (1876), *Estudios sobre educación* (1886), *La persona social* (1899), and *Estudios de filosofía y sociología* (1904). His *Obras completas* fill twenty-two volumes.

Unamuno spoke of Giner as the Spanish Socrates and, while he was attacked with other *krausistas* by Menéndez y Pelayo (q.v., in the *Historia de los heterodoxos españoles*, vol. 3), he was regarded with love and admiration by all of those with whom he came into contact, such as Joaquín Costa, Emilia Pardo Bazán (whose first book he subsidized), and Antonio Machado (qq.v.) who wrote an elegy *A Don Francisco Giner de los Ríos* (*Poesías completas*, 4th edn., 1936, no. CXXXIX) and whose apocryphal philosopher Juan de Mairena (q.v.) is based on Giner.

GIRÓN, DIEGO (1530?–1590), b. Seville. Minor poet. Girón's chief claim to fame is that he continued the Academia de la Alameda de Hércules founded by Juan de Mal Lara (q.v.) in Seville, and was highly respected by other poets of the Seville School. Girón's translations from the fables of Aesop were praised by Rodrigo Caro, and he is known to have translated Horace, Virgil, Seneca, and other Latin writers, and to have written Latin verse himself.

No collection of Girón's verse has ever been made; it is scattered throughout the writings of the period, notably in Herrera's well-known annotations to Garcilaso, and in the *Tratado de la utilidad de las sangrías*, a medical work by Fernando de Valdés to which Girón contributed a dedication in eight *octavas reales*.

Juan de la Cueva (q.v.) composed an *Elegía a la muerte de Diego Girón*.

GIRONDO, OLIVERIO (1891–1965). Argentinian ultraist poet who edited the manifesto of the *avant-garde* magazine *Martín Fierro* (q.v.) in 1924, after publishing the *Veinte poemas para ser leídos en el tranvía* (Argenteuil, 1922). His verse *Calcomanías* (Madrid, 1925) was followed by the prose parable *Espantapájaros* (1932), the short story *Interlunio* (1937) and further poetry: *Persuasión de los días* (1942), *Campo nuestro* (1946), and the heavily surrealistic *En la masmédula* (1954).

GIRONELLA, JOSÉ MARÍA (1917–   ), b. Darnius, Gerona. Novelist. His first book was the early poem *Ha llegado el invierno y tú no estás aquí* (Barcelona, 1945). He married in 1946, promising his wife the Premio Nadal as a wedding present, and fulfilled his promise with *Un hombre* (1947), the Nadal winner of 1946, which was revised substantially in later editions. *La marea* (1949) dealt with World War II and its consequences, but it was with *Los cipreses creen en Dios* (q.v., Barcelona, 1953) that Gironella achieved great popular success. This novel, which deals with the years before the Spanish Civil War, is the first of a chronological pentalogy, involving painstaking historical research as well as Gironella's recollections as an active participant. He continued with *Un millón de muertos* (Barcelona, 1961), on the war itself; *Ha estallado la paz* (Barcelona, 1966), on the immediate postwar period; *Los hombres lloran solos* (Barcelona, 1971); and a projected fifth volume. The novels were written as an explicit reply to the view of the Spanish Civil War presented by foreign novelists such as Hemingway, Bernanos, Malraux, and Koestler, and as such have been criticized by J. L. Alborg: 'es poco menos que si hubiera contestado a una novela con un tratado'. The trilogy was followed by *Mujer, levántate y anda* (1962).

He has written travel books such as *El Japón y su duende* (Barcelona, 1964) and *China, lágrima innumerable* (Barcelona, 1965), and the autobiographical tale on the symptoms of a nervous breakdown *Los fantasmas de mi cerebro* (Barcelona, 1959), which he has adapted for the stage with Julio Manegat. *Gritos del mar* (Barcelona, 1967) and *Gritos de la tierra* (Barcelona, 1970) are collections of articles. *Conversaciones con Don Juan de Borbón* (1968) appeared in a limited edition.

See L. E. Calvo Sotelo, *Crítica y glosa de 'Un millón de muertos'* (1961); and Ronald Schwartz, *José María Gironella* (New York, 1972), in Twayne's World Authors series.

GIRRI, ALBERTO (1918–). Argentinian poet. From his first book, *Playa sola* (1946) to his twelfth, *Envíos* (1967), Girri has avoided rhetoric and conventional phrases, using the resources of surrealism and hermeticism to convey with precision the anguish of solitude, the borders of madness, and the impossibility of love.

Girri has translated from Blake, Eliot, and other English writers. He has adopted the Chinese figure of Lao Tzu to represent the summit of wisdom.

Gitanilla, La, one of the *Novelas ejemplares* (q.v., 1613) by Miguel de Cervantes Saavedra (q.v.).

Raised and taught by the old gipsy who had claimed to be her grandmother, the 15-year-old Preciosa, 'la gitanilla', is the admiration of all who see her or hear her sing. She rejects all the proposals made to her by the men in her band but one day she meets a young man of wealth and good looks who offers to marry her. To test his love, she stipulates that he should join the gipsies as one of them for at least two years. He agrees and is christened Andrés Caballero by the rough and ready community. One day things

take a turn for the worst when a jealous inn girl conceals some jewels in his baggage and then denounces him as a thief. He is on the point of being hanged when Preciosa is discovered to be the only daughter of the local *corregidor*, her real name being Constanza. She had been stolen by the gipsy claiming to be her grandmother. Andrés is revealed as Don Juan de Cárcamo, the inn girl confesses her dishonesty, and Doña Constanza marries Don Juan.

See E. Fey, 'Das literarische Bild der Preciosa des Cervantes' in *Revue Hispanique*, vol. 75 (1929), pp. 459–549; and J. Lowe, *Cervantes: Two novelas ejemplares: 'La gitanilla' and 'La ilustre fregona'* (London, 1971).

GIUSTI, ROBERTO F. (1887–), b. Lucca, Italy. He emigrated with his mother and brother to Argentina in 1895. An essayist and literary critic, he founded the magazine *Nosotros* (1907–44) with Alfredo A. Bianchi.

Mis muñecos (1923) contains short stories of which the best is 'La vida es absurda y cruel', in which a boy who had fallen in love with his schoolteacher meets her again many years later. Giusti wrote influential essays in the three volumes of *Crítica y polémica*, and contributed to the major *Historia de la literatura argentina* edited by Rafael Alberto Arrieta (6 vols., 1958–60).

Gloria (2 vols., 1876–7), one of the *Novelas españolas de la primera época* of Benito Pérez Galdós (qq.v.). Its main theme is religious fanaticism, as in *Doña Perfecta* (1876) and *La familia de León Roch* (1878, qq.v.). The figure of Buenaventura represents latitudinarianism, a heresy much discussed in the book.

Don Juan de Lantigua, a man of strict religious views, lives with his beautiful and intelligent daughter Gloria in Ficóbriga, a sleepy village on the Cantabrian coast. Their only regular visitor is Bishop Ángel, Gloria's uncle. An Englishman called Daniel Morton survives a shipwreck, and is tended at the home of Don Juan. He falls in love with Gloria (who assumes him to be a Protestant), yet finally agrees that they should part. Daniel suddenly returns to Ficóbriga, and, finding Gloria alone, makes love to her, aggravating her anguish by revealing that he is in fact a Jew. Don Juan finds Daniel in Gloria's room, suffers an attack of apoplexy, and dies. Daniel escapes with the Bishop's curse ringing in his ears.

Part II takes place in Easter Week, its urgency of action matching the rising emotional intensity experienced at that time by the truly devout. When it begins (nearly a year having passed), Juan's pious sister Serafina and his more liberal and tolerant brother Buenaventura come to look after the bereaved Gloria, who has had a child by Daniel and is made even more wretched by the taunts of village people. Doña Serafina tries to persuade the young woman to enter a convent, but she is still desperate to see her baby son, who is being brought up in a nearby village. Buenaventura prevails on Daniel to return to discuss Gloria's predicament, and in a moving passage persuades the young Jew to feign to renounce his faith and marry Gloria. But Esther, his fanatical mother, arrives in time to prevent his apparent conversion to Roman Catholicism, so that Gloria decides to take the veil after all, and goes to see her son for the last time. There she meets Daniel, who is attempting to bribe the foster parents to allow him to take the child away. Desolate with grief, Gloria dies in Daniel's arms, after he has promised to raise their son in the Christian home of the Lantiguas. Daniel later dies insane.

Gloria caused immense controversy when it was first published for its attack upon the evils practised in the name of religious belief, and because the Roman Catholics are shown no less intransigent or intolerant than the Jews. *De tal palo, tal astilla* (1879) was an attempted refutation by Pereda (q.v.). Here a Christian girl gives up her love for an enemy of the faith (in this case an atheist), sacrificing human happiness to religious conviction. Galdós's vivid characterization marks a sharp development from *Doña Perfecta*, which like *Gloria* is semi-autobiographical in its portrayal of a tyrannical mother.

Daniel is generally taken to represent the Old Testament, Gloria the New, and their child Jesús a possibility of hope for the world in reconciliation and tolerance between hostile faiths and peoples. Daniel himself recalls Christ in some ways, an ironical reminder that Christ-like qualities are not the monopoly of Christians. Galdós's use of Christ-like figures becomes of even greater significance in such novels as *Nazarín*, *Miau*, *Halma*, and *Misericordia* (qq.v.). The unlikely love affair occurs again in *La de Bringas* and *Misericordia*. He concludes that the only true and mature faith is unselfish love.

Galdós was dissatisfied, incidentally, at having to make his lovers die in such artificial ways, saying to 'Clarín' of Part II: 'it is false and *tourmentée*: I wish I had never written it'. The novel is available in *Novelas*, vol. 1 (1970) of the Aguilar edition of *Obras completas*.

See W. T. Pattison, 'The manuscript of "Gloria"' in *Anales Galdosianos*, vol. 4 (1969), pp. 55–61.

Gloria de Don Ramiro, La, (Madrid, 1908), a novel by the Argentinian Enrique Rodríguez Larreta (q.v.), who spent five years of research to authenticate the background, mainly of Ávila, during the reign of Philip II. The success of the novel lies in the author's ability to write of the Golden Age as realistically as if describing his own period; Larreta was an aristocrat born out of his time and instinctively chose the historical novel as the most appropriate medium.

Don Ramiro, the hero of the novel, is the illegitimate son of a Moorish chief and a Roman Catholic lady whom he had seduced. She later married a Spanish nobleman who died fighting in Flanders. Ramiro too dreams of glory in war, but falls in love with a Moorish girl, Aixa, when sent as a spy to foil a Moorish plot, and momentarily forgets his loyalty to the Christian cause. After complex adventures he denounces Aixa to the Inquisition and sees her burned alive. He becomes a hermit, and encounters a Moor whom he discovers to be his father. Ramiro then goes to America, repents of his sins, and dies.

Larreta's prose is poetic and sonorous, and he uses the Castilian language to create a deliberately archaic setting for his story of conflict between duty and passion.

See Amado Alonso, *Ensayo sobre la novela histórica: El modernismo en 'La gloria de Don Ramiro'* (1942), impugning Larreta's historical accuracy; Martín Aldao, *El caso de 'La gloria de Don Ramiro'* (1943); and Juan Carlos Ghiano, *Análisis de 'La gloria de Don Ramiro'* (1968).

Glosa ('gloss'), (a) a marginal or interlinear note in a medieval MS., clarifying a possible difficulty in the text. Commonly the gloss is a vernacular rendering of a Latin word or expression.

(b) A kind of poetic composition in which a line or lines occurring early on, usually taken from some well-known poem, recur at the end of the poem or at the end of each stanza. The famous ballad on Tristan's death, 'Herido está don Tristán', was particularly popular among the ladies of Queen Isabel the Catholic and several glosses were made upon it by poets of her court. Golden Age poets who wrote *glosas* include Herrera, Ercilla, Lope de Vega, and Calderón.

See *Don Tristán de Leonís* (Valladolid, 1501), edited by A. Bonilla y San Martín (Madrid, 1912), pp. 394–6; and H. Janner, *La glosa en el Siglo de Oro: una antología* (Madrid, 1946), and *La glosa española: estudio histórico de su métrica y sus temas* (Madrid, 1943).

GODÍNEZ, FELIPE (1588–1639?), b. Seville. Jewish playwright in the circle of Lope de Vega (q.v.) whose preference was for biblical drama, hagiographical plays, and *autos sacramentales*. He was tried in Seville in 1624 for allegedly practising his faith in secret, convicted and sentenced to one year's prison and six years' exile.

His biblical plays include *La mejor espigadera* (on Ruth), *Los trabajos de Job, o la paciencia en los trabajos, Judit y Olofernes, Las lágrimas de David,* and *Amán y Mardoqueo, o la horca para su dueño* on the theme of Lope's *La hermosa Ester*.

A play on the life of St. Francis is curiously entitled *O el fraile ha de ser ladrón o el ladrón ha de ser fraile*. His *autos* were generally modelled on those of Mira de Amescua (q.v.); among them are *El provecho para el hombre* and *La Virgen de Guadalupe*.

Aun de noche alumbra el sol, a *comedia de capa y espada* has been attributed to him and published in vol. 45 (1858) of the BAE.

See Adolfo de Castro, 'Noticias de la vida del Dr Felipe Godínez' in *Memorias de la Real Academia Española*, vol. 8 (1902), pp. 277–83.

GODOY, JUAN GUALBERTO (1793–1864), b. Mendoza. Argentinian *gauchesco* poet and journalist, who founded *El Eco de los Andes* in 1824 (reprinted by the Universidad de Cuyo in 1943); *El Iros Argentino* in 1826; and in 1827 *El Huracán*. He emigrated to Chile in 1831, returning to Mendoza in 1856 to work in the Chilean consulate.

His collected works appeared in 1889, without the *gauchesco* poems written before and after his years in Chile. It is his poem *Corro*, unfortunately lost, which is believed to have initiated the vogue of the *gaucho* in literature: it took the form of a dialogue between Col. Francisco Corro and an old man. See GAUCHO LITERATURE.

GODOY, JUAN SILVANO (1850–1926). Educated in Santa Fé, Argentina, Paraguayan diplomat and journalist, who helped to compile the liberal Constitution of 1870. Exiled for political reasons, he spent twenty years in Buenos Aires and also travelled widely in Europe. He acquired a fortune in exile, and donated it to Paraguay in the form of an outstanding art gallery and library. Among his most important books are *Monografías históricas* (Buenos Aires, 1893), *Últimas operaciones de guerra del General José Eduvigis Díaz* (1897), *El concepto de patria* (1898), *El barón de Río Branco* (1912), and *El asalto a los acorazados* (1919). His historical reconstructions suffer from long, imaginary speeches attributed to historical personages. See Lyon, *Godoy* (New York, 1972).

GODOY ALCAYAGA, LUCILA (1889–1957), b. Vicuña, a village in the Elqui valley, N. Chile. Chilean poet. The first Latin American writer to be awarded the Nobel Prize for Literature (q.v.), which she was given in 1945. She used the pen-name 'Gabriela Mistral' in deference to the Italian writer Gabriele d'Annunzio and the French writer Frédéric Mistral.

She attained nationwide recognition in 1914 when her three *Sonetos de la muerte* won the National Poetry Prize. Her exceptional talent and vocation for teaching from the age of 16 led her to high positions, the necessary qualifications being waived in her case, and in 1923 she became Professor of Spanish in the University of Chile. A tragedy in her early life, when a man she was in love with committed suicide after embezzlement, made a deep impact on the tone and subject matter of her work. Federico de Onís drew the attention of the English-speaking world to her work in 1921, describing Mistral as an 'alma tremendamente apasionada, grande en todo, después de vaciar en unas cuantas poesías el dolor de su desolación íntima, ha llenado ese vacío con sus preocupaciones por la educación de los niños, la redención de los humildes y el destino de los pueblos hispánicos'. Her style, in verse as in prose, varies from the concise and classical to the vague and romantic, with lapses in grammar unusual in a writer so well-read. However these lapses only heighten those moments in which Mistral has caught the anguish of loneliness and dread. *Desolación* (New York, 1922; definitive edn., 1954) is her first collection: spontaneity and openness characterize its simple emotional appeal. *Ternura* (Madrid, 1924) consists of poems mostly for children drawn in many cases from the earlier book; thirty new poems were added for the second edition (Buenos Aires, 1945). *Tala* (Buenos Aires, 1938) is hence to be regarded as her second book, and it differs from her first in heightened artifice, and in concentrating on thought and calculation whereas *Desolación* was a work of overriding sentiment. *Lagar* (1954) was her last book. The *Obras completas* (Madrid, 1958; 2nd edn., 1966) have been supplemented by *Poema de Chile* (1967) and other works drawn from unpublished prose and verse notebooks.

The years 1922–38 were spent mostly in Europe, working with Mme Curie and Henri Bergson in the League of Nations. She worked after World War II in a number of U.S. universities, and spent her last years in the home of Doris Dana, whose bilingual edition of Mistral's *Selected poems* (Baltimore, Md., 1971) publishes an adequate cross-section of Mistral's verse, with her personal note of grief, and her cries against social injustice. The *Bibliografía de Gabriela Mistral* (1946) by Norberto Pinilla has now been supplemented by Martin C. Taylor's bibliography in his *Gabriela Mistral's religious sensibility* (Berkeley, Calif., 1968), pp. 162–78. Two works entitled *Homenaje a Gabriela Mistral* appeared shortly after her death, one in Montevideo (1958), and another, much more extensive, in Santiago (1957).

See Margot Arce de Vázquez, *Gabriela Mistral, the poet and her work* (New York, 1964), and Guillermo Rubilar, *Gabriela, maestra y poetisa rediviva* (1972).

Golden Age, see SIGLO DE ORO.

GÓMEZ CARRILLO, ENRIQUE, see GÓMEZ TIBLE, Enrique.

GÓMEZ DE AVELLANEDA, GERTRUDIS (1814–73), b. Puerto Príncipe. Cuban playwright, poet, and novelist. Her passionate life, during which she was twice widowed and experienced many stormy love affairs, has been the subject of several biographies, and has received much of the interest that would otherwise have been concentrated on her varied writings.

From 1836 she lived in Spain, apart from 1859–63, when she returned home and became a force in Cuban literature. With classical roots in the tradition of Quintana and Meléndez Valdés (qq.v.), Avellaneda emerged as a romantic playwright and poet. The religious side of her nature which almost led her into the convent is responsible for the *Devocionario poético* (1867).

The rest of her poetry can be found in the centenary *Obras* (4 vols., 1914–18), the most accessible recent selection being the *Poesías selectas* (Barcelona, 1966). Her best poem is often considered to be the sonnet 'Al partir', written on setting out for Spain.

She began her dramatic career with the historical plays *Alfonso Munio* and *El Príncipe de Viana* (both Madrid, 1844), and experimented with biblical themes, often in grandiloquent language not far removed from the Spanish translations of the Old Testament, in such works as *Saúl* (Madrid, 1849) and *Baltasar* (1858). Her romantic and social experiences gave her ample material for the comedies *Errores del corazón* and *La hija de las flores, o todos están locos* (both Madrid, 1852). The anthology *Teatro* appeared in 1965.

Avellaneda's novels included *Sab* (2 vols., 1841; new edn., Madrid, 1970), a romantic tale of Cuban slavery; *Dos mujeres* (1842), an attack on the institution of marriage; and the historical novel on Mexico, *Guatimocín* (4 vols., 1846).

See Edwin B. Williams, *The life and dramatic works of Gertrudis Gómez de Avellaneda* (Philadelphia, 1924); D. Figarola Caneda, *Gertrudis Gómez de Avellaneda* (1929); E. Cotarelo y Mori, *La Avellaneda y sus obras* (1930); Mercedes Ballesteros, *Vida de la Avellaneda* (Madrid, 1949); and Carmen Bravo Villasante, *Una vida romántica: La Avellaneda* (Barcelona, 1967).

GÓMEZ DE BAQUERO, EDUARDO (1866–1929), b. Madrid. Literary critic and reviewer, writing from 1904 as 'Andrenio'. His main importance is as a book reviewer on *El Imparcial,* succeeding 'Clarín' (q.v.) in this post. Like most Spanish reviewers, he tended to exaggerate the importance of the second-rate, and to avoid mentioning the third-rate altogether, rather than criticize a writer adversely. 'Andrenio' was the most influential regular critic of books in Spain during the first quarter of the present century, preferring the novel to other genres, and he defended his preference in such books as *Novelas y novelistas* (1918) and *El renacimiento de la novela en el siglo XIX* (1924). Other works which retain some interest today include *Pirandello y Compañía* (1928), *De Gallardo a Unamuno* (1926), and *Nacionalismo e hispanismo* (1928). His *Obras completas* (1929–30) appeared in 3 volumes.

See F. de Onís's introduction to A. Alonso, *Antología de ensayos españoles* (1936).

GÓMEZ DE HUERTA, JERÓNIMO (1568?–1643), b. Escalona, Toledo. Poet. After studying humanities at the University of Alcalá and medicine at Valladolid, Huerta translated the first part of Pliny's *Historia naturalis* (1599). While in MS., this work was brought to the notice of Philip II, who commissioned the rest, the whole being published together in 2 volumes (1624–9). Though Huerta also wrote *Problemas filosóficos,* he is known in Spain today for the reprint in vol. 36 of the BAE (1855) of his long poem *Florando de Castillo, lauro de Cavalleros* (Alcalá, 1588). Dismissed by Ticknor as 'a poor romance', the ambitious poem in 13 cantos of *ottava rima* tells how a Spanish knight descended from Hercules is roused from his idle and luxurious life by his great ancestor, and performs worthily in the end. Huerta includes in canto IX a version of the *Amantes de Teruel* (q.v.). Huerta became court physician to Philip IV.

GÓMEZ DE LA SERNA, RAMÓN (1888–1963), b. Madrid. Major Spanish writer in many genres; known affectionately as 'Ramón'. His Pombo *tertulia* ('literary gathering') was frequented by a wide variety of artists and literary people and particularly by the *avant-garde.* In 1936 he fled to Buenos Aires but (although totally uninterested in politics) suffered repercussions from Perón's downfall in 1955. He died in exile.

He published nearly 100 books, all characterized by an originality near to eccentricity.

As Ramón never claimed to have taught anyone anything, the biographies and other extended works seem in retrospect to have less significance than his *jeux d'esprit*, at best brilliantly witty, at worst merely whimsical, that make up his collections of essays and *greguerías* (q.v.). An interesting approach to Ramón is that of Gerardo Diego (q.v.), whose *Lope y Ramón* (1963) compares the fecundity and exuberance of the two in the light of Ramón's biography *Lope viviente* (Buenos Aires, 1954) a rewriting of his *Lope de Vega* (Buenos Aires, 1945). The best bibliography so far is that of Gaspar Gómez de la Serna in *Ramón* (1963).

Ramón produced numerous biographies, including *John Ruskin* (1918), *Oscar Wilde* (1921), *Azorín* (1923), *Goya* (1928), and *Gutiérrez Solana* (1943). His autobiography *Automoribundia* (Buenos Aires, 1948) is an extensive work, highly interesting and often extremely amusing. Its superiority to his novels is due to the fact that he finds himself more extraordinary than any of his invented characters and can thus sustain the reader's interest more easily. He described his life as that of 'a passer-by, an actor, an optimistic and impudent life, ambling towards death with the naïve happiness of one not going in that direction'.

The novels lack shape and consistency, but are full of ideas and imagination. Ramón delighted in the expressive power of Spanish, coining neologisms, refurbishing archaicisms, and using the fund of surrealism then fashionable. The 'major' novels as he himself described them, include *El doctor inverosímil* (1914), *La viuda blanca y negra* (1917), *El incongruente* and *El Gran Hotel* (both 1922), *La quinta de Palmyra*, *Cinelandia* and *El chalet de las rosas* (1923), *El torero Caracho* (1926), and *La mujer de ámbar* (1927).

His plays were perhaps the least successful of his works because he excelled in the monologue; his best works were hastily-written, often out-standingly humorous shorter essays and sketches. These included *El rastro* (1915), *El circo*, *Senos* (both 1917), *Disparates* (1921), *Gollerías* (1926), and *Los muertos y las muertas* (1922; revised and reissued with *Otras fantasmagorías* in 1935).

The *Obras completas* (1956–) are still in progress.

The best general study on Ramón is Rodolfo Cardona's *Ramón* (New York, 1957), which should be supplemented by the life written by his widow, Luisa Sofovich, *Ramón Gómez de la Serna* (Buenos Aires, 1962) and the work by Gaspar Gómez de la Serna mentioned above. In English there is a useful summary by Rita Mazzetti Gardiol, *Ramón Gómez de la Serna* (New York, 1974). José Camón Aznar, *Ramón Gómez de la Serna en sus obras* (1972) is uneven, but indispensable for its references to out of the way material.

GÓMEZ HERMOSILLA, JOSÉ MAMERTO (1771–1837), b. Madrid. Grammarian and critic. Professor of Greek and Rhetoric in the schools of San Isidro, Madrid. He translated the *Iliad* into mediocre verse (1831), and wrote several grammars, including *Principios de gramática general* (1835).

But his reputation is chiefly that of a rigidly neoclassical literary dictator who 'desestimaba y proscribía lo más bello y espontáneo del arte nacional', as Menéndez y Pelayo wrote in *Historia de las ideas estéticas en España*. An *afrancesado* (q.v.), like his friend Leandro Fernández de Moratín (q.v.), he spent the years 1814–20 as a political exile in France, experiences he described in *El jacobinismo y los jacobinos* (1823). He confused perfection with the lack of super-ficial defects in his *Arte de hablar en prosa y en verso* (2 vols., Madrid, 1826; enlarged edn., 2 vols. V. Salvá, Paris, 1842).

Yet his worst errors of judgment were reserved for his *Juicio crítico de los principales poetas españoles de la última era* (2 vols., Paris, 1840) in which he denigrated Meléndez Valdés (q.v.) without attempting to present a balanced opinion, and flattered those responsible for literary decorum in the degree of their adherence to neoclassical ideas. Vol. 1 of the *Juicio crítico* is divided between Leandro Fernández de Moratín and Meléndez Valdés. Vol. 2 deals with the Conde de Noroña, Jovellanos, Álvarez de Cienfuegos, J. M. Roldán, F. de Castro, M. de Arjona, and F. Sánchez Barbero.

GÓMEZ MORENO, MANUEL (1870–1950?), b. Granada. Historian and art historian. He taught at the Centro de Estudios Históricos and the Universidad Central in Madrid and was perhaps best known as a teacher. A member of the academies of language, history, and fine arts, he produced a number of studies for the *Catálogo monumental de España*, including those on Ávila, his native Granada, and Zamora. He edited Hurtado de Mendoza's *Guerra de Granada* (1948), and a number of medieval chronicles, including *Introducción a la Historia Silense con versión castellana de la misma y de la crónica de Sampiro* (1921) and *Las primeras crónicas de la Reconquista: el ciclo de Alfonso III* (1932).

GÓMEZ TIBLE, ENRIQUE (1873–1927), b. Guatemala City. Journalist, critic, and novelist who wrote under the pseudonym 'Enrique Gómez Carrillo'. After failing at diverse studies, he joined *El Imparcial* as a reporter in 1889. When Rubén Darío (q.v.) arrived in Guatemala the following year he hired Gómez Carrillo for his new *Correo de la Tarde*. In 1891 he went to Madrid, editing the *Diccionario Enciclopédico Garnier* and in 1898 went to Paris as correspondent for *El Liberal*, and there met Verlaine, Leconte de Lisle, and other writers who were to influence him throughout his prolific career. His *Obras completas* (1919–26) fill twenty-seven volumes, the most successful being the travel books: *De Marsella a Tokio* (Paris, 1906), *La Grecia eterna* (Madrid, 1906), *La Rusia actual* (Barcelona, 1906), *El Japán heroico y galante* (Madrid, 1912), and *El encanto de Buenos Aires* (Madrid, 1914). His novels were less successful, being derivative and unoriginal, and much inspired by the work of Pierre Louÿs, Anatole France, and Flaubert rather than from life, but the autobiography (*Treinta años de mi vida*, 3 vols.) is of great interest.

GÓNGORA Y ARGOTE, LUIS DE (1561–1627), b. Cordova. Major poet. The son of a notable bibliophile, Góngora came from a cultured home and studied at Salamanca, where he also gambled and whored to such an extent that he left with no degree but a large number of debts. On his return to Cordova he obtained an ecclesiastical benefice through his father's influence. When accused before the bishop in 1589 of gambling, attending theatres and bull-fights, and not singing in the choir, he responded that all was true, but that he could not sing in the choir because he was placed between a prebendary who sang very loudly and continuously and a deaf man who did not know when to stop. Possibly to get rid of an unruly member, the cathedral chapter sent him on missions to various parts of Spain which he recalls in many pleasing sonnets. Anxious to shine at the court of Madrid where Lope was gaining increasing favour, Góngora finally became chaplain to Philip III at the instance of his patron the Duke of Lerma, who was repaid with a fine panegyric.

Góngora became celebrated for twelve ballads in Pedro de Moncayo's anthology *Flor de romances nuevos* (Huesca, 1589) and sonnets and *canciones* in *Flores de poetas ilustres* (1605) by Pedro Espinosa. During his stay in Madrid his animosity was directed especially against Lope de Vega, whom he defeated in angry satires; and against Quevedo, who defeated him. It was in 1609, when the *Polifemo* and *Soledades* were already circulating in manuscript, that he felt the beginnings of premature arteriosclerosis, but he survived until 1627, when struck down by apoplexy as he was preparing for the publication of his complete works. This was *Obras en verso del Homero español, que recogió Iuan López de Vicuña* (1627), improved by *Todas las Obras . . . recogidas por Gonzalo de Hozes y Córdoua* (1633).

The Aguilar *Obras completas* (1932) by J. and I. Millé y Jiménez is usually kept in print and revised. The *Obras poéticas* (ed. by R. Foulché-Delbosc, 3 vols., New York, 1921) was reprinted in 1970.

His predominant themes are the mutability of human fortune and the permanence and loveliness of nature. His sonnet 'Mientras por competir con tu belleza' (1582) transforms Ausonius' 'collige, virgo, rosas' theme not into the warm and sunny Renaissance world of Garcilaso's 'En tanto que de rosa y azucena' but into the baroque darkness of the fear of death. On the other hand his other verses (such as the *romance* 'Mozuelas las de mi barrio') urge us to be merry and enjoy life while we can.

Among his preferred genres were the pastoral, satirical, amorous, and heroic, but the religious poem is comparatively scarce.

Góngora composed in a number of metres: the *silva*, the sonnet, the *romance*, and the *letrilla*, among others. Many of the *romances* and *letrillas* are simple in language and content, but his most characteristic works are written in a *culto* style abounding in Latinisms and Latin constructions. Like most Golden Age writers, Góngora did not aim to be original, but showed his contemporaries how to create a Latinate poetry for his time and achieved his aim admirably, goading Quevedo to his famous parodic sonnet 'Quien quisiere ser culto en solo un día . . .' *Gongorismo* as a term of abuse has come to denote affected rhetoric with useless adornment; but at his most typical he strains for economy and the pictorial phrase—that *admiratio* or surprise caused by a striking metaphor and inventive neologisms.

He wrote 166 known sonnets and there are a further 62 attributed to him without certainty; 121 known *letrillas* and 25 attributed to him; 94 known ballads and 18 attributed; 32 miscellaneous compositions usually referred to as *Otras composiciones de arte mayor*; the plays *Las firmezas de Isabela* and *El doctor Carlino* of scanty significance; and the three long poems: *El Polifemo, comentado por García de Salzedo Coronel* (1629; ed. Dámaso Alonso, 1960, and greatly revised 3rd edn., 3 vols., 1967); *Soledades, comentadas por García de Salzedo Coronel* (n.d. but 1636; ed. Dámaso Alonso, 1927, provoking an international revaluation of Góngora on the tercentenary of his death, 3rd edn., 1956); and the *Panegírico al duque de Lerma* (1617), an admittedly unrewarding, dense, and obscure eulogy of 79 stanzas totalling 632 lines of *octavas reales*.

La fábula de Polifemo y Galatea (q.v., 1613) consists of 504 hendecasyllables in *octavas reales* on the familiar theme of Acis, Galatea, and the vengeance of Polyphemus. In a pageant of colour, music and imagery which was not to be recaptured until the time of García Lorca (q.v.), Góngora creates a lyrical and mythological world inspired indirectly by Ovid and directly by Carrillo y Sotomayor (q.v.).

Góngora's principal fame rests on the incomplete *Soledades* (q.v.). Of the proposed poem in four parts he completed only the 37 lines of the dedication to the Duke of Béjar, the whole

1,091-line *Soledad primera*, and 979 lines of the unfinished *Soledad segunda*.

The first part concerns a shipwrecked youth who is tossed by the waves on to a deserted beach. He climbs up a mountain and eventually reaches a hut where he is tended by the local people. Two young people are being married: the youth attends the various festivities up to the time of the couple's retiring for the night. The second part shows the youth among a seafishing community, listening to tales of their work and taking part in it. However, Góngora's style could hardly be more distant in style from the simple lives of his protagonists: the complexity of imagery and metaphor is extreme. Colour and texture are all, as an enumeration of the nouns soon reveals: *oro*, *plata*, *cristal*, *diamante*, *marfil*, *mármol*, and so forth. A girl's flesh is not 'like a rose' (rósea) but 'a rose' (rosa). An accumulation of such densely-connotatory nouns eventually becomes somewhat tedious for the modern reader, but it must be admitted that the technique in moderation can only be viewed positively as a contribution to the resources of the poet. The controversy which raged at these poems even during Góngora's lifetime was summarized though subjectively—by an opponent—in Menéndez y Pelayo's *Historia de las ideas estéticas*, vol. 2, pp. 324-325.

Góngora is unquestionably one of the greatest Castilian writers of ballads (see *Romances*, ed. J. M. de Cossío, 1927) and sonnets (see *Sonetos*, ed. B. Ciplijauskaité, 1968), though his *letrillas* fall well below the level of Quevedo's, and his *canciones* below Lope's.

There are fine English versions of the *Soledades* (with facing text) by E. M. Wilson: *The Solitudes of Don Luis de Góngora* (Cambridge, 1965).

See M. Artigas, *Don Luis de Góngora y Argote: biografía y estudio crítico* (1925); E. J. Gates, *Documentos gongorinos* (Mexico City, 1950); Dámaso Alonso's works, especially *Estudios y ensayos gongorinos* (1955, 2nd edn., 1961), *La lengua poética de Góngora* (1935; 3rd edn., 1961), and *Para la biografía de Góngora* (1962); W. Pabst, *La creación gongorina en los poemas 'Polifemo' y 'Soledades'* (*Anejo* 80, 1966, to *Revista de Filología Española*); R. Jammes, *Études sur l'oeuvre poétique de Góngora* (Bordeaux, 1967); and E. Orozco Díaz (ed.), *En torno a las 'Soledades' de Góngora* (1969), a collection of 17th-c. criticism.

Gongorismo, a literary movement and style virtually synonymous with *Culteranismo* (q.v.) and named after Luis de Góngora y Argote (q.v.).

GONZÁLEZ, ÁNGEL (1925–), b. Oviedo. Poet. His first books were well received: *Áspero mundo* (1955), *Sin esperanza, con convencimiento*

(Barcelona, 1961), *Grado elemental* (Paris, 1962), and *Palabra sobre palabra* (1965). In brevity which by no means excludes the genial touch, the anti-Romantic González 'canta el dolor o la desesperanza, la gris manquedad de la frustración o la tristeza irremediable del fracaso de los sueños', in the words of Díaz-Plaja.

In a later collection, *Tratado de urbanismo* (1967), the first section, on city life, shows a new sense of anguish mingled with bitter irony. He has since published *Breves acotaciones para una biografía* (Las Palmas, 1971).

See E. Alarcos Llorach, *Ángel González, poeta* (Oviedo, 1969); and José Olivio Jiménez, *Diez años de poesía española, 1960-1970* (1972), pp. 281-304.

GONZÁLEZ, Fray DIEGO TADEO (1733–94), b. Ciudad Rodrigo. Poet. Augustinian prior of the convents of Salamanca, Pamplona, and Madrid. A *tertulia* ('literary club') held in his cell in Salamanca was attended not only by his close friend and disciple Juan Fernández de Rojas (who luckily did not carry out his vow to burn Fray Diego's MSS. on the latter's death) but also by the young Meléndez Valdés and Forner (qq.v.).

His importance was in his influential rejection of the baroque tradition and return to the manner of his admired Fray Luis de León. He wrote presumably platonic eclogues to ladies whom one is supposed to believe mythical shepherdesses, though the 'Mirta' addressed in the burlesque 'El murciélago alevoso' has been supposedly identified. This work is an invective against a bat that dared to distract the mistress of 'Delio' (Fray Diego) while she was writing. Of his didactic work on *Las edades*, only book one (*La niñez*) was published; no others are recorded to have been written.

Some critics believe Fray Diego's best work to be a translation of the Eighth Psalm, and others the *Exposición de Job*. The charming *Llanto de Delio y profecía de Manzanares* is at its best worthy of Luis de León.

The first collection of his poems was made in 1796; his works are also available in vol. 61 (1869) of the BAE. L. Verger edited 'El murciélago alevoso' in *Revue Hispanique*, vol. 39 (1917), pp. 296-301. Previously-unpublished poems and an essay on Fray Diego by Fray E. Esteban appeared in *La Ciudad de Dios* (El Escorial), vol. 25 (1891), pp. 612-7.

See L. Monguió, 'Fray Diego Tadeo González and Spanish taste in the 18th century' in *Romanic Review* (New York), vol. 52 (1961), pp. 241-260.

GONZÁLEZ, ESTEBAN. Hero of the novel *La vida i hechos del Estevanillo González, Hombre de* *buen humor. Compuesto por él mesmo* (Antwerp, 1646), a genuine autobiography in the view of W. K. Jones (*Revue Hispanique*, vol. 77, 1929, pp. 201–45), and of Millé Jiménez who edited the 3rd edition (1655) for Clásicos Castellanos (2 vols., 1946). In the words of A. A. Parker, the *Guzmán de Alfarache* of Alemán (qq.v.), and *Estebanillo González* 'are not only the first and the last [picaresque novels], they are also the two extremes—the one, man's anguished awareness of his need for redemption; the other, man's frivolous insensitiveness to his own degradation' (*Literature and the delinquent*, Edinburgh, 1967, p. 78).

The backcloth to the misadventures of González is the Thirty Years' War. He wanders all over Europe, beginning in Rome and travelling with the Spanish armies in Germany and Flanders, where he robs, drinks, and avoids fighting with callous cynicism. He becomes jester first to Ottavio Piccolomini, Duke of Amalfi, and later to the Governor of the Low Countries. The book is characterized by a mass of ill-assorted episodes often repetitive and relying on single jokes rather than a sense of humour. The accuracy with which places and contemporary persons and events are treated makes it likely that the events, lightly fictionalized, reflect actual experiences of the author, even if his real name was not Esteban González.

A. Carreira and J. A. Cid have produced (1971) the first modern edition based on the *editio princeps*, with interesting views on the author's narrative craft.

GONZÁLEZ, Joaquín V. (1863–1923), b. Nonogasta, La Rioja. Argentinian statesman, writer, and founder of the Universidad de la Plata. His collected works were published in 25 volumes by decree in 1935. *Mis montañas* (1893) described his local Famatina range, its landscapes and festivals, its daily life, and important events. *El juicio del siglo* (1910) was a history written on the centenary of the May Revolution.

He translated the 100 poems of Kabir from the English of Rabindranath Tagore and made available *The Rubáiyát* of Omar Khayyám from the English imitation by Edward FitzGerald.

GONZÁLEZ, Juan Natalicio (1897–1966), b. Villarrica. Paraguayan modernist poet and essayist. A disciple of Juan E. O'Leary (q.v.), González found vital inspiration in the Guaraní poetic and folk tradition, creating the notable *Cuentos y parábolas* (1922) inspired by Guaraní legends, and three series (two in Asunción and one later in Buenos Aires) of the magazine *Guarania*, first founded in 1920. He travelled widely, producing *Baladas guaraníes* (1925) in Paris and the essays: *El Paraguay eterno* (1936),

Proceso y formación de la cultura paraguaya (1938), and *El paraguayo y la lucha por su expresión* (1945). Briefly President of the Republic 1948–9, he was removed by his own supporters and found himself in exile in Mexico, where he produced a novel of social protest against the exploitation of the peasants' land, *La raiz errante* (1953), and two books of poetry: *Motivos de la tierra escarlata* (1952), and *Elegías de Tenochtitlán* (1953).

GONZÁLEZ, Otto-Raúl (1921–), b. Guatemala City. Guatemalan poet and critic of the so-called Generation of 1940. His books of poetry are *Voz y voto del geranio* (Guatemala City, 1943), *A fuego lento* (Mexico City, 1946), *Sombras era* (Mexico City, 1948), *Viento claro* (Guatemala City, 1953), *El bosque* (Quito, 1955), and *El maíz y la noche* (Mexico City, 1959).

González contributed *Panorama de la literatura guatemalteca* to Montezuma de Carvalho's *Panorama das literaturas das Americas* (vol. III, pp. 1017–71) and translated Stephen Spender's poetry into Spanish as *Joven camarada* (Mexico City, 1946). He has long resided in Mexico.

González, Poema de Fernán, see FERNÁN GONZÁLEZ, Poema de.

GONZÁLEZ-ALLER, Faustino (1926?–), b. Gijón. Spanish novelist and playwright who studied law at Salamanca University and journalism at Madrid University before practising law in Madrid for two years. He has worked in Cuba for 2 years as a television news broadcaster and feature writer, and was Chief of the Radio and TV section of the U.N. Department of Information (Iberia/Latin-American Office), 1958–72. He now lives in the U.S.A.

With Armando Sánchez Ocano, González-Aller won the Premio Lope de Vega of 1950 for his play *La noche no se acaba*. The play *Menta* was produced in 1953. He is best known for his novels *Orosia* and *Niña Huanca* (the latter translated by M. S. Peden, New York and London, 1977).

Niña Huanca is dominated by Colonel Félix Arruza, who manipulates a succession of generals and presidents in an unnamed Central-American state bordering Mexico and Belize. The hero is his son, Miguel Ángel Matalax Yanama, and the colonel's wife is Niña Huanca, a beautiful Indian sea-captain. Eventually Arruza is exiled, promises of immediate reform are broken, and the old division remains between 'those who have the right to pluck the low-hanging mangoes' and those who have not.

Technically, *Niña Huanca* is diverse in style and language: scraps of Nahuatl and Dutch, Cantonese and Portuguese are interspersed in a vigorous Castilian owing part of its inventiveness (of matter as well as manner) to the Colombian

Gabriel García Márquez (q.v.). González-Aller is pessimistic about the ability of the ruled to become more demanding, or the rulers to become more generous.

GONZÁLEZ ANAYA, Salvador (1879–1955), b. Málaga. Poet, novelist, and the official historian of Málaga. His memorable novels and *cuadros de costumbres* of his native region worthily continue the tradition established by Estébanez Calderón (q.v.). Beginning as a regional poet in *Cantos sin eco* (1899) and *Medallones* (1900), he quickly made a reputation with his fiction: *Rebelión* (1905); *La sangre de Abel* (1915); *El castillo de vas y no volverás* (1921); *Las brujas de la ilusión* (1923); *Nido de cigüeñas* (1927), set in Écija; *La oración de la tarde* (1929), set in Granada; *Nido real de gavilanes* (1931), set in Baeza; *Los naranjos de la Mezquita* (1933), set in Cordova; *Luna de plata* (1942); and *Luna de sangre* (1944).

He was elected to the Real Academia Española in 1948, the year in which his *Obras completas* appeared. The best bibliography of González Anaya is in J. de Entrambasaguas, *Las mejores novelas contemporáneas, 1930–1934* (Barcelona, 1961), pp. 499–524.

GONZÁLEZ ARRILI, Bernardo (1892–), b. Buenos Aires. Argentinian novelist, short-story writer, and journalist, who became director of *Revista Americana* in 1917. *Mangangá: cuentos criollos* (1927) was a collection of regional stories about the difficulties of scraping a livelihood, as were his next stories in *El pobre afán de vivir* (1928).

He writes with outstanding knowledge of conditions in the far north of Argentina in *La Venus calchaquí*, of the struggle of the working classes of Barracas in *Los charcos rojos*; of politics, which he satirizes, in *Protasio Lucero* (1919); and of religious devotion in *La Virgen de Luján*. He has also written the lives of Sarmiento and Rufino de Elizalde, a minister of Mitre; and an autobiography: *Calle Corrientes entre Esmeraldas y Suipacha* (1952).

González Arrili collaborated with Enzo Aloisi in *Los afincaos: drama bárbaro*, about a feudal landlord. *La invasión de los herejes* is a novel of the colonial past.

GONZÁLEZ DE CLAVIJO, Ruy (d. 1412). The earliest traveller from Spain to reach the Far East and describe it, González de Clavijo is a conscientious chronicler of his three-year journey to and from Samarkand, via Constantinople, Trebizond, and Tehran. Argote y Molina published Clavijo's *Historia del Gran Tamorlán* (Seville, 1582). A much better edition is the 2nd of 1782, while the most useful is also the most

recent: *Embajada a Tamorlán* (ed. F. López Estrada, 1943, in Nueva Colección de Libros Raros y Curiosos), a title more appropriate to the book's subject. The first ambassadors of Henry III of Castile to Tamerlane and Bayazit chanced to be present at the great, decisive battles between these potentates, and Tamerlane returned Henry's sign of respect with some spoils of his victory, including two lovely captives (who are described in the Spanish verse of the period). Henry was gratified by Tamerlane's reciprocation of respect, returning it with a further embassy described by Clavijo, one of his three envoys, from May 1403 to May 1406.

GONZÁLEZ DE ESLAVA, Hernán (1534–1601?), b. Spain. Hispano-Mexican playwright and poet. He reached Mexico in 1559, and produced a number of commissioned dramas for special religious and state occasions, none of much literary value, but interesting for their antiquity. Several of his sixteen colloquies were published in 1610, but even the most interesting of them, such as the curious allegorical *Coloquio del Conde de la Coruña* written in 1580 for the arrival of the Count from Spain, lack all but occasional merit. J. R. Garcidueñas has edited González de Eslava's *Coloquios espirituales y sacramentales* (2 vols., 1958). He also wrote eight preludes, four interludes, and some poetry, all inhibited by the demands of the Inquisition.

See A. Alonso, *Biografía de Fernán González de Eslava* in *Revista de Filología Hispánica*, vol. 2, 1940; and J. J. Arrom, *El teatro de Hispanoamérica en la época colonial* (Havana, 1956).

GONZÁLEZ DE MENDOZA, Juan (1545–1618). Author of the first substantial book on China in Spanish, *Historia de las cosas más notables ritos y costumbres del Gran Reyno de la China* (Rome, 1585; 2nd edn., Valencia, 1585).

GONZÁLEZ DE SALAS, José Antonio (1588–1651), b. Madrid. Humanist. One of the most significant preceptors of his time, Salas composed commentaries on Pliny the Elder, Petronius, Pomponius Mela, and other classical authors, but is best remembered for his neoclassical *Nueva idea de la tragedia antigua . . .* (1633), reissued with biographical and critical notes by Cerdá y Rico (2 vols.) in 1778. Its effect was enhanced by the publication seven years earlier of the first recorded translation into Castilian of Aristotle's *Poetics* (1626), applauded in general terms by Salas.

In the *Nueva idea* Salas translated from the *Trojanae* of Seneca; Quevedo greatly admired these versions and praised Salas in *El Parnaso español, monte en dos cumbres dividido* (1648).

GONZÁLEZ GARCÉS, MIGUEL (1916–), b. Corunna. Galician poet. He worked as a librarian in his native city, and produced a useful anthology, *Poesía gallega contemporánea* (Barcelona, 1974), in which he is well represented.

His earlier books were all in Castilian: *Isla de dos* (1953; 2nd edn., 1964), *Poema del imposible sosiego* (Corunna, 1954), *Siete canciones* (Corunna, 1954), *El libro y el verso* (Corunna, 1958), *Alrededor del mar* (1961), and *El cuervo en la ventana* (Vigo, 1967). He began to publish Galician poems in middle age: *Bailada dos anxos* (Vigo, 1961) and *Nas faíscas do soño* (Vigo, 1972).

Whereas the Castilian verse is unremarkable, the Galician stems directly from the unsophisticated folk song of the Galician countryside the poet knows so well, and achieves beauty and simplicity within its limited scope.

GONZÁLEZ LANUZA, EDUARDO (1900–), b. Santander. He has lived in Argentina since early childhood. Poet, critic, and journalist, he has contributed to *Sur* and the daily *Nación*. His *Prismas* (1924) were written in the so-called *martinfierrista* manner, in the shadow of Gómez de la Serna (q.v.). His *conceptismo* has become less marked with the years, from *La degollación de los inocentes* (1938) and *Puñado de cantares* (1940) to *Transitable cristal* (1943) and the *Oda a la alegría* (1949). Later collections include *Retablos de Navidad y de la Pasión* (1953) and *Cuando ayer era mañana* (1954). He has become independent of all schools, and his piety is closely related to the flow of life rather than to Roman Catholic orthodoxy.

González Lanuza's *Aquelarre* (1928) is a book of short stories reacting against the realist mode then popular. His plays are *El bastón del señor Polichinela* (1935) and *Ni siquiera el diluvio* (1939).

GONZÁLEZ MARTÍNEZ, ENRIQUE (1871–1952), b. Guadalajara, Jalisco. Mexican poet, physician, and diplomat whose celebrated answer to the modernism of Darío occurs in his sonnet: 'Tuércele el cuello al cisne de engañoso plumaje...'; his own symbol is the owl of wisdom against the swan of show and vanity. He practised medicine and worked as a political secretary in the provinces until 1911, then joined other young intellectuals in the Ateneo de la Juventud in Mexico City and became ambassador to Spain, Argentina, and Chile. His two-volume autobiography is *El hombre del búho* (1944) and *La apacible locura* (1951).

His poetry reacts against the surface glitter of Darío's group, becoming reflective, abstract, and serious. His themes are suffering, love, death, and above all optimism in the face of life's

difficulties. His short stories and essays are of relatively little account: what matters is a steadily-improving body of verse: *Preludios* (Mazatlán, 1903), *Lirismos* (Mocorito, 1907), *Silenter* (Mocorito, 1909), *Los senderos ocultos* (Mocorito, 1911), *La muerte del cisne* (1915), *La hora inútil* (1916; merely a selection from his first two books), *El libro de la fuerza, de la bondad y del ensueño* (1917), *Parábolas y otros poemas* (1918), *La palabra del viento* (1921), *El romero alucinado* (Buenos Aires, 1923), *Las señales furtivas* (Madrid, 1925), *Poemas de ayer y de hoy* (1926), *Poemas truncos* (1935), *Ausencia y canto* (1937), *El diluvio de fuego* (1938), *Poemas* (1940), *Segundo despertar y otros poemas* (1945), *Vilano al viento* (1948), *Babel* (1949), and *El nuevo Narciso y otros poemas* (1952). The best edition of his *Obras completas* is that of 1971.

See José Luis Martínez and others, *La obra de Enrique González Martínez* (1951), consisting of 62 critical and biographical studies; José M. Topete, *El mundo poético de Enrique González Martínez* (Guadalajara, Mexico, 1967); and John S. Brushwood, *Enrique González Martínez* (New York, 1969).

GONZÁLEZ PRADA, MANUEL (1848–1918), b. Lima. Peruvian reformer and poet. A link between the post-Romantics and the modernists, he began by translating Schiller and Heine, and reading German philosophers of the Enlightenment, particularly Hegel, Schopenhauer, and Nietzsche, and positivists, including Comte and Herbert Spencer, differing from them only in placing liberty and equality above order and hierarchy, in common with Leslie Stephen. He attacked the notion of the racial inferiority of the Indian and attacked Spanish colonialism and the power of the Church. Three of his collections appeared in his lifetime: *Minúsculas* (1901); *Presbiterianas* (1909), which is mainly anticlerical in tone; and the modernist *Exóticas* (1911). Reluctant to publish, González Prada was published by his son Alfredo (1891–1943): *Trozos de vida* (1933), *Baladas peruanas* (1935), *Grafitos* (1937), *Libertarias* (1938), *Baladas* (1939), and *Adoración* (1946).

His literary and political group originally known as the Círculo Literario developed into the purely political National Union Party in 1891, and he founded the magazine *Germinal*. His party failed to achieve power, however, and González Prada (whose most famous phrase was 'Los viejos a la tumba, los jóvenes a la obra') left for Europe, returning in 1898 to campaign against corruption and nepotism. He was Director of the National Library 1912–18, and continued to write socio-political journalism of a high calibre, seeking clarity and honesty in prose as much as in life and philosophy. He took the anarchists Proudhon and Kropotkin as his masters, and his memorable prose writings in many ways last better than his rather conventional modernist verse: *Páginas libres* (Paris, 1894), *Horas de lucha* on the war against Chile (1908), *Bajo el oprobio* (1933), *Anarquía* (1936), *Nuevas páginas libres* (1937), and *El tonel de Diógenes* (1945).

See L. A. Sánchez, *Don Manuel* (Santiago de Chile, 1930); Jorge Mañach and others, *Manuel González Prada: vida y obra* (New York, 1938); Robert G. Mead, *González Prada, el pensador y el prosista* (New York, 1958); and H. García Salvattecci, *El pensamiento de González Prada* (n.d. [1973?]).

GONZÁLEZ RUANO, César (1902–65). b. Madrid. Novelist, poet, and biographer. He has been a journalist from 1925 on a variety of papers, such as *ABC, Informaciones, Heraldo de Madrid,* and *La Época,* and has worked as foreign correspondent in a number of European capitals. His poetry has appeared as *Poesía, 1924–44* (1944), and he has published a number of biographical sketches, including *Siluetas de escritores contemporáneos* (1949) and *La memoria veranea* (1960).

His fiction up to 1946 has been forgotten, but since that date González Ruano acquired sufficient diversity of tone and style to develop into an artist of some interest, not so much in the transitional *Imitación del amor* (1947) as in the short novel *Ni César ni nada* (1951) in which the conscience is carefully examined by the usual sole protagonist and introspection becomes almost equally rewarding for the reader. Books reflecting this new maturity were *Los oscuros dominios* (1953), *Cita con el pasado* (1954), *Humillación* (1959), and *A todo el mundo no le gusta el amarillo* (1961), a collection containing the title story, 'La carta', and 'La canción del recuerdo'.

See M. Gómez Santos, *César González Ruano* (Barcelona, 1958).

GONZÁLEZ RUCAVADO, Claudio (1865–1925), b. San José, Costa Rica. Novelist, lawyer, and politician, who became a Minister in the Republican government of 1916. With García Monge and González Zeledón (qq.v.), he was one of the first Costa Ricans to write realistic fiction with a local setting. His first novel was *El hijo de un gamonal* (1901), followed by the *costumbrismo* of *Escenas costarricenses* (1906) and *Egoísmo* (1914).

He wrote essays on ethics in politics and education: *Ensayo sobre moral y política* (1911), and a *Proyecto de reforma constitucional: creación del poder docente del estado* (1912).

GONZÁLEZ SUÁREZ, Federico (1844–1917), b. Quito. Ecuadorian priest, historian, and religious controversialist, whose classic *Historia general de la República del Ecuador* (7 vols. in 8, 1890–1903) with an *Atlas arqueológico* (1892) was reprinted in 1931 (7 vols. and atlas).

He openly criticized ecclesiastical abuses; the scandal caused by his revelations reached Rome, where his cause was vindicated. González's *Estudios literarios* appeared in several volumes between 1896 and 1912.

GONZÁLEZ VERA, José Santos (1897–1970), b. San Francisco del Monte. Chilean novelist and short-story writer who took a multitude of jobs, partly to obtain material for his fiction. *Vidas mínimas: novelas breves* (1923) is a half-ironic, half-sympathetic account of tenement life, reflecting the author's own childhood experiences. *Alhué: estampas de una aldea* (1928) is also autobiographical, with an apparently increasing debt to Azorín (q.v.), and centres on village life. *Cuando era muchacho* (1951), explicitly autobiographical, won for its author the 1950 National Prize for Literature and is considered González Vera's best book. *Eutropelia, honesta recreación* (1955) consists of penetrating essays on Latin American writers, among them Manuel Rojas. His subsequent books include *Algunos* (1959) and the short stories *La copia y otros originales* (1961).

See Ester Ljungstedt, *Un prosista chileno: José Santos González Vera* (1970).

GONZÁLEZ ZELEDÓN, Manuel (1864–1936), b. San José. Costa Rican *costumbrista* better known as 'Magón', who began his literary career by contributing the first column on Costa Rican life and manners to *La Patria,* a magazine edited by his cousin Aquileo Echeverría (q.v.). After periods as vice-consul in Bogotá and consul in New York he became ambassador in Washington (1932–36), dying only a few days after his return to San José. His subject is the San José of 1900, and his best short novel is *La propia* (1909), a masterpiece of realism, though rather weakly constructed, and the best example of the use of *costarriqueñismos.* His influence can be seen in the work of such *costumbristas* as Carlos Gagini (q.v.), Manuel de Jesús Jiménez (1854–1916), and Claudio González Rucavado (q.v.).

GONZALO DE CÓRDOBA, see Córdoba, Gonzalo Fernández de.

GOROSTIZA, Carlos (1920–). Argentinian playwright whose work satirizes with humour and occasionally with bleak savagery the contemporary human situation in Buenos Aires. *El puente* (1949) introduces his colloquial style, which has been developed and sharpened in the later plays *Marta Ferrari* (1954), *El reloj de Baltasar* (1956), his most complex achievement *El pan de la locura* (1958), *Los prójimos* (1966) on the cruel indifference of ordinary people, and *¿A qué jugamos?* (1968).

GOROSTIZA, José (1901–   ), b. Villahermosa, Tabasco. Mexican poet who was the most important of the Contemporáneos group. His busy life as a diplomat has limited his work to three books, and the two translations: Simon Gantillon's *Maya* (1930) and *La conversation* by André Maurois (1931, as *La conversación*).

His youthful *Canciones para cantar en las barcas* (1925) show delicacy and purity, with an impeccable sense of style and form. They have nothing in common with the brooding nihilism of the metaphysical poem *Muerte sin fin* (1939), elaborate in the tradition of Valéry and Góngora. Gorostiza, whose complete *Poesía* appeared first in 1964, and augmented in 1971, has been aptly called 'the poet of the intelligence' for his subtlety and complexity. The collected *Prosa* appeared in 1969.

See Ramón Xirau, *Tres poetas de la soledad* (1955); P. Debicki, *La poesía de José Gorostiza* (1962); and M. S. Rubin, *Una poética moderna: 'Muerte sin fin' de José Gorostiza* (1966).

GOROSTIZA, Manuel Eduardo de (1789–1851), b. Veracruz. Mexican playwright of Spanish parentage whose plays (with only one exception) were first performed in Madrid, where the family went in 1794. After active military service he entered politics as an orator at the notorious Fontana de Oro (q.v.) and was exiled in 1821 with Martínez de la Rosa, the Duque de Rivas, and other liberals. He joined the Mexican diplomatic service and in 1836 was appointed ambassador to the U.S.A.; his busy public life led to the virtual exclusion of literature in his latter years. He reworked the still-unpublished 'Emilia Galotti' of Lessing, the Calderón play *Bien vengas mal si vienes solo*, and the Rojas play *Lo que son mujeres*, but his six original plays, which place him in the tradition which runs from L. Fernández de Moratín to Bretón de los Herreros (qq.v.), comprise *Indulgencia para todos* (Madrid, 1818), *Las costumbres de antaño* (Madrid, 1819), *Tal para cual o las mujeres y los hombres* (Madrid, 1820), *Don Dieguito* (Madrid, 1820), *Contigo, pan y cebolla* (London, 1833), and *Don Bonifacio*, first published in the last vol. of the *Obras* (4 vols., 1889–1902) in the Biblioteca de Autores Mexicanos series.

His contribution to the Moratinian tradition was the widening of the range of metres used, the

agility of his dialogue, the accuracy of his portrayal of manners and character, and his excellent wit.

See María Esperanza Aguilar M., *Estudio biobibliográfico de don Manuel Eduardo de Gorostiza* (1932); and Armando María de Campos, *Manuel Eduardo de Gorostiza: su vida, su obra* (1959).

GORRITI, Juana Manuela (1818–92), b. Horcones, Salta. Daughter of the Argentinian independence fighter Dr José Ignacio Gorriti; a novelist of mediocre quality who married the President of Bolivia, Manuel Isidoro Belzú, but was divorced by him shortly thereafter. She spent much of her life in Lima, where she held regular literary evenings and ran a school. Riva Agüero detested Gorriti's romantic fiction: 'son sus obras de las más tediosas, afectadas y tontas que produjo la escuela romántica'.

Her novels include *El ángel caído* and *El pozo de Yocci*, the latter part of *Panoramas de la vida* (1876). *Sueños y realidades* (1865) has the *leyenda El tesoro de los Incas*. Perhaps her autobiographical works are those which are best remembered: *El mundo de los recuerdos* (1886) and *Veladas literarias* (1892).

GOYCOECHEA MENÉNDEZ, Martín de (1877–1906), b. Córdoba, Argentina. Argentinian poet who, after publishing the modernist collections *Los primeros* and *Poemas helénicos*, went to Asunción in 1901 and, as a disciple of O'Leary (q.v.), became a leading Paraguayan nationalist novelist and short-story writer, in a very different mould from the disillusioned Rafael Barrett (q.v.). In the words of Hugo Rodríguez-Alcalá, his nationalism and clericalism led him to become 'más papista que el Papa en el seno de una generación de hero-worshippers'. Goycoechea's remarkable influence on Paraguayan writers dates from the period before *Cuentos de los héroes y de las selvas guaraníes* (1905), which he published after winning a lottery and before leaving his adopted country for the last time.

GOYTISOLO, José Agustín (1928–   ), b. Barcelona. Poet and critic, of Basque and Cuban descent, the brother of Juan Goytisolo (q.v.). He compiled an important bilingual anthology, *Poetas catalanes contemporáneos* (Barcelona, 1968) and an annotated anthology, *Nueva poesía cubana* (Barcelona, 1969).

His own books of poetry include *El retorno* (1955), *Salmos al viento* (Barcelona, 1958), *Claridad* (Valencia, 1961), *Años decisivos* (Barcelona, 1961), and *Algo sucede* (1968). He has translated from, and written essays on, Salvador Espriu, Pavese, Quasimodo, and Pasolini.

GOYTISOLO, Juan (1931–), b. Barcelona. Novelist, who has been an editor with Editions Gallimard in Paris. Outside Spain he is the best-known novelist of his generation. His first book to gain wide recognition was *Juegos de manos* (1954), translated as *The young assassins* (1959), which deals with the problem of juvenile delinquents from well-to-do families who are provided with everything except a reason for their privileged existence. *Duelo en el Paraíso* (Barcelona, 1955), translated as *Children of chaos* (1960), is another study of young people, this time during wartime. The trilogy *El mañana efímero*, from the title of a poem in Antonio Machado's *Campos de Castilla* (qq.v.), consists of *Fiestas* (Buenos Aires, 1958; translated into English in 1960), *El circo* (Barcelona, 1957), and *La resaca* (Paris, 1958). He also wrote the essays *Problemas de la novela* (Barcelona, 1959). Subsequent fiction included the short stories *Para vivir aquí* (Buenos Aires, 1960), and the novels *Fin de fiesta* (Barcelona, 1962; translated as *The party's over*, 1966), and *Reivindicación del Conde Don Julián* (Mexico City, 1969), in which Goytisolo uses the hero's release from decorum under the influence of hashish to deploy a rapidly-broadening linguistic ability. The book ranges freely beyond its nominal theme of exile, but is centred on Goytisolo's gloomy view of his country, from which he lived in voluntary exile in Mexico during the Franco regime.

Goytisolo has also written a travel book *Campos de Níjar* (Barcelona, 1960) and further essays: the highly-praised *Señas de identidad* (q.v., Mexico City, 1966) and *El furgón de cola* (Paris, 1967).

See Kessel Schwartz, *Juan Goytisolo* (New York, 1970) in Twayne's World Authors series.

GOYTISOLO, Luis (1935–), b. Barcelona. Novelist, and the younger brother of José Agustín and Juan Goytisolo (qq.v.). *Las afueras* (Barcelona, 1958) is an *avant-garde* novel introducing several series of characters all with the same names to demonstrate the essential similarity of each succeeding generation in finding disenchantment and bitterness with life, whether they call themselves 'conservative' or 'radical'. Goytisolo's next novel was *Las mismas palabras* (Barcelona, 1963), but he has become best known for *Antagonía*, a tetralogy. The first volume, *Recuento* (Barcelona, 1974), concerns the middle-class upbringing of an ordinary Catalan youth, Raul. Seemingly endless sentences and lack of punctuation are devices which pall in a work as long as this: Goytisolo appears to require the reader to be bored in order to experience the boredom of Raul's routine sexual adventures and his tinkering with Marxist politics. The novel ends with Raul's emergence from jail, where he has spent some time as the result of his political activities, and his departure for the Costa Brava resort of Rosas where he intends to write a novel.

Los verdes de mayo hasta el mar (Barcelona, 1976), the second novel of the tetralogy, consists of the novel which Raul writes in Rosas and notes towards a novel on the tourist industry of the Costa Brava.

The remaining novels of the *Antagonía* sequence are *La cólera de Aquiles* and *Teoría del conocimiento*.

GRACIÁN, Lorenzo, the pen-name used throughout much of his life by Baltasar Gracián y Morales (q.v.).

GRACIÁN Y MORALES, Baltasar (1601–58), b. Belmonte, near Calatayud. Major prose writer, who was educated in Toledo at the expense of his uncle Antonio Gracián, entered the Society of Jesus as a novice at the age of 18, continued his studies in Calatayud and Saragossa, and made his solemn vows in 1635. His first book, *El héroe* (q.v., lost *editio princeps* Huesca, 1647; 1st edn. surviving Madrid, 1653; reprinted Amsterdam, 1653; several available modern edns.) defines with a brevity, unusual for the time, an ideal of the great man as possessing, among other virtues, 'gusto relevante, eminencia en lo mejor, excelencia de primero, gracia en el trato, despejo, simpatía, y sobre todo prudencia'. Signed like all his other books (except pt. 1 of *El criticón* and *El comulgatorio*) with the name Lorenzo Gracián, *El héroe* begins a series of similar works in which Gracián tries to identify true greatness and virtue in men.

El político don Fernando el Cathólico (lost *editio princeps* Saragossa, 1640; 1st edn. surviving ed. by V. J. de Lastanosa, Huesca, 1646; several available modern edns.) eulogises its subject without the slightest attempt at objectivity but has some slight interest for the evolution of Gracián's style.

El discreto (q.v., Huesca, 1646 in two edns.; critical edn. by M. Romera-Navarro and J. M. Furt, Buenos Aires, 1960) is hardly distinguishable from *El héroe* in its regard for prudence above all, the *impavidus vir* of Horace, or the wise man proposed by Machiavelli.

Oráculo manual y arte de prudencia. Sacada de los Aforismos que se discurren en las Obras de Lorenço Graçian (q.v., Huesca, 1647; critical edn. by M. Romera-Navarro, 1954) consists of 300 nuggets of wit and wisdom with brief explanations: prudence is still the guiding factor of human conduct.

Apart from his four political and moral works described above, Gracián produced a conventional religious treatise, *El comulgatorio* (Saragossa,

1655, preceding the Madrid edn. of the same year; new edn. in Colección Crisol, 1958); an important work on literary aesthetics, *Agudeza, o arte de ingenio* (q.v., 1642); and a major philosophical novel written under the anagrammatic pen-name García de Marlones: *El criticón* (Pt. 1: Saragossa, 1651; Pt. 2 (as Lorenzo Gracián): Huesca, 1653; Pt. 3 (as Lorenzo Gracián): Madrid, 1657; critical edn. by M. Romera-Navarro, 3 vols., Philadelphia, 1938).

El criticón (q.v.), which gave Gracián a European reputation, takes certain elements from the picaresque and chivalresque genres he knew very well, but prefers the main allegorical tendency dominating the *Sueños* of Quevedo (q.v.), Juan de Mena (q.v.), Suárez de Figueroa (q.v.), and Fernández de Ribera (q.v.).

Gracián was one of the circle of writers surrounding the Aragonese Maecenas Vicencio Juan de Lastanosa y Baráiz de Vera, and benefitted throughout his life from the practical and moral assistance of Don Vicencio, who secured the publication of his books.

Gracián's *Obras completas* (ed. A. de Hoyo, 1960) contains a good bibliography, as does E. Correa Calderón, *Baltasar Gracián* (1961). See also A. Coster, *Baltasar Gracián* (New York, 1913; Spanish translation, Saragossa, 1947); M. Batllori, *Gracián y el Barroco* (Rome, 1958); Klaus Heger, *Baltasar Gracián* (Saragossa, 1960); W. Kraus, *El sentido de la vida según Baltasar Gracián* (1963); and M. Z. Hafter, *Gracián and Perfection* (Cambridge, Mass., 1968). The first vol. of a new complete edition by M. Batllori and C. Peralta appeared in 1969.

Gracioso, the comedian, or buffoon, in a Spanish play, sometimes a peasant but usually the servant or squire of a knight or gentleman. Deriving ultimately from the Greek comedy of Menander and the Roman comedy of Plautus and Terence, the *gracioso* enters the Spanish theatre roughly at the time of the *Himenea* and *Serafina* of Torres Naharro (q.v.), and not in the plays of Lope de Vega, as he claims in vol. 13 (1620) of his *Comedias*. The *gracioso* can be found in Gil Vicente, and in the *Mozo de los ciegos* of Juan de Timoneda; he reaches his height of characterization not so much in Lope, Rojas, and Tirso, as in their successor Agustín de Moreto (q.v.) and in some (though not all) of Calderón. He frequently comments satirically and even cynically on the main action, but sometimes takes part in the action without asides. If the *gracioso* can to some extent be correlated with the *pícaro* of Golden Age fiction, there is nevertheless no doubt that it is on the stage that he achieves his most complete and satisfying expression.

See Charles David Ley, *El gracioso en el teatro de la Península: Siglo de Oro* (1954).

GRANADA, Fray Luis de, see Luis de Granada, *Fray*.

GRAN CAPITÁN, EL, the usual appellation in Spanish literature of Gonzalo Fernández de Córdoba (q.v., 1443–1515).

Gran conquista de ultramar, an anonymous early *libro de caballería* (q.v.) belonging to the so-called Cycle of the Crusades. Written in or about the early 14th c., it tells the story of the Crusades up to 1271, using material from prose versions of Old French epics including *Helias* (which introduces into Spanish the theme of Lohengrin, the 'Caballero del Cisne'), *Li Caitif*, *La conquête de Jérusalem*, and *La chanson d'Antioche* (on the youthful exploits of Godefroi de Bouillon). The 1,100 chapters are characteristically medieval in their indiscriminate mixture of history and fantasy. The Old French matter had been drawn from the *Historia rerum in partibus transmarinis gestarum* of William of Tyre (d. 1184).

The *Gran conquista* was published in Salamanca in 1503, and was edited by Pascual de Gayangos (q.v.) in vol. 44 (1858) of the BAE.

See G. T. Northup, '"La Gran Conquista de Ultramar" and its problems' in *Hispanic Review*, vol. 2 (1934), pp. 287–302.

GRANDE, Félix (1937–), b. Mérida. Poet and short-story writer. After trying a number of jobs, he turned to literature and is now editor of the *Cuadernos Hispanoamericanos*. He wrote *Por ejemplo, doscientas* (1966) and *Occidente, ficciones y yo* (1968), volumes of short stories and essays, but his chief importance is that of an autobiographical poet. *Biografía* (Barcelona, 1971) contains the poetry previously published in *Taranto* (1961), which was influenced by César Vallejo (q.v.), *Las piedras* (1963), *Música amenazada* (Barcelona, 1966), and *Blanco spirituals* (Havana, 1967), as well as the new prose poems *Puedo escribir los versos más tristes esta noche*. His recent poetry shows a gift for incisive parody, the description of the life of instinct, and a profound preoccupation with the fate of sensuality in a world of men like robots.

GRAN PISCATOR SALMANTINO, EL, the pseudonym under which Diego de Torres Villarroel (q.v.) published his almanacks from 1721. The name was derived from a Milanese astrologer, il Grande Piscatore.

Gran teatro del mundo', 'El, an *auto sacramental* by Pedro Calderón de la Barca (q.v.) written about 1645, first performed (as far as is known) in Madrid in 1649, and first published in *Autos Sacramentales, con quatro comedias nuevas . . . Primera parte* (1655). Lorinser, who translated all of the *autos* into German (*Geistliche Festspiele*, 1856), considered this the first because of its 'incomparable beauty' though Parker (in *The allegorical drama of Calderón*, Oxford, 1943) prefers *La cena del rey Baltasar* (q.v.) for its power and profundity and *No hay más fortuna que Dios* for its greater maturity.

It is the most straightforward in execution and simple in diction, relying on the imperfect analogy between the theatre and the world. The actors are Man, the stage-manager is the World, and the producer is God. Parker points out that the actors are in fact the authors for they recite as they go along without rehearsal (an aspect of freewill); that the producer does not intervene to correct errors in performance; and there is no learning of parts: the actors are merely assigned the parts.

The producer assigns the roles of a poor man, a king, Human Beauty, a rich man, Discretion, a peasant, Divine Grace, and a child—who dies at birth and has no actual part to play. He promises that the best actor shall dine with him after the performance. Divine Grace begins the play within a play by asserting that all must act in accordance with the will of God. But only Discretion and the poor man listen, for all the others are admiring their possessions, their beauty, and their power. But at the moment of leaving the stage all repent their thoughtlessness, except the rich man. Deprived of the attributes given them by the producer, they are all equal in the face of death. The rich man is condemned to hell, the king, the peasant, the child, and Beauty go to purgatory, and the joy of immediate entry into heaven is accorded only to the poor man and Discretion.

There is an accessible edition of this work in the Clásicos Castellanos edition of *Autos sacramentales* (2 vols., 1926–7, ed. A. Valbuena Prat); the best criticism is that of Parker, op. cit. For the staging of this play, see N. D. Shergold, *A history of the Spanish stage* (Oxford, 1967).

GRAU DELGADO, JACINTO (1877–1958), b. Barcelona. Important playwright who ended his days in political exile, and cared little for popularity even in his youth, signing (with a few others) the notorious protest against the national tribute to Echegaray (q.v.) in 1903. An irascible, vain man, with few friends, he attempted single-handed to rescue Spanish drama from dominant commercialism and triviality. His plays failed in Spain in most cases, but were given a better reception in Paris. With A. Gual he adapted an episode from Cervantes' *Quijote* for *Las bodas de Camacho* (1903). Experimenting seriously with all

genres, he wrote a 'sketch for a comedy' in his own words, *El tercer demonio* (1908); a play on Don Juan as a middle-aged man, *Don Juan de Carillana* (1913); and the ambitious tragedies *Entre llamas* (1915), with its well-deployed elements from naturalist, neo-classical, and romantic traditions; and *El Conde Alarcos* (1917), in which the ballad source is developed to a new height. Here Grau Delgado emphasizes the role of the Infanta, 'surgiendo en ella el arrebato dionisíaco de cierto romance ibérico popular y letrado, muy distante de la *diabetes sacarina* que ha padecido la mayoría de la actual literatura teatral española', as he wrote in the prologue to the 1939 edition of the play.

El hijo pródigo (1918) develops in a similarly reflective vein the outline of the biblical story, while the Pirandellian *El señor de Pigmalión: farsa tragicocómica* (q.v., 1923), probably his most secure claim to posterity, is a bitter view of puppets created to perform at the flailing of their master's whip. The master falls in love with Pomponina (who loves only her own beauty) and is eventually killed by Pedro de Urdemalas, a stereotyped figure whose only individuality is in his intelligence and evil.

Grau returned to the Don Juan legend in *El burlador que no se burla* (1930), which is again experimental in the sense of its composition in five distinct sketches without unity. Grau's literary skill (perhaps more than his dramatic sense) caused Valbuena Prat to describe this play as 'el Don Juan más importante del teatro español del XX'.

From 1928 to 1945 Grau dealt with the obsessional theme of superman and his destiny in *El caballero Varona* (1928) and similar plays influenced by German Expressionism. From 1945 to his death in 1958 he experimented with farce, but always with a serious purpose. A useful anthology of Grau's *Teatro* (2 vols.) appeared in Buenos Aires in 1959. He greatly admired Unamuno, compiling a collection of essays entitled *Unamuno y la angustia de su tiempo* (1943).

See Gerardo Rodríguez Salcedo, 'Introducción al teatro de Jacinto Grau' in *Papeles de Son Armadans*, vol. 42 (1966), pp. 13–42.

GREEN, OTIS HOWARD (1898–), American literary historian. He joined the staff of Pennsylvania University in 1923, and was Chairman of the Spanish Department 1938–45. His major work is the seminal *Spain and the western tradition: the Castilian mind in literature from 'El Cid' to Calderón* (4 vols., Madison, 1963–66), which has been translated by C. Sánchez Gil (4 vols., Madrid, 1969). The book omits the *refranero*, the *romancero*, and the *coplas*, as well as Basque, Castilian, and Portuguese literatures. Volume 1 deals with love and chivalry in medieval literature; volume 2 with nature, free-will, reason, and destiny in Renaissance literature; volumes 3 and 4 are more generally concerned with the Renaissance and Baroque in Spain. Green's preparatory studies for this important book included 'Courtly love in the Spanish *cancioneros*', in *Publications of the Modern Language Association of America*, vol. 64 (1949) and *Courtly love in Quevedo* (Boulder, 1952) which has been translated into Spanish (Saragossa, 1955).

Green has studied the Argensola brothers (q.v.), his most notable contributions in this field being *The life and works of Lupercio Leonardo de Argensola* (Philadelphia, 1927) translated by F. Yndurain (q.v., Saragossa, 1945), and *Bartolomé Leonardo de Argensola y el reino de Aragón* (*Archivo de Filología Aragonesa*, Saragossa, 1952).

Greguerías, witty epigrams of a special genre invented in 1911 by Ramón Gómez de la Serna (q.v.), who defined the *greguería* in many ways over the years but most memorably perhaps as 'humour + metaphor = greguería'. Gómez de la Serna states that he chose the word because it is supposed to signify the grunting of piglets behind their sow; it was accepted by the Academy's dictionary in 1960 with the following definition. 'Agudeza o imagen en prosa que presenta una visión personal y sorprendente de algún aspecto de la realidad'. Some examples are 'An excess of fame: defamation'; 'It is only in botanical gardens that trees carry visiting cards'; 'The wheel that keeps rolling away from the car after the crash seems to be going in search of first aid'.

Numerous *greguerías* by Gómez de la Serna have been collected in his *Total de greguerías* (1955).

GREIFF, León de (1895–), b. Medellín. Colombian poet of Swedish-German ancestry. His early influences included Villon and Verlaine, and he became known, with Rafael Maya and Germán Pardo García, as one of the 'decadents'. The books which made a lasting reputation among a small minority public are *Tergiversaciones de Leo Le Gris* (1925), *Libro de los signos* (1930), and *Variaciones alrededor de la nada* (1936). A modern *culterano*, Greiff daringly introduced archaisms, neologisms, onomatopoeia, and a musical sense, and prompted Jorge Zalamea to observe 'yo no tengo memoria ni conocimiento de otro poeta que, como León de Greiff, haya sabido concertar una más permanente, equitativa y competitiva alianza entre música y poesía'. After the *Antología poética* of 1942, Greiff produced *Fárrago* (1955). His *Obras completas* appeared in 1960. It would not be exaggerating to state that a poem such as 'Fanfarría en sol mayor' foreshadowed the rise of sound poetry by more than two decades.

See O. Rodríguez Sardiñas, *León de Greiff: una poética de vanguardia* (1975).

GROUSSAC, Paul (1848–1929), b. Toulouse. An historian, Argentinian by adoption, he arrived in Buenos Aires in 1866 and made his home first in San Antonio de Areco, and later in San Miguel del Tucumán, the 'San José' of his novel *Fruto vedado* (1884). In 1885 he became Director of the National Library, a post he occupied until his death. In 1896 he founded *La Biblioteca*, a distinguished monthly devoted to history, science, and art which, with its successor, *Anales de la Biblioteca* (1900–15), was to raise the level of journalism in Argentina.

Une énigme littéraire (Paris, 1903), on the *Quijote* of Avellaneda, proposed an ingenious hypothesis later demolished by Marcelino Menéndez y Pelayo. The *Estudios de historia argentina* (1918) reprinted articles selected from the *Anales*, while the more personal *Los que pasaban* (1919) shows the humane, agnostic side of the positivist Groussac. Groussac wrote a one-act play called *La monja* (1921) and a historical drama on the Rosas period, *La divisa punzó*, published in 1923, the year his sight failed.

Grupo de Guayaquil, the literary clique of the 1930s that initiated the renaissance of the Ecuadorian novel. Its members were Joaquín Gallegos Lara (1911–), Enrique Gil Gilbert (1912–), and Demetrio Aguilera Malta (1909–), who collaborated to produce the group's manifesto *Los que se van: cuentos del cholo y del montuvio* (1930), as well as the novelists José de la Cuadra, and Alfredo Pareja Diezcanseco. The group is notable for conscientious portraits of Ecuadorian life and landscape coupled with an attitude of protest against social injustice. The group's literary theory can best be summed up in the slogan 'La realidad y nada más que la realidad' (Rojas, *La novela ecuatoriana*, 1948, p. 185).

GUANES, Alejandro (1872–1925), b. Asunción. Paraguayan modernist poet who taught Spanish literature and translated Poe's works into Spanish. He was influenced by Poe, especially in 'Las leyendas' (on the war between Paraguay and the Triple Alliance) and in 'El domingo de Pascua', poems published posthumously in *De paso por la vida* (1936). He became a journalist after abandoning poetry in his youth. A prose collection, *Del viejo saber olvidado* (1926), shows his theosophical interests, and he wrote the play *La cámara oscura* (1906).

Guayaquil, Grupo de, see GRUPO DE GUAYAQUIL.

GUELBENZU, José María (1944–). Spanish novelist whose first novel *El mercurio* is influenced perhaps too strongly by Joyce and other 20th-c. models. *Antifaz* (Barcelona, 1971) indicates that Guelbenzu has found a markedly individual non-realistic style for his novel of bored adolescents in Madrid.

GUEVARA, Fray Antonio de (1480?–1545), b. Treceño. Didactic and ascetic writer of distinguished ancestry who was brought up at the court of Ferdinand and Isabella and was page to Prince Don Juan until Juan died in 1497. In 1504 Guevara became a Franciscan, returning as Court Preacher in 1521 and being appointed Royal Chronicler to Charles V in 1526. He accompanied the king on his expedition to Tunis in 1535, and was raised from the unremunerative bishopric of Guadix to the equally unremunerative bishopric of Mondoñedo in 1537.

A learned writer much influenced by Ciceronian rhetoric and biblical imagery, Guevara achieved a European reputation (particularly in France and Italy) for his *Libro áureo de Marco Aurelio*, which went into 25 printings in Spain alone within the next century. Printed anonymously and without permission in Seville in 1528, it was augmented as *Libro llamado relox de príncipes* (Valladolid, 1529; ed. R. Foulché-Delbosc in *Revue Hispanique*, vol. 76 (1929), pp. 1–319) in the medieval genre of *de regimine principum* (q.v.) and as such went into 16 editions. Guevara knew much of classical antiquity from wide reading and he invented even more; the result is a *mélange* of curious and fanciful learning, obnoxious only to the modern scholar with hindsight for its conceit and presumption.

Similar charges can be levelled at *Epístolas familiares* (Valladolid, 1st ser., 1539; 2nd ser., 1541) a series of 112 essays, usually in epistolary form, which borrow their title and style from Cicero. They were edited by E. de Ochoa in vol. 13 (1859) of the BAE, an edition superseded by that of J. M. de Cossío (2 vols., 1950–2). Guevara here deals with a host of subjects from Holy Writ to famous whores, with advice to an old man who falls in love (don't) and to young lovers.

Década de Césares (1539; ed. J. R. Jones, Chapel Hill, N.C., 1966) is a series of Roman emperors' lives drawn in the main from Herodian, the *Historia Augusta*, and Dio[n] Cassius. *Libro llamado auiso de priuados y doctrina de cortesanos* (Valladolid, 1539) is a handbook for those desirous of obtaining and retaining favour at court or in high society generally. Another work in the group published at Valladolid in 1539 is in the *beatus ille* genre familiar since

Horace: *Libro llamado Menosprecio de corte y alabança de aldea* (ed. Martínez de Burgos (1915) in Clásicos Castellanos), and yet another *De los inventores del marear*, a manual florid and inventive in style for those about to travel by sea.

Guevara's last works were religious in content: *Oratorio de religiosos y exercicio de virtuosos* (Valladolid, 1542) and *Libro llamado Monte Calvario* (Salamanca, vol. 1, 1542; vol. 2, 1549). The selection of Guevara in the BAE (vol. 65, 1873) includes *Marco Aurelio*, the *Relox*, and some of the more memorable *epístolas*. His style was immensely popular, but also found its violent detractors, the most vocal being Pedro de Rúa, who wrote letters to Guevara to ask him to curb his stylistic exuberance in the interest of simplicity and veracity, and finally published *Cartas de Rhúa lector en Soria sobre las obras del Rev. señor Obispo de Mondoñedo . . .* (Burgos, 1549), treated lightly by the bishop concerned. The basic bibliography is by R. Foulché-Delbosc in *Revue Hispanique*, vol. 33 (1915), pp. 301–84.

See R. Costes, *Antonio de Guevara: sa vie et son œuvre* (2 vols., Paris, 1925–6); and J. Gibbs, *La vida de Fray Antonio de Guevara* (Valladolid, 1960).

GUEVARA, José (1928–), b. Huelva. Spanish painter and playwright living in exile in France, like Martín Elizondo and Fernando Arrabal (qq.v.). Guevara is not only bilingual but writes equally successful plays in both languages.

Después de la escalada (1964) is based on the American involvement in Vietnam, but most of its fantasy has since turned into fact and it is seen now less as drama and more as prophecy. *Les téléphones* (1966) is a black comedy of the absurd, owing something to Ionesco and to the prevailing violence reported by the news media. The protagonist is brought into a room full of telephones, and listens as his life and death are discussed over them.

See George W. Wellwarth, *Spanish underground drama* (University Park, Pa., 1972), pp. 134–5.

GUEVARA, Fray Miguel de (1585?–1640). An Augustinian priest whose claim to celebrity is that he included the great sonnet 'A Cristo crucificado' (q.v.) in his MS. *Arte para aprender la lengua matlaltzinga*, dated 1638, inducing Alberto María Carreño, in his *Joyas literarias del siglo XVII encontradas en México* (Mexico City, 1915) to attribute authorship to Guevara. However, as P. Zarco showed in *Ciudad de Dios*, vol. 142 (1923), the sonnet was published in a compilation by one Antonio de Rojas in Madrid, 1628.

See V. Adib, 'Fray Miguel de Guevara y el soneto "A Cristo crucificado"' in *Ábside*, vol. 13

(1949), pp. 311–26; and Mary Cyria Huff, *The sonnet 'No me mueve, mi Dios': its theme in Spanish tradition* (Washington, D.C., 1948). Huff traces the poem to the second half of the 16th c., but cannot identify the author.

GUEVARA, PABLO (1930–), b. Lima. Peruvian poet. His experimental poetry, influenced by Pound and others of Pound's generation, has in turn influenced much of the important Peruvian poetry of the 1960s, including that of some members of the *Estos 13* (q.v.) group. His books include *Retorno a la criatura* (1957), *Los habitantes* (1965), *Crónicas contra los bribones* (1967), and *Hotel de Cuzco*.

GUEVARA DE LA SERNA, ERNESTO (1928–67), known as 'Che' Guevara, b. Alta Gracia, Argentina. Revolutionary *guerrillero* of Guatemala who fought under Fidel Castro until the victorious campaign against Batista in Cuba, and then in Bolivia, where he was killed in action in more guerrilla warfare. Since his death he has become a cult figure among the leftist revolutionary movements of Latin America. After receiving high administrative posts from Castro for his part in achieving Communist power in Cuba, Guevara decided to emerge from bureaucracy to active combat as Garibaldi and Zapata had done before him, with the intention of bringing his great prestige to the impossibly difficult task of defeating the regular army (he was also pressed to leave by the Russians who opposed his economic policies). *Diario de Bolivia* (Havana, 1968) is a moving document of our times on eleven months of monotony in the face of death and torture, and has been translated as *Bolivian diary* (London, 1969).

Guevara's other writings include *La guerra de guerrillas* (Havana, 1960; translated as *Guerrilla warfare*, New York, 1961); *Pasajes de la guerra revolucionaria* (Havana, 1963; translated as *Reminiscences of the Cuban revolutionary war* (New York, 1968); and *¡Venceremos!* (London, 1968), a volume of speeches and writings edited by J. Gerassi.

See Andrew Sinclair, *Guevara* (London, 1970) in Fontana Modern Masters.

GUEVARA VALDÉS, ANTONIO (1845–82), b. San Salvador. Satirical poet and journalist. He trained as a lawyer, and became undersecretary of Finance, War, and the Admiralty from 1871–3. As a journalist, he founded *La Voz de Occidente* in Santa Ana and contributed to *El Constitucional*, *El Faro*, *La Tribuna*, *El Fénix*, and other journals, specializing in linguistics and social questions.

His poems appear in all the anthologies of Salvadorian poetry, such as the *Guirnalda*

salvadoreña of Román Mayorga Rivas (1884), vol. 2, pp. 59–83.

GUIDO Y SPANO, CARLOS (1827–1918), b. Buenos Aires. Argentinian poet, son of General Tomás Guido. In 1840 he left for Brazil and Europe, where his father held various diplomatic posts, and lived in Europe (mainly England and France) until 1851. He was appointed undersecretary in the Ministry of Foreign Relations during the presidency of Derqui, later becoming Director of the Department of National Archives. In 1865 he abandoned politics for writing. His *Hojas al viento: libro lírico* (1871) were followed by *Ecos lejanos* (1895). Guido's *Poesías completas* appeared in 1911. His poetic models and intentions were classical, but he began by writing in the Romantic tradition, and ended as a modernist. *Ráfagas* (1879) is a two-volume collection of his occasional prose.

GUILLADE, XOHÁN DE (*fl.* 1290). Galician troubadour. Forty-seven of his poems appear in the *Cancionero del Vaticano*. Guillade, whose name also occurs as Joham Garcia de Guilhade, is distinguished for his exquisitely delicate love poems, among the finest in medieval Galician, and especially for a charming declaration of first love. See the edition of Guillade's poetry in E. Monaci, *Il Canzoniere portoghese della Biblioteca Vaticana*, with a preface and facsimile (Halle, 1875).

GUILLEM DE BERGUEDÀ, see BERGUEDÀ, Guillem de.

GUILLÉN, JORGE (1893–), b. Valladolid. Important poet who is considered to rank in Spanish where Eliot and Valéry rank in English and French. A member of the so-called Generación del 1927 (q.v.), he went to the U.S.A. as a political exile in 1938, teaching at Wellesley College (Mass.) from 1940 until his retirement in 1957, when he continued to live in Cambridge (Mass.). In 1919 he began to compose a volume that he always conceived as a growing unity and called *Cántico*. The 1st edition (1928) included only 75 poems but the definitive edition (Buenos Aires, 1950) contained 334; there is also an edition by J. M. Blecua (Barcelona, 1971). Essentially serene and optimistic, *Cántico* conveys Guillen's understanding of 'pure poetry' which is, he says, 'todo lo que permanece en el poema después de haber eliminado todo lo que no es poesía' a bland tautology which distorts his achievement: that of refining the essence of experience and feeling and rejecting the merely anecdotal or accidental. He omits explanation, condensing narrative into the sudden illumination.

The trilogy *Clamor* which followed shows a darker side to Guillén's view of humanity: *Maremagnum* (Buenos Aires, 1957), and ... *Que van a dar en la mar* (Buenos Aires, 1960) apparently culminate in the hopeful *A la altura de las circunstancias* (Buenos Aires, 1963), in which the poet seems to have overcome the setbacks of his generation which were never truly his own. *Homenaje* (Milan, 1967) is a work unique in Spanish literature for its dedication to world literature: apart from numerous original poems by Guillén inspired by his wide reading, there are many translations, including those from Arabic, Greek, Latin, Russian, German, and English.

Aire nuestro (Milan, 1968) is a comprehensive collection of his previous work, and *Y otros poemas* (Buenos Aires, 1973) contains later work.

Guillén wrote the essays *Language and poetry* (Cambridge, Mass., 1961; published in Spanish the following year) and has been regarded as a major poet for the last thirty years, yet he received no recognition whatsoever in the land of his birth during the Franco period.

Cántico has appeared in a composite partial translation (ed. N. T. di Giovanni, London, 1965) of variable quality.

See R. Gullón and J. M. Blecua, *La poesía de Jorge Guillén* (Saragossa, 1949); J. Casalduero, '*Cántico' de Jorge Guillén* (1953; reprinted 1974); J. Gil de Biedma, *Cántico: el mundo y la poesía de Jorge Guillén* (Barcelona, 1960); I. Ivask and J. Marichal, *Luminous reality: the poetry of Jorge Guillén* (Norman, Okla., 1969); the important introduction by Oreste Macrí to the bilingual *Opera poética* (Florence, 1972); the special issue (no. 130, January 1974) of *Revista de Occidente*, the publisher of his first book; and B. Ciplijauskaité (ed.), *Jorge Guillén* (1975).

GUILLÉN BATISTA, NICOLÁS (1902–), b. Camagüey. Cuban poet, who studied law in Havana University. The leading poet of the Afro-Cuban movement of the late 1920s and 1930s which sought to blend native Cuban, African, and Spanish song, dance, and music into a new entity. His profoundly influential books include *Motivos de son* (1930), *West Indies Limited* (1934), *Sóngoro Cosongo* (1931), *Cantos para soldados y sones para turistas* (1937), and *Elegías* (1947–8) addressed respectively to Jacques Roumain and Jesús Menéndez. Guillén took the Republican side in the Civil War, on which he wrote the poems in *España* (1937). He became a Communist. His rhythms continued to echo those of the Negroes (he himself is mulatto), and his vocabulary to echo that of the working classes. *El son interno* (1947) showed him at his best, no longer stridently political but even more sensitive than before to native rhythms

and simple values. *La paloma de vuelo popular* (1958) sounded the first artificiality of a writer no longer certain of the exact balance between freedom of sensibility and political commitment.

His subsequent books have included *Prosa de prisa: crónicas* (Santa Clara, 1962), *Balada* (1962), *Tengo* (Santa Clara, 1964), *Poemas de amor* (1964), *El gran zoo* (1967), and *Antología clave* (Santiago, 1971).

See *Nicolás Guillén: nuestro homenaje* (1962) published by the National Library, Havana; Ángel Augier, *Nicolás Guillén* (2 vols., Santa Clara, 1962–4); E. Martínez Estrada, *La poesía afrocubana de Nicolás Guillén* (Montevideo, 1966); and Adriana Tous, *La poesía de Nicolás Guillén* (Madrid, 1971).

GUILLÉN DE SEGOVIA, PEDRO (1413–74?), b. Seville. Poet. Usually known as 'Pero' Guillén, (he was known as 'de Segovia' after his long residence in that city), he was a protégé of Don Álvaro de Luna, after whose fall he was forced to earn his living as a copyist. As he was about to commit suicide he was recommended to Carrillo, Archbishop of Toledo, who employed Guillén as a book-keeper. A poetic jouster with Gómez Manrique (q.v.), Guíllen imitated Dante in *Decir sobre el amor* and reworked the familiar dance of death topos in his satirical *Discursos de los doce estados del mundo*. His other original poems included *Decires contra la pobreza*, *Del día del Juicio*, and *Siete pecados mortales*. Menéndez y Pelayo wrote of Guillén's *Siete salmos penitenciales trovados* (suppressed from the *Cancionero general*) that they are 'casi el único ensayo de poesía bíblica directa que encontramos en nuestra literatura de la Edad Media'.

The first known rhyming dictionary in Castilian is Guillén's *La Gaya, o Silva copiosísima de consonantes para alivio de trovadores*, first edited by O. J. Tallgren (Helsinki, 1907) and latterly by José María Casas Homs and O. J. Tulio (2 vols., 1962).

See H. R. Lang, 'The so-called Cancionero de Pero Guillén de Segovia' in *Revue Hispanique*, vol. 19 (1908), pp. 51–81.

GUIMERÀ, ÀNGEL (1849–1924), b. Santa Cruz de Tenerife. Catalan-language playwright and poet. His parents took him to Catalonia when he was only seven, so he grew up almost exclusively in a Catalan environment, studying in Barcelona and spending the rest of his time in his adopted village of El Vendrell. From 1872 he moved permanently to Barcelona, where in 1877 he was named *mestre en gai saber* ('master troubadour') in the floral games. He published his early work in the magazine *La Renaixença* from 1872–86, collecting his best work as *Poesies* (Barcelona, 1887), in sinewy language and noble sentiments for the new age of Catalan literature which he predicted correctly. *Segon llibre de poesies* (1920) is an unhappy sequel, lacking inspiration and creative power. *Cants a la pàtria* (Barcelona, 1906) is stirring in a rhetorical vein but unrewarding for the modern reader.

Guimerà's principal contribution to Catalan life was his drama, beginning with the fine verse tragedy *Gala Placidia* (1879), *Judith de Welp* (1883), and *El fill del mar* (1886). His stature rose with each play: *Mar i cel* (1888), with masterly characterization and natural situations beyond the level of the German romantic drama which it closely resembled; *Rei i monjo* (1890); *L'ànima morta* (1892); *Les monges de Sant Aymant* (1895), on the legend of Count Arnau; and the first of his modern dramas: *La boja* (1890). The rest of his modern plays are equally absorbing and should be staged more often outside the confines of Catalonia: *Maria Rosa* (1894); *La festa del blat* (1896); and *Terra baixa* (1896), possibly his key play, examining the contrast between the pure heart of the high-mountain dwellers and the low passions of lowlanders. His last period was devoted to abstract ideas, which were often ill-expressed and in any case unsuited to stage presentation. Though a man of great culture, he never felt himself aloof from the masses, by whom he was hero-worshipped.

Obres selectes (Barcelona, 1948) is a broad anthology, but for the range of his dramatic genius the best anthology is *Teatre selecte* (2 vols., Barcelona, 1949–55).

See Juan Givanel, *El teatro de Guimerà* (Barcelona, 1909); Luis Viva, *Guimerà intim* (Barcelona, 1925); and Josep Miracle, *Guimerà* (Barcelona, 1958).

GUIOMAR, the name by which Antonio Machado y Ruiz (q.v.) referred to Pilar Valderrama in *Canciones a Guiomar* and other works in his *Cancionero apócrifo* which first appeared in the *Revista de Occidente* (1926, 1931).

Machado met Guiomar in Segovia, where he spent half his time from 1919. The annotated correspondence of Machado to Guiomar was published by Concha Espina in *De Antonio Machado a su grande y secreto amor* (1951).

GÜIRALDES, RICARDO (1886–1927), b. Buenos Aires. Argentinian novelist, whose first book was a collection of poems, *El cencerro de cristal* (1915). He joined other *avant-garde* writers such as Borges and Rojas Paz in founding *Martín Fierro* and *Proa* (qq.v.). After travels in Europe and the Orient he settled in Argentina; he left Buenos Aires for his ranch, never needing to practise the law he had studied, and it is his recollections of life on and near the La Porteña ranch near S. Antonio de Areco which form the nucleus of

the material for his excellent fiction. *Cuentos de muerte y de sangre* (1915) are hastily-written stories. *Raucho* (1917) is an autobiographical novel, and *Rosaura* (1922) is a delicate love story of a country girl and a city youth. *Xaimaca* (1923) is a prose poem in the style of Villiers de l'Isle Adam, its central theme being a love adventure on a journey from Buenos Aires to Jamaica. It is for *Don Segundo Sombra* (q.v., 1926) that Güiraldes won world fame which he did not live to enjoy. He died in France. *Seis relatos porteños* (1929) appeared posthumously. His ranch became a *gaucho* museum in 1938.

See I. B. Colombo, *Ricardo Güiraldes, el poeta de la pampa* (Buenos Aires, 1952); J. Collantes de Terán, *Las novelas de Ricardo Güiraldes* (Seville, 1959); G. Previtali, *Ricardo Güiraldes* and '*Don Segundo Sombra*' (New York, 1963); and Ivonne Bordelois, *Genio y figura de Ricardo Güiraldes* (Buenos Aires, 1967).

GUTIÉRREZ, EDUARDO (1853–90). Argentinian novelist. The subject of very varied critical assessments, Gutiérrez wrote some thirty novels in serial form for *La Patria Argentina* and similar papers. Many were mediocre, but *Juan Moreira* (1879) created the stereotype of the *gaucho* bully-hero and Jorge Luis Borges praised him as infinitely superior to Fenimore Cooper in the same genre of adventure stories. *Juan Moreira* was adapted as pantomime in 1884 and as melodrama in 1886 by the actor José J. Podestá in the Podestá-Scott Circus.

It seems fair to consider Gutiérrez the originator of the *gaucho* detective story, even if most of his novels were mere pot-boilers. For the story of *Juan Moreira's* adaptation, see Rubén A. Benítez, *Una histórica función de circo* (Buenos Aires, 1956).

GUTIÉRREZ, JUAN MARÍA (1809–78), b. Buenos Aires. Argentinian poet, who was influenced in both literature and politics by the views of Esteban Echeverría (q.v.). Gutiérrez fled to Uruguay like Echeverría, and later travelled in Europe and South America. In 1861 he returned to Argentina as the Rector of Buenos Aires University. His poems include *Los amores del payador* (1838) and *Dos jinetes*. His *Poesías* appeared in 1869.

GUTIÉRREZ DE MONTALVO, GARCI, see RODRÍGUEZ DE MONTALVO, Garci.

GUTIÉRREZ GONZÁLEZ, GREGORIO (1826–72), b. Ceja del Tambo, Antioquia. Colombian poet, lawyer, and politician whose main influences were Zorrilla and Espronceda. His style is simple to the point of prosiness, and he claimed to write not Spanish but Antioquian. His best poems are the charming 'A Julia' (To his wife),

'Las dos noches', and '¿ Por qué no canto?' but the most celebrated is the long *Memoria sobre el cultivo del maíz en Antioquia* (1868), far from the *Georgics* of Virgil though with ostensibly the same rustic theme of farming and the pleasures of the country life. Gutiérrez González is however a man of primitive pleasures unlike the Roman sophisticate and uses common speech, delicate observation, and the occasional spice of earthy humour to enrich a narrative that principally sets out to praise the fertility and beauty of Antioquia province.

GUTIÉRREZ NÁJERA, MANUEL (1859–95), b. Mexico City. Mexican poet and short-story writer who was educated by private tutors at home. He was a prolific journalist, contributing to some forty papers under a variety of pseudonyms, of which the most celebrated was 'El duque Job'. He is a precursor of the modernists for his sensibility, musicality, and sense of colour. An admirer of French literature, he carried French ideas into Spanish forms. None of his three novels was finished, and he was always happier in the short story form, his favourite characters being women and children. The *Cuentos completos y otras narraciones* (1958) are interesting for their subtle humour, wide-ranging imagery, and description of reality.

The first compilation of his *Poesías* (1896) was made by Justo Sierra and this was frequently reprinted. The best current edition is that by Francisco González Guerrero (2 vols., 1953). His moods vary from sunny wit to deep melancholy, and Blanco Fombona called him 'el mayor elegista del romanticismo en América'. In the fine *Odas breves*, Gutiérrez Najera masters the subtle form with taste and bravura. He developed from the early influences of Bécquer, Musset, and Verlaine to an individual style which retains its appeal today.

See N. Walker, *The life and works of Manuel Gutiérrez Nájera* (Columbia, Mo., 1927); C. Gómez del Prado, *Manuel Gutiérrez Nájera: vida y obra* (1964); and B. G. Carpenter and J. L. Carpenter, *Manuel Gutiérrez Nájera* (1966).

GUTIÉRREZ SOLANA, JOSÉ (1886–1945), b. Madrid. Painter and writer. As an artist, he confined his subject matter to bulls, genre scenes set in Spain, and urban landscapes, usually in his native city. His preferred colours were browns and reds; and his draughtsmanship was sombre and stern. Forced into exile because of his opinions, he became increasingly more sceptical of human values and melancholy. Influenced by the tragic themes and attitude of Goya, he was strongly influenced too by the views of the Generación del 1898 (q.v.).

As a writer, his style is equally sombre, bare,

and direct. *Madrid: escenas y costumbres* (2 vols., 1913–18), *La España negra* (1920), *Madrid callejero* (1923), and *Dos pueblos de Castilla* (1925) were collected in *Obra literaria* (1961).

See M. Sánchez Camargo, *Solana* (1945); C. J. Cela, 'Homenaje a don Pepe Solana, escritor, pintor y bajo cantante' in *Cuatro figuras del 98* (1961), pp. 57–100; and W. Flint, *Solana, escritor* (1967).

GUZMAN, IBN (c. 1078–1160), b. Cordova. Poet. A prodigy at the court of al-Mutawakkil of Badajoz, he abandoned court life at the victory of Yusuf ibn Tashfín in 1094, composing for parties and patrons who would pay him for his verses. His *Cancionero* of 149 *zejels* published by A. R. Nykl with a transliterated Arabic text and partial Spanish translation (1933) celebrates love (with boys, girls, and married women), wine and food, and is entertaining and instructive for its undoubtedly genuine autobiographical elements. Like many another reprobate, ibn Guzman ended his days in piety, in his case as an imam.

Emilio García Gómez, who wrote on ibn Guzman in *Cinco poetas musulmanes* (Buenos Aires, 1944), has produced the definitive *Todo Ben Quzmān* (3 vols., 1972).

GUZMÁN, MARTÍN LUIS (1887–), b. Chihuahua. Mexican novelist and journalist. He took an active part in the struggles for power, and abandoned Madero for the revolutionaries of the north, and then left Villa at the victory of Obregón, travelling to Spain via New York, where his first essay was published: *La querella de México* (1915). He continued to write prolifically on political matters, but gradually achieved prominence for his fiction, beginning with the well-known story *El águila y la serpiente* (1928; translated by H. de Onís as *The eagle and the serpent*, New York, 1930), which is semi-autobiographical, like its sequel *La sombra del caudillo* (1929). *Memorias de Pancho Villa* (4 vols., 1938–40), constantly in print since its first publication, attempts to evoke in detail the spirit of the *caudillo*, complementing *Los de abajo* by Azuela (q.v.). Guzmán's *Obras completas* (1961–3) are available in 2 volumes.

See E. Laguette, *La novela de Martín Luis Guzmán* (1963) and E. Abreu Gómez, *Martín Luis Guzmán* (1968).

Guzmán de Alfarache, a major novel by the *converso* Mateo Alemán (q.v.) which began the vogue for the picaresque novel (q.v.). Part I appeared in 1599 and part II (hurriedly following a spurious sequel by 'Mateo Luján de Sayavedra', believed to conceal the identity of Joan Martí) in 1602, with the sub-title *Atalaya de* *la vida umana.* A third part was promised but presumably never written.

A repentant sinner, Guzmán tells the story of his own life from an *atalaya* (watchtower) from which he can see not only the vices and foibles of individuals and social classes, but also Original Sin itself: the ineradicable, unchangeable evil of man's nature. The device of speaking in two voices, one actual and one retrospective, is paralleled by the two diverse attitudes of impulse and repentance, and by the contrast between content (crime and roguery) on the one hand, and form (solemn moralizing) on the other. The style is taut and concise, producing a memorable novel on one level, and the commentary adds a further level on the general problems of delinquency and salvation.

Leaving his sordid home, Guzmán becomes a gambler and petty thief. He emigrates to Italy, and paints sores on his legs to live off charity in Rome. Offered service with a kindly Cardinal, Guzmán scorns the chance of settling down honestly and steals from his master. Dismissed, he steadily amasses a fortune by thievery and returns to Madrid as a wealthy merchant determined to increase his fortune by sharp practice. Once again he is discovered, however, and his fortune disappears.

Guzmán next resolves to live comfortably as a cynical priest, and begins studies to that end. A religious vocation gradually reforms him, until he falls desparately in love with a woman for whom he abandons his theological career, too late realizing that she is a prostitute. After she leaves Guzmán, he decides to pose as a virtuous man; he steals a bag of money and hands it to a priest, who is asked to announce the find from the pulpit in order to discover the rightful owner. Guzmán is consequently acclaimed as a 'saint', but steals from the charitable people who come forward to help him. Found out again, he is brought to trial and sentenced to the galleys, where he undergoes a true moral and spiritual conversion.

Diego de Estrella and Fray Luis de Granada (q.v.) are among the ascetic writers upon whom Alemán drew for the interpolated sermons seen by most scholars as serious warnings against sin, but by some as aimed primarily at making the hero's adventures more acceptable to the censor and the ecclesiastical establishment. The interpolated tales of Osmin and Daraja, and of Don Luis de Castro, are taken from the Italian *Novellino* (XLI).

The immense popularity of the novel throughout Europe, particularly during the 17th c., can be gauged from the fact that James Mabbe's translation (*The rogue*, London, 1622) had reached a fourth impression by 1656. Lesage's *Don Guzman d'Alfarache* (Paris, 1732) was only one of many translations into other languages, in this case 'purgée des moralités superflues' and lacking the final religious conversion of Guzmán, which Lesage took to be a gratuitous ending for the censor's benefit.

Francisco Rico edited the novel in *La novela picaresca española* (Barcelona, 1967), while Luján de Sayavedra's spurious *Segunda parte* appears in vol. 3 (1846) of the BAE with the authentic first two parts.

See E. Moreno Báez, *Lección y sentido del 'Guzmán de Alfarache'* (1948); D. McGrady, *Mateo Alemán* (New York, 1968), in English, mainly on *Guzmán*; Á. San Miguel, *Sentido y estructura del 'Guzmán de Alfarache'* (1972); and M. N. Norval, 'Original sin and the 'conversion' in the "Guzmán de Alfarache"' in *BHS*, vol. 51 (1974), pp. 346–64.

Guzmán el Bueno, the name by which the patriotic hero Alonso Pérez Guzmán is popularly known, from an episode in the *Crónica de Don Sancho el Bravo* (Valladolid, 1554).

The alliance between Muhammad II of Granada and the Arabo-Berber invaders, the Beni Merin, was joined in Tangier by the treacherous Infante Don Juan, brother of King Sancho IV (1284–95), who had taken Tarifa with the King of Granada's help but had refused to cede it to him as previously agreed.

The Aragonese in Tarifa under Alonso Pérez Guzmán were besieged, and the general's son Pedro fell into the hands of Don Juan, who showed the boy to his father and threatened to kill him if Guzmán refused to cede Tarifa. Guzmán replied by throwing down a knife for Juan to use, and the boy was in fact murdered. Mercedes Gaibrois de Ballesteros has established the truth of this tale, which symbolises the Spaniard's ideal of boundless loyalty to one's monarch (who is portrayed as unjust in Vélez de Guevara's play) even if he is wrong. This ideal is observed at its most poignant in the epic of the Cid (q.v.).

The story was retold by Lope de Vega (q.v.) in his poem *La Circe* (1624); by Luis Vélez de Guevara (q.v.) in his stirring play *Más pesa el Rey que la sangre* (reprinted in vol. 45 (1858) of the BAE); by Juan de la Hoz y Mota (q.v.) in *El Abrahám castellano*; and by Nicolás Fernández de Moratín (q.v.) in his tragedy *Guzmán el Bueno* (1777), the last cleverly parodied by Samaniego (q.v.). Perhaps the most successful of all the versions of the story is that by Antonio Gil y Zárate (q.v., 1842), with its sustained tension, fully-rounded characters and sense of period.

I. Millé y Giménez's thesis *Guzmán el Bueno en la historia y en la literatura* was published in the *Revue Hispanique*, vol. 78 (1930), pp. 311–488.

H

Hacedor, El (1960), a miscellany of poems, essays, parables, and stories by the Argentinian Jorge Luis Borges (q.v.).

Borges's own favourite among his books, *El hacedor*, consists of paradoxes, allegories, and other games with words and ideas that more often state a problem or question than solve it. A key motif is nostalgia, and a major pre-occupation the printed word or the book. Echoes of Dante, Homer, and Shakespeare are interspersed with reflections on Buenos Aires and the *gaucho* tradition. The stories, more individual than the poems perhaps, are not only highly cerebral exercises, but also poetic expressions of the fragility of the world and the illusions with which it is permeated.

There is a translation of *El hacedor* entitled *Dreamtigers* (Austin, Texas, 1964).

HALCÓN, MANUEL (1902–), b. Seville. Novelist and short-story writer whose realistic *cuadros de costumbres* are characterized by a deep love for the countryside of Andalusia. He worked as a journalist for *Vértice* and *Semana*. After his first novel *El hombre que espera* (1922) and the stories in *Fin de raza* (Seville, 1927), Halcón spent many years in foreign travel and on his Andalusian estate before publishing his next book, the *Recuerdos de Fernando Villalón, poeta de Andalucía la Baja y ganadero de toros bravos* (1941). Villalón (q.v.) was a relative.

Halcón's fiction matured from the novel *Aventuras de Juan Lucas* (1944), *Cuentos* (1948), and *La gran borrachera* (1953) to the ambitious story of three generations *Los Dueñas* (Barcelona, 1956), written before the publication of a very similar work by Giuseppe Tomasi di Lampedusa (1896–1957), *Il gattopardo*.

His subsequent books are *Monólogo de una mujer fría* (1960), *Desnudo pudor* (1964), and *Ir a más* (1967). Generally speaking, their characterization has become more stereotyped and their plots carry less conviction than in *Los Dueñas*. The first two volumes of his *Obras completas* appeared in 1971–2.

HA-LEVI, JUDAH (b. about 1075–after 1140), b. Tudela, Navarra. Poet and philosopher, who was the most important Spanish poet writing in Hebrew, and among the greatest of all post-biblical Hebrew poets.

Ha-Levi was educated in Granada, where he met Moses ben Ezra (q.v.) and earned his living as a doctor, according to his own admission not particularly competently. He lived in turbulent times, became involved in the conflict between Christians and Muslims, and suffered persecution with other Jews living in Toledo in 1109.

Between 1130 and 1140 he wrote his Arabic *Kitāb al-ḥuyya wa 'd-dalīl fī nusr ad-dīn ad-dalīl* ('The book of the proof and defence of the despised religion'), in which a controversy between religious systems ends with the vindication of Judaism. The influence of Ha-Levi's method can be found in Christian writers, among them Juan Manuel and Ramon Llull (qq.v.) and appears in Spanish literature up to the 18th c.

The *Kitāb* justifies Judaism on the basis of revelation and the witness of each succeeding generation, though it does not deny the virtues of reason within certain limits. Ha-Levi resolves the dilemma of the prophetic inspiration of Israel and the tragedy of the Diaspora, calling for Jewish unity in faith and a return to the Holy Land, a motif forming the crux of his religious poetry, the stirringly eloquent *Sionad*, a collection of over 800 religious poems in the form of the Arabic *qasida*.

In the *Sionad*, Jerusalem is no longer the remote, misty city of Hebrew history, but an actual place of personal redemption. Ha-Levi believed that the Jews could find salvation only by returning to the Holy Land, and he set off there from Spain, via Egypt, where he met the Egyptian Jews and where he may have died (though accounts vary). One legend claims that he was murdered by an Arab horseman at the very gates of the Promised City.

See J. M. Millás-Vallicrosa, *Yehudá ha-Leví como poeta y apologista* (1947); and H. Brody, *Studien zu den Dichtungen Jehuda ha-Levis* (Berlin, 1895); and H. Brody (ed.), *Divan* (Berlin, 1894–1930) in 4 vols. There is a Hebrew text and English translation in *Selected poems of Jehudah Halevi* by N. Salaman (Philadelphia, 1928) and a 3-vol. edition of *Kol shirei Yehuda ha-Levi* (Tel Aviv, 1955) by Y. Zemorah.

A representative selection of his verse appears in English in David Goldstein's *The Jewish poets of Spain, 900–1250* (Harmondsworth, 1971), pp. 117–51.

HA-LEVI BEN LABRAT, DUNASH, see LABRAT, Dunash ha-Levi ben.

Halma (1895), one of the *Novelas españolas contemporáneas* of Benito Pérez Galdós (qq.v.).

The protagonist is Doña Catalina de Artal,

Condesa de Halma-Lautenberg by her marriage to Karl-Friedrich Lautenberg, an attaché at the German Embassy in Madrid. Doña Catalina's spirituality is indicated by her symbolical surname, the pronunciation of Halma being identical to that of *alma* ('soul').

Noble in heart and mind as well as in lineage, Catalina (or Halma as she is known) undergoes terrible hardships and fears after the death of her husband from tuberculosis in Corfu, and eventually returns home to her family in Madrid weak and depressed. On her recovery she renounces high society and turns to asceticism and mysticism. She learns of the simple Christlike priest Nazario Zajarín, whose story is here continued from *Nazarín* (q.v.). Her immense fortune, diminished though it is by the cautious care of the stubborn, mean-minded Conde de Feramor (her elder brother), is eventually settled on an ideal community which Halma founds at Pedralba, partly to save the humble Nazarín from commitment to a lunatic asylum. The latter part of the book is inferior both to *Nazarín* and to *Misericordia*, lacking their wit, irony, and inventiveness. Galdós fails to carry conviction in his description of the love that José Antonio (Halma's vacillating cousin) has for her, and which he tries to convert into platonic admiration. In the first half of the book, on the other hand, Galdós draws a sure portrait of the worldly cleric, Don Manuel Flórez, inspired by Nazarín's example to despise his former artificial manners and conventional religiosity for a true humility which is incomprehensible to those around him at his death.

The best feature of *Halma* is the discussions which rage bitterly on the management of Halma's utopian Pedralba. As the little community is likely to become a public charity, a financial administrator, a doctor, and a priest vie for control over Halma's affairs, persuading her that she cannot see to everything herself. Distressed, Halma seeks the advice of Nazarín, who argues against making Pedralba a public charity and against her pursuit of mysticism. Instead, he urges her to marry José Antonio, who will carry out her every wish to the letter, and continue to offer personal charity. Galdós had decried institutional charity as early as *Marianela* (q.v.).

HALMAR, Augusto d', see Thomson, Augusto Goeminne.

Haravec, an influential magazine founded by Richard Greenwell and David Tipton in Lima. It was shortlived and consisted of five numbers, the first appearing in 1966 and the last in 1968. The title is a Spanish corruption of the Quechua word for 'poet'. See D. Tipton, 'Peru: of poets and poetry' in *Poetry Information (London)*, nos. 9/10 (Spring 1974), pp. 3–7.

An indirect result of the magazine's existence was the publication of the book of translations by Maureen Ahern and David Tipton, *Peru: the new poetry* (London, 1970), including work by Salazar Bondy, Carrillo, Delgado, Belli, Rose, Guevara, Hinostroza, Cisneros, Heraud, Martos, Ortega, and Lauer.

HARIZI, Judah ben Shlomoh (*c.* 1165–*c.* 1234). A Hebrew poet (in Spanish 'Alcharisi'), who lived in Spain, and towards the end of his life travelled in the Middle East, but earned his living as a scholarly translator in Provence. He translated from Arabic into Hebrew such classics as the *Machberoth Ithiel*, being al-Māqamāt of al-Hariri, whose rhymed stories are rendered with great sympathy and skill. Al-Hariri influenced al-Harizi's own rhymed tales in Hebrew, the *Tahkemoni*. Harizi was a disciple of Maimonides, and translated his *Guide for the perplexed* from Arabic into Hebrew at about the same time as Samuel ibn Tibbon, whose version is now recognized as the standard one. Two short poems by Harizi appear in Goldstein's *The Jewish poets of Spain* (Harmondsworth, 1971).

HARO, Juan Fernández de Velasco, Conde de, see Fernández de Velasco, Juan, Conde de Haro.

HARTZENBUSCH, Juan Eugenio (1806–80), b. Madrid. Playwright. The son of a German cabinet-maker who had arrived in Madrid in 1787 and had married a Spanish wife who died of shock on seeing a foreigner persecuted as a spy in the streets of Madrid. Juan Eugenio fled with his father during the worst wave of xenophobia, returning to Spain in 1815. He had been educated in the Jesuit school of San Isidoro from the age of 12 to 15. The dictatorship deprived them of their possessions in 1823, and Juan Eugenio was forced to learn his ailing father's craft to keep them alive.

His reworking of Rojas Zorrilla's *Nuestra Señora de Atocha*, entitled *Las hijas de Gracián Ramírez*, failed on its second night in 1831 and Hartzenbusch was completely unknown when, in 1837 (the year after Antonio García Gutiérrez, q.v., had achieved sudden fame with *El trovador*), his historical play *Los amantes de Teruel* (q.v.) caused a sensation overnight at the Teatro del Príncipe in Madrid. Larra (q.v.), reviewing as 'Fígaro', wrote in generous terms of the new play and the young dramatist, but none of Hartzenbusch's other 68 original plays or adaptations was to impress the public in the same way.

Hartzenbusch explored the dramatic possibilities of the theme of fulfilling one's duty in many of his plays, which excelled in subtle construction but often lacked profound psychological penetration. His other historico-legendary works included *Alfonso el Casto* (1841); a stirring play on the Cid called *La jura en Santa Gadea* (1845), which some critics place above *Los amantes de Teruel*; *La madre de Pelayo* (1846), combining national tradition with Greek mythology; *La ley de raza* (1852), on the *apartheid* law prohibiting marriage between Visigoth and Roman; and *Vida por honra* (1858), on the life of the Conde de Villamediana.

He also wrote plays for children; magical plays, such as *La redoma encantada* (1839) on Enrique de Villena, impaired by poor taste and excessive melodrama; thesis-plays, such as the ferocious diatribe against the Inquisition entitled *Doña Mencía* (1838); and a play in the tradition of Tirso de Molina's *El condenado por desconfiado* (qq.v.) dealing with Judas and Dimas and called *El mal apóstol y el buen ladrón* (1860).

Hartzenbusch also wrote short stories, a novel of little account, and verse fables: 62 collected in *Fábulas en verso castellano* and 102 in *Fábulas en verso castellano* (both 1848), and *Cuentos y fábulas* (2 vols., 1861). He also translated the works of French and German writers, and wrote many *artículos de costumbres*.

As a painstaking editor and advocate of Golden Age drama he produced the following volumes for the BAE: 5 (Tirso de Molina); 7, 9, 12, and 14 (Calderón de la Barca); 20 (Ruiz de Alarcón); and 24, 34, 41, and 42 (part of the works of Lope de Vega). He also edited the *Teatro escogido* of Tirso de Molina (12 vols., 1839–42)

Hartzenbusch was appointed Director of the Biblioteca Nacional in Madrid in 1862, and retired in 1875. His *Obras* (5 vols., 1887–92) were followed by a *Biografía* and a *Bibliografía* (both 1900) by his son Eugenio. *Los amantes de Teruel* and *La jura en Santa Gadea* have been edited for the Clásicos Castellanos (1935) by Álvaro Gil Albacete.

HATZFELD, Helmut A. (1892–), b. Germany. A German Hispanist who studied under Karl Vossler and Ludwig Pfandl (qq.v.) and taught at the Universities of Frankfurt, Heidelberg, and Louvain before emigrating to the U.S.A. on the outbreak of World War II. He taught at the Roman Catholic University in Washington from 1940 and in 1945 he was naturalized an American citizen. His main fields of interest have included stylistics, Cervantes, Spanish mysticism, and the Baroque, while his comparative view of Romance literatures has influenced a generation of Spanish critics such as Amado Alonso (q.v.), who have delved below the surface of Spanish literary forms to the aesthetic roots determining their evolution.

Don Quijote als Wortkunstwerk (Leipzig, 1927) was translated by M. Cardenal as *El Quijote como obra de arte del lenguaje* (Madrid, 1949). His *Romanistische Stilforschung*, which appeared in the *Germanische-romanische Monatsschrift* in 1929, contained a critical bibliographical appendix on stylistics which he kept up to date in successive publications, notably in the *Boletín del Instituto de Filología de la Universidad de Chile*, vol. 4 (1944–6), pp. 7–77.

Hatzfeld has published the important *Estudios literarios sobre mística española* (Madrid, 1955), concerned not so much with doctrine as with style; *Estudios sobre el Barroco* (Madrid, 1964); and a study, *Santa Teresa de Ávila* (New York, 1969).

HAYA DE LA TORRE, Víctor Raúl (1895–), b. Trujillo. Peruvian politician of an aristocratic family who has spent half his life in exile or prison. In 1923 he founded, while exiled in Mexico, the pro-Indian and anti-U.S.A. movement known from its initials APRA as *Aprismo*, standing for the *Alianza Popular Revolucionaria Americana*. He wrote the movement's manifesto *Por la emancipación de América Latina* (Buenos Aires, 1927) which, with *¿Adónde va Indoamérica?* (Santiago, Chile, 2nd edn., 1935), constituted an appeal to Latin American governments to give land back to the Indians (after whom he would rename Latin America), and to nationalize industry in a bid to weaken the domination of the U.S.A.

An idealist, Haya de la Torre has exerted a powerful appeal among the young and the intellectuals. Ciro Alegría (q.v.) and other writers of Bolivia, Ecuador, and Peru (where the Indian problem is generally speaking at its most acute) have given expression to Haya de la Torre's views. Politically, however, his views have been rejected by the ruling classes, though the Aprista's unofficial nominee Bustamante gained a foothold for the movement from 1945 until General Odría's *coup* in 1948. Haya de la Torre was again forced underground, and spent the years 1950–4 in hiding in the Colombian Embassy in Lima. He now lives in Europe.

HAYASECA, Jorge, the anagram which José Echegaray (q.v.) used for his first play, *El libro talonario* (1874).

HAZAÑAS Y LA RÚA, Joaquín (1862–1934), b. Seville. Literary historian and critic. He was a professor at Seville University from 1868, and later Rector.

His works include *Noticias de las academias literarias, artísticas y científicas de Sevilla en los* siglos XVII y XVIII (Seville, 1887), Biografía del poeta sevillano Rodrigo Fernández de Ribera (Seville, 1889), La imprenta en Sevilla, 1475–1800 (Seville, 1892) greatly expanded in a posthumous edition prepared by M. Justiniano (vol. 1, Seville, 1945), Mateo Alemán y sus obras (Seville, 1892), a scrupulous edition of the Obras of Gutierre de Cetina (2 vols., Seville, 1895), and Los rufianes de Cervantes (1906) and Cervantes, estudiante, two studies.

HEBREO, León, see Abarbanel, Judah.

HEIREMANS, Luis Alberto (1928–66?). Chilean short-story writer, poet, and dramatist. The most important of the post-war Chilean playwrights, Heiremans includes in La jaula en el arbol y dos cuentos para teatro (1959), an impressive 'story for the theatre' entitled 'Es de contarlo y no creerlo', in which a modern Don Juan discusses the meaning of his life with a group of angels. Three one-act plays were printed in Mapocho, vol. 3 (1965), and Heiremans has also written Versos de ciego (1960). Luis Domínguez has published Heiremans' Los mejores cuentos (1966).

HENRÍQUEZ, Fray Camilo (1769–1825), b. Valdivia. Chilean patriotic journalist, poet, and dramatist. He was educated in Lima and ordained as a priest in the Order of la Buena Muerte in 1790, but his liberal ideas were denounced to the Inquisition in Lima and he was jailed. On his return to Chile in 1810, he worked unceasingly for Chilean independence, denouncing Spain from the pulpit and blessing independence in 1811. He founded La Aurora de Chile, the nation's first daily (1812–13), and its successor, El Monitor Araucano (1813–14), writing journalism under the pseudonym 'Quirino Lemáchez'. Forced into exile in Buenos Aires, he apostatized and qualified there as a doctor, writing sentimental patriotic dramas such as La procesión de los tontos (1813) and Camila, o la patriota en Sudamérica (1817) which were badly-written, showed no understanding of the human mind and instincts, and were bereft of stage techniques, but had the single, overriding merit of introducing the ideas of Voltaire and Rousseau into Latin America.

His poetry was equally poor in inspiration and construction, relying for its effect purely on the obvious sincerity of its nationalistic sentiments and the author's blind hatred of Spain.

HENRÍQUEZ UREÑA, Max (1885–   ), b, Santo Domingo. Son of Salomé Ureña de Henríquez (q.v.). Diplomat, essayist, and historian. As a young man he went to Cuba, where he became director of the Escuela Normal de Santiago. Among his numerous works are Whistler y Rodin (1906), Los Estados Unidos y la República Dominicana (1919), Rodó y Rubén Darío (1919), and El continente de la esperanza (1939). He also wrote a series of essays, Episodios Dominicanos (first collected in 1951), and edited the important Panorama histórico de la literatura dominicana (Río de Janeiro, 1945). As poets, he and his brother Pedro (q.v.) were notable as pioneers (1901) of the modernist movement in the Dominican Republic, and he compiled Breve historia del Modernismo (Mexico City, 1954). His verses were collected as Garra de luz (1958).

HENRÍQUEZ UREÑA, Pedro (1884–1946), b. Santo Domingo. Son of Dr Francisco Henríquez (in 1916 President of the Republic) and the poet Salomé Ureña de Henríquez (q.v.). After an early book of poems, Aquí abajo (1898), he travelled widely to New York, Havana, Mexico City, and Spain, where he contributed to the Revista de Filología Española. During a distinguished career as critic and teacher, he held the chair of Latin American literature in the University of Buenos Aires from 1925 until his death, apart from the years 1931–3, when he occupied the post of Superintendent of Education in the Dominican Republic. Among his many books, Rodó preferred El nacimiento de Dionisos (New York, 1916), 'one of the loveliest things in contemporary Hispanic-American literature'. In this tragedy, Henríquez Ureña imitated 'the style . . . in use during the period immediately before Aeschylus' (Prologue). His critical labours spanned the years from 1905 (Ensayos críticos), to 1945 (Literary currents in Hispanic America, Cambridge, Mass., 1945, which appeared in Spanish in 1949). His valuable comparative Historia de la cultura en la América Hispánica also appeared posthumously (1947). On his native country he published Literatura dominicana (1917), La cultura y las letras coloniales en Santo Domingo (1936), and El español en Santo Domingo (1940).

Heraldo del Istmo, El, a Panamanian literary review edited 1903–6 by Guillermo Andreve (who had previously edited El Cosmos, 1896–7). Its contributors introduced modernism into Panama: they included Demetrio Korsi and Ricardo Miró (qq.v.), the latter continuing the course of modernism in Panama by founding Nuevos Ritos (1907–17).

HERAUD, Javier (1942–63), b. Miraflores, Lima. Poet, who studied at the Roman Catholic University of San Marcos in Lima. He won there the first prize in the competition El Poeta Joven del Perú, run by the Cuadernos Trimestrales de Poesía, for his book El viaje (1961), and first prize in the Juegos Florales for Estación reunida (1963).

He was killed by Government police while living with revolutionary guerrillas in the remote eastern jungle town of Puerto Maldonado, and his early promise coupled with his violent death converted Heraud into a leftist cult-hero of the Peruvian youth. A prose elegy for Heraud by Washington Delgado (q.v.) appears with a few of his poems in Maureen Ahern and David Tipton's *Peru: the new poetry* (London, 1970).

Heraud's *Poesías completas y homenaje* (1964; 3rd edn., 1975) show that he was never in fact free of several formative influences: Vallejo, Neruda, and above all Antonio Machado. His great virtue is a self-confident tone of voice that manages to avoid stridency. In view of his early death there is a sad irony in his poem *Arte poética* which begins: 'En verdad, en verdad hablando, / la poesía es un trabajo difícil / que se pierde o se gana / al compás de los años otonales.' ('Truly, truly speaking, poetry is something difficult, which is achieved or not achieved with one's autumnal years').

See A. Corcuera and T. G. Escajadillo, *Presencia de Heraud* (1963); and C. A. Ángeles Caballero, *Javier y las voces panegíricas* (1964).

HEREDIA, JOSÉ MARÍA (1803–39), b. Santiago, Cuba. Poet who, while still a child, translated Latin authors. After studying law, he practised as an advocate until he was expelled from Cuba for conspiring against Spanish colonial rule, and returned for only three months, in 1836. A poet of great contemporary fame and influence, Heredia is considered by Manuel Pérez González to be the first Romantic to write in Spanish. His collected poems, of which the best-known are 'Meditación en el teocalli de Cholula' (1820), and an ode 'Al salto de Niagara' (1824) were published first in New York (1825), then, in a better edition, in Toluca (1832). E. Roig de Leuchsenring edited the *Poesías completas* (2 vols., 1940–1) and there is a more recent selection, *Poesías* (1965). Heredia, by nature a Romantic, was nevertheless drawn to the manner of the neoclassical poets of the school of Salamanca. He contributed many stories and essays to periodicals, and wrote derivative plays of little merit: *Los últimos romanos* (1829), *Eduardo IV*, and *Atreo*. His best story, set in the Abruzzi, is the Romantic *Historia de un salteador italiano* (1841).

See Rafael Esténger, *Heredia, la incomprehensión de sí mismo* (1938); J. Balaguer, *Heredia* (Santiago de la República Dominicana, 1939); and M. P. González, *José María Heredia* (Mexico City, 1955).

HÉRÉDIA, JOSÉ MARÍA DE (1842–1905). Cuban poet, born of a Spanish father and French mother, who was educated in France

(1851–9) and lived in Paris from 1861. He studied law, but soon devoted himself solely to poetry, and was one of the first Parnassians (a group including Gautier and Leconte de Lisle), whose ideal of serene images expressed in measured rhythms was exemplified in the 118 sonnets of Hérédia's *Les trophées* (1893). He was elected to the Académie Française in 1894. Hérédia's *Trophées'* five sections: 'La Grèce et la Sicile', 'Rome et les Barbares', 'Le Moyen Âge et la Renaissance', 'L'Orient et les Tropiques', and 'La Nature et le Rêve', seize on a Renaissance binding or a line from a classical text, for example, and weave round that image a delicate sonnet. The influence of Hérédia and the other Parnassians was profound and lasting, notably on the Cuban Julián del Casal (q.v.), the Mexican Rubén M. Campos, the Ecuadorian Francisco Fálquez Ampero (q.v.), and the Colombian Guillermo Valencia (q.v.).

The *Poesías completas* of Hérédia are available in the Colección Sepan Cuantos with an introduction by R. Lazo (Mexico City, 1974).

HEREDIA, JOSÉ RAMÓN (1900–   ). Venezuelan poet of the so-called *Viernes* group, named after an experimental magazine. Heredia's books are *Paisajes y canciones* (1928), *Por caminos nuevos* (1933), *Los espejos de más allá* (1938), *Gong en el tiempo* (1941), and most recently *Maravillado cosmos*. His surrealist leanings are most obvious in his third work.

HEREDIA, NICOLÁS (1852–1901), b. Bani, Santo Domingo. Realist novelist. He lived most of his life in Cuba, and became identified with its life and literature.

Un hombre de negocios (Santiago, Cuba, 1882) is a conventional story, crudely told and influenced by Daudet and Maupassant. *Leonela: narración cubana* (Santiago, 1887) is important for the realism of its Cuban setting, and for the psychological understanding that Heredia reveals of the twin sisters Clara and Leonela.

He also wrote essays, including the controversial, rather harsh, *La sensibilidad en la poesía castellana* (Philadelphia, 1898), a work generally lacking in objectivity.

Hermana San Sulpicio, La (2 vols., 1889), a novel by Armando Palacio Valdés (q.v.), which fulfils the author's stated aspiration to 'move my readers without provoking them to think'.

Set in a vividly-recreated Seville, especially atmospheric in the night scenes, when the Galician poet-doctor Sanjurjo wanders the streets of Andalusia's capital, the novel concerns Sanjurjo's love for a lay sister who is due to renew her vows in a month's time.

Gloria (secular name of the sister San Sulpicio) has another admirer, from Málaga, and Sanjurjo feels torment, hope, and jealousy in turn, while Gloria merely laughs at his infatuation. On leaving the spa of Marmolejo, Gloria, another nun, and her Mother Superior are followed by Sanjurjo, who writes to Gloria but cannot obtain a more revealing reply than 'Sigue Vd. tan gitanillo como antes. Después que salga del convento hablaremos'. Her mother seriously objects to Sanjurjo's infatuation, but Gloria decides to give up her vocation and when her mother takes her back by force to the convent, Sanjurjo rescues her amid the predictable scandal, and the happy ending is not far off.

The book is not as melodramatic as a plot-summary might indicate, but Palacio Valdés is a skilful observer of Andalusian scenes (as he was to show again in *Los majos de Cádiz* (1896)) and the novel has always been extremely popular in Spain despite the decline in the critical esteem of the author since the early years of the century. The best edition is that by C. Berra (Turin, 1960).

HERMINIA, pseudonym of Salome Ureña de Henríquez (q.v.).

HERMOSILLA, JOSÉ, see GÓMEZ HERMOSILLA, José Mamerto.

HERNÁNDEZ, see also FERNÁNDEZ.

HERNÁNDEZ, ALONSO (*c.* 1460–*c.* 1515), b. Seville. Epic poet. He passed the last years of his life in Rome as the protégé of Cardinal Bernardino de Carvajal, and wrote there a poem in *octavas de arte mayor* in imitation of the *Laberinto de fortuna* of Juan de Mena (qq.v.) called *Historia parthenopea* (Rome, 1516), which was edited for publication by his friend Luis de Gibraleón, a Spanish priest living in Naples. It is an epic on the capture of Naples by Gonzalo de Córdoba (q.v.) and remains faithful to the known course of events it describes, which Hernández experienced at first hand.

His other books are lost: they included a book in the manner of Aquinas' *De regimine principum* (q.v.), a life of Christ, and *Siete triumphos de las siete virtudes.*

HERNÁNDEZ, FELISBERTO (1902–64), b. Montevideo. Uruguayan short-story writer whose style is full of surprises, and whose plots abound in Freudian symbolism. His humour is frequently absurd to the point of surrealism, but his grip on reality never quite slackens.

Obras completas (6 vols., 1974) contain *Primeras invenciones*, (1969, containing *Fulano de tal*, first published 1925), *Libro sin tapas* (1929), *La cara de*

Ana (1930), *La envenenada* (1931), *El Fray* (1931), *El caballo perdido* (1943), *Nadie encendía las lámparas* (1946); *Tierras de la memoria* (1965); *Las hortensias y otros relatos* (1967); and *Diario del sinvergüenza, y Últimas invenciones* (1974).

See Lidice Gómez Mango (ed.), *Felisberto Hernández: notas críticas* (1970).

HERNÁNDEZ, JOSÉ (1834–86), b. Chacra de Puyrredón, province of Buenos Aires. The last Argentinian poet of *gaucho* life, in the immensely popular *Martín Fierro* (q.v.). A sickly boy, he was unable to complete his primary education, but read widely on his father's ranch. He enrolled in the army when 19, but left to take up commerce, journalism, and finally politics. In 1863 he wrote the *Vida del Chacho* on the death of that *caudillo*, and later fought against Sarmiento (q.v.), escaping to Brazil in 1870. The following year he published his poem which Leopoldo Lugones (q.v.) claimed as the national epic of Argentina, making a parallel with the *Cantar de mio Cid* (q.v.). The second part of *Martín Fierro* appeared in 1869, with a surprising climax insofar as the theories of his political opponent Sarmiento (regarding the need for *civilización* as opposed to *barbarie*) are now tacitly upheld. His essay *Instrucción del estanciero* (1881) openly recommends combining skilled ranch management with the traditional Creole farming methods.

Only a few years after he had taken part in the struggle of the peasants to limit the central authority of the government of Buenos Aires, propagating his views as a poet, as a soldier, and as a polemical journalist founding the newspaper *El Río de la Plata* (1869), Hernández became a deputy and senator in the central government.

See A. Carretero, *Ida y vuelta de José Hernández* (1972); R. Borello, *Hernández: poesía y política* (1973); and F. Chávez, *La vuelta de José Hernández* (1973).

HERNÁNDEZ, LUISA JOSEFINA (1928–), b. Mexico City. Playwright and novelist whose 'work represents the middle class which is the most important in Mexico', in her own words. Primarily a dramatist, she first achieved recognition with *Aguardiente de caña* (first performed 1951) and repeated the success in 1953 with *Los sordomudos*, whose deaf-mute heroine symbolises the selfishness, pettiness, and lack of understanding in a middle-class family. *Botica modelo* (1954) won the drama prize of *El Nacional*, where it was first published in serial form. Among her other plays are *Afuera llueve* (published 1952), *La llave del cielo* (written 1954), *Los duendes* (first performed 1957), *La paz ficticia* (first performed 1960), and *Popol Vuh* (1966), based on the Maya sacred book *Popol Vuh* (q.v.).

Luisa Hernández's novels include *El lugar*

donde crece la hierba (1959), La plaza de Puerto Santo (1961; dramatized in 1962), the psychological novel Los palacios desiertos (1963), La noche exquisita (1965), and El valle que elegimos (1965). She has made numerous translations of foreign plays into Spanish.

HERNÁNDEZ, MIGUEL (1910–42), b. Orihuela. Poet. Of peasant origin, he obtained a rudimentary education at a state school and later with the Jesuits, but spent most of his early life as a farmboy and goatherd, reading Góngora, Garcilaso, and San Juan de la Cruz, influences that were to remain ever-present in his work. He published some poetry in an Orihuela paper and in Ramón Sijé's magazine El Gallo Crisis (he wrote a memorable elegy for Sijé) and was encouraged by the poets of the Generación del 1927 (q.v.). His first book was a polished exercise in Gongorismo: Perito en lunas (Murcia, 1933), but he first attracted attention with an auto sacramental (q.v.), Quien te ha visto y quien te ve or Sombra de lo que eres (1933). Here Man is seen as a weak creature at the mercy of life's transitory pleasures unless redeemed by the Good Labourer, who is the farmer on one level, the spirit of industry and austerity on another, and Christ on a third.

His forms remain those of Garcilaso in El rayo que no cesa (1936) but his passions are allowed full rein in these poems on love and grief in the face of death. Converted from fervent Roman Catholicism to equally fervent Communism, Hernández served on the Republican side as a soldier and a poet throughout the Civil War. El labrador de más aire: tragedia en verso (q.v., Barcelona, 1937) takes its populist motif from Lope de Vega, but its evangelical communism has nothing in common with Peribáñez (q.v.). Works with a similar aim included La cola, El hombrecito, El refugiado, and Los sentados, collected as Teatro en la guerra (1937); and Viento del pueblo: poesía en la guerra (1937) composed, like the war-poetry of Alberti (q.v.), to be recited to fellow-soldiers. El hombre acecha (1938) and Sin sangriento y otros poemas (1940) are both dramatic collections of his poetry on despair and horror when confronted by man's cruelty to man. A number of other books have appeared since his death, notably the Cancionero y romancero de ausencias (1958), printing the poetry he wrote between 1938 and 1941, when he was in gaol under sentence of death, commuted after international protests to life imprisonment. Cold and hunger caused his death from tuberculosis in the prison hospital at Alicante in 1942. El silbo vulnerado (Buenos Aires, 1949) was a new collection of poems and his prose was assembled in Dentro de luz (1957). Hernández's Obra escogida: Poesía. Teatro (1952) has been super-

seded by Obras completas (Buenos Aires, 1960; 2nd edn., 1973).

His intensely personal and (towards the end of his life) original poetry is far from artless. The deaths of Hernández and García Lorca (q.v.) deprived lyric poetry in Spanish of two of its ablest and most promising creators. Hernández's most influential gift was the ability to combine traditional forms with 20th-c. subjectivity and merciless realism in the portrayal of war. His legend as a peasant, dreamer, and fighter was of seminal influence in the next generation, corresponding with that of García Lorca in Spain and Neruda in Latin America.

See J. Guerrero Zamora, Miguel Hernández, poeta, 1910–1942 (1955); C. Zardoya, Miguel Hernández: Vida y obra. Bibliografía. Antología (New York, 1955); E. Romero, Miguel Hernández: destino y poesía (Buenos Aires, 1958); Juan Cano Ballesta, La poesía de Miguel Hernández (1962); Vicente Ramos, Miguel Hernández (1973); M. Muñoz Hidalgo, Cómo fue Miguel Hernández (1975); and J. Poveda, Vida, pasión y muerte de un poeta: Miguel Hernández (1975).

HERNÁNDEZ, PEDRO (c. 1513– ?), b. Andalusia. Historian and private secretary to Álvar Núñez Cabeza de Vaca (q.v.), Governor of Paraguay during 1540–5. Hernández's Comentarios (Valladolid, 1554), of which the first 13 chapters were written in collaboration with Cabeza de Vaca, is the first Spanish book on the conquest of the River Plate region, and quite naturally takes the part of Cabeza de Vaca against Domingo Martínez de Irala, the governor of Asunción until his death in 1556.

As a historian, Hernández is to be read with caution; the most valuable chapters are those dealing with the life of the Indians, and the desperation with which they fought the conquistadores against overwhelming odds. The Comentarios were reprinted in vol. 22 (1852) of the BAE.

HERNÁNDEZ, RAMÓN (1935–). Spanish novelist. Palabras en el muro (Barcelona, 1968) develops tremendismo (q.v.) as a style within the context of prison life. It can be read allegorically.

El tirano inmóvil (Barcelona, 1971) offers a bitter, disillusioned view of Madrid adolescents. The disabled Bruno attempts to take revenge on a gangster but fails. Like J. M. Guelbenzu (q.v.), Hernández uses documentary methods to make his radical statements.

HERNÁNDEZ CATÁ, ALFONSO (1885–1940), b. Santiago, Cuba. Cuban short-story writer and novelist educated in Spain. He spent some years in the diplomatic service in Europe, but settled in Spain in 1910 as an opponent of the Machado regime in Cuba. His last years were spent in Panama, Chile, and Brazil. He died in an air crash over the bay of Río de Janeiro.

Hernández Catá's fiction rarely touches on Cuba, except for his virulent stories of life under Machado in *Un cementerio en las Antillas* (Madrid, 1933). His style is modernist, and his themes realistic, using the model of Maupassant in *Cuentos pasionales* (1907). His later stories mature in psychological subtlety, as in the collections *Los frutos ácidos* (1915), *Los siete pecados* (1918), *Piedras preciosas* (1927), and *Manicomio* (1931), where his interest in abnormal states of mind becomes an obsession. *Sus mejores cuentos* (Santiago, Chile, 1936) contains selections made by Eduardo Barrios (q.v.). Hernández Catá also wrote a bestiary, *La casa de fieras* (1919), and essays on Martí (q.v.) in *Mitología de Martí* (1928).

His longer novels are less important, since he was unable to sustain a complex plot or differentiate between his many characters shrewdly enough to be convincing. *Pelayo González* (1909) and *La juventud de Aurelio Zaldívar* (1912) show the influence of Felipe Trigo (q.v.) and Oscar Wilde, while the social novel *La muerte nueva* (1922) was ill-conceived, and the Cuban *costumbrismo* of *El bebedor de lágrimas* (1926) has become dated. His last novel was *El ángel de Sódoma* (1927).

Hernández Catá also wrote plays: *La noche clara* and *La casa deshecha*; *Don Luis Mejía* with Eduardo Marquina (q.v.); and two in collaboration with his brother-in-law and fellow-exile Alberto Insúa (q.v.): *El amor tardío* and *En familia*.

HERNÁNDEZ FRANCO, Tomás Rafael (1904–52), b. Tamboril, Dominican Republic. Short-story writer and poet. He wrote sensuous poetry in the Afro-Caribbean manner in *Rezos bohemios* (1921), *De amor, inquietud, cansancio* (1923), *Canciones del litoral alegre* (1936), and *Yelidá* (1942). The best of his three collections of short stories is *Cibao* (1951). Hernández Franco also wrote *La poésie de la République Dominicaine* (Paris, 1923).

HERNÁNDEZ RUANO, Diego (1902–), b. Huelva. Writer of short stories, *Las pequeñas nubes* (1933), and realistic novels in the manner of Alarcón, *El pasado viene* (1956) and *Huellas del buey* (1961). His collection of poems on his native Huelva, *La tierra y yo*, appeared in 1965.

Héroe, El, a didactic work by Baltasar Gracián y Morales (q.v.), which was first published at Huesca (1647) in an edition now lost. The first surviving edition is that of Madrid (1653),

followed the same year by another published in Amsterdam.

As with most of his other works, Gracián signed *El héroe* with the false Christian name 'Lorenzo'. Like *El discreto* (q.v.), the work seeks to 'form a gigantic man through a small book, and to fashion immortal deeds with short sentences'. The great man should restrain his passions, exercise prudence and good taste, and above all dissemble his true powers. He requires good luck, intelligence, and a nimble mind to gain ascendancy over other men. As well as effortless grace he must cultivate virtue first and foremost. 'Greatness cannot be founded upon sin, which is nothing, but upon God, Which is everything. It recks little to be a hero to the world; to be a hero to heaven is worth a great deal'.

Among the editions of *El héroe* are those of A. Coster (Chartres, 1911, a reprint of the 1639 edn.); of A. Reyes, in *Tratados* (1918); of G. Juliá Andreu (Barcelona, 1941); and of J. Costa (Buenos Aires, 1943).

See M. Romera-Navarro, *Estudio del autógrafo de 'El héroe'* . . . (1946), being *anejo* 35 to the *Revista de Filología Española*.

HERRERA, Darío (1870–1914), b. Panama City. Poet, short-story writer, and journalist who travelled widely in South America and settled in Buenos Aires, where he met Leopoldo Lugones (q.v.). Herrera wrote for the daily *La Nación* and for *El Mercurio de América*. His only book, the short stories of *Horas lejanas*, appeared in Buenos Aires in 1903, and his influence on the spread of modernism in Latin America was substantial. His poems, scattered throughout dozens of journals, are considered the prime example of Panamanian modernism, though he is not inspired by national themes. He was the first of many to translate Wilde's *Ballad of Reading Gaol* into Spanish (1898).

HERRERA, Fernando de (1534–97), b. Seville. Poet, called 'el Divino' because of the reputation he enjoyed during his lifetime. In the absence of a university in Seville, he attended one of the *tertulias* (q.v.), that of the Conde de Gelves, where he met the humanist Juan de Mal Lara, the canon Francisco Pacheco (uncle of Herrera's future biographer and editor, the painter Francisco Pacheco), the poets L. Barahona de Soto and Baltasar del Alcázar, and the playwright Juan de la Cueva (qq.v.). In the Count's home, about 1559, he fell in love with the beautiful Countess, and this (probably platonic) love affair afforded him the chief theme for his poetry (see F. Rodríguez Marín's *El divino Herrera y la condesa de Gelves*, 1911). He called Doña Leonor 'Eliodora', 'Luz', 'Lumbre',

'Sirena', 'Aglaia' ('que quiere decir Esplendor'), and other names signifying fire, light, and whiteness, but is chivalrously careful to avoid hinting at her identity, though it was always known to his intimate friends. Even Francisco de Rioja, in his prologue to Herrera's *Versos* (ed. Pacheco, Seville, 1619), refused to name the *amada*, since her second son Nuño Álvarez Pereira Colón y Portugal was still alive.

It has been suspected that in 1571 (when Herrera wrote his joyful *Elegía III*), the Countess offered him hope of affection, and it is known that in 1575 she entrusted him with a will unknown to her husband, but by 1578 (the date of the MS. of the *Rimas inéditas* ed. by J. M. Blecua in the *Revista de Filología Española, anejo* 39, 1948) he was again treated with disdain. The Countess Leonor died in 1591, and Herrera wrote little poetry thereafter, confining himself to prose works which are mostly lost, such as the ambitious *Istoria general del mundo*, which Pacheco claimed was finished in 1590. Lost too are a number of his poems: a pastoral fable concealing his love for the Countess entitled *Los amores de Lausino y Corona*, a translation of Claudian's *De raptu Proserpinae*, and a *Gigantomaquia* again based on Claudian which was already lost by 1619. His *Tomás Moro* (Seville, 1592), now extremely rare, has been edited by F. López Estrada in *Archivo Hispalense*, vol. 12 (1950).

In his lengthy, controversial *anotaciones* to his edition of the *Obras de Garcilaso de la Vega* (1580; see also SÁNCHEZ DE LAS BROZAS, Francisco), Herrera described his poetics (though he never completed a promised *Arte poética*) as the search for 'claridad'. Each idea must be expressed by a single word, and if no word exists for a particular idea, then it must be coined anew. The poet's craft must be learned, and Herrera's constant, thorough revision of his own work must be considered in any discussion of his attacks on other writers. He manages hyperbole with audacity, prefiguring Góngora in his propensity for colours and striking images. He concludes that with Garcilaso the Castilian language has come of age, and can bear the elevation that noble subjects demand. His love poetry is influenced by Petrarch, the *cancioneros*, and Ausias March, while his patriotic *canciones* owe a great deal to the narrative technique of the Old Testament.

He used *liras* (q.v.) for the *Canción al señor don Juan de Austria vencedor de los moriscos en las Alpujarras*, probably written shortly after the victory of 1571, but thereafter his patriotic verse used between 8 and 13 hendecasyllabic lines apart from the odd heptasyllable; the *Canción por la pérdida del Rei Don Sebastián* (on his defeat at Alcazarquivir, Morocco in 1578) first published in 1582 and the *Canción en alabança de la Divina*

Magestad por la vitoria del Señor Don Juan written shortly after the Battle of Lepanto in 1571 and published as an appendix to Herrera's *Relación de la guerra de Chipre* (Seville, 1572). The only edition of his poetry that Herrera prepared for press was *Algunas obras* (Seville, 1582), showing notable changes from his 1572 MS.

O. Macrì's *Fernando de Herrera* (1959) includes a bibliography (pp. 11–20) and an anthology, but the best edition of the *Poesías* is that by J. M. Blecua (2 vols., 1975) as *anejos* of the *BRAE*.

The *Anotaciones* have been edited recently in A. Gallego Morell, *Garcilaso y sus comentaristas* (Granada, 1966). For Herrera's style, see A. D. Kossoff, *Vocabulario de la obra poética de Herrera* (1966). For his prose, see Mary G. Randel, *The historical prose of Fernando de Herrera* (London, 1971); and J. Almeida, *La crítica literaria de Fernando de Herrera* (1976).

HERRERA, FLAVIO (1892–), b. Guatemala City. Novelist, short-story writer, and poet. His legal and diplomatic career has included a period as Guatemalan ambassador to Argentina (1945). He has held the chair of Latin-American Literature in the National University of Guatemala. His first books appeared in 1921: the short stories of *La lente opaca* and the verses in *El ala de la montaña*, but it was the Japanese-style *haiku* and *tanka* in *Trópico* (1931) that brought him international recognition. Another such collection, *Cosmos indio*, appeared in 1938. His short stories (*Cenizas*, Leipzig, 1923) are influenced by Eça de Queiroz, Valle-Inclán, and French writers such as Bourget. Herrera introduced the Creole novel into Guatemala. His first, *El tigre* (Madrid, 1934), is a regional novel in the style of Zola. *Caos* (1949) is a psychological study.

HERRERA, GABRIEL ALONSO DE (1474?–after 1539), b. Talavera de la Reina, the younger brother of Hernando Alonso de Herrera (q.v.). Gabriel was chaplain to Cardinal Ximénez de Cisneros (q.v.), who commissioned him to write a textbook of farming, the *Agricultura general* (Alcalá, 1513), which was then distributed free of charge to farmers. The full title of the book is *Obra de Agricultura, copilada de diversos auctores*, and relies mainly on Greek, Arab, and Latin authorities, adding some observations from Herrera's own experience as a landlord. The book was an accepted classic for two centuries in Spain, and was reprinted by the Sociedad Económica Matritense (4 vols., 1818) and edited by A. de Burgos (2 vols.) in 1858.

HERRERA, HERNANDO ALONSO DE (1460–1527), b. Talavera de la Reina. A humanist who was one of the foremost Latinists of his age in Spain, and taught successively at the universities of Seville, Cordova, Alcalá, and (from 1513) Salamanca.

His *Breve disputa de ocho levados contra Aristótil y sus secuaces* (1517) is a bilingual dialogue opposing some points in Aristotelian philosophy, whose speakers include the author's brother Gabriel (q.v.), Hernán Núñez, Pedro Mártir, and Aristotle himself. It was edited by A. Bonilla y San Martín in *Revue Hispanique* (1920).

He also wrote a *Gramática* and a *Rhetórica* disputing the *Institutiones grammaticae* of Priscian.

HERRERA DE JASPEDÓS, Hugo, pseudonym of José Gerardo de Hervás y Cobo de la Torre (q.v.).

HERRERA PETERE, José (1910–), b. Guadalajara. Novelist, short-story writer, and poet. After producing the short stories *La parturienta* (1936), *Puentes de sangres* (Barcelona, 1938) a *reportaje* on the first phases of the Battle of the Ebro, and the novel *Acero de Madrid* (1938), which shared the Premio Nacional de Literatura with *Entre dos fuegos* by Antonio Sánchez-Barbudo, Herrera Petere emigrated after the Civil War, first to France, then to Mexico, and finally to Geneva, where he settled in 1947. *Niebla de cuernos* (Mexico City, 1940) is a satire on Spanish *emigrados* in France and on the complacency of the French themselves. *Cumbres de Extremadura: novela de guerrilleros* (Mexico City, 1945) employs realism in both dialogue and action to create the figure of the illiterate *guerrillero* Beremundo. *Dimanche, vers le Sud* (Paris, 1956) is a bilingual book of poetry.

HERRERA Y REISSIG, Julio (1875–1910), b. Montevideo. Uruguayan poet of a wealthy Creole family. After he had enjoyed a troublefree childhood and adolescence, his family fell into political disgrace in 1895, and Herrera was forced to earn his living as a civil servant. Believing in 'art for art's sake', he read the French Symbolists before being converted wholeheartedly to modernism (by Rubén Darío, q.v.) and later to *ultraísmo* (see Ultra, Grupo).

He founded *La Revista* (1899–1900) and the shortlived *La Nueva Atlántida* (two numbers, 1907), but his influence was most profoundly felt through the *tertulia* he founded in his Torre de los Panoramas, a room at his home in Montevideo, in 1902. Many young Uruguayan poets and artists visited Herrera there, especially between 1905–7, and it was from his Torre that Herrera issued the following *Decreto* (published in the magazine *Nosotros*, vol. 13, 1914):

'Abomino la promiscuidad de catálogo. ¡Solo y conmigo mismo! Proclamo la inmunidad literaria de mi persona. *Ego sum imperator*. Me incomodo que ciertos peluqueros de la crítica me hagan la barba ... ¡Dejad en paz a los Dioses! Yo, Julio'.

In the absence of real excitement in his life, Herrera invented an autobiography full of poverty, drugs, sickness, and persecution, and his Bohemian attitudes favoured an originality of expression and a quest for the extravagant metaphor at odds with some of his earlier work: *Los éxtasis de la montaña*, elegant sonnets written between 1900–4 and published 1904–7; and the idyllic calm of *Sonetos vascos* (1908), on a part of Spain that he had never seen.

His conversion to modernism is marked by 'Las pascuas del tiempo' (in *Almanaque artístico del siglo XX*, 1901), and signs of surrealism are detectable in *La torre de las esfinges* (1909).

Herrera's doubts and volatile temperament made it difficult for him to create a coherent body of work, but a profound dedication to his craft through periods of neurosis (considered a family weakness by R. Bula Píriz) ensured that his poetry was always exciting, as in *Los parques abandonados* (1909), where pastoral and baroque images mingle unexpectedly.

His *Poesías* (Madrid, 1911) and *Prosas* (1918) preceded more comprehensive editions by Guillermo de Torre, *Poesías completas* (Buenos Aires, 1942; 3rd edn., 1958); by R. Bula Píriz, *Poesías completas* (Madrid, 1951, 2nd edn., 1961, with good bibliography); and in the Colección de Clásicos Uruguayos, *Obras poéticas* (1966).

Herrera's *Obras completas* were published in 5 vols. (1913–14). His sister Herminia wrote *Vida íntima de Julio Herrera y Reissig* for the *Revista Nacional*, no. 63 (1943) and *Julio Herrera y Reissig: grandeza e infortunio* (1949). R. Bula Píriz has written on the biographical background in *Herrera y Reissig* (New York, 1952) and his subject-matter and style have been studied by Y. Pino Saavedra in *La poesía de Julio Herrera y Reissig* (Santiago de Chile, 1932) and by Bernard Gicovate in *Julio Herrera y Reissig and the Symbolists* (Berkeley, Calif., 1957).

HERRERA Y RIBERA, Rodrigo de (1592–1657), b. Madrid. Playwright, who studied with the Jesuits at their Colegio Imperial in Madrid and then lived at court. He was praised by Lope de Vega in the *Laurel de Apolo*, while Cervantes described him (in the *Viaje del Parnaso*) as 'insigne en letras y en virtudes raro'.

His finest play, *Del cielo viene el buen rey* (reprinted in vol. 45 of the BAE, 1858) combines courtly, religious, and symbolic threads in a manner anticipating that of Calderón (q.v.), though Herrera is more frequently associated with the school of Lope. This play has been studied by José Bergamín (q.v.) in *Mangas y capirotes* (1933).

Herrera also wrote *El primer templo de España*; *La fe no ha menester armas, y venida del inglés a Cádiz*; *Lo cauteloso de un guante, y confusión de un papel*; and the satirical *Castigar por defender*. He used the *Crónica de España* (Part 3, chapters 11 and 19) as a source for a rather laboured historical play *El voto de Santiago, y batalla de Clavijo*, a version of which was printed in vol. 33 (1670) of the large collection of *Comedias escogidas* (1652–1704).

HERRERA Y TORDESILLAS, ANTONIO DE (1549–1625), b. Cuéllar, Segovia. Official historian of the Indies and Castile until his death at the age of 76, when he had served Philip II, Philip III, and Philip IV. After 1625 he was succeeded by Tomás Tamayo de Vargas (q.v.).

Most of his writing consists of tendentious studies of near-contemporary history, such as the *Historia de lo sucedido en Escocia e Inglaterra, en quarenta y quatro años que biuió María Escocia* (1589); *Historia de . . . los sucessos de Francia, desde el año de 1585 que comenzó la liga Católica, hasta el fin del año 1598* (1598); and the immensely detailed chronicle of America from the discovery to 1554 contained in his *Décadas o Historia General de los Hechos de los Castellanos en las Islas i Tierra firme del mar Océano* (4 vols., 1601–15), reprinted in 17 vols. by the Real Academia de la Historia (1934–58).

Undiscriminating in his judgment and more verbose than any other historian of his time, Herrera's strength lies in his access to all the official documents of the age, and his diligence in both seeking them out and using them. His numerous other books include the translation *Los cinco primeros libros de los Annales de Cornelio Tácito* (1615) and a history of his own times in 3 vols.: *Primera parte de la Historia general del Mundo . . . desde el año de M.D.LIX hasta el de M.D.LXXIIII* (1601); *Segunda parte . . . desde el año de M.D.LXXV hasta el de M.D.LXXXV* (1601); and *Tercera parte . . . desde el año de 1585 hasta el de 1598* (1612).

See Narciso Alonso Cortés, 'Datos sobre el Cronista Antonio de Herrera' in *Estudios Segovianos*, vol. 1 (1955).

HERVÁS Y COBO DE LA TORRE, JOSÉ GERARDO DE (d. 1742). A priest, lawyer, and professor at Salamanca University. He has been identified as the 'Jorge Pitillas' who wrote *c.* 1741 the elegant *Sátira contra los malos escritores de este siglo*, first published in the *Diario de los literatos de España* (1742) and reprinted by L. A. de Cueto in vol. 61 of the BAE (1869). This *sátira* in *tercetos encadenados* is modelled so closely on Boileau that it employs all the quotations from classical authors found in his work. The *sátira* (often attributed in earlier times to Padre Isla, q.v.) is more important for its theoretical position than for its intrinsic interest, for it exemplifies the current reaction against an enfeebled national tradition, while remaining sufficiently independent to mock at indiscriminate lexical borrowing from French. Its style is sober and moderate. Hervás, who wrote criticism for the *Diario* under the imperfect anagram Hugo Herrera de Jaspedós, did not live to complete further promised *sátiras*.

HERVÁS Y PANDURO, LORENZO (1735–1809), b. Horcajo de Santiago, Cuenca. Polymath and father of comparative philology, he was called 'the Spanish Goethe' by Azorín (q.v.) on account of his encyclopaedic learning. He entered the Jesuit order in 1749, studying at Alcalá until 1756. He taught Latin at Cáceres and classics in the Jesuit college in Madrid. When the Jesuits (q.v.) were expelled from Spain to Italy, Hervás stayed first in Forlì and then in Cesena before establishing himself in Rome in 1783.

His great work, *Idea dell' universo* (22 vols., 1778–90) was written in Italian. The first eight vols. (1778–80) were devoted to physiology, anthropology, and sociology; the next two (1781) to astronomy; the next six to the Earth; the next five to the classification of languages; and the last to the love of God and the other theological virtues.

The Spanish edition was corrected, expanded and largely rewritten as separate treatises: *Historia de la vida del hombre o, Idea del universo* (7 vols., 1789–99); *Viaje estático al mundo planetario, en que se observan el mecanismo y los principales fenómenos del cielo, se indagan sus causas físicas y se demuestran la existencia de Dios y sus admirables atributos* (4 vols., 1793–4); *El hombre físico* (2 vols., 1800); and the epoch-making *Catálogo de las lenguas de las naciones conocidas* (6 vols., 1800–5), publishing new data supplied from Jesuit missionaries the world over, and acknowledged by Max-Mueller, Humboldt, Pallas, and other pioneers in comparative philology as a corner-stone of their research. Hervás wrote grammars of forty languages. When the Jesuits were allowed to return to Spain in 1798, Hervás came to Barcelona, but again suffered common exile in 1801, when Pope Pius VII appointed him Librarian of the Quirinale. His last major work was an attack on the French Revolution in Italian, translated into Spanish as *Causas de la Revolución de Francia en el año de 1789* (2 vols., 1807).

See Fermín Caballero, *Conquenses ilustres* (4 vols., 1868–75), which also deals with Cano (q.v.),

Díaz de Montalvo, and Alfonso and Juan de Valdés (qq.v.).

HIDALGO, ALBERTO (1897–1967), b. Arequipa. Peruvian poet who contributed to *Colónida* in 1916, having founded his own shortlived *Anunciación* (Arequipa, 2 issues, July-August 1915). His immature *Arenga lírica* (Arequipa, 1916) and *Panoplía lírica* (1917) were followed by the futurist, ultraist *Química del espíritu* (1923), published like all his subsequent books in Buenos Aires, where he was living and working as a reporter on *El Mundo*.

Simplismo (1925) was a poetic manifesto proposing the reduction of poetry to pure metaphor, a programme which Hidalgo himself did not follow. He contributed to *Amauta* (q.v.) at this period, and published his *Descripción del cielo* (1928).

His final period is marred by a tiresome cult of the ego imitated from Salvador Dalí: *Dimensión del hombre* (1938), *Carta al Perú* (1953), *Biografía de yo mismo* (Lima, 1959), *Patria completa: Canto a Machu Picchu* (1960), *Historia peruana verdadera* (Lima, 1961), and *Poesía inexpugnable* (1962).

Hidalgo's prose is often as ebulliently iconoclastic as some of his poetry: the novel *El Anticristo* (1957) recalls the *Oda a Stalin* (1945). His *Tratado de poética* (1944) is a belated defence of *simplismo*, the system that he had virtually abandoned years before. He selected the *Antología personal* which was published in Buenos Aires in 1967.

See José Muñoz Cota, *Construcción de Alberto Hidalgo* (Asunción, 1947) and Gyula Kosice, *Peso y medida de Alberto Hidalgo* (Buenos Aires, 1953) for critical studies on his work.

HIDALGO, BARTOLOMÉ (1788–1822), b. Montevideo. Uruguayan creator of *gaucho* literature as we know it today, the chief influence on Ascasubi and Estanislao del Campo (qq.v.). He was a mulatto son of Buenos Aires parents who moved to Uruguay shortly after their marriage. Not a *gaucho* himself, Hidalgo nevertheless portrayed the life of the *gauchos* in their own idiom, and by using their song-models in propaganda for the wars of independence, helped to raise the reputation of the *gauchos*. He wrote predominantly in *cielito* form (q.v.) using the popular rhythms in songs to celebrate the struggles of 1811–16 against Spanish domination.

His *Diálogos patrióticos* (1820–2) consists of *Diálogo patriótico interesante entre Jacinto Chano, capataz de una estancia en las islas del Tordillo, y el gaucho de la Guardia del Monte*, in which the protagonists discuss the quarrels of 'federales' and 'unitarios' in the newly independent nation; *Nuevo diálogo patriótico entre Ramón Contreras . . . y Chano . . .*, on the Spanish expedition to recover her colonies; and *Relación que hace el gaucho Ramón Contreras a Jacinto Chano de todo lo que vio en las Fiestas Mayas de Buenos Aires, en 1822*. The genuinely popular nature of his work is attested by the fact that his poems were bought on the streets by ordinary people.

Hidalgo also wrote a play, *Sentimientos de un patriota* (1816).

See Martiniano Leguizamón, *El primer poeta criollo del Río de la Plata* (Buenos Aires, 1917; 2nd edn., Paraná, 1944); E. F. Tiscornia, *Poetas gauchescos: Bartolomé Hidalgo, Hilario Ascasubi, Estanislao del Campo* (Buenos Aires, 1940); and Nicolás Fusco Sansone (ed.), *Vida y obras de Bartolomé Hidalgo, primer poeta uruguayo* (1944).

HIDALGO, GASPAR LUCAS (1560–1619), b. Madrid. Anecdotist. Almost nothing is known of his life.

He compiled a book of conversational anecdotes in the style of the Italian *novelle* and the *Patrañuelo* of Joan Timoneda (q.v.) entitled *Carnestolendas de Castilla, dividido en la tres Noches del Domingo, Lunes y Martes de Antruexo* (Barcelona, 1605). The stories are often licentious, using as a pretext the liberties permitted during the last three days of carnival in Madrid, and the book was banned by the Inquisition. It was edited by A. de Castro in vol. 36 of the BAE as *Diálogos de apacible entretenimiento, que contiene unas Carnestolendas de Castilla . . .* (1855) and appeared in *Extravagantes: opúsculos amenos y curiosos de ilustres autores* (1884) in the Biblioteca Clásica Española.

The Biblioteca Colombina has three burlesque *apologiae* by Hidalgo in MS.: a defence of long noses, another of horns, and a third of pimples.

HIDALGO, JOSÉ LUIS (1919–47), b. Torres, Santander. Poet and artist. He contributed to the Santander review *Proel* with a group of local poets including José Hierro (q.v.) and published three books in his lifetime: *Raíz: poesías* (Valencia, 1943); *Los animales: poesía* (Santander, 1944), of Franciscan-like affection and semi-mystical simplicity; and eloquent but never strident poems on death from tuberculosis in *Los muertos: poesías* (1947; 2nd edn., Santander, 1954).

L. Rodríguez Alcalde selected a volume of *Obras* (Santander, 1950), and there have been several useful evaluations of his writing: J. L. Blasco's *Escritos sobre José Luis Hidalgo* (Santander, 1956); L. Fernández Quiñones' 'José Luis Hidalgo: su poesía de la muerte' in *Revista de Literatura*, vol. 13 (1958); and 'José Luis Hidalgo' by A. R. Fernández and F. Susinos Ruiz in *Archivum* (Oviedo), vol. 11 (1961).

HIERRO, José (1922–   ), b. Madrid. Poet. He
spent his childhood and youth in Santander,
where he contributed to the magazine *Proel*
(founded and ed. by Pedro Gómez Cántolla)
and trained as an architect.

Hierro is art critic of the Madrid daily *El
Alcázar*. He has insisted that poetry must be
easily understood, and that he is 'un hombre
como hay muchos'. He has experimented with
existential themes and with the epic, but his
most successful poetry uses simple concepts and
colloquial language to imbue the ordinary with
a momentarily new meaning.

His first books *Tierra sin nosotros* (1946) and
Alegría (1947) were reprinted together as
Poesía del momento (1957), the latter having won
the Premio Adonais for 1947. In 1950 he
published the intimate *Con las piedras, con el
viento*, and in 1952 (the year he returned to settle
in Madrid), the important *Quinta del 42*,
containing the well-known poem 'Para un
esteta', which advises a creator (and the critic)
to view his 'work' *sub specie aeternitatis*, with
humility. His *Antología poética* (Santander, 1953)
won the Premio Nacional de Literatura, and
since then he has published *Estatuas yacentes*
(1955), *Cuanto sé de mí* (1957; 2nd edn., 1959),
Poesías escogidas (Buenos Aires, 1960), and
Poesías completas, 1944–62 (1962), supplemented
by the *Libro de las alucinaciones* (1964).

Hija del aire, La (2 pts., 1653?), a semi-
historical play by Pedro Calderón de la Barca
(q.v.).

The theme is overweening ambition, exemplified by Semiramis, Queen of Assyria. She is the
personification of evil, and uses love as a means
to power. She claims lineage from the gods as
the 'daughter of the air' of the title. Calderón
may have used as source material the three-act
La gran Semíramis by Cristóbal de Virués. In
the first part, Semiramis, who has been
brought up by the priest Tiresias in a cave, is
found by the Assyrian general Menón. Menón
frees her from her imprisonment and forgets his
former love Irene, sister of King Nino of
Assyria. Menón takes Semiramis to his country
estate and, on his return to the palace at
Nineveh, describes her great beauty to the king.
Nino falls in love with Semiramis, and vows to
gouge out Menón's eyes if they look once more
upon her. Semiramis is grateful to Menón for
saving her and expects to marry him, but Nino
orders Menón to pretend that his love for her has
vanished. She accepts Nino as a husband, but
only on condition that he does not deprive
Menón of life or liberty. Nino agrees, but still
commands Menón's eyes to be gouged out.

In the second part, Semiramis rules alone
after the death of King Nino. Lidoro, King of
Lydia, comes to claim the throne of Assyria,
stating that his son Irán (whose mother was
Nino's sister Irene) is the true heir to Nino's
kingdom, since Semiramis had poisoned her
husband. Semiramis scoffs at this idea, saying
that she was already in complete control; her son
Ninias is too effeminate to be able to rule a
kingdom. Semiramis wins the ensuing battle
and captures Lidoro. Now the people rebel
against Semiramis and in favour of Ninias. She
abdicates, vowing revenge. Semiramis and her
courtier Friso kidnap Ninias, and she is able to
rule in his place due to their physical similarity.
Lidoro escapes from his prison and in a second
battle, Semiramis is wounded. She sees before
her the victims (Menón, Nino, Ninias) whose
lives she has ruined in her lust for power.

The sub-plots involving amatory intrigue are
complicated by Semiramis' assumption of
Ninias' identity. The imagery of the cave in the
first part and her dress of wild animal skins
presages the violence of her subsequent actions
and the darkness which is to envelop Semiramis'
palace and her soul.

Both parts have been edited by Gwynne
Edwards (London, 1970). See also his articles
on the play's sources and its place in classical
tragedy in the *BHS*, vols. 43 (1966), pp. 177–96
and 44 (1697), pp. 161–94.

HINOSTROZA, RODOLFO (1941–   ), b. Lima.
Peruvian poet. His *Consejero del lobo* (1965)
showed evidence of wide reading (Perse, Joyce)
and a sympathetic grasp of European literary
trends, marking a sharp contrast with the
Indianist preoccupations of the previous generation in Peru.

Hinostroza has since lived in Cuba, France,
and Spain, and has published *Muerte de York*
(Mexico City, 1971) and *Contra natura* (Barcelona,
1971). The latter starts with the student riots in
France of May, 1968 and traces the interconnec-
tion of phenomena, in particular through biology
and psychoanalysis: it is a deeply serious collection of poems.

Hispania, the quarterly journal of the American
Association of Teachers of Spanish and Portuguese, founded in 1917. The current address of
the Association is c/o Wichita State University,
Wichita, Kansas 67208, U.S.A.

**Hispanic and Luso-Brazilian Councils,
The,** were created in 1943 as a British centre for
information on Spain, Portugal, and the
republics of Latin America.

A new library, opened in 1969, has a capacity
of 60,000 vols., and is the largest British lending
library in its special field. The library edits the
annotated, classified, semi-annual *British Bulletin*

of Publications on Latin America, the West Indies, Spain and Portugal (founded in 1949) from the Councils' headquarters at 2 Belgrave Square, London, S.W.1.

Hispanic Review, a scholarly quarterly journal on research in the Hispanic languages and literatures founded in 1933 and published by the Department of Romance Languages, University of Pennsylvania, Philadelphia.

Roughly half of each issue is devoted to scholarly articles and the rest to reviews of major new works in the field.

Hispanic Society of America, a society founded in 1904 by Archer Milton Huntington. It provides at 613 West 155th St., New York, N.Y. 10031, library and museum facilities on the countries where Spanish and Portuguese are or were spoken. (The Hispanic Foundation, also created by Huntington, is a department of the Library of Congress, Washington, D.C.). *A History of the Hispanic Society of America* appeared in 1954. The catalogue of the society's publications issued in 1943 was supplemented by a new list in the magazine *Apollo* (April, 1972).

The library possesses about 150,000 printed books, including 15,000 printed before 1701, of which 250 are incunabula. There are 150,000 separate items in the manuscript collection.

The *Catalogue of the library of the Hispanic Society of America* (20 vols., 1910, 50 copies only) was replaced by the *Catalogue of the library . . .* (10 vols., Boston, 1962) with a *First supplement* (4 vols., Boston, 1970). Other important catalogues are *Printed Books, 1468–1700* (1965) and *Catálogo de los manuscritos poéticos castellanos* (3 vols., 1965–6).

Hispaniola, the name given by Pedro Mártir de Angleria (q.v.) to the country Christopher Columbus called 'la Isla Española' (the Spanish Island), now known as the Dominican Republic, proclaimed 27 February 1844.

Historia troyana polimétrica, a work in prose and verse datable to about 1270 and early attributed to an in fact imaginary historian (Leomarte), but actually taken from the *Crónica general* and the *General Estoria* of Alfonso 'el Sabio' (q.v.) and from Guido della Colonna's *Historia destructionis Troiae*, a prose version of the *Roman de Troie* of Benoît de Sainte-Maure.

It was published by Agapito Rey as *Leomarte, Sumas de historia troyana* (1932), most of its poetic fragments having been edited by A. Paz y Melia (*Revue Hispanique*, vol. 6, 1899, pp. 62–80) and its MSS. and sources studied by A. García Solalinde (*Revista de Filología Española*, vol. 3, 1916, pp. 121–65).

Tres poetas primitivos (revised edn., 1958) includes an edition and study by R. Menéndez Pidal. The unknown poet is the first documented so far in Spain to adapt the strophe to character and theme. The verse metre is *sílabas contadas*.

The two surviving MSS. are in the National Library, Madrid, and the Escorial.

HITA, ARCHPRIEST OF, see RUIZ, Juan, *Arcipreste de Hita.*

HOJEDA, *Padre* DIEGO DE (1571–1615), b. Seville. Mystical poet. Having left Spain as an adolescent against the wishes his parents, Hojeda entered the Dominican order in Peru in 1591 and rose to be Vicar of all the Dominican monasteries in the province of Peru and, as the protégé of the Vicar-General of the Order in Peru, Father Agüero, became Prior of the Lima house. He inflicted such terrible punishment on his body that he was at one time in danger of losing his hearing. When Agüero was replaced by Father Domingo Almería, Hojeda was humiliated by demotion to the grade of monk and exile to Huánuco, a remote village on the edge of the jungle where his weakened body succumbed at the age of 44.

Hojeda's *La Christiada . . . Que trata de la vida i muerte de Cristo nuestro Salvador* (Seville, 1611) is the finest mystical epic in Spanish, using the familiar genre of the epic brilliantly employed by Ercilla in his *Araucana* (qq.v.) to serve a missionary purpose. The book is distinguished by the author's innocent identification of his spiritual anguish and physical torment with the Passion of Christ, and Hojeda's twelve cantos begin not with the Annunciation or the Nativity but with the Last Supper, and end with the Crucifixion. The weakness of the poem lies in its failure to endow the leading characters with a credible personality; its many strengths include imagination, melody, dignity, a sonorous use of baroque diction, and a sensitive use of *octavas reales* in the 15,792 hendecasyllabic lines. While critics have accused him of lacking a sense of drama, it is probably fair to suggest that the theme was believed at the time of writing to carry sufficient inherent drama, and that Hojeda's imagination was governed by admirable restraint.

His sources, by no means solely biblical, included Homer, Virgil, Dante, Ariosto, Tasso, Francisco Hernández Blasco's *La redención universal* (1584), and Marco Girolamo Vida's Latin *Christiad* (1535; cf. M. di Cesare: *Vida's 'Christiad' and Vergilian epic*, New York, 1964). They have been studied by M. E. Meyer in *The sources of Hojeda's 'La Christiada'* (Ann Arbor, 1953).

The poem was reprinted in vol. 17 (1851) of

the BAE, and was edited by Sister Mary Helen Patricia Corcoran (Washington, 1935). A *rifacimento* of the *Christiada* (1841) by Juan Manuel de Berriozábal is not an improvement on the original.

Hombres de maíz (Buenos Aires, 1949), a novel by the Guatemalan Miguel Ángel Asturias (q.v.).

At one level an *indigenista* protest against the exploitation of Indian lands for a quick profit by growing maize, at another level the book makes use of myth and legend in a complex manner which, as Asturias himself later admitted, makes no concession to the reader. The first of the three sections relates the Indians' struggle to preserve their sense of communal identity against the Machojón family, which aims to change their ways by the commercial farming of maize, which is to them a sacred food. The Indian hero Gaspar Ilóm is poisoned by a ruse; a curse is laid on all those who took part in the war against Gaspar, now already a mythical figure.

The second short section is entitled 'María Tecún', after the runaway wife of a blind beggar, and consists mainly of the beggar's search for her. His tale is transformed into a legendary tale in the third and final section.

Apparently unconnected with any previous character, Nicho Aquino, an Indian postman, is the protagonist. He too finds that his wife has disappeared. Having spent some time in jail for drunkenness, Nicho sets out with his dog Jazmín on what is to be his last errand to the capital. He meets an old man who offers to tell him what happened to his wife; he, Nicho and Jazmín fall through reality into a ravine; in a nearby cave Nicho finds a sorcerer who laid the curse on Gaspar Ilóm's enemies; he learns the truth that his wife had fallen into a well, observed only by the dog Jazmín; and goes through many other trials and experiences which can be understood as magical or psychological, but in either case should be read as a poetic evocation of Indian lore about death and the afterlife.

After leaving the cave, Nicho flees to the Atlantic coast and obtains a job in a hotel. One day he meets María Tecún, around whom the legend had grown. The book culminates in the search by a muleteer, Hilario, for Nicho who had wandered near a crag, reputed to lure into the void below any man whose wife had left him.

The novel exemplifies the stages in the development of consciousness defined by Jung's analytical psychology. The novel's inherent difficulties have led to its being less studied than its significance warrants.

See Giuseppe Bellini, *La narrativa di Miguel Ángel Asturias* (Milan, 1966; Spanish edn., Buenos Aires, 1970); and Richard Callan, *Miguel Ángel Asturias* (New York, 1970; in English), pp. 53–84.

HOMERO ESPAÑOL, EL, The title accorded to Luis de Góngora y Argote (q.v.) by Juan Vicuña, who spent the last twenty years before the master died in seeking out all his poems and in 1627 (a year after Góngora's death) published them as *Obras en verso del Homero español*.

HOROZCO, see also OROZCO.

HOROZCO, AGUSTÍN DE (*c.* 1550–*c.* 1620), b. Escalona. Historian, who was in the service of Diego Hurtado de Mendoza (q.v.) until his patron died in 1575. Horozco then went to Cádiz as the town's historian, completing its chronicle in 1598. It was published by the Cádiz Town Council in 1845 with Joaquín Rubio's account of the city's ancient coins.

Horozco is best known for the lively *Discurso historial de la presa que del Puerto de la Maamora hizo la armada real de España, año de 1614* (1615, reprinted in the BAE, vol. 36, 1855). He also wrote lives of the martyred saints Servando and Germano (Cadiz, 1619), benefactors of Cádiz.

HOROZCO, SEBASTIÁN DE (1510?–80), b. Toledo. Proverb-collector, poet, and playwright. Julio Cejador's attribution to him of the *Lazarillo de Tormes* (q.v.) was rejected by Emilio Cotarelo, who edited over 3,000 of Horozco's *Refranes glosados* in the BRAE (1915); most of his proverbs, however, remain unpublished. His *Relaciones* constitute an anecdotal history of Toledo.

Horozco's *Cancionero* was published in 1874 by the Sociedad de Bibliófilos Andaluces. In addition to his poetry, it contains an *entremés*, and three *Representaciones: de la historia evangélica del capítulo nono de San Juan* (which includes amusing scenes enlivened by a *pícaro* called Lazarillo); *de la parábola de San Mateo a los veinte capítulos de su sagrado Evangelio* (first performed in Toledo, 1548); and *de la famosa historia de Ruth*: there is also a *Coloquio de la Muerte, con todas las edades y estados*. There is a new critical edition of Horozco's *Cancionero* (Salt Lake City, 1975) by J. Weiner.

F. Márquez Villanueva's essay 'Sebastián de Horozco y el "Lazarillo de Tormes"' appeared in the *Revista de Filología Española*, vol. 41 (1957), pp. 253–339.

HOROZCO Y COVARRUBIAS, JUAN DE (d. 1608), b. Toledo. Religious writer. The son of Sebastián de Horozco (q.v.) the proverb-collector, and brother of Sebastián de Covarrubias Horozco (q.v.) the lexicographer.

Canon of Seville Cathedral, Archdeacon of Segovia Cathedral, and finally Bishop of Guadix, Horozco compiled one of the most influential emblem books, the *Emblemas morales* (Segovia, 1589), as well as the collection *Paradoxas christianas contra las falsas opiniones del mundo* (Segovia, 1592). In the genre of *De regimine principum* (q.v.) he wrote the *Doctrina de príncipes enseñada por el santo Job* (Valladolid, 1605).

HOSTOS, EUGENIO MARÍA DE (1839–1903), b. Mayagüez. Puerto Rican nationalist, lawyer, and moralist, whose political significance outweighs his literary importance. The 21 vols. of his *Obras completas* (Havana, 1939–1954) are incomplete in 20 vols.; his purely literary works number only six of them: the *Diario* (vols. 1–2), *Páginas íntimas* (vol. 3), *Mi viaje al sur* (vol. 6), *La peregrinación de Bayoán* (vol. 8), and *Crítica* (vol. 11).

From the age of 13 he studied in Bilbao, returning to Puerto Rico for a brief period and then qualifying as a lawyer in Madrid. In 1863 he began his lifelong campaign for the independence of the Antilles (Cuba as well as Puerto Rico) and in the same year published the first edition of the intentionally prophetic *Peregrinación de Bayoán*, a Romantic allegory in the form of an autobiographical novel, in which the hero Bayoán (representing Puerto Rico) hopes to marry a girl representing Cuba, but is prevented from so doing by her father symbolizing Spain, and wanders the earth in despair.

Hostos eventually broke with the Republicans, who refused to grant autonomy to Puerto Rico, and emigrated from Spain to New York, where he joined fellow-separatists from Cuba and Puerto Rico. He tried his hand at many genres, publishing a study of *Hamlet* in which he contrasts the politician Polonius with the poet Hamlet, and a fragment of an epic ode on *El nacimiento del Nuevo Mundo*, but he repudiated literature in the name of morality and logic (in *Moral social*, 1888) and refused to acknowledge his non-political writings. There is a useful *Antología* (Madrid, 1952) by Eugenio Carlos de Hostos.

See J. Bosch, *Hostos el sembrador* (Havana, 1939) and *Eugenio María Hostos: vida y obra. Bibliografía. Antología* (New York, 1940); and Raquel Romeu y Fernández, *E.M. de Hostos, antillano y ensayista* (Madrid, 1959).

HOYO MARTÍNEZ, ARTURO DEL (1917–), b. Madrid. Anthologist, critic, short-story writer, and literary editor for Aguilar, the Madrid publishing house. In *Teatro mundial* (1955) he summarized the plots of 1700 plays. He has edited for Aguilar the selected works of Miguel Hernández (1952), and the complete

works of Federico García Lorca (1954), and Baltasar Gracián (qq.v., 1960), as well as the *Teatro completo* (Mexico City, 1968) of Max Aub (q.v.). He has compiled *Antología del soneto español clásico* (1963) and *Antología del soneto español, siglos XVIII* and *XIX* (1968). He has also written the study *Gracián* (Buenos Aires, 1965), having previously edited Gracián's *Oráculo manual* (1949).

His short stories appeared in *Primera caza y otros cuentos* (1965), *El pequeñuelo y otros cuentos* (1967), and *En la glorieta y en otros sitios* (1972).

HOYOS Y VINENT, ANTONIO DE, *Marqués de Vinent* (1886–1940), b. Madrid. Novelist. He studied in Vienna (where his father was Spanish ambassador), at Oxford and Madrid universities and became one of the most popular erotic novelists of the day, though he stated in an interview with J. M. Carretero in *La Esfera* of 5 May 1916 that 'en mis libros el amor es una cosa horrenda y escalofriante'. In Spain his books were compared with those of Felipe Trigo (q.v.), but his cultivated and imaginative style most closely resembles that of D'Annunzio's *Il fuoco*. He was influenced by 'Rachilde' (the pseudonym of Mme Alfred Valette, née Marguerite Eymery, 1860–1953) and 'Jean Lorrain' (the pseudonym of Paul Duval, 1856–1906).

The thirty long novels and fifty shorter novels by Hoyos are concerned with mysticism, as well as with profane love, often indicating a connection between the two. The setting is that of his familiar aristocratic surroundings, except in *Mors in vita* (1904), *Frivolidad* (1905), *A flor de piel* (1907), and *Los emigrantes* (1909), but Hoyos retains a partly objective view of his characters and their way of life, since his heroes are frequently shown corrupted by vice born of tedium and a lack of charity. His best books are usually considered *Del huerto del pecado* (short stories, 1909), *El horror de morir* (novel, 1914), and *El monstruo* (novel, 1915), the latter an extravagant portrayal of dissolution in which the heroine Helena is grotesquely disfigured by leprosy, yet manages to retain her erotic power over the hero.

Hoyos also wrote essays: *Meditaciones* (1918), *La trayectoria de las revoluciones* (1919), and *América: el libro de los orígenes* (1927). A study of Hoyos is included in *Retratos contemporáneos* (Buenos Aires, 1944) by Ramón Gómez de la Serna (q.v.).

HOZ Y MOTA, JUAN CLAUDIO DE LA (1622–1714), b. Madrid. Playwright of the school of Calderón de la Barca (q.v.). He was made a knight of Santiago in 1653; *regidor* of Burgos; a *procurador* of Burgos in the Cortes, like his father before him, and a minister of the exchequer. As censor of plays, he was apparently the official responsible for sanctioning the performance of his own works.

Among his religious plays are *San Dimas* (which was a source of Hartzenbusch's *El mal apóstol y el buen ladrón*), *Morir en la cruz con Cristo*, and *Joséf, salvador de Egipto*. His best-known *comedias novelescas* are *El villano del Danubio* (drawn from an anecdote of Fray Antonio de Guevara, q.v.) and *El castigo de la miseria*, based on the story of the same title by María de Zayas (q.v.). Hoz y Mota's characterization of the miser Don Marcos is a great improvement on the original, however, and gave Scarron the idea for *Le châtiment de l'avarice*.

El castigo de la miseria is one of the two plays by Hoz y Mota reprinted in vol. 49 of the BAE (1859). The other is his best work, the historical play *El montañés Juan Pascual y primer asistente de Sevilla*, considered by Menéndez y Pelayo to stem from the 'democratic' plays of Lope, but more likely, in Valbuena Prat's view, to derive from Calderón's *Alcalde de Zalamea* (q.v.). This is the source of *Una antigualla de Sevilla* by the Duque de Rivas (q.v.) and *El zapatero y el rey* by José Zorrilla (q.v.).

Hoz y Mota also wrote on the theme of Guzmán el Bueno (q.v.), basing his *El Abrahám castellano y blasón de los Guzmanos* on Luis Vélez de Guevara's *Más pesa el Rey que la sangre*.

His *entremeses El invisible* and *Los toros de Alcalá* were edited by E. Cotarelo y Mori in vol. 17 (1911) of the NBAE.

HUARTE DE SAN JUAN, Juan (1529?–88), b. San Juan de Pie de Puerto, formerly in Spain, now Saint Jean de Pied de Port, France. He left the frontier country in fear of political difficulties, and is known to have studied medicine at Alcalá, where he qualified as a doctor in 1559. He is the writer of only one book, which was of extraordinary influence and fame in its time: the *Examen de ingenios para las sciencias. Donde se muestra la differencia de habilidades que ay en los hombres, y el género de letras que a cada uno responde en particular* (Baeza, 1575). The Inquisition made no objection to the book, but professors at Baeza alleged that Huarte had mocked their disciplines and persuaded the Inquisition to ban it from 1581 (in Portugal) and 1583 (in Spain). But by then it had already appeared in French (Lyons, 1580; there were 25 editions in French, as many as in Spanish), and it was to appear in quick succession in Italian (7 edns., the first being in Venice, 1582), in Latin (3 edns.), in English (translations by Richard Carew, 1594; and E. Bellamy, 1698), in Dutch, and in German (Lessing being the translator).

The main purpose of the book is to indicate which science, profession, or trade should be followed by each person, in view of his aptitudes, hereditary skills, strength, and 'humours'. The souls of all men are equal, according to Huarte, but the four bodily humours: melancholy, blood, choler, and phlegm (corresponding to the four elements: earth, air, fire, and water) occur in different proportions in each man, and other factors influencing his growth and aptitudes include his food and drink, his climate and nationality, the conjunction of the stars at his birth, and his domestic life and education. Perfectly-balanced individuals are mediocrities, and it is necessary to use the special faculties of each man to their best advantage, so that some 'distemper' or imbalance is needed for any exceptional quality in a man. Huarte recommends, in a rudimentary form, aptitude testing in schools, and also career-counselling. The last chapter suggests ways of judging who is best fit to rule, juggling the requirements enough to prove that all of them are to be found in the person of Philip II, to whom the book is dedicated.

The influence of the book has been traced to Bacon, to Pierre Charron (1541–1603), and to Cervantes' *Don Quijote*. Among various aberrations in the book, phrenology is propounded as a science, leading Lavater to praise him as a precursor of that pseudo-science. Several other works were published on the same lines, notably *El sol solo ... y Anatomía de Ingenios* (Barcelona, 1637) by Estevan Pujasol.

Huarte's *Examen* was edited by A. de Castro for the BAE, vol. 65 (1873), while Rodrigo Sanz compared the first edition with the greatly amended one (full of errors) prepared by Huarte's son (Baeza, 1594) in his critical edition for the Biblioteca de Filósofos Españoles (2 vols., 1930).

The standard study on Huarte and his work is Mauricio de Iriarte, *El Dr Huarte de San Juan y su 'Examen de ingenios'. Contribución a la historia de la psicología diferencial* (1931; 3rd enlarged edn., 1948).

Huasipungo (1934), a major social-realist novel by the Ecuadorian Jorge Icaza (q.v.).

Alfonso Pereira, owner of a mountain village where Indians live, is forced by circumstances to leave the city and retire to his village, where his daughter can bear her illegitimate child. He raises money by signing an agreement with a U.S. company which wants to drive a road through the area to open up the country for timber felling. Pereira thus becomes an agent of 'imperialist' interests, and cheats the peasants out of their patches of land (*huasipungos*) with the connivance of the local political boss and the priest. The inarticulate Indians, deprived of the land which is their only means of survival, rebel against Pereira, who calls in the forces of law to massacre the Indians.

Icaza epitomizes the fate of the Indians in the life of Andrés Chiliquinga, whose wife is compelled to nurse Pereira's illegitimate grandchild. Chiliquinga is fined for damage to crops, lamed while working in the forest, and when the family is at starvation point is forced to give his wife rotten meat, which poisons her. Though the book has been accused of overstating its case, there are examples of the evils it attacks in all periods of Latin-American history and all Latin-American nations. Icaza records with brevity and passion the squalor of Indian life and the inevitability of the sudden, instinctive revolt. Chiliquinga's love for Cunshi is a bright moment in a story filled with brutality and superstition. A great *indigenista* novel, *Huasipungo* is by no means purely didactic. It includes descriptions of religious ceremonies, social traditions, and a cockfight, which highlight the Indians' plight. The novel has been reshaped in successive editions, and remains one of the key novels in the Spanish American *indigenista* tradition.

There is a translation, *Huasipungo: the villagers* (Southern Illinois, 1964), with an introduction by Bernard M. Dulsey.

HUDSON, WILLIAM HENRY (1841–1922), b. Quilmes, near Buenos Aires, of New England parents who moved to the River Plate region in 1833, and to Chascomús in the pampas in 1846. His early years were spent exploring the land and wild life where he lived, and in 1868–9 he traversed much of Argentina and Uruguay on horseback during the *gaucho* troubles, and described the 'Guerra Grande' between Rosas and the alliance of the Defensa de Montevideo in his vivid novel *The purple land* (2 vols., London, 1885), which dropped after the first edition from its title *that England lost*, an allusion to the British intention to conquer the area in 1807.

Hudson's mother died in 1859, and his father in 1869, leaving him alone and uneducated except for a few fleeting lessons with private tutors. He visited Patagonia in 1870, producing a sensitive travel book *Idle days in Patagonia* (London, 1893). In 1874 he left Argentina for good, settling in London, where he married a widow who ran a boarding-house. He is buried in Worthing.

He contributed much to our knowledge of natural history in Argentina, especially its bird life, and wrote with Sclater *Argentine ornithology* (2 vols., London, 1888–9), *The naturalist in La Plata* (London, 1892), and *Birds of La Plata* (London, 1920). His *Green mansions* (London, 1904) is a romance of the South American jungle. Hudson's masterpiece is the nostalgic autobiography *Far away and long ago* (London, 1918), in which he praises the wild liberty of the *gaucho* against the ugliness and conformity imposed by the Industrial Revolution.

See Morley Roberts, *William Henry Hudson: a portrait* (London, 1924).

HUERTA, EFRAÍN (1914–), b. Silao, Guanajuato. Mexican poet and journalist. He is closely identified with the magazine *Taller* (1938–41), which viewed literature from a social viewpoint, and while he has written lyrical verse on love and loneliness, he has become associated with ideas of revolution by the proletariat. *Absoluto amor* (1935) and *Línea del alba* (1936), his first collections of poetry, were included in *Los hombres del alba* (1944); his other books are *Poemas de guerra y esperanza* (1943), *La rosa primitiva* (1950), *Poesía* (1951), *Estrella en alto y nuevos poemas*, and *Poemas de viaje, 1949–1953* (both 1956), the latter employing experiences from travels in the U.S.A., U.S.S.R., Hungary, and Czechoslovakia to praise Negro music, attack racial discrimination and capitalist exploitation, and meditate on the possible fate of his own country; this last theme recurs in *¡Mi país, oh mi país!* (1959), which followed *Para gozar tu paz* (1957), and preceded *Elegía de la policía montada* (1959), *Farsa trágica del presidente que quería una isla* (1961), *La raíz amarga* (1962), and *El Tajín* (1963).

Huerta has also written essays on Mayakovski, Tirso de Molina, and Ortega y Gasset.

HUERTA, JERÓNIMO DE, see GÓMEZ DE HUERTA, Jerónimo.

HUETE, JAUME DE (*c.* 1480?–*c.* 1535?), b. Alcañiz? Aragonese playwright. His five-act *Comedia intitulada Tesorina, la materia de la qual es unos amores de un penado por una Señora y otras personas adherentes* (*c.* 1525) and *Comedia llamada Vidriana* (*c.* 1528) were written in the style of Torres Naharro (q.v.), with debts to *La Celestina* (q.v.). These two works, all that survive of Huete, were edited by U. Cronan in 1913 for the Sociedad de Bibliófilos Madrileños.

HUIDOBRO FERNÁNDEZ, VICENTE GARCÍA (1893–1948), b. Santiago. Chilean poet, whose theories led to the formulation of the manifesto *Non serviam* read to the Athenaeum of Santiago in 1914 and the movement known as *creacionismo* (q.v.) in Buenos Aires in 1916. According to this doctrine, the true poet is not the Aristotelean imitator of Nature but the 'creationist', who would 'hacer un poema como la naturaleza hace un árbol'. The books of this period are *Ecos del* *alma* (1910), *Canciones en la noche* (1912), *La gruta del silencio* (1913), *Pasando y pasando: polémicas* (1914), *Adán* (1916), and *El espejo de agua* (1916).

In 1916 he arrived in Paris, and there contributed to *Sic* (1916) and *Nord-Sud* (1917), befriending Pierre Reverdy and other *avant-garde* writers and painters. Though he returned to Chile several times (and his influence was first obvious in the magazine *Pro*, 1933), he only definitively returned to his native land after World War II. He had become so Gallicized that when the Popular Front won their victory of 1938 he said 'Estoy orgulloso de este triunfo. Siempre he dicho que Chile es mi segunda patria'. The books of this period include many in French, and his experimental novels influenced by the word-play of Joyce. The poetry consists of: *Horizon carré* (Paris, 1917), *Tour Eiffel* (Madrid, 1918), *Hallali* (Madrid, 1918), *Ecuatorial* (Madrid, 1919), *Poemas árticos* (Madrid, 1919), *Saisons choisies* (Paris, 1921), *Finis Britanniae* (Paris, 1923), *Automne régulier* (Paris, 1925), *Tout à coup* (Paris, 1925), *Vientos contrarios* (1926), *Altazor* (written in 1919; Madrid, 1931), *Ver y palpar* (1941), *El ciudadano del olvido* (1941), and *Últimos poemas* (1949).

His *Manifestes* were collected in 1925 (Paris). Huidobro's novels are: *Mío Cid Campeador* (Madrid, 1929), *Cagliostro* (written in 1921–2; 1934); *La próxima* (1934), *Papá, o el diario de Alicia* (1934), *Tres inmensas novelas* (1935), and *Sátiro, o el poder de las palabras* (1939). *Temblor de cielo* (written in 1928; Madrid, 1931) is a prose poem, and Huidobro also wrote two plays: *Gilles de Raiz* (written in 1925–6; Paris, 1932), and *En la luna* (1934), the latter a political farce culminating in the collectivist revolution that radicals were dreaming of at the time. The *Obras completas* (2 vols.) appeared in 1964.

As a precursor of *ultraísmo* (q.v.), *creacionismo* sought the striking metaphor and the disconcerting juxtaposition of images seldom or never introduced into poetry before, such as Otto von Zeppelin in *Alerta*. The typographical eccentricities that Huidobro adopted from Apollinaire's *Calligrammes* and made popular formed one of the ingredients of concrete poetry later to become established in Europe and Brazil, in particular.

Huidobro is a key figure in Latin-American poetry for his dedication to 'el poder de las palabras'; for his Bohemian behaviour; his equilibrium between a Spanish, Latin-American identity under a French, European *persona*; his delirious word-building and calculated flair for publicity. Like Joyce, he rebelled against a Jesuit education and chose exile from a provincial background to a metropolis. Like Joyce, he renewed a poetic tradition (the impetus of Darío had vanished) and rejoiced in the hoax

(most of the dates on his works are false) and in the literary humour of the Dadaists.

His immediate disciples (Braulio Arenas (q.v.), Volodya Teitelboim, Eduardo Molina, Eduardo Anguita, and Teófilo Cid) tarnished the reputation of *creacionismo* by their failure to rise to Huidobro's heights. Huidobro's own place is assured as one of the authentic poets of the 20th c.

See H. A. Holmes, *Vicente Huidobro and Creationism* (New York, 1933); the selected *Poesía y prosa* (Madrid, 1957) prefaced by Antonio de Undurraga's essay 'Teoría del creacionismo', of value as a recent statement by Huidobro's principal remaining disciple; E. Caracciolo-Trejo, *La poesía de Vicente Huidobro y la Vanguardia* (1974); and R. de Costa (ed.), *Vicente Huidobro y el creacionismo* (1975).

HUMBOLDT, ALEXANDER, *Freiherr von* (1769–1859), b. Berlin. Explorer and botanist. He studied at Frankfurt on Oder and Göttingen universities and at the Academy of Mining at Freiberg. In 1796 he resigned his appointment in the Prussian Department of Mines to prepare for an expedition to Central America, leaving Paris with the botanist Aimé Bonplan (1773–1858) in December 1798. Travelling slowly through Spain, they eventually set sail from Corunna in May 1799, arriving at Cumaná, Venezuela, on 16 July.

The travels, which took five years, covered Mexico, Cuba, the Orinoco basin of Venezuela, Colombia, Ecuador, and Peru, ending with a short visit to the U.S.A. On his return in 1804, Humboldt was for a short time in Berlin but spent most of the next twenty-three years in Paris, working on the important *Voyage aux régions équinoxiales du Nouveau Continent* (35 vols., 1808–27).

Ideen zu einer Geographie der Pflanzen, nebst einem Naturgemälde (1807) was followed by his most readable book, *Ansichten der Natur* (2 vols., 1808). His study of Mexican politics was *Versuch über den politischen Zustand des Königreichs Neu-Spanien* (1809–14). From 1827 he was required to reside in Berlin, and in 1829 he took part in a scientific expedition to Siberia and Central Asia. From 1834 he was engaged in his monumental work *Der Kosmos. Entwurf einer physischen Weltbeschreibung* (5 vols., 1845–62).

Humboldt's *Gesammelte Werke* (12 vols.) appeared in 1853, and *Mexico-Atlas* (ed. H. Beck and W. Bonacker) in 1969. The best bibliography is that by J. C. Löwenberg, constituting vol. 2 of K. C. Bruhns, *Alexander von Humboldt: eine wissenschaftliche Biographie* (3 vols., 1872).

HURTADO DE MENDOZA, DIEGO DE (d. 1404). Spanish poet, remembered chiefly for a

charming *cossante* (q.v.) included by E. Allison
Peers in his *Critical anthology of Spanish verse*
(Liverpool, 1948).

He was the father of Íñigo López de Mendoza,
Marqués de Santillana (q.v.), and thus related
to the Renaissance humanist of the same name
(see below).

HURTADO DE MENDOZA, Diego de (1503–
75), b. Granada. Humanist, historian, poet and
diplomat. He was a direct descendant of Íñigo
López de Mendoza, Marqués de Santillana
(q.v.), grandson of an ambassador of the Reyes
Católicos at the Holy See, and son of the Conde
de Tendilla who was made governor of Granada
after the capitulation of the Moors in 1492.

Hurtado studied the humanities in Granada
and Salamanca, mastering Hebrew and Arabic
as well as Greek and Latin. He was destined by
his family for the Church, but served instead in
the Spanish armies at Pavia (1525) and Tunis
(1535), distinguishing himself in both campaigns.

He was entrusted with negotiating royal
marriages in England in 1537–8, but his mission
to unite Henry VIII with Charles V's niece (the
Duchess of Milan) and Mary Tudor with Don
Luis of Portugal was unsuccessful. He then
travelled to the Low Countries and was ambassador to Venice 1539–47; there he patronized
the Aldine Press, and continuously commissioned
searches for Greek MSS. on the mainland of
Greece and on Mount Athos. Flavius Josephus,
for example, was first printed from three MSS.
in his great private library.

In 1547 he was sent to Rome to administer a
public rebuke to Pope Julius III in open council
and thereafter was treated almost as Viceroy of
Italy. Governor of Siena at this time, he crushed
a rising and was charged with financial mal-
practices. He requested that the case be examined
fully, but it was not until after his death that a
verdict of innocence was announced in 1578. He
was recalled to Spain in 1554, and when the
severe Philip II acceded to the throne in the
following year, Hurtado's freedom of action was
curtailed.

Philip took the excuse of a court quarrel in
1568 between Hurtado and one Diego de Leiva
to banish Hurtado from the court: first to
Medina del Campo, and later to Granada, where
he joined the king's army in quelling the *morisco*
rising in the Alpujarras (1568–71), a period he
was to recreate from first-hand knowledge in his
remarkable *La guerra de Granada*, published
incomplete in 1610, again (lacking Book III) in
Lisbon (1627) and again, complete but full of
misprints, in 1730 (5th edn., 'con lo que faltaba
en las anteriores', Valencia, 1776). The edition
in vol. 21 (1852) of the BAE is only slightly
superior to that of Luis Tribaldos in 1627, but

B. Blanco-González has re-edited the work in
Clásicos Castalia (1970). It is a crucial book
despite its limited subject and the opinion of
E. Fueter (in *Histoire de l'historiographie*, Paris,
1914) that it 'seems to be a bad translation of
the *Annals* of Tacitus'—for it is the first objective
and impartial military chronicle written by a
Spaniard. Its model is Sallust, rather than
Tacitus, and the latinity of the style is often
oppressive, but Hurtado shows a descriptive
ability and an intellectual honesty that spares
no-one, not even the king. It may have been the
writer's candour that delayed the history's
publication so long.

Hurtado de Mendoza, born in the same year
as Garcilaso de la Vega (q.v.), helped popularize
the Italianate metres of Garcilaso and Boscà,
exchanging verse epistles with Boscà, writing
Petrarchan sonnets, and composing in *octavas
reales* the *Fábula de Adonis, Hipómenes y Atalanta* one
of the most successful essays in the new metres.

His *redondillas* were praised by Lope de Vega,
but his most celebrated poems are indecent, such
as the *Fábula del cangrejo*, revealing another facet
of a writer whose various works included a
translation of Aristotle's *Mechanica* into Spanish.
He was for some time (though is no longer)
considered the author of *Lazarillo de Tormes*
(q.v.) and is almost certainly the Erasmian
satirist who wrote the short *Diálogo entre Caronte
y el ánima de Pedro Luis Farnesio, hijo del Papa
Paulo III* in 1547, the year in which long-
suffering conspirators assassinated the tyrannical
Duke of Piacenza and Parma, Pietro Luigi
Farnese. The dialogue between Charon and
Farnese on the Council of Trent and the abuses
at Rome is both amusing and penetrating, in the
manner of Lucian; it appears in vol. 36 (1855)
of the BAE.

The *Obras* of Hurtado y Mendoza published
by Juan Díaz Hidalgo in 1610 are confined to
poetry. The next selection (of which many are
thought to be spurious) is in vol. 32 (1854) of the
BAE, while the best edition is that of P. Bohigas:
Epístolas y otras poesías (Barcelona, 1944).

There is an exhaustive biography by A.
González Palencia and Eugenio Mele: *Vida
y obras de don Diego Hurtado de Mendoza* (3 vols.,
1941–3). His great private library passed
eventually at his request to the Escurial. A
moving letter written in 1574 (and quoted by
Dormer in *Progresos de la historia de Aragón*,
Saragossa, 1680) shows him dusting his books
for the last time: 'Strange authors there are
among them, of whom I have no recollection,
and I wonder I have learned so little when I find
how much I have read'.

HURTADO DE MENDOZA Y LARREA,
Antonio (1586–1644), b. Castro Urdiales,

Santander. Poet and dramatist at the court of Philip IV, known to his contemporaries as 'el Discreto de palacio'. From 1623 he was a secretary to the king and an intimate of the royal *privado*, the Conde-Duque de Olivares. His plays were written for the king's theatre at Aranjuez, the chivalresque *Querer por sólo querer* (1622) having been written for a royal birthday and acted by the ladies of the court.

The best-known of his plays, *El marido hace mujer y el trato muda costumbre* (1631–2), provided Molière with the theme for *L'école des maris*. *Los empeños del mentir* (after September 1634) gave Le Sage (q.v.) the idea for his *Gil Blas de Santillane*. These two plays, together with the *comedia de figurón* (q.v.), *Cada loco con su tema* (1630), were reprinted in vol. 45 (1858) of the BAE. Hurtado de Mendoza's other plays are *No hay amor donde hay agravio* (before 1621?), *Los riesgos que tiene un coche* (1630–44?), *El galán sin dama* (1635?), *El premio de la virtud* (before 1621?), *Quien más miente medra más* (1631), and *Celos sin saber de quien* (1630–2?).

Mendoza also wrote *entremeses*. Like the work of most other poets of his time, Mendoza's writings were known chiefly through oral tradition and manuscript, and an edition of *El Fénix castellano don Antonio de Mendoza, renacido* (Lisbon, 1690) is clearly extremely corrupt. His elegant devotional verse, the *Vida de Nuestra Señora María Santísima* (Naples, 1672), was highly regarded by Cervantes, who mentions it in the *Viaje del Parnaso* (1614); Lope de Vega praised his verses on the beatification (1620) and the sanctification (1622) of San Isidro. Lope dedicated his verse epistle *La Circe* (1924) to Mendoza.

Some of his secular verse was imitated from Góngora (q.v.), who called him 'el aseado lego' ('the polished layman').

The best edition of his *Obras poéticas* is that by Rafael Benítez Claros (3 vols., 1947). See Gareth A. Davies, *A poet at court: Antonio Hurtado de Mendoza, 1586–1644* (Oxford, 1972), and 'A chronology of Antonio de Mendoza's plays' in *BHS*, vol. 48 (1971), pp. 97–110.

HURTADO DE TOLEDO, LUIS (1523–90), b. Toledo. Playwright. Parish priest of San Vicente, Toledo. Although both works were attributed to him, it has been established with fair certainty that he is the author of neither the *Palmerín de Inglaterra* (now given to the Portuguese Francisco de Morães, 1500–72) nor the *Tragedia Policiana*, the best imitation of *La Celestina* (q.v.), proved now to be the work of Sebastián Fernández (q.v.).

He did write the pastoral *Égloga Silviana*, printed in Valladolid with the 2nd, undated edition of the *Comedia Tibalda* begun by

Perálvarez de Ayllón (q.v.) and completed by Hurtado. He also finished a play by Micael de Carvajal (q.v.), *Las Cortes de la Muerte* (1557), one of the best *danses macabres* ever written in Spain, which was reprinted in the BAE, vol. 35 (1855).

Hurtado has also been credited with the authorship of a *Memorial de algunas cosas notables que tiene la ciudad de Toledo* (1576) and a translation of the *Metamorphoses* of Ovid (Toledo, 1578).

HURTADO DE VELARDE, ALFONSO (1580?–1638), b. Guadalajara. Playwright of the school of Lope de Vega (q.v.), whose *comedia El bastardo Mudarra* inspired Hurtado's own *La gran tragedia de los siete infantes de Lara*, written between 1612 and 1615 and first published in the *Flor de las comedias de España* (1615).

He may be the author of *El triunfo del Avemaría, o la tomada de Granada*, a play by an 'Ingenio de esta Corte' (q.v.) based on another on this theme by Lope.

Hurtado may also be the author of the stirring ballad on the gift of a horse to Juan I at the Battle of Aljubarrota, 'Si el caballo vos han muerto' printed as ballad 981 in the *Romancero general* edition by A. Durán (BAE, vol. 16, 1851), which was interpolated into the play attributed to Vélez de Guevara (formerly to Lope himself), *Si el caballo vos han muerto*.

HURTADO Y VALHONDO, ANTONIO (1825–78), b. Cáceres. Dramatist and civil governor of Albacete from 1859, then, successively, of Jaén, Valladolid, Cádiz, Valencia, and finally of Barcelona, where his courage during an outbreak of cholera in 1865 earned him great respect. He began to compose plays when very young and *La conquista de Cáceres* (1842) was his second success in his home town.

He left for Madrid the same year, turning to journalism and politics. *El romancero de Hernán Cortés* (1847) is a collection of 29 ballads in the manner of the Duque de Rivas (q.v.), which was followed by *El romancero de la princesa* (1852), and *Madrid dramático* (1876; ed. A. González Palencia, 1942), on real and imaginary episodes from the life of Lope de Vega and other playwrights of the Golden Age.

Hurtado wrote a number of plays in collaboration with Núñez de Arce (q.v.): *El laurel de la zubia* (1865) set in 1507, with Queen Isabella anachronistically resolving a conflict as a *dea ex machina*; *Herir en la sombra* (1866), on Antonio Pérez; and *La jota aragonesa* (1866) on the siege of Saragossa.

His best historical play was *Sueños y realidades* (1866), on the wedding of Queen Isabella. Twice a widower, Hurtado resorted to the comforts of spiritualism in his later years: one result was his play *El vals de Venzano* (1872), foreseeably a failure with the public, who were equally unappreciative of his *costumbrista* novels.

HYGINUS, Caius Julius (*fl. c.* 5 A.D.), b. Spain. A pupil of Alexander Polyhistor, he was appointed librarian of the Palatine Library under Augustus, according to Suetonius, and was friendly with Ovid. His writings, now lost, included a treatise *De agricultura*; *De dis penatibus*; *De proprietatibus deorum*; *De familiis Troianis*; and a commentary on Virgil. It is likely that he is the Hyginus who compiled myths as *Genealogiae*, a work familiar as *Fabulae* from the title of its *editio princeps* by Micyllus (Basle, 1535), which is the only extant authority for the text, the MS. having been lost. H. J. Rose published a critical edition (Leyden, 1934) but the original editing by Micyllus was slovenly and it is difficult to reconstruct the original mythography.

I

IBÁÑEZ, Sara de (1910–). Uruguayan poet, who uses strict verse forms in disconcertingly hermetic poems on love, death, and patriotism. Jorge Carrera Andrade has defined her skill in traditional metres such as the sonnet, *décima*, *lira*, and *terceto* coupled with dazzling metaphor and word-play as 'neoculteranismo surrealista'.

Her most important books since *Canto* (1940) and *Canto a Montevideo* (1941), are *Las estaciones y otros poemas* (1957), *La batalla* (1967), and *Apocalipsis 20* (1970).

IBARBOUROU, Juana de (1895–), b. Melo. Uruguayan poet, christened Juanita Fernández Morales, she was educated in a convent, married a young soldier at the age of 18, and went to live in Montevideo.

Her vocabulary is very simple, and her themes are nature and human love: 'Tómame ahora, que aun es temprano / y que llevo dalias nuevas en la mano' is typical of the fresh and sensuous rhythm of *Las lenguas de diamante* (1919), her first book. Her imagery became richer with successive books: *Raíz salvaje* (1922), *La rosa de los vientos* (1930), and *Perdida* (1950), the last appearing in the year that she became President of the Uruguayan Society of Authors. Her popularity throughout Latin America was officially recognized in 1929 when the title 'Juana de América' was conferred on her. She continued to write poetry, publishing *Oro y tormenta* in 1956.

Her prose-poems *El cántaro fresco* (1920) and brief *Autobiografía* (Mexico City, 1957) were not her only writings in prose: she wrote short stories: *Chico Carlo* (1944), a children's play, *Los sueños de Natacha* (1945), and religious books. V. García Calderón wrote an introduction to her *Obras completas* (Madrid, 1953; 3rd edn., 1968) which were compiled by Dora I. Russell, and Jorge Arbaleche selected *Los mejores poemas* (1968).

See Sara Bollo, *La poesía de Juana de Ibarbourou* (1935); Norma Suiffet, *Tres poetas uruguayos: Juana de Ibarbourou, Sara de Ibáñez, Hugo Petragli Aguirre* (1955); and Maria José de Queiroz, *A poesia de Juana de Ibarbourou* (Belo Horizonte, Brazil, 1961).

IBARZÁBAL, Federico de (1894–1954), Cuban poet of persistently Romantic and modernist tendencies who ignored the literary revolutions of Latin America. Of his half-dozen books, the best-known are *Huerto lírico* (1913), *El balcón de Julieta* (1916), *Una ciudad del trópico* (1919), and *Nombre del tiempo* (1946). His poetry developed from adolescent themes such as vague longing towards a recognition of the value of familiar things such as his descriptions of a busy port.

Ibarzábal compiled an anthology of Cuban *Cuentos contemporáneos* (1937) and wrote short stories himself, the finest being *Tam-Tam* (1941), on the traffic in African slaves.

Iberia, the word used by Herodotus to describe the Spanish peninsula. It derives from the Latin *Iberus* (the river Ebro) and, strictly speaking, covers only the territory inhabited by the peoples near the mouth of the Ebro valley.

IBN AL-'ARABI (Spanish: Abenarabi, 1165– 1240), b. Murcia. A *sufi*, whose full name was Abubakr Muhammad ibn al-'Arabi al-Hātimī at-Tā'ī, the greatest mystic of Muslim Spain. His monumental work is *al-Futūhāt al-Makkīa* ('The Meccan Revelations') which is a compendium of spiritual lore, but he wrote copiously on metaphysics, cosmology, psychology, and the Qur'an. His most widely-read book and testament is the *Fusūs al-hikām*, or *Bezels of wisdom* (1229). After Ibn al-Farīd, Ibn al-'Arabi is considered the best of *sufi* poets writing in Arabic. His doctrines have left their mark in Dante and Ramon Llull. Posterity called him 'ash-Shaikh al-Akbar' ('Doctor Maximus') and 'Muhyi ad-Din' ('Reviver of Religion').

IBN AL-KHATIB (Spanish: ABENALJATIB or BEN AL-HATIB, d. *c.* 1374), b. Loja. Poet, and biographer in his *Círculo*, a curious anthology of the lives of men associated with the author's adopted town of Granada. While at the court of Muhammad V in Granada his enemies intrigued against him, causing him to flee to North Africa, where he was captured, brought back to prison, and strangled.

See Emilio García Gómez, *Métrica de la moaxaja y métrica española: ensayo de meditación del 'Gais at-tausih' de Ben al-Hatib* (1975).

IBN BAJJA, ABUBAKR MUHAMMAD, called Avempace (q.v.).

IBN EZRA, see EZRA.

IBN GABIROL, see GABIROL, Solomon ben Judah ibn, called Avicebron.

IBN GAYYAT, ISHAQ BEN YEHUDA, see GAYYAT, Ishaq ben Yehuda ben.

IBN GUZMAN, see GUZMAN, Ibn.

IBN HASDAI, ABRAHAM (d. 1240). Spanish-Hebrew poet and philosopher. His adaptation from the Arabic of the Indian Buddhist tale that became *Barlaam and Josaphat* (1518) was published in Constantinople under the title *Ben ha-Melekh ve ha-Nazir*.

IBN HAYYAN, ABU MARWAN (987–1075), b. Cordova. Historian of Spain, whose two works *al-Matin* (60 vols.) and *al-Muqtabis* (10 vols.) survive only in fragments.

IBN HAZM, ABU MUHAMMAD 'ALI IBN MUHAMMAD IBN SA'ID (994–1064), b. Cordova. By common consent 'the greatest scholar and the most original genius of Moslem Spain' (R. A. Nicholson). By the age of 30 he had become Prime Minister to Abdurrahman V (1023–4), but on the fall of the Ummayads he retired from public life. An adherent of the Zahirite theological sect, Ibn Hazm attacked the most venerable religious authorities of Islam, who virtually 'excommunicated' him and ordered his writings to be burnt. His most valuable work has survived: the *Kitab al-milal wa 'n-nihal* ('The book of religions and sects').

In earlier life he wrote the *Tawq al-Hamama* ('The ring of the dove'), an elegant prose dissertation on aspects of profane love interspersed with mediocre verses. An epitome of the book, which is all that survives, was published in

1953, in a Spanish translation by E. García Gómez, and in an English translation by A. J. Arberry. *Naqt 'arus* has been edited in Arabic by C. F. Seybold and translated into Spanish by L. Saco de Lucena (1974).

IBN SA'ID (*c.* 1210–1274), b. Alcalá la Real. Poet, historian, geographer, and belletrist. His chief work is the *Kitab falak al-adab* ('The book of the sphere of literature'), divided into two parts, dealing respectively with Eastern and Western Arab poets. Extracts from the latter section, dealing with Andalusian writers, have been translated into Spanish by E. García Gómez (1942), and into English by A. J. Arberry (as *The pennants*, 1953).

IBN TUFAIL (*c.* 1105–1185), b. Cádiz. Physician to the Almohad ruler Yusuf. His fame rests principally on his revision of Avicenna's philosophical romance *Ḥayy ibn Yaqzān* ('Alive, son of Awake'), a work of pantheistic mysticism which traces the hero's intellectual development, on a desert island, from ignorance to wisdom. His state of grace is compared with that of Absal, who has come to the desert island to purify his soul in solitude. Ḥayy is persuaded to become a missionary, but on learning that the masses can be swayed only by concrete examples and sensuous allegory, returns to his hermit's life. Ibn Tufail's philosophy influenced Ramon Llull, but it is doubtful whether it was directly known to Gracián, whose *Criticón* (qq.v.) employs a similar theme. E. García Gómez argues that the two books have a common source: the Arabic tale of *The idol, the king, and the king's daughter. Ḥayy ibn Yaqzān* has been translated many times, the first English version being that of Simon Ockley (1708) and the latest Spanish version that of A. González Palencia (1934).

IBN ZAIDUN (1003–1071), according to H. A. R. Gibb, 'the greatest of the Spanish poets [writing in Arabic], both in his early love-songs and in the poetical epistles of his later life.' His best-known epistle, a delightful satire, is to his rival Ibn 'Abdus. Ibn Zaidun became confidential agent to Ibn Jawhar, chief magistrate of Cordova, but fell into disgrace, probably on account of his love for the Ummayad princess Wallada, herself a talented versifier.

ICAZA, JORGE (1906–   ), b. Quito. Ecuadorian novelist, who from 1960 until his retirement, was Director of the National Library in Quito. His first works were plays published in limited editions: *El intruso* (1929), *La comedia sin nombre* (1930), *Por el viejo* and *¿Cuál es?* (1931), *Como ellos quieren* and *Sin sentido* (1932). These were followed by the short stories, *Barro de la sierra* (1933). Later collections of short stories are *Seis relatos* (1952; retitled *Seis veces la muerte*, Buenos Aires, 1954), and *Relatos* (1969).

Icaza's fame as a novelist was established with his first novel, *Huasipungo* (q.v., 1934), an angry indictment of the exploitation of the Indian peasant in the tradition of *Plata y bronce* (1927) by Fernando Chaves (q.v.), and influencing many later writers, among them the Mexican Gregorio López y Fuentes (q.v.) and the Brazilian Jorge Amado (*Cacau*). Icaza's novel *En las calles* (1935) won the Premio Nacional de Literatura. His other novels include *Cholos* (1937); *Media vida deslumbrados* (1942); *Huairapamushcas* (1948); and *El chulla Romero y Flores* (1958).

See J. Eugenio Garro, *Jorge Icaza: vida, obra, bibliografía, antología* (New York, 1948); Enrique Ojeda, *Cuatro obras de Jorge Icaza* (1961); Guillermo Mata, *Memoria para Jorge Icaza* (Cuenca, 1964); and Agustín Cueva, *Jorge Icaza* (Buenos Aires, 1969).

Idearium español (Granada, 1897), an influential meditation by Ángel Ganivet (q.v.) which attempted to penetrate the character of Spain and the Spaniards in history as a method of illuminating the present state of Spain and her future prospects.

For Ganivet, Seneca was the Stoic humanist *par excellence* whose teachings formed the basis of the Spanish national character. With the advent of Christianity, Spain was polarized between the mystical (the exaltation of poetry) and the fanatic (the exaltation of action) and Ganivet teaches as a realist that the future of Spain must take into account Stoic philosophy and Roman Catholicism.

He wrote the book in his early thirties, so much of his historical analysis is tenuous and immature. He divides nations into three classes, for example: continental, peninsular, and insular, and postulates that the first are characterized in their behaviour by resistance, the second by independence, and the third by aggression. His simplistic analysis takes into account no geographical peculiarities within each group; neither does it discuss problems of relationships with other states within the same group, or in others. Yet the *Idearium español* stimulated a great deal of intelligent speculation on the rôle of Spain, and set out the questions which were to preoccupy most writers of the Generation of '98, the year in which Ganivet himself died.

His own conclusions were that Spain's overseas adventures had been mistaken, partly because of the draining of her economic and administrative resources overseas, and partly because her spirit was traditionally combative (*guerrero*) rather than calculatingly militant (*militar*).

The reaction suffered by overextending herself in such expansion he defined as *aboulía* (Greek: 'chronic apathy'), which could only be overcome by renouncing the wealth gained by the exploitation of overseas possessions and returning to the spiritual explorations for which Ganivet believed Spaniards to be ideally suited. 'Vain dreams of glory must be abandoned in favour of a dignified acceptance of everyday reality'. All Spain's efforts should be redirected to internal development, curbing the Spaniards' natural insubordination and failure to co-operate. Ganivet predicted a new Golden Age if Spain resumed her natural rôle as a spiritual and intellectual leader of nations, as had happened during the Islamic conquest.

The *Idearium español* has been translated by J. R. Carey as *Spain: an interpretation* (London, 1946). A recent survey of Ganivet's thought is M. Olmedo Moreno's *El pensamiento de Ganivet* (1965). Other views of Ganivet on the future rôle of Spain can be read in his correspondence with Unamuno (q.v.) published as *El porvenir de España* (1912).

IGLESIAS DE LA CASA, JOSÉ (1748–91), b. Salamanca. Poet of the first Salamancan School, where he was educated and became known for satirical *letrillas*, that circulated in manuscript, in the manner of Góngora and Quevedo. He was given the pastoral name of 'Arcadio' in the group of poets who met as the Parnaso Salmantino (q.v.) in 1774 and, like the others, wrote bucolic poems in the traditional style in addition to satirical verses against the low morals he observed in contemporary Salamanca.

After his entry into the priesthood in 1783, Iglesias turned to more serious writing: *silvas* after Meléndez Valdés (q.v.), *La niñez laureada* (1785) and *La teología* (1790), the only works published in his lifetime. An impressive *canción* on the feebleness of man's architecture confronted with that of Nature, *La soledad*, repeats a commonplace of the time: that of the *alabanza de aldea* and *menosprecio de corte* (q.v.).

His *Poesías jocosas y serias* (2 vols., Salamanca, 1793) first proved his dexterity in the anacreontic: *En tanto que fue niño* and *Batilo, échame vino* are equal to any lighthearted composition by Baltasar del Alcázar or Cristóbal de Castillejo (qq.v.), while his ballads collected as *La lira de Medellín* seem even more effortless than his eclogues and idylls.

The best edition of Iglesias is that in the BAE (vol. 61, 1869) to which R. Foulché-Delbosc added a further selection in *Revue Hispañique*, vol. 2 (1895), pp. 77–96.

See R. P. Sebold 'Dieciochismo, estilo místico y contemplación en "La esposa aldeana"' (a collection of Iglesias' idylls, *letrillas* and eclogues) in *Papeles de Son Armadans*, no. 146 (1968), pp. 119–44.

IGNACIO DE LOYOLA, San (1491–1556), b. Loyola, near Azcoitia, Guipúzcoa. Founder, in 1540, of the Society of Jesus (*la Compañía de Jesús*). His parents are believed to have been Beltrán Yáñez de Oña y Loyola and Marina Sáenz de Licona y Balda. Ignacio's early years were spent as a soldier; he was promoted to Captain under Antonio Manrique, Duke of Medinaceli. He fought under Francisco de Herrera at the defence of Pamplona during the French invasion of 1521, and showed inspiring courage. He was operated on for a leg wound, and thereafter suffered a limp. During his long convalescence he read widely in devotional works, and produced in Spanish, at Manresa in 1522, the *Exercitia spiritualia* (Rome, 1548), which was to become a key work in European intellectual history.

The purpose of these Spiritual exercises (many edns. in Spanish since that of Palma de Mallorca, 1650) is to suppress the desire for the world, and purify the soul by meditation for an encounter with God (see also ASCETIC WRITERS). After focussing the mind's eye on the subject of the meditation ('the composition of place'), the Christian should use 'the three powers of the soul'. These three powers are memory, understanding, and will. The exercise ends with a prayer. Many poems of the late 16th and the 17th cs. have been attributed to the practice of the Ignatian exercises, and the sonnet *A Cristo crucificado* (q.v.) is so close to his precepts that it was for some time attributed to him, although the consensus of opinion has recently turned to Fray Miguel de Guevara (q.v.). The *Exercitia* have been translated into English by J. Rickaby (1915) and W. H. Longridge (1919).

In 1523 he made a pilgrimage to the Holy Land and on his return studied the elements of Latin at Barcelona in 1526 before following courses in theology, physics, and dialectics at Alcalá. There he gathered together a group of students to practise asceticism and poverty. The Inquisition banned these activities, jailed him, and released him only on condition that he refrained from all private or public discussions of religion. Ignacio sought freedom to preach in Salamanca, where he was again imprisoned for a while. He studied at the University of Paris, and eventually graduated in 1534, in which year he made vows of chastity and poverty with a group of friends including S. Francis Xavier, Diego Laínez, Nicolás Bobadilla, and Alfonso Salmerón. Ignacio was ordained in 1537, and he

and his friends, frustrated in their attempts to reach the Holy Land from Venice because of rivalry between Turks and Venetians, put themselves at the service of the Pope, preaching in various Italian cities. Pope Paul III finally approved the Statutes of the Society of Jesus in 1540, and in 1541 the unanimous vote of the members elected Ignacio head of the new religious order. From 1547 to 1550 he compiled the constitution and rules. The Roman and German colleges of the Society were founded before his death. He was beatified in 1556 and sanctified by Gregory XV in 1622.

The *Monumenta Ignatiana* (15 vols.) appeared between 1903 and 1919, while vol. 1 of the *Obras completas* was edited by C. de Dalmases and Ignacio Iparraguirre (1952). P. Iparraguirre has also written *Práctica de los 'Ejercicios' de San Ignacio* (Bilbao, 1946) and *Orientaciones bibliográficas sobre San Ignacio de Loyola* (Rome, 1957).

Ignacio wrote his own *Autobiografía y Diario espiritual* (ed. V. Larrañaga, 1947), but the classic life is the *Vita Ignatii Loyolae* (Naples, 1572) by Pedro de Rivadeneyra (q.v.), the founder's close friend and disciple. The standard modern study is H. Rahner, *Ignatius von Loyola als Mensch und Theologie* (Freiburg, 1964). Heroic poems on the life and work of Ignacio were written by Antonio de Escobar y Mendoza (Valladolid, 1613) and by the Colombian Hernando Domínguez Camargo, the latter's fragment of 400 pages edited and published posthumously by A. Navarro Navarrete (1666).

IGNOCAUSTO, PABLO, the pen-name under which Juan Pablo Forner (q.v.) first published his satire *Exequias de la lengua castellana* (1782).

ILDEFONSO DE TOLEDO, San (607–67), b. Toledo. Ecclesiastical writer, who became Archbishop of Toledo in 657. He was a signatory at two Councils of Toledo in 653 and 655.

His most important work is the *Libellus de virginitate perpetua Mariae, adversus tres infideles*, which was translated into Spanish by Alfonso Martínez de Talavera (1444; MS. in the Escurial), reprinted in Migne's *Patrologia latina*, vol. 96 (Paris, 1850), and edited by V. Blanco García (1937). From this impassioned defence of Mary's perpetual virginity, Ildefonso became known as 'el capellán de la Virgen'. El Greco's painting of Ildefonso with a vision of the Virgin can still be seen in the charity hospital's church in Illescas, halfway between Madrid and Toledo.

Ildefonso also wrote hymns, unpublished homilies, and a surviving section of the Mozarabic liturgy, as well as two letters to Quirico of Barcelona, the biographical *De virorum illustrium scriptis* (in imitation of the *Liber de viris illustribus* of Isidoro, q.v.), and *Liber in cognitione baptismi.*

Ildefonso's style is clear and unpretentious. *The life and writings of St. Ildefonso of Toledo* (Washington, 1942) is a standard work by A. Braegelmann.

Iluminados, see ALUMBRADISMO.

Ilustración, see ENLIGHTENMENT IN SPAIN.

Ilustre fregona, La (1613), one of the *novelas ejemplares* of Miguel de Cervantes (qq.v.).

Two Castilian students of good family, Diego de Carriazo and Tomás de Avendaño, leave home to seek their fortunes as *pícaros*. After some adventures on the road they reach the Inn of the Sevillian (still standing) in Toledo, and when Tomás glances in to spy on the celebrated beauty Constanza, a servant-girl at the inn, he falls in love with her and takes a job in the inn to be near her. Diego becomes a water-seller. Life in Toledo takes up much of the rest of the story; a fight between water-sellers, a *fiesta* with songs and dances typical of the Toledo area, and other *cuadros de costumbres* told with lively wit. The story ends conventionally (as in *La gitanilla*, q.v.) with the discovery that the heroine is, after all, well-born, and with her marriage to Avendaño.

The critical edition of *La ilustre fregona* by F. Rodríguez Marín (1917) has been supplemented by that of A. Burns and J. Gibbs: *Dos novelas ejemplares: Rinconete y Cortadillo y la Ilustre fregona* (London, 1971).

Apart from the many studies of the *Novelas ejemplares* in general, J. Oliver Asín has written 'Sobre los orígenes de *La ilustre fregona*' in the *BRAE*, vol. 15 (1930), and J. Casalduero the 'Notas sobre *La ilustre fregona*' in *Anales Cervantinos*, vol. 3 (1953), where he argues that the love affair and consequent marriage are more significant than the realistic setting on which most commentators have dwelt.

See also Jennifer Lowe, *Cervantes: Two novelas ejemplares: La gitanilla and La ilustre fregona* (London, 1971). The story inspired a *comedia* of the same title by José de Cañizares (q.v.).

IMPERIAL, FRANCISCO (late 14th c.–early 15th c.), b. Genoa? Spanish poet, whose father was a Genoese jeweller who emigrated with his family to Seville. Imperial introduced Dante's hendecasyllable into Spain before Boscán and Santillana. The latter wrote in his *Prohemio e carta que . . . envió al Condestable de Portugal con las obras suyas* (c. 1449): 'Passaremos

a Miçer Francisco Imperial, al qual yo non llamaría deçidor o trovador, mas poeta; como sea, cierto que si alguno en estas partes del Occaso meresçió premio de aquella triunphal e láurea girlanda, loando a todos los otros, éste fué'. ('Let us now pass on to Francisco Imperial, whom I should describe not as "decidor" or "trovador", but rather as "poet", for it is certain that, if anyone in these parts of the world merited the prize of that triumphant laurel wreath, without disrespect to all the rest, he was that man'.)

Though doubts have recently been cast upon his authorship, the work by Imperial that Santillana seems to have been referring to above all others is the Dantesque allegorical poem in sixty *coplas* entitled *Dezir a las syete virtudes*, almost certainly mangled by the copyist in the *Cancionero de Baena*, no. 250 (see BAENA, Juan Alfonso de). In a dream, the poet sees three lovely young women dressed in red (the theological virtues) and four in white (the cardinal virtues), the setting being a heavenly meadow. Unrecognized until the close of the poem, Dante in a long beard emerges to befriend Imperial and to explain the allegory of the women and of the seven deadly snakes who menace them. Dante's curse on Florence is adapted to refer to Seville, and the *dezir* ends on a calm, optimistic note.

Imperial sometimes modifies his sources, but more frequently translates, and he finds the *arte mayor* (q.v.) a cumbersome vehicle when he slips out of the strict Italian hendecasyllables. He quotes effortlessly and correctly from Latin, Arabic, French, and English, showing familiarity not only with classical writers but also with the fashionable *libros de caballería* (q.v.). There is a critical edition by A. Woodford in the *Nueva Revista de Filología Hispánica*, vol. 8 (1954), pp. 268–94, and Woodford has also written 'Francisco Imperial's Dantesque "Dezir a las syete virtudes"': a study of certain aspects of the poem' in *Itálica*, vol. 27 (Chicago, 1950), pp. 88–100.

Another important long poem, the *Decir al nacimiento del rey don Juan* (1405) has been compared with the more celebrated *decir* by D.C. in *Symposium*, vol. 17 (Syracuse, 1963), pp. 17–29.

Imperial's other works include a moving poem on a lady taken prisoner in the Far East by Timur i-Leng and sent by him as a gift to Enrique III of Castile; *Por amor e loores de una fermosa mujer de Sevilla*; and other poems to Isabel Gonçales, mistress of the Conde de Niebla.

His major disciple was the Sevillian Ruy Páez de Ribera (*fl.* 1397–1424), a noble whose sudden destitution provided the theme for poetry on the bitterness of poverty and fate; he also influenced two lesser writers, the *converso* Ferrán Manuel de

Lando (d. 1417?) and Gonzalo Martínez de Medina (d. 1403?).

M. Chaves has written a brief essay: *Micer Francisco Imperial: apuntes bio-bibliográficos* (Seville, 1899). The whole question of Dante's influence in Spain has been traced by Agustín González de Amezúa in his *Fases y caracteres de la influencia del Dante en España* and by R. Rossi in *Dante e la Spagna* (Milan, 1929?).

INCA GARCILASO DE LA VEGA, El, see GARCILASO DE LA VEGA, El Inca.

INCHÁUSTEGUI CABRAL, HÉCTOR (1912–), b. Baní. Dominican Republic poet and diplomat. His early work is dominated by the strident tones of Walt Whitman, later muted by a mild surrealism. His themes are nature, work, justice, and sympathy for the downtrodden, such as prostitutes and the poor.

Incháustegui's *Versos, 1940–1950* (Mexico City, 1950) which gathered together all his best work since *Poemas de una sola angustia* (1940), has been supplemented by *Rebelión vegetal y otros poemas menos amargos* (1956).

INDURAIN, FRANCISCO, see YNDURAIN, Francisco.

Infantes de Lara, Los siete, see SIETE INFANTES DE LARA, LOS.

Infrahistoria, a term invented by Miguel de Unamuno (q.v.) to indicate the largely submerged and unrecorded tradition of humble people, unvisited places, and unimportant events. Writers of the Generation of '98, such as Azorín (in *Castilla,* 1912), were drawn to write *infrahistoria*. It is also the subject matter of travel books by Camilo José Cela (q.v.) such as *Viaje a la Alcarria* (1948) and the partly fictional vignettes of his *El gallego y su cuadrilla y otros apuntes carpetovetónicos* (1949), on everyday life in the insignificant town of Cebreros (Ávila) where Cela spent part of each summer from 1947 to 1950.

INGENIEROS, JOSÉ (1877–1925), b. Palermo, Sicily. Argentinian positivist philosopher, who qualified as a doctor and wrote on psychiatry and criminology. His stance changed from democratic liberalism to socialism over the years.

President Sáenz Peña refused to grant him the chair of Forensic Medicine to which he had been nominated and, bitterly disappointed, Ingenieros left Buenos Aires in 1911, travelling until 1913 through Europe, where he wrote the satirical *El hombre mediocre* (1913).

In 1915 he founded the important *Revista de Filosofía,* and spent much time and money on the preparation of a series of national classics in literature and philosophy: La Cultura Argentina. His best work is *La evolución de las ideas argentinas*: vol. 1 *La revolución* (1918) dealt with the period before the Rosas regime, vol. 2 *La restauración* (1920) with the time of Rosas, and vol. 3 *La organización* (unfinished) with the period after Rosas was overthrown at the Battle of Caseros. Another notable work was *Los tiempos nuevos: reflexiones optimistas sobra la guerra y la revolución* (Madrid, 1921).

The *Obras completas* of Ingenieros were edited by Aníbal Ponce in 24 vols. (1930–40). Sergio Bagú's authoritative *Vida ejemplar de José Ingenieros* (1936; 2nd edn., 1953) has a bibliography of the writings of Ingenieros on pp. 233–50.

INGENIO DE ESTA CORTE, UN, a convenient pseudonym used by many playwrights (often members of the Church or the nobility) to conceal their authorship of plays during and after the time of Lope de Vega. The best of these plays is *El triunfo del Avemaría*, probably inspired by a play by Lope himself, on the struggle over Granada between Christians and Muslims. Luis Astrana Marín has ridiculed the idea, once current, that this latter 'ingenio' was King Philip IV; the author is possibly Alfonso Hurtado de Velarde (q.v.).

The pseudonym was used by Tomás Erauso y Zabaleta (q.v.) on the title-page of his polemical *Discurso crítico sobre el origen, calidad y estado de las comedias de España* (1750).

Ingenioso hidalgo don Quijote de la Mancha, El, see QUIJOTE DE LA MANCHA, El Ingenioso Hidalgo Don.

Inglés de los güesos, El (1924), a novel by Benito Lynch (q.v.).

James Gray, an English anthropologist, lodges at a small ranch called La Estaca while excavating and studying Indian burial grounds. His hosts nickname him 'The Englishman of the bones' (*güesos* being the rural Argentinian pronunciation of *huesos*). The ranch-owner's daughter, Balbina (la Negra), gradually falls in love with him while rejecting the young *gaucho* Santos Telmo, and when the jealous Santos stabs Gray, it is Balbina who nurses the foreigner back to health.

When Gray recovers he finishes his work and returns to Buenos Aires. Despite the pity and affection he feels for Balbina he takes the boat to England. Balbina hangs herself. Lynch's narrative is always taut, with excellent *cuadros de costumbres*, accurate use of pampas dialect and a polished style that seldom, however, jars with the rural setting of the drama. The tragic and impossible love of the passionate, superstitious country girl Balbina for the self-controlled scientist from Europe is a very effective variation on the theme of *civilización y barbarie* so common in *gaucho* literature (q.v.).

Inquisition, Spanish, an institution, quite distinct from the Papal Inquisition of the Middle Ages, founded in 1478 by Pope Sixtus IV at the request of the Catholic Sovereigns, Ferdinand and Isabella. It was established as a result of a desire for racial purity unknown in medieval Spain, when the highest Christian families had intermarried with Jewish families, and when Christian and Muslim princes had at times been allies. Racial intolerance in the 15th c. grew to a point, by 1492, at which Spanish Jews were confronted with the alternative of baptism or exile. Many conformed outwardly but continued to practise Judaism in secret, while others fled.

Similarly, crypto-Muslims became an object of persecution following the rebellion of 1501 which Christians assumed had invalidated the treaty giving Muslims freedom of worship after the Conquest of Granada. Converts to Christianity from Islam were called *moriscos* (q.v.) and from Judaism *conversos* (q.v.) or *marranos*.

Racial purity (*limpieza de sangre*, q.v.) and religious orthodoxy came to be indissolubly connected, and the Inquisition was set up to safeguard these two loyalties, whose force was underestimated and misunderstood abroad. Pedro de Medina, writing *c.* 1540 in his *Libro de grandezas y cosas memorables en España* (1543; 2nd edn., Alcalá, 1548), observed: 'There is and has been in Spain so much zeal for the Holy Catholic Faith that in it is something which is not to be found elsewhere. This is the Holy Office of the Holy Inquisition by which are punished and chastised those who offend against the holy faith. This Holy Office is administered in so excellent a manner that it well shows itself to be guided by God for His praise and honour'.

The Inquisition was not, however, a purely religious organization, but a political instrument wholly controlled by the monarchy to strengthen national unity. The controlling council, or *Suprema*, was a royal council, and all officials of the Inquisition were appointees of the Crown. Thus, the traditional divisions of Spain (Castile, Aragón, Valencia, etc.) ceased to exist for the Inquisition, which governed the whole of Spain, except for the decade from 1507; and the ancient liberties and franchises enjoyed by sections of the community such as the nobles were ignored by the Inquisition, which used its extensive powers for purposes not specifically sanctioned by the Pope on its foundation.

The high degree of efficiency of the Inquisition can be attributed to a number of factors beyond the national solidarity cited by Medina (above). First, large numbers of influential Spaniards were zealous in seeking out suspected persons and urging them to confess. Those who confessed were usually pardoned or given light sentences, but on condition that all 'accomplices' were named and thus caught in an ever-widening net. Another factor was that of secrecy; if anyone disappeared without trace it was assumed that he had been arrested by the Inquisition. There was no defence and no appeal.

In the 16th c., certificates of purity of blood issued by the Inquisition were indispensable to anyone seeking any career. Every so often the Inquisition maintained its hold on the popular imagination by an *auto de fe* (act of faith), or solemn public announcement of its sentences in a manner intended to convey the terror and majesty of the Day of Judgment.

The effect on Spanish literature was far less significant than was the effect on philosophical and religious enquiry. The principal Spanish humanists were imprisoned or went into exile and the Erasmian school, championed at one time by Cardinal Ximénez de Cisneros (q.v.), collapsed. In 1566 Jerónimo de Zurita (q.v.), annalist of Aragón, complained that if his classical knowledge equipped him to correct a reading in Cicero, then the same knowledge enabled him to correct a reading in the Latin Vulgate, which he was prohibited from doing. The voice of Luis de León (q.v.) was heard against the timidity of the universities. As late as 1770, twenty-nine of thirty-three professorial chairs were left vacant since the spirit of enquiry was stifled. By the 18th c. the Inquisition had lost much of its bitter animosity to the Jews and had directed its energies to attacking the Enlightenment in Spain (q.v.).

Proof of the Inquisition's lack of inhibiting impact on Spanish creative literature of the *Siglo de Oro* (q.v.) can be adduced from the fact that the power of the Holy Office was at its zenith precisely at that period when drama, poetry, and the novel were at their height.

See Cecil Roth, *The Spanish Inquisition* (New York, 1964); and Henry Kamen, *The Spanish Inquisition* (London, 1965).

Institución Libre de Enseñanza, a free university, later expanded to include younger pupils, founded by Francisco Giner de los Ríos and other disciples of Julián Sanz del Río (qq.v.) in Madrid, in 1876, after Giner had been deprived of his post at the University of Madrid. The *Boletín* of the Institución first appeared in 1877.

A decree of 1875 bound all teachers to the

strict use of authorized textbooks and in the case of university professors, to submit a synopsis of lectures to their rectors to ensure that they were free from moral or religious error and adhered to the monarchical principle. Castelar and Salmerón immediately resigned on principle and Giner protested to the Prime Minister, Cánovas del Castillo, who arrested him. The British offered to found a free Spanish university for Giner in Gibraltar but he refused and, when released, set up the Institución as an autonomous body free of church or state control.

Its pedagogical methods were not only revolutionary in Spain, but were of European significance. Detailed excursions were planned to mines and important buildings; art classes were given in Madrid galleries; text-books were almost abolished, and the students' own notebooks frequently evaluated; examinations were abolished; and classes were made small enough for personal supervision to become the rule. Open-air games were encouraged, while the traditional Jesuit system of spying was outlawed.

Under ceaseless attack from conservative elements from the moment of its foundation, the Institución became steadily more influential as its methods were seen to result in the formation of citizens more mature, knowledgeable, and tolerant than those completing their studies elsewhere in Spain.

Giner was succeeded as director by Manuel Bartolomé Cossío (q.v.), who preserved the Institución's characteristics of intellectual honesty and open enquiry. After Cossío's period the Institución fell into decline.

Among the founders and teachers were the philosopher Joaquín Costa, the critic and novelist Juan Valera, the playwright José Echegaray (qq.v.), and the poet Ventura Ruiz Aguilera. Most of the pupils came to be associated with the Generación del 1898 (q.v.): they included Unamuno, Ortega y Gasset, Ángel Ganivet, and the Machado brothers (qq.v.).

Giner was also the guiding spirit behind the National Pedagogical Museum (Museo Pedagógico Nacional), directed by M. B. Cossío from its foundation in 1882; the Junta para Ampliación de Estudios e Investigaciones Científicas, founded in 1907 to award scholarships for study abroad, and chaired by Santiago Ramón y Cajal; and the important Residencia de Estudiantes, founded in 1910, over which Alberto Jiménez-Fraud presided.

See Antonio Jiménez Landi, *Don Francisco Giner de los Ríos y la Institución Libre de Enseñanza* (New York, 1959); and V. Cacho Viu, *La Institución Libre de Enseñanza* (vol. 1, 1962–).

Instituto Internacional de Literatura Iberoamericana, founded in 1939, publishes the *Revista Iberoamericana* twice a year from the University of Pittsburgh. It holds biennial meetings in Latin America and the U.S.A.

INSÚA, ALBERTO, pseudonym of Alberto Galt y Escobar (q.v.).

Ínsula, a monthly 'revista bibliográfica de ciencias y letras' in newspaper format issued since January 1946 by the Librería Ínsula, Benito Gutiérrez 26, Madrid 8.

The editor in 1976 was Enrique Canito, and José Luis Cano (q.v.), the poet and critic, has been the secretary since its foundation. *Ínsula* is heavily biased towards *belles lettres* in Spanish, with several long reviews of important new books by established writers in each issue, together with brief notices headed 'Al correr de los libros' and lists of books received in Spanish and other languages. Special issues are occasionally published, such as nos. 300–1 (November-December 1971) on Pedro Salinas (q.v.), and nos. 308–9 (July-August 1972) on Pío Baroja (q.v.).

Intereses creados, Los (1907), a play by Jacinto Benavente (q.v.) based on the traditional Italian *commedia dell' arte* plot, but set in an imaginary land early in the 17th c. The play derives from Benavente's displeasure with his creditors, who made life difficult for him in 1906 and early in 1907, and its cynical thesis is that all men are corruptible and hypocritical. Only a rare and scarcely perceptible thread of true love can bring a hint of redemption to man's sorry situation.

The timid Leandro and the *pícaro* Crispín arrive penniless but well-dressed in an unknown city. They are generous with (borrowed) money to Harlequin and the Captain, and thus gain a reputation for liberality in the city. The aged Doña Sireña is distraught at the thought that she will be unable to pay the musicians and caterers at her forthcoming party, so her niece Colombine promises to seek the aid of her fiancé Harlequin. Crispín intervenes to promise his help and that of his 'master' Leandro if Sirena will persuade the rich Pulchinella to let his daughter Silvia marry Leandro.

Crispín complicates matters by persuading Pulchinella that Leandro is a bad lot, to strengthen Pulchinella's wife's determination to thwart her husband in every conceivable way; and by bribing ruffians to pretend to murder Leandro and spread the rumour that the attempt was the work of Pulchinella, to get rid of his daughter's suitor. Leandro is now ashamed of these tricks and decides to escape, but before he can do so, Crispín brings the lovesick Silvia to

Leandro's house to compromise her and force the wedding.

Then comes a hubbub when creditors, Pulchinella, and a prosecuting lawyer arrive at Leandro's house and threaten ruin. Matters are resolved when Crispín, working on the avarice and self-interest of those present, succeeds in charming and convincing everyone, and Pulchinella finally agrees to the marriage of Leandro and Silvia.

The sequel to this play, *La ciudad alegre y confiada* (1916), lacks irony and spontaneity; both were written against Ortega's statement of 1905 that 'hoy . . . es imposible que una labor de alta literatura logre reunir público suficiente para sustentarse'.

Introducción del symbolo de la Fe (Salamanca, 1583), the devotional masterpiece of Fray Luis de Granada (q.v.). The Dominican's longest work, it was termed by Pfandl an encyclopaedia of the Christian religion in the light of the Spanish conception of the world.

Part 1 is a hymn to the beauty of Creation, and reveals the Franciscan attitude of brotherhood to all animals. From the greatest mountain to the tiniest insect, all testify to the magnificence of God. 'Él que tales voces no oye, sordo es; y él que con tan maravillosos resplandores no os ve, ciego es; y él que vistas todas estas cosas no os alaba, mudo es; y él que con tantos argumentos y testimonios de todas las criaturas no conoce la nobleza de su criador, loco es'. The style is Ciceronian, the language aptly ornate, and the use of imagery from Nature supreme in Spanish literature.

Part 2 deals with the importance of faith, outlines the fundamentals of Christian doctrine, and tells the stories of the martyrs.

Part 3 is concerned with the mystery of Redemption, the twenty fruits of the Cross, and various aspects of biblical and theological knowledge.

Part 4 continues with the account of Redemption understood through biblical prophecy. The beauty of the world is a reflection of God and awareness of it is a path to God.

Part 5 summarizes the foregoing and gives hints on converting the infidel.

The most easily available edition of the *Introducción del símbolo de la fe* is that in Colección Austral.

IPUCHE, PEDRO LEANDRO (1889–), b. Treinta y Tres. Uruguayan poet and short-story writer. In 1909 he moved to Montevideo, where he frequented the *tertulias* of Reyles, Rodó (qq.v.), and other writers.

Until 1930 he concentrated on Creole themes and moods; later he became more attracted to metaphysical speculation and his work moved away from regionalism.

Antología poética (1968) garnered the best work from *Engarces* (1912), *Alas nuevas* (1922), *Tierra honda* (1924), *Júbilo y miedo* (1926), *Rumbo desnudo* (1929), *Tierra celeste* (1938), and *La llave de la sombra* (1949).

Selección de prosas (2 vols., 1968) is a useful anthology of his fiction and essays. His novels are *Fernando Soto* (1931) and *Isla patrulla* (1935); his essays are *El yesquero del fantasma* (1943) and *Alma en el aire* (1952).

IRIARTE Y CISNEROS, JUAN DE (1702–71), b. Puerto de la Cruz de Orotava, Canary Islands. He went to study in Paris at the age of 11 and attended the classes of Voltaire, who profoundly influenced his future development. After some time in London, Iriarte returned to the Canaries, but found life there too tedious and left for Madrid, where he lived under the protection of William Clarke, confessor and librarian to Philip V. He finally found employment as tutor to the children of the Dukes of Béjar and Alba.

He threw himself into the literary life of Madrid, writing criticism for the *Diario de los literatos de España*, such as a defence of Feijóo against the Dominican P. Jacinto Segura (vol. 2, 1737). He eventually became librarian of the Royal Library and the official translator at the Ministry of State, a post in which he was to be succeeded by his nephew Tomás de Iriarte y Oropesa (q.v.).

Elected to the Real Academia Española in 1747, he collaborated on both the Academy's *Gramática* and the great *Diccionario*. He was more adept in Latin versifying than in Spanish, translating Martial and composing a lively poem on bullfighting in Madrid, *Taurimachia matritenses, sive taurorum ludi* (1725). He also wrote a *Gramática latina* (1764).

His principal work as a librarian was the catalogue of *Regia bibliothecae matritensis codices graeci* (vol. 1 only published, 1769). Iriarte's *Obras sueltas* appeared posthumously (2 vols., 1774).

IRIARTE Y OROPESA, TOMÁS DE (1750–91), b. Orotava, Tenerife, Canary Islands. Fabulist, poet, and playwright. He travelled to Madrid at the age of 13 to live with his uncle Juan de Iriarte y Cisneros (q.v.), whom he was to succeed as official translator at the Ministry of State, enjoying an excellent education and attending the *tertulias* (q.v.) of the time, especially that of the Fonda de San Sebastián, where he befriended Cadalso and Nicolás Fernández de Moratín. His first play, *Hacer que hacemos* (1770) was never performed because of the perfunctory character of the hero Don Gil.

His next work under a pseudonym: *Los literatos en quaresma*, by 'don Amador de Vera y Santa Clara' (1773) was a satire in the guise of Lenten homilies composed by a *tertulia* for the edification of the Spanish public. As a product of the Spanish Enlightenment, it is symptomatic of the polemical spirit of the times, and of Iriarte in particular. He defended his friend Moratín against Ramón de la Cruz, attacked the fabulist Samaniego, and the poet Meléndez Valdés, but above all conducted a ceaseless and ill-mannered controversy with Juan Pablo Forner (q.v.), who immediately attacked Iriarte's *Fábulas literarias* (1782) in *El asno erudito* (1782) and lampooned the Iriarte family in the unpublished 'Los gramáticos chinos'. Iriarte replied with *Para casos tales suele tener los maestros oficiales* (1783?).

The polemic, including the text of Forner's *El asno erudito*, can be studied in E. Cotarelo y Mori's fully-documented *Iriarte y su época* (1897). Forner was at one point actually prohibited from publishing further pamphlets without express approval, and Iriarte was denounced to the Inquisition for his Voltairean fable *La barca de Simón*, allegedly disrespectful to the Papacy.

Iriarte's neoclassical verse can be seen at its most characteristic in his didactic poem *La música* (1779), which enjoyed immense popularity when it appeared, running into three impressions in less than a year, one of them subsidized by the State. However his name was made with the skilfully-contrived *Fábulas literarias* (1782; ed. A. Cioranescu, Santa Cruz de Tenerife, 1951; English version by R. Rockliffe, 1851) which, as their title suggests, are not didactic tales in the manner of Aesop, but a sophisticated method of assailing Iriarte's literary opponents. He had already glossed Horace's *Ars poetica* (1777), 'translating' 476 Latin hexameters into 1065 lines of Spanish verse, but now he followed the precepts of Horace in 76 cautionary fables, stressing the need for criticism (III), for the study of the classics (IV), for clarity in style and vocabulary (VI), for combining the useful and the beautiful (VIII), and for simplicity (XV). He also displayed an astonishing mastery over a variety of metres, such as the alexandrine (X), *octavas de arte mayor* (XXXIX), hendeca-syllables stressed on the 4th and 7th syllable, and many more.

Iriarte wrote three *comedias morales* in verse: *El señorito mimado, o la mala educación* (1790, first performed in 1783); *La señorita mal criada* (1788), and *El don de gentes, o la habanera* (1790), all offering an egalitarian view of society, the working middle-class being contrasted with the idle aristocracy. Acquired learning and virtue, he claims, are to be esteemed higher than empty titles and wasted wealth.

He also composed a prose drama, *La librería* (Salamanca, 1790?) and a play for one character (*Guzmán el Bueno*, 1791) to be accompanied by music in the manner of Haydn. José Subirá has studied this aspect of Iriarte's work in *El compositor Iriarte y el cultivo español del melólogo* (2 vols., Barcelona, 1950).

Iriarte's *Colección de obras en verso y prosa* (6 vols., 1787) was revised (8 vols.) in 1805. His *Poesías y fábulas literarias* appeared in vol. 63 (1871) of the BAE and his *Poesías* (1953) were edited by A. Navarro González in the Clásicos Castellanos. Some *Poesías inéditas* (1895) were edited by R. Foulché-Delbosc and there is a *Miscelánea* of unpublished works collected by his brother Bernardo in the Biblioteca Nacional, Madrid. This miscellany is composed principally of plays: two *comedias*, *El malgastador* and *El mal hombre*; and two *dramas*: *Mahoma* and *La pupila juiciosa*.

IRIBARREN PATERNAIN, MANUEL (1903–), b. Pamplona. Novelist and playwright. His early sentimental novel *Retorno* (1932) was an unpromising work. He has since produced *La ciudad* (1939), *San Hombre* (1943), *Pugna de almas* (1945), *Encrucijadas* (1952), and *El tributo de los días* (1968).

Of his popular plays in the *costumbrista* style (*La advenediza*; *La hora íntima*; *Nosotros, los jóvenes*), the most popular so far is *La otra Eva* (1952). Iribarren has also written an excellent biography, *El príncipe de Viana* (Barcelona, 1948).

IRISARRI, ANTONIO JOSÉ DE (1786–1868), b. Guatemala City. A controversialist and novelist, whose personal experiences while travelling inspired the picaresque *El cristiano errante* (Bogotá, 1847; reissued, with a prologue, in 3 vols. by the Guatemalan Ministry of Education, 1960) and the *Historia del perínclito Epaminondas del Cauca* (1863), a satire based on the life of Simón Rodríguez which he published under the pseudonym 'Bachiller Hilario de Alta Grumea'. At the age of 19 he inherited over a million dollars from his father but preferred to take an active part in the politics of the Old World as well as the New, as a convinced liberal. He participated in the Chilean revolutionary struggle, and for a week even became President of Chile (7–14 March 1814). His important *Cuestiones filosóficas* appeared in 1861, and in 1867 the collected *Poesías satíricas y burlescas*. Among his anagrammatical pseudonyms were Dionisio Terraza y Rejón and Dionisio Isrraeta Rejón. He died in Brooklyn, U.S.A., where he was doyen of the diplomatic corps. Menéndez y Pelayo called him 'uno de los hombres de más entendimiento, de más vasta cultura, de más energía política y de más fuego en la polémica que América haya producido'.

IRVING, WASHINGTON (1783–1859), American novelist and essayist. In 1826 he was appointed to the American Legation in Madrid, and wrote there his *History of the life and voyages of Christopher Columbus* (1828). He travelled all over Spain, residing in the Alhambra for several months in 1829, the year when his *Chronicle of the conquest of Granada* (based on Ginés Pérez de Hita, q.v.) was published. The stories and essays in *The Alhambra: a series of tales* (2 vols., Philadelphia, 1832) date from this time. He produced a sequel to his Columbus book in *The voyages of the companions of Columbus* (1831) and his *Diary. Spain, 1828–1829* has been edited by Clara L. Penney (New York, 1926).

His last important book on Spain was *Legends of the conquest of Spain* (1835), when he had already become famous for 'Rip van Winkle' and 'The legend of Sleepy Hollow' in *The Sketch-Book* (2 vols., 1819–20) which he wrote under the pen-name of 'Geoffrey Crayon'.

ISAACS, JORGE (1837–95), b. Cali, Antioquia. Colombian novelist, whose father was an English Jew and whose mother was Spanish. He lived comfortably in Bogotá 1848–59, but was forced to abandon his medical studies when his father was ruined in a civil war, and he took up journalism, editing the conservative *La República* (1867), before accepting a post as consul in Chile. His *Poesías* (1864; ed. A. Romero Lozano, Cali, 1967) are of little account, as they are scarcely more than imitations of Lamartine.

Isaacs is still read today for *María* (1867), the finest Romantic novel produced in Latin America. Paul Groussac described *María* as the 'poema de América'.

He left two historical novels unfinished: 'Fania' and 'Camisa o alma negra', the latter published in the *Boletín de la Academia Colombiana* (vol. 2, 1937). His controversial *Estudios sobre las tribus indígenas del Estado de Magdalena antes de Santa Marta* betrays the pamphleteer rather than the objective ethnographer, and *La revolución radical en Antioquia* (1880) also suffers from partisanship.

See *Vida y pasión de Jorge Isaacs* by Mario Carvajal (Santiago de Chile, 1937); a collective work published in Cali: *Jorge Isaacs, hijo de Cali* (1946); and Germán Arciniegas, *Genio y figura de Jorge Isaacs* (Buenos Aires, 1967). Donald McGrady's *Bibliografía sobre Jorge Isaacs* (1971) contains 490 entries, omitting those in Hector H. Orjuela's *Fuentes generales para el estudio de la literatura colombiana* (1968).

ISAZA CALDERÓN, BALTASAR (1904–   ), b.

Natá, Panamá. Literary critic and philologist. Head of the Spanish Department in the University of Panamá. *El retorno a la naturaleza* (1934) shows the ubiquity of the theme of nature in Spanish literature from the Middle Ages up to the Romantics and beyond. *Estudios literarios* (1957) and *Estampas de viaje* (1959) were followed by *La doctrina gramatical de Bello* (1960), an acute commentary on the influential grammar of the Chilean Andrés Bello.

ISIDORO DE SEVILLA, San (c. 560–636), b. Cartagena. Encyclopaedic writer and last of the Church Fathers. He succeeded his eldest brother and teacher Leandro as bishop of Seville in 601, presided over the Second Council of Seville in 619, and at the fourth national Council of Toledo in 633. His *Regula monachorum* was widely disseminated in the two centuries following its compilation. St. Isidore's significance is not that of an original writer, but that of a compiler who summarized the corpus of classical knowledge, that would otherwise have been lost. His *Originum seu etymologiarum libri XX* (ed. W. M. Lindsay, 2 vols., 1911) was a vast, uncritical work used as a source for quotations by numerous medieval writers, including Alcuin, Bede, and Hrabanus Maurus. Though one of the latest Latin stylists in prose, paradoxically he precipitated the decline of good Latin by banning Virgil, Ovid, and other pagan writers from the libraries in his See (see Eichhorn's *Allgemeine Geschichte der Cultur*, vol. 2, 1799).

St. Isidore's encyclopaedia, which covered all the known sciences and humanities, even discussed boatbuilding, agriculture, and precious stones. It is known most commonly as the *Etymologies* from the philological erudition displayed, frequently incorrect, and often absurd. He was convinced of the mystical significance of numbers in the Bible, and interpreted them in his treatise *De numeris*. Most of his theological writings were against heretics: *Contra iudaeos, Quaestiones adversus iudaeos et ceteros infideles*, and the recently-discovered *De haeresibus*, now edited by A. C. Vega in the series Scriptores Ecclesiastici Hispano-latini Veteris et Mediaevi (El Escorial, 1936). The first *summa theologica* is Isidore's *Sentiarum libri tres*, while the *Liber lamentationum* is Visigothic Spain's remarkable precursor of the 15th-c. *De imitatione Christi* of Thomas à Kempis.

De viris illustribus continues the biographical dictionary of St. Jerome and Gennadius. In the field of history, Isidore's rambling *Chronica maiora* (from the Creation to A.D. 615), also known as the *Chronicon de sex aetatibus*, is less useful than his *Historia gothorum* (both ed. T. Mommsen in the Monumenta Germaniae Historica series, Berlin, 1894).

De ordine creaturarum deals generally with anatomy and biology, while *De natura rerum* (ed. with a French version by J. Fontaine, Paris, 1960) hands down ancient learning on astronomy and meteorology.

The Archpriest of Talavera's *Vidas de San Ildefonso y San Isidoro* was edited by José Madoz (1952) for Clásicos Castellanos. More recent, authoritative works on Isidore are E. Bréhaut's *An encyclopaedist of the Dark Ages* (New York, 1912) and P. Séjourné's *Le dernier père de l'Église, Saint Isidore* (Paris, 1929).

ISIDRO LABRADOR, *San* (12th c.). A peasant who farmed where Madrid now stands, and who is believed to have prayed and attended Mass so assiduously that his fields were neglected and angels descended to plough for him. He was regarded only as the local patron saint until 1598 when Philip III fell ill nearby and Madrid sent Isidro's remains to fend off the king's death. When Philip recovered, the name of Isidro was honoured throughout the country and his cult found its way into literature at once with a long poem *Isidro labrador* by Lope de Vega (q.v.) published in 1599 in five-line stanzas, and no less than three plays also by Lope, the first published in vol. 7 of his *Comedias* (1617), reprinted in vol. 28 of the *Comedias escogidas de los mejores ingenios* (1667), and the other two commissioned by the city authorities of Madrid to be acted in 1622, on Isidro's canonization in that year (vol. 12 of Lope's *Obras sueltas*).

There is another poem on the subject by Joaquín Ezquerra: *Elogio a San Isidro Labrador, Patrón de Madrid* (1779).

ISLA DE LA TORRE Y ROJO, *Padre* José Francisco (1703–81), b. Vidanes, León. Satirical novelist and pamphleteer. A boy of studious temperament, Isla became a novice in the Jesuit monastery at Villagarcía de Campos in 1719, studying at Salamanca and teaching theology in Segovia and Santiago. His first satire was *Juventud triunfante* (Salamanca, 1727) an account of the festivities in Salamanca when two local Jesuits were canonized by Benedict XIII. Much of the satire was taken literally as praise, as was to happen with the first edition of the *Triunfo del amor y de la lealtad. Día grande de Navarra* (Saragossa, 1746), which mocked the nobility and wealthy middle classes of Pamplona. His targets were so flattered that they sent him gifts, at which he added *Dos palabritas del Impresor* to a 2nd edition, revised and enlarged, which appeared in 1747.

His major work, and possibly the most interesting novel of the 18th c., is another satire: *Fray Gerundio de Campazas* (q.v., 2 vols., 1757–68), a long attack on pretentious preachers enlivened by peasant speech, the foolish Fray Blas, and a *gracioso* in the manner of Lope de Vega and his school. The book was banned by the Inquisition in 1760, but its popularity at court and among the laity was so great that the prohibition against reading it was seldom taken seriously. His fame as a preacher (*Sermones morales* appeared in 6 vols., 1792–3) reached Queen María Bárbara of Portugal, who asked him to be her personal confessor. Despite his inordinate delight in food and drink, he refused to leave his cell at Villagarcía, writing to his sister at one point that he hated court life 'más que la muerte'.

On the expulsion of the Jesuits from Spain in 1767, he left Corunna for Civitavecchia, Corsica, and Bologna where he was to end his days. He spent his last years on translations and on *El Cicerón*, a 12,000 line poem of sixteen cantos in *octavas* ostensibly on the life of Cicero, but actually pillorying the follies of contemporary Spain in the form of a parody on the lengthy biographies of saints then fashionable in Roman Catholic Europe. An autograph MS. has been in Boston Public Library since 1844.

Under the anagram Joaquín Federico Is-Salps his translation the *Aventuras de Gil Blas de Santillana, robadas a España, y adoptadas en Francia por Mr. Le Sage, restituidas a su patria y a su lengua nativa por un español zeloso, que no sufre se burlen de su nación* (4 vols., 1787–8), was a hoax on literary nationalism which was taken seriously by some scholars such as Llorente. The fact that Lesage adapted 15 episodes from the *Marcos de Obregón* of Espinel (qq.v.) as well as scenes from plays by Rojas Zorrilla, A. Hurtado de Mendoza, and Diego de Figueroa y Córdoba among others, should not allow the reader to infer that much of *Gil Blas* is not original; literary borrowing was common during the Middle Ages and up to the time of Lesage (q.v.).

The *Obras escogidas* of Isla (including *Fray Gerundio*) were edited by Pedro Felipe Monlau for the BAE, vol. 15 (1850). His letters form the most complete autobiography: the *Cartas familiares* (4 vols., 1786) have been edited by J. M. Reyero (León, 1904), and *Cartas inéditas* (1957) by L. Fernández.

ISRRAETA REJÓN, Dionisio, pseudonym of Antonio José de Irisarri (q.v.).

IS-SALPS, Joaquín Federico, the anagram used by José Francisco de Isla (q.v.) in translating *Gil Blas de Santillane* by Lesage 'back into Spanish'.

IXART Y MORAGAS, José, see Yxart y Moragas, José.

IZA ZAMÁCOLA, Juan Antonio de (1756–1826), b. Dima, Vizcaya. Neoclassical satirist better known by his pseudonym 'Don Preciso' or as Juan Antonio de Zamácola. A provincial scribe in the civil service during the reign of José I, he was in exile in France from 1812 to 1822. He is best known for his burlesques in the tradition of *Eruditos a la violeta* by Cadalso (q.v.): *Libro de moda, o ensayo de las historias de los currutacos, pirracos y madamitas de nuevo cuño* (1795), and *Elementos de la ciencia contradanzaria* (1796).

J. M. de Cossío compiled 'Una biografía de "Don Preciso"' for the *Revista de Bibliografía Nacional*, vol. 5 (1944), pp. 385–406.

J

Jácaras (Arabic: *jakkara*, 'to annoy, molest'), a term the *Diccionario de Autoridades* derives from *xaque*, 'the German word for ruffian'.

In Spanish literature *jácaras* are gay ballads of low life, such as the criminal underworld or brothel; by extension, a 'tall story'. A *jácara* lasting ten or fifteen minutes was often sung between the acts of a Golden Age *comedia* (at first at the request of an actor 'planted' in the pit) to replace the spoken *entremés* (q.v.) or the *baile* (dance). They were written by Quevedo (see Escarramán), Calderón, and Luis Quiñones de Benavente (qq.v.), among others. Six *jácaras* were edited by C. Rosell in his collection of *Entremeses, loas y jácaras* by Benavente (2 vols., 1872–4). Cotarelo y Morí has published a detailed account of the noisy, lewd genre in his *Entremeses, loas, bailes, jácaras y mojigangas desde fines del siglo XVI a mediados del XXVIII* (2 vols., 1911). The modern equivalent of the *jácara* is the *tonadilla*.

JACOB, Porfirio B., pseudonym of Miguel Ángel Osorio Benítez (q.v.).

JACOPIN, Prête, the pseudonym used by the author of the *Observaciones del Prête Jacopin, en defensa de Garcilaso de la Vega*, attacking the edition of the poetry of Garcilaso by Fernando de Herrera. The pseudonym is believed to conceal the identity of Juan Fernández de Velasco, Conde de Haro (q.v.) according to N. Antonio; or Luis Enríquez, Admiral of Castile, according to Ticknor.

JAIME I or **JACME** or **JAUME,** *King of Aragon* (1208–76), called the 'conquistador' from his exploits of expelling the Muslims from the Balearic Islands in 1229–33 and from Valencia, substantially recovered by 1239. He ruled from 1213 to 1276, waging war in Murcia up to 1266 on behalf of his kinsman Alfonso 'el Sabio' of Castile (q.v.) and receiving notable embassies from Michael Palaeologus of Constantinople and the Tartar Khan, as well as beginning a luckless expedition to Palestine in 1268.

Probably a poet although none of his verse has survived, Jaime certainly protected troubadours such as Arnaud Plagnés (who wrote a *chanso* for his queen, Eleanor of Castile) and Guillaume Anélier, who wrote 'Al jove rei d'Aragó, que conferma / Merce e dreg, e malvestat desferma' ('To the young king of Aragón, who defends the just and merciful, and rights the wrong').

Though the authenticity of Jaime's prose chronicle *Chrónica o commentari del Gloriosissim e Invictissim Rey En Jacme, Rey d'Aragò, de Mallorques, e de Valencia* (Valencia, 1557) has been doubted by José Villaroya (Valencia, 1800), it was accepted by Mariana and others. Jaime described his reign thoroughly and without undue bias in the chronicle published by command of Philip II, and also apparently compiled a didactic work in the tradition of medieval wisdom literature: 'Lo libre de la Saviesa', still in manuscript.

JAIMES FREYRE, Ricardo (1868–1933), b. Tacna. Poet and historian. Of Bolivian birth, Jaimes Freyre took Argentinian citizenship in 1916. He founded the influential *Revista de América* (3 issues) in 1894 with Rubén Darío (q.v.), his mentor, and befriended the other great Latin American modernist Leopoldo Lugones (q.v.).

His *Castalia bárbara* (Buenos Aires, 1899) is his finest and most characteristic work, introducing the strange world of German and Scandinavian mythology (its ice, gloom, and timelessness) into the *fin de siècle* Romanticism then enjoying its vogue in Argentina. Leconte de Lisle, Carducci, and above all Wagner, suggested the ethos, characters, and style of poems such as *El canto del mal*.

After publishing *Castalia bárbara*, Jaimes Freyre went to Tucumán, where he taught philosophy and Spanish language and literature for the next thirty years, and wrote many historical works on Tucumán: *Historia de la República de Tucumán* (Buenos Aires, 1911), *El Tucumán del siglo XVI* (Tucumán, 1914), *Historia del descubrimiento de Tucumán, seguida de investigaciones históricas* (Tucumán, 1916), and *Tucumán en 1810* (Tucumán, 1919).

He wrote another book of poetry, *Los sueños son vida* (Buenos Aires, 1917), but it lacked the shock of innovation provided by *Castalia bárbara*. Jaimes Freyre also composed a manual *Leyes de la versificación castellana* (Buenos Aires, 1912), described by Julio Cejador as 'la única teoría verdaderamente científica que existe', which concludes that free verse should be the basis of Spanish poetic writing.

His *Poesías completas* have been edited by E. Joubin Colombres (Buenos Aires, 1944), and by F. Díez de Medina (La Paz, 1957) who claims Jaimes Freyre as a Bolivian writer.

Raúl Jaimes Freyre (Ricardo's brother) has published *Anecdotario de Ricardo Jaimes Freyre* (Potosí, 1953), and there are studies by Emilio Carilla, *Ricardo Jaimes Freyre* (Buenos Aires, 1962); and by E. Ocampo Moscoso, *Personalidad y obra poética de don Ricardo Jaimes Freyre* (Cochabamba, 1968).

JAMÍS, FAYAD (1930–   ), b. Mexico. Cuban poet whose father was an Arab and whose mother was Mexican. He has spent his life since early childhood in Cuba, except for the years 1954–59 when he went to study art in Paris. He now teaches painting in the Escuela Nacional de Arte, and is the chief editor of the Cuban revolutionary *Unión*.

Cuerpos (1966) collected together his previous books: *Brújula* (1949), *Los párpados y el polvo* (1954), *Vagabundo del alba* (1959), *La pedrada* (1962, written in the early '50s), *Los puentes* (1962, written in 1956), and *Por esta libertad* (1962), the last being a work of strident communist propaganda. In his earlier books Jamís unites striking surrealist images with a clever exploitation of popular speech-rhythms.

JARAMILLO ALVARADO, Pío (1889–   ), b. Loja. Ecuadorian historian, sociologist, and politician whose articles in *El Día*, written as 'Petronio', attacked the conservative cause. *La presidencia de Quito* (2 vols., 1938–9) is the first modern historical work produced in Ecuador, while the first sociological work was *El indio ecuatoriano: contribución al estudio de la sociología nacional* (1922; 4th edn., 1954). Jaramillo comes to the conclusion that the cultural life of a nation with an Indian majority must not be confined to a white élite in the capital, a conclusion also reached by González Prada (q.v.) in Peru and Alcides Arguedas (q.v.) in

Bolivia. As a politician, Jaramillo spoke in defence of the Indian, founded the Instituto Indigenista, and stressed the potential of the eastern jungles in his travel book *Tierras de Oriente* (1936).

Jarcha, see KHARJA.

JARDIEL PONCELA, ENRIQUE (1901–52), b. Madrid. Dramatist, novelist, and professional journalist. His forty plays, some written in collaboration, mark him as the leading Spanish humorous dramatist between Pedro Muñoz Seca and Miguel Mihura (qq.v.), especially in his parody of Echegaray (q.v.): *Angelina, o el honor de un brigadier* (1934). Enrique Sordo has described Jardiel's theatre as lying 'entre el *guignol* y la deformación poética', a manner only superficially understood by the public and disagreeable to the critics, whose banal comments not only hurt Jardiel (reputedly leading to his early death from melancholy) but exacerbated the faults in his writing, since he was incapable of self-criticism. 'Construyo la comedia con la exasperación y la deformación y la mecánica hiperbólica de lo humorístico', he stated. *Teatro selecto* (1968) includes *Eloísa está debajo de un almendro, Los habitantes de la casa deshabitada, Madre, Angelina,* and *Los ladrones somos gente honrada,* and excludes the weak last play *Los tigres encerrados en la alcoba*. In his extravagant situations, banal wordplay, and insistence on the absurd and paradoxical as the norm, Jardiel foreshadows Ionesco and Adamov but the chaos in his writings is usually resolved into order, implying that no matter how peculiar events may appear on the surface, there is a reasonable explanation for everything.

He had previously concentrated on the novel, and though he later described *El plano astral* (1922) as 'malísimo', his other four novels were distinguished by black fantasy and an original misanthropic wit reminiscent of Quevedo: *Amor se escribe sin hache* (1929); *¡Espérame en Siberia, vida mía!* (1930); a bitter diatribe against women (and incidentally against men) *Pero, ¿hubo alguna vez once mil vírgenes?* (1931), a 'novela del donjuanismo' in which Don Juan Pedro Valdivia is castigated as 'un idiota. Hace falta ser un idiota completo para vivir pendiente exclusivamente de las mujeres'; and the compelling *La tournée de Dios* (1932), in which a Pope predicts the imminent arrival on earth of God.

Jardiel Poncela's *Obras completas* have been published in Mexico City (3 vols., 1958).

See D. R. McKay, *Enrique Jardiel Poncela* (New York, 1974) in English; and M. Ariza Viguera, *Enrique Jardiel Poncela en la literatura humorística española* (1974).

JARNÉS MILLÁN, Benjamín (1888–1949), b. Codo, Saragossa. Novelist, essayist, and biographer. The 17th child of 22 in a poor tailor's family, he was never sent to elementary school, but at the age of ten he joined a seminary (like his eldest brother portrayed in the biographical novel *Mosén Pedro*, 1924). He left in 1908 without a sense of vocation and then joined the Army Administrative Corps Reserve in 1910, marrying Gregoria Bergua in 1916; and leaving Spain on Franco's victory in 1939. Jarnés returned from Mexico a sick man in 1948, and died the following year in Madrid.

He dedicated himself completely to writing between 1928 and 1936, during which period he produced twenty books and became the most notable novelist of the Generation of 1927, as well as contributing hundreds of essays and reviews to Ortega's *Revista de Occidente* (q.v.).

His first literary success was the experimental novel *El profesor inútil* (1926; 2nd enlarged edn., 1934), in which a Don Juan figure in reverse is pursued by a series of girls, showing the passivity characteristic of most Jarnesian heroes. Already one senses the author's antipathy to the artificiality of 'the well-made novel'. In his admiration for Stendhal he repeatedly inveighed against 'el grupo laborioso—un poco tiznado— de los novelistas *reproductores* de la realidad' and indeed few of his characters are born or die in the course of the novel. Style and intellect, sensitivity and ambiguity, are the aims of Jarnés. In *Teoría del zumbel* (1930), for example, he takes eight pages to describe a car-crash.

Much of his work is semi-autobiographical, like *El convidado de papel* (1928; 2nd edn., 1935), which deals with seminary life in Saragossa; and its sequel *Lo rojo y lo azul* (1932), overtly if ironically Stendhalian in title and concept, on an 'outsider's' life in the army.

Locura y muerte de nadie (1929) appeared in an enlarged edition in Entrambasaguas' *Las mejores novelas contemporáneas* vol. 7 (Barcelona, 1961), for Jarnés constantly added new scenes and fresh dialogues to his published work. Juan Sánchez is an inconsequential hero whose only dream is to become great or famous, whereas everyone mistakes him for a certain Juan Martínez. All else having failed, he commits suicide by falling under a lorry but press reports refer to him merely as 'a pedestrian'. Reminiscent of Augusto Pérez in Unamuno's *Niebla* (q.v.), Sánchez is however a much more human and wittily-conceived figure.

Jarnés's other novels are *Paula y Paulita* (1929), the Arthurian legend *Viviana y Merlín* (1930; 2nd edn., 1936), *Escenas junto a la muerte* (1931), *La novia del viento* (Mexico City, 1940) based on the four stories in *Salón de estío* (1929), and *Venus*

dinámica (Mexico City, 1943) based on the short novel *Don Álvaro o la fuerza del tino* (1936).

Lo rojo y lo azul ended on a note of despair at the widening of apparently irreconcilable divisions within Spain that Jarnés observed in the early 1930s, and as he became more involved with politics, he wrote less creatively, concentrating on biographies and essays. *Sor Patrocinio* (1929; 3rd edn., 1936) deals satirically with the 19th-c. Spanish nun who was the friend and confidante of Isabel II. The *Vida de San Alejo* (1934) was the first book issued by the Spanish P.E.N. Club. Others include *Zumalacárregui* (1931) and *Castelar* (1935) on the 19th-c. politicians; *Doble agonía de Bécquer* (1936); *Don Vasco de Quiroga* (Mexico City, 1942), on a 16th-c. bishop of Michoacán; *Manuel Acuña* (Mexico City, 1942), on the 19th-c. Mexican poet; and *Stefan Zweig* (Mexico City, 1942). Numerous essays are contained in *Ejercicios* (1927), *Rúbricas* (1931), *Feria del libro* (1935), and *Cartas al Ebro* (Mexico City, 1940).

His work has been compared with that of Giraudoux, and there are touches of Miró (q.v.) in the plea for sensual enjoyment as against the ascetic life in *San Alejo* and elsewhere, but Jarnés is primarily an original, creating a homogeneous body of work from a fund of scepticism and irony: a precursor of post-Civil War writers such as Rafael Sánchez Ferlosio (q.v.), whose *El Jarama* offers a similar combination of *ingenio* and *desengaño*, digressing from the linear course of a novel to display the creator's control over his characters.

Jarnés is not widely known in Spain, due to his opposition to the Franco regime, but a recent study *Benjamín Jarnés*, has been written by J. S. Bernstein (New York, 1971) with an annotated bibliography including projects that Jarnés left unfinished.

JÁUREGUI Y HURTADO DE LA SAL, Juan Martínez de (1583–1641), b. Seville. Poet, critic, translator, and painter, who is known to have painted a portrait of Cervantes, probably that in the collection of the Marqués de Casas Torres, showing him as a man of about 65.

While in Rome to study art, Jáuregui assimilated the *terza rima* and translated rather freely Torquato Tasso's *Aminta* (1573) into Spanish (Rome, 1607), a version edited by J. Arce for Clásicos Castalia in 1970. In 1610 he participated in a *justa poética* to celebrate the beatification of San Ignacio de Loyola (q.v.). Jáuregui's *Rimas* (Seville, 1618) are both religious and secular in nature, showing technical mastery of the *terza rima* and a skilful evocation of the Horatian temperament to offset weakness in creative imagination. The prologue is a poetic credo, further elaborated in *Discurso poético contra el hablar culto y oscuro* (q.v.) and the *Antídoto contra la pestilente poesía de las Soledades* (both written 1624, the *Antídoto* first published in 1899), which attack *culteranismo* more moderately than was then the rule in literary polemics. In his *Orfeo* (1624; ed. P. Cabañas, 1948 and I. Ferrer, 1970) an imitation of Ovid which shows his aptitude for classical subjects, Jáuregui was given to the same verbal excesses and neologisms that he censured in others.

In 1625 Jáuregui wrote the *Apología por la verdad* on behalf of the *culterano* preacher Fray Hortensio Paravicino, later to be ridiculed together with his followers in *Fray Gerundio de Campazas* by Father Isla (qq.v.). *Farsalia* (1684), reprinted in 2 vols., 1789) is an exuberant recreation of Lucan's poem. Jáuregui's *Poesías* are available in vol. 42 (1857) of the BAE and the *Obras* (ed. by I. Ferrer de Alba, 2 vols., 1973) in Clásicos Castellanos.

See J. Jordán de Urríes, *Biografía y estudio crítico de Jáuregui* (1899).

JÉREZ, Francisco López de (1504–39), b. Jérez. Historian, who was the secretary appointed by Pizarro to chronicle the conquest of Peru. He accompanied Pizarro on his first journeys to Peru, in 1524 and 1526, and enlisted with him again in 1530, and thus observed at first hand all the events he describes.

Jérez's *Verdadera relación de la conquista del Perú y provincia del Cuzco llamada la Nueva Castilla* (Seville, 1534) is the most detailed, precise, and objective of all the early histories of Peru and thus, despite its comparative brevity, remained useful to scholars up to the time of Prescott (q.v.). Jérez avoids speaking of himself and of his companions, so that his work has the tone of an official report, in total contrast to the more subjective impressions of Bernal Díaz del Castillo (q.v.).

The *Verdadera relación* has been reprinted in vol. 26 (1853) of the BAE, and in vol. 5 (1917) of the Colección de Libros y Documentos Referentes a la Historia del Perú.

JÉRICA or **XÉRICA,** Pablo de (1781–1831 ?), b. Vitoria. Fabulist, who was educated at a Dominican school in his native town and at the University of Oñate. Jérica left Álava (the province of that other fabulist Samaniego, q.v.) to enter a business firm in Cádiz but became embroiled in liberal politics, and was forced into exile in France when Fernando VII proclaimed himself absolute monarch in 1814.

He published *Ensayos poéticos* (Valencia, 1814), *Poesías* (Vitoria, 1822), and *Colección de cuentos, fábulas y anécdotas* (Bordeaux, 1831), reprinted in vol. 67 (1875) of the BAE. Of little originality, his work is often mordant, in epigrams such as

El casamiento a la moda; and humorous, in fables such as *El ratón dentro del queso* and *El ratón y su hijo,* as pointed as anything that Iriarte composed.

Jesuits, Expulsion of the, took place as the result of a decree of Carlos III dated 2 April 1767. Four thousand members of the Society of Jesus were expelled from Spain and Spanish America and sought refuge in Italy, several being distinguished scholars and writers, including José Francisco de Isla, Masdéu, Hervás y Panduro, Juan Andrés, Arteaga, and Francisco Javier Lampillas (qq.v.). Their schools were abolished and their revenues seized.

The immediate pretext of their expulsion was the suspicion that they had instigated the riots of 1766 against the king's Italian minister Esquilache. In fact, the king was determined to strengthen central authority in his hands (including the curtailment of the powers of the Inquisition, which had succeeded in burning only four heretics during his reign) and he was supported by liberals influenced by the French Revolution. The Jesuits had already been expelled from France and Portugal.

Agents of Carlos III (especially Moñino) worked tirelessly in Rome and elsewhere in Italy towards the abolition of the Society of Jesus there and while Pope Clement XIII refused, his successor Clement XIV finally dissolved the Society in 1773 by his Brief *Dominus ac redemptor.*

Carlos IV abrogated his father's decree in 1798, and many Jesuits returned to Spain, but they were expelled again in 1801.

The effect of the expulsion on Italian literature was both profound and lasting, the aesthetic theories of Andrés and Arteaga counteracting the spread of French ideas, and the dissemination of learning assisting the effort of Italian universities to strengthen their departments of theology and classics.

See A. Gallerani, *Jesuitas expulsos de España* (Salamanca, 1887).

JIL, Salomé, the anagrammatic pseudonym of José Milla (q.v.).

JIMENA DÍAZ, see Díaz, Jimena (Ximena).

JIMÉNEZ, see also Ximénez.

JIMÉNEZ, Juan Ramón (1881–1958), b. Moguer, Huelva. Poet and lyrical essayist. He remained free of allegiance to any poetic school or Generation, but is considered the link between Darío and the Generation of 1927, his work evolving from symbolism and modernism to what he called 'poesía desnuda', invoking Intelligence (in 1919) to give him 'el nombre exacto de las cosas' and renouncing as too florid the elaborately poeticized work he had published until then.

He was educated, intermittently, at a Jesuit school and at Seville University. His first poems appeared in literary magazines in Huelva and Seville in 1896-8 and when one of his poems was published in Madrid in 1898, he travelled to the capital, and came into contact with modernism in the shape of Rubén Darío (q.v.). A chronic invalid, 'enfermo de ensueños y de melancolía', as Cansinos Assens wrote, Jiménez spent the years 1901-5 in sanatoria in Bordeaux and Madrid, or visiting Moguer, where he would write in *soledad*, the *leitmotiv* of his first period. He was the unofficial poet in residence at the Institución Libre de Enseñanza (q.v.) at this time, and there met Antonio Machado (q.v.), his favourite poet, and Villaespesa (q.v.), who became his closest friend. He imitated Verlaine, having abandoned Darío and Bécquer, and in 1903 started the magazine *Helios* with Pérez de Ayala (q.v.) and others.

From 1905 to 1912 he spent most of his time alone in Moguer, and the next four years chiefly in Madrid, where he met his future wife Zenobia Camprubí Aymar. A prey to frustration and hopelessness, in 1916 he set sail for a new life in the U.S.A. to marry Zenobia. The *Diario de un poeta recién casado* (1917; title changed in 1948 to *Diario de poeta y mar*) is not only the chronicle of this vital period in his life, but the beginning of a new period in his art, when he was to eliminate purely ornamental adjectives, replace end-rhyme with rhythmical tension, and reduce imagery to the essential, usually bare nouns.

During this time he translated Rabindranath Tagore with his wife, edited short-lived reviews such as *Índice* and *Ley* which published Ortega, Salinas, Lorca, and many others, and authorized a collection of *Poesías escojidas* (New York, 1917), bitterly regretting that his juvenilia had been preserved (unlike those of Machado) and repudiating all work done before 1916 as 'borradores' (rough drafts). The period 1916-27 is one of optimism, when his work begins to become famous and Zenobia assumes the strain of caring for him in illness and in his bouts of creative energy. In 1923 he wrote to the German critic Curtius, 'After 25 years of ceaseless struggle with Beauty, I feel, think and see clearly that this is where I begin', a struggle ending with *La estación total, con las Canciones de la Nueva Luz, 1923-1936* (Buenos Aires, 1946).

On the outbreak of the Civil War, Jiménez fled to the U.S.A., and found temporary homes in Puerto Rico, Argentina, Cuba, Florida, and finally Washington, continuously correcting 'la Obra' as he called his *œuvre*, much as his disciple Guillén (q.v.) was to categorize his own poetry as a single *Cántico*.

Juan Ramón, as he became universally known, was awarded the Nobel Prize for Literature in 1956 but within a few days Zenobia was dead and he survived her by less than eighteen months. His house, Calle Nueva 10, in Moguer is now a library and museum.

His most famous book is *Platero y yo* (q.v., 1914), which he began to write in 1906, using an amiable donkey as a listener while Juan Ramón's *yo* converts the routine life (and deaths) of Moguer into prose poems of sensitivity and great popular appeal. F. Garfias selected his *Primeras prosas* and *Cartas* (both 1962).

The essential poems of his first period, from the *Ninfeas* and *Almas de violeta* (both 1900) to *Estío* (1916) are collected together in *Poesías escojidas* (New York, 1917). [The orthographical eccentricity of 'j' for 'g' before *e* and *i* is consistent in Juan Ramón].

The work of *depuración* can be seen in progress throughout the rest of his life: the 522 poems of the *Segunda antolojía poética, 1898-1918* (1922), the 720 poems of the *Tercera antolojía* (1957), and the unfinished *Dios deseado y deseante*, edited and annotated by A. Sánchez Barbudo (1964).

It may be seen that his example of a life devoted to poetry ended in arid egocentricity, and that the *poesía desnuda* is taken to extremes of banality and naïveté. No poet of his time has provoked more widely-differing evaluations, but there can be little doubt that Jiménez's musical ear and sense of rhythm are faultless in hundreds of poems varying from those like *Mar, nada*, which derive from objective reality, to those in collections like *Animal de fondo* (1947), which adumbrate what he described as pantheistic mysticism, and are often quite unintelligible at first sight.

Among the many studies on the poet are E. Neddermann, *Die symbolistischen Stilelemente im Werke von Juan Ramón Jiménez* (Hamburg, 1935), on his use of French symbolism; G. Palau de Nemes, *Vida y obra de Juan Ramón Jiménez* (1957, 2nd edn., 2 vols., 1974); R. Gullón, *Conversaciones con Juan Ramón Jiménez* (1958) and *Estudios sobre Juan Ramón Jiménez* (Buenos Aires, 1960); A. Sánchez-Barbudo, *La segunda época de Juan Ramón Jiménez, 1916-1953* (vol. 1, 1962; vol. 2: *Cincuenta poemas comentados*, 1963); S. Ulibarri, *El mundo poético de Juan Ramón* (n.d. but 1962); L. R. Cole, *The religious instinct in the poetry of Juan Ramón Jiménez* (1967); Antonio Campoamor González, *Vida y poesía de Juan Ramón Jiménez* (1976); and R. A. Cardwell, *Juan R. Jiménez* (1977).

JIMÉNEZ DE CISNEROS, *Cardinal* FRANCISCO, see XIMÉNEZ DE CISNEROS, *Cardinal* Francisco.

JIMÉNEZ DE ENCISO, DIEGO (1585–1634?), b. Seville. Playwright and poet. A court favourite of Olivares and Philip IV, whose poetry was praised by Cervantes, Lope de Vega, and Pérez de Montalbán. Bances Candamo asserted that Jiménez de Enciso 'empezó las comedias que llaman de capa y espada'.

Unfortunately only ten of his many plays survive, but these include two masterpieces: *El Príncipe Don Carlos* (reprinted in 1927), not only probably the first play on the son of Philip II, but as important as Schiller's *Don Carlos* (1787); and *Los Médicis de Florencia* (to be found in vol. 45 (1858) of the BAE), which deals with the murder of Alessandro dei Medici by his cousin Lorenzo, a sombre and gripping tragedy that, for Pérez de Montalbán, 'ha sido pauta y ejemplar para todas las comedias grandes'.

His other plays are *Los celos en el caballo*; *El casamiento con celos, y el rey don Pedro de Aragón*; the *Fábula de Criselio y Cleón* (1632) known in its time as *Júpiter vengado*; *El valiente sevillano*; a *comedia de santa* called *Santa Margarita*; *La mayor hazaña de Carlos V*, on that monarch's retirement to the Hieronymite monastery of Yuste, in N.E. Extremadura; and *El encubierto* and *Juan Latino*, edited together by E. Juliá Martínez in 1951. Juan Latino is an African Negro brought to Spain as a slave. He learns Latin quickly and gains such a reputation for scholarship that he is appointed private tutor to Doña Ana de Carlobal and finally obtains his freedom from the begrudging Duke of Sesa through the intercession of Don Juan de Austria.

E. Cotarelo y Mori, in *Don Diego Jiménez de Enciso y su teatro* (1914), drew attention to his sensitive delineation of character, his sober and often elegant style, and to the fact that in the surviving plays he avoids comic interludes and prefers a slowly-developing tragedy, with few feminine characters.

JIMÉNEZ DE QUESADA, GONZALO (1503 or 1506–1579), b. Granada or Cordova. *Conquistador* and historian. After having taken a law degree, he practised until 1536 and then went to Italy as a soldier, becoming familiar with Italian poetry.

Fired with enthusiasm for the promised land of El Dorado, he landed in 1536 with Fernández de Lugo on the Colombian coast and while Fernández took his men along the Atlantic coast, Jiménez was appointed general over 900 men and marched for two years through the interior, to found Santa Fe de Bogotá on 6 August 1538 after seizing the Chibcha stronghold Hunza

(now Tunja) and torturing the Chibcha *zaque* Quemuecchatocha. He returned to Spain and was given the title of Adelantado del Nuevo Reino de Granada. Back in Colombia he died of leprosy, left powerless as a result of political intrigue in Spain, in Mariquita on the banks of the river Magdalena.

His story was told by Fray Pedro Aguado (q.v.) in the *Historia de Sta. Marta y del nuevo reino de Granada*, and more recently by P. M. Ibáñez, *Ensayo biográfico de Gonzalo Jiménez de Quesada* (1892); and by Germán Arciniegas (q.v.), *Jiménez de Quesada* (Bogotá, 1939).

While back in Spain, Jiménez came across Paolo Giovio's *Historiarum sui temporis libri XLV* (1550–2) and, incensed by what he believed to be the Italian scholar's scornful strictures against Spanish soldiers in Italy, wrote in reply *El Antijovio*, which has been edited from the copy in Valladolid University by Rafael Torres Quintero (Bogotá, 1952). There is an exhaustive study of the book by V. Frankl, '*El Antijovio*' *de Gonzalo Jiménez de Quesada y las concepciones de realidad y verdad en la época de la Contrarreforma y del manierismo* (1963).

Many of his writings are lost, including much of the respected *Compendio historial de las conquistas del Nuevo Reino de Granada*. He also composed the *Colección de sermones para ser predicados en las festividades de Nuestra Señora* and *Indicaciones para buen gobierno*, relating to advice on administering Indian territories.

Recent work in Jiménez studies includes M. Forero's 'Hallazgo de un libro de Jiménez de Quesada' (*Boletín del Instituto Caro y Cuervo*, vol. 5, 1949, pp. 411–21) and J. A. Garces's 'Identificación de dos manuscritos atribuidos al adelantado Gonzalo Jiménez de Quesada' (*Thesaurus*, Bogotá, vol. 8, 1952, pp. 158–65).

The *conquistador's* eccentricity, his passionate quest for El Dorado, his indignant repudiation of the Italian hendecasyllables (in controversy with Juan de Castellanos) and his wildly fluctuating career of power and adventure mingled with poverty, illness, and illusion make him an excellent subject for fiction. There is a fictional biography of him by L. Galvis Madero (1957), but Arciniegas reminds us that the hero of Cervantes' greatest novel was originally named 'Quijano or Quijada or Quesada'.

JIMÉNEZ DE URREA, JERÓNIMO (1513?–1564?), b. Epila, Saragossa. Aristocrat, professional soldier, and novelist, who is best known for tending the mortally wounded Garcilaso de la Vega (q.v.) at Le Muy (1536).

Jiménez de Urrea's chivalresque novel *Libro del invencible caballero don Clarisel de las Flores* was studied in MS. by G. Borao in his *Noticia de don Gerónimo Jiménez de Urrea y de su novela caballeresca inédita D. Clarisel de las Flores* (Saragossa, 1866), then edited (Pt. 1 only) by J. M. Asensio (Seville, 1879).

Despite its poor quality, his version of Ariosto's *Orlando furioso* (Antwerp, 1549) was very popular, and he made another version (Acuña's, q.v., was the more famous) of Olivier de la Marche's *Le chevalier délibéré: Discurso de la vida humana y aventuras del cavallero determinado* (Antwerp, 1555). *La famosa Epilia* is an imitation of Sannazaro's *Arcadia* (q.v.), and he wrote an epic eulogy on Carlos V as knight errant defending religion in the manner of the *Carolea* of Jerónimo de Sempere (q.v.).

JIMÉNEZ DE URREA, PEDRO MANUEL DE (1486?–1535?), b. Saragossa. Professional soldier and poet, who was the second son of the first Conde de Aranda. In 1516 he was appointed Ferdinand's ambassador in Rome. His *Penitencia de amor* (Burgos, 1514) was probably the first of the many imitations of *La Celestina* (q.v.). His poetry, showing the influence of Petrarch, appeared in a *Cancionero* (Logroño, 1513; Saragossa, 1878). He also wrote *Peregrinación a Jerusalén, Roma y Santiago* (Burgos, 1514).

JIMÉNEZ HUETE, MAX (1900–47), b. San José. Costa Rican poet and artist. After his secondary schooling, he studied painting in England and sculpture, under Bourdelle, in France. His early verse consists of *Gleba* (Paris, 1929), *Sonaja* (Madrid, 1930), and *Quijongo* (Madrid, 1933). Jiménez continued to travel, exhibiting in Havana, and publishing the satirical *El domador de pulgas* (1936), in which the 'Christ of the fleas' dies to redeem his fellows, a sacrifice that turns out to be a vain one as the fleas model themselves not upon their saviour, but upon Man, with all his faults and passions. His best book is the novel *El jaúl*, a series of *costumbrista* sketches on the region of San Isidro de Coronado, where his hacienda was situated. Despite his wealth, Jiménez was the *enfant terrible* of Costa Rican art and letters.

JIMÉNEZ PATÓN, BARTOLOMÉ (1569–1640), b. Almedina, Ciudad Real. Grammarian and critic, and a friend of Lope de Vega.

He became well-known for his *Eloquencia española en arte* (Toledo, 1604), which has been praised by Menéndez y Pelayo for its shrewd opinions on writers in Spanish, though some of his advice to orators is merely ludicrous (such as his belief that one's memory may be improved by anointing the head with a mixture of white wax and bear's grease).

His edition of the *Proverbios de Alonso de Varros* (Baeza, 1605; 1st edn., 1567) contains 1,100 Greek and Latin proverbs rendered into Castilian verse. Jiménez Patón departed from 'el Brocense' (q.v.) in several instances in his *Instituciones de Gramática española* (n.d.), later incorporated into the *Mercurius trimegistus, sive de triplici eloquentia, sacra, española romana* (Baeza, 1621).

Jiménez Patón wrote many minor works, notably *El perfeto Predicador* (Baeza, 1612), *Reforma de trages. Doctrina de Frai Hernando de Talavera ilustrada por Bartolomé Ximénez Patón* (Baeza, 1638), and a continuation of the *Historia de . . . la ciudad* begun by Pedro Ordóñez de Ceballos (Jaén, 1628), in which Patón is described as 'Secretario del Santo Oficio', or Secretary to the Inquisition.

Benito Maestre included a biography of Patón in *El siglo pintoresco*, vol. 1 (1845).

JIMÉNEZ RUEDA, JULIO (1896–1960), b. Mexico City. Playwright, short-story writer, and historian, who was Director of the Centro de Estudios Literarios in the Universidad Autónoma Nacional de México from 1956 to 1960.

His early work, set in colonial Mexico, included *Cuentos y diálogos* (1918), the novel *Sor Adoración del Divino Verbo* (1923) which he later dramatized, and *Novelas coloniales* (1947).

The early plays *Como en la vida* (1918) and *La caída de las flores* (1923) were conventional, but he explored contemporary dramatic techniques in *La silueta del humo* (1927).

Jiménez Rueda's later books were historical: *Historia de la literatura mexicana* (1928; 6th edn., 1957), *Antología de la prosa en México* (1931; 3rd edn., 1946), *Juan Ruiz de Alarcón y su tiempo* (1939), *Letras mexicanas en el siglo XIX* (1944), and *Herejías y supersticiones en la Nueva España* (1946). Of his unfinished *Historia de la cultura en México*, we have the volumes *El Virreinato* (1950), and *El mundo prehispánico* (1957).

Jitanjáfora, an expression employed by Alfonso Reyes (q.v.) to indicate a nonsense-rhyme based on the use of neologisms and word-play. It was inspired by the poem *Verdehalago* by Mariano Brull (q.v.), and occurs in a poem by Reyes:

> *Filiflama alaba cundre*
> *ala alalunea alifera*
> *alveoles jitanjáfora*
> *liris salumba salifera . . .*

JOB, EL DUQUE, pseudonym of Manuel Gutiérrez Nájera (q.v.).

JOHN OF THE CROSS, *Saint*, see JUAN DE LA CRUZ, *San*.

JORDI, JORDI DE SANT, see SANT JORDI, Jordi de.

Jornada ('day'), in Spanish drama, was an 'act' of a play, later referred to as an 'acto'. The term was originally used because no single act was to contain events exceeding the limits of one day (or *jornada*), though any length of time might elapse between acts. Originally in five *jornadas*, the Golden Age play was probably first reduced to three acts by Antonio Díez in his *Auto de Clarindo* (Toledo, 1535?), which has otherwise little interest. Juan de la Cueva (q.v.) is thus quite wrong in claiming (*Ejemplar poético, epístola III*, 508–9) that he was the first to divide plays into fewer than five *jornadas*, even if his drama contributed to the vogue for four-act plays between 1580 and 1585.

JOVELLANOS, Baltasar Melchor Gaspar María de (1744–1811), b. Gijón. Statesman and polymath who was the best prose stylist of his time. His poetic name in Seville was 'Jovino' and he is usually known as Gaspar Melchor de Jovellanos. After studying in Oviedo, Ávila, Osma, and Alcalá he was appointed criminal magistrate in Seville where he joined the circle of the Peruvian governor Pablo de Olavide (q.v.) and became impressed with the views of the Enlightenment. He corresponded with French intellectuals, learnt Italian and English, and campaigned for reforms in economics, education, and justice. He believed that secondary and higher instruction should be in Spanish instead of Latin, advocated the abolition of judicial torture and also of mortmain, by which most land was gradually falling into the hands of the Church. While in Seville he wrote two plays: a tragedy, *Pelayo* (1769), and a sentimental comedy on penal reform: *El delincuente honrado* (1774). On Olavide's fall and the imprisonment of Cabarrús, Jovellanos was downgraded to become an administrator in charge of roads and mines in his native Asturias, and was excluded from power until Cabarrús was freed by Godoy. In 1797 Jovellanos was appointed Minister of Justice and Ecclesiastical Affairs, only to be replaced the following year for his reforming zeal which antagonized the church, the academics, the queen, and Godoy. In 1801 he was arrested and sent as a political prisoner to Majorca, where he spent seven years until, during the brief reign of Ferdinand, he was freed and allowed to return to the mainland. There he joined the central Junta against the French, even after its enforced flight to Seville and Cádiz, and wrote *Memoria en defensa de la Junta Central* (1810) the year before his death.

His *Diarios* (3 vols., Oviedo, 1953–5, ed. Julio Somoza) are considered among the best autobiographical writings in Spanish. The first *Colección de varias obras en prosa y verso* (7 vols., 1830–2, ed. Ramón María Cañedo) is neither complete nor reliable and until recently the best edition was in the BAE (5 vols., 46, 50, and 85–7, 1858–1956), by Cándido Nocedal and Miguel Artola, but a new edition of the *Obras* is at present in progress: vol. 1, *Epistolario* (ed. J. Caso González, 1970); vol. 2, *Escritos de estética*. J. Caso González has produced an extensive selection of *Obras en prosa* (1969) and also an edition of the *Poesías* (Oviedo, 1961).

Jovellanos was also a serene, philosophical poet influenced above all by Fray Luis de León (q.v.). His *Epístola de Fabio a Anfriso* helped to restore some of the subjectivity and sensibility which Spanish poetry had lost and was highly regarded by the Salamancan School, particularly for the description of El Paular, a 14th-c. Carthusian monastery in the Guadarramas.

The basic biography is *Memorias para la vida del Excmo. Señor D. Gaspar Melchor de Jove Llanos* (1814 [i.e. 1820]) by his close friend Juan Agustín Ceán Bermúdez. The most recent survey of his life and work is *Gaspar Melchor de Jovellanos* by John H. R. Polt (New York, 1971).

JOVINO, the poetic name of Jovellanos (q.v.).

Juan, Don, see Don Juan.

Juan II, Crónica de, a chronicle of the life and times of Juan II (1398–1479), who reigned over Aragón and Navarra from 1458 until his death. It is probably the work of the celebrated *converso* Álvar García de Santa María (q.v.), who drew on many earlier chronicles for his compilation. There is an unsatisfactory edition by Galíndez de Carvajal (Logroño, 1517), and an improved one appeared in Valencia in 1779.

Accurate and lively, the chronicle is better written than those in the Alphonsine tradition (see Alfonso 'el Sabio'). The picture given of the great Álvaro de Luna is generally adverse, in contrast to the favourable reports in the *Crónica de don Álvaro de Luna*, written probably by Gonzalo Chacón (d. 1517).

JUANA DE AMÉRICA, the honorific title accorded to Juana de Ibarbourou (q.v.).

JUANA INÉS DE LA CRUZ, Sor (1648–95), b. San Miguel Nepantle, Amecameca, near Mexico City. Mexican poet, playwright, and feminist. At the age of 14, Juana Inés de Asbaje y Ramírez had become so celebrated for her scholarship that the Viceroy's wife, the Marquesa de Mancera, invited her to live at court. An unknown motive (an unhappy love affair or disgust with luxury and frivolity) led her to enter the Carmelite order in August 1667 but she was unable to withstand the rigour of the rule and returned to court in November. In February 1669 she joined the Hieronymite convent in Mexico City because of 'la total negación que tenía al matrimonio' and because of her desire to 'vivir sola, de no tener ocupación alguna obligatoria que embarazase la libertad de mi estudio, ni rumor de comunidad que impidiese el sosegado silencio de mis libros'.

A woman of extraordinary beauty, judging by the portrait by Miguel Cabrera, Juana held open court in her convent, and the Viceregal couple were frequent guests there.

Much of her prose is lost, including a treatise on music, but we have a letter, *Crisis en un sermón*, subtitled *Carta athenagórica* and maliciously made public with an angry letter by the Bishop of Puebla, Manuel Fernández de Santa Cruz, signing himself 'Sor Filotea de la Cruz'. The pretext for his attack was Juana's thoughtful essay on a sermon delivered in 1650 by the great Portuguese Jesuit P. António Vieira (1608–97) concerning the teachings of St. Augustine and St. Thomas Aquinas on Christ's offer of love.

Commanded to give up learning as unbefitting a woman and a nun, Juana composed a dignified *Respuesta a Sor Filotea de la Cruz* (1691), now seen to be a key document in women's emancipation. It has been edited by Emilio Abreu Gómez (1929), and remains one of the most moving prose works in Spanish, with its elegant defence of learning as a proper task for women and its open strictures on a society dominated by men, and on a church dominated by the Inquisition. Criticized for writing secular lyrics and *comedias*, she replies spiritedly that the Holy Office has at least no jurisdiction over those.

But her sensitive spirit was wounded by the public denunciation and in the last few years of her life she sold all her 4,000 books, her musical instruments, and her scientific equipment in aid of the poor, offering her whole life thenceforward to prayer and charitable works. A plague affected Mexico City in 1695, and she fell victim to it while tending the sick.

The first works of Sor Juana to be published were entitled *Inundación castálida de la única poetisa, musa dézima, Sor Juana Inés de la Cruz . . .* (vol. 1, Madrid, 1689; vol. 2, Seville, 1692; vol. 3, Madrid, 1700).

Her longest poem is a *silva* of 975 lines in defence of learning: *Primero sueño*, its title implying that a projected second part was never written. The soul ascends at night in an attempt to understand all Creation in a blinding moment of truth, but fails and returns with increased humility to recognize that patience and diligence constitute the only authentic way to knowledge. The theme is simple, but the style is *culterano* in the manner of the *Soledades* of Góngora (qq.v.);

she introduces neologisms, mythological allusions, effects of colour and music, intentional obscurities, and syntactical complexities. The *Primero sueño* (1680 or 1681), edited by G. Moldenhauer, takes *gongorismo* to new regions. Much of her occasional poetry is trivial, her best work consisting of the ambiguous love poetry (either erotic or mystical, or both, depending on the reader's interpretation) which she wrote in her youth: *canciones*, sonnets, and *villancicos*, as well as the ballads of dreamy adolescence.

Sor Juana's plays consist of two *sainetes*, three *autos sacramentales*, and two *comedias*; one *de capa y espada, Los empeños de una casa* (1683), which puns on the title of a play by Calderón (*Los empeños de un acaso*) and uses a typically complex Calderonian construction to weave a plot, set in Toledo, of disguises and mistaken identity, and the other, *Amor es más laberinto* (1689), spoilt by exaggerated *culteranismo*, and written in collaboration with Juan de Guevara.

Sor Juana's hagiographical *El mártir del Sacramento, San Hermenegildo* and the biblical *El cetro de José* (based on Calderón's *Sueños hay que verdad son*) are of no more than passing interest, but her third *auto sacramental* is of a high order. *El divino Narciso* is a mythological play of great resonance, drawing on the Calderonian *Eco y Narciso* (1661), and at the same time invoking the pre-Columbian Aztec rites of Mexico, in which the Corn God is ritually killed and eaten.

Sor Juana's works, until recently beset by problems of transmission, have now been competently edited by A. Méndez Plancarte, *Obras completas* (1955) and by F. Monterde, *Obras completas* (1969). See also Julio Jiménez Rueda, *Sor Juana Inés de la Cruz en su época* (1951); Jesús Juan Garcés, *Vida y poesía de Sor Juana Inés de la Cruz* (Madrid, 1953); Ludwig Pfandl, *Sor Juana Inés de la Cruz: la décima musa de México* (1963, from the original German): R. Xirau, *Genio y figura de Sor Juana Inés de la Cruz* (1967); E. A. Chávez, *Sor Juana Inés de la Cruz* (1970); F. Arias de la Canal, *Intento de psicoanalisis de Juana Inés* (1972); and M. E. Pérez, *Lo americano en el teatro de Sor Juana Inés de la Cruz* (1975).

JUAN DE ÁVILA, Beato (1500–69), b. Almodóvar del Campo. Religious writer who, after studying at Salamanca and Alcalá, spent most of his life preaching in Andalusia. He was beatified in 1894.

Audi, filia, et vide, written in 1530 and published without his consent in 1556, is a sermon, with asides on the 44th Psalm, written for Doña Sancha Carrillo. It is an ascetic's denunciation of this world and its vanities, and his abasement before the vision of God. Beato Juan de Ávila's *Obras completas* were last edited by L. Sala Balust (2 vols., 1952).

Some 150 letters to correspondents in all walks of life were posthumously gathered together in *Epistolario espiritual para todos estados* (1578) and were last edited by V. García de Diego (Clásicos Castellanos, 1912).

JUAN DE LA CRUZ, San (1542–91), b. Fontiveros, Ávila. Mystical poet and Discalced Carmelite reformer. His father, Gonzalo de Yepes, was nobly born but married the peasant-girl Catalina Álvarez and was disowned by his family, so struggled in poverty, learning the craft of weaving. Gonzalo died when Juan was five, and Catalina took her two sons (one, Luis, having died) to Medina del Campo, where Juan worked in the Hospital de las Bubas, and there came under the protection of A. Álvarez de Toledo, a wealthy merchant who financed his studies at the Jesuit school. Juan entered the Carmelite Order in 1563 with the name of Juan de Santo Matía, the year after Teresa de Ávila (q.v.) had founded in Ávila the first convent of Discalced Carmelite nuns of the Primitive Rule of St. Joseph.

Juan studied at Salamanca University from 1564–8, and in the latter year was appointed subprior (under Antonio de Heredia, also known as Antonio de Jesús) of the new Discalced Carmelite monastery at Duruelo, while in 1572 he became spiritual director of S. Teresa's convent in Ávila. In 1570 he was appointed Rector of the convent in Alcalá, and became active in the Carmelite reform movement until in 1577 he was jailed in Toledo by unreformed monks. He spent nearly nine months in a single cell, with only an hour each day outside and with a compulsory weekly interrogation, during which he was further humiliated.

It was during this period of enforced recollection that Juan composed the three great poems that have made his name immortal in the literature of mysticism: the *Canciones del alma en la íntima comunicación de unión de amor de Dios*, usually known from part of its opening line as *Llama de amor viva* (q.v.); *Canciones entre el alma y el Esposo*, usually known as the *Cántico espiritual* (q.v.); and the *Canciones del alma que se goza de haber llegado al alto estado de la perfección, que es la unión con Dios, por el camino de la negación spiritual*, known from two words in its first line as *Noche oscura* (q.v.).

Like the rest of Juan's prose and poetry, these works are concerned solely with the path to perfect union of the soul with God, and the joys of spiritual love, made remarkably vivid by symbolic reference to carnal love.

He eventually escaped from his prison, and was given asylum in the Hospital of the Holy Cross where his health improved and he tried to write down the poems that had been composed in jail. He then spent some weeks at the Convent of Beas, where he began a detailed prose commentary on his *Cántico espiritual* for Ana de Jesús, prioress of the convent in Granada, and finally arrived at the monastery of El Calvario in northern Andalusia. His enemies within the Carmelite Order persuaded nuns to sign affidavits to corroborate accusations of crime against Juan, and he was persecuted on his deathbed in Úbeda by the prior of the monastery there. He died emaciated, but vindicated in his reforming zeal by the spread of S. Teresa's movement. He was beatified in 1675 and canonized in 1726.

Some of his poems first appeared in *Obras espirituales que encaminan a una alma a la perfecta unión con Dios* (Alcalá, 1618), and the *Cántico espiritual* was first published in Brussels in 1627.

The *Subida del Monte Carmelo* (1578–63) and *Noche oscura* (begun in 1579) are commentaries on the poem *Noche oscura*. Two other prose commentaries were written in 1584: that on the *Cántico espiritual* and that on *Llama de amor viva*, the latter at the request of Doña Ana de Peñalosa. His prose oscillates between straightforward quotations from the Bible and a vigorous, sensitive style that is always more expository than hortatory. He was aware that his poetry condensed his mystical experiences so far that the non-mystical imagination required guidance to follow it, and he achieved the height of his didactic powers in the subtle use of allegory, symbol, and quotation. Even if he lacks S. Teresa's homely Castilian diction, his sublimity manages to persuade the reader of the authenticity of his vision, while demonstrating his economy of words.

His first faltering essays in verse were marked by an unusual sense of melody and economy (he is believed to have written fewer than 1,000 lines altogether). He was aware of Garcilaso's importation of the *lira* from Italy (especially through Sebastián de Córdoba's reworking of Garcilaso *a lo divino*) and in his major poems improved on Garcilaso's handling of it. He was also aware of the *romanceros* and *cancioneros*, and adapted simple songs and ballads for religious purposes, as in ten religious ballads and other verses, of which the most significant are *El pastorcico* (an allegory of a shepherd-boy's death through love which renders a secular poem *a lo divino*) and *Aunque es de noche*, where he first exploits a refrain, one of the most potent of his poetic devices. This great poem is correctly entitled *Cantar del alma que se huelga de conocer a Dios*.

Juan is an unrivalled singer of love and nature, though his main theme is the quest of God. The resonance of his ambiguity lies partly in eroticism and partly in the essentially conventional nature of his pastoral models, here refined and heightened to the point where the eight exclamatory sentences in the four stanzas of the *Llama de amor viva* are apt, and not at all intrusive. *En una noche oscura* can be interpreted as a literal account of his flight from a Toledo monastic gaol, a girl's eloping to join her lover, or simply as the soul's flight from its human prison to *el Amado*: tension is created by all these possibilities.

Juan is a precursor of those modern writers, such as Huidobro or Juan Ramón Jiménez (qq.v.), whose intention is not to describe an event or state of mind but to create it.

The *Obras* of San Juan are available in a critical edition by P. Silverio de Santa Teresa (5 vols., Burgos, 1929–31), which were translated by Edgar Allison Peers (3 vols., 1934–5; revised edn., 1953).

El cántico espiritual (poem and commentary) is in Clásicos Castellanos (1924) but the full text of all the poems is best read with Dámaso Alonso's acute study in *La poesía de San Juan de la Cruz* (only 2nd edn. of 1946 and edn. of 1966 have the texts).

The most sensitive of many English versions is the translation by Roy Campbell, *Poems* (Harmondsworth, 1960). An authoritative biography has been written by P. Crisógono de Jesús Sacramentado: *San Juan de la Cruz* (1929) and translated by Kathleen Pond (New York, 1958). Recent scholarship is summarized in F. Ruiz Salvador's *Introducción a San Juan de la Cruz: el escritor, los escritos, el sistema* in Biblioteca de Autores Cristianos (1968). There is a study of the poems by M. Wilson, *San Juan de la Cruz: Poems* in the Critical Guides to Spanish Texts series (London, 1975).

JUAN DE LOS ÁNGELES, *Fray* (c. 1536–1609), b. Oropesa, Toledo. Mystical writer, who studied at Alcalá and was entrusted with high office in the Franciscan Order. His *Triumphos del amor de Dios* (Medina del Campo, 1590) owing a good deal to Plato's views on love, as well as to St. Bonaventure and Sabunde, was revised and abridged as *Lucha espiritual y amorosa entre Dios y el alma* (1600). The *Diálogos de la conquista del espiritual y secreto reyno de Dios* (2 vols., 1595) influenced by the Northern European mystics, above all by Ruysbroeck and Tauler, has been edited by A. González Palencia (1946). Fray J. Sala has edited the *Obras místicas* of Ángeles in the NBAE, vols. 20–24 (1912–7).

Menendez y Pelayo called Juan de los Ángeles 'uno de los mas suaves y regalados prosistas castellanos'; his style is perhaps inferior only to that of Luis de León (q.v.) in *De los nombres de Cristo*.

Juan de Mairena: sentencias, donaires, apuntes y recuerdos de un profesor apócrifo (1936), a philosophical and poetic miscellany by Antonio Machado (q.v.). A 2nd edition appeared in Buenos Aires (2 vols., 1943).

Machado had already created the persona of 'Abel Martín', a poet-philosopher. Mairena had been invented as a pupil of Abel Martín as early as 1917 (in an Andalusian *copla*) but from 1934 he becomes a recognizable personality. In his general attitudes and maxims he recalls the iconoclastic Baroja and Unamuno; in his poetry he is simply a heteronym for Machado in a predominantly classical vein.

Mairena is stated by Machado to have been born in Seville in 1865, and to have died in Casariego de Tapia in 1909. He is the author of a biography of Abel Martín, an *Arte poética*, a volume of poems, *Coplas mecánicas*, and a treatise on metaphysics, *Los siete reversos*.

There is a partial translation of the book by Ben Belitt, *Juan de Mairena: epigrams, maxims, memoranda, and memoirs* ... (Berkeley and Los Angeles, 1963).

JUAN DE PERSIA, see PERSIA, Juan de.

Juanita la larga (1895), a novel by Juan Valera (q.v.) set in an Andalusian village. Juanita is a seventeen-year-old seamstress, pretty and intelligent; her mother, Juana, is a cook and laundress. The town secretary Don Paco, in his fifties, falls in love with Juanita and courts her, against the wishes of his devout, snobbish daughter Inés, wife of the idle and vicious Don Álvaro Roldán. Inés engages the sympathies of the former monk Anselmo, who attacks Juanita indirectly in a sermon, but the wily Juanita feigns piety and humility to win the approbation of Inés and Anselmo and marries the kind Paco.

Deceptively simple in style, the book is distinguished for its regional flavour (set in Doña Mencía, or 'Villalegre') and sunny optimism; it is generally considered Valera's finest book after *Pepita Jiménez* (q.v.).

Juan Labrador, see LABRADOR, Juan.

JUAN MANUEL, *Príncipe* or *Infante Don* (1282–1348), b. Escalona, Toledo. Prose writer who was the grandson of Fernando III, 'el Santo', nephew of Alfonso X, 'el Sabio', and joint regent during the minority of Alfonso XI. He was unscrupulous in politics, at one time contracting an alliance with the Muslim king of Granada to serve his ends, and brutal to each of his three successive wives. He was however devoted to the Dominican order, and built them a monastery near his fortress in Peñafiel, where he ordered them to keep the original of his

MSS., so that corrupt versions of his works could, if necessary, be amended by reference to the master copy. This concept of the proto-Renaissance literary artist dominates his many works, in contrast to the medieval attitude of his contemporary Juan Ruiz (q.v.), who offered his *Libro de buen amor* for all to amend and improve.

The most important books to have survived are the *Conde Lucanor* (q.v.), a precursor of Boccaccio's *Decamerone*; the *Libro de los Estados* (see ESTADOS), a didactic work, and the *Libro del caballero et del escudero*, written in 1326 and edited by J. M. Castro y Calvo and M. de Riquer in vol. 1 of Juan Manuel's *Obras* (Barcelona, 1955) with the *Libro de las armas*, a meticulous account of the author's ancestry.

In the *Libro del caballero* (ed. by S. Gräfenberg in *Romanische Forschungen*, vol. 7, 1893), a young squire on his way to court is instructed in philosophy, religion, and especially in chivalry by an old knight. Much of the matter is derived from Ramon Llull's *Llibre del ordre de la cavayleria*; from the *Elucidarium* of Honorius of Autun through the Spanish *Lucidario* dating from the reign of Sancho IV; and from the many Alphonsine (see ALFONSO X) works of this nature.

Juan Manuel also wrote a *Libro de la caza* (on falconry); a sober *Tractado de la Asunción* (ed., with the *Libro infinido*, by J. M. Blecua, Granada, 1952); a *Crónica abreviada* (early 1920s), abridging the *Primera crónica general* of Alfonso X, 'el Sabio' (q.v.); and the *Libro infinido*, so-called because the Infante interrupted its writing at chapter 26 to compose *Las maneras de amor* for the monk Juan Alfonso.

The *Libro infinido*, properly *El libro de los castigos o consejos que fizo don Johan Manuel para su fijo*, falls into the category of *De regimine principum* (q.v.). It is a compendium of worldly and spiritual advice addressed to his son Fernando, and draws heavily on the *Libro de los Estados*.

Juan Manuel or a copyist listed his works, so we know what has been lost despite his primitive attempt to create a permanent archive: a *Libro de los cantares* and *Reglas de trovar*; a *Libro de la cavallería* partially surviving as fragments inserted in the *Libro de los Estados*; *Libro de los egennos*; *Libro de los sabios*; and a *Crónica conplida* considered by some scholars (though not by R. Menéndez Pidal) to be the *Chronicon Domini Johannis Emmanuelis* published in E. Flórez's *España sagrada* (vol. 2, 1747) and by G. Baist in *Romanische Forschungen* (vol. 7, 1893).

Juan Manuel is the first Spanish author whose portrait survives. It is as a donor on a painting of S. Lucía in the cathedral of Murcia, where he is shown with his daughter Juana, Queen of Castile. The artist is Barnaba da Modena.

The most convenient collection of his *Obras* is that made by P. de Gayangos in vol. 51 (1857) of the BAE, which includes the *Libro del caballero et del escudero*, *Sobre las armas*, *Libro infinido*, *De las maneras del amor*, *Libro de los Estados*, *Libro de los fraires predicadores*, the *Libro de Patronio* (popularly known as the *Conde Lucanor*), and the *Tractado de la Asunción*.

Don Juan Manuel: biografía y estudio crítico (Saragossa, 1932) by Andrés Giménez Soler is still the authoritative work, and there is a 27-page bibliography in E. Juliá Martínez's edition of *El Conde Lucanor* (1933).

See also R. Ayerbe-Chaux, *El conde Lucanor: materia tradicional y originalidad creadora* (1975).

JUARROZ, ROBERTO (1925–), b. Coronel Dorrego. Argentinian poet. His work seems at first sight to be abstract and intellectual, but his unusually pure diction and finely controlled rhythms produce highly dramatic effects. His main publications are *Poesía vertical* (1958), *Seis poemas sueltos* (1960), *Segunda poesía vertical* (1963), *Tercera poesía vertical* (1965), *Cuarta poesía vertical* (1969).

Juegos de Escarnio, a term found in title 6, law 34 of the first of the *Siete Partidas* (q.v., 1256–1265), of Alfonso X, 'el Sabio' (q.v.), denoting a 'farcical play' (Rennert) or a 'buffoon-play' (Ticknor) which priests are forbidden to act in, attend, or permit to be staged in churches. The law states, however, that this restriction does not apply to miracle plays or mystery plays, or to plays from the Nativity or Resurrection cycles.

Juglaría, Mester de, see MESTER DE JUGLARÍA.

JULIÁN DE TOLEDO, San (642?–690), b. Toledo. Ecclesiastical writer. A *converso* (q.v.), Julián was educated by San Eugenio and became the last great churchman of the Visigothic period. He became Archbishop of Toledo in 680, and presided at each of the four Councils of Toledo (the twelfth to the fifteenth) that sat during his decade as Archbishop.

His writings were listed by Felix, Julian's successor as archbishop (693–700): *Liber prognosticorum futuri saeculi*, the defence of Christianity against Judaism; *De sextae aetatis comprobatione*, which attempts to refute the Talmud, and in so doing shows that the present age is the Messianic age (the sixth); *Liber de contrariis, quod graece Ἀντικειμενων voluit titulo adnotaris*, which attempts to reconcile conflicting passages in the Bible; and other minor works. Felix does not mention the important *Vita S. Ildefonsi* or *Ars grammatica*. Julián's style is superior to the decadent Latin of his period, while his subject matter is evidence in its depth and variety of a mind adapted to scholarship in the midst of ecclesiastical administration. He continued the *De viris illustribus* of St. Jerome, Gennadius, and S. Isidoro de Sevilla (q.v.) and his systematic approach to the study of theology was not superseded even during the Carolingian Renaissance, in the opinion of J. de Ghellinck (*Le mouvement théologique du XIIe siècle*, Louvain, 1914).

Justina, Libro de entretenimiento de la pícara, see PÍCARA JUSTINA, *Libro de entretenimiento de la*.

JUVENCUS (*fl. c.* A.D. 330), a Spanish priest of noble family whose epic on the Gospel story *Evangeliorum libri IV*, consisting of some 3,000 lines, was intended to attract educated readers from the pagan classics. As regards structure and style, his chief debt is to Virgil.

The definitive edition of Juvencus is that by J. Huemer in vol. 24 of the Corpus Scriptorum Ecclesiasticorum Latinorum (Vienna, 1891) but the edition by F. Arévalo (Rome, 1792) is still used for its commentary.

Juventud, a Paraguayan literary review published from 1923 to 1935. It represents the second wave of modernism in Paraguay, as *Crónica* (q.v.) represented the first, and was strongly influenced by Rubén Darío (q.v.). The most prominent *Juventud* poets were Vicente Lamas (q.v.), José Concepción Ortiz, Heriberto Fernández, (q.v.) Raul Battilana de Gásperi (1904–1924), and Pedro Herrera Céspedes (1902–1924). The playwright Júlio Correa (q.v.) was associated with them, and the work of Herib Campos Cervera (q.v.) was first published in *Juventud*.

Juyungo: historia de un negro, una isla y otros negros, a novel by Adalberto Ortiz (q.v.), first published in Buenos Aires (1943) and reprinted as *Juyungo: novela* in Quito (1947).

Racial problems among Negroes, Indians, whites, and half-breeds form the background to the life-story of the Negro Ascensión. Violence, disease, and the exploitation of the poor are seen to affect all races, and eventually the chaos of the universe is reflected in the sudden disappearance from the novel's pages of all the characters but Ascensión, who comes to a tragicomic end.

Ortiz begins each chapter with a poetic section of *ojos y oídos de la selva*, a mannerism which spoils the realistic effect of what follows.

K

Kalila wa Dimna, see CALILA E DIGNA.

Kharja (Arabic. Spanish: *jarcha*, 'going-out' or last verse), the last few lines (usually four) in Mozarabic (the Spanish dialect spoken in areas under Muslim rule) or Vulgar Arabic, or a compound of the two, which conclude a *muwashshaha*, a sophisticated strophic form of a Hebrew or Arabic poem. The function of the *kharja* is comparable with that of the later *estribillo* (q.v.). It was composed or chosen (since many poets did not compose their own *kharjas*) before the *muwashshaha* was begun. The Hebrew and Arabic poets were probably drawing on established traditions of popular verse or song at first; later a good poet might compose his own *kharja* in a popular style and it would then be indistinguishable from the prototype.

The importance of the *kharjas* is that they are the first known lyrics in proto-Spanish, and date from the 10th c., though they are most commonly found in the 11th–12th c. Their existence was discovered by S. M. Stern (q.v.).

The *kharja*'s theme is ordinarily a girl's complaint at the absence of her lover, as in the following example by Tudrus Abu 'l-Afia:

> *Al-sabab bono, garme de ón venis*
> *ya l'-y-sé que otri amas*
> *a mibi no queris.*

(*Aurora buena, dime, ¿de dónde vienes?* | *Ya sé que amas a otra.* | *A mí no quieres*—modern Spanish).
'Good dawn, tell me, where do you come from? I know you love another. You do not care for me'.

The little Spanish love poem which is the *kharja* can be accounted for historically by the fact that, as few women arrived with the Islamic armies, there were many racially-mixed families in Moorish Spain and much of the population became bilingual, speaking Arabic for commercial and administrative purposes, and Spanish in the home; Spanish therefore became the main vehicle for the emotional aspects of life.

It does not necessarily follow from the

kharja's early date that Arabic or Hebrew poetry influenced Peninsular literature, for the *muwashshaha* may itself have been a borrowing from proto-Romance.

See S. M. Stern, *Hispano-Arabic strophic poetry* (Oxford, 1974).

KORN, ALEJANDRO (1860–1936), b. San Vicente, Buenos Aires. Argentinian professor of philosophy at Buenos Aires University (1906–30) whose German *Poemas* (1942) was published, with facing Spanish translations by Ernest Palacio, by the Instituto de Estudios Germánicos in Buenos Aires. His philosophy is Kantian, but displays strong sympathies with Bergson. He was an influential member of the University Reform Movement which began in Córdoba in 1918, and his optimistic work *La libertad creadora* (1920) inspired the next generation of Argentinian writers, especially Francisco Romero (who wrote on his mentor in *Alejandro Korn*, 1940), Vicente Fatone, and Ángel Vassallo.

F. Romero edited Korn's *Obras completas* in 3 vols. (1938–40), the most important being *Influencias filosóficas en la evolución nacional* (1919), *El concepto de la ciencia* (1926), *Apuntes filosóficos* (1935), and *Ensayos críticos sobre arte, ciencias y letras* (1937).

KORNICOFF, P. S., a pseudonym of José María Samper (q.v.).

KORSI, DEMETRIO (1899–1957), b. Panama. Modernist poet and prose writer, whose father was Greek. He was Director of the Biblioteca Colón, married the poet Eloisa M. Sandoval, and was one of the original contributors to *El Heraldo del Istmo* (q.v., 1903–6). His best poetic period is, however, considered to extend from 1933, when he returned from eight years in France, to 1947, when his *Pequeña antología* appeared. This is the period of *Cumbía* (1936), which introduces Afro-Indian themes; *El grillo que cantó sobre el Canal* (1937); and *El grillo que cantó bajo las hélices* (1942), celebrating in popular verses the parish of Santa Ana in Panama City. Korsi seldom exercised self-criticism: his works suffer from repetition of words, images, and ideas, but because they contain folklore material they appeal to a wide variety of readers.

He may have been the inspiration of the Ecuadorian Demetrio Aguilera Malta's (q.v.) hero Pedro Coorsi in the novel *Canal Zone* (Santiago de Chile, 1935).

KOTSKA Y BAYO, ESTANISLAO DE (*fl.* 1830), Spanish historian and historical novelist. As a *costumbrista* he wrote the *Aventuras de un elegante, o las costumbres de hogaño* (Valencia, 1832) but he is best known for his Romantic historical novels *Voyleano, o la exaltación de las pasiones* (1827), *Grecia, o la doncella de Misolonghi* (1830), and *La conquista de Valencia por el Cid* (1831), in which the hero is depicted as a truly perfect knight. *Los expatriados, o Zulema y Gazul* (1834), set in the year 1254, deals with the struggles between Christians and Moors.

Kotska y Bayo's historical knowledge gives his novels their strength, but his style is often unworthy of his themes.

Krausismo, a philosophy of syncretistic idealism propounded by Karl Christian Friedrich Krause (1781–1832) which was brought to Spain by Julián Sanz del Río (q.v.) after his studies under Ahrens in Brussels and Roeder in Heidelberg, and taught by him 1854–67 at Madrid University. The reason for its pre-eminence over other post-Kantian systems is that its *racionalismo armónico* appealed to intellectuals in Spain who wished to retain belief in a divinity without reducing in any way their allegiance to liberal, progressive ideas. Sanz del Río's personal involvement with Krause's *Das Urbild der Menschheit* (1811) made his new edition *Ideal de la humanidad para la vida* (1860) virtually a new work. Krause's doctrine of *Allingottlehre* ('pan[en]theism') asserts that God, as Absolute, contains the whole world within Himself without being contained in it. Humanity unites the human body with a rational awareness of the self. The philosophy of law is involved in the doctrine, since humanity is seen as an organic whole made in the image of God, and law is the form within which the life of humanity develops. Law thus applies not only to the conditions governing human freedom of action, but should also order the whole life of humanity so that each individual and social organism might achieve the desired moral perfection.

The philosophy is fundamentally optimistic, not through underestimation of the problems of life and thought, but because human intelligence and will are considered capable of reaching solutions to them. Religion is essentially negative in Krause: a recognition of the fact of the Divine, but of no practical use in furthering human aspirations.

Sanz del Río's *Lecciones sobre el sistema de filosofía analítica de K. Ch. F. Krause* propagated the German's thought in Spanish as early as 1850, but it was not until 1860 that his version of the *Ideal de la humanidad* appeared, simultaneously with Sanz del Río's *Sistema de la filosofía: metafísica* (Pt. I: *Análisis*). A new generation of Spanish intellectuals achieved liberation from the clerical-scholastic tradition under Sanz; and Giner de los Ríos, Gumersindo de Azcárate, Salmerón (and subsequently Cossío, Lloréns

Torres, and Castillejo) propagated *krausismo* in their turn. The doctrine appealed also to founders and teachers of the Institución Libre de Enseñanza (q.v.), founded in 1876, and found its way into the short story 'Zurita' by Leopoldo Alas and into two major novels by Benito Pérez Galdós (q.v.): *El amigo Manso* and *La familia de León Roch* (qq.v.).

Today the specific doctrines of Krause have disappeared not only in their adopted Spain, but also in their native Germany, yet their pervasive influence on Spanish students of the 1860s and later decades (on Unamuno, for example) constituted the only radical alternative to received ideas, aroused intellectual debate, and made possible a scientific renaissance.

J. B. Trend has studied the consequences of *krausismo* in *The origins of modern Spain* (Cambridge, 1934).

See also Pierre Jobit, *Les éducateurs de l'Espagne contemporaine. I: Les krausistes. II: Lettres inédites de Sanz del Río* (Bordeaux, 1936); and Juan López Morillas, *El krausismo español: perfil de una aventura intelectual* (Mexico City, 1956).

L

La, see under the word following the article, e.g. CELESTINA, La.

LABARTA POSE, ENRIQUE (1863–1925), b. Baio, La Coruña. Humorist. He founded the satirical magazines *Galicia Humorística* (Santiago, 1888) and *La Pequeña Patria* (1891), and collected together his Galician verse in *Bálsamo de Fierabras* (Santiago, 1889). A typical example of his gentle mockery of Galician country people is the poem 'O fin do mundo' in which the author hesitates, then stays behind when everyone else departs, to look after his farm though the end of the world is at hand.

His serious poetry in Castilian lacked inspiration.

Laberinto de Fortuna, El, an allegorical poem in *redondillas* in rhythmical *arte mayor* written by Juan de Mena (q.v.) in 1444 and first published between 1481 and 1488, probably in Salamanca.

From the approximate number of its stanzas (actually 297), Mena's poem has often been referred to as *Las trescientas* or *Las trezientas*. Based generically on Dante's *Divina Commedia*, the poem is influenced by Virgil and above all by Lucan (q.v.), while Mena's use of Ovidian mythology foreshadows Renaissance poetic practice.

El laberinto de Fortuna shows the proper education of man as understood in 15th-c. Spain by means of allegory and visions. The author is lost in a wood, like Dante, and exposed to prowling wild animals. Providence appears in the guise of a beautiful woman and offers to guide him through the dangers that lie ahead, explaining whatever he might be able to comprehend of the mysteries he will encounter. At the spherical centre of the seven zones (where the narrator can see the whole world at one glance), Providence shows him the three great mystic wheels: the past and the future at rest and the present in perpetual motion. Each wheel bears its proportion of mankind.

Mena's Dantean vision ends, and he begins a long catalogue of descriptions of mythological and historical figures, the most interesting being that of the death of the Conde de Niebla in 1436 at the Siege of Gibraltar, the death of the young nobleman Lorenzo Dávalos in 1541, and an eulogy of Don Álvaro de Luna (q.v.), aimed at winning support (especially that of King Juan II) for him. Twenty-four extra stanzas (first published in the Saragossa edn. of 1509) which earlier writers attributed to Mena have been shown by R. Foulché-Delbosc to be by a later hand. Politically, Mena divides the world into evil (not only sin, chance, necromancy but also civil wars and rebellious nobles) and good (associating Providence with Álvaro de Luna and his party).

Among Mena's poetic devices, J. M. Blecua has identified Latin hyperbaton ('divina me puedes llamar Providencia'); Latinate neologisms enriching the common stock of later Castilian (eighty per cent of Góngora's *cultismos* have been traced in Mena's works), such as *exilio* for 'destierro' and *flutuoso* for 'oscilante'; the introduction of words with the uncommon antepenultimate stress (*palabras esdrújulas*) to add variety and sonority (*sulfúreo* and *diáfano*); and continual references to Ovidian mythology.

Mena's Latinized vocabulary combines with his use of the Italianate *terza rima* (introduced by Imperial, q.v.) and other rhyme-schemes to create a wholly original style. *El laberinto de Fortuna* found immediate favour in court circles, and was reported to be the favourite reading of King Juan II.

There is a facsimile of the Seville version of

1495 edited by A. Pérez Gómez (Valencia, 1955), a critical edition by R. Foulché-Delbosc (Mâcon, 1904), a reliable and convenient edition by J. M. Blecua in Clásicos Castellanos (1943), and a translation into modern Spanish by E. González Trillo and L. Ortiz Behety (Buenos Aires, 1939). An essential background book is M. R. Lida de Malkiel's *Juan de Mena, poeta del prerrenacimiento español* (Mexico City, 1950).

Laberinto de la soledad, El (1950) an essay by Octavio Paz (q.v.), subtitled *vida y pensamiento de México*. Paz tries not so much to discover an 'essential' Mexican-ness by discussing what have been isolated as its characteristics (such as the *fiesta* or revolution) as to uncover the masks which conceal the real Mexico. Technological society has made it difficult to love and communicate outside the recognized channels devised and ordained by society. Mexicans must strive to break out of the confines of technological society, and in some ways Paz's sociological imagination resembles that of Blake. Marriage for Paz is a projection of society, and he recommends love outside marriage since this constitutes an attack on society; Mexican reality is made up of 'solitudes' which can only be overcome by such antisocial behaviour. Paz also advocates the ideology of Samuel Ramos (q.v.); his book has influenced a number of creative writers, such as Carlos Fuentes and Vicente Leñero (qq.v.). In 1970 Paz published a long *Posdata* to his book, in which he argued that recent Mexican governments have preserved the authoritarian, paternalistic society inherited from the *conquistadores* and from the Aztecs before them, and that the most important use of the literary imagination today is to attack false idols.

Labrador, Juan, a Spanish folk-hero; the type of the honest and industrious peasant who achieves wealth, happiness, and prosperity by the fruit of his own labours. The most memorable treatment of the subject in Spanish literature is the *comedia* by Lope de Vega, *El villano en su rincón* (qq.v.), in which the character and setting are both French.

Labrador de más aire, El (1937), an *auto sacramental* (q.v.) by Miguel Hernández (q.v.) influenced in theme by the *comedias* of Lope de Vega such as *Fuenteovejuna* and *Peribáñez y el Comendador de Ocaña* (qq.v.) in which peasants rise up against tyrannical noblemen.

In a conventional rural setting, Juan the *labrador* tries to incite the other poor farm labourers to rebel against their exploiting landlords by wielding 'una hoz de rebeldía / y un martillo de protesta'.

But whereas Lope's peasant heroes do not seek to overthrow Society as such and are ultimately pardoned by the King, Juan is murdered for his presumption in questioning the *status quo*. The author, who began as an ardent Roman Catholic, died (of tuberculosis) a convinced communist in prison.

Labrador más honrado, El, a subtitle of the play *Del rey abajo, ninguno* by Francisco de Rojas Zorrilla (qq.v.).

LABRAT, DUNASH HA-LEVI BEN (*c.* 920–*c.* 980), b. Baghdad. Of a distinguished Jewish family, Dunash studied in Baghdad under the great Jewish grammarian Sa'adia ha-Gaon, but when ha-Gaon died in 942, Dunash left for Fez, and is later recorded as a protégé of the minister Hasdai ben Shaprut in Cordova. As a grammarian, Dunash fiercely criticized the Hebrew grammar written by Menahem ben Saruq (another protégé of the generous Hasdai) in his *Teshubot* ('Replies').

He not only introduced the new science of Hebrew grammar into Spain, but also demonstrated the ease with which Hebrew poetry could be written in the Arabic manner. His secular verse was in the style of classical Arabic poetry, while his religious verse was written in the language of the Bible, combining the *puyyut* (q.v.) with the *qasida* and dividing the long monorhymed lines of the Arabic model into shorter monorhyming four-line stanzas conforming to the strophic form of the Psalms. His are the first religious poems by a Jewish writer to have survived in Spain.

His works have been edited by N. Allony: *Dunash ben Labrat: Shirim* (Jerusalem, 1947).

LACUNZA, *Padre* MANUEL (1731–1801), b. Santiago. Chilean Jesuit whose *La venida del Mesías en gloria y majestad* was written in 1790, first published in 1811 under the pseudonym of 'Ben Josaphat ben Ezra', and placed on the index of prohibited books in 1822. Lacunza was a Millenarian, believing the Hebrew prophecy that the world would end after 6,000 years (the Six Days of *Genesis*) and that throughout the seventh millennium justice and virtue would reign supreme.

Expelled with his fellow-Jesuits, Lacunza died in Imola, Italy.

La de Bringas (1884), one of the *Novelas españolas contemporáneas* of Benito Pérez Galdós (qq.v.).

The conflict of this major novel is between Doña Rosalía Pipaón de la Barca and her husband, Don Francisco de Bringas, who both appeared in *Tormento* (q.v.). The theme is a vain woman's passion for keeping up the ostentation of wealth despite being deprived of the necessary money. Bringas is a minor official in the palace bureaucracy of Isabel II. His wife Rosalía and the destitute Milagros, Marquesa de Tellería, squander on clothes and trinkets all the money that they can obtain by taking advantage of Bringas's sudden attack of blindness, and by borrowing recklessly from the usurer Torquemada. Rosalía escapes tragedy by paying Torquemada back with a loan from the high-class prostitute Refugio Emperador, the sister of 'Tormento', whom she despised at the beginning of the novel. *La de Bringas* is a masterpiece of social ironies and psychological insights, ending with the fall of Isabel and, with her, of the Bringas household.

The decline of the methodical Bringas is matched by the rise to power of his spendthrift, unscrupulous wife, marking the gradual triumph of chaos and disorder in the household, echoing the change in the life of the nation. For the weak and ineffectual Prince Consort (also called Francisco) was dominated by the spendthrift Queen Isabel. The Civil Service is represented by the amoral, corrupt Pez, a spirit kindred to Rosalía. The Royal Palace, where much of the action takes place, has an impressive classical façade which conceals a confusing maze within; Galdós compares it with the State, apparently solid and enduring but in reality ramshackle and disordered. A memorable symbol for encroaching chaos is the over-ambitious handicraft on which Francisco Bringas is working as the novel opens; planned as a triumph of order and beauty, it gets out of control and becomes a mere jumble of disparate elements.

The novel has been translated by G. Woolsey as *The spendthrifts* (London, 1951).

See R. Gullón, *La novelística de Pérez Galdós* (1970), especially on the structure of *La de Bringas*.

LAFORET DÍAZ, CARMEN (1921–), b. Barcelona. Novelist and short-story writer. Her family moved to Las Palmas (Canary Islands) when she was two, and she stayed there until she was 18, when she returned to Barcelona to study first arts and then law. She then left for Madrid, where she married the journalist Manuel González Cerezales. She achieved instant recognition for her novel *Nada* (Barcelona, 1944), which was awarded the first Premio Nadal. *Nada* (q.v.) concerns an 18-year-old girl who arrives in Barcelona from the Canary Islands and gradually becomes aware of the tensions in her grandmother's home. The novel is marked by powerful scenes, unusual images, and an acute feminine sensibility. Laforet's mother died when she was 13 and her stepmother became a hated

figure who haunted later novels in one form or another.

La isla y los demonios (Barcelona, 1952) is a more mature work, but perhaps less effective for being more calculated. Marta is the counterpart of *Nada's* Andrea, and most of the other characters of *Nada* recur under different names.

Laforet's conversion to Roman Catholicism in 1951 marks a complete change in her style. The stories in *La llamada* (Barcelona, 1954) and the novel *La mujer nueva* (Barcelona, 1955) reveal heroines deeply affected by religion. Paulina is the explicitly 'Pauline' heroine of *La mujer nueva*, as the title suggests, whose life is radically transmuted by conversion, and *Paralelo 35* (Barcelona, 1967) and the short story 'El viaje divertido' are marked by religious sentimentality. *La insolación* (Barcelona, 1963) is the first novel in the trilogy *Tres pasos fuera del tiempo*. *Gran Canaria* (Barcelona, 1961) is a guide book.

LAGUERRE, ENRIQUE A. (1906–), b. Aguadilla. The major contemporary Puerto Rican novelist. Of rural origins, he describes with tact and sympathy the lives of sugar-cane workers in *La llamarada* (1935). *Solar Montoya* (1941) implicitly proposes new guidelines for agricultural reform, while *30 de febrero* (1943) offers a searching examination of the university system. Laguerre's next two novels are cast in the form of *episodios nacionales* in the manner of Pérez Galdós. *La resaca* (1949) deals with the period 1870–98, and explains the failure of Puerto Rican nationalism due to the apathy of the people. *Los dedos de la mano* (1951) covers the years from 1910 to 1935, incidentally indicting adult maltreatment of children. His subsequent novels include *La ceiba en el tiesto* (1956); *El laberinto* (1959; set in New York and Santo Domingo); and *Cauce sin río* (1962).

Laguerre's essays have been collected in *Pulso de Puerto Rico* (1956), and his *Obras completas* appeared in 2 vols. (1962–3).

LAGUNA, ANDRÉS (1499–1560), b. Segovia. He studied in Salamanca and Paris, and was appointed a physician to Pope Julius III.

According to *Erasme et l'Espagne* (Paris, 1937) by Marcel Bataillon (q.v.), Laguna is the author of *El viaje de Turquía*, first published in the NBAE, vol. 2 (1905). This is a satirical account, in dialogue form, with Erasmian and anticlerical undertones, of a captive's life in Turkey and his adventures on the way. It was not publishable at the time when it was written, but it may have circulated widely enough in MS. to have exerted some influence. The author-hero calls himself Pedro de Urdemalas (q.v.): his two listeners are Juan de Votadiós (the name by which the

Wandering Jew is most often known in Spain) and Mátalascallando. Manuel Serrano y Sanz has claimed to identify these characters as Alonso de Portillo and a priest called Granada.

LAHETJUZAN, Abbé Dominique (1766–1818). A French-born Basque priest who fled to Spain on the outbreak of the French Revolution. He wrote numerous essays on the Basque language, none more curious than the *Essai de quelques notes sur la langue basque par un Vicaire de campagne sauvage d'origine* (Bayonne, 1808), with its ingeniously preposterous etymological explanations in support of his theory that 'le Basque est une langue originale: la divinité de la Genèse le démontre comme vice versa: l'originalité du Basque prouve la divinité de la Genèse'.

LAÍN ENTRALGO, Pedro (1908–), b. Urrea de Gaén, Teruel. Philosopher and psychiatrist. By profession a doctor, he has studied psychiatry in Vienna and has taught the history of medicine in the University of Madrid. Though he has absorbed recent thought from Germany and France, his books begin from the premise that Spain is the spiritual centre of Europe. In *España como problema* (1949; 2nd edn., 2 vols., 1956) and subsequent books such as *La universidad, el intelectual y Europa* (1950) and *Palabras menores* (1952), he has argued that the failure of the Spanish intellectual since the Golden Age has not been (as commonly suggested) the failure to create a viable social and political system, but the failure to persuade the Spanish people that their way of life is already superior to that enjoyed in the rest of Europe, where religion has been displaced as the guiding principle. Laín Entralgo's view of the university is conventional: that it should transmit received knowledge, encourage research, and form the complete human being. *La espera y la esperanza* (1957; revised edn., 1958) is a study of the place of hope in Christian civilization to the time of existentialism.

Laín Entralgo's more important recent works, apart from his magisterial contributions to the history of medicine, are *La empresa de ser hombre* (1958) and *Teoría y realidad del otro* (2 vols., 1961), the latter being an examination of the Self and the Other.

LAMAS, Vicente (1909–). Paraguayan poet. One of the members of the group whose work was published in *Juventud* (q.v.). His poems were collected in *La senda escondida* (1954), in which Lamas successfully describes the landscape and problems of his homeland.

LAMPILLAS or **LLAMPILLAS,** Francisco Xavier (1731–1810), b. Mataró. Spanish literary historian who taught Spanish literature in Barcelona until he was exiled with his fellow-Jesuits from Spain in 1767, when he left for Italy, spending his time partly in Genoa and partly in Ferrara.

Saverio Bettinelli's *Risorgimento d'Italia negli studj* and Girolamo Tiraboschi's *Storia della letteratura italiana* both blamed the decline of Italian literature after 1600 on political subjugation by Spain and the consequent introduction of 'inferior' literary models such as Calderón and Lope de Vega. Lampillas set himself the task of contradicting their statements in the passionate and often over-stated *Saggio storico-apologetico della letteratura spagnuola contro le pregiudicate opinioni di alcuni moderni scrittori italiani* (6 vols., Genoa, 1778–81). This *apologia* of Lampillas helped to change literary opinion in Italy, where it was received with mixed notices, but in its Spanish translation: *Ensayo histórico-apologético de la literatura española* (6 vols., Saragossa, 1782–4; 2nd edn., 7 vols., Madrid, 1789) the book made a profound impact in Spain, appealing to wounded pride and justifying the popularity of Lope and Calderón as opposed to the neoclassical criteria imported from France. The controversy continued for some time, with replies from both Tiraboschi and Bettinelli.

LANDÍVAR, Rafael (1713–93), b. Santiago de los Caballeros, Guatemala. Jesuit, humanist, and poet. He became a Master of Theology at the age of 15 and a Doctor at 16. He took minor orders in Mexico in 1756 and on taking major orders returned to Guatemala in 1762. On the expulsion of the Jesuits from Spanish possessions in 1767, Landívar took refuge in Bologna, where he wrote his *Rusticatio mexicana* (Modena, 1781) in Latin hexameters. Landívar is a Central American neoclassicist, describing the flora, fauna, landscapes, and native industries with Virgilian elegance. Menéndez y Pelayo called him 'one of the most excellent poets to be found among modern Latinists'.

He died penniless in Bologna, but his remains were sent back to Guatemala in 1950.

LANDO, Ferrant Manuel de (1350?–1417?), b. Seville. Poet, and page of Juan I, probably a Jewish *converso* of French ancestry. Thirty-one of his poems appear in the 1851 edition of the *Cancionero de Baena*, and some are reproduced in vol. 4 of Menéndez y Pelayo's *Antología de poetas líricos castellanos*.

As a disciple of Francisco Imperial (q.v.) he popularized Dante's metre and allegorical mode in Spain, indulging in literary polemics with Álvarez de Villasandino, as Santillana testifies: 'fiço buenas canciones en loor de Nuestra

Señora; fiço asymesmo algunas invectivas contra Alfonso Álvarez de diversas materias é bien ordenadas'.

LANGE, NORAH (1906–), b. Buenos Aires. Argentinian poet and novelist of Norwegian ancestry. She has lived in Buenos Aires all her life except for six years in Colonia Alvear, Mendoza, which she has described with exquisite sensitivity in *Cuadernos de infancia* (1937).

In adolescence she joined the *ultraísta* group and met Jorge Luis Borges, who wrote the preface to her first book of poems: *La calle de la tarde* (1925). She contributed to the vanguard magazines of the period, and joined the Florida Street group (q.v.), later writing for *Sur* and *Nosotros*. *Los días y las noches* (1926) and *El rumbo de la rosa* (1930) are her last collections of poetry, but the prose that she published, beginning with the highly subjective semi-novel *Voz de la vida* (1927), is often closer to poetic inspiration than to narrative fiction.

45 días y 30 marineros (1933) follows the twenty-year-old Ingrid, the only woman on the ship, on a voyage from Buenos Aires to Oslo.

Antes que mueran (1944) returns to the theme of childhood and lost days, a lyrical book of regret.

Personas en la sala (1950) and *Los dos retratos* (1956) also move in the dream-world of elegant nostalgia. In her obsession to avoid the vulgar and the cliché-ridden vocabulary of popular writing, Norah Lange has constructed a personal style of clarity and purity, though it is sometimes precious. She is concerned with the landscape of the soul rather than with outward appearances.

There is a penetrating study of her work in Helena Percas's *La poesía femenina argentina* (Madrid, 1958), pp. 485–501.

LANZA, SILVERIO, pseudonym of Juan Bautista Amorós (q.v.).

LARA, JESÚS (1904–), b. Cochabamba. Bolivian novelist, poet, and anthologist. His first collection of verse, *Harahuiy, harahuicu* ('Poet, sing!', 1927), cleverly mixed Quichua words into Spanish poems to strengthen the work's appeal to the Quichua population. In *Poesía popular quechua* (195–?), he compiled a fine anthology of Quichua oral verse with facing Castilian translations. Accused by his detractors of 'racist romanticism', he has indignantly attacked the exploitation of the Quichua in ephemeral journalism and novels which are based on simplistic black-and-white values and stereotyped characters. The revolutionary nature of his fiction has been recognized by the Soviet Government, which (in the late 1960s) published editions of his novels.

The novel *Repete : diario de un hombre que fue a la guerra del Chaco* (Cochabamba, 1938), indicating that the Quichua's enemies are internal as well as foreign, was understandably banned by the Bolivian government. The short *Surumi* (1943) was amplified in the long and involved *Yanakuna* (1952), which reverted to Lara's Indianist theme. *Yawaninchij* ('Our blood', 1959) condemns corrupt politicians, conniving churchmen, and Standard Oil as representative of United States imperialist interests, and demands agrarian reform for the Indian.

His subsequent books, equally militant and one-sided tracts, are *Leyendas quechuas* (1960), *Sinchikay* (1962), *Llalliypacha: tiempo de vencer* (1965), and *Ñancahuazu: sueños* (1969).

LARA, JUSTO DE, pseudonym of José de Armas y Cárdenas (q.v.).

Lara, Los siete Infantes de, see SIETE INFANTES DE LARA, LOS.

LARRA, LUIS MARIANO DE (1830–1901), b. Madrid. Playwright. Son of Mariano José de Larra (q.v.). His niche in literary history is due to some sparkling librettos for *zarzuelas* (q.v.), especially *El barberillo de Lavapiés* (1874) and *El atrevido en la Corte*. Among his extremely popular, though dated, comedies of manners are *La pluma y la espada*, *Bienaventurados los que lloran*, *La viuda de López*, *Los lazos de la familia*, *Batalla de reinas*, and *Flor del valle*.

His play *La oración de la tarde* was alleged to have been copied from *El cura de aldea* by Pérez Escrich, but a literary tribunal presided over by Rodríguez Rubí acquitted Larra of plagiarism.

Larra also wrote some ephemeral plays on historical themes, including *En palacio y en la calle* (on Antonio Pérez), and *Lanuza*.

LARRAMENDI, *Padre* MANUEL DE (1690–1766), b. Andoain, Guipúzcoa. Basque encyclopaedic writer whose misleading *Diccionario trilingüe del castellano, bascuence y latín* (San Sebastián, 1745) and Basque grammar *El Impossible Vencido: Arte de la lengua Bascongada* (Salamanca, 1729) were the principal tools for learning Basque in his time. He taught philosophy and theology in Palencia, Valladolid, and Salamanca, and is especially significant for the impulse he gave to other Jesuit students of Basque: Sebastián Mendiburu (1708–1782) and Agustín Cardaberaz (1703–1770).

He enjoyed controversy, frequently jumping to unwarrantable conclusions on flimsy or non-existent evidence, as in *De la Antigüedad y Universalidad del Bascuence en España* (Salamanca, 1728), in which he claims to prove that Basque is not only the aboriginal language of Spain (which may be true) but also that it was one of the 75 original languages that came into existence after the building of the Tower of Babel. (The Abbé Diharce de Bidassouet declared in his *Histoire des Cantabres* that Basque is in fact the language spoken by God).

Padre Larramendi is remembered best for his loving *Corografía o Descripción general de la muy noble y muy leal Provincia de Guipúzcoa* (1882).

LARRA Y SÁNCHEZ DE CASTRO, MARIANO JOSÉ DE (1809–37), b. Madrid. Essayist and satirist who wrote under a number of pseudonyms: 'El pobrecito hablador', 'El duende satírico', 'El bachiller Juan Pérez de Munguía', 'Andrés Niporesas', the anagram Ramón de Arriala (Mariano de Larra), and most frequently 'Fígaro', after the character made famous by Beaumarchais.

Larra's father was a doctor in the French army, and went into exile with his family in 1814. When Larra returned to Spain in 1817, he could speak only French. In 1828 he abandoned his studies and founded *El Duende Satírico del Día* (5 issues), later producing a similar review, *El Pobrecito Hablador* (14 issues, 1832–3).

With Espronceda, Larra was a guiding spirit of *El Parnasillo*, a *tertulia* (q.v.) meeting at the café of the Teatro del Príncipe, now the Español.

In 1829 he married 'pronto y mal' as he later described his five years with Pepita Wetoret, who bore him three children including Luis Mariano de Larra (q.v.). They separated in 1834, ironically the year that Larra produced his Romantic play idealizing love, *Macías*, a mediocre drama important for its theme of frustrated love ending in death, a theme adopted by most of the Romantic dramatists. He also published a sentimental novel on Macías (q.v.), *El doncel de don Enrique el Doliente* (1834).

Larra's other original play, *El conde Fernán González*, was never performed, and his versions from French plays of the time are of only passing interest.

His major writings are paradoxically the satirical essays that his contemporaries thought ephemeral: the *Artículos* which appeared in his own magazines and in the press of the day and poked fun (often desperately serious) at the Spanish way of life. He attacked procrastination (in the great essay 'Vuelva Vd. mañana'), apathy in public life, corruption in the bureaucracy, bigotry in religion, conservatism in education, nepotism in politics, and the vacuum in intellectual life. But Larra is not merely exercising his wit in dark Quevedesque misanthropy: his intentions are positive; his aim, reform. Even his articles on *costumbrismo* show analysis, rather than mere description, and he is claimed as a predecessor by the Generation of 1898. In his article *De la sátira y los satíricos*, Larra observes that the satirist must be well-equipped intellectually and ethically, aiming at a moral and corrective tone, dealing constructively with the absurdities and vices of his society without malice or evident anger. *El mundo todo es máscaras, todo el año es Carnaval* takes a pessimistic view of Spanish society as a gathering at a masked ball, each mask hiding hypocrisy and evil. In *Entre qué gente estamos* Larra criticizes the ignorant and conceited foreigner who openly derides the shortcomings of Spain while failing to recognize her virtues. *La fonda nueva* rails against bad service in Madrid restaurants. *El castellano viejo* exposes the pretentious Spaniard who preens himself on his pedigree when he has accomplished nothing worthy of it. *Quién es el público y donde se le encuentra* laments the absence of an informed and responsible intelligentsia.

Larra's literary credo is an important document in Spanish Romanticism: in *Literatura: rápida ojeada sobre la historia e índole de la nuestra* (1836) he joined Alcalá Galiano (q.v.) in denouncing the intolerance characteristic of the Golden Age and advocating a new literature to reflect progress in thought and science, and to express the social principles of liberty, truth, and justice.

The obvious motive for his suicide was a quarrel with his mistress Dolores Armijo; the ethos of *Werther* lingered on. But more fundamentally the cause may have been his Romantic reaction to the sudden realization that his political reforms were doomed because mankind is incorrigible and imperfectible.

Zorrilla made his own name with the elegy *A la memoria desgraciada del joven literato Don Mariano José de Larra* read in part by the side of Larra's grave.

Larra's *Obras* appeared in vols. 127–130 of the BAE (1960), but there is a more convenient anthology of *Artículos selectos* by E. M. Aguilera (Barcelona, 1960). Studies on his life and work include *Fígaro* (1918) by C. de Burgos; *Mariano José de Larra* (1936) by J. R. Lomba y Pedraja; *Larra* (1951) by R. B. Moreno; *Fígaro* (1956) by M. Gómez Santos; and J. Escobar, *Los orígenes de la obra de Larra* (1973).

LARREA, JUAN (1895–), b. Bilbao. Poet and critic. As a poet he was involved between 1916 and 1919 in the *creacionista* and *ultraísta* movements, publishing his first poems which show the influences of Apollinaire and Huidobro, in the *avant-garde* magazines *Grecia* (Seville) and *Cervantes* (Madrid) during 1919. In 1924 he moved to Paris, collaborating with César Vallejo (q.v.) in *Favorables París Poemas*, a surrealist magazine which appeared only twice, and he has since since written on the history and theory of surrealism. For many years he directed the Instituto del Nuevo Mundo at the University of Córdoba, Argentina, editing there *Aula Vallejo*, devoted to Vallejo studies.

His first recognition was in Gerardo Diego's *Antología de poetas contemporáneos* (1932), where the editor translated some of Larrea's French poems into Castilian. His most recent books are *Versione celeste* (Turin, 1969), with 106 poems written mainly before 1932 and in French, with Italian translations, and a booklet *César Vallejo frente a André Breton* (Córdoba, 1969), defending the Peruvian for his successful expression of universal love and attacking the Frenchman for having failed to write the poetry his theories would seem to require. Among his prose works is *Rendición del espíritu* (Mexico City, 1943).

LARRETA, ENRIQUE RODRÍGUEZ (1875–1961), b. Buenos Aires. Argentinian modernist novelist. Long periods spent in France and Spain influenced his style (which owes much to Flaubert) and his settings: the Ávila and Toledo of Philip II's reign in his major novel *La gloria de Don Ramiro* (q.v., Madrid, 1908). He owes the treatment of his theme to the example of Walter Scott, while the writing is influenced by Valle-Inclán and Darío. Contemporary Spanish is used for narrative, and archaic Spanish, carefully contrived, for dialogue. An English translation was made by L. B. Walton (New York, 1924).

Larreta's intention in *Zogoibi: el dolor de la tierra* (1926) was to produce a tragedy of the pampas, but the *gaucho* hero Jesús Benavídez plays a minor role and the final effect is to produce a morality in the tradition of Guevara's *Menosprecio de corte y alabanza de aldea* (q.v.). Subsequent novels include *Orillas del Ebro* (1949), which won the Premio Nacional de Novela, *Gerardo* (1953), *En la pampa* (1955), and a complete version of *Gerardo* (1956).

Other books by Larreta include the slow-moving *Tenía que suceder*, in the tradition of *La Celestina* and the plays of Galdós, composed of dialogue without speakers being named; the historical *Las dos fundaciones de Buenos Aires*; the autobiographical *Los días luminosos*; essays on morals and aesthetics entitled *La naranja* (1947); two plays, and a book of sonnets called *La calle de la vida de la muerte*. The *Obras completas* of Larreta (2 vols., 1959) have a prologue by E. de Gandía.

See A. Jansen, *Enrique Larreta, romancier hispano-argentin* (2 vols., Brussels, 1961–2), with a good bibliography.

Las, see under the word following the article, e.g. NAVAS DE TOLOSA, Las.

LAS CASAS, *Fray* BARTOLOMÉ DE (1474?–1566), b. Seville. After studying in Salamanca, he left at the age of 28 for Hispaniola, where he managed his father's ranch. At the age of 38 he trained for the priesthood, having changed his life following a sermon given by a Dominican, and was known thenceforth as the 'Apostle of the Indies'. He requested, and was accorded, the privilege of attempting the peaceful colonization of Cumaná (1520), and when this failed he entered a religious order (1523) and began in 1527 to write the *Historia general de las Indias* about the Spanish conquest, a work left incomplete in 1561. This sober work is very different from his crusading *Brevíssima relación de la destruyción de las Indias* (written in 1542, dedicated to Prince Felipe, and published in Seville in 1552), in which he accuses the Spaniards of systematic and prolonged brutality amounting to genocide. When he sent it to Carlos V, the Emperor gathered a committee of lawyers and theologians to discuss the allegations of Las Casas; the committee, however, rejected his findings.

Las Casas argues that the Indian is by nature virtuous and peaceable, but has been corrupted by an alien civilization: a view of 'the noble savage' long before the phrase became fashionable. Several Americanists believe that he went too far in his denunciation of Spanish colonial policy, damaging a good case, but his essential humanitarianism raises his case above the level of controversy, and should be taken into account when reading apologists for Spain such as Gonzalo Fernández de Oviedo and Juan Ginés de Sepúlveda (qq.v.). Sepúlveda's *Apologia* has been translated from Latin into Spanish by A. Losada with the first publication of Las Casas's reply (1975) with facsimiles of the MSS. Las Casas's *De imperatoria seu regia potestate* has been adapted by L. Pereña and V. Abril as *Derechos civiles y políticos* (1974).

See J. Friede, *Bartolomé de Las Casas, precursor del anticolonialismo, su lucha y su derrota* (1974).

Las de Caín (1908), a *comedia* by the brothers Serafín and Joaquín Álvarez de Quintero (q.v.).

Don Segismundo Caín, a poor but respectable language-teacher in Madrid, is faced with the task of marrying off his five daughters. The anxieties and desperation of every member of the family are brought to the fore in turn, rendering everyone both comic and pathetic. The Quintero brothers retain an atmosphere of family piety and conventional restraints while ridiculing the numerous weaknesses of their characters. The title of the play is a pun on the saying '*pasar las de Caín*', meaning 'to have one hell of a time of it'.

LASTARRIA, José Victorino (1817–88), b. Rancagua. Chilean positivist and novelist, who anticipated Comte's philosophy in many ways and was a member of the Society of Equality, whose secret meetings he attended as 'Brissot', the name of a Girondist.

He founded and edited a short-lived but influential magazine, supporting Bello's classicism, *El Semanario Literario* (31 issues, 1842–3), publishing in its pages contributions by José Joaquín Vallejo, Sanfuentes, Bilbao, and Tocornal. Hugo's *Ruy Blas* was mocked as a 'monstruosidad' but after Sarmiento had vehemently proclaimed that for all Hugo's faults there was no Chilean writer to match him, Lastarria ended by agreeing.

His novels attempted to break loose from Spanish tradition, introducing the Creole element, and Lastarria has been called the founder of Chilean fiction for the historical and semi-autobiographical novels and stories *El mendigo* (1843), *El alférez Alonso Díaz de Guzmán* (1848), and *Antaño y hogaño: novelas y cuentos de la vida hispanoamericana* (1885), a collection which includes 'Una hija', a sympathetic account of the Negroes' plight.

Of his many works, the *Lecciones de política positiva* (1875) mark the culmination of his thought, developing the *Investigaciones sobre la influencia social de la conquista y sistema colonial de los españoles en Chile* (1844). His historical writings (such as the *Historia constitucional de medio siglo*, 1853) foreshadow the semi-scientific methods of Henry Thomas Buckle in attempting to account for historical developments by analysing the geographical and psychological conditions of countries and peoples, but with insufficient data to permit accuracy.

A lifelong Comtean, Lastarria dissented from his French mentor only in opposing Dr. Francia, the republican dictatorship, and Napoleon III's *coup d'état*. His *Recuerdos literarios* (1st ser., 1878, on the period 1836–49; 2nd ser., 1885) are still the best record of Chilean literature in that period.

Lastarria founded the Academia de Bellas Letras in Santiago in 1873. Alejandro Fuenzálida Grandón's *Lastarria y su tiempo* (2 vols., 1911) has now been supplemented by Luis Oyarzún's *El pensamiento de Lastarria* (1953).

LATORRE, Mariano (1886–1955), b. Cobquecura. Chilean novelist of French immigrant stock, an acknowledged master of *criollismo* (q.v.). He worked as a librarian and later taught Spanish literature at the Instituto Pedagógico in Santiago from 1930. In his *Autobiografía de una vocación* Latorre described how 'se despertó en mi un afán casi místico de viajar por todos los rincones de mi tierra,

conocer paisajes y hombres por mis propios ojos y no a través de libros o referencias y, por último, verterlo en novelas, cuentos o ensayos . . .'

Latorre's theme is man's struggle to survive in the inhospitable wildness of Chile's mountains and coastline. His *Paisajes chilenos* (1910) was followed by *Cuentos del Maule* (1912) on fishermen; *Cuna de cóndores* (1918) on Andeans; *Zurzulita* (1920) on the clash between a townsman and villagers; *Ully y otros cuentos* (1924) on the far south; *Chilenos del mar* (1929) on people of the coast; and *Maipú* (1942) on Araucania, among others.

Latorre is significant for the new direction he gave to Chilean literature. His characterization is generally weak, and his descriptions unremarkable, but in books like *Hombres y zorros* (1937) and *Chile, país de rincones* (1955), Latorre conveyed much of his own *afán* for the Chileans and their land. He produced a useful *Antología de cuentistas chilenos* (1938) and a tendentious history, *La literatura de Chile* (Buenos Aires, 1941), which was attacked by Raúl Silva Castro in a booklet of the same title published in 1946.

Sus mejores cuentos (1925) reached a 3rd edition in 1962. *Mariano Latorre: obras, estilo, técnica* (1959) by J. Orlandi and A. Ramírez Cid has not entirely superseded *Mariano Latorre: vida y obra, bibliografía, antología* (New York, 1944) by M. Arce and S. C. Rosenbaum.

LAUER, Mirko (1947–), b. Zatec, Czechoslavakia. Peruvian poet of Czechoslovakian descent. Educated in Lima and Canada, Lauer has worked in Peking. His first book was *En los cínicos brazos* (1967). He achieved wide recognition for his second book, *Ciudad de Lima, 1967–1968* (1968), which had Poundian overtones in diction and rhythm, though rather less in content: 'Y todo tiene que ver con todo: el débil / con su debilidad y el fuerte con su propia fuerza / responderán y darán explicaciones' (from the poem 'Leit Motiv ¡Oh gran ciudad de Lima!').

Lauer's third book, *Santa Rosita y el péndulo proliferante* (1972) is in prose, using techniques from William Burroughs to explore some myths of Latin America. His fourth, *Bajo contínuo* (1975) is poetry.

A collection of 16 translations has been published by David Tipton, *Common grave* (n.d. but 1973). With A. Oquendo, Lauer has compiled an anthology, *Surrealistas y otros peruanos insulares* (Barcelona, 1973), including Moro, Oquendo de Amat, Adán, Westphalen, Eielson, Deustua, Sologuren, and Chariarse.

LAVARDÉN, Manuel José de (1754–1809), b. Buenos Aires. Argentinian poet and playwright, whose 'Oda al majestuoso río Paraná' appeared in the first number of *El Telégrafo Mercantil* (1 April 1801).

His tragedy 'Siripo' (1789) was one of the earliest plays centring on the conflict between the Indian and his conqueror. It dealt with the capture of Lucía Miranda, a theme occurring in Barco de Centenera and Ruy Díaz de Guzmán (qq.v.) which became very popular in the Río de la Plata. Lavardén also wrote two comedies: 'Las armas de la hermosura' and 'Efectos de odio y amor', both lost, like 'Siripo'. He is the author of a curious *sátira* for Buenos Aires and against Lima which first appeared in the *Estudios biográficos y críticos* of Juan María Gutiérrez (q.v.).

See Mariano G. Bosch, *Manuel de Lavardén, poeta y filósofo* (1944).

LAVERDE RUIZ, GUMERSINDO (1840–90), b. Santander. Philosopher, teacher, and poet. An ardent Roman Catholic and opponent of *krausismo* (q.v.), Laverde received Menéndez y Pelayo (q.v.) in Valladolid after he had left Madrid in protest against Salmerón's teachings. Laverde was praised fulsomely in Menéndez's *Horacio en España* and wrote the prologue to his *Polémicas, indicaciones y proyectos sobre ciencia española* (1876, 3rd edn., 3 vols., 1887–8). He signed controversial articles 'L. Ruiz'.

Laverde's poetry, such as 'La luna y el lirio' and 'Paz y misterio', with its misty Scandinavian or Celtic lyricism, is reminiscent of Ossian. He wrote little, since his active life was spent in teaching and administration, but he found time to gather the work *Ensayos críticos de filosofía, literatura e instrucción pública españolas* (Lugo, 1868).

His works have been selected and edited by J. M. de Cossío (Santander, 1951) and there are several articles on him in *Cuadernos de Estudios Gallegos*, vol. II (Santiago, 1956).

Lazarillo de Tormes y de sus fortunas y aduersidades, Vida de, an anonymous short novel which is generally accounted a prototype and precursor of the picaresque genre.

The first known editions are dated 1554 (Burgos, Alcalá, and Antwerp) but there was probably an Antwerp edition of 1553, though no known copy survives. The novel was placed on the Index in 1559 for its vigorous anti-clerical satire, which gave it the reputation of an Erasmian tract, but it continued to be very widely circulated in Spain so that Philip II ordered its expurgation, and the first *Lazarillo castigado* appeared in 1573.

The problem of the work's authorship is still unresolved. In 1605 Padre José de Sigüenza attributed it to Fray Juan de Ortega when a student in Salamanca. In 1607 Valerius Andrea Taxandrus, in his *Catalogus clarorum Hispaniae scriptorum* (Mainz) first ascribed the book to Diego Hurtado de Mendoza (q.v.). These two authors are the likeliest in the recent view of Deyermond, though he also offered the name of the Erasmian dramatist Sebastián de Horozco (q.v.). Morel-Fatio opposed the attribution to Hurtado de Mendoza, suggesting the brothers Valdés (qq.v.) or Cristóbal de Villalón (q.v.). The verdict is still open.

Lazarillo de Tormes is cast in the form of a deceptively straightforward autobiography, divided into seven *tratados* of varying length. Lázaro, a poor boy of criminal origins, is sent to earn his keep with a blind beggar, shrewd, mean, and vicious, who shows him how to survive on his wits. But Lázaro finds so little peace (and less food) that on the point of starving he leaves the *ciego* and offers to help a priest as an altar-boy in exchange for his keep. This is a mistake, for Lázaro escapes 'del trueno y dí en el relámpago, porque era el ciego para con éste un Alejandro Magno, con ser la misma avaricia'. The hilarious vices and follies of the wretched priest are told with gusto, leading some critics to the conclusion that the author was perhaps an Erasmian. Having been dismissed by the priest, Lazarillo passes into the service of a poor *hidalgo* of Toledo, as proud of his nobility as any rich courtier. Like all of the protagonist's masters, the *hidalgo* is not what he seems (the blind man's prayers had been mere showmanship). Forbidden by his ancestry to perform any manual work, the wretched *hidalgo* finally flees his creditors, whereupon Lázaro joins a loose-living Mercedarian friar, then a vendor of Papal bulls, a painter, a chaplain, and a constable. Eventually finding what he claims to be stability and sufficient honour in being appointed town crier, Lázaro reaps the reward of loyal service by marrying the concubine of an archpriest in Toledo and the book ends with his complacent view of a rosy future, which is clearly not as secure as he would believe.

The social satire of the brief novel covers various aspects of contemporary Spain, but is less significant than the religious and philosophical morals to be drawn from it, especially that we are all hypocrites, deceiving ourselves as much as we deceive others. R. W. Truman (*Modern Language Review*, vol. 44, 1969, pp. 62–7) shows that *Lazarillo* parodies treatises praising the virtuous self-made man. It excels most of its successors, the picaresque novels (apart from *El buscón*, q.v.), in the subtlety of the hero's development from childhood to maturity. The writing is more readably concise than in *Alonso, mozo de muchos amos* (q.v.) and less obtrusively moralistic than *Guzmán de Alfarache* (q.v.). Part of the book's appeal to the modern reader lies in its laconic, deft characterization so alien to its pre-Cervantine period, and part in the disparity in length of the *tratados* (II and III are much longer than IV or VI, for example), indicating which parts of his life the 'narrator' believes to have been the most significant. Francisco Rico (*La novela picaresca y el punto de vista*, Barcelona, 1970; 2nd edn., 1973) suggests that the persistent ambiguity of *Lazarillo* is due to moral relativism on the author's part, and/or that the author's self-effacement leaves us without explicit guidance.

Modern editions of the *Lazarillo de Tormes* include those of Cejador (1914; 4th edn., 1941) for Clásicos Castellanos, of R. O. Jones (Manchester, 1963); and of A. Blecua (1974) for Clásicos Castalia.

La segunda parte de Lazarillo de Tormes (Antwerp, 1555, following an early Spanish edition?) is by another, greatly inferior hand. The two parts can be compared in vol. 3 (1846) of the BAE. *El Lazarillo de Manzanares* (1620) written by Juan Cortés de Tolosa satirizes life in Madrid, but without the verve or originality of its model. Another *Segunda parte* (Paris, 1620) was written by Juan de Luna; in this more anti-clerical sequel, Lázaro ends by becoming a religious recluse. The popularity of the original *Lazarillo* can be estimated from the fact that David Rowland's English version (1576) was reprinted at least twenty times. There is a good recent version (with Quevedo's *Buscón*) by Michael Alpert (Harmondsworth, 1969).

R. E. Zwez has edited and modernized three *Lazarillos raros* (1972): *El Lazarillo de Badalona* (1742), *The life and death of Young Lazarillo* (1688), and *El Lazarillo del Duero* (1898), the third by Joaquín del Barco and other two anonymous.

See A. D. Deyermond, *Lazarillo de Tormes* (London, 1975) primarily; and also F. C. Tarr, 'Literary and artistic unity in the "Lazarillo de Tormes" ' in *Publications of the Modern Language Association of America*, vol. 42 (1927), pp. 404–21; S. Gilman, 'The death of Lazarillo de Tormes', *ibid.*, vol. 81 (1966), pp. 149–66; M. Bataillon, *Novedad y fecundidad del 'Lazarillo de Tormes'* (Salamanca, 1968; being the translated introduction to Bataillon's edn., Paris, 1958); J. F. Gatti, *Introducción al 'Lazarillo de Tormes'* (Buenos Aires, 1968); and Derek W. Lomax, 'On rereading the "Lazarillo de Tormes" ' in *Studia ibérica: Festschrift für Hans Flasche* (Berne, 1973), pp. 371–81, suggesting that stress on poverty and clerical immorality may be due to a revolution of rising expectations.

LECETA, JUAN DE, pseudonym of Rafael Múgica (q.v.).

Lectura, La, an important monthly periodical, founded in 1900 by Francisco López Acebal and Clemente de Velasco, which subsequently led to the series Clásicos Castellanos and Pedagogía Moderna.

Lecturas españolas (1912), a collection of essays by 'Azorín' (q.v.).

Dedicated to Larra's memory, this volume is written from a sense of 'curiosity as to what constitutes the Spanish environment—landscapes, literature, art, men, cities, interiors—and preoccupation for a future of prosperity and justice in Spain'. Taken together, these essays on topics as diverse as J. L. Vives, Gracián, Dumas in Spain, music, and Baroja, can be said to represent, with Azorín's other collections of essays, the spirit of the Generación del 1898 (q.v.).

LEDESMA, ROBERTO (1901–), b. Buenos Aires. Argentinian poet who dissociated himself from *vanguardista* tendencies by practising traditional verse-forms such as the sonnet, by concentrating on formal beauty, and by insisting that communication is the first duty of the poet. In the prologue to his translation of Rilke's *Auguste Rodin* (1943) he affirmed his belief that the essence of art resides in 'romper en su núcleo el espantoso aislamiento del espíritu en que Rilke cultivó su angustia'. His collections are *Caja de música* (1925), *Trasfiguras* (1933), *Nivel del cielo* (1943), *Tiempo sin ceniza* (1943), *La llama* (1953), and *El pájaro en la tormenta* (1957).

Ledesma also wrote a novel, *Juan sin Ruido* (1953), which took as its point of departure W. H. Hudson's story 'El niño diablo' and attempted, with some success, to create a universal type with recognizable Argentinian characteristics: Juan, who moves without a sound and arrives without being observed, is a compound of the *payador* and the *gaucho*, the horsebreaker and the guide.

LEDESMA BUITRAGO, ALONSO DE (1562–1633), b. Segovia. Poet who achieved a controversial notoriety with *Conceptos espirituales* (3 vols., 1600–12), and if not Spain's first *conceptista* poet was a more devoted practitioner of *conceptismo* (q.v.) than any poet before him. He was the acknowledged leader of a large number of preachers and writers who filled their works with puns, metaphors, and elaborate verbal conceits of every kind, and whose influence extended as far as Lope (who parodied Ledesma's style) and Quevedo (qq.v.). Some of his ballads appeared in his *Romancero y monstruo imaginado* (1615), while the *Juegos de Noche Buena moralizados* (1611), a Christmas entertainment with medieval songs and *villancicos* transposed *a lo divino*, was placed on the Index of 1667, though reprinted in vol. 25 (1866) of the BAE. *Epigramas y hieroglíficos*

á la vida de Christo appeared posthumously, in
1625.

F. Vindel (1941) attempted to prove that
Ledesma was 'Fernández de Avellaneda' (q.v.),
the alleged author of the false second part of
Don Quijote.

Recent articles on Ledesma include 'Datos
biográficos' (*Estudios segovianos*, vol. 1, 1949, pp.
526–54) by M. A. Quintanilla and another in
the same journal by F. Smieja, 'Ledesma y su
poesía a lo divino' (vol. 15, 1963, pp. 323–48).
Ledesma's *Conceptos spirituales y morales* (3 vols.)
edited by Eduardo Juliá Martínez (1969) was
completed by other editors after Juliá Martínez's
death in 1967. A new edition of the *Romancero
y monstruo imaginado* by Florián Smieja awaits
publication.

See M. d'Ors, *Vida y poesía de Alonso de
Ledesma* (1974).

LEDESMA MIRANDA, RAMÓN (1901–63),
b. Madrid. Novelist, short-story writer, and a
poet who began as a disciple of Darío (q.v.), but
eventually repudiated all his work written prior
to 1930.

Antes de mediodía (1930) was one of the best
Spanish novels of the time, and equally
impressive were *Agonía y tres novelas más* (1931)
and *Evocación de Laura Estébanez* (1933), based
on the death of the well-known actress Rosario
Pino. Then followed the short stories *Saturno
y sus hijos* (1934) and *Almudena* (1944), a
definitive version of *Viejos personajes* (1936) which
was influenced by Fogazzaro and Flaubert (not
by Pérez Galdós as some Spanish critics have
claimed) and improved on Unamuno's treatment of the Cain-Abel story. Cela praised the
novel (in *Arriba*, 24 September 1944) as a work
of European stature.

However Ledesma's most impressive work (if
occasionally prolix) was *La casa de la Fama* (1951),
a chronicle of the decadence of a middle class
family in Almería that had been impoverished
by the collapse of Spain's empire. Ledesma's
last works were *Gibraltar, la roca de Calpe* (1957)
and *Páginas de Andalucía* (1964).

LEGUIZAMÓN, MARTINIANO P. (1858–1935),
b. Rosario del Tala, Argentina. A regional
writer of Basque ancestry whose historical novel
Montaraz was set in Entre Ríos in 1820. Its
strength is in the observation of landscape; its
weaknesses are a heavily romantic plot and
woodenness in the portrayal of characters. His
first book was the regional collection *Recuerdos
de la tierra* (1896), contemporaneous with the
production of *Calandria* (1896), the only one of
his plays to reach the stage. It deals in an original
manner with the legend of the outlaw Calandria,
who died at the hands of the police, a tradition

examined in detail by Groussac in vol. 1 of *El
viaje intelectual*. His short stories in *Alma nativa*
(1906) were well received, but he devoted his
later years to literary and historical topics,
including a study of Hidalgo called *El primer
poeta criollo del Río de la Plata* (1917).

LEIRAS PULPEIRO, MANUEL (1854–1912),
b. Mondoñedo. Galician poet, whose *Cantares
gallegos* celebrated the simple life of Galician
peasants, among whom he lived as a country
doctor, having qualified in Madrid. Though his
style is unoriginal and his diction unadventurous,
Leiras can be read with profit for the authenticity
of his Galician rhythms and an insight into the
varied life of Mondoñedo. The best of his
Poesías (1930) is perhaps '¡Non o sei!'

LEIVA, RAÚL (1916–), b. Guatemala City.
Poet and critic of the so-called Generation of
1940 and a contributor to its important magazine
Acento (q.v.). His poetry has moved from subjectivity (a phase concluding with *El deseo*) to a
recognition of the significance of the Mayan
element in Guatemalan literature. His works
include *Angustia* (1942), *El deseo* (1947), *Danza
para Cuauhtemóc* (1955), *Nunca el olvido* (1957), all
published in Mexico City; and *En el pecado*
(1943), *Sonetos de amor y muerte* (1944), *Muerte
y poesía* (1946), *Mundo indígeno* (1949), *Los
sentidos y el mundo* (1952), and *Oda a Guatemala*
(1953), all published in Guatemala City.

LEIVA or **LEYVA RAMÍREZ DE
ARELLANO**, FRANCISCO DE (1630?–1676?), b.
Málaga. Dramatist of the school of Calderón.
His best-known plays are *Cuando no se aguarda,
y príncipe tonto*, one of the earliest and funniest of
the *comedias de figurón* (q.v.); *El socorro de los
mantos*, a play in the genre de *capa y espada* (q.v.),
attributed in some editions to Carlos Arellano;
and the remarkable *La dama presidente*, in which
a dishonoured woman seeks to revenge herself
on men. All these three are in vol. 47 (1858) of
the BAE. Leiva also wrote a play on the
chivalresque theme of Amadís de Gaula (q.v.),
the religious *Nuestra Señora de la Victoria*, and the
heroic *Albania tiranizada* and *La mayor constancia
de Mucio Scévola. No hay contra un padre razón* is a
gruesome tragedy of a king's vindictiveness.

See N. Díaz de Escovar, *Francisco de Leiva*
(Málaga, 1899).

LEMOS, EL CONDE DE, pseudonym used by
Abraham Valdelomar (q.v.).

LEÑERO, VICENTE (1933–), b. Guadalajara,
Jalisco. Mexican novelist. His first book was *La
polvareda y otros cuentos* (1959), but Leñero made
his name with the accomplished *La voz adolorida*

(1961), in which the narrator's story and dreams are equally effective in establishing credibility. *Los albañiles* (1964) centres on a building site, combining the social observation of a novel of manners with the excitement of a thriller; like the writings of Adolfo Bioy Casares (q.v.) however, Leñero's novel is an intellectual challenge to the reader, since the boundary between guilt and innocence fluctuates so quickly and bewilderingly that the question arises that perhaps there was no murder at all.

In *Estudio Q* (1965), set in a commercial television studio, the hero of a soap opera struggles to define his identity apart from the character he represents. By contrast with his earlier novels, *El garabato* (1967) is a thin, mannered performance, lacking conviction.

LEO JUDAEUS, see ABARBANEL, Judah.

LEÓN, *Fray* BASILIO DE, see PONCE DE LEÓN, *Fray* Basilio.

LEÓN, *Fray* LUIS DE, see LUIS DE LEÓN, *Fray*.

LEONARDO DE ARGENSOLA brothers, see ARGENSOLA, Bartolomé and Lupercio.

LEÓN HEBREO or LEO HEBRAEUS, other names of Judah Abarbanel or Abravanel (q.v.).

LEÓN MARCHANTE, MANUEL DE (1631–80), b. Pastrana, Guadalajara. *Entremesista*, poet, and priest, who studied in Alcalá and wrote the mediocre *Justa poética con que la Universidad de Alcalá celebró el nacimiento del Príncipe Próspero*. He carried on an epistolary romance with his cousin Margarita, a nun in the convent of Santa Fe, and wrote some passable plays, but is now remembered only for some amusing *entremeses*. He is stated to have composed sixteen *entremeses*, three *bailes*, two *jácaras*, and five *mojigangas*. The *entremés Los pajes golosos* concerns two greedy servants whose master laces some food with purgative, telling them it is poisonous. They eat it, sham dead to frighten their master, then reveal the deception. Other trifles of this type are *El abad del Campillo*, *El Pericón*, *El gato y la montera*, and the amusing *Las tres manías*. His *Obras poéticas pósthumas* appeared in 3 vols., the first in 1722, the second in 1733, and the third undated.

See Juan Catalina García, *Escritores de la provincia de Guadalajara* (1899) a biography and bibliography, and A. Méndez Plancarte, *León Marchante, jilguerillo del Niño Dios* (Mexico City, 1948).

LEÓN-PORTILLA, MIGUEL (1926–), b. Mexico City. Mexican cultural historian of the Nahua and other pre-Columbian peoples. He studied at the Loyola University in Los Angeles and the Universidad Nacional Autónoma de México, where he has taught Nahuatl cultural history since 1957. He has been successively Director of the Instituto Indigenista Interamericana, and of the Instituto de Investigaciones Históricas of the University, and as one of the distinguished disciples of Ángel María Garibay (q.v.), has been jointly responsible for the great progress of Nahuatl studies in recent years. He has published the following works: *La filosofía náhuatl estudiada en sus fuentes* (1956; 2nd edn., 1959; trans. by J. E. Davis as *Aztec thought and culture*, Norman, Okla., 1963); *Siete ensayos sobre cultura náhuatl* (1958), *Ritos, sacerdotes y atavíos de los dioses* (1958), *Visión de los vencidos* (1959; translated as *The broken spears: Aztec account of the conquest of Mexico*, Boston, 1963) with P. Garibay, *Los antiguos mexicanos a través de sus crónicas y cantares* (1961), *Imágenes del México antiguo* (Buenos Aires, 1963), *Los maestros prehispánicos de la palabra* (1963), *Las literaturas precolumbinas de México* (1964), *El reverso de la Conquista* (1964), translations of accounts of the Conquest by Aztec, Maya, and Inca authors; *Historía documental de México*, vol. 1 (1964), *Estudios de historia novohispana*, vol. 1 (1966), *Trece poetas del mundo azteca* (1967), and *Pre-Columbian literatures of Mexico* (Norman, Okla., 1969).

LEÓN Y MANSILLA, JOSÉ (d. after 1730), b. Cordova. Minor poet. His *Soledad tercera* (1718) imitates not only Góngora's themes, imagery, and stylistic mannerisms so closely as to lack all personality of its own, but so wholly lacks the master's imaginative flights that its attribution remains secure. León y Mansilla's work exemplifies the great influence of Góngora on the poets of his time.

LEÓN Y ROMÁN, RICARDO (1877–1943), b. Barcelona. Novelist. He spent his childhood in Málaga and thought of himself as an Andalusian. An employee of the Banco de España in Santander from 1901, he was transferred to Madrid in 1910 and lived there for the rest of his life. His novels, such as *Casta de hidalgos* (1908), represent ultra-Conservative, Roman Catholic, and fervently patriotic values as opposed to the radical tradition of Pío Baroja, and were bitterly criticized as being reactionary. León replied to his critics in the essay 'Examen de ingenios', which appears in *La escuela de los Sofistas* (1910), and continued to publish similar novels: *Comedia sentimental* (1909), a sub-Flaubertian extravaganza; *Alcalá de los Zegríes* (1909), on provincial politics; *El amor de los amores* (1917), which has been accurately described as a *Quijote 'a lo divino'; Los centauros*

(1912), on social life in the provinces, and many more. His favourite character is the sober, dignified Castilian *hidalgo*; his females are insipid and insubstantial, and his xenophobia detracts from his work as a whole. He was very popular in his time with an audience who did not understand psychoanalysis (which he ridicules in *Las siete vidas de Tomás Portolés*, 1931) and were impressed by his eloquence (he occasionally used blank verse). *Europa trágica* (3 vols., 1917–19), a collection of stories of World War I, was followed by pre-Civil War novels such as *Cristo en los infiernos* (1943), probably his best book. León's *Obras completas* appeared in 2 vols. in 1944.

Lepanto, a seaport of Central Greece opposite Patras now known as Naupaktos ('shipyards'). In 1571 it was the scene of the great naval battle between the Turks and the Christian 'Holy League' consisting of the Pope's forces allied with those of Venice and Philip II under Don Juan de Austria. The Christian victory was attributed by Sebastián de Nieva Calvo, in *La Mejor Muger Madre y Vírgen, Poema Sacro* (1625), to the miraculous intercession of the Virgin Mary. Odes on the battle were composed by Fernando de Herrera and Bartolomé Leonardo de Argensola (qq.v.). Hierónimo de Cortereal (a Portuguese) wrote a Spanish poem in fifteen cantos in blank verse entitled *Felicíssima Victoria concedida del Cielo al Señor Don Juan d'Austria* (Lisbon?, 1578).

Cervantes, who had joined the Holy League as a common soldier, was wounded twice and permanently lost the use of his left arm at Lepanto. He was taken to the hospital at Messina, and remained there until April 1572. Cristóbal de Virués (q.v.) was also at Lepanto, and described the battle in his epic *Monserrate* (1587).

LERA, Ángel María de (1912–), b. Baides, Guadalajara. Novelist, and journalist on *ABC*, the Madrid daily. The son of a country doctor, he has documented his father's profession in *Por los caminos de la medicina rural* (1966). He tried a number of jobs and failed to win recognition for his first novel *Los olvidados* (1957), but achieved fame overnight with *Los clarines del miedo* (Barcelona, 1958), a novel of two young bullfighters at a country *fiesta*. Crude realism in the manner of Zamacois (q.v.) is characteristic of *La boda* (Barcelona, 1959), *Bochorno* (1960), *Trampa* (1962), and *Hemos perdido el sol* (1963), based on his interviews with Spanish workers in Germany. An exponent of straight story-telling, Lera wrote a Civil War novel, *Las últimas banderas* (1967), to show the Republican point of view without offending the Franco regime, like

Gironella's Civil War trilogy. The sequel to *Las últimas banderas* is *Los que perdimos* (1974).

LESAGE or LE SAGE, ALAIN-RENÉ (1668– 1747), b. Sarzeau, Morbihan. French dramatist and novelist. A diligent translator and adaptor from the Spanish, Lesage altered his sources in such a way as to suit the more 'refined' taste of the 18th c.

The first two volumes of his picaresque novel *Gil Blas de Santillane* (q.v.) were published in 1715, the third in 1724, and the fourth in 1735. The book incorporates fifteen episodes from the picaresque novel *Vida del escudero Marcos de Obregón* (1618) by Vicente Espinel (q.v.) and borrowed from *Empeños del mentir*, a play by Antonio Hurtado de Mendoza (q.v.); and from works by Alonso de Castillo Solórzano (q.v.): *La niña de los embustes, Teresa de Manzanares* (1632), and *Las aventuras del bachiller Trapaza* (1637). P. Francisco José de Isla (q.v.) translated *Gil Blas* into Spanish (1783), claiming ironically that he was restoring it to its native land. Lesage based three other picaresque novels upon Spanish originals: *Don Guzman d' Alfarache* (1732), *Estevanille Gonzalès* (1734), and *Le bachelier de Salamanque* (1736), thought to be a translation of an unpublished picaresque novel (now lost) attributed to the historian and dramatist Antonio de Solís (q.v.).

Lesage is a good-humoured satirist and a clever narrator, excelling in dramatic incident and dialogue, but he fails to comprehend or to express the power of love and the other great passions. He translated Lope de Vega's *comedia Guardar y guardarse* as *Dom Félix de Mendoce* (1700); recast Vélez de Guevara's novel *El diablo cojuelo* as *Le diable boîteux* (1707); and adapted *Dom César Ursin* from Calderón's play *Peor está que estaba*, and *Le traître puni* from Rojas Zorrilla's play *La traición busca el castigo*.

Letrilla, a lyric poem, normally in lines of eight syllables or fewer, usually with the same line (an *estribillo*) concluding each verse. A *letrilla* is often simple and flowing, with religious, amorous, and satirical themes preponderating.

The best *letrillas* have been written by Juan del Encina, Hurtado de Mendoza, Quevedo ('Poderoso caballero / es don Dinero'), Lope de Vega, Góngora, and Meléndez Valdés (qq.v.).

> *Más rápida y sencilla*
> *la amorosa letrilla*
> *parece el leve juego*
> *del niño alado y ciego;*
> *imita su donaire,*
> *su planta fugitiva*
> *deslízase ligera*
> *graciosa nos cautiva—*
> Francisco Martínez de la Rosa.

LEUMANN, Carlos Alberto (1888–1952), b.
Santa Fe. Argentinian novelist, critic, and
journalist who wrote for *La Nación* (from 1910),
for *El Diario,* and for *La Prensa.* His first novel
is also his best: *Adriana Zumarán* (1920; definitive
edn., 1936) is a psychological novel in the
Proustian tradition which, however, lacks irony
and sufficient distance from the upper class
milieu of Buenos Aires in which it is set. It was
followed by *Tres relatos porteños* (1922) and by
more novels in a similar vein: *La vida victoriosa*
(1922); *El empresario del genio* ([1926]) in which
the drama is unfolded in the words of the hero
'inadvertido de las gentes, en la soledad de mi
alma'; *Trasmundo* (1930); and *Los gauchos de a pie*
(1940). His later stories were collected in *El país
del relámpago* (1932).

Leumann's interest in *literatura gauchesca* is
shown by his *La literatura gauchesca y la poesía
gauchesca* (1953); he had earlier published a
critical edition of Hernández's *Martín Fierro*
(qq.v.) in 1945 and *El poeta creador: como hizo
Hernández 'La vuelta de Martín Fierro'* in the same
year.

LEVI, Daniel, a Spanish Jew nominally
converted to Christianity under the name
Miguel de Barrios (q.v.).

Leyendas Marianas, see Marian Legends.

LEYVA RAMÍREZ DE ARELLANO,
Francisco de, see Leiva Ramírez de Arellano,
Francisco de.

LEZAMA LIMA, José (1912–), b. Havana,
where he studied law. Cuban novelist, poet, and
essayist, co-founder of, and contributor to, the
literary magazines *Verbum* (1937), *Nadie Parecía*
(1943), and *Orígenes* (1944–57).

He is one of the moving spirits behind
criollismo (q.v.). Lezama's hermetic poetry is
influenced by Valéry, Claudel, Neruda, Eliot,
and the Spanish baroque. His collections of
verse are *Muerte de Narciso* (1937), *Enemigo rumor*
(1941), *Aventuras sigilosas* (1945), *Dador* (1962),
and *Las eras imaginarias* (Madrid, 1971).
Lezama's *Poesía completa* appeared in 1970. There
are good critical anthologies of his work in
Armando Álvarez Bravo's *Órbita de Lezama
Lima* (1966) and by José Agustín Goytisolo
(Barcelona, 1969). His most complex book is
La fijeza (1949), whose title alludes to the fixed
nature of poetry.

His total devotion to literature, reminiscent
of that of Jorge Luis Borges (q.v.), is seen in his
bookish (even bibliomaniac) essays *Analecta del
reloj* (1953), *La expresión americana* (1957), and
Tratados en la Habana (1958).

Lezama has compiled a definitive *Antología de
la poesía cubana* (3 vols., 1965).

His most sustained work to date is the long,
ambitious novel *Paradiso* (1966). Deploying the
rich resources of modern Spanish at its most
effective, *Paradiso* is an ambitious, predominantly
successful, evocation of a poet's growth through
sensual and spiritual experiences.

LIBERIO, Silvio, pseudonym of Juan Pablo
Forner (q.v.).

LIBERTINO, Clemente, pseudonym of
Francisco Manoel de Melo (q.v.).

Library, Spanish National, see Biblioteca
Nacional, Madrid.

Libro de Alexandre, see Alexandre, Libro
de.

Libro de Apolonio, see Apolonio, Libro de.

Libro de buen amor, El, by Juan Ruiz (q.v.),
Arcipreste de Hita, with the poem of the *Cid*
(q.v.), the most important long poem of medieval
Spain. Three MSS. survive, two (known as
G[ayoso] and T[oledo]) having the version of
1330 and one (known as S[alamanca]) a version
of 1343, though all the MSS. are of later date
(late 14th c.). A palaeographic edition of all
three MSS. was published (Toulouse, 1901) by
Jean Ducamin and there is a recent critical
edition (1967) by Joan Corominas. J. Joset has
edited the *Libro de buen amor* (2 vols., 1974) for
Clásicos Castellanos. The best recent study is by
M. R. Lida de Malkiel, *Two Spanish masterpieces: the 'Book of Good Love' and 'The Celestina'*
(Urbana, Ill., 1962).

El libro de los cantares, as it was known until in
1898 Menéndez Pidal proposed a return to the
author's own title, is a poem of 1,728 stanzas,
interspersing several metres in the predominant
cuaderna vía (q.v.). The prevailing features of the
1330 version are parody, irony, and ambiguity;
the general pattern is the progression of human
life towards death. The changes in the 1343
version are usually towards the didactic, even if
parody remains an essential element: the prose
sermon, for example, belongs to the material
added for the 1343 version.

The *Libro* opens with a prayer to God, asking
for aid in the poet's troubles or *mala presion,*
presumably not a reference to actual imprisonment (see Juan Ruiz); next comes a prose
prologue, which is a parody of a sermon, in
which the author claims that his work, with its
many examples in the form of *loco amor* provides
instances of the kind of sinful conduct that is to

be avoided at all cost. However, 'porque es umanal cosa el pecar', some readers may misuse the work and if they seek *loco amor*, then 'fallarán algunas maneras para ello'. This rather mischievous ambiguity would seem to suggest that Ruiz is in fact parodying contemporary moralizing attitudes on art. After another prayer, invoking divine help in the difficult task of composition, and two hymns to the Virgin, Ruiz tells of a legendary debate in sign language between Greeks and Romans which ends to the satisfaction of both sides, although it then transpires that each has completely misunderstood the other! The speaker for the Greeks was a wise man, the representative of the Romans was a fool; hence we might suppose that the wise as well as the foolish may be equally wrong or equally right in their conclusions about the *Libro de buen amor*—it is an ambiguous book. Still in *cuaderna vía*, Ruiz, citing Aristotle, states that all living things have two basic urges, sustenance and physical love. This has been very true of himself, but 'provar omne las cosas non es por end peor / e saber bien e mal, ë usar lo mejor' (but typically he fails to say which is the better). He describes an alleged adventure of his own in which the lady twice rejects the proposals made by his go-between, on each occasion with a moralizing *exemplum*. There follows a second unsatisfactory affair in which Ruiz loses the girl (a baker's wife) to his go-between. A digression on fate, freewill, and the influence of the stars on human affairs, leads to a third failure in love (the girl rejects him and the verses he offers her) and he consoles himself with another *exemplum*. Then comes a debate with Don Amor, who gives Ruiz advice (derived from Ovid) on how to proceed in matters of love, and urges him to consult Venus; both Ruiz and Amor insert *exempla* into their arguments. Venus, when approached, offers suggestions similar to those made by Amor. There follows the affair of Doña Endrina and Don Melón de la Huerta, as the hero is now called. This derives from the 12th-c. Latin comedy *Pamphilus* (q.v.), which summarizes Ovid's teachings and then shows how they may be applied in practice. Melón manages to seduce the girl, thanks to the aid of the old procuress Trotaconventos who wins over Endrina after an argument in which more *exempla* are exchanged; the lovers finally marry. Next comes yet another love affair: the Archpriest falls in love with a young, rich, beautiful, noblewoman, and employs as his go-between the old woman Urraca (to be identified with Trotaconventos), but the girl falls ill and dies. This episode is followed by a series of mishaps in the Guadarrama mountains involving the Arcipreste and four *serranas* or highland girls, unlike the coy shepherdesses of the *pastorela*

tradition. Three of these turn out to be wild and muscular, and the unfortunate Arcipreste is raped by them. A further parody comes with the mock-epic description of the battle between Lent (Doña Cuaresma) and Carnival (Don Carnal), the subject of many medieval poems. Though defeated and imprisoned, Don Carnal escapes from prison as Lent ends and, accompanied by Don Amor, is triumphantly received by the people, including the clergy (an amusing anti-clerical touch not uncommon in medieval literature). Next Trotaconventos suggests to the Arcipreste that he seek the love of a nun, and, on his behalf, she approaches one called Garoza. They carry on a lengthy debate, again with numerous *exempla* on either side. The end of this affair is ambiguous; the euphemisms Ruiz employs to describe what takes place between himself and Garoza have led some critics to suppose that their love was purely platonic (although, as Corominas points out, no go-between would be needed for this), or that instead of physical love Garoza showed Ruiz the way to the love of God, or that the affair ended with her seduction. Shortly after, she dies and Trotaconventos endeavours to persuade a Moorish girl to become the Arcipreste's mistress, but she refuses. The work concludes with some short passages on Ruiz's poetic art and the variety of his compositions; on the death of Trotaconventos, which leads Ruiz to a bitter denunciation of death itself; a description of the arms the Christian needs to overcome the world, the flesh, and the Devil, is followed by an account of the qualities which make smaller women the most desirable of all; a description of Furón, the Arcipreste's rascally servant; and a characteristically ambiguous indication of how the *Libro de buen amor* is to be understood. Some short songs for beggars (students and blind men) and a number of hymns to the Virgin are followed by the 'Cantiga contra fortuna' and some amusing verses on the consternation of the clergy of Talavera when they receive a letter from their Archbishop forbidding them to keep mistresses on pain of excommunication.

The obvious lack of unity in the *Libro* suggests that it is a collection of verses written at different times and assembled by Ruiz into the work's present form; the 'autobiographical' passages may be, in part, fairly late and a framework in which to fit the rest. Sources of the *Libro de buen amor* include the Scriptures; civil and canon law; Don Juan Manuel (q.v.); Ovid; Goliardic verse; the catechism; treatises on sermons and confession; the *Carmina Burana* (stanzas 490–512) on 'las propriedades que el dinero ha'; the collection of Latin prose fables versified by Walter the Englishman (*fl.* 1177) and known as the *Romulus*; the *Tawq al-*

Hamama of Ibn Hazm (q.v.); the *Libro de Alexandre* (q.v.) for the episodes of the Tent of Love, the Triumph of Love, and the section on the seven deadly sins; and the 12th–13th c. Latin comedy *Liber Pamphili* for stanzas 555–865 describing the seduction of Doña Endrina.

Ruiz was one of the most individual writers before Cervantes (q.v.), his ribaldry interrupted so abruptly by sententiousness that commentators have always been divided on his real intentions. Amador de los Ríos affirms him to be a severe moralist and exemplary cleric. M. R. Lida de Malkiel, too, thinks the Archpriest merely uses the narrator's 'I' to describe events the more vividly, since he himself was never the protagonist. Cejador considers that Ruiz intended to satirize ecclesiastics who persisted in carnal love, or *loco amor*, as opposed to the love of God, or *buen amor*, exemplified by the clerical ideal of celibacy. For Puymaigre, Ruiz is a forerunner of Rabelais; and for Menéndez Pidal, a Boccaccio, mocking the current fashion for didactic literature. According to Menéndez y Pelayo, Ruiz is merely a product of his time: a libertine like his fellows, but a champion of received dogma. The least misleading statement of the book's intention (because the most ambiguous) is probably that in the poem itself: 'E ansí este mi libro a todo omne o muger, al cuerdo e al non cuerdo, al que entendiere bien e escogiere salvación e obrare bien amando a Dios, otrosí al que quisere el amor loco, en la carrera que andudiere, puede cada uno bien dezir: Intellectum tibi dabo, et cetera'.

Whether sincere or hypocritical, Ruiz's encomia of the pleasures of the flesh are splendidly written, filling the book with the bustle and variety of medieval life. He was avidly curious about the life of his time, and the book is enjoyable as well as significant for his dry wit, comprehensive irony, and sheer high spirits which break out at often disconcerting moments. His engaging realism in affairs of love can be gauged from the fact that only two of the twelve *amoríos* end in success. His vocabulary is varied, apt, and above all often popular in a period when literature was more often composed for use in universities ('su ciencia es sobre todo y ante todo ciencia popular, folklore'— Dámaso Alonso). Ruiz uses sayings and proverbs adroitly, convinces in his varied dialogue, and maintains the reader's interest even when he appears to be at his most sententious.

Ruiz wrote predominantly in the *cuaderna vía*, but another fifteen metrical forms were identified by Tomás Antonio Sánchez (q.v.) when he rescued the book from oblivion in his expurgated *Colección de poesías castellanas anteriores al siglo XV*, vol. 4 (1790). Ruiz stated specifically that one of his purposes was to demonstrate and advance the modes of metrical composition.

***Libro de la vida de Barlaam y del rey Josaphat*, see BARLAAM AND JOSAPHAT.**

***Libro del caballero Cifar*, see CABALLERO CIFAR, El.**

***Libro de los engaños*, see SENDEBAR.**

***Libro de los enxienplos del Conde Lucanor et de Patronio*, see CONDE LUCANOR ET DE PATRONIO, Libro de los enxienplos del.**

***Libro de los Estados*, see ESTADOS, Libro de los.**

***Libro del Passo honroso defendido por el excelente cauallero Suero de Quiñones*, see RODRÍGUEZ DE LENA, Pedro.**

Libro de poemas (1921), a selection of 79 early lyrics by Federico García Lorca (q.v.). The earliest poem is dated 1915, but most are from the period 1918–19, before Lorca had arrived in Madrid. In his ingenuous prologue, Lorca offers 'in this book, all youthful ardour and torment and boundless ambition, the precise image of my days of adolescence and youth'.

The preponderant tones of melancholy and innocence were soon to be lost, but already Lorca attempts to understand the passionate Andalusian woman doomed to subservience (and often sterility) who will recur in the important late plays. Lorca's eroticism can be traced to his reading of Darío (q.v.) and the satanic element to Valle-Inclán (q.v.), but the leading influences are Antonio Machado and Juan Ramón Jiménez.

***Licenciado Vidriera, El*,** one of the *Novelas ejemplares* of Cervantes (qq.v.).

Two students of Salamanca University employ a poor, clever 11-year-old, Tomás Rodaja, and pay for him to read law there. Having completed their studies, the new graduates return home to Andalusia, taking Tomás with them. After a few days he starts back on his own, with enough money for the last three years of his course. But on the way he meets Capt. Diego de Valdivia, who persuades Tomás to enlist with him, and they embark at Cartagena for Genoa, and then see Milan, Venice, Florence, Naples, Rome, Ghent, and Brussels.

In Salamanca once again, Tomás is besieged by a rich woman who has fallen in love with him. Seeing that he prefers books to love, she gives him a magic potion which causes the delusion that he is made of glass, and that his name is Vidriera (Glass). He will only sleep on piles of straw and fears to be touched, in case he breaks. His madness leaves his acute intelligence unaffected, and people throng from miles around to hear his barbed wit.

Eventually a Hieronymite monk cures Tomás, who takes the name of Rueda. His fame as a madman deserts him now he is clearly sane, and his promising legal career is once more in ruins. Disillusioned, he leaves for Flanders to rejoin his friend Valdivia, and there loses his life in the army.

Rodaja's delusions have inevitably been compared with Quijote's, but while the *hidalgo's* head was turned by reading novels of chivalry, the madness of the 'Glass Graduate' was artificially induced by a drug, and not by reading law and philosophy.

Menéndez y Pelayo and Pfandl, among others, see the story as a device to string together aphorisms familiar from Timoneda, Mal Lara (qq.v.), and others, but there is a human element in the tale of a sensible man who is heard only when thought mad, and ridiculed even then. There is no way, concludes Cervantes, that the truth can be told so that is is acted on. Rodaja is in the tradition of court fools who are permitted to tell the truth only because of a commonly-held convention that they are mad. The meaning of the exemplary tale is that mankind will simply not listen to those who describe its shortcomings.

El licenciado Vidriera is also the title of Agustín Moreto's best serious play. Moreto (q.v.) differs from Cervantes in showing his hero, Carlos, as feigning madness in order to indict the honour code prevailing in Spain. The play lacks much of the inconsequential sparkle of the story, turning into something of a moral tract against ingratitude.

Cervantes' tale was edited by N. Alonso Cortés (Valladolid, 1916), but the most convenient edition is F. Rodríguez Marín's *Novelas ejemplares* (2 vols., 1914–17) in Clásicos Castellanos.

See G. Edwards, 'Cervantes' "El Licenciado Vidriera": meaning and structure' in *Modern Language Review*, vol. 68 (1973), pp. 559–68.

LIDA, RAIMUNDO (1908–), Argentinan philologist and critic, whose family emigrated from the Austro-Hungarian Empire to Argentina when he was only a few months old. He was a professor at Harvard University from 1952, and the brother of María Rosa Lida de Malkiel (q.v.) and disciple of Amado Alonso (q.v.), with whom he collaborated in various editions and translations. He was active on the

Revista de Filología Hispánica in Buenos Aires, and later re-established it in Mexico City as the *Nueva Revista de Filología Hispánica*. His influence as a scholarly teacher of the highest standards has to some extent overshadowed his own writings, such as *Belleza, arte y poesía en la estética de Santayana* (Tucumán, 1943). His selected essays appeared as *Letras hispánicas* (Mexico City, 1958).

LIDA DE MALKIEL, MARÍA ROSA (1910–62), b. Buenos Aires. Argentinian critic and philologist, the sister of Raimundo Lida (q.v.) and, like him, a disciple of Amado Alonso (q.v.). Her principal works were reappraisals of major significance of Spanish medieval literature. Her first study was *El cuento popular hispanoamericano y la literatura* (1941), which was followed by 'Dido y su defensa en la literatura española' (in *Revista de Filología Hispánica*, vol. 4, 1942 and vol. 5, 1943), *Introducción al teatro de Sófocles* (1944), *Heródoto: introducción y traducción* (1949), *Juan de Mena, poeta del prerrenacimiento español* (Mexico City, 1950), *La idea de la fama en la Antigüedad y en la Edad Media castellana* (Mexico City, 1952), and chapters in H. R. Patch's *El otro mundo en la literatura medieval* (Mexico City, 1956) and R. S. Loomis's *Arthurian literature in the Middle Ages* (Oxford, 1959). Her seminal works on Juan Ruiz and Rojas appeared just before her death: *Two Spanish masterpieces: the 'Book of Good Love' and 'The Celestina'* (Urbana, 1961) and *La originalidad artística de 'La Celestina'* (1962), but she did not manage to complete her projected 'Josefo y su influencia en la literatura española', extracts from which have appeared in *Romance Philology* (Berkeley), vol. 23 (1969–70) and the *BHS* (Liverpool), vol. 48 (1971).

LIHN, ENRIQUE (1929–), b. Santiago. Chilean poet and short-story writer of the Generation of '50, whose first book *Poemas de este tiempo y otro* (1955) revealed a Romantic temperament despairing of the mindless cruelty of the world. *La pieza oscura* (1963) developed an abruptly colloquial technique. Other poems, carefully wrought with baroque rhetoric, add an element of shock to *Poesía de paso, la derrota y otros poemas* (1966), which won the Casa de las Américas prize, and *La musiquilla de las pobres esferas*.

Algunos poemas (Barcelona, 1972) shows him to be the most personal of Chilean poets of his generation. He has also written a brief work *Introducción a la poesía de Nicanor Parra* (1952).

LILLO, BALDOMERO (1867–1923), b. Lota. Chilean short-story writer whose father worked in the mines, where conditions were appalling and child-labour still practised. Lillo went to Santiago in 1898 and became active in the Labour movement. Zola's *Germinal* (1885) made a powerful impression on him, inspiring the mining stories in *Sub terra* (1904) which were the first account in Latin America of man as a victim of industrialization. *La compuerta número 12* shows how a father's desperate need for extra money drives him to take his young son down into the mine; the boy is interested, then alarmed, and when he suddenly realizes that he will have to spend the rest of his life in perpetual darkness, he has to be tied down to the rock to prevent violence. *El pozo, El grisú,* and *El registro* are equally laconic, terrible indictments of man's inhumanity to man.

Lillo's other book, *Sub sole* (1907), is less sombre; and in two of the *cuentos* contained in it, 'El rapto del sol' and 'Las nieves eternas', deserts sociological realism for lyrical impressionism and pathos, and caused less interest because it was less original. *Sub terra* influenced Edwards Bello, González Vera, Alberto Romero, and Nicomedes Guzmán.

Relatos populares and *El hallazgo y otros cuentos del mar* were posthumous collections. A useful *Antología* of Lillo's work was compiled in 1955 by N. Guzmán, and Lillo is studied in *Cuatro escritores chilenos* (New York, 1961), by V. M. Valenzuela.

Limpieza de sangre ('purity of blood', i.e. 'of lineage'), a concept which lay at the heart of investigations by the Inquisition (q.v.) in Spain and elsewhere. Spaniards sought to prove that they were descended from families without Muslims or Jews in their genealogy. *Cristianos viejos* were those with a lineage 'uncontaminated' by those of another faith, while *cristianos nuevos* were those among whose forebears were *moriscos* or *conversos* (q.v.), and whose loyalty to Roman Catholicism and thus to the Spanish monarchy was open to question. Works alleging that even the highest families in the land could count members among the former *judería* and *morería* were written and circulated, but often suppressed (in the case of Cardinal Francisco Mendoza y Bovadilla's *El tizón de la nobleza española* from the 16th c. to the 19th).

Chairs in the Spanish universities and offices in the Inquisition were among the positions reserved for *cristianos viejos*, and the Holy Office derived considerable revenue and influence from the issuance of certificates which enabled applicants to take up such appointments. During its existence the Tribunal of Toledo alone conducted over five thousand such investigations prior to the issue of certificates. Sancho Panza's boast was typical of the equally proud lower classes who declared themselves 'free from any admixture of Jew or Moor'. Bataillon has gone so far as to suggest that the rise of the picaresque novel (q.v.) was due to the nature of a society in which many people felt the need to conceal their origins and live by their wits, a 'respectable' place in society being denied them; the classic instance of this is Pablos in *El buscón* by Quevedo (qq.v.).

In drama the notion of blood purity is of cardinal importance in Golden Age plays such as *El alcalde de Zalamea* by Calderón (qq.v.), and *Peribáñez y el Comendador de Ocaña* by Lope de Vega (qq.v.).

It was as late as the middle of the 19th c. that the legal distinction between *cristiano viejo* and *cristiano nuevo* was formally abolished in Spain, and even then the Xuetas of Majorca were rigidly separated from the other Majorcans.

See Henry Kamen, *The Spanish Inquisition* (London, 1965), and Marcel Bataillon, *Pícaros y picaresca* (1969).

LIÑÁN DE RIAZA, PEDRO (1558?–1607), b. Toledo. Poet and playwright, who studied in Salamanca in 1582–4. His plays, known to his friend Lope de Vega, are apparently lost. He is best known for his *romances artísticos*, conserving the metre of the traditional ballad (eight syllables with assonanced endings in alternate lines) but with the strophic form of the quatrain. His works in this genre, such as *Assi Riselo cantaba*, were long attributed to Góngora.

Some of his sonnets are in the BAE, vol. 42 (1857) and his *Rimas en gran parte inéditas* were edited, rather carelessly, by T. Ximénez de Embrún (Saragossa, 1876). Many of his festive poems have survived in MS. including the satirical poem 'Las bubas'.

LIÑÁN Y VERDUGO, ANTONIO DE (*fl.* 1620), b. Vara del Rey, Cuenca. Novelist. In the view of 'Fr. Julián Zarco', a pseudonym of Fray Alonso Remón (q.v.). His best-known work is the *Guía y Avisos de forasteros adonde se les enseña a huir de los peligros que ay en la vida de la Corte* (1620), composed in the form of fourteen cautionary tales told by an old courtier and a graduate in arts and theology (Fray Alonso?) to a young man of quality. The stories are essentially picaresque in tradition, and while the society of Madrid and its foibles are satirized in the manner later to be exploited by Ramón de la Cruz and Ramón de Mesonero Romanos (qq.v.), the influence of Boccaccio is evident. The best edition is that of Manuel de Sandoval (1923) for the Real Academia Española.

See J. Sarrailh, 'Algunos datos acerca de D. Antonio Liñán y Verdugo' in the *Revista de Filología Española*, vol. 6 (1919), pp. 346–63 and vol. 8 (1921), pp. 15–60.

LINARES RIVAS, Manuel (1867–1938), b. Santiago de Compostela. Judge, member of the Cortes, senator, and dramatist. Though he was interested in the *género chico*, he is best known for his middle-class comedies of manners, which always paint a moral, and were often influenced by Benavente (q.v.). His best plays are generally acknowledged to be *El abolengo* (1904); the political satire *El ídolo* (1906); the didactic *La fuerza del mal* (1914); his plays on the contemporary need for divorce *Aire de fuera* (1903); and the powerful *La garra* (1914). He satirizes the aristocracy in *La estirpe de Júpiter* (1904). His fable *El caballero Lobo* (1910) sees the final victory of the lamb, symbolizing feminine gentleness.

LINDO, Hugo (1917–   ), b. La Unión, El Salvador. Poet, novelist, critic, and short-story writer. *Varia poesía* (1961) contained his best poetry from *Poema eucarístico y otros* (1943) to *Trece instantes* (1959). His principal novels are *El anzuelo de Dios* (1956) and *¡Justicia, señor gobernador!* (1960). Lindo edited a valuable *Antología del cuento moderno centro-americano* (2 vols., 1950–1). *Guaro y champaña* (1955) is a collection of his short stories.

Lindo don Diego, El, a Golden Age *comedia de figurón* (q.v.) by Agustín Moreto y Cabaña (q.v., 1618–69).

In what is often considered the most amusing play of its time, Moreto concentrates his dramatic attention, through the comic servant Mosquito, on the foppish Diego, who rises at 5 a.m. and only finishes his toilet at two in the afternoon. The heroine Inés is in love with the hero Juan, but her father Don Tello forces her betrothal to his nephew Don Diego. Mosquito arranges with Inés's maid Beatriz that she should pretend to be a wealthy, widowed countess and court Diego. The plan succeeds, and the foolish Diego falls into the trap of spurning Inés. Modelled on Guillén de Castro's *El Narcisco en su opinión*, *El lindo don Diego* is a study of a fatuous lady-killer devoid of personal dignity, honour, and social grace. Mosquito is the link between the irreconcilable worlds of Diego and the others, defeating Diego by exploiting his vanity. The plot exists purely to display the character of Diego to the full; his brother Mendo is a polite, sensible, and attractive foil.

There is a convenient edition of the play (with *El desdén con el desdén*, q.v.) by Narciso Alonso Cortés (1916) in Clásicos Castellanos.

LIOST, Guerau de, the pen-name used by the Catalan poet Jaume Bofill i Mates (q.v.).

Lira, a five-line verse of two hendecasyllables (lines 2 and 5) and three heptasyllables rhyming frequently, though by no means invariably, ababb. Apparently first used in the ode *O pastori felici* in Bernardo Tasso's *Amori* (1534), the *lira* is believed to have been introduced into Spain by Tasso's friend Garcilaso de la Vega (q.v.), and is so called after the last word of the first line of Garcilaso's *A la flor de Gnido*:

> *Si de mi baja lira*
> *tanto pudiese el son, que en un momento*
> *aplacase la ira*
> *del animoso viento,*
> *y la furia del mar y el movimiento . . .*

The *lira* was used in Spain by Hernando de Acuña, Francisco de la Torre, and Fernando de Herrera (qq.v.) but its most brilliant application is in the religious poetry of Fray Luis de León and San Juan de la Cruz.

Villegas and others varied the *lira* form by alternating heptasyllables and hendecasyllables ababcc.

LISARDO, pseudonym of Luis de Ulloa y Pereira (q.v.).

LISCANO, Juan (1915–   ), b. Caracas. Venezuelan poet, critic, and folklorist. He lived in Europe (mainly France) from early childhood until 1934, when he returned to Caracas. In 1938 he founded the magazine *Cubagua* with Manuel Salvatierra and Guillermo Meneses, and in 1943 founded *Suma*, and contributed in 1943–6 to *El Hijo Pródigo* and during the 1950s to *Sur*. In 1964 he founded the influential *Zona Franca*, a journal of literature and ideas which Boyd Carter has described as Venezuela's *New York Review of Books*. He has directed the Servicio de Investigaciones Folklóricas Nacionales, publishing the essays *Folklore y cultura* (1950) after his selection *Poesía popular venezolana* (1945). Other essays on literature and politics include *Caminos de la prosa* (1953) and *Tiempo desandado* (1964), while he has written a study of Gallegos entitled *Rómulo Gallegos y su tiempo* (1961).

Liscano is best known as a poet, especially for *Nuevo mundo Orinoco* (1959), a complex structure of images based on the beliefs and life of the Indians.

8 poemas (1939) were followed by *Contienda* (1942), *Del alba al alba* (1943), *Del mar* (1948), and *Humano destino* (1949).

LISENO, the pen-name used in the Parnaso Salmantino by Fray Juan Fernández de Rojas (q.v.).

LISTA Y ARAGÓN, ALBERTO (1775–1848), b. Seville. Poet of the pre-Romantic group of Seville and university teacher. Professor of Mathematics and History at the University of Seville, he was later appointed Dean of the Faculty of Arts. While he was teaching at the Colegio de San Mateo in Madrid (his pupils included Espronceda, Ventura de la Vega, E. de Ochoa, and P. de la Escosura, qq.v.), the authorities closed the college on the grounds that he was advocating revolutionary ideals. He was co-founder of the Free University of Madrid.

His *Poesías* (1822; Paris, 1934) have been supplemented by *Poesías inéditas* (1927), in which the pedestrian, frigid anacreontics by which he had become known were suddenly displaced by fresh ballads, like the neo-Moorish 'Zoraida'. As an *afrancesado* he was forced into exile in France between 1813–17, but his literary masters were always Spanish: Herrera in 'A la muerte de Jesús'; S. Juan de la Cruz in 'Canto del Esposo'. He adapted Pope's *Dunciad* as *El imperio de la estupidez*, and wrote eulogies of Jovellanos and Meléndez Valdés (qq.v.). In fact Lista's place in the transition to Romanticism is similar to that of Meléndez Valdés.

Lista's lectures were intellectual occasions for the youth of Madrid. They were published in *Lecciones de literatura española explicadas en el Ateneo* (1836), *Lecciones de literatura dramática española* (vol. 1, 1839), *Artículos críticos y literarios* (vol. 1, Palma, 1840), and *Ensayos literarios y críticos* (2 vols., Seville, 1844).

J. C. J. Metford's survey *Alberto Lista and the Romantic Movement in Spain* (Liverpool, 1940) set Lista in his period. The most thorough study of the man and thinker is Hans Juretschke's *Vida, obra y pensamiento de Alberto Lista* (1951).

LIZARDI, XABIER DE, pseudonym of José María Aguirre (q.v.).

LLAGUNO AMIROLA, EUGENIO DE (d. 1799), b. Vitoria. Neoclassical translator and editor who prepared the 2nd edition of *La poética* (2 vols., 1789) of Luzán (q.v.) with Luzán's son and translated Racine's *Athalie* (1754) with A. M. Ramírez.

Llaguno Amirola edited Gutierre Díaz de Games's *El Victorial* as *Crónica de don Pero Niño, conde de Buelna* (1782), omitting some passages, and also the *Corónica de Álvaro de Luna* (1784).

His main works, however, were his magisterial edition of Pedro López de Ayala (q.v.) for the Real Academia de la Historia (2 vols., 1779) and an original work of great merit: *Noticia de los arquitectos y arquitectura de España desde su restauración* (4 vols., 1829).

See R. de Apraiz, 'El ilustre alavés don Eugenio de Llaguno y Amirola: su vida, su obra' in the *Boletín de la Real Academia Vascongada*, vol. 4 (1948), pp. 53–95.

Llama de amor viva!, ¡Oh, a mystical poem by San Juan de la Cruz (q.v.) in four six-line stanzas correctly known as *Canciones del alma en la íntima comunicación de unión de amor de Dios*. There are no fewer than eight sentences or phrases in the form of exclamations, and it is in the introductory stanza of this poem that San Juan's allegorical eroticism reaches its zenith:

> ¡ Oh llama de amor viva,
> qué tiernamente hieres
> de mi alma en el mas profundo centro!
> Pues ya no eres esquiva,
> acaba ya si quieres;
> rompe la tela deste dulce encuentro.

San Juan wrote a prose commentary to the poem, *Llama de amor*, for Doña Ana de Peñalosa in 1584, glossing at length the essentially inexplicable nature of his mystical vision.

LLAMPILLAS, FRANCISCO XAVIER, see LAMPILLAS, Francisco Xavier.

Llanto por la muerte de Ignacio Sánchez Mejías, an elegy by Federico García Lorca (q.v.) written in 1934, read aloud at a performance of *Yerma* in 1935, and first published in 1935. It was completed soon after the death of the poet's friend, the bullfighter Sánchez Mejías, who died in Madrid on 13 August 1934, two days after being severely gored at Manzanares.

Sánchez Mejías was himself a playwright, having had his full-length play *Sinrazón* (on illusion and reality) produced in 1928.

Though the poem is in the tradition of the classical *elegía*, the title *llanto* ('lament') sets it apart from its literary ancestors, and turns it into a personal statement of loss. Each of the poem's four parts is in a different stanzaic form. The first, 'La cogida y la muerte', alternates the octosyllabic refrain 'A las cinco de la tarde' with classical hendecasyllables. The second section, 'La sangre derramada', is a eulogy of Sánchez's courage, mainly in octosyllables. The third section, 'Cuerpo presente', is a solemn meditation in alexandrines on the body of Sánchez, and replaces the blood image of the preceding section with the stone. The final section, 'Alma ausente', written in hendecasyllables, denounces the forgetful men who allow the memory of heroes such as Sánchez to suffer oblivion, and swears that the poet will never forget him.

See C. Cannon, 'Lorca's "Llanto por Ignacio Sánchez Mejías"; the elegiac tradition' in *Hispanic Review*, vol. 31 (1963), pp. 229–38.

LLONA, NUMA POMPILIO (1832–1907), b. Guayaquil. Ecuadorian poet educated in Colombia and Peru who spent some years in the diplomatic service in Europe, returning to Guayaquil as Rector of the University in 1882.

By then he had published the *Cantos americanos* (Paris, 1866), the melancholy late Romantic poems of *Noche de dolor en las montañas* (1872), the finest of his contemplative poems in *La odisea del alma* (1876), and the first of several editions *Clamores del occidente* (Lima, 1880) consisting of 100 sonnets, among the finest in Ecuador.

He achieved gratifying public recognition, being crowned for his poetry in 1904.

LLORÉNS TORRES, LUIS (1878–1944), b. Juana Díaz, Puerto Rico. Poet. He studied law and literature in Spain, and published there *Al pie de la Alhambra* (Granada, 1899), but on returning to Puerto Rico he introduced modernism with the Darío-like *Sonetos sinfónicos* in which he practised the aesthetic theories he derived from *krausismo* (q.v.): *pancalismo* (all is beauty) and *panedismo* (all is poetry). He gained extra influence through editing *La Revista de las Antillas*, but he failed to develop from his early stance and *La canción de las Antillas y otros poemas* (1929), like *Voces de la campana mayor* (1935), only ring the changes on conventional love poetry and patriotism. *Alturas de América* (1940) contains his best work. His poetry has been studied by Enrique Laguerre in *La poesía modernista en Puerto Rico* (thesis, University of Puerto Rico, 1942).

Lloréns also published a youthful collection of essays: *América: estudios históricos y filológicos* (Barcelona, 1898).

LLORENTE, JUAN ANTONIO (1756–1823), b. Calahorra. Historian. In 1789 he was appointed principal secretary to the Inquisition but was dismissed two years later for suspected inclinations to French liberalism. Recalled in 1793, with Jovellanos (q.v.) and others he tried to liberalize the Holy Office but failed and was again dismissed. When Joseph Bonaparte became nominal King of Spain in 1809, Llorente was put in charge of the Inquisition's archives and, following Bonaparte into exile, he was able to publish his findings in the celebrated *Histoire critique de l'Inquisition d'Espagne depuis l'époque de son établissement par Ferdinand V jusqu'au règne de Ferdinand VII* (4 vols., Paris, 1817–18) later translated into Italian, and published in 10 vols. in Spain as *Historia crítica de la Inquisición en España* (1822).

Llorente's virtue as a historian is that of comprehensive documentation, though his statistics are questionable. He is prejudiced against the Holy Office, and his materials are incoherently assembled, making systematic study of the work very difficult. Llorente's seminal and influential book was superseded by those of H. C. Lea, *A history of the Inquisition in Spain* (4 vols., 1906–7) and *The Inquisition in the Spanish dependencies* (1908), and more recently by Henry Kamen, *The Spanish Inquisition* (London, 1965).

Llorente also wrote *Observaciones críticas sobre el romance de Gil Blas de Santillana* (1822), accusing Lesage (q.v.) of stealing the original of A. Solís (q.v.).

See A. Morel-Fatio, 'Don Juan Antonio Llorente' in the *Bulletin Hispanique*, vol. 23 (1921).

LLORENTE, TEODOR (1836–1911), b. Valencia. Poet, whose father, from Rincón de Soto in La Rioja, was a relative of J. A. Llorente (q.v.). Until the age of 21 he wrote only in Castilian; then he was persuaded by Mariano Aguilò to write in the Valencian dialect and in 1878 founded Lo Rat Penat, a society of *amadors de la llengua valenciana*. His first collection, *Llibret de versos* (1884–5; 2nd emd., 1909), revealed a Romantic spirit akin to that of the European poets he introduced into Spain: Heine, Schiller, Hugo, and Byron. His translation of Goethe's *Faust, Part I* is still the most reliable in Spanish.

Llorente also published a history of Valencia in 1887 and the *Nou llibret de versos* in 1902.

See Arturo Masriera, *Teodor Llorente* (Barcelona, 1905); and Navarro Reverter, *Teodoro Llorente: su vida y sus obras* (Barcelona, 1912).

LLULL, RAMON (1235?–1316?), b. Palma de Mallorca. Theologian, novelist, and poet. Of a land-owning family from Barcelona who settled the recently-reconquered Majorca, Llull wrote a good deal of poetry in the troubadour style during his youth but this is no longer extant. He is believed to have destroyed it when, aged about 30, he renounced the secular life, devoting all his energies thenceforth to converting non-Christians. He recounts several anecdotes to illustrate his change of heart in memorable terms. At one time he was pursuing a beautiful woman on horseback and followed her into a church, where she opened her robe to reveal a breast eaten away by cancer. He also experienced a repeated apparition of Christ crucified while composing an adulterous love poem.

His method for completing the spiritual conquest of Islam (as Jaime I had completed the military conquest in the Balearics) was to construct a philosophical system that would compel the infidel to acknowledge the superiority of Christianity. To that end he renounced his family ties and fortune and devoted nine years (probably 1265–74) to the study of Arabic,

Islamic theology, Christian theology, and Latin. At his wife's request, he appointed an administrator for his lands and chattels. He then wrote his systematic *Ars magna* or *Ars compendiosa inveniendi veritatem* in a Cistercian monastery.

In the *Libre del Gentil e dels tres Savis*, of this period, a man endowed with natural reason but no religious preconceptions (the *Gentil*) speaks with a learned Jew, Muslim, and Christian. The book was intended for Christian missionaries, and attempted to anticipate their opponents' objections and take advantage of their psychological weaknesses.

After the failure of a missionary college which he founded at Miramar, Llull then aged 45, began his travels and was not to see Majorca again until he was 60. His purpose was to persuade prelates and kings to create monasteries for teaching non-Christian theologies and oriental languages. Unsuccessful in this long struggle, he wrote disillusioned poems such as *Lo desconhort* and the moving *Cant de Ramon*:

> Som home vell, paubre, menyspreat,
> no hai ajuda d'home nat
> e hai trop gran fait emperat . . .

('I am an old man, poor, and laughed to scorn; I have no one to help me, and have taken on too great a task.') He tells how he travelled in 1311 to the Council of Vienna together with a priest who had heard that he was *un gran fantástico*; later he wrote an account of their discussions in *Disputatio Petri clerici et Raymundi Phantastici*, edited by Fr. Mueller in *Wissenschaft und Weisheit* (1935) to mark the seventh centenary of Llull's birth. In fact the Council of Vienna of 1311 did authorize the establishment of schools for oriental languages, though possibly not at Llull's behest. He returned to Majorca and continued to write profusely, begging King Frederick to help with the work of converting Muslims from Sicily. In 1313 Llull is recorded in Sicily, in 1314 in Tunis (protected by the Crown of Aragón) and in 1315, still working as a hated and reviled missionary, he travelled to Bougie to expound the faith. There he was attacked by a mob of infuriated Muslims and left to die. A Genoese vessel took him away from Africa but he died within view of the Majorcan coast.

Llull is the first major poet and prose writer in Catalan; he extended its range and, though most of his writings were in Latin, made the vernacular a respectable medium for literature. He created a new compound of the erudite and the popular in the great *Libre de contemplació* dated 1282, which has been described by Longpré as the most moving work of Christian literature after the *Confessions* of St. Augustine. His works are all imbued with poetry, though only vols. 19 and 20 of the *Obres* are rhymed, and the essential unity of his thought is apparent despite the vagaries of transmission.

His *Llibre del orde de la cavayleria* is the chief source of the *Libro del cavallero et del escudero* of Juan Manuel (q.v.). The epoch-making *Blanquerna* (q.v.) and *Felix*, or *Libre de les meravelles del món* (written in Paris in 1288) are the first novels in Catalan, the latter a didactic adventure which Menéndez y Pelayo has aptly described as a mystic book of chivalry.

The allegorical *Arbre de Filosofia d'Amor* (completed in Paris in 1298) is another compendium, like the *Felix*, in which the author marvels that men will seek knowledge all their lives but take no interest in the search for spiritual love.

Llull's influence on medieval Europe was deep and ubiquitous. See T. and J. Carreras Artau, *Historia de la filosofía española*, vol. 1 (1939), pp. 233–635 and vol. 2 (1943), pp. 9–387; and M. Batllori in 'El lulismo en Italia' in *Revista de Filología*, vol. 2, (1944). The first serious edition of Llull is the *Beati Raymundi Lulli Opera* (8 vols., Mainz, 1721–41), but the best is that by Monseñor Salvador Galmés: *Obres de Ramon Lull* (20 vols. to date; Palma, 1901–). There is the selection *Obras essencials* (2 vols., Barcelona, 1957). A useful compendium of his work, *Obras literarias* (1948), has been rendered into Castilian by M. Batllori and M. Coldentey. Edgar Allison Peers has not only translated much of Llull's work into English but has also produced an accurate and extensive biography: *Ramón Lull* (London, 1929). R. Pring-Mill has studied his philosophy in *El microcosmos lulià* (Palma, 1961). See also J. N. Hillgarth, *Ramon Lull and Lullism in fourteenth-century France* (Oxford, 1971).

Estudios Lulianos is a review of Llull studies issued three times a year from the Maiorensis Schola Lullistica, Aptdo. 17, Palma de Mallorca.

Loa ('praise'), a theatrical prologue used first in a sacred context in the earliest *autos sacramentales* (q.v.), such as the *Loa al sacramento* (preceding an *auto* called *El sacrificio de Abraham* (before 1540), ed. E. González Pedroso in *Autos sacramentales*, BAE, vol. 58, 1965).

The *loa* quickly passed into secular drama, superseding the *introyto* (as Timoneda, q.v., described his prologue) of the earliest playwrights. The *loa* praised the writer, his play, patron, audience, town, or indeed anything else that struck the author's fancy, such as silence, smallness, blackness, or a number. Originally monologues, they developed in time into miniature plays to interest early arrivals while latecomers were finding their seats, like the sketches of Rojas Villandrando or Quiñones de Benavente (qq.v.). Occasionally as in

Calderón's *Los tres mayores prodigios*, the *loa* may be essential to the understanding of the play. Other writers of *loas* include Lope de Rueda, Torres de Naharro, Gil Vicente, Antonio de Solís, Sor Juana Inés de la Cruz, and Lope de Vega (qq.v.).

The best collection of *loas* is found in the *Viaje entretenido* (q.v.) by Rojas Villandrando; the most useful studies are by E. Cotarelo y Mori in vol. I of his *Colección de entremeses, loas ...* (NBAE vol. 17, 1911), and J. A. Meredith's '*Introito' and 'loa' in the Spanish drama of the sixteenth century* (Philadelphia, 1925).

LOBAR, Tomé, an anagram used in *Las letras de cambio* by Bartolomé José Gallardo (q.v.).

LOBO, Eugenio Gerardo (1679–1750), b. Cuerva, Toledo. Poet and soldier who took part in the War of the Spanish Succession on the side of Felipe V, but incurred his monarch's displeasure by his satire *Exhortación politico-cristiana a la nación española*, in which he bewailed the plight of Spain in pedestrian verse. He also took part in the siege of Lérida, which he celebrated in epic *octavas reales*, and in the recapture of Oran in 1732, which he celebrated in the 'Rasgo épico...' (ed. Bauer in *Relaciones de África*, vol. 3).

Of his festive verses, the most witty is a parody: 'Octavas festivas a la derrota de unos pasteles en el Palau', and among his sonnets, the best is a neoclassical composition on sculpture: 'A la estatua del silencio'. Lobo's works were first collected in *Selva de las musas* (Cádiz, 1717), and later in *Obras poéticas* (Cádiz, 1724?) and *Obras poéticas y lyricas* (1738). Some of his *Poesías* appear in vol. 61 (1869) of the BAE.

J. Rubio contributed 'Algunas aportaciones a la biografía y obras de Eugenio Gerardo Lobo' to the *Revista de Filología Española* vol. 31 (1947), pp. 19–85.

LOBO LASSO DE LA VEGA, Gabriel (1559–1615?), b. Madrid. Poet and playwright of a noble family. The *Primera parte del romancero y tragedias* (Alcalá, 1587) included *Manojuelo de romances nuevos*, mediocre ballads subsequently edited by González Palencia, and two tragedies. One, *La destruición de Constantinopla*, was attributed to Lope as part of the *Seis comedias de Lope de Vega* (1603). The other, *La honra de Dido, restaurada*, was transitional between the classical tragedy of the 16th c. and the national drama of Lope.

Influenced by the Latin American epic of Ercilla (q.v.), Lobo Lasso de la Vega produced an epic on the exploits of Hernán Cortés: *Primera parte de Cortés valeroso, y Mexicana* (1588), recast in 1594 with the addition of 13 new

stanzas as *La Mexicana*. This latter version was edited by José Amor y Vázquez in BAE (1970).

He also published *Elogios en loor de tres famosos varones Don Jayme, Rey de Aragon, Don Fernando Cortes, Marques del Valle y Don Aluaro de Baçan, Marques de Santa Cruz* (Saragossa, 1601). With Cristóbal de Mesa, he began the Spanish cult of Tasso's *Gerusalemme liberata*.

LOBÓN DE SALAZAR, Francisco, a priest of the parish of Villagarcía, whose name was used without his consent on the title-page of the *Fray Gerundio de Campazas* of José Francisco Isla de la Torre y Rojo (qq.v.).

LOFRASO or LO FRASSO, Antonio de (1530–90), b. Alghero, Sardinia. Pastoral novelist whose *Los diez libros de Fortuna de Amor* (Barcelona, 1573) was a poor imitation of *La Diana* (1559) by Jorge de Montemayor (q.v.).

Cervantes praised the book satirically in *Don Quijote* I, 6: 'Tan gracioso ni tan disparatado libro como ese no se ha compuesto, y que por su camino es el mejor y el más único de cuantos deste genero han salido a la luz del mundo ...', inducing a teacher of Spanish in London, Pedro de Pineda, to translate and print Lofraso's work in English (2 vols., London, 1740) with a foolish prologue.

LOMAS CANTORAL, Jerónimo de (d. after 1578), b. Valladolid. Poet. A protégé of the Conde de Miranda, Lomas wrote epistles, elegies, sonnets, and epigrams in the style of Petrarch, Bembo, Sannazaro, and Tasso, and his *Obras* (1578), praised by Cervantes in his *Canto de Calíope*, also include verses in traditional Castilian metres influenced by Silvestre and Castillejo (q.v.).

See Enrique Segura Covarsi, 'Don Jerónimo de Lomas Cantoral' in the *Revista de Literatura*, vol. 2 (1952), pp. 39–75.

LONGFELLOW, Henry Wadsworth (1807–82), b. Portland, Maine. American Romantic poet whose translations popularized Spanish literature in the U.S.A. His best-known works include *Hyperion* (1839) a philosophical travelogue deriving from the death of his first wife; *Ballads and other poems* (1841) including 'The wreck of the Hesperus'; and *Hiawatha* (1855).

In 1836 he resigned as Professor of Modern Languages at Bowdoin College (his alma mater) to take up Ticknor's Smith Professorship at Harvard, where he stayed until 1854. He translated the works of many Spanish poets, including Jorge Manrique, Berceo, Juan Ruiz, Lope de Vega, and Tomás de Iriarte and wrote a play, *The Spanish student*, based on Cervantes' *novela ejemplar La gitanilla* (qq.v.).

LOPE DE VEGA CARPIO, see VEGA CARPIO, Lope de.

LÓPEZ, GREGORIO (1546–96), b. Madrid. Religious writer who lived as a hermit in early adolescence until in 1562 he went to Mexico, where he worked in hospitals, lived in the utmost poverty, and died honoured for his poetry. Two of his MSS., *Kalendario histórico* and *Libro de los remedios contra enfermedades*, were seen by Nicolás Antonio (q.v.), but are now lost; a third survives in the Biblioteca Nacional in Madrid: *Manual y advertencias para obispos, sacerdotes y confesores*; while only one of his books has been published: an *Explicación del Apocalípsis* (1678).

López owes much of his celebrity to an absurd legend identifying him with Don Carlos (son of Philip II), on the assumption that the prince's executioner freed him on condition that he left for the New World, changed his name, and never revealed his secret to anybody.

LÓPEZ, LUCIO VICENTE (1848–94), b. Montevideo. Argentinian novelist. After studying law in Buenos Aires, he joined Sarmiento's group on *El Nacional* and became one of the moving spirits behind *Sud-América* in the 1880s. *Recuerdos de viaje* is a travel book on his European tour of 1880–1. *La gran aldea* (1884) is a description of *costumbres bonaerenses* while Buenos Aires was developing from the small town of 1862 into a great city, and counts as one of the major documents of Argentinian realism in the Balzac tradition.

The speed with which it was written is evident in the novel's unevenness, and there are traces of sentimentality, but many notable passages stay in the memory, such as the hero's idyll with Valentina, the death of the narrator's father, and the lively account of commercial life in the capital. López's best-known story is 'El salto de Ascochinga', 'lleno de color y de vida' in Groussac's words. In 1894 López was killed in a duel.

LÓPEZ, LUIS CARLOS (1883–1950), b. Cartagena. Colombian poet and prose-writer. His simplicity, provincial themes, and irony directly challenged the vogue of modernism. *Selección de versos* (Cartagena, 1946) was followed by two broader anthologies: *Lo mejor de Luis C. López* (1961) selected by Germán Espinosa, and *La comedia tropical* (1962) selected by Jorge Zalamea. His vignettes of life in the provinces are collected in *De mi villorrio* (1908), *Los hongos de la Riba* (1909), and *Por el atajo* (1920). López, known as 'el tuerto López', is one poet in *Cinco poetas colombianos* (Manizales, 1964) by

Ebel Botero, the others being Silva, Valencia, Rivera, and Maya.

LÓPEZ, VICENTE FIDEL (1815–1903), b. Buenos Aires. Argentinian novelist and historian, the son of Vicente López y Planes (q.v.). His best novel, in the manner of Walter Scott, is *La novia del hereje* (1854), the first in a long series of Romantic idealizations of the pirate (in this case Francis Drake) which culminated in the works of Byron and Espronceda. The book shows the effect on Lima of Drake's expedition of 1578–9. López's animosity is not directed at Drake, a shadowy figure, nor at the English *hereje* Lord Henderson, but at Fr. Andrés, Inquisitor of Lima, who locks up María, the Protestant Henderson's fiancée.

López's historical work consists of *Introducción a la historia de la República Argentina* (1881), *La Revolución Argentina* (4 vols., 1881), a lengthy *Debate histórico* (1882) in disagreement with Bartolomé Mitre (q.v.), and the *Historia de la República Argentina* (1883–93). He also wrote an epistolary novel, *La gran semana de 1810* (1886), and historical stories collected as *La loca de la guardia*, on the march of San Martín's army of liberation.

LÓPEZ ACEBAL, FRANCISCO (1866–1933), b. Gijón. Dramatist, short-story writer (*De mi rincón*, 1901), and novelist (*Huella de almas*, 1901; *Rosa rústica*, 1909), who founded the important monthly *La Lectura* (q.v.) with Clemente de Velasco. He adapted Pérez Galdós's *El amigo manso* for the stage.

LÓPEZ ALBÚJAR, ENRIQUE (1872–1966), b. Piura. Peruvian short-story writer and novelist. A provincial judge in Huánuco, founder and editor of *El Amigo del Pueblo*, and editor of *La Prensa* (Lima), he eventually became President of Museums and Libraries. His mulatto origin and his position as judge gave him both viewpoint and themes for the realistic *Cuentos andinos* (Huánuco, 1920), which are concerned with psychological understanding of the Indian rather than with his economic exploitation by the colonial regime. Albújar forms part of the Indianist tradition stretching from Abraham Valdelomar and Ventura García Calderón to Ciro Alegría and José María Arguedas (qq.v.). Subsequent collections of short stories are *De mi casona* (1924), *Calderonadas* (1930), and *Nuevos cuentos andinos* (Santiago de Chile, 1937). His *Mejores cuentos* appeared in 1957. Free from the moralizing vein of most of his predecessors, Albújar showed the Indians of the Andes as proud, defiant, and misunderstood. The stories often start with a crime and subsequently describe the circumstances which led to it.

They are usually more successful than his two novels: *Matalaché* (Piura, 1928) and *El hechizo de Tomayquichua* (1953), of which the latter is prefaced with a critical essay by José Jiménez Borja. Both novels are largely concerned with the complex question of race relationships.

López Albújar's earliest stories (so far unpublished in book form) appeared in magazines between 1897 and 1901 and reflect the author's brief attachment to modernism.

See Raúl Estuardo Cornejo, *López Albújar, novelista de Américas* (Madrid, 1961), the autobiographical *Memorias* (1963), and T. G. Escajadillo, *La narrativa de López Albújar* (1972).

LÓPEZ DE AGUILAR COUTIÑO, FRANCISCO, a friend of Lope de Vega (q.v.), and author of a savage pamphlet *Petro de Torres Ramilae* (1617), under the pseudonym of Franciscus Antididascalus, and part-author of the equally bitter *Expostulatio Spongiae* (1618) which defended Lope against the satire *Spongia* (1617) by Pedro de Torres Rámila (q.v.).

Torres Rámila's pamphlet is not extant, having been destroyed by his enemies, but it is known to have contained personal attacks on Lope as well as a denunciation of his dramatic theories and practice insofar as they defy the Aristotelian unities.

LÓPEZ DE AYALA, ADELARDO (1829–79), b. Guadalcanal, Seville. Statesman and dramatist, who was consistently successful in politics, and died while president of the Council of Ministers. He studied law in Seville, where he met the playwright García Gutiérrez and wrote three plays that he took to Madrid with him in 1849: *La corona y el puñal*, *Los Guzmanes*, and *Un hombre de estado*, the last-named being produced with great success in 1851; it is a tragedy on the fate of Rodrigo Calderón, a favourite of the Conde de Lerma brought down by court intrigue and executed in 1621. *Rioja* (1854), on a poet whose love is heroically renounced, closes Ayala's period of nationalistic romanticism, in which by expertly-constructed dialogue he brings to life half-legendary episodes from Spanish history.

His more important plays are contemporary in their treatment of private corruption and public cynicism; Ayala uses satire as a moral whip to lash his less likeable characters, as in *El nuevo Don Juan* (1863), in which the husband's laughter at the seducer symbolises society's relief at the suppression of sexual licence and political anarchy. Both *El tanto por ciento* (1861) and *Consuelo* (1878) stress the need for greater idealism in all spheres of life, while in *El tejado de vidrio* (1856) a seducer's wife takes revenge in

adultery. Ayala embodies the spirit of the Restoration, even though most of his works were written earlier.

He wrote love sonnets and many libretti for *zarzuelas*, of which the best-known is *El Conde de Castralla* (1856). He resisted the Romantic vogue in the theatre, like Manuel Tamayo y Baus (q.v.), who edited Ayala's *Obras completas* (7 vols., 1881–5).

See Conrado Solsona y Baselga, *Ayala: estudio político* (1891); Jacinto Octavio Picón, *Ayala: estudio biográfico* (1892); M. Blasco, *En torno a la figura de don Adelardo López de Ayala* (Seville, 1931); and Luis de Oteyza, *Ayala* (1932).

LÓPEZ DE AYALA, IGNACIO (18th c.). Poet, playwright, and historian who was for some time censor of the public theatres in Madrid. He was a member of the *tertulia* (q.v.) of the Fonda de San Sebastián where he mixed with Cadalso, Iriarte, and his close friend and rival Nicolás Fernández de Moratín (qq.v.).

He completed Diego Hurtado de Mendoza's *Guerra de Granada*, and wrote *Historia de Federico el Grande* and *Historia de Gibraltar* (1782). He used the pseudonym 'Gil Porras de Machuca' to pillory certain aspects of the *Historia literaria de España* by the brothers Rodríguez Mohedano (qq.v.) in his *Carta crítica . . .* (1781). He, himself, in that age of literary polemics, was attacked by Juan Pablo Forner (q.v.) for the sumptuous spectacle he believed necessary for the staging of his tragedy *Numancia destruída* (1775, ed. R. P. Sebold, Salamanca, 1971; see NUMANCIA). The latter, dominated by national fervour, is an artistic failure due to its rhetorical artificiality.

LÓPEZ DE AYALA, PEDRO (1332–1407?), b. Vitoria. Historian and poet, Chancellor of Castile and hence often called El Canciller López de Ayala. The son of a wealthy nobleman (Fernán Pérez de Ayala), Pedro was sent to study with his uncle, Pedro Gómez Barrosa, who had become a Cardinal in 1327. The boy studied Latin and theology but left his uncle in 1353 to attend King Pedro as a page and rose to such eminence that he was entrusted with the Castilian fleet in the war against Aragón.

When Don Enrique invaded Castile, Pedro and Ayala fled from Burgos to the south but, when the nobles recognized Enrique as king, Ayala joined him in 1366. He was taken prisoner by the Black Prince in 1367 but was quickly ransomed. In 1375 he became governor of Toledo and the following year ambassador to Aragón. He advised Juan I against the Battle of Aljubarrota but was overruled and was captured in Portugal, spending about two years in jail and writing there his book on falconry and at least part of the important didactic poem *El rimado de palaçio* (q.v.). On the death of Juan I in 1390, Ayala sat on the Regency Council during the minority of Enrique III but, when the young Enrique assumed the throne in 1393, Ayala returned to his native Álava to complete the *Rimado*, his chronicles, and 'Libro del "Linaje de Ayala"' which remains unpublished. In 1399 Enrique III named him Canciller Mayor del Reino.

His chronicles are largely eye-witness accounts of the time from 1350 to 1390: an early history (compiled not before 1383) termed the shorter history (*abreviada*) by Zurita, and the definitive history (*vulgar*), completed after 1393. They were continued for the period 1390–1460 by Álvar García de Santa María. The *Chronica del rey don Pedro* (Seville, 1495) ... *aumentada con las Cronicas de D. Enrique II y de D. Juan I* was published in Toledo in 1526. Ayala's history has subsequently been edited by E. de Llaguno y Amirola (3 vols., 1779–83) and by C. Rosell in vols. 66 and 68 (1875–8) of the BAE. A selection in 2 vols. has been made by G. Torrente Ballester (1943). His defection to the cause of Enrique de Trastamara led Ayala to write of the life and times of Pedro the Cruel in a critical spirit, but he does not spare Enrique's persecution of the Jews and in general must be considered one of the more impartial of early historians. He translated Books I, II, and IV of Livy (1497) and the Roman historian's penchant for the direct and dramatic style of presentation infected Ayala to the point where Entwistle was able to identify many passages from contemporary ballads in Ayala's 'verbatim' word-pictures. But his inventions are often plausible, and add vivacity to the tale. Politically he still upholds the feudal Christian monarchy in the face of spreading anarchy after the Black Death and civil wars. His sense of human brotherhood is rooted in his Christian upbringing rather than (as some critics would have it) in a proto-Renaissance theory of the pre-eminence of man.

The measure of Ayala's humanistic background can be judged from the range of his translations: the first eight books of the *Cayda de príncipes* from Boccaccio (Seville, 1495), St. Isidore of Seville, St. Gregory, and Boethius.

El libro de las aves de caça (perhaps better known as the *Libro de la cetrería*) was composed in prison and finished in 1386. There is a makeshift edition by E. Lafuente y Alcántara for the Sociedad de Bibliófilos Españoles (1869) and a version in modern Spanish by J. Fradejas Lebrero (Valencia, 1959).

R. Floranes's basic *Vida literaria del Canciller mayor de Castilla don Pedro López de Ayala* (Colec-

ción de Documentos Inéditos, vols. 19–20, 1851–2) has now been supplemented by the Marqués de Lozoya's *Introducción a la biografía del Canciller Ayala* (Bilbao, 1950), Franco Meregalli's *La vida política del Canciller Ayala* (Milan, 1955), and L. Suárez Fernández's *El Canciller Pedro López de Ayala y su tiempo* (Vitoria, 1962). Ayala is one of the subjects of the *Generaciones y semblanzas* of F. Pérez de Guzmán (q.v.).

LÓPEZ DE CARTAGENA, DIEGO (b. *c.* 1480), b. Cartagena or Seville? Erasmian humanist who studied at Alcalá and Salamanca, lived outside Spain for some time, principally in Antwerp and Paris, and was appointed archdeacon of Seville. He taught classics and translated from the Latin. His version of the *Querela pacis, Tractado de cómo se quexa la paz* (Seville, 1520) is the first translation from Erasmus into Castilian. López de Cartagena had already achieved celebrity with his translation of *The Golden Ass* by Apuleius (Seville, 1513).

LÓPEZ DE GÓMARA, FRANCISCO (1512–72), b. Gómara, Soria. Historian. He taught classics at Alcalá, then was ordained as a priest, and went to Rome. On the return of Hernán Cortés, Gómara became his secretary-chaplain and wrote the eulogistic *La istoria de las Indias y conquista de México* (Saragossa, 1552; 2nd edn., Salamanca, 1568) which lacks first-hand knowledge and any pretence at impartiality. Gómara never set foot in the New World but accompanied Cortés on his expedition to Algiers and continued in the employment of his son Martín Cortés after Hernán died in 1547.

Part 1 deals with the discovery and conquest of the New World other than Mexico up to 1552; part 2 is devoted to Mexico. Gómara's style is readable and simple, except for a certain pretentious use of Latin quotations (his models were Sallust and Cicero) and an unquestioning view of Cortés as hero which Bernal Díaz del Castillo (q.v.) angrily rejected. The *Istoria* was immediately reprinted in 1553 (Medina del Campo) and again in 1554 (Saragossa and Antwerp) but it was forbidden to be circulated for its criticism of some decisions of Carlos V.

This ban, coupled with the just popularity of Díaz del Castillo's history, led to the work's oblivion until 1727, when it was reprinted, almost unrecognisably mutilated, by Andrés González Barcia in his Colección de Historiadores Primitivos de las Indias Occidentales. There is an improved edition in vol. 22 (1855) of the BAE, but the best is that of J. Ramírez Cabañas (2 vols., Mexico City, 1943). P. Gibelalde has produced a modernized text (2 vols., Barcelona, 1954). The book was soon translated into Italian (1560), into English

(1578) by T. N[icholas] as *The pleasant historie of the conquest of the Weast India*, and into French (1606).

Gómara also produced a *Choronica de los muy nombrados Omiche y Haradin Barbarrojas*, which appeared in the *Memorial Histórico Español* (1853), and collected materials for a history of the reign of Carlos V which Roger B. Merriman edited with an English translation as *Annals of the Emperor Charles V* (Oxford, 1912).

LÓPEZ DE HARO, DIEGO (*fl.* 1490). Poet, soldier, and diplomat who took part in the conquest of Granada and was Spanish ambassador at Rome. Some of his pleasant shorter poems were collected by Hernando del Castillo in his *Cancionero* (Valencia, 1511), edited in 2 vols. (1882) for the Sociedad de Bibliófilos Españoles, and others appear in R. Foulché-Delbosc's *Cancionero castellano del siglo XV* (in the NBAE, vol. 22 (1915), pp. 735–48) with a pedestrian verse dialogue *Entre la Razón y el Pensamiento*.

The library of the Real Academia de la Historia possesses a 1000-line poem by López de Haro, *Aviso para cuerdos*, in the form of a dialogue between the author and a series of historical or mythical characters (Christ, Muhammad, Julius Caesar, Adam, and Eve).

LÓPEZ DE HARO, RAFAEL (1876–), b. San Clemente, Cuenca. Novelist and playwright whose early work was inspired by the crude naturalism of Felipe Trigo (q.v.). *En un lugar de la Mancha* (1906) established him as a novelist of snobbish and violent themes as in *Dominadoras* (1907), a frank and often unpleasant study in female rapacity, and *Floración* (1909), attacking frigidity in Spanish women. *Poseída* (1911) is described by Cejador as 'un himno sofístico cantado a los instintos bestiales', which summarizes López de Haro's approach.

A collection of *Novelas escogidas* appeared in 1949. There is a bibliography in Joaquín de Entrambasaguas' *Las mejores novelas contemporáneas, 1930–34* (Barcelona, 1961), pp. 3–41.

LÓPEZ DE HOYOS, JUAN (d. 1583), b. Madrid. Schoolmaster who taught Cervantes in Madrid and called him his 'más amado discípulo'. He was parish priest of San Andrés in 1580 but Bataillon believed him an Erasmian who taught a love of tolerance and freedom. He compiled three official acts of homage: *Relación de la muerte y honras fúnebres del SS. Príncipe D. Carlos, hijo de la Mag. del Cathólico Rey D. Philippe el segundo nuestro señor* (1568); *Hystoria y relación verdadera de la enfermedad, felicíssimo tránsito y sumptuosas exequias fúnebres de la Sereníssima Reyna de España doña Isabel de Valoys*

(1569), which included four poems by Cervantes, his earliest known attempt at verse, composed probably before 1568; and *Real apparato, y sumptuoso recebimiento con que Madrid . . . rescibio a la Sereníssima reyna D. Ana de Austria* (1572).

See F. Pérez Mínguez, *El maestro López de Hoyos* (1916).

LÓPEZ DE JÉREZ, FRANCISCO, see JÉREZ, Francisco López de.

LÓPEZ DE MENDOZA, ÍÑIGO, *Marqués de Santillana*, see SANTILLANA, Íñigo López de Mendoza, *Marqués de.*

LÓPEZ DE SEDANO, JUAN JOSÉ (1729–1801), b. Villoslada, Logroño. Anthologist and critic. A librarian in the Biblioteca Nacional in Madrid, he is remembered for the important *Parnaso español* (9 vols., 1768–78) which made known many unpublished MSS. of national writers and caused a polemic with the pro-French neoclassical Iriarte (q.v.), whose rejoinder *Donde las dan las toman* was reprinted in his *Obras*, vol. 6 (1805). López de Sedano replied under the pseudonym of 'Juan María Chavero y Eslava de Ronda' with *Coloquios de Espina* (4 vols., Málaga, 1785).

A further defence of Spanish literature against the prevalent French taste was printed in López de Sedano's *Discurso andante en defensa de algunos puntos de nuestra bella literatura* (1785).

López de Sedano also wrote a tragedy taken from a story in the Book of Judges: *Jahel* (1763).

LÓPEZ DE ÚBEDA, FRANCISCO, b. Toledo. A doctor whose name appears on the title-page of *La pícara Justina* (q.v.) and who is believed by some scholars, including Bataillon, to be the author despite widespread doubts.

LÓPEZ DE ÚBEDA, JUAN (16th c.), b. Toledo. Poet and anthologist. His own poems *a lo divino* converted popular songs to religious use by altering the imagery in the manner of Fray Ambrosio de Montesino (q.v.). They are collected in *Coloquios, glosas, sonetos y romances . . .* (Alcalá, 1580) and *Romance de Nuestra Señora y Santiago, Patrón de España* (Cuenca, 1602). He also prepared two anthologies of religious verse, including some texts by Fray Luis de León (q.v.): *Cancionero general de la doctrina cristiana* (Alcalá, 1579) and *Vergel de flores diuinas* (Alcalá, 1582).

His best poems are to be found in vol. 35 of the BAE (1855).

LÓPEZ DE VILLALOBOS, FRANCISCO (1473?–1549), b. Toledo or Zamora. Didactic prose writer of Jewish ancestry. Court physician to the Duke of Alba, Fernando el Católico, and Carlos V.

His *Libro intitulado Los Problemas* (Zamora, 1543) is divided into two parts: one on astronomy and the other on men and morals. It includes witty essays on *las tres grandes* ('*la gran parlería, la gran porfía, la gran risa*': garrulity, stubbornness, and laughter), in which his targets include old men who marry young girls, old women who wear make-up, and insincere laughter. *Los problemas* appear, with his influential translation from the *Amphitruo* of Plautus (Saragossa, 1515), in the BAE, vol. 36 (1855).

His *Glosa de los dos primeros libros de Plinio* (Alcalá, 1524) sent as a somewhat presumptuous gift to the greatest scholar of the day, Hernán Núñez (q.v.), caused an acrimonious controversy.

Villalobos also wrote a didactic poem of 500 stanzas in *arte mayor* as a textbook on medicine: *El sumario de la medicina* (Salamanca, 1498), edited by G. de Real in 1948 and by María T. Herrera in 1973.

LÓPEZ DE YANGUAS, HERNÁN (*c.* 1470–*c.* 1540), b. Soria. Playwright and proverb-collector. A schoolmaster who took holy orders, López de Yanguas is considered to be the creator of the *auto sacramental* (q.v.) in his *Farsa sacramental* (1520) written in *coplas de arte mayor*.

E. Cotarelo y Mori, who printed and described this *auto* in the *RABM* (vol. 7, 1902, pp. 251–72), also credited López de Yanguas with another *Farsa sacramental* printed anonymously in 1521. Allegory is absent, but symbolism occurs in the presence of the early Church Fathers Jerome, Augustine, Ambrose, and Gregory as shepherds to whom an angel explains the significance of the Eucharist.

Yanguas had already composed an *Égloga ... en loor de la natividad de Nuestro Señor* (probably before 1518) which E. Kohler published in *Sieben spanische dramatische Eklogen* (Dresden, 1911) and a *Farsa del mundo y moral* (about 1518). This latter was reprinted several times. The edition of 1528 was printed by Urban Cronan (a pseudonym of R. Foulché-Delbosc) in his *Teatro español del siglo XVI* (1913) and that of 1551 by Leo Rouanet in his *Colección de autos, farsas y coloquios del siglo XVI*, vol. 4 (1901). The subject of this *Farsa* in *coplas de arte mayor* is the Assumption; the allegorical figures of Appetite and World are among the earliest of their kind.

Yanguas also wrote a *Diálogo del mosquito* first published in Valencia (1521) and in facsimile in Barcelona (1951). It was edited by P. Pérez Gómez (Valencia, 1960) with his *Farsa sobre la felice nueua de la concordia y paz y concierto de*

nuestro felicísimo Emperador ... y del ... Rey d'Francia written to celebrate the short-lived Peace of Cambrai (15 August 1529).

El Nunc Dimittis trovado is a verse dialogue, appended to the *Plácida y Vitoriano* of Encina (q.v.), in which a lover takes leave of his mistress using the liturgical lines heard in Church.

Cincuenta preguntas bivas con otras tantas respuestas (Valencia, 1550), is a collection of proverbs made by Yanguas. His *Obras dramáticas* are now to be found (ed. F. González Ollé, 1967) in *Clásicos Castellanos*.

LÓPEZ DE ZÁRATE, FRANCISCO (1580–1658), b. Logroño. Poet and playwright. He was secretary to the adventurer Rodrigo Calderón who assumed the title of Marqués de Siete Iglesias in the time of Philip III.

In 1624 he composed in 2058 *octavas* the best of the somewhat tedious religious epics then in vogue: *Poema heroico de la invención de la Cruz* (1648), but disregarded the extraordinary story of the Empress Helena and the exploits of Constantine against Maxentius in favour of a colourless account of a contest between Constantine and an imaginary king of Persia on the banks of the Euphrates.

López de Zárate also completed *Tragedia de Hércules* and the more interesting play *La galeota reforzada*, (ed. J. M. Lope Toledo, Logroño, 1951).

His poetry was praised by Cervantes in *Persiles y Sigismunda* (qq.v.). It was first collected in *Varias poesías* in 1619; again as *Obras varias* (Alcalá, 1651); and most recently by J. Simón Díaz (1947) in the Biblioteca de Antiguos Libros Hispánicos. There is an exhaustive study, *El poeta Francisco López de Zárate* (Logroño, 1954) by J. M. Lope Toledo.

LÓPEZ FERREIRO, ANTONIO (1837–1910), b. Santiago de Compostela. Galician historian, archaeologist, and historian. He founded and edited the magazine *Galicia Histórica* and published some fifty monographs on aspects of Galician historiography, the most important being *Fueros municipales de Santiago y de su tierra*. His major work is the eleven-volume *Historia de la Santa A. M. Iglesia de Santiago de Compostela* (1898–1910), which provides fundamental data for Galician history far more extensive than are suggested by the title.

His novels in Galician are *A tecedeira de Bonaval* (Santiago, 1894), *O cartelo de Pambre* (Santiago, 1895), and *O niño de pombas* (Santiago, 1905).

LÓPEZ GÓMEZ, ADEL (1901–), Colombian short-story writer. He has published six volumes of stories, from which *Cuentos selectos* (1956) have been chosen. A *costumbrista* and realist, López Gómez concentrates on developing character to the virtual exclusion of plot. He has written a critical study, *El costumbrismo: visión panorámica del cuento costumbrista en la raza antioqueña* (Manizales, 1959).

LÓPEZ PINCIANO, ALONSO (1547?–1672), b. Valladolid. Doctor, literary theoretician, and epic poet, he was physician to María, sister of Felipe II and widow of Maximilian II.

His dry epic *El Pelayo* (1605) was written in his youth. He versified the *Pronósticos de Hipócrates*, wrongly attributed to the doctor of Cos, and translated the sections from Thucydides dealing with the plague at Athens.

The only 16th-c. work that can be called a complete system of literary criticism is El Pinciano's *Philosophia antigua poética* (1596), ostensibly a commentary in dialogue form on the poetics of Aristotle and Horace and the aesthetics of Plato but in fact a serious and substantially independent work which, in its discussion of the theatre, defends the dramatic unities against the school of Lope de Vega (q.v.). El Pinciano translated Horace into Spanish (1591; reprinted in Lisbon, 1592).

A. Carballo Picazo's is the best edition of *Philosophia antigua poética* (3 vols., 1953) and there is a rather thin study of it by Sanford Shepard: *El Pinciano y las teorías literarias del Siglo de Oro* (1962).

LÓPEZ PINILLOS, JOSÉ (1875–1922), b. Seville. Novelist and dramatist. Having abandoned the study of law for financial reasons, he went to Madrid in 1900 but was dismissed from the Civil Service for 'ideas avanzadas' and earned his living by writing plays and journalism under the pen-name 'Parmeno'.

His first novel was *La sangre de Cristo* (1907), set in the backward village El Candil, in Extremadura. A pig-castrator called Zarramendi arrives and introduces the cultivation of the vine. The villagers harvest the grapes and when the wine is prepared, celebrate a feast to drink the *sangre de Cristo*. The result is mass inebriation, leading to quarrels, fights, and the revelation of dormant hostilities.

Crude realism in both dialogue and situation also marks his later novels: *Doña Mesalina* (1910), *El ladronzuelo* (1911), *Las águilas* (1911), *Frente al mar* (1914), *Ojo por ojo* (1915), *El luchador* (1916), and *Cintas rojas* (1916).

The social, even redeeming mission of López Pinillos' work is equally evident in his plays: *Hacia la dicha* (1910), *La casta* (1912), *El pantano* (1913), *La otra vida* (1915), the violent *Esclavitud* (1918) in which Enrique Borrás created one

of his memorable roles, and *Embrujamiento* (1922).

The pessimism of López Pinillos contrasts notably with the 'well-made plays' of Benavente; López's weaknesses are carelessness in construction and a failure of self-criticism leading to excessive violence.

LÓPEZ POLINARIO, JUANITO, the pseudonym under which Fray Juan Fernández de Rojas (q.v.) wrote his *Impugnación literaria de la Crotalogía*.

LÓPEZ PORTILLO Y ROJAS, JOSÉ (1850–1923), b. Guadalajara, Jalisco. Mexican novelist, short-story writer, and critic. After graduating in law, he travelled in the Middle East, later publishing *Egipto y Palestina, apuntes de viaje* (1874). He then taught law before entering journalism and later politics, as a conservative. He became Governor of Jalisco in 1911, and subsequently Minister of Education and Minister of Foreign Affairs.

La parcela (1898) is, with Luis G. Inclán's *Astucia*, the best novel of Mexican rural life. It is the tale of a bitter quarrel between two wealthy landowners for an insignificant piece of land. The moral, humane Don Pedro eventually triumphs over the slave-driving Don Miguel. The influence of Pereda (q.v.) in the descriptions and dialogue is perhaps too strong. In *Los precursores* (1909), López Portillo defends the social necessity of religious institutions against secular reformers, taking an orphanage as his example. *Fuertes y débiles* (1919) is a comprehensive denunciation of grasping workers and employers in industry and business. López Portillo's *Cuentos completos* appeared in 2 vols. in 1952.

See A. M. Carreño, *El licenciado José López Portillo y Rojas* (1923).

LÓPEZ SOLER, RAMÓN (1806–36), b. Barcelona. Novelist. After studying law at Cervera he worked as a journalist on the *Revista Española* of Madrid (1832), on *El Vapor* of Barcelona (1833), and in 1836 was appointed editor of *El Español* (Madrid).

In 1823–4 he contributed with Bonaventura Carles Aribau, the Italian Monteggia, and others to *El Europeo*, a weekly magazine advocating Romanticism.

In 1828 he began a translation of Sir Walter Scott's *Ivanhoe* (1819) for a projected selected works to be produced in Spanish by a new publishing firm founded by Sanponts and Aribau, but the censor intervened and the work was never finished. A version by P.D.M.X. (Pablo de Jérica?) had already appeared in Perpignan (4 vols., 1826). Scott remained forbidden intil 1829.

López Soler explicitly imitated Scott's novel in *Los bandos de Castilla, o el Caballero del Cisne* (Valencia, 1830) set at the court of Juan II. In his prologue, which constitutes a Romantic manifesto, he states the belief that Scott's technique in the Romantic historical novel can be transposed to Spain with no loss of verisimilitude.

He then published other works in a similar style under the pen-name 'Gregorio Pérez de Miranda': *Kar Osmán, o memorias de la Casa de Silva* (1832); *Jaime 'el Barbudo'* (Barcelona, 1832); *El primogénito de Albuquerque* (4 vols., 1833–4) set in the reign of Pedro I; and *La catedral de Sevilla* (1834), an imitation of Victor Hugo's *Notre-Dame de París* (1831).

The *Memorias del príncipe de Wolfer* (1839) appeared posthumously.

Later and more original writers in the genre of the Romantic historical novel, such as Francisco Navarro Villoslada and Enrique Gil y Carrasco (qq.v.), eclipsed the fame of López Soler.

LÓPEZ VELARDE, RAMÓN (1888–1921), b. Jérez (now Ciudad García), Zacatecas. Mexican poet. He trained as a lawyer and later worked in journalism and the Civil Service. A postmodernist, López Velarde borrowed strikingly dissonant images from the surrealists and was influenced by Herrera y Reissig and Lugones (qq.v.) as well as by Baudelaire and Laforgue. His first book, *La sangre devota* (1916), was full of praise for his province and his adolescent passion for 'Fuensanta' (Josefa de los Ríos), who died in 1917.

His work became more subjective in *Zozobra* (1919). After his death, Xavier Villaurrutia (q.v.) vindicated his dwindling reputation and further books appeared: *El son del corazón* (1932), including the ode 'La suave patria' on the daily life of Mexico, written in 1921; the prose of *El minutero* (1933), *El don de febrero* (1952), and *Prosa política* (1953). The first anthology of his poetry was called *El león y la virgen* (1942) after his own astrological signs: he was born at the conjunction of Leo and Virgo and always took an interest in astrology. A. Castro Leal's edition of his *Poesías completas y El minutero* (1953) reached a 2nd edition in 1957.

See Elena Molina Ortega, *Ramón López Velarde: estudio biográfico* (1952); Allen W. Phillips, *Rámon López Velarde: el poeta y el prosista* (1962); C. Gálvez de Tovar, *Ramón López Velarde en tres tiempos* (1971); and G. López de Lara, *Hablando de López Velarde ...* (1973).

LÓPEZ Y FUENTES, GREGORIO (1897–1966), b. Hacienda El Mamey, Huasteca, Veracruz. Mexican novelist and poet. In 1914 he published poems modelled on Darío's *La siringa de cristal*. Later the same year he was sent to Veracruz to fight the American invaders, an experience recounted in *Campamento* (1931), the thoughts of a group of Mexicans before going into action; in *Tierra* (1932); and in *¡Mi general!* (1934), highly critical of military leaders who seek to impose their views on national politics. This trilogy has been reprinted in *La novela de la revolución mexicana* (2 vols., 1964).

López y Fuentes' best novel is *El indio* (1935), one of the great Indianist classics of Latin America, worthy to stand beside the work of Quiroga, Rivera, Lynch, Icaza, and Alegría (qq.v.). *El indio* (translated by Anita Brenner as *They that reap*, London, 1937) courageously indicts their leaders' failure to improve social conditions for the Indians in the political structure of Mexico.

López y Fuentes edited (1937–45) *El Universal* and published more stories and novels on aspects of life in Mexico. *Arrieros* (1937) is a memoir, rather than a novel, of muleteers and their way of life. *Huasteca* (1939) is a journalistic account of the quest for oil in his native state. *Cuentos campesinos* (1940) contains 31 stories of Veracruz. *Acomodaticio* (1943) is a satirical story of political manoeuvres. His later novels included *Los peregrinos inmóviles* (1944), *Entresuelo* (1948), and *Milpa, potrero y monte* (1951).

LÓPEZ Y PLANES, VICENTE (1789–1856), b. Buenos Aires. Argentinian statesman and poet, whose *El triunfo argentino* (1808) narrated the defeat of the English in 1807 in more than 1,000 hendecasyllables. He is now remembered for composing the Argentinian National Anthem, but a number of his patriotic and Horatian odes also achieved some fame, including 'En la victoria de Maipú', 'A la muerte del general Belgrano', and 'A las delicias del labrador'.

LORCA, FEDERICO GARCÍA, see GARCÍA LORCA, Federico.

Los, see under the word following the article, e.g. PREMIOS, LOS.

Los de abajo (1916), a novel by the Mexican Mariano Azuela (q.v.) first published as a newspaper serial in El Paso, Texas, in 1915. It is the representative work of fiction of the Mexican Revolution, not least for the predominance of its journalistic and documentary interest over style.

After the assassination of President Madero in 1913, Mexico fell abruptly into political anarchy. A rebel peasant, Demetrio Macías, escapes from his house before government forces swoop on the village, and returns to find his wife threatened by them. He escapes with his family and leaves for the Revolution. After the capture of Zacatecas he joins the other victorious rebels in pillaging and rape, lives with a prostitute, la Pintada, whom he eventually abandons, and returns to the violence that he now enjoys for its own sake. A self-appointed general, Macías finally decides to take some leave to see his wife and goes back home with his friends Venancio, Anastasio, and Meco. Returning after home leave he, with all his followers, is ambushed and cut down at the very place where at the beginning of the novel, he and his friends had ambushed government troops. The circular structure of the novel suggests the futility of all that Macías had achieved and of the Revolution generally.

Azuela, who participated in the Revolution under Pancho Villa, writes graphically in the tradition of Zola. He does not idealize the peasant, but illustrates how the spread of violence can release the inherent weaknesses and vices of man, who in his view is essentially egotistic and cruel towards townsmen and peasants alike.

The sadistic ex-waiter Margarito is no better or worse than the former student and journalist Luis Cervantes who joins the Revolution for personal gain, and escapes to the U.S.A. once he has enough money. Alberto Solís is the only true idealist, a character quickly disillusioned by the horror of what he sees. He is eventually killed at the battle of Zacatecas.

Los de abajo has been translated by Enrique Munguía as *The underdogs* (New York, 1929). See J. Rutherford, *Mexican Society during the Revolution: a literary approach* (Oxford, 1971).

LOVEIRA Y CHIRINO, Carlos (1882–1928), b. El Santo, Santa Clara. Cuban novelist and political agitator. After spending much of his childhood in New York, Loveira returned to Cuba in 1898, and there became a railway employee, spending his spare time in the Labour movement. His novels, which derived from Zola and Bourget, were written to redress social, political, and economic injustice. *Los inmorales* (1919) advocated the introduction of divorce; *Generales y doctores* (1920; trans. published in London, 1965) attacked a social structure in which the only means of advancement were the Army and the University; *Los ciegos* (1922) denounced the interference of the clergy in family life; and his best novel, *Juan Criollo* (1928) was a more complex and thorough study of Cuban society in the transition from colony to republic.

LOYOLA, San Ignacio de, see Ignacio de Loyola, San.

LOZANO, Cristóbal (1609–67), b. Hellín, Albacete. Poet, novelist, and dramatist. While a student at Alcalá he fell passionately in love with a girl called Serafina, after whom he named his collection of short novels, *Las Serafinas* (1672).

Las Persecuciones de Lucinda, dama valenciana, y trágicos sucessos de Don Carlos (Valencia, 1638) is a strange fictional compound of hagiography, intrigue, and superstitition, and is inferior to *Soledades de la vida y desengaños del mundo. Novelas y comedias exemplares* (1658), a sequence of four stories told by a hermit of Montserrat and followed by five plays. The Barcelona edition of 1722 replaces the plays with six stories. The work is signed 'Gaspar Lozano Montesinas', a name otherwise unknown and almost certainly assumed.

Lozano also wrote an uninspired ascetic work *David perseguido, y alivio de lastimados* (1652; pt. 2, 1659; pt. 3 Alcalá 1661) which laces the biblical narrative with invented anecdotes; and *Los Reyes nuevos de Toledo* (1667), a legendary-romantic history of the line of Trastamara from Enrique II (1369–79) to the death of Enrique III in 1406. This book was very popular, running through eleven editions in 50 years, and was compiled from 1663 when Lozano was appointed chaplain of the Chapel of los Reyes Nuevos (as the Trastamara monarchs were called) in Toledo Cathedral.

Joaquín de Entrambasaguas published *El doctor don Cristóbal Lozano* (1927) and edited Lozano's *Historias y leyendas* (2 vols., 1943) for Clásicos Castellanos. Lozano's work influenced some Romantic writers, among them Zorrilla and Espronceda (qq.v.).

LUCA DE TENA, Juan Ignacio (1897–), b. Madrid. Playwright. Son of the journalist Torcuato Luca de Tena, first Marqués de Luca de Tena and founder of *Blanco y Negro* and *ABC*. Spanish ambassador in Chile (1940–4) and Greece (1962), Luca de Tena is the author of numerous plays, found in his *Obras completas* (2 vols., Barcelona, 1959).

Perhaps his most interesting play is *El cóndor sin alas* (1951), in which Ricardo Manglano fails to climb the social ladder and become a 'gentleman' because his father is a chauffeur in a wealthy family. Luca de Tena's lack of verisimilitude hampers his effects, especially in *Don José, Pepe y Pepito* (1953), which deals with the problem of jealousy between the generations.

LUCA DE TENA, Torcuato (1932–), b. Madrid. Novelist. Son of Juan Ignacio Luca de Tena (q.v.), with whom he collaborated in dramatizing his first novel *La otra vida del* *capitán Contreras* (Barcelona, 1953), a satirical fantasy. His other novels include *Edad prohibida* (Barcelona, 1958), *La mujer de otro* (Barcelona, 1962), and *La brújula loca* (Barcelona, 1965).

LUCAN, Marcus Annaeus Lucanus (A.D. 39–65), b. Corduba (Cordova). Nephew of Lucius Annaeus Seneca (q.v.). Served as *quaestor* under Nero, at whose command he committed suicide when he fell into disfavour. His *De bello civili* (better known as the *Pharsalia*) is probably the most important Latin epic after Virgil's *Aeneid*. The subject is the civil war between Caesar and Pompey, which ended with the latter's defeat at Pharsalos, in Thessaly, in the year 48. Greatly prized throughout antiquity and medieval times, the book was translated as the *Farsalia* by Juan de Jáuregui in 1614, and published in 1684.

Lucanor, Conde, see Conde Lucanor.

LUCENA, Juan de (d. 1506?), b. Soria? A moralist who was appointed private counsellor by Juan II and sent as ambassador to Rome, where he formed a friendship with Aeneas Silvius Piccolomini, later Pope Pius II. His Ciceronian *Libro de vida beata*, written in 1463 (Zamora, 1483), is an imaginary discussion on happiness between Juan de Mena, Santillana, Lucena, and Alonso de Cartagena, Bishop of Burgos. Ticknor believed that Lucena had derived much of his material from Boethius's *Consolation of philosophy* but it is now known to be an adaptation from Bartolommeo Fazio's *Dialogus de felicitate vitae* (1445).

Lucena also wrote *Epístola exhortatoria a las letras* in extravagant praise of Queen Isabel the Catholic, and both his surviving works were reprinted by A. Paz y Melia in *Opúsculos literarios de los siglos XIV a XVI* (1892).

LUCEÑO Y BECERRA, Tomás (1844–1931), b. Madrid. Popular librettist for the *género chico* (q.v.) in the tradition created by Ramón de la Cruz (q.v.). His first *sainete* was *Cuadros al fresco*, first performed at the Teatro Lope de Rueda in 1870, and this was followed by numerous other libretti, particularly on the manners of Madrid, using shops, squares, and cafés as the settings for a lively display of typical *madrileño* word-play. His plays, selected in *Teatro escogido* (1894), dealt in mildly satirical fashion with bullfighting, the lottery, the flamenco fanatics, political hangers-on, and all the easy targets of city life. Active in the golden age of the *género chico* which coincided with the activity of Ricardo de la Vega and Javier de Burgos, Luceño is still remembered for *La fiesta nacional* (1882), *Los lunes de 'El*

Imparcial' (1894), and *La niña del estanquero* (1897).

LUCERO, Paulino, pseudonym of Hilario Ascasubi (q.v.).

Luces de Bohemia (1920), a play by Ramón del Valle-Inclán (q.v.), serialized in *España* (July–October 1920), and published in book form in 1924.

A rambling, episodic work more like a novel in dialogue than a play, *Luces de Bohemia* parodies the literary Bohemia of Madrid, and many of its characters (like those of the comparable *Troteras y danzaderas* by Pérez de Ayala, q.v.) are based on people whom the author knew. Like the protagonist Max Estrella (Valle-Inclán's friend Alejandro Sawa, q.v.), Valle-Inclán (represented by Bradomín) is angry at the Philistinism of the Spanish people; and he uses a gaoled anarchist as his mouthpiece in declaring that 'In Spain work and intelligence have always been despised. Here everything is controlled by money'.

Set in the Madrid of 1920, the novel follows Max to a bookseller's, a tavern, and a gaol where he has been taken for behaviour insulting to the authorities. There the anarchist tells Max that he expects to be killed according to the *ley de fugas*, whereby the police shoot a 'dangerous' prisoner in cold blood, afterwards claiming that he was killed trying to escape. This prediction is fulfilled.

Max later goes to see the Minister of the Interior, who was indirectly responsible (through the intervention of friends) for his release. This high-ranking official is ridiculed by Valle-Inclán.

Max is accosted by prostitutes in a grotesque park, then comes across a woman carrying a child shot during street fighting. Max dies on his doorstep, and in a graveyard scene parodying that of *Hamlet*, Rubén Darío, and Valle-Inclán's womanizing hero of the *Sonatas*, Xavier de Bradomín, discuss death with two gravediggers.

Pursuing the bizarre, Valle-Inclán makes Max's widow and daughter commit suicide and then tells us that a lottery ticket he had bought turned out to be the winner.

Perhaps the most famous of his *esperpentos* (q.v.), *Luces de Bohemia* includes the statement (Sc. XII) that 'Spain is a grotesque deformation of European civilization' and that consequently 'the tragic sense of life in Spain can also be expressed by a systematically deformed aesthetic'. Max likens this deformation to the reflection of classical heroes in the distorting concave mirrors of the amusement arcades of Madrid's Callejón del Gato.

See A. Zamora Vicente, *La realidad esper-péntica: aproximación a 'Luces de Bohemia'* (1969); and the more general *Visión del esperpento* (1970) by Anthony Zahareas and Rodolfo Cardona.

Lucidario, El (*'Elucidario'*), a book that elucidates or explains matters difficult to comprehend. It is applied principally to a book attributed to Sancho 'el Bravo', but probably compiled in the reign of Sancho IV (1284–95) using as its ultimate source the Latin *Elucidarium* of Honorius of Autun (*c.* 1095). It is divided into 106 chapters whose titles (with the complete text of chapter 1: 'Qual es la primera cosa que ha en el cielo e en la tierra') were printed by Pascual de Gayangos in vol. 51 (1860) of the BAE. The answers are devoted to theology and curious supersititions, especially in natural history, such as 'why male hares become pregnant and give birth, like the females'. Four MSS. were known to Gayangos: all in the Biblioteca Nacional in Madrid. Fr. Juan Eusebio Nieremberg (q.v.) translated 33 chapters of the *Lucidario* into Latin as *Dilucidarium Serenissimi regis castellae et legionis domini sancti*.

See J. Nachbin, 'Noticias sobre el "Lucidario" español y problemas relacionados con su estudio' in the *Revista de Filología Española* vols. 22 and 23 (1935–6); and Richard P. Kinkade, *Los 'lucidarios' españoles* (Madrid, 1968) including a survey and an edition.

Lucinda, the poetic name concealing the identity of Lope de Vega's mistress Micaela de Luján (who cohabited with him 1598?–1607?), the wife of Diego Díez de Castro.

LUGAREÑO, El, pseudonym of Joaquín García Monge (q.v.).

LUGONES, LEOPOLDO (1874–1938), b. Villa María del Río Seco, province of Córdoba. Self-taught Argentinian modernist poet of a stature equal to that of Rubén Darío (q.v.), who greeted his Whitmanesque *Las montañas de oro* (1897) with delight. Lugones wrote poetry of immense variety and prodigious talent, from the baroque sonnets of *Los crepúsculos del jardín* (1905) to the unexpected scientific terminology of *Lunario sentimental* (1909). He turned to realism in the optimistic *Odas seculares* (1910), written in haste to celebrate the centenary of Argentina's independence. Its ode 'A los ganados y las mieses' dealt with the poor and hunted minorities who found refuge in the pampas, the theme of Gerchunoff's stories *Los gauchos judíos* (also 1910). *El libro fiel* (Paris, 1912) was followed by *El libro de los paisajes* (1917), *Las horas doradas* (1922), *Romancero* (1924), *Poemas*

solariegos (1928), and *Romances del Río Seco* (1938). The younger poets of South America used each successive style as a testing-ground. The first edition of his *Obras poéticas completas* appeared with a preface by Pedro Miguel Obligado in Madrid in 1948.

His short stories were excellent, in the full tradition of Argentinian myth and fantasy: *Las fuerzas extrañas* (1906) and *Cuentos fatales* (1924). *El ángel de la sombra* (1926) is a highly artificial novel, evidence of the author's continuing search for new forms.

Lugones began life as a socialist journalist, using the pseudonym 'Gil Paz', writing books on his country's history and traditions, especially the marvellous accounts of *gaucho* history and literature in *La guerra gaucha* (1905) and *El payador* (1911), the latter dealing with the *Martín Fierro* of José Hernández (qq.v.). After a transitional period as a conservative, Lugones became a fascist, defining his position in *La hora de España* (1929), a speech given in Lima during the centenary celebrations of the Battle of Ayacucho. Lugones took his own life with cyanide in 1938.

See J. Irazusta, *Genio y figura de Leopoldo Lugones* (1973), and O. Rebaudi Basavilbaso, *Leopoldo Lugones* (1974).

LUGO Y DÁVILA, FRANCISCO DE (159–?– after 1659), b. Madrid. Novelist, and for a time Governor of Chiapas in Mexico. Lugo's importance lies in his light, amusing *novelas morales* in the manner of Cervantes collected as *Teatro popular* (1622). *El andrógino* recalls *El celoso extremeño* (q.v.) and *La hermanía* is a pale reflection of *Rinconete y Cortadillo*. Lugo's works have been edited by E. Cotarelo (1906).

LUIS, LEOPOLDO DE (1918–), b. Cordova. Poet of the Generation of 1940, and poetry critic of *Ínsula* and *Papeles de Son Armadans*. His first verses were simple and lyrical, near to Cernuda (q.v.). Subsequently he developed an interest in social themes and compiled *Antología de la poesía social española* (1965).

His first book, *Alba del hijo*, appeared in 1946, since when he has published a dozen further selections, of which the best works are presented in *Poesía 1946–68* (Barcelona, 1968).

LUIS DE GRANADA, Fray (1504–88), b. Granada. Preacher and religious writer. Of poor Galician parents who moved to the south after the Reconquest, Luis de Sarriá lost his father when he was five and his mother worked as a laundress in the Dominican monastery of the Holy Cross in Granada. There he was seen by Íñigo López de Mendoza, Conde de Tendilla, who took him into his family as a page. From

1525 he studied in the monastery and from 1528 in Valladolid, where he met Melchor Cano. In Cordova he met the Blessed Juan de Ávila, who exerted a great influence on Luis, and was to be the subject of his best biography. Luis's preaching had become so celebrated for its eloquence and inspiration that in 1543 he was given permission by the Provincial of the Dominican Order to travel freely throughout Spain, preaching wherever he wished.

In 1547 he founded the monastery of Badajoz, where he wrote the *Guía de peccadores* ([*sic*] 2 vols., Lisbon, 1556–7; latest edn., Madrid, 1962) which is his most didactic work, abandoning his usual rhetoric for a plain, often urgent work propounding and advocating the Christian virtues. These included the twelve obligations of a Christian, the twelve privileges to be enjoyed by a Christian, and concluded with the precepts that formed the basis of his ascetic teachings: mortification of the senses, the practice of charity, and the fulfilment of duties to one's self, to others, and to God. It is still disputed whether Luis modelled his *Libro de la oración y meditación* (Salamanca, 1554), on that of Fray Pedro de Alcántara (which is shorter) or vice versa. Like the *Guía*, it is a purely devotional work, without any suggestion of mysticism, yet the Inquisition banned it (despite the Dominican hold over the Holy Office) 1559–76.

Probably disturbed by this official persecution of writers on the inner life, Luis travelled to Portugal where he was generously received and appointed Provincial of his Order. He rejected the archbishopric of Braga to devote his time and energy to preaching and writing in Portuguese, Spanish, and Latin. His *Libri sex ecclesiasticae rhetoricae* (translated into Castilian in 1770) paradoxically defends the notions of clarity and brevity in a speaker, though his own works were distinguished by extensive periods and a rich and sonorous lexicon. He defines the perfect Christian preacher following the methods of pagan mentors such as Quintilian and particularly Cicero, as Rebecca Switzer has shown in *The Ciceronian style of Fray Luis de Granada* (New York, 1927).

In Lisbon he composed the *Memorial de la vida cristiana* (Lisbon, 1565) to which he later wrote *Adiciones* ... (Salamanca, 1574).

His best-known work is the *Introduction del symbolo de la Fe* (q.v. Salamanca, 1583), offering nature imagery more profuse and more vivid than in Luis de León (q.v.), as noted by Mary B. Brentano in *Nature in the works of Fray Luis de Granada* (Washington, 1936). The *Obras completas* of Fray Luis appeared in 1871–2 and in the BAE (vols. 6, 8, and 11) in 1848–9, but the best edition is that by Justus Cuervo (14 vols., Valladolid, 1906–8), while a convenient *Obra*

selecta (1952) is available in the Biblioteca de Autores Cristianos.

J. I. Valenti's *Fray Luis de Granada: ensayo biográfico y crítico* (Palma, 1889) is still useful and has been supplemented by R. L. Oechslin's *Louis de Granada ou la rencontre avec Dieu* (Paris, 1954) and Marcel Bataillon's 'Genèse et métamorphoses des oeuvres de Louis de Granada', in the *Annuaire du Collège de France* (Paris, 1948). One of Azorín's most stimulating essays is the title-essay in *Los dos Luises y otros ensayos* (1921).

LUIS DE LEÓN, *Fray* (1527?–1591), b. Belmonte, Castile. Poet, Biblical translator, and didactic writer. He was one of the creators of Castilian Renaissance prose in *De los Nombres de Cristo, La perfecta casada* (qq.v.), and a long, careful and detailed *Exposición del Libro de Job* (ed. Father Antolín Merino, 1779), which Father Vega has described as an 'autobiografía disimulada' for its spirit of stoical acceptance.

Fray Luis was the eldest son of a distinguished family, which traced Jewish ancestry from his great-grandmother. When his father was appointed *oidor* ('judge') at Granada, Luis was sent to study at Salamanca (from about 1541), where the boy's uncle was Professor of Law. A few months later, Luis joined the Augustinians and was formally accepted into the order in 1544, when he returned to the university and studied theology, first under Melchor Cano (until 1551), and then under Domingo de Soto.

The brilliant Luis graduated as a *bachiller* in about 1557, and a *licenciado* in 1560, and in 1561 was elected to the chair of St. Thomas Aquinas at Salamanca. In 1562 he wrote for a nun, his cousin Isabel Osorio, a translation and commentary on the Song of Songs: *In Cantica Canticorum Salomonis explanatio* (Salamanca, 1580; ed. Jorge Guillén for private publication, 1936), despite the fact that translations from the Bible other than the Vulgate were expressly prohibited by the Church. He tried to keep his version a secret, but the MS. was copied by a servant in the monastery and later brought in evidence against him.

He openly criticized the Vulgate in 1566 (despite the edict of the Council of Trent), clashed in committee with León de Castro, and opposed the awarding of a chair to Bartolomé Medina. His adversaries (particularly the powerful Dominicans) denounced him to the Inquisition, and in 1572 Luis was arrested and kept in confinement until 1576. Orders to torture him were apparently disregarded; he was permitted books as well as paper and candles.

On being pronounced innocent in 1576, Luis returned in triumph, though sick and frail, to occupy his chair at Salamanca and is reported to have opened his first class with the customary (but in this context defiantly ironical) phrase 'Dicebamus hesterna die' ('We were saying yesterday'), but this anecdote is almost certainly a later invention. He was awarded the chair of Moral Philosophy in 1578, and that of Biblical Studies the following year. Elected Provincial of the Augustinian Order in Castile in 1591, he died only nine days later, to the very end a victim of internal enmity within the Church.

Known in his lifetime primarily as a scholar, Luis de León is now read mostly for his poetry, little known and unpublished in his lifetime. It was first issued by Quevedo in 1631 to demonstrate the classical virtues of precision, restraint, and care, as a counterblast to what he considered the excesses of *Gongorismo* (q.v.) Quevedo's edition was imperfect, and his attributions faulty in many cases. Dr. Ángel Custodio Vega has prepared a critical edition of the *Poesías* (1955) in which he admits only 29 as authentic, three of these being close imitations of classical and Italian models.

Luis reworked his poems many times, causing problems of defining precedence. His classical models included Horace and Virgil, and neo-Platonist ideas informed many of his poems. His devotion to the work of Garcilaso led him to study Italian in an effort to judge by the example of Bernardo Tasso how a Horatian ode can be transmuted into the *lira* (q.v.). We know that he translated the courtly work of Bembo and La Casa as well as Seneca, Pindar, and Tibullus, but he departed from classical writers in creating direct, personal poetry of the intellectual and spiritual quests, as S. Juan de la Cruz created a personal, private poetry for his mystical quest.

With San Juan, Fray Luis brought the five-line *lira* to its greatest potential. His early poems were the ode 'La vida retirada', based on Horace's 'Beatus ille', and 'La profecía del Tajo', based on Horace's 'Prophecy of Nereus'.

His later poems are at once more personal and more universal than the conventional 'Vida retirada', and are often dedicated to the friends who stood by him in his turbulent career: 'Oda a Salinas', dedicated to the blind organist of Salamanca Francisco Salinas (q.v.), and demonstrating the power of music; 'Noche serena', written for the otherwise unknown Diego Olarte, and contrasting the majesty of Nature with the transcendence of God; 'A Felipe Ruiz', to the poet-scholar Ruiz de la Torre y Mota, describing an imagined arrival in Heaven, an indication that Luis had not, at least by that time, experienced mystical union; 'En la Ascensión', with its pictorial vision; the imaginative 'Morada del cielo'; the Job-like

resignation and pessimism of 'Al salir de la cárcel' so utterly different from San Juan's 'En una noche oscura' on a similar theme; and a calm denunciation of a miser: 'A un juez avaro'.

Part of Luis's poetic skill lies in his ability to reconcile the pagan Horace with Christian teachings; part in his concise yet passionate eloquence alternating with sections of quietness; and part in the passionate sincerity marking his every utterance. In a fine surviving portrait of the friar by Francisco Pacheco, his eyes are dreamy and his jaw determined: an exact physical likeness of the dour scholar and sensitive poet who emerges from the writings.

The *Obras completas* edited by Fr. Félix García (1944) should still be consulted for the prose works. The best books in English are Aubrey Bell's *Luis de León* (Oxford, 1925) and the popular introduction, *Luis de León* (New York, 1971), by Manuel Durán.

LUJÁN DE SAYAVEDRA, Mateo, pseudonym of Juan Martí (q.v.).

LULIO, Raimundo, the Castilian form of the Catalan name Ramon Llull (q.v.).

LUNA, Álvaro de (1388?–1453), b. Cañete. The powerful adviser to Juan II who became the virtual ruler of Castile until his execution, on a charge of having bewitched the king, in 1453. It was Álvaro who arranged the king's second marriage, with a Portuguese princess who turned the king against his favourite. Luna had become extremely unpopular through his arrogant behaviour towards other noblemen such as the Marqués de Santillana (q.v.), who wrote a diatribe against him called the *Favor de Hércules contra Fortuna* (sent to Juan II) and after the execution composed a tirade in the form of a confession by Álvaro de Luna, *Doctrinal de privados* (1456).

There is a notable panegyric of Don Álvaro by his friend Juan de Mena in *El laberinto de Fortuna* (qq.v.).

Sixteen of Álvaro de Luna's poems appear in the *Cancionero* of Baena, another personal friend, but his principal work is *Libro de las claras y virtuosas mujeres* (1446; ed. M. Castillo, Toledo, 1909), for which Juan de Mena wrote a *proemio*. It defends the cause of women in the celebrated 15-c. controversy on the subject, citing honourable women from the Bible, classical antiquity, and Christianity.

He is not the author of the so-called *Corónica de don Alvaro de Luna*, printed by his great-grandson in Milan in 1546 (ed. J. de Mata Carriazo, 1940). The author of this partisan history of the reign of Juan II was probably Gonzalo Chacón the elder (d. 1517).

LUNA, Juan de (*c.* 1580–after 1630), a teacher of Spanish and author of the bilingual *Diálogos familiares, en los cuales se contienen los discursos, modos de hablar . . . para los que quieren aprender la lengua castellana* (Paris, 1619) and *Arte breve y compendiosa para aprender a leer, escreuir, pronunciar y hablar la lengua española* (London, 1623).

Luna is identified by M. Menéndez y Pelayo with the 'H. de Luna' who composed *Segunda parte de Lazarillo de Tormes* (Paris, 1620) and described himself as an 'intérprete de la lengua española'. The sequel is superior in every way to the previously published and anonymous sequel to *Lazarillo de Tormes* (q.v.), benefitting from the author's absence from Spain in its opposition to the excesses of the Inquisition and the temporal power of the Church. Far more anticlerical than the first part, its style is nearly as witty, concise, and readable as that of its model, but it lacks the same warm humanity.

One of its anecdotes concerns a poor farm labourer asked by an inquisitor for some of his pears. The labourer uproots the tree and sends it with the pears still on it, saying that he prefers the Inquisition to have no cause to call on him a second time.

The text is found with the original and the earlier sequel in vol. 3 (1846) of the BAE and in A. Valbuena Prat's anthology *La novela picaresca española* (1946). The latest edition is by María Inés Chamorro Fernández (1967).

LUNÁTICO, Un, a pen-name used occasionally by Isidoro Fernández Flores (q.v.).

Lunes del Imparcial, Los, the influential weekly magazine edited by José Ortega Munilla (q.v.), which published the works of many writers of the Generation of '98.

LUSSICH, Antonio D. (1848–1928), b. Montevideo. Uruguayan poet, the son of an Austrian sailor. He befriended José Hernández (q.v.) the author of *Martín Fierro* (q.v.) and undoubtedly exerted some influence on him. Lussich fought on the 'Whites' side in the Civil War, and composed three *gaucho* poems: *Los tres gauchos orientales* (Buenos Aires, 1873; ed. in the Colección de Clásicos Uruguayos, Montevideo, 1964); *El matrero Luciano Santos* (Buenos Aires, 1873), interesting for its accurate use of dialect words; and *Cantalicio Quirós y Miterio Castro en el Club Uruguay*, inspired by the *Fausto* of Ascasubi (q.v.).

LUZÁN Y CLARAMUNT, Ignacio (1702–54), b. Saragossa. Critic and minor poet. Of a wealthy noble family, he was sent to Italy at the age of 13 and studied under Giambattista Vico, graduating in law at Catania. On his return he was appointed secretary at the Spanish Embassy in Paris (1747–50), and then occupied high posts in the Spanish Ministry of Finance, the Mint, and the Royal Library. He was a leading member of the private Academia del Buen Gusto (q.v., 1749–51).

He wrote *Memorias literarias de París* (1751) and mediocre verses imitating Herrera ('A la conquista de Orán') and Góngora (the *fábula épica* in *octavas reales*, *Juicio de París*), as well as a dull play, *La virtud coronada* (1742), which was never performed and a translation from Metastasio: *Artajerjes.*

But Luzán's celebrity is due to *La poética, o reglas de la poesía en general y de sus principales especies* (1737; 2nd edn. in 2 vols., Madrid, 1789; ed. L. De Filippo in 2 vols., Barcelona, 1956).

In 1728 he had written a treatise for presentation to the Academy in Palermo, *Ragionamenti sopra la poesia*, which argued the neoclassical case; in *La poética*, he provided the full-scale treatment on which the 18th-c. neoclassical controversy was to be based. It was influenced by Muratori's *Della perfetta poesia italiana* (1706) and *Riflessioni sopra il buon gusto* (1708) as well as by Boileau's Horatian *L'art poétique* (1674) and by other French authors.

Luzán's *Poética* is divided into four books: I. The origin, history, and characteristics of poetry; II. The use and pleasure to be derived from poetry; III. Dramatic poetry; IV. Epic poetry. Poetry he claims, declined after the reign of Philip III. It should strive to imitate Nature in general and in particular. Its aim should be didactic and moralistic. In place of the free imagination, the artist should use his moral sense to ensure stability and order in the state.

The plays of Lope, Rojas, Calderón, and Moreto are praiseworthy in their childish ignorance; they lack cultivation and rigid control by the ordered mind. Herrera is the supreme example of the conscious artist; Góngora is demented. In epic poetry Homer is unequalled as a teacher, since the aim of epic poetry is to display and instil the qualities of the perfect military hero. In drama, there must be a fine balance between utility and pleasure (his motto is *aprovechar deleitando*) as in the work of his friend Montiano and Luyando (q.v.).

Luzán's theories did not find unanimous acceptance; even the fabulist Iriarte believed that Luzán's principles were too strict, and his article in the *Diario de los Literatos de España* was answered by Luzán's *Discurso apologético* (Pamplona, 1741) signed with the anagram Íñigo de Lanuza. Yet his appeal for reason and morality in art was sympathetically received by Spaniards whose taste for French writing generally and neoclassical doctrines in particular was to remain in vogue until the spread of Romanticism.

See Gabriela Makowiecka, *Luzán y su poética* (Barcelona, 1973).

LUZ Y CABALLERO, José DE LA (1800–62), b. Havana. Cuban educator and philosopher. He planned and directed schools, courageously defying the authoritarian measures of the colonial authorities, which included the suppression of a proposed Academia Cubana de Literatura. He was forced to spend much of his life in exile, living in France and the U.S.A. In 1848 he founded El Salvador, the most progressive college in Cuba.

His *Obras* (5 vols., 1945–50) are still popular for *Aforismos* such as 'Más respeto se debe a los niños que a los ancianos', 'Nuestro siglo no es el de oro, sino el del oro', and 'La frialdad, materia prima de la maldad'.

See M. Vitier, *José de la Luz y Caballero, educador* (1956).

LYNCH, BENITO (1885–1951), b. Buenos Aires. Argentinian regional novelist and short-story writer of La Plata region, to which his family

moved in 1890. His first novel *Plata dorada* (1909) failed, but Manuel Gálvez's review of *Los caranchos de la Florida* (1916) brought Lynch's name to the attention of readers. His next books were the city novel *Las mal calladas* (1923) and the important *El inglés de los güesos* (q.v., 1924). *El romance de un gaucho* (1933) was written entirely in *gaucho* slang; Lynch wrote nothing after this, refusing to allow the reprinting of his earlier books, and even to speak to his publishers. His short stories were published in *La evasión* (1922), and *De los campos porteños* (1931). Two short novels appeared in 1925: *El antojo de la patrona* and *Palo verde*. Unlike the idealized *gaucho* figures in *Fausto* or *Martín Fierro*, Lynch's *gaucho* is slow-witted, inarticulate, vindictive, and violent, but his women (Marcelina in *Los caranchos de la Florida*, and Balbina in *El inglés de los güesos*) are by contrast idealized and remote from reality.

LYRA, CARMEN, pseudonym of María Isabel Carvajal (q.v.).

Ll, entries beginning 'Ll' will be found in the order of the English alphabet, between 'Li' and 'Lo'.

M

MACANAZ, MELCHOR RAFAEL DE (1670–1760), b. Hellín, Albacete. A jurist and statesman under Charles II, Philip V, and Ferdinand VI, he was appointed ambassador in France and the Netherlands and suffered imprisonment by the Inquisition in 1748 for trying to curb the power of the Church.

A. Valladares de Sotomayor compiled *Catálogo de las obras de Melchor Rafael de Macanaz* and published Macanaz's *Defensa crítica de la Inquisición* (2 vols., 1788). Macanaz also wrote 'Apologética histórica' (MS. dated 1724), 'Memoria sobre los intereses de la monarquía de España y Nuevo Mundo' (MS. dated 1734) and many other works displaying his erudition (occasionally pretentiously) and his sceptical attitude to the Church. His *Obras escogidas* (Madrid, 1847) appeared in Biblioteca Selecta de Autores Clásicos, and much of his work was published during 1788 in the *Semanario Crítico*.

MACHADO Y ÁLVAREZ, ANTONIO (1848–92), b. Santiago de Compostela. Folklorist who pioneered the study of folklore in Spain, often using the pseudonym 'Demófilo', ('lover of the

people'). He was the father of the poets Antonio and Manuel Machado (qq.v.).

His many works include *Colección de enigmas y adivinanzas* (Seville, 1880), *Bases del folklore español* (Seville, 1881), *Adivinanzas francesas y españolas* (Seville, 1881), and *Colección de cantos flamencos* (Seville, 1881).

He published and edited the Biblioteca de las Tradiciones Populares Españolas (11 vols.: vols. 1–6, Seville; vols. 7–11, Madrid, 1883–6), to which he himself contributed vol. 5: *Estudios sobre la literatura popular* (1884). He founded *El Folklore Andaluz* (1882–3) and later *El Folklore Extremeño*.

MACHADO Y RUIZ, ANTONIO (1875–1939), b. Seville. With García Lorca (q.v.), the most important Spanish poet of his generation, and in Spain the most popular. His father, Antonio Machado y Álvarez (q.v.), was a folklorist. His family left for Madrid when Antonio was 8, and like his brother Manuel (q.v.), he was educated in the Institución Libre de Enseñanza (q.v.).

In 1899 he went with Manuel to Paris to work for a short time as a translator for the publishing house of Garnier, and while there met Oscar Wilde, Moréas, and many of the important French Parnassians and symbolists. It was under their influence, and particularly that of Verlaine, that he wrote the poems in *Soledades* (1902; dated 1903), a collection augmented and revised as *Soledades, galerías, y otros poemas* (1907; 3rd edn., 1943), still indebted to Darío and the modernists.

In 1907 he started teaching French in Soria, giving up his Bohemian life, and in 1909 he married Leonor Izquierdo, the 16-year-old daughter of his landlady. This was his happiest and most fertile poetic period, in which *Campos de Castilla* (q.v., 1912; augmented and revised, 1917) was written. From intimate interior poems, Machado extends his themes to nature and Spain. The influence of the *Romancero* (or corpus of ballads) is strong, especially in *La tierra de Alvargonzález*.

Unable to remain in Soria, where his young wife had died in 1912, Machado moved to Baeza (1913-19), where he completed *Campos de Castilla*. The new second part, which appeared in 1917, accentuated the misgivings voiced by the Generación del 1898 (q.v.) about the decadence and complacency of Spain.

Unlike his brother Manuel, Antonio felt an exile in Andalusia and called up recollections of his childhood to establish a relationship with places he had long chosen to abandon. Dating from the Soria poems, the popular style began to predominate, though even in his modernist phase he had never attempted metrical innovation, being satisfied with a reserved, sober elegance. The final period is that of the aphorism, in which he returns to the *proverbio* of Sem Tob, and emulates the authority of Unamuno, but in wit and brevity, rather than in discursive essays. This last phase is typified by the *Cancionero apócrifo* attributed to 'Abel Martín', himself a teacher of another 'apocryphal professor' whom Machado named 'Juan de Mairena'. *Juan de Mairena* (q.v.): *Sentencias, donaires, apuntes y recuerdos* (1936; 2nd edn., 2 vols., Buenos Aires, 1943) has been translated by Ben Belitt (Berkeley and Los Angeles, 1963).

From Baeza, Machado moved to Segovia in 1919 and there fell in love with Pilar Valderrama. His *Canciones a Guiomar* and other poems for her first appeared in his 'Cancionero apócrifo' in the *Revista de Occidente* (1926, 1931).

He collaborated in writing poetic dramas (and one prose drama) with Manuel Machado (q.v.) but parted from him over the Civil War, going to Valencia in 1936 to write for the Republican *Hora de España*. In 1938 he fled to Barcelona and early in 1939 escaped over the border with his mother and other refugees and died at Collioure, where he was buried.

The *Obras completas* (1947; 4th edn., 1957) contain the works of both brothers except their play *El hombre que murió en la guerra*, which can be found in *Las adelfas* (Buenos Aires, 1947). The Espasa-Calpe *Poesías completas* (1928) contain more than the Losada *Poesías completas* (Buenos Aires, 1943), but both are incomplete and are supplemented by *Prosas y poesías olvidadas* (ed. R. Marrast and R. Martínez-López, Paris, 1964).

The standard biography is M. Pérez Ferrero's *Vida de Antonio Machado y Manuel* (1947). Detailed studies of the poems can be found in A. Sánchez Barbudo's *Los poemas de Antonio Machado* (Barcelona, 1967), and other useful studies are Ramón de Zubiría's *La poesía de Antonio Machado* (1955; 3rd edn., 1966), Segundo Serrano Poncela's *Antonio Machado, su mundo y su obra* (Buenos Aires, 1954), and M. U. Guerra, *El teatro de Manuel y Antonio Machado* (1969).

See also the comprehensive *Bibliografía machadiana* (1976); and R. Gullón and A. W. Phillips (eds.), *Antonio Machado* (1973) in the El Escritor y la Crítica series.

MACHADO Y RUIZ, MANUEL (1874-1947), b. Seville. Poet and, in collaboration with his brother Antonio (q.v.), also a playwright. His father was the folklorist Antonio Machado y Álvarez (q.v.). The family left for Madrid when Manuel was 9, and he was educated there at the celebrated Institución Libre de Enseñanza (q.v.).

In 1899 Manuel went with Antonio to work for a short time with the publishing house of Garnier in Paris, and while there fell under the influence of modernism. His best book, *Alma* (1900), was his first; here his existential pessimism did not overshadow his subjects, and in Felipe IV he found a happy subject for the evocation of painting in verse.

Caprichos (1905) and *El mal poema* (1909) established his reputation. The latter presaged the 'anti-poetry' of the Chilean Nicanor Parra (q.v.) in its frank writing on urban squalor and middle-class complacency. After his marriage to his cousin, Eulalia Cáceres, the quantity and quality of his work declined, and he produced little of note after *Museo* (1910), *Apolo* (1910), and *Cante hondo* (1912).

The collections *Sevilla y otros poemas* (1921), *Ars moriendi* (1921), *Phoenix* (1935), and *Horas de oro* (1938) are slack in inspiration and control. His themes are Andalusia (by whose songs he remained captivated), love, history, and art.

Manuel became more superficial as he grew older, in contrast to Antonio's increasing profundity; his easy sociability led him to the theatre and he became drama critic (from 1915) for *El Liberal*. In the introduction to *Cante hondo* he wrote: 'One day I heard one of my *soleares* being sung by a little flamenco singer in an Andalusian carnival where nobody knew me or could even read; I felt that paradoxical glory of being totally unknown yet completely understood'. His *Obras completas* (5 vols., 1922) were supplemented by *Poesía: opera omnia lyrica* (1942). There is a useful *Antología* (1940) in the Colección Austral.

On the outbreak of Civil War, Manuel became estranged from his Republican brother, but by then they had collaborated in many plays beginning with successful adaptations of Golden Age dramas for the Madrid stage. The poetic drama of the brothers Machado was written relatively late, when Manuel's inspiration had failed, and it is remarkable more for its impact on the young Lorca than for any intrinsic value.

The first such collaboration was *Desdichas de la fortuna, o Julianillo Valcárcel*, a tragicomedy on the manoeuvres of the Conde-Duque de Olivares to obtain power for himself through his bastard son's marriage to Olivares's cousin Juana. In a Romantic fourth act boldly annexed to the three-act Golden Age form, the hero Julianillo dies of love for a commoner. This play was highly successful, and the brothers (whose share in the writing has never been determined accurately) continued with *Juan de Mañara* (1927), another attempt at the still-fashionable Don Juan theme; the modern psychological drama *Las adelphas* (1928); the Andalusian *La Lola se va a los puertos* (1930), *La prima Fernanda* (1931), and *La duquesa de Benamejí* (1932). All of these are in verse, although the last also contains some prose. There is a further work, *El hombre que murió en la guerra*, written about 1928 and revised (probably by Antonio alone) about 1934. It was first performed in 1941, after Antonio's death, its production being an act of some courage at the time.

See Dámaso Alonso, 'Ligereza y gravedad en la poesía de Manuel Machado' in his *Poetas españoles contemporáneos* (3rd edn., 1965, pp. 48–95); G. Brotherston, *Manuel Machado: a revaluation* (Cambridge, 1968); M. U. Guerra, *El teatro de Manuel y Antonio Machado* (1969); and Gerardo Diego, *Manuel Machado, poeta* (1974).

MACHUCA, LICENCIADO, the pen-name used by Francisco Sánchez Barbero (q.v.) in his *Ensayos satíricos . . .* (1820).

MACIAS O NAMORADO (Galician-Portuguese: 'Matthias the enamoured', *fl.* 2nd half of the 15th c.), love-poet, the archetype of the unhappy lover, or *grande e virtuoso mártir de Cupido*, throughout Spanish and Portuguese literature, particularly in Santillana's *El*

infierno de los enamorados, and Lope de Vega's *Porfiar hasta morir* (1638). Larra (q.v.) also dealt with the story in a four-act verse drama *Macías*, and in a historical novel *Doncel de don Enrique el Doliente* (both 1834).

Five poems attributed to him appear in the *Cancionero de Baena* (c. 1445), and some fifteen others are ascribed to him with more or less justification.

Several versions of his story are told. According to one Macías, when required by a jealous husband to stand aside, asserted that he would not stir from the place where his love had once stood, and was instantly killed. Another tale is that when he was a prisoner in the dungeon of Arjonilla, Macías' song of platonic love was overheard by the jealous husband, who shot him with an arrow. This latter version seems to originate from the *Ai sennora, en quen fiança* of Macías himself.

MACÍAS PICAVEA, RICARDO (1847–99), b. Santoña, Santander. Teacher and regional novelist whose concern for Spain was expressed at about the same time and in much the same terms as that of Ángel Ganivet (q.v.), first in *La instrúccion pública en España y sus reformas* (1882) and later in *El problema nacional: hechos, causas y remedios* (1899).

His novel *La tierra de campos* (1897) is a portrait of the Castilian *meseta* and its peasants, with boldly-drawn characters and obvious sympathy for their condition.

MADARIAGA, FRANCISCO (1927–), b. Buenos Aires. Argentinian poet, who spent most of his childhood in the province of Corrientes. A member of the group *A partir de O*, he has published *El pequeño patíbulo* (1954), *Las jaulas del sol* (1960), *El delito natal* (1963), *Los terrores de la suerte* (1967), and *Tembladevales de oro* (1973).

Characterized by the harsh brilliance of its imagery, Madariaga's poetry seeks an intimate contact with reality, particularly that of his native Corrientes, without any form of affectation. Raúl Gustavo Aguirre has written: 'Los poemas de Madariaga tienen a menudo, más allá de sus aparentes desajustes, la coherencia de una pasión salvaje que desliga las palabras de sus relaciones habituales para someterlas a un nuevo y sorprendente sentido'.

MADARIAGA, SALVADOR DE (1886–), b. Corunna. Historian, essayist, literary critic, and novelist. He qualified as an engineer in Paris, and worked on the railways from 1912. On the outbreak of World War I he worked for London's *The Times* and from 1921 in the secretariat of the League of Nations, returning to Geneva in 1935–6 as the Spanish delegate.

He taught Spanish literature at Oxford University during 1928–31 and again later in semi-retirement. He was Spanish ambassador to Washington in 1931 and to Paris in 1932–4. After the end of World War II he lived permanently outside Spain, writing in English and French as fluently as in Spanish. After an early essay on Shelley and Calderón, he became celebrated for his *Guía del lector del Quijote* (1926; translated by himself into English as *Don Quixote, a psychological study* in 1934); *Englishmen, Frenchmen, Spaniards* (1928; Sp. version 1929); *Spain* (1930; Sp. version 1931); and his historical books on Latin America: *Vida del muy magnífico Señor Cristóbal Colón* (1940), *Hernán Cortés* (1941), *Cuadro histórico de las Indias* (2 vols., 1945; in English, *The rise and fall of the Spanish American Empire*, 1947), and *Simón Bolívar* (1949).

Of moderate, liberal, and cosmopolitan leanings, Madariaga found his spiritual home in Britain, while continuing to write and research on the Spanish World. He has composed poetry and plays, but in the field of creative literature he has achieved most in the novel. His first attempt was a humorous fantasy, *La jirafa sagrada* (1924) being an ingenious Utopia set in the year 6922 in Ebania, a matriarchal African Negro state satirizing the (largely English) world. More of a tract than a novel, it preaches tolerance, patience, and reconciliation between nations. *Arceval y los ingleses* (1925) is a similar thesis novel existing to contrast the hero, modelled on Ganivet (q.v.), with English manners. *Sir Bob* (1930) was composed in English. His subsequent novels, all in Spanish, are *El enemigo de Dios* (1936), a religious story deriving from Unamuno's ideas; *Ramo de errores* (1952), a philosophical story; *La camarada Ana* (1954), a political story of the Cold War; and a *novela-fantasía* of totalitarianism, *Sanco Panco* (Mexico City, 1964).

He has also written a sequence of historical novels called *Esquiveles y Manriques* using his knowledge of Latin America: *El corazón de piedra verde* (Buenos Aires, 1942), *Guerra en la sangre* (Buenos Aires, 1957), and *El semental negro* (Buenos Aires, 1961). *Una gota de tiempo* (Buenos Aires, 1958) concerns the Pizarros in Peru.

His autobiographical *Memorias (1921–1936): amanecer sin mediodía* (1974) have been abridged for the English edition as *Morning without noon* (1974).

Madre naturaleza, La (1887), a sequel to Emilia Pardo Bazán's novel *Los Pazos de Ulloa* (q.v.).

MADRID, Fray ALONSO DE, see ALONSO DE MADRID, Fray.

MADRIGAL, ALFONSO DE (1400?–55), b. Madrigal de la Sierra, Ávila. Known as 'El Tostado' after his father, Alonso Tostado. Philosopher, theological writer, and polymath whose prolific output in Latin and Castilian gave rise to the popular saying 'escribir más que El Tostado'. A schoolmaster in Salamanca, he was persecuted by the Dominican Juan de Torquemada and found refuge in Rome, where he impressed Pope Eugenius IV by his knowledge. He joined the Carthusians in the Catalan monastery of Scala Dei but was asked to return to secular life by King Juan II, who recommended him to the Pope for the bishopric of Ávila.

The first edition of his *Opera omnia* (20 vols., Venice, 1507–31) included the *Libro intitulado las catorze questiones del Tostado* edited by Adolfo de Castro as *Cuestiones de filosofía moral* in vol. 65 (1873) of the BAE; a translation of Seneca's *Medea; Sobre el Eusebio; Sobre Sant Matheo;* and *Tratado de como al ome es necesario amar.* He is one subject in *Claros varones de Castilla* (1486) celebrated by Hernando del Pulgar (q.v.). 'Dos obras castellanas de Alfonso Tostado inéditas' were edited by O. García de la Fuente in *La Ciudad de Dios,* vol. 168 (1955).

MAEZTU, RAMIRO DE (1874–1936), b. Vitoria. Philosopher and essayist, whose father was Basque and whose mother was English. After periods in Paris and Cuba, Maeztu returned to Spain, turning to journalism at first in Bilbao and, in 1898, settled in Madrid as one of the Generación del 1898 (q.v.). He lived in England as a press correspondent from 1905 and reported from the Allied Front during World War I, returning to Spain in 1919. Under Primo de Rivera's dictatorship, Maeztu was nominated ambassador to Argentina in 1928. In his earlier writings he is influenced generally by English thought and also especially by that of Nietzsche, as in *Hacia otra España* (1899). Later he proposed the Roman Catholic Church as the model institution in *La crisis del humanismo* (Barcelona, 1919), originally published in English as *Authority, liberty and function in the light of the War.* His last work, *La defensa de la hispanidad* (1934) contradicts his earlier views. It is a collection of essays that had appeared in the conservative magazine *Acción Española,* founded and edited by Maeztu himself, and attacks the *leyenda negra* that alleged brutality and wilful exploitation of Latin America by the Spanish *conquistadores.* In it, Maeztu argues for a return to the monarchical evangelistic enthusiasm of 16th-c. Spain. His works, according to Julián Marías, display 'más pasión que rigor y evidencia', and even in his best literary essays, *Don Quijote, Don Juan y la Celestina* (1926), Maeztu concentrates on the socio-political significance of the characters concerned.

There is a useful bibliography of Maeztu in the special issue of *Cuadernos Hispanoamericanos* nos. 33–34 (1952). The standard biography is *Maeztu* (1955) by Vicente Marrero, who is editing Maeztu's *Obras completas*. Maeztu's own *Autobiografía* appeared in 1962.

MAGALLANES MOURE, MANUEL (1878–1924), Chilean poet, painter, and critic. Alternating between the impressionist and modernist styles in his poems on women, the home, and nature, Magallanes Moure published his first poems in the review *Pluma y Lápiz*, contributed articles on painting to *El Mercurio* and joined the group *Los Diez*. He lived in the Tolstoyan colony of San Bernardo, dissolved in 1907–8, which has been described in Fernando Santiván's *Memorias de un tolstoyano* (1955).

Pedro Prado selected the poems in *Sus mejores poemas* (1926) from *Facetas* (1902), *Matices* (1904), *La casa junto al mar* (1909), and *La jornada* (1910). *La poesía de Manuel Magallanes Moure* (1959) is by Paulinus Stelingis.

MAGARIÑOS CERVANTES, ALEJANDRO (1825–93), b. Montevideo. Uruguayan historical novelist. He was sent to Europe to complete his education and there began a literary magazine. He returned to Montevideo in 1855, founded a literary salon, and in 1858 inaugurated the Biblioteca Americana with his *Estudios históricos, políticos y sociales sobre el Río de la Plata*. He tried his hand at dramas (*No hay mal que por bien no venga*, on a Golden Age theme); an anthology, *Páginas uruguayas: álbum de poesías* (1878); and poems, such as the Indianist *Celiar* (1852). He is best-known, however, for the historical novel *Caramurú* (1848) on the defeat of the Brazilians at the Battle of Ituzaingó, a work that enjoyed great success in its time but is now justifiably forgotten as a badly-written example of Romanticism at its most delirious. Zum Felde has characterized the once lionized figure of Magariños (in *Proceso intelectual del Uruguay*, 1944) as 'el más acabado ejemplo de estéril fecundidad'.

MAGDALENO, MAURICIO (1906–), b. Villa del Refugio, Zacatecas. Mexican novelist and dramatist whose youth was spent in the formative years of the Revolution, which continued to inspire most of his writings. He founded the Teatro de Ahora group with Juan Bustillo Oro, and wrote for it a number of plays, three of them published in *Teatro revolucionario mexicano: Pánuco 137, Emiliano Zapata, Trópico* (Madrid,

1933), but in later years he preferred to write for films. He has also written many essays and literary studies, for example on José María Luis Mora, Martí, and Ricardo Flores Magón. *El compromiso de las letras* is his address on entering the Academia Mexicana de la Lengua in 1957.

Magdaleno is best known for his fiction, and less for stories such as those in *El ardiente verano* (1954) than for novels which show disillusion with the achievements of the Revolution, from *Mapimí 37* (1927) and *Concha Bretón* (with notes on the stories *El compadre Mendoza* and *El baile de los pintos*, 1936), to the important *El resplandor* (1937), a protest against the harsh treatment of Indians after the Revolution. The Indian hero Saturnino Herrera becomes a post-revolutionary leader but ends by exploiting his own village, San Andrés de la Cal, in the Valle del Mezquital. Further novels of protest were equally popular but lacked equal inspiration: *Sonata* (1941), *La tierra grande*, and *Cabello de elote* (both 1949).

See Ruth Stanton, 'The realism of Mauricio Magdaleno' in *Hispania*, vol. 22 (1939), pp. 345–53.

MAGGI, CARLOS (1922–), b. Montevideo. Uruguayan playwright and *costumbrista*. A lawyer on the staff of the Banco de la República, he is a militant supporter of Batlle and the *colorados*, or Liberal Party. His popular essays on Uruguayan life and manners are *Polvo enamorado* (1950), *El Uruguay y su gente* (1963), and *Gardel, Onetti y algo más*. *La trastienda* (first performed in 1958) was a *sainete* obsessed with time, like his first play (staged later) *La biblioteca* (1959), in which a Lorca-like lyricism is cleverly merged with the grotesque vision of Kafka. Another dimension was given to Maggi's dialogue by his use of dialect, whereas his contemporaries were still employing the vocabulary of Greek mythology or, at best, the European *avant-garde*. Maggi showed that he was ready to take his country seriously but, disconcertingly for many critics, not very often. His inventive stagecraft intentionally reduces a potentially serious situation to the grotesque; in this he has learned much from the technique of Ionesco.

His subsequent plays include *La noche de los ángeles inciertos* (1960), which promises to form part of the classic repertory of Uruguayan drama; *La gran viuda* (1961), arguably his weakest play; *El pianista y el amor*, a collage in which a nightclub pianist tells his love story by means of actors who recite from Anouilh, Ionesco, Joyce, Coward, Shakespeare, and others; *Mascarada* (1962), consisting of 'Un cuervo en la madrugada' and the brilliant 'El apuntador', in which an ex-boxer seeks a golden ring to reward the purity of a prostitute; and two more plays devoted to the strange properties of time: *Esperando a Rodó*, an allegory of Uruguay's obsession with the past, symbolized by Rodó (q.v.) and at the same time a parody of Beckett's *En attendant Godot* (*Waiting for Godot*); and *Un motivo*.

The most useful essay on Maggi so far is by Mario Benedetti, in his *Literatura uruguaya, siglo XX* (2nd edn., 1969).

Mágico prodigioso, El, a major religious play by Pedro Calderón de la Barca (q.v.) composed for the Corpus Christi festival at Yepes (Toledo) in 1637. Two versions survive: an autograph in the Biblioteca Nacional, Madrid (ed. Alfred Morel-Fatio, Heilbronn, 1877) and another, more mature, first printed in *Parte veinte de comedias varias nunca impresas, compuestas por los mejores ingenios de España* (1663). A. A. Parker and M. McKendrick have produced an edition of both texts.

The play is set in the year 304, during the imperial reign of Diocletian. Calderón's sources are the *Legenda aurea* of Jacobus de Voragine (1230–98), and two earlier plays: *El esclavo del demonio* by Antonio Mira de Amescua (q.v., an important Faust play from which Calderón took the device of the hero's embracing a skeleton) and *El prodigio de los montes y mártir del cielo, Santa Bárbara* by Guillén de Castro (q.v.).

A pagan student of philosophy, Cipriano, who has arrived at the threshold of the knowledge of the necessity of God's existence by reading Pliny's *Natural history*, encounters the Devil disguised as a traveller who asks the way to Antioch. Cipriano is astonished by the question, since the towers of the city are in sight. Satan says:

> *Esa es la ignorancia,*
> *a la vista de las ciencias*
> *no aprovecharlas*

and proceeds to show the truth of this by diverting Cipriano's search for sacred love into his profane love for the Christian virgin Justina, over whom two young noblemen are fighting. Cipriano offers to intercede on their behalf, but falls in love with her himself. Justina rejects him and in desperation he seeks the Devil's help, offering his soul in exchange for Justina's love. The Devil, unable to overcome her free will, fails to weaken her steadfast purity and can only conjure up a wraith disguised as Justina. When Cipriano embraces it, it turns into a skeleton and he is converted, as the Devil is forced to admit the inferiority of his powers to those of the God in whom Justina trusts.

Justina assures Cipriano of God's mercy and forgiveness if he repents. The governor of Antioch orders them to be executed and they are united in death. The Devil appears to the pagans in an epilogue, forced to confess by God that he was the intruder in Justina's room who had led to her suitors' jealousy and the suspicions of her guardian. God is the 'wonder-working magician' of the play's title, intervening to convert Cipriano through Justina, and saving her too. The sub-plot involving Cipriano's servants Clarín and Moscón and Justina's servant Livia (in which by a process of cynical self-interest the men share the girl's favours on alternate days) parallels the main plot, the immorality of the unprincipled Livia stressing by contrast the righteous conduct of her mistress.

Calderón's most moving passages in this play are perhaps those in which the Devil tempts Justina, and Cipriano praises her beauty.

Whereas in many other Faust plays the protagonist is saved by going back on his promise to the Devil, Calderón avoids this curious cheating the Devil of his due by making the Devil incapable of fulfilling his side of the bargain.

See A. A. Parker, *The approach to the Spanish drama of the Golden Age* (London, 1957), and *Theology of the Devil in the drama of Calderón* (London, 1958).

MAGÓN, pseudonym of Manuel González Zeledón (q.v.).

MAIMONIDES, MOSES (1135–1204), b. Cordova. Spanish-Hebrew writer on law and philosophy. His family left Spain for Fez in 1160 as a result of the religious persecutions under the Almohad dynasty. After living for a while in Acre, Jerusalem, and Hebron, Maimonides settled in Alexandria as Chief Rabbi and physician to the Sultan. The son of a good scholar, from whom he learned mathematics and astronomy, Maimonides wrote an Arabic commentary on the *Mishnah* (1168), following it with the finest of all medieval expositions of Jewish law: the *Mishnah Torah* (1180). His best-known work, however, is his interpretation of Jewish religion in terms of Aristotelian philosophy: the *Dalalat al-haʾirin* (Arabic: 'Guide for the perplexed'), translated into Hebrew in 1190 as *Morah nevukhim*. The book had a deep and lasting influence on Spinoza and many other Jews, but also contributed to the compendia of Thomas Aquinas and other medieval writers (such as Alfonso de la Torre, q.v.) who knew the work either in an anonymous 13th-c. Latin version or in Pedro de Toledo's 15th-c. Castilian translation. The Hebrew literature in the two centuries following the publication of the Hebrew edition of the *Dalalat* is full of commendation and denunciation of the book.

MAITÍN, José Antonio (1804–74), b. Puerto Cabello. Venezuelan poet. During the War of Emancipation he moved to Cuba, where he was befriended by the Colombian writer José Fernández Madrid, and entered the diplomatic service of Colombia. He returned to Venezuela in 1834.

With Abigáil Lozano (1821–66), Maitín is the most popular poet of Venezuelan romanticism, famous for the exquisite octosyllabic *Canto fúnebre a la memoria de la Señora Luisa Antonia de Maitín*. This elegy for his wife is simple and sincere.

In about 1840 he read Zorrilla, who thereafter influenced him. Maitín farmed in the peaceful coastal village of Choroní, celebrated in *Ecos de Choroní* (1844). His *Obras poéticas* appeared in 1851.

Malagueña ('deriving from Málaga; Malagan'), hence, a song from this region of southern Spain; a dance accompanied by the song; and four octosyllabic lines originally intended to be sung. It is of exclusively popular origin.

> '*Los siete sabios de Grecia*
> *no saben lo que yo sé . . .*
> *Las fatiguitas y el tiempo*
> *me lo hicieron aprender.*'
> —Manuel Machado.

Maleficio de la mariposa, El, a two-act play by Federico García Lorca (q.v.) first staged early in 1920, a year after Lorca's arrival in Madrid. The play was weak, and was undoubtedly performed only because Lorca was friendly with Gregorio Martínez Sierra (q.v.) the director of the Eslava Theatre.

A symbolist play in the tradition of Maeterlinck's *L'oiseau bleu* (1909), *El maleficio de la mariposa* concerns a cockroach who is living quietly with his family until a wounded butterfly is brought home. He aspires to the ideal world of the butterfly and gives up the everyday world against his friends' advice, but the butterfly will have nothing to do with him. The ingenuous tone of the play echoes the verse that Lorca was writing at this time (see Libro de poemas) and its failure is understandable when it is compared to contemporary stage productions in Madrid.

MAL LARA, Juan de (1524–71), b. Seville. Humanist. He studied with Hernán Núñez (q.v.) in Salamanca. He founded the important Escuela de Humanidades y Gramática, being succeeded as its director by Diego Girón (q.v.).

Though Mal Lara made his reputation as a teacher, not as a writer, he compiled *La*

Philosophia vulgar (1568; ed. A. Vilanova, 4 vols., Barcelona, 1958), an imitation of the *Adagia* of Erasmus. This collection of proverbs, apologues, and anecdotes was in print for many years and widely quoted, usually without attribution.

'La hermosa Psyche', a MS. in the National Library in Madrid, deals with the familiar Greek myth of Psyche and Cupid, and has been edited in part (*El libro quinto de la 'Psyche'*, Salamanca, 1947) by M. Gasparini, author of the standard *Cinquecento spagnolo: Juan de Mal Lara* (Florence, 1943).

See also F. Sánchez y Escribano, *Juan de Mal Lara: su vida y sus obras* (New York, 1941), with a good bibliography.

MALLEA, Eduardo (1903–), b. Bahía Blanca, Buenos Aires. Argentinian short-story writer, novelist, and essayist. A former editor of the literary supplement of *La Nación*. His first book *Cuentos para una inglesa desesperada* (1926) derived from European models. His essays on the Argentine began with the lecture *Conocimiento y expresión de la Argentina* (1935) read in Italy in 1934, the partly-autobiographical *Historia de una pasión argentina* (1935) probably his most popular book, and *El sayal y la púrpura* (1941).

His reputation in fiction was made by the stories in *La ciudad junto al río inmóvil* (1936), psychological fables set in Buenos Aires. *Roseada está de sueños* (1944) and *El retorno* (1946) are two short novels in sequence. Mallea's fame grew with the publication in 1941 of his finest novel *Todo verdor perecerá* (q.v.), shortly after *Fiesta del noviembre* (1938; translated by Flores and Poore, New York, 1942, and by A. de Sota, London, 1970) and *La bahía de silencio* (1940; translated by Grummon, New York, 1943). Mallea's trilogy on the Ricarte family consists of *Las águilas* (1943), *La torre* (1951), and *La barca de hielo* (1967).

Other novels include *El vínculo* (1946); *Los enemigos del alma* (1950); *La sala de espera* (1953); *Chaves* (1954), in which an introspective man, Mallea's prototype, speaks only one word, 'no', throughout the novel; *Simbad* (1957), about a playwright's personal and artistic crises; *La penúltima puerta* (1969); and *Gabriel Andaral* (1971), another autobiographical novel, the first of a planned saga, which digresses on literature, philosophy, and religion to the exclusion of a conventional plot. *En la creciente oscuridad* (1973) is a novel, and *Los apeles privados* (1974) is described as 'páginas . . . de un diario intelectual'. *Obras completas* (2 vols., Buenos Aires) appeared in 1965.

Most of the younger novelists of Argentina, particularly the 'parricidal' school led by David Viñas (q.v.), have reacted strongly against

Mallea's view that society requires a natural aristocracy of civilized, non-materialistic people if ordinary values and decency are to be preserved.

See H. J. Becco, *Eduardo Mallea: guía bibliográfica* (1959) supplemented by M. J. Pemberton, *Revista Iberoamericana*, vol. 30 no. 58 (1964), pp. 319–23; M. I. Lichtblau, *El arte stilístico de Eduardo Mallea* (1967); Carmen Rivelli, *Eduardo Mallea: la continuidad de su obra* (New York, 1969); and O. H. Villordo, *Genio y figura de Eduardo Mallea* (1973).

MALÓN DE CHAIDE, Fray PEDRO (1530?–89), b. Cascante, Navarra. Augustinian ascetic writer and preacher. A disciple in Salamanca of Fray Luis de León (q.v.) among others, Malón taught (1569–72) in Burgos, then in Huesca (where he wrote his only book), and later in Saragossa. Malón shared with Beato Alonso de Orozco and Fray Luis de Léon the Augustinian view that it was licit to translate the Scriptures into the vernacular as opposed to the prohibition argued by the Dominicans.

Libro de la conversión de la Madalena, en que se esponen los tres estados que tuvo de pecadora, i de penitente, i de gracia (Barcelona, 1588; in vol. 27 (1853) of the BAE, and ed. by P. Félix García (2 vols., 1930) in Clásicos Castellanos) is a paraphrase of the Gospel accounts of Mary Magdalene, with much extraneous and allegorical matter, including digressions on the martyrdom of the saints, fashionable dress, and religious paintings.

The preface in defence of the vernacular is eloquent and Menéndez y Pelayo described *La Magdalena* (as it is familiarly known) as 'the most brilliant, elegant and stately, the most joyful and picturesque work in our religious literature: a book all living colour and oriental pomp, a perennial delight to the eye'. As to Malón's philosophical standpoint, the neo-Platonism of his teacher Luis de León is everywhere evident.

See José María San Juan Urmeneta, *Fray Pedro Malón de Echaide* (Pamplona, 1957), supplemented by D. Carozza, 'Another Italian source for "La Magdalena" of Malón de Chaide' in *Itálica* (Chicago), vol. 41 (1964), pp. 91–8.

MALUENDA, JACINTO ALONSO (1597?–after 1657), b. Valencia. Playwright and poet. Theatre director in Valencia who assumed the duties on the death of his father, Alonso. His poetry appeared in *La coxquilla del gusto* (Valencia, 1629) and *Tropezón de la risa* (Valencia, 1636?), miscellanies of fables, ballads, and festive poetry. His plays (banned in 1646 and permitted again in 1650) included *La*

Virgen de los desamparados, El sitio de Tortosa, and *Santo Tomás de Villanueva*. His work is described at some length in Henri Mérimée's *Spectacles et comédiens à Valencia* (Toulouse, 1913). His *La Magdalena* may have been the *Santa María Magdalena* reported to have been the first play to be performed after the reopening of the Madrid theatres in 1650.

MALUENDA, RAFAEL (1885–1963), b. Santiago. Chilean novelist and editor of *El Mercurio* of Santiago. His realism derives from Maupassant and Zola in scenes of country and city life among the working classes, and also echoes Tolstoy in its social indignation. His *Escenas de la vida campesina* (1909) was followed by the city novels *Los ciegos* (1913) and *Venidos a menos* (1916). The characters in *La Pachacha* (1914) are hens.

Maluenda's strength in psychological delineation is especially notable in his novels about women: *La señorita Ana* (1920), *La cantinera de las trenzas rubias* (1925), and *Confesiones de una profesora* (1927). His *Colmena urbana* (1937) is a crowded canvas dealing with metropolitan life. His last novel was *Arimiño negro* (1942).

MAÑACH, JORGE (1898–1961), b. Sagua la Grande. Cuban critic and historian. Educated in Spain, the U.S.A. and Cuba, Mañach was a contributing editor to the important Cuban avant-garde magazine *Revista de Avance* (1927–30), many of whose writers later turned to politics. *Tiempo muerto* (1928) won a national drama prize, but Mañach is not otherwise associated with the theatre. He won recognition as an essayist in works such as *Glosario* (1924); *Indagación del choteo* (1928); the attack against President Machado *Pasado vigente* (1939); the interpretation of Cuban history *Historia y estilo* (1944); *Examen del quijotismo* (Buenos Aires, 1950); and *Hacia una filosofía de la vida* (1951). For these works he has been called 'el prosador más elegante de Cuba'.

His *Martí, el apóstol* (Madrid, 1933) is one of the most useful biographies of the Cuban leader.

MANCISIDOR, JOSÉ (1894–1956), b. Veracruz. Mexican novelist. A lifelong Marxist, he wrote essays on Lenin, Marx, and other great names of the world communist movement, and several volumes of short stories: *Cómo cayeron los héroes* (1930), *La primera piedra* (1950), and *Me lo dijo María Kainlová* (1956), as well as film scripts and plays, but he will be remembered as a novelist.

La asonada (1931) and *La ciudad roja* (1932) pay less attention to style and construction than to revolutionary fervour, but *Frontera junto al mar*

(1953), which attacks the U.S. Marines' invasion of Veracruz in 1914 from the viewpoint of an eye-witness, has undeniable strength as a narrative. *El alba en las simas* (1953) is a partisan account of the national struggle for Mexican petroleum, which was exploited with American capital.

Mancisidor compiled two useful anthologies: *Cuentos mexicanos de autores contemporáneos* (Mexico City, 1946) and *Cuentos mexicanos del siglo XIX* (Mexico City, 1947).

Mandrágora, an important Chilean review founded in 1938 which published the works of the surrealist Braulio Arenas, Gonzalo Rojas (qq.v.), Jorge Cáceres, and Enrique Gómez Correa. *Mandrágora* ended with its sixth issue (1941), for its leading spirit Arenas abandoned it as reactionary, and founded his own *Leitmotiv.*

MANENT, MARIA (1898–), b. Barcelona. Catalan poet and publisher. In 1925 Manent founded the *Revista de Poesia,* and with Riba, Foix (qq.v.), and others sat on the editorial committee of *Quaderns de Poesia* from 1935.

Manent has been influenced by Verdaguer, Carner (qq.v.), Claudel (in *La branca,* 1918), and has translated poetry from English (*Keats* (1919), *Rupert Brooke* (1931), *Versions de l'anglès* (1938), and *Poesia anglesa i nord-americana* (1955)) as well as from Chinese: *L'aire dourat* (1928), and *Com un núvol lleuger* (1968). Following Chinese models, he has striven for a 'pure' poetry in *La collita en la boira* (1920), *L'ombra i altres poemes* (1931), and *La ciutat del temps* (1961).

His novel *El vel de Maia: dietari de la Guerra Civil, 1936–39* (1975) won the Premi Josep Pla of 1974. Manent's literary criticism includes *Poesia, llenguatge, forma* (Barcelona, 1973), on twelve Catalan poets.

MAÑER, SALVADOR JOSÉ (d. 1751), was the most bitter of the many opponents of Feijoo (q.v.), and he replied to the *Theatro crítico universal* (which began to be published in 1726) with the *Antitheatro crítico . . .* (1729–31). Mañer claimed to have found 70 errors in Feijoo's work. The incensed Feijoo replied with an *Ilustración apologética . . .* (1729), issued against the advice of his friends as he himself confessed, which listed over 400 errors in Mañer's refutation, and showed that most of them were irrelevant and based on misunderstanding.

MANRIQUE, GÓMEZ (1412?–90?), b. Amusco, Palencia. Playwright and poet, who was the uncle of Jorge Manrique (q.v.) and nephew of the Marqués de Santillana (q.v.). An enemy of the powerful Don Álvaro de Luna, Manrique took part in the rebellions against Juan II and

Enrique IV, siding with the Infantes of Aragón. On the losing side at the Battle of Olmedo in 1445, he rebelled again in 1448. In 1465 he defended Ávila against Alfonso and in 1470, with other nobles, forced the king to sign the treaty of Toros de Guisando, by which the future Queen Isabella was recognized as next in line for the Castilian throne. When Enrique died in 1474, Manrique was appointed *corregidor* of Toledo by King Ferdinand.

Manrique's poetry is vigorously satirical, in the *Exclamación y querella de gobernación,* against Enrique IV and Alfonso Carrillo, archbishop of Toledo; amorous in the medieval tradition of courtly love; and allegorical and didactic in *Coplas para Diego Arias de Ávila,* attacking earthly vanities, that were probably the most direct influence on the *Coplas* of Jorge Manrique (q.v.) on the death of Gómez's brother Rodrigo. Typical of his style are the *coplas* vindicating women against the attack in *Coplas que fizo Mosén Pero Torrellas contra las damas:* and an elegy in *arte mayor* worthy of Mena: *Defunzión del muy noble Garci Lasso de la Vega.*

His true originality, however, lay in the nascent drama. His simple, unaffected Christmas play in verse *La representación del Nacimiento de Nuestro Señor* (written between 1467 and 1481) was composed for the nuns at the convent of Calabozanos where his sister was abbess. Dialogue was minimal (180 lines in all, each character offering a short monologue and withdrawing); the shepherds proclaim Jesus as the Redeemer and Gabriel, Michael, and Raphael present Him with the symbols of the Passion: chalice, pillar and rope, scourges, crown of thorns, cross, nails, and lance. The play ends with a lullaby set to a popular air.

Manrique also wrote a short play, *Lamentaciones hechas para Semana Santa,* in which Mary, John, and Mary Magdalene mourn the crucified Christ with the refrain *¡Ay dolor!.* It is an amplified version of the liturgical *Planctus Mariae.*

Other dramatic works of Manrique that survive are allegorical *momos* or masquerades for the birth of his nephew and for the fourteenth birthday of Alfonso, brother of the Infanta Isabel, who had been proclaimed king in 1465. The latter play was composed in 1467, auguring happiness, power, and success to the young king at Arévalo. But Alfonso died the following year without succeeding to the throne and the piece has some piquancy in that it was probably the only occasion on which Isabel performed in public.

A *Regimiento de príncipes* attributed to Manrique and first published in Zamora about 1495 is collected with his other writings in Colección Austral (1947). Manrique's *Cancionero* was edited by A. Paz y Melia (2 vols., 1885) in the

Colección de Escritores Castellanos and as part of the 'Cancionero castellano' in vol. 22 (1915) of the NBAE. There is a brief study, *El poeta Gómez Manrique, Corregidor de Toledo* (Toledo, 1943), by C. Palencia Flores.

MANRIQUE, JORGE (1440–79), b. Paredes de Nava. Poet. Son of the Conde de Paredes, Rodrigo Manrique, Grand Master of the Order of Santiago; nephew of the poet Gómez Manrique (q.v.). A soldier and a poet, Manrique followed his father in taking the part of the Infante Don Alfonso against Enrique IV and after the death of Alfonso supported Isabel. He fought at Calatrava against the Marqués de Villena and helped to lift the siege of Uclés with his father. He died in front of the castle of Garci-Muñoz, fighting against Villena.

Some fifty of his compositions in the courtly tradition deal with love, fortune, and religion in witty, satirical, or conventional styles: Manrique is a poet of his time in his use of frivolity and rhetorical *conceptismo*. The quality that raises his occasional poetry above average *cancioneros* is the authentic melancholy with which he looks steadfastly at death.

The death of his father provoked his best poem: *Las Coplas de Jorge Manrique por la muerte de su padre*, written in 1476 and first published in Seville in 1494. The forty *coplas* in octosyllables with *pie quebrado* celebrate the life of Don Rodrigo in lines sometimes muted, often splendid, which warn against the brevity of life and the vanity of men. The theme of life's transience and of the vanity of earthly pleasures is a medieval commonplace but, if Manrique's theme is unoriginal, his style and execution are not. The strophic form seems at first to be too light and delicate for an elegy, but in fact acts in clever contrast to the argument, which evolves from a medieval indictment of mere earthly ambition to a Renaissance pride in Rodrigo's earthly and spiritual accomplishments. The ideas are expressed with grace and precision, avoiding both an accumulation of adjectives and the customary theologico-moral digressions. The mood is transitional between nostalgic classical humanism and a morbid obsession with the power of death.

> *Recuerde el alma dormida,*
> *avive el seso y despierte*
> *contemplando*
> *cómo se pasa la vida,*
> *cómo se viene la muerte,*
> *tan callando.*

The sense of timelessness in Manrique has impressed writers as diverse as Lope de Vega, Espronceda, and Pedro Salinas, who has written *Jorge Manrique o tradición y originalidad* (Buenos

Aires, 1948). Another good study is V. Borghini's *Giorgio Manrique: la sua poesia e i suoi tempi* (Genoa, 1952). A critical edition of the *Coplas* ... on his father's death was published by R. Foulché-Delbosc (Barcelona, 1902); and Augusto Cortina edited Manrique's *Cancionero* (1929) for Clásicos Castellanos. The *Obra completa* appeared in Buenos Aires in 1940.

MANSILLA, LUCIO VICTORIO (1831–1913), b. Buenos Aires. Argentinian diarist. A colonel in the army, Mansilla was the son of General Lucio Mansilla and his second wife Agustina Rosas, sister of the dictator. In 1852 Rosas was forced into exile by the victory of Caseros and Mansilla faced difficulties, including a three-year exile in Paraná. His literary *œuvre* is an extended but fragmentary autobiography, important for *Una excursión a los indios ranqueles* (2 vols., 1870), and written to justify his imposing an unjust peace on border Indians and his attempt to win them over to Christianity. Though Mansilla may not have been clearly aware of government policy, he obtained a peace treaty with the Indians, who in a few decades were exterminated by the Government's cruel violation of its terms. The political problem of assimilating the Indians was to become a major theme in the later *Martín Fierro* of Hernández (qq.v.), though secondary to the question of assimilating the *gauchos*.

His diaries and essays formed a series of books which include *Entre-nos* (5 vols., 1889–90), *Retratos y recuerdos* (1894; 2nd edn., in Grandes Escritores Argentinos, 1927), *Estudios morales; o sea El diario de mi vida* (Paris, 1896), *En vísperas* (Paris, 1903), and *Mis memorias: infancia, adolescencia* (Paris, 1904; reprinted with preface by Juan Carlos Ghiano, Buenos Aires, 1955 in El Pasado Argentino).

See Enrique Popolizio, *Vida de Lucio V. Mansilla* (1954).

MANSUR, AL- (Arabic: 'the victorious'), an epithet assumed by many Muslim princes, notably the Amir Muhammad of Cordova (939–1002) an enlightened ruler who became king of Andalusia in 996 and greatly extended Muslim power in Spain and Africa. The usual Spanish form is Almanzor.

MANTEROLA, JOSÉ (1849–84) Librarian of the Public Library in San Sebastián and compiler of the first anthology of Basque poetry; the *Cancionero vasco* (3 vols., 1877–80), with biographical, bibliographical, and critical notes.

Manterola founded, and edited until 1884, the important magazine for new poetry in Basque, *Euskal-Erria* (1880–1918).

MANTUANO, PEDRO (1585?–1656), historian.
Secretary to Velasco, Grand Constable of
Castile, Mantuano worked in the government of
Milan. His *Advertencia a la Historia de Iuan de
Mariana* (Milan, 1611; 2nd enlarged edn.,
Madrid, 1613) is an augmented version of
memoranda on alleged errors in the Spanish
history of Mariana (q.v.) originally sent to
Mariana personally and returned with marginal
notes which Mantuano considered insultingly
dismissive. In his published notes he states that
he, at 26, could have compiled a history as
reliable as that of the highly esteemed Mariana.
Both parties have right on their side: for, while
Mantuano's notes on errors are mostly well-
founded, Mariana warned readers that he did
not claim to write a history of Spain accurate in
every detail, 'which would be an endless task:
I have merely striven to put into readable
Latin materials compiled by others'. Tomás
Tamayo de Vargas vindicated Mariana in
Historia . . . de Mariana defendida (Toledo, 1616).
Mantuano's other recorded work is *Casa-
mientos de España y Francia, y viage del Duque de
Lerma llevando la Reyna Christianíssima Doña Ana de
Austria al passo de Beobia . . .* (1618).

MANUEL, *Príncipe Don* JUAN, see JUAN MANUEL,
Príncipe Don.

MAPLES ARCE, MANUEL (1898–), b.
Papantla, Veracruz. Mexican poet and essayist.
He qualified in law at the Universidad Nacional,
and studied French literature and art history
at the Sorbonne. *El arte mexicano moderno* (1945)
has been translated into English.

In 1922 he proclaimed the *estridentismo* movement with Luis Quintanilla, Salvador Gallardo,
Germán List Arzubide (author of *El movimiento
estridentista*, 1926), and Arqueles Vela (author of
El café de nadie, 1926). The movement, not unlike Italian futurism, sought to glorify the
industrial future, with its machines and power.
Andamios interiores (1922) and especially *Urbe*
(1924; translated by John Dos Passos, New
York, 1929) were Maples Arce's main contributions to the poetic movement. He moved
away from *estridentismo* in his later books:
Poemas interdictos (Xalapa, 1927; translated into
French by Edmond Vandercammen, Brussels,
1936), and *Memorial de la sangre* (1947).

His most interesting essays are *Ensayos
japoneses* (1959), deriving from his years as
ambassador to Japan.

MARAGALL, JOAN (1860–1911), b. Barcelona.
Catalan poet, critic, essayist, journalist, and
playwright. In addition to his articles on life and
manners in Catalonia, Maragall was a leading
exponent of *modernisme*, by which he understood

a return to lyricism after a phase of naturalism.
A nature poet, Maragall was the last of the
Catalan romantics, and was influenced by
Ausias March (q.v.) as well as by Novalis and
by Goethe, whose *Römische Elegien* (1888) he
translated.

His five volumes of poems are *Poesies* (1895);
Visions i cants (1900), including the *visions* of
Catalan folk-heroes; *Les disperses* (1903); *Enllà*
(1906); and *Seqüències* (1911), all published in
Barcelona. His early verse concentrated on
personal themes, while his devotion to nature
developed with maturity. The majestic *Cant
espiritual* (1910) beseeches God to let this world
be the second world for Maragall after death.
El comte Arnau (separately ed. Joan-Lluís
Marfany, Barcelona, 1974) was written in three
parts (1900, 1906, and 1911) corresponding to
three phases of Maragall's poetic development:
radical *modernisme*, civic conformism, and
Messianic individualism. His essays in *Elogis*
have been compared with those of Emerson.

Maragall translated the *Homeric Hymns* into
Catalan blank verse and wrote a verse play
Nausicaa (1908–10) on the episode from the
Odyssey, based on Goethe's abandoned project
for a tragedy. His *Notes autobiogràfiques* (1885–6)
revealed a man of warmth and great integrity,
and his correspondence with such figures as
Unamuno, 'Azorín', and Francisco Giner de los
Ríos (qq.v.) is particularly revealing of the
period. *Maragall y su obra* by P. Javier de
Arengs (Barcelona, 1914) has now been supple-
mented by the research of J. M. Corredor in his
Joan Maragall (Barcelona, 1960) and of Arthur
Terry in his *La poesía de Joan Maragall* (1963).
The latest edition of Maragall's *Obres completes*
(11 vols., Barcelona, 1912–13; 1929–31) is that
in 2 vols. (1960–1).

MARAÑÓN, GREGORIO (1887–1960), b.
Madrid. Historian and biographer. By profession a doctor, Marañón was a specialist in
endocrinology, but contributed to the intellectual history of Spain in a series of works reissued in *Obras completas* (from 1966). Among
the most outstanding are *Amiel* (1932), *El
Conde-Duque de Olivares* (1936), *Tiberio* (1939),
Don Juan: ensayos sobre el origen de su leyenda
(1943), *Antonio Pérez* (1947), *El Greco y Toledo*
(1957), and *Los tres Vélez* (1960).

See F. J. Almodóvar and Enrique Warleta,
Marañón, o una vida fecunda (1952), with a
bibliography; Luis Granjel Sánchez, *Gregorio
Marañón* (1960); M. Izquierdo, *Gregorio
Marañón* (1965); and Pedro Laín Entralgo,
Gregorio Marañón (1969).

MARCELA DE SAN FÉLIX, *Sor* (1605–88),
b. Madrid. Poet. An illegitimate daughter of

the actress Micaela de Luján and Lope de Vega (q.v.), who dedicated his play *El remedio de la desdicha* (1620) to her. She took the veil in 1622 and became a Trinitarian. Encouraged by her father, she had begun to write poetry at the age of ten. The *Poesías* and *Coloquios* were edited by M. Serrano y Sanz in vol. 2 of his *Apuntes para una biblioteca de escritoras españolas* (1905).

Marcela, o ¿cuál de los tres? (1831), a comedy by Manuel Bretón de los Herreros (q.v.).

Set in Madrid, the play concerns the rich and beautiful young widow Marcela, who lives with her uncle Don Timoteo. Timoteo suggests that she should remarry, and three suitors quickly call: Don Agapito, an effeminate, vain prig who tries to win her with sweets and chocolates; Don Amadeo, a bashful poet tongue-tied in her presence; and Don Martín, a restless, flamboyant Andalusian captain. Marcela makes fun of all three, having received a formal proposal of marriage from none.

Amadeo attempts to win over Marcela's maid with a madrigal, but she prefers money. Don Timoteo favours the captain. Finally, Marcela receives love-letters from each in turn, and summons them to hear her choice. She rejects Agapito, counselling him to become more masculine if he wants to attract the ladies; she rejects Amadeo, saying that she cannot live with poetry alone; and when it is assumed that she will accept the captain, he too is rejected because she suspects that he is an adventurer. She declares that she rejects them all not out of vanity, but because she is not yet ready to abandon the liberty she enjoys as a young widow.

This delicious comedy of manners, full of wit and charm, is a satire on the Romantic melodrama. It has been edited by J. Hesse (1969).

See A. del Campo, 'Sobre la "Marcela" de Bretón' in *Berceo* (Logroño), 1947, pp. 41–55.

MARCH, AUSIAS (1397?–1459), b. Gandía, Valencia. The first major poet to write exclusively in Catalan and one of the greatest poets in that language. The son of Pere March (q.v.), whose family was raised to the nobility in 1360.

From 1418 he fought under Alfonso V of Aragón in Sicily, Sardinia, Corsica, and Djerba, but *c.* 1425 he abandoned his military career to manage the royal falconry at Albufera. In 1437 he married Isabel, the sister of Joanot Martorell (q.v.), but she died in 1439 and four years later he married Joana Scorna. Joana died in 1454, and it may be her death that is reflected in some of his best poems, the *Cants de mort* XCII–XCVII.

He was influenced by Thomist and other scholastic philosophy, by the Provençal troubadours (particularly by Arnaut Daniel), and by Dante and Petrarch. In Spain his influence was immediate and durable, pervading the work of Garcilaso, Cetina, Montemayor, and Herrera.

Ausias wrote 128 identified surviving poems, of which three quarters deal with some aspect of love, and derive generically from Provençal tradition. But by using Catalan as his medium he removed his poetry from the conventional courtly genre and created a new and individual role as introvert and moralist. Most of his poems are addressed to a married woman, who has been identified with Teresa Bou, whom he calls *plena de seny* ('intelligent' woman) and *llir entre cards* ('lily among thorns'). He sought a pure, spiritual love in his poems to her but recognized the warring need for sensual love. The artist's attempt to reconcile spiritual and carnal love will always result in the triumph of the flesh. The moral problem in his poems, addressed to a dead mistress rather than a wife, is that in analysing his suffering he fears that she cannot be in Paradise, since his sin forbade her entry, and if she is in Hell, it is surely his fault. March is a writer of dramatically concentrated expressiveness, whose strength is in the intellect, rather than in the imagination. His images, commonly described in the first person, are those of a sailor endangered by storms, of a sick man on his deathbed, or of a prisoner in a cell, struggling as a moral and religious being against his avowedly *foll amor*. *Cant espiritual* (CV) is his masterpiece, written in free *estrams* to prevent the slightest formal disruption of sense by metre. A monologue foreshadowing the Hispanic tradition of 'the dark night of the soul', the poem is a confession that March fears God more than he loves Him. He longs to die without committing further sins, yet recognizes how tenuous a hope of salvation he has without sufficient love of God. March's integrity, eloquence, and precision are equal to the depth of his intellectual questioning. Formally, March usually adhered to the rules of versification drawn up by the Catalan troubadour Ramon Vidal *c.* 1200: his metres are the Provençal hendecasyllable with a caesura after the fourth syllable; and the octaves of *coblas croadas* ('crossed rhymes'), and *coblas encadenadas* ('linked rhymes').

The first edition of March was bilingual (Valencia, 1539), but the first virtually complete edition was that of Barcelona (1543). Ausias March was forgotten from 1579 to 1864, and the first critical edition by Amadée Pagès (2 vols., Barcelona) did not appear until 1912–14. Immediately recognized as the founder of Catalan poetry, March has been fully edited by P. Bohigas in Els Nostres Clàssics (5 vols., Barcelona, 1952–9) and there is an *Antologia poètica* of March's work by Joan Fuster with modern Catalan versions (Barcelona, 1959).

MARCH, JAUME (1335?–1410?), b. Barcelona? Catalan poet, the brother of Pere March and uncle of the great poet Ausias March (qq.v.). Among his most celebrated works is 'La joiosa gorda'. At the command of Pedro IV of Aragón (1336–87) he wrote a rhyming dictionary (1371). For an edition of his works, see MARCH, Pere.

MARCH, PERE (1338?–1413), b. Valencia? Catalan poet, the brother of Jaume March and father of Ausias (qq.v.). He was one of the poets who drew up the statutes of the Consistori de la Gaia Ciència in 1393. His works, including the well-known 'Al punt que hom naix, comença de morir', have been edited by Amadée Pagès in *Les coblas de Jacme, Pere i Arnau March* (Castellón de la Plana, 1934; French translation, Toulouse, 1949).

MARCH, SUSANA (1918–), b. Barcelona. Novelist and poet. Her husband is the novelist Ricardo Fernández de la Reguera (q.v.), with whom she has written the *episodios nacionales Héroes de Cuba* (Barcelona, 1962) and *Héroes de Filipinas* (Barcelona, 1963).

The most characteristic of her many novels are *Nina* (Barcelona, 1949), showing how a woman's boundless passion can survive the knowledge of her lover's weakness and even his death; and *Algo muere cada día* (Barcelona, 1955), a sensitive account of the relentless passage of time in a woman's life, told in the first person though not autobiographical.

Poemas (Santander, 1966) is an anthology of her best verse.

MARCHENA RUIZ DE CUETO, JOSÉ (1768–1821), b. Utrera. Poet, who abandoned a religious career in Spain to participate in the French Revolution, was imprisoned by Robespierre, and became secretary to Murat under Napoleon. The most extreme case of Francomania in Spanish literature, Marchena translated Montesquieu, Rousseau, Molière, and Voltaire. He forged *Fragmentum Petronii* (1802?) so brilliantly that he deceived Latin scholars until he himself revealed the hoax. His poem *A Cristo crucificado*, his best-known original work, is not to be confused with the famous anonymous sonnet usually known by that title. Marchena's *Poesías* appeared in vol. 67 (1875) of the BAE. The best edition of his works is *Obras literarias* (2 vols., Seville, 1892–6) by Menéndez y Pelayo, for whom Marchena was 'a student half crazy, with much learning and much wit, but without repose or seriousness'.

Marcos de Obregón, Relaciones de la vida del escudero (1618), a charming novel of adventure and advice by Vicente Espinel (q.v.). The work, obviously to some extent autobiographical, is often described loosely as a 'picaresque' novel (q.v.), but incorrectly, since the elderly narrator is no rogue, even if his hunger and poverty would have tempted a lesser man to become one.

Obregón's first masters are the irritable Dr. Sagredo, and his flirtatious wife, whom he cleverly manages to extricate from a compromising situation with a hairdresser; he then neatly avoids taking a post as tutor to two children whose noble father intends to save money by giving them as little food as possible. He then finds an old friend, now a hermit, who asks for an account of Obregón's life since they last met. Obregón recounts his travels in the Basque country, Saragossa, Valladolid, Madrid, and Seville. He describes his adventures when captured by Barbary corsairs and transported to Algiers, and when he became a slave to a Valencian renegade and subsequently obtained his freedom, travelling through Italy before sailing from Genoa to Barcelona.

Espinel's novel is leisurely in style, well-constructed, and elegantly written, the hero-narrator being more often spectator than actor. The heavy debt of Lesage (q.v.) to *Marcos de Obregón* in his own *Gil Blas de Santillane* (q.v., 1715–35) caused a furious polemic which enhanced the reputation of Espinel's fine novel above the excellent poetry for which he had been best known in his lifetime.

The best edition is that by Samuel Gili Gaya in Clásicos Castellanos (2 vols., 1959–60).

See G. Haley, *Vicente Espinel and 'Marcos de Obregón': a life and its literary representation* (Providence, R.I., 1959).

MARECHAL, LEOPOLDO (1900–70), b. Buenos Aires. Argentinian poet, novelist, essayist, and playwright. An *ultraísta* member of the *Proa* and *Martín Fierro* (qq.v.) circles, Marechal occupied high government posts in education and culture. He was one of the few intellectuals to collaborate with President Perón, repudiating his earlier socialist ideals for Roman Catholicism and nationalism. His poetry falls into two phases: that of *Los aguiluchos* (1922), *Días como flechas* (1926), and *Odas para el hombre y la mujer* (1929), characterized by a plethora of metaphor, sensuality of imagery, and verbal dexterity; and that of the later books. *Cinco poemas australes* (1937) reverts to the spiritual homeland of beauty and truth of the *Odas*, but with *Laberinto de amor* (1936) Marchal turns inward, in search of the self, in the alexandrines which Bernárdez considered 'los más originales y más ricos del idioma'. The strengthening of Marechal's exploration of the Platonic-Augustinian tradition continues in *El Centauro* and *Sonetos a Sophía* (1940) and concludes with *El viaje de la primavera* (1945). *Descenso y ascenso del alma por la belleza* (1939) is the credo which explicates these. His latest anthology is *Antología poética* (ed. Alfredo Andrés, 1969).

Marechal began to explore the novel in a stream-of-consciousness work, *Adán Buenosayres* (1948), which owes much to the *Ulysses* of James Joyce, and reaches much the same élitist public. His subsequent fiction has been equally experimental: *El banquete de Severo Arcángelo* (1965), more of a Socratic dialogue than a plot-confined novel, *Heptamerón* (1966), and *Megáfono o la guerra* (1970). His contribution to the metaphysical or philosophical novel is likely to be seen as increasingly important.

See Rafael F. Squirru, *Leopoldo Marechal* (1961); *Las claves de Adán Buenosayres* (Mendoza, 1966), with articles by J. Cortázar, A. Prieto, and G. de Sola; Alfredo Andrés, *Palabras con Leopoldo Marechal* (1968); and Elbia Rosbaco Marechal, *Mi vida con Leopoldo Marechal* (1973).

Margarita la Tornera, Leyenda de, a Marian legend used by Alfonso X in a charming *cantiga de Santa María* numbered XCIV in the Colección Austral *Antología* (1941) of A. G. Solalinde.

The nun Margarita has run away with her lover after delivering the treasury keys to the Altar of the Virgin and begging Her divine protection. The Blessed Virgin Mary takes her form in her absence and when the repentant nun returns to the convent, having had children, she finds that miraculously she had not been missed since the Virgin has accomplished all her tasks unrecognized. The nun explains what has happened, and the nuns acclaim the miracle. The legend was subsequently used by Lope de Vega (in *La buena guarda*), 'Avellaneda' (in the apocryphal *Quijote*), Vélez de Guevara (in the *auto sacramental La abadesa del cielo*), and Zorrilla (in the poem *Margarita la tornera*).

See A. Cotarelo, *Una cantiga célebre del Rey Sabio* (1904).

María (1867), a Romantic novel by Jorge Isaacs (q.v.) reputed to be the finest of its period produced in Latin America.

Isaacs, a Colombian whose childhood home was in the Cauca valley in the Cordillera Central, first wrote the semi-autobiographical *María* as a play, but converted it into prose narrative at the suggestion of José María Vergara y Vergara.

María is a young orphan who lives in the interior with her distant relatives. Efraín, the son of the family, returns from six years' study in Bogotá and falls in love with the young woman, who returns this idyllic passion. But Efraín is due to complete his studies in England, and María, sensing that she will inherit her mother's epileptic tendencies, fears—correctly—that she will die before they meet again. The cloying sweetness of some passages is redeemed by eloquent descriptions of nature (the real subject of the novel), of the *mulata* Salomé, shallow but delightful, and the account of Efraín's journey.

Critics have traced the theme back to the *Atala* (1801) of Chateaubriand (set in an idealized America like the Colombian setting in Isaacs) and the *Paul et Virginie* (1787) of Jacques-Henri Bernardin de Saint-Pierre. Again, María does in a sense die of love (though Efraín does not die at all) as well as through natural causes. The principal French inspiration is probably Rousseau, since Isaacs always admired the notion of the noble savage, and yearned in the middle of civil wars for a stable, feudal society. His European characters are predictable, and his Indians are hollow, since they think, speak and act like the Europeans. The social message is that adolescent passions must be sacrificed to adult virtues such as responsibility and learning. Efraín returns to reinforce the civilizing mission of the wealthy Christian landowner.

The impact of *María* on the reading public is reflected in the flow of imitations: *Carmen* (1882) by Pedro Castera, *Marianita* (1885) by Vicente Grez, and many more. *María* was translated into English by R. Ogden in 1890.

See the edition in Isaacs's *Obras completas* (Medellín, 1966–); and G. Arciniegas, *Genio y figura de J. Isaacs* (Buenos Aires, 1968).

MARÍA CORONEL DE JESÚS DE ÁGREDA, *Sor*, see ÁGREDA, *Sor* María Coronel de Jesús de.

MARIANA, JUAN DE (1535?–1624), b. Talavera de la Reina. Historian. A Jesuit, Mariana trained for his novitiate under Francisco Borja at Simancas, studied at the University of Alcalá, was ordained in 1561, and appointed professor of theology in Rome. Having taught also in Loreto, Sicily, Paris, and the Low Countries, he returned to Spain and from 1574 lived in Toledo.

His *Historiae de rebus Hispaniae libri XX* (Toledo, 1592) was completed to the full thirty books in the Mainz edition of 1605, by which time his own Castilian version had appeared (2 vols., Toledo, 1601). It made available to Spaniards and (through the Latin original) to the rest of educated Europe, a compendium of Spanish legend and history to the death of

Ferdinand which constituted the main source for many generations. Ticknor has aptly called it 'the most remarkable union of picturesque chronicling with sober history that the world has ever seen', but its 'picturesque' quality led to a detailed list of errors being published by Pedro Mantuano (q.v.) as an attack on the whole book and its author, defended against Mantuano by Mariana's friend Tomás Tamayo de Vargas.

De rege et regis institutione (Toledo, 1599) was construed, rather harshly, as a denial of the divine right of kings. A Spanish translation *Del rey y de la institución de la dignidad real* (1845) was reissued (2 vols.) in 1961.

Tractatus septem (Cologne, 1609), another controversial work, attacked bureaucracy, corruption, and the debasement of the currency in *De monetae mutatione*, and questioned the supposed travels to Spain of St. James in *De adventu Jacobi apostoli in Hispania*; the other essays were *De spectaculis*, *Pro editione Vulgatae*, *De morte et inmortalitate*, *De die mortis Christi*, and *De annis arabum*. Mariana's other known published work is *De ponderibus et mensuris* (Toledo, 1599).

See A. Pasa, *Un grande teorico della politica nella Spagna del secolo XVI: il gesuito Giovanni Mariana* (Naples, 1939); G. Cirot, *Mariana historien* (Bordeaux, 1940); and M. Ballesteros Gaibrois, *El P. Juan de Mariana* (Barcelona, 1944).

Marianela (1878), one of the *Novelas españolas de la primera época* (q.v.) by Benito Pérez Galdós (q.v.).

An unhappy love idyll markedly different from the complex *Doña Perfecta* (q.v.) which preceded it and *La familia de León Roch* (q.v.) which followed.

Marianela ('Nela') is a hideous maidservant to Pablo, a rich youth blind from birth, accompanying him everywhere and describing to him the world's forms and colours in all their beauty. Pablo believes her outward appearance is as lovely as her gentle, affectionate spirit and proclaims her beauty to all who know him. They charitably do not disabuse him.

Doctor Golfín (who reappears in *La de Bringas*, q.v.) arrives in the small town announcing that he can cure blindness, treats Pablo, and after many days declares that soon he will be able to remove the bandages and that Pablo's sight will be restored. Marianela, fearing a horrified reaction from Pablo when he sees her deformation, flees. During her long absence, Pablo falls in love with his cousin Florentina, who one day finds Nela seriously ill from exposure and malnutrition and brings her home without telling Pablo.

One day Pablo visits Florentina in her room, without seeing either Nela or the doctor, and speaks ardently to Florentina. He then notices the other occupants of the room. His recognition of Nela, and her death, are among the most effective passages in Galdós, since his sentimentality even in this situation is never mawkish.

The novel's theme is the clash between progress and science (personified by Dr Golfín, a positivist in Comtean terms); logical thought bereft of a knowledge of reality (personified by Pablo Penáguila, a metaphysician in Comtean terms); and fantasy or illusion (personified by Marianela, representing the theological stage of Comte). Casalduero, in *Vida y obra de Galdós* (2nd edn., pp. 196 ff.), indicates Galdós's debt here not only to Comte, whose philosophy had become popular while Galdós was writing, but also to the *Wilhelm Meister* of Goethe, in which Mignon is the counterpart of Nela.

See L. Blanco, 'Origin and history of the plot of "Marianela"' in *Hispania*, vol. 48 (1965), pp. 463–7; and E. Krebs, *Marianela y Doña Bárbara* (Bahía Blanca, 1967).

Marian Legends, a popular genre in medieval European literature, the legends of the Virgin Mary were first popularized in the Spanish vernacular by Gonzalo de Berceo (q.v.) in his *Milagros de Nuestra Señora* (q.v.), *Duelo que fizo la Virgen*, and *Loores de Nuestra Señora* in the mid-13th c.

Collections of Marian legends were formed in Latin as early as the 11th c., but their number and circulation increased rapidly between the 12th and 14th cs.

Juan Gil de Zamora's Latin prose *Liber Mariae* also appeared in the 13th c., as did Alfonso 'el Sabio's' Galician verse *Cantigas de Santa Maria*. Both were more extensive than Berceo's *Milagros* collection; all three repeat much of the legendary material.

The common sources are utilized by Spanish writers of all periods and in all genres. The legend of the monk whose mystical trance lasts three hundred years is the subject of Alfonso's *Cantiga CIII*; that of the nun who elopes with her lover but repents, only to find on her return that her absence has gone unremarked because her place had been taken by Mary, is the subject of Alfonso's *Cantiga XCIV*, Lope de Vega's play *La buena guarda*, Vélez de Guevara's *La abadesa del cielo*, and *Margarita la tornera* (q.v.) by Zorrilla.

See José A. Sánchez Pérez, *El culto mariano en España* (1944).

MARÍAS, Julián (1914–), b. Valladolid. Philosopher and essayist, who was a disciple of Ortega y Gasset (q.v.), with whom he founded the Instituto de Humanidades in 1948.

Marías has written widely on philosophical themes, including *Historia de la filosofía* (1941), *Miguel de Unamuno* (1943), *Ortega y la idea de la razón vital* (1948), *El existencialismo en España* (1953), *Idea de la metafísica* (1954), and *Circunstancia y vocación* (1960).

Obras completas (1958–71) consist of eight volumes so far. *Antropología metafísica* (1970) is generally regarded as his most original contribution.

MARIÁTEGUI, José Carlos (1895–1930), b. Moquegua. Peruvian left-wing essayist and political activist, who was self-educated but was sent to Europe on a government scholarship during the Leguía dictatorship (1919–30). In Italy he met leading socialists and in Paris befriended Henri Barbusse.

On his return to Peru in 1923 he became a key figure in Haya de la Torre's (q.v.) Alianza Popular Revolucionaria Americana (the *Apristas*) but broke away in 1928 to found the essentially Marxist Peruvian Socialist Party. Though paralysed and confined to a wheelchair, Mariátegui also founded the influential review *Amauta* (1926–30), which published the works of numerous young authors of leftist inclinations, and encouraged social-realist prose writers (César Falcón and others) and socialist poets such as César Vallejo (q.v.).

Mariátegui is the best prose stylist of his generation for clarity of exposition and economy of expression. He attempted to interpret Peruvian life and literature in terms of both the traditional Peruvian Indian communes and the imported doctrines of Marx and Engels. With the poet Vallejo he can be considered the most influential disciple of Manuel González Prada (q.v.). His first book was *La escena contemporánea* (1925), but his most durable essays are *Siete ensayos de interpretación de la realidad peruana* (1928; best edn. is the 2nd, Santiago, 1955) translated by Marjory Urquidi as *Seven interpretive [sic] essays on Peruvian reality* (Austin, Texas, 1971). A useful anthology of Mariátegui's works is that by Benjamin Carrión (Mexico City, 1966) and there is a recent bibliography (1968) by G. Rouillon.

See G. Carnero Checa, *La acción escrita: José Carlos Mariátegui, periodista* (1964); D. Mesegner Illán, *José Carlos Mariátegui y su pensamiento revolucionario* (1974); and H. Aguirre Gramio, *Mariátegui: destino polémico* (1975).

MARÍN, Juan (1900–63), b. Talca. Chilean novelist and short-story writer. After two collections of verse deriving from Huidobro (q.v.), *Looping* (1929) and *Aquarium* (1934), Marín turned to the novel, using his experiences as a doctor in the Chilean Navy and his interest in aviation as raw material for *Un avión volaba...* (1935) and *Paralelo 53 sur* (1936), the latter a convincing account of lawlessness in the remote south. He left the Navy in 1939, having published three more novels, *El secreto del Dr. Baloux* (1936), *Orestes y yo* (1938), and *Alas sobre el mar* (1939). He joined the diplomatic service, with periods in China, El Salvador, Egypt, Syria, Lebanon, and India and during these years wrote essays and travel books. Labour unrest in Chile provided the theme for the novel *Viento negro* (1944). His last novel was *Muerte en Shanghai* (Madrid, 1953).

Marín published two volumes of short stories: *Cuentos de viento y mar* (1949), which included some fantasies; and *Naufragio y otros cuentos* (1953).

See Marilyn L. Terry, *The prose fiction of Juan Marín* (Knoxville, Tenn., 1964).

MARÍN CAÑAS, José (1904–), b. San José, of Spanish parents. Costa Rican novelist, playwright, and essayist. His four novels are *Lágrimas de acero* (Madrid, 1929), the fashionable anti-novel *Tú, la imposible: memorias de un hombre triste* (Madrid, 1931); a savage novel on the Chaco War, *Infierno verde* (Madrid, 1935); and his most mature book, *Pedro Arnáez* (1942). Marín Cañas is by nature a pessimist, preoccupied by the impotence of man facing death, materialism, and economic inequality. His play *Como tú* appeared in 1929, and he wrote a penetrating essay on 'la realidad española' entitled *Pueblo macho* (1937).

MARINELLO, Juan (1898–), Cuban poet and essayist. The author of the exceptional study *José Martí* (Mexico City, 1958), Marinello is a disciple of Martí in his clarity and enthusiasm for Cuba and social justice. Among his many books are *Americanismo y cubanismo literarios* (1932), *Poética: ensayos en entusiasmo* (Mexico City, 1933), *Literatura hispanoamericana, hombres, meditaciones* (Mexico City, 1937), *Sobre el modernismo* (Mexico City, 1959), and *Meditaciones americanas* (Santa Clara, 1963).

Marinero en tierra (1925), the first book of poems by Rafael Alberti (q.v.), which won the Premio Nacional de Literatura of 1924 while still in MS. and brought Alberti instant recognition as a poet of outstanding promise. It was written in and near Madrid while Alberti was in poor health and recollected the boats and sea of Cádiz bay. His nostalgia for the sea is a lament for his carefree youth. The book is full of pleasing imagery and nonsense rhymes.

See S. Salinas de Marechal, *El mundo poético de Rafael Alberti* (1968).

Mariona Rebull (1944), the first novel in the sequence *La ceniza fue árbol* by Ignacio Agustí (qq.v.).

MARLONES, García de, the anagrammatic pen-name used by Baltasar Gracián y Morales (q.v.) in part 1 of *El criticón* (q.v.).

MARMOL, José Pedro Crisólogo (1817–71), b. Buenos Aires. Argentinian novelist, Romantic poet, and dramatist, whose first verses 'Entre cadenas convertir inerte / la primavera de mi triste vida' were written on the walls of a gaol in which he was imprisoned during the Rosas dictatorship. He took opposition to Rosas as his literary theme and in the security of Montevideo wrote in the manner of Byron his *Cantos del peregrino* (complete edn., 1917, latest edn. by E. Brulando de Meyer, 1965), a verse travelogue. Of the twelve Cantos planned, only nos. 1–6, 11 and 12 have come down to us complete, though several more were at least sketched out. They appeared between 1847 and 1857, with a posthumous edition in 1889. Mármol's later verse was published in *Armonías* (1851); he wrote no poetry after 1852. His play *El poeta* (1842) ran for three nights, and *El cruzado* (1851) did not survive the first. Mármol is remembered for his Romantic novel *Amalia* (Barcelona, 1851, latest edn., 1960), which introduced historical fiction into Argentina, and ranks with Jorge Isaacs's *María* (q.v.) as one of the capital works of Argentina in the 19th c. The book is both political and autobiographical and, though its melodrama is overdone, gives a vivid though hastily written picture of life in Mármol's society. When Rosas was overthrown Mármol returned to Buenos Aires and was (1858–71) Director of the Public Library in the city. Rafael Alberto Arrieta edited Mármol's *Poesías completas* (2 vols., 1946–7).

See Stuart Cuthbertson, *The poetry of José Mármol* (*University of Colorado Studies*, vol. 22, nos. 2–3, 1935) and A. Blasi Brambilla, *José Mármol y la sombra de Rosas* (1970).

MÁRMOL CARVAJAL, Luis (1520?–1600), b. Granada. Historian. Mármol took part in the expedition to Tunis (1535) and remained in Africa for twenty-two years, for part of the period a captive. Familiar with Islam and its culture from birth, he was an ideal writer for the two subjects he dealt with in *Descripción general del África, sus guerras y vicisitudes desde la fundación del Mahometismo hasta el año 1561* (3 vols., Granada, 1573–1599) and *Historia del rebelión y castigo de los moriscos del Reyno de Granada* (Málaga, 1600). The latter, an official rejoinder to the version of events given by Diego Hurtado de Mendoza (q.v.) and reprinted in vol. 21 (1952) of the

BAE, was praised by Menéndez y Pelayo but is much less vivid than the histories of Hurtado or Pérez de Hita (q.v.).

MAROFF, Tristán, pseudonym of Gustavo A. Navarro (q.v.).

MARQUÉS, René (1919–), Puerto Rican short-story writer, playwright, and critic. His richly expressive and often poetic stories are imbued with Sartrean existentialism, as in 'El miedo' and 'La muerte' in *Otro día nuestro* (1955), and in *En una ciudad llamada San Juan* (1960).

His first play was *El sol y los MacDonald* (1957, first performed 1950), in which a patrician family of the American South moves towards its doom, a theme drawn from O'Neill and ultimately from Greek tragedy. His most important play so far is 'La carreta', published in *Asomante* (1951–2) in which a peasant family from the Puerto Rican hills is forced by hunger to seek its fortune in the city slums of San Juan and is drawn thence irresistibly to New York, where the Fates continue to pursue them; later, they find readaptation difficult on returning home. A strength of Marqués lies in his ability to convey realism by slang and dialect. His symbolism becomes rather too oppressive in later plays: in *La muerte no entrará en palacio* (1957) a patriotic heroine represents the exploited mother country ruined by foreign greed—a comment on the relationship between Puerto Rico and the U.S.A.; in *Un niño azul para esa sombra* (1958) the theme of political ideals and betrayal is somewhat aridly and schematically worked out; and in *Los soles truncos* (1958) a Chekhovian house decays to symbolize the decay of a social order.

Marqués has shown great aptitude for absorbing European and United States influences into the Puerto Rican context. His plays have been published as *Teatro* (Mexico City, 1959) and his literary manifesto can be read in 'Mensaje de un puertorriqueño a los escritores y artistas del Perú' in *Cuadernos Americanos*, vol. 6 (1955).

MÁRQUEZ, Fray Juan (1565–1621), b. Madrid. Augustinian ascetic writer and preacher. Appointed court preacher in 1616, Márquez was praised by Tirso de Molina, Lope de Vega, and Juan de Mariana, among others, for his elegant prose style. *Los dos estados de la espiritual Hierusalem, sobre los salmos CXXV y CXXXVI* (Medina, 1603), which includes his harmonious verse paraphrases, is less highly regarded than *El Governador Cristiano deducido de las vidas de Moysén, y Iosué, Príncipes del pueblo de Dios* (Salamanca, 1612), a refutation of Machiavelli's *Principe* commissioned by the

Duke of Feria, and popular enough to be translated into both Italian and French.

Márquez's other publications include *Origen de los frailes ermitaños de la Orden de San Agustín* (Salamanca, 1618) and *Vida del Venerable P. Fr. Alonso de Orozco* (1648).

See M. Iracheta, *Antología del P. Juan Márquez* (1948), with a good study of Márquez.

MARQUINA, EDUARDO (1879–1946), b. Barcelona. Catalan playwright and modernist poet who wrote in Castilian. His early poems, such as *Odas* (1900) and *Las vendimias* (1901), are distinguished by formal excellence. In *Canciones del momento* (1910) and *Tierras de España* (1914) Marquina accepts the '98 view of the deterioration of Spain and the Spanish. As a novelist, in *La caravana* (1907), *Almas anónimas* (1908), and *Maternidad* (1917), he is of less account.

It is as a playwright that he is remembered, for the dramatization of popular legends: *Las hijas del Cid* (1908) and *Doña María la Brava* (1909), followed by *En Flandes se ha puesto el sol* (1910), *Alondra* (1918), *La extraña* (1921), and *Teresa de Jesús* (1938). His valuable autobiography is included in the 8-vol. *Obras completas* (1944).

See José Montero Alonso, *Vida de Eduardo Marquina* (1965).

Marranos, Jewish converts to Christianity, see CONVERSOS and INQUISITION, SPANISH.

MARRERO ARISTY, RAMÓN (1913–). Novelist and short-story writer of the Dominican Republic. His short stories in *Balsié* (1938) concerned the rights of the oppressed lower classes and were composed laboriously, with realism and indignation making up for a certain bluntness in imagination. *Over* (1939) is a novel against the exploitation of sugar-cane workers, specifically that of Daniel Comprés by his American manager who is eventually dismissed for extortion. Marrero's fury at injustice is more tightly controlled in this book.

MARROQUÍN, JOSÉ MANUEL (1827–1908), b. Bogotá. Colombian short-story writer and novelist, for a while President of Colombia. His *Blas Gil* (1896), as its Lesage-like title suggests, is a picaresque novel, but Marroquín is above all a writer of *cuadros de costumbres*, such as 'El azote de Bogotá' or 'Las bodas de Camacho', the best collection being *Nada nuevo* (1894). He was a man of austerity and solemnity whose writings are full of vivacity and wit. The best key to the man and writer is the portrait by his son, José Manuel Marroquín Osorio, *Don José Manuel Marroquín, íntimo* (1915).

See also José Joaquín Casas, *Semblanzas: Diego Fallón y José Manuel Marroquín* (1936).

MARSÉ, JUAN (1933–), b. Barcelona. Novelist. He left school at 13 to become an apprentice at a metal workshop. Marsé lived in Paris from 1960 to 1962 and has also been to Cuba and Italy.

His novels are *Encerrados con un solo juguete* (Barcelona, 1959); *Esta cara de la luna* (Barcelona, 1962); *Últimas tardes con Teresa* (Barcelona, 1966), winner of the Premio Biblioteca Breve; and *Se te dicen que caí* (Barcelona, 1973).

Marta y María (Barcelona, 1883), the first significant novel of Armando Palacio Valdés (q.v.).

In a prologue, the author exculpates himself from the predictable charge that he attacks true mysticism or the contemplative life. 'Although I think', he writes, 'that the essence of Christianity is charity and a consequently active life, I understand that even charity is powerless to beatify us without the loving and mystic union of our spirit with that of the Creator'. He compares Cervantes' attack on those who take heroism to absurd extremes with his novel's attack on exalted mystics whose primary motives he believes to be vanity and egotism. In María de Elorza he portrays a younger and more beautiful Doña Perfecta (q.v.) whose morbid religiosity sterilizes her normal affections for fiancé and family. Her Carlist sympathies are shown to be equally harmful.

Marta, by contrast, represents a simpler, less selfish, and more truly Christian attitude to life. Palacio Valdés implicitly reverses Christ's judgment on Martha and Mary. *Marta y María* is one of many Spanish 19th-c. novels which take as their main theme a consideration of what is to be understood by 'true' Christianity.

This serious and important national theme is undermined by Palacio Valdés's treatment, with an artificially happy ending lacking the intellectual rigour which made the works on similar subjects by Galdós so much more rewarding.

Marta y María is available in Colección Austral (1940).

MARTEL, JULIÁN, pseudonym of José María Miró (q.v.).

MARTÍ, JOSÉ (1853–95), b. Havana. Cuban patriot. His secondary education, at the Escuela Superior Municipal de Varones, led him into contact with its headmaster, the separatist Rafael María Mendive. Martí was first identified as a rebel when his correspondence with Fermín Valdés was discovered, and in 1871 he was deported to Spain. After studying in Spain and teaching in Guatemala, Martí was allowed to return on the Peace of Zanjón (1878) but his subversive efforts led to his second expulsion to Spain (1879). He escaped to the U.S.A. and continued to plan for the revolution against Spain. After the landings of March 1895, he was acclaimed supreme leader of the revolution, but was killed shortly afterwards.

As a poet, he is outstanding for *Ismaelillo* (1882), *Versos libres* (1878–82), *La edad de oro* (1889), and *Versos sencillos* (1891), having himself virtually repudiated the rest. The first book is a father's affectionate verses to his son, but is more important as a demonstration of the sincerity and simplicity Martí felt to be lacking in contemporary Spanish poetry. His best verses, however, are those of *Versos sencillos* whose themes are nature and the drama of human life, notably his own.

Martí is a prose-writer as persuasive as he is enthusiastic in journals such as *Revista Venezolana*, the Caracas *La Opinión Nacional*, and *La Nación* of Buenos Aires. His writings are refreshingly free from the clichés of nationalism, and many of his prophecies about integration and independence have proved correct.

The best edition of his *Obras completas* (1963–5) is in 25 vols.

See Carlos Ripoll, *Índice universal de la obra de José Martí* (New York, 1972); *Vida y pensamiento de Martí* (Homage from the city of Havana) (2 vols., 1942); the 871-page *Memoria del Congreso de Escritores Martianos* (1953); Juan Marinello, *José Martí: escritor americano* (Mexico City, 1958); and Carlos Márquez Sterling, *Martí: ciudadano de América* (New York, 1965).

MARTÍ, JUAN JOSÉ (1570?–1604), thought to be the Valencia-born lawyer and author of the spurious continuation of Mateo Alemán's *Guzmán de Alfarache* (qq.v.), published in Valencia (1602) under the pseudonym of Mateo Luján de Sayavedra.

MARTIALIS (known as MARTIAL), MARCUS VALERIUS (*c.* 40–*c.* 102), b. Bilbilis, Hispania Tarraconensis, near the modern Catalayud. Epigrammatist. He lived in Rome from 64–99 and finally returned to Spain. Of his 1500-odd epigrams, possibly the most celebrated is 'Non amo te, Sabidi, nec possum dicere quare: hoc tantum possum dicere, non amo te'. Thomas Brown (1663–1704) based on it his 'I do not love you, Dr. Fell'.

Martial's fifteen books of epigrams constitute a sardonic though not necessarily misanthropic commentary on men and manners of the day. Peter Porter's *After Martial* (London, 1972) contains the most accurately pungent of modern English adaptations.

Martial's influence on Spanish literature can be traced to the writings of Gracián, Baltasar del Alcázar, Ruiz de Alarcón, Ramón de la Cruz, Forner, Iglesias, and Jérica (qq.v.).

Martín, Abel, an 'apocryphal professor' created by Antonio Machado y Ruiz (q.v.) of whom another 'apocryphal professor', Juan de Mairena (q.v.) wrote a biography. According to Machado Abel Martín was born in Seville in 1840 and died in Madrid in 1898. He left a collection of poems, *Los complementarios* (1884) and important books of philosophy: *Las cinco formas de la objetividad, De lo uno a lo otro, Lo universal cualitativo, De la esencial heterogeneidad del ser*.

MARTÍN, TORIBIO, see FERNÁNDEZ DE RIBERA, Rodrigo.

MARTÍN DE BRAGA, *San* (515–580), b. Hungary. Religious and ethical writer. After a period as a monk in Palestine, Martín travelled to the Suevic kingdom now divided between Portugal and Galicia and founded the monastery of Dumio some time after 550. About 570 he was named bishop of Braga. He wrote in simple but correct Latin, and has been described as a Senecan in philosophy, though his Christian attitudes naturally distinguish his writings from those of Seneca and he is better seen as a precursor of S. Isidoro. His works, to be found in vol. 72 of Migne's *Patrologia latina*, include an important compendium of ethical writings composed before 583, *Formula vitae honestae*, with a Platonic basis; *Pro repelenda iactantia*; and *De superbia*.

See C. P. Caspari, *De correctione rusticorum* (Oslo, 1883), for an exhaustive study of the saint.

MARTÍNEZ, LUIS A. (1869–1909), b. Ambato. Ecuadorian novelist. After farming in the coastal belt and writing *La agricultura ecuatoriana* (Ambato, 1903) and *Catecismo de agricultura* (1905), Martínez became an effective Minister of Education. *A la costa: costumbres ecuatorianas* (1904) is a thoughtful thesis novel, which uses Martínez's practical farming experience and work among the poor to attack 'useless' studies (such as the law and the Church) in a powerfully naturalist style. The novel made a great impact with its denigration of the Quito 'idle rich' and praise of the hardworking rural class.

See Augusto Arias, *Luis A. Martínez* (1937).

MARTÍNEZ BALLESTEROS, ANTONIO (1929–   ), b. Toledo. Self-educated *avant-garde* playwright and amateur director. Employed as a Civil Service clerk, he has had ample opportunity to see the workings of the lower reaches of government from the inside but, because of censorship, has placed his disturbing allegories in unnamed countries and makes no overt propaganda. George Wellwarth has written, 'Martínez's pessimism recognizes that a play in which good triumphs over evil is a fantasy, and that a play in which evil triumphs over good is a documentary, and that his plays are documentaries of the political plight of today's world'.

Orestiada 39 (1960) narrates the *Oresteia* in terms of the Spanish Civil War, and concentrates on political allegory. *Los mendigos* (1961) foreshadows Ballesteros' main thematic preoccupation: the faceless and mindless tyranny of bureaucracy over the spirit of the individual, and the death of verbal meanings in totalitarian society, a theme pursued in *En el país de jauja* (1962; translated by H. Salerno and S. Gross as 'The best of all possible worlds' in Wellwarth, *The new wave Spanish drama*, New York, 1970); *El pensamiento circular* (1963); *Las gafas negras del Señor Blanco* (1966), which is a modern morality play; *El camaleón*, another searching examination of the question of personal integrity like the excellent *El héroe* (1965; also in the Wellwarth anthology); three collections of one-act plays: *Farsas contemporáneas* (1969), including 'La opinión', 'Los esclavos', 'Los opositores' and 'El hombre vegetal'; *Retablo en tiempo presente* (1969–70), consisting of 'La colocación', 'La distancia', and 'El soplo', and *Las estampas* (1971), consisting of 'El superviviente', 'Los secuestros', 'Las bicicletas', and 'El orden chino'.

See George E. Wellwarth, *Spanish underground drama* (University Park, Pa., 1972), pp. 38–50.

MARTÍNEZ DE LA ROSA, Francisco (1787–1862), b. Granada. Playwright and politician. In 1805 he was appointed professor of philosophy at Granada University and was a deputy on the extreme liberal wing of the Cortes in 1813, suffering exile for his beliefs 1814–20, returning with more moderate convictions as Minister of State 1820–3, and suffering exile again in France 1823–31. He returned to Spain in 1831 and on the death of Fernando VII in 1833 rose to his former eminence in politics, becoming Prime Minister in 1834, the year in which his best play, *La conjuración de Venecia*, was produced in Madrid.

Though Martínez de la Rosa is unquestionably the founder of Spanish Romantic drama, his early plays showed no trace of the Romantic manner. *La viuda de Padilla* (1812) imitated Alfieri; *Morayma* (1818) is a neoclassical play of scant appeal; *Edipo* (1829) is a pale reflection of Sophocles; and his comedies continue the

tradition of Moratín: *Lo que puede un empleo* (1820), an anti-clerical satire; and the amusing comedy of manners *La niña en la casa y la madre en la máscara* (1821).

While a political refugee in France he fell under the spell of Victor Hugo's Romantic plays, and wrote the first imitation by a Spaniard: *Aben Humeya, ou la révolte des maures sous Philippe II*, first performed with great acclaim in Paris in 1830 and translated by himself for the Paris bilingual edition in the same year. The play was attacked as of no merit by Larra when it reached Madrid in 1836, but by then Martínez de la Rosa had already produced there *La conjuración de Venecia. Año de 1310* (first performed in Paris, 1830; Madrid, 1834), several months before Larra's *Macías* and a year before *Don Álvaro* by the Duque de Rivas (qq.v.). The sources of this play include Sanudo's *Le vite dei Dogi* and Daru's *Histoire de la république de Venise*, but the style is vividly Romantic in its passionate dialogue, on-stage violence, extreme ideals, ebullient crowd scenes noisy with music and dances, rapid changes of fortune caused by mistaken identity, historical and local colour, intrigue and hopeless love. The play is well constructed and comes to an awesome climax.

In addition to these historical plays, Martínez de la Rosa completed a poor novel in the manner of Scott, *Doña Isabel de Solís, Reyna de Granada* (in parts, 1837–46); a biography, *Hernán Pérez del Pulgar él de las hazañas* (1834); an elegant version of Horace's *Epistola ad Pisones* (1819); and an *Arte poética*, modelled on Boileau, which denigrated Lope, Calderón, and Tirso and is to be found in his *Obras literarias* (5 vols., Paris, 1827–30). It has been studied by J. F. Shearer in *The 'Poética' and 'Apéndices' of Martínez de la Rosa* (Princeton, 1941).

His *Obras completas* (5 vols., Paris, 1844–54) has now been superseded by C. Seco Serrano's edition of the *Obras* (8 vols., 1962–3) in the BAE.

The most convenient edition of his best work is J. Sarrailh's: *La viuda de Padilla, Aben Humeya, La conjuración de Venecia* (1933) in Clásicos Castellanos.

Biographies of Martínez de la Rosa have been written by M. Martínez de la Riva (1915), L. de Sosa (1930), and J. Sarrailh, whose *Un homme d'état espagnol* (Bordeaux, 1930) is at once the most authoritative and the most substantial.

MARTÍNEZ DE MENESES, Antonio (1608–1662?), b. Toledo. Playwright of the Calderonian school and poet. Hardly anything of his life is recorded. Much of his work was written in collaboration, such as *La renegada de Valladolid*, a romantic story of a woman who rejects her faith, to regain it at the end, composed with Belmonte and Moreto (qq.v.).

His best play is *Los Esforcias de Milán*, a powerful palace intrigue in which a duchess is disguised as a peasant-girl, and a peasant-boy is heir to the throne of Milan. *El tercero en su afrenta* appears in vol. 47 (1858) of the BAE, and many others in the 17th-c. Colección General de Comedias Escogidas. These include *Juez y reo de su causa*; *El mejor alcalde el rey* (recast like many of his plays from earlier classics); *La campaña de Aragón*; *Amar sin ver*; and *Pedir justicia al culpado*.

MARTÍNEZ DE NAVARRETE, *Fray* MANUEL (1768–1809), b. Zamora, Michoacán. Mexican poet who taught Latin and founded the *Diario de Méjico* (1805), where he published his neoclassical verse on nature and human love influenced by Juan Meléndez Valdés and (in *Noches tristes* and *Ratos tristes*) by Edward Young's *Night thoughts* (1742–5).

Navarrete was a member of the academy called the Arcadia Mexicana, whose members borrowed the names of shepherds as in the anacreontics of Meléndez Valdés (q.v.). Navarrete wrote *Las flores de Clorila* and other works in this style, but is probably at his most effective in the solemn *Poema eucarístico de la Divina Providencia*, in the manner of Fray Luis de León (q.v.).

His works were collected as *Entretenimientos poéticos* (2 vols., 1823, reprinted Paris, 1935) and Carlos María de Bustamante published some of his *Poemas inéditos* in 1929. Francisco Monterde's edition of Navarrete's *Poesías profanas* appeared in 1939.

MARTÍNEZ DE TOLEDO, ALFONSO (1398–? after 1482?), known as 'el Arcipreste de Talavera', b. Toledo. In 1448 he was prebendary of the Cathedral of Toledo. He wrote *Vidas de San Ildefonso y San Isidoro*, and a historical work, the *Atalaya de las crónicas*. But his fame rests on the book conventionally known as the *Corvacho* (or *Corbacho*) despite the author's injunction that it should be called *El Arcipreste de Talavera*. The book, subtitled *Reprobación del amor mundano*, was written in 1438, when Martínez was Chaplain to John II. It is an attack on lust and is divided into four parts, unequal in length and importance. The first is a treatise against worldly love and the second a lively satire against women; the third and fourth contain much contemporary lore on astrology and the humours of men. The *Corvacho* was influenced not by Boccaccio, as the title might indicate, but by French *fabliaux* and the *Llibre de les dones* by the Catalan Francesc Eiximenis (q.v.), a book popular in Barcelona when Martínez was there. Other sources include

the third book of the *De amore* of Andreas Capellanus. The style of *El corvacho* is an intriguing mixture of Latinized and colloquial speech: the former typical of the 15th c.; the latter, looking ahead to the *Celestina* (q.v.), was a device perhaps taken from the practice of introducing vivid popular speech in sermons in order to hold the attention of the congregation.

MARTÍNEZ ESTRADA, EZEQUIEL (1895–1964), b. San José de la Estrada, Santa Fe. Argentinian poet and essayist. His cerebral, allusive poetry engages in 'gymnastics of the dictionary' in opposition to the prevailing violence and popularism of his contemporaries, among them Lugones (q.v.). His hermetic books include *Oro y piedra* (1918), *Nefelibal* (1922), *Motivos del cielo* (1924), *Argentina* (1927), and *Humoresca* (1929), praised by Borges as the work of 'nuestro mejor poeta contemporáneo'.

Martínez Estrada obtained wide recognition as a writer of pessimistic prose analyses of the pampas and the capital: *Radiografía de la pampa* (1933) and *La cabeza de Goliat: microscopía de Buenos Aires* (1940), distinguished by bold metaphors and a view anything but narrow.

Though less known, his fiction is significant, including *La inundación* (1943); *Tres cuentos sin amor* (1956); the short novels *Marta Riquelme* and *Examen sin conciencia* (both 1956), the first on a woman half-angel and half-devil, and the second an ironic tale of quacks and their gullible patients; and *Sábado de gloria* and *Juan Florido* (also both 1956), the first autobiographical and the second a macabre tale of sly humour.

Martínez Estrada produced some experimental drama which has been severely criticized for its lack of theatricality: *Títeres de pies ligeros* (1929), in verse; and *Tres dramas* (1957), comprising *Lo que no vemos morir* (1941), *Sombras* (first published 1941), and *Cazadores*.

Of his literary criticism, perhaps the outstanding examples are the text, commentary, and introduction *Muerte y transfiguración del Martín Fierro* (Mexico City, 2 vols., 1948; 2nd edn., 1958), *El mundo maravilloso de Guillermo Enrique Hudson* (Mexico City, 1951), *La poesía afrocubana de Nicolás Guillén* (Montevideo, 1966), *En torno a Kafka y otros ensayos* (Barcelona, 1967), *Martí revolucionario* (Havana, 1967), *Para una revisión de las letras argentinas* (1967), *Leopoldo Lugones* (1968), *Meditaciones sarmientinas* (Santiago de Chile, 1968), and *Leer y escribir* (Mexico City, 1969).

The most comprehensive bibliography to date is by Carlos Adam: *Bibliografía y documentos de Ezequiel Martínez Estrada* (La Plata, 1968).

See *Homenaje a Ezequiel Martínez Estrada* (Bahía Blanca, 1968); Peter G. Earle, *Prophet in the wilderness: the works of Ezequiel Martínez*

Estrada (Austin, Texas, 1971); and Astur Morsella, *Martínez Estrada* (1973).

MÁRTINEZ MORENO, CARLOS (1917–   ), Uruguayan novelist and short-story writer. His short stories have been collected in *Los días por vivir* (1960), *Cordelia* (1961), and *Los aborígenes* (1964). The title story of the last volume concerns a Latin-American ambassador in Rome who is writing on the primitive peoples of his own country, and his shrewd Italian chauffeur who bewilderingly exemplifies, in the cradle of Mediterranean civilization, the very traits that the ambassador had noted as characteristic of the 'aborigines'.

His best work is the novel *El paredón* (Barcelona, 1963), whose hero Julio Calodoro is faced with the discoveries (in 1958) that the Conservative Party of the *blancos* has lost power in Uruguay for the first time in 93 years, and that his father is suffering from cancer. Julio, disillusioned with middle-class Montevideo, goes to revolutionary Cuba and observes with exemplary impartiality the successes and failures of the Cuban revolution. Half the novel is set in Uruguay and Martínez Moreno has subsequently stated that the theme of the novel is Uruguay.

More recent novels have lacked the serious breadth of *El paredón*. *La otra mitad* (Mexico City, 1966) is a fictional recreation of the story of Delmira Agustini (q.v.), the poet killed by her husband, who himself then committed suicide. *Con las primeras luces* (Barcelona, 1967) is told by a dying drunkard, Eugenio, in a series of flashbacks. Both novels lack originality and inspiration compared with *El paredón*.

MARTÍNEZ MURGUÍA, MANUEL ANTONIO (1833–1923), b. Frexel-Arteixo, Corunna. Galician historian and art-critic. The first president of the Academia Galega, Murguía nevertheless wrote almost exclusively in Castilian. His *Diccionario de escritores gallegos* (vol. 1, Vigo, 1862) has been superseded by the 3-vol. *Diccionario biobibliográfico de escritores* (Santiago, 1951–4) by A. Couceiro Freijomil in the new *Enciclopedia Gallega*. By profession an archivist, Murguía married the important Galician writer Rosalía de Castro in 1858. He edited the magazine *Ilustración Gallega y Asturiana* (1880–3), and his major contribution was the *Historia de Galicia* (5 vols., 1866–80). His other works included the *Galicia* volume (Barcelona, 1888) in the series *España: sus monumentos y artes*, and the essays *Los precursores* (1885).

MARTÍNEZ RUIZ, JOSÉ, a critic, essayist, and novelist better known by his pen-name Azorín (q.v.).

MARTÍNEZ SIERRA, GREGORIO (1881–1948), b. Madrid. Playwright, poet, novelist, actor, and journalist whose work was written in collaboration with his gifted wife María de la O Lejárraga, compiler of a book on their partnership: *Gregorio y yo* (Mexico City, 1953). It is often impossible to distinguish the hand of the husband from that of the wife, but the best-known play they produced, *Canción de cuna* (1910), is a clear evocation of María's youth in Carabanchel. The sentimental vignette of convent life in two acts shows how a foundling girl grows up among nuns and eventually falls in love and leaves them. It constitutes a veiled but nonetheless genuine protest against the conventual rejection of the maternal instinct. Though interested to some extent in social questions (such as feminism), the Martínez Sierras never risked the outspoken or the controversial: their hero in *Don Juan de España* (1921) repents while there is time and abandons his licentious career for charity and sanctity. They wrote some fifty plays altogether, many of them in the manner of their friend Jacinto Benavente (q.v.), and adapted as many translations, including five volumes of Maeterlinck. Their best writings are their one-act plays, some of which have been translated by J. G. Underhill (New York, 1915–23).

Martínez Sierra's book of verse *El poema del trabajo* (1898) was introduced by Jacinto Benavente, in one of whose plays he took a leading role. His later poetry appeared as *La casa de la primavera* (1907).

His poetic novels show a deep feeling for nature: *Almas ausentes* (1900), *Pascua florida* (1901), the well-known *Sol de la tarde* (1904), *La humilde verdad* (1905), *Tú eres la paz* (1906), and *El amor catedrático* (1910). The Martínez Sierras' *Obras completas* (1920–33) appeared in 32 vols. The popularity which their work enjoyed in the early decades of the century has not stood the test of time.

MARTÍNEZ VILLENA, RUBÉN (1899–1934), b. Havana. Cuban *avant-garde* poet and law-graduate. He edited the Grupo Minorista manifesto of 1927 against President Zayas, changing his attitude to poetry then to one of hostility to art for art's sake. Like Vallejo (q.v.), he travelled to the Soviet Union and became a convinced Communist. He was sentenced to death after the General Strike of 1930 but the sentence was not carried out.

La pupila insomne (1936), a posthumous collection, contains much that he professed to reject. His style is simple, sarcastic on occasion in reaction to the delicate early *El cazador* or the imaginative *Insuficiencia de la escala y el iris*, and is at its best in such poems as *El gigante*, an anguished declaration of Promethean man, rendered incapable of greatness by cruel destiny.

MARTÍNEZ VILLERGAS, JUAN (1816–94), b. Gómeznarro, Valladolid. Journalist and minor poet who made a scanty living from articles on *costumbrismo*, and who by reason of scurrilous attacks on politicians such as Narváez and Espartero was obliged to spend much of his life in exile from Spain, mostly in France and South America. He wrote mediocre novels and plays, but his more memorable *Poesías jocosas y satíricas* (1842; 3rd edn., Havana, 1857) contained his amusing epigrams and satires. His *Juicio crítico de los poetas españoles contemporáneos* (Paris, 1854) is unreliable and unbalanced. He shrewdly detected Adolfo de Castro's deception in attempting to pass off *El buscapié* as by Cervantes.

See Narciso Alonso Cortés, *Juan Martínez Villergas* (1910; 2nd enlarged edn., 1913).

MARTÍNEZ ZUVIRÍA, GUSTAVO ADOLFO (1883–1962), b. Córdoba, Argentina. Novelist and statesman who wrote under the pseudonym of 'Hugo Wast'. After a period in politics during which he became Minister of Education (1943–4) and Director of the National Library, he dedicated himself entirely to writing and from 1905 produced a steady stream of novels, the best-known being the historical romances *Tierra de jaguares* (1926–7), *Lucía Miranda* (1929), and *Lo que Dios ha unido* (1945). His Creole novels include *Flor de durazno* (1911) and *Desierto de piedra* (1925). 'Wast' is a religious moralist, his female characters often morally superior to his men. His anti-Semitic *Kahal* (1935) echoed Hitler's propaganda. His *Obras completas* were published in 1957–8 (2 vols.).

Martín Fierro, (1), a narrative poem by José Hernández (q.v.) in two parts: *El gaucho Martín Fierro* (1872) and *La vuelta de Martín Fierro* (1879). For Leopoldo Lugones (q.v.) and others, it is the national poem of Argentina. It consists of 7,210 octosyllabic lines in a variety of stanzaic forms, usually *quintillas*, with an opening line in free verse, but often interspersed with *redondillas*, ballads, and *seguidillas*. The language is colloquial and seeks to reproduce the pronunciation, vocabulary, and syntax of the *gaucho* (*dijunto* for *difunto*; *naide* for *nadie*). The tone is confessional, the worst of Fierro's bitterness having softened with the lapse of time between the events described and the moment of composition.

El gaucho Martín Fierro (in some later editions entitled *La ida de Martín Fierro*) tells how the fiercely independent *gaucho* Fierro was conscripted by a magistrate to fight the Indians. Taken in by promises of generous treatment he goes willingly, eager to defend the land against the 'barbarians'. He finds, however, that soldiers are unpaid, badly fed and clothed, and forced to work on the farms that the officers are sharing out in the region. Such work, as opposed to cattle-rearing, he finds humiliating. (Both parts of the poem expose the abuses of army life.) After one skirmish with the Indians, Fierro deserts after hearing that a campaign to exterminate them is planned. He does this not primarily from an idealistic motive, but from a hatred of army life. Back in the village, he finds that his wife has gone off with another man, his sons have disappeared to make careers of their own, and his house is in ruins. Angered at the society which has caused his misfortunes, Fierro becomes an outcast on the pampas, a *gaucho malo*, who kills a Negro at a dance and later a swaggering bully who starts a quarrel. Fierro meets the *gaucho* Cruz, another victim of injustice, and the two decide to join the Indians: an ironic indictment of 'civilized' society. The golden age of the *gaucho*, lovingly described in the poem, has been lost; now decent treatment can be found only among the pagans.

Hernández's poem sold over 50,000 copies in seven years; *gauchos* identifying themselves with the maltreated Fierro would gather round any *payador* (q.v.) who knew the poem. A sequel was expected, but by the time that *La vuelta de Martín Fierro* appeared in 1879, the *gaucho*'s lifestyle was already waning, the pampas parcelled out to wealthy landlords and intersected by railways. If Martín Fierro's departure was prophetic, then his return was anachronistic, despite the fact that Hernández stresses the social importance of the *gaucho*, as his prefaces show. Hernández's identification with the hero-narrator becomes less convincing, his story long-winded and, above all, the original inspiration is not sustained. Cruz dies during an epidemic which rages through the Indian camp; Martín escapes with a captive woman after having been accused of starting the epidemic by witchcraft.

On returning to 'civilization', Fierro finds his two sons, one of whom has been in gaol and the other a disciple of the amoral *gaucho* Viejo Vizcacha. Fierro also meets Cruz's son Picardía, whose story greatly resembles that of Fierro, and finally the brother of the Negro he had killed tracks him down. A duel with knives is averted when Fierro's sons pacify their elders by persuading them that knives no longer solve problems. Instead they agree to a duel in the form of a *payada* (song contest), which Fierro wins; the Negro departs, still hinting at vengeance. Fierro concurs wryly that his time is over and offers his blessing to the new generation in the hope of peace and justice. In acknowledging that progress is fundamentally good and must be earned by co-operation between social classes, Hernández reverses the conclusion of the first part of his poem, agreeing at last with the view of his old foe Sarmiento (q.v.).

The poem's rhythm enabled it to be memorized easily, and the poem was immediately attractive to country people, who recognized Fierro's problems as their own and often thought of him as a real figure. Sequels and direct imitations include *El hijo de Martín Fierro* by Bartolomé Rodolfo Aprile (1933), *Nemesio* by J. R. Rodríguez Morel (1938), and a series of *gaucho* portraits such as *El gaucho Juan Acero, émulo de Martín Fierro* by Anastasio Culebra (1901).

Many editions of the poem have appeared, among the best being that of Eleuterio F. Tiscornia (1925; 8th enlarged edn., 1953). Walter Owen translated it as *The gaucho Martín Fierro* (Oxford, 1935; reprinted, Buenos Aires, 1960) and Henry A. Holmes as *Martín Fierro, the Argentinian gaucho epic* (New York, 1948). There is a bilingual edition by C. Ward (New York, 1967).

For writers such as Leopoldo Lugones and Borges, Martín Fierro is a symbol of the lost freedom of the rolling pampas and an epic figure of the emergent Argentine nation. The bold colloquialism of the poet's vocabulary and his candour in describing Fierro's savage killing, drinking, and fighting, added a new dimension of realism to the narrative poem (it is not a true epic, despite the frequent claims). Borges has written two *cuentos* on the Fierro cycle; *El fin*, in which the Negro and Martín fight, and Martín is killed; and *Biografía de Tadeo Isidoro Cruz*, an account of Cruz's life up to his encounter with Fierro.

See the substantial bibliography by A. Raúl Cortázar in *Boletín de la Academia Argentina de Letras*, nos. 5–6 (1960), pp. 51–129, supplemented by H. J. Becco in *Cuadernos del Idioma* (Buenos Aires, vol. 2, nos. 5–6, 1966), pp. 109–37 and 123–45. On the poem's language, see F. I. Castro, *Vocabulario y frases de 'Martín Fierro'* (1957). Critical studies include H. A. Cordero, *Valoración de 'Martín Fierro'* (1960); A. Lozada Guidy, *Martín Fierro: gaucho-héroe-mito* (1967); J. B. Hughes, *Arte y sentido de 'Martín Fierro'* (Madrid, 1970); and Nestor A. Fayó, *Contenido histórico-social del 'Martín Fierro'* (1972).

(2), magazines published in Argentina. (a) A literary review published by Alberto Ghiraldo from March 1904. No. 48 appeared in February 1905. (b) A pacifist, anti-clerical magazine of which only three issues appeared in 1919. (c) An important literary journal founded by Evar Méndez in 1924 which ceased publication with nos. 44–5 in December 1927. Created as a

vehicle for the Ultra (q.v.) group (Borges, Caraffa, Eduardo González Lanuza, Pablo Rojas Paz, and others), this third magazine to be entitled *Martín Fierro* also printed the work of other Latin Americans, including J. M. Eguren, Ricardo Güiraldes, Leopoldo Marechal, Pablo Neruda, and Xavier Villaurrutia (qq.v.), and of the leading Spanish writers of the period, such as Alberti and García Lorca. Its willingness to experiment and to mock the literary establishment of Buenos Aires made it the preferred vehicle for many younger writers who would otherwise have found publication difficult. Oliverio Girondo's manifesto (in the fourth issue) condemned the funerary solemnity of the historian, and the professor who mummifies everything he touches. Among the special issues published in 1926–7, one was devoted to Góngora, and another to Gómez de la Serna.

MARTÍN-SANTOS, LUIS (1924–64), b. Larache, Morocco. Spanish novelist. Director of the Psychiatric Sanatorium in San Sebastián until his death in a car accident.

In addition to professional studies: *Dilthey, Jaspers y la comprensión del enfermo mental* (1955) and *Libertad, temporalidad y trasferencia en la psicoanálisis existencial* (Barcelona, 1964), Martín-Santos wrote important short stories and fragments, some collected by Salvador Clotas in the posthumous *Apólogos* (1970), and two major novels, the second remaining unfinished.

Tiempo de silencio (Barcelona, 1962) is a novel set in the Madrid of 1949. Introducing into Spanish the linguistic complexity of James Joyce's *Ulysses*, Martín-Santos borrows his tragic-burlesque milieu also from the *Sueños* of Quevedo and from *La Celestina* (qq.v.). A work of strong negative social criticism, *Tiempo de silencio* also offers a subjective, poetic, and innovatory approach to the novel at odds with the pedestrian social realism then prevalent in Spain, and has been very influential. Pedro, the protagonist of the *Bildungsroman*, never achieves the transformation which the reader is led to expect, but accepts defeat in the face of social or even genetic forces that are inevitably beyond his control. The work is a stylistic *tour de force*, and has been translated into English and several other languages.

Tiempo de destrucción (Barcelona, 1975) is a careful, scholarly attempt by José-Carlos Mainer to gather the fragments of a project on which Martín-Santos was working when he died. In this work, it appears that the protagonist, Agustín, a law student, may achieve his transformation by a careful understanding of his own predicament and that of his Basque society; but *Tiempo de destrucción* is too fragmented, and the novelist's intention too obscure, for any real conclusion to be drawn as to the book's importance to a generation which had already profited by the aesthetic liberation of *Tiempo de silencio*.

MÁRTIR DE ANGLERIA, PEDRO (1459–1526), b. Arona, Anghiera, Lombardy. Italian humanist and historian, whose name has been Hispanicized from Pietro Martire d'Anghiera. He studied in Rome 1478–87, when he was appointed tutor at the Court of the Reyes Católicos at the instance of the Conde de Tendillas. His *Opera* (Seville, 1511) contain Mártir's unoriginal poetical writings, but he was appointed chronicler of the Indies in 1510 and it is his *Decades de orbe novo* (1511–16; printed in Alcalá, 1530) which preserve his fame today. Based on conversations with explorers and correspondence with *conquistadores*, the book is not confined to political or military events, but deals in some detail with flora and fauna, local customs, and religious observances. It suffers from imitating Livy too closely, referring phenomena to their classical counterparts, and making Columbus out to be a latter-day Aeneas. Mártir is the subject of one of the *Tres cronistas de Indias* (Mexico City, 1959) studied by A. M. Salas, the others being Bartolomé de Las Casas and Gonzalo Fernández de Oviedo (qq.v.).

Mártir's other book, *Opus epistolarum* (Alcalá, 1530), has been translated into Spanish by López Toro (1943). It is a first-hand account of events in Spain from his arrival in 1487 to 1525, and includes a description of the conquest of Granada, the city in which the Lombard humanist died.

See J. H. Mariejol, *Pedro Mártir d'Anghiera* (Paris, 1887), and María N. Olmedillas de Pereiras, *Pedro Mártir de Anglería y la mentalidad exoticista* (1974).

MÁRTIR RIZO, JUAN PABLO (1593–1642), b. Madrid. Priest and literary controversialist, he claimed to be a grandson of Pedro Mártir de Anglería (q.v.). His main fame is that of literary opponent to Lope de Vega, against whom he wrote the lost *Spongia* in collaboration with Torres Rámila (q.v.). His own poetry, and translations from the Latin and French, are forgotten, but his prose works were well received, among them an *Historia de la vida de Lucio Annaeo Séneca* (1626), *Norte de príncipes* (1626), *Defensa de la verdad que escribió don Francisco de Quevedo y Villegas* (Málaga, 1628), the *Historia de Cuenca* (1629), and the *Historia trágica de la vida y muerte del duque de Virón* (Barcelona, 1629) on which Pérez de Montalbán (q.v.) based his play *El mariscal de Virón*.

There is a modern edition of the *Norte de príncipes* by J. A. Maravall (1945).

MARTORELL, JOANOT (c. 1420–70), b. Valencia. Novelist. The author of the bulk of *Tirant lo Blanch* (q.v.), the most important of the *libros de caballería* (q.v.) in Catalan.

He lived for some time at the Portuguese court, and probably also for a while at the English court while appealing to the King for support in his quarrel with Joan de Montpalau over Martorell's sister Damiata. His other sister married the Catalan poet Ausias March (q.v.).

MÁS, JOSÉ (1885–1940), b. Écija, Seville. Novelist. A commercial traveller, Más wrote naturalistic novels in the manner of Vicente Blasco Ibáñez (q.v.), as well as criticism and travel books. He grouped his works into loose 'cycles' like Blasco's: 'Novelas de la mujer': *Soledad* (1915), *Sacrificio* (1918), *Esperanza* (1919); 'Novelas sevillanas': *La bruja* (1917), *La estrella de la Giralda* (1918), *La orgía* (1919), *Por las aguas del río* (1921), *Hampa y miseria* (1923), and *La locura de un erudito* (1926); a 'Novela de Galicia': *La costa de la muerte* (1928) and a 'Novela de Castilla': *El rastrero* (1922); 'Novelas alucinantes': *El baile de los espectros* (1916), *Los sueños de un morfinómano* (1921), *La huída* (1927); a 'Novela exótica': *La piedra de fuego* (1924); 'Novelas del campo andaluz': *Luna y sol de la marisma* (1930) and *El rebaño hambriento en tierra feraz* (1935) in which the day-labourers of the Andalusian countryside are portrayed as wretchedly exploited victims of the liberal monarchy, the Primo de Rivera dictatorship, and the regime of Alcalá Zamora alike. They respond to neglect and suffering by rebellion, violence, and crime, resulting in the final act of repression which can only restore a superficial kind of order. The hero, Don Braulio Mejías de Terán, who is made first Count and later Marquis, is a landowner, and the strength of Más's characterization lies in the sympathetic drawing of Mejías, a victim of circumstances like the mob he employs. None of the secondary characters has any real personality; the art of Más lies in his ability to create an atmosphere of political tension. His other novels are 'Novelas docentes': *Yo soy honrada, caballero* (1931) and *En la selvática Bribonicia* (1933), the latter a bitter anti-*Utopia* against Western civilization in which a Central-African country is suddenly colonized for its emerald wealth, and in a few years experiences the invention of private property, envy, adultery, class consciousness, and exploitation that have taken the West many centuries to perfect. Political change brings no improvement; the ending is the reversion of the country to its original state.

Más is no longer widely read, for his books were hastily put together, with little sense of style or discrimination.

MASDEU, Juan Francisco (1744–1817), b. Palermo. Historian and encyclopaedic writer. He entered the Society of Jesus in 1759, and was exiled with the rest of the Order (see Jesuits, Expulsion of the) before he had completed his studies and went to Ferrara, and later Rome. When the Order was dissolved, Masdeu returned to Spain as a secular priest, becoming archivist at León Cathedral. On the fall of Carlos IV, his protector, in 1808, Masdeu accompanied him to Rome, but returned yet again when Pope Pius VII restored the Order. His massive *Historia crítica de España y de la cultura española* (20 vols., 1783–1805) did not extend beyond the 11th c. but was placed on the index for, among other reasons, its scepticism of traditions not fully documented. His *Respuesta...* to his censor Fr. Traggia (1793) defended the work against the Inquisitorial ban. The first two vols. of his encyclopaedic *Historia* appeared in Italian (1781) and have been studied by M. Batllori in 'La edición italiana de la "Historia" del P. Masdeu' in *Hispania*, vol. 3 (Madrid, 1943), pp. 612–30.

Padre Masdeu also composed a *Memorial* (1800) against the French Revolution and an *Arte poética fácil* (1801) in dialogue.

MASFERRER, Alberto (1868–1932), b. Alegría, El Salvador. Journalist. He rebelled against discipline in childhood and later travelled extensively. After a period of teaching he was appointed director of the *Diario Oficial* in 1892. He was consul in Chile (from 1903), and he devoted himself to journalism there, editing first *El Chileño* in Santiago, then *El Mercurio* in Valparaíso. In 1928 he founded the daily *Patria*, using it as a vehicle for his doctrine of the 'Mínimum vital', according to which all men have the right to the primary necessities: food, a home, and an education. He advocated graduated taxation to alleviate the plight of the poor, and to reduce the size of estates. He brought Tolstoy's theories to Central America in his books *Las nuevas ideas* (Antwerp, 1913), *El dinero maldito* (1927), and *El mínimum vital* (1929), the last reappearing with other sociological essays, a bibliography, and a prologue by Francisco Morán, in 1950.

MASIP ROCA, Paulino (1900–63), b. Granadella, Lérida. Novelist, poet, playwright, and journalist. Of republican sympathies, Masip emigrated to Mexico in 1939.

His principal plays are *El báculo y el paraguas* (1930), *La frontera* (1932), *El emplazado* (1949), and *El escándalo* (1952?), but Masip is better known as a novelist. His most important work, classed by Nora with Gironella's *Los cipreses creen en Dios*, is the Civil War novel *El diario de*

Hamlet García (Mexico City, 1944). García is a 'travelling professor of metaphysics' combining odd traits of character (and caricature) from *Quijote, Belarmino y Apolonio*, Ramón de la Cruz, and his Shakespearian namesake. Masip makes his points indirectly, through his protagonist's inability to comprehend the events in the Madrid of 1936.

La aventura de Marta Abril (1953) and the four short novels in *La trampa* (1954) revealed Masip to be essentially a one-book author.

MATA, Andrés (1870–1931), b. Carúpano. Venezuelan poet. Mata evolved from the semi-modernism of Díaz Mirón (q.v.) to a Becquerian romanticism. A writer of intense melodic power, Mata was a nativist employing hypnotic rhythms. The best of the *Poesías completas* (1956, ed. José Ramón Medina) are 'Música triste' and 'Alma y paisaje'.

MATA, Gonzalo humberto (1904–), b. Quito. Ecuadorian biographer, novelist, and controversialist. He is director of the Editorial-Biblioteca 'Cenit' in Cuenca and has been University Librarian of Cuenca. He first made his name with the poems of *Galope de volcanes* (Cuenca, 1932) but his best-known book is the Indianist novel *Sumag allpa* (Cuenca, 1940; the Quechua title means 'Lovely land'), the despairing cry of the dispossessed Indians.

Both his critical and his creative works are strongly felt and passionately expressed, with unconcealed scorn for what Mata considers hypocrisy and complacency. His outspoken ballads against the exploitation of the *sombereras* in *Chorro cañamazo* (Cuenca, 1935) were publicly burned by Remigio Crespo Toral (q.v.), then Rector of the University of Cuenca. His iconoclastic *Zaldumbide y Montalvo* (Cuenca, 1966) led to a bitter polemic following Mata's claim that Juan Montalvo's writing are grossly overrated, partly as a result of Zaldumbide's hero-worship.

Mata's other books include an idiosyncratic biography of an Ecuadorian poet: *Dolores Veintimilla, asesinada* (Cuenca, 1968) and *Historia de la literatura morlaca* (2 vols., Cuenca, 1957–9).

See Margaret H. Dickson, *Gonzalo humberto Mata: su sitial en la novela indianista del Ecuador* (Cuenca, 1963).

MATOS FRAGOSO, Juan de (1608–89), b. Alvito, Alentejo (Portugal). Portuguese dramatist writing in Castilian. Though he wrote indifferent *fábulas*, such as *Fábula burlesca de Apolo y Leucotoe* (1652) and *Fábula de Eco y Narciso* (1655), Matos is best-known as a playwright of the school of Calderón de la Barca (q.v.).

Seven of his plays appear in vol. 47 (1858) of

the BAE, of which the best is *El sabio en su retiro y villano en su rincón, Juan Labrador*, a reworking of Lope's great play and not much inferior. The others are *Ver y creer*; the *comedia de capa y espada El galán de su mujer*; *La dicha por el desprecio*; the witty *Lorenzo me llamo, y carbonero de Toledo; Callar siempre es lo mejor*; and *El yerro del entendido*, based on Cervantes' *El curioso impertinente*.

As was customary, most of his plays were written in collaboration with friends, among them Cáncer, Diamante, Martínez de Meneses, the Figueroas, Moreto, and Andrés Gil Enríquez. His earliest recorded publication is 'La defensa de la fe y príncipe prodigioso' (written with Moreto), which appeared in *El mejor de los mejores* (Alcalá, 1651), and others are to be found in *Comedias escogidas de los mejores ingenios de España*, vol. 9 (1657) and *Primera parte de Comedias* (1658).

Matos wrote *El esclavo del demonio* with Mira de Amescua, and *Caer para levantar* with Cáncer and Moreto. *El traidor contra su sangre*, on the theme of the *Siete Infantes de Lara* (q.v.), is believed to have been the direct inspiration of the Duque de Riva's *El moro expósito*; his other historical plays included *No está en matar el vencer* and *El amor hace valiente y toma de Valencia por el Cid*.

The most interesting of his religious plays is *El marido de su madre*, on the marriage of St. Gregory, Patriarch of Syria, to a woman later discovered to be his mother. It evaded censorship because he declared that Gregory and his 'wife' never consummated their marriage. His other religious plays included *El Job de las mujeres, San Félix de Cantalicio, San Gil de Portugal*, and *La devoción del Ángel de la Guarda*.

H. C. Heaton, has edited *El ingrato agradecido* (New York, 1926).

Matos lacked lyric power and dramatic invention, but his plot construction was ingenious. His language is often laborious and pedantic, but in his finest plays, such as *El sabio en su retiro*, he forgets his mannerism, and writes with fluency and life.

MATOS PAOLI, Francisco (1915–), b. Lares. Puerto Rican poet whose abstract, hermetic poetry has not interfered with his political involvement in the nationalist movement. The immature *Signario de lágrimas* (1931) was followed by notable collections including Creole songs, such as *Cardo labriego* (1937), *Habitante del eco*, *1937–41* (Santurce, 1944), and *Teoría del olvido* (Río Piedras, 1944). In 1952 his unpublished 'Criatura del rocío' (written in 1944) was seized with his other papers by the authorities during the nationalist rising, since Matos Paoli was secretary of the Nationalist Party. His subsequent works include *Canto a Puerto Rico* (1952); the poems on his years in prison *Luz de los héroes* (1954); and *Canto a la locura* (1962), in which his pure poetry has evolved towards Jorge Guillén (q.v.). His main themes are patriotism, religion, and above all metaphysics.

MATTO DE TURNER, Clorinda (1854–1909), b. Cuzco, Peru. Novelist, poet, and playwright. She used the pseudonym 'Carlota Dumont' for some of her works. In *Tradiciones cuzqueñas: leyendas, biografías y hojas sueltas* (2 vols., 1884–6), she was influenced by Ricardo Palma (q.v.), but her best work is the novel *Aves sin nido* (1889), an Indianist protest novel which caused her to be known as the Harriet Beecher Stowe of Latin America. A recent edition (New York, 1968) has a useful prologue by Luis Mario Schneider.

Matto de Turner also published *Don Juan de Espinosa Medrano* (1887); *Bocetos al lápiz de americanos celebres* (1890); the novel *Índole* (1891); *Hima-Sumac* (1892), a play in prose; *Leyendas y recortes* (1893); the novel *Herencia* (1893); *Boreales, miniaturas y porcelanas* (Buenos Aires, 1902); *Cuatro conferencias sobre América del Sur* (1909); and *Viaje de recreo* (Valencia, 1902), on her travels in Spain, France, and England.

See Manuel Cuadros Escobedo, *Paisaje y obra: mujer e historia: Clorinda Matto de Turner* (Cuzco, 1949).

MATUTE, Ana María (1926–), b. Barcelona. Novelist and short-story writer. Her youth was marred by three long and serious illnesses and unpleasant experiences in schools run by French nuns. Her first novel was *Pequeño teatro*, written in 1943 but not revised and published (in Barcelona) until 1954. Her first publication was the novel *Los Abel* (1948), on the recurring theme of the Cain–Abel conflict, but she first achieved recognition with her Civil War novel *Los hijos muertos* (Barcelona, 1958), which was awarded the Spanish Critics' Prize.

Los mercaderes is a trilogy comprising the Premio Nadal-winning *Primera memoria* (Barcelona, 1960), *Los soldados lloran de noche* (Barcelona, 1964), and *La trampa* (Barcelona, 1969). The trilogy's title alludes to those 'merchants' who profit directly or indirectly from the misery of others (Matute points out that the Falange Movement has always advocated private charity rather than socio-economic reforms) and the respective volumes describe the early years of the Civil War, the last few weeks of the War, and contemporary Spain. Of *Olvidado rey Gudu* (1971), Matute states that it represents a new phase in her career, and clearly indicates a subtler sensitivity and a tightening in construction. Her latest novels are *La torre vigía* (Barcelona, 1971) and *El río* (Barcelona, 1973).

Less important novels are *Fiesta al noroeste* (1953), and *La luciérnaga*, which was not licensed for publication; when it was rewritten out of a pressing need for money as *En esta tierra* (Barcelona, 1955), Matute avowed her disenchantment with it. It is an overtly political novel written for the poor and dispossessed against the forces victorious in the Civil War. She has a son by her former husband, Ramón Eugenio de Goichechea, from whom she was legally separated in 1965, and some of her stories for and about children rank among the best in Spanish since World War II: *Los niños tontos* (1956), *Los cuentos vagabundos* (Barcelona, 1956), *El tiempo* (Barcelona, 1957, which includes as the title-story, with its title changed, 'La pequeña vida', 1953), *Tres cuentos y un sueño* (Barcelona, 1961), *Historias de la Artámila* (Barcelona, 1961), and *Libro de juegos para los niños de los otros*.

Her short stories have been collected in *El arrepentido* (the first edn. published by Rocas in Barcelona, 1961, has contents different from those of the second published by Juventud in Barcelona, 1967), and *Algunos muchachos* (1968).

Matute's themes are the conflict between idealism and reality; the tragic effects of the passing of time on each of her characters and in their relationships; the grotesque and the cruel in human existence; loneliness; the defenceless-ness of children and the poor; and the mixture of love and hate that springs up between brothers and lovers. Her style is instinctive, abounding in sudden sprays of adjectives and long, exaggerated descriptions often self-destructive in their cumulative effect. Alborg has criticized her 'rhetorical excesses' and it is true that, in her earlier books, self-criticism was almost absent.

There is a good general account of Matute's literary development by Janet Winecoff Díaz, *Ana María Matute* (New York, 1971), and a more detailed account of her writings by M. E. W. Jones, *The literary world of Ana María Matute* (Lexington, Kentucky, 1970).

MAYA, RAFAEL (1897–), b. Popayán. Colombian poet and essayist. A master of elegance and style, Maya is best known for the subtle and demanding *Navegación nocturna* (1959), original in its expressionist allegories and visions evoking the spirit of God. The third edition of his *Obra poética* (1951) is the most significant collection of his earlier work, adding *Tiempo de luz* to *La vida en la sombra* (1925), *Coros del mediodía* (1928), *¡Después del silencio!* (dialogues in verse, 1938), and *Final de romances y otras canciones*.

Maya is also a considerable prose stylist, among his finest books being *Alabanzas del hombre y de la tierra* (2 vols., 1934–41), *Considera-*

ciones críticas sobre literatura colombiana (1944), *Estampas de ayer y retratos de hoy* (1954), and *De perfil y de frente* (Cali, 1965).

Maya compiled a useful anthology, *La musa romántica en Colombia* (1954).

MAYÁNS Y SÍSCAR, GREGORIO (1699–1781), b. Oliva, Valencia. Humanist. When professor of law at Valencia University, he argued for the increased study of Spanish law at the expense of Roman law. After seven years as an official of the Royal Library, he returned to Oliva in 1740 to write. His *Orador cristiano* (1733), in dialogue form, advocates simplicity in preaching. His masterpiece is the pioneering compilation *Orígenes de la lengua española* (2 vols., 1737; 2nd edn., 1873) and in the same year appeared the first serious (though long superseded) *Vida de Cervantes* (1737) originally intended as a preface to an edition of Cervantes' works in English. As 'Plácido Veranio', he contributed to the *Diario de los Literatos de España* (q.v.). His next major work, following a collection of *Ensayos oratorios* (1739), was *Retórica* (2 vols., Valencia, 1757), the best anthology and study of Spanish prose to appear in the 18th c. His final great work was the *Vida de Virgilio* (5 vols., 1778).

Mayáns y Síscar was a notable correspondent in both Latin and Castilian. Most of his letters (which deal predominantly with history and literature) remain unpublished, but his letters in Latin sent to Cardinal Fleury appeared in 1732, and there is a representative selection in the BAE (vol. 62, 1870).

Mayáns y Síscar produced editions of Gaspar Ibáñez de Segovia Peralta y Mendoza (1741), Luis de León (1761), Sánchez de las Brozas (1766), and Juan Luis Vives (1782), among others.

See A. Morel-Fatio, 'Un erudit espagnol au XVIIIe siècle' in *Bulletin Hispanique*, vol. 17, 1915, pp. 157–226.

Mayorazgo de Labraz, El (Barcelona, 1903), the second novel in the *Tierra vasca* trilogy by Pío Baroja (q.v.).

A sombre novel, resulting in Baroja's words from the 'destruction of (my) romantic illusions' (*Obras*, vol. 1, 1946), probably an ambiguous reference to frustrated love affairs and the state of Spain.

Melodramatic in style like its predecessor, *La casa de Aizgorri* (q.v.), the novel is a modernized morality play with the blind Juan, Lord of Labraz, as the personification of Good and Don Ramiro as Evil. The figure of Ramiro lacks the required grandeur, and is seen merely as a common seducer and petty thief. Labraz turns on his tormentors with the wrath of Christ and becomes a wanderer. An unlikely ending, with

Juan Labraz returning to claim the innkeeper's daughter Marina as his future companion on the shores of the Mediterranean, mars the unity of the novel. Among the autobiographical elements are Marina herself, based on an innkeeper's daughter in the village of Abornícano, and the crossing of Navarre in winter, recalling a trip to Viana with his friend Ramiro de Maeztu (q.v.).

See F. J. Flores Arroyuelo, *Las primeras novelas de Pío Baroja* (Murcia, 1967).

Mayor monstruo, los celos, El, one of the four major tragedies of honour by Pedro Calderón de la Barca (q.v.). It is also widely known as *El mayor monstruo del mundo*.

Mariana, wife of the tetrarch Herod, learns of the prophecy that her husband's dagger will slay her. Herod conspires with Mark Antony against Octavius Caesar, the Emperor, and when Octavius defeats the forces of Herod he captures Mariana's brother Aristobulos and intercepts a box containing a letter proving Herod's treachery and a picture of an unknown woman (Mariana), for whom Octavius conceives a passion.

Ptolemy, a soldier in Herod's army, returns to tell of the defeat; in a vain attempt to console Mariana (whom he had vowed to make Queen of the World), Herod places his dagger at her feet. When the victorious Octavius enters Jerusalem, he carries the portrait of Mariana. Herod sees the picture and suspects Octavius of treachery. He writes a letter instructing Philip and Ptolemy to kill Mariana if he should predecease her. Mariana manages to persuade Octavius to forgive Herod's treachery to him, but (on finding Herod's letter ordering her death) bitterly reproaches her husband. In a quarrel over her picture, Mariana escapes from Octavius when she recognizes Herod's dagger in the Emperor's possession but only after leaving some of her garments scattered on the floor after the struggle. When Herod sees the circumstantial evidence he momentarily suspects her of infidelity but is reassured when he sees her escaping from Octavius. He leaps to her defence, but kills her by mistake, exactly as the prophecy had declared. On discovering his error, he commits suicide by leaping from a window.

Calderón was probably familiar with the plays on the life of Herod by Golden Age predecessors (in particular *La vida y muerte de Hérodes* by Tirso de Molina, q.v.) and with *Antony and Cleopatra* by Shakespeare. Each character has a principal obsession (ambition, jealousy, pride) which leads inevitably to a tragic conclusion. The passions and the emotions of the characters are accentuated, and their ardent sensuality parallels the florid ornamentation of Calderón's poetic language.

Herod's passionate infatuation with his wife leads to civil strife and the wrath of God, who punishes his hubris with death and disgrace. The clever interweaving of political and amorous jealousy in the foreground is accompanied by a romantic parallel sub-plot involving Sirene, Ptolemy, and Libia.

There is an edition of the play by Everett W. Hesse (Madison, Wis., 1955). See the same author's 'El arte calderoniano en "El mayor monstruo, los celos"' in *Clavileño*, vol. 7, no. 38 (1956), pp. 18–30.

MECHÍN, T. P., pseudonym of José María Peralta Lagos (q.v.).

Médico de su honra, El (1637), first performed in 1635, one of the four great tragedies of *honor* by Pedro Calderón de la Barca (q.v.), the others being *A secreto agravio, secreta venganza*; *El mayor monstruo, los celos*; and *El pintor de su deshonra*. It is a new version of a play once attributed to Lope de Vega (q.v.) but now of unidentified authorship (see A. E. Sloman's *The dramatic craftsmanship of Calderón* (Oxford, 1958). The best edition of Calderón's *tragedia* is that by C. A. Jones (Oxford, 1961) and there is a vigorous English translation by Roy Campbell: *The surgeon of his honour* (Madison, Wis., 1960).

Prince Enrique (later Enrique II of the House of Trastámara) falls from his horse and is removed to the home of Doña Mencía with whom he is still in love, despite her earlier rejection of him and her subsequent marriage to the nobleman Gutierre de Solís.

Enrique surprises Mencía in her room and she hides him when Gutierre enters. Enrique departs but drops his dagger, which Gutierre then finds and later identifies as that of the prince.

Gutierre is enraged, but cannot revenge himself on royal blood. He seeks confirmation of his fears by entering Mencía's room under cover of darkness. Mencía, sure that it cannot be Gutierre who acts so stealthily, addresses the intruder as 'Your Highness', thus apparently proving her guilt. Gutierre quickly leaves without betraying his identity. Mencía writes to Enrique that he must leave her alone and she is surprised by her husband while still writing; he discovers the addressee and without waiting for her explanations locks her in her room:

> *El amor te adora, el honor te aborrece,*
> *Y así el uno te mata, y el otro te avisa:*
> *Dos horas tienes de vida; Christiana eres;*
> *Salva el alma, que la vida es imposible.*

Gutierre brings a bloodletter to open her veins so that she may bleed to death, but apparently by accident, Gutierre wishing his vengeance to be in secret, as his 'dishonour' is not publicly known. When King Pedro el Cruel learns of the crime, he pardons Gutierre but compels him to marry his former fiancée Leonor, whom he had deserted, unjustly suspecting her too of infidelity. He specifically demands from the king permission to punish her in the same way if she ever commits a similar offence, and this too the king grants. The moving tragedy reaches its climax, perhaps, in the scene where the bleeding, innocent Mencía lies on her bed below a crucifix. Calderón does not explicitly condone Pedro's verdict on Gutierre, and Menéndez y Pelayo has pointed out that the public would never have condoned an ending in which the husband pardoned the wife in a matter of *honor*, because that pardon is permissible only in afterlife, as symbolized by the crucifix offering hope to the soul of Mencía. The play has often been compared to *Othello* in that an innocent girl is presumed guilty by a jealous husband.

More recent views of the play's moral see it as a subtle attack on the honour code which allows a man to kill his wife on mere suspicion; Gutierre, shedding Mencía's blood to redeem his honour, is not merely mad, but blasphemous, unconsciously parodying Christian teaching on redemption through the blood of the Lamb and transforming vengeance into a kind of perverse religion. Calderón's choice of the King who dispenses justice is subtle too: as Pedro el Justiciero he is just to force Gutierre to marry Leonor, who abominates him, as Pedro el Cruel he is equally cruel to do so, forcing them both to live in misery after curtainfall, whereas the usual dramatic marriage is a resolution denoting harmony and peace. Though earlier writers (and more recently Gerald Brenan) have stressed the play's barbarity, it has now been proposed as a clever indictment of the pathological extremes possible under the *honor* code.

See B. W. Wardropper, 'Poetry and drama in Calderón's "El médico de su honra"' in *Romanic Review*, vol. 49 (1958), pp. 3–11.

MEDINA, FRANCISCO DE (1544–1615), b. Seville. Poet, who studied at Osuna University under Juan de Mal Lara (q.v.). He became a member of the School of Seville, whose poetic manifesto he wrote as a prologue to *Anotaciones a Garcilaso* (Seville, 1580), by his friend Fernando de Herrera (q.v.).

His major original work is the ode 'A Garcilaso', and he was also especially highly regarded for his translations from Latin authors, among them Propertius and Ausonius.

MEDINA, JOSÉ RAMÓN (1921–), b. San Francisco de Maicara. Venezuelan literary critic and poet. His literary history and criticism have included *Biografía de Juan Antonio Pérez*

Bonalde (1954), *Examen de la poesía venezolana contemporánea* (1956), *La nueva poesía venezolana* (an anthology and study, 1959), essays in *Balance de letras* (Merida, Venezuela, 1961), *Antología venezolana* (2 vols., Madrid, 1962), and *Poesía de Venezuela: románticos y modernistas* (Buenos Aires, 1966).

His numerous collections of poetry began with *Edad de la esperanza* (1949). His *Antología poética* appeared in Buenos Aires (1957).

MEDINA, JOSÉ TORIBIO (1852–1930), b. Santiago. Chilean literary historian and bibliographer who qualified as a lawyer but turned to the full-time study of Chilean literature and history. He amassed a great private library (donated at his death to the Biblioteca Nacional in Santiago) and installed a printing press in his own home to produce more than 300 works listed in Guillermo Feliu Cruz's *Bibliografía de don José Toribio Medina* (1931) and Yolanda H. Buffa Peyrot's *Catálogo de la exposición bibliográfica de las obras de José Toribio Medina.*

In addition to his numerous editions of earlier writers (above all that of Ercilla, q.v.), Medina introduced the work of previous historians in a Colección de Historiadores de Chile y Documentos Relativos a la Historia Nacional (1891–1919) and edited the series Documentos Inéditos para la Historia de Chile.

He himself wrote a well-documented but idiosyncratically critical *Historia de la literatura colonial de Chile* (3 vols., 1878); the vast *Diccionario biográfico colonial de Chile* (1906); *La literatura femenina en Chile* (1923); *Diccionario de anónimos y seudónimos hispanoamericanos* (2 vols., Buenos Aires, 1925) corrected and supplemented by Ricardo Victorica in 2 vols. (Buenos Aires, 1928–9), and many monographs of permanent value. He edited two libraries of classics: Biblioteca Hispano-chilena (3 vols., 1897–9) and Biblioteca Hispanoamericana (7 vols., 1898–1907; reissued in facsimile, 1958–62).

There are several major studies of his life and work: *José Toribio Medina: his life and works* (New York, 1941) by Sarah L. Roberts; G. Feliu Cruz's *Medina: radiografía de un espíritu, 1852–1930* (1952); and M. A. Bromsen's compilation *José Toribio Medina: humanist of the Americas* (Washington, 1960).

MEDINILLA, BALTASAR ELISIO (1585–1620), b. Toledo. Poet and prose-writer who was a friend and disciple of Lope de Vega (q.v.). He imitated Lope's *La descripción de la Abadía, jardín del duque de Alba* in *Descripción de Buenavista, recreación en la vega de Toledo* (1617), which he later amplified in a MS. now in the National Library, Madrid. His most celebrated poem is a work of Marian piety in 5 cantos of *octavas reales,* the *Limpia Concepción de la Virgen Nuestra Señora* (1617).

Medinilla's *Obras divinas* survive in a MS. in the National Library. His prose work, of considerable local interest, is *Discurso del remedio de las cosas de Toledo* (Toledo, 1618).

He was killed, in a brawl over a love affair, by Jerónimo de Andrada y Rivadeneyra.

See F. de San Román, *Elisio de Medinilla y su personalidad literaria* (Toledo, 1921).

Meditaciones del Quijote (1914; 2nd edn., 1921), a book of metaphysical essays, rather than a work of literary criticism, by José Ortega y Gasset (q.v.). Its main points are as follows.

The greatest spiritual work produced by Spain is the *Quijote* (q.v.) for the transcendence of its author's environment. Life is not depicted but refracted in the pages of Cervantes, and it is this quality of refraction (necessarily comic or satirical in overall effect) which is lacking in much of Spanish literature. Men are not interested in reading a story which reproduces their circumstances and essential insecurity; they long to discover a being greater than themselves, unaffected by most ordinary events and able to weave his own pattern of security. Men cannot change their past or present circumstances, but they can alter their future, and the decision to become different—or the decision to renounce action—is the crux of human life. [Ortega later claimed to have anticipated Heidegger's existentialism in this section of the book.]

No Spanish work of art possesses a greater power of symbolic allusion to the ultimate purpose of life than the Quijote, yet no work has fewer precedents or fewer internal clues to its interpretation. Cervantes avoids all ideological formulae (extraordinary in a work of the early 17th c.).

The Renaissance imposed on Greek myth and medieval superstition a new value: that of subjective reality. Cervantes takes the reality of Spain, projects myth and miracle into it, and views the whole from a new vantage-point: that of the subjective, in which the three facets of reality, myth, and miracle are forged into a new kind of poetry.

Don Quixote is a hero because he will not agree to act within the social norms of his time, but decides to take a different path. The common man, Sancho Panza, shows the 'normal' reaction of the time to each phenomenon, thus setting Quixote's action in relief, but Quixote, secure in his own interpretation of life and in his determination to accommodate life to his will, is the hero of the novel and of all mankind.

In Plato's *Symposium*, Socrates argues against the comedian Aristophanes and the tragedian Agathon that the poet should unite comedy with tragedy. Ortega concludes that it was left to Cervantes to create the madman and hero who could do so.

MEDRANO, FRANCISCO DE (1569/70–1607), b. Seville. Poet. Strongly influenced by Horace, Medrano is perhaps the finest interpreter of the Latin poet in Castilian after Luis de León. Medrano also imitated Tasso and Ariosto, and Dámaso Alonso has warned that his art and importance 'consisten precisamente en la imitación', so that the work of identifying originals for his 34 odes and 52 sonnets continues. He entered the Society of Jesus in 1584 but abandoned the ecclesiastical life in 1602 to retire to his farm, Mirarbueno, writing poetry and meditating.

Fr. Medrano's work was partly published as pp. 101–80 of the *Remedios de amor* by Pedro Venegas de Saavedra (Palermo, 1617). The edition in vol. 32 (1854) of the BAE has now been superseded by that in the *Vida y obra de Medrano* by Dámaso Alonso (vol. 1, 1948; vol. 2 with Stephen Reckert, 1958).

One of the MSS. of the *Epístola moral a Fabio* (q.v.) bears a marginalium attributing the poem to Medrano, but Alonso has now convincingly vindicated A. de Castro's attribution to Andrés Fernández de Andrada (q.v.).

MEGGET, HUMBERTO (1926–51), b. Paysandú. Uruguayan poet who founded the reviews *Letras* (only one issue), *No*, and *Sin Zona*. He died of tuberculosis after a long illness and his only collection of poems *Nuevo sol partido* (1949) was reissued in 1952, with the addition of 30 extra poems, by Idea Vilariño under the same title. The magazine *Número* also published in 1952 a poetic manifesto in prose by Megget.

Megget's poetry is pessimistic; it employs common words in lyrical, spontaneous metaphors from nature. His sadness is transmuted into wry humour by the power of his imagination. The best essay on his work is by Mario Benedetti, in his *Literatura uruguaya, siglo XX* (2nd edn., 1969).

MEJÍA, PEDRO (1497–1551), poet, historian, and anthologist, whose name was also written Pedro Mexía. Imperial historian from 1548. An Erasmian, Mejía corresponded with Erasmus, and was also much influenced by his *Adagia*, *Colloquia*, and *Enchiridion*.

His important work was the *Libro llamado silua d' varia lección . . . En el qual a manera de Silua, sin guardar horden en los propósitos, se tratan por capítulos muchas y muy diuersas materias, historias, exemplos, y questiones de varia lección y erudición* (Seville, 1540), the Robertis printing being enlarged for the Cromberger printing (Seville, 1540), a few months later. The *Silva de varia lección*, the bedside book of the age, was reprinted 33 times in 150 years. Modelled on the structure of the *Noctes atticae* of Aulus Gellius, the *Silva* borrows its miscellaneous matter from predominantly classical authors, among them Athenaeus, Macrobius, and Pliny (*Historia naturalis*). There is a good bibliography in the edition by J. García Soriano (2 vols., 1933–4).

Mejía was widely respected as court historian to Carlos V. *Relación de las Comunidades de Castilla* (in the BAE, vol. 21, 1852) is a fragment of the *Historia de Carlos V* first edited by R. Foulché-Delbosc (using the pen-name J. Deloffre) in *Revue Hispanique*, vol. 44 (1918), pp. 1–564, but improved in the edition of Juan de Mata Carriazo (1945).

Mejía retold the history of the Roman Empire through the lives of its emperors from Julius Caesar to Maximilian in the *Historia Imperial y Cesárea* (Sevilla, 1545).

See R. Costes, 'Pedro Mejía, chroniste de Charles Quint' in *Bulletin Hispanique*, vol. 22 (1920), pp. 1–36 and 256–68; and vol. 23 (1921), pp. 95–110.

MEJÍA SÁNCHEZ, ERNESTO (1923–), b. Masaya, Nicaragua. Poet, critic, and scholar. Influenced by José Coronel Urtecho (q.v.), he rejected his national traditions, including *modernismo*, and turned to the U.S.A. This did not prevent him from preparing critical editions of Rubén Darío (q.v.): the *Cuentos completos* (Mexico City, 1950) and the *Poesía* (Mexico City, 1952). He has lived in Mexico since 1944, except for two years of study in Madrid, and has written numerous critical essays on such topics as Nicaraguan poetry, on Martí, and Gutiérrez Nájera. His books of poetry include *Ensalmos y conjuros* (Mexico City, 1947), the prose-poem *La carne contigua* (Buenos Aires, 1948), *El retorno* (Mexico City, 1950), *Antología 1946–1952* (Madrid, 1953), *Contemplaciones europeas* (San Salvador, 1957), and *Poemas* (Buenos Aires, 1963).

He compiled the important anthology *Romances y corridos nicaragüenses* (Mexico City, 1946).

MEJÍA VALLEJO, MANUEL (1923– *v*, b. Antioquia. Colombian novelist and short-story writer. His realist novels include *La tierra éramos nosotros* (Medellín, 1945); *Al pie de la ciudad* (Buenos Aires, 1958), a social-protest work incorporating cinematic techniques and the novel-within-novel convention; *El día señalado* (Barcelona, 1964); and *Los negociantes* (Barcelona, 1965).

Many of his prize-winning stories were collected in the impressive *Tiempo de sequía* (Medellín, 1957); later short stories appeared in *Cuentos de zona tórrida* (1967), where characters struggle against all manner of adversity.

Mejía Vallejo has compiled the *Antología del cuento antioqueño* (n.d. but 1961).

Mejor alcalde el rey, El, a play written between 1620 and 1623 by Lope de Vega Carpio (q.v.). Its source is an incident from the *Crónica general* and it is one of those plays (like *Peribáñez y el comendador de Ocaña* or *Los novios de Hornachuelos*) that exalt the nature and power of the monarchy as a method of defending the rights of the peasant from the tyranny of feudal lordlings.

Don Tello, just such a lord, stops a peasant wedding and abducts the lovely bride Elvira to his castle. The humiliated bridegroom Sancho, an untypical peasant, inasmuch as he is of a noble family that has come down in the world, travels to court to obtain an audience with King Alfonso VII, who is shown in a kindly, paternal light. When Tello rejects the letter bearing Alfonso's command and illtreats Sancho, Alfonso decides to return with Sancho in disguise to ascertain the truth of the case.

Elvira enters with her clothes torn and, in lines of great pathos and beauty, accuses Tello of assaulting her. Alfonso,' the best magistrate', marries her to Tello and then executes the presumptuous lord, giving half of his estate to Elvira who is now free to marry Sancho, and bring him great wealth.

Nuño, Elvira's father, is an honourable and dignified peasant, while the swineherd Pelayo, a *gracioso* who sees the world in terms of pig lore, is a masterly creation of trenchant humour. Alfonso is given very few lines, but the ideal of monarchy is stressed throughout the play, possibly with an ironic intention to rebuke the unapproachable, irresponsible Philip III. The play is fluently versified in Lope's best manner, especially the *décimas* in which the loyal Sancho and the sincere Elvira declare their love, and the *romancillo* of Elvira's passionate plea to the king.

The edition by J. Gómez Ocerín and R. M. Tenreiro for Clásicos Castellanos (2nd edn., 1931) is in vol. 1 of the *Comedias*.

MELÉNDEZ VALDÉS, JUAN (1754–1817), b. Ribera del Fresno, Badajoz. He studied law at Salamanca, where he met, and was influenced by, Cadalso (q.v.). He taught there, first Humanities and then Grammar (1778–89), and at the same time took his doctorate in law. His regular visits to Madrid gave him a reputation there, first with the eclogue *Batilo* (1780, the name by which he was known in the Arcadia Salmantina) awarded a prize in 1781 by the Real

Academia Española, then with *La gloria de las artes* (an ode read two years later to the Academia de San Fernando), and finally with the prize-winning play *Las bodas de Camacho el Rico* (1784), and *Poesías* (1785). He became the most celebrated Spanish writer of the day.

He received early promotion as a lawyer but, as the close friend of Jovellanos (q.v.), was subject to political hostility, deprived of his official post, and exiled to Zamora in 1800. He was restored to his post after the mutiny of Aranjuez but he cravenly welcomed the invaders in 1808, and dedicated an ode to Joseph Bonaparte. After receiving favours and official honours from the French, he was forced to emigrate with the other *afrancesados* (q.v.) in 1813 and died in France.

His only major book is *Poesías* (1785; 2nd enlarged edn., 3 vols., 1797), definitively edited by Quintana (4 vols.) in 1820. More poems appeared in vol. 63 (1871) of the BAE, in the *Revue Hispanique* as *Los besos de amor* (vol. 1, 1894, pp. 73–83), and as *Poesías y cartas inéditas* (vol. 4, 1897, pp. 266–313), and in *Poesías inéditas* (ed. by A. Rodríguez Moñino, 1954). His poetry divides into two main types: the erotic-bucolic, of anacreontic inspiration, influenced by Cadalso; and the philosophical, influenced by Jovellanos. He uses the familar themes of his day and traditional metres.

Meléndez's major importance is in his exquisite taste, rhythm, and sensibility at a time when verse was decadent. Among his fine *letrillas* are 'La despedida' and 'El lunarcito'; among the romances, 'Los segadores' and 'El árbol caído'; and among the more successful of the philosophical odes, 'El invierno no es tiempo de meditación' and 'A la presencia de Dios'. His gentle eroticism often borders on the directly sensual, and reveals a Rousseau-like nostalgia for an imaginary golden age, a discontent with the present, and a feeling for nature and landscape.

See W. R. Colford, *Juan Meléndez Valdés* (New York, 1942); G. Demerson, *Don Juan Meléndez Valdés et son temps* (Paris, 1962); and R. Froldi, *Un poeta illuminista: Meléndez Valdés* (Milan, 1967).

MELGAR, MARIANO (1790–1815), b. Arequipa. Peruvian poet, and graduate of San Marcos University. Melgar is considered by some critics a precursor of Latin-American Romanticism, and by others the first Romantic. At the outbreak of the Pumacahua rebellion of 1814, Melgar joined the independence fighters but at their defeat (March 1815) was shot by the Spanish. Many of his poems were burnt by the ecclesiastical authorities because they dealt with sexual love. L. A. Sánchez has described him as

'un Byron inculto y quechua de ambiente seminarizado'. Melgar translated Ovid's *Remedia amoris* as *Arte de olvidar* (1821) and introduced the Quechua *yaraví* (elegy) into Spanish (*Yaravíes*, 1941). Collections of his verse appeared in 1878 (ed. by F. García Calderón), 1944, and 1958.

See María Wiesse, *La romántica vida de Mariano Melgar* (1936); and Ángela Torres Azurra, *Melgar, precursor del romanticismo* (1966).

Mellizos de La Flor, Los, the *gaucho* poem by Hilario Ascasubi (q.v.) better known as *Santos Vega* (q.v.), after the name of its narrator.

MELO, FRANCISCO MANOEL DE (1608–66), b. Lisbon of a Portuguese father and a Spanish mother. Melo is a classic author in both languages, being poet, moralist, playwright, and historian. More celebrated in his lifetime as a soldier, Melo survived the disastrous tempest of 1627, when he was forced to supervize the burial of more than two thousand men who had perished at sea. He served as an officer in the Spanish army in Flanders while Portugal was still annexed to Spain, and took part in the campaign against Catalan rebels in 1640, when he joined the Bragança separatists and was arrested for treason. He was later released and returned to Portugal where, in 1644, he was again gaoled on suspicion of being King João IV's successful rival in love. Melo was exiled to Brazil in 1652 and pardoned in 1657, when he was restored to royal favour and employed in diplomacy.

The aristocratic Melo is, with Quevedo, the greatest writer of his generation in the Iberian Peninsula. He is the model 'discreto', equally adept like Garcilaso at the arts of war and peace. His *auto* entitled *O fidalgo aprendiz* (1676; ed. Mendes dos Remédios, 1898) is an amusing satire on the theme of Molière's *Le bourgeois gentilhomme* (1670), and though his poetry is derivatively gongoresque, both his literary criticism (*Hospital das letras*) and his picaresque fiction (*Relógios falantes* and *Escritório avarento*) are among the most important of the period and are to be found in the Portuguese *Apólogos dialogais* published posthumously in 1721 (and ed. F. Nery, Rio de Janeiro, 1921).

Among his most interesting prose is that in his letters: *Cartas familiares* (Rome, 1664; 2nd edn. selected by M. Rodrigues Lapa, Lisbon, 1942). His witty but repressive *Carta de guía de casados* (1651; ed. Edgar Prestage, 1916) shows him up in a worse light, subordinating women absolutely to the will of their masters. His collected *Obras morales* (2 vols.) appeared in Rome in 1664.

But Melo is best remembered as a historian: for the Spanish *Historia de los movimientos, y separación de Cataluña, y de la Guerra entre . . .*

Felipe el Cuarto . . . y la Deputación general de aquel Principado (Lisbon, 1645), written under the pen-name 'Clemente Libertino', reprinted in vol. 21 (1852) of the BAE, and edited in 1912 by Jacinto Octavio Picón, written in forceful, dramatic prose from first-hand observation; and the Portuguese Epanáforas de vária história portuguesa (1660; ed. Edgar Prestage, 1931), a miscellany of five historical works, including one on his mission at the behest of Olivares to quell a Portuguese uprising against heavy taxes.

See J. Ferreira, Don Francisco Manoel de Melo escreveu a 'Arte de furtar' (Oporto, 1945), and Edgar Prestage's standard study, with a good bibliography: Don Francisco Manuel de Melo: esboço biográfico (Coimbra, 1914; English edn., Oxford, 1922).

MENA, JUAN DE (1411–56), b. Cordova. Poet and prose-writer. Educated in his native city, in Salamanca, and at Rome, where he met several humanists. An intellectual, he remained aloof from the great political quarrels of his time, remaining loyal to Juan II and to Álvaro de Luna despite his friendship with Luna's enemy the Marqués de Santillana (q.v.). He enjoyed Ovid, Virgil, and Lucan, all of whom influenced his literary experiments. Mena occupied several important posts at the court of Juan II, culminating in that of royal chronicler.

About 1442 he made a Castilian version of a poor Latin text of the Iliad, Ilias latina, which he entitled Esta es la Iliada de Homero en romance traducida (Valladolid, 1519) often known as the Omero romançado. He contributed a laudatory prologue to Luna's Libro de las virtuosas e claras mugeres and in the prose commentary to his own poem La Coronación (written 1438, published Salamanca, 1499), renounced his didactic rôle in order to tell a story to give himself the artistic pleasure of creation. He deliberately created a new poetic prose using the more learned vocabulary he had acquired to eliminate common speech rhythms from his elegant version of the vernacular.

His chief importance, however, is that of creating the first 'pure' poetry in Spanish, disregarding the resources of the colloquial language in order to refine a new means of expression. In his contempt for the majority of the reading public he resembles two other writers of Cordova: Lucan and Góngora (qq.v.). He employs periphrasis to avoid a single word for an idea or thing; turns to allegory and mythology as poeticizing devices; and prefers involved syntax. In his early period he writes the traditional verse forms predominate. He writes canciones and decires in the courtly mode with wit, sentiment, and formal virtuosity: such poems, found in the major Cancioneros such as those of

Baena or Stúñiga (qq.v.), offer no originality, either in form or content.

But with El laberinto de Fortuna (q.v.), written in 1444 and first published between 1481 and 1488 (probably in Salamanca), Mena produced a Dantesque allegory in a wholly original style, known from its length as Las trezientas [stanzas]. See D. C. Clarke, Juan de Mena's 'Laberinto de fortuna' . . . (1973). Las cincuenta refers to the allegorical poem of 51 double quintillas in arte menor, La Coronación del Marqués de Santillana (Salamanca, 1499), which begins by describing the torments of Hell and the evils of the times and concludes on Parnassus, with the apotheosis of Mena's friend Santillana (see Inez McDonald's 'The "Coronación" of Juan de Mena: poem and commentary' in Hispanic Review, vol. 7, 1939). The other Italianate-classical work of Mena's mature period is the Claro-escuro, an inventive work in dual metre: coplas of eight-syllable lines for the 'claro' sections and arte-mayor eight-syllable lines and an obscure vocabulary for the 'escuro' sections. Both of these minor works appear in vol. 19 (1912) of the NBAE.

Mena's patron Luna fell in 1453 and Juan II himself died in 1454, so that Mena's political career was at an end. The unfinished Coplas de los siete pecados mortales (Salamanca, 1500) is his first attempt to reach a wider public by adopting a simpler style. The influence is probably the Psychomachia of Prudentius. These Coplas were finished after Mena's death by three poets, one of whom was Gómez Manrique (q.v.). Mena's works appeared first without a title (Saragossa, 1506) and in a corrected edition by Francisco Sánchez (Salamanca, 1582).

The most considerable assessment of his achievement is Juan de Mena, poeta del prerenacimiento español (Mexico City, 1950) by María Rosa Lida de Malkiel (q.v.).

Menard, Pierre, the apocryphal author of nineteen 'visible' works and part of a secret, identical, Quijote, in 'Pierre Menard, autor del Quijote' by Jorge Luis Borges (q.v.). The story was first collected in El jardín de senderos que se bifurcan (1941) and appears in the Obras completas in the volume of Ficciones (1956).

Menard declares: 'Yo he contraído el misterioso deber de reconstruir literalmente [Cervantes'] obra espontánea'.

MENASSA, MIGUEL (1940–), b. Buenos Aires. Poet and short story writer. His method is generally ironical, usually at his own expense, in Poesía junta (1961) and Poemas leídos (1962) to which he contributed, and in his own books. The latter include Pequeña historia (1961), La ciudad se cansa (1963), 22 poemas y la máquina *electrónica, o cómo desesperar a los ejecutivos* (1965), and *Los otros tiempos* (1970), poems inspired by the figure of Captain Cat in Dylan Thomas's *Under Milk Wood*. He is the editor of the *Grupo Cero* magazine in Buenos Aires.

MÉNDEZ PEREIRA, Octavio (1887–1954), b. Aguadulce, Panamá. Panamanian essayist and novelist. He studied at the University of Santiago (Chile) and later travelled in Europe, studying in England. His diplomatic career included terms in Chile, France, and England. Méndez Pereira was instrumental in founding the Universidad Nacional de Panamá (1935) and served as its Rector until 1940. His books ranged from education—*Historia de la instrucción pública en Panamá* (1916)—to biography—*Justo Arosemena* (1919)—and to historical novels such as *El tesoro del Dabaibe* (1934), and its sequel *Tierra firme* (1940), retitled in its second edition *Balboa*. His literary essays were collected under the title *Cervantes y el Quijote apócrifo* (1914), *Dante y la Divina Comedia* (1921), and *Leonardo da Vinci* (1931).

MENDILAHARSU, Julio Raúl (1887–1924), b. Montevideo. Uruguayan poet. A romantic writer on social themes and nature, Mendilaharsu is well-known for the exaltation of his poems about the sea. The best of *Como las nubes* (1909), *Deshogando el silencio* (1911), *El alma de mis horas* (1913), *La cisterna* (1919), and *Voz de vida* (1923) appeared in *Selección de poesias* (1926).

MENDOZA, Antonio, see Hurtado de Mendoza y Larrea, Antonio.

MENDOZA, Bernardino de (1540?–1604), b. Guadalajara. Historian. He accompanied the Duke of Alba to Italy and Flanders in 1567, and compiled the careful, sober *Comentarios de . . . lo sucedido en las guerras de los Payses baxos desde el Año de 1567 hasta el de 1577* (Spanish version, 1592 after the first French edition, translated by Pedro Crespet, had appeared in Paris the previous year). These have been reprinted in vol. 28 (1853) of the BAE.

A respected diplomat, Mendoza was appointed ambassador to England in 1578. His *Theórica y prática de la guerra* (1595) was the work of an expert. He also translated Lipsius and composed *Odas a la conversión de un pecador* included by Cerdá in *Poesías espirituales* (1779).

See Alfred Morel-Fatio, 'Don Bernardino de Mendoza' in his *Études sur l'Espagne* (4th ser., Paris, 1925), pp. 373–490.

MENDOZA, Diego Hurtado de, see Hurtado de Mendoza, Diego.

MENDOZA, Fray Íñigo (c. 1422–c. 1492), b. Guadalajara. Poet. A Franciscan who, according to Menéndez y Pelayo, may have been a converted Jew, he enjoyed the patronage of the Marqués de Santillana (q.v.), whose name he consequently took, as was customary. He was subsequently protected by Queen Isabella. His alleged tendency to flirt with the court ladies provoked this satirical *quintilla* by Vázquez de Palencia: 'Este religioso santo, / metido en vanos placeres, / es un lobo en pardo manto: / ¿cómo entiende y sabe tanto / del trato de las mujeres?'.

The *Vita Christi por coplas* (Zamora, 1482) seems to be a fragment of an uncompleted larger work filled with *villancicos*, edifying stories in ballad form, and other borrowings from folk literature intended to popularize religion. His other poems can be found in the Clásicos Castellanos edition of his *Cancionero* (1968) by J. Rodríguez-Puértolas which supersedes the edition in vol. 19 (1912) of the NBAE. Mendoza also wrote *De las ceremonias de la misa* (Seville, 1499).

See K. Whinnom, 'The printed editions and the text of the works of Fray Íñigo de Mendoza' in *BHS*, vol. 39 (1962), pp. 137–52; and J. Rodríguez-Puértolas, *Fray Íñigo de Mendoza y sus 'Coplas de Vita Christi'* (1968).

MENDOZA, Jaime (1874–1939), b. Sucre. Bolivian essayist, novelist, and poet (*Voces de antaño*, 1938). After qualifying as a doctor, Mendoza worked for a mining company, and wrote *En las tierras de Potosí* (Barcelona, 1911), a moving novel of the miners' plight. Though more pamphlet than novel, it adumbrated the author's view, later amplified, that Indians should not be forced to adopt European ways but by agrarian reform should regain their own lands. Darío called Mendoza the 'Bolivian Gorki' for this book; its sequels *Los malos pensamientos* (1916) and *Páginas bárbaras* (1917) were less carefully written, though the latter has some fine descriptions of the Amazonian jungle. The first of the three stories in the semi-autobiographical *Memorias de un estudiante* (1918) is Mendoza's best work, far superior to *La isla* (1936), a novel on the legend of Manuel María Caballero.

Mendoza spent much of his later life in the legal and social struggle for the Chaco, always counselling a peaceful settlement. These polemics, which won him great honour in his own country, included *El Mar del Sur* (1926), *La ruta atlántica* (1927), *La tesis andinista: Boliva y Paraguay* (1933), *La tragedia del Chaco* (1933), *El macizo boliviano* (1935) which proposed a geographical interpretation of the national character, and *El Chaco en los albores de la conquista* (1937).

See Guillermo Lora, *La frustración del novelista Jaime Mendoza* (1964).

MENDOZA MONTEAGUDO, JUAN DE (1575–1660?), Spanish poet, soldier, and adventurer who left for the New World aged 15 and, after wandering through several countries, enlisted under Francisco de Quiñones in Chile in 1599. The verse chronicle he composed, *Las Guerras de Chile* (1610), has been edited by J. Medina (Santiago de Chile, 1888). As poetry it is negligible, but it provides a valuable picture of Chilean life and society at the turn of the 17th c. Its 8,000 lines are divided into eleven cantos.

See Enrique Blanchard-Chessi, *Sobre Don Juan de Mendoza Monteagudo* (Santiago de Chile, 1899).

MENÉNDEZ PIDAL, RAMÓN (1869–1968), b. Corunna. The leading Hispanist of his age, who concentrated on medieval Spanish language and literature. A disciple of Marcelino Menéndez y Pelayo (q.v.) at Madrid University, he brought to his studies a rigorous analytical scholarship whereas Pelayo had excelled in synthesis and the broad approach.

In 1896 he published *La leyenda de los Infantes de Lara*, awarded a prize by the Real Academia de la Historia. He studied the origins and transmission of the legend of the Siete Infantes de Lara (q.v.) and indicated the path he was to take by adding notes on the primitive Castilian epic, hitherto virtually unexplored.

In 1899 he was appointed Professor of Romance Philology in Madrid, a position he held until retirement in 1939. He became a member of the Real Academia Española in 1901 and in 1904 produced the valuable *Manual de gramática histórica española*. He achieved worldwide recognition with *Cantar de mio Cid: texto, gramática y vocabulario* (3 vols., 1908–12), now superseded in many particulars, but deserving gratitude for its serious approach to the earliest Spanish literary classic. It was revised in 1946 and again in 1956 and the critical text and minimal apparatus appeared in the Clásicos Castellanos (1913).

In 1914 Menéndez Pidal founded the *Revista de Filología Española*, a principal source of scholarship still published by the Instituto Miguel de Cervantes of the Consejo Superior de Investigaciones Científicas. From 1925 to 1939 and then again for some years from 1947 he was a director of the Real Academia Española. *Poesía juglaresca y juglares* (1924) is a major work on medieval poetry. *Orígenes del español* (1926) is an exhaustive study of the languages of Spain up to the 11th c. (75th enlarged edition, 1964). *La España del Cid* (1929) has been translated by

Harold Sutherland (London, 1934; reprinted, 1971) as *The Cid and his Spain*.

His subsequent works included *España, eslabón entre la Cristiandad y el Islam* (1956), *España y su historia* (1957), *La Chanson de Roland y el Neotradicionalismo* (1959), *El dialecto leonés* (Oviedo, 1962), and *Los Reyes Católicos y otros estudios* (Buenos Aires, 1962).

Much of his time after retirement was devoted to editing a multi-volume *Historia de España* for Espasa-Calpe, beginning from prehistoric times.

A comprehensive bibliography by M. L. Vázquez de Parga is in *Revista de Filología Española*, vol. 47 (1964), pp. 7–127. Among his students at Madrid University or at the graduate Centro de Estudios Históricos were Américo Castro, Amado Alonso, Dámaso Alonso, and Tomás Navarro Tomás (qq.v.).

MENÉNDEZ Y PELAYO, MARCELINO (1856–1912), b. Santander. The major Spanish literary historian and critic of the 19th c. His synthesis of learning in such works as his annotated anthologies of the lyric poets and the early novelists remains unsurpassed: his disciples (among them Ramón Menéndez Pidal, Said Armesto, Asín Palacios, Bonilla y San Martín, Blanca de los Ríos, Rubió y Lluch, Serrano y Sanz, and Cotarelo y Mori) were set the task of specializing in fields which their master had opened up.

He combined a magisterial command of Spanish literary history with a phenomenal memory, a humanistic upbringing at the Universities of Barcelona and Madrid, an artistic flair shown in the Spanish and Latin verse he wrote mainly in youth, a bibliographical virtuosity always at the service of his writings but never allowed to dominate them, a superb private library (donated to the city of Santander at his death), a teaching ability second to none, and loyalty to Roman Catholic theology and his native land. These all brought to Spanish literary history a genuine respectability which it had hitherto lacked.

He never lost the love of Latin inculcated at his school in Santander, writing as his doctoral thesis *La novela entre los latinos* (Santander, 1875) and the later *Horacio en España* (1877; 2nd edn., 1885) and a *Bibliografía hispanolatina clásica* (10 vols., 1902), complete to the time of Cicero.

Milà i Fontanals, his foremost professor at Barcelona, was indirectly responsible for the conception and execution of Menéndez's major work, *Historia de las ideas estéticas en España* (1882–91). This, like the rest of his work, discussed issues broader than those implicit in the title, and was not restricted to works and writers in Spanish.

Menéndez took over the editorship of the

NBAE, recognizing the need for popular editions as demonstrated by the sale and general excellence of the parent BAE (1846–80).

He obtained travel grants to study in the major libraries of Portugal, France, and Italy, and achieved there recognition parallel with the fame he already had in Spain. On his return in 1878 he was 21. The Chair of Literary History at Madrid was then vacant, with the death of Amador de los Ríos; as the minimum age for candidates was 25, the Cortes was approached by Cánovas del Castillo with a request to reduce the minimum age to 21. The Cortes agreed and Menéndez got the post. In 1880 he published the first two volumes of the absorbing *Historia de los heterodoxos españoles*, the third appearing in 1882 (the latest edn., of 8 vols., is in the *Obras completas* begun in 1940 and edited by E. Sánchez Reyes). This work studies the evolution of religion in Spain from before Priscillian up to the 19th c. and can be read with great profit even by those opposed to the author's serene, dogmatic viewpoint which usually coincided with the official ecclesiastical viewpoint, though written in an ebullient, exciting style that many a churchman might envy. The chapters on Erasmus and his influence in Spain have proved most fruitful in terms of subsequent scholarship.

Menéndez y Pelayo also wrote *Calderón y su teatro* (1881), five series of *Estudios de crítica literaria* (1884–1908), *Antología de poetas líricos castellanos* (10 vols., 1890–1906), *Ensayos de crítica filosófica* (1892), and the brilliant *Orígenes de la novela* (4 vols., 1905–10), originally written as introductory matter for vols. I, VII, and XIV of the NBAE, and many more. Mention must be made of his prologues and annotations for the edition of Lope de Vega produced by the Real Academia Española (1890–1912) which comprise the six vols. of his *Obras completas* now entitled *Estudios sobre el teatro de Lope de Vega*.

A. Bonilla y San Martín's bibliography of Menéndez in *RABM*, vol. 16 (1912), pp. 238–66, has been supplemented by R. Blanco y Sánchez, *Don Marcelino Menéndez y Pelayo* (1925) and by J. Simón Díaz in *Arbor* (Madrid), vol. 34 (1956), pp. 536–59.

See A. Bonilla y San Martín, *Marcelino Menéndez y Pelayo* (1912); F. G. Andoín, *Un español ejemplar como humanista y como hombre* (1959); F. Lázaro Carreter, *Menéndez Pelayo* (1962); and E. Sánchez Reyes, *Menéndez Pelayo* (Barcelona, 1962).

MENESES, Guillermo (1911–), b. Caracas. Venezuelan novelist and short-story writer. He belongs to the 'Elite' generation, named after an influential magazine and publishing house in Caracas. Meneses was also chief editor of the daily *Ahora* and editor of *El Nacional*'s literary supplement. His fiction concerns the lives of Negroes and mulattoes in their natural setting in Venezuela, but psychological interest often strengthens the simple narrative. His short stories are *La balandra Isabel llegó esta tarde* (1934; this has been filmed in Venezuela); *Tres cuentos venezolanos* (1938); *La mujer, el as de oro y la luna* (1945); and *La mano junto al muro* (1952).

Meneses has written the following novels: *Canción de negros* (1934); a sombre baseball story, *Campeones* (1939), in which only one of the four players escapes alcoholism and syphilis; the racial novel *El mestizo José Vargas* (1942); *El falso cuaderno de Narciso Espejo* (1953); and the satire on military rule, with its consequent corruption of bourgeois life, *La misa de Arlequín* (1962).

Menosprecio de corte y alabança de aldea, Libro llamado (Valladolid, 1539), a work in praise of the rural life by Fray Antonio de Guevara (q.v.). It is one of the group of didactic works (including *Reloj de príncipes* and the *Epístolas familiares*) which gave Guevara European fame.

Guevara attacks the vices of the court and the capital in terms reminiscent of the *Beatus ille* of Horace; among his probable sources was the *De curialium miseriis* (1444) of Pope Pius II, otherwise Aeneas Sylvius Piccolomini.

Guevara argues that country life is cheaper and more healthy, one is not surrounded by hypocrites and place-seekers, and home comforts are easily found. One may dress as one pleases, and have a wider variety of flesh and fish to eat than is possible in the city.

There is a modern edition by P. Pou Fernández (Saragossa, 1969).

MEONIO, Clearco, pen-name of Joaquín Arcadio Pagaza (q.v.).

MERA, Juan León (1832—94), b. Ambato, Ecuador. Novelist, critic, and poet, notable for having produced, in the sentimental *Cumandá* (1879), the first jungle novel of Ecuador, modelled on Chateaubriand and Fenimore Cooper. He began by painting water-colours for sale to travellers, then studied in the studio of Antonio Salas in Quito, where he became a lifelong friend of Julio Zaldumbide (q.v.). It was Mera's *Ojeada histórico-crítica sobre la poesía ecuatoriana* (1868), which first attracted European scholars to the literature of Ecuador.

His works inspired by folklore include a verse legend, *La virgen del sol* (1861), which contrasts the mercenary values of Spanish adventurers with the ancient virtues of the Indians, and the important *Antología ecuatoriana: cantares del pueblo ecuatoriano* (1892). Mera also composed the

Ecuadorian national anthem. Mera's *Novelas cortas* were reprinted at Ambato in 1952.

See Víctor M. Garcés, *Vida ejemplar y obra fecunda de Juan León Mera* (Ambato, 1963).

MERCADER Y CERVELLÓN, Gaspar (*fl.* 1600), b. Valencia? Novelist and historian. Mercader's best book is an excellent pastoral novel, *El Prado de Valencia* (Valencia, 1600; critical edn. by Henri Mérimée, Toulouse, 1907), which includes a large number of poems by his fellow-academics in the Academia de los Nocturnos (q.v.), where he was known as 'Relámpago'.

Mercader's 'Retrato político del Rey Alfonso VIII' appeared in the anonymous *Varios eloquentes libros recogidos en uno* (1726).

MERCEDARIO, El, the name by which Fray Gabriel Téllez (q.v.), or 'Tirso de Molina', was also known.

Mercurio de América, El, the influential Argentine literary review (1898–1900) directed by Eugenio Díaz Romero partly to propagate the modernism expounded by Rubén Darío (q.v.) in his ephemeral *Revista de América*.

The *Mercurio* was the most significant magazine published in Buenos Aires after *La Biblioteca* (1896–8) and before *Ideas* (1903–5).

Mercurio Peruano, El, since the closure of *Cultura Peruana* in 1965, the only non-academic intellectual magazine in Peru. It was founded in 1918 as the organ of the conservatives who belonged to the so-called *Generación Novecentista* led by Riva Agüero. Edited by Víctor Andrés Belaúnde, its aim was to become a 'síntesis de valores nacionales tanto positivos, utilitarios y económicos como teóricos, artísticos y literarios'.

MESA, Cristóbal de (1561–1633), b. Zafra, Badajoz. Poet and translator. Imbued with a love of classical scholarship by his professor at Salamanca University (Francisco Sánchez, 'el Brocense', q.v.), Mesa travelled to Italy, where he met Tasso, and on his return to Spain became chaplain to the Duke of Béjar.

Praised, together with a host of other poets, in *La Galatea* of Cervantes and *El Laurel de Apolo* of Lope de Vega, Mesa wrote three grandiose epics of little importance. They were all dedicated to Philip III, who took no notice. *Las Navas de Tolosa* (1594) describes at great length the battle that finally broke the power of Islam. *La restauración de España* (1607), much shorter, deals with the epic story of Pelayo and his struggle against the Moors. *El Patrón de España* (1612)

concerns the martyrdom of St. James in Jerusalem and the miraculous translation of his body to Spain, its deposition, and subsequent veneration at Compostela.

Mesa's classical education enabled him to write versions from Homer (that of the *Iliad* was never printed), and from Virgil (*La Eneida*, 1615; *Las Églogas y Geórgicas . . .*, 1615, the latter including his poor tragedy *Pompeyo*), but his skill in *ottava rima* and his imagination are unequal to the task.

See *El Criticón* (Badajoz, 1934), no. 2, pp. 33–50, for Mesa's *Epístolas* (ed. with a good bibliography by A. R. Rodríguez-Moñino).

MESA, Enrique de (1878–1929), b. Madrid. Poet, journalist, and dramatic critic. His regional verse of the Guadarrama and Sierra de Gredos is occasionally self-consciously archaic, but often reaches the authentic folk level in the manner of Juan Ruiz or Lope de Vega, two of his models. His favoured themes are love, home, and nature. Mesa's collections of poetry are *Tierra y alma* (1906), *Cancionero castellano* (1911; new edn., 1917), *El silencio de la Cartuja* (1916), and *La posada y el camino* (1928). The prose *Tragicomedia* (1910), *Flor pagana* (1915), and *Apostillas a la escena* are included in the *Obras completas* (1930). There is also an edition of the *Poesías completas* (Buenos Aires, 1941).

MESONERO ROMANOS, Ramón de (1803–82), b. Madrid. *Costumbrista*, or writer in the genre known as *cuadros de costumbres* ('sketches of manners'), realistic or satirical scenes of life in a closely-observed corner of Spain: Andalusia, in the writings of Estébanez Calderón (q.v.) and Madrid in the writings of Mesonero Romanos.

Left wealthy by his banker father, Mesonero Romanos chose to devote himself to the literary life, and specialized in the *cuadros de costumbres* which he raised to a new level of maturity and humorous observation.

Mis ratos perdidos, o ligero bosquejo de Madrid en 1820 y 1821 (1822) are anonymous sketches for the important *Panorama matritense* (3 vols., 1835–38), enlarged with the pen-name 'El Curioso Parlante' as *Escenas matritenses* (q.v., 4 vols., 1842), his acknowledged masterpiece.

Manual de Madrid (1831; with an *Apéndice*, 1835) is a polished guidebook to the city and capital he knew so well.

In 1835 he resuscitated the defunct *Ateneo* and the following year founded the important *Semanario Pintoresco Español* (1836–57), which was the chief vehicle for Spanish *costumbrismo* during its long life, and helped to prepare the public for the novels with an identifiably contemporary setting. The resurgence of interest in local customs was due mainly to the magazine

Cartas Españolas influenced by the French writer Joseph-Étienne Jouy.

Mesonero Romanos defined his technique as 'writing for the general public in a plain style without affectation or carelessness, usually describing, rarely arguing, never causing tears, almost always causing laughter . . . and to sum up attempting . . . to become a true observer'.

Tipos, grupos y bocetos de cuadros de costumbres (1862) takes the biographical and anecdotal approach, while *El antiguo Madrid* (1861) confined itself mainly to streets and houses. His excellent autobiography is *Memorias de un setentón, natural y vecino de Madrid* (1880; enlarged edn., 1881; 2 vols., 1961).

Obras jocosas y satíricas (4 vols., 1862) was supplemented by *Trabajos no coleccionados* (2 vols., 1903–5, with a good bibliography).

The best edition of his *Obras completas* (5 vols., 1967) is that of Carlos Seco Serrano in BAE, vols. 199–203.

Mester de clerecía ('occupation, or art of the clerks, or learned') in a more narrow sense, a body of poetry written mainly or wholly in *cuaderna vía* metre (q.v.) during the 13th c. in the monasteries of Old Castile; the 14th c. *cuaderna vía* poems are quite different. The term first occurs in the *Libro de Alexandre* (q.v.): 'Mester trago fermoso, non es de ioglaria, / mester es sen pecado, ca es de clerezia', which contrasts the art with the *mester de juglaría* (q.v.), despite the fact that they were known to have influenced each other.

Writers of the *mester de clerecía* include Gonzalo de Berceo (q.v.), and the authors of the *Libro de Apolonio*, the *Poema de Fernán González*, and the *Historia troyana* (qq.v.). The last writer to use it was Pero López de Ayala, when it was already changing its character.

Despite its name (indicating a learned origin), the art was recited publicly in the same way as the *mester de juglaría*, and Berceo called himself a *juglar*. Thematically, these works tend to be pious and learned, using classical or biblical sources. However, in the attempt to make their matter palatable to a wide illiterate public, the language became a compound of the Latinate and the popular.

Mester de juglaría ('occupation, or art of the minstrel'), in a more narrow sense, an amorphous body of oral epic and narrative poetry of the 12th, 13th, and 14th cs. preceding, and contemporary with, the *mester de clerecía* (q.v.). Both 'arts' are used by some poets, as for example Juan Ruiz, Arcipreste de Hita (q.v.). Lyrical and dramatic poetry is included in the genre, and it is preserved, or in some cases originated, in the many ballads later collected in the traditional *romanceros*. The *juegos de escarnio* (prohibited by the *Siete Partidas* of Alfonso 'el Sabio', q.v.) were a form of *mester de juglaría* prohibited for their outspokenness. There is no regular rhyme scheme in the *mester*, and no regular metre.

The last major poem of the genre was the 14th-c. *Crónica rimada de Alfonso Onceno*.

See Ramón Menéndez Pidal, *Poesía juglaresca y juglares* (1924); 6th edn., 1957).

METGE, BERNAT (*c.* 1345–1413?), b. Barcelona. Catalan poet and prose-writer whose works were composed during periods of imprisonment between 1381 and 1398. His stepfather was Ferrer Sayol, chief notary to Queen Leonor of Sicily, the third wife of Pere III, called 'el Ceremonioso'. Sayol, a humanist who translated the *De re rustica* of Palladius, probably influenced Metge in the direction of learning.

For obscure reasons, Metge was arrested and imprisoned in 1381, 1388, and again after the death of the king in 1396, but always managed to regain his lost power and was still a royal secretary in 1410, during the reign of Marti I.

During his first period in prison (1381), Metge wrote the allegorical poem *Llibre de fortuna e prudència* in the tradition of Boethius and the *Roman de la Rose*; his second prison term gave him the leisure to produce the *Historia de Valter e Griselda*, the first translation from Petrarch into a Peninsular language.

It is *Lo somni* (written in 1398) that has ensured Metge's fame. Written after reading Petrarch's *Secretum*, *Lo somni* (q.v.) is an apologia of Metge, a debate on the immortality of the soul, a defence of famous women, and much more. The short burlesque *La medecina apropriada a tot mal* was probably written at the same time.

The *Obres completes* of Metge have been edited by M. de Riquer (Barcelona, 1950), but there are separate editions of *Lo somni*, edited by J. M. de Casacuberta (Barcelona, 1924) in Els Nostres Clàssics and the *Obres menores*. (ed. M. Oliver, Barcelona, 1917) in the same series.

MEXÍA, HERNÁN (*fl.* late 15th c.), b. Jaén. Poet. Ten of his poems have survived, of which the most celebrated is the witty and vigorous *Los defectos de las condiciones de las mugeres*, a satire provoked by the verse controversy surrounding the *Coplas de las calidades de las donas* of Torroella (q.v.). It was addressed to Juan Álvarez Gato.

Mexía's works can be read in vol. 19 (1912) of the NBAE. He also compiled *Nobiliario vero* (Seville, 1492) in the genre of self-glorifying genealogies.

MEXÍA, PERO, see MEJÍA, Pedro.

MEXÍA DE LA CERDA, Luis (*c.* 1580–*c.* 1635), playwright. His most celebrated play is *Doña Inés de Castro, reina de Portugal*, first published in *Tercera parte de las comedias* by Lope de Vega. It was based on *Nise lastimosa* by Bermúdez, who wrote under the pen-name 'Antonio de Silva', and it appears in vol. 43 (1857) of the BAE.

Mexía is probably the author of two *autos: Las pruebas del linaje humano* (1621) and *El juego del hombre* in a MS. dated 1625 in the National Library, Madrid.

He is not the 'Luis Mexía' whose *Appólogo* [*sic*] *de la ociosidad y el trabajo* appears in the *Obras* (Alcalá, 1546) of Francisco Cervantes de Salazar (q.v.), who edited and annotated it.

MEY, Sebastián (1586?–1641?), b. Valencia. Fabulist. One of a famous Valencian family which included a printer and the Professor of Greek at Valencia University.

Mey's *Fabulario de quentos antiguos y nuevos* (1613?) included 57 stories and fables, many of them translated from Phaedrus, Aesop, and Italian sources. The whole was edited by M. Menéndez y Pelayo in his *Orígenes de la novela*, vol. 4 (vol. 21 of the NBAE, 1852), and eight of the stories appear in F. C. Saínz de Robles's compendium *Cuentos viejos de la vieja España* (1949).

MEZA Y SUÁREZ INCLÁN, Ramón (1861–1911), Cuban novelist and critic. The best Cuban novelist after Villaverde and before Carpentier. His fiction includes *El duelo de mi vecino, Flores y calabazas* (short stories, 1886), *Carmela* (1886), *Mi tío el empleado* (1887), *Don Aniceto el tendero* (1889), and *Últimas páginas* (1891), of which the most important work is *Mi tío . . .*, a realistic satire on colonial bureaucracy which broadens into an indictment of complacent colonials in Havana.

Meza's criticism was *Eusebio Guilera* (1908), *Julián del Casal* (1910), and *Los González del Valle* (1911).

Miau (1888), one of the *Novelas españolas contemporáneas* by Benito Pérez Galdós (qq.v.).

A magnificent novel, written immediately after the great *Fortunata y Jacinta* (q.v.), *Miau* lacks the density of plot and multiplicity of characters of the earlier book, concentrating instead on one family, that of the unfortunate Ramón Villaamil, nicknamed Miau from the resemblance of the wife Pura and daughters Milagros and Abelarda to cats. Don Ramón is a *cesante*, or victim of the customary civil service upheavals when the favourites of one party supersede those of another. Needing only a few weeks' employment in order to be able to retire on a pension, Villaamil dreams of reinstatement, and writes endless memoranda on administrative reform, one of which (Morality, Income Tax, Aduanas [Customs], and Unification of the national debt) is ridiculed by a treasury official as spelling in their initials the word MIAU. The scrupulously honest Villaamil sees lesser, often corrupt employees reaching positions of power often through the influence of women and friends. Víctor Cadalso, a handsome Mephistophelean figure with the gift of eloquence, who had married Villaamil's daughter Luisa and by his cruelty caused her madness and death, arrives in the family circle from Andalusia.

His son, Luisín Cadalsito, is an epileptic lad of ten profoundly affected by his mother's early death and by his grandfather's desperate search for a job. During his visions he imagines he talks to God, whom he confuses with an old beggar he had once seen, and with his grandfather.

Don Ramón's anxieties lead to fits of insanity and to a desire for suicide to remove himself from the threats of destitution and manipulation. On his last day of life he wanders, at last free of torment, on the outskirts of Madrid, and after a meal which he enjoys more than any other, he shoots himself to liberate both mind and body from the world's wickedness and deprivations. The Villaamil family is brought very convincingly to life throughout, and Galdós's observation of government employees and their offices is wholly authentic.

Miau links a number of Galdós's preoccupations: the Christlike figure of Villaamil, whose qualities are unrecognized by the world at large (cf. the protagonists of *Nazarín, Halma*, and *Misericordia*, qq.v.) and who yet possesses a faintly comic and ironic air reminiscent of Don Quijote; the relationship of madness to innocence and incorruptibility; the hypocrisy of Doña Pura who pawns most of her possessions but gives herself airs (like Rosalía in *La de Bringas*, q.v.); and the solitary nature of the visionary who comes to realize the wretchedness of mankind and the beauties of Nature (a thread that runs from *Fortunata y Jacinta* to *Realidad*).

See R. J. Weber, *The 'Miau' manuscript of Benito Pérez Galdós* (Berkeley, Calif., 1964). The novel has been translated into English by J. M. Cohen (Harmondsworth, 1963).

MICHAËLIS DE VASCONCELLOS, Carolina Guillermina (1851–1925), a German philologist, wife of the Portuguese José Vasconcellos. She specialized in medieval literature of the Iberian peninsula; her books include an edition of the *Romancero del Cid* (Leipzig, 1871), *Tres flores del teatro antiguo español* (1876), the study *Palmerín de Inglaterra* (Halle, 1883), and an edition of the *Cancionero de Ajuda* (1904). In

Portuguese she wrote *Das origens da poesia peninsular* (Lisbon, 1931).

MICHELENA, Luis, a Basque literary historian who has taught at the Seminario de Filología Vasca 'Julio de Urquijo' in San Sebastián and at Salamanca University.

Michelena contributed 'Literatura en lengua vasca' to vol 5 (1958) of the *Historia general de las literaturas hispánicas*, expanding it into *Historia de la literatura vasca* (1960).

He has also published *Textos arcaicos vascos* (1964).

MICRÓS, one of the pseudonyms used by the Mexican short-story writer Ángel de Campo (q.v.).

MIHURA, Miguel (1905–), b. Madrid. Playwright and film scriptwriter. A most successful dramatist of the Madrid light comedy, Mihura began by collaborating with Álvaro de Laiglesia and others. His best play, written in 1932, is *Tres sombreros de copa* (1952), a disconcertingly original work praised by Ionesco for 'combining tragic humour, profound truth and the ridiculous which, as a caricaturing principle, sublimates and elevates the truth of things by enlarging it'.

Francisco Ruiz Ramón has observed that Mihura's subsequent work for the stage has been a continuing, progressive denial of the regenerative values in *Tres sombreros de copa*. The *Obras completas* (1962) show the truth of this statement, and *La bella Dorotea* (1964), and subsequent plays such as *Milagro en casa del los López* (1965), and *Sólo el amor y la luna traen fortuna* (1969) seem to reflect middle-class attitudes rather than authentic inspiration. Mihura's humorous writings can be sampled in the magazine *La Codorniz* which he founded in 1942 and sold a few years later to Laiglesia, his co-author in *El caso de la mujer asesinadita* (1955), or 'The case of the lady who was slightly assassinated'. This play on words is more characteristic of his early period, when one of his *dramatis personae* observes 'I'm getting married, but only a little'.

See F. Ruiz Ramón, *Historia del teatro español, siglo XX* (1971), pp. 350–75.

Milagros de Nuestra Señora, a devotional work in verse by Gonzalo de Berceo (q.v.) on the Marian legends dating from the 13th c. The Latin source is a prose collection of twenty-eight Marian stories similar to, or identical with, an extant collection (see Richard Becker, *Gonzalo de Berceo's 'Milagros' und ihre Grundlagen*, Strasbourg, 1910). Berceo omits four miracles, adds a Spanish one not in the source, and prefaces the work with an allegory: the garden of love (*locus amoenus*) is a perfect meadow representing the perfection of the Blessed Virgin Mary. Mary is shown as a mother caring for her wayward children. The metre throughout is *cuaderna vía* (q.v.), the tone varies from tender to bitter, and the structure is much more careful in some stories (such as the 2nd and the 9th) than in others (the 1st or the 10th).

Editions include those of A. García Solalinde (1922) and Brian Dutton (London, 1971).

See Carmelo Gariano, *Análisis estilístico de los 'Milagros de Nuestra Señora' de Berceo* (1965).

MILÀ I FONTANALS, Manuel (1818–84), b. Villafranca del Panadés. Catalan scholar and poet. Milà, who has been called the founder of modern Spanish scholarship, taught at Barcelona University 1846–84 and counted among his most brilliant pupils Marcelino Menéndez y Pelayo (q.v.), who edited Milà's *Obras completas* (in fact far from complete, 8 vols., Barcelona, 1888–96). A poet in his own right, Milà composed *La cansó del pros Bernat*, described by Menéndez y Pelayo as a 'cantar de gesta en miniatura'. He translated Goethe's *Der König in Thule* as well as odes of Horace, and Dante.

His major contributions to early Romance literary studies are *Observaciones sobre la poesía popular con muestras de romances catalanes inéditos* (1853), later reprinted as *Romancerillo popular catalán* (1882); *De los trovadores en España* (1861; Barcelona, 1966), and *De la poesía heroico-popular castellana* (1874), which related the oldest Spanish ballads for the first time to medieval Spanish epic poetry.

Milà's letters are to be found in *Epistolari* (2 vols., Barcelona, 1922–32).

See J. Rubió y Ors, *Noticia de la vida y escritos de Don Manuel Milà i Fontanals* (Barcelona, 1887); M. Menéndez y Pelayo, 'El Dr. Don Manuel Milà y Fontanals' in his *Estudios y discursos de crítica histórica y literaria*, vol. 5 (1942), pp. 133–75, written in 1908; and A. Rubió i Lluch, *Manuel Milà i Fontanals* (Barcelona, 1918).

MILANÉS, José Jacinto (1814–63), b. Matanzas. Cuban poet and playwright. Influenced by Espronceda and Zorrilla (qq.v.), Milanés was virtually the founder of the Cuban Creole Romantic poem and play. *El Conde Alarcos* (1838) was an immediate success on the stage and was translated into German. His literary life ended with increasing madness from 1843, but in earlier years he had attained wide recognition for his simple but effective lyrics of Creole life such as *La madrugada* and *La fuga de la tórtola*. More interesting than the *Poesías* (1846) are the *Obras completas* (1865) in which his *leyendas* and *cuadro de costumbres El mirón cubano* are included.

MILLA Y VIDAURRE, José (1822–82), b. Guatemala City. Novelist, historian, and journalist, who wrote under the anagrammatical pseudonym 'Salomé Jil'. His historical novels are no longer widely read, but *La hija del Adelantado* (1866) has the distinction of being one of the first of its genre in Latin America. *Los nazarenos* (1867) and *El visitador* (1867) are the others. Milla is appreciated most for his *Cuadros de costumbres guatemaltecas* (3 vols., 1871), good-natured sketches on regional life. In *Un viaje al otro mundo pasando por otras partes, 1871 a 1874* (3 vols., 1875), Milla created the Guatemalan character Juan Chapín, shrewd, cunning, foolish, pretentious, and a little malicious.

His able, well-documented *Historia de la América Central* (5 vols., 1879–1905) covered only the period from 1502 to 1821, but was preceded by a 'Noticia histórica' on the pre-Columbian peoples of the New World, and rectified a number of errors and poor judgments in the *Recordación florida* of Antonio de Fuentes y Guzmán (q.v.). The book was left unfinished at his death, but it was completed by Agustín Gómez Carrillo. The best edition of Milla's *Obras completas* is that of 1935 (12 vols.).

See Walter A. Payne, *A Central American historian: José Milla* (Gainesville, Florida, 1957).

MIÑANO, Sebastián (1779–1845), b. Becerril de Campos, Palencia. Satirist and historian. Prebendary of Seville Cathedral. He lived in France from 1814 to 1816, when he returned to Spain and devoted himself to writing. He contributed most of his satirical *cuadros de costumbres* to the magazine *El Censor*, including *Cartas del madrileño* and *Cartas de don Justo Balanza*.

His most notorious satire, attacking the Spanish absolutist regime, is to be found in *Lamentos políticos de un pobrecito holgazán* (1820), reprinted in the BAE, which sold 60,000 copies in a year, and *Vida, virtudes y milagros del pobre holgazán* (1821). The popularity of Miñano's *cuadros de costumbres* encouraged more important writers (such as Estébanez Calderón and Mesonero Romanos, qq.v.) to specialize in the genre, with greater literary success.

Miñano chronicled the years 1820–3 in *Histoire de la revolution d'Espagne* (Paris, 1825). The Real Academia de la Historia commissioned from him a *Diccionario geográfico y estadístico de España y Portugal* (11 vols., 1826–8).

See E. de Ochoa, *Apuntes para una biblioteca de españoles contemporáneos* (2 vols., Paris, 1840), vol. 2, pp. 373–435.

Mingo Revulgo, Coplas de (c. 1460), an anonymous satirical poem, purporting to be a dialogue between two peasants on the appalling state of Spain. Mingo Revulgo, symbolizing the Spanish people, blames incompetent rulers (the targets are Enrique IV and D. Beltrán de la Cueva) for the dislocation of national life. Gil Arrebato, personifying the aristocracy, points out that the common people must share the blame. The work, first glossed by Juan Martínez de Barros in 1464, influenced the dialogue of Juan del Encina (q.v.) and others. Hernando del Pulgar (q.v.), who wrote a commentary on them (Seville, 1506), praised the *Coplas* so extravagantly that Mariana suspected him to be the author.

The poem comprises 32 nine-line *coplas*, a *redondilla*, and a *quintilla*.

MIRA DE AMESCUA, Antonio (1574?–1644), b. Guadix. Playwright of the school of Lope de Vega (q.v.). Of well-born parents, Mira de Amescua studied in Guadix and Granada, was ordained and in 1609 was named royal chaplain to Granada Cathedral. Finding Madrid more to his taste, he exchanged his chaplaincy for another at court. In 1631 he was appointed archdeacon of his native town and took up the post the following year, occasioning difficulties by his quick temper as he had done also in the playhouses of Madrid.

He is *par excellence* the playwright of the *comedia de capa y espada*, intrigue coupled with excellent versification marred occasionally by inappropriate *culteranismo* setting him stylistically between the simple lyricism of Lope and the sophisticated word-play of Calderón.

A number of Mira's plays are lost or of doubtful authenticity, but enough are known to reveal his versatility, shown by the following groups of works:

Mythological. *Hero y Leandro* and *La manzana de la discordia.*

Religious. *La adúltera virtuosa Santa María Egipcíaca*; *La arpa de David* (critical edn. by C. E. Aníbal, Lancaster, Ohio, 1925); *Vida y muerte de San Lázaro*; *El clavo de Jael*; *El esclavo del demonio* (q.v., Barcelona, 1612; ed. A. Valbuena Prat in *Clásicos Castellanos*, 1928), after *El condenado por desconfiado* by Tirso and *El mágico prodigioso* by Calderón (qq.v.) perhaps the best theological play in Spanish; *El animal profeta San Julián*; and *La mesonera del cielo.*

Historical. *La desdichada Raquel*; *Obligar contra su sangre* and *La rueda de la fortuna* (both in vol. 45 (1858) of the BAE); *El ejemplo mayor de la desdicha* (in *Clásicos Castellanos*, 1926); *Lo que puede el oír misa*; *Ruy López de Ávalos* (ed. N. Sánchez Arce, Mexico City, 1965); *El Conde Alarcos*; *Adversa fortuna de Don Álvaro de Luna* (critical edn. by L. di Filippo, Florence, 1966), and *La segunda de don Álvaro* (critical edn. by N. Sánchez Arce, Mexico City, 1960).

Costumbrista. La Fénix de Salamanca, No hay dicha ni desdicha hasta la muerte, and *Galán, valiente y discreto* (all in vol. 45 (1858) of the BAE); *No hay burlas con las mujeres; La tercera de sí misma; Lo que puede una sospecha*; and *El palacio confuso*, based on the *Menaechmi* theme from Plautus. Perhaps the most charming play of an author distinguished by lightness of touch and Lopesque variety, is *La Fénix de Salamanca* (in Clásicos Castellanos, 1928) in which a young lady disguises herself as a man (a not uncommon device in Golden Age drama), not to repair an insult to herself but from sheer infatuation.

Mira's *autos sacramentales* (of which *Pedro Telonario* is available in Clásicos Castellanos, 1926), are among the finest of their time, prefiguring in their allegorical complexity the great *autos* of Calderón, and originating the device of basing some *autos* on an historic event. *El sol a medianoche*, one of the most impressive, concerns the slavery of human nature, in bondage to Sin, while *La mayor soberbia humana de Nabucodonosor* takes the Assyrian leader and tyrant as a symbol of human arrogance before the might of God.

Mira's versification shows he had learnt much from Lope's example in fluency and variety, including *romances, quintillas*, and *redondillas*.

As a poet Mira is less substantial, as can be seen from his work reprinted in vol. 42 (1857) of the BAE and the *Textos dispersos* in *Revista de Literatura*, vol. 18 (1960).

See E. Cotarelo y Mori, 'Mira de Amescua y su teatro' in *BRAE*, vol. 17 (1930), pp. 467–505, 611–58; vol. 18 (1931), pp. 7–90.

MIRANDA DE VILLAFAÑA, Fray Luis DE (*c.* 1500–*c.* 1575), b. Plasencia. Poet and playwright who landed in South America with Pedro de Mendoza and became involved in Paraguayan politics on the side of Álvar Núñez Cabeza de Vaca, who was imprisoned after the first national revolution. For conspiring to release him, Fray Luis was sentenced to eight months in prison. His *Romance elegíaco* (*c.* 1544) in quatrains, each having one *pie quebrado*, is on the conquest of the Río de la Plata and is one of the first poems on a Paraguayan theme. It influenced his friend and admirer Barco de Centenera (q.v.). It survived thanks to a single copy deposited in the Archivo General de Indias in Seville.

The first play written in Asunción was his seven-act *Comedia pródiga* (Seville, 1554), in *redondillas dobles*, which combines elements from the *Celestina* (the bawd Briana) with the biblical story of the prodigal son. There is no evidence of its performance in Paraguay. J. M. de Álava produced an edition of it in 1868 for the Sociedad de Bibliófilos Andaluces. This popular play

influenced the *Commedia del figliuol prodigo* (before 1588) of Giovanni Maria Cecchi.

MIRÓ, JOSÉ MARÍA (1867–96), Argentinian novelist, author of *La Bolsa*, which he wrote under the pseudonym 'Julián Martel'. The immaturity of the style is outweighed by the originality of the theme—the Buenos Aires Stock Exchange with all its excitement and its questionable deals—and by the contrast between honest Creole values and the poverty of the masses on the one hand, and the opportunism of immigrants and politicians, their wealth easily won, on the other. Miró filled his novel with heavy moral judgments and bitter anti-Semitism.

La Bolsa appeared in book form as late as 1898, seven years after its serialization. The obsession with money recalls Balzac's works, but Miró's style owes more to the Zola of *L'argent*.

MIRÓ, RICARDO (1883–1940), b. Panama City. Generally considered the most important poet of Panama. His father having died while Miró was still a child, the boy left for Bogotá at the age of 14 to study art, returning in 1899 when the revolution broke out. In February 1907 he founded the journal *Nuevos Ritos*, a successor to the defunct *Heraldo del Istmo*. His first collection, *Preludios*, appeared in 1908. In 1909 he went to Barcelona where he met the Italian Futurist Marinetti, and returned to Panama in 1911, resuming the editorship of *Nuevos Ritos*. His next books were *Los segundos preludios* (1916), and the six poems of *Caminos silenciosos* (1929). Miró also wrote some eighteen stories and five plays. His son Rodrigo (q.v.) has become one of the more important literary historians of Panama, editing an *Antología poética* of Ricardo Miró (Guatemala, 1951).

MIRÓ, RODRIGO (1912–   ), b. Panama City. Panamanian essayist and critic. Son of the poet Rodrigo Miró and Isabel Grimaldo Jaén. He has been Director-General of the National Archives and has occupied positions in the diplomatic service. His principal books are *Índice de la poesía panameña contemporánea* (1941), a short essay *La literatura panameña* (1946), a collection of essays on Panamanian literature called *Teoría de la patria* (Buenos Aires, 1947), *El Romanticismo en Panamá* (1948), *El cuento en Panamá* (1950), *Cien años de poesía en Panamá: 1852–1952* (1953), and *Mariano Arosemena* (1960).

MIRÓ FERRER, GABRIEL FRANCISCO VÍCTOR (1879–1930), b. Alicante. Novelist and short-story writer. After attending a Jesuit school in Orihuela, he studied law at Valencia and Granada universities but failed in examinations for the judicature and was obliged to occupy minor positions in city administration in Barcelona and, during the last ten years of his life, in the Ministries of Labour and Education in Madrid. He was never free of the need to earn a living by methods other than writing.

His first two attempts at fiction, *La mujer de Ójeda* (1901) and *Hilván de escenas* (1902), he rightly excluded from his authorized *Obras completas* (12 vols., Barcelona, 1932–49). His style is poetic in its search for the exact word, and the emphasis on music and metaphor. His plot is always subservient to descriptive passages of great eloquence; he is an impressionist with a light touch and an acute sense of colour. His *alter ego* (corresponding to the Antonio Azorín of J. Martínez Ruiz or the Abel Martín and Juan de Mairena of Antonio Machado, qq.v.) is Sigüenza, a dreamy, lyrical figure of the Spanish Levant.

Miró's writings up to the age of thirty were mostly short stories and short novels, such as *Del vivir* (1904), *La novela de mi amigo* (1908), and *Nómada* (1908). His best books appeared during his 30s: *Las cerezas del cementerio* (Barcelona, 1910–11; revised edn., Madrid, 1926); the highly successful *Libro de Sigüenza* (Barcelona, 1916), *Figuras de la Pasión del Señor* (2 vols., 1916–17), the latter imaginary sketches of some of the characters associated by tradition with Jesus, such as Caiaphas, Judas, and Pilate; and *El humo dormido* (1919). Miró's work culminated in *Nuestro Padre San Daniel* (1921) and its second part *El obispo leproso* (1926), both set in Oleza, and especially in the bishop's palace. Gentle satire of the clergy and the *beatas*, though hardly anti-clerical, marks these deft impressions of quiet provincial life, with its intrigues, jealousies, and eccentricities. Miró never recovered the brilliance of these last five novels.

For his bibliography, see J. de Entrambasaguas in *Las mejores novelas contemporáneas*, vol. 4 (Barcelona, 1959), pp. 705–20. See also Vicente Ramos Pérez, *Vida y obra de Gabriel Miró* (1955) and *El mundo de Gabriel Miró* (1964), J. van Praag-Chantraine, *Gabriel Miró ou le visage de Levant, terre d'Espagne* (Paris, 1959), and R. Vidal, *Gabriel Miró: le style, les moyens d'expression* (Bordeaux, 1964).

Mirror for princes, see DE REGIMINE PRINCIPUM.

Misericordia (1897), one of the *Novelas españolas contemporáneas* by Benito Pérez Galdós (qq.v.).

The theme of the novel is the contrast between 'true' and 'false' religion, the former personified by the Christ-like figure of the old servant Benigna, usually known as Benina. Doña Francisca (Paca), her mistress, has become widowed and after reckless spending is now penniless. Benina secretly keeps her by begging, and also helps Francisca's daughter Obdulia. Benina conceals her begging in church porches from her mistress by stating that she is paid as a servant in her spare time by a fictitious priest, Don Romualdo.

A long-awaited legacy (news of which is coincidentally brought by a priest whose name really is Romualdo) finally brings relief to Francisca, and this she shares with Francisco Ponte, a penniless ex-dandy, who searches out Benina and finds her in a poorhouse. However, Juliana (Francisca's daughter-in-law) will not allow Benina back into the house, where she is now a humiliating reminder of the family's former poverty; instead she is fobbed off with a tiny pittance, permission to collect scraps from the kitchen, and a promise that the family will try to get her into the Casa de Misericordia, a charitable institution with a name ironically echoing the novel's title. Benina is heartbroken by this ingratitude, yet she triumphs in the end. Juliana falls victim to the obsession that her children may be fatally ill and only Benina, she feels, can reassure her. She finds that Benina is well and happy, having set up home with Almudena; they are managing on what Benina obtains by begging and on the charity of Don Romualdo. Benina calms Juliana, who is forced to admit that the old, despised servant is indeed 'una Santa'. The novel ends with Benina's final words to Juliana, 'vete a tu casa, y no vuelvas a pecar', which echo Christ's words to the adulterous woman in John 8:11.

The theme of poverty and its connection with charity and selflessness links *Misericordia* with the earlier novels *Nazarín* and *Halma* (qq.v.), and it is of course a recurring obsession in Galdós.

Galdós presents his usual gallery of splendid minor figures, among them the blind Moorish beggar Almudena, who begs Benina to marry him and lead him back to the Orient, where he belongs. Ironically, this blind man is one of the few characters able to 'see' Benina's true goodness. This portrait, like those of Benina, Paca, and Ponte, is drawn from life for, as Galdós wrote in his 1913 preface to the Nelson edition, he spent 'long months' observing and studying at first hand the poor and delinquent in the low quarters of Madrid. He visited doss-houses and brothels accompanied by police or by disguising himself as a municipal doctor, following the authentic naturalistic method. His social commentary is as important here as it is in *Fortunata y Jacinta* (q.v.). Unlike Zola's characters, however, Benina transcends the miseries of life and is not degraded by them, retaining her nobility of character.

See R. H. Russell's article in R. Cardona and A. Zahareas (eds.), *The Christ-figure in the novels of Pérez Galdós* (New York, 1967), pp. 51–78; J. E. Varey, 'Charity in "Misericordia"' in *Galdós studies*, vol. 1 (London, 1970), pp. 164–94; and L. García Lorenzo, '*Misericordia*' de *Galdós* (1975).

Misterio de Elche, see ELCHE, Mystery play of.

MISTRAL, GABRIELA, pseudonym of Lucila Godoy Alcayaga (q.v.).

MITRE, BARTOLOMÉ (1821–1906), b. Buenos Aires. Argentinian statesman and historian. His family emigrated to Uruguay, where he began his distinguished military career. After serving in the Bolivian army he returned to Uruguay to fight against Rosas. He attacked Urquiza's regime in the daily *Los Debates*, a paper he founded in 1852. Exiled by Urquiza, he defeated his enemy at the Battle of Pavón (1861) and became President of the Republic, 1862–68. He founded the newspaper *La Nación* on 4 January 1870. Mitre renounced public life in 1901.

His literary work included the mediocre *Rimas* (1854); translation (Hugo's *Ruy Blas* and Dante's *Divina Commedia*); and a pioneering *Catálogo razonado de las lenguas americanas*. He also wrote *Ollántay: estudio sobre el drama quichua* (Buenos Aires, 1881). *Ollántay* is the masterpiece of Quechua literature (qq.v.).

Mitre's major literary significance lies in his historical writing, much of it based on personal experiences: the *Historia de Belgrano y de la independencia argentina*, which was first written as an entry in the *Galería de celebridades argentinas: biografías de los personajes mas notables* (1857) and issued in a definitive edition in 1887; and the *Historia de San Martín y de la emancipación sudamericana* (1887–90). His *Comprobaciones históricas* (2 vols., 1882) constitute an interesting historical polemic against the views of Vicente Fidel López (q.v.).

The *Obras completas* were directed to be published by act of Congress. His household effects, books, and MSS. form a valuable record of Argentinian politics during the period, and are preserved as the Mitre Museum and Library at San Martín 336, Buenos Aires.

Mocedades del Cid, Las, a chronicle play in two parts by Guillén de Castro y Bellvís (q.v.) first published in 1618 and edited for Clásicos Castellanos (4th edn., 1945) by Víctor Said Armesto. In title and material it draws on a celebrated ballad cycle, *Las mocedades de Rodrigo* (q.v.), on the legends of Rodrigo de Vívar, known as 'el Cid' (q.v.).

In the *Primera parte*, the newly-knighted Rodrigo is prevented from marrying Doña Ximena because her father, Count Lozano, has slapped the face of Don Diego, Rodrigo's father, in a fit of jealousy. Don Diego, too old to avenge himself, commands Rodrigo to do so. Torn between love and duty, Rodrigo prefers to avenge his father, and kills the Count. Ximena, as much in love with Rodrigo as he with her, demands that he be brought to justice but—when he begs her to kill him in reprisal—she cannot bring herself to strike the blow. Eventually he defeats Ximena's champion in single combat, and Ximena agrees to marry him.

This important play is the source of Corneille's *Le Cid* (1636) and Diamante's *El honrador de su padre*, first performed in 1657.

Mocedades de Rodrigo, Las, an epic poem dating from the third quarter of the 14th c., and relating the youthful exploits (*mocedades*) of the Cid. It survives in a single MS. in the Bibliothèque Nationale.

After an account of the life of Fernán González (q.v.) and a digression on the historical rights and privileges of the diocese of Palencia (which the author endeavours to defend and justify), the poem tells of the quarrel between Rodrigo's father and Count Gómez, whom Rodrigo kills. The Count's daughter Ximena asks King Fernando I for justice, but later decides that she wishes to marry Rodrigo. Rodrigo appears before the King and behaves in an arrogant manner quite unlike his conduct in the *Cantar de mio Cid* (see CID). He swears not to see Ximena again until he has been victorious five times in battle. He twice defeats Moorish armies invading Castile, kills a champion of the King of Aragón (who is laying claim to Calahorra), and foils an attempt by some usurpers who had expelled the Bishop of Palencia from his diocese. Before his combat with the Aragonese champion, Rodrigo, returning from a pilgrimage to Santiago, offers his cloak to a leper who reveals himself as St. Lazarus and assures Rodrigo of God's favour in his future exploits. The extent of this divine aid is shown in the fifth battle in which Rodrigo defeats the King of France who, with the Pope, the Patriarch, and the Holy Roman Emperor, had presented Castile with an ultimatum demanding an annual tribute. The text breaks off as a truce is arranged. The *Mocedades de Rodrigo* has even less claim to historical accuracy than the *Cantar de mio Cid*, to which it is artistically inferior.

A lost predecessor to the *Mocedades* was prosified in the *Crónica de Castilla* and the *Crónica de 1344*. It does not appear to have differed greatly from the *Mocedades* in content, apart from presenting Rodrigo's character in a more sympathetic light, and containing no references to the diocese of Palencia. From this lost epic stem the *romances* or ballads on Rodrigo's early deeds, which in turn led to Guillén de Castro's (q.v.) *Las mocedades del Cid*, from which Corneille's *Le Cid* derives.

The text of the *Mocedades de Rodrigo* has recently been edited by A. D. Deyermond (*Epic poetry and the clergy*, London, 1968, pp. 222-7).

MOCHO, *Fray*, pseudonym of José Sixto Álvarez (q.v.).

Modernismo, a complex and as yet imperfectly understood literary movement of the years between 1888, when *Azul* by Rubén Darío (q.v.) was first published, and 1910, when the movement's second phase was at its peak. The *Revista Azul* (q.v., 1894-6) was the organ of the first phase, which includes Manuel Gutiérrez Nájera, Julián del Casal, Salvador Díaz Mirón, José Asunción Silva, Julio Herrera y Reissig, the Spaniard Salvador Rueda, R. Jaimes Freyre, and the early Valle-Inclán of *Sonatas* (qq.v.) among many others.

The second phase, represented by *La Revista Moderna* (1898-1911) and the early Amado Nervo (qq.v.), extends the range of somewhat self-conscious cosmopolitanism established by the first. Members of both phases, inspired by French symbolism and Parnassianism, rejected both the materialism and naturalism typical of Zola, as well as the everyday world, isolating themselves from it in an attempt to create a poetry of timeless values.

Darío and his successors attempted to recreate the atmosphere of the earliest romanticism, creating a world of dream, sensuous imagery, daring metaphor, and nostalgia. In metre and rhyme they were largely innovative, though the majority also returned (as did Darío himself) to medieval and Renaissance forms that had been neglected for centuries.

Modernismo in the Hispanic world began in Central America, later spreading to South America and Spain. Though the movement in its most characteristic form cannot be said to have survived the First World War, as an attitude of mind which rejects imperialism, middle-class values, and materialism it can be said to have survived until today.

See Ricardo Gullón, *Direcciones del modernismo* (Madrid, 1963); P. Gimferrer, *Antología de la poesía modernista* (1969); and L. Litvak (ed.), *El modernismo* (1975).

MOGUEL Y URQUIZA, JUAN ANTONIO (1745-1804), b. Eibar, Guipúzcoa. Basque

novelist and priest, who scarcely moved from his parish throughout his lifetime, Moguel befriended many refugee French priests and seems to have been an *afrancesado* (q.v.) at heart. He translated the *Pensées* of Pascal into Basque.

His *Peru Abarca* (Zarauz, 1955) is perhaps the most successful novel in Basque, first published with a Castilian translation in *Euskalzale 3* (1899) though known in MS. much earlier. It is composed as a series of dialogues, its contrasting characters being a Basque country recluse of undeviating virtue and a jovial, often wayward, street barber called Maisu Juan. Though the work's intention was moral, Moguel gives much incidental information on contemporary language, life, and manners in vigorous Basque.

Moguel's niece Vicenta Antonia (1782-1854) was a fabulist, and his nephew Juan José (1781-1849) wrote an important work of edification in Biscayan dialect, *Baserritar nequezaleentzaco escolia edo icasbidiac* (1816).

See J. Gárate, *La época de Pablo Astarloa y Juan Antonio Moguel* (Bilbao, 1936); and Juan San Martín, *Juan Antonio Moguel eta Urkitza* (Zarauz, 1959).

MOHEDANO, *Fray* PEDRO and *Fray* RAFAEL RODRÍGUEZ, see RODRÍGUEZ MOHEDANO, *Fray* Pedro and *Fray* Rafael.

MOLINA, ENRIQUE (1910-), b. Buenos Aires. Argentinian poet of surrealistic affinities. He has worked as a sailor and spent some time in Peru. His collections are *Las cosas y el delirio* (1941), *Pasiones terrestres* (1946), *Costumbres errantes o la redondez de la tierra* (1951), *Amantes antípodas* (1961), *Fuego libre* (1962), *Las bellas furias* (1966), *Hotel Pájaro* (1967), and *Monzón Napalm* (1968).

Octavio Paz has said that Molina's poetry 'does not describe, but like a knife buries itself in reality'.

MOLINA, LUIS DE (1535-1600), b. Cuenca. Theologian and Jesuit priest, who argued, against the Dominican Domingo Báñez and his supporters, that all human beings are endowed with equal and sufficient divine grace without distinction as to their individual merits, and that salvation depends on the sinner's willingness to receive grace. The controversy began in 1588, and became so bitter that all discussion of it was banned by Pope Paul V in 1607. It is brilliantly dramatized by the *molinista* Tirso de Molina (q.v.) in *El condenado por desconfiado* (q.v.).

MOLINA, TIRSO DE, pseudonym of Fray Gabriel Téllez (q.v.).

MOLINARI, Ricardo E. (1898–   ), b. Buenos Aires. Argentinian poet. *El imaginero* (1927) was an *ultraísta* collection, and the manner of Borges and his group continued to influence *El pez y la manzana* (1929), *Historia de la rosa y el clavel* (1933), and other booklets up to *Mundos de la madrugada* (1943), in which Molinari demonstrated his own individuality with odes nostalgic for lost love and celebrating the fastnesses of his country's deserted south. His later books include *El huésped y la melancolía* (1946), *Esta rosa obscura del aire, 1946–1949* (1949), *Días donde la tarde es un pájaro* (1954), *Unida noche* (1957), *Un día, el tiempo, las nubes* (1964), and *Una sombra antigua canta* (1966).

Among the influences in his more recent work are Góngora, Carrillo de Sotomayor, and Gabriel Bocángel (qq.v.).

See Narciso Pousa, *Ricardo E. Molinari* (1961), with a good bibliography, pp. 105–12; and Julio Arístides, *Ricardo E. Molinari, o la agonía del ser en el tiempo* (1966).

MOLINAS ROLÁN, Guillermo (1889–1945), b. San Miguel de las Misones. Paraguayan poet. Educated in Asunción, he was one of the founders of the literary review *Crónica* (q.v.). He became a drug addict, ruining the career promised by such poems as 'Ofrenda', 'En la fiesta de la raza', and 'Mi lira' which appear in Sinforiano Buzó Gómez, *Índice de la poesía paraguaya* (1943; 2nd edn., 1959). A major influence on Molinas Rolán was Julio Herrera y Reissig (q.v.).

MOLINOS, Miguel de (1628–96), b. Muniesa, Saragossa. Religious writer and the founder of Spanish quietism. Educated by the Jesuits in Valencia, he received the living of S. Andrés there, but in 1665 went to Rome to procure the beatification of Ven. Francisco Jerónimo Simón. There he became a fashionable confessor, summarizing his precepts in the *Guía Espiritual que desembaraza al alma, y la conduce por el interior camino, para alcanzar la perfecta contemplación y el rico tesoro de la interior paz* (Rome, 1675). Molinos suggests that a Christian may find vocal prayer and discursive reflections on sacred themes insufficient for spiritual contentment, and must turn to interior prayers. Few priests, in his view, were equipped to direct the practice of contemplation. The influence of the work was such that for twelve years monks and nuns in many orders threw away their rosaries and took to silent prayer. The *Guía* of Molinos circulated widely in several languages (though not well known in Spain) and it was only in 1685 that Cardinal d'Estrées and the Jesuits in Rome arraigned Molinos for heresy, and in 1687 that the book was proscribed and its author sentenced

to life imprisonment. Apart from his close associates in Rome, many other groups of quietists continued the tradition of Molinos, particularly in France, until they were suppressed.

Molinos wrote another work, *La devoción de la buena muerte* (Valencia, 1662), using the pen-name 'Juan Bautista Catalá', and *La defensa de la contemplación* which was published for the first time, abridged, in José Ángel Valente's edition of the *Guía espiritual* (Barcelona, 1974) in the Rescate series.

See P. Dudon, *Le quiétiste espagnol Michel Molinos, 1628–1696* (Paris, 1921); J. de Entrambasaguas, *Miguel de Molinos: siglo XVII* (n.d. but 1935); and J. Ellacuria, *Reacción contra las ideas de Miguel de Molinos: procesos de la Inquisición y refutación de los teólogos* (Bilbao, 1956).

MONDRAGÓN, Hieronymo de (*fl.* 1590), b. Saragossa. Satirist, lawyer, and prosodist. An Erasmian, influenced by the *Encomium moriae* in his *Censura de la locura humana y excellencias de ella* (Lérida, 1598), which sets out to prove that men by reputation 'sane' are in fact mad, and vice versa.

Some of Mondragón's verse has survived in Carrillo's *Itinerarium ordinandorum* (Saragossa, 1594), and he also published *Arte para componer en metro castellano* and *Prosodia latina en castellano* (both Saragossa, 1593).

MONROY Y SILVA, Cristóbal de (1612–49), b. Alcalá de Guadaira, Sevilla. Historian and dramatist. Though his *Vida del Padre Maestro de Loyola* (Mexico City, 1639) is now very rare, as is his *Epítome de la historia de Troya* (Seville, 1641), Monroy was in his day a noted historian and poet.

It is as a playwright, however, that his reputation has been preserved. His dialogue is effervescent, his lesser characters better observed than was usual, and his facility in versification and wit were much appreciated by audiences of the mid-17th c. His plays were printed in *Doce comedias de diferentes autores* (1646), in vol. 41 of the *Varios . . .* (Valencia), and in the 1652 *Comedias de los mejores autores*. Vol. 49 (1859) of the BAE includes *El ofensor de sí mismo*, *Las mocedades del duque de Osuna*, and *La batalla de Pavía y prisión del rey Francisco*. *Fuenteovejuna* is a reworking of Lope de Vega's play of the same name.

MONTALVO, Juan (1832–89), b. Ambato, Ecuador. Essayist of liberal political views, whose concern for the common people and democracy made him a lifelong enemy of the dictator Gabriel García Moreno. He founded *El Cosmopolita* in 1866 (Quito, 1866–9; reprinted,

Ambato, 1945), but fled three years later when García Moreno staged a *coup*. From the Colombian border town of Ipiales, Montalvo conducted a war of propaganda with his best books. When García Moreno was assassinated on 6 August 1875, Montalvo cried from Ipiales 'My pen killed him', but democracy was short-lived and when the dictator Ignacio de Veintemilla came to power Montalvo attacked him in his *Catilinarias* (Panama City, 1880 and later edns., to the best of which Unamuno wrote a prologue, 2 vols., Paris, 1925).

In *Siete tratados* (2 vols., Besançon, 1882), Montalvo applied maxims from his favourite authors to problems of the day. His finely-wrought but disjointed novel was *Los capítulos que se le olvidaron a Cervantes* (Besançon, 1895; Buenos Aires, 1944).

Roberto Agramonte compiled *Páginas desconocidas* by Montalvo (Havana, 1936); there are more general anthologies by Benjamín Carrión, *El pensamiento vivo de Montalvo* (Buenos Aires, 1961), and by Matilde Calvo de Gangara (Buenos Aires, 1966).

Plutarco Naranjo's and Carlos Rolando's *Estudio bibliográfico* of Montalvo appeared in Quito (2 vols.,) in 1966.

See Darío Guevara, *Quijote y maestro, biografía novelada de Juan Montalvo; o el Cervantes de América* (1947); Piedad Sánchez Jaramillo, *La personalidad de Montalvo como maestro* (1967); and Pablo Fortuny, *Juan Montalvo* (Buenos Aires, 1967).

MONTE, Domingo del, see Delmonte, Domingo.

MONTEFORTE TOLEDO, Mario (1911–), b. Guatemala City. Novelist, short-story writer, and poet. His novel *Anaité* (written in 1939 but not published until 1948), set in the jungles of Petén, struck a blow for realism against the customary idealization of native life in previous Guatemalan fiction. The descriptive passages are of a power comparable to those in *La vorágine*, by the Colombian José Eustasio Rivera (q.v.). Monteforte Toledo's next novel, *Entre la piedra y la cruz* (1948), discussed the plight of the literate Indian torn between the worlds of aborigine and invader. The stories in *La cueva sin quietud* (1949) begin to reveal psychological penetration. His other novels are *Donde acaban los caminos* (1953) and *Una manera de morir* (1957), the latter exploring the conflict between morality and political expediency.

MONTEJO, Esteban (1859–1910?), Cuban slave who fled from the sugar plantations, returning after the abolition of slavery in 1880. He fought in the Cuban War of 1895. The *autobiography of a runaway slave* (Harmondsworth, 1970), was compiled and edited from his recollections by Miguel Barnet.

MONTEMAYOR, Jorge de (1519–61), b. Montemor (Montemayor) o Velho, near Coimbra, Portugal. Author of the greatest pastoral romance in Castilian, *Los siete libros de la Diana* (Valencia, 1559?). His *Diana* (q.v.) can be traced in theme and convention back to Theocritus, the eclogues of Virgil, and to Renaissance works such as Boccaccio's *Ninfale d'Ameto* and Sannazaro's *L'Arcadia* (Naples, 1504; trans. into Castilian, 1547).

Montemayor spent some years as a musician in the service of the Infanta Juana, mother of King Sebastian. In 1554, he accompanied King Philip II to England and probably also to the Low Countries; he was murdered in Piedmont, possibly by a rival in love.

Before he achieved European fame with the *Diana*, he published an *Exposición moral sobre el psalmo 86* (Alcalá, 1548) edited by Francisco López Estrada in the *Revista de la Biblioteca Nacional*, vol. 5, 1944; his first *Cancionero* (Antwerp, 1554) subsequently republished with *Segundo cancionero* (Antwerp, 1558), in which the *Segundo cancionero espiritual* was to be banned by the Inquisition the following year; and a translation of Ausias March (Valencia, 1560). A. González Palencia has edited *El Cancionero* (1932) for the Sociedad de Bibliófilos Españoles.

MONTENGÓN Y PARET, Pedro (1745–c. 1825), b. Alicante. Novelist. A Jesuit novice who was never ordained but chose to go into exile with the Society in 1767, living in Naples and elsewhere. He returned to Spain c. 1798, but was obliged to leave the country again in 1801 and died in his adoptive homeland of Italy.

His novels, no longer widely read, enjoyed something of a vogue. *Eusebio* (4 vols., 1786–8) has an involved plot set mainly in North America and dealing with loves and shipwreck. Its unorthodox position on the importance of fate and its religious tolerance caused it to be withdrawn by the Inquisition; an expurgated edition appeared in 1807. *El Antenor* (2 vols., 1788) concerns the legendary origins of Venice. *La Eudoxia, hija de Belisario* (1793) is a historical novel, concentrating on the education of women and influenced in this by Rousseau's *Émile* (1762). *El Rodrigo, romance épico* (1793) is another historical novel in stilted poetic prose. *Mirtilo, o los pastores trashumantes* (1795) capitalized on a revival of interest in the pastoral novel of Montemayor and his followers. Montengón's style is full of Gallicisms and Italianisms which mar not only his novels but also his translations from Ossian (*Fingal*, 1800) and Sophocles (1820).

Montengón's poetry appears in *Odas* (3 vols., Ferrara, 1778–9), published under the pseudonym 'Filopatro'. His miscellany *Frioleras eruditas y curiosas para la pública instrucción* (1801) has been edited by J. Rodríguez Arzúa (1944) in Colección Cisneros.

See G. Laverde Ruiz, 'Apuntes acerca de la vida y poesías de don Pedro Montengón' in his *Ensayos críticos* (Lugo, 1868).

MONTES DE OCA, Ignacio (1840–1921), b. Guanajuato. Mexican Hellenist, priest, and poet whose main contribution to Spanish literature was a series of translations: *Poetas bucólicos griegos* (1877), *Odas* of Pindar (1881), *La Argonáutica* (2 vols., Madrid, 1919–20), and others still highly regarded. He spent much time in Rome (studying theology there 1860–3) and was Bishop of San Luis Potosí for 36 years from 1885.

His original verses lack vitality and imagination, but his eight vols. of prose *Obras pastorales y oratorias* (1883–1913) reveal the vast reading of a true humanist, quite apart from their pastoral virtues. Most of his poetry was signed 'Ipandro Acaico', his given name in the literary society called the Arcades of Rome.

MONTES DE OCA, Marco Antonio (1932–), b. Mexico City. Mexican poet. He studied at the Universidad Nacional Autónoma de México, but later took a number of different jobs in order to devote himself to the poetry of experience. After beginning as a surrealist in the shadow of Octavio Paz (q.v.), Montes de Oca began to emerge as a poet in his own right, with his own strikingly original style.

There has been a rapid development in technical mastery in his works: *Ruina de la infame Babilonia* (1953; English 2nd edn., 1954), *Contrapunto de la fe* (1955), *Pliego de testimonios* (1956), the collected *Delante de la luz cantan los pájaros* with the as yet uncollected *Ofrendas y epitafios* (1959), *Cantos al sur que no se alcanza* (1961), *Fundación del entusiasmo* (1963), *La parcela en el Edén* (1964), *La vendimia del juglar* (1965), *Las fuentes legendarias* (1966), and *Pedir el fuego* (1969).

Montes de Oca won the Premio Xavier Villaurrutia in 1959 and the Premio Mazatlán in 1966.

MONTESER, Francisco Antonio de (c. 1602–68), b. Alameda, Seville. Playwright. From 1620 he lived in Madrid, moved in theatrical circles, and secretly married the actress Manuela de Escamilla. Though best remembered as a writer of shorter *bailes* and *entremeses* (such as *La hidalga* against snobbery and *Los locos* against vanity, reprinted in the Cotarelo y Mori *Colección* . . . vols. 17–18 (1911) of the NBAE),

Monteser made his name with a burlesque version of Lope de Vega's great tragedy *El caballero de Olmedo*. He followed this with a burlesque *Restauración de España* in collaboration with Antonio de Solís and Diego de Silva. The same writers wrote a parody of Belmonte Bermúdez's *La renegada de Sevilla*.

A witty man of violent temper, Monteser was responsible for some of the finest epigrams in the Duque de Frías's *Deleite de la discreción y fácil escuela de la agudeza* (1743). He was murdered by a servant of the Portuguese ambassador to Madrid.

MONTESINO, Fray Ambrosio de (1448?–1512?), b. Huete, Cuenca. Franciscan poet of the Court of Ferdinand and Isabella. He translated the *Vita Christi* of Ludolphus of Saxony (4 vols., Alcalá, 1502), probably from the Catalan of Joan Ruiz de Corella (Valencia, 1500).

Montesino's own poetry is impregnated with the simple piety and exquisite sensibility of St. Francis and Jacopone da Todi in the popular themes expressed in popular metres of the *Cancionero* . . . (Toledo, 1508; ed. in facsimile by A. Pérez Gómez, Cieza, 1964; and most easily accessible in vol. 35 (1855) of the BAE). The *coplas*, *romances*, hymns, and *villancicos* take rustic motifs and render them most affectingly *a lo divino*. Montesino's *Coplas sobre diversas devociones y Misterios de nuestra Santa Fe Católica* (Toledo, n.d.) has been edited by H. Thomas in facsimile (London, 1936). Montesino also wrote *Epístolas y Evangelios por todo el año* (Toledo, 1512).

MONTIANO Y LUYANDO, Agustín de (1697–1764), b. Valladolid. Dramatist and critic whose key work is the *Discursos sobre las tragedias españolas* (1750–3), which includes his neoclassical tragedies *Virginia* and *Ataulpho* written apparently to prove that Spanish authors could imitate classical models as well as could the French. The first such attempts in the 18th c., they are unusual, too, in portraying the deaths of innocent characters. *Virginia* seems to teach that good nobles should rise against unjust tyrants; neither it nor its companion piece has so far been produced in Spain.

Virginia contrasts the social and moral corruption of the Roman decemvir Appius Claudius with the purity and honesty of Virginia, betrothed to Lucius Icilius. *Ataulpho* pits the order and peace symbolized by Constantius, Rome's ambassador to Gothic Spain, the Roman queen Placidia, and her Gothic king Ataulpho, against the lust for power of Rosamunda, Sigerico, and Vernulpho. The play's dramatic evolution is made by the gradual discovery by the king and queen of the plots against them, and this subtlety, derivative as it is from French models, marks a definite advance on Golden Age practice. Montiano, a disciple of Luzán (q.v.), was 'Humilde' in the Academia del Buen Gusto in Madrid and was a founder and the first director of the Real Academia de la Historia. The melodrama *La lira de Orfeo* (n.p., but Palma, 1742) is undistinguished, as is the poem *El robo de Diana* (1727) and the verses included in vol. 67 (1875) of the BAE, pp. 489–93. Among Montiano's protégés was a more important playwright: Nicolás Fernández de Moratín (q.v.).

See F. Uhagón Guardino, Marqués de Laurencín, *Don Agustín Montiano y Luyando, primer director de la Real Academia de la Historia* (1926).

MONTORO, ANTÓN DE (1404–80?), b. Montoro, Cordova. Satirical poet converted to Christianity under stress who yet retained his pride in his race, unlike Rodrigo Cota of Toledo, whom he attacked for being ashamed of his Jewish ancestry. Though a protégé of Mena and Santillana (qq.v.), Montoro remained a tailor and secondhand clothes-dealer, lamenting his poverty in poetic jousts with Juan Agraz, El Comendador Román, and the Jewish *converso* Juan Poeta of Valladolid. In 1473 he fled from the anti-Jewish riots of Cordova to Seville, where he settled for the rest of his life.

The *Cancionero*, edited by E. Cotarelo y Mori (1900), shows how Montoro chose to reject the Italianate allegorical innovations fashionable in his day, retaining popular metres for his witty but often coarse invective. The *Cancionero de obras de burlas provocantes a risa* (1519) includes two works attributed to Montoro.

MONTÚFAR, LORENZO (1823–98), b. Guatemala City. Politician and historian, whose *Reseña histórica de Centro-América* (7 vols., 1878–87) reflects the author's radical views. Opposing capital punishment and the dominance of the clergy, he supported equal rights and religious tolerance. Montúfar wrote numerous pamphlets and controversial ephemera. His *Memorias autobiográficas* appeared in 1898.

Moradas, Las, by Santa Teresa de Jesus (q.v.), see CASTILLO INTERIOR, El.

MORÃES CABRAL, FRANCISCO DE (1500?–72), Portuguese novelist and secretary to the Portuguese ambassador in Paris. His *Palmeirim da Inglaterra*, written in Portuguese in 1544, belongs to the history of Spanish literature not because it was the best of the peninsular Palmerín cycle (and praised as such in the *Quijote*) but because it first appeared in a Spanish version, by Luis Hurtado (Toledo, 1547–8), while the earliest recorded Portuguese edition is that of 1567.

One of the finest of *libros de caballería* (q.v.), *Palmerín* was edited by A. Bonilla y San Martín (1908) for the NBAE.

See H. Thomas, 'The Palmerín romances' in *Transactions of the Bibliographical Society* (London), vol. 13, 1916.

MORALES, AMBROSIO DE (1513–91), b. Cordova. Historian and antiquary. He studied at Salamanca University with his uncle the humanist Fernán Pérez de Oliva (q.v.), whose works he edited, adding fifteen of his own philosophical discourses.

He continued the *Crónica general de España* (1543) of Florián del Ocampo (q.v.) with his own *La Corónica general de España . . .* (2 vols., Alcalá, 1574–77), a vastly superior work showing the first signs of a scientific approach to history in Spain. As a historian he was called on to defend the *Anales* of his friend Jerónimo de Zurita (q.v.), and did so in *Apología . . .* (Saragossa, 1610). The *Viage . . .* which he undertook at royal command to inventory the MSS., inscriptions, and holy relics of León, Galicia, and Asturias, has been edited by Henrique Flórez (1765; reprinted in the Biblioteca Histórica Asturiana, Oviedo, 1886).

Morales also wrote *Las antigüedades de las ciudades de España . . .* (Alcalá, 1575), lives of SS. Justo and Pastor (Alcalá, 1568), and other works edited by F. Valerio Cifuentes in *Opúsculos castellanos . . . cuyos originales se conservan inéditos en la Biblioteca del Escorial* (3 vols., 1793).

See E. Redel, *Ambrosio de Morales* (Cordova, 1908).

MORALES, CRISTÓBAL DE (*fl.* 1600). An actor to whom some attribute the authorship of a *Comedia de El Caballero de Olmedo* (ed. by E. Juliá Martínez, 1944). It was written in or about 1606 and thus is earlier than the great tragedy of the same title by Lope de Vega which Morley & Bruerton date 1615–26, but which is probably not earlier than 1620.

N. D. Shergold's 'Lope de Vega and the other "Caballero de Olmedo"', written for the E. M. Wilson festschrift *Studies in Spanish literature of the Golden Age* (ed. R. O. Jones, London, 1973), argues a case for Lope's having seen or read the earlier play.

MORALES, TOMÁS (1885–1921), b. Moya, Canary Islands. Poet. He studied medicine on the mainland, returning to practise in 1911. With Rafael Romero (q.v.) and Saulo Torón, Morales was one of the trio of post-modernist poets in the Canary Isles. His most impressive verse is on the sea, and is heavily influenced by

Salvador Rueda and Rubén Darío (qq.v.). His first book was *Poemas de la gloria, del amor, y del mar* (1908), but he is remembered for the 'Oda al Atlántico' and similar word-pictures (compared by Valbuena Prat to the classical seascapes of Claude Lorrain) in his collected poems *Las rosas de Hércules* (Book II, 1919; Book I, 1922). His influence on other Spanish poets of his generation was perhaps due to his insistence that Greek mythology and modern technology are equally acceptable as motifs, a lesson learnt from Whitman.

MORATÍN, LEANDRO FERNÁNDEZ DE (1760–1828), b. Madrid. Poet and important playwright known as Moratín *hijo* to distinguish him from his father Nicolás (q.v.). His poetic name was 'Inarco Celenio', but he used three other pseudonyms: Ginés de Pasadilla, Melitón Fernández, and the anagrammatic Efrén de Lardnaz y Morante. He astonished his father by obtaining an 'honourable mention' at the age of 19 for his heroic ballad on the capture of Granada *La toma de Granada por los Reyes Católicos D. Fernando y Doña Isabel* (1779) submitted to the Real Academia Española in the competition won by Vaca de Guzmán (q.v.). Another 'honourable mention' was awarded to Moratín's *Lección poética: sátira contra los vicios introducidos en la poesía castellana* ... (1782). F. Salvá Miquel edited Moratín's *Poesía lírica* (Barcelona, 1945).

But Moratín would not have survived on his fame as a poet. As a dramatist, though deficient in imagination, he is important for his masterly use of language, exquisite taste, broad culture, excellent wit and satire, and his condemnation of the artificial and hypocritical. He was one of the most significant *afrancesados* (q.v.)., and in 1817 fled to France, and later to Italy, returning temporarily (1820–1) to Barcelona but spending his last years with the Manuel Silvela family first in Bordeaux and then in Paris.

He was the first to translate Shakespeare's *Hamlet* into Spanish direct from English (Ramón de la Cruz's version being from the French) and Molière's *Médecin malgré lui* and *L'école des maris*, the former very freely. Moratín's translation of Voltaire's *Candide* (Cádiz, 1838) is the best in Spanish. His scanty production and his neo-classical style mark him as a writer of a very different age from that of Lope or Calderón. Moratín's five plays are *La comedia nueva o el café* (1792; critical edn. by John Dowling, 1970); *El viejo y la niña* (1795; ed. L. B. Walton, Manchester, 1921); *El Barón* (1803); *La Mogigata* (1804); and the celebrated attack on forced marriages *El sí de las niñas* (q.v., 1805; ed. with *La comedia nueva* by John Dowling and R. Andioc, 1969).

La comedia nueva is a clever satire against what

Moratín considered to be the excesses of the Madrid theatre, which subordinated psychological realism to ostentatious effects and loud rhetoric on plebeian themes. 'A mí me lastima en verdad la suerte de estos escritores', says Moratín through the sagacious Don Pedro, 'que entontecen al vulgo con obras tan desatinadas y monstruosas, dictadas, más que por el ingenio, por la necesidad o la presunción'. He also made attempts at the practical reform of the Madrid stage.

In prose Moratín composed *La derrota de los pedantes* (1789, ed. John Dowling, Barcelona, 1971), against bad writers of the age whose books 'hasta entonces no habían servido de gloria a sus autores, ni de utilidad alguna al género humano'. *Orígenes del teatro español* is a useful history first published in the Real Academia de la Historia edition of Moratín's *Obras* (4 vols., in 6, 1830–1), otherwise to be avoided because of the censor's pencil. The definitive author's text is the 3-vol. *Obras dramáticas y líricas* (Paris, 1825) supplemented by the *Obras póstumas* (3 vols., 1867–8). There are accessible editions of all the works in vol. 2 (1846) of the BAE, and a selection in Clásicos Castellanos (1924).

See F. Lázaro Carreter, *Moratín en su teatro* (Oviedo, 1961); S. Melón R. de Gordejuela, *Moratín por dentro* (Oviedo, 1964); Jorge Campos, *Teatro y sociedad en España, 1780–1820* (1969); R. Andioc, *Sur la querelle du théâtre au temps de Moratín* (Tarbes, 1970); and John Dowling, *Leandro Fernández de Moratín* (New York, 1971) in Twayne's World Authors series.

MORATÍN, NICOLAS FERNÁNDEZ DE (1737–80), b. Madrid. Poet and playwright known as Moratín *padre* to distinguish him from his son Leandro (q.v.). He inherited a court position from his father, and met there the chief writers of the period, among them Iriarte and Cadalso. Spanish by temperament, he was an *afrancesado* (q.v., 'Francophile') and a neoclassic in his literary and theatrical tastes. He considered the theatre to have been degraded by the school of Lope de Vega (q.v.) and by the *autos sacramentales* which were his special target in *Desengaños al Theatro español: respuesta al Romance lizo y llano, y la defensa del Pensador* (1763).

The models he proposed for Spanish playwrights were his own *La petimetra: comedia nueva, escrita con todo el rigor del arte* (1762), a comedy admitted even by his own son (in the prologue to his own *Obras*, vol. 2, 1830) to fall far short of the stated objective, and three tradgedies.

Lucrecia (1763), like his patron Montiano's *Virginia*, is set in the Rome of Tarquin, whose political treachery is matched by his moral treachery in seducing Lucretia. This tract against absolutism shows the fall of the tyrant and the return of just government. Even more interesting is *Hormesinda* (1770), more cautious in its political stance after the Esquilache riots of 1766 but no less strict in its preference of moral standards to blind dogma. *Guzmán el Bueno* (1777) shows a diminution of independence and a return to patriotism and the empty phrase.

Technically, Moratín uses more resources than his immediate predecessors, varying the rhyming hendecasyllabic couplets with unrhyming couplets and interspersing longer speeches with sudden exclamations, clever aphorisms, and a sensitive use of alliteration.

Inferior to his son as a playwright, Nicolás is a superior poet. His works were collected by his son (*Obras póstumas*, Barcelona, 1821); with his plays in vol. 2 (1846) of the BAE; and by R. Foulché-Delbosc (*Poesías inéditas*, 1892). His best work includes a number of ballads: 'Empresa de Micer Jaques Borgoñón', 'Amor y honor', and 'Abdelcadir y Galiana', and the celebrated *quintillas* 'Fiesta de toros en Madrid'. *La Diana, o Arte de la caza* (1765) is a didactic poem on hunting which defends the right of a powerful and just monarch to control society. He revived the use of sapphics after Quevedo's experiments in the previous century. *El Poeta* was the title of his magazine, issued in 1764 to demonstrate the variety and excellence of poetic form and style.

The best life of Nicolás is that by Leandro in vol. 2 of the BAE (see above).

MOR DE FUENTES, José (1762–1848), b. Monzón, Huesca. Autobiographer, poet, and novelist. He trained as a naval engineer, but the literary vocation and love of adventure so evident in his autobiography led him to abandon his profession. The neoclassical *Poesías varias* (3 vols., 1796–1800) show no originality; and the influences of the Rousseau of *La nouvelle Héloïse* and Goethe's *Werther* are evident in his extremely popular novel *El cariño perfecto, o Alonso y Serafina* (1798), known in its 2nd edition (1802) and subsequently as *La Serafina*. Its most recent edition is by the Mor scholar Ildefonso-Manuel Gil (Saragossa, 1959).

Mor's plays *La fonda de París, El egoísta*, and *La mujer varonil* are of little value; it is in fact as an autobiographer that Mor is still read, for the *Bosquejillo de la vida y escritos de don José Mor de Fuentes* (Barcelona, 1836 and later edns. including that of the BAE, vol. 97, 1957).

See the studies by I.-M. Gil, especially 'Vida de don José Mor de Fuentes' in *Universidad* (Saragossa), vol. 37 (1960), pp. 71–116 and 495–566.

MOREIRAS, EDUARDO (1914–), b. Quiroga, Lugo. Galician poet. Imbued with the Hellenic spirit, Moreiras takes the sea for his main theme. He was founder and director of the Vigo magazine *Mensajes de poesía* and has translated Paul Éluard's poems into Spanish (Buenos Aires, 1955).

His earlier books were written in Castilian: *El bosque encantado* (Vigo, 1947), *Éxtasis* (Vigo, 1948), and *Los oficios* (Vigo, 1952); his later books in Galician: *A realidade esencial* (El Ferrol, 1955); *Paisaxe en rocha viva* (Vigo, 1958), and his best book, *Os nobres carreiros* (Vigo, 1970).

Moreiras is well represented in Miguel González Garcés, *Poesía gallega contemporánea* (Barcelona, 1974).

MOREL-FATIO, ALFRED (1850–1924), French Hispanist. One of the founders of the *Bulletin Hispanique* in 1898–9, Morel-Fatio also produced the indispensable catalogue of the Spanish and Portuguese MSS. in the Bibliothèque Nationale (Paris, 1892). Among his critical editions were *El mágico prodigioso* (Heilbronn, 1877) and the *Libro de Alexandre* (Dresden, 1905–6). He collected his major studies in *Études sur l'Espagne* (4 vols., Paris, 1888–1904) and *L'Espagne au XVIe et au XVIIe siècles* (Heilbronn, 1878), and translated *Lazarillo de Tormes* into French.

MORENO VILLA, José (1887–1955), b. Málaga. Poet and art-historian. He studied in Germany and at Madrid University. He belonged to the poetic generation intermediate between that of '98 and that of '27, his major influence being that of his friend Juan Ramón Jiménez (q.v.).

Before 1937 his poems were delicate, intellectual, and often experimental to the point of surrealism. Collections of this period included *Garba* (1913), *El pasajero* (1914), *Luchas de pena y alegría y su transfiguración* (1915), and *Salón sin muros* (1935). After emigrating to Mexico in 1937, he wrote denser, more pessimistic poetry, which he illustrated with his own drawings. These later collections included *Puerta severa* (Mexico City, 1941,) *La noche del verbo* Mexico City, 1942), and the anthology of earlier work, *La música que llevaba* (Buenos Aires, 1949). *Voz en vuelo a su cuna* (Málaga, 1961) is a posthumous volume with a prefatory poem by Jorge Guillén. Moreno Villa edited Espronceda (1923) and Lope de Rueda (1924) for Clásicos Castellanos.

His autobiography is *Vida en claro* (Mexico City, 1944), especially interesting for his years in the Residencia de Estudiantes (1917–37; see INSTITUCIÓN LIBRE DE ENSEÑANZA). The respect felt for him by poets of his generation can be seen in Luis Cernuda's essay in *Estudios sobre poesía española contemporánea* (1957), pp. 153–77.

See J. F. Cirre, *La poesía de José Moreno Villa* (1963).

MORETO Y CABAÑA, Agustín (1618–69), b. Madrid. Playwright of the school of Calderón (q.v.). Of Italian parents, he studied at Alcalá 1634–39 and lived in Madrid in the early and mid-1650s, probably at court. In 1657 he was appointed chaplain to Baltasar de Moscoso, Archbishop of Toledo, who gave him a sinecure in Toledo which permitted him to spend most of his time at court. Unlike many of his contemporaries (such as Lope de Vega) he passed a peaceful and untroubled life, publishing the *Primera parte de Comedias . . .* in 1654 (2nd edn., 1677), the *Segunda parte de las Comedias* in Valencia in 1657, and the *Tercera parte de Comedias* in 1681.

Though his lyrical gift was slight, Moreto was adept at dialogue and plot construction, using skilful verse without verbosity or rhetorical devices.

His masterpiece, *El desdén con el desdén* (q.v.), inspired partly by Lope's excellent *La vengadora de las mujeres*, deals with the attempts of a haughty young noblewoman to humble her suitors, a plot also used in the underrated *El poder de la amistad* (critical edn. by D. E. Dedrick, Valencia, 1968), another *comedia de fábrica*.

Equally popular with audiences in Moreto's time and since is the *comedia de figurón El lindo Don Diego* (q.v.), on a fop who rises to perform his toilet at five a.m., and finishes at about two in the afternoon. Guillén de Castro's *El Narciso en su opinión* is an obvious thematic source for this play, but Moreto's treatment is more subtle and witty. His other *costumbrista* plays include *La fingida Arcadia*; *La confusión de un jardín*, a complex *comedia de capa y espada* drawn from Castillo Solórzano's story *La confusión de una noche*; and *No puede ser el guardar a una mujer*, like Calderón's *La dama duende* an attack on men obsessed by their personal honour.

Moreto's just renown as a comic playwright has overshadowed his undeniable achievements in religious, historical, and legendary drama such as *San Franco de Sena o el lego del Carmen*, which concerns an evil, blasphemous man converted to the true faith. However, Moreto still continues to be as highly regarded an *entremesista* as Quiñones de Benavente and Cervantes (qq.v.).

A good selection of Moreto's more interesting plays (though with unreliable texts) can be found in vol. 39 (1856) of the BAE, while Clásicos Castellanos has better editions by N. Alonso Cortés (1916) of *El lindo don Diego* and *El desdén con el desdén*. Moreto's way with the *auto sacramental* can be seen in vol. 58 (1865) of the BAE, which reprints *La gran casa de Austria y divina Margarita*.

See the bibliographies by E. Cotarelo y Mori in *BRAE*, vol. 14 (1927), pp. 449–94, and by A. M. Coe in *Hispanic Review*, vol. 1 (1933), pp. 236–9. The main studies on his work are Ruth Lee Kennedy, *The dramatic art of Moreto* (Northampton, Mass., 1931–2); E. Caldera, *Il teatro di Moreto* (Pisa, 1960), and Frank P. Casa, *The dramatic craftsmanship of Moreto* (Cambridge, Mass., 1966).

MORGA, Antonio de (*fl.* 1605), Spanish jurist, administrator, and historian. In *Sucesos de las Islas Filipinas* (Mexico City, 1609), Morga attempted to illustrate how Spanish friars had civilized the 'savages'. The Augustinians (1565) had been followed by the Franciscan mission (1577) and the the Jesuits (1581). Morga argued that Filipino material culture was primitive and the spiritual and religious culture non-existent. José Rizal, annotating Morga's work (Paris, 1896) demonstrated Morga's ignorance. There have been two editions in English translation of this key text; one by Encarnación Alzona (Manila, 1962); and another by J. S. Cummins (Cambridge, 1971).

Morga's title is misleading, his work being useful also for its descriptions of China and Japan in the late 16th c.

Moriscos, Muslims converted to Christianity at the time of the Reconquest of the Muslim-held territories of Spain, culminating in the surrender of Granada to Ferdinand and Isabella in 1492.

The expulsion of the *moriscos* in 1609–11 by Philip III, at the instigation of the Duke of Lerma, deprived Spain of some of its most industrious citizens. It is estimated that they constituted some 500,000 of a population then totalling about nine million.

Gaspar Honorat de Aguilar (q.v.) composed an epic poem, *La expulsión de los moros de España* (1610). The play of about 1619, *Los moriscos de Hornachos*, has been incorrectly attributed to Francesc Agustí Tárrega (q.v.).

See Boronat y Barrachina, *Los moriscos españoles y su expulsión* (Valencia, 1901).

MORO, César, the pseudonym of César Quíspez Asín (q.v.), the Peruvian surrealist poet.

MOROSOLI, Juan José (1899–1957), b. Montevideo. Uruguayan short-story writer and novelist. He gave up poetry after publishing *Balbuceos* (1925) and *Los juegos* (1928), and concentrated on the marvellously evocative, gentle stories of people at the end of their tether in *Hombres* (1932; 2nd edn., 1942); *Los albañiles de 'Los Tapes'* (1936); *Hombres y mujeres* (1944);

Vivientes (1953); *Tierra y tiempo* (1959); and *El viaje hacia el mar, y otros cuentos* (1962).

Many of Morosoli's characters are drunkards, prostitutes, and helpless victims of a society both unable and unwilling to understand their plight, or to do anything about it. An early note of irony was quickly replaced by pervasive compassion.

The novel *Muchachos* (1950) is a thread of incidents concerning several boys whom the author conceived as only one: Perico.

MOTILINÍA (Aztec: 'poor'), in Spanish literature, the name assumed by the Spanish Franciscan Fray Toribio de Benavente (q.v.), author of the *Historia de los indios de Nueva España*, completed in 1541.

Mozárabes (Arabic: *must'arab*, 'one who has become Arabicized'), the Hispano-Roman Christians of Andalusia who preferred Islamic domination by the Arab-Berber invaders of 711–12 to the rule of the Visigoths, and so accepted Islamic customs and the Arabic language. The word was *muztárabes* in the time of Alonso VI (1072–1109), but by 1118 it is already recorded as *muzárabes*.

The earliest Spanish poetry consists of lines in mozarabic Castilian appended to learned poems in Hebrew or Arabic characters in the 11th c. (see KHARJA). Mozarabic Spanish was not really a written language at all, and all evidences for its existence are those pieced together from words transcribed phonetically by learned Spanish Muslims or Jews writing in Arabic and Hebrew.

Mudéjares (Arabic: *mudajjān*), the term applied to Muslims remaining in the Christianized territories of Andalusia who were not reduced to slavery (as occurred in the early years of the Reconquest) but were allowed to practise their religion and retain their possessions on the regular payment of taxes. Arabs converted to Christianity were known as *moriscos* (q.v.). The term applied to *mudéjares* in the Kingdom of Aragón was *tagarinos*.

The number of *mudéjares* increased notably during the reign of Alfonso VI (1072–1109), when they were granted civil and religious liberties, including the provision of *shar'ia* law and the subsequent creation of ghettoes known as *morerías*, each with its own Muslim mayor. The so-called *mudéjar* style in architecture (13th–16th c.) combines Christian elements with the use of Arab ornamentation.

Muerte de Artemio Cruz, La (1962), a novel by the Mexican Carlos Fuentes (q.v.), which

has been described by Fernando Benítez as containing 'the greatness, the drama, the sordidness, the purity, and the tenderness of Mexico'.

Through the memories of a political boss on his deathbed, Fuentes gives us a kaleidoscopic study of character and society from the revolutionary period of Mexico to the present. He employs a wide range of narrative techniques which he justifies by claiming that a Latin-American novelist must be both a Balzac and a Butor. The corruption of the protagonist and his loss of ideals mirror the betrayal of the Mexican revolution over the years.

The novel has been translated by Sam Hileman as *The death of Artemio Cruz* (New York, 1964).

MÚGICA CELAYA, RAFAEL (1911–   ), b. Hernani, Guipúzcoa. The most prolific Spanish poet since World War II, who has published as many as five volumes in three years: *Rapsodia éuskara* and *Mazorcas* (1963), *La linterna sorda* and *Dos cantatas* (1964), and *Baladas y decires vascos* (1965). Since *Marea de silencio* (1935) he has published more than twenty-five books.

Contradictions in his poetic viewpoints have been resolved in part by the use of heteronyms (Gabriel Celaya and Juan de Leceta) for contrasting styles. He belonged to the *Espadaña* group (q.v.) and is credited with originating the well-known aphorism: 'poetry is not an end in itself, but a means of transforming the world'. Since his *Poesías completas* appeared in 1969, he has published *Lírica de cámara* (1969), *Operaciones poéticas* (1971), *Cien poemas de un amor* (1971), *Cantos iberos* and *La liga de Arbigorriya* (both 1975). Among his most important prose essays are *Exploración de la poesía* (2nd edn., 1971) and *Inquisición de la poesía* (1971).

Muladí (Arabic: *muwalladi*, 'mixed Arab and foreign'), any Christian who was converted to Islam and lived among Muslims in southern Spain after the overthrow of Rodrigo, the last of the Gothic Kings of Spain, in 711–12.

Mundo es ancho y ajeno, El, an important novel by the Peruvian Ciro Alegría (q.v.) published in Buenos Aires in 1941 and translated by Harriet de Onís as *Broad and alien is the world* (New York, 1941; London, 1942). An important fictional instrument of the policy of APRA (Alianza Popular Revolucionaria Americana), it follows a left-wing and nationalist party line without being avowedly communist. Alegría was an *aprista* gaoled and exiled for his party membership.

The novel is much more than a political

pamphlet, however. Alegría enters the mental world of the Indian (part narrator, part protagonist) Rosendo Maqui, whose organic view of relationships is of no use when confronted by a cynical landowner scheming to steal by legal means the lands traditionally owned by Indians. Rosendo resists, is gaoled, and is killed by prison guards.

In the second half of the book, Rosendo's adopted son Benito continues the struggle for Indians' rights, making them a new commune elsewhere and, because of his literary skills and experience of unions and committees, is able to strengthen the Indians' case for a place in modern society. Troops are sent to bring down the commune and, when the Indians again resist as in the time of Rosendo, the commune is destroyed to the last man.

Alegría's view of the Indian as a noble savage (contrasted with that of Icaza, q.v.) sees simplicity and the rural life as an end in themselves. His idealistic view is noble but ignores the difficulties of governing a modern state, with its bureaucratic apparatus.

Mundo por de dentro, El, the fourth of the *Sueños* of Francisco de Quevedo (qq.v.).

MUÑOZ, EUGENIO (1885–1936), b. Madrid. Novelist and polemicist, whose articles and lectures against the cults of flamenco and bullfighting led to assault, legal proceedings, and even imprisonment. Of penurious parents (he claimed that he had to steal the boots from his father's corpse as his inheritance), he began to write under the name Eugenio Noel, and achieved sudden fame with war despatches to *La España Nueva* from Morocco beginning in 1909 (later collected as *Notas de un voluntario*). His controversial essays found few readers, but his novellas and short stories enjoyed a *succès de scandale* for their daring stylistic mannerisms and for their open anti-clericalism, as in *Vidas de santos, diablos, mártires, frailes* ... (1916). Muñoz wrote one long novel which was undoubtedly his best: *Las siete cucas* (1927).

As the novel opens, Librado and Saturnina live in a village near Salamanca with their unmarried daughters. Their poverty becomes unbearable, and Librado steals and eventually kills to make his fortune. But Saturnina is repelled by the killing and informs the police, who hang her husband. Her honesty makes things worse; her daughters are dismissed from their positions as servants, and the 'siete cucas' resort to prostitution, Saturnina offering all her daughters except the youngest; the ploy is resoundingly victorious; the family rises in local prestige to the point where the doctor, sent to inspect the brothel they run, falls in love with

the youngest daughter and marries her. The sordid aspects of Spanish provincial life are deftly interwoven with none-too-subtle asides on hypocrisy, and digressions on manners, while Muñoz's bitter humour is accurate and to the point.

Joaquín de Entrambasaguas has written a full biography and bibliography of Muñoz in pp. 623–81 of *Las mejores novelas contemporáneas 1925–1929* (Barcelona, 1961). The best source for Muñoz's life is his own *Diario íntimo* (1962).

MUÑOZ, RAFAEL FELIPE (1899–), b. Chihuahua. Mexican short-story writer and novelist. As a journalist aged 16, he met the *caudillo* and *guerrillero* Pancho Villa who was to become a recurrent subject in his writing. Muñoz travelled with Villa until Muñoz chose exile in 1916. *Memorias de Pancho Villa* (1923) was written with Ramón Puente in the year of Villa's assassination. His first novel was ¡ *Vámonos con Pancho Villa!* (Madrid, 1931; widely translated), inferior to *Se llevaron el cañón para Bachimba* (Buenos Aires, 1941), which is set in the state of Chihuahua early in 1912, and concerns Orozco's revolt against the government of Francisco Madero, who had recently come to power on the fall of the dictatorial Porfirio Díaz.

The chief character, Álvaro, is a boy of 13 when the book opens, fighting under a colonel called Marcos Ruiz on the side of Orozco. The boy is captured by the *federales* (government troops) and is returned home to his father. During the war he has matured into manhood, so his experiences have not been entirely futile.

The novel is brutal and sensational in its descriptions of guerrilla action, using rich images and varying the pace expertly from slow-moving descriptions of rural life to rapid cameos of revolutionary warfare.

Muñoz's short stories appeared in *El hombre malo* (n.d. but 1913); *El feroz cabecilla y otros cuentos de la Revolución en el Norte* (1928; the title refers to Villa); and *Si me han de matar mañana* (1934). A volume of his *Obras incompletas, dispersas o rechazadas* appeared in 1967. He wrote a biography of Antonio López de Santa Anna: *Santa Anna* (Madrid, 1936; 3rd edn., 1945, with additional bibliographical material).

See A. Castro Leal, *La novela de la Revolución Mexicana* (1968).

MUÑOZ ROJAS, JOSÉ ANTONIO (1909–), b. Antequera, Malaga. Poet, who qualified in law at Madrid University. His Andalusian sensibility emerges in simple poems cleverly wrought: *Versos de retorno* (Málaga, 1929), *Ardiente jinete* (1934), *Sonetos de amor por un autor indiferente* (Málaga, 1942), *Abril del alma* (1943), *Cantos a*

Rosa (1954), and *Lugares del corazón en nueve sonetos que lo celebran* (Málaga, 1962).

He followed the stories in *Historias de familia* (1945) with two volumes of poetic prose: *Las cosas del campo* (1953) and *Las musarañas* (1957).

MUÑOZ SECA, PEDRO (1881–1936), b. Puerto de Santa María, Cádiz. Playwright. His work, usually vulgar and for a time enormously popular, can be divided into the sentimental, such as *El conflicto de Mercedes*; the parodic, of which the outstanding example is *La venganza de don Mendo*; and the *astracanada* (such as *El verdugo de Sevilla*), a comic genre characterized by a crazy plot with puns and similar word-play. His right-wing propaganda, exemplified by the attack on divorce in *Anacleto se divorcia*, combined with his Philistinism to ensure quick success at the box office. He was soon copied by his collaborators and followers Pedro Pérez Fernández, Enrique García Álvarez, Antonio Paso, and Joaquín Abate y Díaz.

See J. Montero Alonso, *Pedro Muñoz Seca* (1928).

MUNTANER, RAMON (1265–1336), b. Perelada, Gerona. Catalan chronicler. A loyal soldier in the service of the House of Aragón, Muntaner went to Sicily in 1300 and took part in the siege of Messina. He is later found in Greece and Asia Minor, where he commanded a garrison at Gallipoli. In 1325–8 he wrote the *Crònica o Descripcio dels Fets e Hazanyes del Inclyt Rey Don Jaume Primer, Rey Daragò, de Mallorques, e de Valencia* . . . (Valencia, 1558, reprinted Barcelona, 1562).

The 298 chapters are written in an attractive style reminiscent of Froissart. Muntaner makes up for his lack of learning by his acute observation and transparent loyalty. The most interesting sections concern the times of Pere III, the French invasion of Catalonia in 1285, and Muntaner's experiences in the Near Eastern expedition. He is accurate where he is not betrayed by a love of legend. There is a new edition of the *Crònica* (2 vols., 1927–52) by J. M. de Casacuberta and M. Coll i Alentorn.

MUQAFFA', 'ABDULLAH IBN AL- (d. 757), the translator of *Kalila wa Dimna* (Spanish, *Calila e Digna* q.v.), from the Old Persian of Barzuya into Arabic. The work of Muqaffa' enabled the fables to survive in modern European languages.

Muralla, La (1954), a play by Joaquín Calvo Sotelo (q.v.), of social and religious conscience which enjoyed enormous success, recording more than 600 consecutive performances in Madrid's Teatro Larra and hundreds more in provincial cities.

La muralla concerns the dilemma of a rich landowner of Badajoz, Jorge, who lives in Madrid with his family on the proceeds of his rents. Seriously ill, Jorge is tormented by guilt, having expropriated the property after the Civil War, and plans to give it back to its rightful owner. His wife, his daughter, his friends, and his entire acquaintance condemn this action, which is supported only by a Galician country priest.

Calvo Sotelo's purpose was to write 'una radiografía del clima tan de nuestro tiempo', accusing the 'good' Catholic bourgeoisie of idleness and self-seeking. Jorge himself is not portrayed entirely sympathetically; the implication is that his change of heart is dictated more by a wish to save his soul than to restore for its own sake property illegally gained.

MURENA, HÉCTOR ALBERTO, pseudonym of Héctor Alberto Álvarez Murena (q.v.).

MURGUÍA, MANUEL, see MARTÍNEZ MURGUÍA, Manuel Antonio.

Muwashshaha, see KHARJA.

Mystic Writers. *Mística* (Greek: *mystikos*, 'hidden, concealed', from *myein*, 'to close') traditionally consists of the third and last spiritual degree, the 'estado beatífico' of San Juan de la Cruz, and the gifts of grace of St. Thomas Aquinas (see also ASCETIC WRITERS).

Mysticism is a quiet, passive state in which the worshipper attempts to receive the love of God, in contrast to the active mortification and exercises of asceticism.

The most important mystics in Spanish literature are San Juan de la Cruz, Santa Teresa de Ávila, and Sor Juana Inés de la Cruz (qq.v.). Their writings are characterized by the intensely personal, passionate nature of their experiences; they speak of Love and God as interwoven, and their imagery includes a vocabulary of the senses such as touching, tasting, looking, and feeling; their metaphors and symbolism are striking, even to the poets themselves. San Juan is at pains to 'declare' the meaning of each stanza of his highly condensed and allegorical *Subida del Monte Carmelo, Llama de amor viva*, and *Cántico espiritual*.

20th-c. writers have indicated, following Freud, that monks and nuns are liable to periods of exaltation and self-induced frenzy due to sexual frustration and repression, but whether the poetry of the Spanish mystics is due to authentic union with God or to self-induced exaltation, the body of literature is of the highest quality. In addition to the mystics named above, there are the *Triunfos del amor de Dios* (1590) of the Franciscan Fray Juan de los Ángeles, the Erasmian mysticism of Juan de Valdés, the *Guía espiritual* of the quietist Miguel de Molinos, and the sonnet *A Cristo crucificado* (qq.v.).

See E. Allison Peers, *Studies of the Spanish mystics* (1927); P. Groult, *Les mystiques des Pays-Bas et la littérature espagnole du seizième siècle* (Louvain, 1927); and Helmut Hatzfeld, *Estudios sobre mística española* (1968).

N

NACHMAN, MOSES BEN, also called Nachmanides (1194–*c.* 1270), b. Gerona. Religious scholar. For many years Rabbi of Gerona, he led a Cabbalist group there, and was well-known for his mystical tendencies following the tradition of Yehuda ha-Levi, as opposed to the strongly intellectual influence of Maimonides (q.v.). His sense of moral rectitude earned him the title 'Abi ha-hokma' '(the Wise', 'the father of wisdom'). He wrote commentaries on the Pentateuch (*Perush al ha-Tora*) and on the Books of Job and Ruth.

In 1263, King Jaime I invited him, as the highest rabbinical authority, to participate with the *converso* Pablo Cristiano in a public debate in Barcelona. The debate, on the differences between Christianity and Judaism over such questions as the character of Jesus and the date of His Coming, was recorded by Nachmanides in both Latin and Hebrew, and has been studied by J. M. Millás Vallicrosa in *Anales de la Universidad de Barcelona*, vol. 1 (1940), pp. 25–44. Some of Nachmanides' arguments were offensive to the Dominicans, and he was exiled.

Nacimientos, plays and poems on the Nativity of Christ recited or acted at Christmas in Spanish churches, streets, and private houses. Texts of two such works are recorded as early as the 15th c. and are available in R. Foulché-Delbosc's *Cancionero castellano del siglo XV* in the NBAE (1912–15); one is the *Vita Christi* (q.v.) of Fray Íñigo de Mendoza (q.v.), a poem of 4,000 lines of octosyllables; and the other, written by Gómez Manrique (q.v.) between 1467 and 1481, is entitled *Representación del Nacimiento de Nuestro Señor*: it includes a moving procession of martyrs who offer the Child the instruments and symbols of the Passion: the cup of bitterness, column and rope, scourge, crown of thorns, Cross, nails, and lance. Manrique's play follows the *Officium pastorum*, a Nativity story based on St. Luke, with a farcical opening in which Joseph, suspicious of Mary's pregnancy, is rebuked by an angel: it is possible that the tradition of Joseph as a comic figure arose as a

foil to the increasing worship of Mary in the Middle Ages.

Juan del Encina (q.v.) wrote two Christmas plays (acted in 1492), inspiring similar works by Gil Vicente (q.v.) and Jorge de Montemayor (q.v., published in 1554). Lope de Vega is known to have written works in this genre: *Nacimiento de Christo* and possibly the *Auto del Nacimiento de Christo Nuestro Señor* published with other examples of the genre by Cubillo and Valdivielso in *Navidad y Corpus Christi festejado* (1664).

Nativity plays declined in popularity after the reform of the breviary in 1568 and with the growth of the secular theatre.

See also AUTOS DE LOS REYES MAGOS.

Nada (Barcelona, 1944), a novel by Carmen Laforet (q.v.) which won the first Premio Nadal, is autobiographical and concerns lives wrecked by frustration and wilful misunderstandings. Neither Andrea, a mere observer (Carmen Laforet), nor the other characters, truly come to life: a situation viewed by some critics as a fault, and by others as an essential feature of the book's style.

Andrea, a young girl of 18, arrives in Barcelona from the Canary Islands to live in her grandmother's house while studying. The negative qualities of the depressing, squalid, existence led by the family at a time of hardship just after the Civil War account for the book's title ('Nothing'). Andrea gradually becomes aware of the tensions in her adopted home. Her uncle Juan treats his wife viciously on learning that she has had an affair with his brother Román before and after their wedding. Her other uncle, Román, a failed musician, commits suicide. Her aunt Angustias conceals her masochism under a cloak of religion, and after an affair with a married man enters a convent. Even such an apparently happy girl as Andrea's friend Ena flirts with Román to expose his weakness in revenge for gossip linking his name with that of Ena's mother. In a perfunctory dénouement, Andrea is offered work in Madrid, and simply leaves Barcelona and the family.

Though the book was written very quickly—specifically for the first Premio Nadal—*Nada* has not lost its impact, for it characterized the malaise of the post-Civil War generation of Spain more vividly than the fiction of any other writer except Camilo José Cela (q.v.). *Nada* is considered a *tremendista* novel (see TREMEN-DISMO), despite the virtual absence of catastrophes. *Nada* has been compared to *Wuthering Heights* in the sense that its characters from the first page to the last are irrevocably caught in a web of circumstances.

See D. W. Foster, '"Nada" de Carmen Laforet' in *Revista Hispánica Moderna* (New York), vol. 32, 1966, pp. 43–55.

Nadal, Premio, a literary prize awarded annually since 1944 for the best new novel submitted to the publishing house Destino in Barcelona. It was instituted in memory of Eugenio Nadal, a member of the Destino staff, and was first won by Carmen Laforet (q.v.), for her novel *Nada*. Subsequent winners have included José Félix Tapia (1945), José María Gironella (*Un hombre*, 1946), Miguel Delibes (*La sombra del ciprés es alargada*, 1947), Sebastià Joan Arbó (*Sobre las piedras grises*, 1948), Elena Quiroga de la Valgoma (*Viento del norte*, 1950), Luis Romero (*La noria*, 1951), Rafael Sánchez Ferlosio (*El Jarama*, 1955), José Luis Martín Descalzo (*La frontera de Dios*, 1956), Carmen Martín Gaite (*Entre visillos*, 1957), Ana María Matute (*Primera memoria*, 1959), Ramiro Pinilla (*Las ciegas hormigas*, 1960), E. Caballero Calderón (*El buen salvaje*, 1965), Vicente Soto (*La zancada*, 1966), A. Cunqueiro (*Un hombre que se parecía a Orestes*, 1968), F. García Pavón (*Las hermanas coloradas*, 1969), and J. Fernández Santos (*Libro de las memorias de las cosas*, 1970).

Many Nadal winners have subsequently enhanced their reputation. The term 'Nadalismo' was coined by Mariano García in an article 'The modern novel' (*Atlantic Monthly*, vol. 207, no. 1, January 1961) to describe the 'studied addiction to plotlessness and inertia' which in his view was characteristic of novels awarded the Premio Nadal.

'Nada menos que todo un hombre', a *novela ejemplar* by Miguel Unamuno (q.v.) first published in *La novela corta*, vol. 1, no. 28 (15 July 1916) and collected in *Tres novelas ejemplares* (1920).

Alejandro Gómez, the wealthy but low-born husband of Julia, refuses to kiss their son and subjects his wife to mental anguish. Inwardly he comes to love her but feels that to admit this would diminish his masculinity. In despair she tries to find consolation with the Conde de Bordaviella. Gómez's trust in her and his personal vanity are so great that when Julia admits to her affair, he confronts her with the Count and two doctors and forces the Count to admit she is mad, as Gómez's own honour is of course unimpeachable. The doctors realize what is happening but prefer to avert disaster and declare Julia insane. After a time she longs for Alejandro's animal strength and decides to declare that she was never the Count's mistress. In a farcical scene the reunited couple ask the Count's pardon for embarrassing him and invite him to return as a regular visitor but he manages to escape. These emotional crises break down Julia's health, and Alejandro commits suicide, after he has confessed to her, too late, the depth of his adoration.

The terrible irony of the story's title attacks the *machismo* endemic in much Spanish literature.

NAGID, SHEMUEL HA-, see NAGRELLA, Shemuel ha-Levi ben Yosef.

NAGRELLA, SHEMUEL HA-LEVI BEN YOSEF (993–1056), b. Merida. Poet, rabbi, and army general. He was educated in Cordova, but fled in 1013 when the city was sacked by the Berbers, settling in Málaga, where he rose to become secretary first to the *wazir* (vizier, or chief minister) Abu 'l-Qasim ibn al-'Arif and later to Habbūs, King of Granada from 1025 to 1038. He appointed him *wazir* in 1027, when he became known among his fellow-Jews as *ha-Nagid*, 'the prince'. Under Bādis, the successor to Habbūs, he was appointed commander-in-chief of the army and led it many times between 1038 and 1056, against Seville, Carmona, and Almería. His son Yosef was probably the only other Jew to have commanded a Muslim army. A great patron of learning, Nagrella presented money and books to poor scholars and helped Ibn Gabirol after his banishment from Saragossa.

Nagrella's prose works concerned the art of war, politics, and Talmudic exposition, and he wrote a Hebrew grammar, *Sefer na-osher*, now lost. His religious poetry was profoundly influenced by the Bible: *Ben Tehillim* (New Psalms), *Ben Mishlei* (New Proverbs), and *Ben Kohelet* (New Ecclesiastes). D. S. Sassoon edited 1742 of his poems (many others are lost) in the *Divan Shmuel ha-Nagid* (Oxford, 1934), and these are among the finest in the Hebrew language. They include poems on the transience of life and earthly pleasures, and ascetic poetry in the Arabic genre known as *zuhd*, as well as long meditations, rather than descriptions, on military campaigns, such as 'The victory over Ben Abbad' (one of sixteen of Nagrella's works translated by David Goldstein in *The Jewish poets of Spain* (Harmondsworth, 1971)). The content of his poetry was elevated but its form uninspired, originating the proverb 'cold as the snow of Hermon, or the songs of the Levite Samuel'.

Nahuatl Literature, the literature of the Aztecs and other indigenous peoples whose native language was Nahuatl. With Quiche Literature (q.v.) and Maya Literature, it constitutes the major corpus of pre-Columbian literature in Mexico, and has been studied by Padre Ángel María Garibay (q.v.) in his standard *Historia de la literatura náhuatl* (2 vols., Mexico City, 1953-4). The sources of Nahuatl include, among others, the works collected by Bernardino de Sahagún (q.v.) from 1548 to 1560 and three MSS.; the *Manuscrito de cantares*, the *Manuscrito de los romances de los señores de la Nueva España*, and the *Cantares mexicanos*, that were published in 1906.

Nahuatl authors did not distinguish between genres (though most of the surviving material is in poetic form), but between function. Hymns praise the many gods of the Mexican pantheon, such as Huitzilopochtli, the god of war, storms, and the sun, or Coatlicue, the 'white goddess' of life and death. Epics, such as the *Poema de Quetzalcóatl*, extol the soldier kings. Lyrical poems, such as those composed by the poet-king Netzahualcóyotl (q.v.), tell of the transience of life and its pleasures. Nahuatl imagery is often formal, even ritual, in character, every jewel, bird, or flower being associated with a particular quality or emotion.

Padre Garibay's work has been interpreted for English readers by Irene Nicholson in *Firefly in the night: a study of ancient Mexican poetry and symbolism* (London, 1959).

See also Miguel León-Portilla, *Pre-Columbian literature of Mexico* (Norman, Okla., 1969).

Naipes, Los ('playing cards'). In Spanish cards, the suits are *copas* (hearts), *oros* (diamonds), *bastos* (clubs), and *espadas* (spades). The English 'Queen' becomes the *caballo* ('horse').

The most celebrated passage involving cards in Spanish literature occurs in *Don Quijote*, and is associated with the popular phrase *Paciencia y barajar* ('Patience, and shuffle the cards'), with its peculiar resonance of fatalism.

NALÉ ROXLO, CONRADO (1898-1970), b. Buenos Aires. Argentinian playwright, poet, and humorist. His journalism and short stories have appeared under the pen-name 'Chamico', and have been collected in several volumes: *Cuentos* (1941), *El muerto profesional* (1943), *Cuentos de cabecera* (1946), *La medicina vista de reojo* (1952), *Mi pueblo* (1953), and *Las puertas del Purgatorio*

(1968). His children's stories have been equally successful, especially *La escuela de las hadas*. *Extraño accidente* (1960) is a novel.

Nalé's first play was *La cola de la sirena* (1941), in which a fisherman falls in love with a mermaid, who becomes a woman to retain her fascination over him, and thereby loses it. *Una viuda difícil* (1944) is an excellent comedy of Buenos Aires before 1810, also devoted to the puncturing of illusions. *El pacto de Cristina* (1945) is a novel treatment of a wellworn theme: the Devil agrees to help the heroine Cristina to win the love of Gerardo, a Crusader, but when she discovers that the price is the son that would be born to them, she commits suicide. Nalé ironically shows that Gerardo loved her anyway, and that the Devil could not have taken Cristina's soul because it was too pure. Among his other plays are *Judith y las rosas* (1956) and the ironic allegory *El neblí* (1957), the latter contained in the collection *Teatro breve* (1964), which contains also *El pasado de Elisa*.

Nalé's poetry consists of *El grillo* (1923), *Claro desvelo* (1937), and *De otro cielo* (1952). For the most part these works are in traditional forms, such as the sonnet, but there is a clear progression from lightness and joy to melancholy, and a handful of his later poems stand among the finest published in Argentina this century. *Poesía completa* appeared in 1967.

See M. H. Lacau, *El mundo poético de Conrado Nalé Roxlo* (1954).

Narciso en su opinión, El, a play by Guillén de Castro y Bellvís (q.v.) first published in *Parte segunda de las comedias* (Valencia, 1625).

It is one of the witty *comedias de capa y espada* (q.v.) which gave Castro wide renown in the 17th c., and almost certainly inspired *El lindo don Diego* by Moreto (qq.v.). The protagonist, Don Gutierre, is a foolish dandy incapable of inspiring anything but ridicule and scorn in those he tries to impress. There are editions by R. de Mesonero Romanos in vol. 43 (1857) of the BAE, and by E. Juliá Martínez in Castro's *Obras* (3 vols., 1925-7).

NARIÑO, ANTONIO (1765-1823), b. Bogotá. Colombian intellectual who wrote little, but gave a great impetus to the awakening of his country by possessing one of the largest private libraries in Latin America (including many banned books) and by circulating books and pamphlets otherwise inaccessible to the people. The *Declaration of the Rights of Man* was prohibited in Latin America on 13 December 1789. Nariño finally found the text in Galart de Montjoie's history of the Constitutional Assembly and translated it in December 1793, printing it surreptitiously. He was betrayed to the Spanish authorities, who gaoled him for four years in Cartagena (Colombia), for another twelve years in Cádiz, and then exiled him to Africa. Like his contemporary Camilo Torres (q.v.), he became one of the symbols of intellectual and political independence from Spain.

Narváez (1902), the second novel in the fourth series of *Episodios nacionales* by Benito Pérez Galdós (qq.v.). The protagonist is the harsh authoritarian General Ramón Narváez (1800–68), President of the Council of Ministers.

NARVÁEZ, RODRIGO DE (15th c.), a hero of the Reconquest, who won Antequera from the Moors and was made Governor of that town. He is described in *Claros varones de Castilla* by Hernando del Pulgar (q.v.), and is the magnanimous Christian soldier in the anonymous tale of *Abencerraje y la hermosa Jarifa* (q.v.) of which the best version is that published by Antonio de Villegas in his *Inventario* (1565). Narváez is shown helping to unite the Moorish hero and heroine, both prisoners of the Christians, whom he eventually frees.

NASARRE Y FÉRRIZ, BLAS ANTONIO (1689–1751), b. Alquezar, Huesca. Professor of Law at Saragossa University, then royal libarian, and prominent member of the Academia del Buen Gusto and the Real Academia Española (qq.v.) which supported the neoclassical views of Luzán (q.v.) against the *drama nacional* of Lope and his school. He is remembered in Spanish literary history for two notorious judgments. In his reissue of Avellaneda's *Don Quijote* (1732), Nasarre stated in his introduction, which he signed Isidro Perales y Torres, that it was equal to the genuine Part II of Cervantes. He also reprinted the *Comedias y entremeses* of Miguel de Cervantes (1749) on the curious grounds that as the worst plays ever written, they parodied the unnatural excesses of Lope's drama (which Cervantes himself had in fact ridiculed). Nasarre's prologue, entitled *Disertación sobre las comedias de España*, was answered by José Carrillo in the pamphlet *La sinrazón impugnada y beata de lavapies* (1750) and by 'Tomás de Zabaleta' (Marqués de la Olmeda) in his *Discurso crítico sobre el origen, calidad y estado presente de las comedias de España* (1750).

It is possible that Zabaleta's satirical *Discurso* hastened the death of Nasarre as was suggested by his friend and ally Montiano (q.v.) in his *Elogio histórico de Nasarre* (1751).

Nasarre's one uncontroversial contribution to scholarship was his publication of the *Biblioteca universal de la polygraphía española* (1738) of Cristóbal Rodríguez.

NATAS, FRANCISCO DE LAS (16th c.), a priest in the diocese of Burgos who wrote the verse play *Comedia Tidea* (1550). The plot is that of *La Celestina* (q.v.), Beroe being the name of the procuress. Natas, however, contrives a happy ending for his young lovers, Tideo and Faustina. The rhetorical use of language harks back to Encina (q.v.), while the neat construction owes much to Torres Naharro (q.v.). Its coarse language caused the *Tidea* to be placed on the Index of 1559 and again on that of 1583. The play, surviving in a sole MS. in the Royal Library, Munich, was reissued by the Sociedad de Bibliófilos Madrileños (1913).

Natas also wrote a *Comedia Claudiana* (1536) in *coplas* which is no longer extant, and a translation of Book II of the *Aeneid* (Burgos, 1528).

National Library, Madrid, see BIBLIOTECA NACIONAL, MADRID.

Naturalismo ('naturalism'), a literary movement whose major representative is the French novelist Émile Zola. Zola, who preferred the term 'experimental novel', claimed to base his fiction on real knowledge of human nature drawn from direct observation and experimentation. Where *realismo* (q.v.) selects from real life the elements to be included in the work of art, *naturalismo* attempts to include everything, though the necessary shaping and selection in any book of course undermines the attempt. The major naturalist in Spanish fiction is Emilia Pardo Bazán (q.v.), who collected and published an important series of essays on the new style as *La cuestión palpitante* (1883), with a prologue by Clarín (q.v.), who also practised the style. The polemical tone of Pardo Bazán's essays predictably drew a chorus of opposition from those conservatives who contradicted her view that Roman Catholic morality was consonant with naturalist principles. These opponents included Juan Valera (in *Apuntes sobre el nuevo arte de escribir novelas*, 1887), Campoamor, and Alarcón (qq.v.). Blasco Ibáñez continued to write novels in a naturalistic vein into the 1920s.

See D. F. Brown, *The Catholic naturalism of Emilia Pardo Bazán* (Chapel Hill, 1957), and W. Pattison, *El naturalismo español* (Madrid, 1965).

NAVA ÁLVAREZ DE NOROÑA, GASPAR MARÍA DE, see NOROÑA, Gaspar María de Nava Álvarez, *Conde de.*

NAVAGERO, ANDREA (1483–1529), b. Venice. Greek scholar and Latin poet. He was a friend and collaborator of the printer Aldus Manutius, who published an important series of editions of the classics.

Navagero was Venetian ambassador to Spain

during 1522–8, and while the court of Carlos V was at Granada in 1526 he met Joan Boscà (q.v.) and persuaded him to use the varied, flexible forms and metres of Italian poetry. Boscà's experiments, and the more successful ones of Garcilaso (q.v.) were published by his widow in *Las obras de Boscán y algumas de Garcilasso de la Vega repartidas en quatro libros* (Barcelona, 1543). Navagero was thus directly responsible for the popularization in Spain of blank verse, the *terza rima* of Dante, the *ottava rima* of Ariosto, and the *canzoni* and *sonetti* of Petrarch (the experimental Italianate sonnets of the Marqués de Santillana (q.v.) were then still in MS.).

The *Opera omnia* of Navagero did not appear until 1718, but his *Viaggio fatto in Spagna* (Venice, 1563) was long known as a guide to Spanish social life in the early 16th c.: the first translation into Spanish was by Fabié (1879) and there is a later one by José María Alonso Gamo (1951).

NAVARRETE, *Fray* MANUEL MARTÍNEZ DE, see MARTÍNEZ DE NAVARRETE, *Fray* Manuel.

NAVARRETE Y RIBERA, FRANCISCO DE (1592?–1652?), b. Seville. Playwright and novelist, Papal notary at the Court of Madrid, and friend of Lope de Vega (q.v.). His *Flor de sainetes* (1640) printed his *entremeses* and two short novels: *El caballero invisible* and *Los dos hermanos*, the latter written as an exercise in avoiding the vowel a. He also wrote *La carroza con las damas* without using the letter e; *La perla de Portugal* without using i; *La peregrina hermitaña* without o and *La serrana de Cintia* without u. (This is not the only case of its kind in Spanish: Alonso Alcalá y Herrera was another Golden Age novelist who practised the omission of certain vowels and there is a long ballad avoiding the use of o in *La vida de Estebanillo González*, q.v., Antwerp, 1646). The two short novels by Navarrete were reprinted in vol. 33 (1854) of the BAE.

Navarrete wrote another *sainete*, *La casa de juego* (1644), to expose the card-sharpers and confidence tricksters operating in the gambling dens of the time.

NAVARRO, GUSTAVO A. (1898–), b. Sucre. Bolivian revolutionary writer who used the pseudonym 'Tristán Maroff'. He was one of the founders of *Letras de Bolivia* (1946).

Navarro made his name with a satirical novel against the frivolity of Latin-American diplomats in Paris: *Suetonio Pimienta: memorias de un diplomático de la República de Zanahoria* (1924).

He popularized the slogan 'Tierras para el indio, minas al Estado', issuing a series of political pamphlets on Marxist lines: *La justicia del Inca, México de frente y de perfil, Wall Street y hambre, El ingenuo continente americano* and many more. He wrote *La ilustre ciudad*, humorous stories on his native city. His witty history of Bolivia was entitled *Melgarejo y el melgarejismo*, which deals with the illiterate *cholo* bastard who ruled Bolivia with his private army from 1864 to 1871 and was known as 'the scourge of God'.

NAVARRO, PEDRO (16th c.), b. Toledo. Playwright and actor-manager, who wrote *c.* 1580 *Comedia muy exemplar de la marquesa de Saluzia, llamada Griselda* which was preserved in play was based on Viñoles' translation (1510) of Foresti's *Supplementum chronicorum orbis ab initio mundi*. Navarro's play has been edited by C. B. Bourland in *Revue Hispanique*, vol. 9 (1902), pp. 331–54. The play is turgid, poorly-constructed, and overlong, but Navarro was praised by Lope de Vega, who was acquainted with at least five other plays of his.

Cervantes wrote that Navarro 'inventó tramoyas, nubes, truenos y relámpagos, desafíos y batallas' and there is another reference to Navarro's stagecraft in the *Viaje entretenido* of Rojas Villandrando (q.v.).

NAVARRO LEDESMA, FRANCISCO (1869–1905), b. Toledo. Archivist, journalist, and university professor. One of the founders of the Madrid daily *ABC* and the satirical weekly *Gedeón*. His literary essays such as *Lecciones de literatura general* (1901) are now little read, but Navarro was responsible for the best contemporary biography of Cervantes, *El ingenioso hidalgo Miguel de Cervantes* (1905), particularly engaging for the evocative picture of the period he drew from the *Documentos cervantinos* (1897–1902) of Cristóbal Pérez Pastor.

There is an affectionate obituary by Benito Pérez Galdós (q.v.) in *Memoranda* (1906), pp. 5–15.

See also Carmen Zulueta, *Navarro Ledesma: el hombre y su tiempo* (1968).

NAVARRO TOMÁS, TOMÁS (1884–), b. La Roda de la Mancha, Albacete. Philologist. Founder of modern Castilian phonology, Navarro has also written on Basque. He studied first in Valencia and then, under Ramón Menéndez Pidal (q.v.), in Madrid University. During his distinguished academic career he was editor of the *Revista de Filología Española*, director of research on the *Atlas lingüístico de España*, and professor at Columbia University (New York) 1939–52.

Navarro undertook editions of *Las moradas* (1911) by S. Teresa de Jesús and the works of Garcilaso de la Vega (1911) for the Clásicos

Castellanos series before devoting his professional attention to linguistics. Perhaps his most significant works are the *Manual de pronunciación española* (1918), the *Manual de entonación española* (1944), *Estudios de fonología española* (1946), *Métrica española: reseña histórica y descriptva* (New York, 1966), and *La voz y la entonación en los personajes literarios* (Mexico City, 1976). *Tomás Navarro Tomás: a tentative bibliography 1908–1970* was compiled in 1971 by T. S. Beardsley.

NAVARRO VILLOSLADA, Francisco (1818–95), b. Viana, Navarra. Historical novelist. A fanatical Roman Catholic and Carlist, he founded *El Pensamiento Español* in 1860 to propagate his views.

Navarro's literary reputation rests on three imaginative and effective novels inspired by the success of Sir Walter Scott: *Doña Blanca de Navarra, crónica del siglo XV* (1847); *Doña Urraca de Castilla, memorias de tres canónigos* (1849); and *Amaya, o los vascos en el siglo VIII* (3 vols., 1879).

Amaya is concerned with the alliance between Visigoths and Basques against the Arab-Berber invasion. It was too melodramatic for its time, and suffered the further disadvantage of appearing when Galdós was at the height of his achievement and fame.

Navarro's *Obras completas* (1947) exclude his political writings and other journalism.

See B. Q. Cornish, *Francisco Navarro Villoslada* (Berkeley, 1918) and 'A contribution to the historical novels of Francisco Navarro Villoslada' in *Homenaje a don Camilo de Echegaray* (San Sebastián, 1928, pp. 199–234); and J. Simón Díaz, 'Vida y obras de Francisco Navarro Villoslada' in *Revista Bibliográfica Nacional* (1946).

Navas de Tolosa, Las, a battle of 1212 fought to the north of Úbeda in which the forces of Navarra, led by Pedro II of Aragón and Alfonso VII of Castile, defeated the Almohades under Muhammad ibn Yaqub. The Arab defeat turned the tide of Reconquest inevitably in favour of the Christians, who immediately recaptured Úbeda, Baeza, and other towns south of the Sierra Morena, leaving the way open for the total reconquest of Andalusia under Fernando III.

The battle is the subject of *Las Navas de Tolosa* (1594), a feeble epic poem in *octava rima* by Cristóbal de Mesa (q.v.).

Nazarín (1895), one of the *Novelas españolas contemporáneas* of Benito Pérez Galdós (qq.v.).

The protagonist is Nazario Zajarín, a priest intent on emulating the life of Christ in a poor district of 19th-c. Madrid. Preferring to live in poverty, he gives away all he collects in charity except what is needed to keep him alive. The ugly Andara kills another woman and seeks refuge under Padre Nazario's roof, later burning the house down to cover her tracks. Homeless, and accused of illicit relations with la Andara, Nazarín (as he is commonly known) is prohibited from celebrating Mass and, casting off his clerical garb, takes to the road. La Andara recognizes him again and, penitent for her share in his disgrace, follows him as a disciple against his will.

In Móstoles, la Andara persuades Nazarín to visit a child dying of fever; Nazarín touches her on her forehead, and she is later cured. Beatriz, the girl's aunt, treats this as a miracle and also follows him. After many adventures, including attending plague victims and burying the dead, Nazarín and la Andara are recognized by a mayor as the suspects in the murder and arson case and are sent back to Madrid, where Nazarín falls ill with the plague.

Together with *Halma* and *Misericordia* (qq.v.), *Nazarín* is Peréz Galdós's most important religious novel, showing that the anti-clericalism of his other books did not exclude respect for Christ's teachings in the Sermon on the Mount. Nazarín combines the idealism of St. Francis of Assisi, Christ, and Don Quijote.

See *Anales Galdosianos*, vol. 2 (1967) for articles on Nazarín as a Christ-figure by F. P. Bowman, C. Morón Arroyo, and A. A. Parker, reprinted later the same year as a separate volume edited by L. Cardona and A. Zahareas, *The Christ-figure in the novels of Pérez Galdós* (New York, 1967).

NEBRIJA, or NEBRISSA or NEBRIXA, Elio Antonio Martínez de Cala de (1442–1522), b. Lebrija, Sevilla. The greatest of Spanish Renaissance humanists, and held in high esteem by Cardinal Ximénez de Cisneros, under whose direction Nebrija helped in the recension of the Complutensian Bible (q.v.).

Nebrija was the first Latin philologist to improve the teaching of the language, and to lay the foundations for Latin lexicography in Spain. His Castilian grammar was the first of its kind to be published for a Romance tongue, and was used until the 19th c.

Nebrija studied under Pedro de Osma at Salamanca until 1461 when, appalled by the state of classical learning in Spain, he travelled on a scholarship to Bologna, where he remained until 1470, mastering theology, law, medicine, and above all classical philology. He stayed at the home of Archbishop Alonso Fonseca in Seville 1470–3, and by 1475 had arrived in Salamanca, where he was to teach grammar and rhetoric for the next thirty-eight years, only interrupting his teaching to write, 1486–1505 (through the generosity of his patron Juan de Zúñiga, Grand Master of the Order of Alcántara), and to become royal chronicler in 1508–9.

His scorn for those who knew little Latin and less Greek earned him so many enemies that when the Chair of Grammar fell vacant in 1513 he was not appointed, and in disgust left Salamanca for the hospitality of Seville and Alcalá. In Alcalá Cardinal Ximénez de Cisneros honoured the great Greek scholar. The Rector of Alcalá University, Hernando de Balbás, declared that the Cardinal's instructions to him were that Nebrija should 'leyese lo que quisiesse, y si no quisiesse leer, que no leyesse y que esto no le mandaba porque trabajasse, sino por pagarle lo que debía España' ('teach whatever he wanted to teach; and if he should not want to teach, then he need not; and this [salary] was sent him not for him to work, but to pay him for what Spain owed him').

Nebrija's most celebrated work is the *Introductiones latinae* (Salamanca, 1481), the first competent Latin grammar published in Spain, which was based on the teaching method of the Italian humanist Valla. This is not the work commonly known as the *Arte de Nebrija*, which is a rewriting by the Jesuit priest Juan Luis de la Cerda dating from the early 17th c. Nebrija translated his grammar into Spanish in 1486 for Queen Isabel.

He followed this with a 30,000-word Latin-Spanish dictionary: the *Interpretatio dictionum ex sermone latino in hispaniensem* (Salamanca, 1492) and in the same year published his important *Gramática sobre la lengua castellana* (Salamanca). A spurious version was made by the Conde de la Saceda (1744–7). A critical edition of Nebrija's *Gramática* by P. Galindo and L. Ortiz Muñoz was published in 2 vols. in 1946.

His *Interpretación de las palabras castellanas en lengua latina* (1495? reprinted in facsimile by the Real Academia Española (1951)), consisting of 20,000 definitions, was enlarged by the author in 1516 and this 2nd edition has been edited by G. J. Macdonald (1973).

His efforts to standardize Castilian spelling resulted in *Reglas de orthographia en la lengua castellana* (1517; new edn., Bogotá, 1977). He was also interested in history, botany, archaeology, and philosophy.

De liberis educandis, written in 1509 but unpublished until Roque Chabás edited it in the *RABM* (vol. 9, 1903, pp. 56–65), is a manual for educating the young based on suggestions from the writings of Aristotle, Xenophon, Plutarch, Aulus Gellius, and Quintilian.

In addition to numerous minor works, Nebrija wrote commentaries on classical authors such as Sedulius, Persius, and Prudentius.

See F. González Olmedo, *Humanistas y pedagogos españoles: Nebrija* (1942) and *Nebrija en Salamanca* (1944).

NEGREROS, JOSÉ, pseudonym of José Joaquín Ortiz (q.v.).

Negrismo, a Latin-American literary movement deriving ultimately from the *indigenista* tradition but with a specifically Negro aesthetic at its most authentic in poetry based on dance rhythms. In Cuba, where the movement is known as Afro-Cubanism, its leading theoretician was Fernando Ortiz (q.v.).

Since the early 1920s *negrismo* has evolved from the Romantic attitudes and content associated with indigenous writing. Emilio Ballagas (q.v.) made the first anthology and study of black poetry in Latin America in his *Antología de la poesía negra hispanoamericana* (Madrid, 1944) and *Mapa de la poesía negra hispanoamericana* (Buenos Aires, 1946). Other *negrista* writers include the mulatto Nicolás Guillén of Cuba, Luis Palés Matos of Puerto Rico, and Ildefonso Pereda Valdés of Uruguay (qq.v.). Though not a Negro himself, Alejo Carpentier (q.v.) has done much to create interest in Negro art and literature. Gallegos (q.v., *Pobre negro* and *La trepadora*) and the Ecuadorian poet Adalberto Ortiz (q.v., *El animal herido* and the 'Negro novel' *Juyungo*) have also written on Negro themes.

NEGUERELA, DIEGO DE (16th c.), playwright. His only known work, probably written for a wedding *c.* 1530, is the *Farsa llamada Ardamisa* edited by L. Rouanet in the Biblioteca Hispánica, vol. 4 (1900), influenced by Torres Naharro (q.v.) (in the prologue) and by Juan del Encina and Lucás Fernández (qq.v.).

On her way to meet her lover Galirano, Ardamisa is accosted by a series of comic suitors, each interfering at a crucial moment in his predecessor's scene. Galirano meets a friar who praises celibacy, and later plans with the other suitors to win the heroine Ardamisa. The lovesick Portuguese, the cowardly braggart, and other stock figures of 16th-c. comedy also appear.

Much of the play is written in *coplas de pie quebrado*, the rest being in *coplas de arte mayor*.

Neoclasicismo ('neoclassicism'), the prevailing tendency in 18th-c. Spanish literature. It was French in origin, and dates roughly from the accession to the Spanish throne of Philip V in 1700. It was contemporary with the Enlightenment in Spain (q.v.), and many of the *afrancesados* (q.v.) who were originally instrumental in divulgating neoclassicism were also connected with the Enlightenment.

Poetic theorists like the influential Luzán (q.v.) stressed the doctrine of the artist as craftsman, rather than as inspired prophet. Moderation replaces exaltation, and correctness in style and metre outweigh the merits of naturalness and spontaneity. This tendency was by no means ubiquitous in 18th-c. Spain, however, and Feijóo was not alone in viewing it with disfavour.

Neoclassical drama linked theory to practice more effectively; after the alleged baroque excesses of Calderón's imitators, a long-delayed neoclassical spirit first appears in the plays of Luzán's friend Montiano y Luyando (q.v.) in the early 1750s and recurs in those of Montiano's protégé Nicolas Fernández de Moratín (q.v.) and in *Don Sancho García* (1771) by Cadalso (q.v.). These plays preserved the classical unities, and often retain the French spirit typical of neoclassicism in Spain.

Leandro Fernández de Moratín (q.v.) was amongst those involved in the battle for neoclassical control of the Madrid theatres. He was one of the writers whose French ideas and Gallicisms pervaded Spanish literature to such an extent at this period that Forner (q.v.), in his satirical *Exequias de la lengua castellana* (1782), treated the issue of French borrowings as a problem of national importance, and Capmany wrote that 'Half of the Castilian language is buried, because the purest, loveliest, and most useful words have not emerged for fifty years'.

Critics and theorists dominated much of the literature of 18th-c. Spain, which saw the emergence of the essay (Jovellanos, Feijóo, and Cadalso) as a major art-form.

Neoclassicism spread throughout the schools, where it was taught by the Jesuits, to the Academies which sprang up all over Spain at this period (see ACADEMY). Economic and other reforms began to be discussed both in these Academies and in the serious journals such as the *Diario de los Literatos de España* (q.v.) founded in 1737, again on a French model.

See R. E. Pellissier, *The neo-classic movement in Spain during the XVIII century* (Stanford, Calif., 1918).

Neoclassicism, see NEOCLASICISMO.

Neo-Stoicism, a movement better known in Spain as *senequismo* (q.v.).

NERUDA, PABLO (1904–73), b. Parral, Chile. One of the most famous of modern Latin-American poets, whose real name was Ricardo Eliecer Neftalí Reyes, formally changed by deed poll in 1946 to Pablo Neruda, his pseudonym (after the Czech poet Jan Neruda) since 1920. Neruda's mother died when he was very young, and his father (a train-driver) moved to Temuco in the far south of the country, where the boy had his early education and came to know Gabriela Mistral (q.v.). Having worked for two years on *La Mañana*, a local newspaper, he left Temuco in 1920 or 1921 to study in the capital, Santiago, there publishing some of his first poems in the student magazine *Claridad*, and the books *La canción de la fiesta* (1921), *Crepusculario* (1923), and *Veinte poemas de amor y una canción desesperada* (1924), which made his name known throughout Latin America. The last-named book uses nature symbolism to define his attitudes to love, and together with *Tentativa del hombre infinito* (1925–6) marks the first stage in his poetic career.

The next stage is that of his diplomatic service abroad from 1927. He spent six years in South-East Asia, 1934–8 in Spain, returning to Chile in 1943. In 1945 he was elected a senator. While in Spain he founded the important magazine *Caballo Verde para a Poesía* (q.v.), the first issue being dated October 1935 and the last being no. 4 of January 1936 (there was a complete reprint in 1974). His first editorial attacked the concept of 'pure poetry', recommending instead an 'impure poetry' stained by contact with real life. This phase corresponds to the poems in *El hondero entusiasta* (1933), and *Residencia en la tierra, 1925–31* (1933; amplified to 1935, 2 vols., Madrid, 1935). These poems gradually become more opaque as Neruda's perception of death, the passing of time, chaos, and nihilism lead to fragmentation in style, and a rejection of the beautiful in favour of the harsh and elemental. It is his early experiences in the natural world of virgin Temuco which restore a sense of purpose and continuity ('I wrote only to stop myself from dying').

He joined the Communist Party of Chile in 1939, and his work changed direction again: this time to a desire for increased clarity, his only thought being for the 'simple people' in the belief that excessive obscurity in poetry results from class prejudice: a desire to avoid contact with the uncultivated majority. The poet concerned with social questions must write as plainly as possible if he is to enjoy any public at all. This is the period of *Tercera residencia, 1935–1945* (Buenos Aires, 1947) and the *Canto general de Chile* (q.v., Mexico City, 1950, complete), a celebration of America (and Chile in particular) which deals with the continent's flora, fauna, pre-Columbian civilizations (in the section called *Alturas de Machu Picchu*, separately translated as *The heights of Machu Picchu* (London, 1966) by Nathaniel Tarn), as well as social and political comment on the wars of liberation and their effects.

Forced to flee Chile in 1948 for his subversive

activities on behalf of the Communist Party, Neruda travelled in the USSR (where he was awarded the 1950 World Peace Prize), China, and Eastern Europe. He was allowed to return to Chile in 1952, following which he published even more prolifically: *Odas elementales, Nuevas odas elementales*, and *Tercer libro de odas* (Buenos Aires, 1954–6–7), poems intended to shape communist attitudes in Latin America. His *Obras completas* (Buenos Aires, 1957) reached a third edition (2 vols.) in 1968, and have been supplemented by *Fin de mundo* and *La espada encendida* (Buenos Aires, 1969–70). The collection *Estravagaria* (q.v., Buenos Aires, 1968) shows a markedly humorous vein.

Neruda was nominated presidential candidate for the Chilean elections of 1970, but stood down in favour of Dr. Allende, the first Marxist president of Chile, who appointed Neruda ambassador to France.

In 1971 Neruda was awarded the Nobel Prize for Literature. From 1961 he lived much of the time on the Chilean island called Isla Negra, which he left in his will to the copper-workers of Chile. *Memorial de Isla Negra* (1964) is a reflective poetic autobiography consisting of 102 poems in five parts to be read in conjunction with the prose autobiography *Confieso que he vivido* (Buenos Aires, 1974).

The 4th edition of the *Obras completas* (3 vols., 1973) excludes the *Canción de gesta* (1960), two of the five prose sections in *Viajes* (1955), *Maremoto* (1970), an adequate expansion of the fine bibliography contributed to the 3rd edition by Hernán Loyola, and the former preface *Infancia y poesía*. Neruda's play *Fulgor y muerte de Joaquín Murieta* (1967) is only partly successful. Eight new books of poetry were planned for publication on his 70th birthday, and appeared in Buenos Aires posthumously: *La rosa separada* (first published in Paris, 1972); *Jardin de invierno*; *2000*; *El corazón amarillo*; *Libro de las preguntas*; *Elegía*, on Russian themes; *Defectos escogidos*, and *El mar y las campanas*.

See Jaime Alazraki, *Poética y poesía de Pablo Neruda* (New York, 1965); Marta Aguirre, *Las vidas de Pablo Neruda* (1967); Antonio Melis, *Neruda* (Florence, 1971); and Ángel Flores (ed.), *Aproximaciones a Pablo Neruda* (Barcelona, 1973).

NERVO, Amado Ruiz de (1870–1919), b. Tepic, Nayarit. Mexican poet. He studied law and theology. A founding editor of *La Revista Moderna* (q.v.), Nervo began work as a journalist on *El Universal*, publishing his naturalistic novel *El bachiller* (1895) and two volumes of poetry, *Perlas negras* and *Místicas* (both 1898), before leaving for Europe in 1900 to report on the Paris Exhibiton for *El Imparcial*. He lived with Darío (q.v.) in Paris, leading a Bohemian existence

and publishing *Poemas* (Paris, 1901), a book owing much to the influence of M. Gutiérrez Nájera (q.v.), of whom Nervo said 'se lo debíamos todo'; however, French symbolism played an equal part in his poetic development as he employed unusual rhythms and broke the accepted norms of prosody in *La hermana agua* (Madrid, 1901), *El éxodo y las flores del camino* (which also contained prose, 1902), *Lira heroica* (1902), and *Los jardines interiores* (1905). *Almas que pasan*, a collection of short stories, appeared in 1906.

He joined the diplomatic service in 1905, serving in Madrid, Buenos Aires, and Montevideo, but was discharged.

The second phase of his modernist period began with *En voz baja* (1909), and he evolved a Franciscan-like identification with nature (as in *La hermana agua*) which reached its highest point in *Serenidad* (1912), a book which nevertheless includes the Darían 'Rimas irónicas y cortesanas'.

Nervo's final period is marked by a crisis of imagination, as he searches unremittingly but in vain for fresh modes of expression. He attempted a poetry without rhetoric, 'without literature', but produced a body of work without substance or direction, except in a few notable bursts of inspiration. This period saw the publication of *Elevación* (1917), *Plenitud* (prose writings, 1918), *Parábolas y otros poemas* (1918), *El estanque de los lotos* (Buenos Aires, 1919), *La última vanidad* (1919), and also included the posthumously-published *La amada inmóvil* (1922), and *El arquero divino* (1922). His poetry was widely read in his time, but has subsequently become less popular, as have his short stories and novels. His fiction is often tinged with theosophy and most of his poetry is religious. He wrote a serial fantasy *El donador de almas* (1899; first edn. in book form, 1955); a zarzuela, *Consuelo* (first performed in 1899); and criticism, his most important work in this field being *Juana de Asbaje* (Madrid, 1910), on Sor Juana Inés de la Cruz (q.v.).

His *Obras completas* (Madrid, 1920–8 and 1951–2) were last reissued in 1962.

See Genaro Estrada, *Bibliografía de Amado Nervo* (1925); A. M. Herrera y Sierra, *Amado Nervo, su vida, su prosa* (1952); and Manuel Durán, *Genio y figura de Amado Nervo* (Buenos Aires, 1968).

NETZAHUALCÓYOTL (1402–72), poet-king of Texcoco (Central Mexico) during 1433–4. His name means 'Hungry Coyote'. He was present (hiding in a tree) when his father Ixtlilxóchitl, king of the Chichimecs, was killed by soldiers of Tezozómoc, king of Azcapotzalco. The boy-prince fled to his relatives, who managed to plead for his life successfully. When Tezozómoc died, his throne was gained by his son Maxtla after a series of assassinations, and Netzahual-cóyotl's army rose against Maxtla, eventually triumphing in about 1433. He made Texcoco an artistic and intellectual centre of the Aztec empire, establishing an academy of science and music which was described by Hernando de Alvarado Ixtlixóchitl in his *Historia chichimeca* (Mexico City, 1891–2, ch. 36). King Netzahual-cóyotl was a philosopher, astronomer, and engineer, but it seems likely that, of the many poems attributed to him, only a dozen are genuinely his, according to A. M. Garibay's standard *Historia de la literatura nahuatl* (vol. 1, 1953, pp. 488–93). His poetry is of high quality, dealing serenely with the transience of life, and employing the imagery of birds, flowers, and jewels, drawn from Mexican mythology, in psalms similar to those of the Bible. He addresses himself as Yohyontzin in meditations at once humble and sublime. In his views on religion, Netzahualcóyotl, seems to turn away from the polytheistic beliefs of his own time to the monotheism of earlier ages.

Some of his poems have been translated by Irene Nicholson in *Firefly in the night, a study of ancient Mexican poetry and symbolism* (London, 1959) ; there are more detailed studies by Frances Gilmor: *Flute of the smoking mirror: a portrait of Netzahualcóyotl* (Albuquerque, New Mexico, 1949), and by José María Vigil: *Netzahualcóyotl el rey poeta* (Mexico City, 1957).

See also NAHUATL LITERATURE.

NEVILLE, EDGAR, *Conde de Berlanga del Duero* (1898–1967), b. Madrid. Humorous novelist, essayist, film director, and playwright. His five novels are *Don Clorato de Potasa* (1929), subtitled *Andanzas de un hombre que se reía mucho de todo*; *Frente de Madrid* (1942), a documentary deriving much of its interest from its portrayal of post-Civil War attitudes; the humorous middle-class novel *La familia Mínguez* (Barcelona, 1947); the satire on the film industry *Producciones García, S.A.* (1956); and the Chaplinesque *La piedrecita angular* (1957), in which a foundling girl grows into a successful dancer to the despair of her patron, who loves her but cannot follow her into her glamorous new world. *El baile* (1952) is Neville's best play. Among his collections of short stories are *Eva y Adán* (1926), *Música de fondo* (1936), and *El día más largo de Monsieur Marcel* (1966). His *Poemas* were published in 1967.

Niebla, a *nivola* (q.v.) by Miguel de Unamuno (q.v.) first published in 1914.

Using as a backdrop the trivial routine of everyday life in a Spanish country town, Unamuno creates 'out of the mist' a hero without a history, Augusto Pérez, who embodies the power to love. Pérez begins his adult life by falling in love with the mercenary Eugenia, who eventually agrees to marry him (though she does not love him) because he offers to pay off her family's mortgage and find work for her true lover, Mauricio. However, she elopes with Mauricio and Augusto is left disconsolate. He goes to ask Unamuno's advice and, when rebuffed by being told that as Unamuno's fictional creation he is not really free to do anything, he retorts that Unamuno's name will only be remembered if his characters are memorable: they are thus mutually dependent. Angered by this reminder of his mortality, Unamuno decides to kill Augusto, but it is not clear whether he does so. In a prologue, Augusto's friend Goti, himself a novelist, claims that Augusto commits suicide and that Una-muno's version of this ending is untrue; Unamuno's own prologue contradicts this. The novel's technique foreshadows Pirandello's *Sei personaggi in cerca d'autore* and the Borgesian concept of 'el otro, el mismo'.

NIEREMBERG Y OTTIN, *Fray* JUAN EUSEBIO (1595–1658), b. Madrid. Ascetic writer. The son of German parents, Gottfried Nieremberg and Regina Ottin, who had come to Spain with Maria of Austria, the daughter of Carlos V and widow of the Emperor Maximilian II.

Nieremberg studied in the Jesuit Imperial College in Madrid (later teaching there for 19 years), read humanities at Alcalá and theology at Salamanca, and entered the Society of Jesus in 1614 against his father's wishes. His life of teaching and writing in Spain was uninterrupted, though he begged to be sent to Latin America as a missionary. He died as a result of prolonged ascetic practices.

He wrote 73 works, 11 still in MS. and 54 in Latin. His extensive *Epistolario* has been edited in part by Narciso Alonso Cortés (1915) for Clásicos Castellanos. These 'letters' were not correspondence as the name might imply, but memoranda on a wide range of subjects (including divorce, duelling, and the vanity of riches) and, though verbose, they form a valuable record of contemporary social life. Menéndez y Pelayo described Nieremberg's style as 'spontaneous, lively, erudite, and elegant'. It was so highly regarded in his lifetime that it became the custom in many Spanish churches to read extracts from his works to the congregation on Sundays.

All his writings were intended to advocate the Christian virtues, including an example of the genre *de regimine principum* (q.v.), entitled *Obras y días. Manual de Señores y Príncipes* (1629). His version of Thomas à Kempis' *De imitatione Christi* superseded that of Fray Luis de Granada (q.v.). Nieremberg's *Curiosa filosofía, y tesoro de maravillas de la naturaleza, examinadas en varias qüestiones naturales* (1630) is an uncritical compendium of pseudo-scientific lore.

He compiled the splendid *Vida del Santo Padre, y gran siervo de Dios el B. Francisco de Borja* (1644) and the inferior *Vida del glorioso San Ignacio de Loyola* (1631). Nieremberg's most famous work is *De la diferencia entre lo temporal y lo eterno. Crisol de desengaños* (1640). The English translation by Vivian Mullineaux (1672) was plagiarized by Jeremy Taylor in his *Contemplations of the State of Man* (1684). Nieremberg's *Obras escogidas* have been edited by Eduardo Cepeda Enríquez as vol. 103 of the BAE (1957).

Nietos del 1898 ('grandsons of 1898'), the Generación del 1927 (q.v.), which acknowledged the writers of the Generación del 1898 (q.v.) as the source of at least part of their inspiration and ideas.

NIFO or **NIPHO**, Francisco Mariano (1719–1803), b. Alcañiz. The first professional journalist in Spain, Nifo founded fifteen newspapers and periodicals, among them the first *Diario* (1758), *El Correo General, La Estafeta de Londres,* and many other journals translating foreign news for a Spanish audience; Nifo's shrewd knowledge of public taste quickly made him wealthy.

Interested in the drama, he courageously defended Calderón and the *autos sacramentales* (qq.v.) of the Golden Age against the neoclassical theorists of the time. The *Colección de los mejores papeles poéticos y composiciones dramáticas de Don Francisco Mariano Nipho* (2 vols., 1805) induced Menéndez y Pelayo to call Nifo a 'poeta detestable', but Nifo was well inured to insults: Leandro Fernández de Moratín for instance had written of him: ¡Nifo, ¡oh pestilente Nifo! / gran predicador de tiendas, / que desde el año de seis / disparatando voceas. / Tan solo el diablo te pudo / turbar así la cabeza, / y por divertirse hacerte / escritor de callejuela'. Nifo's use of earlier writers for publishable material was instrumental in preserving some important ballads, *entremeses,* and biographical data on Spanish literature that would otherwise have been lost. His treasury is the 7-vol. *Caxón de sastre literato, o percha de maulero erudito, con muchos retales buenos, mejores y medianos, útiles, graciosos y honestos, para evitar las funestas conseqüencias del ocio sin las rigideces del trabajo; antes bien, a caricias del gusto* (1760–1; 2nd edn., enlarged and corrected in 6 vols., 1781–2).

See L. Enciso Recio, *Nifo y el periodismo español del siglo XVIII* (Valladolid, 1956).

NIÑO, Pero, *Conde de Buelna,* whose adventures were chronicled at length by Gutierre Díez de Gámez (q.v.) *El Victorial* (also known as the *Crónica de don Pero Niño*), was begun in 1431 but not published until 1782, in an abridged edition by E. de Llaguna Amirola. It is of great interest for the light it throws on Spanish 15th-c. history. The latest edition was prepared by Juan de Mata Carrizo (Madrid, 1940). Pero Niño also commissioned love songs from Alfonso Álvarez de Villasandino (q.v.).

NIPHO, Francisco Mariano, see Nifo, Francisco Mariano.

NISENO, Fray Diego (17th c.), religious writer, whose *El Político del Cielo* (2 vols., 1637–8) is an interpretation of Divine Providence and Divine Will based on the biblical stories of Isaac and Jacob. He also wrote biographies of St. Basil the Great and St. John the Evangelist in *El Fenis de la Grecia S. Basilio el Grande* (1643) and *El lucero de la tarde, S. Iuan, apostol, evangelista, i profeta* (1649).

His works were translated into Latin by Fr. J. Freylinck as *Opera omnia* (4 vols., Mainz, 1650–1).

Vocal in his attacks on Quevedo's satires, Niseno was believed to have written part of *El tribunal de la justa venganza* (Valencia, 1635) by Arnaldo Franco-Furt, a pseudonym which may also conceal the identity of Juan Pérez de Montalbán (q.v.), whose funeral oration was written by Niseno (1639).

Nivola, a term invented by Miguel de Unamuno (q.v.), whose philosophical novels were denied the status of 'novels' by some contemporary critics.

Víctor Goti, a character in *Niebla* (1914) says that he will change the term *novela* to *nivola,* a new genre, in order that 'nadie tendrá derecho a decir que deroga las leyes de su género' (nobody will have the right to say that he violates the laws of his genre [i.e. since it is a newly invented genre, it can as yet have no rules to be broken]).

Nobel Prize for Literature, a prize instituted in 1901 and awarded each year (with some exceptions) to one (or in some cases two) writers considered by the judges to have made an exceptional contribution to literature.

It has been won by several Spanish-language authors: 1904, José Echegaray (Spain), jointly with Frédéric Mistral (France); 1922, Jacinto Benavente (Spain); 1945, Gabriela Mistral (Chile); 1956, Juan Ramón Jiménez (Spain); 1967, Miguel Ángel Asturias (Guatemala); 1971, Pablo Neruda (Chile); and 1977, Vicente Aleixandre (Spain).

Noche oscura, En una, the popular title of a mystical poem by San Juan de la Cruz (q.v.) written probably in 1577 or 1578. Its correct title is *Canciones del alma que se goza de haber llegado al alto estado de la perfección, que es la unión con Dios, por el camino de la negación espiritual,* and it is also known as *Canción de la subida del Monte Carmelo.*

It consists of eight stanzas of five lines each, beginning:

> *En una noche oscura,*
> *con ansias en amores inflamada,*
> *¡oh dichosa ventura!*
> *salí sin ser notada,*
> *estando ya mi casa sosegada.*

San Juan was imprisoned in a Toledo monastery for eight months in 1577, so that the poem may be true in a literal sense (since he is known to have escaped at night) but the primary theme of the poem is that indicated in the full title: union with God through negation of the self. The exquisite nature imagery, the confident use of the new Italian *lira* metre adapted from Sebastián de Córdoba's rendering of Garcilaso *a lo divino* (1575), the emotional intensity heightened by brevity, and the dreamlike repetition of feminine line-endings, combine to create a work whose only rivals in mystical literature are Juan's other masterpieces: *Cántico espiritual* and *Llama de amor viva* (qq.v.).

Subida del Monte Carmelo (1578–83) is a commentary on the first two strophes of the poem. In the first part San Juan describes the dark night of the senses, recommending mortification as a method of victory; in the second and third parts he describes the dark night of the soul, where faith is the surest guide. *Noche oscura,* begun in 1579, is a sequel to the *Subida* but in the incomplete form in which it has come down to us is limited to the first two strophes and a few lines of the third.

Noches lúgubres, a book in dialogue form by José Cadalso y Vázquez (q.v.), composed late in 1772 or early 1773, first serialized in *Correo de Madrid* (posthumously) in 1789–90, reprinted in vol. 1 of a *Miscelánea erudita de piezas escogidas* (Alcalá, 1792), and first published in separate book-form with his tragedy *Don Sancho García* (Barcelona, 1798).

A dark work, imbued with pessimism and foreboding, it overtly imitates the style of the *Night thoughts* (1742–5) of the English rector Edward Young (1683–1765). The two main characters are Tediato, a wealthy young man, and Lorenzo, a poor grave-digger, who discuss the nature of man, fortune, justice, reason, love, and suicide. Tediato digs up the body of his dead mistress, and seeks death when he is wrongfully imprisoned. The nocturnal setting, poetic style, suspense, and sharp contrast of character combined to make the work of absorbing interest to the Romantics. The work as edited by Nigel Glendinning (1961) for Clásicos Castellanos is clearly incomplete, ending in the middle of the third night, though Glendinning believes that it is complete in the form in which it has come down to us, and certainly the later additions to the third night and the whole of the fourth are spurious. The MS. is lost, the best remaining being a contemporary copy in the British Library.

The latest edition is that by E. Helman (1968) in the Taurus Temas de España series. Cadalso's book was imitated in Mexico by the *Noches tristes y día alegre* (1818), of J. J. Fernández de Lizardi (q.v.).

NOEL, EUGENIO, pseudonym of Eugenio Muñoz (q.v.).

NOGALES, LYDIA, pseudonym of Raul Contreras (?, q.v.).

Nombres de Cristo, De los, a prose dialogue by Fray Luis de León (q.v.) written at least partly between 1572 and 1576, while the author was a prisoner of the Inquisition in Valladolid, and first published in Salamanca (1583).

Marcelo (Fray Luis) is discovered in the quiet Augustinian retreat of La Flecha, on the banks of the Tormes, with his friends Sabino and Juliano. They discuss some of the names by which Christ is known in the Scriptures and explain first of all how these names can be recognized as pertaining to Christ, and secondly in what ways they are appropriate. The names are *Pimpollo* (Bud), *Fazes de Dios* (Faces of God), *Camino* (Way), *Pastor* (Shepherd), *Monte* (Hill), *Padre del Siglo Futuro* (Father of Generations Unborn), *Brazo de Dios* (Arm of God), *Rey de Dios* (King appointed by God), *Príncipe de Paz* (Prince of Peace), *Esposo* (Bridegroom), *Hijo de Dios* (Son of God), *Amado* (Beloved), and Jesús.

Fray Luis's scholastic theory of languages teaches that a thing is perfect in the degree in which it contains all other things, and in this degree resembles the perfection of God, who contains all things. To resemble God is the aspiration of all things. Man's mind is capable of containing all things, but only through their names, thus contributing to the unity of the universe. A word must express as closely as possible the nature of the thing it names. The perfect first language spoken by Adam has since been contaminated, since all other languages are only an approximation to that language. Our understanding of God will only be complete in His presence; until that time we need many names (such as those given to Christ in the Bible) to express some of His many aspects.

The work is a prose masterpiece of the Spanish Renaissance, in which Platonic thought, Ciceronian dialogue, and Christian piety are harmonized. Its doctrinal sources are principally the New Testament and the Church Fathers, but the Old Testament is also employed, and to more varied and telling use than by most other contemporary writers.

The work's originality and lucid elegance supports Luis's contention that theology should and could be taught in the vernacular.

Editions include those by F. de Onís for Clásicos Castellanos (3 vols., 1914–21) and by F. García for Biblioteca de Autores Cristianos (1944).

See H. D. Goode, *La prosa retórica de fray Luis de León en 'Los nombres de Cristo'* (1969).

NORA, EUGENIO G. DE (1923–), b. Zacos, León. Poet, critic, and professor of Spanish at Berne University. His most important critical work is the 3 vol. *La novela española contemporánea (1898–1967)*, which has been revised in a second edition (1963–70). With Victoriano Crémer and Antonio G. de Lama he formed the Espadaña group (q.v.), publishing *Cantos al destino* (1945) and *Amor prometido* (1946), before taking second place in the Adonais Prize of 1947 for his *Contemplación del tiempo*. He won the Boscán Prize of 1953 for *España: pasión de vida* (1954). His latest work marks a departure from his early, social poetry: he treats reality as a mystery, and is more concerned with man's uniqueness than with his role in a group.

NORIEGA VARELA, ANTÓN (1869–1947), b. Mondoñedo, Lugo. Galician poet. He was the first writer in Galician to transcend the sentimental tradition created by Rosalía de Castro (q.v.) in his four books: *De ruada* (1895), *Montañesas* (1904), *A Virxen e a paisanaxe* which contains a hundred popular *cantigas*, and the greatly accomplished *Do ermo* (1920).

Beginning as a writer on rural ways and customs, Noriega Varela was influenced by the pantheism of the Portuguese Teixeira de Pascoaes and later turned to nature lyrics and the *saudade* tradition of poems inspired by real or imagined nostalgia. He early enjoyed the *Georgics* of Virgil, and abandoned clerical studies for teaching in primary schools in the Galician countryside, where he sang of the 'homildade sinxela das cousas, a inxenuidade dos seres imbeles e pobresiños'. His influence has been felt by a number of Galician writers.

NOROÑA, GASPAR MARÍA DE NAVA ÁLVAREZ, *Conde de* (1760–1815), b. Castellón de la Plana.

Poet, playwright, diplomat, and soldier, whose family was of Portuguese origin. The Conde de Noroña is a minor poet of the school of Juan Meléndez Valdés (q.v.). He first achieved recognition with 'Oda a la paz de 1795', published with *silvas* and other odes in *Poesías* (2 vols., 1799–1800).

Noroña's *Ommíada* (2 vols., 1816) is an uninspired narrative poem of over 15,000 lines on the exploits of 'Abd ar-Rahman I, reflecting the Oriental influence on Spanish Romanticism, as do his posthumously-published *Poesías asiáticas puesto en verso castellano* (Paris, 1833), which James Fitzmaurice-Kelly studied in an article in *Revue Hispanique*, vol. 18 (1908), pp. 439–67.

Noroña's tragedy *Madama González* and his comedies *El hombre marcial* and *El cortejo enredador* are uninteresting. His verse is reprinted in vol. 63 (1871) of the BAE.

Noucentisme, a Catalan literary movement named after the 1900s or 20th c., usually taken to date from 1906, the year of Enric Prat de la Riba's manifesto *La nacionalitat catalana* and of the first International Congress of the Catalan Language, followed in 1907 by the founding of the Institut d'Estudis Catalans.

D'Ors (see ORS) and other *noucentistes* aimed to overthrow the alleged 'rusticity' of 19th-c. Catalan literature; though it was impossible literally to restore the Renaissance tradition of Martorell and Rois de Corella (qq.v.), the aim was to create a new humanism fulfilling a similar function to theirs in modern terms. Intellectual rigour, pleasure in craftsmanship, precision in the use of language, and precise metre and poetic structure were the keynotes of the new movement.

Among its leading writers were Guerau de Liost, Carles Riba, and Josep Carner (qq.v.), whose poetry has had a great deal of influence on later Catalan writers.

See Albert Manent, *Josep Carner i el noucentisme* (Barcelona, 1969). See also NOVECENTISMO.

NOVÁS CALVO, LINO (1905–), b. Spain. Cuban writer of short novels and *cuentos*. His first book was *El negrero* (Madrid, 1933), a novelized biography of the slave-trader Pedro Blanco Fernández de Trava (b. Málaga, 1795), which was strongly influenced by the style of Baroja (q.v.), though lacking his firsthand knowledge of the sea. The stories collected in *La luna nona y otros cuentos* (Buenos Aires, 1942) and *Cayo Canas* (1946) were set among the lower classes of Cuba and were experimental in the sense of abandoning realism for the use of gesture, symbol, and silence in a laconic style of great self-confidence.

Two short novels: *No sé quién soy* (Mexico

City, 1945) and *En los traspatios* extend the range of the author's observation, sharpening his psychological penetration.

Novecentismo, a term signifying the spirit of the 20th c. which was borrowed from Massimo Bontempelli's magazine *900*, founded in 1926, and the intellectual currents deriving from futurism. The Catalan critic Eugenio d'Ors introduced the term into Spain, where it has been employed to describe the post-'98 generation of Ortega y Gasset, Valle-Inclán, Pérez de Ayala, Linares Rivas, Martínez Sierra, Pedro Salinas, and others. The common stance of these writers was, at least initially, the makings of a new tradition of European as opposed to national dimensions that would replace tradition with novelty, and the representational with the conceptual.

The term was always pretentious (since literary movements and styles can only be characterized by posterity) and grows less helpful as the progress of its adherents is seen to diverge from the original aim.

See also NOUCENTISME.

Novela pastoril, La, see PASTORAL NOVEL, The.

Novela picaresca, La, see PICARESQUE NOVEL, The.

Novelas ejemplares, short stories by Miguel de Cervantes Saavedra (q.v.) first published in 1613. 'Yo soy el primero que he novelado en lengua castellana', asserts Cervantes in his prologue to distinguish his tales from the foreign models then in vogue. He called them 'exemplary novels' because, despite the doubts of later readers, 'no hay ninguna de quien no se pueda sacar algún ejemplo provechoso'. The twelve *novelas* have been classified as either romantic or realistic, but a more helpful analysis is the following four categories:

1. Picaresque. *Rinconete y Cortadillo, La ilustre fregona, El casamiento engañoso,* and *El celoso extremeño;*

2. Realistic. *Las dos doncellas, La gitanilla,* and *La española inglesa;*

3. Inventive. *El amante liberal, La señora Cornelia,* and *La fuerza de la sangre.*

4. Marvellous. *El coloquio de los perros* and *El licenciado Vidriera.*

A thirteenth novel, *La tía fingida* (q.v.), was attributed to Cervantes but has been conclusively proved spurious.

The style of the exemplary novels is as varied as the thematic material; at the time, the notion of a group of independent tales unconnected by a Boccaccio-like framework novel was virtually

unknown, and the 'ejemplar' motif may have been a mere device to give the set a factitious unity which it does not possess. The romantic novels set in the East or Northern Europe are less interesting than those in which Cervantes describes the society of Spain in his day, particularly Toledo, Madrid, or those cities in Andalusia which he knew well. He rejects the *pundonor* ethic then prevalent, prescribing true nobility and virtue, fidelity in love, and honesty in daily conduct.

The best editions of the *Novelas ejemplares* as a collection are those by F. Rodríguez Marín (2 vols., 1914–17) in Clásicos Castellanos, by R. Benavides Lillo (Santiago de Chile, 1956), by Fernando Gutiérrez (2 vols., Barcelona, 1958), and by A. Roldán (1969).

See F. A. de Icaza, *Las novelas ejemplares de Cervantes* (1901; 2nd edn., 1915); Joaquín Casalduero, *Sentido y forma de las 'Novelas ejemplares'* (Buenos Aires, 1943; 2nd edn., 1962); A. González de Amezúa, *Cervantes, creador de la novela corta española: introducción a la edición crítica y comentada de las Novelas Ejemplares* (2 vols., 1956–8) in Clásicos Hispánicos; and Ruth S. El Saffar, *Novel to Romance: a study of Cervantes' 'Novelas ejemplares'* (Baltimore, 1974). See also entries under individual titles of the *novelas ejemplares.*

Novelas españolas contemporáneas by Benito Pérez Galdós (q.v.), a long sequence of novels, unlike the historical *Episodios nacionales* (q.v.) not overtly based on the political evolution of 19th-c. Spain, but creating a varied gallery of fictional characters who often reappear unexpectedly in several novels. Together they can be read as a social and psychological history of the period in much the same way as the works of Balzac or Dickens. Pérez Galdós wrote these novels in the period of his greatest maturity, and together they represent his most lasting achivement.

The naturalistic novels are *La desheredada* (q.v., 1881), *El amigo Manso* (q.v., 1882), *El doctor Centeno* (q.v., 1883), *La de Bringas* (q.v., 1884), *Tormento* (q.v., 1884), *Lo prohibido* (1884–5), *Fortunata y Jacinta* (q.v., 1886–7), *Miau* (q.v., 1888), and *Incógnita* (1888–9).

The psychological novels consist of *Tristana* (1892) and the sequence built around the usurer Torquemada (q.v.): *Torquemada en la hoguera* (1889), *Torquemada en la Cruz* (1893), *Torquemada en el Purgatorio* (1894), and *Torquemada y San Pedro* (1895).

The idealistic novels are *Ángel Guerra* (q.v., 1890–1), *Nazarín* (q.v., 1895), *Halma* (q.v., 1895), *Misericordia* (q.v., 1897), and *El caballero encantado* (1909).

The dramatic novels, written almost wholly in

dialogue, consist of *Realidad* (1889), *La loca de la casa* (1892), *El abuelo* (1897), *Casandra* (1905), and *La razón de la sinrazón* (1915).

Pérez Galdós classified his earlier novels as *Novelas españolas de la primera época* (q.v.). However, as D. L. Shaw has pointed out in *A literary history of Spain: the nineteenth century* (p. 124), 'Several ingenious attempts have been made to classify Galdós's work, but none is entirely satisfactory'.

Novelas españolas de la primera época, by Benito Pérez Galdós (q.v.).

The author's separate classification of these six novels is not easily defensible, for both *La Fontana de Oro* (1867–8) and *El audaz* (1871) are historical novels more aptly considered *Episodios nacionales* (q.v.); *Doña Perfecta* (q.v., 1876), *Gloria* (q.v., 1876–7), and *La familia de León Roch* (q.v., 1878) are all socio-religious novels belonging to the 'idealistic' group of the *Novelas españolas contemporáneas* sequence; *Marianela* (q.v., 1878) is a psychological novel more appropriately grouped in the same sequence with such works as *El amigo Manso* and *Fortunata y Jacinta* (qq.v.).

Noventa y ocho, Generación del, see GENERACIÓN DEL 1898.

NOVOA, MATÍAS DE (1576?–1652?), b. Toledo. Historian. As aide-de-camp to the future Felipe IV he gained first-hand knowledge of political events during the reigns of Felipe III and Felipe IV. Diffuse and poorly arranged though his *Memorias* are, their only major failure in impartiality is a bias towards the Duque de Lerma, who was responsible for finding Novoa his post.

A. Cánovas del Castillo showed in his *Matías de Novoa. Monografía de un historiador desconocido* (1871) that the *Historia de Felipe III* and the *Historia de Felipe IV* were by Novoa and not by Bernabé de Vivanco, as had been hitherto believed. The MSS. in the Real Academia de la Historia and the Biblioteca Nacional were published in the Colección de Documentos Inéditos para la Historia de España, vols. 60–61 (1875), vol. 69 (1878), vol. 77 (1881), vol. 80 (1883), and vol. 86 (1886).

NOVO LÓPEZ, SALVADOR (1904–), b. Mexico City. Mexican poet of the Contemporáneos group which also included Carlos Pellicer, Jaime Torres Bodet, and Gilberto Owen (qq.v.). He founded the literary review *Ulises* (1927–8), evolving a brisk and often humorous style, with ironical touches, often turning to pessimism and even bitterness. His *Antología, 1925–1965* (1966) retains the best of his poems from *XX poemas*

(1925), the poetic autobiography *Espejo, poemas antiguos* (1933; 2nd edn., 1948 which contains the powerful, despairing additional *Elegía*), *Nuevo amor* (1933), *Poemas proletarios* (1934), and *Poesía* (1961). Jean Franco calls him 'a poet, like the young Borges, of city landscapes'.

Novo's *Nueva grandeza mexicana* (1946) is a sensitive evocation of daily life in Mexico City on the lines of *Grandeza mexicana* (1604), by Bernardo de Balbuena.

Since 1946, Novo has dedicated himself to drama, heading the drama department at the Instituto Nacional de Bellas Artes until 1952, and again since 1956. The intervening years were spent as playwright, producer, and impresario of the Teatro de la Capilla in Coyoacán. He has translated O'Neill, Synge, and other writers. The best of his own plays are his satires: *La culta dama* (1951) on Mexican high society, and *A ocho columnas* (1956) on Mexican journalism. His plays have been studied by M. Muncy in *Salvador Novo y su teatro: estudio crítico* (Madrid, 1971), and A. Magaña-Esquivel has written a more comprehensive study in *Salvador Novo: un mexicano y su obra* (1971).

NUEDA, LUIS (1883–1952), b. Madrid. Essayist and compiler whose enforced idleness during the Spanish Civil War prompted him to systematize his notes for *Mil libros* (1940), a compendium of synopses of the books he had read. The latest edition (2 vols., 1969) is the sixth, revised and enlarged by Antonio Espina, who has strengthened the Latin-American entries in the book. Nueda's comments are not free from bias (cf. the entry on Eugenio Noel (q.v.) and the discussion of his own books) but the range of reading displayed is exceptional. The sixth edition excludes plays, which are dealt with in the companion book from the same publisher: *Teatro mundial*, by Arturo del Hoyo.

Nueda's other books include *De música: epistolario de un melómano* (1920) and a collection of polemical essays entitled *Un libro raro* (1926), useful if only as a guide to the eccentricities of the compiler of *Mil libros*, the nearest Spanish equivalent to Hamerton's more discriminating *Outline of great books*.

Nueva Biblioteca de Autores Españoles, a series of Spanish classics (usually abbreviated NBAE) created by Marcelino Menéndez y Pelayo (q.v.) in 1905 to supplement the Biblioteca de Autores Españoles (q.v., usually abbreviated BAE). It began with Menéndez y Pelayo's own edition and studies, *Los orígenes de la novela* (vols. 1, 1905; 7, 1907; 14, 1910; and 21, 1915). Subsequent contributions have included *Autobiografías y memorias* (vol. 2, 1905) compiled by M. Serrano y Sanz; *Sermones* by Alonso de

Cabrera (vol. 3, 1906); *Comedias* by Tirso de Molina (vols. 4, 1906; and 9, 1907), edited by Cotarelo y Mori; the *Primera crónica general: Estoria de España* (vol. 5, 1906); *Libros de caballerías* (vols. 6, 1907; and 11, 1908) edited by A. Bonilla y San Martín; Fr. José de Sigüenza's *Historia de la Orden de San Jerónimo* (vols. 8, 1907; and 12, 1909); *Crónicas del Gran Capitán* (vol. 10, 1908), compiled by A. Rodríguez Villa; *Historiadores de Indias* (vols. 13, 1909; and 15, 1909), compiled by M. Serrano y Sanz; Cotarelo y Mori's *Colección de entremeses, loas, bailes, jácaras y mojigangas* (vols. 17, 1911; and 18, 1911); R. Foulché-Delbosc's *Cancionero castellano del siglo XV* (vols. 19, 1912; and 22, 1915); Fray Jaime Sala's edition of the *Obras místicas de Fray Juan de los Ángeles* (vols. 20, 1912; and 24, 1917); *Sainetes* of Ramón de la Cruz with prefaces by E. Cotarelo y Mori (vols. 23, 1915; and 26, 1928); and M. Serrano y Sanz's *Orígenes de la dominación española en América* (vol. 25, 1909).

Nuevos, Los, a group of Peruvian poets who began to publish in the early and mid-1960s, but whose works were first published together in *Los Nuevos* (Lima, 1967). The members of the group include Rodolfo Hinostroza (author of the single most important poetry collection of the 1960s in Peru, *Contra natura*, Barcelona, 1971), Antonio Cisneros, Mirko Lauer, and Julio Ortega (qq.v.).

Their key preoccupation is with historical and social conditions in Peru, but treated from a viewpoint (often ironic or symbolic) more cosmopolitan than national. Their chief mentor has been Ezra Pound.

The next poetic generation in Peru is represented by the anthology *Estos 13* (q.v., 1973), edited by José Miguel Oviedo.

Numancia, a Celtiberian town on the upper Duero near Soria which, after withstanding several sieges over some sixty years, finally fell to a Roman army under Scipio Aemilianus in 133 B.C. after an eight-month siege, marking the end of organized resistance to the Roman occupation of Spain. The heroism of the inhabitants of Numancia has inspired a number of Spanish writers: apart from Cervantes' famous play *El cerco de Numancia*, there are less well-known dramas by Rojas Zorrilla and Ignacio López de Ayala (qq.v.); José Cadalso's tragedy *Numancia* has been lost. An unfinished poem in *octava rima* by Lorenzo de Zamora entitled *De la historia de Sagunto, Numancia y Cartago* was published in Alcalá in 1589, and there is also a somewhat feeble epic by Francisco Mosquera de Barnuevo (*La Numantina*, Seville, 1612). A thorough study of the theme of the siege of Numancia in poetry has been published by J. A.

Pérez-Rioja in *Celtiberia* (vol. 4, 1954, pp. 69–103).

NÚÑEZ, ENRIQUE BERNARDO (1895–1964), b. Valencia, Carabobo. Venezuelan novelist and journalist whose best work is the regional novel *Cubagua* (1931). He was historian of the city of Caracas 1945–50 and 1953–64.

Núñez's other novels were *Sol interior* (1918), *Después de Ayacucho* (1920), *La ninfa del Anauco* (1931), *Don Pablos en América* (1932), *La galera de Tiberio* (1938) destroyed by the author but reprinted by the Universidad Central in 1967, and *Bajo el samán* (1963).

NÚÑEZ, SERGIO (1892–), an Ecuadorian novelist who belongs to the school of indigenist writers, with G. humberto Mata and Jorge Fernández (qq.v.). His most characteristic writings, such as the *Novelas del páramo y de la cordillera* (1934), deal with the brutality and amorality of the despotic *gamonales*, or rich landowners of Ecuador. *Un pedagogo terrible* (1927) is a historical novel on the *coup d'état* of 9 July 1925, *Árbol que no da fruto* (1929) is set during the regime of the dictator García Moreno, and *Tierra de lobos* (1939) is another work of fierce, uncompromising realism.

Despite Núñez's occasionally uneven style, his fiction is an important contribution to the Ecuadorian novel of social protest which reaches its zenith in the work of Jorge Icaza (q.v.).

NÚÑEZ ALONSO, ALEJANDRO (1905–), b. Gijón. Novelist and journalist. He lived and worked as a journalist in Mexico 1929–49, then in Rome and Paris before settling in Madrid in 1953 and writing the novels that have made his name: *La gota de mercurio* (Barcelona, 1954) presented as the monologue of a suicidal artist; the crime novel *Tu presencia en el tiempo*; *Segunda agonía* (both Barcelona, 1955) the study of a youth who subjects himself to an eleven-year period of solitude; and a cycle of historical novels on the Roman Empire under Tiberius and the spread of Christianity: *El lazo de púrpura, El hombre de Damasco, El denario de plata, La piedra y el César,* and *Las columnas de fuego* (Barcelona, 1956–62).

Núñez Alonso's other works include a study of a millionaire: *Konko* (Mexico City, 1943, later filmed); a story of a prostitute: *Mujer de medianoche* (Mexico City, 1945), which E. G. de Nora has termed a work of 'naturalismo sentimental'; *Cuando Don Alfonso XIII era rey* (1962); *Gloria en subasta* (1965); *Semiramis* (1965); *Sol de Babilonia* (1967); *Víspera sin mañana* (1971); and *Al filo de la sospecha* (1971), the last on juvenile delinquency.

NÚÑEZ CABEZA DE VACA, ÁLVAR (1490?–1559?), b. Jérez de la Frontera. Grandson of the *conquistador* of the Canary Islands, Pedro de Vera. In 1527 he left Spain with the ill-fated Florida expedition of Pánfilo de Narváez which endured so many shipwrecks and other disasters that only four men survived, one of them Cabeza de Vaca. He wandered for nine years, often captive among Indians, between the Gulf of Mexico and the Gulf of California, experiences which inspired his *Naufragios y Relación de la Jornada que hizo a la Florida con el adelantado Pánfilo de Narváez* (1537), translated by C. Covey as *Adventures in the unknown interior of America* (New York, 1962).

Cabeza de Vaca was subsequently Governor of Paraguay (1540–45) and helped his secretary Pedro Hernández to write his lively *Comentarios* (1554) on this period (reprinted in vol. 22 (1852) of the BAE). A popular edition of the *Naufragios y comentarios* has appeared in the Colección Austral (1942).

NÚÑEZ DE ARCE, GASPAR (1832–1903), b. Valladolid. Poet, playwright, and journalist. He was *La Iberia*'s war correspondent during the African campaign (1859–60), and afterwards entered politics. He joined the Unión Liberal party, and was appointed successively governor of Logroño, deputy for Valladolid, senator at the Cortes, and (in 1883) Foreign Minister. His first plays, which had little success, were *La cuenta del zapatero* (1958) and the play about conscience *Deudas de la honra* (1863); he consequently collaborated with Antonio Hurtado in *Herir en la sombra, La jota aragonesa,* and *El laurel de la Zubia,* but these also failed. He tried the comedy of manners in *Quien debe, paga* (1867), social drama in *Justicia providencial* (1872), and finally achieved renown with a historical piece, *El haz de leña* (1872), on the imprisonment and death of Don Carlos, son of Felipe II. He then concentrated on writing poetry, becoming (in Clarín's trenchant phrase) one of the 'two and a half poets' then writing in Spain, the other one being Campoamor, and the half Manuel del Palacio (qq.v.).

Reacting against what he considered the excessively archaistic and sentimental poetry of Zorrilla (q.v.), Núñez de Arce preferred contemporary themes dealing with the social and political questions of Spain in the years after the Revolution of 1868 which ended the rule of the Bourbons. He became the most popular poet in Spain 1875–90, though he was to suffer public neglect in his last decade of life. *Gritos del combate* (published in 1875 but including poems written over the previous two decades) reveals above all the poet's doubts and uncertainties about many of the social, political, and religious problems of

the time, an attitude strongly expressed in such poems as 'La duda', 'Tristezas', and 'Raimundo Lulio'. Later compositions such as *La última lamentación de Lord Byron* (1879) and *La visión de Fray Martín* (1880; on Martin Luther) continue to deal with the question of intellectual torment. The yearning for certainty also emerges in *La selva oscura* (1879), in which Dante's search for Beatrice is interpreted as an attempt to find some eternal and abiding truth in a transient and unstable world.

His *Discurso sobre la poesía* (1887) is a plea for the defence of poetry in an increasingly materialistic century, and a condemnation of what he considered the excessively prosaic verse of Campoamor. His *Discurso* and his own poetry influenced many subsequent writers, especially Ricardo León and Manuel Reina (qq.v.). He wrote many works intended for recitation, some of them dealing with the great principles of freedom of conscience and liberalism in politics. Of his *Obras dramáticas* (1879), only *El haz de leña* is still read, but his *Poesías completas* (New York, 1920), are the best achievement of Spain's post-Romantic poetry.

See Josefina Romo Arregui, *Vida, poesía y estilo de don Gaspar Núñez de Arce* (1946).

NÚÑEZ DE CASTRO, ALONSO (1627–95), b. Madrid. Historian. His father Juan was a physician to King Philip IV, who appointed Alonso royal chronicler when he graduated from Salamanca University.

Núñez de Castro continued the history by Saavedra Fajardo entitled *Corona gótica, castellana y austríaca* from A.D. 716 to the reign of Henry II, his expanded version being published in Madrid in 1670. His other works include *Espejo christalino de armas para generales valerosos, de desengaños para christianos príncipes* (1648); *Séneca impugnado de Séneca en questiones políticas y morales* (1651); *Vida de las fundadoras del Monasterio del Caballero de Gracia* (1658); a work of propaganda called *Sólo Madrid es Corte* (1658) to support the city's claim to capital status, which it had enjoyed effectively only since 1650; *Historia ecclesiástica y seglar de la cuidad de Guadalaxara* (1658); and *Ley viva de príncipes perfectos* (1673), his second contribution to the popular genre *de regimine principum*. His *Vida de San Fernando* appeared in the Colección Cisneros in 1943. His style is pedestrian, but he made scrupulous use of a wider range of primary sources than was customary at the time.

NÚÑEZ DE CEPEDA, FRANCISCO (17th c.), b. Toledo. A Jesuit priest responsible for a curious reworking *a lo divino* of the *Idea de un príncipe político christiano* by Diego de Saàvedra Fajardo (q.v.) as *Idea del buen pastor representada en empresas sacras* (Lyons, 1682).

His book was reprinted in vol. 35 (1855) of the BAE.

See also A Lo Divino and De Regimine Principum.

NÚÑEZ DE PINEDA Y BASCUÑÁN, Francisco (1607–82), b. Chillán, Chile. Son of the *conquistador* Álvaro Núñez. He studied Latin and theology with the Jesuits, then began a military career, being taken prisoner when wounded by the Arauco Indians of Chile in May 1629. He was protected by chief Maulicán who, at great danger to himself, took the youth unharmed back to his father in November of the same year. The generous treatment he received is reflected in Núñez de Pineda's *El cautiverio feliz y razón de las guerras dilatadas en Chile*, finished in 1673 and published as vol. 3 of the Colección de Historiadores de Chile (Santiago, 1863). The book deals with the customs and manners of his captors in sympathetic detail, but betrays perhaps too close a reading of pastoral novels, books of chivalry, and Christian sermons. *El cautiverio feliz* was a valuable corrective to false tales of the Indians' cruelty and treachery spread by those who never lived among them. There is a modern edition of the book by Ángel Custodio González (1948).

See Alejandro Vicuña, *Bascuñán, el cautivo* (1948); and E. Rodríguez Mendoza, *Francisco Núñez de Pineda y Bascuñán* (1953).

NÚÑEZ DE TOLEDO Y GUZMÁN, Hernán (1475–1553), b. Valladolid. Classical scholar, known as 'El Pinciano' from Pincia, the ancient name of his birthplace and 'El Comendador Griego' from his accomplishment. Hernán Núñez was given one of the 24 scholarships available to Spaniards at the Collegio di San Clemente in Bologna 1490–98, and on his return was appointed tutor to the Mendoza family in Granada until Cardinal Ximénez de Cisneros (q.v.) sought his co-operation in preparing the Complutensian Bible (q.v.). 'El Pinciano' occupied the Chair of Rhetoric at Alcalá and subsequently that of Greek at Salamanca left vacant on the death of Nebrija (q.v.). He also taught Hebrew. Núñez's Greek scholarship was surpassed in the Iberian peninsula only by that of the Portuguese humanist Arias Barbosa (d. 1540), Nebrija's colleague at Salamanca.

His critical editions of Seneca (Basle, 1529), and Pliny (Salamanca, 1544) were well received in humanist circles throughout Europe, and he was also responsible for an edition of Pomponius Mela. He made a Spanish version of Aeneas Sylvius Piccolomini's Latin history of Bohemia. In his youth he published a confused, inadequate commentary on Juan de Mena, entitled *Las CCC del famosísimo poeta Juan de Mena* (Saragossa, 1490). He also left the collection *Refranes, o Proverbios en romance* (Salamanca, 1555) which has been reprinted in the Colección Crisol (1944).

NYKL, Alois Richard (1885–1958), b. Czechoslovakia. Hispanist who studied in Chicago and worked in the Peninsula, then taught at Harvard University 1941–44 and specialized in Hispano-Arabic literature. His first contribution was an edition of *The dove's neckring* (Paris, 1931) by Ibn Hazm, and he also edited the *Cancionero de Aben Guzmán* (1933) and the *Crónica del rey Dom Affomso Hamrríquez* (Cambridge, Mass., 1942).

His major work was *Hispano-Arabic poetry, and its relations with the Old Provençal troubadours* (Baltimore, 1946).

O

OBLIGADO, Rafael (1851–1920), b. Buenos Aires. Argentinian poet. Born into a wealthy family of landowners, Obligado abandoned law and for over 25 years held a literary salon which met in his home on Saturdays and is described by Rubén Darío (q.v.) in his diaries. Obligado founded the Academia Argentina in 1878.

His only book, *Poesías* (Paris, 1885, enlarged 2nd edn., 1906), is distinguished for its patriotism, placing him in the line of nationalist poetry in defiance of new trends from Europe. His concept of a literary language was a combination of *casticismo* and local American usages, provided that the latter were neither obscure nor unacceptable to literate speakers; his own style was sufficiently *castizo* for the Real Academia Española to make him a corresponding member. His best-known poem is one on the established theme of the wandering *payador* Santos Vega (q.v.). He was influenced by Esteban Echeverría (q.v.).

Obregón, Marcos de, see Marcos de Obregón, Relaciones de la vida del escudero, by Vicente Espinel (q.v.).

OCAMPO, FLORIÁN DE (1495?–1558), b. Zamora. Historian who studied under Nebrija (q.v.) at Alcalá de Henares 1509–14. Ocampo is best known for his edition of the *Tercera crónica general* of Alfonso 'el Sabio' (q.v.) entitled *Las quatro partes enteras de la crónica de España* (Zamora, 1541), reprinted frequently, and as late as 1604.

Less successful was Ocampo's *Los quatro libros primeros de la crónica general de España* (Zamora, 1543; enlarged edn., Medina, 1553), a work more ambitious than its title suggests. It includes a survey of world history until Roman times, and uncritically mingles historical facts and legends with Ocampo's own inventions, as well as an unsubtle attempt to prove the antiquity of Spain's ruling Habsburg dynasty. There is an edition of the *Obras* of Ocampo by B. Cano (Madrid, 1791).

OCAMPO, SILVINA (1906–), b. Buenos Aires. Peruvian poet and short-story writer. The title of her poems *Poemas de amor desesperado* (1949) indicates one of her literary preoccupations. Her *Pequeña antología* contains her best verse including material from *Enumeración de la patria y otros poemas* (1942) and *Espacios métricos* (1948). Her surrealistic stories have appeared in *Viaje olvidado* (1937), *Autobiografía de Irene* (1948), *La furia y otros cuentos* (1959), *Las invitadas* (1961), and *Los días de la noche* (1970), constituting an important contribution to the Argentinian vogue of 'literatura fantástica'. She helped to edit, with J. L. Borges and her husband Adolfo Bioy Casares (qq.v.), the important *Antología poética argentina* (1941), and has written a detective story with Bioy Casares called *Los que aman, odian* (1947).

OCAMPO, VICTORIA (1890–), b. Buenos Aires. Editor of *Sur* (q.v.) 1931–70, and essayist. She has introduced two generations of Argentinians to contemporary world literature (especially that of Europe) through the medium of *Sur* and its allied publishing house.

Señora Ocampo's most significant original work is the series of *Testimonios*, of which she has published seven vols. since 1935. The first series was published in Madrid, and the rest in Buenos Aires. The 4th series (1950) was entitled *Soledad sonora*.

She has also written *De Francesca a Beatrice* (1924), *La supremacía del alma y de la sangre* (1935), *La mujer y su expresión* (1936), *Domingos de Hyde Park* (1936), *Emily Brontë* (1938), and *Virginia Woolf, Orlando y cía.* (1938).

OCAÑA, FRANCISCO DE (*fl.* 1603), religious poet of whom nothing is known beyond his being the author of a collection of charming popular songs written on Christian themes, the *Cancionero para*

cantar la noche de Navidad y las fiestas de Pascua (Alcalá, 1603), two of which appear in Justo de Sancha's *Romancero y cancionero sagrados*, vol. 35 in the BAE (1855).

OCANTOS Y ZIEGLER, CARLOS MARÍA (1860–1949), b. Buenos Aires. Argentinian novelist. After a career in the diplomatic service in Brazil, Spain, and Scandinavia, he retired in 1915 to Aravaca, near Madrid, to complete his sequence of twenty Argentinian novels of *costumbres* which had begun with *León Zaldívar* (1888) and concluded with *Fray Judas* (1929). All were published in Spain, with the exception of *Entre dos luces* (1892), *El candidato* (1893), and *La Ginesa* (1894), which appeared in Buenos Aires, and the second in the cycle, *Quilito* (Paris, 1891).

OCHOA, EUGENIO DE (1815–72), b. Lezo, Guipúzcoa. Editor and literary critic, who spent much of his life abroad, in Portugal, England, and France. He took part in the Madrid *tertulia* El Parnasillo, where he became friendly with Ventura de la Vega and Espronceda (qq.v.) and was a member of the Real Academia de la Lengua.

Ochoa edited volumes in the BAE, the *Rimas inéditas de Don Íñigo López de Mendoza* (Paris, 1841), and a sixty-volume Colección de los Mejores Autores Españoles Antiguos y Modernos (Paris, 1835–72); and several *Tesoros: del teatro español* (1835); *de los romanceros y cancioneros españoles* (1836), *de los historiadores españoles* (1840), and *de los escritores místicos españoles* (1847).

Ochoa's bibliographical works were *Apuntes para una biblioteca de escritores españoles contemporáneos en prosa y verso* (1840) and a *Catálogo razonado de manuscritos españoles de la Biblioteca de París* (Paris, 1844), and he wrote critical studies of Hartzenbusch, of the *Cancionero de Baena*, and of Alberto Lista y Aragón (qq.v.), under whom he studied.

His fervently Romantic feelings were given full rein in the short-lived *El Artista* (1835–6), a review he edited with his brother-in-law Pedro Madrazo. He wrote two mediocre plays: *Un día del año 1823* (1835) and *Incertidumbre y amor* (1835), and his translation of Hugo's *Hernani* was a brilliant success. *Ecos del alma* (Paris, 1841) is a volume of derivative melancholy lyric verse. Having translated historical novels by Dumas and Scott, he tried his own hand at the genre in *El auto de fe* (1837), on the death of Don Carlos, son of Philip II, but the result was a Gothic fiasco with far-fetched ingredients including enchanted castles, agonizing screams, and generous bandits.

OCHOA, JUAN DE (1864–99), b. Avilés, Asturias. Novelist and short-story writer. His three short novels *Su amado discípulo* (1894), *Los señores de Hermida* (1896), and *Un alma de Dios* (1898) are characterized by gentle simplicity, a humour akin to that of Palacio Valdés (q.v., whom he met in Madrid on his only extended sojourn there from the provinces), and a marked sympathy for the underdog, such as animals and tramps, observed without undue sentimentality.

From 1892 he wrote stories and political satire for the Madrid journal *La Justicia*, and he also contributed regularly to *El Liberal Asturiano* of Oviedo.

Octava, an eight-line stanza. With eight or fewer syllables to a line, the *octava* is called an *octava de arte menor*, or *octavilla*. With eleven syllables to a line (rhymed ababbcc) it is called the *octava real* (or less commonly *octava rima*, from the Italian *ottava rima*), which entered Spain through the works of Boscà (q.v.); an imitator of Ariosto (1474–1533). It was used by Góngora in his *Fábula de Polifemo*. The *octava real* is also known as the *octava heróica* from its use in epics by such poets as Ercilla, Balbuena, and Virués. Rhyming in any scheme provided the 4th and 8th lines rhyme, the *octava* of nine or more syllables is called an *octava aguda*.

With twelve syllables, the *octava de arte mayor* frequently rhymes abbaacca, and is characteristic of the work of Juan de Mena (q.v.).

Oda (Greek: 'a song accompanied by the lyre'), in Spanish poetry, a lyrical poem, generally qualified by its thematic type, such as the *heroica* (written by Herrera and Quintana), the *sagrada* (S. Juan de la Cruz), the *moral* (Luis de León), the *anacreóntica* (Meléndez Valdés), the *filosófica*, and the *amatoria*. The only feature common to all types of ode is an elevated diction; its metre is not fixed.

OLAVIDE Y JÁUREGUI, Pablo Antonio José de (1725–1803), b. Lima. Peruvian philosopher, poet, and playwright. As *oidor* of the Real Audiencia in Lima, he was accused of misappropriating funds given to help victims of the 1746 earthquake and went to Spain in 1752 to explain his behaviour. While in Madrid he married, and created a salon which disseminated views of the Enlightenment; he also translated plays by Voltaire, Racine, and Regnard, and wrote some himself for his tiny private theatre. Olavide was a friend of Jovellanos (q.v.). For some time Minister in Spain, he was involved in the attempt to counter the rural decline of the Sierra Morena. About 1777 a satire against Olavide and his ideas circulated in MS.: this was the pseudonymous *El siglo ilustrado. Vida de don Guindo Cerezo, nacido, educado, instruido, sublimado, y muerto según las luces del presente siglo,*

allegedly by Don Justo Vera de la Ventosa. His protector, the Conde de Aranda, having fallen, Olavide was tried by the Inquisition in 1778 for his belief in the Copernican theory and disrespect for religious images, and gaoled in Sahagún. In 1780 he escaped to France where he was received with joy by Diderot and the other Encyclopaedists, and adopted as a son of the Republic. He was nevertheless imprisoned under the Terror in 1794, and repudiated the Revolution, returning to Spain in 1798 as a convert to Roman Catholicism. There he published anonymously *El Evangelio en triumpho; o, historia de un filósofo desengañado* (4 vols., Valencia, 1798) using the epistolary technique to present a straightforward account of a sceptic's persuasion by a hermit of the error of his ways.

He wrote the uninspired *Poemas Christianos* (Madrid, 1799) in hendecasyllables, and adapted the Psalms in his *Salterio español; o, versión parafrástica de los Salmos de David, de los cánticos de Moisés y de otros cánticos* (Madrid, 1800). The best study on Olavide is M. Defourneaux's *Pablo de Olavide, ou l'afrancesado* (Paris, 1959). His trial by Inquisition has been edited by Vicente Castañeda in his *Relación del auto de fe contra don Pablo de Olavide* (Madrid, 1916), while there has been a recent edition of his *Obras dramáticas desconocidas* (1971).

O'LEARY, Juan E. (1879–1969), b. Asunción. Paraguayan historian, diplomat, and Director of the Archivo Nacional. He was the propagandist who defended the name of Francisco Solano López in his *Historia de la guerra de la Triple Alianza* (1911), *Nuestra epopeya* (1919), and *El mariscal Solano López* (Madrid, 1925). In opposition to his mentor Cecilio Báez (q.v.), O'Leary created a popular cult of Solano López in a successful attempt to raise the spirit of the Paraguayan people who had been decimated in the disastrous war against Brazil, Argentina, and Uruguay (1865–70). Justo Pastor Benítez has defined O'Leary as 'un predicador que se dirige al sentimiento popular antes que a la razón'. He wrote patriotic poetry: *El alma de la raza* (1898) and *¡Salvaje!* (1902) a poem in praise of the Guaraní Indians, as well as the elegies *A la mi hija Rosita* (1924).

OLIVARES, Gaspar de Guzmán, *Conde-Duque de* (1587–1645), the aristocratic *privado* (or favourite) of King Philip IV, and the effective ruler of Spain 1621–43. Philip III had also accepted government by *privado*, in his case Francisco Gómez de Sandoval y Borja, Duque de Lerma. The public debate on the place of the *privado* in society provoked a series of plays on the rise and fall of royal favourites, which probably began with *Los Guzmanes de Toral* (by Lope de

Vega? c. 1600). Other *comedias* in this genre known as *comedias de privanza* include *No hay dicha ni desdicha* by Antonio Mira de Amescua (q.v.), *Privar contra su gusto* by Tirso de Molina (q.v.), *El conde don Pero Vélez* by Luis Vélez de Guevara (q.v.), *Cómo ha de ser el privado* by Quevedo (q.v.), and *El esclavo en grillos de oro* (1692) by Bances Candamo (q.v.).

The literary importance of Olivares consists in his encouragement of writers (particularly of Calderón) both before and during his rise to power, and in his hostility towards Quevedo, whom he caused to be imprisoned on a charge of subversion between 1639 and 1643. Quevedo's gradual disillusionment with the methods of Olivares is one of the principal causes behind the bitterness displayed in his *Sueños* (q.v.).

OLIVARES, Padre MÍGUEL DE (d. 1786), b. Chillán, Chile. Jesuit historian. His *Historia militar, civil y sagrada, del Reino de Chile* (1864), which aimed to cover the period up to the middle of the 18th c., but extends only to the year 1639, is the best source for a knowledge of indigenous Chilean customs during the Colonial period.

Olivares was a scrupulous writer and described beliefs and customs from firsthand knowledge. His *Breve noticia de la Provincia de la Compañía de Jesús en Chile* was also printed in 1864.

OLIVER BELMAS, ANTONIO (1903–), b. Cartagena. Poet and essayist. Professor of Literature at Madrid University where he specializes in Darío (q.v.). He has edited the *Cantos de vida y esperanza* (1963) and written a masterly study, *Este otro Rubén Darío* (1960).

He married the Cartagena poet Carmen Conde (q.v.) who has edited his *Obras completas* in 2 vols. (vol. 1, 1971).

He has written essays, such as *De Cervantes a la poesía* (1944), under the pseudonym of Andrés Caballero. His poetry includes *Mástil* (1927), *Tiempo cenital* (Murcia, 1932), *Elegía a Gabriel Miró* (1935), and two books of whimsical, ironical, and often searching *loas* (q.v.), *Libro de loas* (1947) and *Loas arquitectónicas* (1951), on the birds, fruit, rivers, and buildings of his native Murcia.

OLIVER I SALLARES, JOAN (1899–), b. Sabadell. Poet and playwright in Catalan. His poetry has appeared under the pseudonym 'Pere Quart'. He edited the *Diari de Sabadell* but was exiled after the Civil War, spending one year in France and seven in Chile before returning to Barcelona, where he worked as literary editor for a publisher.

His poetry is often bitter, satirizing the bourgeois way of life in popular speech influenced

by Brecht. His original plays in Catalan number half a dozen, and he has translated Molière, Chekhov, Shaw, Brecht, and Beckett.

His books of poetry include *Les decapitacions* (1934), *Bestiari* (1937), *Saló de tardor* (1947), *Poemes de Pere Quart* (1949), *Terra de naufragis* (1956), possibly his best book: *Vacances pagades* (1960), and *Dotze aiguaforts de Granyer* (1962). An anthology, *Obra de Pere Quart*, appeared in 1963, followed by *Circumstàncies* (1968).

Ollántay, a Quechua drama of unknown authorship and date considered to be the summit of Quechua literature (q.v.). It has been attributed to Antonio Valdés, a *mestizo* who lived in the 18th c. It has been studied and translated by several scholars in Europe and Latin America since a few fragments first appeared with a commentary in the *Museo Erudito* of Cuzco (1837), where it was attributed to the priest Antonio Valdez. This has now been virtually disproved by the discovery of a MS. from La Paz dated 1735 on which J. D. de Tschudi based his editions of 1875. Rivero and Tschudi suggested (in *Antigüedades peruanas*, 1951) that its composition antedates the Conquest and their view is supported by a number of scholars such as Baudin (*El imperio socialista de los Incas*, Santiago, 1943). Ricardo Palma and Bartolomé Mitre (qq.v.) claim it as a colonial work. Middendorf, Urteaga, and Ricardo Rojas see it as a pre-Columbian tradition rewritten as a play by a Creole or *mestizo*.

Ollanta is a young hero in love with Kusi Qoyllur, daughter of the Inca Pachakútej. Being a plebeian, Ollanta is prohibited by law and religion from marrying into the family of the sun-god Inca, but when his suit for the princess is rejected, he raises his people in rebellion. Ten years pass, and then a little girl of ten, Ima Súmaj, living as an orphan in a Cuzco convent, on hearing strange cries discovers a mourning woman in a hidden cave. This is Kusi Qoyllur, incarcerated by her father for giving birth to Ima, Ollanta's child. The new Inca Túpaj Yupanki sends Rumiñawi to overthrow Ollanta, and during an orgy, he betrays Ollanta's trust by throwing open the gates to the Inca troops. Ollanta is captured and Rumiñawi claims his life from the Inca. The Inca prefers to listen to an old adviser, and pardons all the rebels, naming Ollanta the new governor of Cuzco, and giving him the hand of Kusi Qoyllur.

The play cannot be categorized in European terms: it is neither comedy, tragedy, nor drama. In Quechua it is a *wanka*, a historical play in which suffering is constantly balanced by humour. Song is used in much the same way as the chorus in Greek tragedy. The two lovers are not on stage together until the climax; a feature unknown in Spanish drama of the period.

A Spanish translation of the Quechua text was published by J. M. B. Farfán (Lima, 1952).

Olántay is also the title of a historical play (1939) by Ricardo Rojas (q.v.).

OLLER, NARCÍS (1845–1930), b. Valls, Tarragona. Catalan novelist. Though he spent most of his life as a lawyer in Barcelona and openly treated literature as an amateur pursuit, he became interested in writing on hearing Verdaguer (q.v.) at the Jocs Florals of 1877, and produced some short stories, *Croquis del natural* (1879) in the realist style. His first novel, *La papallona* (1882), dealt with his life as a student and immediately established him as the leading Catalan novelist of his day. *Vilaniu* (1885) is an autobiographical novel of Catalan village life. *La febre d'or* (3 vols., 1890–2), his most substantial book, uses material from his experience as a city lawyer. *La bogería* (1899) is a long story of a psychopath told in the first person. With *Pilar Prim* (1906), Oller moved away from realism towards romantic idealism and then wrote no more fiction, feeling out of key with his contemporaries. His *Memòries literàries: història dels meus llibres* (Barcelona, 1962) do not go beyond 1906.

His *Obres completes* appeared in Barcelona in 1948.

See J. Triadú, *Narcís Oller: resum biogràfic* (Barcelona, 1955).

OLMEDO, JOSÉ JOAQUÍN (1780–1847), b. Guayaquil. Ecuadorian statesman and neo-classical poet. He studied law, though his real interest seems to have been in the classics. He represented his native city in the Spanish Cortes of 1812. When Ecuador rebelled against Spain he was a member of the Junta de Gobierno in Guayaquil, leaving for Peru when the region became part of Colombia. He was a friend of Andrés Bello (q.v.), with whom he played an active part in the movement for Independence. A diplomat who served in France and England, Olmedo became first Vice-President of Ecuador in 1830.

His most famous work is the classically-inspired heroic ode *La victoria de Junín: canto a Bolívar* (q.v., Guayaquil, 1825), inspired by the last battles of the struggle for Independence. Another of his famous odes, on the civil war, was *Al general Flores, vencedor en Miñarica*. Olmedo also translated Pope's *Essay on Man*. His *Obras poéticas* (Valparaíso, 1848) have often been reprinted. His *Poésias completas*, published in Mexico City in 1947, is the same book as the Quito *Obras completas: poesías* (1945), edited by Aurelio Espinosa Pólit, who also edited Olmedo's

Epistolario (1960) and compiled an extensive bibliography appearing on pp. 221–309 of the *Obras completas* above.

See Abel Romeo Castillo, *Olmedo, el político* (Guayaquil, 1946) and *Olmedo y Bolívar* (Guayaquil, 1950); A. Duarte Valverde, *Olmedo* (Guayaquil, 1953); and Darío Guevara, *Olmedo, actor y cantor de la gran epopeya libertadora de América* (1958).

OLMO, LAURO (1922–), b. Barco de Valdeorras, Orense. Playwright, novelist, short-story writer, and poet.

His first published work was the collection of poems *Del aire* (1954). His book of short stories *Doce cuentos y uno más* (Barcelona, 1956) won the Premio Leopoldo Alas, and was followed by *La peseta del hermano mayor* (Barcelona, 1958). He has won considerable critical approval with his novels *Ayer, 27 de octubre* (Barcelona, 1958), which describes a day in the drab lives of the poor inhabitants of a Madrid block of flats, and *El gran sapo* (Barcelona, 1964); however, it is his plays, protests against poverty and injustice, that have really made his name. The best-known of these is *La camisa* (1961), which won the Premio Valle-Inclán, and in which the dilemma of Spain's poor is shown in the decision of Juan, the central character, to stay patriotically in Spain, while his wife chooses to seek a better future abroad. The success of this work was repeated with *La pechuga de la sardina* (1963) in which the tensions arising out of the clash between religious teaching and sexual feeling emerge out of the constant coming and going of prostitutes and *beatas* in a Madrid street. The theme of poverty is again important here.

Olmo's later plays are less impressive. They include *La condecoración* (1965), *El cuerpo* (1966), and *English spoken* (1968), the last described by G. G. Brown as 'a thin and forced contrivance'. Olmo's work nevertheless constitutes an important alternative to the shallow comedies of middle-class life characteristic of Madrid theatres during the Franco period. From 1968, Olmo's work was banned in Spanish theatres. In this time he produced a dramatic presentation of translations from Brecht's poems and songs, and his play *El cuarto poder* was performed at the 17th University Theatre Festival in Parma. In 1977 a play of Olmo's was produced in Barcelona, as a result of the relaxation of theatre censorship after the death of Franco.

OLMOS, FRAY ANDRÉS DE (1500–71), b. Spain. He arrived in Mexico as a missionary in 1524, and learned a number of Indian languages, writing grammars and vocabularies of the Totonaca, Huasteca, and Mexican languages. All his works are lost, except for the *Gramática*

mexicana, finished in 1547 but not published until 1875, in Paris. He was responsible for collecting a series of didactic *Huehuetlatolli* ('Dissertations of the ancients'), the Nahuatl MS. of which is in the U.S.A.

His work with the indigenous people of Mexico was continued by his disciple Fray Bernardino de Sahagún (q.v.).

Fray Andrés also composed a number of religious plays, including an *auto* on the Last Judgment performed annually between 1535 and 1548 at the church of S. José de Naturales, Mexico City.

OÑA, PEDRO DE (1555?–1626), b. Burgos. Ascetic writer of the Mercedarian order who became bishop of Caracas in 1602 and later bishop of Gaeta (Italy) where he died.

His well-written manual of asceticism, *Postrimerías del hombre* (1603), deals with questions of human mortality.

OÑA, PEDRO DE (1570–1643?), b. Los Infantes de Angol, Chile. The first known Chilean-born poet.

García Hurtado de Mendoza, Marqués de Cañete, commissioned Ercilla (q.v.) to commemorate his exploits in Chile, but was displeased with the resulting *Araucana* (q.v.) and requested Pedro de Oña to write another epic that would draw more attention to his prowess. Oña's 16,000-line *Primera parte de Arauco domado* (Lima, 1596) consists of 19 cantos in *octavas reales* rhyming abbaabcc.

Oña's profound feeling for nature is marred by intrusive rhetorical formulae, and by his concentration on those features of the Chilean landscape which might seem familiar to his European readers, rather than on specifically American flora and fauna. A lesser poet than Ercilla, Oña nevertheless improved on his model by excluding theological passages, and by dealing in some detail with the daily life of the *conquistadores.* José Toribio Medina published a critical edition for the Chilean Academy in 1917, and a facsimile edition appeared in Madrid in 1944. Cayetano Rosell edited the poem for the BAE, vol. 29 (1854) and there is the *Estudio del 'Arauco domado' de Pedro de Oña* by S. Dinamarca (New York, 1952).

Oña also wrote a poem on the Lima earthquake entitled *Temblor de Lima* (Lima, 1609), reproduced by J. T. Medina in facsimile on the tercentenary of its publication; *El vasauro* (1635), an extremely longwinded description, in 10,000 lines of *octavas,* of a goblet presented by King Fernando de Aragón to Andrés de Cabrera in recognition of his services to Christianity, which are also described at length (ed. by Rodolfo Oroz in the *Anales de la Universidad de*

Chile (Sección de Filología), vol. 1, 1941, pp. 174–239); and an unfinished eulogy of Ignatius of Loyola, *Ignacio de Cantabria* (Pt. 1, Seville, 1639).

There is an anonymous bibliography of Oña in *Revista del Archivo Nacional del Perú,* vol. 22 (January–June 1958), pp. 160–93.

See E. Matta Vial, *El licenciado Pedro de Oña: estudio biográfico-crítico* (1924), and Gerardo Seguell, *Pedro de Oña: su vida y la conducta de su poesía* (1940).

ONETTI, JUAN CARLOS (1909–), b. Montevideo. Uruguayan novelist and short-story writer of great originality and power; the most outstanding Uruguayan prose-writer of his time. *El pozo* (1939, reprinted in 1965 with an essay by A. Rama) deals with the stifling, parochial atmosphere of Uruguay, behind which Onetti senses only the alien tradition of the *gaucho.* From *Tierra de nadie* (1941) his settings are in Argentina, where he has lived and worked as a journalist, producing a series of pessimistic, lonely, and bitter stories and novels stemming from a disillusioned world-view similar to those of Céline, Faulkner, and Moravia. These books are *Para esta noche* (Buenos Aires, 1943), *La vida breve* (Buenos Aires, 1950), *Los adioses* (Buenos Aires, 1954), *Una tumba sin nombre* (Buenos Aires, 1959), *La cara de la desgracia* (Buenos Aires, 1960), *El astillero* (Buenos Aires, 1961), *Tan triste como ella* (Buenos Aires, 1963), and *Juntacadáveres* (1965).

Onetti's skill as a writer of short stories emerges in *Un sueño realizado y otros cuentos* (Buenos Aires, 1951), *Jacob y el otro* (Buenos Aires, 1960), *El infierno tan temido* (Buenos Aires, 1962, in which the hero of the title-story notes that 'Every morning I register the fact that I'm still alive without feeling either bitterness or gratitude', an existential position similar to that of Beckett's tramps in *Waiting for Godot*).

El astillero (which has been translated as *The shipyard,* New York, 1968) was his first major international success. In it he created an imaginary city of Santa María with its shipyard, itself largely illusory as the anti-hero, Larsen, gradually discovers that the shipyard has no ships, no work, and no employees apart from two men who pay their own wages from the sale of scrap. Frustrated sexuality and the theme of night as an appropriate time for man's activities run through *El astillero* as tenaciously as through *Ulysses.*

Juntacadáveres is an equally powerful novel, set in the period before *El astillero* but concerned with many of the same characters.

His *Cuentos completos* (Caracas, 1968), with only ten stories, have been superseded by a new edition (1974). The *Obras completas* first appeared in 1970, following which Onetti has published *La novia robada*, a short story (Buenos Aires, 1973); *La muerte y la niña* (1973); *Para una tumba sin nombre*, a short story (1974); and *Tiempo de abrazar*, a novel (1974).

There is a bibliography of Onetti by Hugo J. Verani in *Revista Iberoamericana*, no. 80 (July–September 1972), pp. 523–45.

See Reinaldo García Ramos (ed.), *Recopilación de textos sobre J. C. Onetti* (Havana, 1969); Lidice Gómez Mango (ed.), *En torno a Juan Carlos Onetti* (1970); Jorge Ruffinelli (ed.), *Onetti* (1973); and H. F. Giacoman (ed.), *Homenaje a Juan Carlos Onetti* (New York, 1974).

ONÍS Y SÁNCHEZ, Federico de (1886–), b. Salamanca. Literary critic, scholar, and editor, who studied in Madrid under Ramón Menéndez Pidal (q.v.) and taught in Oviedo and Salamanca before taking up an appointment in the Spanish Department at Columbia University (New York) in 1916. After working there for 37 years, he retired to the University of Puerto Rico. He was editor of the *Revista Hispánica Moderna*. Among his many publications are critical editions of the *Vida* of Torres Villarroel (q.v., 1912) and *De los nombres de Cristo* of Luis de León (q.v., 1914) for the Clásicos Castellanos; *Fueros leoneses* (1916) with his colleague Américo Castro (q.v.); *Martín Fierro y la poesía tradicional* (1924); the important *Antología de la poesía española e hispanoamericana, 1882–1932* (1934); and a collection of essays: *España en América* (1955).

OPPENHEIMER, Félix Franco, see Franco Oppenheimer, Félix.

OQUENDO DE AMAT, Carlos (1909–36), b. Puno. Peruvian surrealist poet. He wrote for *Amauta* (1926–30) edited by José Carlos Mariátegui (q.v.) and published one book, *5 metros de poemas* (1929), using inconsequential images and playful puns in the manner of Paul Éluard.

Oquendo was exiled in 1931 and after wandering through Central America, finally settled in Spain, where he died of tuberculosis during the first days of the Civil War.

Oráculo manual y arte de prudencia. Sacada de los Aforismos que se discurren en las Obras de Lorenço Gracián (Huesca, 1647), a didactic work by Baltasar Gracián y Morales (q.v.). No copy of the *editio princeps* is known to survive; the earliest extant edition is that of Madrid, 1653, reprinted at Amsterdam in 1659.

The *Oráculo manual* is a compendium of maxims on conduct and morality drawn directly from the author's other books and indirectly from the broad Western European moral tradition, with special reference to Seneca and the younger Pliny.

Gracián shrewdly and wittily indicates how the average man can rise above the common herd by the cultivation of prudence, patience, good manners, and the careful assessment of those with whom he comes into contact at all levels of society. His conclusion in the 300th maxim is 'In a word, be a saint: that is the sum total of my advice . . . Virtue is real: everything else is but a mockery'.

Didactic literature on the means of attaining Grace and the other delights of Heaven were common in Gracián's Spain; less so were secular works of advice on achieving worldly success comparable with those in Italian by Castiglione and Machiavelli. There is good evidence (Marañón, *Antonio Pérez*, 1952) that Gracián owes something to Pérez (q.v.) as well as to Francis Bacon.

The book's style is extremely simple; though repetitive, approaching the same problem from many different viewpoints, it is never verbose.

L. B. Walton's bilingual edition, *The Oracle*, (London, 1962) is in Everyman's Library. There is a critical edition by M. Romera-Navarro (1954); and another edition by G. M. Bertini (Milan, 1954).

See Monroe Z. Hafter, *Gracián and perfection* (Cambridge, Mass., 1966).

ORDÓÑEZ DE MONTALVO, Garci, see Rodríguez de Montalvo, Garci.

ORELLANA, Gilko, pseudonym of Armando Donoso Novoa (q.v.).

ORIBE, Emilio (1893–), b. Melo. Uruguayan poet, by training a doctor, by profession a teacher of aesthetics, and educational administrator. His first poems were modernist in tone, but Oribe developed an intellectual poetry at the same time as he elaborated a *Teoría del nous* (1934) and his work became gradually more hermetic and disciplined intended for an élite readership until the anthology *Poesía* (1944), which includes work from 1917 (*El castillo interior*) to 1930 (*La transfiguración del cuerpo*) and after.

Rapsodía bárbara (1954) dealt with the Americanist theme, but Oribe returned to his metaphysical style in *Ars magna* (Buenos Aires, 1960), which relies almost purely on the intelligence for its effect.

ORIXE, pseudonym of Nicolás de Ormaechea (q.v.).

ORMAECHEA, Nicolás de (1888–1961), Basque novelist and poet who wrote under the pseudonym 'Orixe'. His most memorable achievement was the long poem *Euskaldunak*, written in the 1930s but not published until 1950, which is a chronicle of the Basque people and their land. His fine translations into Basque include works by St. Augustine and the *Lazarillo de Tormes* (q.v.).

Oro, Siglo de, see Siglo de Oro.

OROSIUS (*fl.* A.D. 500), a priest of Tarragona, a disciple of St. Augustine, and a friend of St. Jerome. He wrote the first Spanish universal history still extant: the *Historia adversus paganos*. King Alfred is reputed to have translated the work into English.

OROZCO, see also Horozco.

OROZCO, *Beato* Alonso de (1500–91), b. Oropesa. Ascetic writer who became an Augustinian in 1522 and spent the next twenty years administering a number of Augustinian communities. He claimed that when he was living in Seville, in 1542, the Virgin Mary addressed him in a dream with the single word 'Write', and from then he never ceased to publish works of asceticism and mysticism which were eagerly read and quoted all over Spain: *Consideraciones acerca de los nombres de Cristo* (Seville, 1544), *Examen de conciencia* (Seville, 1551), *Las siete palabras que la Virgen Sacratísima Nuestra Señora habló* (Valladolid, 1556), *Hystoria de la reyna de Saba* (Salamanca, 1565) an eye-catching title with little connection with the Queen of Sheba, *Victoria del mundo* (1566), the important sermons collected as *Epistolario cristiano para todos los estados* (Alcalá, 1567), *Libro de la suavidad de Dios* (Salamanca, 1576), *Victoria de la muerte* (Burgos, 1583), *Arte de amar a Dios y al prójimo* (Alcalá, 1585), *Guarda de la lengua* (1589), and *Las confesiones del pecador fray Alonso de Orozco* (Valladolid, 1601) among others. His 'De nueve nombres de Cristo', first published by Father Conrado Muiños in *La Ciudad de Dios* (vols. 16–17, 1888), is believed to have inspired Luis de León's work on the same theme, though Muiños asserted the precedence of Luis's work.

Compilations of the Blessed Alonso's writings were made as early as the mid-16th century with the *Recopilación de todas las obras* (Valladolid, 1554–5) and a later edition of the *Obras* was that of Salamanca in 2 vols. (1895–6). He was beatified by Pope Leo XIII in 1882.

See T. Cámara, *Vida y escritos del Beato Alonso de Orozco* (Valladolid, 1882).

OROZCO Y BERRA, Manuel (1816–81), b. Mexico City. Mexican historian and archaeologist. His life as a civil servant was marked by several reverses of fortune, such as imprisonment and poverty, although he also held high positions such as that of Director of the National Museum (1866). He organized and edited the *Diccionario universal de historia y geografía* (7 vols., 1853–5) and *Apéndice* (3 vols., 1855–6), which is still of value for its entries on Mexico. The most important writings of this prolific author were *Geografía de las lenguas y carta etnográfica de Mexico* (1864), *Materiales para una cartografía mexicana* listing 3,400 different maps (1871), *Historia de la geografía en Mexico* (1880), and his voluminous *Historia antigua y de la conquista de México*, published posthumously at government expense in 1880–1 (4 vols. and atlas), in a 2-vol. edition in 1954, and in a 4-vol. edition with an introduction by Ángel María Garibay and a biography and bibliographies by Miguel León-Portilla (qq.v.) in 1960.

His preliminary studies for the unfinished *Historia de la dominación española en México* (4 vols., 1938) supplanted *Historia civil y política de México* by Fr. Andrés Caro (1739–after 1794) which was first published, in a modified and expanded version, by Carlos María de Bustamante in 1836 under the title *Tres siglos de México durante el gobierno español.*

ORREGO LUCO, Luis (1866–1948), Chilean novelist. After studies in Switzerland he returned to edit the Chilean magazines *La Libertad*, *La Época*, and *El Ferrocarril*. He participated in the Revolution of 1891 on the winning side, but was wounded and lost the use of one hand. Thereafter he was given posts in the diplomatic service in Spain, Brazil, and Uruguay, and 1909–12 edited *Selecta*, the best Spanish-language monthly on the arts at that time.

But Orrego Luco aspired to the title of a Chilean Pérez Galdós, writing *Episodios nacionales de la independencia de Chile, 1810: memorias de un voluntario de la vieja patria* (1905) and the series *Recuerdos del tiempo viejo* that openly imitated the Galdosian mixture of historical background and minute psychological portrayal of the landed classes to which Orrego Luco belonged.

This cycle opened with *Playa negra* (1947), on the period 1875–8, and continued with *En familia* (1912), on 1886, *La revolución del 91: al través de la tempestad* (1914), ending with the suicide of Balmaceda after his overthrow in 1891, *Un idilio nuevo* (1900), the famous *Casa grande* (1908) which caused a scandal for its bitter indictment of the corruption, avarice, and immorality of the Santiago rich, and *El tronco herido* (1929), on the period 1925–29.

Orrego Luco also wrote short stories collected

as *Páginas americanas* (Madrid, 1892) and *De la vida que pasa* (1919), and sketches of Spain entitled *Pandereta* (1896).

Falling far short of his idol Pérez Galdós, and not as meticulous a narrator as Blest Gana (q.v.), Orrego Luco nevertheless remains one of the key figures in the development of the Chilean novel in its realist phase.

See V. M. Valenzuela, *Cuatro escritores chilenos: Luis Orrego Luco, Emilio Rodríguez Mendoza, Baldomero Lillo, Federico Gana* (New York, 1961).

ORS Y ROVIRA, EUGENIO D' (1882–1954), b. Barcelona. Essayist, philosopher, art critic, and novelist. He studied at Barcelona University, the Sorbonne, and in Switzerland and Germany. Until 1916 he wrote in Catalan, under the pseudonym of 'Xènius'. Throughout his life his most characteristic genre was the *glosa*, less than an essay, but more than an aphorism. His first *Glossari* (Barcelona, 1906) was expanded in several later editions (the *Glosario* from 1906 to 1910 fills the first volume of his *Obra catalana completa*, Barcelona, 1950) until the *Novísimo glosario* (1946), which ran to over a 1,000 pages.

His best-known work is the allegorical novel *La ben plantada* (1912; translated into Castilian by Rafael Marquina, Buenos Aires, 1913) in which the heroine, Teresa, symbolizes the coming fusion of the Catalan spirit with the classical ideals of grace, harmony, proportion, equilibrium, and craftsmanship.

Always interested in the classical ideal and in reason, D'Ors liked to say, reversing the adage of Pascal, that 'Reason has its feelings that the heart knows nothing of'. D'Ors was one of the leading members of the movement which came to be called *novecentismo* (q.v., Catalan: *noucentisme*, q.v.), which urged the need to harmonize Spain's cultural heritage with that of European enlightenment, Roman Catholicism with a spirit of national enquiry, and the humanities with science.

In his philosophical writings, d'Ors denied the possibility of evolution. He claimed to be the same at the end of his life as in adolescence, and considered that history was not a matter of progress, but of five 'constants' which he called *epifanías* and listed as follows: 1. The epiphany of Man seen both physically and ethically, as exemplified by Socrates and other Greek philosophers and artists; 2. Society, begun by St. Augustine in his *De civitate Dei* and culminating in the Middle Ages; 3. State, begun by Dante, perverted by Machiavelli, and culminating in modern welfare and industrial states; 4. The People, begun by Rousseau, Vico, and Herder and brought to fulfilment in the Marxist cult of the proletariat; and 5. The Age of Culture, by which d'Ors means contemporary civilization.

Each of these *epifanías* can be said to begin at a specific time, but never dies out completely.

His philosophical works include *Religio est libertas* (1908), *Els fenomens irreversibles i la concepció entròpica de l'univers* (1910), *La filosofía del hombre que trabaja y juega* (1914), *Oceanografía del tedio* (1916), *Una primera lliçó de filosofia* (1916), *Las ideas y las formas: estudios sobre morfología de la cultura* (1928), *Estilos del pensar* ([1945]), *El secreto de la filosofía* (1947), and 'El secreto de la cultura' (not yet published).

His prose style is elaborate to the point of Baroque ornament and subtlety in many of his works, but he is sufficiently self-conscious to remain intelligible to the careful reader, and his *glosas* often strike a note of surprise characteristic of the *greguerías* of Ramón Gómez de la Serna (qq.v.). The art criticism of d'Ors, among the most acute in Spanish, includes *Poussin y el Greco* (1922), *Tres horas en el Museo del Prado* (1923), *El arte de Goya* (1928), *La vida de Goya* (1929), *Paul Cézanne* (1930), *Pablo Picasso* (1930), and *Lo Barroco* (1936).

See J. L. Aranguren, *La filosofía de Eugenio d'Ors* (1945); L. Anceschi, *Eugenio d'Ors e il nuovo classicismo europeo* (Milan, 1945); E. Rojo Pérez, *La ciencia de la cultura: teoría historiológica de Eugenio d'Ors* (Barcelona, 1963, with a four-page bibliography); E. Jardi, *Eugeni d'Ors* (Barcelona, 1967, also in Castilian); and P. G. Suelto de Saenz, *Eugenio d'Ors: su mundo de valores estéticos* (1969).

ORTEGA, JULIO (1942–   ), b. Chimbote. Peruvian critic and poet. From the early intimism of *De este reino* (1964) and *Tempo en dos* (1966), his work has evolved into the objectivism of *Las viñas de Moro* (1968). His plays include *Ceremonia y otros actos* (1974). His *Figuración de la persona* (Madrid, 1971) is the most significant study of the vigorous Peruvian poetic scene of the 1950s and 1960s, and is accompanied by a comprehensive anthology, *Imagen de la literatura peruana actual: 1968* (3 vols., 1971). His *La imaginación crítica: ensayos sobre la modernidad en el Perú* (1974) deals with Eguren, Vallejo, César Moro, Arguedas, and Vargas Llosa (qq.v.).

ORTEGA MUNILLA, JOSÉ (1856–1922), b. Cárdenas, Cuba. Spanish journalist and novelist, who was once a seminarist, but abandoned his theological studies. Deputy to the Spanish Cortes for many years, he wrote for *La Iberia*, *El Debate*, *La Patria*, and *El Imparcial* (founding its celebrated 'Hoja de Lunes') among others. With Miguel Moya he began the literary weekly *La Linterna*.

Ortega, father of the famous philosopher José Ortega y Gasset (q.v.), wrote many realist novels in the manner of Pérez Galdós (q.v.) but without his psychological subtlety or power of sustaining a plot. The anti-clerical *La cigarra* (1879) and its sequel *Sor Lucila* (1880) created a stir at the time, but his other novels (such as *Lucio Tréllez*, 1879; or *La senorita de Cisniega*, 1918) are now little read. His collection of *cuentos* are spoken of highly. Ortega showed considerable descriptive skill in his travel books, such as *Mares y montañas* (1887).

ORTEGA Y FRÍAS, RAMÓN (1825–83), b. Granada. Historical novelist whose popularity as a writer of novels issued serially in magazines or pamphlets was due to his melodramatic plots and over-simplified characterization.

An imitator of the serial-writer Manuel Fernández y González (q.v.), Ortega published numerous novels, including *El tribunal de la sangre, o los secretos de un rey* (1867), a book combining his abhorrence of King Philip II and his understanding of the Inquisition as portrayed by Juan Antonio Llorente's study which had appeared in Spanish in 1822; *El siglo de las tinieblas, o memorias de un inquisidor* (1868); *El Cid* (1875); *El testamento de un conspirador* (1880), whose heroine is a daughter of Philip IV; and *El diablo en palacio* (1882), on the life and intrigues of Don Carlos, usually considered his best novel.

ORTEGA Y GASSET, JOSÉ (1883–1955), b. Madrid. Philosopher and essayist. One of the most brilliant stylists writing in Spanish in the first half of the 20th c., son of José Ortega Munilla (q.v.) and grandson of Eduardo Gasset, both journalists. He studied at a Jesuit school at Miraflores (Málaga) then for a year in Deusto and in 1904 was awarded a doctorate by Madrid University (the 'universidad fantasma' as he called it from the absence of intellectual life there) for a thesis on *Los terrores del año mil* (1909).

In 1905 he began his German education in Leipzig and Berlin, and spent most of the next three years in the small Gothic city of Marburg, where neo-Kantian philosophy was taught (with Plato, Descartes, and Leibniz in particular) by teachers such as Hermann Cohen, Paul Natorp, and Ernst Cassirer. It was at this time that he abandoned Roman Catholicism. In 1910, Ortega was appointed to the chair of Metaphysics at Madrid, and it is this central position over a period of 26 years that gave Ortega's thought the seemingly natural pre-eminence it enjoyed for half a century from 1910.

He founded the magazine *España* in 1914, and when it ceased publication in 1923 he founded that pillar of Spanish intellectual life (with a reputation akin to that enjoyed later in Britain by *Encounter*), the *Revista de Occidente* (q.v.). This closed down in 1936 on the outbreak of Civil War, though continued as a publishing

house under the same name and later revived as an intellectual review. In 1917, Ortega was instrumental in founding the Madrid daily *El Sol*. He left Spain in 1936, travelling in Europe and Argentina, and returned in 1945 to live part of the year in Spain and part in Portugal. In 1948 he founded in Madrid a new Instituto de Humanidades, with his disciple Julián Marías.

Marías has stated his belief that Ortega's *Meditaciones del Quijote* (q.v., 1914) forms a metaphysics of human life, as well as a view of Spain's potential, and while this contention may be rather bold for a collection of elegant essays, it is true that much of Ortega's later thought amplifies ideas first adumbrated in this book.

Vieja y nueva política (1914) was followed by *Personas, obras, cosas* (1916), essays written before 1912, such as the important 'Adán en el Paraíso' in which, clearly still an idealist, he first skirmishes with the notion of the I (in this case, the first man) and his relation with the outside world (such as Paradise). The scene for the enactment of the existential drama is already set.

Ortega's brilliant journalism was collected in eight volumes entitled *El espectador: colección de ensayos filosóficos y literarios* (1916–28).

España invertebrada (q.v., 1921) was a historical study of the structure of Spanish society, accounting for the alleged 'spinelessness' of Spain. An aristocrat by persuasion, he accused the Visigothic invaders of Roman Iberia of lacking dynamic leadership, a defect magnified in later centuries.

El tema de nuestro tiempo (1923) is the key work of his early metaphysics in which he finally overcomes dependence on his neo-Kantian upbringing. He elevates life above thought, proposing a form of *razón vital* to replace the pure reason or mathematical reason advocated by his predecessors. Life is a continuous process, and circumstances vitiate and alter the rule of reason in crucial ways. Vital reason (comprising thought and emotion) is to be placed at the service of life, requiring truth in thought, beauty in emotion, and kindness in will.

La deshumanización del arte and *Ideas sobre la novela* (both 1925) consider with neither 'la ira ni el entusiasmo' the *avant-garde* art of the time in its flight from realism. Previously art had usually met with apathy, but never with antagonism. This new art was designed for the minority and was for the first time frankly incomprehensible to the masses. As soon as it loses its human narrative content, art ceases to be understood. Irony is the foremost tool of the new artist, but the sublime is denied him, and his work must be related to sport and the cult of youth and change.

Ortega's book has often been interpreted as a defence of the new art, because he mocks at

19th-c. realism in that, if life is wretched and absurd, there can be no justification for imitating it in art. His view is that, where *Quijote* succeeded by transcending reality, the new art has substantially succeeded by ignoring it. *Ideas sobre la novela* expands the concept of discarding realistic narrative in art in favour of impressionism and in fact by the date of its publication (1925), the book's theory had already been practised by writers such as Gabriel Miró and Valle-Inclán (qq.v.), who broadened the traditional view of a single, omniscient narrator.

Ortega's next books were *Tríptico*: essays on Mirabeau (1927), Kant (1929), and Goethe (1933); and *Espíritu de la letra* (1927).

La rebelión de las masas (q.v., 1929) is a further élitist pamphlet in the style of *España invertebrada*, but Ortega now argues for a United States of Europe to counteract nationalism and the European's declining power in world affairs.

His other works included *La redención de las provincias*; *La decencia nacional* (1930), articles published from 1927 to 1930; *Sobre reforma universitaria. Misión de la universidad* (1930); *Estudios sobre el amor* (1940); *Historia como sistema. Del imperio romano* (1940); and *Teoría de Andalucía y otros ensayos* (1942). Several of his books were published posthumously: *El hombre y la gente* (1957), *¿Qué es filosofía?* (1957), *Idea del teatro* (1958), and *La idea del principio en Leibniz* (1958). His *Obras completas* in 6 vols. reached a 4th edition in 1957–8, and *Bibliografía de Ortega* by Udo Rukser is in the Colección Estudios Orteguianos.

Ortega's philosophical standing and position have been challenged by three Jesuits (J. Iriarte, J. Sánchez Villaseñor, and J. Roig Gironella) and perhaps most thoroughly by the Dominican S. Ramírez, in his *La filosofía de Ortega y Gasset* (Barcelona, 1958). Sánchez Villaseñor in particular treats his work as merely superior journalism.

Ortega has been defended at length by his disciple Julián Marías, in *Ortega: Circunstancia y vocación* (1960), and elsewhere, by V. Marrero in an excellent study *Ortega, filósofo 'mondain'* (1961), and by J. L. Aranguren and Pedro Laín Entralgo. A more moderate position is held by such commentators as J. Ferrater Mora, *Ortega y Gasset: an outline of his philosophy* (New Haven, 1957), who do not question either his coherence or his originality, but prefer to speak of a 'sistema abierto' instead of a philosophical doctrine. The polemic surrounding the achievement of Ortega which began with his death reached its height and ended in about 1960, with the general acknowledgment that his reputation is secure as the most brilliant catalyst of ideas in Spain since Unamuno, that is to say, as a vital force for dissent and discussion in a period

(notably from 1923 to 1939) when controversy was more than usually suspect.

Most of Ortega's works have been translated into English and other principal languages, several of them being available in more than one version.

ORTIZ, ADALBERTO (1914–   ), b. Esmeraldas, Ecuador. Poet, novelist, diplomat, and secretary of the Casa de la Cultura Ecuatoriana. His poems on Negro and mulatto themes which first appeared on the literary page of *El Telégrafo* (Guayaquil) in 1940 created this new genre. His novel *Juyungo* (q.v., 1943), won the Premio Nacional de Novela. Eleven short stories constitute *La mala espalda* (1952). His first anthology of poems was *Tierra, son y tambor* (Mexico City, 1945); his complete poetic works were published in 1959 under the title *El animal herido*.

ORTIZ, AGUSTÍN (16th c.), b. Aragón? The author of an imitation of the *Celestina* (q.v.) entitled *Radiana*, a short five-act *comedia* in *coplas de pie quebrado* showing the influence of both Vicente and Torres Naharro (qq.v.). Written about 1533, it survives in an edition of 1534 and has been edited by R. E. House (Chicago, 1910).

The first act is wholly taken up with the mourning of Lireo, Radiana's father, for his wife, an opening reflecting that of Vicente's *Comedia del Viudo*. Cleriano's servant obtains an audience for his master with Radiana somewhat too easily for convincing dramatic effect. Lireo surprises the lovers, but before he can execute his threat to kill them a priest arrives and performs the marriage ceremony. Radiana herself does not appear until the last act.

ORTIZ, FERNANDO (1881–1969), Cuban anthropologist, and theorist of the Afro-Cuban movement in his two-volume *Hampa afrocubana: Los negros brujos* (Madrid, 1906) and *Los negros esclavos* (Madrid, 1916). He compiled *Glosario de afronegrismos* (1924) and 'Un catauro de cubanismos' in the *Revista Bimestre Cubana*, vol. 17, 1922.

Ortiz's writings inspired the poetry of Nicolás Guillén, José Zacarías Tallet (q.v.), and Ramón Guirao, and, indirectly, the influential anthologies by Emilio Ballagas (1908–54): *Antología de la poesía negra hispanoamericana* (Madrid, 1944) and *Mapa de la poesía negra hispanoamericana* (Buenos Aires, 1946).

ORTIZ, JOSÉ JOAQUÍN (1814–92), b. Tunja. Colombian poet, novelist, and journalist, who occasionally wrote under the pseudonym 'José Negreros'. A Roman Catholic apologist in his essays and poetry, he founded many literary magazines to propagate his views, such as *La Estrella Nacional* (12 issues, 1836), the first of its kind in Colombia.

His *Poesías* (1880) were strongly influenced by Quintana (q.v.), combining a classical style with essentially Romantic subject-matter such as the Conquest, patriotism, and the struggle for Independence. His style is occasionally marred by verbosity, excessive rhetoric, and lapses from rhythmic grace. His *Tragedia Sulma* is an Indianist play suffering from the excessive use of classical models. Ortiz also wrote historical novels in the manner of Sir Walter Scott, and founded the Academia Hispanoamericana.

ORTIZ, Juan Laurentino (1897–), b. Puerto Ruiz, Gualeguay, Entre Ríos. Argentinian poet, considered by the critic Juan Gelman to be Latin America's greatest lyrical poet. Largely self-taught, Ortiz is a profoundly regional writer obsessed by the need to dominate time for self-realization. His first book was *El agua y la noche* (Panama, 1933), followed by *El alba sube* (1937), *El ángel inclinado* (1938), *La rama hacia el este* (1940), *El álamo y el viento* (1947), *El aire conmovido* (1949), *La mano infinita* (1951), *La brisa profunda* (1954), *El alma y las colinas* (1956), and *De las raíces y del cielo* (1958). His collected poems, *En el aura del sauce* (Rosario, 1971), were published in 3 vols.

See A. L. Ponzo, 'Juan L. Ortiz' in *Norte* (Mexico City), no. 273, Sept.-Oct. 1976.

ORTIZ DE MONTELLANO, Bernardo (1899–1949), b. Mexico City, Mexican poet. In 1918 he founded the Ateneo de la Juventud with Pellicer, Torres Bodet (qq.v.), and others, and became the guiding spirit, with Torres Bodet, of the magazine *Falange* (1922–3), before founding the most influential Mexican literary journal of its generation: *Contemporáneos* (1928–31), which he himself edited from no. 9 (February 1929). It concentrated on serious literature, avoiding the ephemeral and drawing on European literature of the time for themes and standards.

Ortiz's own poetry was hermetic, exploring his own dream world and pre-Hispanic values. His *La poesía indígena de México* (1935) attempts to assess the spiritual value of the work on its own merits rather than to concentrate on its historical place in a continuing tradition. The posthumously-published *Sueño y poesía* (ed. Wilberto Cantón, 1952) contains his previous volumes of poetry: *Avidez* (1921), *El trompo de siete colores* (1925), *Sueños* (1933, with the *Primero sueño* of 1931 in which Ortiz predicted the shooting of Lorca that was to take place five years later), and *Muerte de cielo azul* (1937).

He also wrote some puppet-plays, the prose-poems in *Red* (1928) and *Cinco horas sin corazón* (1940), and the stories in *El caso de mi amigo Alfazeta* (1946).

Among his translations was *Miércoles de ceniza* (1946), from Eliot's *Ash Wednesday*. Of his literary criticism, the most important study is *Figura, amor y muerte de Amado Nervo* (1943).

ORTIZ DE ZÚÑIGA Y DE ALCÁZAR, Diego (1633–80), b. Seville. Historian of his native city in *Anales eclesiásticos y seculares de la ciudad de Sevilla* (1677; revised and reprinted by A. M. Espinosa, 1796), one of the spate of city histories published during the Golden Age. He also wrote the genealogy of his own family *Discurso genealógico de los Ortizes de Sevilla* (1670; new edn. by Pérez de Guzmán, 1930).

ORTIZ GUERRERO, Manuel (1897–1933), Paraguayan poet. He was a leper who transcended his affliction in poetry influenced tardily, due to the cultural isolation of Paraguay, by Rubén Darío (q.v.). Despite numerous grammatical errors and slipshod syntax in his Spanish works, Ortiz Guerrero became the most popular poet of his time, and his evocative poetry in Guaraní, notably *Nde rendape ayu*, is free of these linguistic blemishes.

His books in Spanish include *Surgente* (1922) and *Pepitas* (1930): they were collected in *Obras completas* (Buenos Aires, 1952).

OSIUS (256–357), b. Cordova. Bishop of his native city from 295, he attended the Council of Elvira (the Latin Illiberis, near Granada) in the early 4th c. and then travelled to Rome, where he was tortured under Diocletian and Maximian (303) and later helped to convert Constantine.

He presided over the Council of Arles (314), the first ecumenical council (Nicaea, 325), and the Council of Sardis (343). He formulated the Catholic notion of *homousion* on the nature of the Word, as opposed to the Arian doctrine which denied divinity to the Son.

Osius was exiled to Sirmione by Constantius in 356 for refusing to condemn St. Athanasius, who preserved in his *Historia arianorum* a defiant 'Letter to Constantius' in which Osius recalls his sufferings under Constantius' grandfather Maximian. His other writings include resolutions submitted to the Councils of Nicaea and Sardis, and two lost works: *De laude virginitatem* (to his sister) and *De interpretatione vestium sacerdotalium*.

As a saint of the Greek Orthodox Church, his festival is 27 August.

OSORIO BENÍTEZ, Miguel Ángel (1883–1942), b. Santa Rosa de Osos, Antioquia. Colombian poet who used the pseudonyms 'Porfirio Barba Jacob', 'Ricardo Arenales', and 'Maín Ximénez'. His poetic style, originally strongly influenced by Darío, remained modernist, with a pessimistic tinge influenced by Romanticism. He led a deliberately Bohemian life, wandering from one Latin-American country to another, refusing to establish himself permanently, and displaying complete indifference to the systematic collection and publication of his work. His works consequently appeared without revision or selection and are uneven, doubtless including spurious work: *Canciones y elegías* (Mexico City, 1932); *Rosas negras* (Guatemala City, 1933), compiled by Arévalo Martínez (q.v.), who caricatured 'Barba Jacob' in *El hombre que parecía un caballo* (1915); *Canción de la vida profunda y otros poemas* (Manizales, 1935); *El corazón iluminado* (1942); *Poemas intemporales* (Mexico City, 1944); and *Antorchas contra el viento* (1945) compiled by Daniel Arango. *Poesías completas* (1960) were followed by *Obras completas* (Medellín, 1962). He also wrote a mannered autobiography entitled *La divina tragedia*. Osorio died of tuberculosis in Mexico City.

His best poems are those in which breathless diction and violent imagery are impressively combined, as in *La reina* (addressed to his Muse), with its opening confession 'En nada creo, en nada'.

OSORIO LIZARAZO, José Antonio (1900–64), Colombian novelist. A writer of realist fiction in the manner of Zola, Osorio's introduction of *costumbrismo* into each novel helps to balance his concern with social problems. His careful plot-construction is notably more successful than his characterization. His first novel was *La cara de la miseria* (1927), like his later work a pessimistic social chronicle rather than a tragedy. He then published *La casa de vecindad* (1930); *Barranquilla 2132* (1932), Colombia's first science-fiction adventure; *El criminal* (1935), in which a poor journalist stabs his pregnant mistress; *Hombres sin presente* (1938); *Garabato* (Santiago, Chile, 1939), in which a clumsy boy is mocked by his schoolmates and the Jesuit teacher; and *El hombre bajo la tierra* (1944) on the cult of *machismo*, set in a gold-mine. Osorio's stories of crime, sex, drunkenness, and insanity reflect not only the brutality of the lower classes, but equally the callous insensitivity of the middle classes. Generally opposed to the Jesuits and to the conservative elements in Bogotá (as in *Garabato*), Osorio nevertheless wrote a eulogy of the Trujillo regime in the Dominican Republic (*La isla iluminada*, Santiago, Dominica, 1947). *El fundador civil de la República* (*Estudio sobre el general Santander*) appeared in Bogotá (1940).

His best book is *El día del odio* (1952), devoted to the violence in Colombian life, which culminated in the uprising of 1948. The predicament is stated to be the persistent exploitation of the many by the few, and the prediction that the masses will rebel and destroy the society which torments them.

El pantano (1952) concerns a decaying suburb of Buenos Aires whose inhabitants lead an existence degrading both materially and spiritually. *El camino en la sombra* (1965) describes the long slavery of the Indian woman Matilde, and her distress at the death of the family which has taken advantage of her. Osorio is a serious novelist whose work deserves a greater public.

See Charles N. Staubach, 'The novels of Osorio Lizarazo' in *Hispania*, vol. 32 (1949), pp. 172–80.

OSUNA, *El Bachiller* Francisco de, pseudonym of Francisco Rodríguez Marín (q.v.).

OSUNA, *Fray* Francisco de (1497–*c*. 1542), b. Osuna. Ascetic writer who studied in Salamanca, joined the Franciscan order, and travelled in France, Germany, and the Low Countries, where he came under the influence of mystics such as Ruysbroeck and Thomas à Kempis.

His *Gracioso convite de las gracias del Santísimo Sacramento del Altar* (Seville, 1530) and *Norte de los estados* (Burgos, 1541) are his lesser works, the latter (dealing with the single, married, and widowed states) having been reprinted in the *Bulletin Hispanique*, vol. 37 (1935).

Fray Francisco's most important work was his *Abecedario espiritual*, which appeared in six parts. The *Primera parte del abecedario espiritual* (Seville, 1525) deals with the Passion of Christ; the *Segunda* (Seville, 1530) with physical and spiritual preparation to achieve ascetic discipline; the *Tercera* (Toledo, 1527; ed. Fr. Miguel Mir in vol. 16 of the NBAE (1911), on mystical union with God, was the favourite book of S. Teresa de Jesús, and one can still see her annotated copy in the Carmelite convent of S. José in Ávila; the *Ley de Amor Sancto, y cuarta parte* (1530), deals with the nature, mysteries, and practice of love; the *Quinta parte* (Burgos, 1541) consists of guidance for the rich and consolation for the poor; the *Sexta parte* (Seville, 1554) is a treatise on the wounds of Jesus Christ.

Fray Francisco's purity of diction, elevated tone, and stirring eloquence raised the level of discourse among ascetic-mystical writers, preparing the way for later writers such as San Juan de la Cruz (q.v.).

See R. F. de Ros, *Le père Francisco de Osuna* (Paris, 1937) and L. Calvert, *Francisco de Osuna and the spirit of the letter* (Chapel Hill, N.C., 1973).

OTERO, Blas de (1916–   ), b. Bilbao. Poet. Educated by the Jesuits, he has lived in Bilbao,

Barcelona, and abroad. His first book *Cántico espiritual* (Bilbao, 1942) was influenced by San Juan de la Cruz, as the title implies, and his next books continued his quest for God: *Ángel fieramente humano* (1950) and *Redoble de conciencia* (Barcelona, 1951; 2nd edn. with 48 new poems, 1958) collected in *Ancia* (Barcelona, 1958), a title combining the first syllable of the first book with the last of the second. Striking imagery and emotional depth are the virtues of these books, which show a poet disturbed by the anguish of all mankind, 'la inmensa mayoría' which he sets against Juan Ramón Jiménez's purist slogan, 'la inmensa minoría'. Other works of this period were *Antología y notas* (Vigo, 1952), and *Pido la paz y la palabra* (Santander, 1955).

His early poetry resembled that of Miguel Hernández (q.v.), but his more recent work has much in common with that of León Felipe (q.v.). Baroque rhetoric is replaced by a concern for social problems expressed in short, laconic pieces on the misery of Spain and her lack of freedom, but however far Otero's melancholy reaches, there is always a hint of a better future. *Expresión y reunión, 1941–1969* (1969) selected the best of his previous work with some new poems.

See E. Alarcos Llorach, *La poesía de Blas de Otero* (Oviedo, 1955).

OTERO SILVA, MIGUEL (1908–   ), b. Barcelona, Anzoátegui. Venezuelan novelist and poet. A member of the Generation of 1928, whose early social protest poetry *Agua y cauce* (1937) and *25 poemas* (1942) was romantic in form. He abandoned his engineering studies for the political struggle against the dictatorship of Juan Vicente Gómez (1908–1935) and suffered exile as a result. In 1942 he founded the daily *El Nacional*, which fostered the Venezuelan short story by means of its annual competition. He took a degree in journalism at the Universidad Central in 1949, and founded the humorous weekly *El Morrocoy Azul*.

Otero Silva's most significant novels are his sober indictments of the Gómez regime and the exploitation of Venezuelan oil by foreign companies. They begin with *Fiebre: novela de la Revolución venezolana* (1939), where the adventures of the narrator, the rebellious student Vidal, culminate in the horror of a labour camp for dissidents. *Casas muertas* (Buenos Aires, 1955) shows the dead city of Ortiz devastated after the upheavals of the Gómez dictatorship and abandoned by its inhabitants who have gone to scavenge for jobs in the nearby oil-camp. This latter theme is developed in *Oficina no. 1* (Buenos Aires, 1961). Otero's latest novels are *La muerte de Honorio* (1963) and *Cuando quiero llorar no lloro* (Barcelona, 1971).

His essays on art and politics are collected in

El cercado ajeno (1961). His *Poesía completa* appeared in 1973.

See César Tiempo, 'Semblanza de un novelista' in *Espiral* (Bogotá), no. 93 (1964), pp. 21–6.

OTHÓN, MANUEL JOSÉ (1858–1906), b. S. Luis Potosí. Mexican poet. Using Virgil, Garcilaso, and Luis de León as his models, Othón created for Mexico a nature poetry inspired by that of the Golden Age, in reaction to *modernismo* (q.v.). His early work appeared in *Poesías* (San Luis Potosí, 1880). His poetic credo was 'no debemos expresar nada que no hayamos visto; nada sentido o pensado a través de ajenos temperamentos, pues si tal hacemos, ya no será nuestro espíritu quien hable y mentimos a los demás, engañándonos a nosotros mismos'. *Himno de los bosques* (1891) can be said to live up to this criterion in places, but Othón's best book is *Poemas rústicos* (1902), written in the countryside around his birthplace. *Idilio salvaje* (1905) is a moving record in seven sonnets of a middle-aged poet's love for a young girl, an infatuation that he explained to his wife as attributed to the historian Alfonso Toro. His *Obras completas* (1945) include his lesser work, such as short stories, and plays: *Después de la muerte* (1883), *Lo que hay detrás de la dicha* (1886), and *El último capítulo* (1905), an interesting but theatrically feeble encounter between Cervantes and Avellaneda (qq.v.).

There is a recent edition by A. Castro Leal of Othón's *Poesías y cuentos* (1963).

See Rafael Montejano y Aguiñaga's bibliography of Othón in *Fichas de Bibliografía Potosina* (San Luis Potosí), vol. 5, no. 1 (January–March 1959), pp. 3–24); J. A. Peñalosa, *Manuel José Othón, novelista olvidado* (San Luis Potosí, 1952); A. de Valle Arizpe, *Anecdotario de Manuel José Othón* (1958); Baltasar Dromundo, *Manuel José Othón: su vida y su obra* (1959); and Juana Meléndez de Espinosa, 'Manuel José Othón, poeta y mundo' in *Revista de la Facultad de Humanidades* (San Luis Potosí), vol. 2, no. 2 (1960), pp. 169–216.

OVALLE, *Padre* ALONSO DE (1601–51), b. Chile. The first Chilean-born historian and, according to Arturo Torres Ríoseco, the finest Chilean writer of the 17th c. While Procurator of the Chilean sub-province of the Society of Jesus in Rome, he compiled his *Histórica relación del Reyno de Chile y de las misiones y ministerios que exercita en él la Compañía de Jesús* (Rome, 1646), reprinted in the Colección de Historiadores de Chile (vols. 12–13, 1888). It is frankly partial, being written to attract more Christian missionaries to Chile.

OVIEDO Y BAÑOS, JOSÉ (1671–1738), b. Bogotá. Colombian Creole historian of Spanish descent, who spent his childhood in Lima, then travelled to Caracas with his uncle Diego de Baños, Bishop of Caracas. Oviedo became *regidor* of Caracas, and wrote the agreeable but slow moving *Historia de la conquista y población de la provincia de Venezuela* (Madrid, 1723). A second volume was written but never published, and is now lost. Oviedo's painstaking compilation, eloquently narrated, covers the period from the Discovery to the end of the 16th c. Cesáreo Fernández Duro prepared an edition in 2 vols. for the Biblioteca de los Americanistas (Madrid, 1885).

Oviedo's major defect as a historian was to ignore environmental influences on people and events.

Ovillejo, the name given by Francisco de Cascales (q.v.) to a ten-line stanza with three paired rhymes, each pair comprising one octosyllabic and one shorter line, followed by a quatrain (or *redondilla*) of three octosyllables and a fourth line repeating the three short lines. The rhyme scheme is usually aa:bb:cc:cddc.

The first recorded *ovillejos* are three in *Don Quijote* (I, xxvii) and four in *La ilustre fregona* (qq.v.). Zorrilla inserted twelve *ovillejos* in *Don Juan Tenorio* (Act II, scenes 6, 7, and 11). The *ovillejo* has been used with considerable success by Darío, and also for *rima al mezzo*, in which the final rhyme of a line rhymes with the end of the first hemistich of the rest, as in sections of Garcilaso's *Égloga* II.

OWEN, GILBERTO (1905–52), b. El Rosario, Sinaloa. Mexican poet, grandson of a Welsh miner. He served as a diplomat in the United States, Peru, Ecuador, and Colombia. After contributing to *Ulises* (1927–8) he became one of the Contemporáneos group (1928–31) which also included Salvador Novo and Jaime Torres Bodet (qq.v.), and then wrote for *El hijo pródigo* 1943–6.

Owen was a sceptic in religious matters. His poetic influences included Gide, Eliot, and Juan Ramón Jiménez (q.v.). *Poestas y prosa* (1953) is a useful anthology from his prose *La llama fría* (1925) and *Novela como nube* (1928), and from his collections of poetry: *Desvelo* (1925), *Línea* (Buenos Aires, 1930), *Libro de Ruth* (1944), and *Perseo vencido* (1948). *Primeros versos* (Toluca, 1957) contains his earliest poems.

OYUELA, CALIXTO (1857–1935), b. Buenos Aires. Argentinian critic, essayist, and poet of the Generation of 1880. Professor of Spanish and French Literature in the Buenos Aires University. His polemical *Justa literaria* (1883), against his friend Rafael Obligado (q.v.), extended to a vigorous defence of the militant Roman Catholic, classical, and Hispanic position adopted by his intellectual master Menéndez y Pelayo (q.v.) against the contemporary trend towards the liberal, Romantic, and Gallic attitude of Darío and the young *galiparlantes* who surrounded him when he came to Buenos Aires.

Oyuela compiled *Antología poética hispanoamericana* (5 vols., 1919–20). His *Estudios literarios* (2 vols., 1943) reprinted *Estudios y artículos literarios* (1889) and *Estudios literarios* (1915). His original poetry appeared in four volumes: *Cantos* (1891), *Nuevos cantos* (1905), *Cantos de otoño* (1924), and *Cantos nocturnos* (1933). His work is influenced by classical models, by Luis de León (q.v.), and by Leopardi, whom he translated.

OZORES, RENATO (1910–), Panamanian novelist and short-story writer, whose themes and characters are drawn from various social strata, from the playboys and idlers of *Playa honda* (1950), and the historical novel of Panama *Puente del mundo* (1951), to the working classes in *La calle oscura* (1955), whose hero is a boy newspaper-vendor.

P

PACHECO, FRANCISCO (1535–99), b. Jérez. Humanist and Latin poet. Not to be confused with his nephew of the same name (see next entry). He became Canon of Seville Cathedral. His home formed a literary academy with visitors such as his pupil Fernando de Herrera (q.v.), Baltasar del Alcázar (q.v.), and other Andalusian poets.

His Castilian poetry is lost, but there is extant an ode to Garcilaso in Latin which is unimpressive: *Natalis alma lumine candidus.*

PACHECO, FRANCISCO (1564–1654), b. Trigueros, Huelva. Painter, biographer, and poet. The nephew of the humanist of the same name (see previous entry) and father-in-law of the great painter Diego Velázquez.

His first important book was *El libro de*

descripción de verdaderos retratos de ilustres y memorables varones (Seville, 1599), edited by J. M. Asensio (Seville, 1870), much of it based on personal knowledge of the great men of the time, of whom Pacheco met many in his uncle's home. Pacheco's long *Poema de la conquista de la Bética* is mediocre; his best verse consists of the sonnets collected in vol. 32 (1857) of the BAE. He is also remembered for his *Arte de la Pintura, su antigüedad y grandezas* (Seville, 1649), edited by F. J. Sánchez Cantón (2 vols., 1956), though it borrows a good deal from Alberti, da Vinci, and Vasari. In 1619 he produced the first edition of the poetry of Herrera (q.v.), his uncle's pupil and, by intercalating them in his own verse, saved the poetic fragments of Céspedes.

PACHECO, José Emilio (1939–   ), b. Mexico City. Mexican poet, novelist, short-story writer, and literary critic. He has compiled an anthology *La poesía mexicana del siglo XIX* (1965), and works on the literary *Revista de la Universidad de México*.

His early stories in *La sangre de Medusa* (1959) and *El viento distante* (1963) bear the imprint of Jorge Luis Borges (q.v.), but the poems written 1958–62, *Los elementos de la noche* (1963), reveal a powerful poetic personality, delicate yet striking in imagery. *El reposo del fuego* (1966) is a long poem divided into three sections of fifteen poems each, and *Para matar el tiempo* (1969) shows even greater maturity than the second section of *El reposo del fuego*. His latest poems are in *Irás y no volverás* (1973). Pacheco's technically brilliant novel *Morirás lejos* (1967) was succeeded by *No me preguntes cómo pasa el tiempo* (1969), influenced by Samuel Beckett, whose *Comment c'est* Pacheco has translated (Mexico City, 1966). *El principio del placer* (1972) is a collection of short stories.

Pacheco is currently writing for the Mexican cinema. Gordon Brotherston and Edward Dorn have translated a selection of his work as *Tree between two walls* (Santa Barbara, Calif., 1969).

PACHECO DE NARVÁEZ, Luis (*fl.* 1615), Spanish fencing master. The clubfooted Quevedo (q.v.) once disarmed him, remaining Pacheco's lifelong enemy in so doing.

His textbooks on fencing and allied arts of defence were classics: *Libro de las grandezas de la espada . . .* (1600), *Las cien conclusiones, o formas de saber de la verdadera Destreza . . .* (1608), *Engaño y desengaño de los errores que se han querido introducir en la destreza de las Armas* (1635), and the posthumously published *Nueva Ciencia y Filosofía de la Destreza de las Armas . . .* (1672).

PADILLA, Heberto (1932–   ), b. Puerta de Golpe, Pinar del Río. Cuban poet cleverly mixing irony with lyricism, who emigrated to the U.S.A. shortly after World War II, teaching Spanish at Berlitz schools, but returned to Cuba to participate in the Revolution in 1959. He has spent brief periods in England, the U.S.S.R., and Czechoslovakia.

His collection *Las rosas audaces* (1941) made little impact, but *El justo tiempo humano* (1962) was a major addition to Cuban and Latin-American literature. He later published the unremarked *La hora* and *Fuera del juego* (1968), which questioned the assumptions of the Revolution, implying that more than ideology was involved, and caused his brief imprisonment, followed by a humiliating 'confession'. Perhaps his finest poem is the 'Infancia de William Blake'. Antón Arrufat (q.v.), another Cuban writer, was also publicly censured in the 'Padilla affair' at the Havana Cultural Congress of 1968.

PADILLA, Juan de (1468–1522?), b. Seville. Poet. A monk of the Charterhouse of S. María de las Cuevas in Seville, Padilla was often styled 'el Cartujano'. His poem in 150 coplas *El laberinto del duque de Cádiz . . .* (1493) is now lost, but two major works of his have survived. The first is *Retablo del Cartuxo sobre la vida de Nuestro Redentor Jesu Christo* (Alcalá, 1505), which he states having completed in 1500. This popular poem appeared anonymously, but Padilla gave away his identity in an acrostic near the end.

In 1518 he finished his most significant poem, *Los doze triumphos de los doze apóstoles* (Seville, 1521), an allegory in the style of Dante consisting of 1,000 stanzas of nine lines each in *versos de arte mayor*. It was reprinted by Miguel de Riego (London, 1843) with the *Retablo* and included by Foulché-Delbosc in the *Cancionero castellano del siglo XV* (vol. 19 of the NBAE, 1912).

See J. Gimeno, 'Sobre el Cartujano y sus críticos', in *Hispanic Review*, vol. 29 (1961), pp. 1–14.

PADILLA, Fray Pedro de (*fl.* 1585–99), b. Linares, Jaén. Poet. In 1585 he entered the Carmelite Order. His poetry was praised by Lope, and Gallardo wrote that 'está escrito con pureza de dicción, pero con poco espíritu, poca alma poética'.

His writings include *Thesoro de varias poesías* (1580), *Grandezas y excelencias de la Virgen Nuestra Señora . . .* (1581), *Églogas pastoriles . . .* (Seville, 1582), *Romancero . . .* (1583), and *Iardin espiritual* (1585). Padilla's work is found in vols. 10 and 16 of the BAE.

See F. Vegara Peñas, 'Fray Pedro de Padilla' in *Boletín de la Universidad de Granada*, vol. 5 (1933), pp. 43–64.

PADRÓN, Julián (1910–54), b. San Antonio, Monagas. Venezuelan novelist and short-story writer. He studied law, practised journalism (editing *Cuadernos Literarios*, Caracas), and was one of the founders of the review *El Ingenioso Hidalgo*.

His regional novels of eastern Venezuela have an autobiographical foundation. The first was *La guaricha* (1934), in which the Venezuelan landscape is almost the central character. José Mayo and his wife Tilde work hard to achieve success in difficult conditions, rearing three children despite revolution, bad health, and an atmosphere of desperate violence. *Madrugada* (1939) portrays the dawning of adulthood in the life of Bernardo Montes, a sad and lonely village youth. Set on a sugar estate in the Guarapiche valley, *Clamor campesino* (1944) again shows the men and women shaped by the harsh geography of Venezuela.

Primavera nocturna (1950) is a strange novel of the tormented souls of Bernardo and Liana, full of poetry and implicit theories of the interaction of the 'social soul' with the 'personal soul'. *Este mundo desolado* (1954) is a sombre parable of generations inured to farming routine.

Perhaps Padrón's finest book was *Candelas de verano* (1937), a collection of short stories again set in the Venezuelan countryside he knew so well. His *Obras completas* were published (Mexico City) in 1957.

He edited the anthology *Cuentistas modernos* (Buenos Aires, 1945); and, with Artur Uslar Pietri (q.v.), *Antología del cuento moderno venezolano* (2 vols., 1940).

PÁEZ DE RIBERA, RUY (*fl.* 1397–1424), b. Seville. Poet, descended from a noble family. A disciple of Micer Francisco Imperial (q.v.) but unlike him not a direct imitator of Dante. He bewailed many misfortunes in the celebrated *Proceso que ovieron en uno la Dolencia e la Vejez e el Destierro e la Pobreza* on the subject of his lines 'El pobre non tiene parientes ni amigo / Donayre nin seso, esfuerço e sentido'. He also composed *Proceso que ovieron la Soberbia e la Mesura* but is best remembered for his poems in the *Cancionero de Baena* (288–300).

See vols. 2 and 22 of the NBAE and E. B. Place, 'More about Ruy Páez de Ribera' in *Hispanic Review*, vol. 14 (1946).

PAGANO, JOSÉ LEÓN (1875–1964), b. Buenos Aires. Argentinian playwright, critic, and essayist. Long the doyen of drama and criticism in Argentina, Pagano was also a substantial art historian and his 3-vol. *El arte de los argentinos* (1937–40) remains unsurpassed.

Más allá de la vida, first performed in Barcelona (1902) showed a great writer losing control over his inspiration and creative abilities, and this obsession with middle-upper class themes of

art and society led Pagano into conflict with his contemporary Florencio Sánchez, whose success caused Pagano to remark sadly that 'en nuestro país únicamente se aprecia el teatro como manifestación intuitiva de la vida popular'. *El dominador*, first performed in Rome in 1903, shows a Nietzsche-like hero concocting his own diabolical philosophic system. In *Almas que luchan* (Barcelona, 1906), another 'alta comedia', an honest journalist uncovers a financial swindle. His other plays included *Nirvana* (Barcelona, 1906) and *La venganza de Afrodite* (Buenos Aires, 1954), the latter a 'misterio profano en cuatro tiempos'. His drama reviews appeared in *Cómo estrenan los autores* (Barcelona, 1908).

Pagano's theatre is concerned with man's predicament in society as a thinking individual with a conscience. Technically adroit, his plays suffer from absence of vigour and movement. He disdained to write down to the masses, as was then fashionable, yet managed to retain audience appeal. His delicacy of expression and mastery of style can best be seen in essays such as those collected in *Evocaciones* (1964).

See Raúl H. Castagnino, *José León Pagano, monitor del 'Dies Irae'* (1959).

PAGAZA, JOAQUÍN ARCADIO (1839–1918), b. Valle de Bravo, State of Mexico. Mexican poet and translator, who was appointed Bishop of Veracruz in 1895. Possibly the best Mexican poet before Gutiérrez Nájera and Othón (qq.v.), he translated both Virgil and Horace, modelling his style on theirs and using their bucolic and lyrical themes to often piquant effect in sonnets on the Valle de Bravo and in other landscape poems. He used the Arcadian name of 'Clearco Meonio'.

His original works included *Murmurios de la selva* (1887), the ambitious yet uninspired fragments of *María* (1890), and *Algunas trovas últimas* (1893). His *Epistolario* (San Luis Potosí, 1960) has been edited by J. A. Peñalosa.

PALACIO, MANUEL DEL (1831–1906), b. Lérida. Poet. He moved to Soria, Valladolid, Corunna, Madrid, and finally to Granada, where in 1851 he met Alarcón and Fernández y González in the literary group La Cuerda Granadina. The rapidity of his writing diminished its quality, and his satire on behalf of the liberal cause changed direction in later life. This mass of satirical writing has been forgotten due to the ephemeral nature of its targets, and much of it was in collaboration, notably with Luis Rivera, with whom he composed the lampoons *Cabezas y calabazas* (1864) and founded the satirical magazine *Gil Blas* (1864–70).

His other books include *Cien sonetos políticos*

(1870), the *leyendas* called *Veladas de otoño* (1884), and *Melodías íntimas* (1884). He was exiled to Puerto Rico in 1867, but returned the following year and was appointed to the diplomatic corps, first in Italy and subsequently in Uruguay.

In 1889, 'Clarín' claimed scornfully that Spain had only 2½ poets: Núñez de Arce, Campoamor (qq.v.), and the half – Palacio. Palacio, unaccustomed to being the butt of mockery, angrily retaliated with the pamphlet *Clarín entre dos platos* (1889).

See Palacio's *Mi vida en prosa: crónicas íntimas* (1934); and *Homenaje a Manuel del Palacio* (1932), including a contribution by Manuel Machado.

PALACIOS, PEDRO BONIFACIO (1854–1917), b. San Justo, Argentina. Argentinian poet who enjoyed a following comparable to that of his beloved Whitman. Writing as 'Almafuerte', Palacios produced a sequence of misanthropic, megalomaniac poems of titanic defiance: *Confiteor, Gimió cien veces, Vencidos* (all 1904), and *Poesías* (1916). His collected *Obras completas* were edited by A. J. Torcelli (1928). Palacios' facile, flowing style is no longer popular; his extravert personality exerts less and less appeal to younger readers.

PALACIO VALDÉS, ARMANDO (1853–1938), b. Entralgo, Asturias. Spanish novelist. He studied in Oviedo together with 'Clarín' (Leopoldo Alas, q.v.) before going to Madrid University to complete his law studies in 1870. Though he began his literary career as a critic, his taste was unsure and these superficial essays, such as *Los novelistas españoles* (1878) or *La literatura en 1881* (1882), are now forgotten. His views on realism, then a burning topic, were close to those of Valera; he understood the novel to be a work of art which should arouse the aesthetic sensibilities of the reader and resolve given data into an object of beauty. He condemned the 'groseros excesos' of the French naturalists such as Zola.

El señorito Octavio (1881) was an undistinguished début, and it was with his second novel *Marta y María* (q.v., Barcelona, 1883) that Palacio Valdés obtained widespread critical recognition. His María is a younger and lovelier Doña Perfecta (q.v.), through whom Palacio aimed to ridicule religious fanatics, 'en el fondo vanidosos y egoístas'. Palacio Valdés prefers a simple style, lacking the verbal brilliance of Pereda or the extraordinary insights of Pérez Galdós, but is at his best in creating an atmosphere of authenticity in manners and dialogue.

His gradual acceptance of the naturalistic mode reached its climax in *La espuma* (2 vols., Barcelona, 1890), with its shout of angry defiance at the corrupt aristocracy which ex-

ploits miners and their working children; and *La fe* (1892), still banned in Spain for its outspoken attack on exploitation by the Church through its official dogmas and rigid organization of national life at all levels. Meanwhile he had published *José* (1885), like Pereda's *Sotileza* (q.v.) a story of fisherfolk on the north coast of Spain; *Riverita* (2 vols., 1886) and its sequel *Maximina* (2 vols., 1887); *El cuarto poder* (2 vols., 1888), on the new power of the press; and his charming, sunny novel of Andalusia, *La hermana San Sulpicio* (q.v., 1889).

Palacio Valdés's later works were the Andalusian *costumbrista* novel *Los majos de Cádiz* (1896); the tender and humorous *La alegría del capitán Ribot* (1899) set in Valencia; and the 'poema de costumbres campesinas', *La aldea perdida* (1909). After his reconversion to practising Roman Catholicism he wrote *Tristán, o el pesimismo* (1906) and the awkward *Santa Rogelia* (1926), which seems to contradict the sensible position against religious fanaticism taken up in *Marta y María*.

His autobiographical memoirs are *La novela de un novelista* (1921) and there is a curious anti-feminist tract, *El gobierno de las mujeres* (1931). But his reputation has slipped very sharply from its position before World War I, when he was as much admired as Balzac and Tolstoy.

The *Obras completas* (28 vols., 1901–32 and 3 vols., 1925–7) are neither complete nor well edited; better are the *Obras escogidas* (1933 and later impressions), even though they omit the controversial and important novel *La fe*.

See A. Cruz Rueda, *Armando Palacio Valdés: estudio biográfico* (n.d. but 1925; 2nd edn., 1949); J. M. Roca Franquesa, 'La novela de Palacio Valdés: clasificación y analisis' in *Boletín del Instituto de Estudios Asturianos*, vol. 7 (1953), pp. 426–58; M. R. Colangeli, *Armando Palacio Valdés, romanziere* (Lecce, 1962); and M. Pascual Rodríguez, *Armando Palacio Valdés: teoría y práctica novelística* (1976).

PALAFOX Y MENDOZA, JUAN DE (c. 1601– c. 1669), b. Fitero, Navarra. Spanish autobiographer and religious writer. His *Tratados mejicanos* have been newly edited by F. Sánchez Castañer as vols. 217–8 of the BAE. One of the *tratados*, 'De la naturaleza del indio' praises the 'most useful and most faithful vassals of the Indies' and the author's clearsighted sympathy for the newly colonized peoples is reflected in the high position he attained in the Church there, as Bishop of Puebla (1639).

His prose style was over-rhetorical in the complex baroque allegory *El pastor de Nochebuena* (1644), in which a pious shepherd is accompanied by angels through realms of good and evil populated by the personifications of virtues and vices. Palafox was made a candidate for canonization by Charles III. He edited the letters of S. Teresa de Ávila (q.v.) and wrote a fascinating spiritual autobiography: *Vida interior* . . . (Barcelona, 1687). The first edition of his *Obras* (8 vols., Madrid, 1671) was superseded by a second (13 vols. in 14, Madrid, 1762).

See D. Genaro García, *D. Juan de Palafox y Mendoza* (1918).

PALAU, BARTOLOMÉ (b. 1525?), b. Burbáguena, Teruel. Playwright. His first known work is the *Farsa llamada Custodia del hombre* (Astorga, 1547; ed. Léo Rouanet, 1911), written *c.* 1541 in six-line *coplas de pie quebrado* for the Corpus Christi festival. It is in five acts or *jornadas*, and contrasts in allegorical form the paths of good and evil. Palau's *Historia de la Gloriosa Santa Orosia* (*c.* 1550?) is much more important, being the first Spanish play on a theme drawn from national history, and is in six acts or *autos*. He combined the experience of Orosia, ending with her martyrdom in Moorish captivity, with the story of La Cava, Count Julián, and Rodrigo as told in the *Crónica General*. The work has been edited by A. Fernández-Guerra in *Revista Hispano-Americana* (1882).

La farsa llamada salamantina (1552) was edited by A. Morel-Fatio in the *Bulletin Hispanique*, vol. 2 (1900). Probably written for acting by students at Salamanca, it uses some incidents and the atmosphere from Güete's *Tesorina* and the *Himenea* of Torres Naharro, as well as the division into five *jornadas*, the use of *coplas de pie quebrado*, and a comic prologue. Interestingly, the picaresque servant is here no less sordid than his 'sentimental' master.

The least valuable work of Palau is the very popular mystery play *Victoria Christi* (Saragossa, 1569), which is an imitation of Gil Vicente's immeasurably superior *Breve summario da Historia de Deos* (1527).

PALAU CATALÁ, MELCHOR (1843–1910), b. Mataró. Minor poet in both Catalan and Castilian, and literary critic. He was elected a member of the Real Academia Española in 1908.

His popular *Poesías y cantares* (1878) and *Nuevos cantares* (1890), simple in style, concise, and easy to memorize, form one aspect of his poetry; the other comprises his poems on scientific subjects, such as 'La poesía de la ciencia' in the collection *Verdades poéticas* (1879). *De Belén al Calvario* (1876) is a volume of religious verse.

PALENCIA, ALFONSO [FERNÁNDEZ] DE (1423–92), b. Osma. Humanist and satirist who was brought up in the household of Alfonso de Cartagena, and spent a period in the service of Cardinal Bessarion in Italy; his most important assignment was that of chronicler and Latin secretary to King Henry IV from 1456, after the death of Juan de Mena (q.v.). His *Gesta hispaniensia ex annalibus suorum dierum* (also known as the *Décadas*) covering the years 1440–77 has been published in part in Castilian translation by A. Paz y Melia (5 vols., 1904–9). Palencia attacks both Henry IV and Álvaro de Luna in what J. Fitzmaurice-Kelly has described as 'a tale of wrongs borne by an angry witness'. For another view of this reign, see the *Crónica* by Diego Enríquez del Castillo (q.v., 1433–1504?).

A. M. Fabié has edited as *Dos tratados* (1876) Palencia's *Guerra e batalla campal que los perros contra los lobos ouieron* written in 1456 (Seville, 1490?) and *Perfeción del triunfo militar* written in 1460 (Seville, 1490?), satires on political strife and military arrogance respectively.

Palencia's *Universal vocabulario en latín y en romance* (Seville, 1490) was superseded within a few years by the magisterial work of Nebrija (q.v.). He also produced translations: *La primera parte de Plutharco* (Seville, 1491, reprinted 2 vols., 1792) and of Josephus (Seville, 1492).

There is an excellent preface by Mario Penna to a reprint of the second of Palencia's *tratados* in vol. 116 (1959) of the BAE, but the standard work is A. Paz y Melia, *El cronista Alfonso de Palencia: su vida y sus obras* (New York, 1914), which should be supplemented by Ludwig Pfandl, 'Über A. Fernández de Palencia' in *Zeitschrift für Romanische Philologie*, vol. 55 (1935), pp. 340–60.

PALENCIA, CEFERINO (1860–1928), b. Fuente de Pedro Naharro, Cuenca. Minor playwright who took on tour in Spain and Latin America a company led by his wife, the celebrated actress María Álvarez Tubáu. A fluent enough versifier, he moralized in the manner of López de Ayala, excelling in some memorable characterization and atmosphere without ever achieving a durable play.

His works include *El guardián de la casa* (1881), *Cariños que matan* (1882), *La charra* (1884), *Currita Albornoz* (1897), *Pepita Tudó* (1901), *La nube* (1908), and *La bella Pinguito* (1915).

PALÉS MATOS, LUIS (1898–1959), b. Guayama, Puerto Rico. Poet. *Azaleas* (Guayama, 1915) is a derivative modernist collection, but in *diepalismo* he joined José I. de Diego Padró (the 'die' to Palés' 'pal') to create the first Puerto Rican *avant-garde* movement. He became celebrated for his Negro poetry, less for the transitional *Pueblo negro* (1925) than for his *Tuntún de pasa y grifería* (1937); though not himself a Negro, Palés declared through his work that the cerebral civilization of the West should be urgently regenerated by the vitality of the African oral and musical tradition, predicting the end of primitive insight and the dissolution of the Negro spirit in amorphous Americanism unless Puerto Ricans returned to their African origins. There is a useful anthology, *Poesía, 1915–1956* (1964).

See Miguel Enguídanos, *La poesía de Luis Palés* (Río Piedras, 1961).

PALLAIS, Azarías H. (1884–1954), b. León, Nicaragua. Priest, translator, and modernist poet. He was director of the Instituto Nacional de Occidente (a secondary school) 1929–35 and 1937–8, then parish priest of Corinto from 1938. He was often harassed for his open denunciation of exploitation. He said in 1938, with some justice, that he had been 'durante 25 años . . . orientador de las letras nicaragüenses'.

Pallais translated Homer, Horace, Goethe, and Jammes. His own works include *A la sombra del agua* (León, 1917), *Espumas y estrellas* (León, 1918), *Caminos* (León, 1921), *El libro de las palabras evangelizadas* (León, 1923), *Bello tono menor* (León, 1928), *Hesperia* (León, 1936), *Glosas* (León, 1940), and *Piraterías: caminos que están por debajo de la historia* (Madrid, 1951). There is a useful *Antología* (San Salvador, 1963).

See Stefan Baciu, *Poesia, vida e morte de Azarías H. Pallais* (Rio de Janeiro, 1956).

PALMA, Alonso, b. Toledo? Historian. Little is known of 'Bachiller' Palma beyond the fact that he studied at Salamanca. His history of Castile 1385–1478 *Divina retribución sobre la caída de España en tiempo del noble rey Don Juan el Primero* is intended for a popular rather than a learned audience, and was edited by J. M. Escudero de la Peña for the Sociedad de Bibliófilos Españoles (1879).

PALMA, Padre Luis de la (1560–1641), b. Toledo. Jesuit ascetic writer and preacher who taught philosophy and theology at Murcia University. Though he wrote much, he published, but unwillingly, only at the instruction of the Vicar-General of the Jesuits, Muzio Vitelleschi.

His works, in pure and stylish Castilian, include *Historia de la Sagrada Pasión, sacada de los quatro Evangelios* (Alcalá, 1624), *Camino espiritual de la manera que lo enseñaba el bienaventurado Padre San Ignacio de Loyola en el libro de los Exercicios* (Alcalá, 1625), *Práctica y breve declaración del camino espiritual* (1629), and a number of others which were not published in his lifetime but are edited in the BAE, vols. 144, 145, and 160 (1961–3).

See F. X. Rodríguez Molero, 'Mística y estilo de la "Historia de la Santa [*sic*] Pasión" del Padre la Palma' in *Revista de Espiritualidad*, vol. 3 (1944), pp. 295–331.

PALMA, Ricardo (1833–1919), b. Lima. Peruvian writer who created a new literary genre, the *tradición*, beginning from a kernel of fact or superstition and weaving around it a semi-fantastic story running to 3 to 5 pages. His *Tradiciones peruanas* (q.v., 1st ser., 1872) have often been imitated, but always unsuccessfully, for they contain barbed humour, anti-clerical satire, the picaresque, and the witty mingled in a magnificently inimitable style. As a liberal, Palma was exiled to Chile 1860–2 but returned to a position of some influence, including that of secretary to President Balta.

After the Pacific War with Chile he was appointed in 1884 Director of the National Library, which the Chileans had ransacked, and became known as 'el bibliotecario mendigo' for his success in begging books from correspondents all over the world. After great achievements in stockbuilding, he was removed for political reasons in 1912.

Though universally admired for *Tradiciones peruanas*, he published many other books, including *Poesías* (1855); *Anales de la Inquisición de Lima* (1863); *Armonías* (1865); *Recuerdos de España* (1897), on his visit to Spain in 1892; *Anales del Cusco* (1901); and *Papeletas lexicográficas* (1903), with 2,700 words lacking in the dictionary.

His poetry is best read in the *Poesías* (1887) and complementary *Poesías olvidadas* (1963) collected by Alberto Tauro. His daughter Angélica Palma (1878–1935) wrote novels and his biography *Ricardo Palma, el tradicionista* (1933).

Palma's letters have been published in the *Epistolario* (2 vols., 1949), and *Cartas inéditas* (1964).

See Guillermo Feliú Cruz, *En torno a Ricardo Palma* (2 vols., Santiago de Chile, 1933), of which the second volume is a critical bibliography, since supplemented by *Bibliografía* by Raúl Porras Barrenechea (1952); Alessandro Martinengo, *Lo stile di Ricardo Palma* (Padua, 1962); José Miguel Oviedo, *Genio y figura de Ricardo Palma* and *Ricardo Palma* (Buenos Aires, 1965 and 1968); and the critical anthology edited by Ángel Flores, *Aproximaciones a Ricardo Palma* (1973).

Palmerín cycle, a series of *libros de caballería* almost as well known as the Amadís cycle (see AMADÍS DE GAULA). It began with a bad imitation of *Amadís* entitled *El libro del famoso y muy esforçado cavallero Palmerín de Oliva* (Salamanca, 1511), ascribable either to an unnamed woman or to a certain Francisco Vázquez. The same writer is believed responsible for the second book in the cycle, *Primaleón* (Salamanca, 1512), the tale of Polendos and Primaleón, sons of Palmerín, and of Don Duardos, Prince of England. It is from this work that Gil Vicente (q.v.) derived the germ of his important *Dom Duardos*. The third book in the series is the anonymous *Crónica del muy valiente y esforçado caballero Platir, hijo del emperador Primaleón* (1530).

The last work in the cycle has a real significance and literary interest, though rather more in the Portuguese original, written *c.* 1544 by Francisco de Morães Cabral (1500?–1572) and published at Évora in 1567, than in the Spanish translation by Luis Hurtado published as *Palmerín de Inglaterra* (Toledo, 1547), which received praise as 'a thing unique' by Cervantes in *Don Quijote*.

Morães Cabral's work passed through numerous editions, and was translated from the Spanish into French as early as 1553, from the French into Italian in the same year, and into English in 1602.

PALMIRENO, JUAN LORENZO (1514?–1580), b. Alcañiz, Teruel. Erasmian humanist who taught grammar and Greek in the universities of Saragossa and Valencia. He wrote a number of books in Latin and Spanish, including the *Selva de vocablos y frases de medidas y monedas* (Valencia, 1563), *Rhetorica* (2 vols., Valencia, 1564–5), *El estudioso de la aldea* (Valencia, 1568), *Vocabulario del humanista* (Valencia, 1569), *El estudioso cortesano* (Valencia, 1573), and *Campi eloquentiae* (Valencia, 1574).

See C. Lynn, 'Juan Lorenzo Palmireno, Spanish humanist', in *Hispania*, vol. 12 (1929), pp. 243–58.

Pamphilus, the *Liber Pamphili*, also called *De amore*, is a 12th- or 13th-c. Spanish drama, long erroneously attributed to Ovid, surviving in a unique MS. which has been edited by Adolfo Bonilla y San Martín (1917). It was paraphrased as the Doña Endrina episode by Juan Ruiz (q.v.), Archpriest of Hita, in stanzas 555–865 of the *Libro de buen amor* (q.v.).

PANE, IGNACIO ALBERTO (1880–1920), b. Asunción. Paraguayan poet and literary critic. He reacted against the modernism of Darío (q.v.) in his collections of verse *Poesías* (1900) and *Beatriz* (1902). *Poesías paraguayas* (1904) is an anthology of the nation's best verse compiled by Pane, who also wrote in Guaraní.

PANERO, LEOPOLDO (1909–62), b. Astorga. Poet associated with the school of Vivanco and Rosales, broadly satisfied with the Franco regime and leaning towards religious mysticism and conventional forms. Panero studied at Cambridge, Tours, and Poitiers, obtaining a degree in law. His brother Juan (1908–37) was also a poet.

In *La estancia vacía* (1944) he sees God as a refuge, and man as the helpless refugee. His collection *Escrito a cada instante* (1949) won the Fastenrath Prize: it too confronts man and God, involving landscape pantheistically and the prevailing themes of religion and death. Neruda's *Canto general* (1950) formed the pretext for Panero's *Canto personal*. *Carta perdida a Pablo Neruda* (1953), replying to that section of the Chilean's great poem which refers to the Spanish Civil War, but suffering by the comparison. The volume of *Poesías* (1963) is fairly complete.

See Dámaso Alonso, *Poetas españoles contemporáneos* (1952), pp. 333–58; Eileen Connolly, *Leopoldo Panero: la poesía de la esperanza* (1969), the latter omitting the *Canto personal* from consideration; and César Aller, *La poesía personal de Leopoldo Panero* (Pamplona, 1976).

Panza, Sancho, a farm labourer of La Mancha who was finally persuaded by the knight in *Don Quijote de la Mancha* by Miguel de Cervantes (qq.v.) to sally forth as a squire with him, on an ass, with the promise of being appointed governor of an island if Don Quijote managed to conquer one by force of arms. 'Con estas promesas y otras tales, Sancho Panza, que así se llamaba el labrador, dejó su mujer y hijos y asentó por escudero de su vecino' (II, ch. 32).

His wife's name was Teresa. Short, stout, coarse, and illiterate, Sancho was intended at first as Quijote's contrary and complement, but in the course of the novel Cervantes' sympathy with his shrewd peasant increases and the mutual dependence of Sancho and Quijote deepens to some degree of understanding and even mutual influence.

Papeles de Son Armadans, a monthly literary journal founded in 1956 and edited by Camilo José Cela Trulock (q.v.) and still published from La Bonanova, Palma de Mallorca. Its strength has lain in poetry and in special issues on individual writers (such as nos. 185–6 on Miguel Ángel Asturias, q.v.).

Papel Periódico Ilustrado, El, the leading Colombian magazine of its time, founded by Alberto Urdaneta in 1881. It counted among its most distinguished contributors Silva, Torres, and Ismael Enrique Arciniegas, and has been described by J. J. Ortega as 'lujo y ornamento de toda biblioteca colombiana'. It ceased publication in 1888.

Paradox, Silvestre, the hero of two of the three novels in *La vida fantástica* (q.v.), a trilogy by Pío Baroja y Nessi (q.v.).

Paradox, rey (1906), the third novel in the trilogy *La vida fantástica* by Pío Baroja y Nessi (qq.v.).

PÁRAMO, JEREMÍAS, a pseudonym of José María Samper (q.v.).

PARAVICINO, *Fray* HORTENSIO FÉLIX (1580–1633), b. Madrid. Orator and poet. Trinitarian *definidor general* (chairman of governing committee) who travelled much in the course of his duties, especially throughout Spain, Flanders, France, and parts of Italy. He was court preacher to Philip III and Philip IV, and aimed in his sermons to cultivate the same textual richness in style and concept as did Góngora (q.v.), whom he greatly admired. 'He deseado pensar algo de nuevo', he declared, and his sermons were not only full of outward pomp and majesty, but contained cleverly-expressed metaphor and simile. Clearly, his ornate rhetoric was equally easy to parody and to imitate sincerely. Mayáns y Síscar attacked Paravicino's imitators in 1725, but it was left to Padre Isla (q.v.) in his *Fray Gerundio de Campazas* (2 vols., 1758–70) to deflate the style beyond rescue.

Paravicino's sermons were eagerly sought by his contemporaries and frequently reprinted; the most popular included *Sermón de S. Teresa* (1625) and *Sermón de la soledad* (1626).

Posthumous collections were *Oraciones evangélicas de Adviento y Cuaresma* (1636), *Oraciones evangélicas, o discursos panegíricos y morales* (1638), *Oraciones evangélicas . . . en las festividades de Christo Nuestro Señor y su Santísima Madre . . .* (1640), and the collected verse, *Obras póstumas divinas y humanas* (1641) published under the name, 'Félix de Arteaga'.

See Emilio Alarcos, 'Los sermones de Paravicino' in *Revista de Filología Española*, vol. 24 (1937), pp. 162–97 and 249–319.

PARDO, EL, a pen-name used by Estanislao del Campo (q.v.).

PARDO BAZÁN, EMILIA (1851–1921), b. Corunna. Spanish short-story writer and novelist who was created Condesa (Countess) for her literary achievements. She married and moved to Madrid in 1868, but her husband was scandalized by the reputation she made with her naturalistic novels and they later separated. Her earliest literary ideal was Feijóo, a feminist, and she never forgot her campaign to advance female emancipation throughout her distinguished career. She wrote a semi-autobiographical novel

of a medical student, *Pascual López* (1879); a biography of St. Francis (1882); various volumes of literary essays; and a feeble book of poems on the birth of her first child, before causing a sensation in 1883 with *La tribuna*, the first serious contemporary Spanish novel of urban working-class life, set in a Corunna tobacco factory which she studied at first hand over a period of two months, a method then common in France but almost unprecedented in Spain. *La cuestión palpitante* (q.v., 1883) is a provocative defence of realism which criticizes the idealists, discusses the methods of Zola in largely favourable but unfair terms, and concludes by pointing to the 'carácter castizo y propio' of Spanish literature which she claims has always been 'más realista que otra cosa'. She championed the fictional methods of Pérez Galdós and Pereda (qq.v.). Zola repudiated her biased criticism, and Valera (q.v.) published a reply called *Apuntes sobre el arte de escribir novelas* (1886–7), in which he took up the cause of Campoamor, Alarcón, and himself, all targets of the future Countess.

Pardo Bazán's next novels were *El cisne de Vilamorta* (1885), an insubstantial story of the immature poet Segundo, over whom the ill-favoured teacher Leocadia improbably commits suicide; the splendid *Los Pazos de Ulloa* (q.v., 1886) and its sequel *La madre naturaleza* (1887). She set *Insolación* and *Morriña* (both 1889) in Madrid, exploring human sexuality but despite Galdós's attempts to interest her in working-class milieux, limiting her empathy to the well-to-do. During 1891–3 she produced a mass of excellent essays and short stories in the *Nuevo Teatro Crítico* and wrote more than 500 stories in an impressive range of style and theme. She is probably the most important Spanish 19th-c. short-story writer and only the excellence of the novel *Los Pazos de Ulloa* has obscured her other achievements.

Her later novels are neglected because they are unexpected: the religious idealism of *Una cristiana* and *La prueba* (both 1890), the hangman's story of *La piedra angular* (1891); *Doña Milagros* (1894); *Memorias de un solterón* (1896); the study of an artist seeking immortality, *La quimera* (1905), which Unamuno noted as an example of the spirit of '98; and *La sirena negra* (1908), whose hero Gaspar foreshadows 'Antonio Azorín' but possesses a religious serenity denied to members of the Generation of '98.

The *Obras completas* (41 vols., 1891–1912) contain most of her works, but the Aguilar edition (3 vols., 1947–73) includes only the novels, and some 560 of the short stories. The *Apuntes autobiográficos* appeared in the 1st edition of *Los Pazos de Ulloa* but in no other.

The best biography (and the least unsatisfactory bibliography) to date is Carmen Bravo-

Villasante, *Vida y obra de Emilia Pardo Bazán* (n.d. but 1962). Bravo-Villasante has also edited Pardo Bazán's *Cartas a Galdós* (1975).

See also Robert E. Osborne, *Emilia Pardo Bazán: su vida y sus obras* (Mexico City, 1964), and Walter T. Pattison, *Emilia Pardo Bazán* (New York, 1971) in Twayne's World Authors series.

PARDO DE FIGUEROA, MARIANO (1828–1918), b. Medina Sidonia, Cádiz. Antiquarian writing as 'Dr. Thebussem', the 'doctor' referring to a degree in civil and canon law. He corresponded with many writers of the time and the *Epistolario del Dr Thebussen [sic] y Rodríguez Marín (1883–1917) con breves notas de éste último* (1942) sheds considerable light on the period. Essays and books flowed from his pen on cookery (*La mesa moderna*, 1883), philately, heraldry, genealogy, and philology. The *Segunda ración de artículos* (1894) was one of five such miscellanea, occasionally musty in its style and bookishness, but never less than good-humoured and often illuminating.

See Monner y Sanz, 'El Doctor Thebussem' in *Nosotros* (1918).

PARDO GARCÍA, GERMÁN (1902–) b. Ibagué. Colombian poet who lived for some years in Central America. His *30 años de labor del poeta colombiano Germán Pardo García* (Mexico City, 1961) is an anthology of his voluminous writing from *Voluntad* (1930) to *Osiris preludial* (Mexico City, 1960); it was followed by *Los ángeles de vidrio* and *El cosmonauta* (both Mexico City, 1962), *El defensor* (Mexico City, 1964), *Elegía italiana* (Mexico City, 1966), and *Himnos del hierofante* (Mexico City, n.d. but 1969).

PARDO Y ALIAGA, FELIPE (1806–69), b. Lima. Peruvian poet and playwright who studied in Spain at the Colegio de San Mateo under Alberto Lista (q.v.), and was a friend of Ventura de la Vega and Espronceda (qq.v.). He returned to Peru in 1828 and worked in the Santiago de Chile embassy from 1835, shortly after which he was exiled, returning to Lima in 1840. In his last years he was blind and paralysed. He founded the first satirical review of Peru, *El Espejo de Mi Tierra*, in 1840, and was considered by Ventura García Calderón as 'el más famoso de nuestros humoristas', introducing satire not only into his articles and poems, but also into his plays.

His works include three plays: *Frutos de la educación* (1830, reprinted in 1954); *Don Leocadio* and *Una huérfana en Chorrillos* (both 1833); the satirical *letrillas Meditaciones poéticas por M. Alphonse Chunga, bachiller en sagrados cánones en la Universidad de Chuquisaca y membre de l'Institut de Paris* (1835) against Santa Cruz; *Poesías y escritos*

en prosa (Paris, 1869); and *Poesías* (1898). Luis Monguió's edition of Pardo's *Poesías* (Berkeley, 1973) reprints the 57 poems of the 1869 edition with a further 84. Alberto Tauro has collected anonymous sonnets, *letrillas*, and epigrams published in 1834–5 as *La nariz* (1957).

Pardo's brother José Pardo y Aliaga (1820–73) also published a number of poems, but they remain uncollected.

Roselina Cachay Díaz's biobibliography of Pardo appeared in the *Boletín de la Biblioteca Nacional* (Lima), vol. 23, nos. 45-48 (1968), pp. 3-27.

See J. Cornejo Polar, *Dos ensayos sobre Pardo y Aliaga* (1967).

Paredes oyen, Las, a three-act play by Juan Ruiz de Alarcón y Mendoza (q.v.) first performed in 1617 and published in the *Parte primera de las comedias* (1629).

The young widow Doña Ana is courted by the poor, deformed, but honourable Juan, and the false slanderer Mendo. She overhears Juan's praise of her to the Duke and Mendo's detraction of her qualities. Ana spurns the vicious Mendo, who swears revenge and plans to ambush her on the Alcalá road. Juan and the Duke discover the plot and manage to save Ana, who marries Juan.

Ruiz de Alarcón may have taken the plot from *El infamador* by Juan de la Cueva (q.v.) and Lope de Vega's *El triunfo del buen hablar*. The deformity of the virtuous Juan is an autobiographical reflection of the author's pigeon chest and hunched back.

See the introduction and edition by A. Reyes in Clásicos Castellanos (*Teatro*, 1918), and by B. Varela Jácome in Colección Libro Clásico (*La verdad sospechosa . . .*, Barcelona, 1969); and J. Frutos Gómez de las Cortinas, 'La génesis de "Las paredes oyen" de Ruiz de Alarcón' in *Revista de Filología Española*, vol. 35 (1951), pp. 92-105.

PAREJA DIEZCANSECO, ALFREDO (1908–), b. Guayaquil. Ecuadorian novelist and essayist. Compelled from early youth to earn a living, Pareja has distilled his varied experiences into a series of novels beginning with *La muelle* (1933), deriving from his years as a cabin boy in the merchant navy, and continuing with *La Beldaca*, about Ecuador's inland waterways, *Baldomera* (q.v., 1938), *Hechos y hazañas de don Balón de Baba y su amigo don Inocente Cruz* (1939) inspired by Daudet's Tartarin, *Hombres sin tiempo* (Buenos Aires, 1941), and *Las tres ratas* (1944). The prison novel *Hombres sin tiempo* was influenced by Mann, on whom Pareja has written in *Thomas Mann y el nuevo humanismo* (1956). Pareja's *Breve historia del Ecuador* (Mexico

City, 1946) was revised and enlarged for its second edition (2 vols., Quito, 1958). *Los nuevos años* is a sequence of social-historical novels of Ecuador during the last fifty years, and so far three volumes have appeared: *La advertencia* (1956), *El aire y los recuerdos* (1959), and *Los poderosos omnímodos* (1964).

PARIS, GASTON (1839–1903), French medievalist who founded the review *Romania* in 1872 and taught medieval French literature at the Sorbonne.

His *Légendes du moyen âge* (1903) is of great value to Hispanists. The 'Paris' epic theory proposes a predominant French influence for the Spanish minstrels who created the Spanish Romance epic tradition, and a metre of 14-syllable alexandrines. The Menéndez Pidal theory prefers a dominant Germanic influence, and a metre of 16-syllable lines in two hemistichs. The Bédier theory propounds a common Latin origin, while the Ribera theory suggests an dominant Arab-Andalusian substratum.

See J. Bédier, *Bibliographie des travaux de Gaston Paris* (1905).

PARKER, ALEXANDER A. (1908–), British Hispanist who has specialized in Golden Age drama and the Spanish picaresque novel in its European context. He was head of the Department of Spanish in Aberdeen University 1939–53 and subsequently held posts in other British and American universities.

His first important work was *The allegorical drama of Calderón* (Oxford, 1943; reprinted Oxford, 1968), pursuing these studies in 'The chronology of Calderón's *autos sacramentales* from 1647' (*Hispanic Review*, vol. 37 (1969), pp. 164–88) and elsewhere. *The approach to the Spanish drama of the Golden Age* (London, 1957) is extraordinarily fresh and suggestive, despite its brevity.

Parker's other book-length study is *Literature and the delinquent: the picaresque novel in Spain and in Europe, 1599–1753* (Edinburgh, 1967).

Pármeno, Calisto's manservant in *La Celestina* (q.v.) and the pseudonym of José López Pinillos (q.v.).

Parnaso Salmantino, the name of a group of poets who met from 1774 at Salamanca in the cell of the Augustinian priest Diego Tadeo González (q.v.).

The most significant among them were Delio (Fray Diego), Batilo (Juan Meléndez Valdés, q.v.), Arcadio (José Iglesias de la Casa, q.v.), Liseno (Fray Juan Fernández de Rojas, q.v.), and Andrenio (Fray Andrés del Corral).

The Parnaso succeeded the Academia Cadálsica and preceded the Arcadia Agustiniana (qq.v.); the three closely-connected groups were collectively known as the first Salamanca School.

Parnassianism, a French poetic movement of the 1860s and 1870s representing the scientific and positivist spirit of the age in reaction to Romanticism (see ROMANTICISMO).

The Parnassians, who were Leconte de Lisle, Sully Prudhomme, and the Cuban poet José María de Hérédia (q.v.), took their name from a publication called *Le Parnasse Contemporain* (1866). This was followed by a second series prepared in 1869 but published in 1871. The third series (1876) lost much of the first series' character.

The influence of the *movimiento parnasiano* in Spain and Latin America appeared principally in the works of Rubén Darío and Salvador Rueda (qq.v.), though many poets not specifically known as Parnassians occasionally wrote in this vein, among them Manuel Machado, Villaespesa, Lugones, Santos Chocano, Othón, Urbina, Guillermo Valencia, and Gutiérrez Nájera (qq.v.), all associated with modernism in poetry, deriving partly from Romanticism and partly from the perfection of form required by Parnassianism.

The movement was virtually dead by 1905.

Parnassus, Mount, in Greece, a few miles north of Delphi, was connected with the worship of Apollo and the Muses, and thus 'Parnassus' applies by extension to the collectivity of a nation's poets and their writings. Cervantes (q.v.), in his verse *Viage del Parnaso* (1614), based on the poem of the same title by Cesare Caporali, describes the poets known to him in an imaginary ascent of Parnassus. Calderón's *El sacro Parnaso* is an auto sacramental. Quevedo's *Parnaso Español* (2 vols., 1648–70) is an incomplete collection of his own poetry. Castillo Solórzano (q.v.) published his satirical and other light verse as *Donayres del Parnaso* (2 vols., 1624–5).

See also PARNASSIANISM and PARNASO SALMANTINO.

PARRA, NICANOR (1914–), b. Chillán. Chilean poet, who in 1933 entered the Instituto Pedagógico of Chile University and qualified as a teacher of mathematics and physics in 1938. Since 1952 he has been a professor of theoretical physics. His first book was *Cancionero sin nombre* (1937) and he achieved recognition with his second, *Poemas y antipoemas* (1954). He has defined the 'anti-poem' as a traditional poem enriched by surrealist sap, but Parra's Marxist stance and casual, often cynical methods are more complex than that, and his influence in Chilean poetry has been second only to that of Neruda (q.v.), with whom he collaborated in a series of prose *Discursos* (1962). His later poetry has appeared in *La cueca larga* (1958; 'cueca' is a Chilean dance-genre), *Versos de salón* (1962), the unsatisfactory, uninspired *Canciones rusas* (1967), and *Emergency poems* (New York, 1972).

While others write in French, he says (meaning that they are 'refined'), Parra writes in Araucanian and Latin, 'grating verses' that are original. For Parra, an 'anti-poet' is that *persona non grata* who reserves the right to say what he wants to say; yet he is not a political revolutionary (even if his most famous poem, *El pequeño burgués,* sarcastically attacks middle class pretensions): he proclaims himself to be the Individual.

Obra gruesa (1969) is an interim collected works which has been followed by *Poemas* (Havana, 1969) and *Los profesores* (New York, 1971).

Parra has been translated by Jorge Elliott (*Antipoems*, New York, 1960) and by several other hands in *Poems and antipoems* (New York, 1967; abridged for the Cape Editions selection, London, 1968).

See Mercedes Rein, *Nicanor Parra y la antipoesía* (Montevideo, 1970); Hugo Montes and Mario Rodríguez, *Nicanor Parra y la poesía de lo cotidiano* (1970; 2nd edn., 1974); and Ángel Flores (ed.), *Aproximaciones a Nicanor Parra* (Barcelona, 1973).

PARRA, TERESA DE LA (1891–1936), b. Paris. Venezuelan novelist baptized Ana Teresa Sanojo Parra, who later changed her name. Of a wealthy family, she went to Venezuela in adolescence, recording her years there in the continuous autobiographical narrative separately published in the immensely popular *Diario de una señorita que se fastidia* (*La lectura semanal*, 1922); in *Ifigenia. Diario de una señorita que escribió porque se aburría* (Paris, 1924); and in its sequel *Memorias de mamá Blanca* (Paris, 1929; trans. by Harriet de Onís as *Mama Blanca's souvenirs*, Washington, 1959).

Ifigenia is in the form of a long letter. María Eugenia is a young Venezuelan girl who returns from Paris at the age of 18 to find herself 'up for auction to the highest bidder' as a refined and beautiful object. Her friend's marriage has collapsed and she herself falls in love with a married man. A victim no less than her Greek antecedent of the mores of her society, the heroine is a piquant demonstration of the Hispano-Arab attitude to women.

Parra herself never married, though she was much sought after by the Ecuadorian writer Gonzalo Zaldumbide and others. Her last years were spent in distress, suffering from lung complaints, in Switzerland and the Spanish mountain resorts. Her last book was a subtle, self-assured autobiography ostensibly of an old lady feeding off her recollections.

She set a new standard for women's fiction in Latin America, combining a firm regard for her native land with a discreet awareness of French style. Her successors in Venezuela include Ada Pérez Guevara, Trina Larralde, Ana Julia Rojas, and Antonia Palacios. As José Antonio Galaos wrote in *Cuadernos Hispanoamericanos* (1962), Parra was the first 'en descubrir en la mujer criolla una profundidad que va más allá de las violentas turbias pasiones, y quien introdujo en su tierra el refinado espíritu parisiense y la morosidad psicológica, en la que es maestra'.

Parra's *Obras completas* (1965) have been edited by Carlos García Prada.

Her letters have been edited by M. Picón Salas (*Cartas,* 1951) and by Rafael Carías (*Epistolario íntimo,* 1953).

See Ramón Díaz Sánchez, *Teresa de la Parra: clave para una interpretación* (1954; reprinted in part in the *Obras completas* cited above).

Pasajero, see PASSAGERO.

PASAMONTE, JERÓNIMO DE (d. after 1604), autobiographer, of Aragonese origin, Pasamonte fought at Lepanto (1571) and at Tunis (1573), and was a captive of the Moors 1574–92, and on his return to Spain published a lively and spirited account of his experiences, *Vida y trabajos,* edited by R. Foulché-Delbosc in *Revue Hispanique,* vol. 55 (1922) and again in vol. 90 (1956) of the BAE.

PASO, ALFONSO (1926–), b. Madrid. Prolific minor playwright. He began by collaborating with his father, Antonio Paso (q.v.), in light comedies, but then branched out, 'concediendo más y más', in the words of Francisco Ruiz Ramón, 'víctima ya de su público, aunque víctima culpable'. Some thirty of his plays were produced in the period 1953–60 alone, including *Una bomba llamada Abelardo* (1953). Debilitated artistically by the alleged mediocrity of the theatre-going public, Paso has both sought and found wide popularity by means of such plays as *La corbata* (1963), an extended piece of flattery of the middle classes. Up to 1971 he had had no fewer than 160 plays produced.

See Alfredo Marqueríe, *Alfonso Paso y su teatro* (1960); and an interview with A. C. Isasi Angulo in *Bulletin Hispanique,* vol. 74 (1972), pp. 559–75.

PASO, ANTONIO (1870–1958), b. Granada. Prolific minor playwright who began life as a journalist and wrote more than two hundred works for the Spanish stage, often in collaboration with Arniches, Abati, Muñoz Seca, his son Alfonso (q.v.), or others.

Among his popular comedies, *sainetes*, and *zarzuelas* are *El infierno*, *El arte de ser bonita*, *El asombro de Damasco*, *Nieves de la Sierra*, and *La bendición de Dios*.

Paso honroso defendido por el excelente cauallero Suero de Quiñones, Libro del, see RODRÍGUEZ DE LENA, Pedro.

Pasos ('incidents'), single dramatic scenes. The term was used as a synonym for *entremeses* (q.v.) by Joan Timoneda in his collection of *entremeses* entitled *Turiana* (Valencia, 1565). Lope de Rueda (q.v.) wrote thirteen *pasos*, if we exclude the dubiously attributed *Farsa del sordo*. The best are *Las aceitunas* (1548), *La carátula* (1545), and *El convidado* (1546). The genre depends for its effect on humour, clever characterization of a few characters deriving from the stereotypes of the Italian *commedia dell'arte*, a simple plot, and speed of repartee and development. The *bobo* ('clown') of the *pasos* becomes the *gracioso* ('wit') of the later *entremeses*.

Pasos perdidos, Los (Mexico City, 1953), a novel by the Cuban Alejo Carpentier (q.v.), which has been translated by H. de Onís as *The lost steps* (London, 1956).

Its major theme is the contrast between cultured but decadent Europe (represented by the recurring motif of Beethoven's Ninth Symphony); the derivative American capital (such as Caracas) with its nostalgia for Paris; and the primitive life of the jungle. The novel was based on a journey that Carpentier made in Venezuela and takes the form of a journey to find primitive musical instruments for a museum. A secondary theme is the duty of the Latin-American artist to reveal the true and complex nature of his own continent.

The narrator, a composer living in New York but of Latin-American extraction, is accompanied by Mouche, his French mistress, and tries during the course of the journey to find his cultural identity.

The composer is too intellectual to remain in the jungle and goes back, with some misgivings, to New York. Later he attempts to rediscover his lost Eden, but the stone-age tribe has disappeared in a natural catastrophe. The narrator-composer is disoriented: even his dreams are now shattered.

Like many Latin-American novels of the traditional mould, *Los pasos perdidos* is unconcerned with individual psychology, but deals in

types and symbols; dialogue is slight and it is the land that dominates the work.

The novel was written in Batista's reactionary, claustrophobic period in Cuba, and reflects Carpentier's frustration.

See J. Sánchez Brudy, *La temática novelística de Alejo Carpentier* (Miami, 1969).

Passagero. Advertencias utilíssimas a la vida humana, El (1617), a series of dialogues in the manner of Rojas Villandrando's *Viaje entretenido* (q.v.) between the author, Cristóbal Suárez de Figueroa, a goldsmith, a soldier, and a graduate in arts and theology (probably Pedro Torres Rámila, q.v.). The dialogues, divided into chapters called *alivios*, or rests by the wayside, are set on the road from Madrid to Barcelona, where the four companions are going to embark for Italy. The book is a copious source of information about life in Spain and Italy, excelling in descriptions of places, such as Milan and Madrid. Its satirical targets include hypocrisy, *culterano* poetry, contemporary drama, and pretensions to *hidalguía* (nobility). The author claimed to bring readers to *desengaño* (a sharp sense of reality) through his work. *Alivio III* is devoted to actors and the stage, no. IV to the various styles of preaching, no. V to women and marriage, nos. VI–VIII to Suárez's autobiography, and nos. IX–X to the state of Spain. The author's malice (due partly to his parents' neglect of him for his sickly younger brother) is turned against Cervantes, Alarcón, Lope de Vega, Quevedo (qq.v.), and many other writers. *El passagero* is available in two modern editions: that of R. Selden Rose in the Sociedad de Bibliófilos Españoles (1914) and that of F. Rodríguez Marín (1916).

PASTOR, ANTONIO RICARDO (1894–), essayist and banker. Educated at Balliol College, Oxford, Madrid, and Munich, Pastor taught Spanish at Oxford (1920–1), King's College, London (1921–30), and at London University (1930–45). He founded the Instituto de España in London and the Fundación Pastor de Estudios Clásicos in Madrid. He was chairman of the Banco Pastor.

Among his publications were *Un embajador de España en la escena inglesa* (1925) on Count Gondomar; *Spanish chivalry* (1928); *The idea of Robinson Crusoe* (1929); *Aspects of the Spanish Renaissance* (1932); *Breve historia del hispanismo inglés* (1948), less complete than J. C. J. Metford's *British contributions to Spanish and Spanish-American studies* (London, 1950), *Introducción a Toynbee* (1952), and *Cicerón perseguido* (1961).

Pastoral Novel, The. The Spanish genre had Castilian, Galician, and Portuguese antecedents (*serranillas* by the Marqués de Santillana and Juan Ruiz, qq.v.; *églogas* by Encina, Gil Vicente, and Lucas Fernández, qq.v.) but its vogue began with the Castilian translation in 1549 of *Arcadia* (1504) by the Italian novelist Sannazaro, which consists of pastoral scenes and fragmentary tales interspersed with poetry. Feliciano de Silva (q.v.), who knew the Italian original, introduced a pastoral element into both *Amadís de Grecia* (1530) and its sequel *Don Florisel de Niquea* (1532–51), and Torquemada included a pastoral episode (the seventh) in his *Coloquios satíricos* (1553).

The increasing interest in pastoral fiction (and to a lesser degree in pastoral poetry) may reflect a mystical attitude to Nature spread by the 15th-c. Italian revival of neo-Platonism. Nature as a manifestation of cosmic love was taken by pastoral novelists as an appropriate setting for human love between man (seen in Arcadia as a shepherd) and woman (a shepherdess). Major novels exemplifying this tendency include *Los siete libros de la Diana* (Valencia, 1559?) by Jorge Montemayor (q.v.); its important sequel *Diana enamorada* (Valencia, 1564) by Gaspar Gil Polo (q.v.); *La Galatea* (Alcalá, 1585) by Cervantes (q.v.); and *Arcadia* (1598) by Lope de Vega (q.v.).

Many of the pastoral novels are *à clef*; contemporaries were expected to divine which friends or patrons of the author were represented by the pastoral lovers. All the lovers are usually chaste; those who are not may be ridiculed or even punished for their transgression. Weaknesses of the genre include the artificiality of the descriptions of the countryside (often unfamiliar to the courtly authors) and the stereotype characterization enforced, like the limited plot possibilities, by the pastoral convention itself.

The pastoral soon exhausted its potential; among the last novels to be written were *El prado de Valencia* (Valencia, 1600) by Gaspar Mercader (q.v.), *Siglo de oro en las selvas de Erífile* (1608) by Bernardo de Balbuena (q.v.), and *Los pastores del Betis* (Trani, 1633) by Gonzalo de Saavedra (q.v.).

See Juan Bautista Avalle-Arce, *La novela pastoril española* (1959).

PASTOR DÍAZ, NICOMEDES (1811–63), b. Lugo. Poet and autobiographical novelist. His melancholy *Poesías* (1840) are the work of an adroit versifier without genuine inspiration. His readable and careful autobiographical novel *De Villahermosa a la China: coloquios íntimos* (1858) was received badly by critics and public alike, and this apparently unexpected failure so embittered him that he wrote nothing more, entering politics and eventually becoming Rector of Madrid University. A. Ferrer del

Río's edition of Pastor Díaz's *Obras* (6 vols., 1866–8) is being superseded by J. M. Castro y Calvo's edition of the *Obras completas* (1969–) in BAE, vols. 227, 228, and 241.

See J. del Valle Moré, *Pastor Díaz: su vida y sus obras* (Havana, 1911).

Pastorelas (French: *pastourelles*, 'pastoral poems'), poetic encounters between a man of rank and a shepherdess, deriving from 12th-c. Provençal troubadour verse. Strictly a *cantiga de amor*, since the man speaks of his love before the girl replies, the *pastorela* seems to have been considered by the poets themselves as a subgroup of the *cantiga de amigo* genre, which expresses the love of women for men. The Galician-Portuguese *pastorela* generally does in fact use the encounter as a pretext for a shepherdess' song of her love, as in the *pastorela* by Ayras Nunez, no. 869 in the Colocci-Brancuti song-book, edited by E. P. and J. P. Machado, *Cancioneiro da Biblioteca Nacional* (8 vols., Lisbon, 1949–64). Other examples are to be found in C. Michaëlis de Vasconcellos, *Cancioneiro da Ajuda* (2 vols., Halle, 1904). The genre is an antecedent of the *serranillas* (q.v.) or *cantigas de serrana*.

See Mia I. Gerhardt, *La pastorale* (Assen, 1950).

Pastores de Belén, prosas y versos divinos, Los (Lérida, 1612), by Lope de Vega (q.v.), a pastoral novel written in 1611 *a lo divino*, that is to say, in Christian terms, to follow his pastoral novel *Arcadia* (q.v.). It was dedicated to his young son, Carlos Félix.

Though unequal in quality, the *Pastores de Belén* was very popular, running through eight printings in the 17th c. alone. A number of ballads, sonnets, *villancicos*, and other verses enliven a miscellany drawn mostly from biblical sources but also including a *gracioso*, folklore, and a child's game of forfeits. The plot concerns those shepherds who gathered in a valley near Bethlehem before the birth of Jesus, and ends with the flight to Egypt. The Inquisition found some of the interpolations objectionable (among them the story of Susannah and the Elders, and of Absalom and Tamar) and later editions were modified. Lope, in the usual manner of pastoral novelists, promised a second part but never wrote one. The best edition is that by S. F. Ramírez (1930).

A more pious and more tedious pastoral novel *a lo divino*, closely modelled on Montemayor's *Diana* (qq.v.), was written by the Cistercian friar Bartolomé Ponce de León (q.v.).

Patronio, Libro de, see CONDE LUCANOR ET DE PATRONIO, El libro de los Enxiemplos del.

Payador (Quichua: *paclla*, 'a country dweller' or 'peasant'), a *gaucho* guitarist and singer, mainly in Argentina and Chile, who improvised songs of heroes and current events as he travelled about.

One of the best-known *payadores* in literature is Santos Vega (q.v.). *El payador* (1911) by Leopoldo Lugones (q.v.) deals with the *Martín Fierro* of José Hernández (qq.v.).

PAYNO, MANUEL (1810–94), b. Mexico City. Mexican novelist. His adventurous life, including periods as Minister of Finance and periods of exile, served as raw material for his works, the first serial novels to appear in Mexico. *El fistol del diablo* (1845–6) was first published in the *Revista Científica Literaria*, and was enlarged for revised versions in 1859, 1871, and 1887. Despite the sensational and exaggerated narrative, the book is important for its authentic description of customs and speech patterns, in particular for the rich proverbial lore. *Los bandidos del Río Frío* (serialized in 1889–91; ed. A. Castro Leal, 1964) is a long vivid account of Mexican society in the early 19th c. signed 'Un ingenio de la Corte'.

El hombre de la situación (1861) is a *costumbrista* novel which was never serialized. *Tardes nubladas* (1871) are short stories. Francisco Monterde published a selection of Payno's work as *Artículos y narraciones* (1945).

PAYRÓ, ROBERTO JORGE (1867–1928), b. Mercedes, Buenos Aires. Argentinian novelist and journalist, from 1894 on the staff of *La Nación*, on whose behalf he visited Chile (*Cartas chilenas*) in 1895; Patagonia in 1898 (*La Australia argentina*; and northern Argentina in 1899 (*En las tierras del Inti*). Payró spent a number of years in Europe and while in Brussels witnessed the German invasion. He returned to Argentina after World War I. His best books are three novels in the satirico-realistic vein of the Spanish picaresque, with influences of Balzac, Dickens, and Pérez Galdós. *Pago Chico*, a collection of episodes first published in 1908, dealt with political chicanery in the provinces. *El casamiento de Laucha* (1906) brings the ambience of *Guzmán de Alfarache* to Argentina: after many adventures Laucha arrives in Pago Chico, where he marries a rich widow, squanders her money and abandons her. Payró's analogy is between Laucha as an immoral individual, and the systematic corruption and fraud of local cliques and political bosses in general.

Las divertidas aventuras del nieto de Juan Moreira (1910) brings the series to a triumphant climax, the Creole rogue Mauricio Gómez Herrera succeeding in Buenos Aires just as easily as Laucha succeeded in the provinces, by a combination of hypocrisy, lies, and slander.

Payró's historical novels are less important, with the exception of *El mar dulce: crónica novelesca del descubrimiento del Río de la Plata*, a prose epic on the heroic life of Juan Díaz de Solís. Of Payró's plays, only *Canción trágica* (1902) has lasted well.

See Noemí Vergara de Bietti, *Los tres Payró* (Buenos Aires, 1957); S. M. Fernández de Vidal, *Roberto J. Payró* (1962); W. G. Weyland, *Roberto J. Payró* (1962); and Eduardo González Lanuza, *Genio y figura de Roberto J. Payró* (1965).

PAZ, GIL, pseudonym of Leopoldo Lugones (q.v.).

PAZ, OCTAVIO (1914–   ), b. Mixcoac. Mexican poet and essayist. The leading poet of the Taller group (1939–41), which included Alberto Quintero Álvarez, Neftalí Beltrán, and Efraín Huerta, and of the magazine *El Hijo Pródigo*. He joined the diplomatic service in 1943 and subsequently served in France, India, Japan, Switzerland, and elsewhere. He lived in the U.S.A. in 1944–5, and in the latter year participated in the surrealist movement in Paris with André Breton. He was ambassador to India (1962–8), resigning in protest against Mexico's repression of the student movement.

His most important book in prose is *El laberinto de la soledad: vida y pensamiento de México* (q.v., 1950; 2nd edn., 1959), which has been supplemented by a *Posdata* (1970), and translated by L. Kemp (New York, 1962). Subsequent essays have been collected in *El arco y la lira* (1956; translated by R. L. C. Simms as *The bow and the lyre* (Austin, Texas, 1974)), *Las peras del olmo* (1957), *Cuadrivio* (1965), *Puertas al campo* (1966), *Corriente alterna* (1967), *Claude Lévi-Strauss o el nuevo festín de Esopo* (1967), *Marcel Duchamp o el castillo de la pureza* (1968), *Conjunciones y disyunciones* (1969), and *Los signos en rotación y otros ensayos* (Madrid, 1971).

His juvenilia *Luna silvestre* (1933) and *¡No pasarán!* (1936) were followed by the excellent erotic poems of *Raíz del hombre* (1937), *Bajo tu clara sombra* (Valencia, 1937; 2nd edn., Mexico City, 1941), *Entre la piedra y la flor* (1941), *A la orilla del mundo* (1942), *Libertad bajo palabra* (1949; 2nd edn., subtitled *Obra poética 1935–57*, 1960), *¿Águila o sol?* (prose poems, 1951), and *La estación violenta* (1958) in which his well-known 'Piedra de sol' attempts to reconcile opposites: realism and transcendentalism, belief in the word and disillusion with it, the essential loneliness of men and their need for solidarity. This circular poem has as many lines as there are days in the Aztec calendar. Later collections of Paz's poetry include *Salamandra* (1962), *Ladera este* (1969), and an anthology called *La centena. Poemas 1935–1968* (Barcelona, 1969). In 1968 he published two volumes of *poesía espacial: Topoemas* and *Discos visuales*, 'concrete' poetry in the style of Decio Pignatari and the Brazilian Noigandres group. *Configurations* (New York and London, 1971) is a bilingual edition by ten translators, including Paz himself. *El mono gramático* (1974) first appeared in French as *Le singe grammairien* (1972). *Versiones y diversiones* (1974) is a collection of Paz's translations from foreign poets.

Paz's anthology *Mexican poetry* has been translated into English (by Samuel Beckett, Bloomington, Indiana, 1958) and into French (Paris, 1952). Paz has translated visionaries such as Blake, Rimbaud, and Hölderlin with whom he feels a particular affinity.

See Ramón Xirau, *Octavio Paz: el sentido de la palabra* (1970); Rachel Phillips, *The poetic modes of Octavio Paz* (London, 1972); Ángel Flores (ed.), *Aproximaciones a Octavio Paz* (1973); and Ivar Ivask (ed.), *Octavio Paz: the perpetual present* (Norman, Okla., 1973), with a good bibliography.

Pazos de Ulloa, Los, (2 vols., Barcelona, 1886), a novel by Emilia Pardo Bazán (q.v.), at once the best regional novel of the Galician countryside and her finest book. The novel's mood is one of broad pessimism as it chronicles the decline of the rural squirearchy, in sharp contrast to *El sabor de la tierruca* (1881), by José María de Pereda (q.v.).

A wealthy, idle, and cruel squire, Pedro Moscoso, called incorrectly the 'Marqués de los Pazos, takes as his mistress Sabel, the daughter of his sinister steward Primitivo. The keynote of the book is provided by the 'Marquis'' uncle: 'La aldea, cuando se cría uno en ella y no sale de ella jamás, envilece, empobrece y embrutece' ('Village life, when one is brought up in it and never leaves it, makes one vile, impoverished, and brutish'). Primitivo exploits his master's weakness, and with the collaboration of a group of greedy priests comes to dominate the surrounding area. The young priest Julián arrives to put Moscoso's affairs in order, and to thwart him Primitivo uses all available devices, including his daughter's seductiveness, but in vain.

Moscoso returns from the city with Nucha, a gentle bride whom Julián believes will redeem her husband, but she is quickly intimidated by her husband's brutality, Primitivo's vindictiveness, and Sabel's jealousy. Nucha can trust only Julián, and Primitivo quickly exploits their mutual attraction by inventing a slander which causes Julián's abrupt departure from los Pazos. On his way he finds the corpse of Primitivo, who has been killed by a gunman sent by a rival political party. Six months after Julian's abrupt departure from Ulloa he learns that Nucha has died. After an absence of ten years he returns to pray at Nucha's grave, and sees together Perucho, Moscoso's illegitimate 16-year-old son by Sabel, and Manolita, his legitimate 11-year-old daughter by Nucha.

In the book's sequel, *La madre naturaleza* (1887), the young couple fall innocently in love, unaware of the social stigma attaching to incest. Social pressures force Manolita into a convent and Perucho into exile. *La madre naturaleza* justifies its title by splendid descriptions of landscape.

The prologue to *Los Pazos de Ulloa*'s first edition contained *Apuntes autobiográficos* inexcusably never since reprinted.

See Robert E. Lott, 'Observations on … "Los Pazos de Ulloa"' in *Hispania*, vol. 52 (1969), pp. 3–12; and C. Feal Deibe, 'Naturalismo y antinaturalismo en '"Los Pazos de Ulloa"' in *BHS*, vol. 48, no. 4 (1971), pp. 314–27.

PAZ Y MELIA, ANTONIO (1842–1927), b. Talavera de la Reina, Toledo. Editor, palaeographer, and archivist at the Biblioteca Nacional in Madrid. He edited texts of Alfonso Palencia, Rodríguez de la Cámara, and Gómez Manrique (qq.v.), among many others.

A most important contribution was the *Catálogo de las piezas de teatro … en el Departamento de Manuscritos de la Biblioteca Nacional* (1899; 2nd edn., 2 vols., 1934–5).

PEDRO DE ALCÁNTARA, *San* (1499–1562), b. Alcántara, Extremadura. A Franciscan mystic; he studied philosophy at Salamanca. His best-known book is *Petición especial de amor a Dios* (c. 1560). His *Tratado de la oración y meditación* (1533) is now considered to be a précis of Luis de Granada's (q.v.) book of a similar title. As a severe ascetic, San Pedro intended to restore the ancient Rule of St. Francis to its strictest form. He was venerated during his lifetime by S. Teresa, Fray Luis de Granada, and Juan de Ávila (qq.v.), beatified in 1662, and canonized in 1669.

PEDRO DE JESÚS, see ESPINOSA, Pedro de.

PEDRO DE PORTUGAL, *Condestable Don* (*fl.* 1490), poet and playwright. His *Coplas* (Saragossa?, 1490?) are in the manner of Juan de Mena. The Marqués de Santillana (q.v.) wrote his celebrated *Carta* on contemporary poetry for Don Pedro. His 'Sátira de felice e infelice vida' was edited by A. Paz y Melia in *Opúsculos literarios de los siglos XIV a XVI* (1892), pp. 47–101. His 'Tragedia de la insigne reyna Dª Isabel', was edited and introduced by C. Michaëlis de Vasconcellos in *Homenaje a Menéndez Pelayo*, vol. 1 (1899), pp. 637–732; 2nd edn., Coimbra, 1922).

See J. E. Martínez Ferrando, *Tragedia del insigne Condestable don Pedro de Portugal* (1942), with a good bibliography.

Pedro de Urdemalas, a play in three acts by Miguel de Cervantes Saavedra (q.v.), first published in his *Ocho comedias y ocho entremeses* ... (1615).

The plot is similar to that of the *novela ejemplar La gitanilla* (q.v.), developing the atmosphere of the first act of *El rufián dichoso* (q.v.) into a full-length play.

A *pícaro* ('rogue', 'delinquent') goes to live with a troop of gipsies for love of a young girl. Scenes of their lives, vivid with superstition and *cuadros de costumbres*, are further enlivened by gipsy dances and music. Pedro is developed into a rounded character with cynicism, wit, and bitterness in a realistic setting with realistic dialogue. The gipsy girl, however, is discovered to be a niece of the queen and her marriage to Pedro is frustrated. Pedro, for whom a great future has been predicted, merely shrugs his shoulders and decides to become an actor, once in that profession, he argues, one can become 'patriarch, pope and student, emperor and king'. The name 'Pedro de Urdemalas' is not original to Cervantes, though his play gave it further currency, being found in both oral and written traditional tales about any male picaresque wit. It was also the pseudonym of the author of *Viaje de Turquía*, now thought to be Andrés Laguna (q.v.).

See the edition, with a good introduction, by R. Schevill and A. Bonilla y San Martín, in their *Obras completas* of Cervantes (6 vols., 1915–22, vol. 6); J. Casalduero, *Sentido y forma del teatro de Cervantes* (1951); and B. W. Wardropper, in *Suma cervantina* (ed. J. B. Avalle-Arce and E. C. Riley, London, 1971).

PEDROLO, MANUEL DE (1918–), Catalan playwright and novelist, whose plays are concerned with the dilemma of man in an incomprehensible universe.

Cruma (1957) shows a Resident in an empty room, with his daily Visitor. Like Vladimir and Estragon in Beckett's *En attendant Godot*, these two play games to 'pass the time' and keep out thoughts of past and future: even the present is limbo. The *cruma* is an Etruscan unit of measurement whose meaning has been lost, like most Etruscan objects and ideas. In *Homes i No* (1957) two cages with a family in each are guarded by a jailer called No, revealed at the climax to be a prisoner himself. *Darrera versió, per ara* (1958) is a parody of the Fall of Man: a man and woman, trapped in a room by a landlady, having signed a lease including a clause which forbids them to leave the room. *Situació bis* (1958) deals with the

corruption caused by power, again in a jail-like setting. *Sóc el defecte* (1959) is set on a staircase, Ar and Ber walking up and down to solve the meaning of 'climb' and 'descend' which change with each movement. Cir, reading at the foot of the stairs, is equally bemused by his books. In *Tècnica de cambra* (1959) we return to the empty room, where each of seven successive characters finds temporary refuge. *L'ús de la matèria* (1963) is a sinister farce on bureaucracy in the same vein as Václav Havel's better-known *The memorandum* (original and English translation, 1965). At one point the two clerks are ordered to destroy all the papers that engulf their office in the interest of economy, as long as they retain one copy and one duplicate of each.

Pedrolo's novels, less well-known, include *Unes mans plenes de sol* (Barcelona, 1972); *Un camí amb Eva* (Barcelona, 1973); *Espais de fecunditat irregulares* (Barcelona, 1973) with a heroine, Blanca, who strives to liberate herself from the family, and from the religious, sexual, and political taboos of her status; and *Acte de violència* (Barcelona, 1975). His collected essays are *Els elefants son contagiosos* (Barcelona, 1974).

See George E. Wellwarth, 'Manuel de Pedrolo and Spanish absurdism' in *Books Abroad* (Norman, Okla.), vol. 46, no. 3 (Summer, 1972).

PEERS, EDGAR ALLISON (1894–1952), British Hispanist. Professor of Spanish at Liverpool University who specialized in the mystics and Romantics, and founder of the quarterly *Bulletin of Spanish Studies* (1923), now the *Bulletin of Hispanic Studies* whose editor (1977) is Geoffrey Ribbans.

Peers's books include the edition *The poems of Manuel de Cabanyes* (Manchester, 1923); *Rivas and Romanticism in Spain* (London, 1923); 'Rivas: a critical study' in *Revue Hispanique*, vol. 58 (1923), pp. 1–600; *Spanish mysticism* (London, 1924); *Studies of the Spanish mystics* (London, 1926); *Ramon Llull: a biography* (London, 1929) and translations from Llull; *Spain: a companion to Spanish studies* (London, 1929); *St. John of the Cross* (Cambridge, 1932) and translations from John of the Cross; *The Romantics of Spain* (Liverpool, 1934); six books interpreting political conditions for a British reader: *Spanish tragedy* (1936), *Catalonia infelix* (1937), *Our debt to Spain* (1938), *Spain, the Church and the Orders* (1939), *Spanish dilemma* (1940), *Spain in eclipse* (1943); the important *A history of the Romantic Movement in Spain* (2 vols., Cambridge, 1940), abridged as *The Romantic Movement in Spain: a short history* (Liverpool, 1968); and the excellent *Critical anthology of Spanish verse* (Liverpool, 1948).

PELLICER, CARLOS (1899–), b. Villahermosa, Tabasco. Mexican poet, university professor of modern poetry for some years, Director of the Ministry of Fine Arts, specializing in museology, and founding curator of the Museo-Parque de la Venta in Villahermosa. His major contribution to modern Mexican poetry has been an emphasis on music and colour: an 'apoteosis salvaje de los sentidos' to quote Torres Bodet. It is a poetry of affirmation, glorying in nature, which reflects the divine and in life, which overcomes death. Pellicer was awarded the National Literature Prize in 1964.

The complete *Material poético, 1918–1961* (1962) has been supplemented by *Con palabras y fuego* (1963), three poems on Cuauhtémoc; and *Teotihuacán, y 13 de agosto: ruina de Tenochtitlán* (1965).

PELLICER, JUAN ANTONIO (1738–1806), b. Encinacorba, Saragossa. Cervantist and bibliographer who worked in the Royal Library (now the National Library) in Madrid. His major book was the useful *Ensayo de una biblioteca de traductores españoles* (1778), but 'Noticias para la vida de Miguel de Cervantes Saavedra' included in it (the second life of Cervantes, following that of Mayáns y Síscar, q.v.) was poorly written and quickly superseded by an enlarged version prefixed to his monumental annotated edition of the *Quijote* (5 vols., 1797–8) which was quite heavily indebted to John Bowle's edition (3 vols., Salisbury, 1781).

PELLICER DE OSSÁU SALAS Y TOVAR, JOSÉ DE (1602–79), b. Saragossa. Poet and presumed hoaxer. He studied humanities at Salamanca and Madrid, philosophy at Alcalá, and canon and civil law in Salamanca. He was appointed Chronicler of Castile and León in 1624 (at the death of Antonio de Herrera) and of Aragón in 1640 (after the death of Bartolomé Leonardo de Argensola (q.v.)). A specialist in genealogy, he is believed to have invented some of the more flattering details in at least some genealogical commissions.

His *Lecciones solemnes a las obras de don Luis de Góngora* (1630) was a sympathetic approach to Góngora who influenced Pellicer's style in such poems as *El Fénix y su historia natural* (1630) and *La Astrea Sáfica* (1641). Fragments of both appear in vol. 22 (1852) of the BAE.

See Dámaso Alonso, 'Todos contra Pellicer' in *Revista de Filología*, vol. 24 (1937).

Pelo de la dehesa, El (1840), a popular comedy by Manuel Bretón de los Herreros (q.v.), set in Madrid.

Elisa, daughter of the Marquis of Valfungoso, is promised in marriage to Don Frutos Calamocha, who lent Elisa's late father money on condition that he should be able to marry Elisa. The foolish and clumsy Frutos arrives from the provinces and embraces the maid thinking she is Elisa, sleeps in the opera house, and rises for breakfast at six, only to learn that the ladies have not yet returned from a ball. Elisa, who is in love with Don Miguel, agrees with the boorish Frutos that they differ in all respects and would make an ill match, but neither of them can retract the marriage vow previously imposed. Miguel suggests a duel and challenges Frutos to choose his weapon. Frutos selects cudgels!

Finally, Frutos himself proposes that Elisa marry Miguel, and generously tears up the IOU. 'It is not a wedding present', he says, 'but her ransom' and flees back to his quiet country home in Belchite.

The humour lies in the play's situation comedy and the portrayal of contemporary manners in Madrid high society: the ignorance of rich provincials is caricatured without the acid wit of a Molière, and the aim is simply to entertain.

Bretón de la Herreros, while not sparing the fundamentally worthy Frutos, directs his sharpest satire at the decadent *madrileños*: the Marquesa is greedy, Elisa fickle, and Miguel vain and arrogant.

The play respects the neoclassical unities, and is very fast-moving. In the play's sequel, *Don Frutos en Belchite*, after Miguel's death in a duel the widowed Elisa finally marries Frutos.

N. Alonso Cortes edited *El pelo de la dehesa* (1927) for Clásicos Castellanos.

See G. Le Gentil, *Le poète Manuel Bretón de los Herreros et la société espagnole de 1830 à 1860* (Paris, 1909).

PEMÁN, JOSÉ MARÍA (1898–), b. Cádiz. Playwright and poet. He studied law in Seville and Madrid, presenting a doctoral thesis entitled *Las ideas filosófico-jurídicas de la 'República' de Platón.*

An early influence on his poetry was Juan Ramón Jiménez (q.v.); his first collections of poetry were *Poesías, 1923–1937* (Valladolid, 1937), replaced in 1959 by *Poesía: nueva antología, 1917–1959.*

He has written more than 60 plays in four main genres: verse history, thesis drama, farce, and play of manners, in addition to an impressive number of translations and adaptations such as a version of Sophocles' *Oedipus Rex* performed at the Roman theatre of Mérida. His original play *La destrucción de Sagunto* was written for performance in the ruins at Sagunto. His historical plays, beginning with *El divino impaciente* (1933) on the life of St. Francis Xavier, are a vehicle for his conservative views of the position of Roman Catholic, imperial

Spain, as is the *Elegía a la tradición de España* (1931). So far seven vols. of his *Obras completas* (1948–) have appeared.

PEÑALOSA Y MONDRAGÓN, Fray BENITO DE (*fl.* 1629), author of the extravagantly nationalistic *Cinco Excelencias del Español que despueblan España para un mayor potencia y dilatación* (Pamplona, 1620), a book which claims that Spaniards worshipped the True God from the creation of the world, that they practised the laws of God six hundred years before Moses, and evolved a system of philosophy a thousand years before the Greeks. Furthermore, they were in Fray Benito's view the first Gentiles to become Christian.

See A. A. Sacroff, *Les controverses des statuts de pureté de sang en Espagne* (Paris, 1960).

Peñas arriba (1895), a novel by José María de Pereda (q.v.). This masterpiece of Pereda is more a series of *cuadros* than a novel, but is all the more successful for minimizing the plot, which was never Pereda's strong point. His powers are at their height in this gripping, often mystical, story of the transformation of the idle *madrileño* Marcelo into a potential country squire.

Pereda's hero in this work is Marcelo's old uncle, the philanthropic patriarch Don Celso, conservative, pious, noble, and honest. Celso's servant Chisco meets Marcelo in the last small town of the lowlands before they set out together on the last stage of the *madrileño's* pilgrimage to la Montaña: the contrast between Marcelo's friendly reception there and Pepe Rey's reception in Orbajosa (in *Doña Perfecta* by Pérez Galdós, qq.v., to which Pereda replies here in plot, characterization, and themes) is very marked.

Three narrative *cruces* parallel the triple use of the sea in Pereda's *Sotileza* (q.v.). The trapping and killing of bears which are menacing the neighbourhood proves Marcelo's courage and his value to the community as a successor to the ailing Don Celso. The rescue of Pepazos during a snowstorm is followed by the trapping of the rescuers in an avalanche. The final important episode, in a book largely dominated by the description of the Montaña region behind Santander in all its moods, is that of the attempted robbery of Celso's home by the black-mailing husband of Facia, the housekeeper whose mysterious past is a thread running through much of the novel. Pereda identified nature with true religion, and saw Marcelo's redemption in his final rejection of city life. The leisurely pace of the work supports Marcelo's gradual acquiescence in the quiet fulfilment of his duties. The obverse of *Peñas arriba* is *Pedro*

Sánchez (1883), in which a provincial innocent is perverted by city ways.

See J. M. Martínez y Ramón, *Análisis de 'Peñas arriba'* (Torrelavega, 1908); J. M. de Cossío, *La obra literaria de Pereda* (Santander, 1934), with a lengthy analysis of the novel; the largely negative *Pereda o la novela idilio* (1969) by José F. Montesinos; and A. H. Clarke, *Pereda, paisajista* (Santander, 1969).

Pensador, El, the most influential Spanish periodical of the 18th c. It imitated *The Spectator* (1711–14) of Addison and Steele, covering most topics of the day including social justice, education, bullfighting, and superstition, within the limits imposed by the censorship. Founded, edited, and written almost single-handed by José de Clavijo y Fajardo (q.v.), *El Pensador* appeared weekly 1762–7. A second edition in 70 fascicles was published as *El Pensador Matritense* (Barcelona, 1773–4).

Clavijo's neoclassical campaign against Golden Age drama concentrated on *autos sacramentales*, his allies including N. Fernández de Moratín (q.v.). His literary opponents such as Francisco Mariano Nipho and Cristóbal Romea y Tapia were defeated when the *autos* were prohibited by a royal decree of 11 June 1765.

Pensador Mexicano, El, the title of the magazine founded in Mexico City (1812–14) by José Joaquín Fernández de Lizardi (q.v.) and also the name by which he signed much of his voluminous journalism.

Pentasílabos, lines of five syllables each, infrequent in Spanish literature. Castillejo used the metre in a *villancico*, and Jerónimo Bermúdez in a chorus in his tragedy *Nise laureada* (1577): 'Oh, corazones / más que de tigres. / Oh, manos crudas / más que de fieras. / Cómo pudistes / tan inocente, / tan apurada, / sangre verter'.

Most pentasyllabic lines are stressed on the 1st and 4th syllables.

Pepita Jiménez (1874), the first novel of Juan Valera (q.v.), a masterpiece of irony on how people deceive themselves and others, surpassed in Valera only perhaps by *Doña Luz* (1879).

Luis de Vargas, the 22-year-old son of a rich landowner, has a vague vocation inculcated while attending a seminary and plans to become a missionary in distant lands. He spends a short holiday with his father, Don Pedro, whom he finds courting the charming young widow Pepita, aged twenty. She has already met and rejected a number of younger suitors. Luis and

Pepita meet and gradually fall in love, their liaison being protected by the Celestina-like Antoñona, maid to Pepita.

The plot is common enough in Spanish literature, from before Rojas Zorrilla's *Entre bobos anda el juego* to beyond Moratín's *El sí de las niñas*. The first part of the novel consists of letters from Luis to his priest-uncle in which we learn of the struggle between his so-called 'vocation' and his love, at first unconscious, for Pepita. This is a most subtle psychological analysis, equalling the brilliance with which the pretty Pepita is described in the second half of the novel.

The book is influenced by Valera's interest in *krausismo* (q.v.), and is a good example of Valera's *andalucismo* and his use of local colour. His portrayal of nature runs parallel with the 'natural' love of Luis and Pepita.

The novel was translated into a dozen languages during the author's lifetime and sold more than a 100,000 copies. Manuel Azaña (1927) edited the novel for Clásicos Castellanos with a good introduction, but this text has been superseded by that of Robert E. Lott (1974). There is an English translation by H. de Onís (New York, 1964).

See Robert E. Lott, *Language and psychology in 'Pepita Jiménez'* (Urbana, Ill., 1974).

PERALTA, ALEJANDRO (1899–   ), b. Puno. Peruvian poet, who founded and edited, with his brother Arturo, the *Boletín Titicaca*. His poetry, *Ande* (1926) and *El Kollao* (1934), deals with love of the land from the Indian's point of view, and grief at social injustice.

See Alberto Tauro, *El indigenismo a través de la poesía de Alejandro Peralta* (1935).

PERALTA BARNUEVO, PEDRO DE (1664–1743), b. Lima. Peruvian poet, historian, and astronomer. He was educated at San Marcos University, and remained to teach mathematics 1709–43, serving as Rector 1715–17.

Though critics have been extremely harsh on his *Lima fundada o la conquista del Perú. Poema heroico en que se decanta toda la historia del descubrimiento y sujeción de sus provincias por Don Francisco Pizarro* (1732), Riva Agüero (*La historia en el Perú*, 1910) has indicated that 'por sus notas eruditas se puede estimar como un compendio histórico y hasta como un diccionario biográfico'. L. A. Sánchez (*Los poetas de la colonia*, 1921) has pointed out Peralta's rare gift of combining the prosaic with the gongoristic and the reader must forgive faults of versification and taste in appreciating the historiographic values of the book. Peralta's other works include *Desvíos de la naturaleza o tratado del origen de los monstruos* (1695), published under the pseudonym 'José de Rivilla y Pueyo'; the annual *El conocimiento de los*

tiempos (1721–43); *Historia de España vindicada* ... (1730); *Lima inexpugnable* ... (1740).

See Irving A. Leonard, 'A great savant of colonial Peru' in *Philological Quarterly* (Iowa, 1933); Leonard's introduction to Peralta's *Obras dramáticas* (Santiago, 1937), with an appendix of newly-published poems; and L. A. Sánchez, *El doctor Océano* (1967).

PERALTA LAGOS, JOSÉ MARÍA (1873–1944), b. S. Tecla, El Salvador. Engineer, soldier (he studied at Guadalajara Military Academy, Spain), and *costumbrista*. He founded and directed *La Construcción Moderna* the engineering journal, was Minister for War under Dr. Manuel Enrique Aranjo, and was for a time ambassador to Spain.

He wrote humorous articles from 1898 under the pseudonym 'T. P. Mechín'. His best-known works include *Burla burlando* (1923), a collection of satirical pieces; *Brochazos* (1925); a three-act comedy, *Candidato* (1931); and a *costumbrista* novel, *La muerte de la tórtola*.

PEREDA, JOSÉ MARÍA DE (1833–1906), b. Polanco, Santander. Spanish novelist. He was the 21st and youngest child of a country squire's family, of whom only nine survived. His eldest brother Juan Agapito, seeing how the family's finances were waning, sought his fortune in Cuba and succeeded to the extent that José María, 29 years his junior, was generously given the means to become an independent writer at the age of 22, on his brother's eventual return to Spain. The family's strict Roman Catholic atmosphere and class consciousness were never questioned by Pereda in his life or his novels.

Pereda first wrote articles intended to be satirical and humorous; his first significant work was a series of unrelated *cuadros de costumbres* entitled *Escenas montañesas* (q.v., 1864).

A major event of his life was the Liberal Revolution of 1868, which he attacked vigorously in articles between November 1868 and the following June. His political adherence to Carlism and his marriage in 1869 had contrasting effects: one uprooting him on his election as a Carlist deputy to the Cortes in 1871, though scarcely widening his intellectual outlook; and the other giving him the needed stability to write in peace. *Tipos y paisajes* (1871) was generously overpraised by his close friend Pérez Galdós (q.v.), but its nostalgia is oppressive. Pereda also suffers by comparison in *Los hombres de pro* (1872), a political novel written against Pérez Galdós's *La Fontana de Oro* (qq.v.). It was the first of four thesis novels which rarely manage to conceal their tendentious origin, built around insubstantial characters who enact contrived plots predetermined by Pereda's bias.

The other political novel is *Don Gonzalo González de la Gonzalera* (1878) and the two novels about marriage of this period are *El buey suelto* (1877) and *De tal palo, tal astilla* (1879), the latter an ineffectual reply to *Gloria* by Galdós (qq.v.).

In 1881 Pereda published *Esbozos y rasguñas*, a collection of previously-published *cuadros*; and his first important novel *El sabor de la tierruca* (1881), which is a tentative step towards the perfect rural idyll, *Peñas arriba*.

Pedro Sánchez (1883) shows how an untainted youth from the provinces can lose his soul in Madrid; in this and in the next novel *Sotileza* (q.v., 1884), Pereda shows a new stylistic mastery which helps to minimize weaknesses of characterization and plot construction, but his next works lose inspiration and form: *La Montálvez* (1888, another attack on the middle classes of Madrid), *La puchera* (1889), *Nubes del estío* and *Al primer vuelo* (both 1891), and *Pachín González* (1895). But it was in *Peñas arriba* (q.v., 1895) that Pereda, nostalgic for the Montaña of his youth and forgetful of his adolescent trials, created the one great regional novel of the Santander district, a great lexical achievement that makes rewarding reading for its insistence on the need for mystical communion with nature, and strikes a positive note as opposed to the bitter and often unfair criticism of his Madrid books. His inaugural speech in 1897 to the Real Academia Española was on the regional novel, of which he was already an acknowledged master.

There are two unsatisfactory sets of *Obras completas*. The first (1921–30) was published in 17 vols. by Victoriano Suárez and omits *Escritos de juventud* and *Artículos y escritos* which are included in the second (1948–59), published in 2 vols. by Aguilar. The latter, however, omits the author's important prologues. A *Manual de bibliografía perediana* (Santander, 1974) has been compiled by Anthony H. Clarke.

See the best critical study, José F. Montesinos, *Pereda o la novela idilio* (1969); Ricardo Gullón, *Vida de Pereda*; *Cartas a Galdós* (1964) written 1872–1905; and L. H. Klibbe, *José María de Pereda* (Boston, 1975), in Twayne's World Authors series.

PEREDA VALDÉS, ILDEFONSO (1899–), b. Montevideo. Uruguayan poet and essayist, whose sympathy for Negro poetry has resulted in the compilation of the useful *Antología de la poesía negra americana* (1936); and folklore studies, including *Negros esclavos y negros libres* (1941) and *El Cancionero popular uruguayo* (1947). His original verse is included in *La casa iluminada* (1920), *El libro de la colegiala* (1921), and *Música y acero* (1934).

His literary studies are *El arquero* (1924), on

French and Spanish poetry; *El pícaro y la novela picaresca* (1951); and *Cervantinas* (1952). *El sueño de Chaplín* (1930) is a book of short stories.

Peregrino en su patria, El (Seville, 1604), an adventure novel by Lope de Vega Carpio (q.v.) written between 1600 and 1603 on the model of the Byzantine novels and the *Selva de aventuras* written in 1565 by Jerónimo de Contreras (q.v.).

Several couples, whom we first meet together, are separated but are finally reunited after a series of adventures in Spain (Barcelona, Valencia, Saragossa, and Toledo) and abroad, suffering shipwreck, capture by pirates, and various other hardships.

Undoubtedly autobiographical in the treatment of some characters (Nise being Lope's mistress Micaela de Luján and Jacinto being Lope himself), the novel suffers from the under-characterization of others. The important interpolated poems and plays include Lope's first four *autos sacramentales* (*El viaje del alma, Las bodas del alma, La Maya,* and *El hijo pródigo*) which spoil the novel's development. Lope lists 219 of his plays written up to that time and, in the 6th impression, a further 114, a valuable guide to the chronology of his drama. *El peregrino en su patria* appeared in vol. 5 of the *Obras sueltas* (1776–9), and has been edited for Clásicos Castalia (1973) by Juan Bautista Avalle-Arce.

PÉREZ, ABDÓN ANTERO (1871–1926), b. Maracaibo. Venezuelan poet who wrote under the pen name 'Udón Perez'. He studied medicine in Venezuela and Chile without qualifying.

His subject is the Lake of Maracaibo, its natural history and its legends. His style was initially post-Romantic in *Lira triste* (1903) and moved from modernism and Parnassianism in *Ánfora criolla* (1913) to sterile civic verse in later books.

PÉREZ, ALONSO (16th c.), b. Salamanca. Minor poet. His *La segunda parte de la Diana* (Valencia, 1564), a sequel to Montemayor's *Diana* (qq.v.), achieved greater fame than the superior sequel *Diana enamorada* (q.v.) of Gaspar Gil Polo (q.v.), and was often published together with Montemayor's work during the 16th and 17th cs.

Pérez commended his continuation on the dubious grounds that he was Montemayor's friend, and that his own work contains little that is 'not stolen or imitated from the best Latins and Italians'.

He died before his advertised third part was published; it was probably never written.

PÉREZ, *Fray* ANDRÉS, a Dominican monk of León who wrote a *Vida* of San Raimundo de

Peñaforte (1601), *Sermones de Cuaresma* (Valladolid, 1621), and *Sermones de los santos* (1622).

Nicolás Antonio believed him to be the author of *La pícara Justina* (q.v.), an opinion supported by J. Puyol y Alonso in his edition of the novel (3 vols., 1912) for the Sociedad de Bibliófilos Madrileños, but there are probably stronger grounds for believing the author to be Francisco López de Úbeda (q.v.).

PÉREZ, ANTONIO (1540?–1611), b. Madrid. Autobiographer and letter-writer. Secretary of State to King Philip II.

His *Norte de príncipes* (1788) was addressed to the Duke of Lerma, *privado* of Philip. *Vn pedaço de Historia de lo suçedido en Çaragoça de Aragón, a 24 de Setiembre del Año de 1591* (Pau, 1591; ed. A. Pérez Gómez, Valencia, 1959). *Las relaciones* (Paris, 1598; 2 vols., 1849) is an extended *apologia* for his conduct in politics.

His absorbing letters, mannered in style, were first published in Paris (1598) and are accessible in vol. 13 (1850) of the BAE, pp. 463–570.

See J. Fitzmaurice-Kelly, *Antonio Pérez* (London, 1922); G. Marañón, *Antonio Pérez: el hombre, el drama, la época* (2 vols., 1947; 3rd edn., 1951); A. Pérez [Gómez], *Antonio Pérez, escritor y hombre de estado: ensayo de bibliografía razonada* (Cieza, 1959); and Gustav Ungerer, *A Spaniard in Elizabethan England: the correspondence of Antonio Pérez* (2 vols., London, 1975–6), of which the first volume deals with Pérez's first two visits to England and includes his Latin correspondence with the Earl of Essex and Anthony Bacon.

PÉREZ, COSMÉ (*fl.* 1st half of 17th c.), the great comic actor of his day, whose best-known role was that of Juan Rana (q.v.). His niece, Barbara Coronel, was alleged to have murdered her husband with the assistance of her young lover, a prompter, but on Pérez's intercession with the king she was saved from the scaffold.

PÉREZ, JUAN, the 'plain name' of Juan Pérez de Montalbán (q.v.) in the celebrated epigram by Quevedo (q.v.) who directed at the same victim a sarcastic *Carta consolatoria* after one of his plays had been whistled off the stage.

See E. Glaser, 'Quevedo versus Pérez de Montalbán: the "Auto del Polifemo" and the Odyssean tradition in Golden Age Spain' in *Hispanic Review*, vol. 28 (1960), pp. 103–20; and R. A. del Piero, 'La respuesta de Pérez de Montalbán a la "Perinola" de Quevedo' in *PMLA*, vol. 76 (1961), pp. 40–7.

PÉREZ, UDÓN, see PÉREZ, Abdón Antero.

PÉREZ BAYER, FRANCISCO (1714–94), b. Valencia. Educationist and Hebraist. He taught Hebrew at Valencia and Salamanca, and became Director of the Royal Library (now the National Library) in Madrid. With Andrés Marcos Burriel and Velázquez de Velasco, he was commissioned by the Real Academia de la Historia to collect documents, medals, and other primary sources for historical research. Most of his MSS. are in the National Library: the most significant of those published include *Catálogo de la Real Biblioteca de El Escorial* ... (Rome, 1756); the memorial addressed to Carlos III *Por la libertad de la literatura española* (1769), mercilessly exposing the critically low state of university education at the time; and works of Hebrew scholarship.

See L. Juan García, *Pérez Bayer y Salamanca. Datos para la biobibliografía del hebraísta valenciano* (Salamanca, 1918).

PÉREZ BONALDE, JUAN ANTONIO (1846–92), b. Caracas. Venezuelan poet. He spent his adolescence in Puerto Rico, where his father was in exile, but left for the U.S.A. in 1870 and returned to Venezuela in 1890. His versions from Poe (*The raven*) and from Heine (*Lieder*) were well received; his original verse derived as much strength from Anglo-Saxon models as Darío's from the French, and is characterized by neo-Romantic intimism. Perhaps his most interesting poems were 'Primavera', 'Flor', 'Al Niágara', and 'Vuelta a la patria', the last a romantic evocation of town and family written before his return. *Ritmos* (1874) and *Estrofas* (New York, 1877) are superseded by *Poesías y traducciones* (1947) in the Biblioteca Popular Venezolana.

PÉREZ DE AYALA, RAMÓN (1880–1962), b. Oviedo. Novelist, poet, essayist, and diplomat. He studied law at Oviedo University under 'Clarín' (q.v.), and philosophy and literature at the University of Madrid. With Miró, Valle-Inclán, and Baroja (qq.v.), Pérez de Ayala is considered one of the masters of the early 20th-c. Spanish novel. His place as a poet is low: *La paz del sendero* (1903) is an exercise in past modes from Berceo to modernism; *El sendero innumerable* (1916) concentrates on sea-themes and sea-motifs; *El sendero andante* (1921) is similarly permeated by the spirit of rivers.

Pérez de Ayala was much more at home with the essay than the poem. *Las máscaras* (2 vols., 1917–19) is devoted to drama criticism, and his other essays are collected in *Política y toros* (1918), and *Hermann, encadenado* (1917) on his visit to the Italian front in World War I.

The tetralogy of his early novels comprises *Tinieblas en las cumbres* (1907), published under the pseudonym 'Plotino Cuevas'; its sequel *La pata de la raposa* (1911; critical edn. by Andrés Amorós, Barcelona, 1970); *A.M.D.G.* (1910), a bitter indictment of Jesuit education; and *Troteras y danzaderas* (1913), a *roman-à-clef* on Madrid Bohemian life in 1910. All four novels are linked by common characters, in particular by Alberto, Pérez de Ayala's *alter ego*, and they were intended to be continued, as he wryly comments in the prologue, to the last.

He married Mabel Rick (an American) in 1913. He then spent some time on transitional short novels unified by various aspects of the problems of Spain and to that extent influenced by his contemporaries and friends of the Generation of 1898. These short novels are *Prometeo*, *Luz de domingo*, and *La caída de los Limones* (1916; new edn. by J. García Mercadal, 1968), published in a single volume. *El ombligo del mundo* (1924) consisting of a prologue and five short novels, also belongs to this period, and is set in the valley of Congosto and the imaginary village of Reicastro; it is a collection based on rural characters each of whom believes himself and his village to be the 'centre of the universe'.

The major novels turn from autobiography to universality, Pérez de Ayala having learnt from his characters in the early and transitional fiction. They are *Belarmino y Apolonio* (q.v., 1921), *Luna de miel, luna de hiel* (1923) and its sequel *Los trabajos de Urbano y Simona* (1923), and *Tigre Juan* (q.v., 1926) and its sequel *El curandero de su honra* (1926).

Luna de miel, luna de hiel shows how bad education retards the growth to maturity of Urbano and Simona, and how these disadvantages are repaired by their love, sex-life, and the working out of their real nature. It is the least impressive of his major novels partly because the characters are less convincing and the thesis too blatantly biased.

Though always full of humour, Pérez de Ayala is at his best in philosophical satire and the novel of ideas. His language is scintillating, not least in *Justicia* (1928), found in *Obras completas* (vol. 2, 1965), in which a blacksmith is tried for murdering the five women in his household to liberate himself from their tyranny and bigotry. He is condemned to death and executed, despite pleading his innocence and speaking like a psychopath in his own defence. The first 4 vols. of his *Obras completas* (1964–　) have so far appeared with a good preface to vol. 1 by J. García Mercadal.

See Francisco Agustín, *Ramón Pérez de Ayala: su vida y obra* (1927); K. W. Reinink, *Algunos aspectos literarios y lingüísticos de la obra de don Ramón Pérez de Ayala* (The Hague, 1955); M. C. Rand, *Ramón Pérez de Ayala* (New York, 1971) in English; and the detailed studies by Andrés

Amorós, in particular *La novela intelectual de Ramón Pérez de Ayala* (1972).

PÉREZ DE GUZMÁN, FERNÁN (1378?– 1460?), b. Batres. Poet and important prose writer. A nephew of the Canciller Pedro López de Ayala, uncle of the Marqués de Santillana, and grandfather of Garcilaso de la Vega (qq.v.). He was ambassador in Aragón and friend of Bishop Alonso de Cartagena. When Pérez de Guzmán fell into disgrace with King Juan II at the age of 56 he retired from politics and campaigning to his property at Batres, where he spent the rest of his life in study and writing. His verse *Las Setecientas* (Seville, 1506) is a reworking of the *Trescientas* by Juan de Mena (q.v.). His earliest poems appear in the *Cancionero de Baena*; the 'Loores de los claros varones de España' is a verse chronicle in *octavas de arte menor* which first appeared in the *Cancionero del Duque de Híjar* and was reproduced in fragmentary form by B. J. Gallardo in his *Ensayo de una biblioteca española de libros raros y curiosos* (1863–89).

Pérez de Guzmán's elegiac 'Coplas a la muerte de D. Alonso de Cartagena' first appeared in Alonso's *Tractado que se llama el Oracional* (Murcia, 1487) and other poems have been published by H. A. Rennert, *Some unpublished poems* ... (Baltimore, 1897), and C. B. Bourland, 'La Doctrina que dieron a Sarra: poema' in *Revue Hispanique*, vol. 22 (1910), pp. 648–86.

Pérez de Guzmán is above all a dry, succinct, and often ironic prose stylist who takes his tone from Seneca and Tacitus. He compiled *Floresta de Philosophos*, first edited by R. Foulché-Delbosc in *Revue Hispanique*, vol. 11 (1904), pp. 5–154, which borrows heavily from Seneca. His major prose work is *Mar de ystorias* (Valladolid, 1512), an adaptation of Giovanni della Colonna's 14th-c. *Mare historiarum* edited by R. Foulché-Delbosc in *Revue Hispanique*, vol. 28 (1913), pp. 442–622. Its third part is the celebrated series of biographical sketches known as *Generaciones y semblanzas* (q.v.), remarkably successful in creating thumbnail portraits of leading figures of the age, a relatively rare example of the genre of Plutarch's *Vitae parallelae*, but stylistically closer to Tacitus.

See R. Foulché-Delbosc, 'Étude bibliographique sur Fernán Pérez de Guzmán' in *Revue Hispanique* (1906).

PÉREZ DE HERRERA, CRISTÓBAL (1558– 1625), b. Salamanca. Medical adviser to King Philip III and writer on medicine and social welfare who spent the profits from his profession on a poorhouse in Madrid. His first suggestion for reform was the *Discvrso ... a la Católica y Real Magestad del Rey don Felipe señor nuestro, suplicándole* *se sirua de que los pobres mendigantes verdaderos destos sus reynos se amparen y socorran, y los fingidos se reduzgan y reformen* (1595).

He composed *Elogio a las esclarecidas virtudes de . . . Felipe II . . . y de su exemplar y Christianíssima muerte . . .* (Valladolid, 1604), the *Compendium totius medicinae* (1614), and verse *Proverbios morales, y consejos christianos muy provechosos para consejo y espejo de la vida . . .* (1612).

See E. García del Real, 'Cristóbal Pérez de Herrera y la Decadencia de España bajo el Gobierno de los Austrias' in *Las Ciencias*, vol. 14 (1949), pp. 692–715.

PÉREZ DE HITA, GINÉS (1544?–1619?), b. Mula, Murcia? Historical novelist. He wrote *c.* 1592 *Bello troyano,* a verse adaptation of the *Crónica troyana* and another minor work, the *Libro de la población y hazañas de la ciudad de Lorca.*

He followed this with a major historical novel, on the romantic model of *Abencerraje y Jarifa* (q.v.): *Historia de los bandos de los Zegríes y Abencerrajes, caballeros moros de Granada, de las civiles guerras que hubo en ella . . . hasta que el rey don Fernando el quinto la ganó* (2 vols., Saragossa, 1595; Cuenca, 1619). The first part is a remarkable work of fiction on a basis of history but interspersed with frontier and Moorish ballads already circulating out of context and ending with the fall of Granada in 1492. It inspired dozens of imitations, including Washington Irving's *Chronicle of the Conquest of Granada* (1829), and many by French writers, such as *Almahide* (1660) by Mlle de Scudéry, *Zaïde* (1670) by Mme de la Fayette, and *Aventures du dernier Abencérage* (1826) by Chateaubriand. Spanish writers influenced by the book include Fernández y González and Martínez de la Rosa (qq.v.).

The second part is disappointing, paradoxically because Pérez de Hita saw too much of the military action against the *moriscos* at first hand in the Alpujarras to allow his imagination free rein. He describes how the Christians first under the Marqués de los Vélez and then under Don Juan de Austria quelled the *moriscos'* rebellion; he laments the dispersal of the *moriscos* to other parts of Spain and the moving in of 12,000 northerners. There is a good edition of *Las guerras civiles de Granada* (as the book is commonly known) by Paula Blanchard-Demouge (2 vols., 1913–15).

See N. Acero y Abad, *Ginés Pérez de Hita: estudio biográfico y bibliográfico* (1888).

PÉREZ DE LA OSSA, HUBERTO (1897–   ), b. Albacete. Novelist and biographer. He has been connected with the stage all his life and was co-director of the María Guerrero Theatre. His first two novels, *El ancla de Jasón* (1921) and *La lámpara del dolor* (1923), were very poor, while his next two were in the decadent style then in fashion: *El opio del ensueño* and *La santa duquesa* (both 1924), the latter winning the National Literature Prize of 1924 and being translated into English as *María Fernanda* (London, 1931) by E. Allison Peers. Little read nowadays, it combines neo-mysticism with an unintentionally absurd aristocratic atmosphere. *La casa de los masones* (1927) was another weak novel, this time influenced by the later Baroja. So it was an astonished public that greeted two fine neo-realist novels of Barcelona *Obreros, zánganos y reinas* (1928) and *Los amigos de Claudio* (1931), essentially two ways of telling the same story, socio-political in outline but individual in details. His last novel was *El aprendiz de ángel* (1953).

Among Pérez de la Ossa's biographies are *Santa Teresa de Jesús* (1930), *Dantón* (1930), *Orellana y la jornada del Amazonas* (1935), and *Almagro y la epopeya de los Andes* (1936).

PÉREZ DEL PULGAR, HERNANDO, see PULGAR, Hernando Pérez del.

PÉREZ DE MIRANDA, GREGORIO, pseudonym of Ramón López Soler (q.v.).

PÉREZ DE MONTALBÁN, JUAN (1602–38), b. Madrid. Playwright and novelist. The son of the king's bookseller, Alonso Pérez de Montalbán, allegedly of Jewish descent, and who is supposed to have pirated Quevedo's novel *El buscón* (qq.v.). Quevedo visited the sin of the father on the son when baiting 'Juan Pérez' (q.v.) in the following epigram:

> *El doctor tú te lo pones,*
> *el Montalbán no lo tienes;*
> *conque, quitándote el don,*
> *vienes a quedar Juan Pérez.*

Juan Pérez de Montalbán studied theology at Alcalá and was ordained a priest in 1625, later becoming apostolic notary to the Inquisition. With Tirso de Molina and Ruiz de Alarcón (qq.v.), he was one of the more important of the Madrid group of playwrights in the circle of Lope de Vega (q.v.).

He wrote about sixty plays, some in conjunction with his contemporaries; for their chronology see J. H. Parker, 'The chronology of the plays of Juan Pérez de Montalbán' in *PMLA*, vol. 67 (1952), pp. 186–210.

His most notable play is the *Comedia famosa del Gran Séneca de España, Felipe II,* later than Vélez's *El águila del agua* and Diego Jiménez de Enciso's *El príncipe don Carlos* which also deal with the confrontation between Philip II and Don Carlos his son. The character of Carlos is fittingly complex but the main strength of the play is its emphasis on ambience rather than on any melodramatic and superficial denouement. A *Segunda parte* to this play is less melodramatic, but tells with moving power the ageing and death of Philip II. On hearing of the Armada's disaster, he does not blame his own navy, saying 'Yo la envié contra hombres—no contra mares y vientos' (I sent them to fight men—not the elements). The influence of the neo-Stoic movement increases towards the end. Other historical plays by Pérez de Montalbán include *El señor de don Juan de Austria* and *La puerta Macarena*.

The genre in which he excelled was the play of manners. *La más constante mujer* is set in Milan, where Carlo Sforza wins Isabel despite the attentions of the Duke of Milan towards her. *No hay vida como la honra* shows the death of the Conde Astolfo at the hand of Carlos, husband of the lady whom he was attempting to dishonour; Carlos gives himself up, claiming the reward offered for the capture of the murderer and obtaining forgiveness. Others in this genre (also included in vol. 45 (1858) of the BAE) consist of *La toquera vizcaína, Como padre y como rey, Cumplir con su obligación, Ser prudente y ser sufrido*, and *La doncella de labor*, the last on the manoeuvres worked out by Isabel de Arellano to marry Diego de Vargas. Wit, agility, and dramatic tension in these works owe much to Montalbán's mentor Lope de Vega.

His religious plays and pious legends include *Santa Maria Egipcíaca, La gitana de Menfis*, and *Las sacratísimas formas de Alcalá*. He dramatized *Palmerín de Oliva* and *Don Florisel de Niquea*, not recognizing that the qualities of fantasy permitted in the private reading of romances of chivalry would appear ridiculous when translated to the public stage. More successful adaptations from fiction were *La gitanilla* (from Cervantes); *Los amantes de Teruel* (from Boccaccio through Rey y Artieda and Tirso de Molina); and *Los hijos de la fortuna, Teágenes y Cariclea* (from Heliodorus of Emessa through Fernando de Mena's translation).

Montalbán also wrote a number of *autos sacramentales*, the best being *Polifemo*, an allegory in which Galatea is threatened by Evil but saved by the Redeemer, Acis. Montalbán followed Lope in experimenting with most other genres. His poetry was collected in *Orfeo en lengua castellana* (1624; ed. P. Cabañas, 1948) and his short novels in *Sucessos y prodigios de Amor en ocho novelas exemplares* (1624; ed. F. Gutiérrez, Barcelona, 1957), two of which (*La villana de Pinto* and *Los primos amantes*) appear in BAE, vol. 33 (1854). His *novela devota, Vida y purgatorio de San Patricio* (1627) has been edited by M. G. Profeti (Pisa, 1972).

The miscellany *Para todos* (Huesca, 1633)

contains 'exemplos morales, humanos y diuinos, en que se tratan diuersas ciencias, materias, y facultades, repartidos en los siete días de la semana'. It quickly ran through nine editions.

Pérez de Montalbán was also the first biographer of Lope de Vega (q.v.) in *Fama pósthuma a la vida y muerte del doctor fray Lope Félix de Vega Carpio. Y elogios panegíricos a la inmortalidad de su nombre* (1636), which gathered facts and opinions from those who knew Lope.

His plays were collected in two volumes: *Primero tomo de las Comedias . . .* and *Segundo Tomo* (both 1638). On becoming insane shortly before his death, he left unfinished the *Arte de bien morir*.

See G. W. Bacon, 'The life and works of Dr. Juan Pérez de Montalbán' in *Revue Hispanique*, vol. 26 (1912), pp. 1–474; and J. H. Parker, *Juan Pérez de Montalbán* (New York, 1975) in Twayne's World Authors Series.

PÉREZ DE MOYA, JUAN (1513?–1597?), b. Santisteban del Puerto, Jaén. Mathematician and moralist. In 1590 he was appointed a canon of Granada Cathedral. His main literary work was the *Philosophia secreta* (1585; ed. Gómez Baquero, 1928) a deservedly popular work which retold Greek and Roman mythology in a charming manner, with a moralizing epilogue to each tale. Pérez de Moya, who performed a valuable service by producing a number of textbooks on mathematical subjects, also published *Varia historia de Sanctas e ilustres mujeres* (1583) and *Comparaciones o símiles de vicios y virtudes* (Alcalá, 1584).

PÉREZ DE OLIVA, FERNÁN (1494?–1531?), b. Cordova. Humanist who studied at Salamanca and Alcalá, teaching at Salamanca from 1524; he also spent two years in Paris and three in Italy, where he was a protégé of Pope Leo X.

His major work was the *Diálogo de la dignidad del hombre*, first published in the *Obras* (Alcalá, 1546) of Francisco Cervantes de Salazar (q.v.). Reflecting the Renaissance view of man as a second creator, the dialogue is between the pessimist Aurelio, who views man's limitations as crippling; and the optimist Antonio, who sees only his limitless potential. The style is as invigorating as the author's avowed bias to the optimist. Mayáns y Síscar wrote of the dialogue 'si no es oro, es más precioso que el oro mismo'. It has been edited by J. L. Abellán (Barcelona, 1967).

Pérez de Oliva adapted classical plays into Spanish: *La vengança de Agamenón* (Burgos, 1528) from Sophocles' *Electra*, reproduced in facsimile by A. Bonilla y San Martín in *Obras dramáticas del siglo XVI*, vol. 1 (1914); *La comedia de Amphitrión* (n.p., n.d.) from Plautus' *Amphitryon*; and *Hécuba triste*, an adaptation of Euripides'

Hecuba; these three plays were edited, with some poems, by Pérez de Oliva's nephew Ambrosio de Morales in *Las obras* (Cordova, 1586), and the last-named was subsequently edited by J. J. López de Sedano in *Parnaso español*, vol. 6 (1772). There is a critical edition of the *Teatro* by W. Atkinson in *Revue Hispanique*, vol. 69 (1927), pp. 521–659.

Perhaps Pérez de Oliva's most celebrated poem is the elegy in *coplas de pie quebrado* entitled *Lamentación al saqueo de Roma, puesta en boca de Clemente VII*, reflecting the topos of nostalgia familiar from Jorge Manrique (q.v.).

Among his miscellaneous writings were *Tratado en latín sobre la piedra imán, Razonamiento sobre la navegación por el Guadalquivir, Historia de la inuención de las Yndias* (ed. J. J. Arrom, Bogotá, 1965), and the dialogues *Entre el cardenal Martínez Siliceo, la Aritmética y la Fama*.

See P. Enríquez Noreña, *El maestro Pérez de Oliva* (Havana, 1914) and W. Atkinson, 'Hernán Pérez de Oliva: a biographical and critical study' in *Revue Hispanique*, vol. 71 (1927), pp. 309–484.

PÉREZ DE VARGAS, José (1776–1855), b. Massa di Carrara, Italy. Peruvian poet and classicist. He returned to Peru with his family in 1796, and taught Latin. Manuel Beltroy includes him in *Las cien mejores poesías líricas peruanas* (1921), describing him as 'autor de composiciones bucólicas de índole horaciana y estilo fácil'. *El vaticinio* (1826) was an ode to Bolívar. He also published *Poesías* (1845).

Another Peruvian writer of the same name (1703–72), a Jesuit, was exiled with his fellow-Jesuits to Italy and there wrote a compendium on moral law and sermons.

PÉREZ ESCRICH, ENRIQUE (1829–97), b. Valencia. Popular novelist and playwright who capitalized on the success of his master Fernández y González (q.v.) by writing hasty serialized stories for a mass public. He earned colossal sums (up to 50,000 pesetas in a good year) but spent so freely that he died a pauper.

El cura de aldea (1858), a play adapted in 1864 as a novel, was the subject of a case brought against him for alleged plagiarism by Luis Mariano de Larra, the son of Mariano José de Larra (q.v.) and won by Pérez Escrich.

Some of his successful novels, written quickly and without literary pretensions, include *La esposa mártir* (1864), *La mujer adúltera* (2 vols., 1864), *El mártir de Gólgota* (2 vols., 1871), and *La caridad cristiana* (1871).

PÉREZ FERRARI, EMILIO, see FERRARI, Emilio.

PÉREZ GALDÓS, BENITO (1843–1920), b. Las Palmas, Canary Islands. Generally taken to be Spain's greatest novelist after Cervantes. A timid man who took on the responsibilities of a large family after the death of his eldest brother and supported it by his writing, Pérez Galdós arrived in Madrid as a student at 19, and was influenced by the *krausismo* (q.v.) popular at the time, which upheld individual conscience against the ritualism of neocatholicism.

He had an illegitimate daughter, María, and had a brief love affair with Emilia Pardo Bazán, but the prevailing myth of his pathological interest in furtive sex is probably unfounded. He never married, but praised his type of ideal friendship with an older woman (in his case Teodosia Gandarias) in the play *Pedro Minio* (1908). He distrusted marriage as an institution which he believed encouraged infidelity or the fear of it, and constantly preached free love (as in *Realidad* and *Tristana*) though he was opposed to licentiousness. In religion, his attitude of restless enquiry and scepticism contrasts with the faith of his friend Pereda (q.v.), and though he never expressed himself antagonistic to Roman Catholicism, he was the declared enemy of all forms of clericalism, and many of his novels show the malign influence of priests and those who make religion serve their own ends.

Most of his major works fall into three groups: the most important is the varied sequence of *novelas españolas contemporáneas* (q.v.), written for the most part concurrently with the 46 vols. of *Episodios nacionales* (q.v.). The third group is his drama, which began with *La expulsión de los moriscos* and *Un joven de provecho* (written in the aftermath of a brilliant performance of García Gutiérrez's *Venganza catalana* but not produced in his lifetime), and rapidly improved with the dramatization in 1892 of his novel *Realidad* (1889).

According to the author's own classification, the *novelas españolas de la primera época* (q.v.) are included in none of the above categories.

A certain amount of his journalism, autobiographical writings, travel diaries, and drama criticism can be found in the unsatisfactory *Obras completas* (1941, frequently reprinted with varying pagination which hinders reference), but much is missing, most significantly his major statement on his theory of the novel, 'Observaciones sobre la novela contemporánea en España' (*Revista de España*, vol. 15, 1870, pp. 162–72).

He saw Dickens, Balzac, and the Russian novelists gaining quick appreciation and understanding in their own countries, whereas Spanish novelists, he believed, were slow to achieve similar recognition. He accused them of inability

^
no cross-ref to
Misericordia

to portray the life of the times, and their readers of corrupt taste, for preferring foreign novels of dubious merit. He excepted only Fernán Caballero and Pereda from these strictures, urging other writers to take the great issues of the spiritual and sexual problems of the contemporary urban middle classes as their main source of inspiration. His later theoretical writings add little to this viewpoint: a prologue to Pereda's *El sabor de la tierruca* (1881), an address to the Real Academia Española (1897), and a prologue to the 3rd edition of Clarín's *La Regenta* (1900).

Though he translated *The Pickwick Papers* (1868, from the French) and claimed Dickens as a master, he avoided the sense of fantasy and caricature behind most of the Englishman's novels, and often seems closer in such novels as *Nazarín* or *Misericordia*, to Dostoevsky. Though his psychological penetration has rarely been equalled, he virtually ignored several major areas of contemporary life, including education and its backwardness in Spain, agriculture and land reform, and industrial society and its hardships. His strengths include a pure yet vigorous style; a knowledge of madness and schizophrenia (connected with his interest in Don Quijote) which seems uncannily accurate; the effective and systematic device of symbolism (evoking the self-delusion which was in his view a national weakness); and an absorbing sympathy for characters who rise from goodness to saintliness.

Galdós's dramatic works have often been criticized for their essentially novelistic character. He adapted for the stage his own novels *Realidad* (in 1892), *La loca de la casa* (in 1893), *Doña Perfecta* (in 1896), *El abuelo* (in 1904), and others, and his other plays which enjoyed success (such as *Electra*) often did so on account of political or other external reasons. Galdós in his plays was never less than serious, stylish, and thoughtful, all qualities otherwise virtually absent from the contemporary Spanish stage, and his dramatic influence was generally benign.

His last years, from his initial defeat in candidacy for the Academy in 1889 (though he was elected a few months later), were embittered by increasing loneliness and opposition. He resented the patronizing attitude of the young dramatic critics and was wounded that the Generation of 1898 did not consider him their mentor. The award of the Nobel Prize for Literature to Echegaray (a far inferior writer by any reckoning) struck Galdós as a foreign blow to the best Spanish writing of the time. In 1912 he became blind and suffered no less from insolvency in his later years, despite a national subscription which ended in fiasco, though it temporarily alleviated his worst debts and

obligations. Poverty rather than artistic need obliged him to write a third, fourth, and then a fifth series of *Episodios nacionales* from 1898 to 1912, but they were written in great haste, with none of the serene spirit and confidence of his earlier work, as reviewers were uncharitable enough to indicate.

His greatest books were *Fortunata y Jacinta* (q.v.), the group beginning with *El amigo Manso* (q.v.), and the *Torquemada* (q.v.) sequence, though many others of his novels are worthy of comparison with Balzac, Tolstoy, or Dickens.

The so-called *Obras completas* (1941, with several reprints) should be used with caution, and never if a critical edition is available of a given work. A. Ghiraldo produced 11 vols. of Galdos's *Obras inéditas* (1923–33), including *Fisionomías sociales, Arte y crítica, Política española* (2 vols.), *Nuestro teatro, Cronicón* (2 vols.), *Toledo: su historia y su leyenda, Viajes y fantasías, Memorias,* and *Crónica de Madrid.*

See T. A. Sackett, *Pérez Galdós: an annotated bibliography* (University of New Mexico, 1968). Of the numerous studies on Galdós, the following are indispensable: J. F. Montesinos, *Galdós* (4 vols., 1968–); A. Regalado García, *Benito Pérez Galdós y la novela histórica española* (1966); J. Casalduero, *Vida y obra de Galdós, 1843–1920* (1951); S. H. Eoff, *The novels of Pérez Galdós* (St. Louis, 1954); W. T. Pattison, *Benito Pérez Galdós and the creative process* (Minneapolis, 1954); R. Gullón, *Galdós, novelista moderno* (Madrid, 1960); G. Correa, *El simbolismo religioso en las novelas de Pérez Galdós* (1962) and *Realidad, ficción y símbolo en las novelas de Benito Pérez Galdós* (Bogotá, 1967); and H. Hinterhäuser, *Los episodios nacionales de Benito Pérez Galdós* (1963).

Anales Galdosianos has been published since 1966, first from Pittsburgh and now from Austin, Texas.

PÉREZ LUGÍN, ALEJANDRO (1870–1926), b. Madrid. Popular novelist, whose most celebrated work was *La casa de la Troya* (1915), a somewhat sentimental story of student life in Santiago de Compostela, which sold more than half a million copies and was dramatized by Manuel Linares Rivas (q.v.). *Currito de la Cruz* (1921), another work in the *costumbrista* vein, deals with an Andalusian bullfighter. Pérez Lugín's later novels, *La Corredoira y la Rúa* (1923), *La Virgen del Rocío ya entró en Triana* (1926), and *Arminda Moscoso* (1928), are unsuccessful.

Pérez Lugín's expert articles on bullfighting were signed 'Don Pío'.

See José Caamaño, *Ficción y realidad en la 'Casa de la Troya'* (Corunna, 1967).

PÉREZ PASTOR, CRISTÓBAL (1833–1908), b. Horche, Guadalajara. Cervantine scholar, archivist, and historian of acting and printing.

His works on printing included *La imprenta en Toledo* (1887) and *La imprenta en Medina del Campo* (1895), but he is best remembered for the *Documentos cervantinos hasta ahora inéditos* (2 vols., 1897–1901) and *Documentos para la biografía de don Pedro Calderón de la Barca* (1905). His other works included a detailed *Bibliografía madrileña del siglo XVI* (1891–1907) and *Nuevos datos acerca del histrionismo español en los siglos XVI y XVII* (1901–14).

See F. Zamora, 'Un gran bibliógrafo: Pérez Pastor' in *RABM*, vol. 67 (1959), pp. 661–75.

PÉREZ ROSALES, Vicente (1807–86), b. Santiago. Chilean autobiographer. Educated in Mendoza, Argentina, he travelled to France, and then to California for the mining. A businessman and self-confessed smuggler, he was also employed for some time as a colonial agent in southern Chile and wrote of these last experiences during his time as a consul in Hamburg from 1855 in *Essai sur le Chili* (Hamburg, 1857). His other minor works are *Memoria sobre la colonización de la provincia de Valdivia* (1852), *Memoria sobre emigración, inmigración y colonización* (1854), *Manual del ganadero chileno* (1858), and *La colonia de Llanquihue* (1872).

His major work is the autobiographical *Recuerdos del pasado, 1814–1860* (1882; definitive edn., 1886; reprinted 1949), full of life and drama and an important source of our knowledge of early 19th c. Chilean life and times. He wrote a separate travel book on his experiences in California: *Diario de un viaje a California: 1848–1849* (1851).

See E. Rodríguez de Mendoza, *Vicente Pérez Rosales* (1934).

Perfecta, Doña. see DOÑA PERFECTA.

Perfecta casada, La (Salamanca, 1583) is a masterpiece of Spanish-Renaissance didactic prose by Fray Luis de León (q.v.), dedicated to his niece María Varela Osorio on the occasion of her wedding. His principal source is chapter XXXI of the Book of Proverbs, which he annotates literally in detail as opposed to the method of St. Ambrose, who interpreted the passage allegorically to refer to the Church. Luis also refers to the teachings of the Church Fathers (especially Tertullian and Basil), to classical sources, and possibly uses more recent writings (though this is disputed by P. Ángel Custodio Vega in his critical edition of the *Poesías*, (1955)), such as Guevara's *Letra para los recién casados*, Luis Vives, and the *Speculum coniugorum* (Salamanca, 1562) of the Augustinian Alonso Gutiérrez de la Vera Cruz.

Luis satirizes the contemporary (and often universal) affectations and weaknesses of some women, not as an antifeminist, as claimed in J. R. Sánchez's *La perfecta casada según fray Luis de León* (1912), but in order to preach the contrary.

La perfecta casada has been edited by A. Bonilla y San Martín (1917) in the Clásicos de la Literatura Española, the text that is reproduced in most subsequent editions; and by J. López Navarro (1968). *The perfect wife* (Denton, Texas, 1943) is a translation by Alice Philena Hubbard. There is a play entitled *La perfecta casada* by A. Cubillo de Aragón (q.v.).

Peribáñez y el Comendador de Ocaña, a play written *c.* 1606 by Lope de Vega Carpio (q.v.) and first published in *Parte quarta de las comedias . . .* (1614).

Properly considered a double tragedy, the play concerns Fadrique, a basically honourable *Comendador* (not the tyrant more usual in such plays) who falls from his horse and is tended in the home of Peribáñez. There he falls in love with Casilda, wife of Peribáñez, who refuses to betray her husband. Demented with love, Fadrique devises several stratagems to try to meet Casilda alone and though he fails, a popular song is woven around his intentions.

Although Peribáñez rightly believes in his wife's innocence, he kills Fadrique, who had ennobled him for his own ends. It is one of the many Golden Age plays, such as Calderón's *El alcalde de Zalamea* (q.v.), in which a commoner (though in this case a wealthy and respected man) is menaced with dishonour by an *hidalgo*: the contrast between honour as a moral quality and as mere social rank is its central theme. As Duncan Moir writes, Lope's achievements include magnificent poetry and the splendid characterization of Peribáñez, who subtly but strikingly changes in his attitude and his language when he ceases to be just the noble commoner and becomes the ennobled commoner. Peribáñez defends his action before the court of Enrique III (1390–1406). Enrique's queen, moved by his courage, says that his action 'no es delito, sino valor'. The king eventually pardons him.

The play is as unusual and moving in its way as *Fuenteovejuna* (q.v.), another production in which the arrogance of the nobility is subdued by a silent but effective pact between the monarchy and its subjects. Other ideas include the contrast between *aldea* and *corte*, and rash youth (the *Comendador*) and maturity (Peribáñez).

The best of the many available editions of this play is that by Ch. Aubrun and J. F. Montesinos (Paris, 1943). Much of their prologue, together with E. M. Wilson's 'Images et structure dans "Peribáñez"' from *Bulletin*

Hispanique, vol. 51 (1949), pp. 125–59, translated into Spanish, appears in a useful selection of studies, *El teatro de Lope de Vega*, compiled by J. F. Gatti (Buenos Aires, 1962).

See also J. E. Varey, 'The essential ambiguity of "Peribáñez"' in *Theatre Research International* (1976).

Periquillo Sarniento, El, a picaresque novel by José Joaquín Fernández de Lizardi (q.v.), and (according to some literary historians) the first 'true' novel published in Latin America. Originally published in instalments, it first appeared in book form incomplete in 3 vols. in 1816. The fourth volume was prohibited by the censor because of its blunt attack on the Negro slave system, considered by the censor 'inoportuno, perjudicial en las circunstancias, e impolítico por dirigirse contra un comercio permitido por el rey'.

El Periquillo Sarniento first appeared complete in 5 vols. in 1830–1. In the mainstream of Spanish picaresque writing, it is the story, told in the first person to his family, by a *pícaro* on his deathbed. Full of moralizing digressions, the book is far too long, a fault avoided in Fernández de Lizardi's last novel, *Vida y hechos del famoso caballero Don Catrín de la Fachenda* (1832), his favourite.

The style is plain, natural, and full of vigorous Mexicanisms. The plot follows the tradition of *Lazarillo de Tormes* (q.v.) in showing the hero as servant to various masters, and subject to various temptations and misfortunes. Each episode passes judgment on manners and morals, on religion, education, and types of hypocrisy. On the death of his father, el Periquillo squanders a fortune on gambling and women, finally receiving a jail sentence. Once freed, he begins to practise medicine among the Indians, marries but is soon made a widower, and decides on a life at sea. Shipwrecked, he is befriended by a Chinese mandarin. He returns to Mexico and remarries. He finally repents of his wild life and is taken for a saint.

There is a good modern edition of *El Periquillo Sarniento* (3 vols., 1949) by J. R. Spell.

Perqué (Italian: *perché*, 'why?', according to Corominas, though Navarro prefers a Catalan or Provençal origin in spite of the admitted absence of the form in those languages), a verse-form consisting of a series of octosyllabic couplets to ask rhetorical questions usually preceded by a *redondilla* or *quintilla* linked with the verse couplet: abba; ac; cd; de; ef.

The first recorded *perqué* is a satire by Diego Hurtado de Mendoza (q.v.) in the 14th c.; another occurs at the end of B. Torres Naharro's play *Serafina*. Other practitioners of the form include Alonso Núñez Reinoso, Jiménez de Urrea, Garcí Sánchez de Badajoz, Juan del Encina, and Cervantes (who called it *aquelindo* in *El rufián dichoso*). An example of the perqué is as follows: 'Pues no quiero andar en corte / nin lo tengo por deseo, / quiero fer un devaneo / con que haya algún deporte / y qualque consolación: / ¿Por qué en el lugar de Arcos / no usan de confesión? / ¿Por qué la dis-[putación] / faze pro a las devegadas? / ¿Por qué malas peñoladas / fazen falsos los notarios? / ¿Por qué mandan los vicarios / ir frayres de dos en dos? . . .' (Diego Hurtado de Mendoza).

Perros hambrientos, Los, a novel by the Peruvian Ciro Alegría (q.v.), first published in 1938.

The shepherdess Antuca guards her flock with her four dogs. A drought threatens the Peruvian countryside. As it becomes more severe, men turn to violence to stay alive, and 'the hungry dogs' of the title become ferocious like them, eventually massacring the flock with which they are entrusted. Alegría shows the plight of the Indians not only as victims of circumstance, but also as victims of their Spanish masters, and foreign companies.

At last the rain comes, a harvest will be possible in the future, human beings become gentle, and the surviving dog, no longer hungry, reverts to her role as guardian instead of predator.

See A. Cornejo Polar, *La estructura del acontecimiento en 'Los perros hambrientos'* (1968).

PERSIA, JUAN DE (1567?–1640?), the Spanish name adopted by Uruq Bek, son of Sultan Ali Bek on his conversion to Christianity in 1601. He compiled, with the aid of Fray Alfonso Remón, *Relaciones* (1604; ed. N. Alonso Cortés, 1947) concerning Persia, its kings and natural wonders, the wars with the Turks and other peoples, his own journey to Spain, and finally his conversion to Roman Catholicism. There is an English translation by G. Le Strange (1926) in the Broadway Travellers series.

Persiles y Sigismunda, Los trabajos de, a 'Byzantine' novel, subtitled '*historia setentrional*' (1617) by Miguel de Cervantes Saavedra (q.v.); the last book that Cervantes wrote, and long more popular than the superior *Don Quijote* (q.v.). Begun in 1609, *Persiles* was completed hastily, to judge from the fact that the fourth and last book has only 14 chapters, whereas the other three have 23, 22, and 21 respectively.

Cervantes' purpose is to show man's spiritual odyssey by examples of good and evil and, in an exciting though highly improbable sequence of stories, 'enseñar y deleitar juntamente'.

The novel begins in the far north, comes south to Portugal and Spain, and ends in Rome. Persiles and Sigismunda are the perfect hero and heroine, virtuous, chaste, and honourable. He is the son of the Queen of Thule, a land in the uttermost north of Norway, and she the daughter of the Queen of Finland (not the Finland we know but an 'island three hundred leagues away from Thule').

Their marriage is celebrated only after Cervantes has intercalated numerous incidental stories, such as those of the dancing-master Rutilio, Clodio and Rosamunda, Tozuelo and Isabela Castrucho, and Andrés Marulo. Cervantes also inserts dissertations on a variety of matters to which he had given mature thought, including history, ignorance and knowledge, love and women. Though it may be going too far to claim, with W. J. Entwistle, that the subplots constitute the outstanding value of the book, there can be no question but that as a whole the book is disappointing after the success of *Quijote*. The novel was adapted by Rojas Zorrilla (q.v.) as his earliest individual play that can be dated with certainty, being first performed on 23 February 1633: Rojas changes the title to *Persiles y Segismunda*.

The best available edition of the *Persiles* is that by J. B. Avalle-Arce (1969) in Clásicos Castalia.

See P. de Novo y Chicarro, *Bosquejo para una edición crítica de 'Los trabajos de Persiles y Sigismunda'* (1928); Joaquín Casalduero, *Sentido y forma de 'Los trabajos de Persiles y Sigismunda'* (Buenos Aires, 1947); C. Romero, *Introduzione al 'Persiles'* (Venice, 1968); and A. K. Forcione, *Cervantes, Aristotle and the 'Persiles'* (Princeton, N.J., 1970).

Perú Ilustrado, El, a celebrated literary weekly magazine first published on 14 May 1887, when the editor was Abel de la E. Delgado. It quickly built up a reputation as a leading review, attracting Rubén Darío and other writers, including Europeans from outside Peru. From 1889, Clorinda Matto de Turner (q.v.) edited the magazine for a short time, courageously publishing the anti-clerical *Magdala* by the Brazilian Henrique Maximiano Coelho Neto (1864–1934) in the issue of 23 August 1890, after which the editor was burnt in effigy at Cuzco and Arequipa. The review ceased publication in 1892 but was revived in a second series (1893–6), when the leading contributor was José Santos Chocano (q.v.).

PESADO, José Joaquín (1801–61), b. S. Agustín del Palmar, State of Puebla. Minor Mexican poet who was Minister of the Interior in 1838 and of External Affairs 1845–6. Originally a liberal, he later changed to con-servatism. His *Poesías originales y traducidas* (1839) was enlarged in 1849 and 1886. *Los aztecas* (1854) imitates native Mexican poetry. Always subject to classical influences, the Bible, Dante, and Petrarch, Pesado was successful in many semi-derivative works, including the pastoral idyll *Escenas del campo y de la aldea de México* and the incomplete epic poems *Moisés* and *La revelación*. Many of his translations were weak, including those from Virgil, but his version from Tasso's *Gerusalemme liberata* has many felicities. Pesado's short novel 'El inquisidor de México' appeared in *El Año Nuevo* (1838) and has been reprinted with *El amor frustrado* (1838) in *Novelas cortas de varios autores* (1901), pp. 3–87.

See José María Roa Bárcena, *Biografía de don José Joaquín Pesado* (1878) reprinted in Roa Bárcena's *Obras*, vol. 4 (1902), pp. 1–205.

PEYROU, Manuel (1902–), b. San Nicolás de los Arroyos, Buenos Aires. Argentinian novelist and short-story writer. A qualified lawyer, he worked on *La Prensa* for many years His detective stories were among the first and best in Argentina; *La espada dormida* (1944), with the English detective Vane as protagonist; *El estruendo de las rosas* (1948) solves a political crime. The stories in *La noche repetida* (1953) and the novel *Las leyes del juego* (1959) rely on the allegory of life and crime as games. The latter moves confidently in the milieu of Perón's corrupt Buenos Aires, showing how homicide remains uninvestigated where business is involved. The hero Francisco Berthier is a key figure in recent Latin-American literature.

El árbol de Judas (1961) is a book of short stories set in Buenos Aires at the turn of the century. *Acto y ceniza* (1963) is a novel of *vida porteña* during Perón's dictatorship. Later books include *Se vuelven contra nosotros* (1966) the last of the *peronista* trilogy; the short stories, *Marea de fervor* (1967), and a novel *El hijo rechazado* (1969) about a businessman who prefers money to love.

PEZOA VÉLIZ, Carlos (1879–1908), b. Santiago. Chilean poet who was a victim of poverty in early life. He spent a Bohemian adolescence, and his experiences among 'the lower depths' were crucial to his poetry in which the element of social protest was all the more effective for being implicit. He was hurt during the 1906 earthquake in Valparaíso and died from his injuries.

His poetry is modernist though dealing with poverty and misery as principal themes whereas modernism generally idealized humanity. In the posthumous *Alma chilena: poesías líricas, poemas, prosa escogida* (Valparaíso, 1912), the editor E. Montenegro has indicated that Pezoa's work can be divided into three periods: up to 1901; 1902–5; and after 1905, the best being the second. The definitive edition of his *Poesías, cuentos y artículos* (1927) edited by Armando Donoso, has been partly superseded by Raúl Silva Castro's edition of Pezoa's *Obras [y] biografía* (1964).

See Norberto Pinilla's bibliography in *Revista Iberoamericana*, vol. 4, no. 8 (1942), pp. 473–82; and Antonio de Undurraga, *Pezoa Véliz: ensayo biográfico, crítico y antológico* (1951).

PFANDL, LUDWIG (1881–1942). German Hispanist specializing in the literature and life of the Spanish Golden Age. *Spanische Kultur und Sitte des 16. und 17. Jahrhunderts* (Munich, 1924) was a notably clearsighted view of the subject and the Spanish translation by P. Félix García, *Cultura y costumbres del pueblo español de los siglos XVI y XVII* (Barcelona, 1929) has been constantly in print. Pfandl also wrote *Geschichte der spanischen Nationalliteratur in ihrer Blütezeit* (Freiburg/Breisgau, 1929; trans. as *Historia de la literatura nacional española en la Edad de Oro*, 1933, 2nd edn., 1952); *Über das Märchendrama bei Lope de Vega* (Munich, 1942); and *Die zehnte Muse von Mexico. Juana Inés de la Cruz. Ihr Leben. Ihre Dichtung. Ihre Psyche* (Munich, 1946). Among his numerous scholarly articles were an edition of Lope de Vega's 'Los achaques de Leonor' in *Revue Hispanique*, vol. 54 (1922), pp. 347–416 and 'Unveröffentlichte Gedichte der Brüder Leonardo de Argensola' in *Revue Hispanique*, vol. 55 (1923), pp. 161–88.

Pícara Justina, Libro de entretenimiento de la, a picaresque novel published in Medina del Campo (1605). The name on the title-page is that of Francisco López de Úbeda. C. Pérez Pastor has discovered documents proving the existence of a Toledo-born doctor of that name but, since the time of Nicolás Antonio,' López de Úbeda' was believed to conceal the identity of a Dominican monk, Andrés Pérez of León, a view upheld in his edition of the novel by J. Puyol y Alonso (3 vols., 1912). Despite Bataillon's support for the thesis that López de Úbeda is the author (in his *Varia lección de clásicos españoles*, 1964), the attribution remains unproven.

La pícara Justina was written by a born talker with little sense of plot-construction or characterization. He borrows from Timoneda's *Patrañuelo*, Alemán's *Guzmán de Alfarache*, *Lazarillo de Tormes*, and *La Celestina*. It was extremely popular with the sensation-seeking public and was soon translated into Italian (Venice, 1624), and French. The first English version, by J. Stevens, appeared in 1707.

The principal value of *La pícara Justina* nowadays is philological (the introduction of phrases and words in Leonese dialect) and lexicographical, owing to the author's extravagant style and tendency to introduce neologisms. In the words of Mayáns, the author is 'el primer Español que, dejando la propiedad y gravedad de nuestra lengua, abrió el nuevo camino de inventar por capricho, no sólo vocablos, sino modos de hablar'.

A pretentious *Arte poética* introduces each chapter with one of 50 different metres, and a moral or *aprovechamiento* ends each chapter, often with little apparent relevance.

The plot of the novel is thin, contrived, and uninteresting. It is divided into four sections: the rise of Justina the female rogue; her adventures in the *romerías* of Arenillas and León; her travels to Medina de Rioseco and Mansilla; and her rejection of several suitors in favour of a soldier called Lozano. A promised sequel in which she becomes widowed and marries Guzmán de Alfarache was never published, and probably never written.

The notion of a picaresque heroine recurs in *La hija de Celestina; o, la ingeniosa Elena* (1612) by Alonso Jerónimo de Salas Barbadillo (q.v.).

The latest editions of *La pícara Justina* are by A. Valbuena Prat (*La novela picaresca española*, 1944–6), and Carlos Ayala and Jaime Uyá (Barcelona, 1968). In a recent study, *Pícaros y pícaresca: la pícara Justina* (Madrid, 1969), Bataillon suggests that the novel is a *roman à clef* alluding to well-known court figures and satirizing *limpieza de sangre* (q.v.).

Picaresque Novel, The. In Spain, a genre written for the most part during the 16th and 17th cs. and depicting a delinquent's passage through life, frequently with moral or religious comments, and almost invariably told in the first person.

The term *pícaro* is first recorded in 1525 as meaning 'kitchen boy', but by 1545 its connotation was that of 'evil-living' in general, and in 1726 it meant someone 'low, vicious, deceitful, dishonourable, and shameless'.

Novels in this genre, which is generally thought to begin with *Lazarillo de Tormes* (q.v., 1554), are characterized by a low-life milieu, and a shrewd hero (later sometimes a heroine) who may manage to climb the social ladder, and achieve—albeit temporarily—financial and other successes. The true prototype of the Spanish picaresque novel is *Guzmán de Alfarache* (2 vols., 1599–1604) by Mateo Alemán (qq.v.), with which realism became the norm for the Spanish novel. The influence of *Guzmán* in Spain was immediate and widespread; beyond its native borders it found translators and imitators, in Germany (Grimmelshausen's *Simplicissimus*, 1669), in France (Lesage's *Gil Blas de Santillane*,

1715–35), and in England (Defoe's *Moll Flanders*, 1722).

The greatest of Spanish picaresque novels as a work of art is undoubtedly Quevedo's *Buscón* (qq.v., Saragossa, 1626); noteworthy also are the short exemplary novels by Cervantes *Rinconete y Cortadillo* and *La ilustre fregona* (qq.v., both 1613), somewhat in the picaresque manner. Other important examples are *La pícara Justina* (q.v., Medina del Campo, 1605); *Relaciones de la vida del escudero Marcos de Obregón* (q.v., 1618) by Vicente Espinel (q.v.); *Alonso, mozo de muchos amos* (q.v., 1624–6) by Jerónimo Alcalá Yáñez (q.v.); and *Estebanillo González* (see GONZÁLEZ, 1646), an apparently autobiographical work in the historical setting of the Thirty Years' War.

The misconceptions concerning the picaresque spread by F. W. Chandler in his outmoded *Romances of roguery* (New York, 1899; reprinted New York, 1961), and refuted by A. A. Parker in his *Literature and the delinquent* ... (Edinburgh, 1967) include the following: (a) that the picaresque genre arose in Spain mainly because social conditions there were conducive to the existence of delinquents in large numbers (in 1656 there were 40,000 beggars in Paris alone, and large numbers exercised their trade in all other countries of Western Europe); (b) that picaresque novels are primarily comic; (c) that the society portrayed in the novels is more important to the writer than his characters; and, (d) that the novels have no real moral intentions, any moralizing or preaching being satirical or hypocritical. All of these commonly-held notions are wholly or partly incorrect. The picaresque genre emerged as a literary retort to the escapist chivalresque genre. Bataillon sees them at least in part as embodying the tensions caused by the consciousness of 'purity of blood' and the attendant jealousies and hypocrisies.

The genre declined with the growth of *costumbrismo* (q.v.), a phase marked initially by the works of Castillo Solórzano, Salas Barbadillo, and Zayas y Sotomayor (qq.v.), and subsequently by Liñán y Verdugo, Fernández de Ribera, and Francisco Santos (qq.v.).

Many fictional heroes from the late 18th c. have been loosely described as 'picaresque' in the sense of 'roguish' or 'scoundrelly', but the major historical tendency in Spanish literature can be said to have died out in the mid-17th c. with *Estebanillo González*.

See Joseph L. Laurenti, *Ensayo de una bibliografía de la novela picaresca española, años 1554–1964* (1968); A. del Monte, *Itinerario del romanzo picaresco spagnuolo* (Florence, 1957); A. A. Parker, *Literature and the delinquent: the picaresque novel in Spain and Europe, 1599–1753*

(Edinburgh, 1967); and Marcel Bataillon, *Pícaros y picaresca* (1969).

PICÓN, JACINTO OCTAVIO (1852–1923), b. Madrid. Novelist and short-story writer. He studied in France (where he read Dumas and Hugo) and at Madrid University. He excelled as a short-story writer, in *Cuentos de mi tiempo* (1895), *Mujeres* (1911), and similar books.

As a novelist he followed Valera closely, suggesting that his books were intended for entertainment rather than instruction, and paying more heed to his own status as an ironic and detached observer than to the passions and inner lives of his characters.

His books were all set in Madrid. Some earlier novels were anti-clerical in tone, among them *Lázaro* (1882), subtitled *casi novela*; and *El enemigo* (1887). Another group emphasizes the rightness of spontaneous love against forced love, even against artificial ties of marriages where love does not exist: *La hijastra del amor* (1884), *La honrada* (1890), *Dulce y Sabrosa* (1891), *Sacramento* (1910), and *Juanita Tenorio* (1914), the last with a twist all too predictable from its title (Tenorio bring the surname of 'Don Juan'). *Juan Vulgar* (1885) is the ironic study of a student from Andalusia in Madrid.

Picón also wrote some of the most durable art criticism of his time: *Vida y obras de don Diego Velázquez* (1899) and *El desnudo en el arte* (1902).

See H. Peseux-Richard, 'Un romancier espagnol: Jacinto Octavio Picón' in *Revue Hispanique*, vol. 30 (1914), pp. 515–85.

Pie quebrado ('broken foot'), a metrical stanza normally comprising six lines of which the 1st, 2nd, 4th, and 5th are octosyllabic, and the 3rd and 6th tetrasyllabic. The rhyme scheme is variable: abcabc; aabaab; aabccb.

The earliest known *coplas de pie quebrado* date from the 14th c., in Pedro de Veragüe and Juan Ruiz, Arcipreste de Hita: 'Virgen del cielo reyna / e del mundo melezina, / quiérasme oir (muy benina); / que de tus gozos ayna / escriba yo prosa dina / por te servir'. (Juan Ruiz, *Libro de buen amor*, second *cantiga de Gozos de Santa María*, stanza 33.) The above is a variation of the symmetrical *sextilla* (q.v.).

The *coplas de pie quebrado* were popularized by the Marqués de Santillana (q.v.), and have been used by Spanish poets of all generations up to that of Antonio Machado, with great success.

PIFERRER, PAU (1818–48), b. Barcelona. Poet and music critic who died tragically young of tuberculosis. Piferrer collected folk ballads and was one of the moving spirits behind the Catalan Revival. He contributed the sections on Catalonia and the Balearics to *Recuerdos y Bellezas de*

España (1893–43). Of his sixteen surviving poems, the most important are 'Retorno de la feria' and 'Canción de la primavera'.

See R. Carnicer, *Vida y obra de Pablo Piferrer* (1963).

Pilares, the imaginary setting of *Tigre Juan* (q.v.) and its sequel *El curandero de su honra* (both 1926), novels by Ramón Pérez de Ayala (q.v.). Some critics have identified Pilares with Ayala's native town, Oviedo.

PIMENTEL, LUIS VÁZQUEZ FERNÁNDEZ (1895–1958), b. Lugo. Galician poet who studied and practised medicine in his native Galicia. *Barco sin luces* (Lugo, 1960) consists of verses in Castilian, but most of his poems were in Galician. His work first appeared in the magazine *Ronsel* in 1924–5, yet his first published book, *Triscos* (Pontevedra, 1950), did not appear until he was 55 and it was not until after his death that Galicia appreciated him fully, with the collection *Sombra do aire na herba* (Vigo, 1959). Another of his books, 'Cunetas', has so far not appeared. Influences on his work are numerous: French symbolists, especially Laforgue, seem to be paramount. Self-plagiarism abounds, but seems usually to be dictated by each poem's internal needs.

See Miguel González Garcés, *Poesía gallega contemporánea: antología* (Barcelona, 1974), with an introduction to Pimentel and bilingual texts showing his range, from a lullaby owing much to early Galician lyrics, to the delightful melancholy of *Paseo*.

PIÑA, JUAN DE (1566–1643), b. Buendía, Cuenca. Novelist. A devoted friend and admirer of Lope de Vega (q.v.), even to the point of acting as go-between in some of Lope's love affairs, Piña is a minor writer of interest to those concerned with Lopean scholarship. He was a royal scribe to Philip II and his two successors.

His first book was *Novelas exemplares y prodigiosas historias* (1624), containing 'La duquesa de Normandía', 'El celoso engañado', 'Los amantes sin terceros', 'El casado por amor', 'El engaño en la verdad', 'Amor por ejemplo', and 'El matemático dichoso', in addition to the play 'Amar y disimular'. This he followed with *Varias fortunas* (1627), containing 'Las fortunas de don Antonio Hurtado de Mendoza', 'Fortunas del segundo Orlando', 'Fortunas de la duquesa de Milán, Leonor Esforzia', and 'Próspera y adversa fortuna del tirano Guillermo, rey de la Gran Bretaña', in addition to 'Las fortunas del príncipe de Polonia'.

His most entertaining and varied book is the novel *Casos prodigiosos y cueva encantada* (1628) and *Segunda parte . . .* (1629; ed. with a biographical

and critical study by Emilio Cotarelo y Mori, 1907). Piña's narrative power is here at its height, moving easily from the fantasy of the enchanted cave to the realism of Blanca's life in Paris. It is instructive to compare the fiction of Piña with that of Zayas (q.v.).

Pinciano, any *vallisoletano*, or inhabitant of Valladolid. The name derives from the Latin place Pintia erroneously believed to have stood on the site of modern Valladolid. In Spanish literature, 'el Pinciano' generally refers to Hernán Núñez de Toledo y Guzmán (q.v.).

See also LÓPEZ PINCIANO, Alonso.

PINEDA, ANDREU MARTÍ (*c.* 1483–1566), b. Valencia? Religious poet and love poet writing in Catalan who is recorded as a notary 1512–66. His *Procés o disputa de viudes y donzelles* was included in Jaume Roig's *Spill* (1561), but Pineda is best known as a religious poet for his work on the Immaculate Virgin and the Passion of Christ. Fragments of his *Consells a un casat* appear in *Ocho siglos de poesía catalana* (Barcelona, 1969), compiled by J. M. Castellet and J. Molas.

PINEDA, JUAN DE (1515?–97), b. Medina del Campo. Franciscan scholar. *Los treynta y cinco diálogos familiares de la agricultura christiana* (Salamanca, 1589) is a massive work that gives a good idea of a well-read Spanish cleric's view of life in the last quarter of the 16th c. While his laborious style makes for difficult reading, Pineda's learning and vocabulary are impressive. The book was reprinted in vols. 161–3 and 169–70 of the BAE, and last edited in 1919.

Pineda's other books are a *Historia maravillosa . . . de San Juan Bautista* (Salamanca, 1574) and *Los treynta libros de la monarquía eclesiástica o historia universal del mundo* (Saragossa, 1576), in which he refers to, or quotes from, over a thousand authors, according to Hurtado y Palencia.

It was another Juan de Pineda who fought a duel with Alonso de Ercilla (q.v.), author of *La Araucana*. Ercilla was sent to prison and that Pineda joined the Augustinians.

PIÑERA, VIRGILIO (1914–), Cuban playwright, novelist, and short-story writer. Long an exile in Argentina, he published there a novel *La carne de René* (1952) and the stories in *Cuentos fríos* (1956), which show Piñera's view of the torment and absurdity of life. After returning to Cuba, he published another novel, *Pequeñas maniobras* (1963).

PINILLOS, MANUEL (1914–), b. Saragossa. Poet, who studied law at Saragossa University. He was founder and editor of *Ámbito* (1951–62).

His poetry has found continuing inner strength and serenity in solitude, avoiding movements and literary groups which could have robbed it of its quiet individuality. His principal masters are Hölderlin and Rilke. Pinillos has published *A la puerta del hombre* (1948), *Sentado sobre el suelo* (1951), *Demasiados ángeles* (1951), *Tierra de nadie* (1952), *De hombre a hombre* (1952, the winner of the City of Barcelona Prize for 1951), *La muerte o la vida* (1955), *El octavo día* (1958), *Débil tronco querido* (1959), *Debajo del cielo* (1960), *El corral ajeno* (1962), *Aún queda sol en los veranos* (1962), *Esperar no es un sueño* (1962), *Nada es del todo* (1963), *Atardece sin mí* (1964), and *Lugar de origen* (1965).

PÍO, Don, a pseudonym used by Alejandro Pérez Lugín (q.v.) for his articles on bullfighting.

PIQUER, Andrés (1711–72), b. Fórnoles, Teruel. Philosopher and scientist. The uncle of Juan Pablo Forner (q.v.), Piquer studied philosophy and medicine at Valencia University and taught anatomy there. In 1751 he was appointed a royal doctor.

Medicina vetus et nova (1735) caused a good impression, but *Física moderna, racional y experimental* (1745) was the first Spanish book to be solely devoted to physics and gave him an international reputation. He followed this with *Tratado de las calenturas* (1751) and *Filosofía moral para la juventud española* (1755). He earned his nickname 'El Hipócrates Español' with a trilingual translation of Hippocrates (3 vols., 1757–70).

PITA RODRÍGUEZ, Félix (1909–), b. Bejucal. Cuban poet, short-story writer, and essayist who has lived in Europe, Africa, and America. His first collection of poems, *Corcel de fuego* (1948), showed the influences of Vallejo and Neruda (qq.v.), but his second, far more original, *Las crónicas* (1961), was social in inspiration, with surrealist overtones. *Las noches* (1964) intensified his involvement with the Cuban Revolution.

His collections of short stories are *Tobías* (1955), *Esta larga tarea de aprender a morir* (Monticello College, 1960), and *Cuentos completos* (1963). An anthology, *Poemas y cuentos* (1966), has also appeared. His essays include *Literatura comprometida* (1956) and *Carlos Enríquez* (1957).

PITILLAS, Jorge, pseudonym of José Gerardo de Hervás y Cobo de la Torre (q.v.).

PI Y MARGALL, Francisco (1824–1901), b. Barcelona. President of the First Republic (1873–4), historian, and essayist. His major work, *Historia de España en el siglo XIX* (7 vols. in 8, 1902), was edited and partly written by his son Francisco Pi y Arsuaga from materials that Pi y Margall had assembled. His other studies included *Historia de la pintura en España* (1851), *Estudios sobre la Edad Media* (1873), *Las nacionalidades* (1876), *Joyas literarias* (1876), and *Observaciones sobre el carácter de Don Juan Tenorio* (1884). He also wrote an *ensayo dramático* entitled *Rebelión* (1897). *La República de 1873* (1874) outlined his policy and actions while in office.

PLÁ, Josefina (1909–), b. Canary Islands. Poet and playwright, widow of the ceramicist Julián de la Herrería, who died while they were visiting Spain in 1937. Plá has taken Paraguayan nationality.

Having published her first collection of poems in Asunción, *El precio de los sueños* (1934), she returned to Paraguay in 1938, giving an influential radio talk, 'Poetas y poesía moderna', constituting a manifesto of surrealism. Of her copious work, a small collection of poems appeared in *La raíz y la aurora* (1960), to be followed in 1965 by *Invención de la muerte*, and in 1966 by *Satélites oscuros*. Perhaps her best play is the comedy *Aquí no ha pasado nada*, which won the first prize of the Ateneo Paraguayo in 1942. Plá has published the monograph *El teatro en el Paraguay* (1967) as well as the informative *Apuntes para una historia de la cultura paraguaya* (1967). She has recently turned to *cuentos* in *La mano y la tierra* (1963) and won *La Tribuna*'s first prize for her story *El espejo* in 1968. Of her works on the history of art in Latin America many are on Paraguay, including *El barroco hispano-guaraní* (Asunción, 1975).

Plácida y Vitoriano, Égloga de, the most ambitious of the Italianate plays of Juan del Encina (q.v.), father of Spanish Renaissance drama. It was performed in Rome in 1513 and the first surviving published edition is that of Burgos (1520), despite reference by Leandro Fernández de Moratín (q.v.) in *Orígenes del teatro español* to a *princeps* of Rome (1514). It has been edited in the complete *Églogas* by H. López Morales (New York, 1963).

Vitoriano has apparently broken off his courtship of Plácida, who retires to the mountains to die of grief. Vitoriano is advised by his friend Suplicio to find consolation in the arms of Flugencia, but she makes fun of him and sends him away. An old hag called Eritea (based on Celestina, q.v.) then enters and discusses magic love-potions with Flugencia. Vitoriano tells Suplicio that he cannot forget Plácida and goes in search of her, but she has already stabbed herself. Suplicio manages to prevent Vitoriano from suffering the same fate. The next scene,

Vigilia de la enamorada muerta, is a sacrilegious parody of the *Officium defunctorum* in which Cupid is invoked. This treatment recalls the *Liciones de Job* of Garci Sánchez de Badajoz (q.v.) and other compositions of the *Cancionero General*, and also Juan Ruiz's burlesque of the Divine Office in the *Libro de buen amor* (q.v.). Two shepherds now add comic relief. When Vitoriano keeps vigil over the grave of Plácida, and is about to kill himself, Venus appears to explain that Plácida's death was arranged to test his fidelity; she resuscitates Plácida through her brother Mercury, and the play ends in rejoicing. The play is notable because it is probably here that the prologue or *introito* and the *paso* or *entremés* are first introduced. The plot, though it consists of loosely-linked episodes, nevertheless constitutes a great advance over its predecessors. The metres used are *coplas de arte mayor*, octosyllabic *coplas de pie quebrado* of 5-, 7-, 8-, and 10-line strophes, and octosyllabic *coplas* of eight and nine lines.

PLÁCIDO, pseudonym used by Gabriel de la Concepción Valdés (q.v.).

Platero y yo (1914), a series of 137 prose poems (two more were added in the edns. of 1915 and 1916) by Juan Ramón Jiménez (q.v.).

Platero is a donkey whose life, wanderings, and death are narrated in often sentimental, often stark terms to illustrate the activities and personalities of Moguer, Jiménez's native village in Andalusia. Subtitled *elegía andaluza*, *Platero y yo* is essentially autobiographical, showing the author's virtues of imagination, melancholy, and sensitivity. Like most children's classics, it is also a book that can be read with profit and enjoyment by adults.

G. M. Walsh published an English translation in 1922.

PLA Y CASADEVALL, Josep (1897–   ), b. Palafrugell, Gerona. Widely-travelled journalist and historian, writing in Catalan and Castilian. His most important book is the four-volume *Historia de la Segunda República Española* (1941). He has also written *Viaje en autobús* (1942), *Humor honesto y vago* (1942), *El pintor Joaquín Mir* (1944), *Un señor de Barcelona* (1945), and many more. His *Obra completa* reached vol. 25 in 1973. He has an uninhibited curiosity and the faculty of making often trivial experiences interesting.

See A. Manent, *Tres escritores catalanes: Carner, Riba, Pla*. (1973).

Pliegos sueltos ('loose sheets'), a book comprising a few sheets intended to disseminate literary or historical texts among the masses. Its size varies according to its contents so that, although initially it was generally one sheet, that is to say a broadsheet of usual dimensions folded twice to form eight pages, it gradually came to mean also a chapbook of 32 pages and even more.

These broadsheets are of great literary value as the principal vehicle of transmission for medieval ballads and rhymed chronicles during periods when book publishers attached little or no value to these works. Their value decreased as *Romanceros* began to be published. The *pliegos sueltos* known as *relaciones* were the antecedents of the modern Spanish newspapers.

The *pliegos sueltos* are also known as *literatura de cordel* ('writings hanging from a string') from the commercial practice of stringing broadsheets along horizontal strings or cords in stationers' shops or tents on market days.

See F. J. Norton, *Printing in Spain, 1501–1520* (Cambridge, 1966); F. J. Norton and Edward Wilson, *Two Spanish verse chapbooks. Romançe de Amadis c. 1515–19. Juyzio hallado y trovado c. 1510. A facsimile ed. with bibliographical and textual studies* (Cambridge, 1969); Julio Caro Baroja, *Ensayo sobre la literatura de cordel* (1969); A. Rodríguez Moñino, *Diccionario de pliegos sueltos poéticos (siglo XVI)* (1970); and C. Romero de Lecea, *La imprenta y los pliegos poéticos* (1974).

PLUTARCO, a pseudonym of José María Samper (q.v.).

Pobrecito Hablador, El, pen-name assumed by Mariano José de Larra (q.v.).

POCATERRA, José Rafael (1888–1955), Venezuelan novelist. He reacted against the Europeanism of such writers as Díaz Rodríguez, and described in his novels Venezuelan 'people in the street, on corners, in church, in intimate life, from the pavement across the street', but he still learnt much from the methods of Zola in his provincial realist novels.

Política feminista (1912), reprinted as *El doctor Bebé* (Madrid, 1916), concerns a family exalted and destroyed by a political boss for his own ends. It vividly portrays the horror of life during the Gómez dictatorship. *Vidas oscuras* (Maracaibo, 1913), is a panoramic novel on life in Caracas c. 1900. Pocaterra also wrote *Tierra del sol* (1918), the stories *Cuentos grotescos* (1922), the autobiographical *Memorias de un venezolano de la Decadencia* (Bogotá, 1927; reprinted 2 vols., Caracas, 1936), the novel *La casa de los Abila* (1946), and *Despues de mí* (1965), a volume of poems.

See Pascual Plá y Beltrán, 'Cuatro novelistas de Venezuela' in *Cuadernos Americanos*, vol. 18, no. 107 (November–December 1959), pp. 227–46.

Poema de mio Cid, see Cid, Cantar de mio.

Poeta en Nueva York, 1929–30 (Mexico City, 1940), a cycle of poems written by Federico García Lorca (q.v.) while in residence at Columbia University. Directly influenced by Lautréamont's *Les chants de Maldoror* (1868; augmented edn., 1890), which had a belated impact on the surrealists, *Poeta en Nueva York* is an act of defiance by the individual against social and religious institutions which wish to restrain him. Superficially surrealistic in its profusion of unrelated images, the book has been defined as surrealistic in essence by Juan Larrea (in *Letras de México*, vol. 3, 1941–2, pp. 1, 5–6) but Lorca merely uses fantastic, tormented images as a poetic equivalent for what he considered to be the bewildering fantasy of life in rootless North America in the late 1920s.

The poem cycle is in free verse, as befits the chaotic nature of the material. It moves from the Negroes of Harlem and the violence of the city to the countryside of New England where he finds no respite, but merely an inner despair to match the exterior brutality he explored in the city. The last section returns to New York, where his invective against the dehumanization brought about by mechanization completes a powerful statement of the poet's alienation in contemporary society. After *Poeta en Nueva York* Lorca wrote less poetry, devoting himself more to the theatre; only fragments of the work were published in his lifetime (he prepared an edition in 1935) and there is doubt about the number and arrangement of the New York poems.

The translation by Rolfe Humphries (New York, 1940) has been superseded by that of Ben Belitt (New York, 1955), which has an important introduction by Ángel del Río.

See J. Devlin, 'García Lorca's basic affirmation in "Poet in New York"', in *Studies in honor of S. M. Waxman* (Boston, Mass., 1969), pp. 131–40.

Polifemo y Galatea, Fábula, de see Fábula de Polifemo y Galatea.

Política de Dios, Govierno de Christo: Tyranía de Satanás, a political manual by Francisco de Quevedo (q.v.) written in 1617, published incomplete and without consent in Saragossa (1626) and then with its concluding second part in 1655. Quevedo considered it his best book. He probably wrote it quickly, for it shows little sign of planning or revision.

Didactic literature for princes and magistrates has a long history in Spain (see De Regimine Principum) and probably arrived with the Muslims. Juan Márquez's *El governador christiano*

(1612) was a challenge to Machiavelli's *Il principe* (1532), using as its models the biblical stories of Moses and Joshua; it was often reprinted in Spain. Diego Saavedra Fajardo (q.v.) was in Quevedo's circle and may well have used his ideas in *Empresas políticas, Idea de un Príncipe Christiano* (1640), an influential manual. Similar works were written about this time by Antonio López de Vega (*El perfeto Señor*, 1626), Juan Eusebio Nieremberg (*Obras y días: manual de señores y príncipes*, 1629), and Cristóbal de Benavente y Benavides (*Advertencias para reyes, príncipes, y embaxadores*, 1643).

Christ, we are told in *Política de Dios*, was treated as a king by the angels, by the eastern kings, and even by Herod. He was a true king because He reigned over His own soul and only those who imitate Him can become great kings. Quevedo charts the sequence of 'divine political events' in the stories of the woman caught in adultery, the loaves and fishes, the house of Martha, the driving of traders from the temple, the prayer and betrayal in the garden, and so on, offering advice to rulers based on each incident. The duties of a king cover every aspect of his life and behaviour, from the administration of justice and the peace of his kingdom, to the choice of clothes. Corruption must be eradicated from the government and the judiciary, or the king will be condoning the presence of poison in the spring from which his subjects drink.

The king must suppress adulation, preferring to hear complaints. He must never allow his opinion to be overruled, for errors seem slighter emanating from him than from others. A king must guarantee peace while preparing for war. 'Divine politics' is answering good for evil, overcoming by clemency, conquering by peace, turning away anger with patience, and punishing with pity.

POLO, Gaspar Gil (*c.* 1519–85), b. Valencia. Author of *Los cinco libros de la Diana enamorada* (Valencia, 1564), the best pastoral novel in Castilian after the *Diana* of Montemayor (qq.v.). The *Diana enamorada* (q.v.) is often described as a sequel to Montemayor's novel, but it has recently been considered more in the nature of a rejoinder on the philosophical level. Gaspar Gil Polo may have been a professor of Greek at Valencia University (as Valbuena Prat and Cerdá y Rico maintain), but Pfandl and others believe that this was another man of the same name.

Polo was known as a poet before his *Diana enamorada* appeared, being cited as such in Joan Timoneda's ballad *Sarao de amor* (1561).

POLO, Sancho, the pseudonym used by Mexican novelist Emilio Rabasa (q.v.).

POLO DE MEDINA, SALVADOR JACINTO (1603–76), b. Murcia. Poet and fabulist. He was ordained in 1638 and became rector of the Seminary of San Fulgencio in Murcia.

His first book was a miscellany of nature poems and socio-literary comment, *Academias del Iardín* (1630), and his second a long and—despite his assertion that he was 'anti-culterano'—a rather gongoristic poem, *Ocios de la soledad* (Murcia, 1633). *Viage de este mundo al otro* (Murcia, 1636) is an imitation of the *Sueños* of Quevedo (qq.v.), but without his model's memorable acidity. *A Lelio: Govierno moral* (Murcia, 1657), is a treatise on prudence. Most of his poetry, including the comic fables *Apolo y Dafne* and *Pan y Siringa*, are in vol. 42 (1857) of the BAE. J. M. de Cossío edited Polo de Medina's *Obras escogidas* (1931) but the standard edition is the *Obras completas* (Murcia, 1948).

POMA DE AYALA, FELIPE GUAMÁN (1526?– 1615?), b. San Cristóbal de Suntuto, Lucanas. Peruvian of pure Indian stock who compiled between 1587 and 1613 the exhaustive account, *El primer nueva Corónica y Buen Gobierno*, intended to inform the Spanish sovereign of the state of Peru before and immediately after the Conquest. The MS. was taken to Lima but vanished from 1613 until 1908, when Richard Pietschmann discovered it in the Royal Library, Copenhagen. It was first published in facsimile by the Institut de l'Ethnologie (Paris) in 1936, then edited by Arturo Posnanski (Bolivia, 1944), and later by Luis Bustíos Gálvez (2 vols., 1966). It is a work of the utmost value to historians and students of pre-Columbian Peru.

POMBO, RAFAEL (1833–1912), b. Bogotá. Colombian romantic poet. A prolific writer who had written 61 *décimas* by the age of 24 years (collected in *La hora de tinieblas*, 1864) and more than 400 poems altogether. His main theme is love ('Noche de diciembre'), and he wrote Sapphic poems using the pen-name 'Edda la Bogotana'. He covered a wide range of subjects, including the religious 'La casa del cura', the descriptive 'En el Niágara', perhaps the best poem on the falls, the patriotic 'Sucre derrotado', the didactic 'El potro sin freno', and the humorous 'La pareja humana'. Pombo's work falls into three main periods: the sentimentalist years 1851–3; the years in the U.S.A., where he wrote his best poetry and met Bryant and Longfellow; and the final period, until 1912, which was rationalist in outlook and stressed the sonnet form.

The first official edition of his *Poesías* was that in 2 vols., 1916–17, followed by many other anthologies, the best being the *Antología poética*

(1952) in the Biblioteca de Autores Colombianos, and the *Poesías completas* (1957).

See Héctor H. Orjuela, *Biografía y bibliografía de Rafael Pombo* (1965).

PONCE, Fray BARTOLOMÉ (died *c.* 1595), b. Aragón. Cistercian monk and religious novelist, author of the *Primera parte de la Diana a lo divino* (Saragossa, 1581). Being at court in 1559, he explains in his prologue, he found everybody reading the *Diana* of Montemayor (qq.v.), 'la qual era tan acepta quanto yo jamás otro libro en Romance aya visto'. He therefore conceived the idea of a religious adaptation of the work in prose, in achievement not altogether unworthy of its original. Diana here becomes the Blessed Virgin Mary and profane love is transmuted into divine.

Ponce's projected sequel was never published, and may never have been written.

See A LO DIVINO.

PONCE DE LEÓN, Fray BASILIO (1560–1629), b. Granada. Theologian, preacher, and poet. A nephew and disciple of Fray Luis de León (q.v.), and possible author of some of the poems attributed to Luis. He entered the Augustinian order in 1592.

De agno typico (1604) is in part a defence of his uncle. His major work is the collection of Lenten sermons, *Sermones de Cuaresma* (1605–10), which are written in excellent prose enlivened with colloquialisms. His 'Apologia de las obras y doctrina de San Juan de la Cruz' remains in MS., in the National Library in Madrid. Ponce de León's theological treatises in Latin were well regarded during his lifetime, and on his death Francisco Montesdoca published *Fama póstuma* (Salamanca, 1630) in which Fray Basilio was described as 'príncipe de los ingenios y fénix de las ciencias'.

PONDAL ABENTE, EDUARDO (1835–1917), b. Ponteceso, Corunna. Galician poet who also wrote in Castilian. He is considered with Rosalía de Castro and Manuel Curros Enríquez (qq.v.) a leader of the Galician Revival of the 19th c. He studied medicine in Santiago and spent some time as an army doctor, retiring early to the Galician countryside with which he identified himself in his writing. 'The bard of Bergantiños', as Pondal was known, recreated his own Celtic myths, tending towards pessimism and a melancholy pantheism.

Rumores de los pinos (1877) was the first major success of this quiet, reflective poet, but his most famous book was *Queixumes dos pinos* (1886), and especially the long poem *A campana de Anllóns*, which was subsequently corrected and expanded in a separate volume. All these works, together with *O dolmen de Dombate* (1895), were reissued in *Poesías* (1935) by the Academia Galega.

PONS, JOSEP SEBASTIÀ (1886–1962), b. Illa de Riberal, Roussillon. A poet writing in Catalan whose charming verses, reminiscent of Virgil's *Eclogues,* include 'Vall closa' and 'Parpella d'or del vespre' in *Ocho siglos de poesía catalana* (1969) compiled by J. M. Castellet and J. Molas.

PONS I GALLARZA, JOSEP LLUÍS (1823–94), b. Sant Andreu del Palomar. Catalan poet of the Balearics whose neoclassical restraint reflects his conservative position and proud patriotism. His best-known poem is 'L'olivera mallorquina'. His view of the middle-class world is idealized.

PONZ, ANTONIO (1725–92), b. Bechí, Valencia. Travel writer. After studying theology at Valencia University, he went to the Real Academia de Bellas Artes de San Fernando in Madrid, and continued his studies in Rome 1751–60. On his return to Spain he was commissioned to visit the colleges of the expelled Jesuits in Andalusia to make an inventory of their paintings, and he conceived the idea of travelling throughout Spain to record works of art, architecture, and archaeology, eventually widening his notes to include agriculture, commerce, administration, manners and customs, and other matters. From 1771 until his death Ponz visited all Spain except Granada, Almería, Murcia and part of Albacete, Galicia, the coast of Cantabria, and the Balearics, compiling *Viage de España o cartas en que se da noticia de las cosas mas apreciables, y dignas de saberse que hay en ella* (2 vols., 1772–3) under the pseudonym of 'Pedro Antonio de la Puente'. The book was reprinted in 18 vols. (1784–94) under his real name, with the words *o cartas* omitted from the title. Vols. 1–3 are devoted to Castile, 4 to Valencia, 5–6 to Madrid, 7–8 to Extremadura, 9 to Seville, 10–12 to Castile and León, 13 and 15 to Aragón, 14 to Catalonia, and 16–18 to parts of Andalusia. For Asturias, Ponz relied on the assistance of Jovellanos (q.v.), whose letters are reproduced in vol. 50 (pp. 271–311) of the BAE (1858). In 1783 he went to France, England, Holland, and Flanders, publishing a further two volumes of his *Viaje fuera de España* (1785).

Ponz showed a markedly neoclassical taste, neglecting the Gothic and condemning the Baroque. While his style lacks wit and brevity, his book is the most complete factual account of Spain in the second half of the 18th c. and was reprinted in 1947.

Ponz also produced an edition of the *Comentarios de la pintura* (1788) by Felipe de Guevara (d. 1563) from a MS. he found in Plasencia.

Popol Vuh, the holy scriptures of the pre-Columbian Quiché Mayas of Guatemala, preserved in the so-called Chichicastenango Manuscript. A compilation of their rites and symbolism, a history of their migrations, the book also includes some of the poetry of the most powerful native people of the Guatemalan high plateau. Its compiler (Diego Reynoso?) was one of the earliest of the Indians to learn from missionary monks how to write his language in Roman characters, and his work was brought to light by the missionary Francisco Ximénez in the 17th c.

Popol Vuh was translated into Spanish by Miguel Ángel Asturias and J. M. González de Mendoza and published in 1927. Other works of the Quiché Mayas include the *Anales de los Xahil* and the *Rabinal Achi* (qq.v.).

See Margaret McClear, *Popol Vuh: structure and meaning* (New York, 1972).

PORCEL, BALTASAR (1937–), b. Andratx, Mallorca. Catalan novelist, playwright, and journalist who writes in both Mallorquin and Castilian. The best of his travel books are *Viatge literari a Mallorca* (Barcelona, 1967) and *Viatge a les Balears menors* (Barcelona, 1968).

His plays include *Els condemnats* (Palma, 1959) and *La simbomba fosca* (Palma, 1961). Porcel's novels are *Sol negre* (Barcelona, 1963), *Els escorpins* (Barcelona, 1965), *Els Argonautes,* and *Crónica de atolondrados navegantes* (Barcelona, 1973).

PORCEL, JOSÉ ANTONIO (1715–94), b. Granada. Poet. A disciple of Góngora (q.v.), Porcel belonged to the Academia del Trípode in Granada, where he was known as 'El Caballero de los Tahalíes', and to the Academia del Buen Gusto in Madrid, where he was known as 'El Aventurero'.

His major poem is a hunting eclogue in four parts, *El Adónis,* written for his aristocratic circle and published in vol. 61 (1869) of the BAE. Its metre is based on the *terza rima;* its theme is the pastoral tradition of chastity and the difficulty of true love. The BAE volume includes other poems by Porcel, among them 'Fábula de Alfeo y Aretusa' in *octavas reales* and the *fábula burlesca* 'Acteón y Diana'.

See J. M. de Cossío, *Fábulas mitológicas en España* (1952); and E. Orozco, 'Porcel y el barroquismo literario del siglo XVIII' in *Cuadernas de la Cátedra Feijoo* (Oviedo), vol. 21 (1968).

Poridat de Poridades, a medieval collection of *exempla,* or wisdom literature, in the genre of *de regimine principum* (q.v.) which purports to be advice given by Aristotle to his pupil Alexander the Great. It was first compiled, direct from the Arabic unlike most other examples of the genre, during the reign of Alfonso X and appears in the same MS. as the *Libro de los buenos proverbios* and *Enseñamientos et castigos de Alixandre*.

See Lloyd A. Kasten, 'Poridat de las poridades' in *Romance Philology*, vol. 5 (1951–2), pp. 180–90; and the same author's edition (Madrid, 1957).

PORRAS DE MACHUCA, GIL, pseudonym of Ignacio López de Ayala (q.v.).

PORTUGAL, *Condestable Don* PEDRO DE, see PEDRO DE PORTUGAL, *Condestable Don*.

PORTUONDO, JOSÉ ANTONIO (1911–), Cuban critic, literary historian, and university professor. His works include *Concepto de la poesía* (Mexico City, 1944), *José Martí, crítico literario* (Washington, D.C., 1953), *El heroismo intelectual* (Mexico City, 1955), *La historia y las generaciones* (Santiago de Cuba, 1958), *Bosquejo histórico de las letras cubanas* (1960), and *Crítica de la época y otros ensayos* (Santa Clara, 1965).

POSADA, JOSÉ GUADALUPE (1852–1913), b. Aguascalientes. Mexican illustrator of books, numerous chapbooks, and broadsheets. He worked as a lithographer up to 1888, contributing political cartoons to *El Jicote*. From about 1890 he began engraving on type-metal with a many-pointed burin which leaves furrows that print white after the block is inked. It is at this time that he became a staff artist for the prolific publisher Antonio Vanegas Arroyo in Mexico City, producing illustrations of skeletons, executions by firing-squad, disasters, and sensations for hawking in the streets in huge quantities. This is the authentic street literature of Mexico which is neglected in the standard literary histories but concerned much larger numbers of people than the belles-lettres traditionally given prominence. From about 1900 Posada changed his chief technique to relief etching on zinc.

Posada's popular Mexican prints: 272 cuts . . . (New York, 1972) is a selection made by R. Berdecio and S. Appelbaum.

See Frances Toor, Pablo O'Higgins, and Blas Vanegas Arroyo, *Las obras de José Guadalupe Posada, grabador mexicano: monografía* (1930); and *José Guadalupe Posada: ilustrador de la vida mexicana* (1963), published by the Fondo Editorial de la Plástica Mexicana.

Post-Guerra, a Marxist literary and political magazine issued at irregular intervals between 25 June 1927 and August–September 1928 in Madrid. Jointly edited by José Antonio Balbontín and Rafael Giménez Siles, *Post-Guerra*

published new work by writers of primarily working-class origin, including Juan Andrade, J. Loredo Aparicio, and Julián Gorkín. The magazine propounded the need for political revolution at a time of dictatorship; for the participation of intellectuals in government; for art and literature to be used as ideological weapons; and for the dissemination of Marxist ideas. The magazine, which was subject to pre-publication censorship, was abandoned in favour of books, which were then not thus controlled, and between 1929–31 the editors issued books from ephemeral presses such as Oriente, Nosotros, Zeus, Cénit, Hoy, and Historia Nueva. Copies of this rare but then influential journal can be seen in the Biblioteca Nacional, Madrid.

See *Ínsula*, no. 360 (November 1976), p. 4.

POUS I PAGÈS, JOSEP (1873–1953), b. Figueras, Gerona. Catalan novelist and playwright. A socialist by conviction, Pous i Pagès is a master of the acid rural novel born of social frustration and disillusion. His masterpiece is *La vida i la mort d'En Jordi Fraginals* (1912), which Unamuno described as 'novela, toda una novela, no más que una novela', epitomizing the notion of the 'tragic sense of life' in the eventual destruction of the self-willed 'hero'. His other novels included *Per la vida* (1900) and *Quan se fa nosa* (1903).

Pous i Pagès also wrote for the stage: a farce, *Quan passava la tragedia* (1920); and 'straight' plays: *Papallones* (1920), *Primera volada* (1921), *Maria Lluisa i els seus pretendents* (1928), and *Vivim a les palpentes* (1930).

POYO, DAMIÁN SALUCIO DEL, see SALUCIO DEL POYO, Damián.

POZAS, RICARDO (1912–), b. Amealco, State of Querétaro. Mexican novelist and social anthropologist whose *Juan Pérez Jolote* (1952), subtitled *biografía de un tzotzil*, marked a new departure in Latin American fictionalized anthropology. Told in the first person, the story concerns an Indian who runs away from Chamula, a village in the Chiapas highlands, first to work in the plantations and subsequently to fight in the revolutionary forces. The difficulties of his adaptation back into Chamula give the novel its main value; the protagonist is given the job of village school-teacher, because he has learnt Spanish, and he is looked up to by the local people. Yet as a result of the ritual drinking necessary to the performance of village ceremonies, Juan Pérez succumbs to alcoholism as inevitably as his father had done. *Juan the Chamula* (Berkeley, Cal., 1962) is a translation by Lysander Kemp.

Pozas has also written a number of scholarly papers, among them *Los mazatecos* (1957) and *Chamula: un pueblo indio de los altos* (1959).

PRADO, ADRIÁN DE (*fl.* 1620), poet and Hieronymite. His baroque 'Canción real a San Jerónimo en Siria' is drawn boldly and remains long in the memory for its realistic portrayal of St. Jerome by describing a painting of him now lost, imaginary or as yet unidentified. The poem, from the *Cancionero de 1628* (1945 edn. by J. M. Blecua), is reprinted with a ballad, 'Al Santísimo Sacramento', in vol. 35 (1855) of the BAE, and more recently in vol. 1, pp. 281–88 in Blecua's *Floresta de lírica española* (2nd edn., 1968).

PRADO, PEDRO (1886–1952), b. Santiago. Chilean poet, novelist, and essayist. Director of the Museo de Bellas Artes in Santiago, professor of aesthetics and art history, and, in 1927–8, ambassador to Colombia. He founded the group Los Diez in 1915 with, among others, Magallanes Moure, Armando Donoso, and a mythical 'Hermano Errante'. They planned to erect a red tower overlooking the sea as a symbolic retreat but never executed the project. The *Revista Moderna* (1916) was founded by the group as an organ of subjectivism against the prevailing objectivist trend; later Barrios and d'Halmar (qq.v.) joined Los Diez.

An important stylist whose standards impressed many young Chileans, Prado was included by H. Díaz Arrieta in *Los cuatro grandes de la literatura chilena del siglo XX* (1963), the others being d'Halmar, Mistral, and Neruda. His collections of poetry were *Flores de cardo* (1908) which has been described as the last work of modernism in Chile; *El llamado del mundo* (1913), *Camino de las horas* (1934), *Otoño en las dunas* (1940), the sonnets of *Esta bella ciudad envenenada* (1945), *No más que una rosa* (1946), and *Viejos poemas inéditos* (1949).

For some readers, Prado is more important as a novelist than poet, especially for the autobiographical *Alsino* (1920) which achieved an unlikely success through mixing symbolism with Chilean realism. He also wrote a fantasy on Easter Island, *La reina de Rapa Nui* (1914); *Un juez rural* (1924), on provincial Chile; and a prose tragedy possibly better seen as a dramatic poem, *Andróvar* (1925). *La casa abandonada* (1912) and *Los pájaros errantes* (1915) are prose poem collections including a number of parables.

See Olga Blondet's bibliography of Prado in *Revista Hispánica Moderna* (New York), vol. 26, nos. 1–2 (January–April 1960), pp. 81–84; see also J. Arriagada Augier, *Pedro Prado, un clásico de América* (1952); Raúl Silva Castro, *Pedro Prado: vida y obra* (1965); and J. R. Kelly, *Pedro Prado* (New York, 1974).

PRADOS, EMILIO (1899–1962), b. Málaga. Poet. A melancholy, lonely man whose work is tinged with mysticism but not with faith, Prados and his close friend Manuel Altolaguirre (q.v.) founded and published *Litoral* (1927–9), a journal which published early work by García Lorca, Alberti, and Aleixandre (qq.v.).

Prados was influenced by Góngora, Antonio Machado, and Juan Ramón Jiménez. The two strands of his work are the hermetic, especially marked in *Tiempo* (Málaga, 1925), *Vuelta* (Málaga, 1927), and *Cuerpo perseguido* (1928), and the folkloric, culminating in his fine ballads collected in his anthology *Romancero general de la guerra de España* (1937), which appeared at the same time as his personal volumes *El llanto subterráneo* (1936) and *Llanto en la sangre* (Valencia, 1937). At the time of the publication of his *Cancionero menor* (Barcelona, 1937), Prados went reluctantly into exile in Mexico. His books in exile include *Memoria del olvido* (Mexico City, 1940), *Mínima muerte* (Mexico City, 1942), *Jardín cerrado* (1946; 2nd edn., Buenos Aires, 1960), *El dormido en la yerba* (Málaga, 1953), *Antología, 1923–1953* (Buenos Aires, 1954), *Río natural* (Buenos Aires, 1957), *Circuncisión del sueño* (Mexico City, 1957), *La piedra escrita* (Mexico City, 1961), *Signos del ser* (1962), *Transparencias* (Málaga, 1962), and *Últimos poemas* (Málaga, 1965). Prados's *Poesías completas* appeared in Mexico City (1976).

See C. Blanco Aguinaga, 'Emilio Prados: vida y obras' in *Revista Hispánica Moderna* (1960), with a bibliography and select anthology.

PRECISO, DON, pseudonym of Juan Antonio de Iza Zamácola (q.v.).

Premios, Los (1960), a first novel by the Argentinian Julio Cortázar (q.v.), it is an allegory like K. A. Porter's *Ship of fools* (1962) of human life as a sea voyage.

Citizens of Buenos Aires who have won a lottery are given as a prize a free cruise on the ship *Malcolm*. The eighteen passengers include a millionaire, a dentist abandoned by his mistress, and a homosexual; some are searching for the meaning of existence and others are merely passive. Strict rules prohibit them from asking where they are going and from visiting either bridge or stern. One passenger, Medrano, insists on finding out a part of the mystery and is shot, but the other passengers are compelled to sign a statement that he died of typhus, and the ship returns to Buenos Aires. The nine mystical soliloquies of a character called Persio, which are interpolated into the narrative, have been adversely criticized as excessively long and incoherent.

Cortázar refuses to agree that his novel has a

'message', merely messengers, that is to say the human beings he creates and their situation. The book is courageously innovative, its style incorporating neologisms, a metaphysical language that is frequently reminiscent of the essay genre, and startling imagery. Cortázar's attitude is at once ironic and compassionate, though A. Pagés Larraya, in *Ficción* (Buenos Aires, nos. 33–34, 1961, pp. 165–9) has viewed *Los premios* as an anti-Peronista statement.

PRESCOTT, WILLIAM HICKLING (1796–1859), b. Salem, Mass. American historian who began the study of Spanish history in 1824 under the influence of George Ticknor (q.v.) and, despite the loss of one eye and impairment of the other, produced vigorous accounts of his chosen periods in terms of the heroic figures, ignoring most social, economic, and political factors, as was then normal. Within his limitations, Prescott's use of primary sources was exemplary and brought history with an acceptable Protestant bias to readers already attracted to history by the novels of Walter Scott. His works were *History of the reign of Ferdinand and Isabella* (3 vols., 1838); *History of the conquest of Mexico* (3 vols., 1843), his major work, based largely on the account of Bernal Díaz del Castillo (q.v.); *Biographical and critical miscellanies* (1843), published in London as *Critical and historical essays*, including articles on Cervantes and Mme Calderón's *Life in Mexico*; *History of the conquest of Peru* (2 vols., 1847); and the unfinished *History of the reign of Philip II* (vols. 1–2, 1855; vol. 3, 1858; vols. 4–5 incomplete). Prescott's *Works* (22 vols., 1904) were edited by W. H. Munro. The standard life is still that by his mentor George Ticknor, *William Hickling Prescott* (Philadelphia, 1864; 2nd edn., 1875). C. H. Gardiner has edited Prescott's *Literary memoranda* (2 vols., 1961) and abridged the *Conquest of Mexico* (1967).

PRIETO, GUILLERMO (1818–97), b. Mexico City. Mexican poet and essayist. His popular and often patriotic poetry was collected in *Musa callejera* (2 vols., 1883; selected by Francisco Monterde, 1940), and in the first poetical monument erected to the heroes of Independence, *El Romancero nacional* (1885), described by Altamirano as 'la epopeya nacional con todos sus caracteres, con su sabor dramático, su aspecto personal y pintoresco y su verdad histórica, que no tiene necesidad de revestir el brillante atavío de la leyenda para ser admirable'.

A journalist who contributed articles of political, religious, and social interest to *El Siglo XIX* as 'Fidel', he became increasingly anticlerical, as the collection *Los San Lunes de Fidel* (1923) demonstrates. There was also a selection

from his journalism by Yolande Villenave published in 1948. Prieto's autobiography appeared as *Memorias de mis tiempos 1828–1853* (2 vols., 1906; edited by Y. Villenave, 1944). His travel books were *Viajes de orden suprema* (1857) and *Viaje a los Estados Unidos* (3 vols., 1877–8). Selections from Prieto's works include *Prosas y versos*, compiled by L. González Obregón (1955) and *Guillermo Prieto*, compiled by Carlos J. Sierra (1962).

See M. E. Nava Perea, *El costumbrismo de Guillermo Prieto* (1948).

PRIETO, JENARO (1889–1946), Chilean humorist. His most important book is the Pirandellian comedy of identity and deception *El socio* (1928), a subtle satire on Chilean society. In this, Julián Pardo invents a business partner called Walter Davis, whose presence becomes more and more insistent until Pardo commits suicide: the police then hunt Davis as the murderer. *Partner*, a version by Blanca de Roig and Guy Dowler, was published in 1931. An earlier book, *Un muerto de mal criterio* (1926) is in the tradition of Quevedo's *Sueños*, a judge after his own death passing sentences on 'cases' in the next world. *Pluma en ristre* (1925) contained Prieto's best articles from *El Diario Ilustrado*.

Primer Romancero gitano (1928), a collection of eighteen ballads by Federico García Lorca (q.v.) written between 1924 and 1927.

Lorca discounted the *gitano* element by insisting that the book 'is gipsy only in parts; it is essentially an Andalusian portrait with a single true protagonist: Granada, which suffers persecution and can transform its protest into dance'. He mistakenly equated the idea of the gipsy with the idea of unbridled passion and was later irritated when labelled a 'gipsy poet'.

The ballads are such only in form and atmosphere, which owe a great debt to the traditional *romancero*: their language is not in the tradition of the folk *romancero* but follows the *culto* diction and metaphor of Góngora and his successors. Myth and symbol play a major rôle (blue symbolizes innocence and green eroticism) and Lorca's oblique language has led some readers to overlook the true meaning of certain passages (such as the homosexuality of the *Romance sonámbulo*, or the masturbation fantasy of the *Burla de don Pedro a caballo*). Despite the various impersonal, dramatic, and narrative elements, the collection is dominated by Lorca's own lyrical voice and his obsession with sexual passion (symbolized by the fish motif) whether normal (*La casada infiel*), homosexual, or incestuous (a reworking of the biblical story in *Thamar y Amnón*).

See Jaroslaw Flys, *El lenguaje poético de*

Federico García Lorca (1955); and N. D. Shergold (ed.), *Studies of the Spanish and Portuguese ballad* (London, 1973).

Princes, Mirror for, see DE REGIMINE PRINCIPUM.

Príncipe constante, El, a major play by Pedro Calderón de la Barca (q.v.), first performed in 1629, and first published in 1636. Menéndez y Pelayo considered it Calderón's finest religious play.

The three acts take place in 1437, in and around Fez and Tangiers. Fénix, daughter of the King of Fez, is unhappy because for political reasons her father wishes her to marry Tarudante, King of Morocco, a man she does not love. She is in love with Muley, the King of Fez's general, but Muley becomes jealous when he sees that Fénix has a picture of Tarudante.

Two Portuguese princes disembark their troops on the Moorish coast ready to invade; one, Enrique, is nervous and pessimistic, but the other, Fernando, expresses his optimism on the outcome of the expedition. During a battle, Fernando captures Muley but magnanimously releases him on learning of his love for Fénix; Muley then promises to be his slave for life. Soon afterwards the Portuguese army is defeated by the forces of the King of Fez and of Tarudante, and Enrique is sent back to Portugal to announce that they will be freed only if the Christian-ruled town of Ceuta is handed over in exchange.

In Act II, Fénix tells Muley of an old woman's prophecy that her beauty would become the value of a corpse; Muley takes this to mean that if she marries Tarudante, he himself will die of grief and jealousy.

Fernando, awaiting ransom with the other captives, promises them liberty as soon as he himself is ransomed. When the Portuguese ship arrives, it is flying black banners. Fernando takes this to mean that the King of Portugal's answer is 'no' to the exchange, and that he must die a captive: he steels himself to this fate. Then it appears that the banners were a sign of mourning for the late King Duarte; his successor, Afonso, has agreed to the ransom of his brother for Ceuta. Having stoically accepted lifelong captivity, Fernando will not now change his mind. He prefers to remain a slave to the King of Fez, rather than let Ceuta, a Christian town, be handed over to the infidel. This enrages the King, who now treats him as a slave and sets him to work in the palace garden. There Fernando offers flowers to Fénix, who is horrified at the change in his condition. The constant prince warns her that earthly happiness is as transient as the flowers: 'Estas, que fueron pompa y alegría, / despertando al albor de la mañana, / a la tarde serán lástima vana, / durmiendo en brazos de la noche fría'. (These, which were splendour and joy / on waking at the dawn of day, / by evening make a pitiful display, sleeping in the cold night's arms). The faithful Muley offers, despite the dangers, to let Fernando escape, but the Christian refuses to obtain his liberty at the Moor's expense.

In Act III, Muley and then Fénix beg the inflexible King to save Fernando's life. The new king of Portugal, Afonso, arrives to offer a huge money ransom, but in vain: the King of Fez wants only Ceuta, which Fernando will not cede. Afonso departs, threatening war. Fernando, about to die of starvation, meditates on the cruelty of man to man. His ghost then leads a Portuguese invasion force to victory under Afonso and Enrique, and Muley, Fénix and Tarudante are captured. Afonso offers them to the King of Fez in exchange for Fernando. He obtains the prince's corpse and sets them free, thus fulfilling the prophecy; Muley marries Fénix, and Fernando receives Christian burial.

The immediate source of Calderón's play is *La fortuna adversa del Infante Don Fernando* attributed to Lope de Vega (q.v.); a secondary source is possibly Manuel de Faria y Sousa's *Epítome de las historias portuguesas* (1628), recording the Portuguese expedition against Tangiers in 1437.

The play has been interpreted in very different ways by authorities such as Wilson, Entwistle, Sloman, Gulsoy and J. H. Parker, Vieyra, and Spitzer.

Gulsoy and Parker treat the play as a dramatization of the idea of martyrdom; for Ortigoza Vieyra, Fernando is inspired by the spirit of chivalry; for Sloman, Fernando symbolizes the idea of fortitude; for Entwistle the play is an extended *auto sacramental* in which good and evil are the background; for Wilson, Fernando's sincere persistence in his beliefs is evidence of his superiority over inconstant beings. Wardropper's complex analysis (in *Modern Language Review*, vol. 53, 1958, pp. 512–20) possibly corresponds most nearly to Calderón's intention. Both Christian and Moor experience sentiment, but only Fernando, the constant Christian prince, can feel for the sufferings of others and thus aspire to sainthood, while Muley, the constant Moorish prince, is merely good. The Moors seek temporal beauty (Hebrew: 'Ceuta'), a worldly thing, whereas religious beauty (Christianity, in Calderón's view) is the only true beauty and that is why Ceuta must remain Christian. Time, for the Arab, is a dimension of love, feeling, and worldly beauty and power; for the Christian, time is eternal, and his value-system has room for honour and constancy unto death. Fénix the

Muslim is shown attracted by things of the senses and fears the loss of her beauty and the proximity of death; by contrast, the Christian Fernando is shown to be more concerned with his soul's salvation and the life after death. The King of Fez's love of worldly power and glory is also contrasted with the altruism and self-sacrifice of 'the constant prince', a figure comparable in Calderón to the regenerate Segismundo in *La vida es sueño* (q.v.).

The play is also overtly political in its bias against Muslims and their religion.

Calderón's style is influenced by that of Góngora (q.v.), above all in the *romance* 'Entre los sueltos caballos' in the scene between Muley and Fernando on the battlefield in Act I.

The play was used as a source by Dryden for *The Indian Emperor* (1665); the best edition is that by A. A. Parker (Cambridge, 1968).

See E. M. Wilson and W. J. Entwistle, 'Calderón's "El príncipe constante": two appreciations' in *Modern Language Review*, vol. 34 (1939), pp. 207–22; A. E. Sloman, *The sources of Calderón's 'El príncipe constante'* (Oxford, 1950); C. Ortigoza Vieyra, *Los moviles de la comedia 'El príncipe constante'* (Mexico City, 1957); Y. Gulsoy and J. H. Parker, 'El príncipe constante': drama barroco de la Contrarreforma' in *Hispanófila*, no. 9 (1960), pp. 15–29; and Leo Spitzer, 'The figure of Fénix . . .' in *Critical essays on the theatre of Calderón*, ed. B. W. Wardropper (New York, 1965), pp. 137–60.

Proa, a legendary but shortlived Argentinian literary magazine founded by Jorge Luis Borges and Macedonio Fernández (qq.v.). Its 'tres hojas eran desplegables como ese espejo triple que hace movediza y variada la gracia inmóvil de la mujer que refleja', in the words of Borges. An organ of *ultraísmo* (q.v.), it was to appear twice more only, in December 1922 and July 1923, counting among its contributors Salvador Reyes and Guillermo de Torre, as well as its founders.

Proa was reborn in August 1924, the founding editors being Borges (again), Ricardo Güiraldes, Pablo Rojas Paz, and Alfredo Brandán Caraffa, who had all been associated with the magazine *Martín Fierro* (q.v.). The revived *Proa* published works of the young and then unknown Mallea and Arlt (qq.v.) as well as important foreign writers in the original and in translation, among them Joyce, Supervielle, and Scott Fitzgerald. It ceased publication with its 15th number, September 1925.

Propalladia ('the first things of Pallas'), the title of the collected works of Bartolomé de Torres Naharro (q.v.).

Prosas profanos y otros poemas (Buenos Aires, 1896; augmented edn., Paris, 1901), a volume of poems by the Nicaraguan Rubén Darío (q.v.) which marked one of the peaks of modernist writing. Darío was influenced by Parnassianism (q.v.), but also adopted themes and symbols (such as the centaur) from classical literature. The book's metrical novelties and revivals included asymmetry, internal rhyme, and dissonance. The new edition of 1902 included 11 new sonnets, *dezires*, and *layes*. Its impact on the younger generation was far-reaching and is not yet dead, though a reaction against Darío's sensuous, exquisite, and decorative writing (symbolized by the graceful, vague, yet somewhat decadent swan) appeared in a famous sonnet by Enrique González Martínez (q.v.): 'Tuércele el cuello al cisne de engañoso plumaje'.

See Arturo Torres Ríoseco, *Vida y poesía de Rubén Darío* (Buenos Aires, 1944).

Proverbios en rimo del Sabio Salomón, rey de Israel, see SALOMÓN, REY DE ISRAEL, Proverbios en rimo del Sabio.

Proverbs, see REFRANES.

Provincial, Coplas del, an anonymous satirical poem written between 1465 and 1474 in 149 octosyllabic quartets. The target is the court of Enrique IV (1454–74), presented as a corrupt monastery, whose Superior in the order reports on a visitation in a scurrilous manner. An anti-Jewish bias is notable, but even more so is the denunciation of sexual perversion, which apparently had some basis in truth. The *Coplas* have been attributed—without absolute proof—to Alonso de Palencia, to Rodrigo Cota (unlikely), and to Antón de Montoro.

A *Provincial segundo* (1545) was written by Diego de Acuña, and was even more scabrous in its satire than was the model. The text of the original *Coplas* was banned by the Inquisition but continued to circulate in MS. R. Foulché-Delbosc edited 'Coplas del Provincial' in *Revue Hispanique*, vol. 5 (1898), pp. 255–66, and published an essay on the work in vol. 6 (1899), pp. 417–46.

See also MINGO REVULGO, Coplas de.

PRÓXITA, PRÓIXITA or PRÓXIDA, GILABERT DE (*fl.* 1392–1405), Catalan poet of Neapolitan ancestry (from Procida, an island in the Gulf of Naples). His life and work were totally unknown until Martí de Riquer published Próxita's *Poesies* (Barcelona, 1954) in Els Nostres Clàssics. All his twenty-one surviving poems concern love, reviving the courtly love tradition through largely Italian influences.

See M. de Riquer, *Història de la literatura catalana*, vol. I, (Barcelona, 1964), pp. 578–86.

Prudencia en la mujer, La, a *comedia* by Tirso de Molina, the pseudonym of Fray Gabriel Téllez (q.v.).

The play is set during the regency of María de Molina, and its theme is the dispute for control of the realm between the queen-regent (acting on behalf of her son) and Diego de Haro of Vizcaya and the *infantes* Enrique and Juan. María declines the offers of marriage from these three suitors and secures the succession for the future king Fernando IV (1295–1312). Tirso carefully followed his sources (the *Crónica de Fernando IV* and Mariana's *Historia*, among others) except for the clever anachronism of the Queen's banquet which was transferred from the reign of Enrique III (1390–1406).

Ruth Lee Kennedy has argued (in *Estudios*, special no., 1949) that Tirso, a bitter opponent of the new regime, has written a satire on the court of Philip IV and that his attitude is one of disillusion and even of fear.

Tirso cleverly attacks anti-feminist prejudices by presenting his public with a heroine who is strong, wise, and prudent. The play's theme resembles that of the artistically inferior *La república al revés* (q.v.).

C. Samonà has published a new edition of the play (Milan, 1967) and a study, '*La prudencia en la mujer*' *e i problemi del dramma storico barocco* (Rome, 1965).

PUBLICIO, a pseudonym used by Vicente Barrantes y Moreno (q.v.).

PUENTE, *Padre* LUIS DE LA (1554–1624), b. Valladolid. Jesuit ascetic writer whose main preoccupations were prayer and self-mortification. His books were *Meditaciones de los mysterios de nuestra santa Fe con la práctica de la oración mental sobre ellos* (2 vols., Valladolid, 1605), *Guía espiritual* . . . (Valladolid, 1609), *Tratamiento de la perfección del cristiano en todos sus estados* (3 vols., 1612–16), *Directorio espiritual para la Confesión, Comunión y Misa* (1625), and *Sentimientos y avisos espirituales* (1672). His exposition is orderly, detailed, and matter-of-fact. The collected *Obras espirituales* (1690) are in 6 vols. Puente's selected works are found in vol. 111 (1958) of the BAE. The major studies on Puente are those of C. M. Abad, *El Venerable Padre Luis de la Puente de la Compañía de Jesús: sus libros y su doctrina espiritual* (Santander, 1954) and *Vida y escritos del Venerable Padre Luis de la Puente, de la Compañía de Jesús* (Comillas, 1957).

PUENTE, PEDRO ANTONIO DE LA, pseudonym of Antonio Ponz (q.v.).

PUIG, MANUEL (1932–   ), Argentinian novelist of great talent, whose *La traición de Rita Hayworth* (1969) spins out the fantasies of the provincial boy Toto. Translated by S. J. Levine as *Betrayed by Rita Hayworth* (New York, 1971), the novel explores the world of the rootless sons of middle-class immigrants, whose 'traditions', sardonically viewed against the implicit *gaucho* background of Argentinian literature, consist of women's magazines, Hollywood films, radio and TV soap operas, and the banal lyrics of tango and bolero.

Equally comic and yet pathetic is *Boquitas pintadas* (1969), employing the same toneless speech patterns, which has already sold more than 100,000 copies in Argentina alone, and has also won critical acclaim. Puig explores the comic yet pathetic cultural aspirations of the Gentile middle classes in the provinces, using wit and irony without despair.

The Buenos Aires affair (1973), presented in the form of a detective story with a devastating anticlimax, concerns the anguish of two sexual outsiders, Leo and Gladys, each apparently successful in their respective fields of art criticism and sculpture, yet driven insane by their masturbatory obsessions. Puig shows that the prevalent movie ethos of contemporary culture makes sex the key to happiness, and that this value system destroys compassion and love. The impressive use of a wide range of narrative devices (such as stream of consciousness, wittily-observed lists of objects in a room, the ironic use of the footnote, and the *Harper's Bazaar* parody) takes the novel far beyond the traditional scope of the detective tale.

PUJOL, JOAN (*fl.* 1573–1603), b. Matapó. Catalan minor poet, influenced by Ausias March (q.v.). His most important work is an epic poem in three cantos on the Battle of Lepanto, *La singular y admirable victòria que, per la gràcia de nostre senyor Déu, obtingué el sereníssim senyor don Joan d'Àustria de la potentíssima armada turquesca* (Barcelona, 1573), generally known simply as *Lepant*. Pujol concealed his authorship except for an acrostic at the end. The *Visió en somni* has stylistic affiliations with March, but none of his finesse. Pujol also wrote verse commentaries to March's poetry which have been preserved with his epic in MS. 4495 of the Bibliothèque Nationale, Paris.

Etern factor de tota creatura by Pujol has been reprinted by Castellet and Molas in their *Ocho siglos de poesía catalana* (Barcelona, 1969).

See M. de Riquer, *Història de la literatura catalana*, vol. 3 (Barcelona, 1964), pp. 617–24.

PULGAR, HERNANDO DEL (1436?–95?), b. Castile. Annalist to the court, and councillor of state. His *Chrónica de los muy altos y esclarecidos reyes Cathólicos don Fernando y doña Isabel de gloriosa memoria* was first published (Valladolid, 1565) in a Latin translation by Antonio Nebrija (q.v.); the Castilian text appeared later (Saragossa, 1567). It is in the nature of a panegyric, and uses Livy's manner of putting heroic speeches in the mouths of characters. C. Rosell reprinted it in vol. 70 of the BAE (1878). Pulgar wrote a flattering commentary on the *coplas* of *Mingo Revulgo* (q.v.), which led Mariana to the hypothesis that Pulgar was their author. Thirty-two letters were published as *Letras* (Burgos, 1485?) and as *Cartas* in vol. 13 of the BAE (1850).

Pulgar's finest book is the *Libro de los claros varones de Castilla* (Toledo, 1486), twenty-four portraits of noblemen at the court of Enrique IV modelled on the *Generaciones y semblanzas* of Pérez de Guzmán (q.v.). Delightful character-sketches of Garcilaso, the Marqués de Santillana, and other notables of the period at times surpass the model in style, wit, and penetration. There is a critical edition of the book by J. de Mata Carriazo (2 vols., 1943), and another by R. B. Tate (Oxford, 1971).

PULGAR, HERNANDO PÉREZ DEL (1461–1531), called 'Él de las hazañas' for his legendary courage at the siege of Granada, where he gained access to the great Mosque when it was still in Muslim hands, and with a few companions affixed an *Ave María* to the main door, and added the sign of the Cross. A play on this theme, *El cerco de Santa Fe*, was published in Lope de Vega's *Comedias* (vol. 1, Valladolid, 1604) but the popular drama most often staged is *El triunfo del Ave María*, by an unknown 'ingenio de esta corte'. Pulgar served in Italy with Gonzalo de Córdoba (q.v.). The tedious prose *Chrónica*

llamada de las dos Conquistas de Nápoles (Saragossa, 1559) was wrongly attributed in the introduction to Pérez del Pulgar. His *Vida del Gran Capitán* (Seville, 1527) is a much more lively and accurate work, and was reprinted in Madrid in 1834 at the instigation of Martínez de la Rosa as *Hernán Pérez del Pulgar: bosquejo histórico*.

Puntero apuntado con apuntes breves, El (1647), by Juan de Dios del Cid (see DEL CID), a treatise on the cultivation of the indigo plant, which is thought to have been the first book printed on the American continent.

PUYOL Y ALONSO, JULIO (1865–1937), b. León. Historian, literary critic, and essayist. His original works were *Una puebla en el siglo XIII* (Paris, 1904), *Cuentos populares leoneses* (1905), *El Arcipreste de Hita* (1906), *Silva de varia lección* (1909), a reconstruction of the *Cantar de Gesta de Sancho II de Castilla* (1911), a study of the *Crónica particular del Cid* (1911), *Las Hermandades de Castilla y León* (1913), *Vida y aventuras de don Tiburcio de Redín, soldado y capuchino* (1913), *Elogio de Cervantes* (1916), *Los cronistas de Enrique IV* (1921), and he produced a good critical edition of López de Úbeda's *La pícara Justina* (1912).

Puyyut (Greek: *poietes*, 'a maker', 'poet'). Hebrew psalm of the early centuries A.D. written mainly in the Baghdad area, and brought to Spain with the plainsong to which this type of lyric was set. It was then inserted in the Sephardic ritual.

The secular writings of Dunash ben Labrat (q.v.) were intermediate in style between the *puyyut* and the *qasida*.

Q

QUADRADO Y NIETO, JUSEP MARIA (1819–96), b. Ciudadela, Minorca. Archaeologist and archivist of the Balearic Islands, who wrote an interesting social history: *Forenses y ciudadanos: historia de las discusiones civiles de Mallorca en el siglo XV* (1847). Quadrado also wrote some verse and translated three plays of Shakespeare, but he is best remembered for the volumes he contributed to P. Piferrer and Francisco Javier Parcerisa's *Recuerdos y Bellezas de España: Castilla la Nueva* (1848–50), *Asturias y León* (1855–9), *Valladolid, Palencia y Zamora* (1864), *Salamanca, Ávila y Segovia* (1872), *Aragón* (1884). *Islas*

Baleares (Barcelona, 1886) is in the series España: sus Monumentos y Artes.

The best edition of his *Ensayos religiosos, políticos y literarios* is the 2nd in 3 vols. (Palma, 1893–4).

QUART, PERE, pseudonym of Joan Oliver (q.v.).

Quechua Literature, the Quechua Indians of Peru are descended from the Incas, and their language is still spoken by the majority of Peruvian Indians. Spanish words deriving from

Quechua include *chinchilla, coca, cóndor, guanaco, guano, llama, pampa, puma,* and *quinina.*

Quechua literature was entirely oral, since the Incas had no system of writing, and naturally a vast proportion has been lost. Jorge Basadre compiled a *Bibliografía de la literatura quechua* and included an anthology in vol. I of the Biblioteca de Cultura Peruana (Paris, 1938). A collection, *Fábulas y ritos de los Incas,* found by C. R. Markham, was translated into English (London, 1873), and into Spanish by M. Jiménez de la Espada (Madrid, 1879), and by C. de Molina (Lima, 1943). J. M. B. Farfán has published *Poesía folklórica quechua* (Tucumán, 1942) and the important *Colección de textos quechuas del Perú* (Lima, 1952).

The main genres of Quechua literature are love songs and hymns dealing with love, agriculture, and war; plays; and stories, often fables. The heroic hymns are written in a verse-form called *jailli,* the most familiar being inserted in Book 2, ch. 27 of the *Comentarios reales* of the Inca Garcilaso de la Vega (q.v.). It explains the falling of rain, hail, or snow on the earth as the result of a trick played by her brother on the Princess of Heaven, whose pitcher is smashed on her way from the spring in the sky, where the invisible Inca god Wiraqocha had ordered her to draw water.

Other poetry is preserved in *El primer nueva coronica i buen gobierno* of Felipe Guamán (also spelt Huamán) Poma de Ayala (1526–1614) found in Copenhagen by R. Pietschmann in 1908 and published by Paul Rivet (Paris, 1936).

Quechua drama includes *Ollántay* (q.v.); *Atauwallpa,* still performed by the people of the Cliza valley; the pre-Columbian *Usqha Páuqar* conserved by Indians of Bolivia; and two post-Conquest plays: *El pobre más rico* and *Uska Páuqar,* both *autos sacramentales* (q.v.).

QUEIPO DE LLANO, José María, *Conde de Toreno* (1786–1843), b. Oviedo. Liberal historian. After witnessing the uprising of the Dos de Mayo in Madrid and taking sides against the French, he fled to Oviedo, where his accounts of the massacres helped to stiffen national resistance. The Junta de Asturias sent him to England to seek help from the Government. On his return to Oviedo in December 1808 he continued his political activities, later moving to the Junta Central, which was in Seville but later transferred to Cádiz, and was representative of the Juntas of León and Asturias to the central government. He urged the calling of the Cortes, and was elected deputy of his province at their first general assembly in 1810, even though he had not reached the legal minimum age of 25. On the return of Fernando, Queipo's libertarian views

led to his proscription, and he went first to Portugal, then in July 1814 to England; after the Cent-Jours he settled in Paris, going back to Spain after the Revolution of 1820. When absolutism was restored following the invasion of 1823 he went back to Paris, writing there his *Historia del levantamiento, guerra y revolución de España* (in French, 5 vols., Paris, 1835–8; in Spanish, 3 vols., Paris, 1836–8; revised by the author, 4 vols., 1848), one of the few contemporary classics which obtained a place in the BAE (vol. 64, 1872).

As a consequence of the amnesty of 1832 he returned to Madrid in 1833, becoming Minister of Finance the following year and holding the office of President of the Council from June to September 1835, after which he went into voluntary exile and died in Paris.

His *Discursos parlamentarios* (1872) and *Diario de un viaje a Italia* (1882) were posthumously published, and he also left the incomplete 'Historia de la dominación de la Casa de Austria'.

QUEROL, Vicente Wenceslao (1836–89), b. Valencia. Poet writing in Catalan and Castilian on conventional themes such as religion, family life, and patriotism. By profession a lawyer and director of the railways, he was also a founder of the Juegos Florales in Valencia.

His patriotic odes were once widely known, but now he is remembered rather for the three serenely Horatian *Cartas de María,* and the equally muted but effective elegy *A la muerte de mi hermana Adela.* Quintana (q.v.) influenced Querol's *Canto épico, o la guerra en África.* His *Rimas* (1877) were revised by his friend Llorente (q.v.) for a posthumous edition (1891) and were reissued in 1924 as *Poesías.*

See L. Guarner, *Poesía y verdad de Vicente W. Querol* (1976).

QUESADA, Alonso, pseudonym of Rafael Romero (q.v.).

QUEVEDO Y VILLEGAS, Francisco Gómez de (1580–1645), b. Madrid. Poet, satirist, moralist, and novelist. One of the greatest and most prolific writers that Spain has produced, he has never been as popular as Cervantes or Lope de Vega, partly because of his often demanding style (see Conceptismo) and partly because of his vitriolic temperament remarkable even in an age when poetic differences were often carried into the sphere of personal abuse. His childhood was unhappy; he suffered from a club-foot and shortsightedness and hated his mother, a lady-in-waiting to the queen. His father was secretary to Princess María, daughter of Carlos I.

After a good university degree at Alcalá, where he studied classical and modern languages and philosophy 1596–1600, he went on to study theology at Valladolid, where he took up an appointment at court and quickly became famous for eighteen poems (including the *letrilla* 'Poderoso caballero/es don Dinero') published in Pedro Espinosa's *Flores de poetas ilustres* (Valladolid, 1605). At this time he began his friendship with Cervantes, and lifelong enmity with Góngora (qq.v.). Having decided against taking Orders, he returned to Madrid with the court in 1606, causing a sensation shortly after his arrival by scornfully knocking off the hat of the great fencing-master Luis Pacheco de Narváez, who became another implacable foe.

Between 1603 and 1608 he wrote the picaresque novel *Historia de la vida del Buscón, llamado Don Pablos, exemplo de Vagamundos, y espejo de Tacaños* (Saragossa, 1626; another edn. later the same year, Barcelona), commonly known as *El buscón* (q.v.). In 1606 he wrote *El juicio final*, first of the five *Sueños* (q.v.) which constitute a terrible indictment of contemporary vice and hypocrisy, following it with *El alguacil endemoniado* in 1607, *El sueño del infierno* in 1608, *El mundo por de dentro* in 1612, and in 1621–2 *El sueño de la muerte*. These 'visions' were not approved by the censors, and did not appear until 1627, by which time MSS. of them and most other works by Quevedo were circulating very widely and several spurious works had already been published in his name. His first publication was in fact the long-forgotten *Epítome a la historia de la vida exemplar, y gloriosa muerte del bienaventurado F. Thomás de Villanueva* (1620).

The story has long been current that in 1611 Quevedo murdered a man who had insulted a lady in the Madrid church of San Martín, and had to flee to his patron the Duke of Osuna, viceroy in Sicily. A. González Palencia has claimed in his *Del 'Lazarillo' a Quevedo* (1946, pp. 257–71) that Quevedo could not have committed a murder in Madrid because he was absent from the city at the time, but whatever the truth behind the legend, he was definitely in Sicily in 1613, as a secret agent and administrator for the Viceroy, the Duke of Osuna. In 1618 he became a knight of the Order of Santiago for services to the fraternity of the Esclavos del Santísimo Sacramento. As a devotee of Santiago he wrote a pamphlet against the proposal to elevate St. Teresa to equal status with St. James (*Su espada por Santiago*, 1629).

The period of Quevedo's intervention in Italian affairs, to bolster Spanish interests in the central Mediterranean at the expense of Venice, culminated in the night of 19 May 1618, when the Venetian secret police attempted to assassinate all suspected political adversaries of the state. Quevedo was one of the few who escaped; owing to his mastery of Italian, he eluded two assassins disguised as a *lazzarone*. The Venetians spread a rumour that Osuna, Viceroy of Naples since 1616, was planning to take over authority independently of Spain, and when Quevedo failed to vindicate his patron's character at the court of Madrid, Osuna no longer trusted him and ordered him to remain in Spain. Osuna was gaoled in 1620, and when Olivares came to power on the accession of Philip IV in 1621, Quevedo was confined to his estate at La Torre de Juan Abad, where he spent his time in pursuing the debtors among his tenants and in writing.

He defended Osuna after his disgrace and imprisonment, but approved of Olivares' reforms and had no compunction in trying to ingratiate himself with the court favourite by dedicating to him the *Política de Dios, Govierno de Christo: Tyranía de Satanás* (q.v.). Olivares was softened, and Quevedo returned to royal favour, even giving lodging to Philip IV (1624) on a journey from Madrid to Andalusia. In 1632 he was appointed a secretary to the king (a post which was little more than a sinecure) and in 1634 succumbed to pressure from the Duke of Medinaceli to marry the widowed Doña Esperanza de Aragón, an arrangement terminated to their mutual relief in 1636. In 1639 Philip IV found under his napkin the famous anonymous verse memorandum denouncing corruption under Olivares. Quevedo, identified as the writer, was gaoled until the fall of Olivares in 1643, but was too ill and embittered to return to court, and retired to La Torre de Juan Abad, dying in Villanueva de los Infantes in 1645.

Repenting of his tumultuous youth, near the end of his life he wrote many religious books and pamphlets now little read, such as *La constancia y paciencia del santo Job* (1641), *Providencia de Dios* (1642), and *Vida de San Pablo Apóstol* (1643), his last full-length work.

Though the *Política de Dios* is his most significant political book, he wrote eighteen more, including *España defendida* (1609), *Mundo caduco y desvaríos de la edad* (written 1621, but first published in 1852), *Grandes anales de quince días* (written 1621, but first published in 1788), *Lince de Italia o zahorí español* (written in 1628, but first published in 1852), *El chitón de las taravillas* (1630), and *La vida de Marco Bruto* (1631–44), which is based on Plutarch's account.

Apart from *Los sueños* and *El buscón* (qq.v.), Quevedo wrote a library of satirical squibs and pamphlets covering the whole range of human iniquity and folly: *Genealogía de los modorros* (1597), *Orígenes y definiciones de la necedad* (1599), *Vida de la Corte y oficios entretenidos de ella* (1599), *Premáticas y aranceles generales* (1600), *El Caballero de la Tenaza* (1606), *Premática de las cotorreras* (1609), *Libro de todas las cosas y otras muchas más* (1627), *El entremetido, la dueña y el soplón* (1627–35), and *La hora de todos y la fortuna con seso* (a MS. copy of 1645 exists), the last a series of sketches outlining the motives and ambitions of the principal foreign powers: England, the Netherlands, Genoa, Venice, and the Muslim Empire, first published pseudonymously in 1650.

Quevedo is above all a stylist, whose daily exercise in writing Spanish verse and prose led him to complete mastery of common and uncommon usage, to playing havoc with grammar, meaning, and word-construction to excite and entertain his cultivated public. His lexicon is unequalled among writers in Castilian, benefitting from his easy familiarity with the underworld and court of Madrid, the classical and modern languages, the Bible and the Church Fathers.

Quevedo's most celebrated literary polemics against Góngora and *culteranismo* (q.v.) are *La aguja de navegar cultos. Con la receta para hacer 'Soledades' en un día* (q.v., 1613) and *La culta latiniparla. Catecismo de vocablos para instruir a las mujeres cultas y hembrilatinas* (1626). That his bilious satires against Góngora were directed as much by personal dislike as by literary criteria is suggested by the sonnet 'Ten vergüenza, purpúrate, don Luis', which ends:

> *Peor es tu cabeza que mis pies.*
> *Yo polo, no lo niego, por los dos;*
> *Tú puto, no lo niegues, por los tres.*

and by an *Epitafio* written for 'Gongorilla', as he called him in a *silva*, before the death of Góngora.

On a more responsible level, Quevedo attempted to counteract Góngora's growing reputation by editing and prefacing the works of Fray Luis de León and Francisco de la Torre (qq.v.).

His own poems were not published in his lifetime, but were assembled posthumously by his friend Jusepe Antonio González de Salas, who published six of the nine sections, or 'musas': *El Parnaso español, monte en dos cumbres dividido* (1648), publishing six of nine sections, while the other three *Las tres musas últimas castellanas* (1670) were published by his nephew Pedro Aldrete Quevedo.

While these two anthologies contain over a thousand poems, they nevertheless omit much of Quevedo's verse and attribute to him poems subsequently given to Argensola, Esquilache, and others. He is not only one of the most prolific poets in world literature: he is also one of the most varied in excellence, capable of the fine love lyric 'A Flora', a malicious caricature such

as 'Érase un hombre a una nariz pegado', the sonnet 'Faltar pudo a su patria el grande Osuna', a Senecan *silva*, the nostalgic poem of old age 'Miré los muros de la patria mía', the biting sonnet '¡Cómo de entre mis manos te deslizas!', and witty *jeux d'esprit* in the style of Baltasar del Alcázar (q.v.). His *poesía festiva* includes hundreds of ballads, *letrillas* (q.v.), and a number of the low-life *jácaras* (such as that on the bully Escarramán, q.v.) that were later imitated by Lope de Vega and many others.

One of the finest Quevedo scholars was Luis Astrana Marín (q.v.) who edited the *Obras completas* (3rd edn., 2 vols., 1943–5) and the *Epistolario completo* (1946), as well as writing *Ideario de don Francisco de Quevedo* (1940). The *Obras completas* are being newly edited by J. M. Blecua, who has so far produced four vols. of the *Obra poética* (1963–72).

See J. O. Crosby, *Guía bibliográfica para el estudio crítico de Quevedo* (London, 1976).

Quietismo, a doctrine, also known as *Molinosismo* after the theologian Miguel de Molinos (q.v.), affirming that the way to Divine Grace is through passivity rather than active works. Prohibited in Spain, the doctrine was propagated and widely accepted in France and Italy during the last years of the 17th c.

Molinos advocated disinterested love, with neither hope of reward nor fear of punishment. Prayer was transformed from a struggle to meditate into a state of pure contemplation, as in some Eastern religions, principally Buddhism. A spiritual void permitting God's will to work undisturbed replaced the more active *vías de perfección* described by earlier Spanish mystics. *Quietismo* was always of less importance in Spain than in France, where it evoked a celebrated polemic between its advocate Fénelon and its opponent Bossuet.

Quijote de la Mancha, El ingenioso hidalgo don, a novel in two parts (1605 and 1615) by Miguel de Cervantes Saavedra (q.v.).

A false sequel to the first part, printed at Tarragona in 1614, was entitled *Segundo tomo del Ingenioso Hidalgo don Quijote de la Mancha, compuesto por el licenciado Alonso Fernández de Avellaneda, natural de la villa de Tordesillas*. Due to the literary rivalry between Cervantes and Lope de Vega (q.v.), it has been conjectured that 'Fernández de Avellaneda' is a pseudonym concealing either Lope's name or that of one of his close associates, such as Alonso del Castillo Solórzano (of Tordesillas) or Alonso Ledesma. The work is, however, inferior, and Ramón Menéndez Pidal shrewdly observes that 'Avellaneda no parece que escribió otro "Quijote" sino para darnos una medida probable del valor propio de Cervantes'.

The same critic suggested (in *De Cervantes y Lope de Vega*, 1940) that the *Quijote* was inspired by an *Entremés de los romances* (*c.* 1591) in which a simple peasant goes mad after reading too many ballads of extraordinary deeds.

In the prologue to Part I, at several points in the novel, and at the end of Part II, Cervantes asserts that the whole book 'es una invectiva contra los libros de caballerías' (see CABALLERÍA, Libros de) and there is no reason to doubt that this was partly his intention.

Yet scholars have also attributed other motives to Cervantes, understanding his purpose in writing the *Quijote* as (1) the idealist, which sees exemplary values in the hero's idealism; (2) the cautionary, which sees Cervantes essentially as a moralist illustrating the progressive purging of the hero's chivalresque illusions; and (3) the perspectivist, which sees the book as an example of the tension between the real and the ideal.

Quijote's obsession with knight-errantry causes him to behave in a manner perfectly intelligible in the light of the psychological knowledge of the time: the deluded mono-maniac is incapable of distinguishing reality from illusion; yet. Cervantes in fact shows the everyday world to be ambiguous, baffling, complex, and fascinating.

Cervantes discusses the art and practice of novel-writing (Pt. 1, ch. 47). His own practice is extremely varied, encompassing the pastoral, lyrical, picaresque, autobiographical, satirical, and chivalresque modes among others. His discussions of human affairs generally are penetrating and far-ranging, on arms and letters, love, politics, religion, and a thousand other matters which have absorbed generations of readers who would not perhaps have read more solemn treatises on any of these subjects.

Quijote can be viewed as the first important European essay in the realistic mode as opposed to the over-simplified yet fantastic world of the chivalresque novel which Cervantes knew very well and criticizes in detail in the bookburning episode in Part I and elsewhere. He saw great possibilities in the *libros de caballería* (variety, action, psychological analysis), but condemned most examples of the genre for failing to realize the genre's potential, and tried to succeed in *Don Quijote* in the very ways in which they had failed.

Like all great works of art, the novel can bear the weight of most interpretations, and has been called upon to do so. Thus Ruskin, on realizing the extent to which Cervantes here appears to attack the roots of idealism, concluded that the book was aimed at undermining the sacred principles of humanity and he consequently rejected it. Arthur Efron, in *Don Quijote and the*

Dulcineated world (Austin, Texas, 1971) suggested that there is no fundamental opposition between the knight and his surroundings and that, for him, quijotesque idealism (which he calls dulcineísmo) weakens any quest, and Dulcinea is a 'dead weight'. Cervantes seems not to attack virtues such as love and honour *per se*, but rather to derive humour from the follies of a man who longs to become a warrior and lover when he is really incapable of becoming either.

Part I consists of 52 chapters. Alonso Quijano is an elderly minor nobleman living an ordinary existence in a quiet village of La Mancha. Gradually his head is turned by reading many romances of chivalry; he models himself on Amadís de Gaula (q.v.), with reminiscences of many other similar figures, such as Cirongilio de Tracia (from the novel of that title by Bernardo de Vargas, 1545) and the Caballeros 'de la Triste Figura' and 'de los Espejos' from *Don Clarián* (1524 and 1528), and sets out on his adventures.

The book begins to quicken the reader's interest more with the knight's second expedition and the introduction of his squire Sancho Panza, originally a cowardly, greedy boor but developing in the course of the novel into a fully-rounded and sympathetic character of good sense and concern for his eccentric master. With the possible exception of his poor nag Rocinante, the other 697 characters, including the 'fair' Dulcinea del Toboso upon whose behalf Quijote imagined he set out, are insignificant compared with Quijote and Panza; yet there are memorable character-sketches of figures such as the hussy Maritornes, the convict Ginés, the barber, the priest, and Sansón Carrasco.

'The tale of foolish curiosity' has undoubted weakness for its inconsistent morality and psychology, as has the Cardenio–Lucinda–Dorothea story interrupting the course of the novel in chapters 24 and 28, and the goatherd's tales in chapters 12 and 51. But the richness of the language, drawing on proverbial lore, duplication and accumulation, repetition and euphemism, led to the creation of what is generally known as 'la lengua cervantina', often imitated but never rivalled.

With its uncertainties, changes of direction, and interpolated short stories, Part I bears all the marks of a hitherto unsuccessful writer unsure of himself and of his work's reception. Cervantes even pretends that he is not the author, but is merely translating an Arabic account by the wise Cidi Hamete Benengeli. The great success of Part I, however, gave him more confidence.

Part II, published ten years afterwards, and finished in haste after the appearance of its spurious rival, has seventy-four chapters and is far superior to Part I, with no separate tales sewn in without regard to unity. Here is the expedition to El Toboso, the Cave of Montesinos, the prophesying ape and the puppet show of Maese Pedro, the visit to the Duke and Duchess, the governorship of Sancho, the adventure with the hogs, Quijote's final return home, cured of his folly at last, and his death.

Among the book's sources were the many *libros de caballería* which Cervantes specifically mentions and parodies; the anonymous *Entremés de los romances*; Ariosto's *Orlando furioso*; and Erasmus's satire *Encomium moriae* (1509).

Among the better annotated editions of the *Quijote* are that of the Academy (4 vols., 1780), that of Diego Clemencín (1833), the critical edition by Clemente Cortejón (6 vols., 1905–13), the five critical editions by F. Rodríguez Marín (8 vols., 1911–13; 6 vols., 1916–17; 4 vols., 1916–17; 7 vols., 1927–8; and 10 vols., 1947–9); M. de Riquer (1943; 2nd edn., 1950); J. García Soriano and J. García Morales (1951).

Shelton's contemporary English version has the advantage of being written in a language as varied and rich as Cervantes' own, but lacks the necessary quality of accuracy; the best in English is now that by J. M. Cohen (Harmondsworth, 1950; many reprints).

The tens of thousands of books and articles on every conceivable aspect of *Quijote* cannot be reduced to a handful: consult the author bibliographies cited under CERVANTES. However, it is necessary to be familiar with Joaquín Casalduero, *Sentido y forma del 'Quijote', 1605–1615* (1949; 2nd edn., 1966); J. Ortega y Gasset, *Meditaciones del 'Quijote'* (1914); Salvador de Madariaga, *Guía del lector del 'Quijote'* (1926); Américo Castro, *El pensamiento de Cervantes* (1925); Helmut Hatzfeld, *El 'Quijote' como obra de arte del lenguaje* (1949; 2nd edn., 1966); R. L. Predmore, *El mundo del 'Quijote'* (1958; translated as *The world of Don Quixote*, Cambridge, Mass., 1967); Helmut Hatzfeld, *Don Quijote: Forschung und Kritik* (Darmstadt, 1968); P. E. Russell, '"Don Quixote" as a funny book' in *Modern Language Review* vol. 64 (1969), pp. 212–326; and E. C. Riley, *Cervantes' theory of the novel* (Oxford, 1962).

Quiñones, Libro del Passo honroso defendido por el excelente cavallero Suero de, see RODRÍGUEZ DE LENA, Pedro.

QUIÑONES DE BENAVENTE, LUIS (1593?–1651), b. Toledo. Priest, friend of Lope de Vega, and writer of *entremeses, loas*, and *jácaras* (qq.v.). His popular, satirical short plays fall into the line of development from Lope de Rueda to Ramón de la Cruz (qq.v.). Hannah E. Bergman, in her important *Luis Quiñones de Benavente y sus entremeses* (1965) has divided his works into the realistic and the fantastic, the former being *comedias* in miniature and the latter his sung *entremeses*.

His friend Manuel Antonio Vargas collected in 1645 a number of his works written between 1630 and 1640, and stated in his preface that Benavente no longer wrote for the stage. This book is *Iocoseria, Burlas veras, o reprehensión moral, y festiva de los desórdenes públicos. En doze Entremeses representados, y veinte y quatro cantados*. Cayetano Rosell edited 2 vols. of *entremeses*, *Colección de piezas dramáticas* (1872–4) and E. Cotarelo y Mori published 142 works attributed to Benavente in his *Colección de entremeses, loas, bailes . . .* in the NBAE (vols. 17–18, 1911), and suggests a total of 900 such playlets in all. Tirso de Molina (q.v.) had already estimated his works as 300 by the age of thirty in his play *Tanto es lo más como lo de menos*. Cotarelo's views have recently been impugned, many works attributed to Benavente now being given to others. Since his name was synonymous with the best of *entremeses* during his lifetime, it is likely that many works bearing his name are not his, and others not published by Cotarelo have since been given to him.

A typical *entremés, El miserable*, takes from Quevedo's novel *El buscón* that caricature of avarice Cabra the schoolmaster, and exaggerates his meanness even further in the picture of Don Martín de Peralvillo, who scolds his wife for breathing out when she could have used her breath more economically on a lamp.

Benavente's *entremeses*, performed in the intervals between acts of most *comedias* acted between 1620 and 1650, reminded the audience of their own foibles.

See Hannah E. Bergman's edition of the *Entremeses* (Salamanca, 1968), her study of them (1965), and her *Luis Quiñones de Benavente* (New York, 1972) in Twayne's World Authors series.

QUINTANA, MANUEL JOSÉ (1772–1857), b. Madrid. Poet and dramatist. He studied in Salamanca under Meléndez Valdés (q.v.), whose influence, like that of Álvarez de Cienfuegos (q.v.), is apparent in his earliest work *Poesías* (1788). He was a close friend of Jovellanos (q.v.).

Quintana was praised in his lifetime (and in fact crowned publicly in 1855 by Isabel II, his former pupil) for his thirty-four patriotic poems written between 1795 and 1808 of which the best are probably the odes *A la invención de la imprenta* (1800) and *A la expedición española para propagar la vacuna en América 1803–4* (1806), the narrative *Al combate de Trafalgar* (1805), and the stirring battle-cries written in 1808, *Al armamento de las provincias españolas contra los franceses* and *A España después de la revolución de marzo*. Quintana largely excluded such themes as religion, love, and Nature from his poetry, being much more interested in scientific and patriotic achievements. In the War of Independence he took the national side and occupied high positions, editing the *Semanario Patriótico* and in 1808 publishing a collection, *Poesías patrióticas*. On the restoration of Fernando VII in 1814, Quintana was jailed in the citadel of Pamplona. He was released and honoured from 1820 to 1823, confined again until 1828, and on Fernando's death in 1833 hailed as a national hero, receiving among other posts those of Presidente de Instrucción Pública, and tutor to the young queen Isabel II. He wrote two neoclassical plays to prove the methods advocated in his *Las reglas del drama* (1791), a didactic poem in the tradition of Horace's *Ars poetica* and Boileau's *L'art poétique: El duque de Viseo* (1801), a tragedy based on M. G. Lewis's *The castle spectre* (1798), and *Pelayo* (1805).

His excellent prose style can be enjoyed in *Vidas de españoles célebres* (vol. 1, 1807; vol. 2, 1830), on the lives of the Cid, Guzmán el Bueno, Roger de Lauria, the Prince of Viana, the Great Captain, Núñez de Balboa, Álvaro de Luna, Pizarro, and Bartolomé de Las Casas.

Though Quintana lived through the Romantic period, he was little affected by it. His *Obras completas* were published in the BAE, vol. 19 (1852) and vol. 67 (1872); there is another edition (3 vols.) of 1897–8.

QUINTERO brothers, see ÁLVAREZ QUINTERO brothers.

Quinteto, in Spanish metre, a verse of five lines of *arte mayor* (q.v.). The scheme abbab was used with success by Campoamor (q.v.). The hendecasyllabic *quinteto* ending abcdd was introduced by J. M. Heredia in 'A mi caballo'. With the final line heptasyllabic, this form was used by Cadalso, Iglesias de la Casa, and Juan Meléndez Valdés (qq.v.).

Quintilla, in Spanish metre, a verse of five octosyllabic lines in which no three consecutive lines may rhyme. The commonest rhyme-scheme is abaab, and the others: aabab, aabba, ababa, ababb, abbaa, abbab.

The *quintilla* was formed by adding a line to the *redondilla* (q.v.) and until fairly late it was described (by Rengifo among others) as the *redondilla* of five lines. Its heyday was the 15th c., and its most illustrious practitioner Juan de Mena (q.v.).

A *quintilla real* is a verse of five hendecasyllabic lines.

QUIROGA, HORACIO (1878–1937), b. Salto, Uruguay. Short-story writer. The early death of his father in a shooting accident made a deep impression on him. His first literary influences were the modernists (in particular Lugones, q.v.) and Poe. After a few months in Paris he returned to Montevideo and published the modernist poems of *Los arrecifes de coral* (1901). He accidentally killed one of his friends and left for Buenos Aires, where he met Lugones and took part in an expedition to study the Jesuit ruins in the tropical region of Misiones. Quiroga was attracted by the primitive life he observed there, and went to live in the Chaco as a cotton planter, and then in Misiones. Neglected by the rising generation in Buenos Aires, Quiroga committed suicide when he learnt he was suffering from cancer. A son and a daughter of his also committed suicide, and it is likely that his father did as well. He has been called the American Kipling, but whereas a definite similarity of subject-matter exists, Quiroga succeeds to a greater extent in conveying the helplessness of man in the face of elemental forces in nature and himself. He shows how animals survive where man is an alien, bringing Poe's technique of the horror story to situations where it is most effective: a fight between snakes; the danger of minor defects of character which, harmless in the city, may prove fatal in the wilds, or the tragedy of men losing control through alcohol or hysteria. Quiroga is one of the earliest of the cultivated writers of regional stories; apparent defects in technique are seen to result from the complexity of the stories, for Quiroga was a pioneer in the genre. All his collections of short stories were first published in Buenos Aires. They include *El crimen del otro* (1904), *Los perseguidos* (1905), *Cuentos de amor, de locura y de muerte* (1917), published after his wife had committed suicide in 1915, *Cuentos de la selva para niños* (1918; translated by A. Livingstone, New York, 1922), *El salvaje* (1920), *Anaconda* (1921), *El desierto* (1924), *La gallina degollada y otros cuentos* (1925), *Los desterrados* (1926), *Pasado amor* (1929), and *Más allá* (1935).

See Walter Rela, *Horacio Quiroga: repertorio bibliográfico anotado, 1879–1971* (Buenos Aires, 1972); and N. A. S. Bratosevich, *El estilo de Horacio Quiroga en sus cuentos* (Madrid, 1973).

QUIROGA, JUAN FACUNDO (1790?–1835), a *gaucho caudillo* of the Argentine pampas, known also as 'El Tigre de los Llanos', whose life and times formed the pretext for the wide-ranging discussion of the problem of *civilización y barbarie* by Domingo Faustino Sarmiento (q.v.) in his *Vida de Juan Facundo Quiroga* (1845).

QUIROGA, PEDRO DE (c. 1540–c. 1595), a Spanish missionary in Peru whose *Coloquios de la verdad* (1583?; ed. G. Zarco, 1922) consist of four dialogues between an Indian, a Spaniard, and a hermit on the conquest of Peru. Quiroga leans heavily for his facts and prejudices on the well-known work by Bartolomé de Las Casas (q.v.), entitled *Relación de la destruyción de las Indias*.

QUIROGA DE LA VÁLGOMA, ELENA (1921–   ), b. Santander. Novelist. She spent much of her life up to 1950 on her father's estate in Barco de Valdeorras (Orense). After *La soledad sonora* (1949), an unsatisfactory achievement, Elena Quiroga won the Premio Nadal of 1950 with *Viento del norte* (published 1951, in Barcelona as were all her subsequent novels) and in 1950 married Delmiro de la Válgoma, a historian, and has since lived in Madrid.

Viento del norte concerns an elderly Galician nobleman who marries a young servant who only after his death, caused partly by grief at her unconcern, realises that she really loved him. *La sangre* (1952) is a saga of four generations of family life told by a tree, and bears a resemblance to the *Historia de una escalera* of Antonio Buero Vallejo (q.v.). *Algo pasa en la calle* (1954) falls into the category of *tremendismo* (q.v.). *La enferma* (1955) deals with the psychosomatic illness of a woman abandoned by her lover. *La careta* (1955) explores the stream of consciousness in the manner of William Faulkner. Three short novels published in *Plácida la joven y otras narraciones* (1956) were followed by a remarkable *tour de force: La última corrida* (1958), a novel in dialogue on the lives of three *toreros*. Elena Quiroga has also written *Tristura* (1960) and *Escribo tu nombre* (1965).

QUIRÓS, PEDRO DE (*c.* 1600–67), b. Seville. Poet. Provost of the Minorites in Salamanca and subsequently Vicar-General of the Order in Spain.

His sonnet 'A Itálica' and his madrigal 'Tórtola amante' have been familiar in anthologies since Amador de los Ríos first published them in 1838. Quirós's love poems occasionally equal those in *La Dorotea* of Lope de Vega (qq.v.) and his religious eclogue 'Al nacimiento de Cristo' is extremely moving. M. Menéndez

y Pelayo edited his *Poesías divinas y humanas* (Seville, 1887).

QUÍSPEZ ASÍN, CÉSAR (1904–56), Peruvian surrealist poet and essayist, who lived in Paris throughout the heyday of surrealism (1925–33), and wrote principally in French, using the penname César Moro. He lived in Lima 1934–38, in Mexico City 1938–48, and in Peru again from 1948 until his death. His books are extremely scarce: *Le château de Grisou* (Mexico City, 1943), *Lettre d'amour* (1944), *Trafalgar Square* (1954), and *Amour à mort* (Paris, 1957), the last-named collecting together his French poems from the last Lima period. He also wrote a number of poems in Spanish while in Mexico; these include 'La tortuga ecuestre' and 'La vida escandalosa de César Moro'. *Los anteojos de azufre* is a prose collection from the same period. His collections of essays are *El uso de la palabra* (1935) and *El obispo embotellado* (1936), and later he was an important contributor to the 8 issues of Emilio A. Westphalen's excellent review *Las Moradas* (1946–8). There is a good selection of Moro's work in *Surrealistas y otros peruanos insulares* (1970) compiled by A. Oquendo and M. Lauer.

André Coyne has been entrusted with the posthumous publication of Moro's work. See his 'César Moro: el hilo de Ariadna' in *Ínsula*, nos. 332–3 (July–August 1974). There are translations by Philip Ward from the French and Spanish entitled *The scandalous life of César Moro* (New York, 1976) with a biobibliographical introduction.

Quixote, Don, see QUIJOTE DE LA MANCHA, El ingenioso hidalgo don.

QUTIA, ABU BAKR IBN AL- (Spanish: ABENAL-CUTIA, d. 997), b. Cordova. Historian, whose mother was a Goth (Arabic: *qutia*) of royal blood. His important history of Spain up to 'Abd ar-Rahman III (912–61) has been edited by Pascual de Gayangos, and published with the translation of Julián Ribera y Tarragó (q.v.) as *Historia de la conquista de España* (1926).

QUZMAN, IBN, see GUZMAN, Ibn.

R

RABASA, Emilio (1856–1930), b. Ocozocoautla, Chiapas. Mexican novelist and jurist responsible for major texts on Mexican constitutional law. In 1888 he founded *El Universal* with Rafael Reyes Spíndola.

His reputation as a novelist rests on four works of his youth written under the pseudonym 'Sancho Polo': *La bola* (1887), in which a local revolution in the imaginary township of San Martín de la Piedra is the setting for a conflict between the young idealist Juanito Quiñones and the unscrupulous *cacique* Cabezudo, who appear also in the other three; *La gran ciencia* (1887), on corruption in the state capital; *El cuarto poder* (1888), on the misuse of the press' power by political interests in Mexico City; and *Moneda falsa* (1888), on the realization by the central characters of their inability to cope with the pressures and intrigues of life in the capital, and their return home to the countryside.

La Guerra de los Tres Años (1931; ed. by Emmanuel Carballo, 1955), which first appeared serially in *El Universal*, deals with the power of the Church and the difficulties in the way of reform.

Rabasa is the first realist novelist of Mexico, being influenced by the naturalism of Zola and particularly by the construction and style of Pérez Galdós's fiction. He deals with the middle classes ironically and humorously, and usually with affection. Though mistrusting politicians, Rabasa offers in these four novels (forming a tetralogy around the opposing figures of Juanito and Cabezudo) hope for improvement in Mexican society. His influence helped bring about the abandonment of Romanticism and *costumbrismo* in the Mexican novel. A fine prose stylist, he is much weaker in his psychological analysis than in his convincing picture of the inner workings of a corrupt political system.

See F. Tena Ramírez, *Silueta de don Emilio Rabasa* (1935); Vicente Liévano, *Emilio Rabasa* (Tuxtla Gutiérrez, 1946); and M. A. Hakala, *Emilio Rabasa* (1974).

Rabinal Achí, a ballet-drama of the Quiché Indians of Guatemala which is still performed at festivals. The musical play's theme is the heroic legend of the princes of Rabinal. The MS. was discovered towards the middle of the 19th c.

See the Spanish translation published, with an introduction by Francisco Monterde, as *Teatro indígena prehispánico: Rabinal Achí* (Mexico City, 1955).

RAIMUNDO, (1124–51), *Archbishop of Toledo,* member of the Cluniac order, and founder of the so-called 'school of translators' in Toledo: a group of scholars whose work of disseminating Arabic, Hebrew, and Graeco-Roman sources was to be continued by Alfonso X 'el Sabio' (q.v.). The converted Jew Juan Hispalense translated books by Avicenna, al-Ghazali, Avicebron, and others into the vernacular, and Dominicus Gundisalvus of Segovia translated from the vernacular into Latin. These and their compatriots were well known as teachers in Europe at that time, and students came to learn from them from England (Adelard of Bath and Michael Scotus), Germany (Herman), and Italy (Gerard of Cremona). Medieval Spanish writers drew on the literatures thus interpreted and it is through the School of Toledo that western Europe first came to learn of Arab achievement in medicine, philosophy, grammar, astronomy, and other disciplines.

See A. González Palencia, *Don Raimundo y los traductores de Toledo* (Madrid, 1942).

RAMÍREZ, Ignacio (1818–79), b. San Miguel de Allende, Guanajuato. Mexican poet, freethinker, and controversialist who wrote under the pseudonym 'El Nigromante' and has been called the Mexican Voltaire. A member of the Academia de San Juan de Letrán, while still a student he caused consternation when he defended the proposition 'There is no God; natural beings sustain themselves independently'. He subsequently wrote and lectured widely in support of his positivist beliefs. The magazine *Don Simplicio* was banned in 1848 for publishing his anti-conservative article *A los viejos* in its opening issue. A Romantic in politics, he nonetheless wrote neoclassical poetry, such as the sonnet 'Al amor' and the tercets 'Por los desgraciados' and 'Por los gregorianos muertos'. His *Obras* (2 vols.), were published in 1889, being reprinted in 1952.

RAMÍREZ DE ARELLANO, Feliciano, *Marqués de la Fuensanta del Valle* (19th c.), literary scholar whose extensive private library is now incorporated in that of the Hispanic Society of America and listed in an important catalogue (20 vols., New York, 1910). With José Sancho Rayón he published the valuable *Colección de libros españoles raros o curiosos* (24 vols., 1871–1896), including the *Cancionero de Stúñiga* (1872) which was hitherto known only in the MSS. of the National Library, Madrid, and the Biblioteche Marziana and Casanatense in Italy.

RAMÍREZ or REMÍREZ DE ARELLANO, Luis (17th c.), b. Villaescusa de Haro, Cuenca. Poet and plagiarist, whose memory is recorded as being phenomenal. Espinel wrote in his *Marcos de Obregón* (qq.v.) that Ramírez would sit through a *comedia*, and then go home to write down every word without errors or omissions. Suárez de Figueroa (*Plaza universal de todas ciencias y artes*, Perpignan, 1630) declared that Ramírez needed three consecutive visits: the first to master the plot; the second to study the variety of the composition, and the last to memorize the exact words. In this way it is claimed that Ramírez learnt Lope's *La dama boba*, *El príncipe perfecto*, and *La Arcadia* (based on his pastoral novel of the same name). Once, when Lope's *El galán de la membrilla* was being performed by Sánchez's company, the actors were interrupted and prompted wrongly so often by the manager that the audience protested. Sánchez replied that someone in the audience (Ramírez) would have the play by heart in three evenings unless it was abridged and distorted, and the audience then forced Ramírez to leave the theatre before the play continued.

Blatant plagiarism of this type was also prevalent in Shakespeare's England (cf. Malone's *Historical account of the English stage*, 1801).

His *Última línea de la vida y avisos para la muerte* ... (Saragossa, 1640), contains his own work and poetry by Lope de Vega, Calderón, Rojas Zorrilla, Mira de Amescua, and others.

RAMÓN, Fray Alonso, see REMÓN, Fray Alonso.

Ramonismo, see GÓMEZ DE LA SERNA, Ramón.

RAMOS, José Antonio (1885–1946), b. Havana. Cuban playwright, essayist, and journalist. In 1932 he sought exile in Mexico from the dictator Machado, but was reinstated in his diplomatic career after Machado's fall the following year. His socialist theatre of ideas, the most important body of work in its genre during the first generation of the Republic, owes much to Ibsen. His best play, *Tembladera* (1918), deals with the question of the sale of sugar plantations to foreigners and misuse of the proceeds. He wrote on feminism and social justice in plays such as *Libertá* (Madrid, 1911), *Satanás* (1913), *Calibán Rex* (1914), *El hombre fuerte* (1915), the symbolic *En las manos de Dios* (1933), and the Pirandellian *La leyenda de las estrellas* (1935).

His *Manual del perfecto fulanista* (1916) is a liberal polemic on the political problems of Cuba in his day. His novels were less successful than his other writings.

Fermín Peraza's bibliography of Ramos was published in *Revista Iberoamericana*, vol. 12, no. 24 (June 1947), pp. 335–400, a special issue on Ramos.

See José Antonio Portuondo, 'El contenido político y social de las obras de José Antonio Ramos' in *Revista de la Biblioteca Nacional José Martí*, vol. 60, no. 1 (January–April 1969), pp. 5–58.

RAMOS, Samuel (1897–1959), b. Zitácuaro, Michoacán. Mexican thinker and essayist, whose Adlerian analysis *El perfil del hombre y de la cultura en México* (1934) attacked the alleged propensity of Mexicans to imitate foreign systems, such as the federalism of the U.S.A. or French positivism, and suggested that the passion for rewriting the Constitution led to the theoretical rejection of political realities and made reality itself illegal, thus fostering an ambivalent attitude to life and action. Ramos named sincerity as the single attribute to be cultivated by Mexicans, and proposed psychoanalysis as their cure. Ineffective though this panacea may seem, *El perfil* was the most penetrating essay on Mexico until the appearance of *El laberinto de la soledad* by Octavio Paz (qq.v.) and has influenced several important creative writers, such as Carlos Fuentes (q.v.).

Subsequent works by Ramos included *Diego Rivera* (1935), *Mas allá de la moral de Kant* (1938), *El caso Stravinsky* (1939), *Hacia un nuevo humanismo* (1940), *Veinte años de educación en México* (1941), and *Historia de la filosofía en México* (1942).

RAMOS CARRIÓN, Miguel (1845–1915), b. Zamora. Journalist and popular comic writer of *zarzuelas* (q.v.). His best-known works include *La tempestad* (1882), *La bruja* (1887), and *El rey que rabió* (written, like many of his more durable works, with Vital Aza, q.v.), and he wrote a number of light comedies such as *Cada loco con su tema* (1874) and *León y leona* (1874). He founded the weekly *Las Disciplinas*, to which he contributed under the pseudonym of 'Boabdil el Chico'. His *Prosa escogida* appeared in 1916.

Rana, Juan, a popular *gracioso*, or comic hero of the *entremeses* (q.v.), apparently invented as 'Pedro Rana' by Cervantes in *Los alcaldes de Dagazo*, but most frequently portrayed by Luis Quiñones de Benavente (q.v.).

Juan Rana appears in no less than 43 extant Golden Age *entremeses*, most of them by Quiñones de Benavente. Dressed in cap and smock, he was often a rustic mayor, laywer, or doctor. Among his characteristics were a peasant shrewdness, ignorance, avarice, cowardice, and gluttony. The part of Juan Rana was played so frequently by the actor Cosme Pérez that for many playgoers and the public at large the two identities coalesced.

RAQUEL, a Jewess of Toledo with whom Alfonso VIII (1158–1214) fell in love. Her story was the subject of plays by Lope de Vega (q.v., *La Raquel hermosa*), Antonio Mira de Amescua (q.v., *La desdichada Raquel*), and Vicente García de la Huerta (q.v., *Raquel*, 1772) the last translated into Italian *versi sciolti* (Bologna, 1782) by his brother Pedro, one of the exiled Jesuits. The Austrian Franz Grillparzer (1791–1872) wrote a play on this subject called *Die Jüdin von Toledo* (1873), which has been translated into English by G. H. and A. P. Danton.

Raquel is also the name of one of the two Jews (the other being Vidas) in the *Cantar de mio Cid* (q.v.).

Rayuela (1963), the second novel by Julio Cortázar (q.v.), translated into English as *Hopscotch* by G. Rabassa (London, 1966), which caused a great stir for its portrayal of the anti-hero and for its unusual structure. Cortázar explicitly repudiates the conventional form of narrative, symbolizing in its erratic order of reading the illogical progress of men through life and the irrational search for meaning and truth through the traditional chronological sequence. In his prefatory note he points out that 'the book is many books but above all two books'; that 'book one' consists of chapters 1–56 which may be read in numerical order; that 'book two' includes as well as the narrative a number of extracts from newspapers and philosophical works, stressing the essentially absurd nature of life; and that 'book two' begins with ch. 73 and continues with chs. 1, 2, 116, 3, 84, 4, 71, 5 . . . Thus the reader participates in the creation of the novel, exactly as he is expected to do in *62. Novela para armar* (1968).

The whole work is an elaborate game. Oliveira, the Argentinian, and his mistress Maga, live in existentialist Paris, agreeing never to arrange a meeting, but preferring to run into each other by chance. Oliveira mutilates his copy of the standard Academy dictionary because he prefers to invent games with language with private systems of meaning. He mocks such concepts as nationalism which set up arbitrary divisions among men, and rejects the conventional in life and art. He is astonished at the quotidian absurdity of existence, including the strangeness of food; the use, colour, and shape of clothes (reminiscent of Beckett's interest in pockets); and the peculiar 'boxes' in which people choose to live and keep their dogs. The ridiculous character Ceferino, who has insane dreams of reorganizing the world on a purely logical basis, is a clear victim of 'la manía clasificatoria del homo occidentalis' and the antithesis of the anarchic, illogical Oliveira.

A weakness of *Rayuela* is that Cortázar's stunning wordplay is at odds with his essentially juvenile sense of humour, but his influence is likely to remain strong among young writers of Latin America.

See R. Brody, *Julio Cortázar: 'Rayuela'* (London, 1976) in the Critical Guides to Spanish Texts series.

Raza de bronce (1919), a novel by the Bolivian Alcides Arguedas (q.v.), and his finest work. This is a sympathetic, balanced, and careful fictional account of the Aimará Indians and their traditional conflict with white society. Since the Aimará are so slow to adapt to the society and culture of their Hispanic exploiters (such as landowners, priests, or central government bureaucrats), the only chance for success in life of future generations is miscegenation, and in the meantime rejection of all outside interference.

The plot concerns the Indians' long journey from the highlands to the valley to sell their produce and to buy seed. In the second part of the novel the Indians are shown to be exploited by brutal, avaricious, and sensual whites. Their boss is less than generous with them, the priest deceives them, and a pregnant girl, Maruja, is raped by the son of the landowner. An Indian uprising is put down by the army.

It is the first really important novel to emerge from Bolivia. Arguedas, a professional historian whose facts are beyond dispute, cleverly combines known customs and rites with a poetic view of the Indians' identification with the land they inhabit, and inserts an Indian legend into the novel without loss of coherence. Before Arguedas it was inconceivable to write of the Aimará as a people with their own rights and their own culture, and his contribution to the *indigenista* novel won continental fame for its integrity and skilful blend of fantasy and realism.

See Gordon Brotherston, 'Alcides Arguedas as a "Defender of Indians" in the first and later editions of "Raza de bronce"' in *Romance Notes* (Chapel Hill, N.C.), vol. 13 (1971), pp. 41–47.

Razón feita de amor (early 13th c.), an anonymous lyric poem generally considered to be the earliest extant in Castilian, and probably deriving from an earlier poem in French. Together with a burlesque verse dispute between Water and Wine, it is in a MS. of the Bibliothèque Nationale, Paris. The name of Lupus de Morus is at the end of the MS., but he was more likely copyist than author. The poem is popular or *juglaresco* in style, with sensuous imagery and vivid dialogue between two lovers. It was published (with the related *Denuestos del agua y el vino*, q.v.) by Morel-Fatio in *Romania*, vol. 16 (1887); by Menéndez Pidal in *Revue Hispanique*, vol. 13 (1905); and by G. H. London in *Romance Philology*, vol. 19 (1965-66).

See Mario de Pinto, 'La "Razón de amor" e il problema della sua unità' in *Due contrasti d'amore nella Spagna medievale* (Pisa, 1959); and Arsenio Pacheco, '¿Razón de amor o Denuestos del agua y el vino?' in *BHS*, vol. 51 (1974).

Real Academia Española de la Lengua (Royal Spanish Language Academy, usually known simply as La Academia, 'the Academy'), the first official academy (many private 'academies' existed earlier) founded in 1713 by Juan Manuel Fernández Pacheco, Marquis of Villena, and Duke of Escalona, and given its royal charter on 3 October 1714. The objective, as set out in the charter, was that of cultivating and improving the national (or Castilian) language, and to that end to produce a dictionary which would distinguish the words and phrases employed by the best Spanish writers from the slang and colloquial terms to be excluded from good writing. Their authoritative *Diccionario de autoridades* (6 vols., 1726-39) is still of value. The lesser *Diccionario*, first published in one volume in 1780, reached its 19th edition in 1970.

The Academy's membership was fixed at 24 in 1715, raised to 36 in 1874, and in addition to those of director and secretary, the posts of censor, librarian, and treasurer have been created. The Academy's official *Ortografía* first appeared in 1741 and the official *Gramática* in 1771, both having been under continuous revision ever since.

Its duties also included the sponsoring of authoritative classic texts. In 1780 appeared the monumental *Quijote* and in 1917 the facsimile edition of the *Obras completas* of Cervantes, including the fifteen vols. of the *Obras dramáticas* (1890-1913) edited by M. Menéndez y Pelayo and the 13 vols. of the new edition by E. Cotarelo y Mori (1916-30). The Biblioteca Selecta de Autores Clásicos Españoles began publication in 1866 (as Biblioteca Clásica Española), including such authors as Ercilla, Lucas Fernández, Ruiz de Alarcón, Lope de Rueda, González del Castillo, and Manuel del Palacio.

Among the most distinguished directors of the Academy have been Martínez de la Rosa, the Duque de Rivas, Rodríguez Marín, Asín y Palacios, Menéndez Pidal, and Dámaso Alonso (qq.v.).

The quarterly *Boletín de la Real Academia Española* first appeared in 1914.

Realismo ('realism'), a literary tendency which attempts to portray life as it is, opposed to idealism or Romanticism (see also ROMANTICISMO). Though it is of universal and perpetual importance as one of the major literary modes, in Spanish literature it is said to be the dominant style of the later 19th c., in reaction to the earlier Romanticism, and to make the novel the principal literary genre of that period. The great realist authors are Benito Pérez Galdós, Pereda, and Pedro Antonio de Alarcón (qq.v.); Armando Palacio Valdés (q.v.) is a less significant figure.

The characteristics of realistic fiction are minute detail in human psychology and natural scenery, the inclusion of real contemporary events, language suited to the region or district where the book is set, and behaviour natural to ordinary people and society in general. (See also COSTUMBRISMO).

Spanish realism is very much *sui generis*; by the standards of French realism, neither Pereda nor Alarcón is a 'realist' since they are committed to preserving *decoro*, and to an orthodox moral, social, and religious code, lacking the objectivity of Flaubert. The French concept of realism is approached in the mature work of 'Clarín' and Pérez Galdós.

Realism has played a major part in the Spanish-American novel, from the precursors (Cambaceres and Blest Gana, qq.v.) to the Indianist and regionalist novels of Azuela, Manuel Gálvez, Martín Luis Guzmán, J. R. Romero, Manuel Rojas, J. E. Rivera, Quiroga, Güiraldes, Gallegos, Arguedas, Icaza, and Alegría (qq.v.).

'Magic realism' is the term associated with writers such as Gabriel García Márquez (q.v.), whose apparently realistic narrative is broken by apparently incongruous or bizarre events and apparitions.

Realismo in an exaggerated form leads to *naturalismo* (q.v.), though of course there is no clear demarcation between the two notions, which are based on critics' and writers' differing ideas of what constitutes the norm in human conduct.

See Alfonso Sastre, *Anatomía del realismo* (Barcelona, 1965); and G. Ara, *La novela naturalista hispanoamericana* (Buenos Aires, 1965).

Rebelión de las masas, La (1929), a sociopolitical polemic by José Ortega y Gasset (q.v.) against the apathy and vulgarity he had already detected among the masses of Spain in *España invertebrada* (q.v., 1921). Ortega's complaint is that 'ya no hay protagonistas: sólo hay coro' in the intellectual life of the nation, and he views the rebellion of the masses as the most crucial danger facing not only Spain, but also the entire western world. Ortega's solution is control by a benevolent élite.

'Hombre-masa' is a socio-intellectual, rather than a political concept, comprising all those who allow others to control their lives, behaving and thinking for preference 'like the rest'. The natural aristocrat is a man who requires more from himself than others do, even though he cannot always fulfil his own strict programme for self-development. The vulgar man often recognizes his own vulgarity, but claims that he has a right to be vulgar and to impose his vulgarity of thought, and taste, and behaviour on the others. The enormous popularity of Ortega's book can be judged by the fact that it has averaged a new impression for every year since its original publication.

REBOLLEDO, BERNARDINO DE (1597–1676), b. León. A professional soldier of aristocratic parentage, he served with distinction against the Turks, and in the Thirty Years' War, during which he was created Conde de Rebolledo. When peace was declared in 1647, he was appointed ambassador to Denmark (1648–62) and there he wrote the prose *Discurso de la hermosura y el amor* (Copenhagen, 1652), which Menéndez y Pelayo called 'the swan-song of Platonism in Spain', and the three *Selvas*: the didactic poem on the art and practice of war, *Selva militar y política* (Cologne, 1652); the attack on Protestantism, couched as an eulogy of the Danish royal family, *Selvas dánicas* (Copenhagen, 1655); and the *Selva sagrada* (1657), translating the Psalms and the Lamentations of Jeremiah.

His poetry was exceptional for its time in taking no account of Gongorism. *Ocios* (Antwerp, 1650) was expanded into *Obras poéticas* in 3 vols., which includes his tragicomedy *Amar despreciando riesgos* and the *Entremés de los maridos conformes*. His poetry lacks originality in general, and is modelled upon that of the Argensola brothers (qq.v.).

Redondilla ('roundelay'), a stanza of four octosyllabic lines rhyming abba. Possibly of Portuguese origin, the *redondilla* was used in Alfonso el Sabio's Galician poetry, and in the *Libro de buen amor* (q.v.). A *redondilla menor* is a hexasyllabic stanza. The *redondilla* is common in verse drama, especially in that of Espronceda.

Refranes (*refrán*, 'refrain'), originally a line or couplet ending a verse of a poem or song and usually making an appropriate moralizing statement; later any proverbial utterance. Proverbs appear in Spain as early as Seneca (q.v.), but they reach the zenith of their literary significance in the Golden Age, when Cervantes employs them, usually out of context to stress the incongruity of his characters' homely reactions to fantastic situations. Gerarda, in Lope de Vega's *Dorotea* (V, i) says of proverbs: 'Estos son todos los libros del mundo en quinta essencia. Compúsolos el uso y confirmólos la experiencia'. Proverbs are even more abundant in Gerarda's prototype, the heroine of *La Celestina* (q.v.), and are found as early as the *Poema del mio Cid* (see CID) and later in the *Libro de buen amor* (q.v.) and *El corbacho*. An extant *entremés* reprinted by Northup in *Ten Spanish farces* (London, 1924) consisting of 192 proverbs cleverly woven into 269 lines has been attributed by J. M. Asensio (1870) to Cervantes, by F. Guerra to Quiñones de Benavente and by C. Vidal de Valenciano (Barcelona, 1883) to Quevedo.

The Marqués de Santillana (q.v.) was the first to collect proverbs: his hundred *Refranes que dizen las viejas tras el fuego* (Seville, 1508) assembled at the behest of Juan II has recently been edited by G. M. Bertini in *Quaderni Ibero-Americani* (Turin, vol. 3, 1955, pp. 13–23). There followed three curious letters by B. de Garay made up of proverbs: *Dos cartas en que se contiene, como sabiendo una señora que un su servidor se querría confesar* (1541), a work imitated by Quevedo in his *Cuento de cuentos*.

Pedro Vallés's *Libro de refranes* (1549) gathered 4,300 proverbs, but during the Golden Age it was the 6,000 *refranes* collected by Hernán Núñez de Toledo (1555) that became the most familiar source-book for writers, and this was reprinted eight times. Juan de Mal Lara (q.v.) used Núñez's work for *La philosophia vulgar* (1568), which glosses proverbs taken from numerous contexts, but has not been edited in modern times. Sebastián de Horozco's *Recopilación de refranes y adagios comunes y vulgares de España* has still only been published in part (by Cotarelo y Mori in the *BRAE*, 1915–17). The best collector was probably Gonzalo Correas (d. 1631), whose *Vocabulario de refranes* was written about 1626 and first published by Mir in 1906 (2nd edn., 1924).

J. M. Sbarbi compiled the bulky but unscholarly *Refranero general* in 10 vols. (1874–8), and the *Refranes del Quijote* have been studied by José Coll y Vehí (Barcelona, 1874), while Francisco Rodríguez Marín sought to supplement the work of Correas with *Más de 21,000 refranes castellanos* (1926), *Doce mil seiscientos refranes más* (1930), *Los 6,666 refranes de un última rebusca* (1934), and *Todavía diez mil setecientos refranes más* (1941). Julio Cejador y Frauca's posthumously-published *Refranero castellano* appeared in 3 vols. (1928–9). A *Diccionario histórico de refranes castellanos* has been in preparation by F. C. Hayes and R. S. Boggs in the U.S.A. since 1934.

REGAÑADIENTES, El Bachiller, pseudonym of Juan Pablo Forner (q.v.).

Regeneracionismo, the doctrine, propounded by reformists such as Joaquín Costa y Martínez (q.v.), of the Europeanization of Spain, and the abandonment of loyalty to traditions such as that of El Cid and the allegedly outdated *pundonor* code.

Regenta, La, a novel by Clarín (pseudonym of Leopoldo Alas y Ureña, q.v.), published in 2 vols. in 1884. Clarín's best novel, *La Regenta* is a Flaubertian analysis of life in Vetusta, as he calls his adopted home-town Oviedo.

Ana Ozores, an orphan reared, after her father's death, by her aunts Anuncia and Agueda, marries an affable ex-judge thirty years her senior, Don Víctor Quintanar. Sexually frustrated, Ana (nicknamed 'La Regenta') turns to mystical reading and works of devotion under the guidance of a sly, ambitious priest, Fermín de Pas, a canon (Magistral) of the Cathedral, who has become powerful in Vetusta even over the bishop, whose former housekeeper was Fermín's mother. Ana realizes that Fermín has fallen in love with her, and avoids his company. In desperation she allows herself to be seduced by Vetusta's Don Juan, Don Álvaro Mesía. Jealous and spiteful, Fermín looks for an opportunity to reveal Ana's love-affair to Don Víctor, who challenges Álvaro to a duel and is killed. The cowardly Álvaro leaves Vetusta.

The melodramatic plot (Víctor reads Lope and Calderón; Ana reads religious writers such as S. Teresa and Fray Luis de León) is outweighed by the extraordinary naturalism in the treatment of *tertulias* and cathedral matters, intrigue and gossip. If Ana remains shadowy, Víctor and Mesía are memorable characters, while many lesser figures are brilliantly sketched, among them the free-thinker Pompeyo Guimarán who calls for a confessor on his deathbed; the malicious Doña Visita Olías; the Celestina-type Petronila Riazares, and the wretched Santos Barinaga, whose trade in church trinkets is ruined by Fermín's clever mother.

Several writers have suggested that *La Regenta* owes much to Zola, but Clarín differs from him in rejecting determinism and positivism, and excluding popular speech. Ana's resemblance to Emma Bovary was stridently proclaimed by Luis Bonafoux y Quintero in *Yo y el plagiario Clarín* (1888) and more temperately by Carlos Clavería ('Flaubert y *La Regenta*') in his *Cinco estudios de literatura española* (Salamanca, 1945). Certainly Clarín reveals a profound disillusionment with the life and people of Vetusta in his detailed chronicle of their jealousy, hatred,

hypocrisy, selfishness, and illwill, and his attitude does recall that of Flaubert towards the provincial bourgeoisie in *Madame Bovary* and *Bouvard et Pécuchet.*

See A. Brent, *Leopoldo Alas and 'La Regenta'* (Columbia, Mo., 1955); J. Becarud, *'La Regenta' y la España de la Restauración* (1964); J. Ventura Agudiez, *Inspiración y estética en 'La Regenta' de Clarín* (1970); and J. D. Rutherford, *Leopoldo Alas: 'La Regenta'* (London, 1974) in the Critical Guides to Spanish Texts series.

REINA, Casiodoro de (1520–c. 1584), b. Granada. Translator of the 'Bear' Bible (Basle, 1569), so called because of the emblem of a bear tasting honey on the title-page which has been traced to the Bavarian printer Mattias Apiarius, 'the bee-keeper'.

Reina, of Moorish descent, turned Protestant and fled from Spain in 1557, spending the next twelve years on the first complete translation of the Bible into Castilian: *La Biblia, que es, los sacros libros del Viejo y Nuevo Testamento. Trasladada en Español.* It was revised in 1602 by Cipriano de Varela, and the 1569 edition was reissued in facsimile by the Bible Society of Madrid (1970).

M. Menéndez y Pelayo (q.v.) was the first scholar to stress Reina's achievement in his *Historia de los heterodoxos españoles* (vol. 5, 1882).

See also A. G. Kinder, *Casiodoro de Reina* (London, 1975), in English.

REINA Y MONTILLA, Manuel (1856–1905), b. Puente Genil, Cordova. Poet, who was elected to Parliament in 1886, made a senator in 1893, and became Civil Governor of Cádiz. He was founder and editor of the important literary review *La Diana* (1882–4), which published translations of many French and German writers, as well as Poe and Longfellow.

He anticipated some of the novelties of *modernismo* (q.v.) in *Andantes y allegros* (1877), the Gautier-inspired *Cromos y acuarelas* (1878), *La vida inquieta* (1894), *Poemas paganos* (1896), and *El jardín de los poetas* (1899). The influence of Núñez de Arce and Alfred de Musset, whom he translated, is notable in the posthumous *Robles de la selva sagrada* (1906). E. de Ory's *Manuel Reina: estudio biográfico* (Cádiz, 1916) collected many *inedita* and B. Belmonte compiled the selection *Sus mejores versos* in 1928.

REINOSO, Félix (1772–1841), b. Seville. Poet and priest. One of the founders of the neoclassical Academia de Letras Humanas (1793). He wrote an interesting poem in two cantos on the model of *Paradise lost: La inocencia perdida,* often pedestrian but brilliant in a few passages. He was also the author of a curious apology for the *afrancesados* (q.v.) who collaborated with

Napoleon: *Examen de los delitos de infidelidad a la patria imputados a los españoles bajo la dominación francesa* (Auch, 1816), translated by H. Wood as *Who is the liberator of Spain?* (1846).

Reinoso's *Obras* have been edited in 2 vols. by A. Martín Villa and F. de B. Palomo (1872–9), and as vol. 67 of the BAE (1875).

REMÓN or RAMÓN, *Fray* ALONSO (1565?–1635?), b. Vara de Rey, Cuenca. Playwright and Mercedarian friar who was appointed chronicler of his Order. It is said that he wrote 200 plays, but only seven survive, including one written with Lope de Vega (q.v.): *¡ De cuándo acá nos vino!* The others are *Las tres mujeres en una*, *El santo sin nacer y mártir sin morir*, *El hijo pródigo*, *El sitio de Mons*, *La ventura en el engaño*, and *El español entre todas las naciones y clérigo agradecido*. José López Tascón has attributed to Remón the well-known *comedia El condenado por desconfiado* (q.v.), generally ascribed to Tirso de Molina (see TÉLLEZ,*Fray* Gabriel), his successor as chronicler of the Orden de la Merced, but there is no more support for this view than for the suggestion of P. Julián Zarco Cuevas that Remón is the 'Antonio de Liñán y Verdugo' (q.v.) who wrote *Avisos y guía de forasteros*.

Remón's other works include *La espada sagrada y arte para los nuevos predicadores* (1616), *Vida del Caballero de Gracia* (1620), *Entretenimientos y juegos honestos* (1623), *Gobierno humano sacado del divino* (1624), *La casa de la razón y el desengaño* (1625), *Laberinto político* (1626), the detailed *Historia general de la Orden de la Merced* (2 vols., 1618–33), and the first edition of the *Historia verdadera de la Conquista de Nueva España* (1632) by Bernal Díaz del Castillo (q.v.) into which, according to C. Sáenz de Santa María (*Missionalia Hispánica*, vol. 12, 1956, pp. 561–7) Remón may have interpolated his own material.

Renacimiento, El (1869), the first significant journal in Mexican literary history. It made its début as a non-political organ, founded by Ignacio Manuel Altamirano (q.v.) on 2 January 1869 'con el objeto . . . de que haya en la capital de la República . . . un foco de entusiasmo . . . para la juventud estudiosa de México'.

For the first time, Mexican writers were paid for their contributions: famous names in its pages included those of Pesado, Montes de Oca, and Roa Bárcena, and nearly a hundred more. It closed, completing Altamirano's serial novel *Clemencia*, with its issue 52 for Christmas 1869, but its example was highly effective in generating a series of competitors of an equivalent, if not superior, standard.

The reason for *El Renacimiento's* demise was ostensibly the increase in the price of a roll of imported newsprint from 8.60 pesos to 12.68, but that increase was itself politically motivated to inhibit freedom of expression.

RENGIFO, JUAN DÍAZ, see DÍAZ RENGIFO, Juan.

RENNERT, HUGO ALBERT (1858–1927), American Hispanist, whose distinguished career at Pennsylvania University produced major contributions on Golden Age drama, particularly *The life of Lope de Vega, 1562–1635* (Glasgow, 1904), revised for a Spanish version (Madrid, 1919) in collaboration with Américo Castro (q.v.), and *The Spanish stage in the time of Lope de Vega* (New York, 1909). His most important book was probably *The Spanish pastoral romances* (Baltimore, 1892).

He edited Góngora, Pérez de Guzmán, Juan Rodríguez del Padrón, Lope's *Sin secreto no hay amor*, and the only two extant plays of Miguel Sánchez 'el Divino': *La isla bárbara* and *La guarda cuidadosa* (Boston, 1896).

Repertorio Americano, El, the leading 20th-c. literary periodical of Costa Rica, published in San José 1919–59, the last issue (no. 1186) being in homage to the late Joaquín García Monge (q.v.), the magazine's founder and editor throughout. Originally superseding the Colección Ariel series as the leading voice of the Costa Rican *avant-garde*, *El Repertorio Americano* later came to represent the national voice of literature, and also assumed the character of the *Revista de Occidente*, expanding into the fields of sociology, economics, and politics. All the principal literary figures of Spain and Spanish America appeared in its pages, and there were articles on Antonio Machado, Nervo, Juan Ramón Jiménez, Isaacs, Kipling, and Poe, among many more.

Another magazine with the same title was edited and published in London by Andrés Bello (q.v.) in 1826–7, succeeding his *La Biblioteca Americana* (1923).

RÉPIDE, PEDRO DE (1882–1947), b. Madrid. Historian and novelist of life in Madrid. While a student in Paris he became librarian to the exiled Isabel II until she died in 1904, and later wrote her biography, *Isabel II, reina de España* (1932). *Alfonso XII* (1936) is another biography. Among his Madrid novels were *Del Rastro a Maravillas* (1907), *Noche perdida* (1908), *Madrid de los abuelos* (1908), *Paquito Candil* (1909), and *Costumbres y devociones madrileñas* (1914). His quaint style, with its archaic terms, quickly went out of date, and Répide published no more novels after 1920, though a collection of his *Novelas madrileñas* appeared in 1951. *Estampas grotescas* (1925) is a volume of verse.

República al revés, La, a *comedia* by Tirso de Molina, the pseudonym of Fray Gabriel Téllez (q.v.).

This early work, foreshadowing the more successful *comedia de intriga La prudencia en la mujer* (q.v.) in its praise of women as prudent and just in governing, is set during the reign of Constantine IV. Porphyrogenitos, an ambitious youth who usurps the throne of his mother Irene, repudiates his wife for a concubine, lets the criminals out of the jails, and encourages immorality.

Irene seeks refuge in the mountains, where decency, personified by the shepherd Tarso, still prevails. A popular insurrection restores Irene to the throne and, when faced with the problem of punishing her treacherous son, she neither pardons him nor condemns him to death, but blinds him.

RESENDE, Garcia de, the compiler of a *Cancioneiro geral* (Lisbon, 1516), produced in imitation of Hernando del Castillo's *Cancionero general* of 1511.

Of the 286 Portuguese poets included, twenty-nine are also represented by a total of 107 poems in Castilian. Garcia himself has verses in the form of a monologue on the death of Inés de Castro (q.v.). Few of the poems have any merit, and the work leans away from the Galician-Portuguese folk tradition and towards the allegorical school of Mena and Santillana (qq.v.). A. M. Huntington produced a facsimile of the *editio princeps* (New York, 1942) and there is an edition by Kausler (2 vols., Stuttgart, 1846–52).

See J. Ruggieri, *Il Canzoniere di Resende* (Geneva, 1931).

Retablo, a Church reredos or altarpiece, frequently decorated with carved wooden figures. *Retablo* later came to signify a religious play with wooden puppets, and later any puppet show.

Juan de Padilla uses the term figuratively in his poem *Retablo de la vida de Christo*, finished in 1500 (Toledo, 1505) and it reappeared in its sense of 'puppet-show' in Cervantes' *entremés* on village gullibility *El retablo de las maravillas*. See also *Don Quijote* II, xxv, xxvi.

In modern times the word has been used by Luis Rosales in his *Retablo sacro del nacimiento del Señor* (1940); by José García Nieto in his *Retablo del ángel, el hombre, y la pastora*; ironically by Camilo José Cela in his *Nuevo retablo de don Cristobita* (Barcelona, 1957), and in a variant form by García Lorca in *El retablillo de don Cristóbal* (1931).

Revista Azul, La, the most important Mexican literary magazine of the first modernist movement, founded by Manuel Gutiérrez Nájera (q.v.) and Carlos Díaz Dufoo. It appeared from 1894 to 1896, attracted most of the important writers in Hispanic America, and translated works by figures of world importance, such as Gautier, Whitman, and Tolstoy. Succeeded by *La Revista Moderna* (q.v.), the magazine was also widely circulated in Spain.

Another *Revista Azul*, edited by Manuel Caballero, appeared briefly in 1907.

Revista de Cuba (1877–84), the most important Cuban literary magazine of its time. Founded by J. A. Cortina, it ceased publication with his death, and was succeeded by the *Revista Cubana* (1885–94), edited by Enrique José Varona. There was a later *Revista Cubana*, issued from 1935 to 1958, which changed its name to *Nueva Revista Cubana* in 1959, and ceased publication in 1962.

Revista de Filología Española, a scholarly quarterly founded in 1914 by Ramón Menéndez Pidal (q.v.) to publish learned articles on aspects of Hispanic language and literatures, with a particularly useful bibliographical section on those subjects. It is published by the Instituto Miguel de Cervantes, Madrid.

Revista de Guatemala, the most significant post-war literary magazine to appear in Guatemala, it was published in three distinct series, with government support 1945–8 and 1951–2, and finally 1959–60 with the independent resources of its founder and editor, Luis Cardoza y Aragón.

It was particularly strong in its Mexican contributors. Its wide cultural range comprised bibliography, sociology, criticism, philosophy, and history, and typical articles were Raúl Leiva's 'Federico García Lorca: aspectos de su poesía', and 'La poesía mexicana contemporánea' by J. L. Martínez.

Revista de las Indias, the leading Colombian review, founded by the Ministry of Education and edited by Germán Arciniegas 1936–51. It replaced *Senderos* (1934–5), founded by Daniel Samper Ortega as the organ of the National Library in Bogotá. It devoted special issues to Federico García Lorca, Balzac, Goethe, Quevedo, and Carrasquilla, and published most of the great names in contemporary Latin American literature, including Abreu Gómez, Guillén, Neruda, Pellicer, Reyes, and Salinas. Among important authors translated were Blake, Cocteau, Eliot, Frost, and Valéry.

Revista de las Indias was replaced in 1951 by *Bolívar*, which ran for a further twelve years.

Revista de Occidente, Spain's leading 20th-c. intellectual and literary review, founded by José Ortega y Gasset (q.v.) in 1923 to replace his *España*. The tendency of the magazine, issued monthly until July 1936, was to introduce European thought in general, and German ideas in particular, to a markedly isolationist intellectual climate. The associated Revista de Occidente publishing house was responsible for disseminating translations of Freud, Spengler, Heidegger, Worringer, Husserl, and Bertrand Russell, among many others.

The *Revista de Occidente* was revived in April 1963 by José Ortega Spottorno, and dedicated the 100th issue of its new series to *Letras argentinas*, guest-edited by Victoria Ocampo, the editor of *Sur* (qq.v.).

Revista de Occidente, Generación de la, a name frequently given to the group (more often termed the 'Generación del 1927', q.v.), from the title of the journal in which many of them first made their name.

Revista Interamericana de Bibliografía, a quarterly review of new books from Central and South America, published since 1951 by the Organization of American States, Washington.

Revista Moderna, La, apart from *La Revista Azul* (q.v.), possibly the most important literary magazine published in Mexico. It was founded by the poets Amado Nervo (q.v.) and Jesús E. Valenzuela, and appeared between 1898 and 1911, during the second period of modernism (see MODERNISMO). Among its leading contributors were José Juan Tablada, Balbino Dávalos, Francisco de Olaguíbel, Efrén Rebolledo, and Rubén M. Campos.

See Carole Adele Holdsworth, *A study of the 'Revista Moderna'* (thesis, Northwestern University, Illinois, 1966).

Revista Nacional, the major 20th-c. literary magazine of Uruguay. The *Revista Nacional* of the Ministry of Public Instruction in Montevideo was edited from 1938 (its first publication) for a total of 186 issues until 1956 by Raúl Montero Bustamente, who had edited the Montevideo *Vida Moderna* 1900–1903.

Its editor 1956–65 was José Pereira Rodríguez, who continued the broadmined policy initiated by Montero Bustamante of covering philology, sociology, popular science, history, and politics. Most Uruguayan writers of note appeared in its pages.

Revista Nacional de Cultura, a major Venezuelan journal, founded by Mariano Picón Salas in 1938, and still appearing. Published initially by the Ministry of Education, it passed with issue no. 167 of January 1965 to the Instituto Nacional de Cultura y Bellas Artes. Reinaldo Leandro Mora, then Minister of Education, recorded in its 25th anniversary issue (no. 161, Autumn, 1963), that 'cada tendencia literaria o estética, cada género, cada noticia o reseña cultural de general interés, encontró en la *Revista* adecuado instrumento de divulgación'. Allowing for pardonable hyperbole, this claim is substantially true. Among its editors have been Manuel F. Rugeles and J. L. Salcedo-Bastardo. Several special issues were devoted to individual themes or writers: for instance no. 178 of November–December 1966 was dedicated to Rubén Darío (q.v.).

Revista Nacional de Literatura y Ciencias Sociales, La, the best of the 19th-c. literary magazines produced in Uruguay, published 1885–91. Raúl Montero Bustamante called it 'el órgano que realmente defendió y puso en valor crítico las nuevas corrientes literarias y preparó así el terreno para la futura cruzada, ... verdadera cátedra que alcanzó autoridad magisterial'.

It published not only the best work of national writers such as Elías Régules, M. E. Vaz Ferreira, and Víctor Arreguine, but also the work of numerous foreigners, among them Darío, Lugones, Blanco-Fombona, and Gómez Carrillo. Its chief contributors were two of its modernist editors: Víctor Pérez Petit (whose work was published in 33 issues) and José Enrique Rodó (in 21), but the main tendencies of the magazine were *fin-de-siècle* romanticism and classicism.

Revista Nueva, La, the only significant literary review to emerge from Panama. It was edited by José Dolores Moscote and Octavio Méndez Pereira, and published 1916–19 in the hope of creating 'un órgano de cultura que, en su más genuino alcance, sea algo como el *idearium* de la patria panameña'.

During its short life it attracted many of the leading Spanish American writers of the time, though preferring Panamanian authors.

REVUELTAS, José (1914–), b. Durango. Mexican revolutionary writer. He was sent to a reformatory when 15 and deported for Communist activities to the Islas Marías at the age of 20, experiences described in *Los muros de agua* (1941). His fame spread quickly with the appearance of *El luto humano* (1943), written almost cinematically as a series of Faulkner-like interior monologues inserted into an account of the attempts of some peasants to save themselves from drowning in a flood. After this novel, which won the National Literary Prize, Revueltas published two books of short stories: *Dios en la tierra* (1944) and *Dormir en tierra* (1960), and more novels: *Los días terrenales* (1949), *En algún valle de lágrimas* (1956), *Los motivos de Caín* (1957); and *Los errores* (1964), perhaps the most successful of his novels which aim to *épater le bourgeois*.

In 1961 Revueltas left the Communist Party and helped to found the new Spartacus Leninist League, but quickly repudiated that party also.

Revueltas' *Obra literaria* (2 vols.) was collected in 1967, with a useful epilogue by José Agustín (vol. 2, pp. 631–648).

See James E. Irby, *La influencia de William Faulkner en cuatro narradores hispanoamericanos* (1957), pp. 40–131.

REY DE ARTIEDA, Andrés (1549–1613), b. Valencia. Dramatist and poet. A professional soldier who was wounded at Lepanto. He was known as 'Centinela' to fellow-members of the Academia de los Nocturnos (q.v.).

Rey de Artieda's four-act tragedy *Los amantes* (Valencia, 1581) is the first Spanish play on the theme of the *amantes de Teruel* (q.v.). It is also the first serious portrayal of tragic love on the Spanish stage, concentrating on the universality of the experience rather than on the biographical circumstances (as in the case of Tirso or Pérez de Montalbán, qq.v.). Three other plays, none now extant, have also been ascribed to him: *Los encantos de Merlín*, *El príncipe vicioso*, and *Amadís de Gaula*. His poetry was first published in the miscellany *Discursos, epístolas y epígramas de Artemidoro* (Saragossa, 1605), in which he satirizes the rising star, Lope de Vega (q.v.), by whom he was to be eclipsed. The six satirical *epístolas* include one against sportsmen, and another in ironical defence of the manners of the time.

His sonnets are the best of the *Poesías* reprinted in vols. 25 (1866) and 42 (1867) of the BAE.

See John G. Weiger, *The Valencian dramatists of Spain's Golden Age* (New York, 1976), pp. 21–30.

REYES, Alfonso (1889–1959), b. Monterrey, Nuevo León. One of Mexico's most distinguished men of letters, whose prolific writings have caused Octavio Paz (q.v.) to call him 'un grupo de escritores'. After legal studies, Reyes devoted himself professionally to studying and teaching literature, going to Madrid in 1914 to work under Ramón Menéndez Pidal (q.v.) at the Centro de Estudios Históricos. He joined Mexico's diplomatic service in 1920, becoming ambassador in 1927, serving in Argentina, 1927–30 and 1936–7, and in Brazil, 1930–6.

Apart from creative work, in particular poetry, he has written important essays, especially on the Greek and Latin classics and on Spanish Golden Age literature. His *Obras completas* began to appear in 1955, and will probably run to at least 27 volumes.

His essays and literary criticism include *Cuestiones estéticas* (Paris, 1910), *El suicida* (1917), *Visión de Anáhuac* (q.v., San José, Costa Rica, 1917), *Retratos reales e imaginarios* (1920), *Cuestiones gongorinas* (Madrid, 1927), *Idea política de Goethe* (1937), *La crítica en la edad ateniense* (1941), *La experiencia literaria* (Buenos Aires, 1942), *Grata compañía* (1948), *En torno al estudio de la religión griega* (1951), and *Los nuevos caminos de la lingüística* (1960).

Reyes's poetry, influenced by Góngora and Mallarmé, has been collected in *Obra poética* (1952).

Ifigenia cruel (1924) is a dramatic poem with prose commentary. *El plano oblicuo* (1920) contains 'La cena', an interesting fantastic *cuento* of 1912.

Diario 1911–1930 (Guanajuato, 1960) is a useful biographical source for the period. The influence of Reyes on the younger generation of writers and critics has been immense thanks to his high intellectual stature and wide range of interests.

See Ingemar Düring, *Alfonso Reyes humanista* (Madrid, 1955); A. Cardona Peña, *Alfonso Reyes en la poesía* (1956); Manuel Olguín, *Alfonso Reyes ensayista* (1956), with a good bibliography; and J. W. Robb, *El estilo de Alfonso Reyes* (1965).

REYES, Matías de los (1575?–1641?), b. Madrid. Novelist and playwright. Reyes, who was a tax collector, never achieved fame for his literary work which was outside the influential circles of his time.

El Curial del Parnaso (1624) is a didactic novel of less interest than *El Menandro* (Jaen, 1636), a curious amalgam of Byzantine novel, Italian *novella*, *comedia*, and picaresque novel. *Para algunos* is linked by its technique to the dialogues of the Renaissance.

Reyes's plays are of indifferent quality, though *El agravio agradecido* is perhaps the most satisfactory Spanish adaptation of the *Amphitryon* of Plautus; the others include *Dar al tiempo lo que es suyo*, *Los enredos del diablo*, *Él que dirán y donaires de Pedro Corchuelo*, and *Di mentiras y sacarás verdad* (Jaén, 1629). The influence of Lope and Tirso is marked.

See Carroll B. Johnson, *Matías de los Reyes and the craft of fiction* (Berkeley, 1973).

REYES, Ricardo Eliecer Neftalí, original name of Pablo Neruda (q.v.).

Reyes Católicos ('the Catholic Sovereigns'). In Spanish history and literature, the usual epithet for Queen Isabella I of Castile, who was born in 1451 and reigned 1474–1504, and King Fernando V, born in 1452, who reigned in Aragón from 1479 and when his queen died in 1504 became regent of Castile until 1516. They married in 1469. Their reign was characterized by the same expansionist drive as the time of Elizabeth I in England. Important events included the Reconquest of Granada (1480–92), the discoveries of the New World (1492–1503), the conquest of Naples, and the internal unification of Castile, Aragón, and (in 1512) Navarra.

REYLES GUTIÉRREZ, CARLOS CLAUDIO (1868–1938), b. Montevideo. Uruguay's leading novelist. A millionaire on the early death of his father in 1886, Reyles travelled the world, staying long enough in his mother's native Seville to capture the atmosphere for *El embrujo de Sevilla*. Reyles's disinterested methods of exploiting his estate ended in the dissipation of his considerable fortune, following which he accepted a lectureship at Montevideo University, subsequently working for the national radio network. His first books were the Zolaesque *Por la vida* (1888), now lost because Reyles removed all copies from circulation, including those on legal deposit in the National Library, probably because of embarrassing autobiographical elements, and *Beba* (1894). His psychological short stories *Primitivo* (1896), *El extraño* (1897), and *El sueño de rapiña* (1898) were collected as *Academias* and, like most of his short stories, were later expanded into novels: the first into *El terruño* (1916), and the second into *La raza de Caín* (1900), an interesting precursor of Unamuno's *Abel Sánchez* (qq.v.) in its picture of a jealous intellectual, here the Stendhalian Guzmán.

Juan Valera (q.v.), writing in *El Liberal* (Madrid), praised *Primitivo*, but harshly condemned *El extraño*; Reyles replied in the same periodical.

His short story 'Capricho de Goya', published in *La Nación* (Buenos Aires) in 1900, was turned into the *costumbrista* novel *El embrujo de Sevilla* (1920), a book somewhat overpraised by Unamuno, and translated as *Castanets* by J. Leclercq (New York, 1929). Critics are divided in their preferences: Benedetti has suggested that Reyles's most successful novel may be *El terruño*, in which an amusing contrast between Tocles, an ineffective intellectual who plans a reply to *Also sprach Zarathustra* called *Así respondió Pérez González*, and his mother-in-law Mamagela, ends in victory for the latter, whose philosophy consists of three maxims: 'Estar bien con Dios; no vivir a costillas del prójimo; y tener el intestino corriente'.

Reyles expanded the *cuento* 'Mansilla y El Pial' into an interesting novel of the hacienda: *El gaucho Florido* (q.v., 1932), in which the view-

point of the landowner is exceptionally fairly presented.

'Una mujer pasó', is another *cuento* developed at novel-length and retitled, *A batallas de amor . . . campos de pluma*, which appeared posthumously.

Walter Rela's bibliography, *Carlos Reyles*, appeared in 1967. *Carlos Reyles* (1957) by L. A. Menafra corrects the excessively laudatory *Reyles* (1943) of J. Llerena Acevedo de Blixen. See also Gervasio Guillot, *La conversación de Carlos Reyles* (1966).

RIBA BRACÓNS, CARLES (1897–1959), b. Barcelona. Catalan poet and scholar, who was active in the Bernat Metge Foundation from 1942, publishing Greek and Latin classics with Catalan translations. Professor of Greek at the Autonomous University of Barcelona until 1939, Riba then went into exile until 1942. He was personally responsible for the editions of Homer's *Odyssey*, Virgil's *Eclogues*, Plutarch's *Vitae parallelae*, and complete editions of Sophocles and Euripides. His finest poetry, *Primer llibre d'estances* (Barcelona, 1919) and its sequel *Estances: Llibre segon* (Sabadell, 1930), are classical and formally disciplined. His exile àfter the Civil War produced *Tres suítes* (1939), and *Elegies de Bierville* (1942), influenced by Goethe, which have been put into Castilian by Alfonso Costafreda. Riba's other translations include *Versions de Hölderlin* (1944) and *Poemas de Kavafis* (1962). After returning to Catalonia he published *Del jòc i del fóc* (1946); *Salvatge cor* (1952), a sonnet sequence; and *Esboç de tres oratoris* (1957). Vol. 1 of his *Obres completes* (1965) consisted of *Poesia i narrativa*.

In the Catalan resurgence from about 1912 Riba had already exercised some influence with Folguera, d'Ors (see ORS), and Carner (qq.v.), but his prestige had grown much greater by the time he returned from exile in the late 1940s, and Espriu, Rosselló-Pòrcel, Joan Petit, Eduard Valenti, and many others reveal a profound debt to him in their best work.

A bilingual anthology of his work (Catalan and English) was produced by Joan Gili (Oxford, 1964).

See A. Manent, *Tres escritores catalanes: Carner, Riba, Pla* (1973) and *In memoriam Carles Riba* (Barcelona, 1973).

RIBERA Y TARRAGÓ, JULIÁN (1858–1934), b. Carcagente, Valencia. Professor of Arabic at Saragossa University, and later in Madrid. With his teacher Francisco Codera he edited the ten-volume Bibliotheca Arábigo-Hispana (1882–93). He specialized in Muslim law and learning in Spain and wrote *La enseñanza entre los musulmanes españoles* (1893), *Bibliófilos y bibliotecas de la España musulmana* (1896), *La épica entre los*

musulmanes españoles (1915), and the collection
Disertaciones y opúsculos (1928). He translated the
Crónica of Ibn al-Qutia (q.v.), and edited
al-Khushani's *Historia de los jueces de Córdoba* and
the *Cancionero* of Ibn Guzman (1912), from which
he demonstrated the coexistence of Romance
dialect with literary Arabic among the *mozárabes*.
Ribera's *Música de las 'Cantigas'* (1922) shows how
music in Muslim Spain derived from local,
classical, and oriental sources, and influenced
the music of the Provençal troubadours.

RIDRUEJO, DIONISIO (1912–75), b. Burgo de
Osma, Soria. Poet. He spent his early years in
Segovia where he became a leading Falangist;
later, however, he turned to the democratic
opposition. His poetry uses the classical forms of
Garcilaso, particularly the sonnet, but he has
also used *versos sueltos* to good effect. *En once años*
(1950), a volume of selected poems, won the
Premio Nacional de Literatura. The collected
poems *Hasta la fecha* (1961) have been supplemented by *Cuaderno catalán* (1965).

His prose works are *Tiempo de reencarnar* (1958),
La Europa que se proyecta (1958), *Dentro del tiempo*
(1960), *En algunas ocasiones* (1960), *Escrito en
España* (1962), *España* (1963), *Cataluña* (1968),
Cuaderno de Roma (1968), and *Guía de Castilla la
Vieja* (2 vols., 1968).

See Hans-Peter Schmidt, *Dionisio Ridruejo, ein
Mitglied der spanischen 'Generation von 36'* (Bonn,
1972).

Rimado de palaçio, El, a long poem by the
Chancellor of Castile, Pedro López de Ayala
(q.v.) and, with *El libro de buen amor* (q.v.), one
of the two major poems in *cuaderna vía* of the
14th c.

It survives in two complete MSS., one in the
Biblioteca Nacional and the other in the
Escurial, while fragments of a third are extant
in the Bibliothèque Nationale, Paris. A. F.
Kuersteiner's edition of López de Ayala's *Poesías*
(2 vols., New York, 1920) includes both versions,
together with other poems, and supersedes
F. Janer's inadequate edition in vol. 57 (1864)
of the BAE. A representative selection has been
edited by Kenneth W. J. Adams (Salamanca,
1971).

The *Rimado* was written over a number of
years, partly in prison, and makes use of *arte
mayor* and juglaresque short metres in addition to
the preponderant *cuaderna vía*. The first section of
the poem is a confession based on the manuals
produced after the fourth Lateran Council.
Ayala then launches into a long and thorough
indictment of contemporary Spain with all the
bitterness of a prisoner, beginning with the
corrupt and lax clergy, the feckless monarchy
and hypocritical royal favourites, and sparing

neither the merchant class nor the military who
all conspire to suck the 'sangre de los pobres
cuytados'. More serious and less forgiving in his
satire than Juan Ruiz (q.v.), López de Ayala is
also less boisterously amusing.

There follows a section on Egidio de Colonna's
De regimine principum (q.v.), which gave rise to an
important genre in the Spanish Middle Ages.
The second section is religious, consisting of
songs in various metres, prayers, and his
thoughts on the Great Schism which had
divided the Church since 1378. The third
section is an adaptation in *cuaderna vía* of
Gregory the Great's *Moralia* on the Book of Job,
two works which Ayala studied over a long
period, as Francesco Branciforti has shown in
his edition of Ayala's translation *El libro de Job*
(Florence, 1962) and *Las flores de los Morales de
Job* (Florence, 1963).

See also Helen L. Sears, 'The "Rimado de
Palacio" and the "De regimine principum"
tradition of the Middle Ages' in the *Hispanic
Review*, vol. 22 (1952), pp. 1–27.

Rinconete y Cortadillo (1613), one of the
twelve *Novelas ejemplares* (q.v.) by Cervantes
(q.v.) written not later than 1605, since it is
mentioned in the first part of *Don Quijote* (q.v.).

Two youths, Pedro Rincón and Diego
Cortado, strike up a friendship in an inn of the
Alcudia region, and decide to travel as *pícaros* to
Seville. They rob some travellers on the road
and, while employed as an errand-boy in the
city, Diego snatches a purse from a sacristan.
He is seen by another thief, who informs the pair
that all of their profession must be licensed by
Monipodio, boss of the Sevillian underworld.
The manage to pass the test, and are admitted
to the fraternity. Monipodio introduces them to
notorious thieves and assassins such as la
Gananciosa, Chiquiznaque, el Repolido, and la
Cariharta. In the deft account of this assembly,
more properly a *cuadro de costumbres* than a *novela*
(a term Cervantes borrowed from the Italian
'novella'), an officer of the law enters to request
the purse stolen by Diego from a friend of his,
and a gentleman enquires whether his enemy
has been dispatched as arranged. The use of the
term 'exemplary' is here notably ironic, since the
members of the Seville underworld are shown to
observe external forms of religious observance
and consequently believe themselves to be good
Christians.

That the work reflects the author's own
experiences of Seville at the end of the 16th c. is
suggested by Luis de Zapata de Chaves's (q.v.)
Miscelánea (1592) edited by Gayangos in the
Memorial Histórico Español (1859) and also by
G. C. Horsman (Amsterdam, 1935).

The critical edition by Francisco Rodríguez

Marín (Seville, 1905) should be read in conjunction with the edition by J. M. Alda Tesán (with *Coloquio de los perros*, Salamanca, 1970). A translation, 'Big Sharper and Little Snip' by J. M. Cohen appears in *Blind man's boy* (London, 1962).

See J. L. Varela, 'El realismo cervantino en "Rinconete"' in *La transfiguración literaria* (1970), pp. 53–89.

RIOJA, FRANCISCO DE (1583?–1659), b. Seville. Poet, librarian to Philip IV, and royal chronicler of Castile. Favoured by Olivares, Rioja accompanied him into exile, and retired to his native city when Olivares died. Like many of his contemporaries, Rioja published nothing in his lifetime.

Partly on account of his experiences at court, partly through the influence of Herrera (q.v.), transience, the folly of ambition, and *desengaño* or disillusionment with the world are important elements in Rioja's poetry; Rodrigo Caro's *Canción a las ruinas de Itálica*, and Andrés Fernández de Andrada's *Epístola moral a Fabio* (q.v.), both on the theme of mutability, have been incorrectly ascribed to him. His best-known works today are perhaps his *silvas* in which (like, e.g. Góngora) he employs flowers as symbols of ephemeral happiness and beauty doomed to fade ('Al jazmín', 'Al clavel', 'A la rosa', etc.). A certain stoicism is noticeable in his attitude towards life. The influence of Góngora may be seen in some of his sonnets, although others are more moralizing in tone, and he wrote some *canciones morales*, including 'A la constancia' and 'A la riqueza'. The collection *Poesías inéditas* first appeared in 1797. *Poesías* was edited in 1867 by C. A. de la Barrera y Leirado, who later published *Adiciones a las poesías* (Seville, 1872). Adolfo de Castro edited Rioja's *Poesías* for vol. 32 (1857) of the BAE.

Ríos profundos, Los (Buenos Aires, 1958), a novel by the Peruvian José María Arguedas (q.v.).

Through an evocation of his childhood and adolescence described in terms of 'magic realism', Arguedas portrays the conflict between an imposed culture (the Hispanic) and a natural one (the Indian), concluding that the Indian way is not only superior, but the only true culture of Peru. Mario Vargas Llosa, in his prologue to the Havana edition of 1965, stresses that 'the Indian is not obsequious, servile, deceitful, hypocritical, but his conduct might be so in certain circumstances and by necessity'. The autobiographical character (Ernesto) rebels against his harsh school environment and his headmaster Linares. Though the theme of the present and future of Peru seen through a

microcosm resembles that of Vargas Llosa's *La ciudad y los perros* (qq.v.), the book's style is closer to that of Azorín (q.v.).

Sex is an obsessive feature of Arguedas's conception of Peruvian life. His characters include a prostitute (repeatedly abused for her mental deficiency), a bully, a thief, and Ernesto's one real friend Antero. Ernesto leaves his school in Abencay abruptly when an epidemic reaches the town, and returns to his detested uncle. Paradoxically, Arguedas seemed to find an optimistic future for Peru in this otherwise sombre work.

See Sara Castro Klarén, 'Las fuentes del narrador en "Los ríos profundos"' in *Cuadernos Americanos*, vol. 30, no. 175 (March–April 1971), pp. 230–8.

RÍOS Y NOSTENCH, BLANCA DE LOS (1862–1956), b. Seville. Literary scholar. She studied under Marcelino Menéndez y Pelayo (q.v.) and specialized in the drama of Tirso de Molina (q.v.). She edited his *Obras dramáticas completas* (3 vols., 1946–58), in which she argued convincingly in favour of the ascription to Tirso of *El condenado por desconfiado* and *El rey don Pedro en Madrid*. Her critical writings include *Estudio biográfico y crítico de Tirso de Molina* (1889), *Del siglo de oro: estudios literarios* (1910), *Las mujeres de Tirso* (1910), *De la mística y de la novela contemporánea* (1910), *De Calderón y su obra* (1917), and '*La vida es sueño' y los diez Segismundos de Calderón* (1926).

Professor Ríos also wrote poetry: *Esperanzas y recuerdos* (1881) and *La novia del marinero* (1886), as well as the *costumbrista* novel *Melita Palma* (1901).

RIQUELME, DANIEL (1857–1912), Chilean reporter and writer of *costumbrista* sketches, articles, and short stories. He fought in the Pacific War (1879–84) between Chile and both Peru and Bolivia, and thereafter became a popular chronicler of life during the War. *Chascarrillos militares* (1885), containing 13 stories, was expanded as *Bajo la tienda: recuerdos de la campaña del Perú y Bolivia, 1879–1884* (1888). Some of his periodical articles appeared as *Artículos escogidos de Inocencio Conchalí* (1903). His style is surprisingly light (and even comic) compared with much contemporary journalism on the War.

See Domingo Melfi, *Estudios de literatura chilena* (1938), pp. 49–63.

RIQUER, MARTÍ DE, *Conde de Casa Dávalos* (1914–), b. Barcelona. Literary historian and critic. Professor of Romance Literatures at Barcelona University and author of the monumental *Història de la literatura catalana* (6 vols., Barcelona, 1964–).

Among the works he has edited are *Tirant lo Blanch* (1947) in Catalan and (1947–9) in Castilian; *El cavallero Zifar* (2 vols., Barcelona, 1953); Boscà's *Obras poéticas* (with A. Comas and Joaquim Molas, Barcelona, 1957); Bernat Metge's *Obras* (1959); and the *Obras completas del trovador Cerverí de Girona* (1947).

His many books and learned articles on medieval studies are already considered classic: they include *La lírica de los trovadores* (Barcelona, 1948); *Los cantares de gesta franceses (sus problemas, su relación con España)* (1952), and *Caballeros andantes españoles* (1967).

Riquer has edited (Barcelona, 1943) the *Tesoro de la lengua castellana o española* of Covarrubias (q.v.), and the best popular text of the *Quijote* (3 vols., Barcelona, 1944). He has been a member of the Real Academia Española since 1965. His 'Discurso de recepción', entitled *Vida caballeresca en la España del siglo XV* was published with an appendix listing his works.

RISCO AGÜERO, VICENTE MARTÍNEZ (1884–1963), b. Orense. Novelist, medievalist, and ethnologist. Risco was one of the main inspirers of the Galician revival in the 20th c., with essays, his *Historia de Galicia* (1952), novels, and poetry in Galician, including *O porco de pe* (Corunna, 1928).

His novel *La puerta de paja* (1953) was written in twenty days in a burst of inspiration. It is an allegory reminiscent of Calderón's *La vida es sueño* (q.v.) in which Risco's Segismundo, Baldonio, the civil and ecclesiastical ruler of the medieval fantasy realm of Nerbia, repudiates his former life of tyranny, blasphemy, and licence; however, while Nerbia had prospered under his autocratic rule, under the virtuous and high-principled Cardinal Arnulfo who replaces him the peasants and the noblemen rise in revolution and bring chaos and misery on themselves. *La puerta de paja* is not wholly didactic; fantasy and erudition mingle in scenes such as the discussions of four medieval physicians.

Risco also wrote *Historia de los judíos desde la destrucción del Templo* (1944) and a *Biografía de Satanás* (1948) which was reworked in 1956 as *Satanás: historia del diablo*.

RITTER AISLÁN, EDUARDO (1916–), Panamanian poet. His books include: *Umbral* (1940), *Crisálida* (1941), *Nenúfares* (1944), *Mástil* (1947), *Poemas* (1949), *Espigas al viento* (1951), *Rosicler* (1955), and *Silva de amor* (1957).

RIVADENEYRA, RIBADENEYRA, or RIBADENEIRA, PEDRO DE (1527–1611), b.

Toledo. His real name was Pedro Ortiz de Cisneros, but he preferred his maternal grandmother's name. Ignatius Loyola, whom he met in Rome, persuaded him to join the Society of Jesus, and this influence changed Rivadeneyra's life. He wrote a biography of Ignatius in Latin (1572) which he later translated into Spanish (1583) and was entrusted by the founder with the Jesuit mission to Belgium (1556), during which period he collected materials for his *Historia ecclesiástica del Scisma del Reyno de Inglaterra* (vol. 1, 1588; vol. 2, 1593).

His ascetic *Tratado de la tribulación* (1589) offers serene advice on Senecan lines to Spaniards grieved and bewildered by the defeat of the Armada; the book was edited by Mir in 1879.

Padre Rivadeneyra, known to St Ignatius as 'Perico', wrote a vigorous refutation of Machiavelli in his *Tratado de la religión; y, virtudes que deue tener el Príncipe Christiano, para gouernar y conseruar sus estados* (1595). He also compiled the *Flos sanctorum; o, libro de las vidas de los santos* (2 vols., Madrid, 1599–1601).

RIVA PALACIO Y GUERRERO, General VICENTE (1832–96), b. Mexico City. Mexican statesman, novelist, and short-story writer, whose historical fiction influenced by Dumas and Manzoni enjoyed great popularity in its day.

Calvario y tabor (1868) is an eye-witness account of how the French invaders were thrown back. *Virgen, monja, casada, y mártir* (1868), *Martín Garatuza* (1868), *Las dos emparedadas* (1869), and *Memorias de un impostor* (1872) are novels of the Mexican Inquisition based on archives that Riva had collected in 1861 by command of the government.

Los piratas del golfo (1869) is a Romantic novel in the style and on the theme of Walter Scott's *The pirate* (1821), which had already inspired *La novia del hereje* (1854), a novel by the Argentinian Vicente Fidel López (q.v.) written *c.* 1840. The posthumously-published *Cuentos del general* (Madrid, 1896) is widely considered Riva's best book. With Roa Bárcena (q.v.), he founded the Mexican short-story tradition. *La vuelta de los muertos* (1870) is a novelized biography of Cortés. *Mis versos* (1893) is a collection of poems.

RIVAS, Duque de, see SAAVEDRA REMÍREZ DE BAQUEDANO, Ángel de, *Duque de Rivas*.

RIVAS BONILLA, ALBERTO (1891–). b. Santa Tecla, El Salvador. Poet, journalist, and *costumbrista*, sometimes writing as 'Sebastián Salitrillo'. He belongs to the Generation of 1920 (with Arturo Ambrogi and Salarrué, qq.v.), a school which created the modern Salvadorian short story. His prose works include *Andanzas y malandanzas* (1936) a picture of rural life in

San Salvador as seen through the eyes of a wretched dog on a hacienda, and *Me monto en un potro* (1943), a collection of *cuentos*, mostly humorous. He has also written some three-act comedies: *Celia en vacaciones* (1937), *Una chica moderna* (1945), and *Alma de mujer*.

RIVERA, José Eustasio (1889–1928), b. Neiva. Colombian novelist and poet. Of a lower-middle class family, Rivera qualified as a teacher and lawyer, practising in the interior of Colombia, where he observed the life of the plains. He was elected to the National Congress and later became an inspector of oil-fields, an experience which enabled him to see at first hand the corruption of national politicians and their acquiescence in their country's exploitation by foreign interests. In 1922 he visited the Amazon jungle as secretary of a boundary commission.

A book of sonnets *Tierra de promisión* (1921) was elegant, but failed to satisfy Rivera because it omitted the cruelty and desperation of men at the mercy of natural forces, and described only the beauties of Colombia. In consequence he wrote the influential novel *La vorágine* (q.v., 1924), presented as the autobiography of Arturo Cova, an urban intellectual horrified by the barbarism of jungle life. This novel came to represent the Latin American's awareness of his real environment, and his need to come to terms with it. *La vorágine* was the most significant Colombian novel until *Cien años de soledad* by Gabriel García Márquez (qq.v.). Rivera's biography has been written by Eduardo Neale Silva as *Horizonte humano* (Mexico City, 1960).

See M. Ferragu, *Les colombianismes du vocabulaire et de la syntaxe dans l'œuvre de José Eustasio Rivera* (Paris, 1954); R. Charrá Tobar, *José Eustasio Rivera en la intimidad* (1963); and L. C. Herrera Molina, *José Eustasio Rivera, poeta de promisión* (1969).

RIVILLA Y PUEYO, José de, a pen-name adopted by Pedro de Peralta Barnuevo (q.v.).

RIZAL Y MERCADO ALONSO, José Protasio (1861–96), b. Calamba. Philippine novelist, whose writings in Spanish supported Philippine independence in the tradition of Luis Rodríguez Varela. His native language was Tagalog.

Noli me tangere (Berlin, 1886) shows the attempts of the hero Ibarra to introduce primary education to a village in the Philippines. The authorities of church and state and the local *caciques* frustrate these attempts, spread rumours about Ibarra, and eventually imprison him. Rizal's dialogue and social observation are accurate, and the book helped to awaken the social conscience of his generation. *El filibusterismo*

(Ghent, 1891) is according to the author a sequel, but the hero is different in a cynical, disillusioned way, and though the novel is technically superior to *Noli me tangere*, the creative impetus is weaker. Rizal is the subject of *Lineage, life and labours of José Rizal* by A. Craig (1914) and *Hero of the Philippines* (1923) by C. E. Russell and E. B. Rodríguez.

ROA BÁRCENA, José María (1827–1908), b. Xalapa, Veracruz. Mexican short-story writer, novelist, historian, and poet. A conservative and monarchist in politics, Roa Bárcena lived in Mexico City from 1853, devoting himself to business and literature. With Vicente Riva Palacio (q.v.), he was the founder of the Mexican short story, excelling in social observation. A selection of his *Relatos* edited by J. Jiménez Rueda appeared in 1941 (2nd edn., 1955).

He wrote *Ensayo de una historia anecdótica de México en los tiempos anteriores a la conquista* (1862) and *Recuerdos de la invasión norteamericana* (1883). Roa Bárcena is the author of biographies of Gorostiza (1876) and Pesado (1878). His *Poesías líricas* (1859) were followed by the verse *Leyendas mexicanas* (1862) and *Últimas poesías líricas* (1888). A good linguist, he translated from Horace, Virgil, Schiller, Byron, and Tennyson. His *Obras* were first collected in 6 vols. (1897–1910), and vol. 1 of *Obras poéticas* appeared in 1913.

Juan B. Iguíniz's *Bibliografía de novelistas mexicanos* (1926) lists Roa Bárcena's fiction (pp. 311–14); a list of his verse by Renato Rosaldo appears in *Revista Iberoamericana*, vol. 9 (1945), pp. 381–9.

See Elvira López Aparicio, *José María Roa Bárcena* (1957).

ROA BASTOS, Augusto (1917–   ), b. Neiva. Paraguayan novelist and poet of the Generation of 1940, with Herib Campos Cervera and Josefina Plá (qq.v.). He has been a journalist, worked in radio, travelled in Europe, and was cultural attaché to the Paraguayan Embassy in Buenos Aires. Exiled to Buenos Aires after the civil war of 1947, he renounced his *neo-gongorista* poetry, publishing of his vast works only a pamphlet of verses, *El naranjal ardiente* (1960), and turned to the short story and the novel. His first stories were *El trueno entre las hojas* (1953) vying in the violence of their social protest with the work of his mentor Miguel Ángel Asturias (q.v.). His great novel *Hijo de hombre* (1960) is an epic of Paraguayan history from the dictatorship of José Gaspar Rodríguez Francia (who was proclaimed dictator in 1816 and died in 1840) to the end of the Chaco War, 1932–35, in which he fought. The evil committed by man against his neighbour is partly redeemed by the heroism of the meek and poor, and by the suffering of the weak and defenceless. The novel's seven parts may be read separately, but together they form a work of sustained power. Roa Bastos has subsequently published collections of short stories: *El baldío* (Buenos Aires, 1966) in which he searches for real and metaphysical truths; the partial anthology of his work *Los pies sobre el agua* (Buenos Aires, 1967; *Madera quemada* (Santiago, 1968); *Moriencia* (Caracas, 1969); and *Cuerpo presente y otros textos* (Buenos Aires, 1972).

Yo el Supremo (Buenos Aires) is another reworking in novelized form of the history of Paraguay, concentrating this time on the figure of Francia himself. In a work of stylistic beauty and innovation, Roa Bastos re-evaluates the earlier, almost wholly adverse historical assessments of Francia's role as founder and father of the Paraguayan nation and shows how it is possible to view Francia as an administrative genius who subdued the internal oligarchy and foreign interests.

See D. W. Foster, *The myth of Paraguay in the fiction of Augusto Roa Bastos* (Chapel Hill, N.C., 1969); and H. F. Giacoman (ed.), *Homenaje a Augusto Roa Bastos* (New York, 1973), a critical anthology.

Rocinante, Don Quijote's aged, skinny horse, 'a name which seemed [to Don Quijote] both grand and sonorous, and also to express the common nag he had been before arriving at his present state: the first and foremost of all the world's horses' (*Quijote*, Pt. I, ch. i).

See Hugo Emilio Pedemonte, 'Del Rocinante que cabalgó Don Quijote' in *Norte* (Mexico City), no. 274 (November–December 1976), pp. 46–9.

RODERICK or RODRIGO, *King of the Goths*. In 711, the Christian empire of Spain was in the hands of Roderick, a usurper who had exiled the sons of Witiza, rightful heirs to the throne. They called on the governor of Ceuta, a Spanish possession on the north coast of Africa, to bring a force of Arabs and Berbers under Jabal Tariq (after whom Gibraltar was named) and overthrow Roderick. The two armies met near Guadalete, not far from Cape Trafalgar, and the Visigothic forces under Roderick were defeated. Roderick either died fighting, or in the hills after the battle. Tariq then went to attack Roderick's capital, Toledo, leaving some forces, and Visigoths hostile to Roderick, to take Cordova. The traitors took some time to realize that the Arabs had no intention of returning home after accomplishing the mission for which their services had been recruited.

The story is told in three forms: in ballads, such as 'Las huestes de don Rodrigo' (translated by Lockhart in his *Ancient Spanish ballads*,

London, 1823), and 'Después que el rey don Rodrigo' in plays, such as Lope de Vega's *El último rey godo de España*; and most frequently in legends, the first to survive being the semi-fictional narrative *Crónica del Rey Don Rodrigo* (by Pedro del Corral, q.v.), of which the first extant edition was published in Seville in 1499. Its bizarre tournaments and incredible feats echo the *libros de caballería* (q.v.) which had been popular for a couple of centuries; the whole Arthurian tradition; and the primitive *Amadís*.

According to one popular version, a vault in Toledo was forbidden ground to kings of Spain, who were required to add another padlock to it when succeeding to the throne. Roderick managed to enter, however, and found paintings of Muslims, with an inscription declaring that the first king to look upon the likenesses would lose his throne to such men. According to another story, Roderick seduced La Cava, the daughter of Count Julián, governor of Ceuta, who despatched a force of Moors in revenge, and it was then that the battle of Guadalete took place. The defeated Roderick fled to Viseu, and there sought guidance from a hermit, who dictated that he should enter a tomb filled with snakes as penance.

The most exhaustive treatment of the legend is R. Menéndez Pidal's *Floresta de leyendas heroicas españolas: Rodrigo, el último godo* (3 vols., 1925–8). The theme was adapted by Sir Walter Scott in his poem *Vision of Don Roderick* (1811), by Walter Savage Landor in *Count Julian* (1812), and by Robert Southey in *Roderick, the last of the Goths* (1814).

RODÓ, José Enrique (1871–1917), b. Montevideo. Uruguayan essayist, whose best-known book was *Ariel* (q.v., 1900). In 1895 he founded the influential *Revista Nacional de Literatura y Ciencias Sociales* (q.v., not to be confused with the *Revista Nacional*, q.v.). Rodó lived most of his life in Montevideo, devoting himself to literature, and his house in Calle Cerrito became a cultural centre of Uruguay. He was greatly influenced by Renan, Comte, and Spencer, as well as by Plato, Marcus Aurelius, and Montaigne. Rodó died in Sicily while on a long-planned journey to Italy.

In addition to the important *Ariel*, he also published *Los motivos de Proteo*, on the ethics of renewal in the spirit of Henri Bergson's creative evolution, the significant essay *Rubén Darío* (1899), and two other volumes of essays: *Él que vendrá* and *El mirador de Próspero* (both 1913). Most of his work was published posthumously: *El camino de Paros: meditaciones y andanzas* (1918), *Hombres de América* (1920), *Nuevos motivos de Proteo* (1927), and *Los últimos motivos de Proteo* (1932).

His *Obras completas* (Madrid, 1957) have been edited by Emir Rodríguez Monegal. *Rodó: estudio crítico y antología* (Buenos Aires, 1971), is a usefully annotated selection by Emilio Oribe.

See Arturo Scarone, *Bibliografía de José Enrique Rodó* (2 vols., 1930); *Parábolas* (a critical anthology with essays by Mario Benedetti and others, 1972); Clemente Pereda, *Rodó's main sources* (San Juan, Puerto Rico, 1948); E. Rodríguez Monegal, *José Enrique Rodó en el Novecientos* (1950); Glicerio Albarrán Puente, *El pensamiento de Rodó* (Madrid, 1953); M. Benedetti, *Genio y figura de José Enrique Rodó* (Buenos Aires, 1966); and Arturo Ardao, *Rodó: su americanismo* (1970).

RODRIGO, *Rey de los Godos*, see RODERICK or RODRIGO, *King of the Goths*.

RODRÍGUEZ, GONZALO, *Arcediano de Toro* (*fl.* 1380). Poet. Nothing is known of his life, beyond the fact that he was a witness to the Treaty between Castile and Portugal in 1383 on the occasion of the marriage of Juan I to the daughter of Ferdinand.

A number of his poems, in Galician and Castilian, are included in the *Cancionero de Baena* (q.v.) nos. 311–17, and are mostly on the theme of love. The most interesting is perhaps a *Testamento* in *arte mayor* (q.v.), a contribution to a tradition whose best-known example is Villon's *Petit Testament*. This is in the *Cancionero de Baena* (no. 18), but is there attributed to Alonso Álvarez de Villasandino.

RODRÍGUEZ, LUIS FELIPE (1888–1947), Cuban short-story writer and novelist. His family was very poor, and he was forced to do manual work before writing fiction of social protest. His humorous semi-autobiographical novel *Cómo opinaba Damián Paredes* (1916) was followed by *La conjura de la ciénaga* (1924), given definitive form in *Ciénaga* (1937), which makes up for the absence of action by a moving allegory revealing sympathy for the exploitation of peasants on the large estates or *latifundios*. His regional short stories are even more effective: *La Pascua de la tierra natal* (1923), and *Relatos de Marcos Antilla* (1932), the first of a projected series.

RODRÍGUEZ, MARIO AUGUSTO (1919–), b. Santiago de Veraguas, Panama. Short-story writer and poet who has written feelingly about the plight of the lower classes in *Campo adentro* (1947) and *Luna en Veraguas* (1948). His impassioned *Canto de amor para la patria novia* (1957) is thought to be one of the most successful songs of praise to a Central American motherland.

Rodríguez also writes for a popular daily newspaper.

RODRÍGUEZ ÁLVAREZ, ALEJANDRO (1900–65), b. Tineo, Asturias. Playwright using the pseudonym 'Alejandro Casona'. Theatre director from 1932 of the touring company called La Barraca (q.v.). He went into exile in 1937 and lived in Buenos Aires from 1939 until 1962 when he returned to Asturias.

His first success as a writer came with *La sirena varada* (first performed 1934), notable for the interplay between levels of illusion and reality. He has contributed to the attempted renovation of the Spanish theatre with his individual humour and lyricism, and his version of *Inés de Castro* is at least equal to all previous ones except that of Luis Vélez de Guevara (q.v.). His best play is generally considered to be *La dama del alba* (1944), a fantasy in which La Peregrina (Death) performs a miracle, restoring life through falling asleep for the first time; the sentimental story is full of Asturian folklore. *La barca sin pescador* (1945) deals with the contract that Ricardo a ruined businessman makes with the Devil, by which Ricardo must murder a simple fisherman to obtain his wish. Ricardo is saved by the power of love. Casona's *Obras completas* (Mexico City, 1954) also include *Prohibido suicidarse en primavera* (1937) and *Los árboles mueren de pie* (1949).

RODRÍGUEZ BUDED, RICARDO (20th c.), Spanish playwright whose works swing disconcertingly from realism to farce as a mirror of Spanish society. *La madriguera* and *Un hombre duerme* were both first performed in 1960. The first is almost exclusively realist in depicting life in a sordid tenement shared by several families with access to a common kitchen. Buded shows how society makes embittered criminals and warped personalities by the deprivation of decent housing and lack of privacy. The second adds the element of farce to the situation of a homeless married couple who act out their imaginary life once a week round a table in a café. *El charlatán* (first performed in 1962 at the Teatro Goya) is a clever symbolist farce on the cruel exploitation of a girl by her parents, building an atmosphere of deceit and fear. All three have appeared in the Colección Teatro.

RODRÍGUEZ CERNA, JOSÉ (1889–1952), b. San Luis de Jilotepeque, Guatemala. Journalist who wrote for Spanish, Guatemalan, and Mexican newspapers. His numerous collections of such articles include *El libro de las crónicas* (1914), vignettes of Guatemala entitled *Tierra de sol y de montaña* (Barcelona, 1930), and *Bajo las alas del águila* (1942). *Un pueblo en marcha:*

Guatemala (Madrid, 1931) is a general study of his homeland.

RODRÍGUEZ DE LA CÁMARA, JUAN (*c.* 1390–*c.* 1450), b. El Padrón. Also known as Rodríguez del Padrón. Novelist, poet, priest, and nobleman. Possibly a page at the court of Juan II; he may also have been among the entourage of Cardinal Cervantes at the Council of Basel (1431–49).

El siervo libre de amor (1439–40) is a largely autobiographical novel in which he inserted a sentimental tale, 'Estoria de los dos amadores Ardanlier e Liesa'. The story of the two lovers ends tragically, with the death of Liesa and Ardanlier's subsequent suicide. The tale may be partly autobiographical and partly drawn from the story of Inés de Castro; it is thought that Rodríguez may have spoken indiscreetly with a lady of the court, who immediately and irrevocably rejected him, upon which he sought refuge in the mountains of Galicia, and in 1445 entered the Franciscan monastery of El Herbón, Corunna.

Rodríguez's poems appeared in a number of the *Cancioneros*, notably that of Baena and the *Cancionero General* (see CASTILLO, Hernando del).

Among his main works are *Cadira del honor*, a treatise on nobility; and *El triunfo de las donas*, a work in defence of women against such attacks on them as the *Corbacho* of Alfonso Martínez de Toledo (q.v.). Rodríguez also translated part of the *Heroides* of Ovid, as *Bursario*.

His *Obras* (1884) were edited by A. Paz y Melia for the Sociedad de Bibliófilos Españoles (reprinted, Buenos Aires, 1943), and the same editor's *Opúsculos literarios de los siglos XIV a XVI* (1892) published Rodríguez's *Dezir que fizo contra el amor del mundo*.

See three articles on Rodríguez de la Cámara by M. R. Lida in *Nueva Revista de Filología Hispánica*, vol. 6 (1952), pp. 313–51; vol. 8 (1954), pp. 1–38; and vol. 14 (1960), pp. 318–21; and C. Samonà, *Per una interpretazione del 'Siervo libre de amor'* (Rome, 1960).

RODRÍGUEZ DE LENA, PEDRO (15th c.), author of the *Libro del Passo honroso defendido por el excelente cauallero Suero de Quiñones*, abridged for publication by Juan de Pineda (Salamanca, 1588). A facsimile of the first edition appeared in New York in 1902. The work is an eyewitness account of events also related in the *Anales* of Zurita (q.v.) and in the *Crónica de Juan II* concerning a challenge made by Suero de Quiñones, who vowed to defend the bridge of San Marcos de Órbigo, near León, with nine friends for a whole month from 10 July 1434 against all knights travelling to the shrine at Santiago. Of the 68 contenders to cross the bridge, one—an Aragonese—was killed, and nine of the defenders, including Suero himself, were wounded in the 627 jousts. The judges proclaimed that Quiñones had won the right to remove an iron chain that he wore every Thursday around his neck as a token of bondage to his lady, this in spite of the fact that only 177 lances had been broken, whereas Suero had vowed to continue wearing the chain until the total reached 300. He himself had fought on four occasions only during the entire month. The *Passo honroso* is curious as a contemporary account of one of numerous bizarre adventures enacted in imitation of the *libros de caballería* (q.v.). The *Crónica de Juan II* (1433) records at least five such tournaments which took place about that time. The dating of the *Passo honroso* has been studied by W. Mulertt in *Homenaje a Miguel Artigas* (vol. 2, Santander, 1932).

The tournament is the subject of *El paso honroso* (1812) by the Duque de Rivas (q.v.), and of the poem *Esvero y Almedora* by Juan María Maury (Paris, 1840).

See Martí de Riquer, *Caballeros catalanes y valencianos en el Passo Honroso* (Barcelona, 1962) and *Caballeros andantes españoles* (1967).

RODRÍGUEZ DEL PADRÓN, JUAN, see RODRÍGUEZ DE LA CÁMARA, Juan.

RODRÍGUEZ or GUTIÉRREZ ORDÓÑEZ DE MONTALVO, GARCI (*c.* 1440–*c.* 1500), a *regidor* of Medina del Campo. He edited and adapted the original *Amadís de Gaula* (q.v.), adding a fourth book which he apparently began *c.* 1492, and a fifth, the *Sergas de Esplandián* concerning the adventures of the hero's son. The *Sergas* are perhaps the best of the many sequels to *Amadís*, and were reprinted in the BAE, vol. 40 (1857).

RODRÍGUEZ FREILE, JUAN (1566–1640?), b. Bogotá (then Santa Fe de Bogotá). Colombian social historian. The Creole son of a *conquistador*. His only book is his anecdotal, often malicious *Conquista y descubrimiento del Nuevo Reino de Granada*, finished in 1636 and widely known in MS., but not published until 1859. The edition of 1884 is given the title by which it is popularly known: *El carnero de Bogotá*. Of little scholarly value, the book is however very amusing, with its love intrigues, ambushes, fights, and moralizing in the manner of *La Celestina* and the *Libro de buen amor* (qq.v.). Rodríguez's Freile misogyny is possibly derived from the latter work, rather than reflecting his own convictions.

The best edition of *El carnero* is that by Miguel Aguilera (1963) in the Biblioteca de Cultura Colombiana. *El carnero* has been translated by

W. C. Atkinson as *The conquest of New Granada* (London, 1961).

See Alessandro Martinengo, 'La cultura literaria de Juan Rodríguez Freile' in *Boletín del Instituto Caro y Cuervo* (Bogotá), vol. 19, no. 2 (May–August 1964), pp. 274–99.

RODRÍGUEZ GALVÁN, Ignacio (1816–42), b. Tizayuca, Hidalgo. Mexican poet and playwright. A background of poverty combined with an exaggerated Romanticism has produced such arrogant, bitter verse, as *La profecía de Guatimoc,* which denounces European and U.S. imperialism, Mexican politicians, and even God.

His *Poesías* (1851) is in two vols., of which the second includes three plays on colonial Mexico: *La capilla* (written in 1837); *Muñoz, visitador de México* (1838); and *El privado del virrey* (1841). This work was reprinted (with a biographical essay) as *Obras* (1876) and again as *Poesías* (1883).

RODRÍGUEZ MARÍN, Francisco (1855–1943), b. Osuna. Literary scholar, Member of the Spanish Academy, and Director of the National Library, Madrid. He occasionally used the pen-name 'El bachiller Francisco de Osuna'. His major work is the definitive annotated *Don Quijote* (q.v., 1911), expanded into 10 vols. (1947–9), but he published much else, including editions of *El diablo cojuelo* by Luis Vélez de Guevara (q.v.), the poetry of Baltasar del Alcázar (q.v.), and the *Flores de poetas ilustres* of Pedro de Espinosa (q.v.). He produced the monumental collection *Cantos populares españoles* (5 vols., 1882–3; 2nd edn., 1951) and wrote an important biography of Barahona de Soto (q.v., 1903). His main contributions to lexicography are *Dos mil quinientas voces castizas y bien autorizadas que piden lugar en nuestro léxico* (1922). A *Biografía y bibliografía de D. Francisco Rodríguez Marín* by G. M. del Río y Rico appeared in 1947.

RODRÍGUEZ MOHEDANO, *Fray* Pedro and *Fray* Rafael, Franciscan friars and brothers who worked most of their lives to complete *Historia literaria de España* but only managed to get as far as Lucan (q.v.). An edition of 10 vols. in 11 (1766–91) was succeeded by another of 9 vols. in 10 (1779–85).

Their history was criticized systematically by Ignacio López de Ayala (q.v.), in his *Carta crítica . . .* (1781) written under the pseudonym of the Bachiller Gil Porras de Machuca. The brothers replied with *Apologia del tomo V* (1779) and J. Suárez de Toledo supported them with his *Defensa de la 'Historia literaria de España'* (1783). López de Ayala's side was taken by C.

Berruguete y Maza in *Reflexiones críticas . . .* (1783).

RODRÍGUEZ-MOÑINO, Antonio (1910–70), b. Calzadilla de los Caños, Badajoz. Literary critic, historian, editor, and Librarian of the Lázaro Galdiano Foundation in Madrid. He continued the work of the great bibliographer Bartolomé José Gallardo, whose *Correspondencia* he published. Among his hundred and more publications, his most important work as an editor was *Las fuentes del Romancero General* (12 vols., 1957) and, as an author, *Historia literaria de Extremadura* (vol. 1: *Hasta la Reconquista*, 1942; vol. 2: *Edad Media y Reyes Católicos,* 1950), and *El primer manuscrito del 'Amadís de Gaula'* (1957).

His cataloguing of manuscripts and printed-book collections has been of inestimable service to scholars.

ROIG, Jaume (*c.* 1405–1478), b. Valencia. Catalan poet, a physician at the court of Alfonso V, who wrote a long satirical poem against women called the *Llibre de Consells* (*c.* 1460), also known as *L'Espill, o Llibre de les dones.* Despite its anti-feminist spirit, the book gives a good picture of contemporary life. There is a critical edition by R. Chabás (1905), and a translation into Castilian by R. Miquel y Planas (1936–42).

See V. G. Agüera, *Un pícaro catalán del siglo XV: el Spill de Jaume Roig y la tradición picaresca* (1975).

ROÍS DE CORELLA, Joan (*c.* 1433–97), b. Valencia. A Catalan poet influenced by classical and Italian models. His humanism took the unusual form of inventing Greek writers and then compiling letters which he attributed to them. While his best poem is generally considered to be his 'Oració a la Sacratíssima Verge Maria', he is also well known as a love poet.

See the selection of his verse in *Ocho siglos de poesía catalana* (1969), selected by J. M. Castellet and J. Molas.

ROJAS, Fernando de (*c.* 1465–1541), b. Puebla de Montalbán, Toledo. Novelist. He studied in Salamanca, and was induced by racial discrimination to move from his native town to Talavera, where he became mayor, and where he died. His Jewish parents had been forcibly converted, and it has been argued that his novel in dramatic form *La comedia* (later more familiar as *La tragicomedia*) *de Calisto y Melibea,* is a roman-à-clef on the *conversos* in Spain. The novel, the most important literary work produced in 15th c. Spain, is popularly known as *La Celestina* (q.v.). Foulché-Delbosc denied the ascription to Rojas until conclusive biographical data were discovered and published by M. Serrano y Sanz (*RABM*, vol. 7, 1902, pp. 245–99) and by F. del Valle Lersundi (*Revista de Filología Española*, vol. 12, 1925, pp. 385–96 and vol. 16, 1929, pp. 366–88).

ROJAS, GONZALO (1917–   ), Chilean university lecturer and poet of the so-called Generation of 1938, whose work is a reaction against baroque rhetoric. *La miseria del hombre* (1948) and *Contra la muerte* (1964) are both obsessed with death, and even more with loneliness, darkness, and nightmares. His world view is pessimistic, and even his lyrical passages tend to be melancholy.

ROJAS, RICARDO (1882–1957), b. Tucumán. Argentinian literary historian and poet. The first professor of Spanish literature in Buenos Aires University. His essay *Blasón de plata* (1909) was the first Argentinian statement of the view that even in Argentina, where few indigenous cultures survive, the influence of the land must be taken into consideration in any account of the country's past, present, and future. He believed that there was a certain power in the soil of Argentina—a natural force—which would make even gringo immigrants into true Argentinians. In his essay *La restauración nacionalista* (1910) Rojas, while approving of the assimilation of European culture, proposed a return to the true Indo-Spanish tradition submerged during the tide of 19th-c. immigration. To this end he wrote detailed lives of San Martín (*El santo de la espada*, 1933), Sarmiento (*El profeta de la pampa*, 1945), and the play *Ollántay* (q.v., 1939). He collected local myths and customs in *El país de la selva* (1904; 2nd edn., 1946), and also wrote *Archipélago*, *Tierra del Fuego* (1942), and the verse play *La Salamanca: misterio colonial* (1943). The work for which he is best remembered is the pioneering and often controversial *Historia de la literatura argentina* (4 vols., 1917–22; latest edn., 9 vols., 1960) which boldly proclaimed the epic stature of *Martín Fierro* (q.v.).

Rojas began by publishing poetry, *La victoria del hombre* (1903), which reflected Romantic influence, like *La sangre del sol* (1915). Modernism made its mark on two other collections: *Los lises del blasón* (1911) and *Cantos del Perséfona*, written *c.* 1911 but not published until the revised edition of *La victoria del hombre* which appeared in 1951.

H. J. Becco's bibliography of Rojas appeared in *Revista Iberoamericana*, vol. 23, no. 46 (July–December 1958).

See Jorge M. Furt, *La obra de Rojas . . .* (1928) and *Lo gauchesco en 'La literatura argentina' de Ricardo Rojas* (1929).

ROJAS GONZÁLEZ, FRANCISCO (1904–51), b. Guadalajara, Jalisco. Mexican anthropologist, novelist, and short-story writer. He spent the years 1920–35 in the diplomatic corps, serving in Guatemala and the U.S.A., and then joined the Instituto de Investigaciones Sociales of the Universidad Nacional Autónoma to study the Indian communities throughout Mexico. Apart from his scientific publications, he wrote many short stories using (often rather obtrusively) his personal experiences; the best is the posthumously-published *El diosero* (1952), the inspiration of *Raíces*, one of the finest Mexican films. His previous collections were: *Historia de un frac* (1930), *. . . y otros cuentos* (1931), *El pajareador* (1934), *Sed* (1937), *Chirrín y la celda 18* (1944), and *Cuentos de ayer y de hoy* (1946). He wrote two novels: *La negra Angustias* (1944), on a woman revolutionary leader, and *Lola Casanova* (1947), on the lives of Indians in the state of Sonora.

ROJAS HERAZO, HÉCTOR (1921–   ), Colombian novelist and poet. He has published four collections of verse and two novels, the first being *Respirando el verano* and the second *En noviembre llega el arzobispo* (1967), in which the plot consists of incoherent and coincidental happenings without a connecting thread, a reflexion of the illogical quality of life itself. L. A. Sánchez has termed Rojas Herazo the finest Spanish-American novelist of the present time as regards style, language, and lyrical inspiration.

ROJAS SEPÚLVEDA, MANUEL (1896–1973), b. Buenos Aires, of Chilean parents. Short-story writer and novelist. On returning to Chile as a youth he worked as a house-painter, electrician, railway construction-worker, and in the port of Valparaíso. Since 1931 he has been director of the University of Chile Press. His direct, vigorous prose expresses solidarity with the poor, deprived, and delinquent. Rojas was influenced by Faulkner and Hemingway in his early stories: *Hombres del sur* (1926) and *El delincuente* (1929), but his individuality asserted itself in the autobiographical *Lanchas en la bahía* (1932), *La ciudad de los Césares* (1936), *El bonete maulino* (1943), and the important novel *Hijo de ladrón* (1951), translated by F. Gaynor as *Born guilty* (New York and London, 1955). This is a deliberately harsh essay in social realism which nevertheless employs sophisticated techniques of time reversal and interior monologue. Its influence has been greater than that of any other Chilean novel.

Later novels by Rojas are *Mejor que el vino* (1958) and *Punta de Rieles* (1961), the latter returning to a favourite preoccupation: that of the power of a woman to alter a man's life irrevocably for good or evil. Rojas's *Obras completas* appeared in 1961, since when he has published *Manual de literatura chilena* (1964) and the novel *Sombras contra el muro* (1964). *El vaso de leche y sus mejores cuentos* appeared in 1959.

ROJAS VILLANDRANDO, Agustín de (*c.* 1572–*c.* 1625), b. Madrid. Actor and dramatist. His most important work is a delightful picaresque novel, *El viaje entretenido* (q.v., 1603), laced with theatrical gossip. It relates the adventures and conversations of four friends: Rojas himself, the actor Agustín Solano, and the two actor-managers Nicolás de los Ríos and Miguel Ramírez, and is based on Rojas's experiences as a strolling player from *c.* 1600 to 1603. The best edition is by Jean-Pierre Ressot (1972) in Clásicos Castalia.

A living *pícaro*, Rojas was taken prisoner at La Rochelle while serving as a soldier; he later joined pirate ships sailing against the English; travelled in Italy and elsewhere; sought sanctuary after killing a man in Málaga and persuaded a strange woman to pay 300 ducats for his pardon, then begged alms to support her; wrote sermons in payment for meals; and eventually left Granada in 1600 for the stage. In 1610 he appeared in Zamora to claim a title of nobility, and is last heard of in 1618, when he again laid claim to the privileges due to him as an *hidalgo*.

As well as 40 or 50 *loas* (q.v.) which are included in *El viaje entretenido*, Rojas wrote the play *El natural desdichado* (edited by J. W. Cromwell (New York, 1939) from an autograph MS. in the National Library in Madrid). This has been considered an antecedent to Calderón's *La vida es sueño* (qq.v.).

El buen repúblico (Salamanca, 1611) is a satire on government banned by the Inquisition for the allegedly superstitious nature of its content.

See N. Alonso Cortés, 'Nuevos datos biográficos' in *Revista Castellana*, vol. 7 (1923) and 'Varia fortuna de Agustín de Rojas' in *Boletín de la Biblioteca Menéndez y Pelayo*, vol. 24 (1948).

ROJAS ZORRILLA, Francisco de (1607–48), b. Toledo. Dramatist. After desultory university studies, he arrived in Madrid, and was first noted as one of the eighty-nine court poets contributing a sonnet in praise of Philip IV published in 1631 in the *Anfiteatro de Felipe el Grande*. He is considered a member of the so-called *ciclo calderoniano* because of his close association with Calderón (extending to joint authorship of several plays) and because of Calderón's clear influence on his work, especially in the fifteen inferior *autos sacramentales* written when he was in need of money, such as *La viña de Nabot* and

El gran patio de palacio (probably his last, written in three days during 1647). He collaborated with other playwrights too, notably with Pérez de Montalbán in *El monstruo de la fortuna*.

Two collections of his plays appeared in his lifetime: the *Primera parte de la Comedias* (1640), and the *Segunda parte de las Comedias* (1645). The first volume contained: *No hay amigo para amigo*, *No hay ser padre siendo rey* (in which an Abel–Cain situation is set in Poland), *Donde hay agravios, no hay celos*, *Casarse por vengarse* (an immature but popular play of *honor*), *Obligados y ofendidos* (an intriguing *honor* play in which two noblemen are each in love with the other's sister), *Persiles y Segismunda* (a stage version of Cervantes' novel presented in El Pardo in 1633), *Peligrar en los remedios*, *Los celos de Rodamonte*, *Santa Isabel, reina de Portugal*, *La traición busca castigo*, *El profeta falso Mahoma*, and *Progne y Filomena*.

The second volume contained *Lo que son las mujeres* (a brilliant play on many aspects of love, satirizing affectation at court), *Los bandos de Verona*, *Entre bobos anda el juego* (the first complete *comedia de figurón*, q.v.), *Sin honra no hay amistad*, *Nuestra Señora de Atocha*, *Abrir el ojo* (an amusing comedy about the ladies of the court, sometimes reprinted as *Abre el ojo*), *Los trabajos de Tobías*, *Los encantos de Medea*, *Los tres blasones de España*, *Los áspides de Cleopatra* (in MacCurdy's view the most poetic tragedy of love in Golden Age drama), and *El más impropio verdugo por la más justa venganza*, a particularly 'modern' drama of gratuitous violence by Alejandro the rebel against his own father.

Other plays by Rojas Zorrilla were published later. *Del rey abajo, ninguno: García del Castañar* (q.v., Saragossa, 1650) is on the question of honor. *El Caín de Cataluña* (Alcalá, 1651) returns to the Abel–Cain motif of *No hay ser padre siendo rey*. Of his other plays, the most interesting is *Cada cual lo que le toca*, in which Rojas shows a seduced wife, Isabel, not only punishing her seducer herself, but also becoming reconciled with her husband, a denouement which according to Bances Candamo (q.v.), shocked the public, who hissed the closing scene.

The fecundity of Rojas is surprising, considering that he probably enjoyed only 14 years of creative work before his sudden death. In one year alone (1635), it is recorded that seven of his plays (including *El catalán Serrallonga*, written with Luis Vélez de Guevara and Antonio Coello, qq.v.) had their first performances at court.

Rojas was a splendid stylist, and seldom falls into what he considered the verbal excesses of the school of Góngora, which he satirizes in *Sin honra no hay amistad*. His plots are more carefully worked out than those of Lope, and it is clear that his moral attitudes were more stringent than those prevalent at the time. His creation of the full-length *comedia de figurón* in *Entre bobos anda el juego* (q.v.) is a memorable achievement: Don Lucas de Cigarral is the pompous fool, familiar from the *entremeses* (q.v.), who seeks to marry the young heroine, and fails.

His *Comedias escogidas* were edited by R. de Mesonero Romanos as vol. 54 (1861) of the BAE. Cotarelo y Mori's *Don Francisco de Rojas Zorrilla: noticias biográficas y bibliográficas* (1911) is still useful, but Américo Castro has denied Cotarelo's attribution to him of *Saber de una vez*, *El alcalde Ardite*, and *La prudencia en el castigo*. R. R. MacCurdy's important *Francisco de Rojas Zorrilla and the tragedy* (Albuquerque, New Mexico, 1958) has been supplemented by his *Bibliografía crítica* of Rojas in *Cuadernos Bibliográficos* no. 18 (Madrid, 1965), and by his recent editions of *Morir pensando matar* and *La vida en el ataúd* (Clásicos Castellanos, 1961) and *Lucrecia y Tarquino* (Albuquerque, 1963).

The influence of Rojas on French writers was particularly noteworthy. *No hay amigo para amigo* gave Lesage (q.v.) the inspiration for *Le point d'honneur*, and *Entre bobos anda el juego* (also known as *Don Lucas del Cigarral*) influenced *Dom Japhet d'Arménie* by Scarron and *Don Bertrand du Cigarral* by Thomas Corneille, who turned to other light comedies by Rojas for ideas.

ROKHA, PABLO DE, pseudonym of Carlos Díaz Loyola (q.v.).

Romancero gitano, Primer, see PRIMER ROMANCERO GITANO, by Federico García Lorca (q.v.).

Romances ('ballads', hence *Romancero*, 'a collection of ballads', and by extension the whole corpus of Spanish ballads). Essentially of anonymous folk origin, the Spanish ballad (in the generally accepted theory of Manuel Milá i Fontanals) developed after the decline of the epics, deriving from them the verse-form for ballads in general, the subject for very many, and even the detailed content for a few.

The earliest datable printed editions are of *c.* 1530 but it is known that ballads circulated as early as 1421 and it is probable that many were known earlier. These songs were sung in the form of *cantares de gesta*, often unified in theme and style, often surviving in isolation from a parent text of greater length now lost. The first indigenous epics are also the sources of the first Spanish ballads (the Cid, Fernán González, Siete Infantes de Lara, Bernardo del Carpio, qq.v.), but ballads may have been composed on epic themes concurrently with epic poems, or they may have been inspired by epics.

The ballad metre is octosyllabic, with assonance on even lines:

> *El pie tenía de oro,*
> *y almenas de plata fina;*
> *entre almena y almena*
> *está una piedra zafira:*
> *tanto relumbra de noche*
> *como el sol a mediodía.*
>
> —Anonymous ballad known as *Rocafrida*.

There are two usual ways of classifying Spanish ballads: the traditional classification into *romances viejos* (such as the historic; the frontier, or Moorish; the chivalresque; the lyric; and the novelesque); the 16th-c. so-called *romances antiguos* or 'learned', composed in the main by literate poets on the basis of either the chronicles or the *romances viejos*; and the *romances artificiosos*, deliberately affecting an antique mode, and written by poets of 16th c. and later. The classification proposed by W. J. Entwistle consists of the historical (deriving directly from a datable event); the literary (including the epic, deriving indirectly from an event through a chronicle or epic); and the adventure ballad, usually concerned with love, revenge, or adventure, with no known historical connection. Examples of the first kind are those on the Cid and the Moorish frontier wars; the second kind includes the lyric ballad of Lope de Vega (q.v.) such as 'A mis soledades voy' or the 'Amarrado al duro banco' of Luis de Góngora (q.v.); the third kind includes the ballad of Conde Alarcos or that of Durandarte.

The language of the *romances* is often consciously archaic, with frequent echoes from the epic tradition, formulaic, impersonal, and sober in its limited use of adjectives and heightened expression. A sign of their fragmentation (which can have a beautiful effect) is in the enigmatic beginning and ending of a ballad in the middle of a much longer action: 'Conde Arnaldos' is an example of a (wilful?) ending halfway through a tale which Menéndez Pidal succinctly called 'saber callar a tiempo' ('knowing when to stop'). It is believed that in most cases a ballad was composed by a sole author, but that during transmission it suffered accretions, and more commonly omissions, which render its surviving form effectively a collaborative work. They were sung at court, circulated in chap-books throughout Spain from the early 16th c., and early fixed in the form we know (unlike the Yugoslav examples recorded by A. B. Lord in *The singer of tales*, Cambridge, Mass., 1960) by collectors of the *romanceros* in the 16th c. The scholarly publication of *romances* from Andalusia, Catalonia, Galicia, and Portugal began in the 19th c., but they were assumed to have become extinct in Castile until Menéndez Pidal discovered a 15th-c. ballad known in Osma (May 1900), thus beginning the hunt which has so far revealed thousands of surviving ballad-texts. They have been recovered from the Canary Islands, Rhodes, and Morocco; and Judeo-Spanish ballads have been studied with great care and in detail by S. G. Armistead and J. H. Silverman.

In the Golden Age, Quevedo, Góngora, and Lope are outstanding practitioners of the literary ballad; Meléndez Valdés is the great balladmaker of the 18th c.; Zorrilla and the Duque de Rivas are important in the 19th; A. Machado and García Lorca in the 20th.

See R. Menéndez Pidal, *Romancero hispánico* (2 vols., 1953); A. Rodríguez-Moñino, *Las fuentes del Romancero General* (12 vols., 1957); E. M. Wilson, *Tragic themes in Spanish ballads* (London, 1958); Paul Bénichou, *Creación poética en el romancero tradicional* (1968); Diego Catalán, *Siete siglos del romancero* (1969) and *Por tierras del romancero* (1970); N. D. Shergold (ed.), *Studies of the Spanish and Portuguese ballad* (London, 1973); and Giuseppe di Stefano, *El Romancero* (1973).

Romances of Chivalry, see CABALLERÍA, Libros de.

Romanticismo ('Romanticism'), a literary tendency opposed to *realismo* (q.v.). Though it is of universal and permanent significance as one of the major literary modes, in Spanish literature it is said to be the dominant movement of the period 1820–50. According to one view, it arose in Spain only after the French Revolution but Sismondi described Spanish literature as 'wholly Romantic and chivalric' (in *De la littérature du Midi de l'Europe*, Paris, 1829, vol. 3, pp. 497–8) and, for A. W. von Schlegel, Spanish drama up to the age of Calderón was 'almost entirely Romantic' (*Über dramatische Kunst und Literatur*, Heidelberg, 1809, 12te. Vorlesung, II, ii, 12–13).

A conflict arose between neoclassicism (advocated by José Joaquín de Mora) and Romanticism as represented by Calderón and his allegedly absolutist-theocratic ideas (advocated by J. N. Boehl von Faber, q.v.). This controversy, which took place in 1814, was followed in 1823 by Monteggia's article on *romanticismo* in *El Europeo* (Barcelona) and López Soler's defence of Boehl in the following issue. In 1828 Agustín Durán made the last defence of so-called 'historical romanticism' in his *Discurso sobre el influjo que ha tenido la crítica moderna en la decadencia del teatro antiguo español* (newly ed. by D. L. Shaw, Exeter, 1973). He claimed that the Siglo de Oro ('Golden Century') had been the true Romantic century, associated the literary movement with the Roman Catholic and absolutist

monarchical traditions then enjoying a revival under Fernando VII, and failed to understand Romantic themes and techniques.

It was Antonio Alcalá Galiano (q.v.), in his preface to Rivas's *El moro expósito* (Paris, 1834), written in 1833, who rejected the artificial notion of historical Romanticism and proposed that contemporary Romanticism was quite different: Byron, and to a lesser extent Scott, Hugo, and Dumas were the writers who exemplified the new movement.

The main themes of Romanticism were the 'inner commotions' (Alcalá Galiano) of the new philosophical poetry written by Ángel de Saavedra (q.v., Duque de Rivas), Espronceda, and others; anguish in the face of passing time and the inexorability of death; love as the only true principle of life (as in García Gutiérrez's play *El trovador* and Hartzenbusch's play *Los amantes de Teruel*); spiritually in love (as in the heroines in Espronceda) gradually giving way to an erotic tendency in writers such as Juan Arolas; and the inevitability of love thwarted by fate leading to death (the prototype in the Romantic era being Larra's *Macías*).

The technique of *Macías* exemplifies one type of Romantic play, which attempts to observe the classical unities and at the same time to imitate the characteristic *comedia* of the Golden Age, though without sub-plot or *gracioso*. *Los amantes de Teruel*, risking bathos with its melodramatic plot, constantly reiterates the Romantic formula of love-unto-death within a lyrical atmosphere.

Gertrudis Gómez de Avellaneda (q.v.) represents the Romantic writer identifying extreme attitudes of love still described as 'romantic' in her life with those in her poetry. Subjective, strongly emotional, and unafraid of metrical innovation, Avellaneda in her poems such as 'Soledad del alma' and 'La noche de insomnio y el alba' offers a formula now recognizably Romantic.

Zorrilla, in his Romantic verse, shows typical faults of haste, grandiloquence over natural expression, and unrestrained imagination over true feeling. His strengths are also typical: lightness of touch, expert use of colour in imagery, total dedication to poetic values and integrity, and mastery over a variety of verse-forms and rhythms.

The Spanish Romantic novel was the latest major genre to develop, since in 1799 the Government had imposed a total ban on the publication of prose fiction, and even translations of Sir Walter Scott's novels were officially forbidden until 1829. The first native historical novels are R. Húmara Salamanca's *Ramiro, Conde de Lucena* (1823) and Antonio López Soler's *Los bandos de Castilla* (1830), which has a preface in the form of a Romantic manifesto.

The first generation of Spanish Romantics included Quintana, L. Fernández de Moratín, and Boehl von Faber; the second, Lista, Gallardo, Gallego, and Martínez de la Rosa; the third, Fernán Caballero, Bretón de los Herreros, Estébanez Calderón, Mesonero Romanos, and the Duque de Rivas; the fourth, Espronceda, Larra, Hartzenbusch, López Soler, Balmes, García Gutiérrez, Avellaneda, Zorrilla, and Campoamor.

See E. Allison Peers, *History of the Romantic Movement in Spain* (2 vols., Liverpool, 1940), abridged in one vol. (Liverpool, 1949); Emilio Carilla, *El romanticismo en la América hispánica* (2nd edn., 2 vols., Madrid, 1967); Hans Eichner (ed.), *'Romantic' and its cognates: the European history of a word* (Manchester, 1972); Guillermo Díaz-Plaja, *Introducción al estudio del romanticismo español* (Buenos Aires, 1953); and I. L. McClelland, *The origins of the Romantic Movement in Spain* (2nd edn., Liverpool, 1975).

ROMERA-NAVARRO, Miguel (1888–1954), b. Almería. Literary critic and historian. He became a naturalized United States citizen in 1927 and taught at the University of Texas. His many works on Gracián include critical editions of *El criticón* (3 vols., Philadelphia, 1938–40) and the *Oráculo manual y arte de prudencia* (Madrid, 1954), and *Estudios sobre Gracián* (Austin, Texas, 1950).

He also wrote *Historia de la literatura española* (Boston, 1928, 2nd edn., 1949), *Miguel de Unamuno* (Madrid, 1928), and *La preceptiva dramática de Lope de Vega y otros ensayos sobre el Fénix* (Madrid, 1935).

ROMERO, Elvio (1927–), b. Asunción. Paraguayan poet, possibly the best-known of his generation, and influenced by Herib Campos Cervera (q.v.). His poetry of social protest includes *Días roturados* (Buenos Aires, 1948) based on the civil war of 1947, *Resoles áridos* (1950), *Despiertan las fogatas* (Buenos Aires, 1953), and *El sol bajo las raíces* (Buenos Aires, 1955). His love poetry is collected in *De cara al corazón* (1961) and the impressive *Un relámpago herido* (Buenos Aires, 1967). A representative selection of his work appears in *Antologica poética* (Buenos Aires, 1956). Among his critical works is *Miguel Hernández: destino y poesía* (Buenos Aires, 1958).

ROMERO, José Rubén (1890–1952), b. Cotija de la Paz, Michoacán. Mexican novelist and short-story writer. He took part in the Revolution and also helped to draft the Constitution. After working on *El Universal* (Mexico City) he was appointed consul in Barcelona in 1930, and became successively ambassador in Brazil (1937) and Cuba (1939), retiring in 1944.

His early prose works are *Cuentos rurales* (Tacámbaro, 1915) and *Mis amigos, mis enemigos* (1921). His fiction is often autobiographical: after two volumes of *costumbrista* reminiscences on provincial life (*Apuntes de un lugareño*, 1932, and *Desbandada*, 1934) came *El pueblo inocente* (1934), in which Romero's own childhood in a small country town serves as model for the experiences of the young protagonist 'el niño Daniel'. *Mi caballo, mi perro y mi rifle* (Barcelona, 1936) is a novel of the Revolution not unlike that of *Los de abajo* by Mariano Azuela (q.v.), in its pessimistic view that very little had been achieved despite great loss of life and property.

La vida inútil de Pito Pérez (1938) is Romero's most famous novel and arguably his best. The central character of this picaresque work had already appeared in *Apuntes de un lugareño* and *El pueblo inocente*; now Romero devotes a whole book to this amoral and dishonest drunkard with his cynical comments on religion and politics. Romero's sympathetic portrayal of a character representative of the whole class of *desgraciados* or unfortunates make this his most significant work.

He later published *Anticipación a la muerte* and *Una vez fui rico* (both 1939); *Algunas cosillas de Pito Pérez que se me quedaron en el tintero* (1945); and *Rosenda* (1946), a sad love story (with his typical touches of humour) in which the many good qualities of Mexican womanhood are portrayed with an affection and understanding lacking in many of his compatriot authors. Romero wrote a biography, *Álvaro Obregón* (1935); a number of books of verse; and several essays and lectures, including *Breve historia de mis libros* (Havana, 1942). His *Obras completas* (1957; 2nd edn., 1963) have been supplemented by a volume of *Cuentos y poesías inéditos* (1963), compiled by W. O. Cord with a select bibliography.

See John F. Koons, *Garbo y donaire de Rubén Romero* (1942); David Arce, *José Rubén Romero: conflicto y logro de un romanticismo* (1952); and Inés Muñoz Domínguez, *José Rubén Romero, novelista* (1963).

ROMERO, Luis (1916–), b. Barcelona. Novelist and modern historian. After the Civil War he travelled throughout Spain as an insurance agent, and in 1950–1 lived in Buenos Aires, where he wrote *La noria* (Barcelona, 1952), winner of the Premio Nadal for 1951. Nora has pointed out that *La noria* shows the influence of *La colmena* by Cela (qq.v.) and Joyce's *Ulysses*, both in vogue while Romero was in Argentina. The author himself has described it as a novel without a hero: 37 principal characters and many others of lesser importance illustrate aspects of one city: Barcelona.

Romero subsequently published *Carta de ayer*

(1953) and *Las viejas voces* (1955), but it was not until *Los otros* (1956) that he found his most personal vein, concentrating on the interior life rather than on the social problems that interest the majority of his contemporaries.

He has since produced *Esas sombras del trasmundo* (1957), short stories; and the novels *La Nochebuena* (1960), *La corriente* (Barcelona, 1962), and *El cacique* (Barcelona, 1963).

Tres días de julio (1967) is a detailed documentary on the outbreak of the Spanish Civil War. *Desastre en Cartagena* (1971) deals with the rebellion in Cartagena in March 1939. *El final de la guerra* (1977) is a further significant contribution to the history of the war, concentrating on events of the period February to March 1939 which determined the Republican defeat.

ROMERO, RAFAEL (1886–1925), b. Las Palmas. Poet, writing under the pseudonym 'Alonso Quesada'. With his friends Tomás Morales (q.v.) and Saulo Torón, he was one of a trio of post-modernist poets in the Canary Isles, and represents there the spirit of the Generación del 1898 (q.v.). *El lino de los sueños* (1915) is tinged with melancholy, the poet's financial and other difficulties seeming to be reflected in the irony and resignation of his poetry. In his prose *Crónicas de la ciudad y de la noche* (1919), Romero condemns the inertia and spiritual emptiness of his countrymen. *La umbría* (Madrid, 1922) is a three-act dramatic poem.

Los caminos dispersos (1944) consists of his later poems, published posthumously, in which he comes near to the mood of Antonio Machado (q.v.).

ROMUALDO VALLE, ALEJANDRO (1926–), b. Trujillo. Peruvian poet, who writes 'social poetry' (influenced by Neruda) as well as more purely lyrical works (inspired by Guillén). His clarity occasionally descends to banality, as when he writes 'He venido a decir sencillamente / que esto es un árbol y esto es una piedra'. His anti-rhetorical *Edición extraordinaria* (1958), which followed a collected *Poesía, 1945–54* (1954), caused a polemic and divided Peruvian poets into camps supporting the colloquial diction and free verse of Romualdo (Heraud, Cisneros, Calvo (qq.v.), and others), and the traditional school claiming that Romualdo's book represented the end of poetry, 'el sacrificio de la poesía'.

Romualdo then left for Cuba, where he published *Como Dios manda* (1967).

Roncesvalles, Cantar de, a 13th-c. ballad of which the surviving hundred lines were edited by Ramón Menéndez Pidal (1917) and revised with a study in *Tres poetas primitivos* (Buenos Aires, 1948, pp. 47–49). The metre is irregular, like that of the *Cantar de mio Cid* (q.v.); the language is Castilian, though with Navarro-Aragonese elements.

The extant fragment, which is the first known survival in Spanish of the Carolingian cycle, recounts Charlemagne's discovery of the corpses of Bishop Turpin, Oliver, and finally Roland. The version of historical events differs substantially from that in the *Chanson de Roland*.

See J. Horrent, *Roncesvalles: étude sur le fragment de cantar de gesta conservé à l'Archivo de Navarra, Pampelune* (Paris, 1951); R. H. Weber, 'The diction of the "Roncesvalles" fragment' in *Homenaje a Rodríguez-Moñino*, vol. 2 (1966), pp. 311–21; and M. de Riquer, 'El "Roncesvalles" castellano' in his *La leyenda del Graal . . .* (1968), pp. 205–20.

ROSALES CAMACHO, LUIS (1910–), b. Granada. Poet and literary critic. A member of the Real Academia Española. His collection *Abril* (1935) marked a return to the style of Garcilaso, in reaction to neo-Gongorism, in common with his friends and contemporaries the Panero brothers and Luis Felipe Vivanco (qq.v.). Rosales's typically Andalusian, lyrical grace is allied to a preoccupation with religious themes that often appears to derive from his private dream-world rather than from the experience of Christianity, as in *Retablo sacro del nacimiento del Señor* (1940). A revised version of his largely autobiographical *La casa encendida* (1949) appeared in 1967. This followed a collection of *Rimas* (1951), which won the Premio Nacional de Poesía.

The best of his critical works are *Cervantes y la libertad* (2 vols., 1960), *Pasión y muerte del conde de Villamediana* (1964), and *El sentimiento del desengaño en la poesía barroca* (1966). He collaborated with Vivanco in the drama *La mejor reina de España*.

ROSALES Y ROSALES, VICENTE (1894–), b. Jucuapa, El Salvador. A poet and journalist whose work is midway between modernism and the new poetry. On returning from travels in Central America, he became chief editor of *El Día*. His *Antología* (1959) took classical allusiveness from *Sirenas cautivas* (1918), lyrical landscapes from *El bosque de Apolo* (1929), and mingled the derivative harmonies and onomatopoeia of *Euterpología politonal* (1938) with the highly personal tone of *Pascuas de oro* (1947).

ROSENMANN TAUB, DAVID (1926–), Chilean poet. After making an unimpressive début with *El adolescente* (1941), Rosenmann Taub grew in stature with each successive book: *Cortejo y epicinio* (1949), *Los surcos inundados* (1951), and *La enredadera del júbilo* (1952), and eventually joined the literary group known as Taller 99. A good view of his ambitious, deeply pondered later writing can be found in the final section of his contribution to *Antología de la poesía chilena contemporánea*, compiled by R. E. Scarpa and H. Montes (Madrid, 1968).

ROSILLO, Claudio Bachiller, a pseudonym used by Pedro Estala (q.v.).

Rosita la soltera, Doña, see Doña Rosita la soltera.

ROSSELLÓ-PÒRCEL, Bartomeu (1913–38), b. Palma de Mallorca. A pupil of Gabriel Alomar (q.v.) at Barcelona University, he was already familiar with Latin, English, French, and Italian at the time of his early death from tuberculosis. His melancholy lyrics in Catalan were collected in *Obra lírica* (Palma, 1949) from *Nou poemes* (1933), *Quadern de sonets* (1934), and the posthumously-published *Imitació del foc* (1938).

RUBIÓ I LLUCH, Antoni (1856–1936), b. Valladolid. Catalan historian and literary critic. Son of the Catalan poet Joaquim Rubió i Ors, pupil of Milá i Fontanals (q.v.), whom he succeeded at Barcelona University, and fellow-student of Marcelino Menéndez y Pelayo (q.v.). He taught Catalan literature at the Institut d'Estudis Universitaris Catalans in Barcelona and edited its publications.

His principal works are on the history of Catalan culture in Catalonia and overseas: *La expedición y dominación de los catalanes en Oriente juzgadas por los griegos* (1883), *Documents per l'història de la cultura catalana mig-eval* (2 vols., 1908–21), *La cultura catalana en el regnat de Pere III* (1917), and *Joan I humanista i el primer periode de l'humanisme català* (1919).

RUEDA, Lope de (c. 1505–1565), b. Seville. Playwright and actor-manager, who began life as a gold-beater, but joined a band of strolling players and eventually became an *autor de comedias* ('actor-manager'). In 1551 he acted for the future King Philip II in Valladolid, and he is known to have performed subsequently at Benavente (1554), Segovia (1558), Seville (1559), Toledo and Madrid (1561), Seville (1564), and Cordova (1565).

Joan Timoneda (q.v.), his friend and editor, published three series of Rueda's works posthumously. These collections are *Las quatro comedias y dos colloquios pastoriles* (1567); *Compendio llamado el deleytoso, en el qual se contienen muchos passos graciosos* (1567); and *Registro de representantes a do van registrados por I. Timoneda muchos*

y graciosos pasos de Lope de Rueda y otros diuersos autores (1570).

Rueda's *comedias* include *Eufemia* (derived, like Shakespeare's *Cymbeline*, from Boccaccio's *Decamerone*); *Los engañados* (derived from the anonymous Italian *Gl' ingannati* first performed in Siena, 1531); *Armelina* (drawn from Raineri's *Altilia* and Cecchi's *Il servigiale*); and *Medora* (drawn from Giancarli's *La Cingana*, 1545).

These plays are all in prose; their weakness is slowness in action and development, *Eufemia*, in eight scenes, does not present the dramatic problem until the sixth. The interpolated *pasos* (q.v.) enliven this and his other works and foreshadow the comic sub-plots and interludes (*entremeses*, q.v.) of later Golden Age plays.

Los engañados is also significant for the introduction into Spain of a favourite Golden Age motif: the woman disguised as a man (probably in any case played by a boy in early productions). Rueda's adaptation of secular Italian models indicated a possible new direction for the largely ecclesiastical drama then dominant in Spain. His acting was so superior to that of most of his contemporaries that Cervantes praised him very highly, especially for his comic roles of the Biscayan, the rascal, the fool, and the coloured woman. His company and its plays attracted the important actor Ganassa to Madrid 1574, as an indirect result of which the first permanent theatre (the Teatro de la Cruz) opened in Madrid in 1579.

Discordia y cuestión de amor is a verse play; the amusing *Diálogo sobre la invención de las calzas*, also in verse, is a discussion between two footmen. Rueda wrote several pastoral dialogues: *Prendas de amor* in verse, and *Camila* and *Tymbria* in prose.

His principal contribution to the drama, however, consists of some forty *pasos*, or short farcical interludes, of which twenty-four survive, fourteen of them interpolated in his *comedias*. The other ten are *La carátula* (1545), *El convidado* (1546), *La tierra de Jauja* (1547), *Las aceitunas* (1548) in which a peasant and his wife wrangle over the price they will ask for olives not yet planted, *Los criados*, *Cornudo y contento*, *Los lacayos ladrones*, *La generosa paliza*, *Pagar y no pagar*, and *El rufián cobarde*. These *pasos* impressed Cervantes and they impress us even now for their joyful vitality, the spirit of the absurd taking hold of a shrewd peasantry.

Imitators of Rueda include Andrés de Prado (*Cornelia*), Sebastián de Horozco (two *entremeses*), Alonso de la Vega (*Seraphina* and *Tholomea*), and Diego de Neguerela (*Ardamisa*) (qq.v.).

V. Tusón's critical bibliography *Lope de Rueda* appeared in 1965.

Editions of Rueda's works include those by E. Cotarelo y Mori (*Obras*, 2 vols., 1908); José Moreno Villa (*Eufemia, Armelina*, and *El deleitoso*

(1958) for Clásicos Castellanos; A. Cardona (*Teatro completo*, Barcelona, 1967); and F. González Ollé (*Los engañados* and *Medora*, 1973).

See E. Cotarelo y Mori, *Lope de Rueda y el teatro de su tiempo* (1898); S. Salazar, *Lope de Rueda y su teatro* (Santiago de Cuba, 1911); and L. Sáez Godoy, *El léxico de Lope de Rueda* (Bonn, 1968).

RUEDA SANTOS, SALVADOR (1857–1933), b. Málaga. Poet and essayist. Self-taught, and almost illiterate until eighteen, he was later given employment on the Madrid *Gaceta* by Núñez de Arce (q.v.). His first book, *Noventa estrofas* (1883) anticipated some of the modernist innovations of Rubén Darío (q.v.) and his exuberant style evolved through *Aires españoles* (1890) to his first important work, *En tropel: cantos españoles* (1893), with a preface by Darío and a new landscape—that of Asturias. Most of his poetry was highly coloured, spontaneous, and musical, though at times superficial and occasionally lacking in artistic good taste. His *Poesías completas* (Barcelona, 1911) were supplemented by *Cantando por ambos mundos* (1914). His prose *costumbrista* writings dwelt on Andalusia, like most of his poetry: *El patio andaluz* (1886), *El cielo alegre* (1887), *Granada y Sevilla* (1890). His novels and plays were less successful. There is a posthumously-published *Antología poética* (Buenos Aires, 1944).

See M. Prados y López, *Salvador Rueda: el poeta de la raza* (Málaga, 1941); and D. Vázquez Otero, *Salvador Rueda* (Málaga, 1960).

Ruedo ibérico, El, an unfinished cycle of historical novels by Ramón del Valle-Inclán (q.v.), who visualized a series of nine volumes divided into three parts which were to interpret events in Spain from the downfall of Isabel II in 1868 until the Spanish-American War of 1898.

Two of the novels were completed (*La corte de los milagros*, 1927; and *Viva mi dueño*, 1928), a third was not (*Baza de espadas*, 1958), and others survive in fragmentary form (such as 'El trueno dorado', which was serialized in part in the newspaper *Ahora* from 19 March to 23 April 1936).

Though the two unfinished novels are a detailed and often shrewd evocation of Isabel's Spain in 1868, it has been observed by a number of critics (among them Pedro Salinas) that Valle-Inclán's real intention was to circumvent the harsh censorship of the dictatorship of Primo de Rivera by concealing in his historical novels an attack on political and military corruption in the Spain of his own time.

In episodic and panoramic descriptions of Madrid, its court and its middle and lower classes, Valle-Inclán castigates the majority of his characters; he has sympathy only for the Prime Minister, Narváez, whose illness and death form the background of *La corte de los milagros*. Isabel herself is dismissed as a weak-willed, sensual nonentity who is a mere puppet in the hands of an alleged miracle-working nun, Sor Patrocinio, who is in turn a pawn of the extreme right-wing Neo-Catholics.

In *Viva mi dueño* a group of high-ranking army officers is planning a revolt against Isabel. This novel is circular in construction like its predecessor. Books one and nine move rapidly from one centre of activity to another; books two and eight dwell on the conspiracy in Madrid and the court; books three and seven are set in Cordova, and deal with the Cuban revolutionary agent Fernández Vallín; books four and six concern the Queen; and the central fifth book, set in the Andalusian town of Solana del Maestre, compares the lawlessness of the provinces with the chaos caused by power-hungry generals in Madrid. The unfinished *Baza de espadas* and the fragments of the remaining volumes of *El ruedo ibérico* make it clear that Valle-Inclán's obsession with circular time, and his rejection of a purely chronological interpretation of events, were to remain a dominant feature in his plot-construction. *Baza de espadas* begins (books one and two) in Cádiz, and takes further the discussion of the uprising planned against Queen Isabel II. Book three is set on a London-bound ship which is carrying the anarchist Bakunin and some Spanish republican conspirators. Book four, set in England, shows the agreement of Juan Prim to participation in the conspiracy, and the rejection of it by the veteran Carlist general Cabrera. The last book returns us to Cádiz.

The cycle is of major importance for Valle-Inclán's exuberant use of language, so brilliantly allusive that translation presents great difficulty. His writing is 'un habla total' (to quote Juan Ramón Jiménez), fusing without loss of unity such varied speech patterns as criminal slang, aristocratic affectation, lyrical effusions (often ironic), Americanisms, his own neologisms, and rustic Galician.

With *Tirando Banderas* (q.v.), *El ruedo ibérico* is the most mature and rewarding achievement of Valle-Inclán's prose fiction.

See J. Franco, 'The concept of time in "El ruedo ibérico"' in *BHS*, vol. 29 (1962), pp. 177–87; Julián Marías, *Valle-Inclán en "El ruedo ibérico"* (Buenos Aires), which is concerned largely with Valle-Inclán's interpretation of Spanish history in the 19th c.; and A. Sinclair, *Valle-Inclán's 'Ruedo Ibérico': a popular view of revolution* (London, 1977).

Rufián dichoso, El, a verse play in three acts by Miguel de Cervantes Saavedra (q.v.)

published in his *Ocho comedias y ocho entremeses* ... (1615).

A *comedia de santos* ('religious play'), it is based on fact. Cristóbal de Lugo, the central character, leads a life of debauchery in Seville, but is converted, repents, and dies a holy man in Mexico. His adventures could be described as those of a Quijote *a lo divino*. Act 1 is a *cuadro de costumbres* of low life reminiscent of *Rinconete y Cortadillo* (q.v.). Acts 2 and 3 are inferior, since Cervantes was less familiar with the pious than with the picaresque, and he was reduced to quoting disconnected episodes for the reformed Lugo almost verbatim from his source, the *Historia de la fundación y discurso de la provincia de Santiago de México* ... (1596) by Fray Agustín Dávila.

An unrepentant sinner, Doña Ana de Treviño, refuses to confess at the hour of her death, and the scene in which Fray Cristóbal persuades her to repent is the most satisfactory element in the latter part of the play. Act 2 begins with an allegorical dialogue in which Comedia and Curiosidad show the transformation of Lugo, who will henceforth be seen as a friar.

See J. Casalduero, *Sentido y forma del teatro de Cervantes* (1951); and Alberto Sánchez, 'Conexiones temáticas de la comedia cervantina "El rufián dichoso"' in *Homenaje al Professor R. Sánchez Escribano* (1969), pp. 121–41.

RUFO Y GUTIÉRREZ, JUAN (1547?–1625?), b. Cordova. Poet and writer of maxims. He studied at Salamanca University. The son of a dyer, he was persistently in debt throughout his life, because of gambling, until he inherited his father's business and himself turned dyer. Rufo fought against the invasion in 1568.

La Austriada (1584; reprinted in vol. 29 of the BAE in Rosell's edition, 1854) is an epic poem, somewhat overpraised by Cervantes, on Don Juan of Austria. The first 18 cantos of the 24 are a rhymed version of *La guerra de Granada* by Hurtado de Mendoza (q.v.).

Rufo's principal work is *Los seyscientos Apotegmas* ... *Y otras obras en verso* (Toledo, 1596), which has been edited by A. G. de Amezúa (1923), and in Clásicos Castellanos by A. Blecua (1972). These witty maxims influenced not only his son Luis (1581–1653), who published a further anthology *Los quinientos apotegmas*, but also Fray Juan de la Cerda, Fray Tomás de Llamazares, and Baltasar Porreño.

The rest of Juan Rufo's poetry was published by Adolfo de Castro in vol. 42 (1857) of the BAE.

RUFUS, CANIUS (1st c. A.D.), b. Gades (Cádiz), but lived at Rome during Domitian's rule. A writer of elegies, epigrams, and tragedies. A close friend of Martialis (q.v.), who declared that Canius Rufus lavished on Domitian's Rome 'a torrent of grace, sweetness, and joviality'. His wife (or lover) was Theophila (q.v.).

RUGELES, MANUEL FELIPE (1904–59), b. San Cristóbal. Venezuelan poet and editor for many years of the *Revista Nacional de Cultura*, founded in 1938.

An *Antología poética* (Buenos Aires, 1952) has been superseded by *Poesías. Antología general*, selected by O. Sambrano Urdarreta (San Cristóbal, 1961). Both collections give prominence to Rugeles's *Puerta del cielo*, considered by some critics the finest group of sonnets produced in Venezuela.

Ruido, Comedias de ('noisy plays') so called in Spanish Golden Age drama because they required many properties and mechanical devices. In *El passagero* (q.v., 1617), Suárez de Figueroa (q.v.) defined them as plays that '(apart from those about kings of Hungary or princes of Transylvania), deal with the life of some saint and employ all kinds of machinery and stage artifices to attract the rabble'. They are thus also called *comedias de caso, de teatro, de cuerpo, de fábrica, de tramoya, mitológicas*, and, where appropriate, *de santos*. They include historical and mythological plays (of which Lope de Vega (q.v.) alone wrote more than 200) and were usually notable for rich costumes and exotic settings. The opposite category is that of the simpler *comedias de capa y espada* (q.v.).

RUIZ, JUAN, *Arcipreste de Hita* (1283?– 1350?), author of the *Libro de buen amor* (q.v.), with the *Poema de mio Cid* the most important long poem to survive from medieval Spain. Nothing is recorded of Ruiz's life apart from what emerges from his book, and Manuel Criado de Val (*Teoría de Castilla la Nueva*, 1960) has suggested that any dates or facts found in the poem might be interpolations, and that even the name 'Juan Ruiz' might be a pseudonym or a later invention.

If the text is reliable, Ruiz was born at Alcalá de Henares, was educated at Toledo (where he could have come into contact with the Islamic culture so evident throughout his book), and by the year 1330 had finished the first recension of the *Libro de buen amor* at Hita, a village in the Alcarria thirty miles east of Alcalá, where he was archpriest. By that time he was already well known for his popular songs (as for instance those in stanzas, 1513–14).

It has been suggested that Ruiz composed either the 1330 version or the enlarged 1343 version of the *Libro* while in a Toledo prison on the orders of the Archbishop, but modern scholars have suggested that his references to imprisonment should rather be interpreted metaphorically, meaning for instance that the poet was perhaps a 'prisoner' of old age or infirmity.

RUIZ, L., pseudonym of Gumersindo Laverde Ruiz (q.v.).

RUIZ DE ALARCÓN Y MENDOZA, JUAN (1580–1639), b. Mexico City. Playwright. From a well-to-do family, he left for Spain in 1600 to continue his education at Salamanca, graduated in 1602, spent the years from 1606–8 with his relative Gaspar Ruiz de Montoya in Seville, then went back to Mexico City.

In 1611 he returned to Spain, living in Madrid, working at the Council for the Indies (where he attained high office) from 1614 until his death, and writing (between 1615–25) the twenty-five plays for which he has been considered one of the half-dozen greatest dramatists of the Golden Age. Pigeon-chested and hunchbacked in an age intolerant of physical deformities, he was cruelly pilloried by Lope, Góngora, Vélez de Guevara, Pérez de Montalbán, the cleric Mira de Amescua (who helped to cause the failure of Alarcón's only religious play *El Anticristo*, first performed in 1623) and especially by Quevedo, who wrote 'Los apellidos de don Juan crecen como los hongos; ayer se llamaba Juan Ruiz; añadiósele el Alarcón, y hoy se ajusta el Mendoza, que otros leen Mendacio. Así creciese de cuerpo, que es mucha carga para tan pequeña bestezuela' ('The names of John grow overnight like mushrooms; once he was John Ruiz; then Alarcón; today Mendoza, which others read "mendacious". His body should grow in like manner, for the weight of his names is too great a burden for so little a beast').

Most of his plays were published, in two collections, during his lifetime. The *Parte primera de las comedias* (1628) consists of eight plays: *Los favores del mundo*, a moral lesson with a hero named Ruiz de Alarcón; *La industria y la suerte*, a *comedia de enredo* ('play of intrigue'); *Las paredes oyen* (q.v.), a pathetic cry of rebellion from the hunchback writer against those who mock his deformity; *El semejante a sí mismo*, a *comedia de enredo*; *La cueva de Salamanca*, a fantasy; *Mudarse por mejorarse*, on the fickleness of lovers; *Todo es ventura* (of doubtful attribution); and *El desdichado en fingir*, another moral drama.

The *Parte segunda de las comedias* (Barcelona, 1634) contains thirteen plays: *Los empeños de un engaño*: *El dueño de las estrellas*, a history of Lycurgus of Sparta; *La amistad castigada*, an equally unsuccessful evocation of Dion's Sicily; *La manganilla de Melilla*, a play about Christians taken captive by Moors who are finally defeated

by a stratagem (*manganilla*); *Ganar amigos*, which introduces the noble and generous Don Fadrique, one of the noblest characters on the Castilian stage, whose honour is saved by men he has befriended when he is slandered before King Pedro the Cruel; *La verdad sospechosa* (q.v.), his most famous play and the source of Corneille's *Le menteur* and Goldoni's *Il bugiardo*; *El Anticristo*, a play using as sources the Apocrypha and early Christian traditions; *El tejedor de Segovia* (ed. A. V. Ebersole, 1974), in two parts, of which probably only the second is by Ruiz de Alarcón, and dealing with the revenge of a nobleman against his father's murderers; *Los pechos privilegiados*, in which loyalty to one's sovereign involves the betrayal of a woman; *La prueba de las promesas*, on a story from *El conde Lucanor* (q.v.); *La crueldad por el honor*, based on an anecdote from the annals of Aragón by Zurita (q.v.), in which a prince is forced to choose between honesty and loyalty to his sovereign; and *El examen de maridos*, which had been published in 1630 (with *Ganar amigos* and *La verdad sospechosa*) as the work of Lope de Vega (q.v.) and stems from the same source as Shakespeare's *The merchant of Venice*.

All these and six additional *comedias* were published in vol. 20 (1852) of the BAE: *La culpa busca la pena y el agravio la venganza*; *No hay mal que por bien no venga* (like *El examen de maridos* a masterpiece of social observation); *Quién engaña más a quién*; *Quien mal anda en mal acaba*, on the Faustian theme of a pact with the devil to obtain a woman's love; *Siempre ayuda la verdad*; and *Algunas hazañas del Marqués de Cañete*.

Ruiz de Alarcón was in advance of his time in careful, almost classical, plot-construction and psychological penetration, though with little of his contemporaries' fertility of invention, verbal brilliance, or creative energy, and in his satire on contemporary manners he anticipates Moreto and Leandro Fernández de Moratín (qq.v.). Ruiz de Alarcón's *Obras completas* have been edited by A. Millares Carlo (3 vols., Mexico City, 1957–68).

See W. Poesse, *Ensayo de una bibliografía de Juan Ruiz de Alarcón* (Valencia, 1964); Serge Denis, *La langue de Juan Ruiz de Alarcón* (Paris, 1943); Antonio Castro Leal, *Juan Ruiz de Alarcón, su vida y su obra* (1943); Alva V. Ebersole, *El ambiente español visto por Juan Ruiz de Alarcón* (Valencia, 1959); C. O. Brenes, *El sentimiento democrático en el teatro de Juan Ruiz de Alarcón* (Valencia, 1960); and Ellen Claydon, *Juan Ruiz de Alarcón, baroque dramatist* (Chapel Hill, N.C., 1970).

RUIZ IRIARTE, VÍCTOR (1912–), b. Madrid. Playwright. President of the Sociedad General de Autores de España. He has written more than forty plays combining fantasy with realism, and concerned more with dialogue than action. His style is generally comparable with that of Alejandro Casona (q.v.). He has translated into Spanish authors such as Terence Rattigan.

Tres comedias optimistas (1947) contains *Un día en la gloria* (1943), *El puente de los suicidas* (1944), and *Academia de amor* (1943). His later plays include *Don Juan se ha puesto triste* (1946), *El cielo está cerca* (1947), *Los pájaros ciegos* (1948), and his first success: *El landó de seis caballos* (1950), a lyrical entertainment in Ruiz Iriarte's habitually optimistic vein. Subsequently he has written an amusing satire of European court life in the 18th c. in *El gran minué* (1951); *Una investigación privada* (1958); and *Esta noche es la víspera* (1959). A collection of his numerous plays for television has been published under the title of *La pequeña comedia*.

RULFO, Juan (1918–   ), b. Sayula, Jalisco. Mexican novelist and short-story writer, whose family lost their substantial wealth in the Revolution. He spent his childhood in the provinces, which form the background to his semi-autobiographical fiction. He was Director of the publications department of the Instituto Nacional Indigenista.

Rulfo's first short stories appeared in *Pan*, a magazine published in Guadalajara, and edited by Juan José Arreola (q.v.) and Antonio Alatorre. Fifteen of them were collected in *El llano en llamas* (1953; translated as *The burning plain* by G. de Schade, Austin, Texas, 1968), but Rulfo is best-known for *Pedro Páramo* (1955; translated by L. Kemp, New York, 1959).

Pedro Páramo is one of the few Latin American novels successfully to lay bare the inner lives of country people. Rulfo's characters here are dead, existing merely as faint voices in the air of an abandoned village, but his evocative powers combine with techniques (such as the fluidity of time and the interior monologue) borrowed from Faulkner to create a recognizable Mexico. Rulfo's hero is obsessed with the past (in this case the years from Porfirio Díaz's regime to that of Obregón), lonely, and incapable of genuine communication with others.

See A. Benítez Rojo (ed.), *Recopilación de textos sobre Juan Rulfo* (Havana, 1969); R. Roffé, *Juan Rulfo: autobiografía armada* (1973); and H. F. Giacoman (ed.), *Homenaje a Juan Rulfo* (New York, 1974).

S

SAAVEDRA, Gonzalo de (*fl.* 1633), b. Cordova? Novelist. Little is known of his life, except that he spent some time as governor of one of the provinces of Southern Italy. His style as a writer is decadent and affected. His mediocre *Los pastores del Betis* (Trani, 1633), probably written in Italy, has the distinction of being probably the last true pastoral novel (q.v.) written in Castilian.

SAAVEDRA, Miguel de Cervantes, see Cervantes Saavedra, Miguel de.

SAAVEDRA FAJARDO, Diego de (1584–1648), b. Algezares, Murcia. Political writer and diplomat. He spent his life in the diplomatic service from the age of 22 to his retirement, 40 years later, in Italy. Many of his writings have disappeared, among them *Guerras y movimientos de Italia de cuarenta años a esta parte*, *Suspiros de Francia*, and *Ligas de Francia con holandeses y sueceses*. Of those extant, the most characteristic is the *Idea de un príncipe político christiano. Representada en cien Empresas* (Munich, 1640; ed. in Clásicos Castellanos, 3 vols., 1927–

30), the finest Golden Age treatise on statecraft after the *Política de Dios* (1625–55) of Quevedo and the works of Gracián (qq.v.). Each chapter is preceded by a detailed graphic symbol or '*empresa*' (i.e., emblem) intended to express in pictorial form the statements and conclusions of that chapter; it was a genre much in favour but treated with a new seriousness by the diplomat. A Christian reply to the allegedly secular cynicism of Machiavelli, it assumes a Senecan simplicity in contrast to the Ciceronian style of Gracián. The *Idea* is also available in vol. 25 (1866) of the BAE, which contains most of Saavedra Fajardo's surviving works.

The *Introducciones a la política y razón de Estado del Rey Católico don Fernando* (1631) propose the name of King Ferdinand as the ideal of the Catholic prince but in the tradition of justice and virtue laid down by Aristotle. More interesting is the pseudonymous *Juicio de Artes y Sciencias. Su autor Don Claudio Antonio de Cabrera* (1655), commonly known as the *República literaria*, reprinted in Alcalá (1670) and edited for Clásicos Castellanos (1922) by V. García de Diego. This is a witty survey, in the form of a dream, of books and writers ancient and (more particularly) modern; Menéndez y Pelayo compared it favourably with both Forner's (q.v.) *Exequias de la lengua castellana* and Leandro Fernández de Moratín's (q.v.) *Derrota de los pedantes*.

Corona gótica, castellana y austríaca (1646) is a virtually worthless essay on the history of the Visigoths in Spain. The second and third parts, much more useful, were added later by Alonso Núñez de Castro.

Locuras de Europa (1748) is a fine Lucianesque dialogue between Mercury and Lucian, written just before the author's death, to defend Spain and Roman Catholicism against the intrigues of nations opposed to them for political and religious reasons.

The first edition of Saavedra Fajardo's *Obras completas* appeared in Antwerp (4 vols., 1677–8) and the latest in Madrid, edited by Ángel González Palencia (1946), though the best edition of *República literaria* is now that of John Dowling (Salamanca, 1967).

See M. Fraga Iribarne, *Don Diego de Saavedra y Fajardo y la diplomacia de su época* (Murcia, 1956, but 1955); J. C. Dowling, *El pensamiento político-filosófico de Saavedra Fajardo* (Murcia, 1957); and F. Murillo Ferrol, *Saavedra Fajardo y la política del Barroco* (1957).

SAAVEDRA GUZMÁN, ANTONIO DE (*fl.* 1599), b. Mexico City. Mexican poet who, while on the voyage of 70 days to Spain, composed the long narrative chronicle poem *El peregrino indiano* (Madrid, 1599). In 2,039 *octavas reales* he recounts the exploits of Cortés in Mexico. Compared by Beristaín with the *Pharsalia* of Lucan, the work was condemned by Clavijero for containing 'nothing poetical except the metre' and by Menéndez y Pelayo for its indigestible aridity, being worthy of note only for its extreme rarity and for being the first known printed book by a poet born in Mexico.

Trivial, monotonous, and marred by many clichés, the work was nevertheless reprinted in Mexico City in 1880 with a preface by J. García Icazbalceta.

SAAVEDRA REMÍREZ DE BAQUEDANO, ÁNGEL DE, *Duque de Rivas* (1791–1865), b. Cordova. Romantic poet and playwright. His early *Poesías* (1813; 2nd enlarged edn., 2 vols., 1820–1), and plays *Ataúlfo* (1814) and *Lanuza* (1822) were neoclassical, still under the influence of Quintana and Meléndez Valdés (q.v.), but while he was in exile on Malta he met the English man of letters John Hookham Frere (1769–1846), who introduced him to the works of Shakespeare, Scott, and Byron.

The Duque de Rivas adopted the new

Romantic style, producing *El faro de Malta* (1828) and the greatly superior *El moro expósito, o Córdoba y Burgos en el siglo décimo* (2 vols., Paris, 1834), edited in the Colección Crisol in 1945. A novel in verse like Scott's *Marmion* (1808), this *leyenda* of 12 *romances* is composed in assonanted hendecasyllables. He later wrote *Romances históricos* (1841; 2 vols. in Clásicos Castellanos, 1912).

Rivas is best known for the first and perhaps the finest of Spanish Romantic dramas, *Don Álvaro, o la fuerza del sino* (first performed in Madrid, 1835; new edn. by R. Navas Ruiz in Clásicos Castellanos, 1975), which caused an almost immediate triumph on the stage and was used for the libretto of Verdi's opera *La forza del destino* (1862). It has remained in the repertoire, unlike Rivas's other plays, such as *Aliatar* (1816); *Doña Blanca* (1817), the only MS. of which was destroyed in 1823; *El Duque de Aquitania* (1817); *Malek-Adhel* (1818); *Arias Gonzalo* (1826?); and *Tanto vales cuanto tienes* (1840, but written in Malta 12 years earlier).

El desengaño en un sueño (1842) is, however, a reaction against *Don Álvaro* and Romanticism, its central character, Lisardo, being a grotesque from the Golden Age *comedia* who seems to attack the cosmic rebellion evident in much Romantic drama. Rivas explicitly turned his back on his former 'doctrinas disolventes, impías y corruptoras' in a speech to the Real Academia Española (1860).

Rivas's *Obras completas* (7 vols., 1894–1904) are also available in the Colección Castellanos (5 vols., 1854–5) and in the BAE (3 vols., 1957).

See E. Allison Peers, 'Ángel de Saavedra, Duque de Rivas: a critical study' in *Revue Hispanique*, vol. 63 (1923), pp. 1–600, and *Rivas and Romanticism in Spain* (London, 1923); and G. Boussagol, *Ángel de Saavedra, duc de Rivas: sa vie, son œuvre poétique* (Toulouse, 1926), with amendments in *Bulletin Hispanique*, vol. 30 (1928), pp. 328–9.

SABAT ERCASTY, CARLOS (1887–), b. Montevideo. Uruguayan poet. He began in the decadent, Parnassian mode, but burnt these early writings in 1912.

Pantheos (1917) was his pantheistic reaction to Romanticism, but he soon abandoned that style and turned to Whitmanesque vitalism in three series of *Poemas del hombre* (1921), continued in *Poema del hombre: Libro del mar* (1922), and *Poema del hombre: Libro del amor* (1929), a sequence interrupted by *Églogas y paisajes marinos* (1923). *Los adioses* (1929) is a book of sonnets which obtained a mixed reception.

Sabat Ercasty subsequently published *Los juegos de la frente* (1929), *Libro del amor* (1930), *Lírida* (1933), *El demonio de Don Juan* (1934),

Sinfonía del río (1939), *Himno a Rodó. Oda a Rubén Darío* (1939), *Himno a Artigas* (1946), *Las sombras diáfanas* (1947), *Libro de la ensoñación* (1947), *Libro de la Eva inmortal* (1948), *Poema del hombre* (1952), *Prometeo* (1952), *Retratos del fuego*, a portrait of M. E. Vaz Ferreira (q.v., Santiago de Chile, 1954), *El charrua Veinte Toros* (1957), *Retratos del fuego*, a portrait of C. Vaz Ferreira (q.v., 1958), *Chile en monte, valle y mar*, sonnets on Chilean themes (Santiago de Chile, 1958), *Libro de los mensajes* (1958), *Lucero el caballo* (1959), *Euridice, la joven del canto* (1959), *El mito de Prometeo* (1960), and *Himno de mayo* (1964).

On Sabat Ercasty's influence on Pablo Neruda (q.v.), see Giovanni Meo Zilio, *De José Martí a Sabat Ercasty* (1967), pp. 186–252. See also G. L. Haws, *El Prometeo uruguayo* (1969).

SÁBATO, ERNESTO (1911–), b. Rojas, Province of Buenos Aires. Argentinian novelist and essayist. He qualified and worked as a physicist, but his vocation as a writer was equally strong, and in 1940 his first article appeared in the magazine *Sur* (q.v.). He was appointed Professor of Theoretical Physics at La Plata University in 1940 but like many other liberals was forced to resign his post in 1945.

His first book was *Uno y el universo* (1945), a brilliant literary and philosophical work, using aphorisms, paradox, and irony in discussing creation, man, death, the infinite, and other such elusive metaphysical questions. In *Hombres y engranajes* (1951) and *Heterodoxia* (1953) he propounds similar problems of modern man, alienated and often despairing; Sábato regards the contradictions and dangers of his statements and their consequences as a necessary step towards an understanding of the complex human condition evolving from the time of the Middle Ages. Among the ideas in *Heterodoxia*, for instance, are the alleged Platonism of Sartre; the relationship between authors and their fictional characters; the value of the metaphor; a refutation of the alleged rationalism of the Jews; and a discussion of the progress of language in literature and science. Subsequent essays include *El caso Sábato* (1956) and *El otro rostro del Peronismo* (1956), the former in political justification of himself and the latter against torture and censorship; *Tango: discusión y clave* (1963); *El escritor y sus fantasmas* (1963); *Tres aproximaciones a la literatura de nuestro tiempo* (Santiago de Chile, 1968), on Robbe-Grillet, Borges, and Sartre; *La convulsión política y social de nuestro tiempo* (1969); and *Claves políticas* (1974).

Sábato's novels are considered even more important: *El túnel* (q.v., 1948), *Sobre héroes y tumbas* (q.v., 1961), and *Abaddón el exterminador* (1974). They are psychological novels employing an existential and philosophical basis, but

with sufficiently strong characterization and construction to absorb disparate material such as essays, asides by the author on his own writings and influences (such as Faulkner), and hallucinatory glimpses of Buenos Aires reminiscent of Marechal (q.v.).

Obras: ensayos (1970) contains much of his non-fiction up to 1970. There is a bibliography by Fred Petersen in *La Palabra y el Hombre* (Xalapa, Mexico), vol. 48 (July–September 1969), pp. 425–35.

See Angela Dellepiane, *Ernesto Sábato: el hombre y su obra* (New York, 1968); H. D. Oberhelman, *Ernesto Sábato*, in Twayne's World Authors series (New York, 1970); M. A. Correa, *Genio y figura de Ernesto Sábato* (1971); H. F. Giacoman (ed.), *Homenaje a Ernesto Sábato* (New York, 1972); and Joaquín Neyra, *Ernesto Sábato* (1973).

SABINES, JAIME (1925–), b. Tuxtla Gutiérrez, Chiapas. Mexican poet. He studied in the capital, but his roots are in the Chiapas countryside and his sensibility rebels against what he considers to be an essentially hostile bourgeois urbanism. His early books were *Horal* (Tuxtla Gutiérrez, 1950); *La señal* (1951); a sequence (addressed to his unborn son) called *Tarumba* (1956); and *Diario semanario y poemas en prosa* (Xalapa, 1961). These were collected with new and some older poems in *Recuento de poemas* (1962). His latest work is *Doña Luz* (1969).

SABUCO Y ÁLVAREZ, MIGUEL (1529?–1588), b. Alcaraz. Philosopher. His collection of philosophical dialogues, *Nueva filosofía de la naturaleza del hombre, no conocida ni alcanzada de los grandes filósofos antiguos: la qual mejora la vida y salud humana* (1587), was attributed on the title-page to Oliva Sabuco (1562–1625), his daughter, but José Marco Hidalgo, in his *Biografía de doña Oliva de Sabuco* (1900), proved that the author was Miguel Sabuco. Two of the dialogues were reprinted in vol. 65 (1873) of the BAE, and a complete reprint appeared in 1935.

Sabuco's main thesis is that all evils proceed from the brain, and that the passions are to be preferred to reason. His miscellany includes remarks on medicine, meteorology, philosophy, and hygiene, not without a touch of irony to relieve the dogmatizing.

SACO E ARCE, XOAN ANTONIO (1836–81), b. S. Martiño de Alongos, Orense. Galician poet and scholar who taught Greek at Pontevedra and produced *Gramática gallega* (1866), the first respectable Galician grammar.

His own poems, collected in *Poesías* (Orense, 1878), were however, with the exception of nine in Galician, all in Castilian, most being delicate, and religious in theme.

He left two unpublished MSS. at his death: 'Literatura popular de Galicia' and 'Colección de coplas, romances, cuentos y refranes gallegos', the latter partly published in the *Boletín Provincial de Monumentos de Orense*.

SÁENZ DÍEZ SERRA, NARCISO, see SERRA, Narciso Sáenz Díez.

Saeta, (Latin: *sagitta*, 'arrow'), a brief unaccompanied song chanted in religious processions, especially during Easter Week. The stanzas vary from two to six octosyllabic lines. Its best examples come from Andalusia.

Sáficos ('sapphics'), a verse form adapted to Castilian from Horace and Catullus. The *estrofa sáfica* consists of three hendecasyllabic lines (the *sáficos* proper) and a five-syllable *adónico*. Esteban Manuel de Villegas and the Marqués de Santillana (qq.v.) are among the finest practitioners of the form.

SAFINIO, the first pen-name of Serafín Estébanez Calderón (q.v.).

SAGARRA, JOSEP MARIA DE (1894–1961), b. Barcelona. Catalan playwright, poet, and novelist. A friend of Alcover, Carner, and Maragall, he remained isolated from the *noucentisme* of Carner and Guerau de Liost, writing traditional verse such as the lively 'Balada de Luard, el mariner'. His poems are collected in *Primer llibre de poemes* (1914), *El mal cassador* (1916), *Cansons d'abril y de novembre* (1918), *Cansons de taberna e d'oblit* (1922), *Cansons de rem y de vela* (1924), *El comte Arnau* (1928), and *El poema de Nadal* (1931). He wrote many plays, among them *Juan Enrich* (1918), *El jardinet de su amor* (1922), and *Març al Prior* (1926). They were Romantic in style, inspired by the Catalan dramatist Ignacio Iglesias, and Sagarra's play *L'Hostal de la Gloria* won the Iglesias prize of 1932.

His novels are in the realist tradition: *Paulina Buxaren* (1919), *Els ocells amichs* (1923), *All i salobre* (1929), *Café, copa i puro* (1929), and *Vida privada* (1932), winner of that year's Crexells Prize.

SAHAGÚN, *Fray* BERNARDINO RIBEIRA DE (1499?–1590), b. Sahagún. Historian and philogist. A Franciscan missionary, he left for Mexico in 1529 and (after translating documents from Aztec into Nahuatl) wrote the pioneering *Historia general de las cosas de Nueva España* (first published in 1892 and in a revised edition in 4 vols. by Ángel María Garibay, q.v., 1956).

Fray Bernardino's importance lies in his discovering at first hand and discussing the ancient mythology and culture of Mexico, and in publishing a native version of the Spanish conquest. He wrote numerous religious books in both Spanish and Nahuatl, but most are known only through references in other writers' works. The only book he published in his lifetime was *Psalmodía cristiana*.

SAID ARMESTO, VÍCTOR (1871–1914), b. Pontevedra. Literary critic and literary historian who taught Galician-Portuguese literature at the Universidad Central in Madrid. Apart from his study *Las mocedades del Cid* (1913), Said Armesto specialized in comparative literature, his major contributions being *La leyenda de don Juan* (1908) and *Tristán y la literatura rústica* (1911).

Sainete (diminutive of *saín*, a 'piquant sauce'), a term probably first used in 1639 to describe the one-act sketches which came to constitute the main type of *género chico* (q.v.). To begin with, the *sainete* did not differ essentially from the comic *paso* popularized by Lope de Rueda (q.v.) or the *entremés* of writers such as Quiñones de Benavente (q.v.), but gradually it acquired music and elaborated its observation of typical scenes and characters of urban life, particularly in the Madrid *sainete* of Ramón de la Cruz (q.v.). Its dialogue contrasts the rough and colloquial realism of the streets to the rhetoric and romanticism of the three-act *comedia* or *tragedia* with which it was always presented. Always beloved by audiences, the *sainete* retains its appeal even today.

SAINZ, GUSTAVO (1940–), b. Mexico City. Mexican novelist and short-story writer. After publishing some short stories in magazines, Sainz had a critical success with his autobiographical, *avant-garde* novel *Gazapo* (1965), which semi-satirically shows the aimlessness of adolescence and early adulthood in Mexico City through long, pointless telephone calls, letters, and diaries.

He followed this with an autobiography *stricto sensu*: *Gustavo Sainz* (1966) and the important novel *La princesa del palacio de hierro* (1974) which won the Premio Xavier Villaurrutia.

SAÍNZ DE ROBLES, FEDERICO CARLOS (1898–), b. Madrid. Anthologist and compiler of reference books, mainly in the field of Spanish literature. His main works are the anthology *Cuentos viejos de la vieja España* (1941), *Historia y antología de la poesía española* (1943), *Historia y antología del teatro español* (7 vols., 1942–3), *Ensayo de un diccionario de la literatura* (3 vols.,

1947; 3rd edn., 1964), and *Los movimientos literarios* (1955).

His son, Federico Carlos Sáinz de Robles y Rodríguez (b. Madrid, 1927), has published biographical and critical studies of Camus and Gogol, and the useful *Historia y antología de las Utopías* (1964).

Saker Ti, Grupo ('The Dawn Group'), a Guatemalan literary movement founded in 1947 by Huberto Alvarado (q.v.). The main influences were Valéry, Rilke, Joyce, Kafka, and the surrealists, but Saker Ti writers also read 'committed' authors: Marx, Engels, Aragón, Guillén, Neruda, and Vallejo. Many of the more notable participants in the less radical Grupo Acento (q.v.) eventually joined Saker Ti. The members included Rafael Sosa, Olga Martínez Torres, Werner Ovalle López, Melvin René Barahona, Oscar Edmundo Palma, and Oscar Arturo Palencia.

SAL, JUAN DE LA (*c.* 1550–*c.* 1620), b. Seville. Letter-writer. A Bishop of Bône (Algeria), formerly Hippo Regius, who wrote seven interesting letters to the Duke of Medina Sidonia, reprinted in vol. 36 (1855) of the BAE, discussing among other matters a certain Francisco Méndez who, having declared that he would die on a certain day and being proved wrong by his survival, in fact succumbed several months later, allegedly of mortification.

SALARRUÉ, pseudonym of Salvador Salazar Arrué (q.v.).

SALAS BARBADILLO, ALONSO JERÓNIMO DE (1581–1635), b. Madrid. Novelist, playwright, and poet. He succeeded his father as business agent of Nueva España in 1603. Of quarrelsome disposition, he wounded a nobleman and was gaoled, writing a satire against his judges and gaolers, for which he was exiled for two years. On his return to Madrid he became friendly with Miguel de Cervantes, Valdivielso (qq.v.), and other writers.

He wrote a great deal in his early life, but later became deaf and abandoned literature, apart from the two works published in 1634 and 1635.

His poetry survives in an epic poem, *Patrona de Madrid restituyda* (1609); *Rimas castellanas* (1618); and *Triunfos de la Santa Juana de la Cruz* (1621). Three sonnets and a dozen epigrams are available in vol. 42 (1857) of the BAE; his epigrams are masterly, especially that on the matron wishing to appear young by wearing many jewels: 'Alumbra más que la esfera / de diamantes adornada; / Calle tan bien empedrada / sin duda que es pasajera'.

Salas also wrote *entremeses* such as *El buscaoficios* and *El caprichoso en su gusto y la Dama setentona*; thirteen of them appear in Cotarelo y Mori's edition for vol. 17 (1911) of the NBAE.

Salas Barbadillo created a sensation with his picaresque novel *La hija de Celestina* (Saragossa, 1612), overtly imitating the *Celestina* (q.v.) but with an originality of its own based on the clever satire of contemporary types in Madrid and on the sympathetic and subtle characterization of its heroine, after whom the book was subsequently usually known as *La ingeniosa Elena*. Elena's husband, the complaisant Montúfar, is murdered by her lover and she is then judicially murdered in her turn. This work, imitated in France by Scarron and drawn on by Molière, was edited by J. López Barbadillo (1907).

Salas Barbadillo's other works, whether in narrative or dialogue form, usually displayed a gift for satire and wit that made enemies of his acquaintances and admirers of all others. They included *El cavallero puntual* (1614) and its *Segunda parte . . .* (1619), edited with the play *Prodigios de Amor* by E. Cotarelo y Mori in Colección de Escritores Castellanos (1909); *Corrección de vicios* (1615), eight tales in prose and three in verse, edited by E. Cotarelo y Mori with *La sabia Flora Malsabadilla* (1907), a novel in dialogue about a gipsy girl who succeeds in marrying a nobleman; *El cavallero perfecto* (1620; ed. P. Marshall, Boulder, Colorado, 1949); *Casa del placer* (1620; ed. E. B. Place in University of Colorado Studies, 1949), which is the first true Spanish imitation of Boccaccio's *Decamerone*, a collection of stories, with plays and poetry; *La escuela de Celestina y el hidalgo presumido* (1620); the splendid picaresque tale *El subtil cordovés Pedro de Urdemalas* (1620); *El sagaz Estancio, marido examinado* (1620), a dramatic novel in the genre of the *Celestina* and Lope de Vega's *Dorotea*, with witty caricatures of figures such as the doctor and the miser; the prose fable *La peregrinación sabia* (1621), edited with *El sagaz Estancio* by F. A. de Icaza in Clásicos Castellanos (1924); *La sabia Flora Malsabadilla* (1621); the comic novel *El necio bien afortunado* (1621) and *El cortesano descortés* (1621), edited together in the Sociedad de Bibliófilos Españoles, vol. 31 (1891); *Las fiestas de la boda de la incasable mal casada* (1622), a satire on the pert young misses about Madrid in Salas's day; *Don Diego de Noche* (1623), a masterpiece of nine nocturnal adventures; and the works of his increasing deafness: *La estafeta del Dios Momo* (1627), 64 satirical epistles; *El curioso y sabio Alexandro, Fiscal, y Iuez de vidas agenas* (1634; reprinted in vol. 33 (1854) of the BAE); and *Coronas del Parnaso, y platos de las Musas* (1635).

The only other accessible works by Salas Barbadillo are the 3-act play *Comedia famosa titulada galán tramposo y pobre*, a moral satire in the manner of Mira de Amescua (q.v.) reprinted in vol. 45 (1858) of the BAE, and 'Textos dispersos' edited by J. Simón Díaz, in the *Revista de Literatura*, vol. 32 (1968), pp. 153–67.

A complete edition of the work of this engaging satirist is still awaited, to restore him to the high reputation he justly enjoyed during his lifetime.

See M. A. Peyton, *Alonso Jerónimo de Salas Barbadillo* (New York, 1973) in Twayne's World Authors series; and L. Brownstein, *Salas Barbadillo and the new novel of rogues and courtiers* (1974).

SALAVERRI, VICENTE A. (1887–). Though born in Spain, Salaverri is a naturalized Uruguayan. He started as a modernist, then turned to novels of city life, and finally to novels of country life. His peasants are neither poetic nor heroic, but generally realistic. Salaverri's short stories are collected in *La vida humilde* (1912), *La locura del fauno* (1921), *Cuentos del Río de la Plata* (1921), and *El manantial* (1927). Among his novels are *El corazón de María* (1919), *La mujer inmolada* (1920), *El hijo del león* (1922), *Deformarse es vivir* (1924), and *Este era un país* (1927).

SALAVERRÍA, JOSÉ MARÍA (1873–1940), b. Vinaroz, Castellón de la Plana. Essayist. His *Vieja España* (1907) raised hopes of a penetrating analysis of Spanish woes in subsequent books, with suggested solutions for reform. Instead, Salaverría abandoned his stance reminiscent of the Generation of 1898 and gradually assumed a position on the far right, defending all things Spanish, whether good or bad, in books such as *Las sombras de Loyola* (1911), *A lo lejos: España vista desde América* (1914), *La afirmación española* (1917), *Alma vasca* (1920), *Santa Teresa de Jesús* (1921), *Los paladines iluminados* (1925), and *Sevilla y el andalucismo* (1929).

His novels, plays, and travel books are mediocre.

SALAVERRY, CARLOS AUGUSTO (1830–91), b. Piura. Self-taught Peruvian Romantic poet and playwright, he belonged to the Bohemia literary group. His plays were described by J. de la Riva Agüero as 'lamentables equivocaciones', but he was considered the most outstanding of Peru's lyrical poets of his period, though displaying the usual Romantic defects of monotony and over-abundance.

Among his collections of poetry were *Diamantes y perlas* (1869), a title wryly described as 'scarcely modest' by Menéndez y Pelayo;

Albores y destellos (1871; 2nd edn., 1958), which adds *Cartas a un ángel* to his earlier collection; and *Misterios de la tumba* (1883), a philosophical poem. *Poesía* (1958) is a recent collection of his best work.

See Alberto Ureta, *Carlos Augusto Salaverry* (1918).

SALAZAR, AMBROSIO DE (1575?–after 1640), b. Murcia. Grammarian and man of letters. Teacher of Spanish and interpreter to King Henri IV and tutor to the Dauphin, later Louis XIII; he spent some time away from the court and Paris, teaching Spanish in Rouen, but returned to the capital in 1615 as secretary to Queen Anne of Austria.

His industry as anthologist produced *Almoneda general de las más curiosas recopilaciones de los reinos de España* (Paris, 1612), *Espejo general de la gramática en diálogos*, and the miscellany drawing on Santa Cruz's *Floresta* which Salazar called *Las clavellinas de recreación* (both Rouen, 1614), *Flores diversas y curiosas* (Paris, 1620), *Thesoro de diversa lición* (Paris, 1636), based on Mejía's *Silva*, and many more.

See A. Morel-Fatio's *Ambrosio de Salazar et l'étude de l'espagnol en France sous Louis XIII* (Paris, 1901).

SALAZAR ARRUÉ, SALVADOR (1899–), b. Sonsonate, El Salvador. Better known by his pseudonym Salarrué. A poet, novelist, and painter, he studied at the Corcoran School of Art, Washington, D.C. (1917–19), and belongs with Ambrogi and Rivas Bonilla (qq.v.) to the so-called Generation of 1920. He writes of the common people, and the countryside of Cuzcatlán in his short stories *Cuentos de barro* (1934), much more subtly than most contemporaries. His many books include the legend *El Cristo negro* and the regional novel *El señor de la burbuja* (both 1927), the short stories *Eso y más* (1940), *Trasmallo* (1954), and *La espada y otras narraciones* (1960).

SALAZAR BONDY, SEBASTIÁN (1924–64), b. Lima. Peruvian poet, playwright, essayist, critic, and short-story writer, of French and Jewish-Czech ancestry. He lived for some time in Buenos Aires, contributing to *La Nación*.

His plays include *Pantomimas* (1950), *Rodil* (1953), *No hay isla feliz* (1954), *Un cierto tic-tac* (1956), and *Seis juguetes* (1958).

He became notorious for his bitter attack *Lima, la Horrible* (Mexico City, 1964), portraying the grand, colonial city of baroque monuments as a hideous monster of grubby shanty towns and pockmarked hills. But he is remembered most for his poetry: *Voz desde la vigilia* (1944),

Cuaderno de la persona oscura (1946), *Máscara del que duerme* (1949), *Los ojos del pródigo* (1951), *Vida de Ximena* (1960), and *Confidencias en alta voz* (1960). L. Loayza's selection of Salazar Bondy's poetry in the Colección Ocnos is entitled *Sombras como cosas sólidas y otros poemas* (Barcelona, 1974).

SALAZAR DE ALARCÓN, EUGENIO DE (1530?–1612?), b. Madrid. Poet and letter-writer. An *oidor* (judge) in Mexico, Santo Domingo (now the Dominican Republic), and Guatemala, he was appointed minister to the Council of the Indies in 1601.

An Erasmian satirist in surviving letters reprinted in vol. 176 (1964) of the BAE, he also wrote some melodious songs now in vol. 42 (1857) of the same series: 'Canto del cisne' and the *canción* beginning '¡Varias y lindas flores…!'.

SALAZAR Y TORRES, AGUSTÍN DE (1642–75), b. Almazán, Soria. Dramatist and poet. Having won a prize in boyhood for declaiming and expounding Góngora's *Soledades* at a Jesuit college in Mexico, Salazar remained under Góngora's influence throughout his short literary career, especially in the servile imitation *Soledad*. His best poetry is found in *Las estaciones del día*, in *Cythara de Apolo, varias poesías divinas y humanas que escribió don Agustín de Salazar y Torres* (2 vols., 1681–94, of which the second contains his plays). Some of his poetry has been reprinted in vol. 42 of the BAE, and vol. 49 in the same series reprints the plays *Elegir al enemigo* and *El encanto es la hermosura*, finished on his deathbed, on the Celestina theme. Among his other plays are *Sin armas vence el amor*, *Thetis y Peleo*, *Los juegos olímpicos*, and *El mérito es la corona, y encantos de amor*, many others appearing in vols. 22, 38, and 41 of Comedias Escogidas de los Mejores Autores.

SALCEDO CORONEL, JOSÉ GARCÍA DE (1592?–1651), b. Seville. Poet, and defender of Góngora, who studied in Seville and Alcalá, and travelled to Italy as captain of the guard of the Duke of Alcalá, Viceroy of Naples and Governor of Capua.

His own verse was printed in *Rimas. Primera parte* (1624), *Ariadna* (1624) a poem in octaves, and *Cristales de Helicona, o Segunda parte de las Rimas* (1642), but he was perhaps more significant to Spanish literary history for his annotated, laudatory *Obras de don Luis de Góngora, comentadas* (1635–8).

SALINAS, FRANCISCO (1530–90), blind professor of music and organist at Salamanca University, immortalized by Fray Luis de Leon (q.v.)

in the neo-Platonic 'Oda a Salinas' (*c.* 1570), which opens:

> *El aire se serena*
> *y viste de hermosura y luz no usada,*
> *Salinas, cuando suena*
> *la música extremada*
> *por vuestra sabia mano gobernada …*

('The air becomes serene, and puts on beauty and unearthly light, Salinas, when your skilful hands draw out that ineffable music …').

Salinas was a dozen years senior to Fray Luis and one of his closest friends. E. Allison Peers has called the ode 'the greatest poem ever written in Spanish on music' and denies any symbolical content.

Salinas' *De musica libri septem* (1577) was considered the best treatise on music then available in Spain.

SALINAS, PEDRO (1891–1951), b. Madrid. Poet, playwright, and critic who spent his childhood and adolescence in the Spanish capital. He was *lecteur* at the Sorbonne 1914–17, and professor at Seville University 1918–28, when he was transferred to the national tourist office in Madrid. He ran successful residential language courses for foreigners there until 1933, when he created the Universidad Internacional Menéndez y Pelayo of Santander, where he worked until the outbreak of the Civil War in 1936.

Like so many of his contemporaries, he left Spain after the War never to return, and his later poetry is seen by most critics as a cry of disillusionment and nostalgia. He was the eldest member of the generation which included García Lorca, Cernuda, Prados, Alberti, Aleixandre, Dámaso Alonso, and Altolaguirre (qq.v.). He defined poetry as 'una aventura hacia lo absoluto', but he was never close to the 'pure poetry' advocated by Jiménez and at least in his earlier, more optimistic works showed a zest for technological inventions, unlike his good friend Jorge Guillén (q.v.).

His poetry falls into three periods. The first contrasts appearance and reality: *Presagios* (1923), *Seguro azar* (1929), and *Fábula y signo* (1931). The second period sees his major accomplishment: the distinguished love poetry of *La voz a ti debida* (trans. by W. Barnstone, Albany, N.Y., 1976) as *My voice because of you*); *Razón de amor* (1936); and the still incompletely-published *Largo lamento*. The third period condemns industrial society in the disillusionment of long and bitter exile: *El contemplado* (1946), *Todo más claro* (1949), and the posthumously-published *Confianza* (1954).

Poesías completas (1955), prepared by Juan Marichal, has now been superseded by Soledad

Salinas de Marichal's new edition (Barcelona, 1971), which incorporates *Volverse sombra y otros poemas* (1957).

His plays were overshadowed by the excellence of his poetry, but there is a collected *Teatro completo* (1957), of which the most interesting item is *Caín, o una gloria científica*, haunted like much of his later poetry by dread of the atomic bomb.

Salinas produced much important criticism, including *Reality and the poet in Spanish poetry* (Baltimore, 1940; reissued with a lecture on Salinas by Jorge Guillén, 1966); *Literatura española: siglo XX* (1941; enlarged edn., Mexico City, 1949); *Jorge Manrique, o tradición y originalidad* (Buenos Aires, 1947); and *La poesía de Rubén Darío* (Buenos Aires, 1948).

See Carlos Feal Deibe, *La poesía de Pedro Salinas* (1965); Alma de Zubizarreta, *Pedro Salinas: el diálogo creador* (1969); O. Costa Viva, *Pedro Salinas frente a la realidad* (1969); the special Salinas issue of *Ínsula* (Madrid, November–December, 1971); J. Crispin, *Pedro Salinas* (New York, 1974) in Twayne's World Authors series; and A. P. Debicki (ed.), *Pedro Salinas* (1976) in the Colección El Escritor y la Crítica.

SALINAS DE CASTRO, JUAN DE (1562?–1643), b. Seville. Poet. He studied at Logroño and Salamanca, travelled in Italy, and was appointed to a canonry in Segovia. Inheriting great wealth from his father, he devoted much of his time and money to the Hospital of St. Cosimus and St. Damian in Seville. His poetry began in the Renaissance style, with echoes of Italian and classical writers, but on his return to Spain he came under the influence of *culteranismo*, though he is not a mere imitator of Góngora. His poetry avoids the heroic and patriotic, even dismissing romantic passion in favour of a comfortable, worldly life.

His works were collected and published between 1647 and 1650 by José Maldonado Dávila de Saavedra. Some of Salinas' poetry appears in vols. 32 and 42 (1854–7) of the BAE, but the most complete edition of the *Poesías* is that published by the Sociedad de Bibliófilos Andaluces (Seville, 1869).

See Henry Bonneville, *Le poète sevillan Juan de Salinas, 1562?–1643: vie et œuvre* (Paris, 1969).

SALISACHS, MERCEDES (1916–), b. Barcelona. Novelist. Of a wealthy family, she was educated successively in a convent and at a commercial school. She is widely travelled, and is married to a Barcelona industrialist.

Her first novel, *Primera mañana, última mañana* (1955; 2nd edn., 1968) was published under the pen-name 'María Ecín'. Among her subsequent works are *Carrera intermedia* (1956), *Una mujer llega al pueblo* (1957), *Más allá de los raíles* (1957), *Adán helicóptero* (1957), *Pasos conocidos* (1957), *Vendimia interrumpida* (1960), *La estación de las hojas amarillas* (1963), *El declive y la cuesta* (1966), *La última aventura* (1967), *Adagio confidencial* (1973), and *La gangrena* (1975).

In the view of J. L. Alborg, 'Salisachs has given clear evidence that she is an intellectual woman of an intelligence better endowed for abstraction than for the concrete, equipped more with ironic and satirical powers than with love for the ordinary, alert more to ridicule than to the portrayal of sentiment'.

SALITRILLO, SEBASTIÁN, pseudonym of Alberto Rivas Bonilla (q.v.).

SALOM, JAIME (1925–), b. Barcelona. Playwright. By profession a doctor, Salom has made a great success with a number of plays, including *El mensaje* (Bilbao, 1955), *El triángulo blanco* (Barcelona, 1960), *Verde esmeralda* (1960), *Culpables* (1961), *La gran aventura* (1961), *Juegos de invierno* (1964), *El baúl de los disfraces* (1964) on the relentless passage of time, *Falta de pruebas* (Barcelona, 1964), *Motor en marcha* (Barcelona, 1964), *Espejo para dos mujeres* (1965), *Parchis-Party* (1965), *La casa de las chivas* (Barcelona, 1968), *Los Delfines* (1969), and *Nueve brindis por un rey* (1975).

See A. Marquerie, *Ensayo crítico del teatro de Jaime Salom* (1973).

Salomón, rey de Israel, Proverbios en rimo del Sabio, a 14th-c. poem in 56 irregular stanzas of *cuaderna vía* (q.v.) discovered by Rafael de Floranes (q.v.) and first published by Paz y Melia in *Opúsculos literarios de los siglos XIV a XVI* (1892). Essentially a résumé of the Book of Ecclesiastes (whose attribution to Solomon is responsible for the poem's Spanish title), the poem also draws on other books of the Bible. The 'author' is stated to have been Pero Gómez, who may however have been merely the copyist. Some scholars have indicated that the poet may have been attacking the decadent Castilian society of the 14th-c. through these aphorisms and moral epigrams, which offer in their fragmented style no coherent comment on the troubled times and the lot of the common people.

The *Proverbios del sabio Salomón* influenced both Juan Ruiz (q.v.), Arcipreste de Hita, and Rodrigo Yáñez, author or copyist of the *Poema de Alfonso XI* (see ALFONSO XI, Poema de).

SALUCIO or SALUZIO DEL POYO, DAMIÁN (*c.* 1550–1614), b. Murcia. Playwright of the school of Lope de Vega (q.v.).

His plays were published in *Tercera parte de las comedias de Lope de Vega y otros autores* (Valencia,

1611) and *Flor de las comedias de España: quinta parte* (1615).

One of them was on a religious theme: *La vida y muerte de Judas*, and several on historical themes: *La privanza y caída de don Álvaro de Luna*, *La próspera fortuna* . . . and *La adversa fortuna de Ruy López de Ávalos el Bueno* (both published in vol. 43 (1857) of the BAE).

See Justo García Soriano, 'Damián Salucio del Poyo' in *BRAE* (1926).

SALVADOR, HUMBERTO (1909–), b. Guayaquil. Ecuadorian novelist and short-story writer who narrates urban problems of Quito in both literal and psychoanalytic terms. A prolific writer, he also edited *La Semana*, organ of La Casa de la Cultura Ecuatoriana. After the short stories in *Ajedrez* (1929), he wrote a novel, *En la ciudad he perdido una novela* (1930) influenced by Pirandello and Proust, and another collection of short stories *Taza de té* (1932). The novel *Camarada* (1933) depicted the working classes. Unlike Icaza or Aguilera Malta, Salvador is not content to let the action speak for itself, but comments and moralizes openly at intervals; he deals in social stereotypes rather than in personalities, so that books like *Trabajadores* (1935) have understandably reached a wide public in Russian. He has also written *Los fundamentos del psicoanálisis* (1947) and compiled the useful two-volume *Antología de la moderna poesía ecuatoriana* (1949?).

SALVADOR, TOMÁS (1921–), b. Villada, Palencia. Novelist. His first novels, *Garimpo* (1952) and *La virada* (1954), were written with José Vergés. Later novels include *Hotel Tánger* (1955), *Diálogos en la oscuridad* (1956), *Lluvia caliente* (1958), *El agitador* (1960), and *El atentado* (1960), all published in Barcelona.

His books are on delinquency, crime, and adventure, but there are no elements of puzzle or detection.

SALVAT-PAPASSEIT, JOAN (1894–1924), b. Barcelona. Catalan poet. Self-taught, Salvat earned a living by manual labour, then entered radical journalism *c.* 1914, writing on social injustice in *Los Miserables* and *Justicia*, the articles collected in *Humo de fábrica* (1918), using the pen-name 'Gorkiano' after Maxim Gorky. In 1917 he edited an ephemeral 'hoja de subversión social' (to use his own phrase) entitled *Un Enemic del Poble*.

His poetry is very different from his prose, often ironic and playful as in the poem 'Bodegó', and often romantic. His collections were *Poemes en ondes hertzianes* (1919), *L'irradiador del port i les gavines* (1921), *Les conspiracions* (1922), *La gesta estels* (1922), *El poema de la rosa als llavis* (1923),

the posthumous *Óssa menor* (1925), and the collected *Poesies* (1962).

SAMANIEGO, FÉLIX MARÍA (1745–1801), b. La Guardia. Fabulist. Early in life a friend of Iriarte, Samaniego later became his enemy, writing the anonymous and undated *Observaciones sobre las 'Fábulas literarias'* against Iriarte, and satirizing Iriarte's *La música* in *Coplas para tocarse al violín*.

For his *Fábulas en verso castellano* (2 vols., 1781–4), Samaniego's preferred models were Phaedrus, Gay, and La Fontaine, and he was influenced by Voltaire, and by *encyclopédiste* ideals in general. His other works have appeared in *Obras inéditas o poco conocidas* (Vitoria, 1866) and *Obras críticas* (ed. J. Apraiz, Bilbao, 1898).

There is a modern edition of the *Fábulas* by Ernesto Jareño (1969). Quintana's judgement was that 'Iriarte cuenta bien, pero Samaniego pinta; el uno es ingenioso y discreto, el otro, gracioso y natural'.

SAMAYOA CHINCHILLA, CARLOS (1898–), b. Guatemala City. Short-story writer, essayist, and historian, who is best-known for his collections of Guatemalan folk tales and legends. The first was *Madre Milpa* (1934), followed by *Cuatro Suertes* (1936), and *La casa de la muerte* (1941). Harriet de Onís has translated *Madre Milpa* and other stories in an anthology entitled *The emerald lizard* (Indian Hills, Colorado, 1957). Samayoa Chinchilla has been Director of the Guatemalan National Library and of the Institute of Anthropology and History.

SAMPER, JOSÉ MARÍA (1828–88), Colombian poet, novelist, and biographer. The husband of Soledad Acosta de Samper (q.v.), a better novelist than he was. Among Samper's more familiar pseudonyms are 'Plutarco', 'P. S. Kornicoff', and the near-anagram 'Jeremías Páramo'.

A passable versifier in *Flores marchitas* (1849), *Ecos de los Andes* (1860), and *Últimos cantares* (1864), Samper belonged to the Mosaico group of J. M. Vergara, E. Díaz Castro, and others. His novels included *Martín Flórez* (1866), *El poeta soldado* (1881), and *Los claveles de Jula* (1881). His biographies of Colombian notables were collected in *Galería nacional de hombres ilustres y notables*, vol. 1 (1879). A selection of his numerous articles was published in his lifetime as *Miscelánea o colección de artículos escogidos* . . . (Paris, 1869) and another more recently as *Selección de estudios* (1953).

SAMPER ORTEGA, DANIEL (1895–1943), Colombian essayist and novelist. He compiled many anthologies of poetry, oratory, and fiction.

His novels grew in stature with experience: *Entre la niebla* and *La marquesa de Alfandoque* (both 1923), *La obsesión* (1926), and finally *Zoraya* (1931), based on the amours and repentance of José Solís, 18th-c. Viceroy of Nueva Granada, and judged by Gómez Restrepo to be very nearly the Colombian equivalent of Argentina's *La gloria de Don Ramiro* by Larreta (qq.v.).

Samper Ortega wrote a good many essays, some collected in *Al galope* (1930) and *Escritos* (1936), and *Colombia: breve reseña de su movimiento artístico e intelectual* (Madrid, 1929).

SÁNCHEZ, FLORENCIO (1875–1910), b. Montevideo. The major Uruguayan playwright. A self-taught Creole of poor parents, he joined the anarchist movement after the Revolution of 1897, becoming a director of the International Centre of Social Studies, an anarchist group. He wrote many of his plays in Buenos Aires, where they were performed. He knew Ibsen, D'Annunzio, and other playwrights of his generation, and knew also how to set naturalistic theatre in the Argentina and Uruguay of his time, appealing to popular audiences yet never writing down to them. Sánchez also wrote *El conventillo* and *El cacique Pichuleo*, zarzuelas with music by Francisco Payá.

His first works were *Puertas adentro* and *Ladrones*, but his first plays to be performed (both 1902) were the *sainete La gente honesta* and the one-act *Canillita*, a reworking of *Ladrones*. His best work was written from 1903 to 1907, beginning with *M'hijo el dotor* (1903), contrasting the ideals and morals of a conservative old *gaucho* with his radical city-educated son, and *Barranca abajo* (1905), in which Don Zoilo loses his lands and is attacked by his wife, his sister, and his daughter Prudence, defended only by his ironically named daughter Robustiana, who dies during the course of the play of tuberculosis, the disease which killed Sánchez himself.

Plays first produced in 1904 were the one-act *Cédulas de San Juan*, the two-act *La pobre gente*, and the three-act *La gringa*, possibly his most celebrated play, which shows how the easy-going *gaucho* Cantalicio loses his farm to the hard-working Italian immigrants, but saves his livelihood through marrying his son to an Italian girl, the *gringa* of the title.

After these rural plays, Sánchez set his 1905 productions in the city. These are *Los muertos* and *En familia*, the first a tragic masterpiece and the second a dramatic comedy.

In 1906 the one-act *El desalojo* and the city drama *El pasado* were first performed, and in 1907 the one-act *La tigra*, the city comedy *Nuestros hijos*, and the city drama *Los derechos de la salud*. Though the last two are generally considered thesis plays, Sánchez's most remark-able quality is his impartiality, understanding the impatience and vision of youth as clearly as the routine and acceptance of the aged. His anatomy of the *gaucho* is accurate and sympathetic but by no means biased. His social observation is intuitive. He uses problems of money and property to characterize attitudes to greed and laziness rather than for the mere sake of the story. Sánchez is a democratic dramatist and excels in depicting social problems and creating theatrical tension and characterization. While all of his types are authentically of the Río de la Plata, they are also universal. His work has been collected in *Obras completas* (2 vols., Buenos Aires, 1968). Walter Rela has compiled a bibliographical guide, *Florencio Sánchez* (1967).

See R. F. Giusti, *Florencio Sánchez, su vida y su obra* (1920); Wilfredo Jiménez, *Pasión de Florencio Sánchez* (Buenos Aires, 1955); Jorge Cruz, *Genio y figura de Florencio Sánchez* (Buenos Aires, 1966); and Tabaré J. Freire, *Florencio Sánchez, artesano del sainete* (Porto Alegre, 1966).

SÁNCHEZ, FRANCISCO (1552–1632), b. Túy. Spanish sceptical philosopher. The son of a Jewish doctor, he qualified as a doctor himself, practising first in Montpellier, then in Rome, and finally teaching medicine in Toulouse. Apart from numerous medical books, commentaries on Aristotle, and the Latin poem *Carmen de cometa*, he wrote the important *Tractatus de multum nobili et prima universali scientia, quod nihil scitur* (Lyons, 1581), translated by M. Menéndez y Pelayo as *Que nada se sabe* (1923?). He attacks the syllogism, and questions any received dogma that cannot be tested by the senses. Before Descartes he found that the act of thinking creates more rather than fewer doubts: 'quo magis cogito, magis dubito'. His scepticism reflects the notion of *que sais-je?* expressed by his contemporary, Montaigne.

SÁNCHEZ, FRANCISCO, called 'el Brocense', see SÁNCHEZ DE LAS BROZAS, FRANCISCO.

SÁNCHEZ, GUILLERMO (1924–), b. Bocas del Toro, Panama. Poet and novelist writing under the pen-name 'Tristán Solarte'. His poetry in *Voces y paisajes de vida y muerte* (1950) and *Evocaciones* (1955) has been influenced by classical and North American models. His novel *El ahogado* appeared in 1957.

SÁNCHEZ, LUIS ALBERTO (1900–). b. Lima. Peruvian critic and literary historian, who taught literature at the Universidad de San Marcos before being appointed deputy director of the National Library (1928–31), when he was Deputy in Parliament for Lima province. He was active in the Peruvian Aprista Party and has suffered several terms of exile, mainly in other Latin American countries and the U.S.A., for his political beliefs.

His literary histories include *Los poetas de la Revolución* (1919), *Los poetas de la Colonia* (1921), *La literatura peruana* (3 vols., 1928–36; 6 vols., 1950–1; 5 vols., 1966), *Panorama de la literatura actual* (1934; 2nd edn., 1936), *Índice de la poesía peruana contemporánea* (1938), *La literatura del Perú* (1939), and *Proceso y contenido de la novela hispano-americana* (Madrid, 1953; 2nd edn., Madrid, 1968). Sánchez has edited the *Obras completas* (Mexico City, 1954) of José Santos Chocano (q.v.) and written *Aladino* (Mexico City, 1960) on Santos Chocano.

See Vidal Galindo Vera, *Contribución a la bibliografía de Luis Alberto Sánchez* (1963).

SÁNCHEZ, MIGUEL (*c.* 1545–after 1615), b. Valladolid. Poet and playwright. Secretary for some time to the Bishop of Osma and Plasencia. He was known as 'el Divino' for his exquisite religious poetry, but he also wrote some memorable ballads, especially that beginning 'Oíd, señor don Gaiferos', in vol. 10 (1849) of the BAE.

Sánchez has been suggested as the author of the great anonymous but probably contemporary sonnet 'A Cristo crucificado' (q.v.) once attributed with less likelihood to Fray Luis de León (q.v.).

His two surviving plays are remarkably uninventive and leaden by comparison with his verse. *La guarda cuidadosa* is in vol. 43 (1857) of the BAE; a better edition by H. A. Rennert, with Sánchez's *La isla bárbara*, appeared in Boston, Mass., in 1896.

SÁNCHEZ, NÉSTOR (1935–), Argentinian novelist. Influenced by Cortázar's *Rayuela*, his *Nosotros dos* (1966) tells the story of an adolescent boy who becomes involved with prostitutes and a literary anarchist in a vain and ironic search for respectability. *Siberia Blues* (1967) is set in a sleazy bar which is visited by many city types, with the central character again a semi-autobiographical figure. Cela's *La colmena* seems to be an influence here. In *El amor, los Orsinis y la muerte* (1969) the feeling of chaos in Sánchez's earlier fiction is intensified.

SÁNCHEZ, TOMÁS ANTONIO (1723–1802), b. Ruiseñada, Santander. Editor, scholar, polemicist, and pioneering archaeologist.

His greatest importance in the field of Spanish literature lay in his publishing, for the educated public of his day, the *Cantar de mío Cid* (1779), works by Gonzalo de Berceo (1780), the *Poema de Alexandre* (1782), and the works of the Arch-

priest of Hita (1790) in the Colección de Poesías Castellanas Anteriores al Siglo XV. These editions are superseded now, but were of great significance when first issued. Sánchez, one-time Director of the Royal Library (which was to become the National Library) in Madrid, also collaborated with J. A. Pellicer and Rafael Casalbón in a new edition of Nicolás Antonio's *Bibliotheca Hispana Nova* (1788).

He mocked Forner (q.v.) in *Carta de Paracuellos* (1789) and (after Forner's own reply) again in *Defensa de don Fernando Pérez* (1790).

SÁNCHEZ BARBERO, FRANCISCO (1764–1819), b. Moriñigo, Salamanca. Poet and scholar. He soon abandoned his religious studies, preferring the secular poetry of the School of Salamanca, and becoming a member of the circle which included Meléndez Valdés, Jovellanos, and Forner.

As a journalist in 1813 he founded *El Constitucional* in Madrid and came into conflict with the absolutist regime of Ferdinand VII, who confined him first for 19 months, during which Sánchez completed a new Latin grammar, and later gave him a sentence of 10 years, during which he died.

Principios de retórica y poética (1805) departs from the ideas of Luzán (q.v.) in declaring individual passions and imaginations to be the sources of true eloquence, and in preferring Filangieri's ideas to those of the French neoclassical preceptists favoured by Luzán. His *Saúl: melodrama sacro* was inspired by Vittorio Alfieri and his tragedy *Coriolano* by Shakespeare's play.

The posthumously-published *Ensayos satíricos en verso y prosa por el Licenciado Machuca* (1820) included Sánchez's satire on the Inquisition in the form of a parody of Garcilaso: 'La muerte de la Inquisición: Égloga sepulcral. Flanesio y Rancinoso'.

See A. Gil Sanz, 'Don Francisco Sánchez Barbero' in *Semanario Pintoresco Español* (1851), pp. 82–84 and 89–91.

SÁNCHEZ DE ARÉVALO, RUY or **RODRIGO** (1404–70), b. Arévalo. Teacher and political writer. An absentee bishop and governor of Rome's Castel Sant' Angelo under Pope Paul II. In his historical works, such as the *Compendiosa historia hispánica*, he imitated Alfonso de Cartagena. He addressed his monarch in the *Vergel de los príncipes*, 'en que fabla de honestos deportes e virtuosos exercicios en que los ínclitos reyes se deuen exercitar', these occupations consisting of arms, hunting, and music; it was published in vol. 116 (1959) of the BAE and edited by F. R. de Uhagón (1900).

His *Speculum vitae humanae* (Rome, 1468) was

translated as *Espejo de la vida humana* (Saragossa, 1491). His important work on political theory was *Suma de la política*, edited by J. Beneyto (1944).

See T. Toni, 'Don Rodrigo Sánchez de Arévalo, 1405 [*sic*]–1470' in *Anuario de Historia del Derecho Español*, vol. 12 (1935), pp. 97–360; R. H. Trame, *Ruy Sánchez de Arévalo, 1404–1470, Spanish diplomat and champion of the Papacy*, Washington, 1958); and Juan María Laboa, *Rodrigo Sánchez de Arévalo* ... (1973).

SÁNCHEZ DE BADAJOZ, DIEGO (*fl.* 1525–49), b. Extremadura. Curate at Talavera, Badajoz. Important playwright who took the drama of Vicente, Encina, and Fernández much further by making the theological argument more complex, the use of allegory more consistent, and by introducing more characters. He cleverly combines social satire, comedy, and morality. The *Recopilación en metro* (Seville, 1554) includes 28 plays. There was a facsimile reprint by the Real Academia Española (1929), followed by very poor editions by V. Barrantes (2 vols., 1882–6), and an excellent edition by Frida Weber de Kurlat (Buenos Aires, 1968). Most of Sánchez's plays, written for church performance, deal with the Nativity, the Eucharist, and the Incarnation. His modifications of the pastoral eclogue mark the late prehistory of the *auto sacramental*, and some of his themes are equally as interesting as his technique, for example the equality of 'old' and 'new' (or converted) Christians in the *Farsa de Isaac*.

See also Gladstone R. Fluegge, *Four 'farsas' by Diego Sánchez de Badajoz* (Toronto, 1953).

SÁNCHEZ DE BADAJOZ, GARCI (1460?–1526?), b. Écija. Poet of great fame and reputation, as Lope de Vega indicated in his prologue to *Isidro* (1599): '¿Qué cosa se iguala a una redondilla de Garcí Sanchez, o de don Diego de Mendoza?'. Sánchez was also praised as a master of style by Juan de Valdés (q.v.) in his *Diálogo de la lengua*.

The best of his 'paradoxical and tormented poems', to cite A. D. Deyermond, is 'Enderezada a su amiga recontando un sueño que soñó', published in the *Cancionero general* (1511). Reputedly chained down due to a madness induced by love, Sánchez apparently died insane. Technically highly accomplished, he mastered Dante's metre in the *Infierno de amor* and the metre of Manrique's *Coplas* for the 'Lamentaciones de amores' which was never published in the *Cancionero general* (even in later editions) but can be found in Usoz's *Cancionero de obras de burlas provocantes a risa* (n.d., but 1841).

See J. Martín Jiménez, *Cancionero de Garci Sánchez de Badajoz* (Seville, 1948), which includes

a biography; and P. Gallagher, *The life and works of Garci Sánchez de Badajoz* (London, 1968).

SÁNCHEZ DE CEPEDA Y AHUMADA, TERESA, the secular name of Santa Teresa de Ávila or Jesús (q.v.).

SÁNCHEZ DE LAS BROZAS, FRANCISCO (1523–1601), b. Las Brozas, Cáceres, hence his common epithet 'el Brocense'. The major humanist of his time, and successor to Nebrija (q.v.) at Salamanca University. His *Verae brevesque grammaticae latinae institutiones* (1562) improved on Nebrija's methods of teaching Latin, and he later wrote a grammar in verse, the *Arte para saber latín* (1595), as well as translations of Ovid (*Ibis*, 1546), Virgil (*Eclogues*, 1591), and Persius. *Minerva, o de la propiedad de la lengua latina* has been translated into Castilian by F. Riveras Cárdenas (1976). He also wrote original poetry in Latin. His *Grammatica graecae compendium* appeared in 1581. Menéndez y Pelayo described el Brocense as 'padre de la gramática general y de la filosofía del lenguaje'.

His major philosophical works are the *Paradoxa* and the commentary *Doctrina de Epicteto* (Salamanca, 1600); his rhetorical works include *De arte dicendi* (1556) and the *Organum dialecticum et rhetoricum cunctis discipulis utilissimum et necessarium* (Lyons, 1579); while his scientific writings include the *Declaración y uso del reloj español* (Salamanca, 1549), *Pomponii Melae de situ orbis* (1574), and the *Sphera mundi* (1579).

A friend of Luis de León (q.v.), el Brocense took a great deal of interest in Spanish poetry, commenting on the *Obras* (Salamanca, 1582) of Juan de Mena, and indicating sources and models in his edition *Obras del excelente poeta Garci-Lasso de la Vega* (Salamanca, 1574). The Castilian friends of Sánchez de las Brozas felt aggrieved when the Sevillian Fernando de Herrera ('el divino') did not even mention the earlier edition in his own lengthy commentary on Garcilaso (1580). In a bitter controversy, Juan Fernández de Velasco, Conde de Haro (writing as the 'Licenciado Prete Jacopín') ridiculed Herrera's pedantry, illogicality, and irrelevance. The quarrel is documented in J. M. Asensio's edition of Herrera's *Poesías inéditas* (Seville, 1870).

El Brocense was indicted by the Inquisition on charges of suggesting that errors were to be found in translations of the Bible and of attacking the excessive idolatry of sacred images. He was confined to the house of his son Lorenzo while the case was being heard, but died before the verdict was given.

See Antonio Tovar and M. de la Pinta Llorente, *Procesos inquisitoriales contra Francisco*

Sánchez de las Brozas (1942); Gregorio Mayáns y Síscar's edition of el Brocense's *Opera omnia una cum eiusdem scriptoris vita* (4 vols., 1776); P. U. González de la Calle, *Francisco Sánchez de las Brozas: su vida profesional y académica* (1912); and Aubrey Bell, *Francisco Sánchez el Brocense* (Oxford, 1924).

El Brocense is not to be confused with the sceptical philosopher Francisco Sánchez (q.v., 1552–1632).

SÁNCHEZ DE TALAVERA, Ferrant (d. after 1443), poet of the *Cancionero de Baena* whose name also occurs as 'Calavera'. He was apparently in favour for some time at the court of Enrique III, but then fell into disgrace or was disappointed in some hope, and thereafter attacked the court for unfulfilled promises never exactly specified.

He conducted a celebrated argument with the Canciller Ayala on free will, writing 'Y desta quistión se podía seguir / una conclusión bien fea atal: / que Dios es causa e ocasión de mal' ('and from this argument an ugly conclusion might well be drawn: that God is the cause and occasion of Evil').

His sceptical, pessimistic *dezyres* have a strangely modern ring; the best are *Vanas maneras del mundo* and *A la muerte del Almirante Ruy Díaz de Mendoza*, of which the latter is a moving variation on the medieval topos of earthly vanities, and important as an immediate antecedent of Jorge Manrique's *Coplas*.

SÁNCHEZ FERLOSIO, Rafael (1927–), b. Rome. Novelist. His father was the poet and novelist Rafael Sánchez Mazas (q.v.) and his mother Italian. In 1950 he married the novelist Carmen Martín Gaite, who won the Premio Nadal of 1957 for *Entre visillos* (Barcelona, 1958), her account of the life of girls in a provincial city. Sánchez Ferlosio is considered one of the most notable Spanish writers of his time.

Industrias y andanzas de Alfanhuí (1951; annotated edn. by S. C. and A. H. Clarke, London, 1969, with good bibliography), in the author's phrase an 'historia llena de mentiras verdaderas', is a fantasy in which *Alice's adventures in Wonderland* and the *Arabian Nights* are fused. The first chapter, 'concerning a weathercock that hunted lizards and what a child did with them', introduces the boy Alfanhuí, who is later expelled from school for writing in a hitherto unknown alphabet and thereafter meets a puppet who has escaped from a theatre, finds a tree that sprouts flat birds instead of leaves, and enjoys many similar experiences in a rich, poetic book belonging partly to the picaresque tradition of Lazarillo,

and partly to the dream-world of Kenneth Grahame or J. M. Barrie.

El Jarama (Barcelona, 1956) is even more successful. It captures the mood of a summer Sunday during which eleven youngsters from Madrid bathe and picnic by the river Jarama. The day is boring; one couple kiss, and a member of the party is drowned at the end. Sánchez Ferlosio's style is subtly adapted to each mood, the language veering accurately from *madrileño* slang to the author's precise descriptions of nature and the ordinary characters, whose pointless remarks set up in the reader a feeling of vague irritation, as if half-listening to a train conversation about people he does not know. Whereas Moravia's novel on boredom, *La noia*, is knowing and too calculated, *El Jarama* obtains much of its effect from an impression of spontaneity. G. G. Brown has referred to the novel's 'symbolic depths and its subtle recourse to realms of mystery and poetry'. *El Jarama* won the Premio Nadal for 1955 and has been translated by J. M. Cohen as *The one day of the week* (1962).

Subsequently Sánchez Ferlosio has written *Semana primera* and *Semana segunda* (1974) in the cycle *Las semanas del jardín*.

See E. Riley, 'Sobre el arte de Sánchez Ferlosio' in *Filología* (Buenos Aires, 1963), vol. 9, pp. 201–21, on *El Jarama*; and M. Salgado, 'Fantasía y realidad en "Alfanhuí"' in *Papeles de Son Armadans* (Palma, 1965), vol. 39, pp. 140–52.

SÁNCHEZ MAZAS, Rafael (1894–1966), b. Madrid. Novelist and poet. He lived in Italy for some time, and married there. He belonged to the influential Roman Catholic group of *Cruz y Raya* and wrote much journalism. He was appointed a minister in 1939 and a member of the Real Academia Española in 1940. His poetry was issued only in limited editions and is scarce, but he is well known for two widely-separated autobiographical novels on the theme of adolescence evolving into maturity. Their titles are *Pequeñas memorias de Tarín* (Bilbao, 1915) and *La vida nueva de Pedrito de Andía* (1951) and they are possibly more distinguished than the similar autobiographical works of Azorín, Jarnés, Miró, Sender, and Unamuno (q.v.). His son is the novelist Rafael Sánchez Ferlosio (q.v.).

SÁNCHEZ MEJÍAS, Ignacio, see Llanto por la Muerte de Ignacio Sánchez Mejías.

SÁNCHEZ QUELL, Hipólito (1907–), b. Asunción. Paraguayan historian educated for the legal profession, who became a diplomat, minister of state, Director of the National Archive, President of the Supreme Court, and professor of history and sociology at Asunción

University. His books include *Estructura y función del Paraguay colonial* (1944) and *Triángulo de la poesía rioplatense* (Buenos Aires, 1953).

SÁNCHEZ VERCIAL, CLEMENTE (1370?–1426?). Doctrinal writer and compiler, and a canon of León Cathedral. Between 1400 and 1421 he compiled the anonymously-published *Libro de los exenplos*, the best of the medieval genre known as *Alphabeta exemplorum* published incomplete by P. de Gayangos in vol. 51 (1860) of the BAE. A. Morel-Fatio discovered the missing A–B section and published the complete work in *Romania*, vol. 7 (1878), pp. 481–526, a total of 467 tales intended for preachers; it was critically edited by J. E. Keller (1951 [but 1961]). According to A. H. Krappe ('Les sources du "Libro de exemplos"', *Bulletin Hispanique*, vol. 39, 1937, pp. 5–54), Sánchez Vercial translated the *Disciplina clericalis* almost entire, with elements from the *Vitae patrum*, St. Isidore, *Barlaam and Josaphat*, and the *Gesta Romanorum*.

From 1421 to 1425, he compiled *Sacramental*, a devotional work, which was published about 1470 in Seville, according to Vindel the first book printed in Spain. It was translated into Catalan as *Lo sagramental* (Lérida, 1495).

SANCHO JIMÉNEZ, MARIO (1889–1948), b. Cartago, Costa Rica. Essayist, polyglot, and private librarian. According to Abelardo Bonilla, he is the best prose stylist that Costa Rica has so far produced. Among his most notable books are *Viajes y lecturas* (1933), the ironic *Costa Rica, Suiza centroamericana* (1935), and *El pueblo español* (1937).

SANDOVAL, Fray PRUDENCIO DE (1553–1620), b. Valladolid. Benedictine chronicler who became Bishop of Túy in 1608 and in 1612 Bishop of Pamplona. He continued the chronicles of Florián de Ocampo and Ambrosio de Morales, but is useful only for the numerous documents he inserted, for he lacked a critical sense, interspersing legends with established facts, and was unaware of the need to check unsupported assertions by authors, among them Guevara (an unpublished MS.) and Mejía, whom he copied, without acknowledgment.

His most substantial books are *Historia de la vida y hechos del Emperador Carlos V* (2 vols., Valladolid, 1604–6), often reprinted in the 17th c. and most recently in 1847–9 (9 vols.); and *Historia de los Reyes de Castilla y de León* (Pamplona, 1615), usually known as the *Historia de los cinco reyes*, the five rulers in question being Fernando I, Sancho II, Alfonso VI, Doña Urraca, and Alfonso VII.

See Vicente Castañeda, *El cronista Fray Prudencio de Sandoval: nuevas noticias biográficas* (1929).

SANDOVAL Y ZAPATA, LUIS (*fl.* 1640–45), Mexican poet. Among his works are a *Relación fúnebre* on the beheading of the two brothers Ávila in the central square of Mexico City; the gongoristic sonnet 'A la materia prima', in which he compared the transformation of flowers into an image of the Virgin to the metamorphosis of the mythical phoenix; *Poesías varias a Nuestra Señora de Guadalupe* (1645), and a *Panegírico a la paciencia* (1645), eulogizing (in the words of Carlos González Peña) the very quality needed to finish reading the poem.

Sandoval's works can be sampled in A. Méndez Plancarte's anthology *Poetas novohispanos*, vol. 2 (1944), pp. 102–15.

See A. Méndez Plancarte, 'Don Luis de Sandoval y Zapata' in *Ábside* (Mexico City, 1937), no. 1, pp. 37–54; and José Pascual Buxó, 'Sobre la relación fúnebre a la infeliz trágica muerte de dos caballeros' in *Anuario de Letras* (Facultad de Filosofía y Letras, Mexico City, 1964), vol. 4, pp. 237–54.

SANFUENTES, SALVADOR (1817–60), b. Santiago. Chilean playwright and poet. He rose from the post of secretary of the Universidad Nacional to become Minister of Justice and State (1847–51).

A disciple of Andrés Bello and imitator of Mora in the verse *tradición El campanario* (1842), he published a collection of similar *Leyendas y tradiciones* (1850), but is best known for his plays, which bridge neoclassicism and Romanticism in Chile. The most celebrated of them is *Juana de Nápoles* (1863). His least happy venture was the long poem *Ricardo y Lucía o la destrucción de la Imperial*, in 17,626 hendecasyllables. He also translated Racine and Molière, and wrote an historical work, *Chile desde la batalla de Chacabuco hasta la de Maipo* (1850). *Obras escogidas* appeared in 1921.

See M. Amunátegui, *Don Salvador Sanfuentes* (1892).

Sangre, Limpieza de, see LIMPIEZA DE SANGRE.

SANÍN CANO, BALDOMERO (1861–1957), b. Rionegro. Colombian who lived for a time in England and Germany and is considered in Latin America a model scholar of the Anglo-Saxon type.

His wide reading produced critical essays on many authors, among them his friend José Asunción Silva (q.v.), Bergson, Goethe, Bourget, and Jorge Isaacs whose complete poetry Sanín

Cano edited. His books were *La civil manual y otros ensayos* (Buenos Aires, 1925), *Indagaciones y imágenes* (1926), *Crítica y arte* (1932), *Ensayos* (1942), *Letras colombianas* (Mexico City, 1944), *Tipos, obras, ideas* (Buenos Aires, n.d. but 1949), the autobiographical *De mi vida y de otras vidas* (1949), and *El humanismo y el progreso del hombre* (Buenos Aires, 1955).

See R. Posada Franco, *Baldomero Sanín Cano y otros ensayos* (Palmira, 1958).

SAN JOSÉ, JERÓNIMO DE (1587–1654), b. Mallén, Saragossa. Carmelite poet and historian, known in the world as Jerónimo de Ezquerra y Rosas. A disciple and admirer of the Aragonese poet Bartolomé Leonardo de Argensola, he composed an exquisite sonnet on the theme of *vita brevis* entitled 'Vita nostra vapor admodicum parens', reprinted in J. M. Blecua's *Floresta de lírica española* (2nd edn., 1968, vol. 1, p. 300) from San José's *Poesías selectas* (Saragossa, 1876).

During his lifetime, San José published *Historia del Carmen Descalzo* (1637), *Vida de S. Juan de la Cruz* (1641), and *Genio de la historia* (Saragossa, 1651).

J. M. Blecua has edited *Cartas* by San José in *Archivo de Filología Aragonesa*, vol. 1 (1945).

San Manuel Bueno, mártir (1933), a short novel by Miguel de Unamuno (q.v.) published with three other short novels.

Don Manuel Bueno is a priest unable to believe in the basic doctrines of the Roman Catholic Church who nevertheless devotes his whole life to the welfare of his parishioners. Manuel is based on Unamuno's childhood friend, the priest Francisco de Iturribarría who, like Manuel, had attended the seminary in Vitoria, only to return to the place which he never again left (Bilbao in the case of Iturribarría; Valverde de Lucerna in the case of Manuel).

Manuel is the Spanish form of Immanuel ('God with us') and the priest's close friend and disciple (the author's persona) is Lazarus, whom he helps to 'resurrect' from the death of unbelief to a life of compassionate deception. The story is told by Angela Carballino, writing the life-story of Manuel, who is being assessed for beatification by his Bishop. She is the sister of the atheist Lazarus, who returned from the New World to remove his family from the 'rural, feudal, priest-ridden town', but stayed as a close friend and confidant of the honest, compassionate Manuel.

Unamuno's priest, whose lost faith only strengthens his sense of social obligation, recalls a priest in the story 'Karl' in the *Reminiscencias tudescas* (1902) by the Colombian Santiago Pérez Triana which Unamuno had reviewed, and another in *El Vicario* (1905) by Manuel Ciges Aparicio (q.v.).

Unamuno stated his belief that *San Manuel Bueno* formed the third part of a trilogy that began with *Del sentimiento trágico de la vida en los hombres y en los pueblos* (1913) and continued with *L'agonie du christianisme* (1925, in the French translation by Jean Cassou), first issued in Spanish in 1931 as *La agonía del cristianismo*.

Unamuno's most considerable work of fiction in the view of some critics, *San Manuel Bueno* is surprising for its apparent conservatism: he seems to be regretting in this late work the belligerence and iconoclasm of his popular reputation.

See C. Blanco Aguinaga, *El Unamuno contemplativo* (Mexico City, 1959); C. Aguilera, 'Fe religiosa y su problemática en "San Manuel Bueno, mártir" de Unamuno' in *Boletín de la Biblioteca Nacional* (Mexico City, 1964), vol. 40, pp. 205–307; and P. Fernández, *El problema de la personalidad en Unamuno y en 'San Manuel Bueno'* (1966).

SAN PEDRO, DIEGO DE (c. 1437–c. 1498). Novelist probably of Jewish descent. He administered Peñafiel not later than 1452 (and subsequently other Castilian towns) on behalf of Pedro Girón, Master of the Order of Calatrava, and his sons. He is a cardinal figure in the development of the Spanish novel of courtly love, and his poems of grace and sentiment appeared in all editions of the *Cancionero general* of Hernando del Castillo (q.v.).

The *Tractado de amores de Arnalte e Lucenda* (Burgos, 1491) tells the story of two unhappy lovers and can best be read as a precursor of *La cárcel de amor* (q.v., Seville, 1492), another novel of unhappy love but greatly superior in style and complexity. Samuel Gili y Gaya's edition of the *Obras* of San Pedro in Clásicos Castellanos (1950) also contains the *cancionero* poems and the tedious *Sermón ordenado porque dixeron unas señoras que le desseauan oyr predicar*, but omits *Las siete angustias de Nuestra Señora* (Medina del Campo, 1534, of which no copy is known; and 1540?) and a religious work conventionally known as *La pasión trovada*, probably printed in Salamanca in 1496, which has been studied and published in facsimile by A. Pérez Gómez (*Revista de Literatura*, vol. 1, 1952, pp. 147–83) and more recently studied by D. S. Severin in 'The earliest version of Diego de San Pedro's "La pasión trobada"' in *Romanische Forschungen*, vol. 81, 1969, pp. 176–92.

R. Foulché-Delbosc's reprint of the *editio princeps* of *La cárcel de amor* (1904) is still usable, though Gili y Gaya's is preferable, but his edition of *Arnalte e Lucenda* (1911) was based on the inferior Burgos reprint of 1522 and is now superseded. There is a facsimile edition of *Arnalte* by the Real Academia Española (1952).

See K. Whinnom, *Diego de San Pedro* (New York, 1974) in Twayne's World Authors series.

SAN PEDRO, HIERÓNIMO DE, see SEMPERE, Jerónimo de.

SANTA CRUZ, MELCHOR DE (1520–80), b. Dueñas. Anthologist and editor who brought together two major collections of authentic and attributed sayings by real people, classifying his collections according to the category of speakers, for example kings, dukes, travellers, and tradesmen. Many of these stories are still current, long after their source has been forgotten.

The *Floresta española de apotegmas, o sentencias sabia y graciosamente dichas de algunos españoles* (Toledo, 1574) was reprinted in 1910 by the Sociedad de Bibliófilos Españoles, but *Los cien tratados de notables sentencias assí morales como naturales* (Toledo, 1576) has not so far been reprinted.

SANTA CRUZ Y ESPEJO, FRANCISCO JAVIER EUGENIO, see ESPEJO, Eugenio Francisco Javier.

Santa Hermandad, La ('the holy brotherhood'), name of the original *hermandades* or groups of commoners formed to resist extortion of noblemen. In 1476 Ferdinand and Isabel organized this disparate praeto-police force into a militia of two thousand horsemen to protect the more sparsely-populated districts of Spain from bandits. They were assigned to communities roughly on the basis of one horseman for every hundred inhabitants.

See M. Lunenfeld, *The Council of the Santa Hermandad: a study of the pacification forces of Ferdinand and Isabella* (1971).

SANTA MARÍA, ÁLVAR GARCÍA DE, see GARCÍA DE SANTA MARÍA, Álvar.

SANTAYANA, JORGE RUIZ (1863–1952), b. Madrid. Philosopher and essayist, known generally as 'George' Santayana, since all his works were written in English. He spent his childhood from the age of 3 to 16 in Ávila, but was educated at Harvard and Oxford, and at 26 was appointed professor of philosophy at Harvard.

His first book was *Sonnets and poems* (1894), and he continued to compose formally perfect, reflective verse throughout his long life. But he first achieved a reputation with *The sense of beauty* (New York and London, 1896), declared by Muensterberg to be the finest work on aesthetics published in the U.S.A. He then published *Interpretations of poetry and religion* (New York and London, 1900) and the important philosophical work *The life of reason, or the phases of human progress* (New York and London, 1905). *Three philosophical poets* (Cambridge, Mass. and London, 1910) dealt with Lucretius, Dante, and Goethe.

In 1912 Santayana received a large legacy, gave up his chair, and moved to Oxford to write and study, but after World War II spent some time in Paris, before finally settling in Rome.

Scepticism and animal faith: introduction to a system of philosophy (1923) was followed by *The realm of essence* (1927), *The realm of matter* (1929), *The realm of truth* (1938), *The realm of spirit* (1940), and *Realms of being* (1940). His autobiography is a sequence of novels: *The last Puritan* (1935), *Persons and places* (1945), and *The middle span* (1947).

Santayana is not a major philosopher, creating a new system; he is rather a critic of existing systems. He criticizes the attempt to impose unity as alien to the human experience of the real world. His view is moral and aesthetic, contemplating the universe in the hope of discovering some of its many aspects but certain that he will not discover them all.

See M. K. Munitz, *The moral philosophy of Santayana* (1939); Brownell and others, *The philosophy of Santayana* (1940); and Raimundo Lida, *Arte y poesía en la estética de Santayana* (1943).

'¡Sant Iago y serra!' 'St. James and close [the] ranks!', the Spanish battle-cry. St. James is the patron saint of Spain.

SANTIBÁÑEZ PUGA, FERNANDO (1886–), b. Arauco. Chilean novelist, short-story writer, and journalist, who joined the Tolstoyan experiment in southern Chile with Magallanes Mauro, d'Halmar, and Pedro Prado (qq.v.), and wrote the classic description of it in *Memorias de un tolstoyano* (1955). He first made his name, as 'Fernando Santiván', with the stories in *Palpitaciones de vida* (1909) and has written others in *El bosque emprende su marcha* (1946), but it is as a novelist that he is primarily known. *Ansia* (1911) is an autobiographical tale of his early days as a writer, struggling to make his name in the face of indifference; *El crisol* (1913) and its sequel *Robles, Blume & Cía.* (1923) on urban life; the absurd, melodramatic *La hechizada* (1916); the realistic novel of life in southern Chile, *Charca en la selva* (1934); *La camará* (1945); a novel on the life of the national hero Bernardo O'Higgins, *El mulato Riquelme* (1951); and *Bárbara* written four decades earlier.

His most interesting book is the autobiographical novel *Confesiones de Enrique Samaniego:*

recuerdos literarios (1933), elaborated for republication in 1958. His *Obras completas* (1965) are in 2 vols.

SANTILLANA, Íñigo López de Mendoza, *Marqués de* (1398–1458), b. Carrión de los Condes, Palencia. Humanist, poet, and literary critic. The son of Diego Hurtado de Mendoza, Admiral of Castile, who died in 1404, when Íñigo was sent to live with his wealthy grandmother Doña Mencía de Cisneros, patroness of arms and learning. He served at the court of Aragón 1412–18, forming an important friendship with Enrique de Villena and marrying in 1416 Catalina de Figueroa. He began to form the great private library which passed through the safekeeping of the Dukes of Osuna to the Biblioteca Nacional in Madrid. The contents and making of this important humanistic undertaking have been studied by Mario Schiff in *La bibliothèque du marquis de Santillane* (Paris, 1905) and by Arturo Farinelli in his *Italia e Spagna* (Turin, 1929). López de Mendoza showed great prowess in the Battle of Olmedo in 1445, and it was in that year that he became Marquis of Santillana and Count of Real de Manzanares. Santillana collected classical MSS. (though he could read neither Greek nor Latin) and commissioned translations into Spanish of the *Iliad*, the *Aeneid*, and Seneca's tragedies.

He did know Italian, French, Catalan, and Galician, however, and wrote at least one early song in Galician. His cultural interests were wide, and his literary curiosity such that he composed (1449) what is generally considered to be the first work of literary criticism in modern Spanish, the *Prohemio é carta que el Marqués de Santillana envió al condestable de Portugal* prefacing a selection of his own poems sent at the request of Don Pedro de Portugal. His classification of poetry is threefold: the sublime (poetry in Greek and Latin), the mediocre (poetry in vernacular languages written by the cultivated), and the low (ballads and popular songs without formal rules). But the *Prohemio* is an important plea to a potential Maecenas for his patronage of poetry in the Iberian peninsula and his public recognition of the significance of patronage in the development of civilization. Santillana's own poetry marks the transition between the feudal, Christian, and chivalresque world and the Renaissance mood imported from Italy; it was characterized by a resurgence of interest in pagan elements from literature and mythology, individuality, and conscious elegance of expression. Santillana commissioned Villena's translation of the *Divina Commedia* (finished in 1428), a copy of Petrarch's *Canzoniere* in the original, and himself wrote 42 Petrarchan *Sonetos, fechos al itálico modo* from 1438 until the

end of his life. These sonnets are adventurous, being the first written in Castilian, but are not yet attuned in style or rhythm to their new medium. In this allegorical, Italianate vein Santillana also composed *Comedieta de Ponça* (begun in 1436) on the Genoese victory over Alfonso V of Aragon off Ponza in 1435 (ed. by J. M. Azáceta, Tetuán, 1957), the 22 *octavas* in *arte mayor Defunssión de Don Enrique de Villena*, and the *Infierno de los enamorados*, and such minor works as the Petrarchan *Triunfete de amor*.

Santillana's moral and didactic poems include the *Proverbios de gloriosa doctrina e fructuosa enseñanza*, some hundred stanzas in *pie quebrado* composed for Prince Enrique; and two attacks on Don Álvaro de Luna (q.v.): *Diálogo de Bías contra Fortuna* (Seville, 1502) written in 1448 to console his cousin the Conde de Alba, gaoled by Luna, in which the Stoic philosopher Bias, one of the Seven Sages of Greece, debates with Fortuna, a subject also dealt with by Santillana's political opponent Juan de Mena in *El laberinto de Fortuna* (qq.v.); and the *Doctrinal de privados*, 53 stanzas of 8 octosyllabic lines written in 1454 in the form of a public confession of his sins by de Luna in the spirit of Augustine's *Confessions* and deriving part of its impact from both saint and sinner and also to be understood as figuring Everyman.

Santillana is appreciated today, however, for his songs in the troubadour tradition of Provence and Galicia which V. García de Diego has edited in Clásicos Castellanos as *Canciones y decires* (1913). The earliest of them are lyrical, like the 'Querella de amor', but his style soon evolved into the Italianate mould introduced by Imperial, the lyrical element gave way to narrative, and his charming spontaneity was occasionally lost.

It is not certain that he compiled the *Refranes que dicen las viejas tras el fuego* commonly attributed to him and edited by R. Foulché-Delbosc as 'Urban Cronan' in *Revue Hispanique*, vol. 25 (1911), pp. 114–219. His poetry can be read in Foulché-Delbosc's *Cancionero castellano del siglo XV*, vol. 1 (1912) in the NBAE. The critical edition of his *Obras* by J. Amador de los Ríos (1852) has not yet been entirely superseded but the best edition of the *Poesías completas* is that by M. Durán (1976—in progress) for Clásicos Castalia.

See D. W. Foster, *The Marqués de Santillana* (New York, 1971); M. Menéndez y Pelayo's chapter in *Poetas de la corte de don Juan II* (Buenos Aires, 1943); *Prose and verse* edited by J. B. Trend (London, 1940); R. Lapesa, *Los decires narrativos del Marqués de Santillana* (1954) and *La obra literaria del Marqués de Santillana* (1957); and Josefina Delgado, *El Marqués de Santillana* (Buenos Aires, 1968).

SANTIVÁN, Fernando, pseudonym of Fernando Santibáñez Puga (q.v.).

SANT JORDI, Jordi de (*c.* 1385–*c.* 1424), b. Valencia. Poet and court chamberlain to Alfonso V of Aragón. His music and Petrarchan love songs in the Valencian dialect of Catalan mark the high point of the Catalan Renaissance. He accompanied Alfonso in 1420 on expeditions to Corsica and Sardinia and is recorded in Naples during 1422–3, when he was imprisoned for about a month by the *condottiere* Sforza. He is known to have died unmarried before 30 January 1425.

The virtuosity of his 'Cançió d'opòsits' with words taken from Petrarch's sonnet 90 was praised by Santillana. 'Presoner' is a poem with neither presumption nor abasement imploring the king's help. The melancholy of his 'Comiat' and 'Enyorament' avoid the sentimentality prevalent at the time. 'Estat d'honor' is a poem dedicated to the idea of ennoblement by secular love. Milà y Fontanals claimed to have identified Sant Jordi's *reyna d'honor* with Queen María herself; Riquer prefers the widowed Queen Margarita de Prades. The best edition of his works is that by M. de Riquer (Barcelona, 1935) in the Els Nostres Poetes series.

SANTOB DE CARRIÓN, see Shem Tov Ardutiel.

SANTOS, Francisco (*c.* 1631–*c.* 1700), b. Madrid? Writer of picaresque novels whose work marks the decadence of the genre, lacking the vitality and inspiration of his predecessors; his style is often contorted and dense, reminiscent more of Gracián than of Quevedo's *El buscón* (qq.v.). Santos himself cited Lope de Vega as the supreme poet and Quevedo as the supreme prose satirist. Torres y Villarroel reported that 'los libros de Santos, aunque encaminados a la enmienda de costumbres con la representación de los vicios, y llenos de reprensiones y severidades morales, han sido bien recibidos por todo linaje de gentes'.

The most comprehensive collection of his work is the *Obras en prosa y verso* (1723), containing 15 satirical novels. A new edition of his *Obras selectas* (1976—in progress) is being produced by M. Navarro Pérez for the Instituto de Estudios Madrileños. In his anthology *Novela picaresca en España* (1943–6), Ángel Valbuena Prat reprinted *Periquillo, él de las gallineras* (1668), the life of a *pícaro* who, like the original Lazarillo, serves part of his apprenticeship as a blind man's boy.

The first recorded novel by Santos is *Día y noche de Madrid, discursos de lo más notable que en él se passa* (1663), reprinted in vol. 33 (1854) of the BAE, eighteen discourses on the life and manners of Madrid portrayed in dark colours, to scourge the evils of contemporary life. Le Sage used much material from this book for the second part which he added to his translations of Guevara's *El diablo cojuelo* in *Le diable boîteux*.

Santos also wrote *Las tarascas de Madrid, y tribunal espantoso* (1665); *Los Gigantones en Madrid por defuera, y prodigioso entretenido. Festiva salida al Santo Christo del Pardo* (1666); *El no importa de España, loco político, y mudo pregonero* (1667), edited with *La verdad en la potro* for Támesis Books by J. Rodríguez-Puértolas, (1973); *El diablo anda suelto, verdades de la otra vida soñadas en ésta* (1677?); *El sastre del campillo* (n.d. but 1685); *La verdad en el potro y Cid resucitado* (1686); *Cárdeno lirio, Alva sin crepusculo, y Madrid llorando* (1690); *La tarasca de parto en el mesón del infierno, y días de fiesta por la noche* (Valencia, 1696); and *El arca de Noé, y campana de Belilla* (Saragossa, 1697).

See C. J. Winter, 'Notes on the works of Francisco Santos' in *Hispania*, vol. 12 (1929), pp. 457–64.

SANTOS CHOCANO, José (1875–1934), b. Lima. Peruvian modernist poet. In 1893–4 his angry verses against the dictator Cáceres led to imprisonment and the death sentence. He was freed in March 1895 and appointed state printer, publishing his early poetry in *Iras santas* and *En la aldea* (both 1895). He married the first of his three wives in 1896 (never obtaining a legal divorce) and spent 1901–8 in the diplomatic corps in Central America, Colombia, and Spain. The years from 1908 were full of adventures: he founded *La Prensa* in Guatemala City, arrived in 1912 in Mexico as a friend of Madero and was jailed in 1913 on Madero's assassination; he spent 1915–18 with Pancho Villa; he returned in 1919 to Guatemala as a friend of the dictator Estrada Cabrera and on the latter's fall in 1920 was saved from execution only by foreign intervention; he was crowned Poet Laureate of Peru in 1922; in 1925 he killed an ideological opponent and was jailed until 1927; during 1928–34 he lived in Santiago, rewriting his poetry and planning to retrieve hidden treasure, and he was killed in a tram in Santiago by an unknown assailant.

His poetry is full of grandeur and a sense of destiny rarely absent from his life: hyperbole, daring metaphor, and a semi-epic torrent of words and images. He won literary prizes with *El canto del siglo* (1901) and *La epopeya del Morro* (1899), the second extant in a fragment of some 500 lines from a total of over 1600. As he himself wrote, 'Debí yo haber nacido no en esta edad sin gloria, sino en un tiempo heroico que nunca volverá . . .' and Chocano's mania for action and adventure marred much of his hastily-written work prior to his Santiago years, and even they were filled with poverty and distress. His influences were Darío (in the modernist phase), Walt Whitman, and Victor Hugo, and his life was spent in the inner circles of autocrats such as Pancho Villa and Estrada Cabrera.

L. A. Sánchez's edition of the *Obras completas* (Mexico City, 1954) is the best available; the most sensitive selection and commentary on Chocano is that by Francisco Bendezú in *Sus mejores poemas* (1962); the mistitled *Páginas de oro de José Santos Chocano* compiled by his son Eduardo (1944) is a hotch-potch of rejected juvenilia across which the author had plainly written 'NO' in enough places for his feelings to have been made clear. His most interesting prose works are *Idearium tropical* (1922), with essays on the necessity of dictatorship, the U.S.A., and the Mexican Revolution; and *Memorias: las mil y una aventuras* (Santiago de Chile, 1940), a work of high romance but often severely misleading as to fact and history.

The best study of Chocano is Luis Alberto Sánchez, *Aladino, o vida y obras de José Santos Chocano* (Mexico City, 1960). In English there is a useful, brief *José Santos Chocano* (1970) by P. W. Rodríguez-Peralta in Twayne's World Authors series.

Santos Vega, o Los mellizos de La Flor, rasgos dramáticos de la vida del gaucho en las campañas y praderas de la República Argentina (1778–1808) (Paris, 1872), a long narrative *gaucho* poem by Hilario Ascasubi (q.v.). The bulk of the poem was written hurriedly between September 1871 and April 1872, two earlier parts (totalling 1,080 lines) having appeared in 1850–1. The final version, mainly in octosyllables, consists of 12,604 lines. Ambitious in plan, *Santos Vega* is an uneven picture of *gaucho* life in the Viceroyalty of Río de la Plata in a series of fragments of which the most successful are Canto X (*La madrugada*) and Canto XIII (*El malón*).

Santos Vega, an old *gaucho* very different from the popular picture of the young and handsome *payador* (see VEGA, Santos), tells a married couple whom he knows of the two twins of La Flor ranch: the vicious, deceitful Luis and his peaceful, honest brother Jacinto. Ascasubi wrote of ranch life and the *gauchos* he had known, to preserve his recollections of a world virtually unaffected by city happenings, in a language appropriate to his characters and with few anachronisms.

See the edition of 1915, with an introduction by Carlos O. Bunge; that of 1919 (pp. 8–27) with various critical assessments; and that of

Jorge Luis Borges and Adolfo Bioy Casares in *Poesía gauchesca* (vol. 1, 1955). See also GAUCHO LITERATURE.

SANZ DEL RÍO, JULIÁN (1814–69), b. Torre Arévalo, Soria. Philosopher. He studied in Granada and Madrid, where he became professor of the History of Philosophy. In 1843 he received a government scholarship to pursue his studies overseas, thus becoming one of the earliest Spaniards in modern times to travel exclusively for purposes of study. (In 1559 Philip II had made unauthorized study abroad, except in Italy and Portugal, a capital offence).

Sanz was not impressed with his teachers in Paris, but under Ahrens in Brussels and later Roeder in Heidelberg, he learnt the doctrines of *krausismo* (q.v.) which were to revolutionize intellectual life in Spain from 1860 until the end of the century.

In 1854–67 he taught small classes of the well-informed (instead of the huge classes of the uninitiated) not philosophy but how to become philosophers; and educators like Giner de los Ríos and philosophers such as Azcárate (qq.v.) carried his theories into practical effect in pedagogy and politics. See also INSTITUCIÓN LIBRE DE ENSEÑANZA.

In 1860 he published both *Ideal de la humanidad para la vida* and the first part of his *Sistema de la filosofía: metafísica* (Pt. II, 1874; the work remained incomplete). His style was so obscure that the young Menéndez y Pelayo (q.v.) described it (in vol. 3 of his *Historia de los heterodoxos españoles*, 1882) as 'an Eleusinian mystery concealed by gibberish, a fetid skeleton with whose sterile caresses we have been soliciting and exciting the passions of the youth of Spain for so many years'.

Sanz also wrote *Lecciones sobre el sistema de filosofía analítica de Krause* (1850), *Análisis del pensamiento racional* (1877), and *Filosofía de la muerte* (1877).

SANZ-LAJARA, J. M. (1917–). The most celebrated novelist of the Dominican Republic, Sanz-Lajara has also written important travel essays interspersed with short stories: *Cotopaxi* (1949), *Aconcagua* (1950), and *El candado* (1959).

The novel *Caonex* (1949) reveals his strong attachment to his native country. His subsequent novels include *Viv* (1961) a tragic love story, and *Los rompidos* (1963).

SANZ Y SÁNCHEZ, EULOGIO FLORENTINO (1822–81), b. Arévalo. Poet and dramatist. He studied at the University of Valladolid. His Romantic drama *Don Francisco de Quevedo* (1848; edited by R. Selden Rose, Boston, 1917) obtained great success with its unhistorical portrait of Quevedo as a Romantic creator beset by *Weltschmerz*, but *Achaques de la vejez* (1854) was soon forgotten by critics and public alike and, in his chagrin at this critical failure, Sanz refused to write more for the stage. Fragments of *La escarcela y el puñal* were published (1851) in the *Semanario Pintoresco Español*, the magazine which had published his poetry in 1843. Sanz's best-known poem is the 'Epístola a Pedro', a verse letter to his editor on a visit to the neglected tomb of Enrique Gil (q.v.), which Menéndez y Pelayo judged worthy of a place in *Las cien mejores poesías de la lengua castellana*. Sanz fused in his poems the popular (as did his contemporary Trueba) and the Germanic (as did Selgas), for he had spent two years (1854–6) in Berlin and translated fifteen poems of Heine which appeared in *El Museo Universal*.

His work is apparently still uncollected.

See J. M. Díez Taboada, 'Eulogio Florentino Sanz, 1822–1881' in *Revista de Literatura*, vol. 13 (1958), pp. 48–78.

SARABIA, JOSÉ DE (*fl.* early 17th c.). Poet, who often used the pseudonym 'Trevijano'. Secretary to the Duke of Medina Sidonia.

His best-known work is the address, to a woman, usually referred to as 'Canción real a una mudanza' which begins 'Ufano, alegre, altivo, enamorado' attributed to Antonio Mira de Amescua (q.v.) in *Poesías varias de grandes ingenios* (Saragossa, 1654), and elsewhere attributed to Bartolomé Leonardo de Argensola (q.v.).

The poem appears in many anthologies, among them José M. Blecua's *Floresta de lírica española* (2nd edn., 1968), pp. 289–92.

SARDANÁPALO, CRISÓFILO, pseudonym used by Alejandro Tapia y Rivera (q.v.) when writing *La Sataniada* (Madrid, 1878).

SARDUY, SEVERO (1937–), b. Havana. Cuban novelist and poet whose experimental *Gestos* (Barcelona, 1963) owed much to the French *nouveau roman* while remaining faithful to his own tropical setting of myth, colour, movement, and violence.

De donde son las cantantes (Mexico City, 1967), first published in French as *Écrit en dansant*, is a more traditional novel, in which a singing Negress comes to self-knowledge during the Cuban Revolution. *Escrito sobre un cuerpo* (Buenos Aires, 1969) is a collection of critical essays. *Cobra* (Buenos Aires, 1972) is a novel. *Big bang* (1974) is a collection of experimental poetry. Sarduy has also produced collections of poems in limited artist's editions: *Flamenco* (with Erhardt, Stuttgart, 1969) and *Mood indigo* (with Leonor Fini, Stuttgart, 1970).

The best bibliography of Sarduy's writings so far is by Roberto González Echevarría in *Revista Iberoamericana*, no. 79 (April–June 1972), pp. 333–43.

See Emir Rodríguez Monegal, 'Conversación con Severo Sarduy' in *Revista de Occidente*, no. 93 (1970), pp. 315–43; and Jean M. Fossey, 'Severo Sarduy' in her *Galaxia latinoamericana* (Las Palmas, 1973), pp. 221–52.

SARMIENTO, DOMINGO FAUSTINO (1811–88), b. San Juan, Argentina. President of Argentina from 1868 to 1874. Self-taught except for a little tuition by a priest, he worked as a shop assistant in youth, learning languages and reading in his spare time. He became involved in politics and went into exile in Chile 1831–6 and 1840–52, with intervals travelling in Europe and the U.S.A. He was particularly influenced by contemporary French radicalism and was impressed by the gigantic potential of the U.S.A., attributing its commercial and political successes to the moral qualities inherited from Puritan forebears. He read de Tocqueville's *De la démocratie en Amérique* (2 vols., 1835), a work which influenced *Facundo*. This polemical essay, known in full as *Civilización y barbarie: vida de Juan Facundo Quiroga, y aspecto físico, costumbres, y hábitos de la República Argentina* (q.v., 1845) was a powerful plea for urbanization and industrialization, completely opposed to the traditional *gaucho* culture of the pampas. While still in exile he produced *Mi defensa* (1843) justifying his opposition to the Argentine dictator Rosas; a travel book, *Viajes por Europa, África y América* (1849–51); and the autobiographical *Recuerdos de provincia*.

He was a strong reformist president of his country, retiring when exhausted in 1874, but continuing to devote his remaining energies to popular education. *Conflictos y armonías de las razas en América* (1883) attributes the problems of Latin America to inherent racial defects, recommending large-scale immigration of Europeans and investment in large industrial complexes.

Sarmiento's *Obras* (Santiago, 1885–1914) run to 53 vols.

The latest bibliography of Sarmiento is by Horacio Jorge Becco in *Humanidades* (Córdoba, Argentina), vol. 37, 1961, pp. 119–45.

See Ricardo Rojas, *El profeta de la pampa: vida de Sarmiento* (1946; 5th edn., Buenos Aires, 1951); A. W. Bunkley, *The life of Sarmiento* (Princeton, 1952); Leopoldo Lugones, *Historia de Sarmiento* (1960); Carlos D. Quiroga, *Sarmiento . . .* (1961); Félix Weinberg, *Vida e imagen de Sarmiento* (1963); and Porto Lobos, *Sarmiento y sus detractores* (Córdoba, Argentina, 1966).

SARMIENTO, *Fray* MARTÍN (1695–1772), b. Villafranca del Bierzo, León. Benedictine scholar and private librarian known until 1710 as Pedro José García Balboa. He devoted his life from 1750 entirely to writing and to assisting Feijóo (q.v.) with writing his books. Sarmiento's library consisted of about 8,000 vols. His greatest bibliographical achievement was the discovery of the two Rome *Cancioneros*. By far the greater part of his MSS. remain unpublished to this day, including the useful 'Onomástico etimológico de la lengua gallega'. *Índice de una colección manuscrita de . . . Sarmiento, seguido de varias noticias bibliográficas del mismo* (1888) was compiled by M. Gesta y Leceta from the 23 vols. in the Natural History Cabinet in Madrid.

The more important of his two published works is the *Memoria para la historia de la poesía y poetas españoles* (1775), which is the first and only volume of the *Obras póstumas* planned. The only book Sarmiento published in his lifetime was the *Demostración crítico-apologética en defensa del 'Theatro crítico universal'* (2 vols., 1732), an immediate reply to S. J. Mañer's attack on Feijóo entitled *Anti-Theatro Crítico* (1729–31). Sarmiento had assisted Feijóo in many points of detail and felt personally aggrieved by Mañer's often petty complaints against what was generally recognized as a work of major significance.

See A. López Peláez, *El gran gallego Fr. Martín Sarmiento* (Corunna, 1895) and *Los escritos de Sarmiento y el siglo de Feijóo* (Corunna, 1901).

SARRAILH, JEAN LOUIS (1891–1964), French Hispanist. Rector of the Université de Paris and director of the Institut Français in Madrid. His major works on the 18th and 19th cs. are *Un homme d'état espagnol: Martínez de la Rosa* (Bordeaux, 1930), the essays *Enquêtes romantiques. France-Espagne* (Paris, 1933), and the important *L'Espagne éclairée de la seconde moitié du XVIIIe siècle* (Paris, 1954) translated as *España ilustrada de la segunda mitad del siglo XVIII* (2nd edn., Mexico City, 1975).

SASTRE, ALFONSO (1926–), b. Madrid. Playwright of social commitment in the tradition of Camus and Sartre. His wife E. Forest has written *Diario y cartas desde la cárcel* (1975, with facing French translation; English translation, Harmondsworth, 1975). His first collection of plays, *Teatro de vanguardia* (1948), consists of *Ha sonado la muerte* and *Comedia sonámbula* (both written with Medardo Fraile, 1946), *Uranio 235* (1946), and *Cargamento de sueños* (1948). *Escuadra hacia la muerte* (1953), a pacifist play (subsequently banned) set in a bunker during 'the next war', was first performed by the Teatro Popular Universitario, which Sastre had helped

to organize. *La mordaza* (1954), possibly influenced by O'Neill's *Desire under the elms* (though Sastre himself specifically confesses a debt to Arthur Miller), concerns a hero who tries to seduce his daughter-in-law and then kills a man seeking revenge for a crime committed by the hero. Sastre then wrote *La sangre de Dios* (1955), *Muerte en el barrio* (1955), *El cuervo* (1957), *La cornada* (1959), and *En la red*, on the independence movement in Algeria. His plays were rarely performed in Spain on account of their subversive qualities of dissent, pacifism, and compassion for the under-privileged, but their publication has been permitted and *Teatro selecto* (1966) included *Escuadra hacia la muerte, La mordaza, Ana Kleiber, La sangre de Dios, Guillermo Tell tiene los ojos tristes,* and *En la red*.

Plays written since vol. 1 of Sastre's *Obras completas* appeared in 1968 include: *La sangre y la ceniza o Diálogos de Miguel Servet* (written in 1965), *El banquete* (1965), *La taberna fantástica* (1966), *Crónicas romanas* (1968), *Ejercicios de terror* (1970), *Las olas magnéticas* (1971), *Asalto a una ciudad* (based on a play by Lope, 1971), *¡Askatasusa! (Libertad)* (1971), and *El camarada oscuro* (1972). *El escenario diabólico* is a play of terror written in 1958 but not published until 1973.

Leonard C. Pronko has translated five of Sastre's plays into English: *Escuadra hacia la muerte* in *The modern Spanish stage* (New York, 1970); *La cornada* in *Masterpieces of the modern Spanish theatre* (New York, 1967); *Ana Kleiber* in *The new theatre of Europe* (New York, 1962); *Prólogo patético* in *Modern international drama* (Philadelphia, 1968); and *Guillermo Tell tiene los ojos tristes* in *The new wave Spanish drama* (New York, 1970).

Sastre has also written criticism and essays, notably *Drama y sociedad* (1956), translated for the special issue of the *Tulane Drama Review*, vol. 5, no. 2 (1960) devoted to his work; *Anatomía del realismo* (Barcelona, 1965; 2nd edn., 1974); and *La revolución y la crítica de la cultura* (Barcelona, 1970).

Sastre's short stories are collected in *Las noches lúgubres* (complete edn., 1973).

See A. C. van der Naald, *Alfonso Sastre, dramaturgo de la revolución* (1973); and F. Donahue, *Alfonso Sastre: dramaturgo y preceptista* (1973).

SAWA, ALEJANDRO (1862–1909), b. Málaga. Minor novelist and journalist who was connected with the *Generación del 1898* (q.v.) by age though not by ideology. He led a Bohemian existence in Madrid and Paris, dying blind and insane in abject poverty.

Zola's influence dominates his novels, which include *La mujer de todo el mundo* (1885), *Crimen legal* (1886), *Declaración de un vencido* (1887), *Noche* (1889), *Un criadero de curas* (1890), *La sima de Igusquiza* (1897?), and *Iluminaciones en la sombra* (1910).

Valle-Inclán (q.v.), in his play *Luces de Bohemia* (q.v.), used Sawa as the model for his hero, Max Estrella.

Sayagués, the dialect spoken in and around the village of Sayago, in Zamora province; in Spanish literature, the conventional but inaccurate term used for artificial rustic speech found in the *Coplas de Mingo Revulgo* (q.v., *c.* 1464), in the shepherd scene of Fray Íñigo de Mendoza's *Vita Christi*, and in the plays of dramatists predating Lope, such as Juan del Encina, Lucas Fernández, and Gil Vicente. In *Mingo Revulgo*, the dialect was used to give local colour, but it was later employed for almost exclusively comic ends, and departed radically from the known speech of Sayago.

See John Lihani, 'Some notes on sayagués' in *Hispania*, vol. 41 (1958), pp. 165–9; and Charlotte Stern, 'Sayago and sayagués in Spanish history and literature' in *Hispanic Review*, vol. 29 (1961), pp. 217–37.

SCHACK, ADOLF FRIEDRICH (1815–94), b. Schwerin. German poet and orientalist. He specialized in Calderón studies, but contributed two general works of great value: *Geschichte der dramatischen Literatur und Kunst in Spanien* (3 vols., Berlin, 1845–54; 4 vols., Frankfurt, 1854; trans. E. de Mier, 5 vols., Madrid, 1885–7; reprinted (4 vols. in 3), 1975), and *Poesie und Kunst der Araber in Spanien und Sizilien* (1865; trans. by Juan Valera, 1881).

SCHINCA, MILTON (1926–), b. Montevideo. Uruguayan poet using the occasional pseudonym (in the weekly *Marcha*) 'Alberto Salvá'. The fifteen poems of his first book *De la aventura* (1961) are already mature, and deal mainly with nostalgia and loneliness, the best being a subtle, ironic poem on death entitled 'Propiedad reservada y sus fundamentos'. This was followed by *Esta hora urgente*(1963) and a long confessional poem, *Mundo cuestionado* (1964), which has been described as an important encounter with chaos.

SCORZA, MANUEL (1928–), b. Lima. Peruvian poet and novelist. A political activist, Scorza founded the Movimiento Comunal del Perú to defend the peasants, and as Secretary-General travelled to Cerra de Pasco, where the massacres of Rancas, Yanahuanca, and Ambo had been carried out under the Creole government of Manuel Prado. Scorza, who lives in Paris and teaches at the École Normale Supérieure, has added a new dimension to the Latin-American novel of social protest.

His social indignation is obvious from his first poems, *Las imprecaciones* (Mexico City, 1955), which won the National Literary Prize for 1956. Later books of poetry include *Los adioses* (1958), *Desengaños del mago* (1961), *El país de los reptiles*, and *Réquiem por un gentilhombre* (1962).

Scorza has also compiled the anthology *Satíricos y costumbristas* (1957), but it is for his passionate novels that he has achieved renown. They form a sequence called *La epopeya de la lucha por la tierra en la América Indígena: una novela en cinco baladas* (5 vols., Caracas, 1977). It is well to bear in mind that Scorza has warned us that 'mis libros más que literarios son éticos' for all his characters (with a few exceptions) are not only historical but in most cases even bear their real names. His first novel is *Redoble por Rancas* (Barcelona, 1970), quickly translated into more than a dozen languages. Written conversationally and using many colloquialisms, the book is impressive in its authenticity yet, like García Márquez (q.v.), Scorza is never reluctant to use the apparently fantastic or magical elements thought to be significant ingredients of Indian life. His second novel is a further chapter in the 'Silent War' between the Creoles and Indians which the author claims has already taken half as many lives as the Battle of Junín: *Historia de Garabombo, el invisible* (Barcelona, 1972). The others are *El jinete insomne*, *Cantar de Agapito Robles*, and *La tumba del relámpago*.

Sefardí (Hebrew: *Sephardi* from *Sepharad*, 'Spain'), the Spanish term for a Spanish or Portuguese Jew or his descendant. Sephardic Judaism dominated Jewish culture from about 600 A.D. until the expulsion of the Jews from Spain at the end of the 15th c. Writing mainly in Arabic (even on religion), the Sephardim contributed to the corpus of Judaic thought new ideas in algebra, astronomy, geometry, mechanics, medicine, metaphysics, music, and many other disciplines.

Communities of Sephardic Jews are found today in the United States, Latin America, England, Greece, the Netherlands, and Turkey. The *Encyclopaedia Britannica* estimated that there were some 500,000 Sephardim in 1968, as compared with 1.5 million Oriental Jews and 11 million Ashkenazim (northern Jews).

SEGARRA, PABLO, pseudonym of Juan Pablo Forner (q.v.).

SEGOVIA, TOMÁS (1927–), b. Valencia, Spain. Mexican poet. He moved to Mexico in 1940, later studied at the Universidad Nacional Autónoma de México, and edited the *Revista Mexicana de Literatura*. After travelling in Europe, he lived in Montevideo 1963–6 but has returned to Mexico. His poetry tries to bring order from the prevailing chaos: *La luz provisional* (1950), *Siete poemas* (1955), *Apariciones* (1957), *Luz de aquí* (1958), and *El sol y su eco* (Xalapa, 1960).

He has written a novel on adolescence, *Primavera muda* (1954), and a play set in 11th-c. Spain, *Zamora bajo los astros* (1959).

Seguidilla (probably from *gente de la vida seguida*, 'travelling people'), a four-line stanza of alternate 6/7- and 5-syllable lines with the rhyme or assonance scheme abab, the 1st and 3rd lines being occasionally unrhymed. The form was established in the 16th c. on the basis of traditional folk lyrics: among its principal practitioners were Timoneda, Horozco, Lope de Vega (in *Los pastores de Belén* for instance), Sor Juana Inés de la Cruz, José Benegasi (in his burlesque *San Benito Palermo*), and modern writers up to the time of Federico García Lorca and Joaquín Romero Murube. If an *estribillo* of three lines is added, it becomes a *seguidilla compuesta*.

An example of a *seguidilla* is:

> *Pisaré yo el polvico*
> *atán menudico,*
> *pisaré yo el polvo*
> *atán menudo.*
> —Cervantes.

SEGURA, JUAN DE (*fl.* 1548–55), novelist. Author of the first epistolary novel in Spanish and, according to R. O. Jones, the first such in the whole of Europe: *Proceso de cartas de amores* (Toledo or Alcalá?, 1548; critical edn. E. B. Place, Evanston, Ill., 1950). The story tells of an unhappy lover who diffidently declares his love, of the development of the courtship by correspondence, and the despair of the girl when the family take her to a new home. Though the epistolary vogue was not long coming, there was no immediate sequel to this important book.

Segura also wrote the conventional religious works *Libro de institución cristiana* (Burgos, 1554) and *Confesionario* (1555).

SEGURA Y CORDERO, MANUEL ASCENSIO (1805–71), b. Lima. Peruvian dramatist and *costumbrista* of Spanish descent. He first fought with his father against the army of independence, but later changed sides. J. de la Riva Agüero has claimed that Segura's regional theatre was worthy of comparison with the best *sainetes* of Ramón de la Cruz (q.v.). His dialogue is natural and flowing, and his depiction of rural customs carefully authentic.

Of his fourteen plays, the best-remembered are *La saya y el manto* (1841), attacking the hypocrisy of the politicians of his day; and *Ña Catita* (1845; revised, 1856), a Creole *Celestina* (q.v.). The *Comedias* were reprinted in 1924 in 2 vols. F. Panizo y Orbegozo published *Dos tesis sobre Manuel A. Segura* (1901) on two unpublished plays of Segura: 'Percances de un remitido' and 'Las tres viudas'.

See also Luis Humberto Delgado, *Manuel Ascensio Segura y el teatro peruano* (1939).

SELGAS Y CARRASCO, JOSÉ (1822–82), b. Lorca, Murcia. Poet, named 'poeta de las flores' after his favoured theme. After the extravagance of the early Romantic poems, his own poetry has a moderate note of quiet tenderness and melancholy in *La primavera* (1850), *El estío* (1853), *Flores y espinas* (1882), and *Versos póstumos* (1883). His poems show the influence of German *Lieder*.

He founded the satirical, conservative magazine *El Padre Cobos* and collected his humorous articles in several books which have stood the test of time no better than his popular novels such as *Deuda del corazón* (1872) or *La manzana de oro* (1873).

See E. Díez de Revenga, *Estudio sobre Selgas, poeta, novelista, satírico* (Murcia, 1915), and E. Aranda Muñoz, *Selgas y su obra* (Murcia, 1954).

SELVA, SALOMÓN DE LA (1893–1959), b. León. Nicaraguan poet, essayist, and journalist. From the age of 13 he studied in the U.S.A. and began his literary career in English with *Tropical town and other poems* (New York, 1918) but soon abandoned English. *El soldado desconocido* (Mexico City, 1922) is a partly fictional account in verse of his experiences in the British forces during World War I. Selva's later work is more intellectual, turning away from the influence of the great Nicaraguan poet Darío (q.v.) to classical Rome for his inspiration in *Evocación de Horacio* (Mexico City, 1949) and *Evocación de Píndaro* (1957). He finally settled in Mexico in the later 1930s and died in 1959 as ambassador of Nicaragua in Paris.

See Orlando Cuadra Downing's anthology *Nueva poesía nicaragüense* (Madrid, 1949), pp. 173–215.

Selva de aventuras (Barcelona, 1565), a novel by Jerónimo de Contreras (q.v.) in the Byzantine tradition established by Heliodorus.

The noble Luzmán, in love with Arbolea who has decided to give up the world and retire to a nunnery, seeks consolation in a journey lasting ten years. Vivid descriptions of Italy and many verses are interpolated into the structure of the *Selva*.

After all his adventures, Luzmán is taken captive by Algerian corsairs; once ransomed, he discovers that Arbolea has taken her vows and becomes a hermit, spending the rest of his life in charitable works. The symbolic notion of the purification of the soul by suffering is implicit throughout. The novel was translated into French by Gabriel Chapuys (Lyons, 1580) and reprinted in vol. 3 of the BAE (1846 and reissues).

SEMPERE, JERÓNIMO DE (*fl.* 1554–60), b. Valencia? Novelist also known as 'Hierónimo de San Pedro'. With the intention of driving out profane books of chivalry long before Cervantes professed the same desire in *Don Quijote*, Sempere produced two books of chivalry *a lo divino*, with Christ as the Knight of the Lion, Satan as the Knight of the Serpent, John the Baptist as the Knight of the Desert, and the apostles as Knights of the Round Table. In the *Libro de caballería celestial del pié de la Rosa Fragante* and the *Segunda parte de la cavalleria de las hojas de la Rosa fragante* (2 vols., Valencia, 1554), Sempere portrayed in allegorical terms the story of the Old Testament down to King Hezekiah, and from Hezekiah to the Resurrection of Jesus respectively. Ticknor adds that a third volume, 'promised under the name of "The flower of the rose" never appeared, nor is it now easy to understand where consistent materials could have been found for its composition; the Bible having been nearly exhausted in the two former parts. But we have enough without it.'

Sempere may be the merchant Jheronimo Sentpere recorded by Gayangos as presiding at a Valencian poetry festival in 1533.

He was certainly a poet, being the author of the *Carolea* (1560), a historical chivalric poem on Carlos V, which shows the king as a knight of religion with much the same magniloquence as Jerónimo Jiménez de Urrea's hero in the contemporary *Carlos virtuoso*.

SEMPERE Y GUARINOS, JUAN (1754–1830), b. Elda, Alicante. Historian of law, literature, and institutions who was President of the Supreme Tribunal before the War of Independence, and consequently exiled thereafter. While in France he pursued his historical studies in such works as the *Histoire des Cortes d'Espagne* (Bordeaux, 1815), but he owes his place in the literary annals to the prologue and translation of Muratori's *Riflessioni sopra il buon gusto intorno le scienze e le arti* (Venice, 1708) which he produced in 1782, since the Spanish version helped to spread Muratori's neoclassical ideas on the need for fantasy to be regulated by the intellect; and to an expansion of that prologue entitled *Ensayo de una biblioteca española de los mejores escritores del reinado de Carlos III* (6 vols., Madrid, 1785—9).

SEM TOB DE CARRIÓN, see SHEM TOV ARDUTIEL.

Señas de identidad (Mexico City, 1966), a novel against the Franco regime written in exile by Juan Goytisolo (q.v.).

The years since the 1930s are remembered by Álvaro Mendiola, who had left his conservative family in Barcelona in October 1952, no longer able to tolerate the police state that Spain had become since the Civil War, but returned home to Barcelona with a liberal girl-friend, Dolores, in early 1963. Álvaro then revisits the scenes of his youth and in an amalgam of flashback and interior monologue recalls university friends such as the nihilist Sergio and the disillusioned Falangist Enrique. Goytisolo describes the 'lost decades' of Primo de Rivera, Ledesma, the depression, public works programmes, the false statistics of economic recovery and progress, the increase of tourism to assist economic viability, and the continuous censorship of news and thought. Lyrical passages of great beauty are set beside caricatures of Spanish stereotypes, and political commentaries beside metaphysical questions. The novel has been translated as *Marks of identity* (1969).

See Kessel Schwartz, *Juan Goytisolo* (New York, 1970), in Twayne's World Authors series, pp. 95–107.

Sendebar (also *Sindbad*, *Sindibad*, and *Syntipas*), the title of the first substantial collection of *fabliaux* to penetrate European literature from two principal sources: (a) a lost Pahlavi original surviving in an Arabic version and translated at the instruction of Fadrique, brother of Alfonso 'el Sabio' in 1253 as *Libro de los engannos et de los assayamientos de las muggeres*; (b) the Greek *Syntipas*, source of the *Dolophatos* or *Libro de los siete sabios de Roma* (trans. by Marcos Pérez, Burgos, 1530), a version of which had earlier been translated from Latin by Diego de Cañizares.

As with the *Calila e Digna* (q.v.), *Sendebar* is a collection of Oriental tales stressing worldly shrewdness in place of the Christian morality in contemporary European medieval tales. In one story, a vindictive concubine falsely accuses the king's son of attempted seduction, and, as the youth is mysteriously struck dumb for seven days, seven sages come forward to defend him. The concubine then repeats her accusation, and the youth's muteness vanishes. He vindicates himself to the king, who condemns the woman to death. The 26 *fabliaux* often reflect the low status of women in the early Orient, and their widespread popularity may incidentally reflect the same condition in early medieval Spain. M. Menéndez y Pelayo (q.v.) estimated *Sendebar*,

Calila e Digna, and *Barlaam y Josaphat* to be the three capital books entering Spanish literature from the East.

See B. E. Perry, 'The origin of the "Book of Sindbad"' in *Fábula*, vol. 3 (1959–60), pp. 1–94; *Tales of Sendebar: an edition and translation of the Hebrew version of the Seven Sages* (ed. Morris Epstein, Philadelphia, 1967); A. H. Krappe's 'Studies on the Seven Sages of Rome' in *Archivum Romanicum*, vol. 8 (1924), pp. 386–407, vol. 9 (1925), pp. 345–65, vol. 11 (1927), pp. 163–76, vol. 16 (1932), pp. 271–82, and vol. 19 (1935), pp. 213–26; and A. González Palencia, *Versiones castellanas del 'Sendebar'* (1946).

SENDER, RAMÓN J. (1902–   ), b. Alcolea de Cinca, Huesca. Spanish novelist, considered by Baroja and others to be the most significant of his generation. He appears as 'Manuel' in André Malraux's novel *L'espoir* (1937). Having fought in Morocco (1922–4), he took a job on *El Sol* until 1929, when he started to write for *La Libertad* and other left-wing papers. After periods of exile in Guatemala and Mexico, he moved to the U.S.A. to teach Spanish Literature.

His first novel *Imán* (1929) deals with the tragedy of the Moroccan war from the viewpoint of the ordinary soldier. Then came the trilogy *Los términos del presagio*, consisting of *Orden público* (1931), a denunciation of police brutality; *Viaje a la aldea del crimen* (1933), a similar work set in Cádiz; and *La noche de las cien cabezas* (1934), a work in the same nightmare genre as Quevedo's *Sueños*. *Siete domingos rojos* (1932; reworked as *Las tres sorores*, 1974) culminates in a strike, and is written in the manner of Upton Sinclair. In *Mister Witt en el cantón* (1935), Sender first revealed his inventive powers and psychological understanding, and won the National Prize for Literature for that year. *Contraataque* (1938) is about the Civil War. *El lugar del hombre* (1939) was an even greater success, dealing with the reactions of a community to the sudden reappearance of Sabino García, a poor labourer allegedly murdered fifteen years earlier by two other labourers. *Mexicayotl* (1940), the miscellaneous stories and legends of Mexico, were followed by the darkly symbolic *Epitalamio del prieto Trinidad* (Mexico City, 1942) which deals with a revolt in a Mexican penal colony, and the mutinous consequences, when the chief warder Trinidad is murdered on his wedding-day. Sender's fictionalized autobiographical series, first announced collectively as *La jornada*, is known now as *Crónica del alba*, after the first book (Mexico City, 1942). It also comprises *Hipógrifo violento* (Mexico City, 1954), *La quinta Julieta* (Mexico City, 1957), *El mancebo y los héroes* (1960), *La onza de oro*, and *Los niveles del existir*.

He has also written lives of S. Teresa and Hernán Cortes, travel books, and plays, the most notable of which is *El diantre*; tragicomedia (Mexico City, 1958). His other books include the existentialist *Proverbio de la muerte* (1939), rewritten as *La esfera* (Buenos Aires, 1947), *El verdugo afable* (Santiago de Chile, 1952), *Réquiem por un campesino español* (New York, 1960) his best work so far, *Examen de ingenios: los 98* (New York, 1960), *La llave* (Montevideo, 1960), *Las imagenes migratorias* (Mexico City, 1961), *El bandido adolescente* (Barcelona, 1965), *La aventura equinoccial de Lope de Aguirre* (1967), the 2-volume historical novel *Bizancio* (1968), *En la vida de Ignacio Morel* (1969), *Tánit* (Barcelona, 1970), *Zu, el ángel anfibio* (1970), the novels *Una virgen llama a tu puerta* (1973), *Cronus y la señora con rabo* (1974), *Jubileo en el zócalo* (1974), the collection of poems *Libro armilar de poesía y memorias bisiestas* (1974), the novel *La mesa de las tres Moiras* (1974), *Novelas ejemplares de Cíbola* (1975), *El futuro comenzó ayer: lecturas mosaicas* (1975), and the trilogy of Nancy novels: *La tesis de Nancy* (1962), *Nancy, doctora en gitanería* (1974), and *Nancy y el Bato loco* (1975). The first volume of Sender's *Obra completa* (Barcelona, 1976) consists of *Bizancio* and *Tres novelas teresianas*.

See J. Rivas, *El escritor y su senda: estudio crítico y literario sobre Ramón Sender* (Mexico City, 1967) and M. Peñuelas, *Conversaciones con Ramón J. Sender* (1970).

Senderos, see REVISTA DE LAS INDIAS.

SENECA, LUCIUS ANNAEUS (4 B.C.–A.D. 65), b. Corduba (Cordova). Playwright and Stoic philosopher. The second child of Lucius (or Marcus) Annaeus Seneca (q.v.). Educated in Rome, Seneca became a senator under Caligula and Claudius, but was exiled to Corsica during Claudian times. On Nero's accession, Seneca was recalled and wrote his lampoon *Apocolocyntosis*, or *Pumpkinification of the Divine Claudius*. He became an adviser to Nero but was dismissed from office and committed suicide at Nero's command.

His nine tragedies include rhetorical reworkings on the themes of Medea, Hippolytus, and Oedipus. An *Octavia* attributed to Seneca is now, however, believed to be the work of a near contemporary. His high position in the state and tolerance of Nero's vices ill accord with his philosophical views on virtue and simplicity. Seneca's *Naturales quaestiones* was used as a physics textbook well into the Middle Ages.

For his influence in Spain see K. A. Blüher, *Seneca in Spanien: Untersuchungen zur Geschichte der Seneca-Rezeption in Spanien vom 13. bis 17. Jahrhundert* (1970).

SENECA, Lucius (or Marcus?) Annaeus (*c.* 54 b.c.–*c.* a.d. 38), called Seneca the Elder, b. Corduba (Cordova). Rhetorician. The father of the more famous Lucius Annaeus Seneca. He divided his life between Rome and Spain. His principal works, apart from the history of Rome which has all but disappeared, are the *Controversiae*, imitated by Luis Vives, and the *Suasoriae*, two of which were translated and continued by Quevedo.

Senequismo, the neo-Stoic system of moral philosophy named after Lucius Annaeus Seneca (q.v.). The system resembles Stoicism in its aspiration to virtue, justice, and the good. Human liberty is defended against the practice of slavery (*Ep.* 44); vengeance is proscribed (*De ira*, II); and co-operation is extended to all men (*De ira*, I), including one's enemies (*De vita beata*, 20).

Seneca was rediscovered by the Spanish humanists of the 15th c., and his works are constantly cited in the literature of the period. Poetry, too, is full of *senequismo*; the Senecan Fernán Pérez de Guzmán (q.v.) praises his master Alfonso de Cartagena (q.v.) as 'aquel Séneca / a quien yo era Lucilo'. *Senequismo* became fashionable in the works of Santillana, 'El Tostado' (Alfonso de Madrigal), Álvaro de Luna, Hernán Núñez el Pinciano, Navarrete, Quevedo, Gracián, and Saavedra Fajardo (qq.v.), and influenced writers as diverse as Diderot and Goethe. Taken to extremes, the system becomes *cinismo* (cynicism) advocating self-sufficiency and the reduction of one's needs to a minimum.

Señor de Pigmalión, El (1923), a play by Jacinto Grau Delgado (q.v.), subtitled *farsa tragicocómica*, and first published in *La Farsa*, no. 40 (1923).

In the imaginary city of Aldurcara, the theatre is being prepared for an unusual show: Pigmalión and his lifelike puppets, which like him feel human passion and are subject to the other human laws. Pigmalión's dream is to surpass his previous creations, and also mankind, by making a puppet without any defect. This doll is Pomponina, with whom Pigmalión has fallen in love, though he realizes that she loathes him.

The local dignitaries assemble in the theatre for a preview, and the Duke of Aldurcara is enchanted by Pomponina, whom he seeks in vain to buy from Pigmalión. An hour later, on the silent stage, the dolls emerge from their boxes. The coquettish Pomponina is attracted by the money offered her by Mingo Revulgo (q.v.), and the other 'characters' all show their human traits: Lindo his sentimentality, Juan el Tonto his foolishness, and Pedro de Urdemalas

(q.v.) his malice. The Duke stealthily elopes with Pomponina, offering her a life of luxury, and the other puppets take their chance to escape.

In fury, Pigmalión pursues his dolls and the Duke with a whip. On finding them, he terrifies all but Urdemalas, who smiles insolently, and takes advantage of Pigmalión's turned back to shoot his master. Pigmalión feigns death, and all the characters again run away, except for Juan el Tonto. Pigmalión wipes the blood away and holds out his hand to Juan to be helped to his feet. The shrewd and vindictive 'Fool' now takes vengeance on his master by beating him on the head with the same shotgun until Pigmalión dies, a victim of his own puppet.

With influences as diverse as Cervantes and Pirandello, Grau contrives a play combining traditional figures of the *commedia dell' arte* and Spanish folklore with the eternal failings of human weakness and arrogance; lifelike puppets and puppetlike humans; and the relationship between an artist and his inventions. Pigmalión's dying words are a reflection on the 'sad fate of the hero, continually humiliated, in his arrogance, by the puppets of his fantasy'. The play also attacks contemporary theatre-managers for their reluctance to stage anything intellectually demanding, and indeed it was not performed in Madrid until 1928, five years after its Paris première.

Señor Presidente, El, a novel by the 1967 winner of the Nobel Prize for Literature, the Guatemalan Miguel Ángel Asturias (q.v.). Its kernel is the story *Los mendigos políticos*, begun in Guatemala in 1922 and completed in Paris in the early 1930s. It was published in 1946, remodelled after the fall of the dictator Jorge Ubico, and attracted much critical attention with the appearance of its second edition in 1948.

Guatemala's dictator Estrada Cabrera (1898–1920) is the shadow behind the book, but it transcends one regime and one country, distorting symbolically a city and its inhabitants to portray the horrors of domination by one man in all places and at all times. The United States' support of the regime, parallels between modern Guatemala and Mayan legends, hallucinations, interior monologues, sadism, and violence form some of the varied themes and style of a work which intersperses the ever-present evil with tantalizing prospects of hope. *The President* (London, 1963) is a translation by F. Partridge.

See G. Martin, 'El señor Presidente and how to read it' in *BHS*, vol. 47 (1970), pp. 223–43.

Sentimiento trágico de la vida en los hombres y en los pueblos, Del (1913), a long philosophical essay by Miguel de Unamuno (q.v.). The essence is his belief that the idea of God is not the cause, but the consequence, of man's longing for immortality. It is this need that constitutes the tragic sense of life.

Theologically unorthodox, Unamuno rejects rationalism, believing that immortality is attainable because man needs it so strongly. Man differs from animals not so much in his capacity for reason as in his capacity for feeling, and it is feeling, he argues, that made possible Kant's leap from his *Kritik der reinen Vernunft* to the *Kritik der praktischen Vernunft*. Immortality will be denied to those who do not seek it strongly enough. He concludes by opposing faith in Roman Catholicism, rationalism, or any other system; doubt and wonder alone are tenable philosophical positions.

There are translations by J. E. C. Flitch (London, 1921), by P. Smith (1958), and by Anthony Kerrigan (London, 1973).

Sepharad (Hebrew: 'Spain'), see SEFARDÍ.

SEPÚLVEDA, JUAN GINÉS DE (1490?–1573), b. Pozo Blanco, Cordova. Having studied classics in Cordova, Alcalá, and Bologna, he wrote a biography of Gil de Albornoz, founder of the Spanish College in Bologna. He translated the *Politics* of Aristotle (Paris, 1548) and entered into controversy with Erasmus, and subsequently with Fray Bartolomé de Las Casas (q.v.), whose pro-Indian *Destrucción de las Indias* he answered with dialogues entitled *Democrates alter; sive, de justi belli causis*, a document published and translated into Spanish by Menéndez y Pelayo in the *Boletín de la Real Academia de la Historia*, vol. 21 (1892). When he returned to Spain, Carlos I named him court historian, and he wrote the conscientious *De rebus gestis Caroli V* (1556) and *De rebus gestis Philippi II* (1564) in limpid Latin praised as 'Ciceronian' by Menéndez y Pelayo.

Sepúlveda gave evidence in the emperor's tribunal against Las Casas's allegations of brutality by the Spaniards in Hispaniola, quoting Aristotle's justification for subjugating inferior races. The Crown officially repudiated Sepúlveda's policy, and ordered the conversion of the American Indians to be attained by peaceful methods, passing laws in 1542 and 1573 that incorporated the ideas of Las Casas, though retaining some of Sepúlveda's views.

His *Opera* in Latin were collected by F. Cerdá y Rico (1780).

See A. F. Bell, *Juan Ginés de Sepúlveda* (Oxford, 1925); Teodoro Andrés Marcos, *Los imperialismos de Juan Ginés Sepúlveda en su 'Democrates alter'* (1948); A. Losada, bibliography in the *Revista Bibliográfica y Documental* (vol. 1, 1947, pp. 315–93); *Epistolario* (ed., 1966); *Juan Ginés de Sepúlveda a través de su Epistolario, y nuevos documentos* (1973); and *Juan Ginés de Sepúlveda: estudios y su crónica indiana en el IV centenario de su muerte* (Valladolid, 1976).

SEPÚLVEDA, LORENZO DE (*fl.* 1551), ballad-writer who versified the ancient Castilian chronicles in his popular and influential *Romances nuevamente sacados de Historias Antiguas de la Crónica de España* (Antwerp, 1551), several times enlarged, to the extent of 156 ballads in the edition of 1584.

His ballad 'En Sant Pedro de Cardeña' became famous in the 19th c. as the source of *Le Cid et le juif* by Théophile Gautier (1811–1872). The *Comedia llamada de Sepúlveda* based on Ariosto's *Il negromante* and Secchi's *Gl' inganni* (1547) is not in fact attributable to Lorenzo.

Sepúlveda's ballads were reprinted in vols. 10 and 16 (1849–51) of the BAE.

SEPÚLVEDA LEYTON, CARLOS (1894–1941), b. Santiago. Chilean novelist. He was brought up in the slums of Matadero, Santiago, and became a teacher. These two autobiographical elements form the basis for his novels: *Hijuna* (1934), on the childhood of his hero Juan de Dios from about 1905; *La fábrica* (1935), on the ignorance and prejudice of his teacher-training period; and *Camarada* (1938), on his period as a teacher up to *c.* 1930, on the germs of social revolution, and on his part in a strike by teachers. The earnest effort to understand the situation instead of bitterly condemning it makes this trilogy one of the most serious fictional treatments of Chile this century.

See Jaime Valdivieso, *Un asalto a la tradición. Sepúlveda Leyton: vida y obra* (1963).

SERÍS, HOMERO (1879–1969), b. Granada. Bibliographer and literary scholar. He was a disciple of R. Menéndez Pidal (whose bibliography he compiled in 1931) and of A. Morel-Fatio. Head of the Department of Bibliography in the Centro de Estudios Históricos in Madrid 1925–36, he emigrated to the U.S.A. during the Spanish Civil War and became a naturalized U.S. citizen in 1941.

He was Director of the Centro de Estudios Hispánicos at Syracuse University (New York) from 1945 until his retirement, and produced an indispensable tool for Hispanists: the *Manual de bibliografía de la literatura española* (Part 1 only published, 2 vols., New York, 1948–54).

SERPA, ENRIQUE (1899–), Cuban poet, realistic novelist, and short-story writer. His short stories include *Felisa y yo* (1937) and *Noche de fiesta* (1951), his novels *Contrabando* (1938) and the less successful *La trampa* (1956). His poetry marks the transition from modernism to ultraism in *La miel de las horas* (1925) and *Vitrina* (1940).

SERRA, NARCISO SÁENZ DÍAZ (1830–77), b. Madrid. Playwright. He wrote over forty plays, some Romantic in a style not far removed from that of José Zorrilla (q.v.), as in *El reloj de San Plácido* (1858) or the earlier *Con el diablo a cuchilladas* (1854), some *costumbrista* in manner, and some influenced by Spanish classical drama. He also adapted some Golden Age plays, such as Tirso de Molina's *Amar por señas*. Serra is best remembered for plays on Cervantes: *El loco de la guardilla. Paso que pasó en el siglo XVI* (1863) and its sequel *El bien tardío* (1867), for *La boda de Quevedo* (1854), and for *¡Don Tomás!* (1858), though all his plays are hastily written, lose a great deal in the reading, and are unequal in quality and vulgar in tone.

His poetry was collected in *Poesías líricas* (1848) and *Leyendas, cuentos y poesías* (1876).

See N. Alonso Cortes, *Quevedo en el teatro y otras cosas* (Valladolid, 1930), pp. 129–202.

Serranilla, a song or poem, usually in the form of a six- or eight-syllable *romance*, *villancico*, or *canción*, purportedly written by a townsman of some learning such as a knight or cleric on encountering a highland girl or *serrana*. Of Luso-Galician ancestry, the Spanish *serranilla* (which has its counterparts in most European languages), was parodied by Juan Ruiz, Archpriest of Hita, in the *Libro de buen amor* (qq.v.); the most celebrated examples are those of the Marqués de Santillana (q.v.). It is analogous to the *pastorelas* (q.v.), which some practitioners imitated. It influenced poets of the *Cancionero*, was set to music by composers of the Golden Age, and recurs in 20th c. poets such as Enrique de Mesa.

> *Non creo las rosas*
> *de la primavera*
> *sean tan fermosas*
> *nin de tal manera,*
> *fablando sin glosa*
> *si antes supiera*
> *de aquella vaquera*
> *de la Finojosa.*
> —Marqués de Santillana.

SERRANO PONCELA, SEGUNDO (1912–   ), b. Madrid. Literary historian and novelist. He emigrated in 1939, first to the Dominican Republic, later to Puerto Rico and Venezuela. A self-declared disciple of Américo Castro (q.v.), Serrano Poncela has been influenced by the

essays of Unamuno and Machado (q.v.), whom he studied in *El pensamiento de Unamuno* (Mexico City, 1953) and *Antonio Machado: su vida y su obra* (Buenos Aires, 1954).

His other critical essays include *El secreto de Melibea* (1959), *Dostoiewski menor* (1959), and *Del Romancero a Machado* (Caracas, 1962). E. G. de Nora has indicated the pre- or pseudo-existential nihilism of his short stories and novels. The titles are *Seis relatos y uno más* (Mexico City, 1954), the erotic *La venda* (Buenos Aires, 1956), *La raya oscura* (Buenos Aires, 1959), *La puerta de Capricornio* (Buenos Aires, 1960), *Un olor a crisantemo* (Barcelona, 1961), and *Habitación para un hombre solo* (Barcelona, 1963).

SERRANO Y SANZ, MANUEL (1868–1932), b. Ruguilla, Guadalajara. Historian and literary critic. Professor of History at the University of Saragossa. Among his most significant publications were *Apuntes para una biblioteca de escritoras españolas desde 1401 a 1833* (2 vols., 1893–5), *Noticias biográficas de Fernando de Rojas . . .* (1902), the compilation of the important collection *Autobiografías y memorias* forming vol. 2 (1905) of the NBAE, and *Orígenes de la dominación española en América* (1918), also in the NBAE.

See the essays in homage in *El erudito español don Manuel Serrano y Sanz* (1935) offered by the city of Sigüenza.

Sextilla, a variant of the *sextina* (q.v.) but in *arte menor*, that is with lines of fewer than nine syllables (usually eight), except that one of the lines may be hendecasyllabic. The rhymescheme is variable, but is most frequently ababab. The most common stanza forms are a quartet and a couplet, or a couplet and a *redondilla*, as in this example:

> *Yo haré dudar del cariño*
> *que muestra al tímido niño*
> *el corazón maternal;*
> *y haré vislumbre al través*
> *de su amor el interés*
> *como su vil manantial*
> —Espronceda.

Sextina, a six-line stanza of hendecasyllables (with an occasional heptasyllable in later writers) first found in the work of the Provençal poet Arnaut Daniel, but introduced into Castilian from the Italian models of Petrarch ˙and Sannazaro. Rhyme is not by different words with a similar ending, but by the same words repeated throughout six stanzas, the sixth line ending with the same word as the first line of the sixth stanza, the fifth like the second, and the fourth like the third (see Juan de la Cueva's 'Ejemplar poético' in *El infamador*, 1924, p. 232). The rhyme scheme is variable.

A *sextina doble*, such as that sung by Arsileo in the fifth book of Jorge de Montemayor's *Diana* (qq.v.) adds a further six stanzas of six lines each:

> *¡ Ay, vanas esperanças quantos días*
> *anduve hecho siervo de un engaño,*
> *y quán en vano mis cansados ojos*
> *con lágrimas regaron este valle!*
> *pagado me an amor y la fortuna*
> *pagado me an, no sé de qué me quexo.*

The *sextilla* (q.v.) is a variant of the *sextina*.

SHEM TOV ARDUTIEL (Spanish: SANTOB or SEM TOB, 1290?–1369?). Rabbi of Carrión de los Condes. Pedro the Cruel was noted for his tolerance towards the Jews, and Shem Tov addressed to him a collection of *Proverbios morales* drawn from biblical and Talmudic sources. These aphorisms (a genre called *musar* in Hebrew) consist of 686 stanzas in heptasyllabic *cuartetas*, and were the first of their kind written in Spanish. Shem Tov later translated them into Hebrew for the Jewish community.

The succinct *Proverbios morales* were praised by the Marqués de Santillana, who imitated them. They survive in three MSS.: one in the National Library in Madrid; one in the Escorial, edited by F. Janer for the BAE, vol. 57 (1864) and of which a critical edition has been produced by I. González Llubera (Cambridge, 1947); and one in Cambridge University, published by I. González Llubera in *Romance Philology*, vol. 4 (1950–1), pp. 217–56. A. García Calvo's edition (1974) contains a version in modern Spanish to accompany the original.

Shem Tov also wrote, in 1345, a rhymed prose *Disputa entre el cálamo y las tijeras*, and translated into Hebrew the liturgical work of Israel ben Israel.

Sí de las niñas, El (1805), a social satire by Leandro Fernández de Moratín (q.v.) against arranged marriages, a common theme in his drama. Probably written after a draft play *El tutor*, now lost, this is the masterpiece of Moratín, and one of the finest of Spanish neoclassical plays.

The action is set in an inn in Alcalá, from seven in the evening to five the following morning, and thus observes the classical unities of time and place. The sexagenarian Don Diego awaits the arrival from her convent of Francisca, whose mother has arranged a marriage with him. Diego's servant Simón believes that the marriage is to be between Francisca and Carlos, Don Diego's nephew. The charming Francisca is then contrasted with her scheming mother, the thrice-widowed Doña Irene. Francisca in fact loves the 'student' Don Félix de Toledo, whom she had met in Madrid. Don Félix arrives, serenades Francisca, and throws her a letter, but in the dark neither she nor her mother, who has been spying on the young couple, can find it. Don Diego picks it up and discovers that his bride-to-be loves another man. No martinet, he seeks an explanation from the frightened Francisca, and learns that 'Félix' is none other than his nephew Carlos. Irene seeks to excuse the behaviour of her daughter but Diego forgives Francisca and consents to her marriage to Carlos, saying 'esto resulta del abuso de la autoridad, de la opresión que la juventud padece; éstas son las seguridades que dan los padres y los tutores, y esto es lo que debe fiar en el sí de las niñas . . .'. Francisca's 'admirable' convent upbringing has, through no fault of her own, turned her into an insincere and deceitful woman.

The plot, used earlier by Lope de Vega in *La discreta enamorada* and by Rojas Zorrilla in *Entre bobos anda el juego*, is based on an experience of Moratín's own, when he fell in love with Francisca Muñoz Ortiz but through his timidity lost her to a soldier much younger than himself.

The attack on self-delusion and deception which Moratín thought common vices in the Spain of his time is perhaps overshadowed by the powerful anticlerical tone influenced by Voltaire (whose *Candide* he had translated, Cádiz [but probably Valencia], 1838). The play both teaches and exemplifies Moratín's view that literature should combine entertainment with a moral lesson. The play was phenomenally successful with the public, but caused disquiet in some ecclesiastical circles and in an attempt to make political capital from the discrediting of a work by Moratín, as the protégé of Manuel Godoy, a certain Bernardo García was induced by powerful friends to write *Carta crítica de un vecino de Guadalajara sobre la comedia 'El sí de las niñas' . . .* against Moratín and two poets (Arriaza and Quintana) who had written odes on the Battle of Trafalgar. García's *Carta*, which remained unpublished after discussion between nominees of the Inquisition, specifically opposed Moratín's critique of convent education, and generally takes Moratín to task for alleged inconsistency and lack of verisimilitude. Faced with opposition from García and others, Moratín angrily determined to write nothing more for the stage.

Many editions are available, including one in Clásicos Castellanos (1933), and one by John Dowling and R. Andioc (with *La comedia nueva*, q.v., 1969).

See Joaquín Casalduero, 'Forma y sentido de

"El sí de las niñas"' in *Nueva Revista de Filología Hispánica*, vol. 11 (1957) pp. 36–56; Alfredo Lefebvre (ed.), *El teatro de Moratín* (Santiago de Chile, 1958); and Ch. V. Aubrun's essay on the play in 'Homenaje a Ángel del Río' (pp. 29–35) in *Revista Hispánica Moderna*, vol. 31 (1965).

SIERRA, JUSTO (1848–1912), b. Campeche. Mexican historian and educationist. The son of Justo Sierra O'Reilly (q.v.), he qualified as an advocate and entered radical journalism, contributing vigorous political articles, poems, and stories to many newspapers and magazines, such as *El Renacimiento*, in which his novel *El ángel del porvenir* (1873) first appeared.

The death in 1880 of his beloved brother Santiago, also a writer, made a great impression on him, persuading him to turn to serious works of sociology, history, and education. He was Minister of Education 1905–11, during which period he founded the National University (1910). He was appointed ambassador to Spain in 1912, but died very shortly after taking up his duties.

The *Obras completas* (1948–9) of Sierra fill 15 vols. His most outstanding works are the *Evolución política del pueblo mexicano* (1940), which had previously appeared in the collective *México: su evolución social*, vols. 1–2 (1900–2) and has been translated by C. Ramsdell as *The political evolution of the Mexican people* (Austin, Texas, 1969); *Cuentos románticos* (Paris, 1896: 3rd edn., 1946), described by the author as 'poemillas en prosa' and forming with the novels of Altamirano (q.v.) the transitional point at which the Mexican novel assumes a purely literary (as opposed to a socio-political) importance; and the *Poesías* (1937) compiled by Margaret Dorothy Kress. There is an accessible edition of Sierra's *Prosas* (1939; 3rd edn., 1963) selected by Antonio Caso.

Apart from stressing the need for national education at all levels, Sierra was notable for his insistence on integrating the Indian into all aspects of Mexican life.

See Agustín Yáñez, *Don Justo Sierra* (1950).

SIERRA O'REILLY, JUSTO (1814–61), b. Tixcacaltuyú, Sotuta, Yucatán. Mexican historical novelist and journalist. The father of Justo Sierra (q.v.). He graduated as a lawyer in 1838 and practised from 1839 as a judge in courts of first instance. He created the local press in Yucatán with a series of four newspapers: *El Museo Yucateco* (1841–2), in which he published his novel *El filibustero: leyenda del siglo XVII* (1841 and later edns.); the *Registro Yucateco* (1845–9), in which he published his novel *Un año en el Hospital de San Lázaro* (1845–6); *El Fénix* (1848–51), in which his novel *La hija del judío* (1849

and later edns.) appeared under the anagram José Turrisa; and *La Unión Liberal* (1855–61).

These romantic novels introduced the fashion of serials into Mexico, borrowing the technique and the historical setting from Dumas and Sue. Posthumous editions of Sierra O'Reilly's works appeared in 1905 (*Obras*) and 1960 (*Páginas escogidas*, ed. by Carlos J. Sierra).

Siete Infantes de Lara, an epic poem based on real events of the year 985, during the reign of Garci Fernández (970–95), and celebrating a heroic period in the history of Castile. It was composed originally not much later than 1000, and has been reconstructed in part by R. Menéndez Pidal from the chronicles of Castile.

The subject of the poem is a family feud, subsequent betrayal, and vengeance. The seven princes of Lara (or Salas) attend the wedding of Doña Lambra and their uncle Ruy Velázquez, and during unruly scenes which develop into a battle, Doña Lambra angrily denounces the Infantes for offending the ceremony and thus herself.

Though peace is eventually restored, Lambra succeeds in persuading her husband to send a message in Arabic to Gonzalo Gustios (father of the Infantes) which will cause Gustios to be killed. Velázquez feigns to take the Infantes out on a mission against the Moors: they are killed and their heads sent to Cordova, where the Moorish king shows them to the imprisoned Gustios. A sequel to this tragic tale centres on the figure of Mudarra the Avenger (another son of Gustios from his union with a Moorish woman) who finally succeeds in killing both Velázquez and Lambra.

The chronicler of the *Estoria de España* (also known as the *Primera crónica general*), compiled in the second half of the 13th c. under the guidance of Alfonso 'el Sabio' (q.v.), made extensive use of epic poems, and acknowledged these borrowings openly. One such epic was the *Siete Infantes de Lara*, existing in at least two other versions, one composed in the second half of the 13th c. or early in the 14th, and another (according to Menéndez Pidal) incorporated in the prose *Estoria de los Godos*. As C. C. Smith writes, 'The tale of insult, family feud, treachery, and vengeance seems to preserve features of a remote Spanish past in which Germanic customs hold sway and Christian restraints are absent'.

A number of ballads were composed on episodes in the legend, including 'Pártese el moro Alicante', 'A Calatrava la Vieja', 'Ya se salen de Castilla', and 'A cazar va don Rodrigo'.

Among the plays inspired by the story are *Los siete Infantes de Lara* (1579) by Juan de la Cueva (q.v.), based on *La Estoria del noble caballero el*

Conde Fernán González con la muerte de los siete Infantes de Lara; the anonymous *Famosos hechos de Mudarra*; Lope de Vega's *El bastardo Mudarra y los siete Infantes de Lara*, imitated by Alfonso Hurtado Velarde in *La gran tragedia de los siete Infantes de Lara* (*c.* 1615), imitated in its turn by Juan de Matos Fragoso in *El traidor contra su sangre* (1650). Another work of the year 1650 is *Los siete Infantes de Lara*, written jointly by Jerónimo Cáncer and Juan Vélez de Guevara.

In poetry the theme was treated by the Duque de Rivas (in *El moro expósito*), and by other Romantic poets.

See R. Menéndez Pidal, *La leyenda de los Infantes de Lara* (1896; 2nd edn., 1934); A. M. Espinosa, 'Sobre la leyenda de los Infantes de Lara' in *Romanic Review*, vol. 12, 1921, pp. 135–45; M. Menéndez y Pelayo, 'La leyenda de los Infantes de Lara por Menéndez Pidal' in his *Estudios y discursos de crítica histórica y literaria*, vol. 1 (Santander, 1941, pp. 119–42); and the relevant chronicle texts and reconstructed epic in R. Menéndez Pidal's *Reliquias de la poesía épica española* (1951), pp. 181–239.

Siete Partidas, Las (1256–63), the legal encyclopaedia drawn up under the supervision of Alfonso X (q.v.), to codify Castilian legal practice. Among the collaborators were Jacobo (or Jacomé) Ruiz, *el maestre de la ley*; Juan Alfonso, Archdeacon of Santiago; and Fernán Martínez. The *Partidas* follow Roman law in general and the *Institutes* of Justinian in particular; they are also influenced by Aristotle, Seneca, St. Isidore, and others. Apart from its purely legal worth, the book attains great dignity of thought and expression in examining the common good, and the right behaviour of kings. A fairly satisfactory edition was prepared and published by the Academia de la Historia (3 vols., 1807).

See J. M. Dihigo, 'Las Siete Partidas: estudio lingüístico' in *Revista de la Facultad de Letras y Ciencias* (Havana), vol. 33 (1923), pp. 1–71.

Siglo de Oro ('Golden Century', Golden Age), (a) a Golden Age is considered among poets to be that period of time and location governed by the god Saturn, in which men lived together in peace and harmony. (b) More restrictedly, a period in which art and letters flourish in a particular civilization. (c) In Spain, the period (from *c.* 1500 to *c.* 1681) which saw the publication of the major works by such writers as Cervantes, Juan de Valdés, Antonio de Guevara, Garcilaso de la Vega, Montemayor, Gaspar Gil Polo, Luis de León, Juan de la Cruz, Fernando de Herrera, Quevedo, Espinel, Góngora, Lope de Vega, Gracián, Calderón, Gil Vicente, Torres Naharro, L. Leonardo de Argensola,

Vélez de Guevara, Ruiz de Alarcón, Tirso de Molina, and Rojas Zorrilla (qq.v.).

The varied literature of the Golden Age is scarcely susceptible to generalization, but the majority of writings are characterized by religious fervour, with the influence of Erasmianism in the earlier decades of the period; by patriotism, and a new interest in early Spanish ballads and epics; by a heightened realism that has its roots in *La Celestina* and the *Libro de buen amor* (q.v.); and by a neo-Stoic thread that can be traced back to the influence of Seneca (see SENEQUISMO).

There is no general agreement as to the opening or closing year of the so-called Golden Century which most critics consider covers at least two hundred years. R. Trevor Davies, in *The Golden Century of Spain* (London, 1956), defines the period as 1501–1621; others limit it to the 16th c., or suggest that it begins with the coronation of the Catholic Sovereigns in 1474 and ends at 1700.

E. M. Wilson and D. Moir's *The Golden Age: Drama* (London, 1971), suggests the period 1492 to 1700, but perhaps the most widespread acceptance of a definition is that of Merimée's: 1517–1681. This period comprises three ages: 1517–98, or the reigns of Charles V and Philip II; 1598–1635, ending with the death of Lope de Vega and considered by Merimée to be the apogee of the Golden Age; and 1635 to 1681, ending with the death of Calderón and considered by Merimée the time of relative decadence.

See Ludwig Pfandl, *Spanische Kultur und Sitte des 16. und 17. Jahrhunderts* (Munich, 1924; translated by P. Félix Garcia, Barcelona, 1929); A. González Palencia, *La España del Siglo de Oro* (Stanford, Calif., 1939); R. Vilches Acuña, *España de la Edad de Oro* (Buenos Aires, 1946); and F. Pietri, *La España del Siglo de Oro* (1960).

SIGÜENZA, *Padre* JOSÉ DE (1544?–1606), b. Sigüenza. Historian and poet, who succeeded Arias Montano (q.v.) as librarian of the Escorial. He eventually became Prior of the Monastery there; Unamuno has described his *Historia de la Orden de San Jerónimo* (3 vols., 1595, 1600, 1605) as the 'Escorial of Spanish prose', in its flat, humourless but finally impressive solidity. The first volume is a life of St. Jerome. The third contains the best description of the Escorial yet and, with the second, has been reprinted (as vols. 8 and 12) in the NBAE (1907–9). The MS. of the first, entitled *Historia del Rey de los Reyes y Señor de los Señores Jesus Xristus, heri et hodie*, is in the Escorial.

Sigüenza's poems were edited by L. Villalba in *Ciudad de Dios* (vol. 99, 1914).

See M. A. Menger, *Fray José de Sigüenza, poeta*

e historiador, translated by G. Méndez Plancarte (Mexico City, 1944); and L. Rubío González, *Valores literarios del Padre Sigüenza* (1976).

SIGÜENZA Y GÓNGORA, CARLOS DE (1645–1700), b. Mexico City. Mexican scholar and poet, who was related on his mother's side to Luis de Góngora. One of the outstanding intellectuals of his time, he was appointed to the chair of Mathematics in Mexico University in 1672, and when he retired in 1694 he continued to write important works. He bequeathed his library and scientific instruments to the Jesuits, though he had left the Society of Jesus early in life and had attacked the Jesuit Kino who declared, among other hypotheses, that comets were an evil sign. Sigüenza replied in his *Libra astronómica y filosófica* (1690; ed. Bernavé Navarro, 1959) that the citation of authorities is invalid in science. Many of the historical writings completed after his retirement were not published in his lifetime, and were destroyed when the United States invaded Mexico in 1847.

His poetry is undistinguished but copious: *Primavera indiana: poema sacro-histórico* (1668; reprinted 1945), on the Virgin of Guadalupe, in 69 *octavas reales*; and *Oriental planeta evangélico: epopeya sacropanegírica* (1700), on the mission of St. Francis Xavier. The *Triumpho parthénico* (1683) compiles more than 500 compositions presented to Mexico University in a competition of 1682 to honour the Immaculate Conception, an anthology condemned by González Peña as lacking 'no sólo el buen gusto y la poesía, sino la sensatez y el decoro literario'.

Sigüenza's most popular book was *Los infortunios que Alonso Ramírez padeció en poder de ingleses piratas* (1690; reprinted, Madrid, 1902), a novel which mingled the traditions of the Byzantine adventure novel and the proto-picaresque style of *Lazarillo de Tormes* (q.v.). An epic poem on Cortés, *Piedad heroica de don Fernando Cortés* (1689), has been edited by Jaime Delgado (Madrid, 1960). Other modern editions include *Obras* (1928), *Poemas* (Madrid, 1931) compiled by I. A. Leonard and introduced by E. Abreu Gómez, and the *Obras históricas* (1944; 2nd edn., 1960).

See I. A. Leonard, *Don Carlos de Sigüenza y Góngora* (Berkeley, 1939); J. Rojas Garcidueñas, *Don Carlos Sigüenza y Góngora* (1945); and B. Santillán González, *Don Carlos Sigüenza y Góngora con unas notas para la bibliografía científica de su época* (1956). Some *Documentos inéditos* of Sigüenza have been edited and annotated by Irving A. Leonard (1963).

SILLÓ Y GUTIÉRREZ, EVARISTO (1841–74). Spanish poet. *Una fiesta en mi aldea* (1867) revealed a gentle poet of meditation and tranquillity.

Silló's work was published posthumously in *Poesías* (Valladolid, 1897).

Silva, an Italian verse form combining hendecasyllabic and heptasyllabic lines irregularly, with a variable rhyme scheme.

One of the best Spanish writers of *silvas* is Francisco de Rioja (q.v.), though Góngora also used the form for his *Soledades*.

SILVA, ANTONIO DE, the pseudonym used in his plays by Frai Jerónimo Bermúdez (q.v.).

SILVA, CLARA (1905–), b. Montevideo. Uruguayan poet and novelist. Her books of poetry began as intensely personal lyrics with *La cabellera oscura* (1945) and *Memoria de la Nada* (1948), continued with the sonnets on the conflict between mortal and divine love in *Los delirios* (1955) and the religious poems of *Las bodas* (1960), and turned to popular rhythms on traditional themes in *Guitarra en sombra* (1964).

Silva's novels have also moved some way from her obvious leanings towards the French *nouveau roman* in *La sobreviviente* (1951) to *El alma y los perros* (1962) and the excellent *Aviso a la población* (1964), spoiled only by an improbable denouement. It tells the story of a murderer who seems more sympathetic than police, warders, or judges, and seems to share a point of departure with the novel *Eloy* by Carlos Droguett (q.v.).

See Mario Benedetti, *Literatura uruguaya: siglo XX* (2nd edn., 1969).

SILVA, FELICIANO DE (1492?–1558?), b. Ciudad Rodrigo. Novelist. He married the daughter of a Jewish *converso* despite the difficulties, recording this love-match in the poignant *Sueño de Feliciano de Silva* at the end of part 1 of *Amadís de Grecia* (1530), a work which is in the full tradition of the romances of chivalry and is one of the first to include pastoral elements, taking as its model the *Arcadia* (1504) of Sannazaro. In this sequel to *Amadís de Gaula* (q.v.), the shepherd Darinel is in love with the proud shepherdess Silvia, who is none other than the abducted daughter of Lisuarte of Greece. Don Florisel de Niquea also becomes a shepherd, temporarily, to win her love. There is an even odder pastoral intrusion in Silva's *Segunda comedia de Celestina* (1534), perhaps the most successful early imitation of the great *Celestina* (q.v.). Celestina is here resuscitated, to the amazement of Elicia, Areusa, and the reader; the sequel maintains the original's anti-clerical tone.

Silva's second *Celestina* is far superior to his romances of chivalry, rightly mocked by Cervantes for their outlandish heroics and contorted style. They included *La crónica de los muy* valientes y esforçados e invencibles cavalleros Don Florisel de Niquea y el fuerte Anaxartes (Valladolid, 1532) in two parts; the Tercera parte . . . (Medina del Campo, 1535); and the Quarta parte . . . (Salamanca, 1567).

M. I. Chamorro has recently edited the Amadís de Grecia (1968).

See E. Cotarelo y Mori, 'Nuevas noticias biográficas de Feliciano de Silva' in the BRAE (1926); and Sydney P. Cravens, Feliciano de Silva y los antecedentes de la novela pastoril (Chapel Hill, N.C., 1976).

SILVA, José Asunción (1865–96), b. Bogotá. Colombian poet, described by Juan Valera (q.v.) as 'el más delicado y profundo de los líricos hispanoamericanos'.

The son of Ricardo Silva the costumbrista, and a member of the Mosaico group, Silva spent an influential period in France (and elsewhere in Europe) from 1884. A spate of misfortunes quickly depressed him however: the death of his father in 1887, the loss of his MSS. in a shipwreck, financial ruin which had loomed even during his father's lifetime, his frustration in a society where his artistic pretensions caused him to be isolated as an eccentric, the death of his sister Elvira in 1891, and the increasing persecution by his creditors, were cumulative factors which finally drove him to suicide.

He chose the favoured Romantic themes of love and death, the Nocturno III being especially evocative of death's constant proximity. His first period, that of youth, coincided with the influence of Bécquer: his second was the mature period of intellectual excitement in France, when he brought back to Colombia such important works as those of Schopenhauer and the contemporary French poets; the third period is that of growing despair.

Silva's works have never become outmoded: among modern editions are the Poesías completas: seguidas de prosas selectas (Madrid, 1951), the Obra completa (2 vols., Buenos Aires, 1968), and two Colombian editions, the Obra completa (1956) in the Biblioteca de Autores Colombianos and the Obras completas (1965) published by the Banco de la República.

The autobiographical novel De sobremesa (1887–1896) was rewritten after the original had been lost at sea, and is of great importance for understanding Silva's art and mind.

See Alberto Miramón, José Asunción Silva: ensayo biográfico con documentos inéditos (1937; 2nd edn., 1957); Juan Carlos Ghiano, José Asunción Silva (Buenos Aires, 1967); E. Camacho Guizado, La poesía de José Asunción Silva (1968); and Betty T. Osiek, José Asunción Silva: estudio estilístico de su poesía (1968).

SILVA, Víctor Domingo (1882–1960), b. Coquimbo province, Chile. Chilean novelist and journalist, poet and playwright, who won the National Literary Prize in 1954. His poetry consists of Hacia allá (1905), El derrotero (1908), La selva florida (1911), the patriotic ballads on the war at sea El romancero naval (1912), Odas y arengas (1913), and Poesías (1914). Silva's poetry is often careless, and too abundant, seeking popularity at the expense of quality.

The most interesting of his fiction is the pair of historical novels on the Araucanian Indians and their conquest, El mestizo Alejo (1934) and La criollita (1935); he also wrote Golondrina de invierno (1911), Palomilla Brava (1923) also known as Pepe Lucho and Papelucho, its sequel El cachorro (1937), and Los árboles no dejan ver el bosque (1948).

His plays include Nuestras víctimas (1912), La vorágine (1919), Las aguas muertas (1921), and Lucesita en la sombra (1926).

SILVA VALDÉS, Fernán (1887–), b. Montevideo. Uruguayan poet and short-story writer. His first poetic period reflected the fashionable 'decadent' style in Ánforas de barro (1913) and Humo de incienso (1917), but he made a truly original contribution with the ultraist Creolism of Agua del tiempo (1921) and Poemas nativos (1925), calling his innovations 'nativism'. With Intemperie (1930) he moved to popular verse forms, particularly the ballad, while Romances chúcaros (1933) and Romancero del Sur (1939) consisted purely of ballads of high quality. There is a useful Antología poética (1943).

Silva Valdés was also an accomplished prose-writer: Leyendas (1936), Cuentos y leyendas del Río de la Plata (1941), Leyendas americanas (1945), Cuentos del Uruguay (1945), and Lenguaraz (1955); he also wrote prose and verse for children.

SILVELA, Manuel (1781–1832), b. Valladolid. Playwright and historian. He collaborated with the French invaders of 1808, as did his friend and mentor Leandro Fernández de Moratín (q.v.); when the French withdrew the two left for Bordeaux, and in 1827 for Paris. He wrote two plays influenced by Moratín: Don Simplicio de Utrera and El reconciliador. His works were collected in Obras póstumas (2 vols., 1845), with a biography by his son F. A. Silvela, and Obras literarias (1890) in Colección de Escritores Castellanos.

See the obituary by a son, Francisco Silvela y de Le-Vielleuze, 'Necrología del Excmo. Sr. Don Manuel Silvela' in Memorias de la Real Academia Española, vol. 8 (1902), pp. 220–35.

Manuel Silvela is not to be confused with his nephew Manuel Silvela y de Le-Vielleuze

(1843–1905) who edited the works of Leandro Fernández de Moratín.

SILVESTRE, GREGORIO (1520–69), b. Lisbon. Poet. The son of João Rodrigues, doctor to João III of Portugal, Silvestre lived for many years in Granada. He was organist of the cathedral there, and was host (1567–9) to the Antequera poet Barahona de Soto (q.v.). His early poetry employed octosyllables for medieval themes, but with the triumph of Renaissance themes and the hendecasyllabic metre, Silvestre successfully adapted to these.

Silvestre's Renaissance poetry was in the mythological mode: *Fábula de Dafne y Apolo, Fábula de Píramo y Tisbe,* and *Fábula de Narciso,* though he also wrote fine religious verse and sonnets.

Silvestre's *Obras* (Granada, 1582) were first collected by his heirs and P. de Cáceres y Espinosa, and there have been later editions by A. R. Rodríguez-Moñino (in *Cruz y Raya,* 1935, pp. 75–113) and by J. del Rosal (Barcelona, 1940).

See A. Marín Ocete, *Gregorio Silvestre: estudio biográfico y crítico* (Granada, 1939).

SIMANCAS, DIEGO DE (*fl.* 1525–75), b. Cordova. Autobiographer, After studying in Valladolid and Salamanca, he was appointed to the Inquisition and wrote *De catholicis institutionibus* (Valladolid, 1552), in fact little more than an analysis of heresy and its forms. He became Bishop of Zamora and conducted against other churchmen various undignified campaigns of vilification, including his celebrated *La vida y cosas notables del senor obispo de Zamora Don Diego de Simancas.* This MS. in the Biblioteca Colombina, copied in 1685, was 'dictado por la soberbia', in the words of M. Serrano y Sanz, for it contains a protracted attack on Archbishop Carranza and lacks all signs of Christian humility.

Serrano y Sanz edited Simancas' autobiography in vol. 2 (1905) of the NBAE.

Símbolo de la Fe, Introducción del, see INTRODUCTION DEL SYMBOLO DE LA FE.

SIMÓ, ANA MARÍA (1943–), Cuban short-story writer. She was the most talented of an *avant-garde* group, El Puente, now disbanded. Her first book was *Las fábulas* (1962), consisting mainly of black fantasies. Two stories were translated as 'A deathly sameness' and 'Growth of the plant' for J. M. Cohen's anthology *Writers in the new Cuba* (Harmondsworth, 1967).

SIMÓN DÍAZ, JOSÉ (1920–), b. Madrid. The doyen of Hispanic bibliographers. He has compiled the exhaustive *Bibliografía de la*

literatura hispánica (in progress, 1950–), abridged before completion in the essential *Manual de bibliografía de la literatura española* (Barcelona, 1963; 2nd edn. with *Adiciones, 1962–4,* 1966, and supplementary *Adiciones, 1965—1970,* 1972). Among his major bibliographical works is the standard *Ensayo de una bibliografía de las obras y artículos sobre la vida y escritos de Lope de Vega Carpio* (1955), written with Juan de José Prades; with a supplement of *Nuevos estudios*... (1961). A founding member (1951) of the Instituto de Estudios Madrileños, he has been its President since 1964. He is director of *Cuadernos Bibliográficos* and director of the bibliographical section of the Instituto Nacional del Libro Español.

Simplismo, see HIDALGO, Alberto.

Sinalefa ('synalœpha'), a term in Spanish phonetics denoting changes in the sounds of adjacent words caused by the grouping of two or more vowels as one metric syllable.

Before the 17th c., synalœpha does not, however, occur in cases involving the aspirated h (i.e., those cases in which Spanish h < Latin f, e.g. ha*z*aña, her*m*oso, h*o*ja, huir).

SINÁN, ROGELIO, pseudonym of Bernardo Domínguez Alba (q.v.).

SIN CIELO, JUAN, pseudonym of Alejandro Carrión (q.v.).

Sindbad, see SENDEBAR.

Smith Professorship, Harvard University, a chair established at Harvard in 1816 following a bequest by Abiel Smith and intended for a professorship of the French and Spanish Languages and Literatures. Among the most distinguished holders of the chair have been George Ticknor (1819–35), author of a standard *History of Spanish literature* (3 vols., 1849; many later edns.), Henry Wadsworth Longfellow (1836–54), James Russell Lowell (1854–91), and J. D. M. Ford (1907–43).

Sobre héroes y tumbas (1961), a novel by the Argentinian Ernesto Sábato (q.v.).

The source of the novel is the actual death by shooting of a man, Fernando Vidal Olmos (a perverse and sadistic paranoiac) at the hands of his only daughter Alejandra, who then committed suicide by setting fire to their home on 24 June 1955. Vidal Olmos had written, shortly before he was killed, a manuscript called *Informe de ciegos.* Sábato, on the basis of these few details, reconstructs not only a sequence of possible events leading up to the double death, but also a possible text of the *Informe*.

The long novel incorporates satire, the absurd, black comedy, characters imaginary and real (Borges, for instance, is portrayed), a conflicting time sequence, complex mythological and psychoanalytical symbolism, and a language deliberately cultivating ambiguity and imprecision to reflect the uncertainty of the characters and the hallucinatory Buenos Aires in which they live.

Bruno, the novel's optimistic commentator, listens to Martín Castillo's account of his adolescent failure to understand Alejandra (who killed her father in the prologue). Similarly, Bruno had failed to understand Alejandra's mother, Georgina. Martín is desolated by the suicide of Alejandra, but finds love and kindness with Hortensia, a woman of the lowest social class. We learn that Alejandra had an incestuous relationship with her father and had been torn by feelings of guilt and anguish which could only have ended in suicide. The title refers to the heroes and tombs of the Olmos family, descended from an English officer (Patrick Elmtrees) and his Argentinian wife. The Olmos family had opposed Rosas as they now oppose Perón. Sábato implies that, by wiping out the satanic Vidal Olmos and then herself as a murderess, Alejandra has given Buenos Aires and Argentina another chance. Martín, young and now hopeful with a wife of honest peasant stock, represents a new and better land.

See the interview with Sábato in *Mundo Nuevo*, no. 5 (1966), pp. 5–21; and essays by E. B. Cersósimo and A. B. Dellepiane in H. F. Giacoman (ed.), *Homenaje a Ernesto Sábato* (New York, 1972).

Sobre los ángeles (1929), the fifth and finest book of poems by Rafael Alberti (q.v.), who here finds his authentic voice. He rejected the classical verse forms (the sonnet, ballad, and tercet) of such books as *Cal y canto*, subordinating form to poetic purpose, passing within the same work, as he recalled in *La arboleda perdida* (p. 271), 'from the controlled, disciplined short line . . . to a longer line, more adaptable to the movement of my imagination at the time'.

The source of the collection was a powerful emotional crisis and a worsening physical condition: the author is 'Rafael the tormented', as Salinas described him in *Ensayos de literatura hispánica* (3rd edn., 1967, p. 368), in complete contrast to the author of the quiet, simple verses of *Marinero en tierra* (q.v.) dedicated to, and praised by, Juan Ramón Jiménez. Usually labelled 'surrealistic', *Sobre los ángeles* uses striking yet neither random nor dream images. The angels of most of the poems represent forces

governing aspects of Alberti's inner nature: while the majority are evil, representing bitterness, jealousy, or melancholy, others are good, representing hope or peace. The brutality of the 'cruel angels' ensures that nature, ravaged by violent winds, will never bloom into leaf or flower and that the birds will never again be able to fly freely. Like Rimbaud, Alberti believed in the theological geography of heaven and hell and spent his own 'season in hell', recording his experiences with such energy and imagination that *Sobre los ángeles* has come to be recognized as one of the major poetic documents of the century.

Less can be said for its sequel *Sermones y moradas* (1930), deriving from the same emotional crisis, 'a volley of acrid recriminations and strident self-justifications which, seething anarchically in endlessly flowing lines, fail to engage completely our emotions or involve us in his difficulties' (C. B. Morris, *A generation of Spanish poets, 1920–36*, Cambridge, 1969, p. 213).

Concerning the angels is a translation by Geoffrey Connell (London, 1967).

See C. B. Morris, *Rafael Alberti's 'Sobre los ángeles'* (Hull, 1966); and S. Salinas de Marichal, *El mundo poético de Rafael Alberti* (1968).

SOLARTE, TRISTÁN, pseudonym of Guillermo Sánchez (q.v.).

SOLDEVILA, CARLES (1892–   ), b. Barcelona. Catalan playwright, essayist, novelist, and journalist. His plays include *Civilizats tan-mateix* (1921), *Deu hi fa mes que nosaltres* (1922), *Vacantes reals* (1923), *Bola de neu* (1928), *Leonor o el problema domestic* (1928), and *Necessitem senyoreta* (1935). Among his works of fiction are *L'Abrandament* (1917), *Una atziagada i altres contes* (1921), *Eva* (1931), and *Moment musical* (1936).

SOLDEVILA, FERRANT (1894–   ), b. Barcelona. Historian and playwright, brother of Carles Soldevila (q.v.). Professor of Catalan History in Barcelona University 1931–38, after which he emigrated to France. He later returned to Spain. Among his major contributions to historical studies are *Jaume I* (Barcelona, 1926), *Recerques i comentaris* (Barcelona, 1929), *História de Catalunya* (3 vols., Barcelona, 1934–5), *Les dones en la nostra História* (Barcelona, 1936), and *L'esprit d'Oc et la Catalogne* (1942).

His plays include *Matilde d'Anglaterra* (Barcelona, 1923), *Guifre* (Barcelona, 1949), and *L'hostal de l'amor* (Barcelona, 1951).

Soledades, an incomplete long poem by Luis de Góngora y Argote (q.v.) in *silvas*, a free combination of seven- and eleven-syllable lines.

The work, upon which Góngora's principal

fame rests, was intended to be in four parts, but he wrote only the dedication to the Duke of Béjar (37 lines), the whole of the *Soledad primera* (1,091 lines), and 979 lines of the unfinished *Soledad segunda*. Though the work circulated in MS. from about 1612 or 1613, it was not published until 1627, in Juan López de Vicuña's *Obras en verso del Homero español*. The next editions were by Gonzalo de Hoces (1633), and García de Salcedo Coronel (q.v.), *Obras de don Luis de Góngora comentadas* (3 vols., 1636, 1644, 1648).

The four 'solitudes' were probably intended to deal in turn with the countryside, the sea-shore, the woods, and deserts, and to possess a number of common or parallel features. In the first *Soledad* a young prince is shipwrecked, a symbol of the defects of life at court (folly and arrogance) which lead a man to abandon his God-given element (the land) and venture forth upon the seas. The poem presents by way of contrast the innocence and beauty of the countryside in all its variety and is thus an example of the *Menosprecio de corte y alabanza de aldea* genre (see also Fray Antonio de GUEVARA) so common in Golden Age literature. The harmony of the truly moral life is shown in various scenes involving music, song, and dance.

Góngora's narrative is of an importance secondary to that of his lyrical and metaphysical poetic world, the beauty of which (as Dámaso Alonso has written) 'is stylised and simplified in order to be reduced to well-drawn outlines, to agile foreshortenings, to harmonious sonorities and to splendid colours. By means of a continual and complicated metaphorical play the object tends to lose its individuality and to be entered in a metaphorical category. We do not look for sea-water, fresh water, water from a fountain or lagoon in the *Solitudes*: crystals is the label that covers all. But *crystals* is also used to describe the beautiful limbs of a woman.' Similarly, the Straits of Magellan become 'an elusive silver hinge joining two oceans', and a marriage-bed 'a field of feathers for the strife of love'.

The unfinished poem immediately became the object of unrestrained praise and censure, and was bitterly lampooned by Quevedo (q.v.). Apart from the useful commentary by Salcedo Coronel, there were others by Pellicer, Díaz de Rivas, and Salazar Mardones.

Among Góngora's many imitators, of whom none reached his level, were Soto de Rojas and Bocángel (qq.v.), and as late as 1711 a third 'solitude' was published by León y Mansilla (q.v.). Alberti's 'fragment' *Soledad tercera* (actually a 'paráfrasis incompleta') appears in his *Cal y canto* (q.v.).

Though Darío (q.v.) emphasized the unique importance of Góngora in Spanish Baroque poetry, it was not until the tercentenary celebra-

tions of 1927 that the foundations of serious scholarship on the *Soledades* were laid. The best edition of the poem is that by Dámaso Alonso (1927), with an introductory study and a prose version in modern Spanish; another, with facing English translation, is by E. M. Wilson (Cambridge, 1965).

See Dámaso Alonso, *La lengua poética de Góngora* (1950); Eunice Joiner Gates, *Documentos gongorinos* (Mexico City, 1960), containing the *Discursos apologéticos* of Pedro Díaz de Rivas and Juan de Jáuregui's *Antídoto*; W. Pabst, *La creación gongorina en los poemas 'Polifemo' y 'Soledades'* (1966); and E. Orozco Díaz, *En torno a las 'Soledades' de Góngora* (1969), a collection of 17th-c. criticism on the poem.

SOLER, BARTOLOMÉ (1894–), b. Sabadell, Barcelona. Novelist and autobiographer whose restlessness brought him experiences of great value to his writing even if, in Nora's view, 'the absence of taste or a refined artistic instinct became more and more obvious with every succeeding book, though his beginnings had been brilliant'. He earned a precarious living as an actor in Spain and Latin America, but won great success with his first novel *Marcos Villarí* (Barcelona, 1927), finally published after many rejections. This was followed by *Germán Padilla* (1927), *Almas de cristal* (1940), *Pitusín* (Barcelona, 1941), *Karú-Kinká* (Barcelona, 1946) set in Patagonia, *Tamara* (Barcelona, 1953), and *Los muertos no se cuentan* (Barcelona, 1961). He capitalized on his success in fiction by writing an autobiographical trilogy, of which the most interesting volume was the second: *La cara y la cruz del camino* (Barcelona, 1963); and he turned his dramatic skills to writing in *Tres comedias* (1951).

See G. Paolini, *Bartolomé Soler, novelista* (Barcelona, 1963).

SOLÍS, DIONISIO, the pen-name of Dionisio Villanueva y Ochoa (q.v.).

SOLÍS Y RIVADENEIRA, ANTONIO DE (1610–86), b. Alcalá de Henares. Historian, playwright, and poet. He studied at Alcalá and Salamanca, eventually succeeding León Pinelo as Official Chronicler of the Indies. However, he left the court and was ordained a priest in 1667 (following the tradition of other Golden Age playwrights such as Lope, Calderón, Tirso, and Moreto). He refused when asked to complete the *autos* left uncompleted by Calderón at his death, and indeed wrote no more poetry or drama, but concentrated on a second part of his official history, which was to remain incomplete and unpublished. The first part is a noble work of literary historiography: *Historia de la conquista de*

México, población y progressos de la América septentrional, conocida por el nombre de Nueva España (1684), reprinted in vol. 28 (1853) of the BAE. The time-span is from the journey of Juan de Grijalva in 1518 to the final surrender of Montezuma in 1520, and Solís's attitude is that of hero-worship, with Cortés unequivocally at the centre of the narrative throughout. Solís adds little not already known to the accounts of López de Gómara, Díaz del Castillo (qq.v.), and others, but his work is a model of Castilian prose, and the story is constantly gripping.

Solís was also a playwright, composing twelve works on his own, and many others in collaboration with friends such as Coello, Calderón, Francisco de Monteser, and Diego de Silva. *Amor y obligación*, which made his reputation at the age of 17, has been edited by E. Juliá Martínez (1930), who has analysed the plot/character structure common to most of Solís's plays. Three of the five main characters are young men and two young ladies. Man 1 loves and is loved by Lady 1. Man 2 also loves Lady 1. Lady 2 loves Man 1 and she is jealous of Lady 1. Man 3 provides a further complication, courting one of the ladies but finally being discovered as her relative.

A lively, witty dramatist equipped with a vein of self-mockery, Solís is at his best in the satirical *El amor al uso*, one of the four plays in vol. 45 (1858) of the BAE, together with *Un bobo hace ciento*, *El doctor Carlino*, and *La gitanilla de Madrid*. Nevertheless, Solís never emerged from the influence of Rojas Zorrilla and Calderón as a playwright, or indeed from that of Góngora as a poet, as is proved by the *Varias poesías sagradas y profanas* (1692), edited in 1968 by M. Sánchez Regueira, and available in selection in vol. 42 (1857) of the BAE.

Little has been written on Solís as poet and playwright.

See L. Arocena, *Antonio de Solís, cronista indiano: estudio sobre las formas historiográficas del Barroco* (Buenos Aires, 1963).

SOLITARIO, EL, pseudonym adopted throughout the later part of his literary life by Serafín Estébanez Calderón (q.v.).

SOLOGUREN, JAVIER (1921–), b. Lima. Peruvian poet and anthologist who studied at San Marcos University in Lima (1940–4), the Colegio de México (1948–50), and the Catholic University of Louvain (Belgium, 1971–2). He has spent several years teaching literature, won the José Santos Chocano national poetry prize in 1960, was a founding director of La Rama Florida (which has published more than 140 titles), and is an editor of the Lima magazine *Creación y Crítica*.

His first publication was *El morador*, a *separatum* with *Historia* no. 8 (1944), and his first book *Detenimientos* (1947). *Dédalo dormido* was a *separatum* with *Cuadernos Americanos* (Mexico City, 1949), followed by the booklet *Bajo los ojos del amor* (Mexico City, 1950). Then followed a long silence, broken by the *separatum Otoño*, *endechas* with *Mercurio Peruano* (1959), and several books; *Estancias* (1960; 2nd edn., with English version, 1961), *Vida continua* (1966; 2nd edn., 1971), *Recinto* (1968), and *Surcando el aire oscuro* (Madrid, 1970).

Among his anthologies are *La poesía contemporánea del Perú* (with J. E. Eielson and Sebastián Salazar Bondy, 1957) and *Poesía del Perú* (Buenos Aires, 1964).

See Luis Hernán Ramírez, *Estilo y poesía de Javier Sologuren* (1967); and Armando Rojas, *Obra poética de Javier Sologuren 1944–50* (1972) and a second volume covering 1959–70 (1973).

SOLÓRZANO, CARLOS (1922–), b. Guatemala City. Playwright and director. A resident of Mexico City since 1939, he studied at the Universidad Nacional Autónoma de México, obtaining a doctorate in 1948, and then specialized in drama at the Sorbonne (1949–51). Appointed director of the university theatre at UNAM (1952–62), he introduced to Mexico such European *avant-garde* dramatists as Beckett, Ionesco, and Ghelderode.

His first completed play was *Doña Beatriz, la sin ventura* (1951), markedly different in style from the regional realism then dominating the Spanish-American stage. This was followed by *El hechicero* (1954), and *Las manos de Dios* (1956), a play on the theme of rebellion and submission which teaches that each man must avoid the sin of submitting to the alien or repressive.

The study *Teatro latinoamericano del siglo XX* (Buenos Aires, 1961) was followed by the anthology *El teatro hispano-americano contemporáneo* (2 vols., Mexico City, 1964) and a study of his own national drama, *Teatro guatemalteco* (Madrid, 1967).

More recently, Solórzano has turned to the novel. *Los falsos demonios* (1966) concerns the social problem of how a subjugated man can achieve something in a repressive community and studies the psychological dilemma of identifying and fulfilling one's basic desires.

Sombrero de tres picos, El (1874), by P. A. de Alarcón (q.v.), subtitled *Historia verdadera de un sucedido que anda en romances, escrita ahora tal y como pasó*, a long short story originating from the old ballad *El molinero de Arcos*.

Lucas the miller knows that the mayor, Don Eugenio de Zúñiga y Ponce de León, is in love with his wife, but believes her faithful, despite his own ugliness. One night, on his way to present himself at the town hall of a neighbouring village, he observes the mayor's constable going to his mill and feels jealousy for the first time. On arrival he is told to wait until the morning but, after feigning sleep, returns to his mill. The door is open, and the mayor's three-cornered hat and his clothes are in front of a blazing fire. What can he do to save his honour? He puts on the mayor's clothes and remembers that the mayor's wife is pretty, too. During the miller's absence, his wife Frasquita had heard cries of 'I'm drowning!' and had opened the door to find the mayor soaking, having fallen into a ditch. Having tried to seduce her (and been indignantly rejected), he dropped to the ground in a faint. Frasquita had run to the village to fetch the constable and doctor. The constable Garduña had helped the mayor to bed, put his clothes in front of the fire to dry and gone back to the village. It was at this point that Lucas had returned.

The villagers now come to the mill and help Don Eugenio into the miller's clothes, accompanying him back to his own house. There, the mayor's wife replies that he must be an impostor, since the 'mayor' has been in his own bed and asleep for an hour. Frasquita weeps and the mayor is furious. His wife draws Frasquita aside and lets her into the secret, but Don Eugenio will never know what occurred.

Alarcón's tale, written in the space of only two weeks, presents village life of Andalusia with abundant liveliness and good humour. The dramatic qualities of the work induced Falla to make a ballet of it, and Hugo Wolf an opera. Emilia Pardo Bazán (q.v.) called it 'el rey de los cuentos españoles', partly because it is free from Alarcón's usual unevenness, and partly because the suspense is maintained until the very end.

The novel has been edited (1975) by V. Gaos for Clásicos Castellanos.

Somni, Lo, (1398), a series of four dialogues in Catalan written by Bernat Metge (q.v.) while imprisoned for the third time in 1396. It was composed after reading Petrarch's *Secretum*, a powerful confessional dialogue, and bears the imprint of that work.

In the first dialogue, King Juan I appears to Metge in a dream flanked by Orpheus the god of music and Teiresias the Greek soothsayer. Metge disputes the immortality of the soul, but finally professes to be convinced. Sources of this important dialogue included the Church Fathers, Thomas Aquinas, and Petrarch.

The second dialogue deals tactfully with problems of the day, but pressing Metge's claim to freedom. The third, influenced by Boccaccio, tells the stories of Teiresias and Orpheus. The

fourth, equally derivative as to sources but written with polish and restraint, is a defence of famous women, concluding with praise of the new queen, María de Luna.

Lo somni has been edited by J. M. de Casacuberta (Barcelona, 1924) in Els Nostres Clàssics.

SOMOZA Y MUÑOZ, JOSÉ (1781–1852), b. Piedrahita, Ávila. Spanish *costumbrista*, poet, and historical novelist. He was a liberal like his friends Quintana, Jovellanos, and Meléndez Valdés (qq.v.). In 1829 he returned from Madrid to Piedrahita, where he devoted his time entirely to writing. Of his verse, the most celebrated examples are the ode 'A fray Luis de León' and the fine sonnet 'A la laguna de Gredos', while *El capón* (1844) is his best historical novel.

The sketches of provincial life he collected in *Memorias de Piedrahita* (1837) and *Recuerdos e impresiones* (1843) anticipated the essays of Mesonero Romanos (q.v.). During his lifetime he published *Obras poéticas* (4 vols., 1834–7) and *Obras* (2 vols., 1942, one of poetry and one of prose). J. R. Lomba de la Pedraja edited Somoza's *Obras en prosa y verso* (1904) with a good introduction.

See also Azorín's *Leyendo a los poetas: José Somoza* (Barcelona, 1914).

Sonatas, a tetralogy of novels by Ramón del Valle-Inclán (q.v.) comprising *Sonata de otoño* (1902), *Sonata de estío* (1903), *Sonata de primavera* (1904), and *Sonata de invierno* (1905).

Compared with his mature works, such as *Tirano Banderas* and the cycle *El ruedo ibérico* (qq.v.), the *Sonatas* are mannered period pieces which seem trivial today, but are important as a reflection of their age's concern with symbolism (music, the seasons), impressionistic writing, and the decadent hero (reminiscent partly of the Übermensch of Nietzsche and partly of des Esseintes in Huysmans's *À rebours*). Xavier de Bradomín, this central figure, is partly autobiographical here and becomes more obviously the author's *alter ego* in the play *Luces de Bohemia* (q.v.) and in the novels forming the cycle *El ruedo ibérico* (q.v.). Bradomín is a womanizing Galician marquis described by the author as 'an ugly, sentimental, Catholic Don Juan', though he is also clearly an ironic creation, and expresses himself ironically.

The four memoirs begin with *Sonata de primavera* (the third to be published), set *c.* 1830, when Bradomín was an officer in the Pope's service. He is sent to inform Monsignor Gaetani, a bishop, that he has been given a Cardinal's hat, but Gaetani dies before he can receive it. Princess Gaetani, sister-in-law of the bishop, invites Bradomín to stay with her and her five daughters, of whom the eldest, María Rosario, is about to enter a convent.

Bradomín plans to seduce María Rosario (who symbolizes the Virgin Mary and the power of good) but her mother learns of this and arranges for him to be killed one night in the palace gardens. When this attempt fails, she tries to rob him of his virility by magic. The gentle María Rosario learns of this further scheme and, shocked, sends a friar to warn Bradomín to make his escape back to Rome. His valet and coachman are both helplessly drunk, however, and Bradomín is forced to prolong his visit until the next day. Then he resumes his attempted seduction; alarmed, María Rosario seeks the company of her youngest sister, María Nieves. María Nieves then mysteriously falls to her death from the window-ledge where she is sitting; María Rosario goes mad as a result.

Valle-Inclán contrasts the death of experience (Gaetani) with the death of innocence (María Nieves); religion with satanism; and eroticism with purity. His style is decorative, even exquisite.

In *Sonata de estío*, Bradomín visits Mexico ostensibly to inspect his family estates but in fact to forget a love affair. He encounters a Creole woman, Niña Chole, and seduces her before finding out that she is married to General Bermúdez, who finds her and carries her back home after lashing her face with his whip. Bradomín, on reaching his estate, finds that his steward has given refuge to a band of outlaws. That night he hears a disturbance and the following morning discovers that they had kidnapped none other than Niña Chole, with whom Bradomín is now reconciled. Several carefully-placed humorous incidents prove that Valle-Inclán does not intend the reader to take Bradomín or his adventures too seriously.

Sonata de otoño is a meditative work, as befits its autumnal title. Sacrilegious, openly erotic, and even satanic, the novel is set in the Galician palace of Brandeso, where Bradomín's former mistress and cousin Concha is dying of consumption. Bradomín visits her, and while he is there Concha's two daughters by her estranged husband arrive with her cousin Isabel.

One night Concha visits Bradomín, who persuades her to sleep with him. She dies in his arms, whereupon Bradomín decides to inform Isabel of what has happened. When he enters Isabel's bedroom, she begs him to keep silent lest Concha hear them and, partly to avoid humiliating Isabel, Bradomín satisfies her then returns to his own room to carry Concha's corpse back to her bedroom. Bradomín's irony and aristocratic nihilism are the keynote of this beautifully-written work.

Sonata de invierno departs from the refined decadence of the earlier *Sonatas* and concentrates on the political and social issues of Galicia during the second Carlist War (1872–6). Bradomín serves Charles VII, whose wife Margarita tells the Marquis that the King is surrounded by traitors in the pay of the guerrilla leader Manuel Santa Cruz. Bradomín finds that one of Margarita's ladies-in-waiting is his former mistress María Antonieta. During a mission on the Pretender's behalf, Bradomín and his party are attacked, and Bradomín is so badly wounded in the left arm that he is taken to a convent for the arm to be amputated. There he is nursed by a timid girl who turns out to be Maximina, his illegitimate daughter by María Antonieta. This discovery does not prevent his trying to seduce her; when she finds out the truth, Bradomín suspects that she will commit suicide. Bradomín bids farewell to María Antonieta, whose husband has suffered a stroke and is on the point of death.

Apart from the relatively late incident concerning incest, which seems gratuitous in context, this is the most sombre novel in the tetralogy, as befits a work symbolizing winter.

See Amado Alonso, *Estructura de las 'Sonatas' de Valle-Inclán* (written for first publication in 1928 and reproduced in his *Materia y forma en poesía*, 1955, pp. 257–300); A. Zamora Vicente, *Las 'Sonatas' de Ramón del Valle-Inclán* (1951; 2nd edn., 1955), which concentrates on the tetralogy's modernist elements; and E. S. Speratti-Piñero, 'Génesis y evolución de "Sonata de otoño"' in *Revista Hispánica Moderna* (New York, 1959), vol. 35, pp. 57–80.

SOTELA, Rogelio (1894–1943), b. San José. Costa Rican poet and critic, best known for his works on the national literature: *Valores literarios de Costa Rica* (1920), *Escritores y poetas de Costa Rica* (1923), *Literatura costarricense* (1927 and later edns.), and *Escritores de Costa Rica* (1942). His poetry is full of rhetoric (especially the 'Oda a Costa Rica') with sound prevailing over meaning in *La senda de Damasco* (1918) and subsequent collections.

Sotileza (1885), a major novel of the sea by José María de Pereda (q.v.), set mainly in the port of Santander.

The orphan-girl Silda, known as 'Sotileza' because of her delicacy, is transferred from the brutal guardianship of Mocejón and Sargüeta to the kindly family of Mechelín and Sidora, who live in the same building as her previous foster-parents. A central character in the first part is Padre Apolinar, a schoolteacher and exemplary priest who is a more convincing creation than the priests in Pereda's *Don Gonzalo González de la Gonzalera* (1878) and *De tal palo, tal astilla* (1880).

He sympathizes with Silda to the extent of helping with her education and the transfer of her guardianship; he builds up a respect for her ugly and illiterate fellow-pupil, the orphaned Muergo; and he clothes Muergo at his own expense.

Another boy in Apolinar's class, Andrés, is the son of a sea-captain; a conflict arises between the captain, Pedro Colindres (popularly known as Bitadura), and his wife Andrea, as to their son's career. Bitadura wants the boy to become a ship's officer, while his wife urges her husband's employer, Venancio Liencres, to take him into his office as a clerk. Andrea wins, and Andrés enters the office, where he befriends Venancio's son, Antolín. Andrés, Muergo, and another boy called Cleto, all seem to be fascinated by Sotileza, who nevertheless remains indifferent to them, obsessed as she is by her lack of parents.

The boys' rivalry comes to a head when an innocent meeting between the infatuated Andrés and the embarrassed Sotileza is deliberately described as a dishonourable assignation by Sargüeta and her daughter Carpia. Bitadura is shocked and suggests to Mechelín that his son should marry Sotileza to 'put things right'; but Sotileza angrily protests her innocence and affirms that nobody should make her marry against her will. Andrés goes to sea and takes command of the ship during a storm when the captain is knocked unconscious, an experience which makes him a man at last. He returns to Santander and marries his childhood friend Luisa. Cleto proposes to Sotileza, who accepts him; she feels that, though he is not yet ready for marriage, three years as a conscript in the Navy may mature him.

As a sympathetic study of the lower classes whom he did not know very well, *Sotileza* is a remarkable achievement, inferior in Pereda's writings only to *Peñas arriba* (q.v.).

The debate over the 'naturalism' of the novel, never clearly resolved, occupied both Pereda and his critics. One of these, 'Clarín' (Leopoldo Alas y Ureña, q.v.), praised the book for its naturalism, which Pereda in a prologue denied that it possessed.

The language of the novel is more popular than that of Pereda's next great novel, *Peñas arriba*. Its style is similar to that of the Madrid novels of Pérez Galdós, and in particular perhaps to that of *Misericordia* (q.v.).

There is a good translation by Glenn Barr (New York, 1959).

See José Fernández Montesinos, *Pereda o la novela idilio* (1969), esp. pp. 149–77; 'Clarín', *Nueva campaña 1885–1886* (1887), pp. 135–49; and on Pereda's alleged naturalism, Walter T. Pattison, *El naturalismo español* (1969), pp. 63–83.

SOTO DE ROJAS, Pedro (1584–1658), b. Granada. Poet. Canon of San Salvador, Granada, he managed to combine his clerical duties with frequent visits to the court, where he became a friend, admirer, and disciple of Góngora (q.v.). He was a member of the Academia Selvaje of Madrid, to which he delivered *Discurso sobre la poética*. His first known poetic exercise included lines on bull-fighting in a celebration of a *fiesta* (1609). Later works included *Desengaño de amor en rimas* (1623) and *Los rayos de Faetón* (1639), displaying the exotic imagery and metaphor that he was to bring to a culmination in his extravagant *Paraíso cerrado para muchos, jardines abiertos para pocos* (1652), a *culto* masterpiece. The *Obras* were recently edited by A. Gallego Morell (1950).

SOTO MORALES, Manuel (1901–   ), b. Talca. Chilean *criollista* novelist and short-story writer using the pseudonym 'Lautaro Yankas'. He wrote mainly on country life, in the tradition of Mariano Latorre (q.v.). His books included *La bestia hombre* (1924), *Marina* (1926), *Mujer de laja* (1930), *Flor Lumao* (1932), *La llama* (1940), *La ciudad dormida* (1943), *Rotos* (1945), *El cazador de pumas* (1947), and *El vado de la noche* (1955).

Spanish Inquisition, see Inquisition, Spanish.

Spanish National Library, see Biblioteca Nacional, Madrid.

Speculum principis, see De Regimine Principum.

Spongia, a lost diatribe against the dramatic theories and practice of Lope de Vega by Pedro de Torres Rámila (q.v.) known only from Lope's reply, *Expostulatio Spongiae.*

SPOTA, Luis (1925–   ), b. Mexico City. Mexican novelist and journalist. The son of an Italian immigrant and a Spanish aristocrat, he left school after primary studies and earned his living at a variety of trades, among them seamanship and bullfighting, but he has spent most of his life in journalism, from 1943 on *Excelsior*, a leading Mexican newspaper.

He has published more than a dozen novels, among them *Murieron a mitad del río* (1948), on the exploitation of labourers on the frontier; *Más cornadas da el hambre* (1950; translated by Barnaby Conrad as *The wounds of hunger*, New York and London, 1958); *Casi el paraíso* (1956), an indictment of Mexican high society; *Las horas violentas* (1958), on corrupt trade union leaders; *La carcajada del gato* (1964), in which a man imprisons his family at home, based on a true incident reported in the Mexican press; *Los sueños del insomnio* (1966); and the cycle *La costumbre de poder*, consisting so far of *Retablo hablado* (1975), *Palabras mayores* (1975), and *Sobre la marcha* (1976).

STERN, SAMUEL MIKLOS (1920–69), b. Tab, Hungary. Hebrew and Arabic scholar at Oxford University who was the discoverer of the *kharjas* (q.v.) first published in *al-Andalus*. His article *Les vers finaux en espagnol dans les muwaššah hispano-hebraïques* (1948) was subsequently expanded into a book: *Les chansons mozarabes* (Palermo, 1953; reprinted, Oxford, 1964). J. D. Latham's and H. W. Mitchell's 'Bibliography of S. M. Stern' appeared in *The Journal of Semitic Studies*, vol. 15 (1970).

A posthumously published collection of Stern's *Studies on Hispano-Arabic strophic poetry* has been edited by L. P. Harvey (Oxford, 1974).

STORNI, ALFONSINA (1892–1938), b. Sala Capriasca, Switzerland. Argentinian poet, teacher, and journalist. She committed suicide by drowning in the Mar del Plata on learning that she was suffering from an incurable disease.

After the juvenilia of *La inquietud del rosal* (1916) she railed against men, for their physical dominance over women and lack of sensibility, in a number of books. Her style matured from *El dulce daño* (1918) to *Irremediablemente* (1919), and from *Languidez* (1920) to the romanticism of *Ocre* (1925), in which her frustrated eroticism is most marked. In the *avant-garde El mundo de siete pozos* (1934) she begins to overcome her antagonism towards men, and develops in *Mascarilla y trébol* (1938) towards the abstract and intellectual.

Her *Obra poética completa* (1961) reached a third impression in 1968.

See Arturo Capdevila, *Alfonsina: época, dolor y obra de la poetisa Alfonsina Storni* (1948); C. Fernández Moreno, *Situación de Alfonsina Storni* (Santa Fe, Argentina, 1959); Carlos Alberto Andreola, *Alfonsina Storni* (1974); and R. Phillips, *Alfonsina Storni: from poetess to poet* (London, 1975).

STÚÑIGA, LOPE DE (1415?–1465). Poet, after whom the so-called *Cancionero de Stúñiga* was named, presumably since he was the first poet anthologized in it. His poems, influenced by Provençal and Italian writers, are predominantly amorous in nature: they are to be found in the National Library in Madrid (some thirty in two MSS.), in the *Cancionero* of Gallardo (17 more), and in the *Cancionero general* of 1511 (a further 9).

Stúñiga also wrote some political poems, such as the *decir* 'Sobre la cerca de Atienza'; and some moral, such as 'Esforzando a sí mismo

estando preso'. The authenticity of his courtly sentiments is never in doubt, for he accepted the invitation from his cousin Suero de Quiñones to participate in the celebrated *Passo honroso* in 1434 (see RODRÍGUEZ DE LENA, Pedro), in which he is believed to have acquitted himself valiantly. He took sides against Count Álvaro de Luna.

There is no direct evidence that Stúñiga was ever in Naples, but the *Cancionero de Stúñiga* consists mainly of works by poets of the court of Alfonso V, who ruled Naples from 1443 until his death in 1458. Among this poetic circle were Juan de Dueñas, Juan de Andújar, a certain Carvajal or Carvajales, and Juan de Tapia. Much of their verse consisted of love songs to ladies of Naples, but their forms remained Spanish: *decires* and *canciones* of courtly love, and *serranillas* both parodic (reminiscent of Juan Ruiz's *Libro de buen amor*, qq.v.) and idealized (like the later examples by the Marqués de Santillana, q.v.). The remarkable absence of Italianate innovations in the Stúñiga *Cancionero* has led to the assumption that Alfonso V deliberately kept the Italian humanists at his court separated from the Spanish poets.

There are three MSS. of the *Cancionero de Stúñiga*: that in the Biblioteca Nacional, Madrid, edited by M. Fuensanta del Valle and J. Sancho Rayón (1872) in the Colección de Libros Españoles Raros o Curiosos; that in the Biblioteca Casanatense (Rome); and that in the Biblioteca Marziana (Venice).

See F. Vendrell Gallostra, *La corte literaria de Alfonso V de Aragón y tres poetas de la misma* (1933); and Eloy Benito Ruano, 'Lope de Stúñiga: vida y cancionero' in *Revista de Filología Española*, vol. 51, 1968, pp. 17–109.

SUÁREZ, CONSTANCIO S., a writer employed by the Mexican publisher Antonio Vanegas Arroyo, now chiefly remembered for his illustrator José Guadalupe Posada (q.v.).

SUÁREZ, FRANCISCO (1548–1617), b. Granada. Jesuit writer who entered the Order in 1564 and was ordained in 1572. He taught philosophy in Segovia (1572–4) and then theology at Valladolid, Alcalá, Salamanca, and Coimbra. The complete Latin edition of his works is in 26 vols. (Paris, 1856–61); among his more important works were the *Ius gentium*, possibly the earliest theoretical exposition of public law; the *De incarnatione verbi* (1590); *Disputationes metaphysicae* (1597); *De Deo uno et trino* (1606); and *De legibus* (1612).

Suárez's most important writings are being edited in the Biblioteca de Autores Cristianos (1951–), with prologues by Romualdo Galdós.

See P. Raul de Scorraille, *El Padre Francisco de Suárez*, translated by P. Pablo Hernández (2 vols., Barcelona, 1917).

SUÁREZ BRAVO, CEFERINO (1825–96), b. Oviedo. Satirist, playwright, and journalist. He joined the Carlists, and emigrated to Paris after the Second Carlist War, but returned in 1876.

He caused a sensation with his play *Amante y caballero*, performed when he was 17; his verse is agreeable and his Romantic tendency not too extravagant; Hartzenbusch considered his play *¡Es un ángel!* among the best of his time, and *Enrique III* (1847) was also successful.

His satirical works remain largely uncollected in book form, except for *Perfiles senatoriales* and *España demagógica* (1873). His stirring, controversial novel of the Carlist troubles, *Guerra sin cuartel* (1885), was severely condemned in a detailed review by L. Alas ('Clarín') in his *Nueva campaña 1885—1886* (1867).

SUÁREZ DE DEZA, ENRIQUE (1906–), b. Buenos Aires. Playwright of Spanish parents, who was educated in Spain. By profession a lawyer, he has become a popular playwright since his early success with *Ha entrado una mujer* (1925), and has written for films. He has experimented with many genres, including the *farsa de buen humor* (*¡Catalina, no me llores!*, 1945), the thesis play (*Aquellas mujeres*, 1946), the dramatic comedy (*Ambición*, 1945), and the dramatized novel (*La millona*, 1937). The influence of Wilde has permeated his career, and he has been sensitive to changes in public taste, reflecting it rather than leading it.

SUÁREZ DE DEZA, VICENTE (*fl.* 1663), playwright and poet. A courtier of Queen Mariana of Austria. His works were printed in *Parte primera de los donaires de Terpsícore* (1663), containing two burlesque plays and forty shorter pieces, among them *sainetes, bailes, entremeses,* and *mojigangas*. His plays were light pieces, often almost nonsensical, with a tendency to licentiousness, and mockery of the 'low' or 'vulgar'.

SUÁREZ DE FIGUEROA, CRISTÓBAL (1571 ?– 1644), b. Valladolid. When about 17 he went to Italy, where he qualified as a lawyer and translated Guarini's pastoral novel *Il pastore Fido* (Naples, 1602), returning to Spain in 1604. A bitter, jealous, and unpleasant character, he was very hostile to more successful writers of the day. In 1623 he returned to Italy with the Duque de Alba, and died there.

His own pastoral novel, *La constante Amarilis: prosas y versos* (Valencia, 1609), was one of the most effective in this genre. In this the sage

Menandro has been identified as Juan Andrés Hurtado de Mendoza, and Amarilis as María de Cárdenas, daughter of the Duque de Maqueda.

España defendida: poema heroyco (1612) is an epic of 1400 octaves on Bernardo del Carpio. Suárez also wrote *Plaza universal de todas Ciencias y Artes* (1615), in great part translated from Tommaso Garzoni's *La piazza universale di tutte le professioni del mondo* (Venice, 1610), but his most significant book is *El Passagero. Advertencias utilíssimas a la vida humana* (q.v., 1617), valuable as a record of the society of its time, followed by *Varias noticias importantes a la humana comunicación* (1621), a series of twenty essays on miscellaneous subjects.

See J. P. Wickersham Crawford, *The life and works of Cristóbal Suárez de Figueroa* (Philadelphia, 1907) translated into Spanish by N. Alonso Cortés (Valladolid, 1911); A. R. Rodríguez Moñino, 'Bibliografía inédita de Cristóbal Suárez de Figueroa' in *Revista del Centro de Estudios Extremeños* (Badajoz, 1929), vol. 3, pp. 265–85.

SUÁREZ Y ROMERO, ANSELMO (1818–78), b. Havana. Cuban novelist who studied law, practised as an advocate, and later lived for eleven years in adverse conditions in Surinam studying life on the sugar plantations. Domingo Delmonte (q.v.) suggested that he should write a novel revealing the tragic plight of the slaves, and the result was one of the earliest abolitionist tracts in fiction: *Francisco* (New York, 1880: written 1838 or 1839) subtitled ironically by Delmonte 'the plantation: or the joys of the fields'. The Cuban Mario Zambrana used the theme and even the same title for another anti-slavery novel published in Santiago de Chile in 1873.

SUBERCASEAUX, BENJAMÍN (1902–), Chilean novelist and essayist. Much of his early life was spent abroad, mainly in France, where he studied psychology.

He made a great impression with an account of an aristocratic childhood in the autobiographical novel *Niño de lluvia* (1938) revised as *Daniel* (1942). Previously he had published the short novels *Mar amargo* (1936) and *Rahab* (1938). His most memorable work of literary criticism was *Contribución a la realidad* (1939). *Chile o una loca geografía* (1940) should no longer be misread as a wayward historical geography, but as a fantasy on national character or, in the words of L. A. Sánchez, 'una pesquisa o buceo psicológico y aventurero en el alma de la tierra y el hombre chilenos'. Subercaseaux's best novel is *Jemmy Button* (1950; trans. by M. and F. del Villar, New York, 1954), a subtle fictionalized account based on the actual experiences of a Victorian expedition which set out from England and took back from Tierra del Fuego three Indians to be 'civilized'.

SUEIRO, DANIEL (1931–), b. Ribasar, Corunna. Novelist. He studied law and practises journalism, but first achieved recognition, after his stories *La rebusca y otras desgracias* (Barcelona, 1958) and his novel *La carpa* (1958), with the short stories comprising *Los conspiradores* (1960), which won the National Literature Prize for that year. Subsequent works have shown Sueiro's ability to transcend the somewhat provincial level of post-war Spanish fiction: *La criba* (Barcelona, 1961), *Toda la semana* (Barcelona, 1964), *Estos son tus hermanos* (Mexico City, 1965), *La noche más caliente* (Barcelona, 1965), and in particular the notable *Corte de corteza* (1969) which depicts the so-called horrors of modern Western civilization. He has been influenced by Pío Baroja (q.v.). Among his most recent books is the collection of short stories *El cuidado de las manos . . ., o de como progresar en los preparativos del amor sin producir averías en la delicada ropa interior* (1974).

Sueños y discursos de verdades descubridoras de abuso, vicios y Engaños, en todos los Oficios y Estados de Mundo, Los, a series of five satirical prose sketches by Francisco de Quevedo (q.v.), first published in Barcelona in 1627 (2nd edn. in Saragossa later in 1627).

They comprise *El juicio final* (written in 1607), *El alguacil endemoniado* (1607), *El sueño del infierno* (1608), *El mundo por de dentro* (1612), and *El sueño de la muerte* (1621–2). Some of their titles were changed when they were reissued, censored in the religious passages, as *Juguetes de la niñez y traversuras del ingenio* (1629); *El juicio final* was entitled *El sueño de las calaveras; El alguacil endemoniado, El alguacil alguacilado*; the vision of Hell was called *Las zahurdas de Plutón*; and the vision of Death, *La visita de los chistes*.

Some writers make the *sueños* six in number by adding *La hora de todos y la fortuna con seso* (written in or after 1635 and first published posthumously in 1650); seven, by adding the *Discurso de todos los diablos, o infierno enmendado* (Gerona, 1628), which is actually a continuation of the *Política de Dios* (q.v.); or even eight, by attributing to Quevedo a work certainly by another hand: *La casa de los locos de amor*.

In *El sueño de las calaveras,* an angel wakes the dead, who file past Jupiter and explain their conduct to Jupiter enthroned: an avaricious man justifies his weakness by claiming that he hoarded all he could find only in order to love God more than everything else put together. Luther, Judas, and Muhammad mingle with ladies of easy virtue, doctors, tailors, priests, and merchants to provide Quevedo with varied targets for his satire.

El alguacil alguacilado introduces a demon who complains bitterly at having to inhabit the body of a constable, and describes the other inhabitants of Hell and their respective torments.

Las zahurdas de Plutón are the pigsties and hovels of Hell, where Quevedo inspects the various kinds of malefactor castigated in the earlier visions, again expounding their vices and excesses.

Quevedo's guide in *El mundo por de dentro* is an old man who is identified as Disillusion, showing the reality behind each set of appearances: a widow's mourning, female 'beauty', aristocratic wealth: the scene is the largest street in the world, known as Hypocrisy, where almost everyone has a house, flat, or room. This despairing vision is among the most moving expositions of pessimism in Spanish literature, and gave rise to many imitations, such as *Los anteojos de mejor vista* (c. 1625) by Rodrigo Fernández de Ribera (q.v.) and *El diablo cojuelo* (1641) of Luis Vélez de Guevara (q.v.).

The *danse macabre* of *La visita de los chistes* shows one by one the enemies of man in the presence of Death: World, Devil, Flesh, Ingratitude, Discord, and the others, together with a bizarre collection of characters who are the originals of proverbial names or expressions such as Mateo Pico, el bobo de Coria, don Diego de Noche, and Pero Grullo.

See I. Nolting-Hauff, *Visión, sátira y agudeza en los 'Sueños' de Quevedo* (1974).

Superrealismo, see SURREALISMO.

Sur, a major bi-monthly literary review founded and edited in Buenos Aires by Victoria Ocampo (q.v.). It had a sequence of 350 issues (1931–70). In its place, the editor announced the publication twice a year of a book devoted to a particular theme, or of an anthology.

A Latin-American counterpart of the North American *Partisan Review* in its uncompromisingly intellectual stance, *Sur* published works by most of the significant Argentinian writers of the period, though in its first 20 years it published only 182 Latin-American and 41 Spanish writers as against contributions by 217 authors from other countries, notably France, England, and the U.S.A. *Sur* introduced to Latin America Aldous Huxley, D. H. Lawrence, Greene, Orwell, Camus, Sartre, and Jung. In Argentina it reflected the taste of a steadily-widening group of intellectuals such as Jorge Luis Borges, Adolfo Bioy Casares, Silvina Ocampo, Eduardo

Mallea, H. A. Murena, Guillermo de Torre, Manuel Peyrou, Juan Rodolfo Wilcock, Alberto Girri, Macedonio Fernández, and Ernesto Sábato (qq.v.).

Issues 303–5 constituted a cumulative index covering the period up to 1966.

Victoria Ocampo's 'Vida de la revista "Sur"': 35 años de una labor' appeared in *Revista de Occidente* (February 1967), pp. 129–50.

Surrealismo ('surrealism'), a movement which began in Paris *c.* 1923 and was led by André Breton, who issued manifestos in 1924, 1930, and 1934 which developed to take account of new ideas. The aim of the early surrealists was to recreate a preconscious or dream state reconciling images considered contradictory by the conscious mind. Their emphasis on automatism shocked those who believed that art should be carefully controlled. Spanish and Spanish-American writers, among them the Peruvian César Moro (q.v.), moved in Parisian surrealist circles and contributed to the movement's magazines such as *La Révolution Surréaliste* (1924–9) and *Le Surréalisme au Service de la Révolution* (1930–3). P. Ilie, in *The surrealist mode in Spanish literature* (Ann Arbor, 1968) argues that 'surrealism' is to be understood as a prevailing tendency rather than as a strict ideology, but C. B. Morris claims in *Surrealism and Spain, 1920—1936* (Cambridge, 1972) that such a definition is unhelpful, and makes a much sharper definition. Lorca's *Poeta en Nueva York*

(1940, but written 1929–30) has been claimed for surrealism, but it seems more likely that he was expressing as accurately as he could the apparently fantastic, grotesque, and chaotic images that he found in New York. Alberti, Aleixandre, and Cernuda (qq.v.) experimented more or less seriously with the new technique, which had a greater impact on films (Buñuel, q.v.) and on painting (Dalí, q.v.) than on literature.

Other surrealists writing in Spanish include Juan Larrea, Emilio Prados, José Moreno Villa, and Antonio Espina, while among the many who experimented briefly with the idea were Gerardo Diego, Dámaso Alonso, and Manuel Altolaguirre.

The surrealists had in common a rebellious contempt for Church, State, and conventional morality, and were keen to explore without constraint the ambivalence of violence and ecstasy, or pain and pleasure. Barcelona was as important a meeting-place for surrealists as was Madrid, and the influence of the movement on the Catalan Foix (q.v.) is especially evident.

Useful anthologies are V. Bodini's *I poeti surrealisti spagnoli* (Turin, 1963) and M. Lauer & A. Oquendo's *Surrealistas y otros peruanos insulares* (Barcelona, 1973).

Superrealismo, a less common form of the word, is also the title of a novel by 'Azorín' (q.v.) published in 1929, which is a dilution of the original concept in terms of Azorín's personal vision.

T

Tabaré, a Romantic, epic poem in fourteen cantos by the Uruguayan poet Juan Zorrilla de San Martín (q.v.). It was written from 1879 to 1887, first published in 1888, with revisions in 1892 and 1918, and in its definitive version in 1923. The dedication to the author's wife Elvira is a famous tribute.

Tabaré, the *mestizo* son of an Indian chief and his captive Spanish wife Magdalena, is baptized when young in the river Uruguay. He later falls in love with Blanca, sister of the *conquistador* Don Gonzalo de Orgaz, because she reminds him of his mother. When Blanca is abducted by the Indian chief Yamandú, Tabaré rescues her but is murdered by Gonzalo, who takes Tabaré to be the abductor. Zorrilla does not attempt narrative realism: the poem is a Christian meditation on the disappearance of the Charrúa Indians, extirpated by their Spanish conquerors.

The influence of Bécquer is very strong; that of José Zorrilla and Núñez de Arce less so.

TABLADA Y OSUNA, JOSÉ JUAN DE AGUILAR ACUÑA (1871–1945), b. Mexico City. Poet and art critic. During his career in journalism, he is believed to have written more than 10,000 articles for *El Universal*, *El Imparcial*, *El Mundo Ilustrado*, and other papers, and was active in shaping *La Revista Moderna* (q.v., 1898–1911). After a visit to Japan in 1900, he introduced the *haiku* verse-form into Latin America, modified to suit the Castilian tradition. He was a tireless innovator in many styles, encouraging experimentation among younger Mexican writers. His first book of verse was *El florilegio* (1899; enlarged in 1904). He was exiled to New York in 1914 (for collaborating with General Huerta) and the *zapatistas* destroyed his fine art collection. He returned to Mexico in 1918, working in the diplomatic service until 1920, when he resigned and returned to the U.S.A.

Al sol y bajo la luna (1918) was a fuller collection of his poetry, while *Un día* . . . (1919) consisted of *haikai*. His later poetry appeared in *Li-Po y otros poemas* (1920), *El jarro de flores* (1922), and *La feria* (1928). *Los mejores poemas de José Juan Tablada* (1943) was his last anthology. Among his many contributions to art criticism, possibly the most outstanding is the *Historia del arte mexicano* (1927).

Tablas Alfonsíes, a translation of astronomical tables compiled by az-Zarqali (q.v.).

Tablas poéticas (Murcia, 1617), a dialogue on the art of poetry by Francisco Cascales (q.v.) in the manner of the *Philosophia antigua poética* (1596) of Alonso López Pinciano (q.v.).

Cascales followed the *Poetics* of Aristotle and, to some extent, the *Ars poetica* of Horace. He condemned contemporary epic verse and much of the drama, the only exception being that of Lope de Vega, whom he praised as 'the most distinguished writer of dramatic verse in Spain today, giving that verse whatever wit, elegance, splendour and presence it possesses'.

See Antonio García Berrio, *Introducción a la poética clasicista: Cascales* (Barcelona, 1975).

TABOADA, LUIS (1848–1906), b. Vigo. Humorist and *costumbrista* writer. His work is characterized by light satire of the Madrid middle class in such collections as *Errar al golpe* (1885), *Madrid en broma* (1890), *Siga la fiesta* (1892), *Madrid alegre* (1894), and *La viuda de Chaparro* (1899). His autobiography, *Memorias de un autor festivo* (1900), also deals with political events of the previous half-century.

'Clarín' (q.v.) wrote on Taboada in his *Nueva campaña, 1885–6* (1887), pp. 279–87.

TAFUR, PERO (1410?–1484?), b. Cordova. Travel writer. A descendant of Pedro Ruyz de Córdoba, he grew up in the household of Luis de Guzmán, Maestre de Calatrava, and took part in the wars of the time. In Autumn 1435 he began his travels from Sanlúcar de Barrameda and, arriving in Genoa, travelled in Italy, Switzerland, France, and Germany before setting out for the Holy Land. His journeys, which lasted until 1439 and took him to Rhodes, Cyprus, and Egypt and Judaea, were recalled long after with gusto and a fine sense of humour in *Andanças y viajes por diversas partes del mundo avidos*, edited from an incomplete 18th-c. MS. by M. Jiménez de la Espada (1874) in the Colección de Libros Españoles Raros y Curiosos, and again by J. M. Ramos (1934).

Tafur is at pains to impress the reader with the reception he was accorded by the King of Germany, the Pope, and the Sultan of Constantinople, but the book is well worth reading for the descriptions of places and the numerous legends included throughout the narrative. There is a detailed study of the book by J. Vives in *Analecta sacra Tarraconensia*, vol. 19 (1946), pp. 123–216.

TALAVERA, *Arcipreste de*, see MARTÍNEZ DE TOLEDO, Alfonso.

TALAVERA, FERRANT DE, see SÁNCHEZ DE TALAVERA, Ferrant.

TALAVERA, *Fray* HERNANDO DE (1428–1502), b. Talavera de la Reina, Toledo. He studied in Salamanca, and became the first Archbishop of Granada, appointed on 2 January 1492, the date of the completed Reconquest. Of the Hieronymite Order, he was confessor to Queen Isabel, but he claimed that his sermons were intended for 'la más simple viejecita' and employed simple images to convey his message. His *XXIV capítulos sobre el tratado del vestir, calzar, comer y beber* (1480?) show clearly, though incidentally, the manners of the time.

His attempt to have the Bible translated into Arabic as a means of propagating the faith among the Muslims in his see was frustrated by Cardinal Ximénez de Cisneros (q.v.), but it is known that Fray Hernando learnt some Arabic himself.

His ascetic writings prefigured those of S. Teresa de Ávila (q.v.), concentrating on the necessity of clear exposition for a popular audience, particularly in his influential *Breve e muy provechosa doctrina de lo que deue saber todo christiano* (1496). His works were edited by M. Mir for vol. 16 of the NBAE (1911).

See A. Fernández de Madrid, *Vida de Fray Fernando de Talavera* (1931); and Fidel Fernández, *La España imperial: Fray Hernando de Talavera, confesor de los Reyes Católicos* (1942). See also ASCETIC WRITERS.

TALLET, JOSÉ ZACARÍAS (1893–), Cuban poet of the Generation of 1930 whose sensual poem 'La rumba' (in *Atuei*, August 1928) marked him with Nicolás Guillén (q.v.) as one of the first Afro-Cuban poets. Afro-Cubanism is a movement of Negro and white poets who believe the essential Cuban culture to be that of the Negro, and so use African rhythms in a non-intellectual poetry. The theoretician of the movement was Fernando Ortiz (q.v.).

Tallet's only collection, *La semilla estéril*, is permeated with pessimistic irony; though his easy good humour often breaks through, it is none the less effective when seen as a Stoic acceptance of life's lack of purpose.

TAMAYO, FRANZ (1880–1956), b. La Paz. Bolivian poet, playwright, and educationist. The son of Isaac Tamayo, whose *Habla Melgarejo* (published under the pen-name 'Thajmara') anticipated by twenty years the spread of Indianist ideology in Latin America. With Freyre and Reynolds, Tamayo was one of the triad of important modernist poets in Bolivia. He founded the daily *El Fígaro* and achieved such popularity that in 1935 he was nominated President of the Republic, but the Army refused his nomination. He soon outgrew the Hugoesque *Odas* (1898), producing the philosophical poem in *cuartetos Los nuevos Rubayat* (1927), *Scherzos* (1932), and *Epigramas griegos* (1945). A classicist, he wrote *Horacio y el arte lírico*, and his drama in *Tetralogía* (1937) reveals the extent of his debt to classical models: 'La Aquileida', 'Aquiles y Briseida', 'Los Argonautas', and 'La Prometeida'. These were followed by the lyrical tragedy *Scopas* (1939).

Tamayo's visionary optimism in his *Creación de la pedagogía* (1910) helped to counter the pessimism of the *indianista* novel *Pueblo enfermo* (1909) by Alcides Arguedas (q.v.). While agreeing with Arguedas that the Indian was the ultimate and true source of Bolivian nationality, Tamayo felt hopeful that his way of life—and the future of Bolivia—would be preserved. *¡Buscad la energía en vez del oro!* was his celebrated exhortation to Bolivia. In the Nietzschean-influenced *Proverbios* (1917) and *Nuevos proverbios*, he reiterated the faith in superman: 'How melancholy, how marvellous: behind the truth, there is always another truth even more true'.

See the critical biography *Franz Tamayo: hechicero de Ande* (Buenos Aires, 1944), subject of a heated polemic between Tamayo and the author, Fernando Díez de Medina.

TAMAYO DE VARGAS, TOMÁS (1588–1641), b. Madrid. Scholar, bibliographer, and from 1625 on the death of Antonio de Herrera y Tordesillas (q.v.), official historian of Castile. He studied and taught at Toledo University, and wrote a number of minor works on the important families and the religious history of Toledo.

In 1616 he began an acrimonious controversy with Pedro Mantuano (q.v.), who published an extensive and detailed attack on the Spanish history of Mariana (q.v.) in *Advertencia a la Historia de Iuan de Mariana . . . En que se enmienda gran parte de la Historia de España* (Milan, 1606; 2nd enlarged edn., Madrid, 1613). Tamayo's reply was *Historia general de España del padre doctor Juan de Mariana defendida* (Toledo, 1616). The controversy has been studied by A. González Palencia in 'Polémica entre Pedro Mantuano y Tomás Tamayo de Vargas con motivo de la Historia del Padre Mariana' in *Boletín de la Real Academia de la Historia*, vol. 84 (1924), pp. 331–51.

Tamayo went to Venice as secretary to the Spanish Ambassador in 1621; when he returned he was made a council-member of the Inquisition. He prepared an edition of the works of Garcilaso, entitled *Garcilaso de la Vega, natural de Toledo, Príncipe de los Poetas Castellanos* (1622), and he was friendly with both Góngora and Quevedo.

As a bibliographer he compiled one of the most useful works to appear before the time of Nicolás Antonio (q.v.): *Junta de libros la mayor que España ha visto en su lengua* which survives in 3 MSS. (the most accessible being that of the Biblioteca Nacional in Madrid) but not in a printed version, though according to Vanegas it was published in Madrid in 1624. León Pinelo declared that a work by Tamayo entitled *Catálogo de los escritores que hay en la lengua castellana* was also published, but there are no extant copies of this, which Serís suggests may have been simply an index to the above *Junta*.

TAMAYO Y BAUS, MANUEL (1829–98), b. Madrid. Playwright. One of the most significant dramatists of the 19th c. His parents, José Tamayo and Joaquina Baus, were both actors and he acted when young, writing for the stage from the age of 11, when he translated a French play, first performed by his parents as *Genoveva de Brabante* the following year, and his career was thus decided. He adapted Schiller's *Die Jungfrau von Orleans* as *Juana de Arco*, first performed by his parents in Madrid (1847).

His first original work, *El cinco de agosto* (1848), was badly received so he returned to Schiller, adapting *Kabale und Liebe* as *Angela* (1852). His tragedy in the manner of Alfieri, *Virginia* (1853), was a popular success, being a blend of Romanticism with a classical theme, and his important preface outlined his views on tragedy. His next works were the historical dramas *La ricahembra* (1854, written in verse with Aureliano Fernández-Guerra) and *La locura de amor* (1855) a prose account of Juana de Mendoza, 'la Loca'. *Hija y madre* (1855) is a forgotten melodrama, but with *La bola de nieve* (1856) he broke new ground, denouncing the Spanish obsession with jealousy. Other thesis plays followed, ·in which for the first time Tamayo felt able to subdue his innate sense of theatricality in the interests of social morality. In *Lo positivo* (1862) he reduced the characters to four, concentrating on a satire of the middle class love of money. *Lances de honor* (1863) attacks the custom of duelling. *Los hombres de bien* (1870) reduces the action to the minimum; he repudiates in long speeches the ideas of Renan and satirizes the liberals who succumb to Renan. A fervent Roman Catholic and conservative, Tamayo was offended by the public's lack of interest in his crusading drama, and never wrote again after the failure of *Los hombres de bien*. He worked as a secretary for the Real Academia Española and later as Director of the Biblioteca Nacional.

His finest play, *Un drama nuevo* (1867), combines his passion for the theatre with that sombre sense of the evil of jealousy in *La bola de nieve*. It was written under the pseudonym 'Joaquín Estebánez', and is considered by some critics to be the best play written in 19th-c. Spain. It is set in Elizabethan England, and the protagonists are Shakespeare's company of actors. The hero, who plays Yorick, is jealous on stage and off of his wife's love for a younger actor. The envious Iago-figure of Walton feeds Yorick's suspicions and the play (together with the play within a play) ends in tragedy. Tamayo's psychological need to borrow subjects and characters from other writers is successfully resolved in echoes from *Hamlet*, *Othello*, and Kyd's *Spanish tragedy*.

A. Pidal y Mon edited Tamayo's *Obras* in the Colección de Escritores Castellanos (4 vols., 1898–1900). N. Sicars y Salvadó's *Don Manuel Tamayo y Baus: estudio crítico-biográfico* (Barcelona, 1906) has been superseded in part by *El teatro de Tamayo y Baus* (1965) by R. Esquer Torres.

See also G. Flynn, *Manuel Tamayo y Baus* (New York, 1973) in Twayne's World Authors series.

TAPIA, EUGENIO DE (1776–1860), b. Ávila. Liberal journalist and historian, who lived in England 1806–8 to study the language and English law. He was joint editor of the *Gaceta* in Cádiz during the Napoleonic invasion. Imprisoned by the Inquisition on a charge of conspiracy in 1812, he was released in 1813 when the charge was dropped. He went into exile in France in 1823, and returned to honours in 1831; he was Director of the Biblioteca Nacional in Madrid 1843–7.

His mediocre poems were printed in vol. 67 (1875) of the BAE. Among his serious verses are 'Oda a Quintana' (he published *El Semanario Patriótico* from Cádiz with Quintana) and the ballads 'La vejez' and 'El mar en estío'. His *Historia de la civilización española desde la invasión de los árabes hasta la época presente* (4 vols., 1840) was until recently widely consulted in Spain.

See Valle y Bárcena, *Biografía de Eugenio de Tapia* (1859).

TAPIA, JUAN DE (15th c.), a poet of the court of Alfonso V in Naples. His work, almost exclusively love poetry, has been preserved in two *cancioneros*: those of Stúñiga (q.v.) and of the Royal Palace, Madrid. Some of his work is autobiographical, including the poems written while a prisoner of war after the Battle of Ponza. His most affecting poem is 'Estando ausente de su amiga', reprinted with others in vol. 5 of Menéndez y Pelayo's *Antología de poetas líricos castellanos*.

Tapia is one of the subjects of F. Vendrell Gallostra's *La corte literaria de Alfonso V de Aragón y tres poetas de la misma* (1933).

There is also a Tapia (Christian name unknown) who is one of the poets of the *Cancionero General*, but he is probably not the same man.

TAPIA Y RIVERA, ALEJANDRO (1827–82) Puerto Rican playwright, poet, and novelist of the Romantic age. His first play, on Elizabeth and Essex, *Roberto d'Evreux* (written in 1848) was banned for its familiar treatment of royalty, but was performed in 1856 when reworked. He matured as a historical dramatist in *Bernardo de Palissy* (first performed 1857) and *Camoens* (published in Madrid, 1868; reworked in 1876), on the Portuguese poet's love for Catalina Ataide.

Vasco Núñez de Balboa (first performed 1872) was a failure, but Tapia caused a stir with two thesis plays: *La cuarterona* (Madrid, 1867) on racial prejudice, and *La parte del león* (written in 1878 and first performed in 1880) on equality in marriage.

Tapia wrote an allegorical burlesque epic with serious undertones, *La Sataniada: grandiosa epopeya dedicada al príncipe de las tinieblas, por Crisófilo Sardanápalo* (Madrid, 1878; 2nd edn., 1945; reprinted Barcelona, 1967) judged somewhat too harshly by the severely orthodox Menéndez y Pelayo, who criticized the subject matter and ignored the often magnificent invention. Tapia's fiction is typically Romantic, based loosely on historical themes but inventing Byronic heroes and heroines. *La palma del cacique: leyenda histórica de Puerto Rico* (Havana, 1862) is one such, and others are *Cofresí* (1876) a pseudo-historical idealization of a Puerto Rican pirate deriving from *La novia del hereje* (1854) by Vicente Fidel López (q.v.); and the two short novels in *Misceláneas* (1880), 'Enardo y Rosael' and 'A orillas del Rhin'.

His most interesting novels are *Póstumo el transmigrado* (Madrid, 1872) and the less successful *Póstumo el envirginiado* (Madrid, 1882), partly-satirical explorations of the theme of the transmigration of souls, in the first of which the soul of Póstumo inhabits the body of his enemy.

Tapia's *Conferencias sobre estética* (1881) confesses to a modified acceptance of the theories of Schelling and Hegel. As an historian, he helped to compile a useful collection of documents of the 15th–18th cs. entitled the Biblioteca Histórica de Puerto Rico, but his most enjoyable book is still *Mis memorias* (1928; 2nd edn., 1946), which is also a contemporary cultural history of Puerto Rico.

Tarasca, the figure of a dragon or sea-serpent carried by men at the head of a Corpus Christi procession in Spain. It was usually surmounted by a figure of the Whore of Babylon (whom the Toledans called Anne Boleyn, according to the *Semanario Pintoresco*, 1841, p. 177). It is mentioned in the *comedias* of Pérez de Montalbán (q.v., 1638).

Tarascas were used to best effect on the Spanish stage by Francisco Santos (q.v.) in three allegories against Spanish apathy and insensitivity: *Las tarascas de Madrid y tribunal espantoso* (1664), *Los gigantones de Madrid por defuera* (1666), and *La tarasca de parto en el mesón del infierno y días de fiestas por la noche* (1671).

There are two drawings of *tarascas* (dated 1674 and 1683, the latter signed by Jusepe Caudi) as figs. 27–8 of N. D. Shergold's *A history of the Spanish stage from medieval times until the end of the seventeenth century* (Oxford, 1967).

TÁRREGA, FRANCESC AGUSTÍ (1554–1602), b. Segorbe?, Valencia. Canon of Valencia Cathedral, poet, and playwright of the Valencian group (which included Guillén de Castro and Aguilar). A member of the Academia de los Nocturnos (q.v.), where he was known as 'Miedo'. He wrote a dozen plays, of which two survive only by title. Eight of them are published in *Doze comedias famosas de quatro poetas naturales de . . . Valencia* (Valencia, 1608), and three were reprinted in *Norte de la Poesía Española* (Valencia, 1616). Four were edited by R. Mesonero Romanos (q.v.) in vol. 43 of the Biblioteca de Autores Contemporáneos (1857).

Tárrega's religious play *La fundación de la Orden de Nuestra Señora de la Merced* concerns the conversion of a great sinner to sainthood, and may have been a source of Calderón's *La devoción de la Cruz* (qq.v.). *Los moriscos de Hornachos* was edited by C. B. Bourland in *Modern Philology*, vol. 1 (1903), pp. 547–61 and vol. 2 (1904), pp. 77–90, but the attribution to Tárrega (upheld from the 17th c. up to J. Simón Díaz in the 20th) is clearly wrong since the play reveals a knowledge of events years after his death. Jean-Marc Pelorson dates the play to 1619 and attributes it to a court dramatist in the circle of Lope de Vega (see 'Recherches sur la "comedia" "Los moriscos de Hornachuelos" in *Bulletin Hispanique*, vol. 74, 1972).

La sangre leal de los montañeses de Navarra

is a partly-historical, partly-legendary drama managed with skill, and *La duquesa constante* is equally convincing. Most of Tárrega's plays are clumsily constructed, such as the patriotic *El cerco de Pavía y prisión del rey Francisco*; the historical *El cerco de Rodas* and *Las suertes trocadas y el torneo venturoso*; *La condesa Constanza*; *La gallarda Irene*; and *La perseguida Amaltea*.

Tárrega's works lack the imaginative flights of Lope de Vega, and are marred by an excessive use of puns and other verbal conceits, but *La enemiga favorable* suffers least from these defects, being praised by the canon in *Don Quijote*, Pt. 1, ch. 48. An intrigue at the court of Naples shows Laura in love with the King, and urging him to poison the Queen. Later, in disguise, she defends the Queen, falsely charged with infidelity; the lack of verisimilitude is outweighed by superior versification. Tárrega wrote an interlude, *El baile de Leganitos*, to accompany this play in which two lackeys squabble over a maidservant, and one is ducked in the public fountain.

El prado de Valencia (not to be confused with the miscellany of the same title produced by the Academia de los Nocturnos) is a merry, inconsequential *cuadro de costumbres* set in Valencia and uses Tárrega's first-hand knowledge of the city.

Tárrega was also a poet, contributing verses to the *Relación de las fiestas que el Arzobispo y Cabildo de Valencia hicieron en la traslación de la Reliquia del glorioso San Vicente Ferrer a este santo templo* (Valencia, 1600).

See J. Serrano Cañete, *El canónigo F. A. Tárrega poeta dramático del siglo XVI: estudio biográfico-bibliográfico* (Valencia, 1889), an edition limited to only 60 copies; and J. G. Weiger, *The Valencian dramatists of Spain's Golden Age* (New York, 1976), pp. 50–80, in Twayne's World Authors series.

Tartaro, in Basque legend, the equivalent of Homer's Cyclops. 'A huge one-eyed giant, occasionally a cannibal, but not without a rough *bonhomie* when satiated with food and drink. Intellectually far below the feebler race of mankind, he is invariably beaten in his contests with them, notwithstanding his enormous strength: he loses all his wagers and is generally lured on to commit involuntary suicide' Wentworth Webster, *Basque legends* (London, 1878).

TAS(S)IS Y PERALTA, JUAN DE, Conde de *Villamediana* (1582–1622), b. Lisbon. Court wit and baroque poet, a disciple of Góngora (q.v.). He grew up at court, but was exiled from Madrid to Valladolid for gambling heavily in 1608. While travelling to Italy he met the poet Marino. Villamediana returned to Madrid in

1617 but was exiled again, to Andalusia in 1621, for his savage epigrams, such as: '¡Qué galán que entró Vergel / con cintillo de diamantes! / Diamantes que fueron antes / de amantes de su muger'. His fame as a libertine is due mainly to his attempted seduction of Isabel of Bourbon, the pretty queen of Philip IV. It is said that during an extravagant performance of his play *La gloria de Niquea* (based on an episode from *Amadís de Grecia*), he set the theatre at Aranjuez on fire in order to take Isabel in his arms while rescuing her. During a tournament in Madrid he covered himself with silver *reales* and punningly dedicated his exploits to the queen in the saying 'son mis amores reales'. He was killed by an unknown assassin one night when returning home from the palace with his friend Luis Haro, and it is suspected that the motive was royal jealousy.

It has been suggested that Villamediana's *Fábulas* are more gongoristic than Góngora's; there is no doubt that these verbal fireworks (*Faetón*, *Apolo y Dafne*, *Fénix*, *Europa*, and *Venus y Adonis*) are wrought for richness of texture rather than for meaning, and they are often mere echoes of his master. The two hundred or so sonnets in the *Obras* (Saragossa, 1629; Madrid, 1631; and enlarged, Saragossa, 1634) are somewhat more original, especially the best, 'A la muerte de la reina Margarita'. *Poesías* were reprinted in the BAE, in vol. 42 (1857; new edn., 1950).

See E. Cotarelo y Mori, *El Conde de Villamediana* (1886), a biography with some previously unpublished poems. *Son mis amores* (Barcelona, 1944) is the title of A. Albert Torrella's fictional biography of Villamediana.

Teatro crítico universal . . ., see THEATRO CRÍTICO UNIVERSAL . . ..

Teatro Universitario 'La Barraca', see 'BARRACA, LA'.

TEJEDA Y GUZMÁN, LUIS JOSÉ DE (1604–80), b. Córdoba del Tucumán, Argentina. Poet, generally considered the first of any importance in the country now called Argentina. His life is divided into two by his imprisonment (1660–2) and the confiscation of his possessions. In 1663 he took refuge in the Dominican order.

The *Romance de su vida* dates, like most of the work he retained, from the last years of his life. In it, he asks pardon for a frivolous adolescence, infidelity in marriage, and his blustering arrogance as a soldier. His MS. *Libro de varios tratados* is the only work known to have survived from the 17th-c. bishopric and university town of Córdoba del Tucumán.

Because of the shortage of printing presses in Spanish America, where printing was officially discouraged, many works circulated only in MS. and have since been lost.

TÉLLEZ, Fray GABRIEL (1583–1648), b. Madrid. Playwright. The most important disciple of Lope de Vega (q.v.); better known by his pseudonym 'Tirso de Molina'.

Blanca de los Ríos (q.v.), the foremost Tirso scholar and editor of the standard *Obras dramáticas completas* (3 vols., 1946–59), discovered a baptismal certificate dated 9 March 1584 for one Gabriel, father incognito, mother Gracia Juliana. She believes this to refer to Tirso, whom she alleges to be the bastard son of the Duke of Osuna, offering as literary evidence the passage in *El melancólico* defending the honour of illegitimate sons. Her thesis has been rejected by Fray Miguel L. Ríos and Padre Manuel Pinedo Rey, partly because it would have been impossible for a bastard to have enjoyed preferment in the Mercedarian order without a special dispensation, and though there is ample evidence of his progression in the order (which he joined in 1600), there is no record of any dispensation, and partly because any suspicion of his illegitimacy would have been seized on gleefully by rival playwrights.

Téllez studied at Alcalá and professed in 1601 at Guadalajara, where he continued his studies. He probably lived almost continuously in Toledo during 1605–15, and his first plays were probably written then, for in his miscellany *Los cigarrales de Toledo* (q.v.), written in 1621, he stated that he had written 300 *comedias* in the previous fourteen years. He travelled widely, enjoying in particular Galicia and Portugal, the setting of many of his plays. In 1614 he was in Aragón, probably in exile for satirizing the nobility of Castile. In 1616 he went to Hispaniola (now the Dominican Republic) for two years, and in 1620 we hear of him in Madrid. The Council of Castile admonished him in 1625 for depicting vice too vividly on the stage, and required him on pain of excommunication to write nothing secular again. Thereafter we have only three surviving *comedias*: *La huerta de Juan Fernández* (1626), *Las quinas de Portugal* (dated 1638 on the autograph MS. in Madrid), and a reworking of *En Madrid y en la casa*.

His last years (1632–48, the first seven in Barcelona) were spent in the service of his order, and on his appointment as Mercedarian chronicler in 1637 he wrote *Historia general de la Orden de Nuestra Señora de las Mercedes*, discovered by Blanca de los Ríos in the library of the Real Academia de la Historia and edited (2 vols., 1974) by Fray Manuel Penedo Rey. He was generally known to his contemporaries as 'El Mercedario'.

Two other prose works by Tirso were published in his lifetime, a Boccaccio-inspired miscellany written before his official warning and entitled *Los cigarrales de Toledo* (the 'cigarrales' being weekend retreats in the countryside near Toledo) published in 1624 and reprinted in the Colección Crisol in 1954; and the less exuberant *Deleytar aprovechando* (1635), a similar compendium. The first takes its form and some of its anecdotes from *Il Decamerone*, and shows how a group of friends while away the summer, each telling a story in his own *cigarral*, the best being the risqué *Los tres maridos burlados*. Interpolated *comedias* include the celebrated *El vergonzoso en palacio* (q.v.) and *El celoso prudente*.

Deleytar aprovechando (unavailable in a modern edition) is a series of stories and plays told by three pious couples who prefer to leave the city while the carnival is on. Apart from three *autos*, there is a sustained historical novel called *El bandolero*, on the conversion of S. Pedro Armengol.

Tirso wrote some four hundred plays, of which about 86 survive (though some of these are of dubious attribution). Five collections appeared in his lifetime: *Doze Comedias nueuas del Maestro Tirso de Molina: Primera parte* (Seville, 1627), *Segunda parte* (1635), *Parte tercera* (Tortosa, 1634), *Quarta parte* (1635), and *Quinta parte* (1636). The BAE published 36 in vol. 5 (1848) and the NBAE a further 45 in vols. 4 and 9 (1906–7). María del Pilar Palomo has re-edited the plays as vols. 236–9 and 242–3 of the BAE.

Tirso's drama can be divided broadly into the religious, the historical, and the plays of character and intrigue.

Religious Plays. His *autos sacramentales* are mere reflections of those of Lope de Vega. Only four can be ascribed to Tirso with any certainty: *El colmenero divino* (possibly his first work), *No le arriendo la ganancia*, *Los hermanos parecidos* (a transposition of the *Menaechmi* of Plautus *a lo divino*), and *El laberinto de Creta*. The first three appear in his *Deleytar aprovechando* (1635). Tirso's biblical plays are often lyrically charming, but lack dramatic gusto. The best is *La mejor espigadera*, on the story of Ruth and Naomi, with sensitive use of popular poetry in the love scene of Ruth and Boaz. Others are *La mujer que manda en casa*, *La viña de Nabot*, the incest play *La venganza de Tamar*, *La vida y muerte de Herodes*, *Los cabellos de Absalón*, and the interesting *Tanto es lo de más como lo de menos*, which blends the parables of the prodigal son and the wealthy miser. His plays on the lives of saints include a trilogy called *La santa Juana* on a local 16th c. Toledan *beata* who has not yet, in fact, achieved formal sainthood; *La ninfa del cielo*; and *La dama del olivar*, reminiscent of Lope's *Fuenteovejuna* (q.v.). Tirso's most significant religious plays are

El condenado por desconfiado (q.v.), and the play that introduced the Don Juan (q.v.) theme into European literature: *El burlador de Sevilla y convidado de piedra* (q.v.).

Historical Plays. Lope de Vega wrote 200 historical plays, so it is strange that his pupil Tirso wrote so few, even if one, *La prudencia en la mujer* (q.v.) has been termed by Menéndez y Pelayo 'el mejor drama histórico de nuestro teatro'. Tirso's concealed attacks on the court of Philip IV are repeated in two *comedias* that Blanca de los Ríos believes were written in collaboration with Quevedo in 1615: *Próspera fortuna de Don Álvaro de Luna* and *Adversa fortuna de Don Álvaro de Luna*. Other historical plays include *La república al revés* (q.v.), *Los lagos de San Vicente*, and a trilogy on the Pizarros: *Todo es dar en una cosa* (on Francisco), *Amazonas en las Indias* (on Gonzalo), and *La lealtad contra la envidia* (on Hernando).

Plays of Character and Intrigue. Though *Marta la piadosa* is commonly likened to Molière's *Tartuffe*, the main theme is not the scheming hypocrisy of a lecher, but the wiles of a girl determined to marry the man of her choice; she cannot do this openly, against the patriarchal temper of the times, so is forced to use deceit, which succeeds. The best-known *comedia de intriga* is *El vergonzoso en palacio* (q.v.). Others include the witty *Don Gil de las calzas verdes*, employing Tirso's favourite comic device of disguising women as men; *El amor y la amistad*, *El celoso prudente*, and *Cómo han de ser los amigos*.

Given Tirso's fecundity, second in Golden Age drama only to that of Lope de Vega, it is remarkable that his plays are so well constructed, and that so many of his principal characters are not only memorable, but even universal: Don Juan Tenorio of *El burlador de Sevilla*, María of *La prudencia en la mujer*, Irene of *La república al revés*, Rugero of *El melancólico*, Marta in *Marta la piadosa*, Paulo in *El condenado por desconfiado*, and Madalena in *El vergonzoso en palacio*. Though Tirso is less fluent or lyrical as a versifier than Lope, he is usually more judicious in his choice of words: he is a master of Castilian, controlling every nuance to obtain the effective result, whether in the comic scenes of *Don Gil de las calzas verdes* or in the complex morality play of *El burlador de Sevilla*. Though a baroque writer, influenced at least in *El burlador de Sevilla* by Góngora, he nevertheless eluded the excessive *culteranismo* of Gracián, excelling in dialogue that harmonizes with the action.

With Tirso, the *comedia de intriga* evolves beyond Lope and, until Tirso, the mother figure does not emerge clearly and fully on the Spanish stage, and his affection for parents (the father Anacleto in *El condenado por desconfiado*) seems to stem not only from the natural gentleness of a

Mercedarian, but partly from that long and profound formal education that Lope was denied, and partly too from listening to confession, with its insights into personality, motives, and behaviour.

See Serge Maurel, *L'univers dramatique de Tirso de Molina* (Poitiers, 1971); Ruth Lee Kennedy, *Studies in Tirso* (3 vols., vol. 1: *The dramatist and his competitors, 1620–1626*, Chapel Hill, N.C., 1974, others in progress); and H. W. Sullivan, *Tirso de Molina and the drama of the Counter-Reformation* (1976).

Tema de nuestro tiempo, El (1923), metaphysical essays by José Ortega y Gasset (q.v.).

Ortega, in this early work, proposes a form of *razón vital* ('vital reason') to replace the neo-Kantian pure reason or mathematical reason advocated by some of his predecessors. *Razón vital* comprises thought and emotion, and is so called because it is to be placed at the service of life, requiring beauty in emotion, truth in thought, and kindness in will.

The work is generally considered to be Ortega's most significant and durable contribution to philosophical debate. His emphasis on 'becoming' leads to the view that any 'truth' which is set or static immediately ceases to be truthful.

Tensón, a poem intended for a poetical contest between two or more poets. Alternative titles such as *joc inamorat, joc d'amor, contenso,* and *torneyamen* show that love was the most common theme of troubadours in Provence, notably by Guillaume de Machaut and Alain Chartier.

The *tensón* is composed of a variable number of stanzas each of six, seven, or eight octosyllabic or decasyllabic lines. The second contestant to compose is bound to follow the rhyme-scheme of the first; the decision is made by a jury often composed of ladies. The first Spanish lyric compositions *Razón feita de amor* and *Denuestos del agua y el vino* derive, according to Zenker's *Die provenzalische Tenzone*, from the *tensones* of Provence.

Tercerilla, a three-line stanza of *arte menor*; that is, of two to eight syllables of one or more rhythmic stresses. The rhyme-scheme abb is the commonest in *letrillas* (q.v.) of the 17th c., but aba also occurs. Antonio Machado has used the *tercerilla* with assonantal rhyme.

Terceto, a stanza of three lines deriving from the Italian *terza rima* in which Dante's *Divina Commedia* is written. It was introduced into Castilian by Boscà and used frequently by Garcilaso, by Meléndez Valdés in his elegy 'El deleite y la virtud', by Cadalso in his ode 'A la

fortuna', and by the Guatemalan Rafael García Goyena (1766–1823) in his satirical 'Fábula de los animales congregados'.

The lines of a *terceto* are normally hendecasyllables. If the rhyme scheme is aba, bcb, cdc, the *tercetos* are *encadenados*; but it may also be aba, cdc, efe, or the monorhyme aaa, bbb, ccc. Pérez de Guzmán referred to his monorhymed *tercetos* as *trinadas*.

Tercetos have also been written in octosyllables, notably by Rubén Darío, and in the *fábula* 'El murciélago' of Hartzenbusch.

Álvarez Gato used *tercetos* in maxims such as the following from the *Cancionero del siglo XV*: 'Procuremos buenos fines, / que las vidas más loadas / por los cabos son juzgadas.'

See also the authors mentioned above.

TERESA DE ÁVILA or JESUS, Santa (1515–82), b. Ávila or Gotarrendura, a village near Ávila. Her secular name was Teresa Sánchez de Cepeda y Ahumada; she was born into the nobility. Inflamed by reading the lives of saints, she ran away from home with her brother Rodrigo at the age of seven to achieve martyrdom by converting the infidel, and later began to write, again with her brother, an imitation of the romances of chivalry then in vogue. Having spent some time in the Augustinian convent at Ávila, she became a Carmelite at the age of 19. Her health was always poor, due to the severe asceticism of her early years, and she suffered headaches, insomnia, and attacks of fever.

She set out conscientiously to reform the Carmelite order, and managed to reform or found in collaboration with San Juan de la Cruz (q.v.) thirty-two convents throughout Spain, mainly in Castile and Andalusia. The first convent of Discalced (Barefoot) Carmelites she founded was that of San José in Ávila (1562) and during the next three years she wrote at the request of her spiritual director Francisco de Soto y Salazar her autobiographical *Vida*, a book denounced to the Inquisition by the conservative Carmelites who resisted reform. They tried to bring about her deportation to Latin America, but managed only to secure her confinement to Toledo, where she wrote *El castillo interior* (q.v., also known as *Las moradas*), a major milestone in Western mystical literature. Her friends were even more powerful than her enemies, however, and the Jesuits, together with Fray Luis de León, the theologian Domingo Báñez (qq.v.), and above all San Juan de la Cruz resisted attempts to silence Teresa. She travelled indefatigably, despite physical debility, and honestly set forth her occasional religious doubts. She wrote tirelessly, revealing a frank and pleasant personality combining masculine energy with feminine sensibility. Her *Libro de las fundaciones*

(Brussels, 1613; last reprinted in Clásicos Castellanos, 2 vols., 1940) describes her work of reform, while *Libro de las relaciones* narrates her progress to confessors, among them Fray Pedro de Alcántara. One of the most deplorable losses in Spanish literature is that of her correspondence with San Juan de la Cruz, but more than four hundred other letters were published by J. de Palafox y Mendoza in *Cartas* (2 vols., Saragossa, 1658).

El camino de perfección (q.v., Évora, 1583) is a spiritual guide for the ascetic, a more coherent work than the *Avisos espirituales . . . dados a todas las religiosas sus hijas* (Cordova, 1598). She also wrote on the Song of Songs: *Conceptos del amor de Dios sobre algunas palabras de los Cantares de Salomón* (Brussels, 1611). It is possible that some of the many poems attributed to S. Teresa that do not appear in her published writings may in fact be hers, though most scholars limit her works to seven, of which the finest is by common consent 'Vivo sin vivir en mí'.

Teresa's mysticism is simple, pure, and spontaneous, easily understood by the average believer yet susceptible of multiple interpretations by the theologian. Beatified in 1614, Teresa was canonized in 1622, and her influence has spread far beyond the Carmelite Order that she reformed.

An edition of *Los libros de la Madre Teresa de Jesús* was published in 3 vols. in Salamanca (1588), but the standard edition is that of P. Silverio de Santa Teresa (9 vols., Burgos, 1915–24) and reference should be made to the Biblioteca de Autores Cristianos edition (3 vols., 1951–9), especially for the bibliography.

Of the many biographies of this key figure in Occidental religious life, see P. Silverio de Santa Teresa, *Vida de Santa Teresa* (5 vols., Burgos, 1935–7), Crisógono de Jesús, *Teresa de Jesús* (Barcelona, 1936), Marcelle Auclair, *La vie de Sainte Thérèse d'Ávila* (Paris, 1950; English translation, 1953), R. Hoornaert, *Sainte Thérèse d'Avile* (Bruges, 1951), E. Allison Peers, *Mother of Carmel* (London, 1945), a sensitive short study.

TERRAZAS, FRANCISCO DE (1525?-1600?), a Creole, the earliest recorded Mexican poet, who wrote nine sonnets in the Italian manner on the cruelty and beauty of his beloved, an amatory epistle in *tercetos* (q.v.), ten *décimas*, and fragments of an epic poem in imitation of Ercilla's *Araucana* (qq.v.) called *El Nuevo Mundo y su conquista*, written c. 1580 and first published in Baltasar Dorantes de Carranza's *Sumaria relación de las cosas de la Nueva España* (1902), written between 1601 and 1604. Terrazas was apparently well-known in Spain before 1584, when Cervantes wrote in his *Canto de Caliope* that Terrazas was one of the 'entendimientos

sobrehumanos de la región antárctica'. *El Nuevo Mundo* idealizes the primeval innocence of the Indians before the conquest in the tradition of Las Casas (q.v.). It was edited by A. Castro Leal as vol. 3 of the Bibliotheca Mexicana (1941). The best essay on Terrazas is by Joaquín García Icazbalceta in his *Obras* (1896), reprinted in 1962.

TERRAZA Y REJÓN, DIONISIO, pseudonym of Antonio José de Irisarri (q.v.).

Tertulia, a literary clique or *salon* which gradually replaced the more formal literary academies on the 18th c. The word is first recorded in an *entremés* of Quiñones de Benavente in the first half of the 17th c. In his *Geschichte der dramatischen Literatur und Kunst in Spanien* (Berlin, 1846, vol. 3, pp. 25–6), Schack derived the word from the nickname of that part of the early theatres where the educated classes and clergy sat. They were known as *tertuliantes* from their frequent citing of the Christian apologist Quintus Septimius Florens Tertullianus (c. 160–c. 220), called Tertuliano in Castilian, and their *tertulia* (originally known as the *desván*) was an upper circle, or gallery.

Early *tertulias* met in private houses, especially those of the nobility, such as the Marqués de Molíns and the Duque de Rivas.

The best-known 18th-c. *tertulia* was the Fonda de San Sebastián, in which neoclassical theories were propounded by Cadalso, Nicolás F. de Moratín, and Iriarte. The *sainete Las tertulias de Madrid* (first performed in 1770) by Ramón de la Cruz satirized those who attended the gatherings merely for the refreshments, gossip, and perhaps to flirt.

Romanticism favoured the spread of the *tertulia*. Fernández de la Vega's Tertulia del Liceo was founded in 1837 in his own home, and both Menéndez y Pelayo and Emilia Pardo Bazán in more recent times opened a *salon* for the literary. But since 1830 most *tertulias* have been held in cafés, clubs, and in the offices of literary magazines, such as (from 1923), the *Revista de Occidente tertulia* presided over by José Ortega y Gasset.

In 1830, the first *tertulia* held in public, El Parnasillo, met at the Café del Príncipe in Madrid; among the *tertuliantes* were Mesonero Romanos (whose *Memorias de un setentón*, 1880, give a graphic account of the meetings), Antonio Gil y Zárate, Larra, Espronceda, Ventura de la Vega, and Manuel Bretón de los Herreros. La Hijuela del Parnasillo met in the Café Suizo, another *tertulia* was established in 1846 in the Café del Recreo, and a revolutionary group met under cover of the *tertulia* La Fontana de Oro, whose members included Antonio

Alcalá Galiano. La Fontana de Oro was described in the novel of that title (1890) by Benito Pérez Galdós, whose *episodio nacional La estafeta romántica* (1899) also described the world of the *tertulia*. Other well-known *tertulias* were held at the Café de la Esmeralda, with Barrantes, Luis de Eguilaz, Cánovas del Castillo, and Fernández y González; La Cuerda Granadina included Riaño, P. A. de Alarcón, and Fernández Jiménez, and at the end of the 19th c. the famous Bilis Club met at the Café Levante, Café Inglés, and elsewhere: 'Clarín', Taboada, Palacio Valdés, Selles, and others drew many humorists together, and from these meetings arose the magazine *Madrid Cómico*.

In the 20th c., Jacinto Benavente founded the *tertulia* at the Café Gato Negro; the *ultraístas* and surrealists met in the Café de Platerías, and the Café de Pombo was immortalized in Ramón Gómez de la Serna's book of recollections *Pombo* (1918).

See E. M. Williams, *The development of the literary tertulia* (1935), Cornell University thesis.

Tesis andina, La ('the Andean thesis'), as expressed by the Bolivian novelist Jaime Mendoza (q.v.) in his book *La tesis andinista: Bolivia y Paraguay* (1933), and his subsequent *El macizo boliviano* (1935), is that the Andean climate and terrain were paramount in moulding the personality of the Andean peoples, and that it is impossible to understand the history and development of the Andean countries without a knowledge of the geographical background. This argument is developed from the view of Alcides Arguedas (q.v.).

Theatro crítico universal: discursos varios en todo género de materias, para desengaño de errores comunes (9 vols., 1726–40), essays by Fray Benito Jerónimo Feijóo y Montenegro (q.v.). *Theatro*, nowadays *Teatro*, is used in the sense of 'panorama' or 'conspectus', and the 118 discourses provide an encyclopaedic view of 18th-c. Spain as seen by an enquirer strongly influenced by the Erasmian movement and the French Enlightenment. As was to be expected, given the strongly conservative age in which it was written, controversy raged around the *Theatro* until 1750, when a royal decree of Fernando VI prohibited further attacks on Feijóo.

There is no unabridged modern edition of the *Theatro*. The fullest is the 4-vol. edition in the BAE, and a 3-vol. selection by A. Millares Carlo is available in Clásicos Castellanos (1923-5).

THEBUSSEM, DOCTOR, the pen-name of Mariano Pardo de Figueroa (q.v.).

THEODULF (*c.* 760–821), b. Northern Spain. A poet of the Gothic people, who wrote in Latin and was highly respected for his learning at the court of Charlemagne, who appointed him Bishop of Orleans.

He was imprisoned by Louis the Pious in 818, and while incarcerated he composed the 'Gloria, laus et honor', a section of which is used in Palm Sunday processions. He wrote many other poems, including 'Ad Carolum regem'.

See C. Cuissard, *Théodulfe, évêque d'Orléans* (Orleans, 1892).

THEOPHILA (1st c. A.D.), b. Gades (Cádiz). A poet and philosopher of Greek origin, she was associated (wife or lover?) with the poet Canius Rufus (q.v.), and belonged like him to the Stoic group. She is the 'noble Theophila, eloquent sage' of Martial's eulogy. None of her work appears to have survived.

THOMSON, AUGUSTO GOEMINNE (1880–1950), b. Valparaíso. Chilean novelist who wrote under the name 'Augusto d'Halmar'. With two friends he founded a Tolstoyan colony in San Bernardo devoted to literature and agriculture, an experiment described by one of the friends, Fernando Santiván, in *Memorias de un tolstoyano*. The colony broke up when d'Halmar was appointed consul in India, 1907–8. His first book *Juana Lucero* (1902) had told a prostitute's story in a compound of Zolaesque naturalism and Tolstoyan idealism. D'Halmar's travels altered his literary attitudes, and he adopted an elegant, philosophical style for *La lámpara en el molino* (1914). He went to Europe as a war correspondent during World War I, writing travel sketches in the manner of Pierre Loti and publishing the exotic *Nirvana* (1918). While in Spain he followed Azorín's (q.v.) *Ruta de Don Quijote* in his own observations, *La Mancha de Don Quijote* (1934), but it was the Sevillian novel *Pasión y muerte del cura Deusto* (1924) that made his name famous.

Like Larreta (q.v.) before him, and Reyles (q.v.) after him, d'Halmar was captivated by Seville, and the city made a creative writer out of an amateur. In 1934 he returned to Chile as director of the Museo Municipal de Bellas Artes in Valparaíso, and in that year his *Obras completas* began to appear, and his novel *Capitanes sin barco* was published.

In 1942 he was awarded the inaugural National Literary Prize of Chile.

Tía fingida, La, a *novela ejemplar* attributed by some scholars to Cervantes (q.v.).

The plot concerns an 'aunt' calling herself Doña Claudia de Astudillo y Quiñones, who arrives in Salamanca accompanied by her 'niece' Esperanza, whose virginity had already been traded three times. Two students and a friend of theirs discover the profession of Doña Claudia, who is sent to gaol. One of the students forgets the past and marries Esperanza. The tale was never included in the *Novelas ejemplares* of Cervantes until Arrieta published it in 1814; the style is considered by some to be Cervantine, while the fact that it was discovered in an old MS. with *Rinconete y Cortadillo* and *El celoso extremeño* added some weight to that case. Nowadays the attribution is generally rejected.

TICKNOR, GEORGE (1791–1871), b. Boston. The first North American to distinguish himself in Hispanic studies. After travelling in Spain and elsewhere in Europe 1815–19, he became Smith Professor of French and Spanish at Harvard University, where he remained until 1835. He collected a large and valuable library of early Spanish and Portuguese books while writing his detailed and bibliographically valuable *History of Spanish Literature* (3 vols., New York, 1849; 6th American edn., corrected and enlarged, 1891; reprinted, 1965). Pascual de Gayangos corrected and improved the first edition in his 4-vol. Spanish translation (Madrid, 1851–7). Often superseded in its critical judgments, and notably intolerant of Roman Catholic faith and practice, Ticknor's *History* is nevertheless still of use for its reference to rare books.

Ticknor's books were donated to the Boston Public Library, whose librarian, James L. Whitney, produced a *Catalogue of the Spanish library and of the Portuguese books, bequeathed by George Ticknor to the Boston Public Library* (Boston, 1879).

TICK-TACK, one of the pseudonyms used by the Mexican humorist Ángel del Campo (q.v.).

TIEMPO, CÉSAR, pseudonym of Israel Zeitlin (q.v.).

Tierra Nueva, an important literary magazine sponsored by the National University of Mexico between 1940 and 1942. Its fifteen issues were edited by Leopoldo Zea (q.v.), Alí Chumacero, Jorge González Durán, and José Luis Martínez, and it encouraged contributions from writers of all styles and opinions, including Abreu Gómez, Cuesta, González Martínez, Juan Ramón Jiménez, Neruda, Revueltas, and Reyes (qq.v.).

See J. F. Garganigo, '"Tierra Nueva": su estética y poética' in *Revista Iberoamericana*, vol. 31 (July–December 1965) pp. 239–50.

Tierra vasca, a trilogy of novels by Pío Baroja y Nessi (q.v.) comprising *La casa de Aizgorri* (Bilbao, 1900), *El mayorazgo de Labraz* (Barce-

lona, 1903), and *Zalacaín el aventurero* (qq.v., Barcelona, 1909).

Tigre Juan (1926), and its sequel *El curandero de su honra* (1926), were the last major novels by Ramón Pérez de Ayala (q.v.). Both parts have divisions with musical headings. The work is in sonata form, with primary and secondary themes, moving first slowly, then rapidly, with a final coda.

Like *Belarmino y Apolonio* (q.v.), *Tigre Juan* is set in the small university town of Pilares, which is the author's native Oviedo. 'Tigre' Juan Guerra Madrigal, a merchant, scribe, and blood-letter, falls in love with Herminia, the grand-daughter of a stallholder in the market-place. Despite the difference in their ages, Juan brings her gifts and courts her. Herminia believes she is in love with Vespasiano, a travelling salesman with the reputation of a Don Juan, and plans to escape with him before her wedding day. Tigre Juan takes the leading role in a town performance of Calderón's *El médico de su honra* (q.v., the choice of which has a symbolic significance in the novel), and after Vespasiano quietly leaves town, Herminia and Juan are married.

On Vespasiano's next visit, Herminia feels the impulse to leave the powerful, awe-inspiring Juan for the salesman, who reluctantly agrees but abandons her, after hypocritically stating that he cannot betray his friend Juan. Herminia returns to Pilares, very ill, and his friends try to convince Juan of her innocence. Juan lets his own blood, but Herminia is now reconciled to life with him and persuades him to stop the haemorrhage. After the tragedy, they find happiness, and a son is born to them. The personality of Juan Guerra Madrigal is shown by the contradictory names Pérez de Ayala gives him: he is a virile man of quick temper, but sentimental, and with a great need for love.

In *La Regenta* (q.v.), Leopoldo Alas (writing as 'Clarín') had first implied that Don Juan's behaviour may have resulted from his effeminacy. Pérez de Ayala, who studied under Alas at the University of Oviedo, develops this idea, drawing on a knowledge of Freud to express the idea that Don Juan is the archetype of men with weak heterosexual urges and a strong sense of sexual inadequacy which forces them to perpetual novelty. As G. G. Brown explains, the young Colás's analysis of Don Juan as a child who never grew up provides the further Freudian explanation that the nature of a man's first relationship with a woman (his mother) affects all others.

As the ironic title of the book's sequel suggests, the major character of *El curandero de su honra* is the figure who takes the part of the 'offended husband' (Tigre Juan) both in real life, and in amateur theatricals (Gutierre in *El médico de su honra* by Calderón). Pérez de Ayala's critique of traditional Spanish values, from the standpoint of the *Generación del 1898* (q.v.), involves the caricaturing of such types as the inveterate seducer or Don Juan figure (here Vespasiano) and the furious man of honour or Gutierre figure (here Tigre Juan). Each is shown to lack the true maturity of manhood. Pérez de Ayala's earlier novels dealt with the need to reject *parecer* in favour of *ser*, and here too Tigre Juan is from one viewpoint a quixotic figure, living in a world of fantasy and myth in Part I, and working out his salvation in the real world guided by love and reason in Part II.

The subconscious plays a major rôle in these two novels, even in such incidents as the *couvade*, Juan's attempt at breast-feeding, and in the recognition of the father's 'maternal' instincts. Honour, love, marriage, and the place of women in society all receive serious consideration.

Both parts were translated together as *Tigre Juan* (New York and London, 1933) by Walter Starkie.

TIMONEDA, JOAN (*c.* 1520–1583), b. Valencia. Ballad-collector, short-story collector, playwright, bookseller, editor, and publisher (but not printer). He was responsible for editing and publishing the works of Alonso de la Vega (q.v., 1566) and Lope de Rueda (q.v., 1567 and 1570).

In 1559 (not 1517, as printed) he published *Las tres comedias*, of which the first two were skilful adaptations from the *Amphitryon* and *Menaechmi* of Plautus, and the third probably imitated Ariosto's *Il negromante*. This last is the *Comedia de Cornelia*, though the heroine is usually named 'Carmelia' in the text. Timoneda declared in his preface that his intention was to harmonize the use of prose as in *La Celestina* (q.v.) with the dramatic quality of Torres Naharro (q.v.).

In 1565, as 'Joan Diamonte' (an anagram), he published six verse plays and five *entremeses* in a book called *Turiana*, the first three plays being dated 1564. These *comedias* and *farças* are 'Filomena', 'Paliana', 'Aurelia', 'Trapacera' (the best of them), 'Rosalina', and 'Floriana'. J. P. Wickersham Crawford (in his *Spanish drama before Lope de Vega* (Philadelphia, 1922; 2nd edn. corrected with a bibliographical supplement, 1967) considers these plays inferior to anything Timoneda signed and hence probably not his own work.

Timoneda also wrote five *autos sacramentales*: three collected in *Ternario spiritual* (1558), one is included also in *Ternario sacramental* (Valencia, 1575), and reprinted in vol. 58 of the BAE (1865). The best, 'La oveja perdida', has been edited by A. Sanvisens in *Autos sacramentales eucarísticos* (Barcelona, 1955).

Timoneda compiled four collections of ballads, roughly grouped typologically: *Rosa de amores*, *Rosa española*, *Rosa gentil*, and *Rosa real* (Valencia, 1573), which have been reprinted in vol. 10 of the BAE.

He also compiled several *cancioneros*, including the *Dechado de colores* (Valencia?, 1573?), apparently surviving only in a copy lacking the title-page in the Vienna National Library; the *Villete de amor* (Valencia, 1565?); the *Enredo de amor*; the *Guisadilla de amor*; and the *Truhanesco* (all Valencia, 1573).

But today Timoneda is best remembered for his collections of stories, anecdotes, and jokes. *El sobremesa y alivio de caminantes* (Saragossa and Medina, 1563; enlarged edn., Valencia, 1569) is a collection of stories, mainly from Italian authors (Bandello, Boccaccio, Morlini, and others) and from such miscellanies as Guevara's (q.v.) *Epístolas familiares*. Another such compendium is *El buen aviso y portacuentos* (Valencia, 1564). The best-known of all is the *Primera parte de las patrañas de Joan Timoneda*, affectionately known to all subsequent generations of readers as *El patrañuelo* (Valencia, 1565), reprinted with *El sobremesa* in vol. 3 of the BAE (1846) and edited at least seven times since 1946, notably by Rafael Ferreres in Clásicos Castalia (1971). Timoneda's sources are extended to Ariosto and Masuccio Salernitano for this amusing compilation.

A three-volume edition of Timoneda's *Obras* has been prepared by E. Juliá Martínez (1947–8).

See Josef Romeu i Figueras, *Joan Timoneda i la 'Flor de Enamorados'* (Barcelona 1972), in which Timoneda is attributed with the compilation of an important *cancionero* which he probably published in 1556–7 but is now apparently lost.

Tirano Banderas (1926), a novel by Ramón María del Valle-Inclán (q.v.). The first *esperpento* (q.v.) novel, it is set in an imaginary Latin-American country, Tierra Caliente, in the second half of the 19th c. and gives an impressionistic view, in brilliant Spanish, of life under a dictator. Its immediate sources were Valle-Inclán's second visit to Mexico in 1922, and two Mexican chronicles dealing with the rebellion of one Lope de Aguirre against the Spanish king. The caricature was intended to be equally applicable to the Spanish dictator Primo de Rivera (ruled 1923–30).

The author fiercely defends the right of the Mexican Indian to his own land, echoing his defence of the Galician peasant in his earlier work. The tyrant Santos Banderas (his name symbolizing the dual tyranny of church and army) is described by the idealist Roque Cepeda as 'a serpent from Genesis'.

See V. A. Smith, *Valle-Inclán: 'Tirano Banderas'* (London, 1971) in the Critical Guides to Spanish Texts series.

Tirant lo Blanch, the finest medieval *libro de caballería* (q.v.) in Catalan. Begun *c*. 1460 by Joanot Martorell (q.v.), it was finished after his death by Martí Joan de Galba (q.v.) and first published in Valencia in 1490 (facsimile edn., New York, 1904). The first Castilian version appeared in Valladolid in 1511. Martí de Riquer (q.v.) published a critical edition (Barcelona, 1947) and *Nuevas contribuciones a las fuentes del Tirant lo Blanch* (Barcelona, 1949). According to Riquer, the first 39 chapters were based on a manual of chivalry called *Guillem de Vàroic* which may be a youthful work by Martorell himself, derived from an Anglo-Norman verse romance *Gui de Warewic* together with plagiarisms from the *Llibre de l'Orde de Cavayleria* of Ramon Llull (q.v.). Chapters 40–415 were also written by Martorell, then Galba finished the book and added chapter-headings throughout. Martorell's statement that the work was translated from English into Portuguese and then Valencian has been taken to refer to the first 39 chapters only.

Though it began as a manual of chivalry, Martorell's book was soon transformed by his sensual, ironic, temperament into an animated series of adventures, often erotic, that never stray far from the possible. Cervantes praised the book in *Don Quijote* (Pt. 1. ch. 6) for the human qualities of its protagonists: 'aquí comen los caballeros, y duermen y mueren en sus camas, y hacen testamentos'. Parody leavens the exploits of the knights-errant, as in the battle with Vilesermes (ch. 67), the scene of the Last Judgement (ch. 239), and the sermon (ch. 276).

The Breton knight Tirant travels to England for a royal tournament. From there he finds his way to France and Sicily, takes part in the defence of Rhodes against the Turks, and then in Constantinople we witness the *amorío* of the Empress and her squire Hipòlit, who eventually marry (like Tirant and his beloved Carmesina, daughter of the Emperor of Constantinople). Tirant becomes a famous general and commander of the Byzantine armies by the end of the book. When the Empress dies, Hipòlit marries the young princess of England, and inherits not only from Tirant (who has died in bed, as Don Quijote does later), but also from the Emperor of Constantinople.

The book reads oddly at times, since Martorell inserts whole passages from earlier writers, and paraphrases Dante, Petrarch, Boccaccio, the *Voiage of Sir John Maundevile*, Rodríguez de la

Cámara, Llull, Metge, Guillem de Cervera, and the true story of Roger de Flor's oriental expedition as told in the *Crónica* of Muntaner (q.v.).

TIRSO DE MOLINA, pseudonym of Fray Gabriel Téllez (q.v.).

TOB, SEM, see SHEM TOV ARDUTIEL.

Todo verdor perecerá (1941), a novel by the Argentinian Eduardo Mallea (q.v.).

Ágata Cruz, the daughter of a Protestant Swiss doctor, marries a hopelessly unsuccessful farmer who dies when she opens the doors and windows of her house to let the cold wind exacerbate his pneumonia. She planned a double death, but survives and runs away from the hated farm to Bahía Blanca (Mallea's home town), where she enjoys her first love affair with the lawyer Sotero. This affair is quickly forgotten by Sotero who returns to Buenos Aires, but his desertion strikes Ágata as an enormous loss, and she returns to the place where she was born, unbalanced and lonely beyond friendship. The title is drawn from Isaiah; it expresses the desolation of a widow without vocation or companionship, together with the desolation of the land that widows and impoverishes her. The novel is the most successful that Mallea wrote, with its memorable portrait of Ágata. There is an English translation by John B. Hughes, *All green shall perish* (London, 1967).

Tolosa, Las Navas de, see NAVAS DE TOLOSA, Las.

Tonadilla, a *tonada* was a ballad-like poem, often obscene, performed in the intervals between the acts of *autos sacramentales* (q.v.), and a *tonadilla*, or gay little *tonada*, came to signify an operetta, with two, three, or four characters, lasting about 15 minutes, which used popular airs such as the *jácara* or *seguidilla*. It was often given, like an *entremés* (q.v.), between the acts of serious plays in the first quarter of the 18th c., but it reached its height of popularity from 1770, when the *zarzuela* (q.v.) declined, until about 1790, when the *zarzuela* was revived.

The standard compilation is *La tonadilla española* (3 vols., 1928–30) by José Subirá.

TOPET, PIERRE, see ETCHAHOUNIA, Pierre Topet d'.

TORENO, *Conde de*, see QUEIPO DE LLANO, José María, *Conde de Toreno*.

Tormento (1884), one of the *Novelas españolas contemporáneas* of Benito Pérez Galdós (qq.v.).

Tormento is a sequel to *El doctor Centeno* (q.v.), and follows the fortunes of Felipe Centeno in the service of the wealthy Agustín Caballero, as kind as he is shy. In the household of Caballero's cousin, the model bureaucrat Francisco Bringas, Amparo Sánchez Emperador is working as a servant. In *El doctor Centeno*, Amparo had given herself to the schoolmaster-priest Pedro Polo (Felipe's former teacher) and now views her one lapse from chastity with revulsion, though Don Pedro is still passionately in love with the now orphaned 'Tormento', as he calls her, and continues to pester her.

Don Agustín, who has often seen her in his cousin's home, comes to love Amparo and eventually offers her his enormous wealth in marriage. Amparo, overcome with joy, cannot bring herself to tell her future husband about her past and, hearing that 'friends' are going to disclose her secret, tries to poison herself, but fails as a result of a trick played by Felipe Centeno.

When Amparo does tell Don Agustín the truth, he makes light of the matter, much to the concern of Rosalía de Bringas and Polo's sister Marcelina. Amparo and Agustín begin a liaison, though they do not marry.

The novel has been read symbolically, Amparo symbolizing Spain. She turns from the priest (clerical reaction) to happiness with the man of business (progress and enlightenment).

TORO, *Arcediano de*, see RODRÍGUEZ, Gonzalo, *Arcediano de Toro*.

Torquemada, a series of darkly satirical *cuadros de costumbres* by Benito Pérez Galdós (q.v.), comprising *Torquemada en la hoguera* (1889), *Torquemada en la cruz* (1893), *Torquemada en el purgatorio* (1894), and *Torquemada y San Pedro* (1895).

Torquemada is a miserly pawnbroker, not in the humorous tradition of Molière's Harpagon in *L'avare* or in the severely realist strain of Balzac's Père Grandet, but in the profoundly psychological mould of a Flaubertian character. He is a human being with a soul, whose redeeming characteristic (and for Galdós this is paramount) is a true love for his family, and the novelist's success lies in the extent to which he manages to claim the reader's sympathy for Torquemada, as his rise to banker, senator, and finally marquis fails to bring him happiness.

Torquemada, like Ángel Guerra in the novel of that title (q.v.), both loses a beloved child and falls under the influence of a woman, undergoing thereby a change of personality. Torquemada's evolution is outward, social, and negative, whereas Ángel's is inward, individual, and positive.

TORQUEMADA, ANTONIO DE (1530–90), b. León? Humanist. During his lifetime he was well-known for the *Iardín de flores curiosas, en que se tratan algunas materias de humanidad, Philosophía, Theología y Geographía, con otras cosas curiosas y apazibles* (Salamanca, 1570), a miscellany of facts, fiction, myths, and superstition drawn from dozens of authors as various as Aristotle and Albertus Magnus, the Spanish chronicles, and books of chivalry. Cervantes derided the book, but he used Torquemada's plagiarized tales of Iceland and Friesland for his own *Persiles y Sigismunda* (q.v.).

The *Jardín* was widely read in Castilian, was translated into French in 1582, into Italian in 1596, and Lewes Lewkenor translated it into English as *The Spanish Mandeuile of miracles, or the garden of curious flowers* (1600). It has been edited by A. G. de Amezúa for the Sociedad de Bibliófilos Españoles (1943).

As in the *Jardín*, the curate in *Don Quijote* also consigned to the flames Torquemada's absurd *libro de caballería* (q.v.) called *Historia del invencible caballero don Olivante de Laura* (Barcelona, 1564), but his seven Lucianesque dialogues can be read with some pleasure in the NBAE, vols. 7 (1907) and 21 (1915). These are *Los colloquios satíricos, con un colloquio pastoril, y gracioso al cabo dellos* (Mondoñedo, 1553), dedicated to Antonio Alfonso de Pimentel, Count of Benavente, for whom Torquemada worked as secretary. These dialogues against gluttony, excessive interest in clothes and personal adornment, gambling, quack doctors, and ignorant apothecaries, are interspersed with fiction, as in the *Patrañuelo* of Joan Timoneda (q.v.) and the *Coloquio de los perros* of Cervantes himself (qq.v.).

See J. H. Elsdon, *On the life and work of the Spanish Humanist Antonio de Torquemada* (Berkeley, California, 1937).

TORQUEMADA, *Fray* JUAN DE (1563–1624), b. Spain. Arriving in Mexico as a boy, he became an Augustinian priest in 1583 and rose to become Provincial of the Order. His *Monarquía indiana* was finished in 1612, published in Seville in 1615, and was reissued in Madrid (3 vols.) in 1723. A facsimile of the 1615 edition with an introduction by Miguel León-Portilla (q.v.) appeared in Mexico City in 1969.

Torquemada's book is a compilation of earlier and better authorities, such as Sahagún, Motilinía, Andrés de Olmos (qq.v.), and above all Mendieta from whose hitherto unpublished *Historia eclesiástica indiana* he plagiarized whole chapters, altering Mendieta's words only where the *conquistadores* were criticized in an attempt to justify their actions. Yet Torquemada's book assumed great significance at the time, in that it was one of the few early accounts (with those of José Acosta and Juan de Cárdenas) accessible to his contemporaries. Torquemada also wrote a number of religious plays.

TORQUEMADA, Tomás de (1420–98), Dominican Inquisitor-General appointed by Ferdinand and Isabel in 1483. Though Torquemada did not institute the Inquisition, it was during his eighteen-year control that the Inquisition became a byword for barbarous torture and unexplained deaths. In Torquemada's time, 2,000 heretics were burnt alive and a further 17,000 mutilated in some way. He drew up the *Copilación de las Instrucciones del Officio de la Sancta Inquisición hechas por el muy Reverendo Señor Fray Thomas de Torquemada* first published in Latin in 1592. The term 'Torquemada' has since been synonymous with heartless cruelty.

TORRE, Alfonso de la (1410?–1460?), b. Burgos? Graduated in Arts and Theology at Salamanca. As a political opponent of Don Álvaro de Luna, Torre fled to the Kingdom of Aragón on the success of his enemy. He was well received there, and composed love-poems (*coplas, canciones, decires,* and *esparzas*) which were published in the *Cancioneros* of Valencia (1511), Seville (1540), and Antwerp (1573). He was author of the *Visión delectable de la filosofía y artes liberales* (there are numerous variants of the title) written *c.* 1440, and published in Burgos about 1485. The *Visión* is an encyclopaedia using as source-material the *Guide to the perplexed* of Maimonides (q.v.), a logical treatise by al-Ghazali, Isidore of Seville's *Etymologiae*, and the works of Avempace (q.v.), Alain de Lille (12th c.), and Martianus Capella (4th c.). The first part deals with the liberal arts, metaphysics, and natural science, while the second covers moral philosophy. By one of those ironic coincidences that bedevil medieval bibliography, Torre's *Visión* was translated into Italian in 1556 by Domenico Delfini, and in 1663 rendered back into Spanish, as Delfini's own work, by Francisco de Cáceres, who thought that he was introducing a novelty into Spain.

TORRE, Claudio de la (1898–), b. Las Palmas, Canary Islands. Playwright, novelist, and film director. Educated in England, he was the first Reader in Spanish at Cambridge University (1920–1). He directed films 1931–4, and in 1932 married the writer Mercedes Ballesteros Gaibrois, with whom he wrote the play *Quiero ver al doctor* (1941). He directed radio drama on Radio Nacional 1941–4, and from 1954 to 1960 directed the Teatro Nacional María Guerrero. His best-known plays are *Un héroe contemporáneo* (1926), *Tic-tac* (1930), *Hotel Terminus* (1944),

El río que nace en junio (1950), and *La caña de pescar* (1959).

He wrote a tragicomic novel *En la vida del señor Alegre* (1924) about an Englishman hopelessly entangled in Spanish society in Seville in 1915, and a more pretentious but less successful novel of pre-war life in the Canaries, *Alicia, al pie de los laureles* (1940).

TORRE, Francisco de la (1534?), a Petrarchan poet of whom nothing certain is known, and in the view of Alonso Zamora Vicente who has edited la Torre's *Poesías* (1944) for the Clásicos Castellanos, it is not even certain that such a poet existed. The *Obras* of a certain 'bachiller Francisco de la Torre' were published by Quevedo in 1631, shortly after he had published the poems of Fray Luis de León (q.v.), leader of the Salamancan school to which de la Torre can be said to belong. But Quevedo erred in assuming this writer to be the 'bachiller la Torre' praised by Boscá, and the matter was confused even further by Luis José Velázquez, whose essay in another edition of la Torre's *Poesías* (1753) suggested that Quevedo himself was the author and denied independent existence to la Torre. Fernández-Guerra y Orbe in a *Discurso en la Academia de la Lengua* (1857) claimed that la Torre was a real person, adducing from internal evidence that he was born in Torrelaguna, studied in Alcalá, spent some time in Italy, possibly as a soldier, and that when he died he was a priest. J. P. Wickersham Crawford (in vol. 2 of the *Homenaje a Menéndez Pidal*, 1935) also attempted to reconstruct la Torre's life from his work.

Certainly the volume of work that goes by the authorship of 'Francisco de la Torre' is Salamancan in inspiration, and differs substantially from the known poetry of Quevedo. One long poem and nearly a hundred short poems (two-thirds being sonnets) are characterized by lyrical melancholy, absorption in nature, and a pagan approach to love in allegorical *canciones* such as 'La cierva herida' and 'La tórtola', somewhat marred by an abundance of adjectives, which slow down the movement and seem inserted for their sonority. While the influence of Virgil, Horace, Petrarch, and Garcilaso is clear, some of the sonnets are direct translations: ten from Benedetto Varchi (1502–65) and two from Giambattista Amalteo (1505–73). 'Claras lumbres del cielo' is a well-constructed ode, but perhaps his most successful poetry is to be found in the eight eclogues collectively called *La bucólica del Tajo*.

TORRE, Guillermo de (1900–), b. Madrid. Critic, poet, and translator, who invented the term *ultraísmo* and then led the Grupo Ultra (q.v.), writing *Manifiesto vertical ultraísta* (1920). His early poetry was collected in *Hélices* (1923), but his reputation was established by defending *avant-garde* movements in *Literaturas europeas de vanguardia* (1925), *Itinerario de la nueva pintura española* (1931), and *La aventura estética de nuestro tiempo* (1961). Torre has translated Max Jacob and Verlaine, and edited the *Obras completas* of Federico García Lorca.

TORRELLAS, PEDRO, see TORROELLA, Pere.

TORRENTE BALLESTER, GONZALO (1910–), b. El Ferrol, Corunna. Novelist, playwright, and critic. After studying and teaching at Santiago de Compostela University, he became drama critic on the Madrid daily *Arriba*, and is currently teaching at the University of Albany, New York.

Torrente Ballester's important *Panorama de la literatura española contemporánea* (1956) and *Teatro español contemporáneo* (1957; 2nd edn., 1968) have obscured his power as an original novelist. *Javier Mariño* (1943) is a serious yet ironic quest for self-knowledge set in Paris during World War II. *El golpe de estado de Guadalupe Limón* (1946) is a remarkable novel set in a Latin-American republic, its Creole heroine being one of the most original creations in Spanish literature. The author's intention is partly satirical, but he raises the problems of the relation of reality to fantasy, myth to history, and the ethics of power. *Ifigenia* (1950) was a short novel on the sacrifice of the innocent in politics in the series *Historias de humor para eruditos*. A subsequent series, *Los gozos y las sombras*, consists of *El señor llega* (awarded the Premio, March 1957), *Donde da la vuelta el aire* (1960), and *La Pascua triste* (1962). Later novels are *Offside* (1969) and *Fragmentos de apocalipsis* (1977).

As a playwright, Torrente Ballester has used insights derived from psychoanalytic theory in a poetic drama, *El viaje del joven Tobías* (Bilbao, 1938); the cinema influenced the conquest-play *Lope de Aguirre*; and Greek mythology influenced *El retorno de Ulises* (1945).

TORREPALMA, *Conde de*, see VERDUGO CASTILLA, Alfonso, *Conde de Torrepalma*.

TORRES, CAMILO (1766–1815), b. Popayán. Colombian federalist politician who openly sought legal redress for inequalities in Colombia. Torres was shot for insurgency, and his head was displayed to the crowds as a grim warning. Diego Fallón has said, 'La independencia de Colombia no la hizo la espada de Bolívar sino la lengua de Torres'.

His work has been lost except for two memoranda. The first is to Antonio de Narváez, who represented Colombia in the Spanish Parliament when the Viceroy forbade Torres to attend, and is entitled *Instrucción para el diputado del Reino*. The second is the *Representación del Cabildo de Bogotá a la Suprema Junta Central de España* (1809), better known as the *Memorial de agravios*, in which Torres cogently argued the case for Creole rights.

TORRES, CAMILO (1929–66), the pseudonym used by a Colombian revolutionary Roman Catholic priest killed by government troops in a guerrilla skirmish on 15 February 1966. He chose to use the name of the Creole freedom-fighter Camilo Torres (see above) and not unexpectedly suffered the same fate. *Revolutionary priest: the complete writings and messages of Camilo Torres* has been edited by John Gerassi (London, 1971).

TORRES BODET, JAIME (1902–74), b. Mexico City. Poet and novelist. He lived abroad as a diplomat 1929–40, 1943–6, and 1952–8. He was a very active Minister of Education and was Director-General of Unesco 1948–52, years documented in his autobiographical *Memorias* (in progress, vols. 1–5, 1970–74).

He participated with Bernardo Ortiz de Montellano (q.v.) in the reviews *La Falange* (1922–3) and *Contemporáneos* (1928–31). His early book *Fervor* (1918) was influenced by French symbolism, but the years of self-discovery 1922–5 saw the publication of six books of poetry, followed by the collection *Poesías* (1926). He continued to write and publish prolifically, concluding his surrealist phase with *Destierro* (1930); his best book being *Cripta* (1937). *Selected poems* appeared in a bilingual edition (Indianapolis, 1964), then a collection *Poesía* (1965) showed his progress to a hermetic stance, his subtle and mysterious works often owing something to surrealism.

A critical anthology called *Contemporáneos* (1928) was followed by the essays *La escuela mexicana* (1944). His *Obras escogidas* (1961) reprinted the autobiographical *Tiempo de arena* (1955) and two further volumes of his *Memorias* have been published.

He has also written fiction of minority appeal: his experimental novel *Margarita de niebla* (1927) was followed by *La educación sentimental* (1929), *Proserpina rescatada* (1931), *Primero de enero* (1934), *Sombras* (1937), and *Nacimiento de Venus y otros relatos* (1941), all works of extreme sensibility and delicacy of style, in some ways presaging the *nouveau roman* of Sarraute and Duras.

See B. K. Miller, *La poesía constructiva de Jaime Torres Bodet* (1974).

TORRES NAHARRO, BARTOLOMÉ DE (1485?–1524?), b. La Torre de Miguel Sesmero, Badajoz. Playwright and poet. He was possibly educated at Salamanca, ordained as a priest, then became a soldier, and was captured by Barbary pirates and sold into slavery in Algiers. After being ransomed, he travelled to Rome, where he found a protector in Cardinal Bernardino de Carvajal, also from Extremadura, who suffered excommunication by Pope Julius II in 1510. Torres's first play was the *Comedia Seraphina* (1508?, later known as *Serafina*) and his second, *Trofea*, was performed in front of Pope Leo X in 1512, and the *Tinellaria* in 1516.

Seven of his plays and a number of his poems were collected in a volume entitled *Propalladia* (Naples, 1517), 'the first things of Pallas', as opposed to the maturer work that he hoped to publish later. There is a copy of this edition in the Royal Library in Copenhagen, that in the Biblioteca Nacional in Madrid being incomplete. *Propalladia* was reissued in Seville (1520) with another *comedia, Calamita*, and again in Naples (1524) with the romantic *Aquilina* added. The edition by M. Cañete in 2 vols. (1880–1900) has an important prologue by M. Menéndez y Pelayo in vol. 2. The best edition is that of J. E. Gillet (Bryn Mawr, 1943–61) in 4 vols.

Naharro's *Prohemio* to the *Propalladia* is the first extant theoretical essay on the Spanish drama. He begins by defining as a *comedia* a play that ends happily; others are *tragedias*. He defends the Horatian five-act model, calling the acts *jornadas*, a term revived at the end of the 16th c. by Virués and Cueva (qq.v.). He divides the *comedia* thematically into *comedias a noticia* (realistic) and a *fantasía* (purely imaginative), categorizing his own *Soldadesca* and *Tinellaria* in the first group, and *Serafina* and *Himenea* in the second.

He was the first Spanish dramatist to attempt realistic character-drawing on the stage, and to introduce foreign languages or dialects. Three of his plays have foreigners as characters, and there are as many as five dialects in the *Tinellaria*.

Of the seven *comedias* in the first known edition of the *Propalladia*, a *Diálogo del Nascimiento* and the *comedia Trofea* are merely eclogues in the manner of Juan del Encina (q.v.).

By contrast, the two *comedias a noticia* are first-rate realistic *cuadros de costumbres*. In *Soldadesca*, a Spanish captain is recruiting soldiers for the Pope's army. Some are veterans of the war with Tripoli (1510) and long for war and a change in their fortunes. Girls of easy virtue, an Italian innkeeper, and a poor friar come to life in gay, often crude dialogue. *Tinellaria* shows the pressures under which cooks have to work. Naharro's scene is set in a cardinal's *tinello* or kitchen, where the servants are dominated by Barrabás, the chief steward, a corrupt, thieving rascal who has risen from scullion by devious paths.

The *comedia Jacinta* is an elegant entertainment written for Isabella d'Este (called here 'Divina'), who visited Rome in the winter of 1514–15.

Naharro's four *comedias a fantasía* are *Seraphina* and *Himenea* (in the 1517 edn.), *Calamita* (in the 1520 edn.), and *Aquilina* (in the 1524 edn.).

Seraphina is an extravaganza set in Rome, where Floristán has just married the Italian Orfea. In Valencia he had promised to marry Seraphina, who comes to Rome and challenges Floristán to make good his vow. The deceitful friar Teodoro agrees to try to annul his marriage, but Policiano, Floristán's brother, suddenly arrives in the hope of marrying his former fiancée Orfea, and the problem is resolved artificially. The main interest of the play is the anti-hero Lenicio, a sketch of the coward and wit who will recur in Lope de Vega (q.v.) and in *El desdén con el desdén* by Moreto (q.v.).

Himenea's success is due partly to that of the 12th, 14th, and 15th acts of *La Celestina* (q.v.), from which it is drawn. Himeneo is the rather colourless Calisto type, consumed with romantic passion for Febea, while his cynical servants Eliso and Boreás exploit his weakness for their own ends. Naharro's innovation is a brother for Febea, and this *honor* element makes *Himenea* the first of the countless *comedias de capa y espada* that were to fill the theatres a hundred years later. Nicolás Fernández de Moratín (q.v.) praised its observance of the three unities, and the verse form used (twelve-line stanzas, the eleventh in *pie quebrado*) is equally successful.

The plays were considered too Erasmian for circulation, and so were put on the index of Valdés (1559), but after slight changes they were resissued in 1573.

Naharro's poetry is traditional, and it has surprised many commentators that this innovator in drama did not introduce the Italian hendecasyllable into Spanish long before Boscà (q.v.). Naharro's poetry, published in the *Propalladia*, consists of four ballads, three 'Lamentaciones de amor', and 'Psalmo en la gloriosa victoria que los españoles ovieron contra los venecianos'.

TORRES RÁMILA, PEDRO DE (1583–1658), b. Villarcayo, Burgos. Professor of Latin at Alcalá who was taken as the model for the 'scholar' in Cristóbal Suárez de Figueroa's dialogue *El passagero* (q.v.) and—possibly at Suárez's instigation—waged a literary war against Lope de Vega (q.v.) in his virulent satire *Spongia* (1617). Lope's friend Francisco López de

Aguilar Coutiño replied as 'Franciscus Antididascalus' in *Petro de Torres Ramilae* (1617) and again, with Alfonso Sánchez de la Ballesta (Professor of Hebrew at Alcalá), and possibly with Lope himself, in *Expostulatio Spongiae a Petro Turriano Ramila nuper evulgatae* (1618), written under the collective pseudonym 'Julio Columbario'. The attack on Lope was so scurrilous that all the copies (some printed as by 'Juan Pablo Martín Rizo' and others as by 'Petrus Ruitanus Lamira', his Latin anagram) were sought out and destroyed by Lope's allies. The episode has been documented by Joaquín de Entrambasaguas in 'Una guerra literaria del Siglo de Oro' in *Estudios sobre Lope de Vega*, vol. 1 (1946).

Sánchez's view is that the arts are based on the observation and delineation of nature, that the rules of art are susceptible to change, that Lope has changed them and in so doing has not only created a new art-form (see ARTE NUEVO DE HACER COMEDIAS) but has also excelled every other poet past or present.

There is an allegorical treatment of this battle in Lope's *La Filomena* (1621), in which the nightingale represents Lope and the thrush Torres Rámila: 'Pero los dioses luego decretaron / la sentencia en favor de Filomena, / y a su eterno silencio condenaron / el tordo, que hoy con tal vergüenza suena; / y que si hablare, por piedad mandaron / que sólo sea, del delito en pena, / lo que aprendiere con mortal fatiga, / sin saber lo que dice, aunque lo diga'.

TORRES VILLARROEL, DIEGO DE (1693–1770), b. Salamanca. Autobiographer, satirist, and poet. One of eighteen children, he studied little but took to the road, becoming in turn apprentice hermit in Tras os Montes, dancer in Coimbra, bullfighter in Lisbon, musician, and failed smuggler. He took minor orders in 1714, but abandoned his clerical career (though he was to be ordained later, in 1745). In 1721 he began to print a series of *Almanaques* under the name 'el Gran Piscator Salmantino', and though in later life he ridiculed these *pronósticos* and those who consulted them, he made a great deal of money from their sale, especially after he predicted the death of Luis I in the almanac of 1724, and the French Revolution in a *décima* in the almanac of 1756. He wrote extensively on witchcraft and was employed by the Condesa de Arcos in exorcizing her house in 1723, after which he was invited to remain there as her guest for two years.

In 1726 Torres won the open competition for the vacant chair of Mathematics at Salamanca University, and though he was deprived of the chair for several years pending investigation into allegations of dishonesty, he regained it in 1734.

His first collection of poetry, *Ocios políticos, en poesías de varios metros* (1726), includes some of the best burlesque poetry since his acknowledged master Quevedo (q.v.), together with religious *villancicos* (such as *Al nacimiento de Jesús*, at odds with the tradition of simplicity connected with this theme), and many sonnets of varying quality. L. A. de Cueto collected these poems in vol. 61 of the BAE (1869). Quevedo's influence was even more marked in the *Sueños morales* (1727 and 1728), which he subtitled *visiones y visitas de Torres con Francisco de Quevedo*. These are based almost entirely on the style and attitudes of the *Sueños* (q.v.) of Quevedo, denouncing doctors, lawyers, and the moral iniquities of the period. The first is *La barca de Aqueronte*, recently published by Guy Mercadier (Paris, 1969), from an autograph MS. dated 1731 in which the devil interrupts the narrative to describe Torres in scathing terms. The remaining *Sueños* are *Residencia infernal de Plutón, Correo del otro mundo, Sacudimiento de mentecatos, Historia de historias*, and *El soplo de la justicia*. Torres's severity is the more cynical for his own avowal of thieving and chicanery, and whereas Quevedo's denunciations are bitterly righteous, Torres adds caricature to caricature as though his motive were pure mockery. As the *Diario de los Literatos de España* (q.v.) wrote of his prose, 'también se desazonan los manjares por abundancia de sal, que, en siendo mucha, muerde y no sazona'. Among his many other works in prose collected in the 14-volume edition of Torres's *Obras* published by subscription (Salamanca, 1752), were the life *Sor Gregoria de Santa Teresa* (1738) and a dialogue *El ermitaño y Torres*, in which the protagonists discuss alchemy, chemistry, and medicine, and Torres offers a favourable opinion of the *Quijote* of Avellaneda (q.v.).

Several short plays collected as *Juguetes de Talía* (1738) fail through a lack of action or plot and an excess of long-winded dialogue.

His main claim to fame is an autobiography considered among the most important in the Spanish language. This is the *Vida, ascendencia, nacimiento, crianza y aventuras del doctor don Diego de Torres y Villarroel*, divided into six *trozos*, of which the first four (each describing a decade in his life) appeared in 1743, the fifth in 1751 or 1752, and the sixth in 1758. Torres's *Vida* has to be read in the context of the picaresque novels so popular in the preceding century; of the reforming literature of Isla and Feijóo (qq.v.) contemporary with Torres; and of the *Confessions* of Rousseau which were to dignify the genre some years later. Again, the model is the 'disillusion' of Quevedo, and nobody is given any significance apart from the author, who shows scant respect even for himself. He bewails the ignorance, corruption, and superstition of the age, offering his own devotion to mathematics as one solution to the general malaise. There is a useful edition of the *Vida* (1912) by Federico de Onís in the Clásicos Castellanos, which should be checked by reference to the edition of Guy Mercadier in Clásicos Castalia (1972), and an excellent translation, *The remarkable life of Don Diego* (London, 1958) by W. C. Atkinson.

See A. García Boiza, *Don Diego de Torres Villarroel: ensayo biográfico* (1949); Joaquín de Entrambasaguas, 'Puntualizando un dato en la biografía de Torres Villarroel' in *Miscelánea Erudita* (1957), pp. 35–7; M. C. Peñuelas, 'La vida de Torres Villarroel: acotaciones al margen' in *Cuadernos Americanos*, vol. 20 (1961), pp. 165–76; S. Kleinhaus, *Von der 'novela picaresca' zur bürgerlichen Autobiographie* (1975); I. L. McClelland, *Diego de Torres Villarroel* (New York, 1976) in Twayne's World Authors series; and G. Mercadier, *Diego de Torres Villarroel: masque et miroirs* (3 vols., 1976).

TORROELLA or TORRELLA(S), PERE (1416?–1453?), b. Saragossa. A poet at the court of Alfonso V in Naples. His work was published in the *Cancionero de Stúñiga* (see STÚÑIGA). In addition to *esparças*, *lahors*, and *complantes*, he wrote the attack on women *Coplas de las calidades de las donas*, which is often reprinted with the replies of his adversaries (such as Juan del Encina or Suero de Rivera) at the end. According to a legend told in the *Tractado de Grisel y Miravella* of Juan de Flores, resentful women tore him limb from limb.

Torroella's uninspired *Coplas* were the model for Hernán Mexía's (q.v.) far superior *Coplas en que descubre los defectos de las condiciones de las damas.*

See P. Bach y Rita, *The works of Pere Torroella* (New York, 1930).

TORUÑO, JUAN FELIPE (1898–), b. León, Nicaragua. Critic, poet, and novelist. He founded and edited the magazine *Darío* 1919–23, in which latter year he went to El Salvador. His criticism includes *Orientaciones de la poesía y literatura hispanoamericana* (1925), *Poesía aborigen* (1945), *Poesía negra* (1953), *Desarrollo literario de El Salvador* (1957), and a literary survey of Nicaragua from 1900 to 1950 in Montezuma de Carvalho's *Panorama das literaturas das Américas* (vol. 3, pp. 1093–1202).

Toruño's poetry includes *Senderos espirituales* (1922), *Ritmos de vida* (1924), *Hacia el sol* (1940), and *Arcilla mística* (1946). He has published two novels: *La mariposa negra* (1928) and *El silencio* (1938), and a collection of short stories: *De dos tierras* (1947).

TOSTADO, EL, see MADRIGAL, Alfonso de.

Trabajos de Persiles y Sigismunda, Los, see PERSILES Y SIGISMUNDA, Los trabajos de.

Tradiciones peruanas, sketches by Ricardo Palma (q.v.).

Originally published in magazines, from *El Diablo* (1848) to *El Constitucional* (1867), the first series of *Tradiciones peruanas* appeared in book form in 1872, when they had already become popular. The *tradición* is a genre new to Spanish with Palma. A kernel of fact or legend is taken as the basis for a story of 3 to 5 pages, on average, varying in historical foundation and accuracy from the documented fact with merely literary perfection added to the totally new invention, narrated with such tongue-in-cheek verisimilitude that it rivals the much later Borges *ficción*.

Further series of *Tradiciones peruanas* appeared in 1872, 1874, 1875, 1883, 1885, 1906, and 1910, and *Tradiciones en salsa verde* were left incomplete at his death. The period covered by these sketches runs from pre-Conquest times to his own, with a great preference for the viceregal period, which he clearly loved and imaginatively recreated with the least effort.

Palma's prose style is exquisite, his manner satirical, mocking superstition and taking nothing very seriously, least of all convents, social climbers, and hypocrisy. Often anticlerical and picaresque, he uses anecdote and ballad fragments to good effect, varying pace as well as tone.

The *Tradiciones peruanas completas* (1957) have been neatly abridged, with a study, by Raimundo Lazo, in *Tradiciones peruanas* (Mexico City, 1969) for the Sepan Cuantos . . . series.

Trafalgar, the naval battle fought on 21 October 1805 between the British fleet of 27 ships of the line and four frigates under Nelson, and the Spanish and French fleet under Villeneuve consisting of 33 ships of the line and five frigates. The result was an overwhelming victory for the British, during which Nelson was killed.

Trafalgar (1873) is the first novel in the first series of Benito Pérez Galdós's cycle *Episodios nacionales* (qq.v.). The fourteen-year-old hero Gabriel Araceli is present at the Battle of Trafalgar on board the Spanish flagship *Santísima Trinidad.* Pérez Galdós's evocation of the battle is the finest account of Trafalgar in Spanish literature (which does not normally dwell on military defeats) and has been studied by C. Vázquez Arjona in his 'Cotejo histórico de cinco Episodios nacionales de Benito Pérez Galdós' in *Revue Hispanique*, vol. 68 (1926), pp. 321–551.

Tremendismo, a trend in post-World War II Spanish novel writing of which the outstanding exponent is Camilo José Cela (q.v.). The authors achieve their effects by a technique culminating in violence and terror, which parallels the rise of violence in contemporary film-making. They show the impact of unfavourable social and religious environment on moral behaviour, deriving in one line of descent from Zola, and in another from Baroja and Unamuno (qq.v.). The masterpiece of *tremendista* fiction is considered to be Cela's *La familia de Pascual Duarte*; another example is *Nada* by Carmen Laforet (q.v.). *Tremendismo* is intimately connected with *existencialismo*.

Guillermo Díaz-Plaja's *El reverso de la belleza* (Barcelona, 1956) deals with the origins of *tremendismo*.

TREND, JOHN BRANDE (1887–1958), the first Professor of Spanish at Cambridge University (1933–52) and a music critic. He excelled in popularizing and, though he contributed numerous articles to critical journals, he will be best remembered for *The origins of modern Spain* (Cambridge, 1934) on the liberal educators of the post-1869 period; *The civilization of Spain* (London, 1944), *Bolívar and the independence of Spanish America* (London, 1945), *The language and history of Spain* (London, 1953), *Lorca and the Spanish poetic tradition* (Oxford, 1956), and *Portugal* (London, 1957). His contributions to musicology included articles in Grove (3rd edn., 1927), 'Catalogue of the Music in the Biblioteca Medinaceli, Madrid' in *Revue Hispanique*, vol. 71 (1927), pp. 485–554, *A picture of modern Spain : men and music* (London, 1921), *Luis Milán and the vihuelistas* (Oxford, 1925), *The music of Spanish history to 1600* (Oxford, 1926), and *Manuel de Falla and Spanish music* (New York, 1929).

Trend was responsible for the 2nd edition of *The Oxford book of Spanish verse* (Oxford, 1940) and the translation *Fifty Spanish poems* by Juan Ramón Jiménez (Oxford, 1950). Eight of the pamphlets printed privately for him by Severs of Cambridge were reissued more or less revised in *Lorca and the Spanish poetic tradition*.

Treno ('threnody'), in Spanish poetry, a dirge, or elegiac song on a personal or public catastrophe, generally in the form of an *oda* or *silva* (qq.v.).

Quevedo translated the Lamentations of Jeremiah as *Trenos*. In the Visigóthic-Mozarabic liturgy, the *treno* is a prayer sung in the Lenten Mass after the first lesson but before the sermon.

Trent, The Council of, sat intermittently (at Trento in the Tyrol) from 1545 to 1563, when its decrees were finally published. Its purpose, which was achieved, was to establish the lines of

development within the Roman Catholic Church aimed at countering the effects of the Reformation, and the deliberations of the Council were confirmed by Pope Pius IV in 1564. The Spanish delegation were vocal and active throughout, and greeted the final results with satisfaction; their role has been studied by C. Gutiérrez in *Españoles en Trento* (Valladolid, 1951).

Under Philip II (1556–98), Spain became closed to new currents of ideas arising beyond her frontiers and any form of intellectual novelty was suspect. A law of censorship (in existence since 1502) was strengthened in 1558 and a book needed the *aprobación* (approval) of the censors before publication. The importation of foreign books without a royal licence was even made a capital offence. The Inquisition published its first index of banned books in 1551, and in 1584 its first expurgatory index of books which were permitted to circulate after their offending passages had been deleted.

The volume of 16th-c. fiction did not immediately decline after Trent; though it was not expected that didactic or exemplary fiction would suffer, it was widely felt that literature of entertainment value would diminish sharply, if not die out altogether. This did not occur, though it is highly probable that potentially offensive subjects were treated in a more oblique manner and that such novels gained in subtlety what they lost in liberty of expression. Religious books did not gain in strength relative to book production in other fields, as J. M. Sánchez has shown in his *Bibliografía aragonesa del siglo XVI* (2 vols., 1914) for Aragón, where religious books accounted for 63% of all books produced 1501–50, but only 50% in the period 1551–1600.

The demand for edification, while not discouraging fiction, did encourage literary realism, though this tendency was already in evidence before the Council of Trent in such works as *La lozana andaluza* by Francisco Delicado (q.v.).

As regards theological publications, the effect of the Council's decrees was felt immediately, as can be seen for instance in the 1567 edition of Martín de Azpilcueta's *Manual de confesores y penitentes*, which maintains that the Will must not remain passive, but must actively seek to receive the Grace of God through good works.

The Trentine decisions on faith and discipline have been largely undisputed in the Roman Catholic Church up to the present time.

See Charles Dejob, *De l'influence du Concile de Trente sur la littérature et les beaux-arts chez les peuples catholiques* (Paris, 1884).

Trescientas, Las, a title commonly given to Juan de Mena's *Laberinto de Fortuna* (qq.v.), deriving from the approximate number of its stanzas.

TREVIJANO, a pseudonym used by José de Sarabia (q.v.).

TRIANA, José (1933–), Cuban playwright, whose rapid evolution has brought him international recognition. *Medea en el espejo* (1960) was followed by *El parque de la fraternidad* (1962); *La muerte del ñeque* (1963), interesting for its use of Cuban folklore; and *La noche de los asesinos* (1965), a sombre allegory in which three children play at murder. This last play won the Casa de las Américas prize and was produced in London in 1967.

TRIGO, Felipe (1865–1916), b. Villanueva de la Serena, Badajoz. Popular novelist, who is classed with Zamacois (q.v.) as an erotic novelist. Though his professed intentions were high and moral, Trigo was read for his love-stories and earned a great deal of money from them: 100,000 pesetas for *Las ingenuas* (1901). Trigo committed suicide at the height of his popularity in 1916. The success of his sub-Kiplingesque début, set in India, was the first of many: *La sed de amar* (1901), *Alma en los labios* (1902), *Del frío al fuego* (1903), *La altísima* (1903), *La bruta* (1904), the novel of hypocrisy and honour, *Sor Demonio* (1905), the autobiographical account of a medical student *En la carrera* (1906) completed by *El médico rural* (1912) set in Andalusia, where Trigo had worked as an army doctor; and many others.

See Manuel Abril, *Felipe Trigo* (1917), on his life and work; J. P. Ton, *Felipe Trigo* (Amsterdam, 1952), a critical study; and A. T. Watkins, *Eroticism in the novels of Felipe Trigo* (New York, 1954).

TRIGUEROS, Cándido María (1736–c. 1801), b. Orgaz, Toledo. Playwright, poet, and priest, who lived for long periods in Seville, where he was a prominent member of the Academia de Buenas Letras. He used pseudonyms for most of his works, such as the *Teatro español burlesco o Quixote de los por el M. o Crispín Caramillo* (1802) or the *Poesías de Melchor Díaz de Toledo* (1776), a fictitious 16th-c. author whose diction was, however, too archaic for the period, so that the hoax was soon discovered.

Trigueros followed the moribund fashion of the philosophic poem and the epic in *El poeta filósofo, o poesías filosóficas en verso pentámetro* (7 pts., Seville, 1774–8), and *La Ríada* (Seville, 1784), the latter an epic in four cantos, on a calamitous flood that had recently hit Seville, which Vargas ridiculed in a letter and Forner mocked in a pamphlet written under the

pseudonym 'Antonio Varas'. The failure of *Los menestrales* (1784), a social drama, led Trigueros to adapt Golden Age dramatists for the taste of the time, and it was this that brought him his most lasting renown. While reworking *La estrella de Sevilla* by Lope de Vega (?) as *Sancho Ortiz de las Roelas* (1800) and Lope's *Los melindres de Belisa*, Trigueros tightened the construction of his models and became inspired in his lyrical composition. Menéndez y Pelayo stated that in his adaptations Trigueros 'dió y ganó la primera batalla romántica treinta años antes del Romanticismo', in common with his contemporary Dionisio Solís (q.v.). His tragedy *El Viting* (or *El Witingo*) was produced in Madrid in 1770.

The other work by Trigueros that deserves mention is *Los Enamorados o Galatea y sus bodas. Historia pastoral comenzada por Miguel de Cervantes Saavedra, abreviada después y continuada, y últimamente concluída* (4 vols., 1798), for which he used the abridgment already made by Jean-Pierre Claris de Florian.

TRIGUEROS DE LEÓN, Ricardo (1917–), b. Ahuachapan, El Salvador. Poet, critic, and impressionistic prose-writer, esteemed above all for the sonnets in *Presencia de la rosa* (1945). For many years editor of the literary supplement to *El Diario de Hoy*, he was subsequently appointed director of the publications department of the Salvadorian Ministry of Education. His first books of verse were *Campanario* (1941) and *Nardo y estrella* (1943); his critical essays were collected in *Labrando en madera* (1947) and *Perfil en el aire* (1955). His *Pueblo* (1960) is a volume of impressions of provincial life.

TRILLO Y FIGUEROA, Francisco de (1620?–1675), b. Corunna. Poet and historian. He left Galicia at the age of 11, and thenceforth spent most of his life in Granada, except for 1640–3, when he was fighting in Italy and Flanders. He wrote a feeble epic in the *culterano* style called *Neapolisea: poema heroyco, y panegírico al Gran Capitán, Gonzalo Fernández de Córdoba* (Granada, 1651), but he is at his best in the light, humorous, and occasionally obscene verses, including many *letrillas* and *romances*, collected as *Poesías varias, heroycas, satíricas y amorosas* (Granada, 1652) deriving most frequently from Góngora (q.v.), but also employing deftly and ironically the thieves' cant of the time, known as *germanía* (from *hermano, hermandad*, 'brother', 'brotherhood'). This collection includes fine translations from Anacreon. Trillo's poems were edited by A. de Castro in vol. 42 (1857) of the BAE and by A. Gallego Morell in the Biblioteca de Antiguos Libros Hispánicos (1951). As an historian, Trillo published nothing in his lifetime but left a number of MSS., one of which, a history of Corunna, is kept in the British Library. The rest include *Historia y antigüedades del reino de Galicia, Blasones y cruces de la nobleza de España, Historia política del Rey Católico,* and *Epítome de la historia del rey Enrique IV de Francia.*

See Antonio Gallego Morell, *Francisco de Trillo y Figueroa,* a supplement to the *Boletín de la Universidad de Granada* (1950).

Trinada, the monorhymed *terceto* of Pérez de Guzmán (qq.v.).

Trobes en lahors de la Verge Marie, Les, a collection of hymns to the Virgin Mary, 41 in Valencian dialect, 3 in Castilian, and 1 in Italian compiled by Bernardo Fenollar and including work by Jaume Roig and Joan Roís de Corella (qq.v.).

The importance of this book is that it was probably the first book printed in Spain, appearing from the press of Alfonso Fernández de Córdoba in Valencia (1474).

Trotaconventos ('convent-trotter'), the unsavoury epithet given to the *alcahueta* or go-between Urraca in the *Libro de buen amor* of Juan Ruiz (qq.v.) the Archpriest of Hita. After the hero (sometimes referred to as Fita (i.e. Hita) or el Arcipreste, sometimes as Don Melón de la Huerta) has failed to win the attention of the pretty widow Doña Endrina, he takes the advice of the goddess Venus and employs Trotaconventos to pursue Endrina on his behalf (stanzas 910–949).

She is successful, and later in the book (stanzas 1318–31) suggests that the nun Doña Garoça could be induced to accept him as her 'buen servidor'. Doña Garoça dies, and Trotaconventos also dies shortly afterwards, to be discovered by the reader enthroned with the martyrs in heaven for her sufferings on earth, one of the many examples of rich irony throughout the poem.

The figure of Doña Urraca was given further depth and psychological understanding as la Celestina (q.v.) in the prose drama by Fernando de Rojas (q.v.).

Trovador, El, a five-act Romantic play in prose and verse by Antonio García Gutiérrez (q.v.) first performed in 1836, when it made his name famous overnight.

Set in Aragon in the 15th c., the play centres on the tragic hero Manrique and the ministering angel Leonor.

Three servants are discussing an old tale. Their late master had two sons; Juan was aged 2, and Nuño (now Count de Luna) was 6 months when an old gipsy woman entered the castle and gazed fixedly at the elder boy. From that day he began to waste away and, since the old Count thought the gipsy had put the evil eye on his son, he ordered her to be burnt at the stake. The boy's health improved but one day he disappeared and the gipsy's daughter was suspected. A boy's skeleton was eventually found among the ashes at the place where the gipsy had been burnt.

Another of the servants tells how Nuño, in love with the Queen's lady-in-waiting Leonor who rejects him, obtains the key to her room, and is about to enter when the serenade of the troubadour Manrique is heard. Leonor emerges from her room to listen to her beloved Manrique and takes the Count for Manrique in the darkness. Manrique is enraged at the conduct of his betrothed, but is reconciled to her. Leonor's brother Guillén demands that Nuño marry Leonor, but she vows to enter a convent before she would marry Nuño. Nuño surprises Manrique and in their ensuing duel he is gravely wounded, and Manrique again disappears, believed after a year to be dead. Leonor is on the point of entering a convent.

Manrique learns from his 'mother' Azucena in the gipsy camp that she destroyed her own child instead of the Count's in a horrible mistake of miscarried vengeance. Manrique is thus discovered to be his hated rival's brother; but Azucena then retracts her words. He secretly enters Leonor's convent, where his beloved wrestles with the dilemma of her faith and her love, at last falling prey to the latter. A servant bursts in and tells them that Azucena has been seized. Manrique runs off to save her but he too is captured. Doña Leonor begs Nuño to save their lives, agreeing to become his wife if he will show mercy. He consents and they proceed to Manrique's cell, where the troubadour rejects the pact. Leonor, who has taken poison to avoid the fate of such an unhappy marriage, dies in Manrique's arms. After hearing the blade sever the troubadour's head from his body, Azucena triumphantly shouts to Nuño that Manrique was his own brother, and to her mother in the next world that now she is avenged, dying in her turn.

Such was the tremendous success of this work, that the author was made to come on stage to acknowledge the applause of the public: the first recorded event of this type in the Spanish theatre. Verdi used the play as the source for his opera *Il trovatore* (1853) with equal success.

There is a good edition by J. Lomba y Pedraja (1941) in Clásicos Castellanos.

TRUEBA Y COSSÍO, Joaquín Telésforo de (1799–1835), b. Santander. Novelist and playwright. He emigrated to England in 1823 because of his opposition to Spanish absolutism, and there wrote novels and plays in English, most of which he later translated into Castilian. *The romance of the history of Spain* (1827) retells a number of legends in the Romantic style then in vogue. He wrote the first Spanish Romantic historical novel, in the style of Sir Walter Scott: *Gómez Arias* (1828; Spanish edn., 1831). His later novels were *The Castilian* (1829), *The exquisites* (1831), and *The incognitos* (1831). In 1834 he returned to Spain, where his *La España romántica*, a version of *The romance . . .*, appeared in 4 vols. in 1840. A. González Palencia edited another version in 1942.

Trueba also wrote plays in the manner of Scott, such as *Elvira*, and in the manner of Leandro Fernández de Moratín (q.v.), such as *Call again tomorrow* (1832). Menéndez y Pelayo's study of Trueba, vol. 6 in the series Estudios de Crítica Literaria (Santander, 1876), was his first publication in book form.

TRUEBA Y DE LA QUINTANA, ANTONIO DE (1819—89), b. Montellano, Biscay. Self-taught poet, short-story writer, and novelist. Working in Madrid as an artisan, he wrote *El libro de los cantares* (1851), praising the simple life and faith of his home province in plain language and easy rhythms, and became known in Biscay as 'Antón él de los cantares'. He then entered journalism, writing a historical novel, *El Cid Campeador* (1851), and another on the Basque country, *La paloma y los halcones* (1865). His later novels were *El gabán y la chaqueta* (1872), and *Redentor moderno* (1876). In 1862 he was appointed archivist and chronicler of Biscay Province, and thenceforward lived there, writing *Bilbao* (1878) and *Arte de hacer versos al alcance de todo él que sepa leer* (1881). His poetry, influenced by Bécquer, includes *El libro de las montañas* (1868) and, like most of his writings, is moralistic in tone.

Trueba's most characteristic works are his collections of short stories; moralizing, sentimentally optimistic, and lexically poor, they nevertheless reveal a delightful personality. They are *Cuentos populares* (1853), *Cuentos de color de rosa* (1859), *Cuentos campesinos* (1860), *Cuentos populares* (1862), *Cuentos de vivos y de muertos* (1866), *Cuentos de varios colores* (1866), *Cuentos del hogar* (1875), and the posthumous *Cuentos populares de Vizcaya* (1905). Trueba's *Obras* were reprinted in 11 vols. (1905–24), and P. A. M. Escudero edited the selection *Cuentos y cantares* (1959).

See A. González Blanco, *Antonio de Trueba* (Bilbao, 1914).

TRULOCK, JORGE CELA (1932–), b. Madrid. Novelist and short-story writer. He is on the staff of *Papeles de Son Armadans* (q.v.) and

Cuadernos Hispanoamericanos. Cartas a la novia (1969) is a collection of short stories, but his reputation rests on his novels: *Blanquito: peón de brega* (Valladolid, 1958), *Las horas* (Barcelona, 1958), *Trayecto Circo-Matadero* (1965), *Compota de adelfas* (Barcelona, 1968), and *Inventario base* (1970). In this last book, Trulock brings the *nouveau roman* into Spanish. He has attempted to withdraw his own personality from the drab scene of seven people in a small flat concerned to the point of absurdity with the minutiae of everyday life. A child becomes ill and is ignored among events such as eating and television-watching. Trulock achieves his effects by understatement and irony, in direct contrast to the writing of his brother, Camilo José Cela (q.v.).

TUDENSE, EL, familiar appellation of Lucas de Túy (q.v.).

TUERTO LÓPEZ, EL, the nickname of Luis Carlos López (q.v.).

Túnel, El (1948), a novel by the Argentinian Ernesto Sábato (q.v.).

A working-out of Sábato's metaphysical ideas in fictional form, the book aims to show the alienation of his generation through the example of the schizophrenic painter Juan Pablo Castel, who writes his memoirs in prison, where he is serving his sentence for murder (a situation not unlike that of Duarte in Camilo José Cela's *La familia de Pascual Duarte*, q.v.). Sábato gradually reveals the workings of Castel's mind and his relationships with the other characters. The plot consists of the events following an exhibition in which Castel showed the painting *Maternidad*, ignored by critics and public alike except by María Iribarne, who is married to Allende, a blind man. Castel feels that she understands the painting and can therefore understand him: he pursues her with desire and eventually seems to kill her when he rips his painting to shreds. However, the existence of María outside Castel's own mind is in doubt: she may be only a figure on the canvas, and both the murder and the trial may be illusory. Castel symbolizes modern man in his confusion, loneliness, and existential despair. As B. Gibbs has written (*Hispania*, vol. 48, 1965, pp. 429–36), 'Castel's maniacal addiction to reason [and] the associative process [is] in itself symptomatic of the protagonist's mania' and leads to his self-condemnation and eventual tragedy.

See Marcel Coddou, 'La estructura y la problemática existencial de "El túnel"' in *Atenea* (Concepción, Chile, April–June 1966), vol. 162, no. 412, pp. 141–68; T. C. Meehan, 'Ernesto Sábato's sexual metaphysics: theme and form in "El túnel"' in *Modern Language Notes*, no. 83 (March 1968), pp. 226–52; and Carmen Quiroga de Caballero, *Entrando a 'El túnel' de Ernesto Sábato* (Barcelona, 1971).

TURCIOS, FROYLÁN (1875–1943), b. Juticalpa, Olancho. Honduran short-story writer, novelist, and poet. His career was divided between journalism and diplomacy. *Flores de almendro* (Paris, 1931) was a collection of modernist poems selected from earlier books of prose and verse: *Mariposas* (1895), *Renglones* (1899), *Hojas de otoño*, and *Tierra maternal* (1911).

Some critics consider his best work two novels influenced by Poe: *Annabel Lee* (1906) and *El vampiro* (1910), but the Honduran settings of his *Cuentos del amor y de la muerte* (Paris, 1930) combine well with a D'Annunzian exoticism to produce stark little stories in which the terror and mystery of Poe still penetrate.

TURMEDA, ANSELM (1352?–after 1423), b. Palma, Majorca. A Franciscan friar who studied first in Lérida, and 1377–87 in Bologna. He fled one night with a nun and another friar to Tunis, and though his companions later returned to Spain, he became a Muslim and as 'Abdullah at-Tarjumān lived from 1387 in Tunis serving the Bey of Tunis as chief customs officer. As a poet, his best-known work is the *Elogi dels diners*, and his allegorical *coplas* were published in 1398 as *Cobles de la divisió del regne de Mallorques*. He imitated a 13th-c. Italian poem in the *Llibre de bons amonestaments*, which was still being used as a Catalan school-text in the 19th c. His best-known work is the prose *Disputa de l'ase* written in 1417 or 1418 after a 10th-c. Arabic apologia. The *Disputa* was first published in Barcelona in 1509 (no known copy survives), in Lyon (1548), and in Paris (1554). It was edited from French sources by R. Foulché-Delbosc in the *Revue Hispanique*, vol. 24 (1911), and again by M. de Epalza, *La Tuhfa: autobiografía y polémica islámica contra el cristianismo* (Rome, 1971). The autobiography he wrote in Arabic in 1420, *Tuhfat al-arib fi 'r-radd ala ahl as-salib*, was translated into French by J. Spiro as *Le présent de l'homme lettré pour refuter les partisans de la croix* (Paris, 1886).

See Agustín Calvet, *Fr. Anselm Turmeda*,

heterodoxo español (Barcelona, 1914), and the useful résumé of his life and works in vol. 2 of Riquer's *Història de la literatura catalana* (Barcelona, 1964).

TURRISA, JOSÉ, an anagram used by the Mexican novelist Justo Sierra O'Reilly (q.v.).

TÚY, LUCAS DE (*c.* 1160–1249), b. León. Historian. On returning from travels in Italy, Cyprus, Constantinople, and the Holy Land, he was commissioned by Queen Berenguela to write *Chronicon mundi* (Frankfurt, 1608), written in Latin in 1236 and translated towards the end of the century as *Coronica de Spana por Luchas de Tui*, with additions bringing the account up from 1236 to 1252. Lucas, often called 'el Tudense' because he was Canon Regular of San Isidro at Túy and Bishop of Túy from 1239 until his death, also wrote *Milagros de San Isidro* and a tract against the Albigensians entitled *De altera vita fideique controversiis adversus Albigensium errores libri III* (Munich, 1612).

His history was based largely on Sampiro and Pelayo, and is at its best when describing events seen at first hand. One of the most important features of the *Crónica del Tudense* is the interpolation of *cantares de gesta* (such as that of Bernardo del Carpio) paraphrased in prose. The book is credulous, though less so than many contemporary writings, and suffers from a lack of critical judgment. The *Chronica mundi* was edited afresh by J. Puyol in 1920.

Tzántzico, Grupo, an Ecuadorian literary and political movement of protest which arose in the 1960s as a reaction to alleged literary and social deterioration. Members of the Tzántzico movement held recitals, happenings, debates, and performances of plays and poetry-readings. The name *tzántzico* is derived from the Jívaro Indians' word for 'head-shrinker'.

Pucuna is the movement's journal. Its members are the playwright Simón Corral, the poet Alfonso Murriagui (b. Quito, 1930), the poet and short-story writer Ulises Estrella (b. Quito, 1940), Rafael Larrea, Antonio Ordóñez, and others. Both Murriagui and Estrella are represented in Aldo Pellegrini's *Antología de la poesía viva latinoamericana* (Barcelona, 1966).

U

UGARTE, Manuel (1878–1951), b. Buenos Aires. Argentinian diplomat, journalist, travel-writer, and short-story writer, who lived for many years in Paris, where he published *Crónicas parisienses*, *Crónicas de bulevar*, and *La novela de las horas y de los días*. The nostalgic *Cuentos de la pampa* (1903) and *Cuentos argentinos* (1908) are his most important short stories.

He wrote polemically on many subjects, notably against the influence of the U.S.A.

As a critic, he is too generous in his judgments to be reliable, as in the capricious anthologies *La joven literatura hispanoamericana* (Paris, 1906) and *Las nuevas tendencias literarias* (1908). His *Poesías completas* (Barcelona, 1921) included the *Vendimias juveniles* (1907).

ULLOA Y PEREIRA, Luis de (1584–1674), b. Toro, Zamora. A *culterano* (q.v.) poet (using the pseudonym 'Lisardo') and playwright. A protégé of Olivares, in 1627 he was appointed *corregidor* of León.

His *Versos* (1659) were reissued in expanded form in 1674 as *Obras: prosas y versos*. His *comedias* included *Porcia y Tancredo* (1662), *Pico y Canente*, *No muda el amor semblante*, and *La mujer contra el consejo*. His most important poem is *Raquel* (1650), printed in vol. 29 (1854) of the BAE, on the love of Alfonso VIII for the 'Jewess of Toledo'. The theme of *Raquel* (q.v.) may have been borrowed from Lope de Vega's play *La Raquel hermosa*.

Ulloa's most curious prose work is a detailed refutation of Antonio de Guevara's *Menosprecio de corte* (q.v.) entitled *Epístola a un cavallero amigo, que vivía en Sevilla*, praising the cultivated life at court as opposed to the dull, sluggish pursuits of countrymen.

M. Artigas has edited Ulloa's *Memorias familiares y literarias* (1925). See also Josefina García Aráez, *Don Luis de Ulloa y Pereira* (1952).

Ultra, Grupo, a group of seven poets, influenced by Mallarmé, who signed the *Manifiesto vertical ultraísta* (1920) after having created the *ultraísmo* movement the previous year. They were Guillermo de Torre (q.v.), who invented the name, Xavier Bóveda, César A. Comet, Pedro Garfías, Fernando Iglesias Caballero, J. Rivas Panedas, and J. de Aroca. Their manifesto urged a total break with the past, and the creation of the 'pure' poem, free from any erotic element, and lacking any kind of narrative or formal, logical structure. The magazine *Ultra* appeared in 1921–2. Jorge Luis Borges became associated with the group, and it has benefited from the reputation of his later, very different poetry. *Ultraísmo* was the pretext for Ortega y Gasset's famous essay *La deshumanización del arte* (q.v.), first published in book form in 1925. The *ultraísta* group was related to *creacionismo* (q.v.).

See Guillermo de Torre, *Historia de las literaturas de vanguardia* (1965).

Ultraísmo, see ULTRA, Grupo.

Ulyssipo, in imprints, Lisbon.

Ummayads, a family of the Quraish tribe (to which the Hashimite family of the Prophet Muhammad also belonged) which included a number of caliphs, beginning with Mu'awiya, successor to Ali, and ending with Marwan, who was beheaded in 750.

The Ummayads originally ruled from Damascus, but when Marwan was killed the whole of his family perished with him except the grandson of Hisham (724–43), Abd ar-Rahman, who escaped to Spain and founded the Spanish dynasty at Cordova in 755, routing the Goths.

The Ummayads of Spain reached their zenith in the reign of Abd ar-Rahman III (912–61). The last Caliph of Cordova was Hisham III (1027–31).

UNAMUNO Y JUGO, Miguel de (1846–1936), b. Bilbao. Philosopher, essayist, novelist, poet, and playwright. A distinguished senior member of the *Generación del 1898* (q.v.). He was for many years Rector of Salamanca University and from 1931 held the chair of History of the Spanish Language. Though a Basque, he came to identify himself equally with Castile in his writings, and in his desire to rediscover the Spanish landscape, greatly influenced Antonio Machado (q.v.). In early life he was strongly attracted to Hegel's dialectic, and practised the art of paradox throughout his life. He read Spencer and the positivists, attempting at this time to explain his faith by recourse to reason. After a religious crisis he studied Kierkegaard, William James, and Bergson, especially their ideas on faith, reason, and intuition. The central tenets of his philosophy were: belief in man as an end in himself rather than as an instrument of God; belief in the immortality of the soul; and denial of the validity of any inflexible philosophical system. He hated all labels, but stated that the label he could accept most readily would be 'ideoclast', a breaker in of ideas like boots, making them his own by wearing and using them. Much of his significance in Spanish thought and literature derives from his attacks on dogma, religious or anti-religious.

His *Obras completas* first appeared in 9 vols. (1928–30) and have subsequently been revised and reissued in 6 vols. (1950–8), the sixth being *La raza y la lengua: colección de escritos no recogidos en sus libros* (1958). Among his most influential books are the philosophical travelogues *Por tierras de Portugal y España* (1911) and *Andanzas y visiones españolas* (1922). He wrote many hundreds of essays, some of great value, such as those collected in *Mi religión y otros ensayos* (1910) and *Soliloquios y conversaciones* (1911). The most important of all are probably five essays first printed in *La España moderna* (1895) and collected as *En torno al casticismo* (1902); *La vida de Don Quijote y Sancho* (q.v., 1905); *Del sentimiento trágico de la vida en los hombres y en los pueblos* (q.v., 1913); and *La agonía del cristianismo* (1925).

His fiction and poetry have been variously judged. The fiction was attacked on publication as being excessively didactic, after the auto-biographical *Paz en la guerra* (1897), on the Carlist siege of Bilbao in 1874. *Amor y pedagogía* (1902) is a tragicomedy on the futility of bringing up children on scientific lines, to which some critics denied the name of novel. Unamuno thereupon coined the term *nivola* (q.v.). *Una historia de amor* (1911) was followed by the short stories of *El espejo de la muerte* (1913) and *Niebla* (q.v., 1914), the latter an interesting experiment anticipating Pirandello. Then came *Abel Sánchez: una historia de pasión* (q.v., 1917); *Tres novelas ejemplares y un prólogo* (1920), consisting of 'Nada menos que todo un hombre' (q.v.), 'Dos madres', and 'El marqués de Lumbría'; *La tía Tula* (1921); and *San Manuel Bueno, mártir, y tres historias más* (q.v., 1933), which besides the title story includes 'La novela de Don Sandalio, jugador de ajedrez', 'Un pobre hombre rico', and a revision of 'Una historia de amor'. *Cómo se hace una novela* (first published in Jean Carson's French version, Paris, 1926; Buenos Aires, 1927) is a useful insight into his technique.

Unamuno's poetry was voluminous, his themes ranging from the Castilian landscape to his familiar yearning for immortality; where his search for truth led to a religious conclusion, his work is reminiscent of Luis de León (q.v.). His first books of verse, *Poesías* (1907) and *Rosario de sonetos líricos*, are generally accounted unsuccessful, but his long poem *El Cristo de Velázquez* (1920), despite *longueurs*, achieves impressive sonority, particularly the second poem in Part II and the twenty-third in Part III. His later

books of verse were *Rimas de dentro* (1923), *De Fuerteventura a París* (1925) which includes some prose, the love poems *Teresa* (1923), and the *Romancero del destierro* (1927). From 1928 to 1936 he composed the 1,775 poems for *Cancionero: diario poético*, edited by F. de Onís (Buenos Aires, 1953), while a further *Cincuenta poesías inéditas* have been introduced by Manuel García Blanco (Palma de Mallorca, 1958) and more un-collected poems appeared on pp. 365–425 of *Don Miguel de Unamuno y sus poesías* (Salamanca, 1954), by M. García Blanco, who succeeded to Unamuno's chair at Salamanca.

Of Unamuno's plays, edited by M. García Blanco in *Teatro completo* (1959), the best-known is *Sombras de sueño*, in four acts, first performed and published (in *El Teatro Moderno*, vol. 6) in 1930, which is a revision of *Tulio Montalbán y Julio Macedo*, based on Unamuno's short story of the same title which appeared in *La Novela Corta*, vol. 5, no. 260 (1920). *El otro* deals with the theme of *Abel Sánchez* (q.v.), *Fedra* adapts the play by Euripides to modern life, and *El hermano Juan* is a reworking of the Don Juan figure in the spirit of '98. Unamuno's finest achievement as a translator is his free rendering of Seneca's *Medea*. See Andrés Franco, *El teatro de Unamuno* (1971).

Bibliografía crítica de Miguel de Unamuno by P. H. Fernández (1976) includes material published up to 1975.

See also Julián Marías, *Miguel de Unamuno* (1943); *Cuadernos de la Cátedra de Miguel de Unamuno* (Salamanca, 1954–); Martin Nozick, *Miguel de Unamuno* (New York, 1971), in English; A. Jiménez Hernandez, *Unamuno y la filosofía del lenguaje* (1973); A. Sánchez Barbudo (ed.), *Miguel de Unamuno* (1974); F. Wyers, *Miguel de Unamuno: the contrary self* (London, 1976); and R. Díez, *El desarrollo crítico de la novela de Unamuno* (1976).

UNDURRAGA, ANTONIO DE (1911–), b. Santiago. Chilean poet and essayist. As a disciple of Huidobro, he has remained faithful to *creacionismo* (q.v.), in his own poetry, in his magazine *Caballo de Fuego* (1946–), and in his *Manifiesto del Caballo de Fuego y poesías* (1945). His important essay 'Teoría del creacionismo' forms the preface to a collection *Poesía y prosa* by Vicente Huidobro (Madrid, 1957). Undurraga's books include the poems *La siesta de los peces* (1938), *Morada de España en ultramar* (Valparaíso, 1939), *Antología poética* (1942), *Transfiguración en los párpados de Sagitario* (1944), *El arte poético de Pablo de Rokha* (1945), *Red en el Génesis* (1946), *Zoo subjetivo* (1947), *Poesía y efigie de Pezoa Véliz* (1951), and an *Atlas de la poesía de Chile* (1958).

He has edited *La Araucana* by Ercilla (q.v., Buenos Aires, 1947).

University Theatre 'La Barraca', see 'BARRACA, LA'.

URABAYEN, FÉLIX GUINDOERENA (1884–1943), b. Ulzurrun, Navarra. Essayist and novelist of the Toledo region, where he taught in the Escuela Normal. His novels, such as *Toledo: piedad* (1920) and *La última cigüeña* (1921), showed an attitude to Spain unaffected by *noventayochismo* (see GENERACIÓN DEL 1898). Urabayen continues to live enraptured by Spain's ideal history and romanticized landscapes, as in *Por los senderos del mundo creyente* (1929), the paths in question being the five great aisles of Toledo Cathedral. The rest of the essays in this book are devoted to a lyrical account of Toledo and environs: Yepes, los Cigarrales, Almorox, and the castle of Escalona.

El barrio maldito (1925) is a novel of the Barrio de Lozate, a mile from Arizcun in the Baztan valley, *maldito* because it was the dwelling of the *cagots* (Basque: *agotak*), who are descended from leper colonies and were not allowed to intermarry with the Basques until the end of the 19th c.

URBANEJA ACHELPOHL, LUIS MANUEL (1874–1937), b. Caracas. Venezuelan novelist and short-story writer. One of the first *criollista* writers, he interrupted the plot of his earlier novels to describe nature, in the manner of Pereda (q.v.), but in his later work turned to the naturalism of Zola. Unlike Blanco-Fombona or Gallegos (qq.v.), he avoids political and even social themes, concentrating on the world of the Creole in such stories as '¡Ovejón!'.

His principal works were *Los abuelos* (short stories, 1909), *En este país* (novel, 1916), *El tuerto Miguel* (novel, 1927), and *La casa de las cuatro pencas* (novel, 1937).

URBINA, ISABEL DE, the first wife of Lope de Vega (q.v.), the 'Belisa' of his poetry.

URBINA, LUIS GONZAGA (1868–1934), b. Mexico City. Mexican poet, critic, and essayist. He was Director of the National Library, a diplomat, and a university professor.

His poems were first published in the *Revista Azul* (1894–6) of Gutiérrez Nájera (q.v.), his poetic predecessor. Urbina has been called 'el último romántico'. His juvenilia appeared in *Versos* (1890), and his development was continuous through *Ingenuas* (Paris, 1902), *Puestas de sol* (Paris, 1910), and *El glosario de la vida vulgar* (Madrid, 1916), to *Lámparas en agonía* (1914), *El corazón juglar* (Madrid, 1920), *Los últimos pájaros* (Madrid, 1924), and *El cancionero de la noche serena* (1925).

Urbina wrote six prose books, of which three were devoted to travels in Spain, and the others

to literary essays and reviews, including the useful *La vida literaria de México* (1917; new edn. by Antonio Castro Leal, 1946). His *Poesías completas* were edited for publication in 2 volumes by Antonio Castro Leal (1946; 2nd edn., 1964, including *Retratos líricos*).

See M. del Socorro López Villarino, *Luis Gonzaga Urbina, el poeta y el prosista* (1956); and Gerardo Sáenz, *Luis Gonzaga Urbina, vida y obra* (1961).

URDEMALAS, PEDRO DE, see PEDRO DE URDEMALAS.

UREÑA DE HENRÍQUEZ, SALOMÉ (1850–97), b. Santo Domingo. Dominican poet, wife of Francisco Henríquez, President of the Republic. She published her first verses when fifteen under the pseudonym 'Herminia'. *Poesías* (1880; another edn. Madrid, 1920) is distinguished for patriotic sentiment. Doña Salomé founded the Instituto de Señoritas in 1881, the first ladies' college in the country. She was the mother of two important writers: Max and Pedro Henríquez Ureña (qq.v.).

URETA, ALBERTO J. (1885–), b. Lima. Peruvian poet. His melancholy verses, influenced by Francis Jammes (1868–1938), were collected in *Rumor de almas* (1911), *El dolor pensativo* (1917), *Poemas* (1925), *Las tiendas del desierto* (1933), and *Elegías a la cabeza loca* (Paris, 1937).

URÍA Y RÍU, JUAN (1891–), b. Oviedo. Professor of Spanish History at Oviedo University. His monographs on medieval Asturias are mostly concerned with literature: *Juglares asturianos* (1940), *Notas para la historia de los judíos en Asturias* (1944), and *Notas para el estudio del mozarabismo en Asturias*.

With L. Vázquez de Parra Iglesias (q.v.) and J. M. Lacarra he has written the authoritative *Las peregrinaciones a Santiago de Compostela* (3 vols., 1948–9).

URIBE, DIEGO (1867–1921), b. Bogotá. Colombian poet whose best work, influenced by Bécquer (q.v.), consists of a series of elegies written for his beloved wife, *Margarita* (Paris, 1898). His subsequent *Hielos* (Paris, 1898) contains poems on the wretched, from the captive eagle and the caged tiger to the blind man.

Obras poéticas escogidas (1967) was issued to celebrate the centenary of Uribe's birth.

URIBE ECHEVERRÍA, JUAN (1908–), Chilean critic and folklorist, who compiled the *Cancionero de Alhué* in which he shows that popular songs of the Alhué region of Chile derive from Spanish songs of the 15th and 16th cs. He has written *La novela de la revolución mexicana* (1935),

Cervantes en las letras hispanoamericanas: antología y crítica (1949), and *Estudios sobre José Ortega y Gasset* (1955). He has also compiled the *Antología para el sesquicentenario, 1810–1960* (1960).

URIBE PIEDRAHITA, César (1897–1951), b. Antioquia. Colombian bacteriologist, art critic, anthropologist, and novelist. His most important book was *Toá: narraciones de caucherías* (Buenos Aires, 1933) a realistic chronicle of rubber plantations in the Amazon forests thinly made fiction by the introduction of a love affair between Toá and the semi-autobiographical hero Antonio de Orrantia.

In *Mancha de aceite* (1935), Uribe attacks the foreign-dominated oil industry which he considers to have exploited Latin American interests. It is a better-constructed novel than *Toá* and less markedly influenced by Rivera's *La vorágine* (q.v.), but it generates less excitement because of the author's failure convincingly to evoke the atmosphere of oil exploration.

URQUIJO E IBARRA, Julio (1871–1950), b. Deusto, Vizcaya. Basque historian and philologist. He founded the *Revista Internacional de Estudios Vascos* in 1907, the review *Euskalerriaren Alde* (with Aguirre, Campión, and Echegaray) in 1911, and the Academia de la Lengua Vasca in 1918. The Seminario de Filología Vasca in San Sebastián has been named after Urquijo.

Among his principal editions are the *Obras vascongadas del doctor labortano Joannes d'Etcheberri* (1907) and *El refranero vasco: los refranes de Garibay y refranes en vascuence compuestos por Esteban de Garibay* (San Sebastián, 1925).

URQUIZA, Concha (1910–45), b. Morelia, Michoacán. Mexican poet. Resident in New York 1928–32, she returned to Mexico as a postulant to enter the religious life and taught for a time in San Luis Potosí.

Her *Obras* (1946), edited with an introduction by Gabriel Méndez Plancarte, reveal her as a natural mystic unsure whether to abandon the world. She was drowned on an excursion to Baja California.

URRUTIA Y MONTOYA, Ignacio José de (1735–95), b. Havana. Cuban historian. His sound historical judgments and extensive research were marred by verbose, incoherent presentation in his important *Teatro histórico, jurídico, y político-militar de la Isla Fernandina de Cuba y principalmente de su capital la Habana* (1791) and the unfinished *Compendio de memorias para escribir la historia de la Isla Fernandina de Cuba.*

USIGLI, Rodolfo (1905–), b. Mexico City. Mexican playwright and critic. His father was Italian and his mother Polish. The most

important contemporary dramatist of Mexico. His *Teatro completo* has already appeared (2 vols., 1963–6). His plays include *El Apóstol* (1931), the melodrama *Estado de secreto* (1936), the realistic middle-class comedy *Medio tono* (1937), *El gesticulador* (q.v., 1937), *La mujer no hace milagros* (1939), *Vacaciones* (1940, the year he founded the Teatro de la Media Noche), and the social satire of the upper classes *La familia cena en casa* (1949). His most popular work is *Corona de sombra* (1947, 3rd edn., 1959), an historical tragedy based on the period of Maximilian in Mexico, in which the historian Erasmo Ramírez interviews the insane Empress shortly before her death. His later plays include *Los fugitivos* (1950), *El niño y la niebla* (1951), *Aguas estancadas* (1952), and *Un día de estos...* (1954).

Corona de luz (1965) is about Bartolomé de Las Casas (q.v.), and the cult of the Virgin of Guadalupe. He has also written *Ensayo de un crimen* (1944); *Anatomía del teatro* (1967) a volume of dramatic criticism; and *Conversaciones y encuentros* (1974).

See Margarita Mendoza López's biobibliographical note in *Teatro: Boletín de Información e Historia,* no. 3 (November 1954).

USLAR PIETRI, Arturo (1906–), Venezuelan novelist and short-story writer. He has been Minister of Education and Minister of Foreign Affairs. His first book was *Barrabás y otros relatos* (1928), but his best is the novel *Las lanzas coloradas* (Madrid, 1931) a subtle account of Bolívar's time which concentrates on the ordinary people caught up in the fluctuations of war; impressively unbiased politically, the book is a major document in modern Venezuelan fiction. Among Uslar Pietri's later books are the short stories in *Red* (1936), and *Antología del cuento moderno venezolano* compiled with Julián Padrón (1940); a fictionalized biography of the *conquistador* Lope de Aguirre, *El camino de El Dorado* (Buenos Aires, 1947); *Letras y hombres de Venezuela* (Mexico City, 1948); the short stories *Treinta hombres y sus sombras* (Buenos Aires, 1949); *De una a otra Venezuela* (1950); *Apuntes para retratos* (1952); *Tierra venezolana* (1953); the short stories *Tiempo de contar* (1954); *El otoño en Europa* (1954); *Breve historia de la novela hispanoamericana* (1954); *Pizarrón* (1955); the novel *El laberinto de fortuna* (2 vols., Buenos Aires, 1962–4); *Pasos y pasajeros* (Madrid, 1966); *Vista desde un punto* (1971); *Manos* (1973); and *La otra América* and *El globo de celares* (both 1975).

See the introduction to the otherwise outdated *Obras selectas* of Uslar Pietri (1953); José Luis Vivas, *La cuentística de Arturo Uslar Pietri* (1963); and Domingo Miliani, *Uslar Pietri, renovador del cuento venezolano* (Mexico City, 1965).

V

VACA DE GUZMÁN, José María (1744–1803), b. Marchena. Minor poet. He studied law at Alcalá, where he eventually became Rector. In 1789 he was appointed counsellor to the court.

A. González Palencia, in a chapter 'Don José María Vaca de Guzmán, el primer poeta premiado por la Academia Española' in his book *Entre dos siglos* (1943), has described how Vaca de Guzmán's epic *Las naves de Cortés destruídas* (1778) was awarded the Real Academia's prize above the composition submitted by Nicolás Fernández de Moratín (q.v.), and in the following year his heroic ballad *Granada rendida* (1779) won the prize against the entry of Leandro Fernández de Moratín (q.v.). Vaca de Guzmán's collected *Obras* (1789–93) appeared in 3 vols. His works can be found in vol. 29 (1854) and vol. 61 (1869) of the BAE.

His brother Gutierre Joaquín wrote a satirical novel in English, *The travels of Henry Wanton* (2 vols., 1769–71, with a continuation in 2 vols., 1778).

VACA GUZMÁN, Santiago (1847–96), Bolivian novelist and critic, of Indianist sympathies, who has written on Bolivian literature in general and Andean poetry in particular, affirming that 'nuestro porvenir literario está en la riqueza y variedad del suelo boliviano . . .'. Vaca Guzmán uses language unoriginally to tell thin plots, and his books are of value more to the historian of Bolivian writing than to the general reader or literary critic.

His novels are in the Romantic tradition, beginning with the melodramatic *Ayes del corazón* (1867) and the description of a suicide, *Días amargos: memorias de un pesimista* (1886). *Sin esperanza* (1891) is the story of a priest who is unable to prevent the murder by her husband of the woman he loves. *Su Excelencia y Su Ilustrísima* (1899) deals with 16th-c. Paraguay, concentrating on the enmity between the Bishop of Asunción and the Governor.

VALCÁRCEL, Gustavo A. (1921–), b. Arequipa. Peruvian novelist, essayist, and poet. A journalist for the magazine *Panorama Internacional* (Novosti Agency) in Lima. *Sus mejores poemas* (1960) collect early work, mainly 'pure' poetry, and the later verse influenced by Vallejo which turns to melancholy predictions and social involvement. Valcárcel's *Ensayos* (1960) were published to coincide with the 2nd edition of *La prisión* (1951), a novel of prison life under the

dictator Manuel Odría in which Froilán, a student, is wrongly gaoled instead of his namesake but is happy to die rather than undergo further sexual and spiritual humiliation by his warders and fellow-prisoners.

Valcárcel's subsequent works include *Artículos literarios* (1960); *Reportaje al futuro* (1963), a sympathetic account of travels in the U.S.S.R.; *Pido la palabra* (1965), poems; *Perú: mural de un pueblo* (1965), Marxist views on pre-Hispanic Peru; and *Poesía extremista* (1967), a volume of poems drawing on his political beliefs.

VALCÁRCEL, Luis E. (1893–), b. Ilo, Moquegua. Peruvian essayist and short-story writer. His earlier books were intemperate in their passionate defence of the Indian way of life: *Los problemas actuales* (1916) and the influential *Tempestad en los Andes* (1927), described by Estuardo Núñez as 'at once a message, pamphlet, programme and prophecy concerning the incorporation of the Indian into the life of the nation'.

More solid, judicious contributions were the *Historia de la cultura antigua del Perú* (2 vols., 1943–9) and *Ruta cultural del Perú* (Mexico City, 1945), in which the best chapters are those devoted to religion (where he criticizes the uprooting of indigenist ways of thinking by Christian missionaries) and to education (where he attacks academic schooling of the western type in Indian society, and advocates mass literacy based on technical and agricultural needs). Elsewhere he proposes widespread land reform, the mechanization of agriculture, and the development of heavy industry.

His later books include *Tradición, planeamiento y urbanismo* (1954), *La vida rural en el Perú* (1957), *El estado imperial de los Incas* (1961), and *Historia del Perú antiguo a través de la fuente escrita* (3 vols., 1964).

VALDELOMAR, Abraham (1888–1919), b. Ica. Peruvian short-story writer and poet. Valdelomar, who often used the pseudonym 'El Conde de Lemos', spent his childhood in Pisco, and his authentic regionalism marks a first step away from modernism. He is the first important Creole writer of fiction in Peru, anticipating neo-realism and influencing many of the next generation. Two early short novels of his in the style of D'Annunzio are now little read: *La ciudad muerta* and *La ciudad de los tísicos* (both 1911), the former a 'decadent' story of the viceroys and cities of colonial Peru; the latter a 'modernist mystery story of consumptive love affairs and refined, decadent and sexually perverse pursuits', in the words of Kessel Schwartz.

His first full-length book was *La Mariscala* (1915), a fictional biography of Doña Francisca Zubiaga, wife of General Agustín Gamarra; his second was the highly successful *El caballero Carmelo* (1918), containing stories of the Peruvian coast and of the Inca period, and others with foreign settings. He travelled in Europe in 1913, and from then on contributed assiduously to *La Prensa* of Lima. He founded and edited the magazine *Colónida* in 1916, continuing the experimental, anti-academic trend begun by *Contemporáneos* in 1909 and *Cultura* in 1915, and publishing the works of Mallarmé and other European writers unfamiliar in Peru. *Belmonte el trágico* (1918) was an essay on the aesthetics of bullfighting. *Los hijos del sol* (1921) was a posthumously-published collection of short stories on the Indians of Peru. Valdelomar's *Obra poética* has been edited by Javier Cheesman (1958), and there is an edition, *Cuentos y poesía*, by A. Tamayo Vargas (1959).

See L. F. Xammar, *Valdelomar: signo* (1940), C. Ángeles Caballero, *Vida y obra de Abraham Valdelomar* (1964), Earl A. Aldrich, *The modern short story in Peru* (Madison, Wis., 1966), and L. A. Sánchez, *Valdelomar o la 'Belle Époque'* (Mexico City, 1969).

VALDÉS, ALFONSO DE (1490?–1532), b. Cuenca. Satirical *converso* writer, who corresponded with Erasmus and Melanchthon and has been called 'more Erasmist than Erasmus'. The brother of Juan de Valdés (q.v.). A secretary to Charles V, he left Spain with the court in 1529.

His two prose works are among the most powerfully-written of their century and, first published in 1530, were reprinted four times up to 1547. Valdés was denounced to the Inquisition for them, but escaped punishment and died of the plague in 1532.

The anonymously published *Diálogo de las cosas ocurridas en Roma*, or *Diálogo de Lactancio y un arcediano* defends the Emperor's sacking of the Holy See in 1527, and through the mouth of Lactancio attacks simony, avarice, indulgences, and the outward show of the Church.

Formerly attributed to Juan de Valdés (q.v.), the *Diálogo de Mercurio y Carón* has been shown by Marcel Bataillon (in 'Alfonso de Valdés, auteur du "Diálogo de Mercurio y Carón"', *Homenaje a R. Menéndez Pidal*, vol. 1, 1925, pp. 403–15), to be unquestionably by Alfonso. Influenced by Lucian as regards form, and by the medieval Dance of Death topos as regards theme and treatment, Valdés divides his dialogue into two

books. Book I is negative, attacking a smug preacher, a callous duke, a bishop more interested in income than prayer, a king whose first thought is for his own survival and prestige rather than for his people, and a hypocrite. Book II is positive, describing prelates and secular rulers who carry out their duties according to the spirit rather than the letter.

Both dialogues have been edited by José F. Montesinos (1928–9) for Clásicos Castellanos. Other works by Valdés were issued posthumously: commentaries on the Epistle of St. Paul to the Romans (1556) and on the First Epistle to the Corinthians (1557) and two translations first published in 1880: *El Salterio traducido* and *El Evangelio según San Mateo*, together with 40 of the *Ciento y diez consideraciones divinas* (1539).

See M. Carrasco, *Alfonso et Juan de Valdés: leur vie et leurs écrits réligieux. Étude historique* (Geneva, 1880).

VALDÉS, CARLOS (1928–), b. Guadalajara, Jalisco. Mexican short-story writer and novelist. His activities are literary and academic and include contributing to many magazines; with Huberto Batis he edited the review *Cuadernos del Viento*.

Ausencias (1955) is the first of his collections of fantastic and often sad short stories, the others being *Dos ficciones* (1958), *Dos y los muertos* (1960), and *El nombre es lo de menos* (1961), the last showing flashes of humour.

Los antepasados (1963) is a chronicle novel of a family through four generations. from 1823 to 1917. Valdés has also written the autobiographical *Crónicas de vicio y la virtud* (1963).

VALDÉS, GABRIEL DE LA CONCEPCIÓN (1809–44), Cuban poet, known as 'Plácido', whose mediocre verse was overshadowed by his tragic life and death. He was executed on a charge of conspiracy in 1844.

Brought up in an orphanage, Valdés lacked formal education: he was inspired to become a poet by reading the work of Martínez de la Rosa (q.v.), to whom he addressed 'La siempreviva', which was included in an *Aureola poética* offered to Martínez by Valdés's fellow Cuban poets. Martínez praised Valdés's poetry and encouraged him to write the ballad 'Jicoténcal', the *letrillas* 'La flor de la piña' and 'La flor de la caña'. *Poesías de Plácido* (1838) was his first collection and *El veguero* (1842) his second. S. A. de Morales collected 260 hitherto unpublished poems for *Poesías completas* (1886), and a *Poesías completas* of 1930 includes a further 210 *inéditas*. There is a critical edition, *Los poemas más representativos de Plácido* (1976), by F. S. Stimson and H. E. Robles.

See L. Horrego Estuch, *Plácido, el poeta infortunado* (1960); I. Bar-Lewaw, *Plácido: vida y obra* (Mexico City, 1960); and Frederick S. Stimson, *Cuba's Romantic poet, the story of Plácido* (Chapel Hill, N.C., 1964), with a good bibliography, pp. 146–50.

VALDÉS, JUAN DE (*c.* 1491–1541), b. Cuenca. Humanist, and *converso* brother of Alfonso de Valdés (q.v.). He studied at the University of Alcalá, and was influenced by Erasmus in his *Diálogo de doctrina cristiana* (Alcalá, 1529; facsimile edn. by M. Bataillon, Coimbra, 1925), which was denounced for heresy. Fearing the Inquisition, Valdés left for Italy, where he taught for some years in a select circle, introducing Reformation ideas. His *Alfabeto cristiano* (1546; ed. Benedetto Croce, Bari, 1938) is a dialogue affirming justification by faith. *Ciento y diez consideraciones divinas* (1539), written with Alfonso, teaches salvation by interior illumination.

His major work is the *Diálogo de la lengua* (q.v., written about 1535 but not published until 1737; ed. by J. F. Montesinos in Clásicos Castellanos, 1928), which is a discussion of the evolution and style of modern Castilian, advocating simplicity and directness of expression. His taste is impeccable, preferring the *Celestina* and *Amadís de Gaula* to the extravagant *libros de caballería* (qq.v.) then in vogue.

See M. Carrasco, *Alfonso et Juan de Valdés: leur vie et leurs écrits religieux. Étude historique* (Geneva, 1880); D. Ricart, *Juan de Valdés y el pensamiento religioso europeo en los siglos XVI y XVII* (Mexico City, 1958); and José C. Nieto, *Juan de Valdés and the origins of the Spanish and Italian Reformation* (Geneva, 1970).

VALDÉS Y TORO, LUCAS DE, b. Cordova. A surgeon whose curious masterpiece, printed in Cordova (1630) on four unpaginated leaves, is entitled *Tratado en que se prueba que la nieve es fría y húmeda.*

VALDIVIELSO, JOSÉ DE (1560–1638), b. Toledo. Poet and playwright. Chaplain to the Archbishop of Toledo and to the Infante Don Fernando, and a close friend of Lope de Vega (q.v.).

Valdivielso was admired for his lengthy sacred epic, the *Vida, excelencias y muerte del glorioso Patriarca, y Esposo de Nuestra Señora San Ioseph* (Toledo, 1604?) and the unsuccessful heroic poem *Sagrario de Toledo* (1616), but he is strongest in his *autos sacramentales*, such as *El villano en su rincón* and *La serrana de Plasencia*, published in *Doze autos sacramentales y dos comedias divinas* (Toledo, 1622), reproduced in vol. 58 (1865) of the BAE, but best studied in the *Teatro completo* (vol. 1, 1975; in progress) edited

by R. Arias y Arias and R. V. Piluso. His poetry appears in vols. 35 (1855) and 49 (1857) of the same series. J. Simón Díaz has edited 'Textos dispersos' in *Revista de Literatura*, vol. 19 (1961), pp. 125–68 and vol. 20 (1962), pp. 407–36. Valdivielso's baroque 'folk poetry' is deceptively simple, with striking images that were borrowed by Lorca. He produced only the first part of his *Romancero Espiritual . . .* (Toledo, 1612). This facet of his varied work has been studied by J. M. Aguirre in *José de Valdivielso y la poesía religiosa tradicional* (Toledo, 1965).

VALDIVIESO, JAIME (1929–), Chilean novelist and short-story writer who has written *El Tonillito* (1961) a revised version of *El muchacho* (1958); then achieved wide recognition with *Nunca el mismo río* (1965), a brilliant experimental novel written in an introspective style; *La condena de todos*; and *Un asalto a la tradición: Sepúlveda Leyton: vida y obra* (1963), on the Chilean novelist Carlos Sepúlveda Leyton (1894–1944).

VALENCIA, GUILLERMO (1873–1943), b. Popayán, Antioquia. Colombian poet. Of a wealthy family, he spent several years in Paris, where he met Mallarmé, and also Oscar Wilde, whose *Ballad of Reading Gaol* he translated (Popayán, 1932). He was a diplomat, but found his *métier* as a translator.

His original work was strictly classical for the most part, yet paradoxically he was also drawn to the Parnassian movement (best exemplified in his 'Los camellos' and his finest inspiration is found in 'San Antonio y el Centauro', an eclectic poem fusing classicism and modernism. *Ritos* (1899; 2nd edn., 1914) was the only book of poetry he published in his lifetime, though *Catay, poemas orientales* (1929) was a useful contribution in the field of translation.

The *Obras poéticas completas* (Madrid, 1948) attempt to include translations, but is generally unsound (see the *Fe de erratas . . .* (1949) by C. López Narváez and others); the *Antología poética* (1952) is preferable.

See Sonja Karsen, *Guillermo Valencia, Colombian poet* (New York, 1951); and Oscar Echeverri, *Guillermo Valencia: estudio y antología* (Madrid, n.d. but 1965).

VALENCIA, PEDRO DE (1555–1620), b. Zafra, Badajoz. A celebrated humanist, he studied Greek with 'el Brocense' and Hebrew with Arias Montano. During his lifetime he was respected for his *Academica sive de judicio erga verum ex ipsis primis fontibus* (Antwerp, 1596). Recent Góngora criticism has pointed to his influence (detrimental, in the view of E. M. Wilson) on the first versions of the *Soledades* and the *Polifemo* in a private criticism later published as 'Censura de Las Soledades y El Polifemo y obras de don Luis de Góngora, hecha a su instancia' (*RABM*, July 1899). This critique was made to persuade his friend to turn to a lighter, simpler form of verse and Góngora accepted the need for eliminating certain passages, and reducing certain obscurities. Valencia's views were made public only when Francisco de Cascales (q.v.) made his more violent criticisms.

See M. Menéndez y Pelayo, *Ensayo de crítica filosófica* (1918) for biographical and bibliographical details on Valencia.

VALENCIA DE LEÓN, Fray Diego (1350?–1412?), a Franciscan poet of the *Cancionero de Baena* belonging to the traditional Castilian school. A contemporary of Francisco Imperial (q.v.), Valencia was held in equally high esteem for his knowledge and poetic skill. The 'Pregunta . . . por qué son los fidalgos' includes an element of social criticism. 'En un vergel deleitoso' is considered by Menéndez y Pelayo to be the best love poem of the Baena anthology. Fray Diego also wrote *cantigas de burlas* for a León woman known as 'la Cortabota', and for others.

See Wolf-Dieter Lange, *El fraile trobador: Zeit, Leben und Werk des Diego de Valencia de León* (Frankfurt, 1971).

VALENTE, José Ángel (1929–), b. Orense. Poet, whose main preoccupations are exile, deprivation, death, and contemporary Spain. He works for an international organization in Geneva, having studied modern languages in Madrid 1947–53 and lectured on Spanish studies at Oxford 1955–58. His books are *A modo de esperanza* (1955), which won the Adonais Prize of 1954, *Poemas a Lázaro* (1960), which won the Critics' Prize of 1961, *Sobre el lugar del canto* (1963), *La memoria y los signos* (1966), *Siete representaciones* (1967), *Breve son* (1968), the sarcastic *Presentación y memorial para un monumento* (1970), *El inocente* (Mexico City, 1970), and *Punto cero* (Barcelona, 1972). Valente has translated the works of Manley Hopkins and Kavafis.

Keith Botsford published English versions of eight of Valente's poems in *Modern Poetry in Translation* (London, 1970), no. 6.

VALERA, Diego de (1412?–1488), historian, courtier, and moralist at the court of Juan II, who was present on the expedition to the Kingdom of Granada in 1431 and at the Battle of La Higuerela.

Valera's best work is the *Crónica cierta y verdadera de los católicos príncipes el Rey don Fernando e la Reina doña Isabel de esclarecida e gloriosa memoria*,

usually known as the *Crónica de los Reyes Católicos*, edited by Juan de Mata Carriazo as *Anejo VIII* of the *Revista de Filología Española* (1927). Carriazo characterized Valera as 'el caballero inquieto, docto y andariego de los días de Juan II, el prudente moralista y hombre de consejo de los malos tiempos de Enrique IV' who, in the times of the Catholic Monarchs, 'se revela . . . como un político bien documentado, de mirada sagaz, de admirable amplitud de pensamiento'.

Mario Penna edited a number of other works by Valera for vol. 116 (1959) of the BAE: *Tratado de las epístolas*; *Tratado en defenssa de virtuossas mugeres*; *Espejo de verdadera nobleza*; *Tratado de las armas*; *Tratado de providencia contra fortuna*; *Breviloquio de virtudes*; and *Doctrinal de príncipes* written for Fernando (see also DE REGIMINE PRINCIPUM).

As a historian, Valera used selections from earlier writers, adding sections (occasionally intrusive) from his personal experiences and from contemporary documents. A declared enemy of Don Álvaro de Luna, Valera wrote his celebrated *Suplicación* against him.

VALERA Y ALCALÁ GALIANO, Juan (1824–1905), b. Cabra, Cordova. Novelist and critic. Graduated in law at the Colegio del Sacro Monte at Granada. Of an aristocratic family, Valera spent three years from 1847, unsalaried, with the Duque de Rivas in the diplomatic service. He became a salaried diplomat when he moved to Portugal in 1850, and to Brazil in 1851. His distinguished career ended in Vienna, where he represented the Spanish Government as ambassador 1893–5. Valera made a late and unhappy marriage to a girl half his age.

As his first book, *Ensayos poéticas* (1844), showing a heavy influence of Espronceda, was destroyed—but for a few copies—before publication, Valera's first published work must be considered the *Poesías* of 1858. This was followed by literary criticism in *De la naturaleza y carácter de la novela* (1860) and the two-volume *Estudios críticos sobre literatura, política y costumbres de nuestros días* (1864). The series of novels, in which his talents finally matured, began with *Pepita Jiménez* (q.v., 1874), possibly the most immediately successful novel of the Spanish 19th c.; *Las ilusiones del doctor Faustino* (1875); *El comendador Mendoza* and *Pasarse de listo* (1877), and *Doña Luz* (q.v., 1879), a year that also saw Valera's *Tentativas dramáticas*). Progressive blindness isolated him from the world during his last decade of life, but he continued to dictate literary and critical essays and other works, including the outstanding novel *Juanita la Larga* (q.v., serialized 1895; published 1896). Valera translated and bowdlerized *Daphnis and Chloe*; and rendered into Spanish parts of Goethe's *Faust*, a poem discussed in Valera's *Sobre el Fausto*. A serious and conscientious critic, inclined to leniency, Valera was among the first to praise the *Azul* of Rubén Darío.

See Cyrus C. DeCoster, *Bibliografía crítica de Juan Valera* (1972); J. Krynen, *L'esthetisme de Juan Valera* (Salamanca, 1946); A. Jiménez, *Juan Valera y la Generación de 1868* (Oxford, 1955); J. F. Montesinos, *Valera o la ficción libre* (1957); J. Merino, *Valera desde hoy* (1968); P. C. Smith, *Juan Valera* (Buenos Aires, 1969); and Cyrus C. DeCoster, *Juan Valera* (New York, 1974) in Twayne's World Authors series; and Cyrus C. DeCoster (ed.), *Genio y figura de Juan Valera* (1975).

VALLADARES Y SOTOMAYOR, ANTONIO (*fl.* 1780–90), scholar and dramatist who edited the 34-vol. *Semanario erudito, que comprende varias obras inéditas, críticas, morales, instructivas, políticas, históricas, satíricas y jocosas de nuestros mejores autores antiguos y modernos* (1787–91), which was continued in 1816 as the *Nuevo semanario erudito*.

His plays, which numbered more than a hundred, were very successful in their day but are now forgotten with the possible exception of *El vinatero de Madrid* (1784). His other works included *Vida interior de Felipe II* (1788), *Historia de la isla de Puerto Rico* (1788), a novel in nine volumes *La Leandra* (1797–1807), and *Almacén de frutos literarios* (1804).

See A. Alcayde y Vilar, *Don Antonio Valladares de [sic] Sotomayor: autor dramático del siglo XVIII y la comedia 'El vinatero de Madrid'* (1915).

VALLADOLID, JUAN DE (1403?–1452?), b. Valladolid. A blind poet of very humble origin, a converted Jew, and called 'Juan Poeta' (Juan the Poet) for his recognized mastery of verse. A minstrel, astrologer, and satirical writer, Juan spent some time at the courts of Mantua and Milan. On his return to Spain by sea, he was captured by Barbary pirates and taken to Fez, where he was held to ransom. He maintained a running verbal battle with the Manrique family. Two satires by Pedro Manrique are directed against Juan, the better being 'Coplas a Juan Poeta cuando le cautivaron sobre el mar y lo llevaron allende'. Gómez Manrique, a much more significant writer, also wrote satires against Juan, among them two in *pie quebrado*: 'En nombre de una mula', and 'Razonamiento de un rocín a su paje'. Satires were also written by Antón de Montoro (1404–1480?). Juan's best-known poem is a set of *Coplas* addressed to Don Álvaro de Luna. Most of his surviving work is collected in the *Cancionero de Stúñiga* and in the *Cancionero de obras de burlas provocantes a risa*.

See E. Motta, 'Giovanni di Valladolid alle corti di Mantova e Milano, 1458–1473' in the *Archivio Storico Lombardo* (Milan), vol. 7 (1890), pp. 938–80; and E. Levi, 'Un juglar español en Sicilia: Juan de Valladolid' in his *Motivos hispánicos* (1933), pp. 75–109.

VALLE, ADRIANO DEL (1895–1958), b. Seville. Poet. Dámaso Alonso, in his introduction to Valle's *Arpa fiel* (1940), reprinted on pp. 168–78 of Alonso's *Del siglo de oro a este siglo de siglas* (1962), wrote that Valle's work 'es vera y actual continuadora de la brillante tradición barroca española del siglo XVII'.

Valle often lacks inspiration, but like most Andalusian poets concentrates on expressing a feeling for colour, and he uses his lexical dexterity in the manner of Quevedo. His books are *Primavera portátil* (Paris, 1934), *Lyra sacra* (40 copies only, Seville, 1939), *Los gozos del río. Homenaje a Debussy* (Barcelona, 1940), *Arpa fiel* (1940), *Sonetos a Italia* (1942), *Misa de alba en Fátima y Gozos de S. Isidro* (1955), *Égloga de Gabriel Miró y Fábula del Peñón de Ifach* (1957), and *Oda náutica a Cádiz* (Cadiz, 1957). The best selection is *Las mejores poesías* (Barcelona, 1955).

See R. Gómez de la Serna, *Nuevos retratos contemporáneos* (Buenos Aires, 1945), pp. 108–19.

VALLE, HÉCTOR DEL, pen-name of Fernando García Vela (q.v.).

VALLE, JOSÉ CECILIO DEL (1780–1834), b. Choluteca. Honduran statesman and journalist who drafted the *Acta de Independencia de Centro América* (Guatemala City, 1821) and edited the influential *El Amigo de la Patria* (1820–22) in Guatemala City, where his family had moved in 1789. He was loyal to the colony until 1821, when he retired on the declaration of Agustín de Iturbide as Emperor of Mexico. Iturbide appointed Valle Minister of Foreign Affairs in 1823 against his will. Nominated president of Guatemala in 1834, he died before taking office. The first edition of his *Obras* contained only his *Escritos políticos* (Tegucigalpa, 1914 [but 1906]; the second was complete in 2 vols. (Guatemala City, 1929–30).

See Rafael Heliodoro Valle (q.v.), *Bibliografía de don José Cecilio del Valle* (Mexico City, 1934) and the anthology *El pensamiento económico de José Cecilio del Valle* (1958).

VALLE, LUIS DEL, pseudonym used by Enrique José Varona (q.v.).

VALLE, RAFAEL HELIODORO (1891–1959), b. Tegucigalpa. Honduran poet, historian, and essayist. He moved to Mexico in 1907 and lived there most of his life, teaching at the Universidad Nacional Autónoma and later running the

Bibliography Section of the Ministry of Education. He was Honduran ambassador in the U.S.A. 1949–55.

His many writings included *El rosal del ermitaño: cuentos de monjas y de arrepentidos* (Coyoacán, 1911), *Como la luz del día: poemas de pasión, amor y sacrificio* (1913), *Ánfora sedienta: poemas* (Mexico City, 1922), bibliographies of José Cecilio del Valle (Mexico City, 1934), Ignacio Manuel Altamirano (Mexico City, 1939), Hernán Cortés (Mexico City, 1953), and Porfirio Barba-Jacob (Bogotá, 1961), *Índice de la poesía centroamericana* (Santiago, Chile, 1941), *Iturbide: varón de Dios* (Mexico City, 1944), an anthology called *Semblanzas de Honduras* (Tegucigalpa, 1947?), *Cristóbal de Olid, conquistador de México y Honduras* (Mexico City, 1950), and *Historia de las ideas contemporáneas en Centro-America* (Mexico City, 1960). Valle's poetry is delicately lyrical, suggestive, and musical, if not profound.

See E. Romero de Valle, *Recuerdo a Rafael Heliodoro Valle en los cincuenta años de su vida literaria* (Mexico City, 1957).

VALLE-ARIZPE, ARTEMIO DE (1888–1961), b. Saltillo, Coahuila. Mexican novelist and historian. A career diplomat, he is credited with creating the historical novel of the Mexican colonial period, alternating his fictional writings with historical monographs. His archaic style was cultivated to reflect the period in both narration and dialogue, growing gradually more idiosyncratic.

The important fictional series of *Tradiciones, leyendas y sucedidos del México Virreinal* began with *Del tiempo pasado* (1932) and ended with the tenth book, *Piedras viejas bajo el sol, Inquisición y crímenes* (1952). A prolific writer of fiction, he also wrote *Ejemplo* (Madrid, 1919), *Vidas milagrosas* (1921), *Doña Leonor de Cáceres y Acevedo, y Cosas tenedes* (Madrid, 1922), *Tres nichos de un retablo* (1936), *Lirios de Flandes* (1938), *Cuentos del México antiguo* (1939), *El Canillitas* (1942), and *La movible inquietud: en México y en otros siglos* (1948). Of his *Obras completas*, vol. 1 appeared in 1959 and vol. 2 in 1962.

VALLE-INCLÁN, RAMÓN MARÍA DEL (1866–1936), b. Ramón Valle Peña at Villanueva de Arosa, Pontevedra. Major novelist and playwright, who was brought up in rural Galicia. After leaving Santiago University without his degree in law, he worked in journalism in Madrid, and then visited Mexico City in 1892, where he worked briefly on *El Universal* and *El Correo Español*. William L. Fichter has edited his journalism as *Publicaciones periódicas ... anteriores a 1895* (Mexico City, 1952). His first book was a collection of mediocre short stories, *Femeninas*

(Pontevedra, 1895), following the publication of which he settled in Madrid, where he led a Bohemian existence and befriended the Barojas, Darío, Benavente, and Azorín, among others. In a café brawl he received a slight wound which turned septic, and his left arm had to be amputated. His modernist period, strongly influenced by Darío, culminates in *Epitalamio* (1897) and the *Sonatas* tetralogy (q.v.): *Sonata de otoño: memorias del Marqués dé Bradomín* (1902); *Sonata de estío* (1903, the same year as two collections of short stories, *Corte de amor* and *Jardín umbrío*); *Sonata de primavera* (1904, the same year as the poetic novel *Flor de santidad* set in 19th-c. Galicia); and *Sonata de invierno* (1905). Taken together, these *sonatas* are an elegant achievement owing much to Darío stylistically; their decadent hero is reminiscent not only of the Don Juan type, but of Nietzsche's Übermensch and of des Esseintes in Huysmans's *À rebours*. They are period pieces which Valle-Inclán was later to dismiss as 'literature fashioned from literature', but they are readable for the fascinating play element and their superb style.

In 1907 he married the actress Josefina Blanco, and visited Navarra to meet veterans of the Second Carlist War and to gather material for his cycle of novels on that period, *Los cruzados de la causa*, *El resplandor de la hoguera*, and *Gerifaltes de antaño* (1908–9). In 1910 he stood as a right-wing candidate for the Cortes, but failed, as he was to fail later as a left-wing candidate after he had dropped his Carlist, pro-aristocratic, and modernist views. In 1916 he travelled to France as war correspondent for *El Imparcial*, rejecting there his naïve glorification of war. *La pipa de kif* (1919) is a book of poems intensifying the play element notable in the *Sonatas*. 'Might not this grotesque muse / ... which exasperates the dull rhetoricians / with its spasmodic shouts / and jumps about showing its legs, / be the modern muse?', exemplifies the mood of his play *Farsa y licencia de la reina castiza* (1922).

His second visit to Mexico in 1921 provided the atmosphere for his first *esperpento* (q.v.) novel, *Tirano Banderas* (q.v., 1926), a truly original work on the theme of dictatorship. He had caused a stir the previous year with two plays: *Divinas palabras* (translated as *Divine words* by T. Faulkner, 1977), set in rural Galicia; and the *esperpento Luces de Bohemia* (q.v., serialized in *España*, July–October 1920). In 1922 he published *Cara de plata*, the last of the trilogy *Comedias bárbaras* which also included *Águila de blasón* (1907) and *Romance de lobos* (1908), plays on the Galician patriarch Don Juan Manuel Montenegro, the last of which shows the souring of Valle-Inclán's attitude towards the old aristocracy.

Los cuernos de don Friolera (1921) is one of the three works to which he actually gave the subtitle *esperpento*, and is a bitter attack on military morals and the decadence of Spain. His habit of publishing fragments of long works in advance gives the reader exceptional insight into his methods of composition: this is especially important in the case of the symbolism and gnosticism of the cycles such as *El ruedo ibérico* (q.v.), a projected nine-volume sequence ostensibly attacking Isabel II and her court but (given the severity of Primo de Rivera's censorship) actually making oblique comments on the corruption and brutality of his own time. Only two volumes of *El ruedo ibérico* were completed: *La corte de los milagros* (1927) and *Viva mi dueño* (1928); a third is unfinished (*Baza de espadas*, serialized in *El Sol* from 1932); and fragments of two others survive: *Fin de un revolucionario* and *El trueno dorado* (the latter edited with notes by G. Fabra Barreiro, 1975).

In 1930 three *esperpentos* were collected as *Martes de carnaval*. He divorced his wife in 1932 and the following year, poor and in bad health, he was given work by the Republican government as director of the Spanish Academy of Fine Arts in Rome, a position he was too ill to occupy. He died outside the Church, a professing communist but apparently nearer to anarchism, in 1936, since when his reputation has risen steadily.

The *Opera omnia* (22 vols., 1912–28) have been superseded by *Obras completas* (2 vols., 1954). There is a generous *Obras escogidas* (1958) with a prologue by G. Gómez de la Serna.

In 1966 his centenary celebrations produced two books of importance: *Estudios reunidos en conmemoración* (La Plata, 1967); and *Ramón del Valle-Inclán: an appraisal of his life and works* (ed. A. N. Zahareas, New York, 1968). Since then the rate of new publications and scholarly interest in Valle-Inclán has greatly increased, quickly outdating José Rubia Barcia's *A bibliography and iconography of Valle-Inclán* (Berkeley, 1960) and Robert Lima's *An annotated bibliography of Ramón del Valle-Inclán* (Philadelphia, 1972).

Introductions to his work include Melchor Fernández Almagro, *Vida y literatura de Valle-Inclán* (1943; revised edn., 1966); Verity Smith, *Ramón del Valle-Inclán* (New York, 1973; written in 1966–7) in Twayne's World Authors series; Manuel Bermejo Marcos, *Valle-Inclán: introducción a su obra* (Salamanca, 1971); and A. Risco, *El demiurgo y su mundo* (1977).

Valle-Inclán's deeply serious attitude to the drama has been explored by E. González López in *El arte dramático de Valle-Inclán* (New York, 1967) and by Sumner N. Greenfield in *Valle-Inclán: anatomía de un teatro problemático* (1972).

VALLEJO, César Abraham (1892–1938), b. Santiago de Chuco. Major Peruvian poet whose importance was underestimated during his lifetime. He grew up in the mountains of North Peru, one of a large family. He attended university in Trujillo during 1913–15, studying literature and writing a thesis, *El romanticismo en la poesía castellana*, and he studied law 1915–17.

In 1918 he went to Lima, and there published his Christian poems *Los heraldos negros* (1918) dominated by the modernismo of Darío and Valdelomar (qq.v.). The book was virtually ignored. On returning to his home in 1920 he was involved, probably innocently, in political disturbances and was imprisoned for $2\frac{1}{4}$ months. This period of confinement produced *Escalas melografiadas* (short stories, 1922) and much of his important second book of poems, *Trilce* (1922; 2nd edn., Madrid, 1930), the title being derived from *triste* and *dulce* ('sad' and 'tender'). *Trilce*, which has been translated by David Smith (New York, 1971) shows Vallejo's surrealistic experiment in neologism and typography. *Fabla salvaje* (1923) is a mediocre psychoanalytical novella on love, jealousy, and madness among the Peruvian Indians.

From 1923 until his death in 1938, Vallejo lived in Paris, with visits to Russia in 1928 and 1929, and occasional visits to Spain. He lived with his wife Georgette in poverty, producing the *Poemas humanos* (Paris, 1939; translated by Clayton Eshleman, New York, 1968), the novel *Tungsteno* (Madrid, 1931), and the complex poem *España, aparta de mí este cáliz* on the Spanish Civil War, first issued in a special number of the review *Nuestra España* in 1938, and then in book form (Mexico City, 1940).

Tungsteno is an unsatisfactory social-realist novel because Vallejo, who was to join the Communist Party in 1931, treated each of his characters as a type, and the 'reportaje novelado' rarely rises to a level higher than anti-U.S. propaganda. *Paco Yunque* (1951) is a sentimental tale of an Indian boy, but Vallejo's mastery over words deserted him in his fiction.

His poetry has been edited by Roberto Fernández Retamar, *Poesías completas* (Havana, 1965), and by F. Moncloa, *Obra poética completa* (1968), superseding the Buenos Aires edition of 1949. His fiction is collected in *Novelas y cuentos completos* (1967).

Vallejo attacks Catholic colonial culture that many South Americans still even unconsciously support, turning violently from the Christocentric poems in *Los heraldos negros* to the idiosyncratic Marxism of *Poemas humanos* which is paradoxically imbued with extreme individualism. As a *mestizo*, he felt himself a victim of racial discrimination; as a convinced Communist, he felt the workers' movement endangered by the

Spanish Civil War. The poems are a desperate cry for justice, for order in a world of chaos. It is possible that Vallejo's unquestioned mastery of most poetic styles may have made possible the flowering of Peruvian poetry in the 1950s–70s; he has certainly had a direct influence on Belli and Ortega (qq.v.) among others. Vol. 3 of Vallejo's *Obras completas* is the *Obra poética completa* (1974).

See Luis Monguió, *César Vallejo, vida y obra, bibliografía, antología* (New York, 1951); Eduardo Bazán, *César Vallejo: dolor y poesía* (Buenos Aires, 1958); Juan Espejo Asturrizaga, *César Vallejo: itinerario del hombre* (1965); Alberto Escobar, *Cómo leer a Vallejo* (1973); A. Ferrari, *El universo poético de César Vallejo* (1974); J. Ortega (ed.), *César Vallejo* (Madrid, 1975); and F. Martínez García, *César Vallejo: acercamiento al hombre y al poeta* (1976).

VALLE (Y) CAVIEDES, Juan del (1652?–1697?), b. Porcuna, Andalusia. Poet and playwright. He was taken to Peru when very young, and returned to Spain at the age of 20 for only 3 years. The son of a wealthy business man, he squandered his inheritance and died an alcoholic.

His allegories are *Entremés del amor alcalde, Baile del amor médico,* and *Baile del amor tahur.* A *conceptista* poet and disciple of Quevedo, he wrote satirical verse (such as *Guerras físicas, proezas medicinales,* against doctors), religious verse (including a *Carta* to Sor Juana Inés de la Cruz, q.v.), and even mystical and lyrical verse. Earlier editions of his works have been superseded by Fr. Ruben Vargas Ugarte's edition of the *Obras* (1947).

See L. F. Xammar, *La poesía de Juan del Valle y Caviedes* (1946); Glen L. Kolb, *Juan del Valle y Caviedes: a study of the life, times, and poetry of a Spanish colonial satirist* (New London, Conn., 1959); and Daniel R. Reedy, *The poetic art of Juan del Valle Caviedes* (Chapel Hill, N.C., 1964).

VALVERDE, José María (1926–   ), b. Valencia de Alcántara, Cáceres. Poet of love, serenity, and religion which he treats with ironic detachment. Valverde belonged to the Juventud Creadora group of poets, and contributed to the reviews *Garcilaso* and *Mensaje.* After teaching appointments in the universities of Rome and Barcelona, he emigrated for political reasons and is now teaching literature in North America; some of his more interesting poems deal with this occupation.

His first book of poems was *Hombre de Dios* (1947). His second collection, *La espera* (1949), won the Primo de Rivera Prize. The poems of his middle age have become more rueful and less self-centred. *Enseñanzas de la edad: poesía 1945–*

1970 (Barcelona, 1971) includes all of his earlier work that he wishes to preserve and a new collection called *Años inciertos.* His style is direct and even colloquial at times. The tone is meditative, and the content rarely deviates from the existential search for God, and man's condition in a strange world. He has translated Hölderlin. His writings on literature include *Guillermo de Humboldt y la filosofía del lenguaje* and *La literatura de Hispanoamérica* (Barcelona, 1977).

VANEGAS ARROYO, Antonio, a leading Mexican publisher of ballads, broadsheets, and songs who employed the outstanding folk artist José Guadalupe Posada (q.v.).

VANEGAS DEL BUSTO, Alejo, see Venegas del Busto, Alejo.

VARAS, Antonio, pseudonym of Juan Pablo Forner (q.v.).

VARELA, Antón Noriega, see Noriega Varela, Antón.

VARELA, *Padre* Félix, b. Havana. Cuban philosopher partly responsible for the educational reforms of the second decade of the 19th c. He was elected to the Cortes of 1821, but was unpopular with the absolutist regime of Fernando VII for his passionate patriotism, and fled to the U.S.A.

Influenced by Descartes and Condillac, his books taught young Cubans how to think, and to express themselves with clarity, brevity, and energy. They include *Instituciones de filosofía* (1812–14) and *Lecciones de filosofía* (1818–20). His most original work was *Cartas a Elpidio sobre la impiedad, la superstición y el fanatismo* (New York, 1835–8), of which the letters on fanaticism were probably never written, since none of them is in fact published in this collection.

VARELA, Florencio (1807–48), b. Buenos Aires. Argentinian liberal journalist and poet, the sixth child of Jacobo Adrián Varela and Encarnación Sanjinés. He was the younger brother of Juan de la Cruz Varela (q.v.), whom he accompanied into exile in Montevideo on the fall of Rivadavia in 1829. The series, *Escritos políticos, económicos y literarios,* were collected by Luis L. Domínguez in 1859. His *Autobiografía* appeared in Montevideo in 1848. He founded *El Comercio del Plata* in Montevideo in 1845. Varela was a classical stylist of the Romantic generation, his best-known work being the ode 'A la libertad de Grecia'.

VARELA, Juan de la Cruz (1794–1839), b. Buenos Aires. Argentinian journalist and poet, the eldest of ten children, and the brother of Florencio Varela (q.v.). In the service of President Rivadavia, he edited the pro-Government *El Centinela, El Mensajero Argentino*, and *El Granizo*. He fled to Montevideo in 1829 with other enemies of the dictator Rosas (such as Gutiérrez and Alberdi, qq.v.) and died there ten years later.

His most important poems are 'Sobre la invención y libertad de la imprenta' and the propagandistic 'Profecía de la grandeza de Buenos Aires', but he destroyed most of his poetry, including the earliest love lyrics and most satirical barbs of his Buenos Aires period. A Latinist by early training, he incorporated versions from Horace and Virgil in his published works, and his neoclassical tragedies were *Dido* (1836) based on the *Aeneid*, and the less success-ful *Argía* (1837), inspired by Alfieri. The best edition of his *Poesías* is in the Colección de Clásicos Argentinos (1943).

VARGAS LLOSA, MARIO (1936–), b. Arequipa. Peruvian novelist of international stature. He attended the Leoncio Prado military school in Lima, graduated from the Universidad de San Marcos there, obtained a doctorate in Madrid in 1958, and lived in Paris until 1966. He taught at London University (Queen Mary College, later moving to King's) and is now resident in Barcelona. He has also lived and taught in the U.S.A.

His novels are exclusively concerned with his own perception of Peru, which is in the some-what pessimistic tradition of S. Salazar Bondy's essay *Lima la Horrible*, though he has generalized that 'the world is *always* wrong; life should *always* change'. Novelists are, in his own words again, 'los profesionales del descontento, los perturbadores conscientes o inconscientes de la sociedad, los rebeldes con causa, los insurrectos irredentos del mundo'.

His first work was the play *La huída* (1952), followed by interesting but unexceptional short stories, *Los jefes* (1958) set in Lima and Piura. It was with the extraordinary *tour de force La ciudad y los perros* (q.v., Barcelona, 1962) that Vargas Llosa achieved prominence. Set in the Leoncio Prado military school that he knew so well, the novel was technically fascinating, switching narrators in a manner at first bewil-dering to the reader, but later most rewarding, since Vargas Llosa believes in giving the reader little more data than the characters have them-selves.

La casa verde (q.v., Barcelona, 1966) is another accomplished novel of great complexity, the 'casa verde' being a brothel, yet in another sense the jungle around the trading post of Santa María de Nieva, and in another the green earth, itself.

Los cachorros: Pichula Cuéllar (Barcelona, 1967) is a novella of adolescence. The hero, castrated as a boy in an accident, tries to develop to a sort of manliness but is unable to live up to the Latin American ideal of *machismo* and is eventually killed in a car crash. An ironic case-study of erotic frustration, the novel is a poetic parable (but in colloquial language) on difficulties of social and sexual adjustment, which is to be read as a comment not only on Cuéllar but also on the Peru (and the world) in which he lived and died. For Vargas Llosa, young Cuéllar personi-fies his country, for which even love may not ultimately be sufficient.

Conversación en 'La Catedral' (1969) is a densely-structured novel set during the period of the dictator Manuel Odría (1948–56), shown here as a time of hypocrisy and corruption. The scene is a sleazy riverside bar ironically called 'La Catedral', and Vargas Llosa's description of Lima at night recalls the equally powerful scenes of Havana by night in *Tres tristes tigres* by the Cuban Guillermo Cabrera Infante (q.v.). Rapidly flickering dialogue at first dazzles the reader like neon lights in a big city: the Faulknerian device is outstandingly successful in showing certain aspects of illusion and reality in raw confusion. The novel reveals the truth below respectability in business and government, showing an almost deterministic approach within a wholly modern narrative form. Vargas Llosa is perhaps the most interesting Peruvian novelist, dealing with the themes of loss of innocence and the collapse of ideals with increasing sophistication.

His latest works include *Pantaleón y las visita-doras* (1973); an absorbing critical work, *Historia secreta de una novela* (Barcelona, 1972); a study of Flaubert's *Madame Bovary* entitled *La orgía perpetua* (1975); *Día domingo* (2nd edn., Buenos Aires, 1976); and *La Tía Julia y el escribidor* (Barcelona,1977).

See José Miguel Oviedo, *Mario Vargas Llosa: la invención de una realidad* (Barcelona, 1970), with a good bibliography; L. A. Díez, *Mario Vargas Llosa's pursuit of the total novel* (1970); H. F. Giacoman (ed.), *Homenaje a Mario Vargas Llosa* (New York, 1971); *Agresión a la realidad* (Tenerife, 1972), critical essays by María Rosa Alonso and others; L. A. Díez (ed.), *Asedios a Vargas Llosa* (Santiago, 1972); J. L. Martín, *La narrativa de Vargas Llosa* (Madrid, 1974); and C. M. Fernández, *Aproximación formal a la novelística de Vargas Llosa* (1977).

VARGAS PONCE, JOSÉ DE (1760–1821), b. Cádiz. Historian and poet. Naval officer. His best-known work is a *Declamación contra los abusos introducidos en el castellano . . .* (1791). His histori-cal work is concerned mainly with the Spanish

Navy. The BAE vol. 67 (1875) publishes much of his poetry, which is predominantly burlesque, as in the *octavas reales* of *Proclama de un solterón a las que aspiren a su mano* (Marseilles, 1827).

His correspondence has been studied by, among others, J. Guillén y Tato in *Perfil humano del capitán de fragata de la Real Armada don José de Vargas Ponce a través de su correspondencia epistolar, 1760–1821* (1961).

VARGAS TEJADA, Luis (1802–39), b. Bogotá. Colombian poet, playwright, and polemicist. He was involved in an unsuccessful conspiracy to assassinate Bolívar on 25 September 1828. The plotters met in his house; after the plot's failure, Vargas Tejada sought refuge in the Ticla hacienda for more than a year, then fled farther away, and was drowned while crossing one of the eastern rivers.

His *Monólogo de Catón en Utica* (Bogota?, 1826?) was considered the best hendecasyllabic ballad of its time, and was recited by Colombian students as a hymn to liberty. He was probably the pro-masonic author of the *octavas Contestación al Gallo de San Pedro que leyó su autor en una tertulia,* the *décimas Contestación del Pollo masón al Gallo anti-masónico* (n.d. but both 1823), and may have been the author of *Fábulas políticas* against Bolívar also attributed to José Scarpetta Roó (author of the burlesque poem *La Boliviada*).

Of his five recorded tragedies, only two are known to survive: *Sugamuxi* (1826) and *Doraminta* (1827). His *sainete Las convulsiones,* based on *Le convulsioni* by Francesco Albergatti Capacelli, has been translated into English in *Plays of the Southern Americas* published by the Dramatists' Alliance of Stanford University (1942).

Poesías de Caro i Vargas Tejada (2 vols., 1857) devotes vol. 2 to the poetry of Vargas Tejada.

VARGAS VILA, José María (1860–1933), b. Bogotá. Colombian novelist whose novels, ungrammatical and badly constructed, enjoyed a tremendous popularity. Rafael Maya's view was that Vargas Vila 'desconocía por completo el arte de novelar' and nowadays his books are forgotten. A defiant atheist and violently opposed to the U.S.A., Vargas Vila was a man of great energy and prejudice. His first novel was *Aura, o las violetas* (1886), followed by many more, including *Flor de fango* (1895), his own favourite *Ibis* (1899), *Las rosas de la tarde* (1900), *La caída del Cóndor* (1913), *María Magdalena* (1917), *El huerto del silencio* (1917), *Salomé* (1918), and *El Minotauro* (1919) which dealt with abortion, politics, and exile.

See A. Andrade Coelho, *Vargas Vila: ojeada crítica de sus obras* (Quito, 1912); and Victoriano Luis Besseiro, *Un hombre libre: Vargas Vila, su vida y su obra* (Buenos Aires, 1924).

VARONA, Enrique José (1849–1933), b. Camagüey. Minor Cuban poet and prose-writer, whose collected *Obras* began publication in 1936 but are not yet complete.

His verse includes *Odas anacreónticas* (1868) and *Poesías* (1878). *Poemitas en prosa* (1912) was influenced by Rabindranath Tagore. In prose he wrote, under the pseudonym 'Luis del Valle', *Estudios literarios y filosóficos* (1873), *Artículos y discursos* (1881), *Desde mi belvedere* (1907) consisting of 56 articles written mainly in New York between 1894 and 1906, and *De mis recuerdos* (1917).

VASCONCELOS, José (1882–1959), b. Oaxaca. Mexican philosopher, statesman, and sociological writer. The title of his *Todología* (1952) is a neologism for his 'study of everything', which is in fact more of a philosophical system than an encyclopaedia. He qualified as an advocate in 1907, campaigned for Madero and Villa, was nominated Rector of the National University on the triumph of the Revolution, and was made Secretary of Public Education, 1921–24. He later went into exile in the U.S.A. and Europe. After failing in his final bid to become President, he edited the Biblioteca México until his death.

Influenced early by Schopenhauer, and later by Bergson, Vasconcelos produced a series of stimulating works: *Pitágoras, una teoría del ritmo* (1916); *El monismo estético* (1918); the highly controversial but fascinating *La raza cósmica* (1925) and *Indología* (1926), both of which predicted that Spanish America, and in particular the Indian race, will inherit the future; *De Robinsón a Odiseo* (1935); and one of the masterpieces of Latin-American autobiography, the tetralogy *Ulises criollo* (1935), *La tormenta* (1936), *El desastre* (1938), and *El proconsulado* (1939). His *Obras completas* (1957–61) are in 4 vols.

See G. De Beer, *José Vasconcelos and his world* (1966).

VAZ FERREIRA, Carlos (1872–1958), b. Montevideo. Uruguayan philosopher of the Generation of 1900. He became Rector of Montevideo University. A positivist of the John Stuart Mill school, he followed Mill's inductive logic in *Lógica viva* (1910) and later was influenced by William James and Henri Bergson. He was given to Socratic self-questioning, and his students much appreciated ideas such as those in *Fermentario* (1938), a deliberately fragmentary record of his thought. His first book was the precocious *Psicología experimental* (1897); this was followed by *Cuestiones escolares* (1902), *Ideas y observaciones* (1905), *Los problemas de la libertad* (1907), *Moral para intelectuales* (1908), *La exageración y el simplismo en pedagogía* (1908),

Lecciones sobre pedagogía (1918), *Estudios pedagógicos* (1921), *Sobre los problemas sociales* (1922), and the radical *Sobre feminismo* (1933).

VAZ FERREIRA, María Eugenia (1875–1924), b. Montevideo. Uruguayan poet of exquisite sensibility and unusual intensity; her belated Romantic poetry of subjective melancholy gradually changed, as she developed, to symbolist rhythms and Parnassian opulence of imagery. A disciple of Heine, she drew her themes from beauty (in 'Oda a la belleza'), night, twilight, and the sea. The posthumous publication of *La isla de los cánticos* (1925) was followed by that of *La nueva isla de los cánticos* (1959).

Her two plays, 'La piedra filosofal' (first performed in 1908) and 'Los peregrinos' (1909), were unsuccessful, neither achieving publication.

VÁZQUEZ, José, the pen-name of Cadalso (q.v.) in his *Los eruditos a la violeta* (1772).

VÁZQUEZ DE PARRA IGLESIAS, Luis (1908–), b. Madrid. Deputy Director of the Museo Arqueológico Nacional in Madrid. His most significant contribution to medieval studies was the monumental *Las peregrinaciones a Santiago de Compostela* (3 vols., 1948), written with J. Uría y Ríu (q.v.) and J. M. Lacarra.

VEGA, Alonso de la (*c.* 1510–*c.* 1565), b. Seville. Playwright, who was for some time an actor in the company of Lope de Rueda (q.v.). Joan de Timoneda (q.v.) published Vega's three prose plays: *Las tres famosísimas comedias del ilustre poeta y gracioso representante Alonso de la Vega* (Valencia, 1566). There is a modern edition by M. Menéndez y Pelayo (*Tres comedias*, Halle, 1905).

The *Comedia Tholomea* is a thin play on the resemblance between two men, both called Tolomeo. The *Tragedia Serafina* is an unsuccessful compound of pastoral and mythological elements marred by inept comic insertions. Vega's best extant work is the *Comedia de la duquesa de la rosa*, inspired by Bandello's story *Amore di Don Giovanni di Mendozza e della Duchessa di Savoja* and the seventh *patraña* of Timoneda.

VEGA, Bernardo de la (1560–1625), b. Seville. Poet, novelist, and travel-writer. His chivalresque poem *La bella Cotalda y cerco de París* induced Cervantes to place him in the army of bad poets infesting the holy mountain in his *Viaje del Parnaso*, while the priest in *Don Quijote* (Pt. I, ch. vi) consigned his novel *El pastor de Iberia* (1591) to the flames without comment. Vega also wrote the much more interesting

Relación de las grandezas del Perú, Mexico y Los Angeles (Mexico City, 1601) about his journeys in Latin America, where he eventually became a priest.

VEGA, Garcilaso de la, see Garcilaso de la Vega.

VEGA, Ricardo de la (1839–1910), b. Madrid. Playwright and civil servant, the son of Ventura de la Vega (q.v.). Possibly the most distinguished of the many *género chico* writers. *La canción de la Lola* (1880), with music by Valverde and Chueca, was his most popular work until 1886, the year of *Pepa la frescachona, o el colegial desenvuelto*, a colourful *sainete*. His characters were the men and women of Madrid in their familiar settings, providing for the middle class light entertainment such as *El señor Luis el tumbón, o Despacho de huevos frescos* (1891; first published in 1894) and *La verbena de la paloma, o El boticario y las chulapas, y Celos mal reprimidos* (1894) with music by Bretón, this time set among the lower classes, a *sainete* performed more than 25,000 times.

See J. Deleito y Piñuela, *Origen y apogeo del género chico* (1949) and P. Lozano Guirao, *Vida y obras de Ricardo de la Vega*, a dissertation for the University of Madrid, 1959.

Vega, Santos, a *payador* or *gaucho* minstrel who, in Argentinian legend, had been outsung in a contest by the Devil, and thenceforth travelled like a soul in purgatory throughout the countryside.

His story was told first by Bartolomé Mitre, then by Hilario Ascasubi (see Santos Vega), Eduardo Gutiérrez, and Rafael Obligado (qq.v.).

VEGA, Ventura de la (1807–65), b. Buenos Aires. Playwright, whose full name was Buenaventura José María Vega y Cárdenas. He left Argentina for Spain in 1818, after his father died. Educated at the Colegio de San Mateo, he became a pupil of Alberto Lista (q.v.) and later taught literature to Isabel II, having made his name at the age of 19 by translations of the Song of Songs (1825) and of the Psalms (1826).

His plays reveal the influence of various dramatists, but his favourite manner was that of Leandro Fernández de Moratín (q.v.). He adapted many plays from the French (Dumas, Hugo, Scribe) but his best work was in the theatre of social criticism, continuing the work of Bretón and anticipating Adelardo López de Ayala and Benavente (qq.v.) in his drawing-room comedies. Such a play is *El hombre de mundo* (1845), a four-act play first performed privately, which deals with the professed 'man of the world' who is tormented by jealousy of his wife. From this verse play came the popular saying 'Todo Madrid lo sabía, todo Madrid menos él'.

See J. H. Mundy and Edgar Allison Peers, *Ventura de la Vega and the Justo Medio in drama* (Liverpool, 1940); J. Montero Alonso, *Ventura de la Vega: su vida y su tiempo* (Madrid, 1951); and J. I. Luca de Tena, 'Semblanza literaria y social de Ventura de la Vega' in *BRAE*, vol. 45 (1965), pp. 385–93.

VEGA CARPIO, LOPE DE (1562–1635), b. Madrid. Spain's most important and prolific dramatist, and one of the world's leading writers for the stage. In the posthumously-published *Égloga a Claudio* (1637), which contains much critical and bibliographical data, Lope states that more than 100 of his plays had been written in less than a day each, and that the total exceeded 1,500 plays, though only a third of this total survive today. And whereas Cervantes concentrated most of his world-view and abilities into a single work, the fecund 'Fénix' (as Lope de Vega Carpio was often called) expressed himself fluently and poetically in numerous works, many of them non-dramatic, such as *La Dorotea* (q.v.), *La Arcadia* (q.v.), or lyric verse.

Lope was born to Félix, a man of Santander, who escaped from his family in Valladolid to settle himself in Madrid with a Greek girl called Helen; his wife followed the couple to Madrid and managed to separate them.

Lope's early years are obscure, though Pérez de Montalbán wrote in the *Fama póstuma* (*Colección de obras sueltas*, vol. 20, 1779) that Lope could read Spanish and even Latin easily at the age of five but, not yet able to write, dictated poetry to the boys who could. The Madrid school he attended was run by Vicente Espinel (q.v.), the celebrated author of the *Vida del escudero Marcos de Obregón*, after which he graduated to the Jesuits' School, where he was taught grammar and rhetoric, and to the Academia Real, where he probably learnt mathematics and astronomy.

He entered the service of Jerónimo Manrique, Bishop of Ávila, to whom he dedicated several poems, and probably studied in Alcalá University 1577–1581 at the bishop's expense; it is also possible that, having left Alcalá without finishing his studies due to a love affair, he spent some time at Salamanca University before enlisting in the Marquis of Santa Cruz's expedition to conquer Terceira, the only one of the Azores to resist Spanish administration after the annexation of Portugal. On his return after two months, Lope fell wildly in love with Elena Osorio (wife of the actor Cristóbal Calderón and daughter of the actor Jerónimo Velázquez), the 'Filis' of numerous lyrics and the 'Dorotea' of *La Dorotea*.

Their affair lasted five years, and continued clandestinely even after Elena's mother forbade Lope to see her as he was to be replaced by an influential, wealthy nephew of Cardinal Granvela. In 1587 some scurrilous poems against the Velázquez family were ascribed to Lope, he was imprisoned, and sentenced to eight years of exile from the capital, and two years from Castile. But he defied the threat of death by returning to Madrid to seduce Isabel de Urbina, an aristocrat. Their marriage was arranged by proxy, since Lope was legally barred from entering the city. A few weeks later, on 29 May 1588, Lope set sail with the Armada after a casual affair in Lisbon, and on board the *San Juan* wrote poems to Isabel as 'Belisa' as well as part of his chivalresque poem *La hermosura de Angélica*. He survived the fate of many of his companions, and on returning to Spain went with Isabel to Valencia, where he achieved renown as a ballad-writer (1588–91) and wrote his early plays, sending them to the impresario Gaspar de Porres in Madrid. In 1590 (when he was permitted to enter the kingdom once more), he moved to Toledo as secretary of the Duke of Alba. These five years, mostly spent at the ducal residence of Alba de Tormes, permitted him to become better acquainted with the university life of Salamanca which he portrayed in the play *El dómine Lúcas*, later taken as a model in a better play of the same title by José de Cañizares (q.v.). This is also the period of Lope's *La Arcadia*, the literary source being Sannazaro and the atmosphere that of Alba de Tormes. In 1594 his wife died in giving birth to their second daughter, who also died, and the following year Lope returned from Alba to Madrid, having benefited from a reprieve requested by Jerónimo Velázquez. But in 1596 Lope was again harassed, this time for illicit union with the widow Antonia Trillo. In 1598 he married Juana de Guardo, for money rather than for love according to his jealous rivals, because before that he had written love poems to 'Camila Lucina', the actress Micaela de Luján, and after his second marriage he lived with her while Juana lived in Toledo: he had five children by Micaela and three by Juana. The scandal was heightened by his prolific, transparent love poetry to Micaela (which disappeared in 1608). In 1610 he moved house permanently from Toledo and Seville to Madrid, living with his patient wife and family there for the rest of his life, and composing there his most enduring works. In 1613 Juana died, shortly after the death of their son Carlos Félix at the age of 7. He then brought his illegitimate children Marcela and Lope Félix to live with him and, even while indulging in various illicit affairs, prepared for ordination as a priest in 1614. This turn of events can hardly be considered hypo-critical in Lope, for a man of such towering passions was capable too of extraordinary self-abasement. In 1616 he fell passionately in love with Marta de Nevares Santoyo (a woman of 26 with a good education, married to a coarse businessman), and celebrated her love with a cascade of love poems—and a daughter. Her husband had barely realized that all Madrid was laughing at him, when he died unexpec-tedly, and Lope cruelly celebrated this turn of events with joking verses. Marta went to live with Lope, who continued his astoundingly prolific work. Marta gradually became blind, Micaela's daughter Marcela left Lope's home for the Convent of the Barefoot Trinitarians, and in 1628 Marta lost her reason, and died in 1632. Lope's fame was growing, but his poverty was never relieved. Lope Félix, Micaela's son, was drowned on a pearl-fishing expedition. Antonia Clara, Marta's daughter, was seduced at the age of 17 by Cristóbal Tenorio, a protégé of the Conde-Duque de Olivares, causing Lope the same grief that he caused so many others. Lope died in 1635, his funeral paid for by the Duque de Sessa, whose correspondence with Lope remains our most vital private source for the poet's thoughts and feelings.

Lope de Vega's life and loves gave ample scope for the most varied autobiographical treatment in his work; this element is most pronounced in *La Dorotea*, a major novel in dialogue based partly on the *Celestina* and partly on his own life.

His poetry, of whatever form (and he practised most), is full of lyricism: he is supreme in sonnets, ballads, and songs (*canciones*), and even his epics, novels, and many plays are full of lyrical fragments and full lyrics which stem from his life and not, as with the verses of so many of his contemporaries and followers, from mere imitation or artifice. The transparent mundane loves and ardent repentance shown alternately in the *Poesías líricas* (2 vols. in Clásicos Castella-nos, 1926–7, expertly edited from the vast reserves by José F. Montesinos) are expressed in a torrent of music, simple, vivid, and unquestion-ably authentic. *La Vega del Parnaso* (1637) con-tains his lyrical poetry collected by his friends and relatives, but Lope did not consider himself purely a 'poet' like Garcilaso or his literary enemy Góngora (q.v.).

His ballads, which he was to continue writing all his life, are especially abundant in his early period, when he sang with freshness and ardour of his barely-disguised love for Elena Osorio, exile, marriage to Isabel de Urbina, and other affairs. They were scattered in early collections, and many were brought together in the *Romancero general* of 1600 and 1604. They are

about 50 in number. His religious ballads were compiled for *Rimas sacras* and the *Romancero espiritual*.

His sonnets are more numerous than those of any other writer in Spanish, and of outstanding excellence, benefiting from the rigid format and being divided, usually, into two dramatic parts, of rising tensions (the quartets) and lowering tensions (the tercets). Lope's first 200 sonnets appeared with the Italianate *La hermosura de Angélica* and the epic *Dragontea* in *La hermosura de Angélica con otras diversas rimas* (1602). His major influence, especially in those sonnets dedicated to Micaela de Luján, was that of Petrarch.

A hundred sonnets form the major part of *Rimas sacras* (1614), possibly his most successful religious work.

Lope's remaining poetic work includes epistles, eclogues, odes, and songs. The epistles, many published in *El jardín de Lope de Vega* (1621–4), tell us much of his life, his family, and his opinions, usually literary. The best of the eclogues is *Amarilis* (1633), written after the death of his beloved Marta de Nevares. Of the songs, the best-known is '¡Oh libertad preciosa!' in *La Arcadia*, one of the frequent imitations of Horace's *Beatus ille*.

His didactic narrative poems include *Laurel de Apolo*, in which he discusses with great brevity, and often unfairly, more than 280 Spanish and Portuguese poets, and many French and Italian. *La Gatomaquia*, a splendid burlesque of the literary epic, was first published in the *Rimas divinas y humanas del licenciado Tomé de Burguillos* (1634; ed. by J. M. Blecua, Barcelona, 1976). The story concerns the wicked cat Marrama-quiz, intent on frustrating the love of Micifuf for Zapaquilda. Marramaquiz ambushes the wedding party, seizes Zapaquilda, and cedes her only when his castle is surrounded by the ultimately victorious friends of Micifuf. Less happy in execution are the tedious mythological poems so popular in their day such as *La Circe* (with more than 3,000 lines) and *La rosa blanca*, composed in praise of the daughter of the Conde-Duque de Olivares.

Lope's epic in ten cantos on Sir Francis Drake, *La Dragontea* (Valencia, 1598; 2 vols., Burgos, 1935), is a very long-winded attack on Drake, Hawkins, Queen Elizabeth I, Protestantism, and England, and shows the religious, political, and nationalistic chauvinism of Lope at its most typical. Lope's enemy Góngora remarked: 'What a small streak of lightning for such a loud clap of thunder!', again showing that Lope's strength is in the intimate, popular, and lyrical and not in the bombastic, recherché, and epic. *El Isidro* (1599) is another work which has not stood the test of time. In praise of the patron saint of Madrid, it is repetitive (especially about the saint's humble origins and illiteracy) and tedious in its *quintilla* rhyme-scheme.

Lope's Italianate epics consist of twenty cantos each: *La hermosura de Angélica* (Seville, 1602), indebted to Ariosto and interesting for the revelation of his love for Micaela de Luján; and *La Jerusalén conquistada* (1609), indebted to Tasso but differing from its original in placing Spain squarely at the geographical centre of the Christian struggle against the Saracen.

The novels rarely surpass those of other writers of the day. For example, *La Arcadia* (1598) follows the established tradition of Montemayor and Gil Polo, excelling in descriptions of nature, but otherwise of interest only for the pseudo-literary problem of identifying the real people portrayed by the main characters.

El peregrino en su patria (Seville, 1604) is in the moribund tradition of the Byzantine novel, with four *autos sacramentales* inappropriately inserted, and an important autobibliography listing 219 plays written by Lope up to that date.

Los pastores de Belén (1612) was described by the author as an *Arcadia a lo divino*, but in retrospect it seems superior for the popular elements in metrical forms and characterization.

Lope's four *Novelas a Marcia Leonardo* (by which name that of Marta de Nevares is disguised) were apparently written at her request urging her lover to emulate the success of Cervantes' *novelas ejemplares*. *Las fortunas de Diana* was included in *La Filomena* (1621) and three more in *La Circe* (1624): *La desdicha por la honra*, *La prudente venganza*, and *Guzmán el bravo*. These novels offer a curious testimony of Lope's love for Marta, since he frequently 'talks' to her while the fiction is in progress.

La Dorotea (1632) is incomparably Lope's best and most mature prose work, of absorbing autobiographical interest and yet a work of literature that shows clear origins in the *Celestina* tradition and the *honor* plays. The intercalation of poetry is well achieved, adding elegance and melancholy to the course of the plot.

Lope's plays form the basis of a national theatre; even without the contributions of Calderón, Rojas Zorrilla, and 'Tirso de Molina' (qq.v.), Spanish drama of the Golden Age would rival that of any country in the world. His incredible fecundity drew on themes of every description and from many countries and periods. The fact that he is at his most lyrical and dramatic when writing within the Spanish historical and religious tradition should not detract from an understanding of his universality.

His dramatic theories are to be found in the *Arte nuevo de hacer comedias* (q.v., 1609), read before a Madrid literary society to justify his mature fame as a popular playwright.

Such justification was needed against the perpetual attacks on his *drama nacional* by such writers as Francisco de Cascales (q.v.), for the neoclassic movement had begun as early as 1605 and gained strength for the rest of the first quarter of the century (see J. de Entrambasaguas, 'Una guerra literaria del Siglo de Oro' in his *Estudios sobre Lope de Vega*, vol. 1, 1946, pp. 63–580, and vol. 2, 1947, pp. 7–411).

In later life, Lope frequently professed himself dissatisfied with his plays, stating that he had to write five large sheets (*pliegos*) every day to earn his living, and wrote quickly for money. Though there is some truth in this, his high lyrical quality and keen dramatic sense turned whatever he wrote for the stage into a memorable event, and those scholars who have read a majority of the 501 plays attributed to Lope are constantly rewarded. He published a selection of his plays only relatively late in life, and then merely for the immediate purpose of rejecting pirated versions or plays by other hands attributed to him as the most popular playwright of the day. The *partes* of his collected plays which appeared without his personal sanction were I–VIII (1604–17); he then published parts IX to XX, and his son-in-law Luis de Usátegui parts XXI–XXV. But most of the plays have come down to us in defective acting editions if at all. There is no complete edition of the surviving plays. M. Menéndez y Pelayo's *Obras completas de Lope de Vega* (15 vols., 1890–1913) contains only drama, and is not even completed by the continuation in 13 vols. (1916–30) by E. Cotarelo and Mori. Many of the texts are unsatisfactory. An incomplete but still large collection of Lope's non-dramatic works appeared in the *Colección de las obras sueltas* (21 vols., 1776–79). A selection of the secular plays are in vols. 24, 34, 41, and 52 and some religious plays in vols. 58 and 157 of the BAE, but again Lope has not been well served by his editor, here Juan Eugenio Hartzenbusch (q.v.). Reliable critical editions of single plays are gradually appearing but the common reader's current best selection is the *Obras escogidas* edited by F. C. Saínz de Robles (1946, vol. 1, the plays; vol. 2, some poetry, prose, and fiction). A new edition of the *Obras completas* (vol. 1, *Obras no dramáticas*, 1965) is being undertaken by J. de Entrambasaguas, author of *Vivir y crear de Lope de Vega* (1961).

Difficulties of attribution and the cautious attitude of modern scholars have reduced the number of extant *comedias* definitely by Lope to 314. Of the 187 others attributed to him, 27 are probably his, 73 possibly his, and 87 probably not his.

In their valuable *Cronología de las comedias de Lope de Vega* (1968), S. Griswold Morley and

Courtney Bruerton have established Lope's chronological development by analysing the different types of strophe in the authentic, dated plays (with other evidence) to give tentative dates to otherwise undated plays, and to eliminate from the corpus those works which in their opinion do not appear to be his.

One classification of his plays, by theme, is that of M. Menéndez y Pelayo, but this has been challenged many times and seems less valuable now than when it was first propounded. The most important category consists of *comedias de capa y espada*, amorous cloak-and-dagger plays. These are basically plays of intrigue familiar since Plautus and Terence, and Lope is a supreme exponent in such examples as *Los melindres de Belisa* (1606–8), in which a wilful girl and her snobbish mother fall in love with a man they believe to be a slave, and *La dama boba* (q.v., 1613; ed. by D. Marín, 1976). Others of this kind are *El acero de Madrid*, *La noche toledana*, and—possibly his last play—*Las bizarrías de Belisa*.

Bances Candamo called the aristocratic version of the cloak-and-dagger play the *comedia de fábrica* and, if we accept his distinction, then the best of this type is *El perro del hortelano* (1613–15), which in the popular saying 'no come ni deja comer' (the dog in the manger, neither eating nor allowing others to eat). This refers to the Countess of Belflor, who is in love with her secretary Teodoro but snobbishly decides she cannot marry him, yet forbids his marriage to Marcela. Teodoro's servant, the *gracioso* Tristán, brilliantly saves her master's life and the Countess's love by telling her aristocratic suitors that Teodoro is in fact a Count. Diana is not convinced by the lie, but the irony which was lost on neither Lope nor his audience was that by lying, Teodoro would be able to marry a Countess and thus become a true Count. Honour is thus itself called into question. Others in this genre are *La moza de cántaro* (before 1618; partly revised, 1625), and *La hermosa fea* (*c.* 1630) in which a haughty noblewoman is won by a prince's feigned disdain, her beauty being repeatedly insulted.

His plays based on poems or romances of chivalry include *El marqués de Mantua* (*c.* 1600) and *La mocedad de Roldán* (*c.* 1601).

Lope wrote many plays on biblical themes and on the lives or legends of popular saints. Churchmen were revolted by the sight of often dissolute actors impersonating biblical characters, but there is no doubting the pious intention of Lope, Calderón, Tirso, and other contemporary writers on biblical themes. Perhaps Lope's finest play of this type is *La hermosa Ester* (1610), dramatizing the book of Esther. Others are *La historia de Tobías* (1606–15) and *El robo de Dina* (1615–22) on Shechem's rape of Dinah and the vengeance of Jacob's sons.

Plays about saints include *Lo fingido verdadero* (*c.* 1608) on the conversion and martyrdom of St. Genesius under Diocletian; *El divino africano* (*c.* 1610) on the conversion of St. Augustine; and the astonishing, amusing *La buena guarda* (1610), in which a nun's elopement with her lover is not noticed since an angel, rewarding her for unceasing devotions to the Virgin Mary, takes the nun's place until she returns.

Lope's immense range as a historical dramatist can be judged by his choice of themes, from ancient Persia–*Contra valor no hay desdicha* (*c.* 1625–30)—to Neronian Rome–*Roma abrasada* (*c.* 1598–1600)—and contemporary Eastern Europe—*El Gran Duque de Moscovia y El emperador perseguido* (1606?). But most of his plays on historical themes concern the Peninsula, and lessons to be drawn from past errors. These include *El postrer godo de España* (1599–1603) from Visigothic times; *El bastardo Mudarra* (1612) on the *Siete Infantes de Lara* (q.v.) story; *El Duque de Viseo*, a great universal tragedy with a Portuguese setting; and *Fuenteovejuna* (q.v., 1612–14), perhaps Lope's most famous single work, which is a paean to justice and 'honour for everyman, no matter what his social status', again based on a historical incident.

Other plays on peasant honour and the pleasures of rural life (played almost solely in the *corrales* of Madrid) include *El mejor alcalde, el rey* (q.v., 1620–3), *El villano en su rincón* (q.v., 1611), and the marvellously subtle *Peribáñez y el Comendador de Ocaña* (q.v., 1605–8?).

Some specialists claim that Lope's finest play is *El caballero de Olmedo* (q.v., 1615–26), a tragedy stemming from *La Celestina* and a haunting popular refrain.

The uncritical *Ensayo de una bibliografía de las obras y artículos sobre la vida y escritos de Lope de Vega Carpio* (1955) by J. Simón Díaz and J. de José Prades is the most exhaustive available and has been supplemented by *Nuevos estudios, adiciones al Ensayo . . .* (1961). More useful for the period cited because of its critical annotation is *Lope de Vega studies, 1937–1962* (Toronto, 1964) by Jack H. Parker and others.

Lope's letters have been edited by Agustín de G. Amezúa in *Lope de Vega en sus cartas* (4 vols., 1935–43). Books on Lope are generally not as distinguished as those on Cervantes or other major writers of the Golden Age. The best are Hugo Albert Rennert's *Life of Lope de Vega* (Glasgow, 1904) as revised by Américo Castro in the Spanish edition, *Vida de Lope de Vega* (1919); Karl Vossler's *Lope de Vega und sein Zeitalter* (Munich, 1932; translated by R. Gómez de la Serna, 1933; 2nd edn., 1940, as *Lope de*

Vega y su tiempo); and Alonso Zamora Vicente's *Lope de Vega, su vida y su obra* (1961).

M. Menéndez y Pelayo's *Estudios sobre el teatro de Lope de Vega* (6 vols., Santander, 1949) must now be read with Morley and Bruerton's *Cronología de las comedias de Lope de Vega* (1968). Countless articles in the scholarly journals testify to the inexhaustible fascination and problems of Lope's writings, authentic or dubious. A short but essential selection of such articles has been collected by José F. Gatti in *El teatro de Lope de Vega* (Buenos Aires, 1962), concentrating on *Peribáñez, Fuenteovejuna*, and *El villano en su rincón*.

See F. M. Clark, *Objective methods for testing authenticity and the study of ten doubtful comedies attributed to Lope de Vega* (Chapel Hill, N.C., 1971); and H. Gerstinger, *Lope de Vega and Spanish drama* (1974).

VEGAS SEMINARIO, FRANCISCO (1903–   ), b. Piura. Peruvian short-story writer and novelist in the *criollista* tradition. His quick, careless writing is in the manner of Dumas and Manzoni, but lacks craftsmanship or innovation. His stories of the jungle, coast, and sierra are collected in *Chicha, sol y sangre* (1946) and *Entre algarrobos* (1955). His first novel was *Montoneras* (1953), set in the Peru of 1893–5. It was succeeded by the cynical tale of political intrigue and deception *El honorable Pinciano* (1957) and *El retablo de los ilusos* (1960).

But Vegas Seminario achieved wider recognition for a detailed fictional defence of Marshal Lamar in the Peru of 1825–34, the trilogy consisting of *Cuando los mariscales combatían* (1959), *Bajo el signo de la Mariscala* (1960), and *La gesta del caudillo* (1961).

VEINTIMILLA DE GALINDO, DOLORES (1821–57), b. Quito. A Romantic poet whose works were posthumously collected in *Producciones literarias* (1908). At the age of 18 she married a Colombian doctor, Sixto Galindo, and accompanied him to Guayaquil and Cuenca. She took part in literary debates in these towns, causing controversy in Cuenca when she agitated for the acquittal of the condemned native parricide Tiburcio Lucero. Slander quickly gathered about her; pamphlets were circulated to defame and support her, and the 'Sappho of Ecuador' as she was known was so profoundly affected by the rumours that she took her own life.

VELA, DAVID (1901–   ), b. Guatemala City. Literary critic and historian. He was chief editor of *El Imparcial* 1926–31 and 1935–44, becoming director in 1944. His best-known book is *Literatura guatemalteca* (2 vols., 1943–4), but he has also written an interesting novel: *Un personaje sin novela* (Mexico City, 1958), in which his hero is merely a pretext for discussions on philosophical, political, and other topics.

VELA, EUSEBIO (1688–1737), playwright who was born in Spain but emigrated to Mexico. Most of his fourteen *comedias* are lost, but *Tres comedias* (1948) includes texts and studies of *Si el amor excede al arte, ni amor ni arte a la prudencia*, about Telemachus on the isle of Calypso; *Apostolado en las Indias y martirio de un cacique*, a patriotic extravaganza in praise of Cortés, St. James, and Franciscan missionaries; and *La pérdida de España por una mujer*, yet another play on Rodrigo, last of the Goths. All are in three acts, and all take the Calderonian model to excess, using spectacle, machinery, and crowd scenes to offset a lack of wit and dramatic polish, characteristic of the fading Golden Age.

See Armando de María y Campos, *Andanzas y picardías de Eusebio Vela* (1944).

VELA, FERNANDO GARCÍA (1888–   ), b. Oviedo. Essayist. A disciple of José Ortega y Gasset (q.v.), he was secretary of *Revista de Occidente* (q.v.) from 1923. He has translated from French literature and from German philosophy. Among his volumes of essays are *El arte del cubo y otros ensayos* (1927), *El futuro imperfecto* (1934), *El grano de pimienta* (1950), and *Circunstancias* (1953). Using the pen-name 'Hector del Valle', Vela has written biographies of Mozart and Talleyrand (both 1943).

VELARDE, JOSÉ (1849–92), b. Conil, Cádiz. Minor poet who collaborated with Juan A. Cavestany in the historical play *Pedro el Bastardo* (1888). *Teodomiro, o la Cueva de Cristo* (1879) is a 'legend' (*leyenda*) imitating those by Zorrilla (q.v.). Originally a pure lyric poet, Velarde experimented with the didactic and realistic modes. *Voces del alma* (1884), harshly reviewed by Leopoldo Alas ('Clarín'), is a selection of his work, superseded by *Obras poéticas* (2 vols., 1887).

VELASCO, *Padre* JUAN DE (1727–92), b. Riobamba. Ecuadorian Jesuit priest, anthologist, and historian. Exiled in 1767 by order of Carlos III with the other Jesuits, Velasco went to Faenza and, trusting to his own memory and imagination, produced *Historia del reyno de Quito* (1789) which Benjamin Carrión somewhat disparagingly called 'the first novel of Ecuador'. In this fanciful account, the Emperor Huayna Cápac marries Queen Shiri of Quito for love, thus making peace between their countries. Their son Atahuallpa conquers his stepbrother Huáscar, a child of a loveless, arranged marriage. The political symbolism is neither subtle nor convincing, but satisfied Velasco's uncritical audience.

Velasco's *Colección de poesías varias, hecha por un ocioso en la ciudad de Faenza* (1790) contained Spanish, Latin, and Italian poems by exiles, including Ramón Viescas, the brothers Ambrosio and Joaquín Larrea, Mariano Andrade, José Orozco, and himself.

VELÁZQUEZ DE VELASCO, Alfonso (*c.* 1560–*c.* 1620), b. Valladolid. Playwright and poet who spent some time as a soldier in Italy and Flanders. He imitated the odes of Fray Luis de León (q.v.) in *Odas a imitación de los siete salmos penitenciales de David* (Antwerp, 1593), but is remembered chiefly for his imitation of *La Celestina* (q.v.), *La Lena, o el celoso* (Milan, 1602), a clever, sophisticated comedy deriving much from the author's own picaresque adventures in Europe. In the view of M. Menéndez y Pelayo, *La Lena* is 'the best prose *comedia* composed by a Spaniard at the turn of the 16th century'. It has been edited by E. Ochoa in his *Tesoro del teatro español* (1838).

VELÁZQUEZ DE VELASCO, Luis José, *Marqués de Valdeflores* (1722–72), b. Málaga. Historian and poet. The protegé of the Marqués de la Ensenada, he obtained a commission to collect data for his work *Historia monumental de España*, and from 1752 amassed 67 vols. of documents. He was involved in Ensenada's downfall, was imprisoned 1766–72, and died from apoplexy shortly after his release.

As a critic he was a disciple of Luzán (q.v.), affirming French dramatic principles against the Spanish theatre of the Golden Age in *Orígenes de la poesía castellana* (Málaga, 1754). J. A. Dieze's copiously annotated German translation (1769) is far more useful than the Spanish original.

Velázquez was the first to collect the poems of Francisco de la Torre, but attributed them to Quevedo. His own poems are reprinted in vol. 67 (1875) of the BAE and his neoclassical literary views in vols. 33 (1854) and 42 (1857).

His other works include *Anales de la nación española desde el tiempo más remoto hasta la entrada de los romanos* (Málaga, 1759) and *Noticia del viage de España hecho de orden del Rey* (1765).

See the remarks by J. Sempere y Guarinos on pp. 139–53 of vol. 6 of his *Ensayo de una biblioteca española de los mejores escritores del reinado de Carlos III* (6 vols., 1785–9).

VÉLEZ DE GUEVARA, Juan (1611–75), b. Madrid. Playwright, like his father Luis (q.v.). *Los celos hacen estrellas*, his important early *zarzuela* with music by Juan Hidalgo, has been edited by N. D. Shergold and J. E. Varey (with J. Sage) for Támesis Books (London, 1970).

His *comedias* include *El mancebón de los palacios, o agraviar para alcanzar* (in BAE, vol. 47, 1852),

and *Encontráronse dos arroyuelos, o La boba y el vizcaíno*.

He wrote a burlesque with Cáncer (q.v.) on the theme of the *Siete Infantes de Lara* (q.v.).

Among Vélez's amusing *entremeses* are *Entremés del sastre* and *Los holgones*.

His best-known work as a poet is a sonnet in homage to Velázquez, on the latter's equestrian portrait of Philip IV, beginning 'Pincel, que a lo atrevido y a lo fuerte . . .'.

VÉLEZ DE GUEVARA, Luis (1579–1644), b. Écija. Playwright, poet, and satirist. The father of the playwright Juan Vélez de Guevara (q.v.). His early works were signed Vélez de Santander. Vélez was credited by his contemporary José Pellicer with over 400 plays, of which more than eighty survive. Vélez graduated in Arts in Osuna (1596), entering the service of the Archbishop of Seville, Cardinal Rodrigo de Castro. On the Cardinal's death in 1600, he turned soldier, travelling in Spain, Algiers, and Italy before finally returning to Madrid to join the service of a succession of noblemen. Cervantes (in his *Viaje del Parnaso*) calls him 'lustre, alegría y discreción del trato cortesano'.

He wrote *entremeses* (*La burla más razonada* and *Antonia y Perales*), *autos sacramentales* (collected in 1931 by Lacalle), and biblical plays, such as *La hermosura de Raquel* and *La Magdalena*. His style was so closely modelled on that of Lope de Vega that difficult problems of the attribution of authorship arise (Aníbal considers *La estrella de Sevilla* to be Vélez's, for example).

His *comedia La serrana de la Vera*, notable for its tenderness, intensity of emotion, and blending of aristocratic and popular motifs, is considered by Valbuena Prat to be greater than Lope's *comedia* of the same title which inspired it.

Other notable plays by Vélez are *El ollero de Ocaña, El diablo está en Cantillana, El embuste acreditado y el disparate creído*, the last-named being the subject of a critical edition (1947) by A. G. Reichenberger; and *Virtudes vencen señales* (critical edn. by M. G. Profeti, Pisa, 1965). A special fame attaches to Vélez's moving historical dramas *Más pesa el Rey que la sangre* on the loyalty of Guzmán el Bueno (q.v.), and *Reinar después de morir*, the most effective dramatization of the love of Prince Pedro of Portugal for Inés de Castro (q.v.). *La creación del mundo* has been edited (Athens, Georgia, 1974) by H. Ziomek and R. W. Linker; *El amor en vizcaíno* and *El príncipe viñador* (Saragossa, 1975) by H. Ziomek; and *El verdugo de Málaga* (Saragossa, 1975) by M. G. Profeti.

Vélez wrote a satirical novel in the tradition of Quevedo's *Sueños* (q.v.), and *Los anteojos de mejor vista* (1620–5) by Fernández de Ribera (q.v.). This novel, *El diablo cojuelo* (q.v., 1641), is divided not into chapters but 'strides'; it enjoyed a considerable vogue in its day. From it Lesage drew theme and substance for his inventive *Le diable boiteux*.

See F. E. Spencer and R. Schevill, *The dramatic works of Luis Vélez de Guevara: their plots, sources and bibliography* (Berkeley, Cal., 1937); and M. G. Profeti, 'Note critiche sull' opera di Vélez de Guevara' in *Miscellanea di Studi Ispanici* (Pisa), 1965, pp. 47–174.

VÉLEZ LADRÓN DE GUEVARA, Francisco Antonio (1721–after 1781), Colombian poet. A writer in several manners, he produced one of the first-known Spanish poems published in Colombia, *Octavario a la Inmaculada Concepción de la Virgen María N.S.* (Cartagena, 1774), but his usual manner is that of an elegant society versifier in the rococo style then popular in Europe.

See Manuel José Forero, *La poesía de F. A. Vélez Ladrón de Guevara* (1969), issued as a separatum to *Thesaurus* (Bogotá), vol. 24, no. 1.

VENEGAS or VANEGAS DEL BUSTO, Alejo (1495?–1554?), b. Toledo. Ascetic writer and scholar. He wrote *Tractado de Orthografía y acentos en las tres lenguas principales* (Toledo, 1531), but is celebrated for *Agonía del tránsito de la muerte con los auisos y consuelos que cerca della son prouechosos* (Toledo, 1537), an ascetic work written for Doña Ana de la Cerda on the death of her husband, who had been Venegas del Busto's protector. Venegas is here seen as a disciple of the Senecan tradition which regarded life as a preparation for death. The work was edited by P. Miguel Mir in vol. 16 (1911) of the NBAE. Venegas' *Primera parte de las Diferencias de libros que ay en el universo* (Toledo, 1540) divides books into four classes: those on God, those on Nature, those on morals, and those on religion. He was not in fact a priest, having married before completing his theological studies, and he remained a poor man all his life, with a large family.

Venganza de Tamar, La, a biblical tragedy in three acts by Tirso de Molina, the pseudonym used by Fray Gabriel Téllez (q.v.). The play was first published in *Parte tercera de las comedias de Tirso de Molina* (1634).

A skilled theologian, Tirso is shrewd in his selection and handling of Old Testament source-materials, and his dramatic treatment is frequently in accordance with interpretations made by Jewish and Christian commentators. His best play in the Old Testament genre, *La venganza de Tamar*, deals with the episode of Amnon's love for his half-sister Tamar, his seduction of her, and his punishment of being stabbed at a banquet by the servants of his half-brother Absalom, eager to inherit the throne of their father David.

The episode is outwardly simple, but is made moving and memorable by the subtle character-ization of the neurotic Amnon; little by little he is overtaken by a passion which he is powerless to reject. Absalom is not a disinterested avenger, but a self-serving egoist. A. K. G. Paterson, in his edition of the play (Cambridge, 1969), has shown that its main themes are guilt, justice, and mercy. It is superior not only to Lope de Vega's Old Testament tragedies, but also to *Los cabellos de Absalón* by Calderón, which took as its second act Tirso's third act, almost intact, and then carried the story on to the death of Absalom.

VERAGÜE, Pedro de (c. 14th c.), a catechistic writer who signed himself 'Pedro de Beragüe' in the last line of the Escurial MS. which also contains the works of Sem Tob (q.v.). His verse catechism, the earliest in Spanish, is known variously as the *Tractado de la doctrina* (in the Escurial MS.), the *Espejo de doctrina* (Seville, 1520?), the *Doctrina de la discrición* (in the BAE, vol. 57, 1864), and the *Doctrina de la descrición* in R. Foulché-Delbosc's edition in *Revue Hispanique*, vol. 14 (1906)). It consists of 154 octosyllabic monorhyming tercets followed by a tetrasyllabic *quebrado*.

VERÁSTEGUI, Enrique (1950–   ), b. Lima. Peruvian poet. *En los extramuros del mundo* (1972) was an important first book, showing a keen appreciation of the expressiveness of Spanish, and a wide range of cultural references from Brueghel to Ezra Pound.

Verástegui is one of the thirteen poets whose works appeared in the anthology *Estos 13* (1973).

VERA TASSIS Y VILLARROEL, Juan de (1636–after 1701). Editor, prose-writer, and playwright. His main significance lies in his being the first to attempt publication of the complete plays of Calderón de la Barca (q.v.). Five volumes of his plays had appeared in Calderón's lifetime (1636–77), but the last incurred the author's displeasure, because he disowned four of the ten plays (the titles had been altered without his consent) and two were not in fact his. Vera Tassis then issued a 'true' fifth part as *Verdadera quinta parte de comedias ...* (1682), following with a sixth and a seventh part in 1683 and an eighth in 1684. He then reissued the first five which had originally appeared from other editors (1686–9) making a total of nine; a promised tenth part failed to appear because of Vera's death. E. W. Hesse has indicated changes made by Vera Tassis to the Calderonian texts in *The Vera Tassis text of Calderón's plays, Parts I–IV*

(Mexico City, 1941), and N. D. Shergold's 'Calderón and Vera Tassis' (*Hispanic Review*, vol. 23 (1955), pp. 212–8) shows the changes made by Vera in the stage directions. Vera alleged that he was an 'íntimo amigo' of Calderón but Cotarelo, in his biography of Calderón, rejects this claim, stating his belief that they were not even acquainted. Vera Tassis also wrote a number of now forgotten plays, including a wedding eulogy for Carlos II and María Luisa of Bourbon, *Epitalamio real* ... (1680), and such prose works as *Historia del origen, invención y milagros de la Sagrada Imagen de Nuestra Señora de la Almudena* ... (1692), attacked for its credulity and inaccuracy by Cano y Olmedilla, who was taken to task in Vera's *El triunfo verdadero y la verdad defendida en la historia del origen ... de la Almudena* (1701).

See E. Cotarelo y Mori, *Ensayo sobre la vida y obras de don Pedro Calderón de la Barca* (1924).

VERA Y SANTA CLARA, Amador de, the pseudonym under which Tomás de Iriarte y Oropesa (q.v.) wrote his satire *Los literatos en quaresma* (1773).

Verbena, (a) the verbena plant sacred to the ancient Iberians, and still used in folk medicine; (b) an open-air folk festival held on the eve of certain religious festivals, notably those devoted to SS. Anthony, Peter, and John.

VERBITSKY, Bernardo (1907–), b. Buenos Aires. Argentinian neo-naturalistic novelist and short-story writer, and literary critic on the evening *Noticias Gráficas*. Recurring themes in his work are the obsessions and difficulties of adolescence, especially in the Jewish community of Buenos Aires, and the desperation of slum life and suburbia, broadening out in his novel *Un hombre de papel* (1967) to global hysteria at the prospect of total annihilation by atomic war.

Es difícil empezar a vivir (1941) shows the Jewish youth Pablo Levinson embroiled in life's false values during 1930–3. The student activism portrayed in this novel is continued in *Esos años* (1947), which shows Buenos Aires during 1937–42. *Una pequeña familia* (1951) takes the story into Peronist days. *La esquina* (1953) describes an adolescent whose cynicism is ultimately conquered by sincere love, a theme similar to that of *Calles de tango* (1953). Adolescence again dominates the short novel *Vacaciones* (1957), while in *Villa miseria también es América* (1957) and *La tierra es azul* (1961), Verbitsky implies that the pace of life's disintegration is accelerating.

The autobiographical element is equally marked in the short stories of street life in Buenos Aires, *El café de los Angelitos y otros cuentos porteños* (1950).

Verdad sospechosa, La, a moral comedy by Juan Ruiz de Alarcón y Mendoza (q.v.), which appeared in the *Parte segunda de las comedias* (1634) but had been published in 1630 and attributed to Lope de Vega.

Don García, a handsome young man whose only vice is that of lying freely, leaves his university studies at Salamanca on learning of the death of his elder brother Gabriel. On arriving at court he meets two ladies, Jacinta and Lucrecia, and falls in love with Jacinta, pretending to be a rich merchant from the Indies. Don Beltrán, his father, proposes an advantageous match with a woman of great wealth and beauty (in fact Jacinta herself) but Diego eludes the proposal by explaining that he had married secretly while in Salamanca. Complications lead to García's being married to Lucrecia, while Jacinta gives her hand to Juan, a former admirer. The moral lesson on deceit and lying achieved with deft wit and irony is lost in Corneille's derivative *Le menteur*, which is given an unconvincingly happy ending. Editions of the play have been made by A. Reyes (with *Las paredes oyen*, 1918) for Clásicos Castellanos; by E. Emmanuele (Naples, 1961); and by A. V. Ebersole (1976) for Colección Letras Hispánicas.

VERDAGUER, Jacint (1845–1902), b. Folgueroles, Barcelona. Major Catalan poet of his time whose importance lay in the success of two epic poems, which established Catalan as a modern literary language capable of subtlety, depth, and variety. At the age of 11, Verdaguer began studies at the Seminary of Vich, and was regularly awarded prizes at the Jocs Florals from 1865. Ordained in 1870, Verdaguer suffered from bad health which led him to serve as chaplain on transatlantic ships during 1873–5, a period producing the prose *Excursiones y viajes* (1887) and *Dietario de un peregrino a Tierra Santa* (1889). In 1875 he became chaplain to the Marqués de Comillas and in 1877 won first prize at the Jocs Florals with the epic *Atlàntida*, in which he drew on Plato, Nieremberg, and early chroniclers of American exploration to show how Columbus's discovery of the New World restored the cosmic order upset by the disappearance of Atlantis. The triumph of this poem, unfashionably long but irresistible to Catalan nationalists for the beauty of its language, led Verdaguer to create another epic, *Canigó* (1885), on the legendary origins of Catalonia. Shorter poems were collected in the charming *Cants mistics* (1879), *Flors del Calvari* (1896), and *Aires del Montseny* (1901), the last perhaps the most childlike of his books in its Franciscan simplicity.

Involvement in exorcism and excessive acts of charity were among the factors that led to a bitter polemic with Bishop Morgades, and

Verdaguer suffered persecution, suspension from the priesthood, and banishment to the hermitage of La Gleba near Vich. Weakened by fasting, he died in 1902. More than ten thousand sympathizers and admirers paid homage at his burial. The *Bibliographie de Jacint Verdaguer* (New York, 1912) by R. Dubois has not been brought up to date. Sebastià Joan Arbó's standard biography *Verdaguer* (Barcelona, 1952) has been translated from the Catalan by Joan Fuster as *La vida trágica de Mosén Jacinto Verdaguer* (Barcelona, 1970).

VERDUGO CASTILLA, ALFONSO, *Conde de Torrepalma* (1706–67), b. Alcalá la Real, Jaén. Poet and diplomat, he was a member of the Real Academia Española, the Real Academia de la Historia, and the Academia del Buen Gusto, where he was known as 'el Difícil'. Most of his lyric poetry is lost, as is *La libertad del pueblo de Israel por Moisés*, but it is possible to judge his frigid academicism from the mythological poem *El Deucalión* (1770), published in J. J. López de Sedano's *Parnaso* and again in the BAE, vol. 29 (1854). 'El juicio final' is one of the poems in vol. 61 (1869) of the BAE. More impressive are his ballads 'Al incendio de Roma por Nerón' and 'A César mirando la cabeza de Pompeyo'. 'El diluvio', a long poem on the Flood, uses his favourite themes of death and melancholy. His period as ambassador in Vienna (1755–60) has been studied in *Cuadernos de Historia Diplomática* (Saragossa), vol. 4, 1958, pp. 155–75 by N. Marín López, author of 'La obra poética del Conde de Torrepalma' in *Cuadernos de la Cátedra Feijóo* (Oviedo), 1963, no. 15, pp. 7–56.

VERGARA, JUAN DE (1492–1557), b. Toledo. Humanist and teacher of philosophy at the University of Alcalá. Cardinal Ximénez de Cisneros (q.v.) entrusted him and Bartolomé de Castro with the textual comparison for the Complutensian Bible (q.v.). Cisneros also commissioned translations from Aristotle, and at the time of his benefactor's death Vergara had already completed *De anima*, the *Physics* and most of the *Metaphysics*. He then became secretary to Archbishop Alonso de Fonseca, who prided himself on replying to Pope Leo X in Latin as elegant as that of Bembo. A good friend and persistent correspondent of Erasmus, Vergara was arrested by the Inquisition and imprisoned for much of the period 1533–47. His principal original work is the *Tratado de las ocho Questiones del Templo* (Toledo, 1552), reprinted by Cerdá y Rico in *Clarorum hispanorum opuscula selecta et rariora* (1781).

Vergara's brother Francisco was professor of Greek at Alcalá and was the first to translate the Byzantine novel *Aethiopica* of Heliodorus into Castilian; his version was never published and is now lost, and the influence of *Aethiopica* on Cervantes' *Persiles y Sigismunda* and other Byzantine novels in Spanish is due to later translations.

Vergonzoso en palacio, El, a comedia by Tirso de Molina, the pseudonym of Fray Gabriel Téllez (q.v.). The play was written in 1611 and revised for publication in Tirso's miscellany *Los cigarrales de Toledo* (q.v., 1621). Originally a failure, the play came to rank among his most popular comedies. It is particularly notable for the generous eulogy of his friend and mentor, Lope de Vega (q.v.).

Young Mireno, a poor shepherd who dresses as an *hidalgo*, is accepted when so disguised into the court of the Duke of Aveiro. He is appointed secretary to Madalena, the Duke's daughter, and the couple fall in love. Despite Madalena's encouragement the young man is too shy to propose; when he finally does so, he is discovered to be the nobly-born Dionís, son of the falsely-accused and unjustly-imprisoned Duke of Coimbra. There is an interesting sub-plot in which Madalena's sister falls in love with her own portrait in masculine dress, taking it for a picture of a handsome youth.

In Américo Castro's view, the wilful independence of Madalena stems from Erasmian ideas. The concept of the daring woman is common in Tirso, recurring most notably in *La gallega Mari-Hernández*, in which a peasant-woman falls in love with, and succeeds in marrying, a nobleman.

El vergonzoso en palacio has been edited for Clásicos Castilia (1971) by Francisco Ayala.

Versos sueltos ('blank verse'), a verse form without assonance or rhyme, which was unknown in early epic and ballad poetry in Spain, but was popularized there by Francisco de Figueroa (q.v.) in *Tirsi* (1526).

Versos sueltos were also used by Boscà (q.v.), whose *Leandro* (1543), took the legend of Hero and Leander from Musaeus, and the *versi sciolti* form from Trissino.

However, full rhyme and the *asonante* are so remarkably easy in Spanish that there has never been much technical inducement for poets to use blank verse. Figueroa (in his *Passagero*) claims that only Garcilaso, among the Spaniards, had cultivated the form with any success, and Castillejo says of those writing in blank verse 'usan de cierta prosa / Medida sin consonantes'.

Vetusta, the setting of many of the novels of 'Clarín', the pen-name of Leopoldo Alas y Ureña (q.v.). Vetusta is Oviedo, where he spent most of his life.

Viaje entretenido, El (1603), a picaresque novel by Agustín de Rojas Villandrando (q.v.) filled with theatrical gossip and information on the state of the Spanish travelling companies at the turn of the century. It tells the adventures (with long conversations and between forty and fifty *loas*, q.v.) of Rojas and three friends: the actor Agustín Solano and the actor-managers Miguel Ramírez and Nicolás de los Ríos. Although Rojas had only two or three years' experience as a strolling-player his style is so lively and his curiosity so warm and pervasive that the book is one of the most entertaining in all Spanish literature, and it influenced not only Scarron (*Le roman comique*) but even Goethe (*Wilhelm Meister*).

Rojas deals at length with the poor troupes of actors doing 'one-night stands' at villages and country towns, sleeping rough and eating only occasionally. Modern editions include those of A. Bonilla y San Martín (2 vols., 1901), M. Menéndez y Pelayo in vol. 21 of the NBAE (1915), J. García Morales (1945), and Jean Pierre Ressot (1972) in Clásicos Castalia.

VIANA, ANTONIO DE (*c.* 1578–after 1650), b. La Laguna, Canary Islands. Epic poet. He went to Seville to take holy orders, but returned in 1605 with a wife and in the same year published his well-known epic poem *Antigüedades de las Islas Afortunadas de la Gran Canaria, conquista de Tenerife y aparecimiento de la Imagen de la Candelaria* (Cordova, 1604), unreliably reproduced in the Canaries in 1905, and reliably by F. Löher (Stuttgart, 1883). In free verse, intercalated with *octavas reales*, the poem is a *mélange* of historical incident and romantic legend, culminating in a love story which brings together the Guanche and Castilian peoples. The play was the direct and only source of Lope de Vega's play *Los guanches de Tenerife y conquista de Canarias*. Viana practised medicine in Italy and Spain, producing the *Espejo de cirugía* (Seville, 1636).

See María Rosa Alonso, *El poema de Viana: estudio histórico-literario de un poema épico del siglo XVII*, a supplement to *Cuadernos de Literatura*, (1952; 2nd edn., Santa Cruz de Tenerife, 1968).

VIANA, CARLOS DE ARAGÓN, *Príncipe de* (1421–61), b. Peñafiel, Valladolid. Historian. The son of Juan II of Aragón, who imprisoned him and whom he was accused of having poisoned. His mother was Blanca de Navarra. He was a disciple of Alfonso de la Torre and friend of Ausias March (q.v.). He spent some time in Naples, at the court of his uncle Alfonso V.

Carlos compiled an interesting *Crónica de los reyes de Navarra* (Pamplona, 1843), which takes the story of the kingdom up to the times of Carlos III, his grandfather; and he translated the *Nicomachaean Ethics* of Aristotle.

See Desdevises du Dézert, *Don Carlos d'Aragon, prince de Viane* (Paris, 1887).

VIANA, JAVIER DE (1868–1926), b. Montevideo. Uruguayan naturalistic short-story writer and journalist who was among the first to chronicle Creole life in Uruguay from his wide experience of life as medical student, cattleman, revolutionary, and Congressman. A good descriptive writer, Viana possibly weakened his impact by exaggerating the negative aspects of a *gaucho*'s existence: brutality, promiscuity, alcoholism (Viana himself was to die an alcoholic). A welcome antidote to the romantic picture of a clean-living God-fearing *gaucho*, his writings have a solidly autobiographical background. The eleven stories in *Campo* (1896) are set in the Uruguayan countryside and offer a one-dimensional picture of a bestial society; *Gaucha* (1899) is a mediocre novelette of murder, rape, and arson; *Gurí y otras novelas* (1901) contains seven short stories of improved technique; followed by historical stories in *Crónicas de la Revolución del Quebracho* and *Con divisa blanca* (1902), *Macachines* (1910), *Leña seca* (1911), *Yuyos* (1912), *Abrojos* (1919), *Sobre el recado* (1919), *Paisanas* (1920), *La Biblia gaucha* (1925), and *Pago de deuda, Campo amarillo y otros escritos* (1936).

The continuing popularity of his *gaucho* tales is shown by the range of recent reprints: *Selección de cuentos* (2 vols., 1965), *Sus mejores cuentos cortos* (1968), and *Los mejores cuentos* (Buenos Aires, 1969).

Viana also wrote for the stage, though his drama was less successful than his fiction. His plays include a *sainete*, *Pial de volcao* (1914), and two three-act plays in the naturalistic style: *La Nena* (1905) and *La dotora* (1907).

See Tabaré Freire, *Javier de Viana, modernista* (1957); María E. Cantonnet, *Los vertientes de Javier de Viana* (1969); and John F. Garganigo, *Javier de Viana* (New York, 1972) in Twayne's World Authors series.

VICARIO, VICTORIANO (1911–66), Chilean poet. He was self-taught, and followed Neruda (q.v.) in the use of striking metaphor and symbol. *El lamparero alucinado* (1936) was highly derivative, and Vicario is remembered more as the author of *Fábulas de Prometeo* (1942).

See Tomás Lago, *Tres poetas chilenos* (1942); the other two poets were Nicanor Parra and Óscar Castro (qq.v.).

VICENTE, GIL (1465?–1536?), major Portuguese- and Spanish-language playwright born in the Portuguese countryside, probably in the province of Beira Alta, but possibly in the town of Guimarães. His bilingualism has been studied extensively by Paul Teyssier in his *La langue de Gil Vicente* (Paris, 1959). Teófilo Braga thought that Gil Vicente, goldsmith to Queen Leonor, was a cousin of the playwright but Anselmo Braamcamp Freire has insisted on their identity, and it is probably as a goldsmith that he was attracted to the court at Évora in 1490, for the wedding of the Crown Prince and Isabel, daughter of the Catholic Monarchs Ferdinand and Isabella of Spain. He became director of pageants, actor, and above all playwright, excelling in a wide variety of secular and religious genres, particularly the farce and the chivalric play, the lyric song and the religious *auto*. As a goldsmith Vicente is best known for the Belém monstrance (in Lisbon's Museu Nacional da Arte Antiga) made with gold brought from Goa and Malacca. In 1509 he was appointed overseer of gold- and silver-craft in Portugal and in 1513 Master of the Royal Mint until 1517.

António José Saraiva has claimed that Vicente is the most eloquent representative of a dying medieval Portuguese dramatic tradition, but I. S. Reváh claims him as the founder of a Renaissance theatre. His materials were in the main old, but his treatment was often original, spontaneous, and sparkling, even if 'incorrect' by academic standards. Of his 44 surviving plays, 16 are completely in Portuguese, 11 completely in Spanish, and 17 bilingual, and would have been intelligible to the bilingual court. His dialogue also contains *sayagués* (q.v.), comic Jewish, comic Moor, and comic Negro elements deriving from current travels and discoveries, and the plays are often distinguished by lyrical interludes, a feature unrivalled in the Peninsula until the time of Lope de Vega (q.v.).

His first surviving play is the *loa* of 1502 offered to King Manuel and Queen Maria on the birth of Prince João, the *Visitação*, or *Monólogo do vaqueiro*, in which a rustic shepherd, speaking the *sayagués* introduced to the stage by the Salamancan Juan del Encina, comes to congratulate Queen Maria in her bedchamber. The *Auto pastoril castelhano* (1502) shows again the impact of Encina's style and language, and Valbuena Prat has in fact divided Vicente's work into two (before and after 1520) on the principle that the early works are heavily derivative, while in the later works a definite personality emerges. In both the *Visitação* and the *Auto pastoril* as well as the *Auto dos Reis Magos* (1503) it is quite clear that Vicente played a leading rôle, as he may have done in the 1504 *Auto de S. Martinho*. It is presumed that his work in gold occupied him for the next four years, until the appearance of the best of his farces in 1508, *Quem tem farelos?* a splendid comedy of

national customs, continued in the *Auto da India* (1509), which reflects not altogether favourably on the effects of the discovery of India on national morals and work habits. In the 1510 *Auto da fe*, a Portuguese-speaking Faith converts two Spanish-speaking peasants, who are joined by a third in a final song.

In 1512 Vicente wrote two plays with characters inspired by those in the *Celestina* (q.v.): the *Farsa do velho da horta*, ridiculing an old man looking for a young mistress; and the hilarious *Auto dos físicos*, in which a priest falls ill with unrequited love and suffers at the hands of a series of outrageous doctors, who finally give him up and leave him to a priest-confessor, who confesses that he has himself been in love for many years. For Mia A. Gerhardt it is 'one of the masterpieces of Spanish theatre of the 16th c.'

The *Auto da Sibila Casandra* is an interesting play on the prophetess who refuses to marry, since she believes that God has chosen her for the Messiah's mother. Based on Andrea da Barberino's *Guerino meschino*, the play ends with the humbled sybil worshipping at the crib of Jesus. By contrast, the *Auto da Fama* (1515) is an allegorical paean to Portuguese overseas adventure. Fame is wooed in turn by a Frenchman (speaking garbled French), an Italian (again speaking his own barely-recognizable tongue), and a Spaniard (speaking Castilian), but she rejects them all and settles for Portugal.

In 1516 Vicente produced an *Auto dos quatro tempos*, and the first of a celebrated trilogy: *Auto da barca do Inferno*, like its successor *Auto da barca do Purgatório* (1518) in Portuguese. However, *Auto da barca da Glória* (1518?) is in Spanish. The theme is the medieval dance of death, and the judging of souls ready for Hell or Paradise according to their deeds on Earth. Purgatory is reserved for peasants guilty of venial sins who will be able to work out their salvation. The *Auto da alma* (1518) is a pilgrim's progress drawing on Lucian's *Dialogue of the dead*.

In 1521 Vicente wrote *Comedia de Rubena*, a sketch for *Dom Duardos* called *Comédia do viúvo*, which began as a farce and ended as an impressive comedy, and the festival pageant *Cortes de Júpiter*, comparable to the masques of the English court.

Vicente's work for 1523 included the *Farsa de Inês Pereira* and a Christmas play for the court at Évora, the *Auto pastoril portugués*. One of the most original of Vicente's plays is the *Farsa do juiz da Beira*, a diverting series of judicial paradoxes. By contrast, the conventional *O templo do Apolo* (1526) is a palace piece for the wedding of the Emperor Carlos V and Isabel, daughter of Manuel I. Many other court plays of lesser importance were performed in 1527:

Não de amores, Comédia sôbre a Divisa da Cidade de Coimbra, Tragicomedia pastoril da Serra da Estrêla, as well as the comic *Farsa dos almocreves*. In 1529 Vicente produced a slapstick farce, *O clérigo da Beira*, which degenerated into a private court game; the brief medieval anti-Jewish *Diálogo sobre a Resurreição*; and the important court pageant *O triunfo do Inverno*, a fascinating compound of the folkloric (the *salvagem*-Inverno- and the *velha*-Brásia Caiada), the popular (two Spanish yokels), the farcical (a henpecked blacksmith and his shrewish wife), and the mythological (sirens). The climax is a prince's grand entry on a pageant-wagon representing the garden of virtues.

Vicente's mastery of the stage, its style, and its language, was now at its peak, but he was constantly being fettered by palace requirements for occasional pieces, so that the *Auto da Lusitânia* (1532) begins with a lively sketch of a courtier wooing a tailor's eldest daughter, but falls away into an unconnected allegory of Portugal's overseas glory. The *Auto da Mofina Mendes* (1534) is a highly successful play which has attracted especial interest because of its Erasmian opening scene ridiculing scholastic friars, which was deleted from later editions of Vicente's works by order of the Inquisition. The *Auto da Cananeia* (1534) exemplifies the power of the Lord's Prayer if applied with faith, understanding, and perseverance. Vicente's last play was the *Floresta de engaños* (1536), based on a series of tricks and deceptions.

His two plays of chivalry, both written in Spanish, fall into a special category for their length and complexity. *Dom Duardos* (1522) is his longest play, selecting a few crucial episodes from the romance of chivalry *Primaleón* (Salamanca, 1512; Seville, 1524), a continuation of *Palmerín de Oliva* (Salamanca, 1511), itself a close imitation of the prototype *Amadís de Gaula*. The theme of Vicente's play is the courting of Princess Flérida of Constantinople at her father's court, where Dom Duardos is disguised as a gardener. There is an edition by Dámaso Alonso (Madrid, 1942).

Amadís de Gaula (1523?) selects a few important episodes from the romance and does not appear to be ironic, despite Waldron's claim in his edition (Manchester, 1959).

Vicente's works were conscientiously published by his son Luis as *Copilação de todas las obras* (Lisbon, 1562), and a facsimile from retouched negatives has been issued by the National Library (Lisbon, 1928). Owing to the edition's royal patronage, the Inquisition left the book uncensored. Two editions of the complete works have appeared this century: that of Mendes dos Remedios (3 vols., Coimbra, 1907–14) and the more reliable edition by Marques de Braga (6

vols., Lisbon, 1942–4; 2nd edn., 1961), following the order of the original *Copilação*.

The *Obras en español* (Buenos Aires, 1943) have been edited by R. E. Molinari, and the *Obras dramáticas castellanas* (Madrid, 1962) are edited in Clásicos Castellanos by T. R. Hart. *Farces and festival plays* (Eugene, Oregon, 1972) is an edition by T. R. Hart of the farces *Auto da India* and *Quem tem farelos?* and the festival plays *Frágua de amor* (1524), *Cortes de Júpiter*, and *O triunfo do Inverno* (1529).

The original *Copilação* of Luis Vicente omits only one play of unquestioned authenticity: the *Auto da festa* (1525) published by Conde de Sabugosa (Lisbon, 1906).

See L. M. de Castro e Azevedo's *Bibliografia vicentina* (Lisbon, 1942); Aubrey Bell's brief but important *Gil Vicente* (Oxford, 1921); the standard work by Anselmo Braamcamp Freire, *Vida e obras de Gil Vicente, 'Trovador, mestre da Balança'* (Oporto, 1920; 2nd edn., Lisbon, 1944); and Jack Horace Parker, *Gil Vicente* (New York, 1967), a useful survey in Twayne's World Authors series.

VICETTO, BENITO (1824–78), b. El Ferrol. Galician novelist, historian, and journalist. His painstaking *Historia de Galicia* (7 vols., El Ferrol, 1863–73) did much to help the rediscovery of Galician cultural autonomy in the second half of the 19th c., as did his colourful novels which are influenced by Sir Walter Scott, and his journalism for *El Clamor de Galicia* and the *Revista Galaica*.

Among his novels are *El caballero verde* (1844), *Los hidalgos de Monforte* (1857), *Rojín Rojal, o el paje de los cabellos de oro* (1857), *Los reyes suevos de Galicia* (Corunna, 1860), *El caballero de Calatrava* (1863), and *El último Roade* (1868).

Victoria de Junín canto a Bolívar, La, an heroic ode by José Joaquín Olmedo (q.v.), on a theme suggested by Bolívar himself. It was begun in August 1824, when Olmedo heard of the battle of Junín, but it was not until December of the same year, when the victory of Ayacucho was proclaimed, that he decided on the poem's final, heroic form.

In the poem Huainacápac, the last all-powerful Inca emperor, appears and prophesies the triumph of Bolívar's forces. The poem comprised 900 lines in its definitive version, and was very different from Olmedo's habitual neoclassical verse. It was published in Guayaquil in 1825, in London and Paris in 1826, and in most South American capitals in the course ·of the next decade.

VICUÑA CIFUENTES, JULIO (1865–1936), Chilean folklorist and post-modernist poet. He translated from Horace and Virgil as well as from modern writers, but his main work consisted of studies in folklore: *Instrucciones para recoger de la tradición oral romances populares* (1909), *Coa, jerga de los delincuentes chilenos: estudio y vocabulario* (1910), *Romances populares y vulgares recogidos de la tradición oral chilena* (1912), and *Mitos y superstición recogidos de la tradición oral chilena* (1915).

Characteristically, his late poetry, *La cosecha de otoño* (1929; Madrid, 1932), shows a preference for the simple and popular in contrast to the prevailing *modernista* trend.

VICUÑA MACKENNA, Benjamín (1831–86), b. Santiago. Chilean historian and critic. After taking part in the revolution of 1851, he fled Chile and lived for some time in the U.S.A. and Canada. On his return he campaigned bitterly once more in *El Mercurio*, was imprisoned in 1858 and exiled in 1859, living first in England and then in Spain. On returning to Chile he became chief editor of *El Mercurio* from 1863 and spent much of his time in writing important historical works. J. Hunneus Gana declared that he is 'acaso, el más original de todos los historiadores de América, él de mayor fecundidad y él de talento más vivo'. R. Briceño enumerates 160 books by Vicuña Mackenna in his *Catálogo de las publicaciones ... de Vicuña Mackenna* (1886) including *El ostracismo de los Carreras* (1857), *Vida de don Diego Portales* and *El general don José de San Martín* (both 1863), the exemplary *Historia crítica y social de la ciudad de Santiago, 1541–1868* (1869), the account of the Pacific War in *Las campañas de Tarapacá, Tacna y Lima* (1881), *Chile: relaciones históricas* (1887), *Diego de Almagro: estudios críticos sobre el descubrimiento de Chile* (1889), and *El Washington de Sur: Sucre* (1893).

See Pedro Pablo Figueroa, *Vida y obras de don Benjamín Vicuña Mackenna* (1886).

Vida de Don Quijote y Sancho, según Miguel de Cervantes Saavedra, a long essay by Miguel de Unamuno (q.v.) first published in 1905 and translated by H. P. Earle (1927).

Unamuno concludes his *Sentimiento trágico de la vida* (q.v.) by declaring that while other civilizations leave behind them books or institutions, Spain's legacy is great souls, and while he cites S. Teresa, he also indicates the pre-eminence of Quijote. Don Quijote continues to exist in order to overcome Unamuno's fear that his reason will laugh his faith out of court.

In his *Vida de Don Quijote*, Unamuno treats the hero as a mystic on a level with S. Ignacio de Loyola (q.v.), a Basque like Unamuno. The idealist Quijote and the realist Sancho are not opposites, nor even 'two halves of an orange', but

one person seen from two different aspects. Quijote's life is a quest for immortality through the fame he will achieve by exploits performed to the glory of Dulcinea. Unamuno's approach to the book is severely anti-biographical; he seldom mentions Cervantes, and at one point goes so far as to state that Cervantes was born simply to create Quijote, just as Unamuno was born to comment on the creation: the author himself is of less interest than his works. The book is as essential to an understanding of Unamuno's dialectic, existentialist philosophy as it is to his view of man's yearning for immortality, expressed in the life of Quijote and Sancho.

Vida es sueño, La, one of the greatest plays of Pedro Calderón de la Barca (q.v.), written in 1635 and first published in *Parte treinta de comedias famosas de varios autores* (Saragossa, 1636).

Rosaura, disguised as a man and accompanied by her servant Clarín, becomes lost on her way from Moscow to Poland on a secret mission aimed at restoring her lost honour. She hears the lament of Segismundo, a prisoner in a tower, and she takes pity on this man who seems even more wretched than herself. Clotaldo, Segismundo's keeper, appears and gives orders for the strangers to be imprisoned too: he has orders to execute all those who speak with Segismundo.

Segismundo is in fact, without realizing it, the son of King Basilio, who was told by a horoscope that Segismundo would be a cruel and vengeful prince. Rosaura surrenders her sword to Clotaldo, telling him that a mystery surrounds it; her mother told her to show it to the nobles of Poland, one of whom would recognize it and aid her. Clotaldo remembers how he gave the sword to his mistress Violante: Rosaura is thus his 'son' but he keeps silent out of fear. Rosaura and Clotaldo are brought before the King but are pardoned as Basilio is in the act of revealing his secret to the court, declaring that out of fairness to his son he will test the prophecy by placing him on the throne; if Segismundo is proved unworthy he will return to the tower and to captivity, and Basilio's nephew and niece Astolfo and Estrella will rule instead as king and queen.

Clotaldo restores the sword to Rosaura and learns that his 'son' is really a woman and that she has been dishonoured by Astolfo; he is now obliged to avenge her dishonour.

A typical Calderonian conflict between love and duty thus arises when, in Act II, Astolfo saves Clotaldo from death at the hands of Segismundo. Clotaldo cannot now take rightful vengeance on his rescuer. Rosaura, in Act II, has transformed herself back into a woman;

she calls herself Astrea, maintains that she is a niece of Clotaldo and is appointed lady-in-waiting to Estrella. Segismundo, drugged, now awakes to find himself proclaimed prince and heir to the kingdom of Poland; he rounds furiously on Clotaldo for 'treachery' in keeping him locked up; rejects the homage of Astolfo; calls his father tyrant for the harsh treatment meted out to him in the past; and kills a courtier whom he finds annoying.

Believing that the prediction has fulfilled itself to the letter, King Basilio orders a fresh narcotic to be given to Segismundo, who is returned to his cell. When Segismundo awakes, Clotaldo tells him that he has been dreaming.

For Segismundo the experience has been a salutary *memento mori*. When he reawoke in the cell, he thought for a moment that he was dead and in his grave awaiting judgment. This terrifying ordeal has made him *desengañado*: he has been forcefully reminded that a life of sin is followed by punishment after death. This life on earth is short and intangible as a dream; spiritual values alone endure.

Act III begins with the sensational news that the people have rebelled on learning of their prince's fresh imprisonment: they wish him free, to rule over them as a Polish prince, instead of the foreigner Astolfo. Segismundo, freed by the rebels and proclaimed king, fears that he is dreaming again.

Segismundo's great test comes now. He had been drawn to Rosaura in the palace scene and had tried to rape her; he was drawn to her not only because of her beauty but also he subconsciously recalled having seen her earlier in his dungeon. Rosaura now joins his revolt to take revenge on Astolfo, since Clotaldo cannot help her in this respect. With her in his power, Segismundo is tempted to give way to his passions; however, Clotaldo, discussing his cruel actions performed in the palace 'dream', had suggested that 'aún en sueños no se pierde el hacer bien' and Segismundo, though he suspects that this present experience is also but a dream, decides to act honourably towards the girl and overcomes his passions. He argues, in a speech on his dilemma between love and duty, that a prince's duty is to protect his subjects and not dishonour them. In the battle with Rosaura against Basilio and Astolfo, Segismundo is the winner; mercifully he spares the life of the tyrant his father; and kneels at Basilio's feet. Astolfo is obliged to marry Rosaura to restore her honour, as he had seduced her and then left her for Estrella. Segismundo marries Estrella and keeps the throne.

A major theme of the play is the idea of free will versus predestination; Basilio believes that the horoscope is inexorably correct in its predic-

tion, and though he admits that by God-given freewill 'un magnánimo varón' can 'vencer las estrellas' he will not take the risk in the case of his own son and imprisons the prince. The stars, in Calderón's view, show only what is certain to occur *if* a man follows the instincts of his baser nature. By being locked in a cell in a tower, cut off from the rest of mankind, Segismundo becomes a 'monstruo', as the symbolism of his animal-skins show, and he is thus almost forced to act and react in the bestial way that his father had sought to avoid. Nevertheless a tiny spark of humanity does remain (symbolized by a flickering lamp in his cell), and when he is begged by Rosaura to spare her and Clarín, he does so.

Basilio's arrogance in denying his son his rights as man (free-will) and prince (the throne) is paralleled by Clarín's arrogance in thinking he can escape death: he is the victim of a stray bullet as he tries to hide on the battlefield instead of doing his duty as a soldier.

The many oriental sources of *La vida es sueño* include legends of the Buddha and the Arabic *Alf layla wa layla* (*The Thousand and One Nights*). The magnificent verse and dramatic expertise match the exalted theme of this remarkable play, in which the typical Spanish Baroque themes of worldly disillusion and the vanity of earthly things are memorably displayed.

Calderón's *auto sacramental* of the same title was published with the *comedia* by G. M. Bertini (Turin, 1949). Editions of the *comedia* alone include those by Milton A. Buchanan (Toronto, 1910), E. W. Hesse (New York, 1961), and A. E. Sloman (Manchester, 1961). There are good points in Arturo Farinelli's annotated edition, *La vita è un sogno* (2 vols., Turin, 1916).

See P. Cepeda Calzada, *La vida es sueño* (1964); essays by Wilson, Dunn, Hesse, Sloman, and Whitby reprinted in Bruce Wardropper (ed.), *Critical essays on the theatre of Calderón* (New York, 1965); and V. Bodini, *Segni e simboli nella 'Vida es sueño'* (Bari, 1968). Edward and Elizabeth Huberman have translated the play as 'Life is a dream' in Ángel Flores's anthology, *Spanish drama* (New York, 1962).

Vida fantástica, La, a trilogy of novels by Pío Baroja y Nessi (q.v.), comprising *Aventuras, inventos y mixtificaciones de Silvestre Paradox* (1901), *Camino de perfección* (1902), and *Paradox, rey* (1906).

The first and third volumes are devoted to Silvestre Paradox, an inventive and impractical man living in a Madrid attic with a dog, a snake, and a stuffed bustard. Baroja confesses in his memoirs (*Obras*, vol. 7, p. 651) that the exploits of Paradox and his friend, the reformed bibliomaniac Avelino Diz de la Iglesia, owe a good deal to Baroja's own youthful adventures. The partners establish an Eternal Life Insurance Company which, for a small premium, says sufficient prayers to ensure entry into Heaven for policy-holders too busy to pray themselves. This success and others lead to temporary solvency, which vanishes when Paradox's servant and secretary Pelayo absconds with all but the stuffed bustard.

Paradox dislikes socialism, democracy, and the rule of the masses, and hates the criminality and vice of Madrid. He is chaste and moral, though moving in permissive Bohemian society. Paradoxically, he feels nausea at the sight of people and things, yet is endlessly inventive and proclaims the indestructibility of his spirit in the face of an indifferent universe. A secondary character in this novel is the artist Fernando Ossorio, who as a medical student becomes the central character in *Camino de perfección*. Ossorio is based on a student acquaintance of Baroja, 'an avid reader of Baudelaire and somewhat decadent and satanic'. The work was influenced by Max Nordau's *Entartung* (1892–3, available in Spain from 1894 in its French translation *Dégénération*), which attempted to show that the greatest creative artists of the 19th c. were barren, hysterical madmen. Ossorio is Nordau's typical degenerate, his sense of tedium leading to hysteria accentuated by sexual obsessions. Ossorio seeks liberation by wandering across Castile, visiting old churches in spite of his lack of faith. He is eventually converted to a philosophy of optimism, reflecting Baroja's conversion to Nietzschean affirmation after his friend Paul Schmitz (Max Schultze in the novel) had read him some of Nietzsche's letters. Ossorio marries his cousin Dolores; their first child (symbolizing negation and Nordau) is born prematurely and dies; their second (symbolizing affirmation and Nietzsche) is robust and lives.

In *Paradox, rey*, Paradox and Don Avelino set out from Valencia on another quest, this time to Tangier, but their ship sinks on its way to establish a Jewish colony in the Republic of Cananí, and crew and passengers are taken as captives to Bu-Tata, capital of Uganga. When the tyrannical King Kiri is assassinated, Paradox is made king and immediately proclaims total liberty: 'Let us live the free life, without restraint, without schools, without laws, without teachers . . .' and sets up a fairground roundabout in the main square of Bu-Tata.

Paradox's Utopia is abruptly brought to an end by a French invasion, followed by such European benefits as tuberculosis, alcoholism, and prostitution. The invaders and the group of adventurers accompanying Paradox symbolize various aspects of Spanish or European society that Baroja enjoyed satirizing, particularly the aristocracy, the clergy, and the military. The work, largely in dialogue, is a triumph of fantasy and social satire: its ebullience was attributed by Baroja to a mood he called *robinsoniano* (like that of Robinson Crusoe), in which things and people are seen in a fresh, youthful light of adventure.

Vidalita, in *gaucho* literature (q.v.), a popular verse-form of four- or six-line stanzas of four, six, or eight syllables each, usually rhyming in the second and fourth, or third and sixth respectively.

Like the *cielito* (q.v.), the *vidalita* takes its name from a refrain-word. The dominant mood is melancholy, as in the following anonymous extract:

> *Palomita blanca,*
> *vidalita,*
> *pecho colorado,*
> *dile que me muero,*
> *vidalita,*
> *porque me ha olvidado.*

Vida Moderna, the most important Uruguayan literary magazine of its period. Edited by Raúl Montero Bustamante 1900–3, it was briefly revived in 1910–11. The contributors in its first period included E. Díaz Romero, Eduardo Acevedo Díaz, Jules Supervielle, and M. Goycoechea Menéndez.

Several of the contributors were influenced by Baudelaire, and all acknowledged him as the most persistent influence on Uruguayan poetry during the preceding twenty years.

Montero Bustamante also edited the short-lived *Revista Literaria* (six issues, 1900) and the important *Revista Nacional* (from 1938).

VIEJO PANCHO, the pseudonym of José Alonso y Trelles (q.v.).

VIERA Y CLAVIJO, José (1731–1813), b. Realejo Alto, Tenerife, Canary Islands. Historian. He studied in the Dominican convent of Puerto de la Cruz, and lived in La Laguna 1757–70, obtaining much respect for his sermons. He then left for Madrid to publish his history of the Canary Islands, entering the service of the Marqués de Santa Cruz, with whom he resided and travelled through Europe. He published notes of his journeys in *Extracto de los apuntes del Diario de mi viage desde Madrid a Italia y Alemania . . . por los años de 1780 y 1781* (Santa Cruz de Tenerife, 1848) and *Apuntes del Diario e itinerario de mi viage a Francia y Flandes . . . en los años de 1777 y 1778* (Santa Cruz, 1849). His main historical work is the excellent *Noticias de la Historia general de las Islas de Canarias* (4 vols., 1772–83; revised edn. in 8 vols., Santa Cruz,

1941; definitive edn. by E. Serra Ráfols, 3 vols., Santa Cruz, 1950–2).

As a didactic poet Viera is less well-known. *Los ayres fixos: poema didáctico* (1780) was completed by *La máquina aerostática*, a sixth canto, in 1784. *La elocuencia* (Las Palmas, 1841) is another, published posthumously.

See the entry for Viera in J. Sempere y Guarinos, *Ensayo de una biblioteca española de los mejores escritores del reinado de Carlos III* (6 vols., 1785–9), vol. 6, pp. 153–8.

VIGILA, monkish chronicler of the *Albeldense* MS. See CRONICONES.

VILARIÑO, IDEA (1920–   ), b. Montevideo. Uruguayan poet. Her first book is the immature *La suplicante* (1945), but the simplicity of that work gives way to the hermeticism of *Cielo cielo* (1947) and later collections: *Paraíso perdido* (1949), of which only the title poem is new; *Por aire sucio* (privately published, 1950; first commercial edn., 1951); her best achievement, *Nocturnos* (1955), with its newly-found serenity replacing the anguish in the face of suffering and death predominant in the earlier work; and *Poemas de amor* (privately published, 1958; first commercial edn., 1962).

Her themes are disillusionment with aduithood (in *Paraíso perdido*), rebellion, and the sparse chances of success in love or life (as in 'Ya no').

VILINCH, the pseudonym used by the Basque Romantic poet Indalecio Bizcarrondo (q.v.).

VILLAESPESA, FRANCISCO (1877–1935), b. Laujar, Almería. Minor poet and playwright. His first work showed the earliest modernist influence in Spain: *Intimidades* and *Flores de almendro* (both 1898), *Luchas* (1899) and *La musa enferma* (1901); later he turned to Romantic figures such as Zorrilla for inspiration. Throughout his life he was inspired by Moorish art and culture, especially that in Granada. He travelled across Latin America as a theatrical impresario, earning a great deal of money and squandering it, returning to Spain poor. His weaknesses are vulgarity, uncritical fecundity, and repetition even in his best work such as *Tristitia rerum* and *El jardín de las quimeras* (both 1909). His *Poesías completas* appeared in 1953. His drama, in the words of Cejador, 'resulta poco dramático por la falta de densidad y sobra de lirismo'. His most characteristic play is perhaps *El Alcázar de las Perlas* (first performed 1911), written according to Villaespesa 'to magnify the spirit of Granada lyrically as an Arab of Granada would have written'. The volumes in *Novelas completas* (1951) are little read, but are still available in Colección Crisol.

See J. Álvarez Sierra, *Francisco Villaespesa: vida, episodios y anécdotas de este genial poeta* (1949).

VILLALOBOS, FRANCISCO LÓPEZ DE, see LÓPEZ DE VILLALOBOS, Francisco.

VILLALÓN, CRISTÓBAL DE (c. 1505–58), A. González Palencia has declared that this name conceals the identities of three or perhaps even four writers: the first wrote *Tragedia de Mirrha* (Medina del Campo, 1536) edited by Foulché-Delbosc in the *Revue Hispanique* (vol. 19, 1908); the second wrote a dialogue called *La ingeniosa comparación entre lo antiguo y lo presente* (Valladolid, 1539) and *El provechoso tratado de cambios y contrataciones de mercaderes y reprovación de usura* (Valladolid, 1541); the third compiled *Gramática castellana* (Antwerp, 1558) which attacks Nebrija's methods of teaching Latin; yet a fourth wrote the *Viaje de Turquía* (attributed by Bataillon to Andrés Laguna, qq.v.), *Diálogo de las transformaciones de Pitágoras*, and *El crotalón* (q.v.) Another work attributed to Villalón, *El scolástico*, was first printed in its entirety in 1967. José Fradejas Lebrero argued convincingly in favour of a single Villalón in the *Revista de Literatura* (July–December 1956).

VILLALÓN, FERNANDO, Conde de *Miraflores de los Ángeles*, b. Arcos de la Frontera, Seville. Poet. After concentrating on regional and folk themes in *Andalucía la baja* (1927), Villalón turned to the classics with *La toriada* (1928) showing the influence of Góngora and Herrera. *Romances del 'Ochocientos': poesías* (Málaga, 1929) is a collection of his ballads, marked by an affection for the style and themes of Federico García Lorca (q.v.). His *Poesías completas* appeared in 1944.

See Manuel Halcón (q.v.), *Recuerdos de Fernando Villalón* (1941).

VILLAMEDIANA, JUAN DE TASSIS PERALTA, *Conde de*, see TASSIS PERALTA, Juan de, *Conde de Villamediana*.

Villancicos, a verse form deriving from the Arabic *zéjel* (q.v.), and used by Spanish court poets of the early Renaissance. A popular song with a refrain, it was most commonly used in celebrations of Christ's nativity, and even now in popular parlance a Christmas carol is often known as a *villancico* rather than as a *canción de Navidad*.

Variants include the *villancicos eclesiásticos* used for various other liturgical purposes; the secular *serranillas* or *villancicos propios de caminantes* used for themes involving travelling; *serranillas* imitating Provençal *pastourelles*; and others deriving from Galician-Portuguese *pastorelas*.

Many Spanish poets have written in this attractive yet simple verse-form, among them Juan del Encina, Valdivielso, and Lope de Vega (qq.v.). The example that follows is by the subtle Valencian diplomat Joan Escrivá (q.v.):

> ¿Qué sentís, coraçón mío?
> ¿No dezís?
> ¿Qué mal es él que sentís?
> ¿Qué sentistes aquel día
> quando mi señora vistes
> que perdistes alegría
> y descanso despedistes?
> ¿Cómo a mí nunca volvistes?
> ¿No dezís?
> ¿Dónde estáis que no venís?
>
> ¿Qu'es de vos qu'en mí n'os hallo?
> ¿Coraçón quién os agena?
> ¿Qu'es de vos que, aunque callo,
> vuestro mal tan bien me pena?
> ¿Quién os ató tal cadena?
> ¿No dezís?
> ¿Qué mal es él que sentís?

See A. Sánchez Romeralo, *El villancico* (Madrid, 1968).

Villano en su rincón, El, a play in praise of rural life and country virtues by Lope de Vega Carpio (q.v.), written about 1611 and first published in the *Séptima parte de las comedias* (1617).

Lisarda, daughter of the wealthy French farmer Juan Labrador (a figure from folklore), changes her clothes for those of a fine lady and goes to Paris from the countryside, accompanied by her cousin Belisa. There she attracts the noble courtier Otón, who gives her a diamond and makes her promise to meet him again. Otón sends his servant Marín to discover more about Lisarda, whom he finds to be at home in the country at Belflor, two leagues from Paris. Juan Labrador, her father, lives in harmony with the changing seasons and has become rich by careful husbandry; he has no desire to go to court or to obtain favours from the King of France, for he considers himself to be king of his own corner of France. So when his son Feliciano tells him that the king's hunting party has arrived in the village, Juan Labrador neither wishes nor intends to meet the king. The king finds on the village church an inscription 'Yace aquí Juan Labrador, / que nunca sirvió a señor, / ni vió la corte ni al rey, / ni temió ni dió temor; / ni tuvo necesidad, / ni estuvo herido ni preso, / ni, en muchos años de edad, / vió en su casa mal suceso, / envidia ni enfermedad'.

Thinking this inscription to be an epitaph, the king is astonished to find Juan still alive and hearty. Otón, in the royal retinue, discovers Lisarda in her country dress, and makes an assignation with her for that evening.

While Otón returns to Juan's village disguised as a peasant, the king also returns (dressed as a hunter) and, introducing himself to Juan as the Governor of Paris, requests lodging for the night. Juan offers hospitality, laughingly rejecting his guest's praise of life at court by listing the happiness of peace and tranquillity in the country. To test Juan's loyalty, the king sends Otón back with a letter requesting a hundred thousand escudos, which Juan instantly provides; then with another requesting the services of Feliciano and Lisarda, his children. With a heavy heart, Juan agrees to this as well, and the king, who has learned of Otón's love for Lisarda, gives Feliciano the title of 'caballero', marries Lisarda to Otón, and appoints Juan Labrador as his major-domo.

Lope's sources for the play included the folk story of Juan Labrador, the type of the honest and industrious countryman, and the third of the *Colloquios satíricos* (Mondoñedo, 1553) by Antonio de Torquemada (q.v.). The actual occasion for the writing of the play was the journeys undertaken by Anne of Austria to marry Louis XIII of France and by Isabel de Borbón to marry Philip IV of Spain. Though the play begins as a dramatic illustration of the popular Golden Age (and medieval) theme of *Menosprecio de corte y alabanza de aldea* (q.v.), it concludes as a kind of *auto sacramental a lo profano* to show the omnipotence of God's viceroy on earth, the king.

The most memorable character is intended merely to demonstrate his type: Juan Labrador, whose dignity, wisdom, and unquestioning loyalty could be considered models for the ideal citizen.

There are two editions by A. Zamora Vicente, the first of 1961, and the second (with *Las bizarrías de Belisa*) of 1963 in Clásicos Castellanos.

See Marcel Bataillon, 'El villano en su rincón', in his *Varia lección de clásicos españoles* (1964), pp. 329–72.

VILLANUEVA Y OCHOA, DIONISIO (1774–1834), b. Cordova. Playwright. He used the pen-name 'Dionisio Solís'. Friendly with Leandro Fernández de Moratín (q.v.), he however preferred the 'patriotic' side when Moratín joined the French invaders in 1808. He married the great actress María Ribera, and worked as a prompter, adapter, and translator of works by Alfieri, Kotzebue, Chénier, Voltaire, and others. His own plays are derivative and have been forgotten by producers and public alike: *Las literatas, Tello de Negra, La pupila,*

Blanca de Borbón on the unfaithful wife of Pedro the Cruel, and *Camila* are some of the titles.

His sonnets, fables, *villancicos*, *cantilenas*, odes, and epistles have been collected in vol. 67 (1875) of the BAE.

VILLAR PONTE, Antón (1881–1936), b. Viveiro, Lugo. Galician playwright, novelist, and essayist. He founded the regional Irmandades da Fala in 1916 and wrote stirring calls for regional cultural autonomy in essays such as *Nacionalismo galego: a nosa afirmación regional*. After qualifying as a pharmacist at Santiago University he practised in Fox, went to Madrid as a journalist, then to Cuba, and finally returneḍ to Galicia in 1916. With Ramón Cabanillas Enríquez (q.v.) he wrote *O mariscal* (1926), an historical-legendary play, and then began to publish plays of his own, of which the most enduring are *O tríptico teatral* (Santiago, 1928), consisting of *A patria do labrego*, on *caciquismo*; *Almas mortas*, on emigration; *Entre dous abismos*, on superstition; and *Os evanxeos da risa absoluta* (Santiago, 1934), a folk-play of great charm and vivacity.

VILLARROEL, Diego de Torres, see Torres Villarroel, Diego de.

VILLARROEL, Gaspar de (1587?–1665), b. Quito. Bishop of Santiago (Chile) and subsequently of Arequipa. He spent ten years in the Iberian peninsula, then on his return defended the Creoles' rights against the prejudice and injustices shown by Spaniards in the viceregal court.

Of his many books, the most important is *Govierno eclesiástico-pacífico y unión de los dos cuchillos, pontificio y regio* (2 vols., Madrid, 1656–7 and later edns.), in which he attempts to resolve dilemmas arising from the dispute between civil and ecclesiastical authorities. Theoretical canons are supported by ingenious anecdotes, often partly autobiographical.

See Rubén Vargas Ugarte, *El Ilmo. Don Gaspar de Villarroel* (Lima, 1939) and *Tres figuras señeras del episcopado americano* (Lima, 1966), pp. 1–63; José López Ortiz, *El regalismo indiano en el 'Gobierno eclesiástico-pacífico'* (Madrid, 1947); and Gonzalo Zaldumbide, *Fray Gaspar de Villarroel, siglo XVII* (Puebla, Mexico, 1960), a useful selection and study.

VILLAURRUTIA, Jacobo de (1757–1833), b. Santo Domingo (now Ciudad Trujillo). Dominican man of letters who began his education in Mexico and completed it in Europe as a protégé of Cardinal Lorenzana. Arriving in 1772, he stayed in Spain twenty years, graduating in law. He translated a French compilation of moral reflections as *La escuela de la felicidad* (Madrid, 1786) under the pseudonym 'Diego Rulavit y Laur' and published in the same year the oddly-assorted *Pensamientos escogidos* of Marcus Aurelius and Friedrich II of Prussia. He edited *El Correo de los Ciegos* (1786–7) in Madrid, but is best known for his version of Frances Sheridan's *Memoirs of Miss Sidney Bidulph* (3 vols., London, 1761; continued in 2 vols., London, 1767) taken from the French and entitled *Memorias para la historia de la virtud* (Alcalá, 1792).

On his return to Spanish America, Villaurrutia was appointed *oidor* ('judge') in Guatemala (1792–1804), editing the *Gacetas*, and in 1805 founded with Carlos María de Bustamante (1774–1850), the first daily paper recorded in Latin America, the *Diario de México*.

VILLAURRUTIA, Xavier (1903–50), b. Mexico City. Mexican poet and playwright. With José Gorostiza (q.v.), the most important of the group associated with *Contempóraneos* (1928–31). Influenced by López Velarde (q.v.), his poetry has been divided into three phases: the first of puns and other verbal dexterities, the second of the dominance of intellect over emotion, and the third of the dominance of emotion. His range of mood is extremely varied, from merry to deeply religious; his range of themes is limited with a few exceptions to suffering, death, darkness, and similar preoccupations. His *Primeros poemas* were collected in *Ocho poetas* (1923), his first separate publication being *Reflejos* (1926). Then followed the series of nocturnes for which Villaurrutia is still best remembered: *Nocturnos* (1933), *Nocturno de los ángeles* (1936), *Nocturno mar* (1937), *Nocturno rosa* (1937), *Nostalgia de la muerte* (Buenos Aires, 1938; 2nd definitive edn., 1946), *Décima muerte y otros poemas no coleccionados* (1941), the last-named influenced by Rilke, and *Canto a la primavera y otros poemas* (1948). Villaurrutia is often claimed as a surrealist poet, though much of his work shows only a slight influence of surrealism.

He studied drama at Yale University in 1935–6, his first plays being five sketches, *Autos profanos* (1943), for a minority audience. His three-act plays, composed later, included *Invitación a la muerte* (1940), *La hiedra* (1941) and *La mujer legítima* (1942), *El yerro candente* (1944), *El pobre Barba Azul* (1946; first performed in 1947), *Juego peligroso* and *El solterón* (both 1949; first performed in 1950).

Poesía y teatro completos (1953) has now been superseded by the *Obras* (1966) which also contain his prose and a bibliography by Luis Mario Schneider.

See Eugene L. Moretta, *Poetic achievement of Xavier Villaurrutia* (Cuernavaca, Mexico, 1971), and A. Snaidas, *El teatro de Xavier Villaurrutia* (1973).

VILLAVERDE, CIRILO (1812–94), b. Pinar del Río. Cuban novelist and journalist. For some time an advocate, he conspired against Spain, but managed to escape to New York in 1849, where he continued to support the separatist movement, editing *La Verdad* in New York and *El Independiente* in New Orleans. Pardoned in 1858, he returned to Cuba, but later had to escape again, and died exiled in New York. He wrote the classic Cuban anti-slavery novel, *Cecilia Valdés* (Part 1, Havana, 1839; Part 2, New York, 1882). In his prologue he states that his models were Balzac, Scott, and Manzoni, and he succeeded in reducing the element of propaganda to an acceptable level, as opposed to Zambrana or Suárez y Romero (q.v.), who treated slavery as a central theme. Pérez Galdós 'never believed that a Cuban could write anything so good'. The incestuous relationship occurring in *Cecilia Valdés* recurs in two short novels published in the *Miscelánea de Útil y Agradable Recreo* (1837): *La peña blanca* and *El ave muerta*. He wrote many minor novels, such as *El penitente* (1844), now little read. In 1845 he published *Compendio geográfico de la Isla de Cuba*.

There is a good bibliography and study by Olga Blondet Tudisco and Antonio Tudisco in their edition, *Cecilia Valdés* (New York, 1971). See also J. J. Geada, *Un novelista pinareño: Cirilo Villaverde* (1929); Robert J. Young, *La novela costumbrista de Cirilo Villaverde* (Mexico City, 1949); Emeterio S. Santovenia, *Personajes y paisajes de Villaverde* (1955); and J. C. Sánchez, *La obra novelística de Cirilo Villaverde* (Madrid, 1973).

VILLAVICIOSA, JOSÉ DE (1589–1658), b. Sigüenza. Burlesque poet. After studying law in Cuenca, he practised in Madrid, and from 1622 worked for the Inquisition. *La Moschea: poética inventiva en octava rima* (Cuenca, 1615) is a burlesque epic in twelve cantos imitating the *Moschaea* of Teofilo Folengo published in 1521, itself an imitation of the Greek *Batrachomyomachia* ('Battle of frogs and mice'), a parody formerly attributed to Homer but actually much later in date.

Villaviciosa's mock epic tells of the war between flies and their allies including mosquitoes and horseflies on the one hand, and on the other ants and their confederates, among them spiders, bedbugs, lice, and fleas. The latter party wins. Homer, Virgil, and Ovid are potent influences, but there are reminiscences of many other classical and modern authors, especially of Dante. The poem is reprinted in vol. 17 (1851) of the BAE, and was studied by A. González

Palencia in a chapter of his *Historias y leyendas* (1942).

VILLEGAS, ALONSO DE (1534–1615), b. Toledo. Playwright and hagiographer, called 'Selvago'. Chaplain of the Toledan *mozárabes*. He is famous for the anonymous five-act *Comedia llamada Selvagia* (Toledo, 1554) reprinted in the Colección de Libros Raros y Curiosos (1873). Apart from Lope de Vega's *Dorotea* (qq.v.), the *Selvagia* is the best imitation of the *Celestina* (q.v.) and the author, whose name is proved by an acrostic, was affectionately called 'Villegas Selvago' after his hero.

A prolific hagiographer, Villegas compiled a five-volume *Flos sanctorum* (Toledo, 1580–1603) and individual lives of a number of saints: *Vida de San Isidro Labrador* (1592) and *Vida de San Tirso* (Toledo, 1595) among others. His *Vitoria o Triunfo de Iesu Cristo* (1600) is only one of many pious books popular in their day.

VILLEGAS, ANTONIO DE (1512?–c. 1551), b. Medina del Campo. Poet and novelist whose name has been associated, probably fictitiously, with the Moorish tale of *Abencerraje y de la Hermosa Jarifa* (q.v.), because an early version appears in his *Inventario* (Medina del Campo, 1565), a book licensed by the ecclesiastical authorities in 1551. F. López Estrada, who has collaborated with J. Keller in an edition of *El Abencerraje* (Chapel Hill, N.C., 1964), has published 'Estudio y texto de la narración pastoril "Ausencia y soledad amor"' from the same collection in the *BRAE*, vol. 29 (1949), pp. 99–133. Other contents include *canciones*, *coplas*, a thin retelling of the story of Pyramus and Thisbe, *Fantasía y comparaciones de amor*, and *Definición de los celos*. The *Inventario* has been edited by F. López Estrada (2 vols., 1955–6) in the Joyas Bibliográficas. A most penetrating study of Villegas by Marcel Bataillon is entitled '¿Melancolía renacentista o melancolía judía?' in *Homenaje a Archer M. Huntington* (1952).

VILLEGAS, ESTEBAN MANUEL DE (1589–1669), b. Matute, Nájera, Logroño. Poet. After the brothers Leonardo de Argensola (qq.v.), the most important member of the so-called Aragonese school. Little of his life is known, except that he married c. 1626, practised law, and was exiled by the Inquisition from Nájera, Logroño, and Madrid for four years from 1659.

His epic poems were failures, but the splendid versions and imitations from Anacreon inspired a number of 18th-c. writers, among them Meléndez Valdés and Iglesias de la Casa (qq.v.). He also translated some *Odes* of Horace better than any previous Spaniard, and produced a version of Boethius' *Consolatio philosophiae* (1665) in his old age. He is still appreciated for the *Eróticas o amatorias* (2 vols., Nájera, 1618), reprinted in vols. 42 and 61 (1857, 1869) of the BAE but more conveniently read in the Clásicos Castellanos edition (1913) by N. Alonso Cortés.

VILLEGAS SELVAGO, Alonso de, see Villegas, Alonso de.

VILLENA, Enrique de (1384–1434), b. Iniesta, Cuenca. Translator, astrologer, and writer on cookery. A false claimant to the title of Marqués de Villena, he divorced his wife María de Castilla to obtain honours from King Enrique III (whose concubine she had become). The king offered him a knighthood in the Order of Calatrava but later withdrew it. Villena was reputed a great gourmand and womanizer, and he was deprived of his goods and chattels late in life for alleged sorcery. After this he retired to Iniesta to devote himself to magical studies. At Villena's death Juan II ordered his library to be burnt but the Bishop of Segovia, Fray Lope de Barrientos, saved some important texts, using them in his own *Tractado de las especies de adivinanza*. Villena's story has been dramatized by Lope de Vega, Hartzenbusch (qq.v.), and others. Villena's greatest claim to literary fame is the first complete version in a peninsular language of Dante's *Divina Commedia*, an enterprise which made possible a great increase and deepening of Italianism in Castilian letters. Villena made the first complete version of the *Aeneid* (1427) into Castilian, and also translated Cicero's *Rhetoric*.

The *Arte de trovar* (1433) is a compilation largely based on Provençal poetic models; it has been edited by F. Sánchez Cantón in the *Revista de Filología Española* (1919).

Los doce trabajos de Hércules (Valencia, 1417) is a moralizing Christian-pagan allegory in Catalan which Villena himself later translated into Castilian. Villena's occult studies can be examined in Millás's edition of his 'Tratado de astrología' in the *Revista de Filología Española*, vol. 27 (1943), and his book on the evil eye, *Libro de aojamiento, o fascinología*, in *Revue Hispanique* (1917).

In 1423 he composed his best book, a gleeful and well-informed cookery book and manual of carving entitled *Arte cisoria, o Tractado del arte de cortar con el cuchillo*, first published in 1766 by the library of San Lorenzo, and reprinted in Barcelona in 1879.

See E. Cotarelo y Mori, *Don Enrique de Villena: su vida y obras* (1896).

VIÑAS, David (1929–), b. Buenos Aires. Argentinian novelist, essayist, and short-story writer. A professed Marxist, he has used the novel as a weapon to change attitudes towards existing institutions. The short stories in *Las malas costumbres* (1963) do not show Viñas at his best, for his vision is essentially panoramic and needs the novel's length to succeed. *Cayó sobre su rostro* (1955) takes as its hated hero Antonio Vera, a landowner who finds sexual and political victims among exploited Indians. *Los años despiadados* (1956) describes the deception of the young Rubén Marcó (and of the common people whom he represents), in the early years of Péron's rule. *Un dios cotidiano* (1957) is an autobiographical account of how the young teacher Carlos Ferré fails as a teacher in a Salesian College of Buenos Aires during the 1930s; the hypocrisy that students learn from political and religious leaders is implicitly blamed for this. *Los dueños de la tierra* (1959) is a powerful, committed novel on the exploitation of Indians, chronicling the years 1892, 1917, and 1920. *Dar la cara* (1962) emphasizes the negative aspects of Argentina during the failed 'Revolución Libertadora' of 1956; this was followed by *Las malas costumbres* (1963); *En la semana trágica* (1966) attacks police brutality against strikers in 1919; *Los hombres de a caballo* (Havana, 1967) is a novel of the Argentine military expedition of 1964 against *guerrilleros* in Peru, sardonically contrasting the military ideals of honour, duty, and courage with the daily life and experiences of the officer Emilio Godoy. Viñas's latest novel is *Cosas concretas* (1969).

Viñas is a vigorous essayist and literary journalist, occasionally using the pseudonym 'Raquel Weinbaum'. His books in this genre include *De Sarmiento a Cortázar: literatura argentina y realidad política* (1964); *Laferrère: del apogeo de la oligarquía a la crisis de la ciudad liberal* (Rosario, 1965); and *Grotesco, inmigración y fracaso* (1973), on the Argentinian playwright Armando Discépolo (q.v.).

VINCENZI, Moisés (1895–), b. Tres Ríos, Costa Rica. A philosopher and essayist, he has written more than fifty books (including four novels). Some of the best known are *Crítica trascendental* (1920), *Ruinas y leyendas: metafísica de la libertad* (1921), *Principios de crítica filosófica* (Paris, 1928), and *El hombre y el cosmos* (1961).

VINYOLI, Joan (1914–), b. Barcelona. Catalan poet. He was drawn to poetry by the work of Rainer Maria Rilke, and contributed translations from Rilke, Hölderlin, and Goethe to Catalan magazines. He was noticed by Carles Riba, and in Riba's circle met Rosselló-Pòrcel, Teixidor, and others. His education had been cut short before he could enter university by the outbreak of Civil War, so he is largely self-taught. His poetry is existentialist, melancholy, and seeks to escape from reality, especially in the earliest collection *Primer desenllac* (1937). Rilke's influence gradually disappears in *De vida i somni* (1948) and *Les hores retrobadas* (1951), and in *El callat* (1956) and *Realitats* (1963) the concrete presence of daily life makes itself amply felt. His recent books include *Encara los paraules* (Barcelona, 1973). Vinyoli's *Poesia completa 1937–75* (Barcelona, 1975) has an introduction by Joan Teixidor. *Vent d'aram* (1976) won both the Premi de la Crítica and the Premi 'Serra d'or' for 1976.

VÍQUEZ, Pío (1850–99), b. Cartago, Costa Rica. Journalist and poet, he founded and ran *El Heraldo* (1893–) until shortly before his death, contributing daily columns on national and foreign affairs. In 1903 a selection of his writing entitled *Miscelánea: prosa y verso* was compiled by R. Machado Jáuregui and T. Zúñiga Montúfar.

VIRUÉS, Cristóbal de (1550?–1614?), b. Valencia. Epic poet and playwright. Virués is reported to have fought as a soldier at Lepanto and Milan. His long anti-Reformist poem in *octavas reales*, *El Monserrate* (1587), deals with the legend of the hermit Juan Garín, and was successful both in a popular sense (*El Monserrate segundo* (Milan, 1602) being its sequel) and in a critical sense (Cervantes preserved it from destruction in the bookburning scene of *Quijote*). It is reprinted in vol. 17 (1851) of the BAE.

Virués wrote plays from *c.* 1575 to 1590 but they were not published until 1609, when they appeared as *Obras trágicas y líricas del capitán Cristóbal de Virués*. These are *La gran Semíramis*, *La cruel Casandra*, *Atila furioso*, *La infelice Marcela*, and *Elisa Dido*. They are more properly described as melodramas than tragedies.

See C. V. Sargent, *A study of the dramatic works of Cristóbal de Virués* (New York, 1930), and John G. Weiger, *The Valencian dramatists of Spain's Golden Age* (New York, 1976), pp. 30–49 in Twayne's World Authors series.

Visión de Anáhuac, one of a projected series of essays by Alfonso Reyes (q.v.), first published in San José, Costa Rica (1917), and often reprinted, on the national spirit of Mexico and the Mexican mission on earth. After evoking the pre-Columbian world of Tenochtitlán and the court of Montezuma, Reyes suggests that it is as absurd to attempt to recreate the indigenous tradition obliterated by the *conquistadores* as to perpetuate their dream of a purely Castilian Mexico.

Mexico, he argues, has always been a con-fluence of different racial strains: this, and their common mental attitude to the natural environment of Mexico, constitutes the strength of Mexicans. Recognition that they share the same physical surroundings creates a common identity for Indian, *mestizo*, and Spaniard alike.

Visita de los chistes, the fifth of the *Sueños* of Francisco de Quevedo (qq.v.).

VITALE, Ida (1928–), b. Montevideo. Uruguayan poet, translator of poetry and plays, and critic. Her distinctive *œuvre* up to 1960 included only fifty poems, most of them subjective and even other-worldly, though not mystical. Her central theme is time, regarded as holy, cruel, and all-powerful: a characteristic poem, about the conjunction of summer and autumn, is 'Paso a paso'. Her books are *La luz de esta memoria* (1949), *Palabra dada* (1954), and *Cada uno en su noche* (1960), the last containing the best of her earlier work with 19 new poems.

VITIER, Cintio (1921–), b. Havana. Cuban poet, anthologist, and critic. His important anthologies include *Diez poetas cubanos, 1937–1947* (1948), *Cincuenta años de poesía cubana, 1902–1952* (1952), and *Los poetas románticos cubanos* (1962).

His poetry is divided sharply into two phases: the lyrical, erudite pre-revolutionary period of *Extrañeza de estar* (1943), the collected *Vísperas* (1953), and his best book to date, the revelatory *Canto llano* (1956) which deals with poetic theory among other matters; and the bombastic post-revolutionary poems, which began badly, but during the mid-1960s achieved excellence in *Testimonios* (1968), committed poetry as fine as the 'pure poetry' of *Canto llano*.

Viudo Rius, El (1945), the second novel in the sequence *La ceniza fue árbol* by Ignacio Agustí (qq.v.).

Viva mi dueño (1928), the second novel in the cycle *El ruedo ibérico* by Ramón del Valle-Inclán (qq.v.).

VIVANCO, Luis Felipe (1907–75), b. San Lorenzo del Escorial. Poet and literary journalist, who trained as an architect. His dominant theme is God, and even his love poems are tinged with religious symbolism in his first book, *Cantos de primavera* (1936). Readings in Claudel and Jammes (whom he has translated) influenced his style towards a greater openness to religious experience, expressed in free, irregular metre. *Tiempo de dolor* (1940) was probably his best book. Later collections are *Continuación de la vida*

(1949), *El descampado* (1957), *Memoria de la plata* (1958), the so-called 'autobiographical legend', *Los ojos de Toledo* (Barcelona, 1953), and *Lecciones para el hijo* (1961).

Los caminos (*1945–65*) has been reissued with *Continuación de la vida*, *El descampado*, and *Lugares vividos* (1974) and there is a good selection made by J. Mª. Valverde, *Antología poética* (1976).

VIVES, JUAN LUIS (1492–1540), b. Valencia, Renaissance polymath, who wrote in Latin. A *converso* (q.v.) who probably lived abroad as a consequence, he studied in Paris 1509–12, in which latter year he went to Bruges as tutor to the Valldaura family, and married Margarita Valldaura in 1524, afterwards being appointed Professor of Humanities at Louvain. Here he met Erasmus, who was to become his close friend and encouraged him to compose an elaborate commentary (1522) on St. Augustine's *De civitate Dei*. On Nebrija's death in 1622, Vives was offered his chair at Alcalá, but refused it. Instead he accepted an invitation to visit the court of Henry VIII of England, where he was tutor to the Princess Mary, and it was for her that he wrote *De ratione studii puerilis epistolae duae* (1523). While in England, he lectured on philosophy at Corpus Christi College, Oxford. On opposing Henry's divorce from Catherine of Aragón he lost the king's favour and was confined to his house for six weeks. On his release, he returned to Bruges (1527), where he wrote many works, some directed against the Aristotelianism current at the time. His emphasis on the need for direct experience for true knowledge (in *De causis corruptarum artium*) predates the *Organon* of Bacon. Among his other important works are *De disciplinis*, *De prima philosophia*, and *De institutione féminae christianae* (which was to inspire Luis de León (q.v.) when writing *La perfecta casada*), soon translated into Spanish (1528) and English (1540).

Vives opposes the extremes of individualism in *De subventione pauperum* and communism (of the Anabaptist variety) in *De communione rerum*. His charming dialogues for use in schools, the *Exercitatio lingua latinae*, deservedly achieved wide distribution over a long period.

The important *Introductio ad sapientiam* (1524) was rendered into English by Morysone as *An introduction to wysdome* (1540).

A recent edition of Vives's *Obras completas* in Spanish has been published by Lorenzo Riber (2 vols., 1948).

See Carlos G. Noreña, *Juan Luis Vives* (The Hague, 1970), in English.

Vorágine, La (1924), a novel by the Colombian José Eustasio Rivera (q.v.), written after he had spent some time as the secretary of a Colombian boundary commission's expedition to the Amazon jungle. Rivera's only novel, *La vorágine* was the first novel to emerge from outside the Colombian aristocracy, and was considered the major novel of Colombia before *Cien años de soledad* by Gabriel García Márquez (qq.v.).

It is the semi-fictional, semi-autobiographical account by an urban intellectual, Arturo Cova, of his life among the cowboys on the plains, and the terrible conditions suffered by Indians working in the rubber industry of the jungle. Cova, forced to flee Bogotá with his mistress, gradually recognizes the force of jungle law, and adapts to it in order to survive. The melodramatic plot is never unbelievable, because the setting is naturalistically exotic; the social commentary is just, humane, but never obtrusive, while the lyrical power of the writing convinces because the hero-narrator is in fact a well-known poet. The climax is impressive in showing the clash between *civilización* and *barbarie* which Colombians of the future will have to resolve.

See Trinidad Pérez (ed.), *Recopilación de textos sobre tres novelas ejemplares* (Havana, 1971), the other two novels studied being *Don Segundo Sombra* and *Doña Bárbara* (qq.v.).

VOSSLER, KARL (1872–1949), b. Hohenheim. German philologist, Romance scholar, and, towards the latter part of his career, a distinguished Hispanist; both his *Lope de Vega und sein Zeitalter* (1932) and *Poesie der Einsamkeit in Spanien* (1935) having been translated into Spanish (1933 and 1941 respectively). Many of his lectures and articles have been collected in Colección Austral volumes, notably the *Introducción a la literatura española del Siglo de Oro* (Madrid, 1934; 2nd edn., Buenos Aires, 1945), the somewhat disappointingly superficial *Fray Luis de León* (Munich, 1943; Madrid, 1946), and the stimulating miscellany *Escritores y poetas de España* (Buenos Aires, 1947), which includes a useful essay on Sor Juana Inés de la Cruz (q.v.).

W

WAST, Hugo, pseudonym of Gustavo Adolfo Martínez Zuviría (q.v.).

WESTPHALEN, Emilio Adolfo (1911–), Peruvian surrealist poet and editor who now lives in Rome. His volume of work though small has nevertheless been influential in promoting the surreal in subsequent Peruvian writing. *Las ínsulas extrañas* (1933) and *Abolición de la muerte* (1935) contain 18 poems in all; they are concerned mainly with the reality of impalpable mystery and the curiously half-waking life of apparently inanimate objects. 'Andando el tiempo' and 'Una cabeza humana' are typical examples of his work.

Westphalen published no poetry after 1935, but edited two magazines still regarded with respect: the eight numbers of *Las Moradas* (1947-9), and the longer-lived *Amaru* (1967–71), whose purpose was to purify poetry of all but 'su esencia irracional, el automatismo síquico, y la verdad poética', to quote E. Núñez.

WÉYLAND, Walter Guido (1914–), b. Rosario de Santa Fe. Argentinian novelist, short-story writer, and literary journalist who wrote his early, now repudiated, works as 'Silverio Boj'. These were his first novel, *El pequeño monstruo* (Tucumán, 1938) and *Ubicación de Don Segundo Sombra y otros ensayos* (Tucumán, 1940). In Jujuy and later in Tucumán he wrote his important novel *Áspero intermedio* (1941; 2nd edn., 1949) and contributed to the local *¡Ya!* and *El Orden*. But since 1943 he has lived in Buenos Aires, writing for *La Nación* and producing a single collection of short stories, *Belgrano 'R'* (1953). A novel, *El fuego sombrío*, was announced before 1961 but is apparently still unpublished. Wéyland's themes are adolescence and provincial life, often interacting. His style is naturalistic, close to that of his compatriot and contemporary Bernardo Verbitsky (q.v.).

WHITE, Joseph Blanco, see Blanco White, José María.

WILCOCK, Juan Rodolfo (1919–), b. Buenos Aires. Argentinian writer in several languages, and one of the so-called Generation of 1940, with Roberto Paine, Enrique Molina, María Granati, and César Fernández Moreno. In Spanish he has published *Libro de poemas y canciones* (1940), followed by *Persecución de las musas menores* (1945), *Ensayos de poesía lírica* (1945), *Los hermosos días* (1946), and *Sexto* (1953).

In Italian his books so far are *Caos* (short stories, Milan, 1961), *Luoghi comuni* (poetry, 1961), *Fatti inquietanti del nostro tempo* (1961), *Teatro in prosa e in versi* (Milan, 1962), and *La parola morte* (1968), the last a sequence of poems on the end of the world.

Wilcock has translated from Christopher Marlowe and James Joyce (*Finnegans Wake*).

WILDE, Eduardo (1844–1913), b. Tupiza, Bolivia, his family having fled from the Rosas regime in Argentina. Realist novelist and humorist of the so-called Generation of 1880. He qualified as a doctor in 1870 and taught anatomy, but his social concern led him into politics. He was Minister of Education (1882–6), subsequently abandoned public life (1889–98), travelled in North America, Europe, the Near East and Far East, but returned when Roca became Minister of the Interior, and was appointed ambassador in Madrid and the Low Countries. His father was James Wellesley Wilde, a relative of the Duke of Wellington, and Wilde's familiarity with English literature led him to adopt themes and stylistic mannerisms from Dickens in his serious novels, in his short stories, and in his humorous books. Literature was always peripheral in his life, and many of his writings are fragmentary, but he will be remembered for short stories collected under the ironic, mock-reproachful title of *Tiempo perdido* (Buenos Aires, 2 vols., 1878) and *Prometeo y Cía.* (1899), and a vigorous novelized autobiography, *Aguas abajo* (1914). Wilde was the first serious Argentinian writer for children. A Spencerian positivist in philosophy and a liberal in politics, Wilde was at his most pleasantly discursive in the travel books *Viajes y observaciones* (Buenos Aires, 2 vols., 1892) and *Por mares y tierras* (Buenos Aires, 1899), published in both sets of the *Obras completas*, one in 19 vols. (1917–39) and another in 15 vols. (1923–).

There is a recent anthology of Wilde's short stories: *Tini y otros relatos* (Buenos Aires, 1960), and a later selection edited by Teresita Frugoni de Fritsche (Buenos Aires, 1973). Wilde's selected *Escritos literarios* appeared in Buenos Aires in 1952.

Yolanda H. Buffa Peyrot's bibliography of Wilde appeared in *Bibliografía Argentina de Artes y Letras*, no. 31 (Buenos Aires, 1967).

See Florencio Escardó, *Ensayo sobre Eduardo Wilde* (Buenos Aires, 1943; 2nd edn., 1959); and Gastón Gori, *Eduardo Wilde* (Santa Fe, 1962).

WILSON, Edward Meryon (1906–77), b. Kendal. British Hispanist educated at Cambridge, who was Cervantes Professor of Spanish at King's College, London, from 1945 to 1953, and for the next twenty years occupied the Chair of Spanish at Cambridge University.

Wilson achieved recognition for his sensitive verse translations, *The Solitudes of Don Luis de Góngora* (Cambridge, 1931; rev. edn., 1965, the latter with facing text). With Jack Sage he wrote *Poesías líricas en las obras dramáticas de Calderón. Citas y glosas* (1964), inaugurating the now well-known Támesis monograph series. With F. J. Norton he wrote *Two Spanish verse chap-books* (Cambridge, 1969), and edited *Romance de Amadís c. 1515–19* and *Juyzio hallado y trobado, c. 1510.* He wrote the chapter on Calderón in R. O. Jones's standard *A literary history of Spain, vol. 3: The Golden Age: drama, 1492–1700* (London, 1971).

See R. O. Jones (ed.), *Studies in Spanish*

literature of the Golden Age presented to Edward M. Wilson (1973), which includes a six-page list of his publications.

WYLD OSPINA, Carlos (1891–1958), b. Antigua. Guatemalan novelist, poet, and short-story writer. A journalist for more than thirty years, he directed *El Independiente* (Mexico City) 1913–14, the *Diario de Los Altos* (Quezaltenango) 1915, jointly directed *El Pueblo* (1920–1), edited *El Imparcial* (1922–5), and directed the *Diario de Centro América* from 1947, after a parliamentary career in 1932–5 and 1937–42.

Beginning as a poet, with *Las dádivas simples* (1921), he made his name as a writer of fiction: *El solar de los Gonzagas* (1924, a novel); *La tierra de las Nahuyacas* (1933), regional stories; and another novel: *La gringa* (1935). Wyld Ospina also published an essay on three Guatemalan dictators, *El autócrata* (1929), and a second book of poems: *Los lares apagados* (1957).

X

XAMMAR, Luis Fabio (1911–47), b. Lima. Peruvian poet and critic. His poetry was collected in *Las voces armoniosas* (1932), *Wayno* (1937), and *Alta niebla.* As a critic he concentrated on Peruvian literature, with studies of Ricardo Palma and Concolorcorvo (qq.v.). His books also included *Valores humanos en la obra de Leónidas Yerovi* (1938) and *Valdelomar-signo* (1940). In 1939 he brought out the review *3* with Arturo Jiménez Borja and José Hernández.

XENIUS, pseudonym of Eugenio d'Ors y Rovira (see Ors y Rovira).

XÉRICA, Pablo de, see Jérica, Pablo de.

XIMENA DÍAZ, see Díaz, Jimena or Ximena.

XIMÉNEZ, see also Jiménez.

XIMÉNEZ, Maín, pseudonym of Miguel Ángel Osorio Benítez (q.v.).

XIMÉNEZ DE CISNEROS, Cardinal Francisco (1436–1517), b. Torrelaguna, Madrid. Grand Inquisitor and Civil Administrator of Spain, he succeeded in spreading the power of the Inquisition to Oran, the Canaries, and Cuba, although before his appointment he had opposed the establishment of the Inquisition.

In 1506 he founded the university of Alcalá, where he recruited the team of scholars for the Complutensian Bible (q.v.). In 1513 he sponsored the publication of Gabriel Alonso de Herrera's *Agricultura general* and its distribution among the largely illiterate farming community.

Employed by Philip IV to obtain the Cardinal's beatification, Pedro de Quintanilla attempted to demonstrate, in his curious *Oranum Ximenii virtute catholicum* (Rome, 1658), that from the date of his death to 1657 the Cardinal had intervened with the aid of miracles to extend Roman Catholicism from Oran through Africa and the Americas.

XIMÉNEZ DE RADA, Rodrigo (1170?–1247), b. Puente de la Reina, Navarra. Historian and Archbishop of Toledo. At the command of Ferdinand III of Castile, he wrote the *Historia gothica, vel De rebus Hispaniae*, better known as the *Crónica del Toledano*, which covered the period from the Gothic invasion to 1243 and was edited by A. Paz y Meliá in the Colección de Documentos Inéditos para la Historia de España, vol. 88 (1887). The popularity of the vernacular version paved the way for the later histories commissioned by Alfonso X (q.v.).

Ximénez de Rada also wrote *Historia arabum* (critical edn. by J. Lozano Sánchez, 1974), *Historia romanorum,* and *Breviarum historiae catholicae.*

XIMÉNEZ DE SANDOVAL Y TAPIA, FELIPE (1903–), b. Madrid. Novelist, translator, journalist, and biographer. His novels include *Tres mujeres más equis* (1930), *Los nueve puñales* (1936), the pro-Falange *Camisa azul* (1940), *El hombre y el loro* (1951) whose plot recalls that of David Garnett's *Lady into fox*, the Galdosian *Manuela Limón* (1951), and the Dickensian *Las patillas rojas* (1954).

He has written the well-known *Biografía apasionada de José Antonio* (1941); other biographies of Don Juan de Austria, Catherine of Aragón, A. Alcalá Galiano, Columbus, and Cadalso; and two books on Spanish Trappists: *A las puertas del cielo* (1958), which is descriptive, and *La comunidad errante* (1960), which is historical.

His interpretation of Spanish history, *La piel de toro* (Barcelona, 1948) was subtitled *cumbres y simas de la historia de España*.

XIRAU, RAMÓN (1924–), b. Barcelona. Philosopher and literary critic, who has lived and taught in Mexico since 1939. He has written *Método y metafísica en la filosofía de Descartes* (1946), *Duración y existencia* (1947), *El péndulo y la espiral* (1959), and an *Introducción a la historia de filosofía* (1964).

From 1953 to 1964 he was deputy director of the Centro Mexicano de Escritores and editor of its *Boletín*. He was the co-founder and editor of *Diálogos*. His literary studies include *Tres poetas de la soledad* (1955), *Poesía hispanoamericana y española* (1961), and *Poetas de México y España* (1962). He has written poetry in Catalan, including *Les platges* (Barcelona, 1974).

Y

YAGÜE DE SALAS, JUAN, the forger of the earliest version of *Los amantes de Teruel* (q.v.).

YAN, MARI, pseudonym of María Flora Yáñez de Echevarría (q.v.).

YÁÑEZ, AGUSTÍN (1904–), b. Guadalajara, Jalisco. Mexican novelist, short-story writer, and scholar. Governor of the State of Jalisco 1952–9, Subsecretary to the President 1962–4, and Minister of Education 1964–70; Yáñez has written the six volumes, *Discursos al servicio de la educación pública*. He has also written a great deal on Mexico and its literature: *El pensador mexicano* (1940), *Genio y figuras de Guadalajara* (1941), *Flor de juegos antiguos* and *Mitos indígenas* (both 1942), *El contenido social de la literatura iberoamericana* (1944), *Alfonso Gutiérrez Hermosillo y algunos amigos* (1945), *El clima espiritual de Jalisco* (1945), and *Don Justo Sierra* (1950).

Al filo del agua (1947), the tenth of his novels, was the first to gain wide attention. It deals with a backward village in Jalisco the year before the Mexican Revolution of 1910. Damián Limón murders his father and sweetheart, then in 1910 María, the priest's niece, runs away with the rebels of Rito Becerra. Yáñez shows how these episodes are related, borrowing Faulkner's stream-of-consciousness technique. *La creación* (1959; 3rd edn., 1963) elaborates an episode in the previous novel: Gabriel's relationship with Victoria and María. Here Yáñez uses the theme of art as a creative force, whereas religious superstition represents a destructive force in *Al filo del agua*, which has been considered the finest Mexican novel of the century. *Ojerosa y pintada* (1959) tells the story of a day in the life of a Mexico City taxi-driver. *La tierra pródiga* (1960) deals with tradition and modernization in the hot lands of coastal Mexico, while *Las tierras flacas* (1962) charts the gradual disappearance of feudal power between 1920 and 1925. Yáñez has subsequently published *Tres cuentos* (1964) and *Los sentidos del aire* (1964).

See J. J. Flasher, *México contemporáneo en las novelas de Agustín Yáñez* (1969); A. Rangel Guerra, *Agustín Yáñez* (1969); Linda M. Van Conant, *Agustín Yáñez, intérprete de la novela mexicana moderna* (1969); and H. F. Giacoman (ed.), *Homenaje a Agustín Yáñez* (New York, 1973), a critical anthology.

YÁÑEZ, RODRIGO (*fl.* 1348), the copyist or writer of the *Poema de Alfonso XI* (q.v.).

YÁÑEZ DE ECHEVARRÍA, MARÍA FLORA (1901–), b. Santiago. She has also written as 'Mari Yan'. Chilean *criollista* writer influenced by Mariano Latorre (q.v.). Her novels and short stories show a keen appreciation of Chile's natural beauties and native cultures: *El abrazo de la tierra* (1933), *Espejo sin imagen* (1936), *Las cenizas* (1942), *El estanque* (1945), *La piedra* (1952), the short stories in *Juan Estrella* (Madrid, 1955), and *¿Dónde están el trigo y el vino?* (1963).

She has also compiled the *Antología del cuento chileno moderno* (1958, 2nd edn., 1965).

YANKAS, Lautaro, pseudonym of Manuel Soto Morales (q.v.).

YEPES, José Ramón (1822–81), b. Maracaibo, Venezuelan poet, novelist, and sometime Minister of the Navy. He went into exile several time to avoid imprisonment. His best poetry is perhaps that describing Lake Maracaibo. Creole ballads such as *Balada marina* also form an important part of his *Poesías* (Maracaibo, 1882). His fictional treatment of Indian legends in *Anaida* and *Iguaraya* (each dealing with the rivalry of two Indians seeking the same girl) was influenced by Chateaubriand.

YEPES Y ÁLVAREZ, Juan de, the secular name of San Juan de la Cruz (q.v.).

Yerma, a play by Federico García Lorca (q.v.) first performed in 1934. It is the central play in the rural trilogy that opens with the supernatural, fantastic *Bodas de sangre* and closes with the documentary, realistic *La casa de Bernarda Alba* (qq.v.).

Yerma (her name means 'the barren one') is married by her family to Juan, who is fertile but uninterested in children. Yerma, in love with Víctor, is also fertile but condemned to live without the children she desperately wants. The element of the supernatural (such as the inevitability of fate) is perhaps better integrated into the action here than in *Bodas de sangre*. In a drama which succeeds on the several levels of poetic speech, symbolism, and popular drama, her agony of stifled maternity finds its outlet in the murder of Juan. 'I have killed my child' she cries in despair. As in the rest of this trilogy, Lorca complains bitterly against the exploitation of women in Spain, keeping the character of Yerma intentionally schematic to broaden the area of his indictment.

See C. Calvin, 'The imagery of Lorca's "Yerma"' in *Modern Language Quarterly*, vol. 21 (1960), pp. 122–30; R. Skloot, 'Theme and image in Lorca's "Yerma"' in *Drama Survey*, vol. 5 (1966), pp. 151–61; and P. Sullivan, 'The mythical tragedy of "Yerma"' in *BHS*, vol. 49 (1972), pp. 265–78.

YEROVI, Leónidas N. (1881–1917), b. Lima, Peruvian journalist, poet, and dramatist. His often humorous *Poesías líricas* (1917) show a belated Romantic strain during the rise of modernism, which he parodies. His work was reprinted in vol. 9 of the Biblioteca de Cultura Peruviana (Paris, 1938).

Yerovi's *zarzuelas* and *comedias de costumbres* such as *La gente loca* are still popular.

YNDURAIN, Francisco (1910–   ), b. Aoíz, Navarra. Professor of Spanish Language and Literature in the University of Saragossa. He has published some *Contribuciones al estudio del dialecto navarro-aragonés* (Saragossa, 1945). He has edited Quevedo's *Sueños* (Saragossa, 1943) and Vélez de Guevara's *Reinar después de morir* (Saragossa, 1944), and has written on Gracián, San Juan de la Cruz, Palau, and the modern Spanish novel.

He has also compiled an *Antología de la novela española* (1954) and written *El pensamiento de Quevedo* (Saragossa, 1954).

YNSFRÁN, Pablo Max (1894–   ), Paraguayan poet and founder-member of the literary review *Crónica* (q.v.). *Parnaso paraguayo* (Barcelona, 1924) contains his 'Cántico inmortal' and 'La parábola de la selva'.

A member of parliament in 1924 and subsequently ambassador to Washington, Ynsfrán was a member of the cabinet of General José Félix Estigarribia, whose illustrated memoirs he produced in English as *The epic of the Chaco War . . ., 1932–35* (Austin, 1950).

Ynsfrán was exiled by the dictator General Higinio Morínigo in 1940, and went to the U.S.A. His books include *El Paraguay contemporáneo* (1929) and *La expedición norteamericana contra el Paraguay, 1858–59* (Mexico City, 1958).

Yoçef, Coplas de, an example of *aljamía* (q.v.) literature. A 14th-c. poem on the story of Joseph in Egypt, it is written in Spanish but in Hebrew script. Unlike the *Poema de Yuçuf* (q.v.), it follows the Bible rather than the Qur'an.

The *Coplas* survive in a 15th-c. MS. (with the *Proverbios morales* of Shem Tov Ardutiel, q.v.) which has been edited by I. González Llubera (Cambridge, 1935).

Yuçuf, Poema de, until the recent discovery of the *kharjas* (q.v.), thought to have been the earliest surviving example of *aljamía* (q.v.) literature.

Its 312 stanzas were written in *cuaderna vía* (q.v.) by an anonymous Aragonese *morisco*, probably in the early 14th c. One of the two MSS. is in the Biblioteca Nacional, Madrid; the other is in the Academia de la Historia, Madrid. The story of Joseph in Egypt is laboriously told from rabbinical legends and the twelfth *sura* of al-Quran. The final stanzas are lacking, and the work's main interest is philological. The *Poema de Yuçuf* has been edited by R. Menéndez Pidal in *RABM* (1902), and by W. W. Johnson (1974).

YUNQUE, Álvaro, pseudonym of Arístides Gandolfi Herrero (q.v.).

YXART Y MORAGAS, José (1852–95), b. Tarragona. Drama critic of the Catalan Renaissance. His first book was in Catalan: *Lo teatre català: son passat, present y porvenir* (1879); and his later books in Castilian: the five-volume

chronicle, *El año pasado: letras y artes en Barcelona* (Barcelona, 1886–90); and *El arte escénico en España* (1893).

See M. de Montoliu, *José Yxart, el gran crítico del renacimiento literario catalán* (Tarragona, 1956).

Z

ZABALETA, Juan de (*c.* 1610–*c.* 1670), b. Madrid. Playwright (influenced by Calderón, q.v.) and *costumbrista* (influenced in his style by Gracián, q.v.). His ugliness caused him ridicule, his poverty suffering, and his gout blindness.

His principal works are witty and informative descriptions of Madrid society in *El día de fiesta por la mañana* (1654) and *El día de fiesta por la tarde* (1660), which have been reprinted together in E. Correa Calderón's *Costumbristas españoles* (1950–2).

Zabaleta's didactic works were *Problemas de filosofía moral* (1652), *Errores celebrados en la antigüedad* (1652, edited by David Hershberg in Clásicos Castellanos, 1972), and *Milagros de los trabajos* (1667).

Of his plays, *El ermitaño galán* is an advance in style and simplicity on its model by A. Mira de Amescua (q.v.), *La mesonera del cielo. El hijo de Marco Aurelio* is one of a Roman cycle he did not live to complete, and *Osar morir da la vida* deals with the redemption of a sinner. Among his other works are *Historia de Nuestra Señora de Madrid* and *Historia y vida del Conde Matisio*.

ZABALETA, Tomás Erauso y, see Erauso y Zabaleta, Tomás.

Zahurdas de Plutón, Las, the third of the *Sueños* of Francisco de Quevedo (qq.v.).

Zalacaín el aventurero (1909), the final and most successful novel in the *Tierra vasca* trilogy by Pío Baroja (q.v.). The others are *La casa de Aizgorri* (1900), dramatizing the conflict of industry with agriculture, and *El mayorazgo de Labraz* (1903), sketches in the life of a provincial *hidalgo* in a decaying Basque town.

Martín Zalacaín grows up in the countryside around the Bidasoa with his cynical uncle, and the rich young Carlos Okando, who is rejected by Martín's sister Ignacia. Zalacaín flirts with Linda and Rosita, but his heart is set on Catalina, the sister of Carlos. Baroja's breathless narrative rushes through smuggling, the second Carlist war, a gaolbreak, elopement and

marriage with Catalina, and a terrible climax serving Baroja's professed theories of cruelty and pessimism rather better than it serves psychological truth. The disconcertingly abrupt style is intentional, indicating Baroja's concept of the disjointed nature of reality.

ZALAMEA, Jorge (1905–69), Colombian essayist, playwright, and novelist; cousin of Eduardo Zalamea-Borda (q.v.). Zalamea and Alberto Lleras Camargo gathered round themselves a group named Los Nuevos after the magazine they published. They met in a *tertulia* (literary discussion group) at the Café Windsor of Bogotá which, with León de Greiff (q.v.) at the head, included Luis Vidales, Silvio Villegas, Eliseo Arango, José Camacho Carreño, and Augusto Ramírez Moreno.

Zalamea's dialogue-novels, or 'comedias para leer', were the Freudian *El regreso de Eva* (1927) and *El rapto de las Sabinas: farsa romántica* (1941), published with *Pastoral* and *Hostal de Belén.* The essays on Colombian life and national identity, which Zalamea published in Colombian and foreign journals, made his name a household word. *Minerva en la rueca y otros ensayos* (1943) contains essays on English literature and travels in Italy and Mexico.

El gran Burundún Burundá ha muerto (1952) is an impressive, surrealistic prose poem on tyranny which reaches the conclusion that animals are superior to men. The dictator (a figure reminiscent of Jarry's dictator) states that comprehensible speech is the root of all evil; when his coffin is opened, the mourners find a huge parrot shrouded in newsprint.

La metamórfosis de Su Excelencia (1949) is another story dealing with violence and dictatorship, themes obsessive in Colombian literature, as Zalamea himself has indicated in 'La actual literatura de Colombia' (in *Panorama de la actual literatura latinoamericana*, Madrid, 1971, proceedings of the Congreso Cultural in Cuba, 1968).

Zalamea, who founded the journal *Crítica* in 1949, won the Cuban Casa de las Américas prize for his essays *La poesía ignorada y olvidada* (1965), and in 1968 was awarded the Lenin Literature Prize.

ZALAMEA-BORDA, EDUARDO (1907–63), Colombian novelist; cousin of Jorge Zalamea (q.v.). *Cuatro años a bordo de mí mismo* (1934), subtitled *Diario de los cinco sentidos*, is ostensibly an account of life on the lonely salt-flats of La Guajira, his experiences among the Indians, and his return to the city. But these are merely the pretexts for a 'magic-realist' story of Indian women, violence, and death expressed in prose of the utmost sensuality.

See Ricardo A. Latcham, 'Perspectivas de la novela colombiana actual' in *Atenea* (Chile, February 1946), vol. 83, no. 248, pp. 200–35.

ZALDUMBIDE, GONZALO (1884–), b. Quito. The son of Julio Zaldumbide (q.v.), he is arguably the most distinguished *literato* Ecuador has produced this century. Among his numerous works of literary criticism are studies of Barbusse, d'Annunzio, and Ventura García Calderón, but he is best known for *Cuatro clásicos americanos: Rodó, Montalvo, Fray Gaspar de Villarroel, P. J. B. Aguirre* (1947).

It was a lecture, *De Ariel* (1903), stimulated by the work of Rodó, that first made Zaldumbide's name. Shortly afterwards he spent seven years in Europe, mainly in Paris. He served for many years in the diplomatic service, including periods in Havana, Caracas, Bogotá, Buenos Aires, and Río. Zaldumbide's important novel *Égloga trágica* was written in 1910–11, and partially published in magazines 1912–16, but it did not appear as a book until 1956. In 1960–1 the Ecuadorian Department of Education published a two-volume selection by Humberto Toscano, *Páginas de Gonzalo Zaldumbide.*

ZALDUMBIDE, JÚLIO (1833–87), b. Quito. The most important Romantic poet of Ecuador, and a translator of Byron, Moore, Alfieri, and Foscolo. He was a contemplative, melancholy writer whose best-known poems recur throughout the anthologies: *Canto a la música* (1865), *Eternidad de la vida, La mañana, El mediodía,* and *La tarde* (1892). No collected edition of his poetry has so far appeared.

ZAMACOIS, EDUARDO (1876–1954), b. Pinar del Río, Cuba. Spanish novelist and journalist, whose family moved to Brussels when he was four, and to Paris when he was five. In 1886 he went to study in Spain, founding later in Barcelona the weekly *Vida Galante* and in Madrid *El Cuento Semanal* (1907) and *Los Contemporáneos* (1909). His novels fall into two distinct periods, the first devoted to *amor galante* (a euphemism for erotic love) exemplified by *Punto negro* (1898)

and *El seductor* (1902), and the second more broadly based in realism. The watershed between the two phases is *El otro* (1910), one of his best books. The others include *La virtud se paga* (1923), *Memorias de un vagón de ferrocarril* (1924), *Los muertos vivos* (1932), and *El delito de todos* (1935). The other best-selling novelist of his time who cultivated the erotic novel was Felipe Trigo (q.v.).

ZAMÁCOLA, JUAN ANTONIO DE IZA, see IZA ZAMÁCOLA, Juan Antonio de.

ZAMBRANO, MIGUEL ÁNGEL (1899–), b. Riobamba, Ecuador. Poet. His desolate night thoughts were first collected in *Diálogo de los seres profundos* (1956 and later edns.). Zambrano has taken part in politics and legislation; he was responsible for the *Anteproyecto del Código del Trabajo.*

ZAMORA, ALONSO DE (1660–1717), b. Bogotá, Colombia. A *mestizo* historian of the Dominican order. His *Historia del Nuevo Reino y de la Provincia de San Antonio en la religión de Santo Domingo* (1701) is an important source for the ecclesiastical and social history of Colombia. It has been reprinted as *Historia de la Provincia de San Antonio del Nuevo Reino de Granada* (Caracas, 1930).

ZAMORA, ANTONIO DE (c. 1664–1728), b. Madrid. Playwright. His work is divided into religious plays, historical plays, and *comedias de figurón* (q.v.) such as *El hechizado por fuerza* (satirizing the foolish and avaricious Don Claudio), and *Don Domingo de Don Blas.*

Among his historical plays are *Cada uno es linaje aparte* and *La doncella de Orleáns*; on religious themes he wrote *Judas Iscariote* (similar in treatment to Ruiz de Alarcón's *El Anticristo*) and *El lucero de Madrid y divino labrador San Isidro.*

Zamora's finest play deals with the Don Juan legend: *No hay plazo que no se cumpla ni deuda que no se pague y convidado de piedra*, less subtle than Tirso de Molina's version, but more realistic than Zorrilla's (qq.v.). Zamora leaves the ending in doubt, permitting the possibility of the libertine's redemption.

His *Comedias nuevas con los mismos saynetes con que se executaron* (2 vols., 1722) was reprinted in vol. 49 of the BAE. Zamora also wrote *autos sacramentales* (q.v.) in the style of Calderón (q.v.). The first mention of his *La honda de David* dates from 1695.

ZAMORA VICENTE, ALONSO (1916–), b. Madrid. Philologist (former pupil of Ramón Menéndez Pidal) and literary critic. He has written the standard *Dialectología española* (1960,

2nd edn., 1967) and numerous works on philological subjects.

His critical writings include: *Presencia de los clásicos* (Buenos Aires, 1951), *Las 'Sonatas' de Ramón del Valle-Inclán* (Buenos Aires, 1951; 2nd edn., Madrid, 1955), *La novela picaresca* (Buenos Aires, 1961), *Lope de Vega: su vida y su obra* (1961), *Camilo José Cela* (1962), and *Lengua, literatura, intimidad* (1966).

He has produced scholarly editions of the *Poesías* of Francisco de la Torre (1944), the *Oración apologética de España y su mérito literario* of Juan Pablo Forner (Badajoz, 1945), the *Poema de Fernán González* (1946) and, in collaboration with M. J. Canellada de Zamora, two plays by Tirso de Molina, *El amor médico* and *Averíguelo Vargas*.

Among his collections of *cuentos* are *Smith y Ramírez* (1957), *La voz de la tierra* (1958), and *Primeras hojas* (1959).

J. Urrutia has edited a special issue (nos. 209–10) of *Papeles de Son Armadans* (1973) devoted to Zamora Vicente.

ZAPATA, MARCOS (1845–1913), b. Ainzón, Saragossa. Dramatist who lived in Argentina from 1890 to 1898. A former law-student inured to poverty, Zapata gained a brief, overwhelming success with his historical play *La capilla de Lanuza* (1871), performed three years after his arrival in Madrid. He remained poor all his life, partly because publishers took advantage of his straits, and partly because of his slowness in composition, a characteristic epitomized by his saying 'hay años en que no se le ocurre a uno nada'.

El castillo de Simancas (1873) suffered from lack of self-criticism after his early success which he was never to recapture in *La corona de abrojos* (1875) or *El solitario de Yuste* (1877). The government ban on *La piedad de una reina* (1887) restored some of Zapata's lost celebrity; the next 'political' first night in Madrid was to be the *Electra* of Pérez Galdós (q.v.).

He wrote fine libretti for *zarzuelas* (q.v.), the best being *El anillo de hierro* (1878), *Camoens* (1879), and *El reloj de Lucerna* (1884).

ZAPATA DE CHAVES, LUIS DE (1526–95), b. Llerena. Courtier and page at the court of Philip II. He spent thirteen years writing the 22,000 lines in *octavas reales* that make up the fifty cantos of his panegyric *Carlos famoso* (Valencia, 1566) a pedestrian chronicle that Cervantes attributed to Luis de Ávila and consigned to the flames in the book-burning scene in *Don Quijote*.

Zapata wrote a verse 'Libro de cetrería', still unpublished, and produced a mediocre translation of Horace's *Ars poetica* (Lisbon, 1592).

His burlesque epic between the cats and the rats is the first known in its genre in Spanish.

His only memorable book was the diverting *Varia historia* of court anecdotes, written *c.* 1590, which was edited as *Miscelánea* by Pascual de Gayangos in the *Memorial Histórico Español*, vol. 11 (1859). For Rodríguez Moñino, the *Miscelánea* is one of the hundred best books in Spanish literature. It is an excellent source for the social history of its time, and was subsequently edited by G. C. Horsman (Amsterdam, 1935).

ZÁRATE, AGUSTÍN DE (*c.* 1506–*c.* 1565), historian of Peru, and secretary to the Royal Council of Castile for more than fifteen years; he was sent by Carlos I in 1543 with the Viceroy Núñez Vela to investigate the Treasury in Peru; was an eye-witness to Gonzalo Pizarro's insurrection, but remained loyal to the Emperor. His enjoyable *Historia del descubrimiento y conquista del Perú y de las guerras y cosas señaladas en ella, acaecidas hasta el vencimiento de Gonzalo Pizarro y de sus secuaces que en ella se rebelaron contra Su Majestad* was first published in Antwerp (1555). The first edition printed in Spain was that of Seville, 1571, and it has several times appeared in English, most recently in the version of J. M. Cohen (Harmondsworth, 1968). Zárate's *Censura de la obra de 'Varones ilustres de Indias' de Juan de Castellanos* has been reprinted in vol. 4 of the BAE. Though biased towards the policies of Carlos, Zárate's book is not as partisan as the pro-Pizarro work by Francisco López de Jérez (q.v.).

ZÁRATE, FERNANDO DE, pseudonym of Antonio Enríquez Gómez (q.v.).

ZARDOYA, CONCHA (1914–   ), b. Valparaíso, Chile. Literary critic and poet. Among her critical works are *Miguel Hernández* (New York, 1955), *Historia de la literatura norteamericana, 1607–1950* (Barcelona, 1956), and *Poesía española del siglo XX* (4 vols., Madrid, 1974). She has translated and edited Walt Whitman (*Obras escogidas*, Madrid, 1946; 2nd edn., 1955) and has written on Charles Morgan, Gil Vicente, and Ercilla. Her own poetry is of lyrical simplicity, beginning with *Pájaros del Nuevo Mundo* (Madrid, 1945). Her later books include *Donde el tiempo resbala* (Montevideo, 1966) and *Hondo sur* (Barcelona, 1968).

ZARQALI, az-, b. Cordova. Astronomer. His original observations were modified and enlarged by Jewish astronomers by royal command at Toledo (1252–62), chosen for its central position and clear skies. They were translated as the Alphonsine Tables (*Tablas alfonsíes*) under Alfonso X of Castile (q.v.). Through their accurate measurement of planetary movements and eclipses, the Tables greatly extended the king's reputation as a patron of learning. A revised version by the Frenchman Jean de Lignières remained in use in Western Europe until the Renaissance.

Zarzuelas, musical comedies in one to three acts, first composed by Pedro Calderón de la Barca in conjunction with composers such as Juan Risco. Calderón's first *zarzuela* was probably either *El mayor encanto amor* (1635), written for the opening of the Buen Retiro Palace in Madrid, or *El jardín de Falerina*. The earlier *zarzuelas* were mostly written for outdoor performance; they obtained their name from La Zarzuela, a hunting lodge near the Pardo Palace, where these plays were performed about 1656.

The distinctive quality of the *zarzuela* was the increasing importance of the musical element, alternating aria and recitative. They were often occasional in nature, such as Calderón's *La púrpura de la rosa* (1660), which took the legend of Venus and Adonis to allegorize the peace with France and the marriage of the Infanta Maria Teresa to Louis XIV. They were highly stylized in structure and language. The themes were usually mythological, understood in a symbolic or allegorical sense.

The *zarzuela* never lost its popularity. In the 19th c., it evolved into the self-contained three-act *zarzuela*, differing in its length from the merely occasional character of the earlier examples, and the shorter *género chico* (q.v.).

See E. Cotarelo y Mori, *Ensayo histórico sobre la zarzuela* (1933).

ZAVALA MUNIZ, JUSTINO (1898–), b. Cerro Largo, near Melo, Uruguay. Novelist. His important trilogy employs the *gaucho* in his changing circumstances as a true and symbolic expression of Uruguay's history from the mid-19th c. up to 1930. *Crónica de Muniz* (1921) vindicates the character of the author's grandfather Justino Muniz, a rural *caudillo* accused of treason. *Crónica de un crimen* (1926) is haunted by the figure of 'The Hawk', a murderous *gaucho*, and the book gains extra power from the author's obvious admiration for the outlaw. *Crónica de la reja* is a gently ironic anti-climax, in which the exploits of the past are now quietly told over a shop-counter. Zavala Muniz writes in the manner of Benito Lynch and Carlos Reyles (qq.v.).

ZAYAS Y SOTOMAYOR, MARÍA DE (1590–1660?), b. Madrid. Novelist and poet, who lived most of her life in Saragossa. Her short novels of love and intrigue were published during her lifetime in two collections: *Novelas amorosas y exemplares* (Saragossa, 1637), which all end happily; and *Parte segunda del sarao, y entretenimientos honestos* (Barcelona, 1647), which all end unhappily. These novels are artificially linked together somewhat in the manner of the *Decamerone*: they are told on successive evenings to amuse a sick woman, and bring the picaresque genre into the aristocracy.

María de Zayas was praised as a poet by Lope de Vega and Castillo y Solórzano. She wrote a play called *La traición en la amistad*. Her novels have been edited by A. González Amezúa (1948).

See Irma V. Vasilevski, *María de Zayas y Sotomayor: su época y su obra* (New York, 1972).

ZEA, LEOPOLDO (1912–), Mexican philosopher. One of the editors of *Tierra Nueva* (q.v., 1940–2), he also published a number of essays in *El Hijo Pródigo* (1943–6). He has discussed the evolution of thought in Mexico in numerous influential studies, including *El positivismo en México* (1942; English translation, Austin, Texas, 1974), *Apogeo y decadencia del positivismo en México* (1944), *Dos etapas del pensamiento hispanoamericano* (1949) which has been translated by J. H. Abbott and L. Dunham (Norman, Okla., 1963), *La filosofía como compromiso* (1952), *Conciencia y posibilidad del mexicano* (1952), *La filosofía en México* (1955), *El Occidente y la conciencia de México* (1956), and *Dependencia y liberación en la cultura latinoamericana* (1974). Zea's view is that formerly Mexico had undergone changes without awareness (*conciencia*) and that now a knowledge of the forces shaping the nation will help it to avoid believing in a new Utopia. Zea has been Director of the Centre of Latin American Studies in the Universidad Nacional Autónoma de México.

ZEITLIN, ISRAEL (1906–), b. Ekaterinoslav (now Dnepropetrovsk), Ukraine. Domiciled in Argentina, he writes under the pseudonym 'César Tiempo', and worked for the Buenos Aires newspapers *Crítica* and *El Sol*. He was associated with the Boedo Street group of socially-concerned writers whose work appeared in the magazine *Claridad*, later called *Los Pensadores*. His poetry of satire and prophecy attacks his fellow Jews. Zeitlin's principal works are the *Libro para la pausa del sábado* (1930), *Sabatión argentino* (1933), and *Sábadomingo* (1938).

Zéjel, a type of poem usually of Mozarabic origin and generally octosyllabic. It was similar in form to the Castilian *villancico* (q.v.) and the name *zéjel* is nowadays synonymous with the Castilian word *estribote*.

The most usual arrangement of the *zéjel* in Castilian poetry (though many variations exist) is that in which the rhymed couplet (*estribillo*) is followed by a variable number of stanzas, each consisting of a rhymed triplet called a *mudanza* or *cuerpo* and ending in a fourth line rhyming with the *estribillo* and known as the *vuelta* (aa:bbba).

In contradistinction to the classical Arabic *muwashshaha* (q.v.), the *zéjel* (or *zajal*) is in colloquial Arabic and was used throughout the Arab World, and as far as Central Asia, where it remains popular to this day.

The best-known exponent of the *zéjel* was Ibn Guzman (q.v., *c.* 1078–1160).

ZENEA, JUAN CLEMENTE (1832–71), b. Bayamo, Cuba. Poet. His elegies and romantic love poems for Adelaida Menkeu, *Cantos de la tarde* (1860), were strongly influenced by Alfred de Musset and Lamartine. Zenea was executed in 1871 for continuous propaganda against Spain, and his *Poesías póstumas* appeared in the same year, followed in 1872 by an edition of his *Poesías completas* (New York). *Nueva colección de poesías* was published in Havana in 1909.

Among the many studies of his life and work is J. M. Carbonell's *Juan C. Zenea, poeta y mártir* (Havana, 1929).

ZENO-GANDÍA, MANUEL (1855–1930), b. Arecibo. Puerto Rican novelist. By profession a doctor, he used his everyday contacts with ordinary people to produce an outstanding tetralogy, *Crónicas de un mundo enfermo*, on Puerto Rican life before and during the first years of the American occupation of 1898. The first to appear (though the second written) was *La charca* (1894), on the misery and sloth observed in rural life; *Garduña* (1896), written first, showed the depths of human depravity on a sugar plantation; *El negocio* (1922) dealt with corruption and commercial life in a Puerto Rican city after the American occupation; *Redentores* (1925) is a denunciation of collaborators with the American 'redeemers', and prophesies the birth of a Puerto Rican government.

Zeno-Gandía also published some Romantic verse in *Abismos* (1885), which was never able to surpass its models Campoamor and Núñez de Arce. In the *Crónicas* he surpassed in sensitive naturalism the less successful work of his model Émile Zola. He also published two short novels: *Rosa de Mármol* (1889) and *Piccola* (1890), written some nine years before their publication and lacking, in their derivative Romanticism, the essential creative power which was to sustain Zeno-Gandía in his *Crónicas*.

See F. Manrique Cabrera, 'Manuel Zeno-

Gandía, poeta del novelar isleño' in *Asomante* (San Juan, 1955), vol. 11, no. 4, pp. 19–47.

Zifar, El Caballero, see CABALLERO CIFAR, El.

ZORRILLA DE SAN MARTÍN, JUAN (1855–1931), b. Montevideo. Uruguayan poet. He returned from studies in Santa Fé (Argentina) and Santiago (Chile) in 1878, and in 1880 was appointed Professor of Literature in Montevideo University. He was exiled to Buenos Aires by General Santos for his political propaganda in the daily *El Bien Público* and there wrote his best work, the Romantic verse drama *Tabaré* (q.v.). On his recall to Uruguay he was appointed to the diplomatic service, and spent some time in Portugal, Spain, and France. On his eventual return to Montevideo, he took up the teaching of art history.

Apart from *Tabaré*, he wrote *Notas de un himno* (1876), and *La leyenda patria* (1879) an ode in the tradition of Olmedo's *A la victoria de Junín* (q.v.). His speeches were famous in their day: they included *El mensaje a América* on the anniversary of Columbus' landing in America, and he also wrote history (in *La epopeya de Artigas*, 1910), letters on his travels (*Resonancias del camino*, 1895), and numerous essays. The sixteen vols. of his *Obras completas* appeared in 1930.

See Rimaelvo A. Ardoino, *La prosa de Juan Zorrilla de San Martín* (1945); Alfonso M. Escudero, *Zorrilla de San Martín y Chile* (Santiago de Chile, 1955); Roberto Ibáñez, *Originales y documentos de Juan Zorrilla de San Martín* (1956); and Domingo L. Bordoli, *Vida de Juan Zorrilla de San Martín* (1961).

ZORRILLA Y MORAL, JOSÉ (1817–93), b. Valladolid. Romantic poet and playwright. He abandoned the study of law in Toledo to devote himself to literature. In 1850 he went into voluntary exile in France and during 1855–66 in Italy, partly because of his father's disapproval, and partly owing to incompatibility with his wife, Matilde, sixteen years his senior. After Matilde died he married again, this time a much younger woman. Though extremely popular, he was always poor and obtained no financial recognition apart from a state pension in 1884. In his candid but rather fanciful autobiography, *Recuerdos del tiempo viejo* (Barcelona, 1880; enlarged edn. in 2 vols., 1882–3), he declares with complete truth that even in old age he had never been able to grow up.

From 1837, when his first *Poesías* appeared, his fluent verse obtained immense popularity throughout the Spanish-speaking world. He is at his best in interpreting 'old Spain' through her ballads and legends, in books like *Cantos del trovador* (3 vols., 1840–1) and the evocative *Granada* (Paris, 1852), planned in three vols., of which only the first two were executed. This is a history in verse of Granada's legends up to the Reconquest, with much of the skill and zest of Lope de Vega (q.v.). *La leyenda del Cid* (Barcelona, 1882) shows Zorrilla to be even more of a Golden Age writer *manqué*; while he is seldom flagrantly unhistorical, his emphasis on the picturesque scene or dramatic incident places him in the direct line of descent from Lope and Tirso de Molina, and he did in fact write *comedias de capa y espada* (q.v.) such as *Más vale llegar a tiempo que rondar un año* and *Cada cual con su razón* as well as historical plays and two unsuccessful classical tragedies. But the work for which Zorrilla has become especially popular is the seven-act *Don Juan Tenorio: drama religioso fantástico en dos partes* (1844) which is the most famous Spanish play of its century and is still performed in Spanish theatres during the first week of November. Written in lively verse, it is a fast-moving sentimental melodrama epitomizing the Romantic movement in the contrast between the cynical libertine and Doña Inés, and is by far the most effective successor to Tirso's *Burlador de Sevilla* (q.v.). Its happy ending, of redemption for the sinner through the love of a pure woman, also incidentally satisfied the Spanish playgoing public.

Zorrilla himself scoffed at the early *Don Juan Tenorio*, preferring the three-act *Traidor, inconfeso y mártir* (1849), a verse play on the trial of the pastry-cook of Madrigal (1595) who claimed to be King Sebastian of Portugal. But possibly Zorrilla's best play is *El zapatero y el rey* (Bordeaux, 1840) a reworking of *El montañés Juan Pascual y primer asistente de Sevilla* by Juan Claudio Hoz y Mota (q.v.), in which a cobbler kills his father's murderer, who is an aristocrat. The murderer had been given a token punishment after bribing the judge; the king, equally lenient, condemns the cobbler to make no shoes for a year. Part 2 of this play (1843) is about a completely different subject: the death of Pedro I in 1369 at the hands of his brother, the Infante Don Enrique.

Zorrilla wrote too much, too quickly, and had too few ideas of his own to rank with the greatest of Spanish writers. But, at the cost of trivializing the legend of Don Juan, he at least rendered it accessible to many of his compatriots who would otherwise not have come to know of it. An edition of his *Obras completas* begun in 1884 in Barcelona did not proceed past vol. I, but there have been several subsequent editions, notably that of Narciso Alonso Cortés (2 vols., Valladolid, 1943), who has written the standard book on him: *Zorrilla: su vida y sus obras* (3 vols., Valladolid, 1916–20; 2nd edn., 1942).

See also G. Díaz-Plaja and others, *Estudios románticos* (1975), being papers read at the 1st and 2nd Semanas Románticas (1972–3) at the Casa-Museo Zorrilla established in the poet's honour in Valladolid.

ZUM FELDE, ALBERTO (1889–   ), b. Bahía Blanca, Argentina, but moved to Uruguay, his parents' homeland, when one year old. A notable critic and literary historian, he was for several years Director of the National Library of Uruguay. His many books include *Proceso histórico del Uruguay y esquema de su sociología* (1920), *Proceso intelectual del Uruguay y crítica de su literatura* (1930; 2nd enlarged edn., 3 vols., 1940), *Índice crítico de la literatura hispanoamericano* (2 vols., 1955–58), and *La narrativa en Hispanoamérica* (1964).

ZÚÑIGA, FRANCESILLO DE (*c.* 1503–1532), b. Béjar? A dwarf, originally a poor tailor, he became court fool to Carlos V. His scandalous *Corónica istoria* (1527) so angered some of his victims that an assassin was hired to murder him in his home at Navarredonda. The book has been reprinted with Zúñiga's *Epistolario* by Adolfo de Castro in vol. 36 (1855) of the BAE. J. Menéndez Pidal published some of Zúñiga's 'Cartas inéditas' with a study in the *RABM* (Madrid), vols. 20 (1909) and 21 (1910).

ZÚÑIGA, LUIS ANDRÉS (1878–   ). b. Camayagüela, Honduras. Honduran fabulist and Director of the National Library, Tegucigalpa. He was Rubén Darío's (q.v.) private secretary in Paris, where he edited the literary magazine *Mundial*. He has written the biography *Rémy de Gourmont* (Paris, 1912) and a 'drama nacional en tres actos' called *Los conspiradores* (1914; 2nd edn., Mexico City, 1954).

His collection *Fábulas* (1917; 3rd edn., 1946) in prose and verse is considered the finest of its genre in Central America. The July–August (1964) issue of *Honduras Literaria* (Universidad de Honduras) was dedicated to Zúñiga.

ZÚÑIGA Y ÁVILA, LUIS DE (1510?–1573), b. Plasencia. Courtier and close personal friend of the Emperor Carlos V. He was appointed ambassador to Rome in 1539, and accompanied Carlos on his campaigns in Tunis (1535), and Germany (1546–7). He wrote, mainly on the spot and using the Emperor's views and knowledge, the interesting *Comentario de la guerra de Alemania* (Venice, 1548; frequently translated and reprinted) which appears in vol. 21 (1852) of the BAE. Though Zúñiga does not praise his patron more outrageously than was usual in such books, Carlos said of him that he was a better chronicler than Alexander the Great enjoyed, even if his themes were less august.

ZUNZUNEGUI, Juan Antonio de (1901–), b. Portugalete, Vizcaya. Novelist and short-story writer. He went to a Jesuit school in Orduña, and then studied law and literature in Deusto, under Unamuno in Salamanca, and in Madrid. A brief period in the business community of Bilbao disillusioned him, and his view of money as an evil influence in human affairs is reminiscent of Balzac's. His first short stories appeared in the series known as *Cuentos y patrañas de mi ría: Vida y paisaje de Bilbao* (1926), *Tres en una, o la dichosa honra* (1935), *El hombre que iba para estatua* (1941), and *Dos hombres y dos mujeres en medio* (1944).

Zunzunegui has described his novels as a 'fleet'; among the 'larger vessels' the first is *Chiripi* (1925), one of the earliest novels about Association Football. Then followed *El chipli-chandle* (a corruption of the English 'ships' chandler', 1940) about the Basque *pícaro* Joselín; *¡Ay ... estos hijos!* on family life in Bilbao; the satire *El barco de la muerte* (1945), in which townspeople murder an undertaker who gloats on their mortality; and the novels on bankruptcy (*Ramón o la vida baldía* and *Beatriz o la vida apasionada*) collectively entitled *La quiebra* (1947).

La úlcera (1949) is a short novel on a man's psychological dependence on his ulcer; when cured of it he dies of grief and the local people turn against his doctor. *Las ratas del barco* (1950) is a Galdosian panorama hinging on the difficulties of love between those from different social classes. *El supremo bien* (1951), his best work to that date, attacks three generations of a Madrid family who waste their supreme possession— their lives. *Esta oscura desbandada* (1952) deals with the economic and moral crisis in post-war Madrid. *La vida como es* (Barcelona, 1954), according to Cano and Torrente Ballester his best novel, offers a realistic portrait of Madrid's underworld similar to *La busca* by Pío Baroja (q.v.). Zunzunegui's subsequent books have been remarkable more for their social criticism than for their creative imagination, as in *El hijo hecho a contrata* (Barcelona, 1956) and *El camión justiciero* (Barcelona, 1956). In the latter, a

swindler is crushed by a rubbish lorry in his finest hour. In these and later novels, Zunzunegui emulates the *Episodios nacionales* of Pérez Galdós (qq.v.). *Los caminos de El Señor* (Barcelona, 1959) was followed by *Una mujer sobre la tierra* (Mexico City, 1959), banned in Spain. Interesting short stories were collected in *La poetisa* (1961). *El premio* (1961) is a lengthy satire against Spanish literary prizes; ironically it won the National Prize for Literature. Subsequent novels have included *El camino alegre* (Barcelona, 1963), *Don Isidoro y sus límites* (Barcelona, 1963), *Todo quedó en casa* (Barcelona, 1964), and *Un hombre entre dos mujeres* (Barcelona, 1966). Zunzunegui's *Obras completas* reached vol. 8 in 1976.

ZURITA, Jerónimo de (1512–80), b. Saragossa. Historian. With Morales (q.v.), Zurita is considered one of the founders of Spanish historiography. His father was one of the physicians of the court, and in 1506 accompanied Ferdinand to Italy, where he examined archive material.

Zurita was educated at the University of Alcalá, and in 1548 was appointed first Chronicler of Aragón, a position he filled conscientiously by compiling his six-volume *Anales de la Corona de Aragón* (Saragossa, 1562–80), to which an index volume was added in 1604. The best edition is the third, in 7 volumes (Saragossa, 1610–21). Zurita's history runs from the Arab invasion to 1516 and is more usefully critical than any previous work in its genre. Though his prose style is undistinguished, Zurita began the scientific approach to historiography in Spain by travelling to examine contemporary documents at first hand, weighing rival accounts of events, and omitting much of the supernatural and pious material considered necessary by his predecessors; his was the first Spanish history to avoid beginning with Noah, for instance. His successor was the poet Bartolomé Leonardo de Argensola (q.v.), who narrated in considerable detail the events of the period 1516–20. Francisco Diego de Sayas wrote a continuation (1667) covering the period to 1525.

Zurita's magnificent private library is now in the Escurial.

See A. Canellas, *Fuentes de Zurita* (1974), in the Colección Fuentes Históricas Aragonesas.